Religions of the World
Second Edition

Religions of the World

Second Edition

A COMPREHENSIVE ENCYCLOPEDIA OF BELIEFS AND PRACTICES

Volume Four: I–M

J. GORDON MELTON
MARTIN BAUMANN
Editors

TODD M. JOHNSON
World Religious Statistics

DONALD WIEBE
Introduction

ABC-CLIO

Santa Barbara, California • Denver, Colorado • Oxford, England

Library of Congress Cataloging-in-Publication Data

Religions of the world : a comprehensive encyclopedia of beliefs and practices / J. Gordon Melton, Martin Baumann, editors ; Todd M. Johnson, World Religious Statistics ; Donald Wiebe, Introduction. — 2nd ed.
    p.   cm.
  Includes bibliographical references and index.
  ISBN 978-1-59884-203-6 — ISBN 978-1-59884-204-3
  1. Religions—Encyclopedias.   I. Melton, J. Gordon.   II. Baumann, Martin.
  BL80.3.R45   2010
  200.3—dc22   2010029403

ISBN: 978-1-59884-203-6
EISBN: 978-1-59884-204-3

14 13 12 11 10   1 2 3 4 5

This book is also available on the World Wide Web as an eBook.
Visit www.abc-clio.com for details.

ABC-CLIO, LLC
130 Cremona Drive, P.O. Box 1911
Santa Barbara, California 93116-1911

This book is printed on acid-free paper ∞
Manufactured in the United States of America

Contents

A–Z List of Entries

Note: Core essays are indicated with the symbol ◆; country essays are indicated with the symbol ■.

Volume Two

Volume Three

Volume Five

Presbyterian Church of East Africa

Presbyterian Church of Ghana

Presbyterian Church of India

Presbyterian Church of Korea (HapDong)

Presbyterian Church of Korea (TongHap)

Presbyterian Church of Liberia

Presbyterian Church of Mozambique

Presbyterian Church of Nigeria

Presbyterian Church of Pakistan

Presbyterian Church of Rwanda

Presbyterian Church of the Sudan

Presbyterian Church of Vanuatu

Presbyterian Church of Wales

Presbyterian Church (U.S.A.)

Presbyterian Reformed Church in Cuba

Presbytery of Liberia

Priory of Sion

Progressive National Baptist Convention of America

Protestant Christian Batak Church

Protestant Christian Church–Angkola

Protestant Christian Church of Bali

Protestant Christian Church of Nias

Protestant Church in Indonesia

Protestant Church in Sabah (Malaysia)

Protestant Church in Southeast Sulawesi

Protestant Church in the Moluccas

Protestant Church in the Netherlands

Protestant Church in Timor Larosa'e

Protestant Church in Western Indonesia

Protestant Church of Algeria

Protestant Church of Senegal

Protestant Evangelical Church in Timor

Protestant Evangelical Church of Guinea

Protestant Methodist Church of Benin

Province of the Episcopal Church in Rwanda

■ Puerto Rico

Pure Brightness Festival

Pure Land Buddhism

Purim

Putuo Shan

Qadiriyya Rifa'i Sufi Order

Qadiriyya Sufi Order

■ Qatar

Qigong

Quanzhen Daoism

Rada Religion

Radhasoami

Raelian Movement International

Ramadan

Ramtha's School of Enlightenment

Rastafarians

Rawze-e-Sharif

Reconstructionist Judaism

Reform Baptists (Russia)

Reform Judaism

Reformed Christian Church in Slovakia

Reformed Christian Church in Yugoslavia

Reformed Church in America

Reformed Church in Romania

Reformed Church in Zambia

Reformed Church in Zimbabwe

Reformed Church of Alsace and Lorraine

Reformed Church of Christ in Nigeria

Reformed Church of France

Reformed Church of Hungary

Reformed Churches in the Netherlands (Liberated)

Reformed Denomination

Reformed Ecumenical Council

Reformed Presbyterian Church of Equatorial Guinea

Reformed/Presbyterian Tradition

Volume Six

Religions of the World
Second Edition

A COMPREHENSIVE ENCYCLOPEDIA
OF BELIEFS AND PRACTICES

Volume Four: I–M

I

I AM Religious Activity

The I AM Religious Activity is a spiritual and educational group founded in 1932 by Guy W. Ballard (d. 1939) and his wife Edna Ballard (d. 1971). The group falls within the Ancient Wisdom family of religious organizations that includes Theosophy, Bridge to Freedom, the Arcane School, the Holy Order of MANS, and Church Universal and Triumphant. As such it is a significant precursor group to the New Age movement of the late 20th century. The purpose of the Activity is to assist humankind at a critical juncture in its history by publishing heretofore hidden spiritual teachings from higher planes of existence. These teachings emanated from the Ascended Masters, also known as the Great White Brotherhood, and were communicated in more than 3,000 discourses given to the Ballards. Guy Ballard claimed that these masters were a mystical brotherhood of advanced initiates who have responsibility for the spiritual evolution of humanity.

The most important of the Ascended Masters for the I AM Activity is Saint Germain, who is believed to have appeared to Guy Ballard in 1930 while Ballard was hiking near Mount Shasta in Northern California. Saint Germain declared Ballard to be the Messenger of the Great White Brotherhood for the Seventh Golden Age, a coming millennial era of spiritual enlightenment. Ballard's description of his calling to messengerhood and of the teachings he received during his encounters with Saint Germain were published in 1934 under the titles *Unveiled Mysteries* and *The Magic Presence*. Ballard used the pen name Godfre Ray King in these books. He published other discourses from the Ascended Masters in *The I AM Discourses* (1936).

These three titles continue to be the core of teaching materials for the Activity.

The parent organization for the I AM Activity is the Saint Germain Foundation, which was led by Guy Ballard until 1939 and by Edna Ballard until 1971. Since 1971 the Foundation, with its worldwide headquarters in Schaumburg, Illinois (a Chicago suburb), has been under the guidance of a board of directors. The board oversees both the Foundation and the Saint Germain Press. The press claims that it publishes the Ascended Masters' words in their original form, free from the revisions that have occurred in I AM Activity splinter organizations such as Bridge to Spiritual Freedom, Summit Lighthouse, and Church Universal and Triumphant. Among the press's offerings are complete editions of the Ballards' books, DVDs and videos, contemplation music, and paintings of the Ascended Masters. The Saint Germain Foundation is represented throughout the world by 300 local groups termed "I AM" Sanctuary, "I AM" Temple, "I AM" Study Groups, or "I AM" Reading Rooms. These groups are fully autonomous but are chartered by the Saint Germain Foundation's board.

The basic teachings of the Activity include knowledge of the "Mighty I AM Presence," the use of God's creative name, the "I AM," and the use of the Violet Flame. The "Mighty I AM Presence" is the individualized presence of God in each person. It can be contacted during meditation and can be used to create positive outer conditions through the practices of affirmation and decreeing. Affirmations are short sentences that affirm an ideal spiritual state and give thanks for blessings to come. In decreeing, a person calls forth the visible manifestation of a spiritual condition or seeks to dissolve a negative condition using the Name of God, "I AM." Through progressive attunement with the God Presence Within, a person can balance out negative karma and gain Ascension back to a state of Divine Realization. The most powerful dictation calls on the Violet Consuming Flame, a highly charged spiritual force revealed by Saint Germain, to pass through the body and around it, thereby clearing a person's spiritual and physical bodies from past imperfections.

The Saint Germain Foundation has always affirmed the special role of the United States in bringing the Seventh Golden Age to fruition. It is highly patriotic and proudly displays the American flag at its worship centers and during special events such as the "I AM COME!" pageant that is presented annually at the G. W. Ballard Amphitheater in Mount Shasta, California. The pageant was created, produced, and directed beginning in 1950 by Edna Ballard. It presents the life of Jesus and focuses on the Gospel miracles and the Ascension. The I AM Religious Activity is the oldest and most conservative of the groups that have their roots in the work of the Ballards.

Phillip Charles Lucas

See also: Arcane School; Church Universal and Triumphant; Meditation; Shasta, Mount; Western Esoteric Tradition.

References

Braden, Charles Samuel, *These Also Believe: A Study of Modern American Cults and Minority Religious Movements*. New York: Macmillan Company, 1956.

King, Godfre Ray. *Unveiled Mysteries*. Chicago: Saint Germain Press, 1934.

King, Godfre Ray. *The Magic Presence*. Chicago: Saint Germain Press, 1935.

Saint Germain [through Guy W. Ballard]. *The "I AM" Discourses*. Chicago: Saint Germain Press, 1935.

Saint Germain Foundation. http://www.saintgermainpress.com/. Accessed June 15, 2009.

Ibadhi Islam

The Ibadhites, who constitute the major Muslim group in the state of Oman, continue to espouse the empha-

The front gate and fort tower of the Ras Al-Hadd Castle, Oman. (dbimages/StockphotoPro)

ses originally championed by the now defunct Kharijites, a group that emerged as the Muslim community was still maturing in the seventh century CE. The prophet Muhammad was succeeded by a succession of close followers who were appointed to the office of caliph and led in the growth of the Arab Muslim Empire. Some of the early followers of Islam felt that the growth had come at the price of bringing many into the faith who did not even accept the bare essentials of belief and practice, the so-called Five Pillars—acceptance of Allah and his prophet Muhammad, fasting, almsgiving, daily prayers, and the pilgrimage to Mecca. The Khariji (or successionists) argued that the new converts must live exemplary lives or forfeit their right to be called Muslims.

Caliph Uthman (644–656) opposed the Kharijite position and in its stead favored the position of another group, the Murji'ah, who argued that one must withhold judgment on any individual's moral laxity and leave that judgment to Allah in the next life. Those who broke the provisions of the Muslim law (the *sharia*) were to be punished appropriately, but their status as Muslims was not to be called into question. The issue reached a crisis point when Uthman was himself accused of stealing money. The Kharijites argued that he was henceforth not a Muslim and demanded his ouster from office. Uthman was subsequently killed during a Kharijite riot in Mecca.

Uthman was succeeded by Ali ibn Abi Talib (d. 661), the Prophet's son-in-law. The Kharijites were supportive of Ali, but withdrew their support when he attempted to reconcile his rulership with the challenge from the Umayyads, who eventually established themselves in the caliphate. The Kharijites accused Ali of compromising with evil and turned against him. Most were killed when Ali defeated them, but a small number survived to keep the Kharijite vision alive.

In the meantime, a half century earlier, Islam had spread to Oman. About 630, the Prophet sent a letter to the two brothers who ruled Oman jointly at that time. They embraced Islam and then became allies in the Arab conquest of Persia. The connection to the Kharijites came through Abdullah ibn Ibadh, a seventh-century Omani who shared many of the Kharijite beliefs. In the eighth century, an effort arose to transform Oman into an ideal Muslim country along the lines of Kharijite principles. Also, it was decided that an imam would be chosen to lead the community.

The first Ibadhi imam, Julanda bin Mas'ud, was elected in 751. He died in battle soon afterward and not until 801 was a successor, Warith bin Kaab, named. The final establishment of the imamate was followed by a period of peace, stability, and prosperity that lasted for some three centuries. Sohar emerged as one of the great seaports in the Muslim world, and the Omanis became responsible for the spread of Islam to the countries farther west (North Africa) and south (along the African coast).

The Ibadhis are distinguished by their creation of an allegorical interpretation of most of the anthropomorphic images in the Koran, especially statements about Allah, paradise, and the doctrines concerning the last days. Thus they believe that the coming day of resurrection, for example, should be understood as the gradual coming of Allah's order on Earth. They are most concerned with the commission of major sins (things forbidden in the Koran) and believe that such sins must be repented of in this life, or the person will not be able to enter paradise. There are a variety of differences between the Ibadhis and the Sunnis on particulars in regard to prayer and fasting.

The Ibadhis trace their history to the Kharijites, but consider some Kharijite opinions too extreme. Most important, Ibadhis do not believe that sinful Muslims are not Muslims. They use the term *kufr ni'mah* (ungrateful) to designate Muslims who commit major sins or fail to practice the faith they profess.

The great majority of Ibadhis reside in Oman. The sultan serves as head of the community, and its administration and coordination is carried out through the government's Ministry of Awqaf (endowments) and Religious Affairs. The endowment moneys are administered by the ministry for the upkeep of mosques and for the benefit of the community. The ministry also oversees Muslim schools, coordinates travel to Mecca for pilgrims, and makes provisions for the observation of the annual fast of Ramadan. The ministry headquarters are in Muscat. Smaller communities of Ibadhis reside in Zanzibar, Algeria, Tunisia, and Libya. An unofficial but helpful Internet site on Ibadhis can be accessed at http://www.angelfire.com/ok5/ibadhiyah/index.html.

J. Gordon Melton

See also: Ali ibn Abi Talib; Islam; Muhammad.

References

Ennami, Amr Khalifa. *Al-Ibadhiyah.* Muscat: Ministry of Awqaf and Religious Affairs, Sultanate of Oman, n.d. http://www.angelfire.com/ok5/ibadhiyah/index.html. Accessed April 24, 2009.

Lewicki, T. "The Ibadhites in Arabia and Africa." *Journal of World History* 13, no. 1 (1971): 51–131.

Maamiry, A. H. *Oman and Ibadhism.* New Delhi: Lancers Books, 1989.

Wilkinson, J. C. *The Imamate Tradition of Oman.* Cambridge: Cambridge University Press, 1987.

Ibn Hanbal, Ahmad

780–855

Ahmad ibn Hanbal is recognized as the founder of one of the four schools of Islamic law and an expert in the collection of *hadith* about the Prophet Muhammad. He is also famous for the persecution he endured from several Iraqi caliphs during a time of inquisition known as *al-mihnah*. Ibn Hanbal resisted their advocacy of the theory that the Koran was a created document. This view was connected to the Mutazilite movement and in particular the campaign of the Abbasid caliph al-Mamun.

Ibn Hanbal is said to have begun studies of the hadith at the age of 15. He traveled widely to learn from the hadith scholars in Mecca, Medina, Yemen, and Syria. His mistreatment over Mutazilite doctrine began in 833 and lasted until 848, when the traditionalist view that the Koran was eternal was readopted by the political powers in Baghdad. During the years of trial Ibn Hanbal was flogged and imprisoned but remained a champion of the orthodox position.

His most important written legacy was his collection (Musnad) of reliable hadith about the Prophet Muhammad. This is said to have been completed about 842. Two of his sons were said to have heard their father dictate his entire hadith corpus. During his lifetime he was known more for his piety than his jurisprudence. His status as the founder of a distinct school came with his written material on law, which is actually minimal by later standards. He argued that law has to be based on the Koran and the traditions and sayings of Muhammad and that jurists should thus resist any codifications that create distance from the holy book and holy traditions.

The Hanbalite School originated after the other three Sunni schools were established. There are reports of Ibn Hanbal having close ties with al-Shafii, the founder of the Shafiite School, but this is a questionable tradition. The rise of the Hanbalite School owes most to the work of Abu Bakr al-Khallal (d. 923 CE), who collected the teachings of Ibn Hanbal in 20 volumes. While the Hanbalite School remained the smallest of the four schools, it influenced the great Muslim jurist Ibn Taymiyah (1263–1328). He in turn impacted the Wahhabi movement of the 18th century, which shapes the Islam of contemporary Saudi Arabia.

James A. Beverley

See also: Hanafite School of Islam; Malikite School of Islam; Muhammad; Shafiite School of Islam: Wahhabi Islam.

References

Hurvitz, Nimrod. *The Formation of Hanbalism: Piety into Power.* London: Routledge, 2002.

Melchert, Christopher. *Ahmad ibn Hanbal.* Oxford: Oneworld, 2006.

■ Iceland

Iceland is an island nation located in the North Atlantic, north and west of Norway and Scotland and southeast of Greenland. It was home to just over 300,000 people as of 2009. The land area is approximately 39,770 square miles.

Although formally integrated into mainstream Western religious traditions, religious life in Iceland from the period of the settlement to the present has had unique characteristics that can be easily misunderstood by outsiders. The Icelandic case is particularly valuable for comparative studies because Iceland has undergone rapid, thorough modernization, but it does not have—and never has had—racial-ethnic diversity, regionalism, or rigid status hierarchies. In addition, the absence of a pre-European Native population means that there is not a double layer of cultural traditions that have intertwined and must now be carefully dissected. It has undergone, as has the rest of the modern world, a rural-urban transition. Unlike the rest of the West, however, this was not a transition from village to city, but from individual farmsteads to cities and towns. Iceland has also undergone the important transition from colony to nation. From the standpoint of the history of religions, too, Iceland has not only in the past been relatively isolated from events affecting the world-system, but also is one of the few thoroughly Protestant socio-cultural systems not to have been exposed at one point or another to Calvinism or post-

ICELAND

Puritan piety. If we are careful to note the distinction that sociologist Max Weber has made between the traditionalist Lutheran and the modernist Calvinist contributions to the Protestant ethic, much of the paradoxical character of the Icelandic religion-society-culture complex is rendered comprehensible.

Although there may well have been Christian monks from Ireland in Iceland in the eighth century, they had fled by 874 CE, when Ingólfur Arnarson cast overboard his high-seat pillars, consecrated to the Nordic gods, and vowed to settle where they came ashore. Yet it is also clear from the ancient documents of Iceland (Edda and Saga) that the early settlers included both atheists and persons who might at least have had rudimentary Christian persuasions.

The story of Iceland's conversion to Christianity in 1000 is unique in the annals of the faith. It is also a paradigm for the study of Icelandic religious consciousness. A conflict had been brewing between the independent Pagan Icelanders and Ólafur Tryggvason,

the king of Norway, who had accepted the Christian faith and subsequently took upon himself the obligation to bring the Icelanders under the sway of the new teaching. The stage was set for a potential confrontation at Alþingi (the Icelandic Parliament), as Christian and Pagan parties each began to gather strength and as each declared that it would not live under the law of the other. The Christians then chose Hallur Þorsteinsson (Síðu-Hallur) to proclaim their law. However, apparently unwilling to be responsible for dividing the people, he instead brought the question before the Lawspeaker, þorgeir Ljósvetningagoði, himself a Pagan, whom the Pagan party had already authorized to speak on its behalf. Þorgeir took the case and then went "under the cloak": he lay down for a day and a night, pulled his cloak over him, and spoke to nobody, nor did anybody speak to him, probably in an attempt to attain hidden knowledge in some ancient Pagan tradition. When he finally mounted Law Rock to deliver his decision, it was for conversion, but with a series of

ficially "absolute" imposition of celibacy upon the higher clergy by the First Lateran Council in 1123, the defender of the Catholic position against Lutheranism 400 years later in Iceland was a bishop living openly in the married state, and his sons were national heroes. As was true with the Scandinavian Reformation generally, ecclesiastical changes were minimal: monasteries were abolished, but vestments and a formal sung liturgy were retained, with many of the clergy simply continuing in their parishes as before.

One crucial concession for Icelandic history was obtained at this point: namely, that conducting worship in the common tongue meant the use of Icelandic, not Danish. This decision made the church the central institution for a distinctively national life-world for Iceland during the colonial period.

Religion in Iceland has historically been a matter of the hearth. The home was the principal place of worship and teaching, with the church building serving

Church in Seydisfjordur, Iceland. Ninety-six percent of Icelanders are members of the evangelical Lutheran church. (Corel)

limitations, one of which was that the worship of the old gods could continue in private.

Iceland accepted Christianity by a freely taken decision that weighed the options in light of international political and economic considerations but also in terms of domestic tranquility. Iceland became a vassal state to the king of Norway in the 13th century and was passed to Denmark in the 14th. Formally, then, it was part of the Western (Roman Catholic) Church until the time of the Reformation. But even the old church's strictures lay rather lightly in Iceland. For instance, when Iceland was required to submit to Danish Lutheranism, the principal holdout for Catholicism was Jón Arason, the bishop of Hólar. The effect was a rebellion and martyrdom for Jón, but the twist of Icelandic irony that slides in here was that the leaders of the rebellion were Jón's sons. In short, in spite of the of-

Hallgrimskirkja, located in the capital Reykjavik, is one of the tallest buildings in Iceland and is named after Hallgrimur Petursson, an Icelandic poet and minister. (iStockPhoto.com)

Iceland

Religion	Followers in 1970	Followers in 2010	% of Population	Annual % growth 2000–2010	Followers in 2025	Followers in 2050
Christians	200,000	295,000	95.6	0.94	319,000	331,000
Protestants	185,000	263,000	85.4	0.27	280,000	287,000
Independents	12,000	18,000	5.8	3.78	22,000	25,000
Roman Catholics	1,000	7,200	2.3	6.04	8,500	10,000
Agnostics	1,900	8,000	2.6	4.34	11,000	15,000
Spiritists	600	1,400	0.5	1.02	1,600	1,700
Atheists	1,000	1,200	0.4	1.02	1,500	1,800
Hindus	60	780	0.3	1.02	1,000	1,400
Baha'is	300	650	0.2	1.01	900	1,200
Buddhists	0	560	0.2	1.01	700	900
New religionists	100	280	0.1	1.05	400	550
Ethnoreligionists	100	310	0.1	1.05	400	700
Muslims	0	270	0.1	1.03	400	550
Total population	**204,000**	**308,000**	**100.0**	**1.02**	**337,000**	**355,000**

primarily as the focal point for central life events. In this sense, every trip to church was a pilgrimage. Since Iceland was not a village but a farm society, the church was not the quasi-political center of village life but the pilgrimage center of family life. Particularly important for the development of a distinct Icelandic spirituality was the institution known as *kvöldvaka*, or the "evening wake," born of a combination of Iceland's literary cultural heritage, which made reading a valued pursuit, and cosmological circumstance: the winter noonday moon, the concomitant of the "midnight sun" touted by today's summer tour brochures, provided many hours to while away. Kvöldvaka was at once church, school, and theater for each farmstead. It also provided the vital link between saga consciousness and modernity, mediated by Christian literature.

Iceland obtained internal freedom from Denmark in 1874, and changes came to its religious life. The birth of institutionalized "religious freedom" was occasioned by the Church of Jesus Christ of Latter-day Saints in the Westman Islands—a saga recounted in the form of a historical novel, *Independent People*, by Iceland's Nobel laureate, Halldór Laxness. Beginning in 1905 there was also a series of dramatic spiritualistic phenomena associated with the "boy medium," Indriði Indriðason, and uniquely among mainstream Western Christian traditions, spiritualistic theory and practice were integrated into sectors of the Lutheran state church, so much so that it has been estimated that half the Icelandic clergy by the mid-1930s were sympathetic to Spiritualism, and when they were first allowed to elect their own bishop in 1938, they chose a man sympathetic to the Spiritualist movement. *Icelandic Spiritualism* makes the case that Iceland's tradition of spiritual phenomena stretching back to and through the conversion experience at Law Rock—a tradition described in the book as "saga consciousness"—provided a cultural substructure for distinctly modern innovations of "new men" at the helm of Icelandic society in the church, journalism, and politics. Later in the 20th century, Spiritualist influences in the national church seem to have waned into obscurity.

But Spiritualism and Mormonism are not the only "new religions" to have appeared in Iceland. Nýall, a unique Icelandic religion, founded by Dr. Helgi Pjeturss in about 1919, combined elements of Spiritualism, Theosophy, Icelandic nationalism, Eddic poetry and the sagas, and the latest scientific research of the period. It antedated both the Church of Scientology and the flying saucer religions but included elements that later appeared in each. The Theosophical Society also had a wide following; indeed, it had the highest per capita membership in the Icelandic population of any nation in the world in 1947. Beginning in 1972 an Icelandic neo-Pagan religion, Ásatrú, applied for legal status as a registered religious body, and in 1973 official recognition was granted. The chief *godi* was hence a legitimate "minister of religion" in the state's eyes, and the Ásatrúarmenn receive tax support in proportion to their numbers, which is at this time is between 200 and 300, or about 0.1 percent of the population.

The great majority of the country's population remains in the state church, the Evangelical Lutheran Church in Iceland. Weekly practice remains the province of a small minority, but baptisms, confirmations, weddings, and funerals retain historic significance, with participation at rates running from 75 to 99 percent of the population. There is also a Free Lutheran Church with a few congregations. The principal distinction between the two is the method by which pastors are selected. In the state church, the entire geographical parish (but not those who are members of other religious bodies) may vote on the selection of a new pastor (who is paid by the state), regardless of their participation in the affairs of the church, whereas the selection of pastors among Free Lutherans is limited to active church members (who also pay the pastor's salary). Free Lutheran pastors, however, remain part of the pastors' synod of the state church. The Roman Catholic Church has had a renewed presence since the turn of the 20th century, with a cathedral and resident bishop. There are also groups of the Pentecostals, Baha'i Faith, Seventh-day Adventist Church, Christian Brethren, and Jehovah's Witnesses; recent immigration has also brought new immigrant Buddhists and Muslims.

William H. Swatos Jr.

See also: Baha'i Faith; Christian Brethren; Church of Jesus Christ of Latter-day Saints; Church of Scientology; Evangelical Lutheran Church in Iceland; Jehovah's Witnesses; Roman Catholic Church; Seventh-day Adventist Church; Spiritualism.

References

Aðalsteinsson, Jón Hnefill. *Under the Cloak*. Stockholm: Almquist and Wiksell, 1978.

Hjálmarsson, Jón R. *History of Iceland: From the Settlement to the Present Day*. Reykjavik, Iceland: Iceland Review, 1993.

Hood, John F. C. *Icelandic Church Saga*. London: SPCK, 1946.

Kristjansson, Gunnar. *Churches of Iceland: Religious Art and Architecture*. Reykjavik: Iceland Review, 1988.

Petursson, Petur. *Church and Social Change: A Study of the Secularisation Process in Iceland 1830–1930*. Reykjavik: University of Iceland Press, 1997.

Swatos, William H., Jr., and Loftur Reimar Gissurarson. *Icelandic Spiritualism: Mediumship and Modernity in Iceland*. New Brunswick, NJ: Transaction, 1996.

Swatos, William H., Jr., and Loftur Reimar Gissurarson. "*Pagus et urbanus* in Iceland: Conjunctions and Disjunctions in Neo-Pagan Religion." In *Alternative Religions among European Youth*, edited by Luigi Tomasi. Aldershot, UK: Ashgate, 1999.

Vesteinsson, Orri. *The Christianization of Iceland: Priests, Power, and Social Change 1000–1300*. New York: Oxford University Press, 2000.

Ife

Ife (aka Ile Ifa), an ancient city in southwest Nigeria, northeast of Lagos, is believed by the Yoruban Ibo people of Nigeria to be the place where creation occurred. Here the emissary of the Orisha Olodumare, the Supreme God (the one who has the fullness of everything), took the materials given by Olodumare that were spread out to create the Earth, separating the land from the water. Archaeologists have suggested that the city is at least 1,000 years old, while the surrounding region has been inhabited for another 1,000 years.

The Yorubans divided themselves into various groups, each with royal leadership. Each of the royal families believe that they have descended from the first king of Ife, Oduduwa. After Oduduwa's death, his children left the city to found their own kingdoms. Oduduwa is believed to have had several sons (16 in number) who later became powerful traditional rulers of Yoruba land.

Through the centuries, Ife existed as a city-state whose paramount importance was its role as the original sacred city and the dispenser of basic religious teachings, including the divining technique known as

Ifa, an indispensable tool in defining the course of one's life. At Ife one finds the acknowledgment of a basic pantheon of Yoruba gods, estimated variously to number 201, 401, 601, or more. Some divinities are said to have existed when Olodumare created the Earth, while others are outstanding individuals who have been deified. Among the more popular deities are Shango (god of thunder and lightning), Ifa (or Orunmila, god of divination), and Ogun (god of iron and of war). These deities have been brought to the Americas by the practitioners of what became Santeria.

The old Yoruban kingdoms have been superseded by the post-colonial Nigerian government, but the royal leadership persists at a less formal level. The kings (who united political and religious power) of the Oni people of Ife and the Alafin people of Oyo, farther to the north, are still the most highly respected Yoruba kings and religious leaders in Nigeria. Ife is home to the palace of the Oni.

Ife was largely destroyed in 1849 and rebuilt in 1882. Today, approximately 300,000 people live in Ife.

J. Gordon Melton

See also: Pilgrimage; Santeria.

References

Abimbola, Wande, ed. *Yoruba Oral Tradition.* With a contribution by Rowland Abiodun. Ile-Ife, Nigeria: Department of African Languages and Literature, University of Ile-Ife, 1975.

Bascom, William. *Ifa Divination: Communication between Gods and Men in West Africa.* Bloomington and London: Indiana University Press, 1969.

Dennett, Richard Edward. *Nigerian Studies; or, The Religious and Political System of the Yoruba.* London: Cass, 1968.

Forde, Cyril Daryll. *The Yoruba-speaking Peoples of Southwestern Nigeria.* London: International African Institute, 1962.

Iglesia ni Cristo

The Iglesia ni Cristo is very critical of the Roman Catholic Church (the majority church in the Philippines) and firmly believes itself to be the only one "true" church. It was founded by Felix Manalo Isugan (1886–1963), born to a Roman Catholic family in the Philippines, who subsequently joined successively the Methodist Church, the Christian Church/Churches of Christ, and the Seventh-day Adventist Church. In 1913, however, he felt called by God to establish his own church, which was officially incorporated on July 27, 1914 (its coinciding with the beginning of World War I would later be interpreted as a prophetic sign). The name Manalo gave to his church was simply Iglesia ni Cristo (Church of Christ), but its followers were known as Manalists in the Philippines.

Following a prophetic tradition in the Philippines, Manalo is venerated as the *sugo*, or the last prophet of God, as well as the angel from the East mentioned in Revelation 7. Manalists reject the traditional doctrine of the Trinity as potentially polytheistic, believing instead in a messianic role of Jesus Christ but not that he was God himself. They are also conditionalist and do not believe in the immortality of the soul, which in their view remains "sleeping" in the grave until the Last Judgment (a doctrine derived from Seventh-day Adventists). Manalists also give a literal interpretation to the biblical command not to eat blood, a serious matter in the Philippines where a popular dish known as *dinuguan* is prepared with cooked animal blood.

Although beginnings were difficult, a spectacular expansion followed in the wake of World War II. Membership in the Philippines currently exceeds 3 million. Smaller constituencies also exist in Europe (5,300 members, with regional headquarters in Italy) and the United States.

An international journal in English distributed by the church carries the title *God's Message.* The headquarters for international missions are situated at 1617 Southgate Avenue, Dale City, CA 94015. There is an international website for members only: www.inc-world.org.

*Massimo Introvigne, PierLuigi Zoccatelli
and Verónica Roldán*

See also: Christian Church and Churches of Christ; Seventh-day Adventist Church; United Methodist Church.

References

Tuggi, A. Leonard. *Iglesia ni Cristo: A Study in Independent Church Dynamics.* Quezon City: Conservative Baptist Publishing, 1976.

Iglesia ni Cristo church, Manila, Philippines. (Catherine Karnow/Corbis)

Tuggi, A. Leonard. "Iglesia ni Cristo: An Angel and His Church." In *Dynamic Religious Movement: Case Studies of Rapidly Growing Religious Movements around the World,* edited by David J. Hesselgrave, 85–101. Grand Rapids, MI: Baker Book House, 1978.

Ignatius of Loyola

1490–1556

Ignatius of Loyola was the founder of the Society of Jesus, the Jesuits, an order within the Roman Catholic Church known for its dedication to learning and missionary work. The Jesuits also took a special oath to place themselves unhesitatingly at the behest of the pope.

Ignatius, of noble Basque lineage, was born in the family castle in the Guipuzcoa Province of Spain. As a youth he was sent to the court of King Ferdinand and Queen Isabella of Spain, where he was trained for the army, which he joined in 1517. In 1521, he suffered an injury to his leg that left him partially crippled for the rest of his life and virtually ended his military career. While recuperating from his wound, he read two books, a volume on the lives of the saints and a biography of Christ, which helped him reorient his life.

Upon regaining his health, he took a vow of chastity, formally resigned from the military, and assumed the garb of a pilgrim, after which he moved into a cave and began a year-long retreat (1522–1523) to develop his understanding of living the Christian life. At the end of the year, he journeyed to Rome and then on to the Holy Land, where he tried his hand at converting Muslims. He also began work on the *Spiritual Exercises*, a manual for spiritual growth/development, which is still widely used both in and beyond the Order. To the present, Order members make an annual retreat, during which they practice these exercises.

In 1528 he began his formal study of theology, which over the next six years led him to visit successively Barcelona, Alcala, Salamanca, and Paris. By the time he completed his studies, in the summer of 1534, he had formulated plans for a new religious order that would become the Society of Jesus. He had also brought around him a small group of trusted companions. Even before the Order was formalized, James Lainez, Alonso Salmerón, Nicholas Bobadilla, Simón Rodriguez, Peter Faber, and Francis Xavier (1506–1552), among others, assumed vows of poverty and chastity and agreed to begin missionary work in the Holy Land. They began the preparation for their journey.

In 1537, Loyola was ordained as a priest, and the following year the group met with Pope Paul III (r. 1534–1549). By this time, travel to Jerusalem was blocked by a war, and they settled in Venice awaiting an end to hostilities and the issuance of the pope's bull that completed the formalities constituting the Society of Jesus.

The group elected Ignatius the military-like Order's first general. He subsequently traveled throughout Europe and to the Holy Land, before settling in Rome, where he worked until his death on July 31, 1556. The order he founded would become a global body, leading to the development of Catholicism in many parts of the world. In 1542, Ignatius dispatched Francis Xavier to India. He would become the pioneer of the Asian development and herald the Order's and the church's first incursions into Southeast Asia, Japan, and ultimately China.

Ignatius was beatified in 1609 by Pope Paul V (r. 1605–1621) and canonized in 1622 by Pope Gregory XV (r. 1621–1623).

J. Gordon Melton

See also: Francis Xavier; Jesuits; Roman Catholic Church; Saints.

References

de Dalmases, Candido. *Ignatius of Loyola: Founder of the Jesuits*. St. Louis: Institute of Jesuit Sources, 1985.

Donnelly, John Patrick. *Ignatius of Loyola: Founder of the Jesuits*. London: Longman, 2003.

Egan, Harvey D. *Ignatius Loyola the Mystic*. Wilmington, DE: Michael Glazer, 1987.

Ignatius of Loyola. *Inigo: Original Testament: The Autobiography of St. Ignatius Loyola*. Trans. by William Yeomans. London: Inigo International Centre, 1985.

Ignatius of Loyola. *Spiritual Exercises and Selected Works*. Ed. by George Ganss. Classics of Western Spirituality Series. New York: Paulist Press, 1991. Multiple editions available.

Ravier, Andre. *Ignatius of Loyola and the Founding of the Society of Jesus*. San Francisco: Ignatius Press, 1987.

Independence, Missouri

Located in Jackson County, Missouri, the city of Independence was founded in 1827. In 1831, Independence became home for immigrants coming from the northeastern United States who were followers of the Mormon prophet Joseph Smith Jr. Smith, claiming divine revelation, chose Independence as the center place of Zion. The church soon bought a tract of about 63 acres west of the courthouse for building a temple. The temple would be the central structure of this New Jerusalem and the place to which Jesus Christ would make his Second Coming. Smith also suggested that Jackson County was the location of the biblical Garden of Eden. Today several denominations based on the religious work of Joseph Smith Jr. have a presence or make their headquarters in Independence.

An important town on the American frontier, Independence soon became the trailhead for the Santa Fe, Oregon, and California trails. Riverboat navigation on the Missouri River in the early years stopped at Independence. Fur traders coming from the west sent their goods east and resupplied their needs here. Immigrants heading west bought their supplies and equipment in Independence. Into the 1860s, the traffic heading west continued to bring Independence great prominence on the American landscape as well as economic prosperity.

During the Civil War, two battles were fought in Independence (1862 and 1864), both of which resulted in victories for the Confederacy. The aftermath of the war and the rise of nearby Kansas City, Missouri, caused Independence to lose both its prosperity and prominence, but it continues to be the county seat. President Harry S. Truman grew up in Independence and was active in county politics for many years.

The history of the Mormon efforts to colonize Independence was short-lived in the 1830s, lasting about two years. By early 1833 some 1,200 of Smith's followers had settled in the city and bought about 2,000 acres. They believed they were literally building the "city of God." But relations between the original citizens and the Mormon immigrants were tense. These tensions erupted in mob violence in July 1833. An angry mob attacked the church's printing and publishing house and destroyed the press and scattered the type. Mobs also destroyed the Gilbert and Whitney store. The Mormon population was forcibly evicted from Jackson County by the end of 1833.

Upholding a fervent belief in the geographical location of the center place of Zion, three different denominations tied historically to Joseph Smith Jr. occupy sections of the original tract of land bought by Smith's organization in 1831. This property is intersected by Walnut Street and River Boulevard in Independence. Most of the denominations with foundations in Joseph Smith Jr.'s work view this acreage as sacred.

The first group of Joseph Smith Jr.'s followers to return to Independence arrived in 1867. Two years later they bought 2 lots located on the original 63-acre tract that Smith chose as the place for the temple of Zion. This group, now known as the Church of Christ, was organized formally in 1863 when they selected Granville Hedrick as president and prophet of the church. Sometimes called the Church of Christ (Temple Lot), Hedrick's followers believe themselves to be a "remnant" of the original church of Joseph Smith Jr. Their world headquarters building and local meetinghouse are located on a 2-acre tract of land in the northwestern section of the 63 acres, at the northwest corner of the intersection between Walnut and River.

Occupying land at the southeast corner of Walnut and River is the visitors' center, meetinghouse, and mission offices of the Church of Jesus Christ of Latter-day Saints. Headquartered at Salt Lake City, Utah, this church was formed by those who followed Brigham Young in the aftermath of Joseph Smith Jr.'s assassination in 1844. This denomination was formally organized in 1847, when they selected Brigham Young as president of the church, as they made their way west across the continent from Illinois to what is now Utah. They too understand Independence, Missouri, as the site of the New Jerusalem and a sacred place for the Second Coming of Christ.

On the northeast and southwest corners of the sacred intersection are the international headquarters buildings of the Community of Christ. This denomination was formed by members of Smith's original church organization who remained in the Midwest after Smith's death. They formally organized in 1860 when they accepted Smith's eldest son, Joseph Smith, III, as the president of the church. The first members of this denomination returned to Independence in the late 1860s. The first congregation of the denomination located at Independence was organized in 1873. The Community of Christ, then known as the Reorganized Church of Jesus Christ of Latter-day Saints, made Independence its international headquarters in 1920. The denomination began building a multistoried, domed auditorium in 1926 to provide a place for church conferences and offices for church officials. Seating more than 5,000 people, the auditorium housed the headquarters offices of the church from the 1940s into the early 1990s, when it was joined across the intersection by the newly erected temple. The temple also houses offices for church officials, with space for worship and leadership education.

Several other denominations based on the teachings of Joseph Smith Jr. also make their headquarters in Independence and Jackson County. Many of these believe all or part of the 63-acre tract of land is sacred space. These groups do not accept the temple built by the Community of Christ as legitimate and look to the day when a "true" temple will be built on that land. Some of these denominations were formed by disaffected members of the Community of Christ, while others were formed by disaffected members of the Church of Christ (Temple Lot).

Steven L. Shields

See also: Church of Jesus Christ of Latter-day Saints; Community of Christ; Smith, Joseph, Jr.

References

Campbell, Craig S. *Images of the New Jerusalem: Latter Day Saint Faction Interpretations of*

Independence, Missouri. Knoxville: University of Tennessee Press, 2004.

Dyer, Alvin R. *The Refiner's Fire: The Significance of Events Transpiring in Missouri.* Salt Lake City, UT: Deseret Book Company, 1968.

Flint, Bert C. *An Outline History of the Church of Christ (Temple Lot).* Independence, MO: Board of Publication of the Church of Christ (Temple Lot), 1979.

Scherer, Mark A. *The Journey of a People: The Era of Restoration 1820–1844.* Independence, MO: Herald Publishing House, 2009.

Independent Church of Australia

The Independent Church of Australia, a relatively new expression of Western Esotericism, was founded in Perth, Australia, in 1969. It has an eclectic perspective, with ritual and liturgy derived from both Roman and Protestant Christianity and teachings inspired by both New Thought and Theosophical traditions, especially the Unity School of Christianity and the Christian Community founded by Rudolf Steiner.

The Reverends Mario Schoemaker (1929–1997) and Colin Reed (1944–1999) opened the first church center and in 1971 created the church's educational arm, the Institute of Metaphysics. It is the church's belief that Jesus was a divine being who took on human form and who, having passed through death, now inhabits the spiritual atmosphere of the planet. The church teaches that each member has an essential divine nature. Their task is to nurture the "Christ within" and pursue a path of development toward a mystical unity with God. The Cosmic Mass (similar to that of the Christian Community) is celebrated weekly, as is a service focused upon spiritual healing.

The Institute's curriculum introduces students to occult metaphysics, the metaphysical interpretation of the Bible, psychism, mysticism, and the Christian mysteries. With his more advanced students, in 1988 Schoemaker founded the Order of the Mystic Christ. As students develop psychically they are directed to the gaining of a mystic vision of the Christ. The Order has its own distinctive set of chants and meditations. Many members of the Order reside in metropolitan Melbourne, where members can supplement their personal program of spiritual practice and study with bimonthly gatherings.

The Independent Church of Australia is headquartered in Victoria (a suburb of Melbourne). In 2009, it reported four centers in Australia, two in New Zealand, and one in the Netherlands. The church uses the several textbooks written by Schoemaker, including *The New Clairvoyance* and *A Short Occult History of the World*, and the many tapes of his talks and classes.

Independent Church of Australia
32 Trevallyn Close
Montrose, Victoria 3765
Australia
http://www.ica.org.au

J. Gordon Melton

See also: Meditation; Steiner, Rudolf; Unity School of Christianity/Association of Unity Churches.

Reference

Independent Church of Australia. http://www.ica.org .au. Accessed March 23, 2009.

■ India, Contemporary Religion in: Asian Religions

The cultural, linguistic, and religious diversity of South Asia and of India in particular reflects a long history of encounter and dialogue among the various groups of people, communities, and traditions that share common religious concepts but whose religious identities cannot be reduced to those commonly shared elements. With 827,578,868 persons, approximately 80 percent of the Indian population identify themselves as Hindu. Thus, Hinduism is the largest religious tradition in India. However, as it is clear from the study of this complex religion, diversity in ritual, worship, and theological/philosophical outlooks makes it difficult to understand it as a monolithic tradition. The diversity of Hinduism can be traced to the Vedic period (ca. 1200–200 BCE), when already variously connected but individual ritual-schools (*shakhas*) present us with a variety of interpretations of the meaning Vedic sacrifice. It is also toward the end of the Vedic

Tibetan pilgrims chant under the shade of the Bodhi tree in Bodhgaya, India. (Corel)

period, around the fifth century BCE, that Buddhism and Jainism emerge out the Vedic religious milieu expounding new religious ideas while continuing to reinterpret common South Asian religious concepts, such as *karma*, *samsara*, and spiritual salvation (*moksha*, *nirvana*) in new ways. Jainism continued through the centuries, while Buddhism was all but obliterated early in the second millennium BCE. They would be joined in the modern world by Sikhism. One of the youngest religions in India, Sikhism is rooted in Guru Nanak's experience of One Supreme Being (Ekankar) as the Eternal Reality and Creator through whose grace spiritual liberation (moksha) may be achieved in one's lifetime.

Religious pluralism in India has also been shaped by contact with non-indigenous peoples that have come into the subcontinent as a result of migrations or have been driven by economic, political, and religious ideologies. Included are Zoroastrianism, Christianity, Islam, and Judaism (covered in a separate entry below).

Buddhism Although India is the birthplace of Buddhism, by the 13th century the institutions that supported the doctrines taught by the Buddha had virtually disappeared. The 2001 census of India counted 7,955,207 individuals, less than one percent of the population, who identified as Buddhist.

Society and culture in India around the sixth century CE was undergoing a radical transformation. The late Vedic texts, the Upanishads, indicate the transition from small chiefdoms to a period of urbanization not seen in South Asia since the Indus Valley period (3500–1200 BCE), and the concurrent shift from an agricultural-based economy to one primarily based on commerce and trade allowed for a broader distribution of goods as well as wider dissemination and debate about religious ideas and institutions. It is during this period that the great religious tradition founded by Siddhartha Gautama (ca. 563–483 BCE), known as the Buddha (the Awakened One), appears on the cultural horizon of North India, according to the Tripitika in Pali (generally referred to as the Pali canon), the earliest Buddhist texts.

After having attained enlightenment (*nirvana*) under the Bodhi tree, located in modern-day Bodhgaya, the Buddha established the Buddhist monastic community of monks and nuns (*Sangha*), which has taught the heart of the *dhamma* (Sanskrit: *dharma*) for approximately the last 2,500 years. Although the Buddha's teaching of the Four Noble Truths contains the essential path for the spiritual transformation of the individual person, he did not lay down a system for his community to follow; rather, he presented a set of general principles of conduct for monks, nuns, and novices. These general principles are collected in the Vinaya pitika, whose guiding principles is to overcome excessive desire (*tahna*) by cultivating contentment in the company of others who are aiming for the same goal. Soon after the *parinirvana*, or final passing of the Buddha, the first Council of Arhats was held at Rajagaha, where the attending monks agreed upon the contents of the Sutta and Vinaya portions of the Tripitika. The Second Council was held approximately 70 years later at Vesali, where a number of issues regarding monastic practice became the focus of discussion, such as whether a monk should accept money.

Various perspectives on fundamental questions of Buddhist doctrine, such as the status of the self, the question of personal continuity, and the concept of causality developed within the various monastic fraternities. By the third century BCE, three schools of thought had crystallized within the Sangha: the Personalists (Puggalavadins), the Pan-realists (Sarvastivadins), and the Distinctionists (Vibhajjavadins). These three early schools of Buddhist thought developed within the elder (Sthaviras) monastic fraternities, which were distinguished by the time of the Second Buddhist Council from the Mahasanghika, or the greater assembly. The monastic fraternities connected with the Vibhajjavada

perspective were primarily found in South India and eventually became established in Sri Lanka (formerly Ceylon), where they referred to themselves as Theravada, 'the tradition of the elders' (the Pali equivalent to Sanskrit Sthaviravada), one of the two major branches of Buddhism today.

At the Second Buddhist Council, the question of following one's teacher's practice against the practice established in the Vinaya was a controversial one. The elder (*sthaviras*) monks, primarily from western India, concluded that it was at times permissible to follow the practice of one's teacher, but there was no clarification of the details and application of the decision. According to non-Theravada sources, the majority of eastern monks disagreed on this issue and held their own council at Pataliputra, where the schism of the Sangha is said to have begun. At their council, the various Mahasangika monastic fraternities, centered in the capital city of Pataliputra and in the southern cities of Amaravati and Nagarjunakonda, generally argued against the Sthaviravada position that the Sutta and Vinaya of the Tripitika were the final authority regarding the Buddha's teachings. According to non-Theravada sources, there were five major points of contention regarding the status of the *arhat*, the ideal perfected individual who achieves freedom from the bonds of desire by following the teachings of the Buddha: (1) the arhat was capable of being seduced by another; (2) the arhat could be subject to ignorance; (3) the arhat may have doubts; (4) the arhat may be instructed by another person; (5) entry into the path of the Buddha may be accompanied by sorrow. The so-called five points of Mahadeva are an explicit critique of the arhat and the Theravada fraternities.

Many of the doctrines and practices of the Mahasangika monastic fraternities have much in common with those in the Mahayana traditions of Buddhism, which arose sometime between 150 BCE and 100 CE as contained in many of their sutras composed in Sanskrit, which claimed be the word of the Buddha. In addition to questioning the status of the arhat and the limitation of the Buddha's teaching to the Tripitika, the Mahasangikas also stressed the transcendental nature of Buddhahood as not being limited to the historical Buddha. Recent scholarship has questioned the understanding of the later Mahayana tradition as developing from within Mahasangika groups and suggests that Mahasangika positions may have been influenced by already existing proto-Mahayana groups.

Theravada Buddhism survives today primarily in Sri Lanka and parts of Southeast Asia (Myanmar, Laos, and Thailand), while Mahayana Buddhism spread beyond the borders of India through trading routes to Central Asia as well as through seafaring trade into China, Japan, Cambodia, Korea, Japan, and Tibet.

The ascendancy of Buddhism in India and its spread to Central, East, and Southeast Asia cannot be understood apart from the intimate relationship between political power and religion. In the sixth century BCE, the political landscape of North India was made up of small kingdoms and tribal confederations. Following Alexander the Great's (ca. 356–323 BCE) invasion of North India and after the decline of Persian power in the region, Magadha emerged as the first major kingdom in the Gangetic plain to assert control over a large part of the subcontinent. By 303 BCE, Chandragupta Maurya (r. 324–301 BCE) had consolidated power over the territory extending from eastern Afghanistan to Bengal and south to the Narmada River, in modern-day Gujarat. The Mauryan Empire spread into the Deccan Plateau to modern-day Mysore and the Tamil region under Bindusara (r. 297–272 BCE). However, it was Ashoka (r. 269–232 BCE) who completed the first unification of India after his conquest of Kalinga (modern-day Orissa).

The close affinity and dependence between the Sangha and political authority for the Sangha's economic sustenance, as well as the king's need of the legitimating authority of the Sangha, have been an important aspect in the history and spread of Buddhism. After an initial period of bloody conquest during the early part of his reign, Ashoka converted to Buddhism. After his conversion, Ashoka made the Buddha's dhamma a guiding principle of this great empire by institutionalizing Buddhist doctrine, as is evident in the language of his edicts, which show a close affinity to Buddhist religious language and provided the ideological underpinning for his empire. Ashoka outlawed animal sacrifices in the royal court, as well as killing animals in royal kitchens. Although somewhat critical of Vedic ritual practices, Ashoka never outlawed any particular religious practice of any other religious com-

munities. Indeed, many of his edicts show that there was royal support for all major religious traditions of this time—Buddhism, Vedism, Jainism, and Ajivikas. The tradition of royal support for religious institutions, regardless of the personal adherence of the ruler, may be traced to the early Mauryan rulers, including Ashoka.

The sectarian split along doctrinal lines between the Theravada and Mahayana traditions with the subsequent identification of monastic identity along doctrinal lines began at the Council at Vesali and was crystallized by 100 CE. For the next 800 years, Buddhism continued to survive in India alongside other religious communities in the various kingdoms that came into being with the end and the subsequent fragmentation of the Mauryan Empire. Royal patronage of Buddhist institutions declined after the death of Harsha (606–647 CE).

A crucial blow to Buddhist institutions in India came with the rise of Islamic political power in India that was inaugurated by raids into areas of Baluchistan, Sind, Punjab, and Gujarat by the armies of Mahmud of Ghazni in 997 CE. There were several factors, both internal and external, that contributed to the decline and eventual disappearance of a thriving Buddhist community in India, including the assimilation of Buddhist ideas and practices into Hinduism with its focus on religiosity connected to locality through the enormous web of sacred narratives of pilgrimage sites, the nearly exclusive dependence of Buddhist monastic institutions on royal patronage, and the isolation of monastic institutions from village communities. With the conquest of the Gangetic Plain by Muslim Turkish-Ghurids and the destruction of the two great Buddhist universities at Nalanda in 1197 and Vakramashila in 1203, the institutional foundation of Buddhism in India was shattered. Although Tibetan pilgrims in the early 1200s noted pockets of surviving monks and a few monasteries, by the 13th century Buddhism had institutionally been driven out of India.

The consolidation of British hegemonic authority in India and the subsequent policy of religious tolerance gave rise to movements to reintroduce Buddhist institutions. One such movement began at end of the 19th century, when Sri Lankan monk Anagarika Dharmapalan (1864–1933), inspired by the efforts of the

Theosophical Society, established the Maha Bodhi Society in 1891. The aim of the Dharmapala's movement was to revive Buddhism in India by restoring the most important Buddhist pilgrimage sites, including the Mahabodi Temple at Bodhgaya. Dharmapala used the existing legal system and sued the Brahmans who had controlled the site for several centuries to regain control over other Buddhist pilgrimage sites including Kushinagar, the site of the Buddha's parinirvana.

The most significant effort to revive Buddhism in India was the re-conversion campaign led by Bhimrao Rami Ambedkar (1892–1956) to lead 600,000 untouchables (*dalits*) into the Buddhist tradition. Ambedkar saw Buddhism as an effective ideology to fight and abolish discrimination based on caste status. In 1955, he founded the Buddhist Society of India (Bharatiya Bauddha Mahasabha). He completed his final published work, *The Buddha and His Dhamma*, in 1956. He converted to Buddhism in a public ceremony along with some 300,000 others in 1956. Although the number of converts to Buddhism remains relatively low, members of Dalit Buddhist movements have continued to campaign in order to regain control of traditional Buddhist sites.

In the 21st century, the most visible strand of Buddhism in India is the Vajrayana, or Tibetan, branch of Buddhism. After troops from the army of the People's Republic of China amassed on the Tibetan border beginning in 1950 and Communist collectivization was instituted, the 14th Dalai Lama, Tenzin Gyatso (b. 1937), the spiritual and political leader of the Tibetan community, escaped from Chinese troops into India in 1954. The Tibetan exile community has made its home in Dharmasala in the Kangra District of the state of Himachal Pradesh.

Jainism With 4,225,053 adherents, or 0.4 percent of the population, according to the 2001 census of India, Jainism is the fifth largest religion in India. In North India, Jains are found primarily in the state of Gujarat, Madhya Pradesh, and Rajasthan as well as farther south in Maharashtra and Karnataka. Jainism emerged out of the same historical context as Buddhism, namely, the late Vedic period. Jains understand their tradition to stretch back into prehistory, having been transmitted in a series of 24 ford makers (*tirthankaras*) who

A group of Jain priests gathers at Ranakpur Temple in Rajasthan, India. (Corel)

have periodically taught the Three Jewels, the uncreated teachings of right faith, right knowledge, and right practice. The historical tradition may be traced to the Mahavira (ca. 540–468 BCE), the 24th tirthankara, who is said to have taught Five Great Vows: restraint from violence, restraint from lying, restraint from taking what has not been given, restraint from possession, and restraint from sexual relations.

Jainism understands everything in the universe to be constituted of two eternal and ultimate real entities, life-monad or soul (*jiva*) and nonsentient matter (*ajiva*). Ajiva provides the conditions and mechanism through which jiva functions. In this view, jiva is understood to be restricted in its motion especially by *karma*, which is regarded as physical substances that sticks to the jiva in the same way as dust. Karma is the inescapable result of actions, which are conceived to harm living beings. The aim of the teachings of Mahavira is to stop the accumulation of new karma and to eliminate accumulated karma, so that the jiva may experience pure knowledge and bliss in its naturally unencumbered, liberated and disembodied state at the top of the universe.

Jain thought and practice is inseparable from the ascetic idea, which is the foundation of both the Jain lay community and the monastic community. For Jain monks, nuns, laymen, and laywomen, the goal of liberation from the entanglements of karma can only be achieved through the gradual increase of restraint and purification. The religious life of laymen and laywomen is understood in the Jain sacred texts to be a less potent form of asceticism. Only by restraining body and mind is it possible to attain the correct view of reality that provides the initial push toward the strict path of spiritual purification of monks and nuns.

Two distinct monastic traditions—Digambara (sky-clad) and Svetambara (white-clad)—associated with the teachings of Mahavira are historically attested as early as the fourth century BCE. Although there were other sects among the Jains, such as the Yapaniya, the Digambara and Shvetambara have remained historically the monastic foci of the Jain community. The schism between these two groups is predicated on several issues, including the content of the Jain scriptural canon (Agama), styles of monastic practices, the question of female religiosity and liberation, and the question of whether the fully omniscient being (kevalin) needs food.

The most visible distinction between Digambara and Shvetambara monks is their understanding of the great vow of restraint from possession. Nudity as the ultimate detachment from possession is traceable to Mahavira himself, who is said to have refused to cover himself with garments. Digambara monks affirm nudity as a marker of their monastic identity. Shvetambara monks recognize nudity as the ultimate expression of non-possessing, but point to textual passages that advise a monk to limit the wearing of clothes by minimizing the number of garments.

Inseparable from the split over garments and nudity is the question of spiritual capacity of women, another point of contention between the two traditions. The fully developed Digambara doctrine holds that because female nudity is socially unacceptable, women therefore cannot fully participate in the naked ascetic path. Furthermore, they argue that women's physical and emotional character makes it impossible for them to genuinely engage in the intense path necessary for spiritual purification. Although by this argument, women can never do evil to the same extent as men, it also follows that they are inherently unable to carry out the good acts necessary for liberation. Only by being reborn as a man can a woman engage the ascetic path. Later Digambara secondary arguments appealed to human physiology in order to exclude women from the path: by their very biological basis, women constantly generate and destroy (and therefore harm) life-forms within their sexual organs. Shvetambara oppose this view by appealing to scriptures, which show that since the time of the first tirthankara, Rishabha, women monastics outnumbered monks. Shvetambara also maintain that the 19th tirthankara, Malli, was a woman. The Kalpasutra also points out that at the time of Mahavira's death, the community centered on his teachings included two and a half times more female ascetics than male ascetics.

Within the Digambara and Shvetambara branches there have been subsequent fragmentations based on doctrinal disputes, including the interpretation of image-worship as well as the practice of wearing a mouth piece (muhpatti) in order to minimize the destruction of air-bodies and tiny insects that may be accidentally harmed through the mere biological process of breathing. Sub-lineages within the two main branches were historically connected to influential teachers who claimed to be restoring the original teaching of Mahavira.

Lay Jains engage in a variety of popular religious practices, including image worship (puja), temple rituals, and pilgrimage, activities that from the point of view of an observer makes Jains and Hindu nearly indistinguishable on the surface. The focus of Jain devotional ritual is not directed toward a deity or meant to mediate a relationship between the sacred and profane. Rather, the focus of Jain devotion, whether through puja in the home or as part of larger temple rituals, is a celebration of the heroic lives of the tirthankaras and jina (literally "conquerors," who have conquered samsara), in order to direct the focus the mind on the qualities which the image of the jina embodies. Devotional rituals, including image-worship, songs, and prayers, are meant to remind the Jain householder of the ultimate centrality of the Five Great Vows as the only way to overcome samsara. Thus, the religious life of Jain householders, instead of leading the householder away from the monastic idea of complete restraint, only serves to magnify the centrality of progressive renunciatory progress toward liberation.

Sikhism   Sikhs account for 19,215,730, or 1.9 percent, of the Indian population according to the 2001 census of India. Sikhism emerged as a distinct religious tradition within the broadly defined context of northern Indian Sant tradition, also known as the Nirguna Sampradaya. The devotional songs composed by famous Sants, including Kabir (1440–1518), Mirabai, and Dadu, incorporated the religious language of Vaishnava devotionalism (*bhakti*) and Sufism to emphasize the transformative personal experience of the transcendent deity who is beyond qualities and form. Like many devotional traditions in India around this period, Sant traditions focus on the signing of hymns, the recitation of mantras, and the singing of devotional songs (*bhajans*) as important practical elements for spiritual transformation.

The Sikh tradition is rooted in the uniquely transformative experience of its founder, Guru Nanak (1469–1539), who at the age of 30 received a revelation that designated him to honor and sing the praises of the One Supreme God. Nanak's experience of the divine was influenced by the vocabulary of both Hindu devotional movements, theological/philosophical schools, and the Muslim understanding of Oneness (*tawhid*) of God. Informed by this religious milieu, Nanak understood his experience in terms of both traditions, but at the same time maintained its uniqueness. After visiting Hindu and Muslim pilgrimage sites (*tirtha*), Nanak established the village of Kartapur, in modern-day Pakistan, as the location of the newly emerging community of Sikhs (derived from the Sanskrit word *shishya*, disciple) who were attracted to his charismatic personality and teachings.

The core of Nanak's teaching was the assertion of One Supreme Being (Ekankar), eternal and everlasting, who took on no physical manifestation. The Supreme

Bangla Sahib Gurudwara, New Delhi's main Sikh temple. (Corel)

INDIA

God may be known only through the grace of the *guru* (teacher), a concept that encompasses four essential doctrinal points: (1) guru as the Eternal Guru, the Supreme God; (2) guru as the personal guru; (3) guru as the Guru Granth Sahib, also known as the Adi Granth, the sacred texts of Sikhism; and (4) guru as the Guru Panth, the community of Sikhs as well as the doctrine of the community. Sikhism opposes any anthropomor-

phic representation of the Supreme God, insisting that it is beyond gender, transcendent (*nirguna*), but simultaneously immanent (*saguna*) as embodied in the Divine Name (*nam*), in the words (*bani*) of the sacred texts, and in the person of the guru and other saints.

The daily life of Nanak's early community of Sikhs centered on agricultural activity meant to sustain the town of Kartapur. The *gurumuk* (one oriented

India

Religion	Followers in 1970	Followers in 2010	% of Population	Annual % growth 2000–2010	Followers in 2025	Followers in 2050
Hindus	426,370,000	891,520,000	73.1	1.53	1,029,209,000	1,154,330,000
Muslims	62,877,000	168,250,000	13.8	1.69	210,000,000	250,000,000
Christians	20,598,000	58,367,000	4.8	3.12	86,790,000	113,800,000
Protestants	8,062,000	21,100,000	1.7	2.41	27,000,000	33,000,000
Roman Catholics	8,433,000	21,700,000	1.8	3.47	28,000,000	34,000,000
Independents	3,382,000	18,200,000	1.5	3.05	35,000,000	50,000,000
Ethnoreligionists	19,230,000	45,488,000	3.7	1.61	48,000,000	50,000,000
Sikhs	10,287,000	22,900,000	1.9	1.63	27,200,000	31,200,000
Agnostics	2,000,000	15,400,000	1.3	1.67	24,000,000	32,000,000
Buddhists	3,779,000	8,500,000	0.7	1.73	10,500,000	12,800,000
Jains	2,582,000	5,521,000	0.5	1.63	6,500,000	7,400,000
Atheists	700,000	1,990,000	0.2	1.68	2,600,000	3,300,000
Baha'is	730,000	2,000,000	0.2	1.71	2,400,000	3,000,000
Chinese folk	60,000	171,000	0.0	1.63	250,000	400,000
Zoroastrians	90,000	65,000	0.0	−1.45	40,000	30,000
Jews	9,000	10,000	0.0	1.63	10,200	10,500
Total population	**549,312,000**	**1,220,182,000**	**100.0**	**1.63**	**1,447,499,000**	**1,658,270,000**

toward the guru) focused on the cultivation of a three-fold spiritual relationship with the nam, society, and self. For Nanak, disciplined worldly activity was a requirement for the ultimate union of the self with Aral Purakh (Timeless One). The early Sikh tradition incorporated the pan-South Asian religious concepts of karma and samsara into its worldview, but made both subservient to the monotheistic doctrine expressed in the Adi Grant. Karma is not an unalterable and unavoidable law of cause and effect, as in Hinduism or Jainism, but is subject to the divine order (*hukam*) instituted by the Supreme One. Divine grace can shatter cause and effect and free the individual from samsara.

The religious life of Sikhs has been shaped by the teachings of Guru Nanak, and also by the transmission and innovations instituted by the lineage of the Sikh gurus from Nanak up to the 10th and last guru, Gobind Singh (1666–1708), who closed the Sikh canon, terminated the line of personal gurus, and shifted ultimate authority to the sacred texts by establishing the Adi Granth as the eternal guru for all Sikhs.

From the middle to the end of the 16th century the Mughal Empire under Emperor Akbar (1542–1605) was relatively tolerant of various religions. The third guru, Amar Das (1479–1974), who had served in the court of Akbar, was granted land in the region between the Sutlej River and the Ravi River, where the city of Amritsar, the spiritual center of the Sikh tradition, was built. There he built the Harimandir (Golden Temple) one of the oldest and most important *gurudwars*. Following the death of Akbar, the Sikh community was caught up in the political machinations and the subsequent shifting currents of political and religious ideology within the Mughal Empire. The fourth guru, Arjan (1563–1606), was arrested by Akbar's son, Emperor Jahangir (1569–1627) for aiding his son Khusrau Mirza (1587–1622) in a plot to depose him. Arjan never admitted his guilt nor abandoned his faith in the face of Jahangir's policy of terror and conquest, and was eventually tortured to death.

Conflicts with the Mughal authorities intensified during the period of the guruship of Gobind Singh (1675–1708). After the public execution of the ninth guru, Tegh Bahadur (1621–1675), fear of persecution spread among the community of Sikhs and led to a general movement to conceal Sikh identity. In reaction to both of these events, Gobind Singh reorganized the community around visible markers of Sikh identity and created the Sikh Khalsa, the community of pure ones. The five K's—uncut hair (*kesh*), a comb for the top-knot (*kangha*), a saber (*kirpan*), a steel bracelet worn on the right wrist (*kara*), and knee-length soldiers' shorts (*kachh*)—are mandatory for members of the Khalsa. Gobind transformed the Sikh religious community into a religio-military order. In this transformation Sikhism abandoned certain religious emphases that had been important in its founding, including the strict interpretation of the concept of nonviolence (*ahimsa*).

The congregational life of Sikhs as well as their individual daily religious routines is centered on the Guru Granth Sahib. Congregational service takes place in the gurudwara and consists of singing passages from the Granth as well as hymns (*kirtans*). It also includes a sermon (*katha*) on the meaning of a particular section of the Granth delivered by the *granthi* (reader) or by a Sikh scholar (*gyami*). After a joint recitation of petition prayers and the reading of the divine command, sanctified food (*karah prasad*) is distributed among the devotees. Sikhs engage in the meditation on the Divine Name (nam) immediately after rising in the morning and taking an early morning ritual bath. After recitation of the five daily prayers, the individual or family read a randomly chosen passage from the Adi Granth, which is considered to be the divine commandment (*vak laina*).

The central place of the Guru Granth Sahib is also observed in Sikh lifecycle rituals. The naming ceremony for a newborn involves the selection of a name that begins with the same letter as the first composition on the left-hand page of a randomly opened section of the Granth. In addition, males receive the surname Singh, "Lion," while females are given the surname Kaur, "princess." These names became middle names especially among Sikh communities in North America, who use traditional caste names as last names. The initiation ceremony (*amrit sanskar*) for a Sikh boy may take place at any point in time when the initiate is willing and able to join the Khalsa community. During the ceremony, the initiate drinks five times from *amrit*, sweetened water stirred with a double-edged sword, which is also sprinkled in his eyes and poured on his head five times. The initiate takes on the five K's along with a turban as visible markers of his identity as a Sikh. In diaspora contexts, especially in North America and Europe, some Sikhs choose to cut their hair but maintain their Sikh identity through the continued used of the name Singh or Kaur. *Sahaj-dhari*

Sikhs maintain traditional ritual practices such as the meditation upon the Divine Name, but disregard the five K's. Sikhs have been one of the most economically successful communities of the various Indian religion and many Sikhs have immigrated to Western countries over the last century.

Carlos Lopez

See also: Ambedkar Buddhism; Asceticism; Ashoka; Bodh-Gaya; Buddha, Gautama; Buddhism; India, Contemporary Religion in: Asian Religions; India, Contemporary Religion in: Middle Eastern Religion; India, Hinduism in: Ancient Vedic Expressions; India, Hinduism in: Medieval Period; India, Hinduism in: Modern Period; Jainism; Kusinagara; Maha Bodhi Society; Mahavira; Mahayana Buddhism; Monasticism; Nanak, Guru; Pilgrimage; Sikhism/Sant Mat; Theravada Buddhism; Tibetan Buddhism; Vaishnavism; Women, Status and Role of; Zoroastrianism.

References

Ahmad, Imtiaz, and Helmut Reifeld. *Lived Islam in South Asia: Adaptation, Accommodation, and Conflict.* New Delhi: Social Science Press, 2004.

Baird, R. D. *Religion in Modern India.* 2nd ed. Delhi: Manohar Publications, 1989.

Bauman, Chad M. *Christian Identity and Dalit Religion in Hindu India, 1868–1947.* Grand Rapids, MI.: William B. Eerdmans Publishing Company, 2008.

Grewal, Jagtar Singh. *The Sikhs: Ideology, Institutions, and Identity.* New Delhi: Oxford University Press, 2009.

Hardy, F. *The Religious Culture of India: Power, Love, and Wisdom.* New York: Cambridge University Press, 1993.

Long, Jeffrey D. *Jainism: An Introduction.* London: I. B. Tauris, 2009.

Neill, S. C. *A History of Christianity in India.* 2 vols. Cambridge: Cambridge University Press, 1984–1985.

Young, Richard F. *India and the Indianness of Christianity: Essays on Understanding: Historical, Theological, and Bibliographical in Honor of Robert Eric Frykenberg.* Grand Rapids, MI: William B. Eerdmans Publishing Company, 2009.

■ India, Contemporary Religion in: Middle Eastern Religions

Hinduism is, of course, the largest religious tradition in India. The diversity of Hinduism can be traced to the Vedic period (ca. 1200–200 BCE), and it is toward the end of the Vedic period, around the fifth century BCE, that Buddhism and Jainism emerge out of the Vedic religious milieu. Religious pluralism in India, however, was also shaped by contact with non-indigenous peoples that have come into the subcontinent as a result of migrations or have been driven by economic, political, and religious ideologies. Practitioners of Zoroastrianism, a tradition that shares much with the ancient religion of the Rig Veda, have made a home in India since their arrival in the Gujarat region in the early part of the 10th century CE. The origin of a relatively small community of followers of Judaism in India can be traced to Jewish merchants and traders from the Middle East as far back as the ninth century. Diversity also characterizes the history of Christianity in India, a community that accounts for approximately 3 percent of the population, according to the 2001 census of India. While the three major ecclesiastic traditions—Eastern Orthodox, Roman Catholic, and Protestant—are well established in India, the oldest communities of Indian Christians trace themselves to Saint Thomas, one of Jesus' disciples, who visited India during the first century CE and established a church connected to the Syrian Orthodox Church. Islam, the second largest religion in the world, entered the subcontinent through two routes. Before the military raids of Mahmud of Ghazni into the areas of modern-day Baluchistan, Sind, and Gujarat in search of the long reputed wealth of al-Hind (India), Arab traders had established contact with the coast of southern India and, in the context of commerce and trade, were successful in gaining converts.

Christianity Christianity is the third largest religious community in India, with 24,080,016 adherents, or approximately 2.3 percent of the population according to the 2001 census of India. The members of three major branches of the Christian tradition—Eastern Orthodox, Roman Catholic, and Protestant—are found throughout India. The largest Christian churches are the Roman Catholic Church, the Church of South India, the Malankara Syrian Orthodox Church, the Church of North India, the Council of Baptist Churches in Northeast India, the United Evangelical Lutheran Church in India, the Methodist Church in India, the New Apostolic Church, and the Samavesam of Telugu Baptist Churches. The majority of Christians in India are located primarily in the states of Kerela, Tamilnadu, and Andhra Pradesh.

The oldest ecclesiastical Christian tradition in the subcontinent is the Eastern Orthodox tradition, represented by the Indian Orthodox Church, the Orthodox Syrian Church of the East, the Armenian Apostolic Church, and the Chaldean Syrian Church. These traditions claim a historical connection to Saint Thomas, who established a church in India during the first century. However, the earliest attestation of Christians in southern India appears in the historical record only in the end of the second century CE. Roman Catholicism arrived in India with Vasco de Gama (1460–1524) in 1498. Catholic missionary activity by Franciscans and Dominicans was headquartered in Goa, a small town on the west coast of India, south of Mumbai. Protestant missionary activity in India began in 1706, with the arrival of German missionaries sent by the king of Denmark. They established the first Protestant congregation in Tharangampadi, in Tamil Nadu, south of Chennai. These early Protestant missionaries translated the Bible into Tamil. With the eventual arrival of more Western Protestant missionaries, the network of Protestant congregations expanded throughout India.

The importance of corporate worship in Christianity has remained a central element of the religious life of Indian Christians. However, Indian Christians have incorporated several linguistic and regional peculiarities that have given rise to authentic patterns of worship, liturgical practices, and church architecture that incorporate individual rituals, traditional rites of passage (*samsakaras*), and family ceremonies. Eastern Orthodox and Catholic traditions introduced the use of vernacular language for liturgy, the use of local musical traditions, and the adoption of Indian architectural styles in the construction of churches. While Protestant churches have been more cautious about incorporating local language and cultural practices into worship, they have also adapted the liturgy to traditional patterns

After fasting for Lent, a congregation of 1,000 Christians, carrying small crucifixes, follows the scene of Christ carrying the cross along the major paths of the city of Jabalpur, 2009. (Dr. Sandeep Jain/Dreamstime.com)

of worship in India: entry (*pravesha*), awakening (*prabodha*), remembering and offering (*smarana-samarpana*), sharing the Body and Blood of Christ (*darshana*), and blessing (*prashena/prasada*).

The religious life of Indian Christians is also informed by home-based religious practices, many of which have adapted traditional Hindu *samskaras* (rites of passage). Indian Christian weddings follow the same pattern as Hindu weddings, which includes a set of rituals to be observed as part of the pre-wedding sequence, marriage day, and post-wedding days. As in Hindu weddings, the *tilaka* (marks of auspiciousness) ceremony is performed as part of the pre-wedding day rituals in which tilakas are applied on the head of the bride and the groom in their respective homes, using *kumkum* and turmeric paste. The bride and relatives from both families are made to wear green glass bangles.

In addition to home-based worship, the community celebrates Christmas and Easter, as well as church anniversary festivals, which commemorate the consecration of the local or regional churches. Roman Catholic churches have incorporated elements of Hindu temple rituals and *puja*, including the procession of the statue of the Virgin Mary. Like Hindus crowding to get *darshan* (religious sight) of the consecrated image (*murti*) of the deity being brought to see devotees, Indian Christians gather around to gain grace from seeing the procession of the Virgin Mary.

The Bible has occupied an important place in the religious life of Indian Christians, but early on both the Orthodox Christians and Catholics paid less attention to the translation of the text than to the collected body of liturgical practices, incorporating the focus on orthopraxy that has always permeated the Hindu tradition. The translation of the Bible into the vernacular languages of India was primarily a concern of Protestant missionaries, who named their translation the Veda or Vedagma. Some missionaries referred to the Bible as the "fifth Veda," thus linking their sacred text to the antiquity and prestige of the Veda.

In the 20th century, there were several efforts to connect and unite the hundreds of different Christian communities throughout India. These efforts had some notable success, leading to the formation of the Church of South India (1947) and the Church of North India (1970), which brought together Anglicans, Presbyterians, Congregationalists, Brethren, British and Australian Methodists, and the Disciples of Christ. A number of the Lutheran groups formed the United Evangelical Church in India.

Islam   Today, Muslims form the second largest religious community in India, with some 138,188,240 adherents, or approximately 13.4 percent of the population, according to the 2001 census of India. Inspired by the universality of the message of the Koran, the early Muslim community based in Medina expanded and within 100 years Muslim armies had conquered substantial portions of the Iberian Peninsula, ancient Iraq, and Asia Minor. The first serious military incursion into South Asia took place in 711 CE, when the Umayyad governor of Iraq sent a military force into Sind as result of pirate attacks on Arab ships that passed near the mouth of the Indus River. With the decline and subsequent disintegration of the Abbasid Caliphate (ca. 750–1258), independent Muslim-dominated kingdoms were in competition with each other for territorial and economic gains. An independent Turkish Islamic kingdom was founded in 962 by a Samanid warrior slave, who seized the Afghan fortress of Ghazni. His grandson, Mahmud of Ghazni (971–1030), undertook a series of raids into Thanesar, Mathura, Kanauj, Nagarkot, and Somnath in modern-day Gujarat in search of wealth. By the time of his death, Mahmud had annexed the Punjab region into his empire. By 1175, Ghazni had fallen to Turk Ghurids under the leadership of Sultan Muhammad of Ghur (1162–1206). The Ghurids took Peshawar from the Ghaznavid forces in 1179, Lahore in 1189, and Delhi in 1193. The sultan left his lieutenant Qutb-ud-din Aybak (d. 1210) to consolidate control over North India with Delhi as the capital city and eventually founded the Sultanate of Delhi upon Muhammad of Ghur's death in 1206. The Sultanate expanded its territory through campaigns of suppression against the Hindu Rajput confederacy as well as through tactics of persuasion and tolerance. Shams-ud-din Iletmish (1211–1236) consolidated his power by winning the support of Turkish military bureaucrats by continuing the system of grants of revenue from landed areas as well as by extending the status of "protected People of the Book" (*dhimmi*) to all Hindus, leaving local Hindu rulers in control of their domain as long as they paid land revenue to the sultan's treasury.

In 1398, the Mongol conqueror Tamerlane (ca. 1336–1405) invaded northern India. Although he did not stay long, the plundering of the Punjab and the sacking of Delhi left the Sultanate in ruins and created a political vaccum that led to the fragmentation of a once powerful empire. In the aftermath of the Mongol invasion, two dynasties claimed control of the Delhi Sultanate, the Sayyids (1414–1451) and the Lodis (1451–1526). In 1526, Babur (1483–1530), Timur's great-grandson, seized Delhi and established the Mughal dynasty after defeating a Rajput confederacy under the banner of Rana Sanga (r. 1509–1528) in 1527 and the remnant force of Mahmud Lodi in 1529.

Upon his ascension to the throne, Babur's son Humanyu (1508–1556) faced opposition from his father's Afghan general, Sher Khan Sur. By 1540, Sher Khan had driven Humayun into Persia, and after declaring himself king proceeded to implement reforms of the revenue system and administrative appointments in order to consolidate imperial power, which would continue under the Mughal's upon Humanyun return to India in 1555.

Under Akbar (1542–1605), Muslim rule extended over most of the subcontinent. Akbar's policies hinged on his understanding of the pluralistic character of Indian society and the necessity of cooperation with Hindu chiefs and kingdoms in order to maintain a functional empire. He established political alliances with Hindu chiefs through marriage and also abolished the tax levied on Hindu pilgrims and the *jizya* tax levied on non-Muslims. Akbar included Muslims as well as individuals from other major ethnic, regional, and religious groups, incuding Hindus, as part of the various

Quawat, Islam mosque, Delhi, India. (Corel)

ranks of the *mansabdari* system of administration. Indeed, the second most powerful person in Akbar's administration, the minister of revenue (*diwan*), was Raja Todar Mal, a Hindu. Although king Akbar enforced Islamic law (*shariah*) as interpreted by learned scholars (*ulama*) and enforced by judges (*qazi*), at the local levels Hindu law (*dharma*) was applied and decisions of village *pañchayat* councils were generally accepted as final.

Akbar's general understanding of the pluralism and the necessity of religious tolerance continued under his son Jahangir (1569–1627) and his grandson Shah Jahan (1628–1658). However, the last great Mughal emperor, Aurangzeb (1618–1707), systematically undermined the attitude of religious tolerance that Akbar had implemented in the administration of the empire in favor of stricter enforcement of Islamic religious law. Aurangzeb appointed "censors for public morals" (*muhtasibs*) to assure that Islamic law was obeyed and that prayers (*salat/namaz*) were being performed. He outlawed Hindu religious festivals, denied

permits to build new Hindu temples, and reinstituted jizya in 1679.

The transmission of Islam into South Asia has not been limited to contact of the Native population with Muslim military forces. Indeed, another major conduit for Islam to the broader populations has been Sufism. Although not rejecting the straight path to God laid down in the Koran and systematized in the later schools of Islamic law, Sufis emphasize the internal, ecstatic communion with God motivated by pure love. The Sufi path (*tassawuf*) encapsulated in the poems of the great Sufi saints brim with a language of devotion that not only describes the ineffability of the divine but also provides the paradigmatic model of the devotee. The language of Sufi poetry resonated with the *bhakti*-focused traditions and literary works that similarly focused on the ecstatic experience of the deity achieved through loving devotion with the ultimate aim of communion with the divine. In popular practice, the tombs (*dargah*) of Sufi saints function as sites of popular Muslim religiosity that are understood as charged with superhuman power and charisma (*barakah*). Muslims, as well as Hindus, Sikhs, and Christians, share the understanding that such superhuman or divine power can be accessed through devotion in order to cure the sick or help women become pregnant.

The religious life of Muslims in India as elsewhere in the world is structured around the practices that express the core beliefs found in the Koran and clarified by the various schools of Islamic law. The five universal obligations to Allah serve to structure the life of Muslims: declaration of faith (*shahadah*), daily worship (*salat/namaz*), fasting during the holy month of Ramadan (*swam*), obligation to share wealth (*zakat*), and pilgrimage to Mecca (*hajj*). The commemoration of the martyrdom of Husayn, the Prophet's grandson, as well as the celebration of the birth and death of Sufi saints, is also an important aspect of Muslim religiosity in India. Of the four schools of Shariah, the Maliki and Hanafi schools have had significant adherents in India.

The advent of British hegemony in South Asia saw the developments of Muslim reform movements that promoted different visions of Islam and Muslim life. Muhammad Iqbal (ca. 1877–1983) envisioned the reformation of Muslim society on the basis of *ijtihad* (independent reasoning) as both a way to revive past ideals and to modernize Islam by bringing modern democratic ideals into Muslim life and soceity. Ahl-e Sunnat wa'l-Jama'ah (People of the Way and the Community), founded by Ahmad Riza Khan (d. 1921), sought to reform Islam by focusing on the life of the Prophet as a model of indiviual responsibility. The Muhammadan Anglo-Oriental College was founded by Sayyid Ahmad Khan (d. 1898) as an alternative for Indian Muslim students to the British schools or the Islamic *madrasahs* of the times. Sayyid Ahmad rejected some of the traditional subjects taught in the madrasahs as no longer relevant to society, but the Islamic orientation of education that was compatible with the rationalism that underpinned Western education and thus remained an essential feature of the college. For Sayyid, the Koran and Western science were inherently compatible.

The Ahmadiyya Muslim movement and the Ahmadiyya Anjuman Ishaat Islam Lahore, heirs of the 19th-century Muslim revival movement begun by Mirza Ghulam Hazrat Ahmad (1835–1908), were founded in India (in what is now Pakistan) and have gone on to become important international movements, though thought of as heretical by the majority of Muslims.

Judaism According to the 2001 census of India, 0.6 percent of the population is identified as belonging to "other religions and persuasion." Indian Jews are included among this statistically small group. Although visibly small in numbers, Jewish communities have been found in India perhaps as early as Saint Thomas's arrival to the subcontinent in 52 CE. A popular legend among Christian communities in Kerala tells how upon his arrival in India, Thomas encountered a young woman, who was a flute-player, "by race a Hebrew," among the participants in the wedding celebration of the local king. According to this popular story, the girl eventually converted to Christianity. Indian Jews belong to one of three communities located primarily in India, but also found in Burma: the Bene Israel, the Cochin Jews, and Baghdadi Jews. The number of these already small communities has shrunk over the centuries. In 1947, Indian Jews numbered approximately 23,000 but have steadily declined in numbers since.

The contact between local communities in India with Jews from the traditional territory of Israel is attested by linguistic evidence in the biblical book of Kings as well as tales told in the Talmud regarding trade with Hoddu (India). Documents from Egypt also indicate trade relations between the Near East and South Asia during the ninth century. Individual Indian Jewish communities maintain legendary accounts, tracing their origins back to biblical times.

The Bene Israel communities connect themselves through time to Israel as being members of the lost 10th tribe, who escaped persecution by their oppressors by sailing from Israel. The present community's ancestors were shipwrecked on the Konkan coast of Maharashtra and became part of the economic life of the community as oil pressers, known as *Sahnwar telis* (Saturday oil pressers), because they would not work on Saturday, the traditional Jewish Sabbath. Having lost their sacred books as well as the guidance of rabbis, they continued to recite the *Shema* (Deuteronomy 6:4), observe Jewish holidays and related fasts, and carry out the ritual of circumcision of newborn males. Over centuries, they have adopted Marathi as their mother tongue and have also incorporated Urdu, Persian, and Arabic words, especially those related to kingship and religion. They reincorporated the sacred text, the Hebrew Bible, primarily through the translation activities of Christian missionaries. By the 1840s Jewish prayer books had been translated into Marathi.

The community of Cochin Jews on the Malabar Coast of India is attested in a land grant to Syrian Christians in the mid-ninth century. Cochin Jews claim that the seed of their community arrived along with Saint Thomas in 52 CE. The community moved from Cranganore, known to medieval travelers as Shingly, to Cochin in present-day Kerala in 1344. Jewish traders that followed Vasco De Gama's arrival in the subcontinent eventually settled in Cochin and had established a synagogue by 1568. Because of their contact with Portuguese and Dutch Jews, Cochin Jews have used the standard Sephardic prayer books.

The third major group of Indian Jews consists of immigrants from Baghdad and other major centers of Iraq who arrived in the subcontinent beginning in the early 1700s and originally settled in Surat and later moved to Mumbai and Calcutta. Baghdadi Jews spoke Arabic from the time of their arrival in India, but eventually adopted English as their primary language, with little attempt to adopt native Indian languages, except for a working knowledge of Hindustani.

Indian Jews observe major Jewish festivals and commandments (*mitzvah*), reflecting the centrality of monotheism of Judaism. Among the Bene Israel, Rosh Hashanah, Yom Kippur, Simchat Torah, and Pesach are the most important festivals in which the entire community participates. Local Hindu traditions have influenced the religious life of all Indian Jews. In addition to celebrating major Jewish festivals and the traditional ritual of circumcision, Bene Israel Jews observe the hair-shaving ceremonies for newborns and also go on pilgrimages. They believe that the prophet Elijah (Eliyahoo Hannabi) departed on his chariot from the village of Khandall in Kondan, which has become an important pilgrimage center for them. During Sukkot, Cochin Jews decorate their *pandals* (*sukka*) with painted coconut leaves. The Simchat Torah celebrations have incorporated singing, handclapping, and dancing in local Shingli style as well as the partaking of alcoholic drinks and refreshments. Baghdadi Jews have incorporated a number of local practices meant to protect the life of a mother and newborn child by wearing garlands and hanging amulets on a newborn's bed, including garlic, nutmeg, and pinning the name of God onto the baby.

With the formation of the state of Israel in 1948, many Indian Jews left India to settle in Israel. Nearly 50,000 Bene Israel, the majority of Cochin Jews, and a few Baghdadi Jews live in Israel today. Small Jewish communities remain in India, but they continue to diminish in size as religious intermarriage continues to rise. As numbers continue to dwindle, fewer individuals can lead prayer services and establish the required quorum of 10 men (*minyan*). It has become more difficult to maintain a cohesive community, which has resulted in the neglect and closing of many synagogues. In 1979, the Council of Indian Jewry was established in order to represent the interests of the various small Jewish communities in India.

Other Religious Communities   Beyond the major world religions, there are a number of other religious traditions, ancient and modern, as well as religious movements that are found in contemporary India. Zoroastrians, or Parsis, as they are called in India, practice an ancient religion that served as the state religion under various Persian rulers, most notably Cyrus the Great (559–530 BCE). Zoroastrianism was dislodged from its prominent place in Persian culture and society as result of the conquests of Alexander the Great (356–323 BCE), whose successors suppressed the religion. It was re-established in the second century CE, but it was permanently displaced from traditional Persia as a result of the destruction of the Sassanid Empire by Muslims in the seventh century. Zoroastrianism survives in isolated regions of the world today, most prosperously in Mumbai, India, where there are approximately 200,000 adherents.

In the years since independence, numerous religious movements have emerged in India, including indigenous forms of older traditions. In addition to the numerous movements focused on a particular charismatic guru, there have been movements to unite the many independent Christian churches in India.

The Indian Constitution guarantees religious freedom for all religious groups, especially as they engage in purely religious affairs. The government operates on a principle of separation of religion and state affairs. It raises no money to support religion and does not allow religion to be included in the curriculum of state-supported schools. It is also a crime to promote enmity between groups based on religious prejudice. Although the Constitution provides a secular context for a religiously diverse society, old tensions have manifested in recent decades due to attempts to use the religious language and institutions for political purposes, especially in separatist movements.

Carlos Lopez

See also: Ahmadiyya Anjuman Ishaat Islam, Lahore; Ahmadiyya Movement in Islam; Bene Israel; Church of North India; Church of South India; Cochin Jews; Council of Baptist Churches in North East India; Dominicans; Eastern Orthodoxy; Franciscans; India, Contemporary Religion in: Asian Religions; India, Hinduism in: Ancient Vedic Expressions; India, Hinduism in: Medieval Period; India, Hinduism in: Modern Period; Malankara Orthodox Syrian Church; Mar Thoma Syrian Church of Malabar; Methodist Church in India; New Apostolic Church; Pesach; Pilgrimage; Ramadan; Roman Catholic Church; Rosh Hashanah; Samavesam of Telegu Baptists Churches; Sufism; Syrian Orthodox Church of Malabar; Syro-Malabar Catholic Church; Syro-Malankara Catholic Church; United Evangelical Lutheran Church in India; Yom Kippur; Zoroastrianism.

References

Ahmad, Imtiaz, and Helmut Reifeld. *Lived Islam in South Asia: Adaptation, Accommodation, and Conflict.* New Delhi: Social Science Press, 2004.

Baird, R. D. *Religion in Modern India.* 2nd ed. Delhi: Manohar Publications, 1989.

Bauman, Chad M. *Christian Identity and Dalit Religion in Hindu India, 1868–1947.* Grand Rapids, MI: William B. Eerdmans Publishing Company, 2008.

Hardy, F. *The Religious Culture of India: Power, Love, and Wisdom.* New York: Cambridge University Press, 1993.

Neill, S. C. *A History of Christianity in India.* 2 vols. Cambridge: Cambridge University Press, 1984–1985.

Young, Richard F. *India and the Indianness of Christianity: Essays on Understanding: Historical, Theological, and Bibliographical in Honor of Robert Eric Frykenberg.* Grand Rapids, MI: William B. Eerdmans Publishing Company, 2009.

■ India, Hinduism in: Ancient Vedic Expressions

The subcontinent/country of India is unique in a variety of ways. It is home to 1,166,100,000 people, making India the second largest country in the world, with slightly more than 17 percent of the world's population. Historically, a variety of kingdoms and dynasties have ruled different portions of the subcontinent—great and small. Definitively for the present, the British came to rule India in the 19th century and from their colonial state, the present countries of India, Pakistan, and Bangladesh were carved. The present state of India includes some 1,269,219 square miles of territory. Its lengthy southern shoreline bounds the Arabian Sea, the Indian Ocean, and the Bay of Bengal. Around its northern border is Pakistan, China, Nepal, and Myanmar. Bangladesh borders India on three sides.

India is also the home base to the religion we popularly call Hinduism. Though India has a substantial number of Muslims and Christians, and is home to the Sikh and Jain communities, 75 percent of the population are Hindus, almost 800,000,000 people. The Indian Hindu community is the source of the global Hindu community.

The formative stages of what we term Hinduism today occurred over several millennia and remain somewhat obscure due to a lack of written records. For the archaeological research and the few documents that have survived, the Hindu community can be seen as emerging through several distinctive periods discussed below as the Prehistoric, Vedic, and Classical. Later developments are discussed in a separate entry.

"Hinduism" is the relatively modern English term that designates the religious traditions and faith

Illustration depicting Alexander the Great (Iskandar) meeting the Brahmans, 1719. (The British Library/StockphotoPro)

practiced by the largest majority of people in South Asia, especially India, as well as sizable diaspora communities in Africa, Europe, and the United States. However, when the question "What is Hinduism?" is asked, one is led immediately into the problem of defining a Hindu, Hinduism, and religion. Historically, it is nearly impossible to pinpoint a set of essential markers, such as a creedal statement, a founder figure, a universally accepted set of authoritative texts, or a unified belief system, worldview, or cosmology by which Hinduism may be understood as a monolithic tradition. The term "Hinduism" as representing a world religion is itself problematic, because it is not a word from any of the indigenous languages of South Asia, including Sanskrit, Middle Indic languages (Pali, Ardhamagadhi, etc.), or modern Indo-Aryan languages (Bengali, Gu-

jarati, Hindi, etc.), that means "religion." Hinduism is the name given to a collection of beliefs, practices, and traditions by outsiders. This modern term was formed by adding the suffix -ism to the base word hindu, which was adopted into European languages from the Persian translation for the name of the largest and most prominent river in Northwest India, the Indus (Sanskrit: Sindhu, Pali: Hindu). By 1050, Muslims referred to the land beyond the Indus as al-Hind and to the people who lived there, who were not "People of the Book," as Hindus. For European traders and missionaries of the 17th century, "Hindu" came to signify both the people and the range of religious traditions, practices, and beliefs of persons who did not self-identify as Christians, Jains, Jews, Muslims, or Sikhs. As such, Hinduism does not designate a fixed creed, unified set of ritual traditions, institutional form, or group of exclusive practitioners or believers. Religious identity in South Asia has been traditionally affirmed with reference to multiple markers, such as doctrinal belief, sectarian affiliation (Vaishanava, Shaiva, Shakta), ritual practices, occupations, personal and religious lineage (parampara), ancestral village, and birth groups (varna, jati). Thus, from the beginning of its usage by Europeans, the term "Hinduism" has had a tangled history. One can think of "Hinduism" as an umbrella term that refers to particular configurations of linguistic, literary, anthropological, and archaeological evidence. The various traditions that are included under the term "Hinduism" share several characteristics, none of which can be considered as being essential, including the acceptance of the sacred status and authority of the Veda, its authoritative transmitters and interpreters, the Brahmans, and the body of ritual traditions contained therein.

One way to study Hinduism historically is by examining the textual and archaeological evidence, which spans a period of nearly 3,000 years. For the earliest period, the evidence consists of materials found in archaeological assemblages, including bricks, pottery, standardized weights, and inscriptional evidence. Beyond archaeological evidence, which is virtually lacking from ca. 1200 to 500 BCE, the bulk of the evidence for the history of Hinduism is textual. Although the texts cannot be accurately dated, their language, content, and other internal evidence have led to a relative linguistic chronology of Hindu texts that helps to ground the historical study of the tradition. The linguistic chronology overlaps with the Hindu understanding of the traditional chronology of the sacred texts. Most scholars divide the history of Hinduism into five periods: the prehistoric period (prehistory–1500 BCE), the Vedic period (ca. 1500–200 BCE), the classical period (ca. 400 BCE–600 CE), the medieval period (ca. 600–1600 CE), and the modern period (ca. 1600–present). The latter are treated in separate entries in this encyclopedia, "India, Hinduism in: Medieval Period," and "India, Hinduism in: Modern Period."

Prehistoric Period (prehistory–1500 BCE)   The earliest advanced civilization known from archaeological evidence in South Asia is the Indus Valley civilization, or the Harappan civilization. This urban civilization flourished from ca. 2800 to 1300 BCE in the western part of South Asia and extended approximately 386,000 square miles throughout present-day Afghanistan, Iran, Pakistan, and India. The Indus civilization is characterized by sophisticated city planning, a system of water delivery and waste removal, granaries, a common weight system, and the use of writing. Although there is clear evidence of a system of writing, the language encoded in the Indus script remains unknown, and without access to the language, a reconstruction of the religion of the Indus must be deduced from material culture that has been excavated.

Excavations of Indus sites have yielded a large number of terra-cotta figurines that suggest parallels to mother goddess cults in Baluchistan, the Northwest Frontier Territory, and the Aegean area. Many of these figurines are female, as can be concluded from the exaggerated breasts and thighs, in addition to elaborate headdresses. These features suggest that one aspect of the religion of the Indus Valley was a concern for fertility. These figurines have been found throughout the various levels of excavation, which also suggests that goddess worship was a constant and popular feature in the Indus region. In addition to a mother goddess cult, there is evidence for a cult of a great male god. The evidence for this male deity comes primarily from a number of steatite seals, which also provide evidence of writing. The best known of these seals, identified by Ernest J. Mackay as seal #420, depicts a male figure

seated in a pose that is similar to the lotus position that is used in the modern practice of yoga. This male figure wears a headdress with buffalo horns. In other similar seals, it also appears that the male figure has three faces or is wearing a three-faced mask. In some seals, the figure, possibly ithyphallic, is sometimes seated on a raised platform and often surrounded by animals, including an elephant, rhinoceros, water buffalo, and tiger.

These artistic motifs have led scholars to propose that this Indus figure might be an early representation of the Hindu god Shiva, who was known in the Rig Veda by the name Rudra. In this earliest Hindu text, one of Rudra's epithets is "the lord of animals" (*pashupati*). In the later classical texts and images of Shiva, he is regularly depicted as seated in the lotus position, clearly engaged in meditative activity. He is regularly called "the great meditator" (*mahayogi*), which draws attention to Shiva's intimate connection with asceticism, meditation, and the practice of yoga. The epithet *sadashiva* underscores the various dimensions of Shiva's personality, which is artistically represented in sculpture and painting by Shiva's multiple faces or heads. Finally, Shiva's natural manifestation is the *linga*, a cylindrical shaft that often sits on a pedestal called the *yoni* (womb). Symbolically, the linga is said to represent two aspects of Shiva: eroticism and the potentiality for procreation on the one hand, and the ascetic, world-renouncing dimension, which is exemplified by sexual restraint.

Despite the numerous terra-cotta goddess figurines and seals depicting a great male god, there has been little else excavated that sheds light on the public dimension of Indus religion. There are no structures excavated that may be said to have a clear religious function, except perhaps the Great Bath of Mohenjo-daro. It is a large tank, with steps at the north end that descend into the tank. No other similar structures have been excavated at other Indus sites. The presence of steps going down into the tank suggests that it was probably used for ritual bathing by people who had access to the upper city. The ritual function of the structure may be also supported by the presence of bathing rooms on the eastern side of the building housing the tank.

It is possible to read many of these Indus artifacts as representing a point of origin for many important

The Great Bath at Mohenjo-Daro, third to second millenium BCE. (J. M. Kenoyer, Courtesy Dept. of Archaeology and Museums, Government of Pakistan)

religious concepts, practices, and deities of Hinduism. However, many scholars have questioned such readings as perhaps expressing an unsupported assumption of cultural continuity. Regardless of the exact nature of Indus religion and religiosity, the archaeological record suggests that the Indus civilization came to an end sometime around 1500–1000 BCE. How a civilization as expansive and complex as the Indus suddenly comes to end has been a question that has preoccupied scholars since the discovery of the earliest Indus sites. Hypotheses about the demise of the Indus civilization have been shaped by later Hindu religious texts, as well as contemporaneous political ideologies. The earliest proposal for the demise of the Indus was the result of reading the archaeological evidence in light of the Rig Veda. Several hymns of the Rig Veda depict a struggle between a group of speakers of Sanskrit, who refer to themselves as noble ones (*arya*), and the *dasu/ dasyus*, who are often described in the texts as being dark-skinned, having large noses, and constantly being defeated in battle by the arya with the help of the great Vedic god Indra. The so-called Aryan Invasion Theory proposes that the Indus civilization and its people were wiped out by the invading arya, who were nomadic, cattle-raiding warriors. The horse-driven chariot, which was a significant component of their civilization, came to be understood as providing the technological superiority that made it possible for the Indus civilization to be wiped out. Beyond the textual evidence, there is no archaeological evidence of an invasion. Contemporary scholars of the Indus civilization have come to understand the late phase of the Indus civilization as a period of cultural transformation resulting from several forces, one of which was the influence of migrating populations, possibly of Indo-Aryan speakers, as may be indicated by Painted Gray Ware pottery found in the region.

Vedic Period (ca. 1500–200 BCE) Literary as well as some archaeological evidence from outside and inside of South Asia suggests the immigration of a new group of people into the northwest regions of South Asia. These newcomers have been identified as the composers and transmitters of the Vedas and the dominant culture in South Asia for the next two millennia. The "racial" character of the arya composers of the Veda is uncertain at best, but they spoke a language that was different from that of the Indus civilization. Vedic or Vedic Sanskrit belongs to the Indo-Iranian branch of the Indo-European language family, which includes the majority of the languages spoken in Europe, Central Asia, the Iranian Plateau, and northern parts of the Indian subcontinent. The genetic relationship of these languages has been established through the analysis of phonology, morphology, syntax, and lexical items that show a common linguistic structure that has only been reshaped by the study of sound changes/phonological developments. The question of the homeland of the arya remains a disputed one among archaeologists, linguists, and scholars of South Asian religions. However, it is clear from the large body of primarily religious literature found in South Asia from ca. 1200 BCE on that their social and religious ideologies became dominant, probably absorbing much of the previously existing culture, as can be seen from a large number of non-Sanskrit words in the Rig Veda.

The texts produced by these new immigrants into the subcontinent are called the Veda. The word *veda*, cognate with Greek *(w)oida*, English *wit*, and German *Wissen*, reflects the character of these texts as containing sacred knowledge. The Veda consists of poetry dedicated to the various deities, ritual injunctions, and prose explanations of various religious rituals. The post-Vedic, medieval Hindu tradition characterizes the Veda as *shruti* ("that which has been heard"), which is considered to be eternal, to have no human author, and to have been originally heard by the ancient seers (*rishis*), who preserved and transmitted them. Shruti is distinguished from *smriti* ("that which is remembered"), a genre of authoritative religious texts that have been composed by human authors.

The Veda consists of four separate collections—Rig, Sama-, Yajur-, and Atharva—characterized by the type of material and its usage in the classical Vedic rituals. Each Vedic collection is further subdivided into four sections—Samhita, Brahmana, Aranyaka, and Upanishad. The Samhita is the oldest section of each collection, consisting primarily of poems used in the performance of rituals. The Brahmanas present a type of exegetical commentary on the poetic formulas, or *mantras*, used in ritual activity. The Aranyakas, which stylistically are very much like the Brahmanas, focus on more secret and dangerous rituals that must be learned, recited, and performed in the wilderness (*aranya*) outside the village along with their more sophisticated, cosmic interpretations. The last section of each Veda, the Upanishads, continues to apply the same method of ritual exegesis as the Brahmanas and Aranyakas in order to set out the hidden connection between the cosmos, ritual, and the individual human being. The Upanishads are also called Vedanta ("the end of the Veda") as they stand at a moment of transition between the archaic ritual-based religion of the Veda and the new religious ideas and institutions that characterize Hinduism. The Vedic texts were transmitted and preserved orally by ritual schools (*shakhas*) for a long period before they were written down.

The Rig Veda Samhita is the oldest and most authoritative text of the Hindu tradition. It is a collection of 1,028 hymns composed by various clans of poets, which have been arranged into 10 books. The hymns praising the various Vedic deities were used in religious rituals, which included the kindling and worship of the sacred fire (*Agni*), preparation of a special drink called *soma*, and specific rituals such as the horse sacrifice, and domestic rituals, including marriage and death rites. The Sama Veda contains a collection of chants (*samans*), primarily verses from the Rig Veda that have been set to melody, which are sung during the soma ritual. The Yajur Veda is the largest of the four Vedic collections and consists of mantras called *yajus*, which were recited during rituals. The Atharva Veda, the fourth Veda, is distinguished from the other three Vedas mainly in terms of content. It largely represents the popular side of Vedic culture and religion and contains spells for healing illness, the removal of demons, love-spells, speculative hymns about cosmic forces, as well as material relevant to domestic rituals, such as marriage, initiation, and death. Unlike the other three Vedas, its content is not directly relevant to shrauta rituals.

Like all dates in ancient India, the date of the Rig Veda is by no means certain, but linguistic and internal evidence suggests that the text was composed ca. 1200–1000 BCE. The date of iron in South Asia (ca. 1000–900 BCE) helps to narrow down the date, since the Rig Veda mentions only metal or yellow metal (copper), as opposed to the Atharva Veda, which speaks about the black metal (iron). In addition, the Mitanni texts of Syria and Iraq (ca. 1450–1350 BCE) specifically mention the names of the most important Vedic deities (Indra, Mitra, Ashvins, and Varuna) as part of the treaty between a Hittite king and a Mitanni king. It also includes a manual on chariot horses by a Mitannian named Kikkuli, which contains many Indo-Aryan technical terms about horse training.

The hymns of the Rig Veda presume a complex mythological system that provides the context for the other Vedas, as well as later Hindu texts. It mentions several gods, many of whom belong to chronologically distinct groups or generations. The Sadhyas and Vishvadevas are distinguished from the Adityas, the younger generation of gods who are the focus of praise in the Rig Veda. The Adityas are counted as seven (sometimes eight) gods that in part represent important Vedic social and religious concepts, including tribal agreements (Mitra), arya-hood (Aryaman), luck (Bhaga), and lot (Amsha). The generational difference is also seen in the division of gods (*devas*) and *asuras*, the latter title often applied to gods that belong to the pre-Aditya generation, such as Varuna. In the Vedic text, the asuras slowly morph into a group of beings who stand in permanent opposition to the devas, and by Epics and Puranas are understood to be the demonic enemies of the gods. Among the 33 gods of the Rig Veda, the majority are male deities, with only few goddesses mentioned, including Ushas (dawn) and her sister, Ratri (night). The most important gods are Agni and Indra, to whom the majority of hymns are dedicated. Varuna, Mitra, Surya, Vishnu, Rudra, the Maruts, and the twin gods, the Ashvins, also play important roles in Vedic mythology.

Agni is the personification of the sacred ritual fire, which is the most important feature of the Vedic religion. As the ritual fire and the priest of the gods, Agni is the intermediary between the human world and the heavenly, divine sphere. He transports offerings to the gods, who consume the trans-substantiated offering in the form of smoke or aroma (*medha*). Indra, the king of the gods, plays a major role in the cosmogony of the Rig Veda and ranks second in importance only to Agni. It is Indra who separates heaven and earth, releases the dawns from the cave (*vala*), and frees the life-giving waters being held back by Vritra, the demonic power of chaos against the ordering power of the gods. Indra is able to carry out his demiurgic activity through the invigorating power of soma, which is both a deity and a plant/drink. Soma, extracted by means of pressing stones and mixed with milk, is said to have an intoxicating and exhilarating effect that stimulated the ancestors (*pitris*) to ritual activity and confers immortality on gods and men. Like Indra, Varuna is also regularly referred to as king of the gods. However, whereas Indra represents the martial or royal dimension of kingship, Varuna is primarily connected with the moral sphere as the god who looks down upon people to see if they are acting out truth (*satya*), and are not actively engaging in deceit (*druh*). He is intimately connected with *rita*, the active moral-cosmic force of truth according to which the cosmos properly operates.

Although Vishnu is one the most important deities in the Hindu tradition, in the Vedas he plays a minor role, primarily as Indra's charioteer and helper in his battle with Vritra. His independent act in the mythology of the Vedas is as the god who takes three wide steps with which he measures out triple world (*trivikrama*). In the Rig Veda, the universe is conceived as consisting of three levels—Earth, the middle space/atmosphere, and the heavens. In taking these three wide strides, Vishnu traces and encompasses the totality of the universe. His first stride covers the Earth, the second stride traces the middle region between the heavens and Earth, and his final step encompasses the heavens and everything beyond.

Like Vishnu, Rudra, who is called Shiva in post-Vedic texts, is also one of the major gods of the Hindu tradition whose role in Vedic mythology starts out small and slowly expands. Rudra, whose name is probably connected with the howling storm, is often depicted as an ambivalent deity. He is praised as a healer and remover of infirmity while simultaneously being asked not to harm the poet, his family, and cattle. Hymns to the Vedic gods generally consist of explicit praise of their great deeds followed by a request for the standard Vedic wishes: wealth in the form of cattle, long life/immortality, progeny (especially sons), and fame. However, hymns dedicated to Rudra do not follow this paradigm, and instead ask Rudra not to be angry and to direct the effect of his anger toward others. Poetic material dedicated to Rudra in later Vedic texts attempt to change the character of this god by attributing a number of epithets that highlight the benevolent side of his personality, including Shiva ("friendly one"), Maheshvara ("great lord"), and Shankara ("the maker of happiness").

Compared to their importance in the later Hinduism, the few goddesses mentioned in the Rig Veda seem relatively unimportant and anthropomorphically underdeveloped in the mythology and religion of the Veda. There are very few hymns dedicated to goddesses. Goddesses primarily represent natural or abstract concepts, such as Ushas (dawn), Ratri (night), Vac (sacred speech), and Shraddha (confident intention in the efficacy of ritual; faith). The goddess who receives most hymns in the Rig Veda is Ushas, the dawn, whose appearance announces the coming of the Sun, a new day, and the possibility of life.

Unlike the majority of hymns of the Rig Veda, which are primarily dedicated to the gods and focus on praise of their deeds, the hymns in the 10th book focus on speculation about the source and nature of the universe. Rig Veda 10.129, the famous Nasadiya Hymn, sets out a series of questions about the source of the universe. "Neither existence nor non-existence was there at that time" (10.129.1). The hymn goes on to deconstruct the possibility of anyone knowing "that" which was at the beginning before the duality of being and non-being. It culminates with the denial that even the overseer of the cosmos might know "that."

The well-known Purusha Hymn (10.90) provides an insight into the ritual ideology of the Vedas as well as a glimpse in the sociological dimension of Vedic religion. The universe is said to have arisen from the ritual dismemberment of *purusha*, a man of infinite size, who encompasses the universe on all sides. In the beginning, there was only purusha, who was so immense that only one-quarter of him constitutes all being. We are told that the gods, the Sadhyas, and the rishis offered a sacrifice with purusha as the oblation,

and from that sacrifice the entire ordered universe came into being; his eye became the sun, his mind the moon, his breath the wind, from his head came the heavens, and from his feet the Earth. The Veda itself was one of the first products of this sacrifice. The four classes (varnas) of human beings came from different parts of his body: the Brahmans, the priestly class from his mouth, warriors (Kshatriyas) from his arms, the agriculturalists and merchants (Vaishyas) from his thighs, and the Shudras, the class that supports the other three, came from his feet. The importance of this hymn for understanding Vedic religion as well as the later Hindu tradition is enshrined in the last verse: "The gods sacrificed with the sacrifice to the sacrifice. These were the first rites. These powers reached heaven, where the ancient Sadhyas and the gods are located" (10.90.16). Not only is ritual the source of the universe and human society, but it is the means by which the gods attained heaven and immortality. The implication is that without access to ritual, immortality is not possible. Thus, the gods were themselves mortal before reaching heaven by means of ritual.

The central practice of the Vedic religion was sacrifice. The Vedas show a complex system of ritual practices carried out by priests on behalf of the sponsor of the sacrificer (*yajamana*) and his wife. Each Veda contains liturgical material that is necessary for these sacrifices, each performed by a priest that specializes in one particular Veda. Thus, at minimum, any sacrifice required a priest from each of the Vedas. Sacrifices were divided into two broad categories, sacred (*shrauta*) rituals and domestic (*grihya*) rituals. Shrauta rituals required three sacred fires: the householder's domestic fire (*garhapatyagni*), the southern fire (*dakshinagni*), and the offering fire (*ahavaniyagni*). These sacred fires were lit by a man who was qualified to take on the responsibility of become a yajamana. First, he must be a member of one of the three upper social classes (varnas), who has undergone the traditional education in the Veda. Second, upon completion of his Vedic education and only after having married, could he opt to establish his sacred fires, which he was then obligated to maintain through regularly offering sacrifices for the rest of his life.

There are two general types of shrauta rituals, *haviryajñas*, which involved offerings of milk products into the sacred fires, and *somayajñas*, which involved the main offering of soma. Animal sacrifice, which was a normal part of the Vedic ritual system, is considered a haviryajña. Vedic sacrifices vary in complexity and duration. Sacrifices were carried out by priests employed by the yajamana, who were paid a sacrificial fee. Although the yajamana did not play an active role in the ritual performance, the Vedas expressly state that the benefits produced by the sacrifice are accrued by the sacrificer and his wife. Domestic rituals only require one sacred fire, usually the yajamana's home fire, which was established at the time of the marriage ceremony. Domestic rituals are performed to mark points in the life of an individual that must be ritually established, such as Vedic initiation (*upanayana*), marriage, and funerary rites.

It is in the exegesis of the sacrifice that the texts give further details about the religious concepts and themes central to the religion of the Veda. The performance of sacrifice had several aims. Certainly, the performance of a complex and expensive ritual like the Agnicayana, which lasted 12 days and required 17 priests, would produce for the sponsor of the sacrifice a great deal of social and political currency in terms of prestige. The texts also speak about the cosmic and soteriological dimensions of sacrificial activity.

The cosmic dimension of Vedic ritual may be understood in terms of the relationship between humans and the gods mediated by ritual. In ritual, human beings make offerings of food to the gods, which are trans-substantiated by the sacrificial fire into two components, aroma (*medha*) and life force (*asu*). The gods consume the aroma. In return, they give back rain, which makes life and the ritual cycle possible. The texts often say that human beings offer sacrifices because the gods have no food in heaven. Sacrifice also involves offerings to the departed ancestors (*pitris*) of the yajamana, who like the gods have no food in heaven, and must be kept alive, lest they should fall back to Earth. In return, the ancestors give back progeny to the sacrificer. The ritual exegetes also understand a third cycle of exchange in which human poets offer praise to the prototypical ancient poets (*rishis*), who in return provide renewed inspiration for the composition of new poetry.

Vedic exegetes also understood the sacrifice to have a soteriological function. As the hymns of the Rig Veda make clear, the poet hopes to live a long life (*ayus*), to the ideal age of 100. Upon death, the wish expressed in all Vedic texts is that one will be immortal in the place one's wishes are fulfilled. That place is called by different names: home, the highest heaven, and the place of the ancestors and Yama, the first mortal who found the way to the heavenly abode. Immortality is conceived as a permanent stay in that world, where one does not die, which is achieved through the accumulation of merit that results from the correct performance of sacrifices. It is by means of accumulated ritual merit that the yajamana constituted his new heavenly body. Eternal life in heaven, unencumbered by death, was conceived in terms of a body that was sustained by the continuing ritual activity of subsequent generations of the yajamana's descendants.

The belief in immortality as a permanent condition is found throughout the Vedic texts alongside competing ideas about the nature of the afterlife. The Brahmanas speak about the second death (*punarmrtyu*) and the ritual means to avoid it. Although the texts are not explicit about what the second death entails, the contexts in which this concept is discussed suggest that the second death was understood to take place in the heavens. Since the texts state that the way to avoid it is by the correct knowledge of ritual, the implication must be that the result of the second death must also lead to the situation in which rituals can be performed, which must be as a human being rather than a departed ancestor in heaven. By the time of the Upanishads, punarmrtyu has disappeared from the discussions about the afterlife and the new concept of rebirth (often popularly called reincarnation) has entered the soteriological vocabulary of Vedic thinkers.

The Upanishads, the last section of each Veda collection, were composed ca. 800–300 BCE. Like the Brahmanas and Aranyakas, the Upanishads continue the tradition of exegesis whose aim was to understand the meaning of sacrifice. They focus on the correct understanding of the hidden correspondences or identities (*bandhu*, *upanishad*) whose knowledge was necessary for the ritual to be efficacious. This method of exegesis of the Brahmanas aimed to establish the hidden identity between the elements of sacrifice and their cosmic counterparts. The Upanishads take this analysis one step further to elucidate the secret correspondences between the sphere of ritual (adhyayajna) and the macrocosm (adhidevata), and expand it to include the connection to the individual person (adhyatma). It is the search for the three-way identity between macrocosm, mesocosm, and microcosm that drives the speculative exegesis of the Upanishads.

The Upanishads introduce new perspectives on all questions regarding Vedic rituals. Upanishadic discussions about ritual take place in various contexts, including debates among priests, which occasionally include women debaters (Gargi), debates between kings and priests, and discussions between Vedic teachers and their students. Specific teachings are often attributed to various well-known teachers, especially Yajñavalkya, or a famous king, such as King Janaka. It is in the context of ritual discussions that the Upanishads address broader questions about the nature and origin of the universe, the nature of human beings, the body, death, and the afterlife, and introduce new doctrines such as rebirth, transmigration, karma, and moksha.

Whereas the picture in the older Vedic texts is of a permanent blissful afterlife, the Upanishads introduce the belief that immortality in the heavenly world is temporary and eventually leads to rebirth. Rebirth is described primarily in biological and ecological terms, in which after an unspecified period of time, the person falls back down to Earth as rain and eventually re-enters the ecological food chain. He eventually becomes the food consumed by a man, which eventually becomes his semen, and is reborn in the womb of his wife. The idea that immortality was limited only by the amount of one's accumulated ritual merit is taken to its logical conclusion: immortality achieved by ritual was not real. Immortality is only truly achieved by the knowledge of brahman, which leads to the world of the gods, which is said to be beyond samsara, the cycle of birth, death, and rebirth.

The triumph of rebirth ideology over the older notion of a permanent, blissful heavenly existence occurs at the same time as the concept of sacrificial action (karma) is being reconceived. The older concept of ritual action and its effect (immortality) was already being questioned in the conceptualization of punarmrtyu, "the repeated death," which had to be prevented in order to attain an immortal heavenly existence. The effects of actions beyond ritual were also being questioned in the Brahmanas. The violent killing of animals, which was required in sacrifice, came to be understood to lead to an afterlife in which human beings became the sacrificial victims of the sacrificial animals that they killed in sacrifice. Anxiety about the afterlife and the effects of killing led to the conception of an inverted afterlife in which the sacrificer became the sacrificed. It is in this context that Yajñavalkya introduces a new understanding of karma that becomes central to Hinduism. All actions (karma), not simply ritual actions, have automatic, inescapable results that affect not only one's present situation but also one's next rebirth. Although the Upanishads do not present a systematic exposition of karma and rebirth, they introduce the new concepts that are elaborated into a consistent theory of retribution and rebirth in later Hindu narratives, as well as by schools of Indian philosophy.

In dealing with the search of the threefold secret identity that links macrocosm, mesocosm (the sphere of ritual), and microcosm, the Upanishads focus on two concepts as the secret correspondence par excellence, namely brahman and atman. In the Rig Veda, brahman means both formulation of truth and the power that is activated by that formulation. By the time of the Upanishads, it comes to represent not only the essential identity among all things, but the ultimate source of all seeming diversity. All things are ultimately reducible to that is which real, brahman. Brahman is both the top of the hierarchical chain of being and foundation of the chain. Yajñavalkya calls it the imperishable, which is beyond conceptualization and which makes the ritual efficacious. Brahman emerges as the hidden ritual identity that must be known and without which all sacrifices are unproductive. Thus, the Upanishads raise knowledge of the ultimate ritual identity, brahman, beyond ritual itself: it is knowledge of brahman that ultimately leads to the highest goal, moksha, release from the cycle of birth, death, and rebirth and complete freedom from conditionality.

In addressing the question of the secret ritual identity from the point of view of the individual person, the

Upanishads systematically deconstruct the human person into the various vital powers (*prana*) of the body (breathing, thinking, seeing, hearing, and speaking) only to conclude that upon which all vital powers depended and with which they are identical is the self (atman). The atman is identical with the vital functions of the body, but is none of the individual vital functions, and as such is the ultimate source of the human person. The highest teachings of the Upanishads establish knowledge of the identity of brahman and atman as the efficacious, liberating knowledge that leads to freedom from rebirth, conditionality, and suffering. They distinguish ritual knowledge from knowledge of brahman and atman and attribute the latter to those who dwell in the wilderness and have renounced Vedic sacrificial activity through the internalization of ritual.

Carlos Lopez

See also: India, Contemporary Religion in: Asian Religions; India, Contemporary Religion in: Middle Eastern Religions; India, Hinduism in: Classical Period; India, Hinduism in: Medieval Period; India, Hinduism in: Modern Period; Jainism; Meditation; Pilgrimage; Sikhism/Sant Mat; Temples—Hindu; Women, Status and Role of; Yoga.

References
General
Doniger, Wendy. *The Hindus: An Alternative History.* New York: Penguin Press, 2009.

Flood, Gavin, ed. *The Blackwell Companion to Hinduism.* Oxford: Blackwell, 2003.

Lorenzen, David N. *Who Invented Hinduism?: Essays in Religion in History.* Delhi. Yoda Press, 2006.

Michaels, Axel. *Hinduism: Past and Present.* Princeton, NJ: Princeton University Press, 2004.

Mittal, Sushil, and Gene Thursby, eds. *The Hindu World.* New York: Routledge, 2004.

Mittal, Sushil, and Gene Thursby, eds. *Studying Hinduism: Key Concepts and Methods.* London and New York: Routledge, 2008.

Sharma, Arvind, ed. *The Study of Hinduism.* Columbia: University of South Carolina Press, 2003.

Wolpert, Stanley A. *A New History of India.* 8th ed. New York: Oxford University Press, 2009.

Prehistoric
Allchin, F. Raymond. *The Archaeology of Early Historic South Asia: The Emergence of Cities and States.* Cambridge: Cambridge University Press, 1995.

Bryant, Edwin. *The Quest for the Origins of Vedic Culture: The Indo-Aryan Migration Debate.* Oxford; New York: Oxford University Press, 2001.

Kenoyer, Jonathan M. *Ancient Cities of the Indus Valley Civilization.* Karachi and New York: Oxford University Press; Islamabad: American Institute of Pakistan Studies, 1998.

Possehl, Gregory L. *The Indus Civilization: A Contemporary Perspective.* Walnut Creek, CA: Altamira Press, 2002.

Vedic Period
Bodewtiz, H. H., *The Daily Evening and Morning Offering (Agnihotra) according to the Brahmanas.* Leiden: Brill, 1976.

Cohen, Signe. *Text and Authority in the Older Upanishads.* Leiden: Brill, 2008.

Jaminson, Stephanie. *Sacrificed Wife/Sacrificer's Wife: Women, Ritual, and Hospitality in Ancient India.* New York: Oxford University Press, 1996.

Jamison, Stephanie, and Michael Witzel. "Vedic Hinduism." In *The Study of Hinduism,* edited by A. Sharma. Columbia: University of South Carolina Press, 2003.

Macdonell, Arthur A. *Vedic Mythology.* Strassburg, K. J. Trübner, 1897.

Smith, Brian K. *Reflections on Resemblance, Ritual, and Religion.* Delhi: Motilal Banarsidass, 1989.

Staal, Frits, ed. *Agni: The Vedic Ritual of the Fire Altar.* Berkeley, CA: Asian Humanities Press, 1983.

■ India, Hinduism in: Classical Period

The classical period (ca. 500 BCE–600 CE) of Indian Hinduism was marked by transition from the religion of the Veda to a form of Hinduism based on the worship of various new deities that displaced the great Vedic deities, sectarian affiliations with new forms and expression of worship, and new philosophical/theological systems.

The Upanishads, the youngest layer of Vedic texts, the Vedanta, not only introduce new ideas but, when read in their historical and social context, show internal developments and changes with Vedic religion or Vedism. The term "Vedism" is used by scholars to show both the continuities and discontinuities between the ancient religion of the Vedas and the classical Hinduism of the Puranas. The transition from the ritual-based traditional religion of the Veda to the classical Hinduism of worship of various new deities based on new sacred stories that displace the great Vedic deities (Indra, Varuna, Mitra), sectarian affiliations with new forms and expressions of worship (*puja*, temple building, chanting of *bhajans*, pilgrimage), and new philosophical/theological systems that reach back to the Veda for their intellectual foundation can be seen in the religious text composed in the classical period—the great Indian epics, the Ramayana and the Mahabharata, and in the vast body of literature that expound *dharma*. These texts document how the sacrificial system of the Vedas, rather than being eliminated, was re-imagined under the overarching principle of dharma. At the same time that ritualism was transformed into an ideology that encompassed both ritual and moral behavior, the epics show the integration of new ideologies with the religious ideas that had become firmly established, such as *atman*, *brahman*, *karma*, *moksha*, rebirth, and *samsara*.

By the third century BCE, the Vedic concept of dharma had been expanded from its limited connection in the Veda as specific ordinances and sacrifices that supported and continually maintained the cosmic order (*rita*), the regulative principle of the natural and cosmic order. Dharma was reformulated as the all-encompassing cosmic ordering principle, whose scope extended beyond sacrificial and ritual activity but embraced all socio-cultural practices as being inseparable from the cosmic order. Dharma emerged as the central topic of religious discourse in the two great Indian epics, the Mahabharata and Ramayana, and in the four principal genres of literature on dharma—Dharma Sutras (ca. third to first centuries BCE), Dharma Shastras (ca. first to ninth centuries), the body commentarial literature (beginning ca. ninth century), and later

A scene from a printed version of the Mahabharata, an epic collection of mythological tales based on Hindu spiritual beliefs. (Apurva Patel and Marketa George)

Nibandhas (beginning ca. 12th century), digests that collected and topically organized extracts from various sources on dharma. This body of literature, which expounds the complexities of dharma and its application, although religiously authoritative, is not considered *shruti*. *Smriti* texts are understood to have been produced by human agency and as such represent a genre of knowledge that includes Vedic teachings and practices of dharma that have been lost or forgotten.

The two great Indian epics, the Ramayana and the Mahabharata, although technically not revealed texts are believed to have been divinely inspired and as such are considered as authorities only to relative lesser degree than the Veda. In the daily lives of Hindus, these two narratives play a far more important role than the Veda, which most people have neither learned nor studied. The encyclopedic nature of the epics, especially the Mahabharata, has gained them the status of "fifth Veda." It is primarily through the narratives about the heroes and heroines and the many interspersed stories linked to the main story line from which, as children, Hindus learn about the nature of dharma—social and religious duty, morals and ethics.

The Ramayana (ca. 750–500 BCE) is the shorter of these two great narratives, consisting of approximately 50,000 verses and attributed to the sage Valmiki. As its name reflects, the main story is about the life and adventures of Rama, the young prince who is heir to the throne of King Dasharatha of Ayodhya. The night before Rama's consecration as king, Rama, joined by this wife Sita and his brother Lakshmana, voluntarily goes into exile as a result of a royal promise his father, King Dasharatha, had made to his youngest wife, Kaikeyi. As a result of the machination of Rama's old nurse maid, Manthara, Kaikeyi became afraid that under Rama's rule her son Bharata would be mistreated. She demands fulfillment of the royal promise, which, as king, Dasharatha is unable to refuse. She insists that Rama be exiled for 14 years and that her son Bharata be consecrated as king. Bharata has no desire to rule and tells Rama that he will rule only in his stead until he returns from exile. Bound by his word, Dasharatha accedes and eventually dies of a broken heart, after having banished his beloved son. Knowing the dharma of a king and the importance of the king's word, Rama accepts his banishment. While in exile, the demon king Ravana becomes enamored by Sita and abducts her. This key event sets up the rest of the story; in order to return to Ayodhya and reclaim his rightful place as king, Rama must regain Sita. On the way to Lanka, the island home of Ravana, Rama and Lakshmana gather not only allies, including King Sugriva and his commander, Hanuman, but also obtain divine knowledge and weapons. After battling Ravana's armies and laying siege to Lanka, Rama eventually defeats Ravana in combat, regains Sita, and returns to Ayodhya to reclaim his rightful place as king. Upon their return, the people express serious misgivings about Sita's chastity and purity during her forcible stay in Lanka. In order to placate his subjects and consolidate his kingship, Rama asks Sita to undergo a test of fire, which she successfully completes, thus publicly establishing her chastity and purity. However, rumors of her potential misconduct while in Lanka return again and, as king, Rama is obliged to banish Sita, who unbeknownst to him is pregnant with twin sons. While in exile, Sita meets the sage Valmiki, who takes her to his forest hermitage (*ashram*) where eventually she gives birth to Kush and Lavana. Shortly thereafter, after Sita returns to Ayodhya for the completion of Rama's Ashvamedha (horse sacrifice), she implores her mother, the Earth, to take her back into herself.

At its core, the Ramayana expounds the complexity of dharma, especially as it applies to the connection of the well-being of the world and the fulfillment of the king's dharmic duties. The main characters of the narrative—Rama, Sita, Lakshman, Hanuman, Kausalya, Dasharatha—embody social and moral ideals in the Hindu tradition. Rama, the star of the epic, is depicted as the ideal male human being, whose very actions are continually praised as proper dharma, even in cases in which his actions may appear to be dubious (shooting Valin from behind, banishment of Sita, etc.). His decisions and actions encapsulate the dharma of a son, husband, brother, friend, warrior, and especially ruler/king. Together with Sita, he is part of the paradigmatic married couple. Sita is portrayed as the ideal, devoted wife who obeys and follows her husband through all perils and refuses to break her oath of marriage, even at the expense of her own life. At the same time, Sita is also depicted as a strong-willed and wise woman who is skilled in the subtleties of dharma, especially when she presents a nearly unimpeachable argument to her husband as to why it is her duty to follow him into exile, although Rama does not wish her to go. Hanuman, Rama's faithful friend, represents the ideal devotee, who is said to have Rama and Sita enshrined in his heart.

The power and significance of the Rama story has given birth to numerous versions of the retellings, each reflecting literary attempts to address problematic aspects of the characters and story as understood in changing religious, political, and economic contexts. Next to Valmiki's Ramayana, the most well-known re-telling includes Tulsida's (ca. 1570) Ramacarita in Hindi, Kampan's (ca. 1100) Iramavataram in Tamil, and Adhyatma Ramayana in Sanskrit, which is part of the Brahmananda Purana (ca. fourth century BCE to fifth century CE).

The Mahabharata (ca. 400 BCE–400 CE) attributed to the legendary author Vyasa, whose name means "the editor," is the longest extant poem in the world, consisting of 100,000 stanzas in its critical edition. Like the Ramayana, it is a compendium of dharma. The text refers to itself as "the fifth Veda" and expounds its encyclopedic application with the declaration that whatever is not found in the Mahabharata is not to be found elsewhere. The main story line concerns the struggle for succession to the throne of the Kuru dynasty between two sets of cousins, the Pandavas and the Kauravas. While on a hunting trip, King Pandu is cursed by a *gandharva*, after having killed him and his lover while they were making love in the form of gazelles. The childless Pandu is cursed to die if he should ever enjoy the pleasure of love-making with his wives, Kunti and Maitri. Kunti reveals that she knows a sacred mantra that allows her to call upon any god to father a child while maintaining her virginity. Pandu asks Kunti to call on the gods Dharma, Vayu, and Indra, to father respectively, Yudhishthira, Bhima, and Arjuna. Using Kunti's mantra, Maitri calls upon the twin gods, the Ashvins, and gives birth to the twins Nakula and Sahadeva. The five princes are collectively known as the Pandavas. Meanwhile, with the help of his uncle, the sage Vyasa, Pandu's elder brother Dhritarashtra, who was born blind and thus was unable to become king, and his wife Gandhari obtained 100 children known as the Kauravas, the eldest being Duryodhana.

After Pandu's death, Dhritarashtra becomes king, with the explicit understanding that Yudhishthira would inherit the throne. However, as the main plot unfolds, the audience witnesses the repeated attempts of the Kauravas, led by Duryodhana, to usurp and even kill the Pandavas. The enmity of the Kauravas toward the Pandavas reaches its height during Yudhishthira's royal coronation ceremony. Part of the coronation ritual for the king involves a dice game in which the soon-to-be king plays and defeats his adversary. Duryodhana asks his uncle Shakuni, who is well known for his skills at playing dice, to play against Yudhishthira in his stead. As the match progresses, Yudhishthira loses every throw of the dice until he has lost all his possessions. He then wagers his brothers Nakula, Sahadeva, Arjuna, and Bhima and also loses them to Shakuni. After having wagered and lost himself, he wagers Draupadi, the Pandavas' common wife, who had been wedded to Arjuna, but who became their common wife as result of Arjuna honoring Kunti's command to share all things he may have obtained with his brothers. Draupadi is forced to appear in front of the participants, even though she is in seclusion associated with her menstrual period. Like Sita, Draupadi questions the dharmic status of being wagered by Yudhishthira after he had already lost himself. After much debate, King Dhritarashtra resolves the conflict by restoring all property to Yudhishthira. After the Pandavas had left the ceremony, Duryodhana challenges Yudhishthira to one last throw of the dice. The loser and his family

would go into exile for 12 years followed by an additional year, which had to be spent incognito, and if they were discovered the entire cycle of 13 years would be repeated. Upon completion of the exile period, their rightful portion of the kingdom would be restored. Yudhishthira loses the dice game and together with his brothers and wife is forced into exile.

Upon their return from exile, Dhritarashtra, manipulated by Duryodhana, refuses to restore the Pandavas' kingdom. The great war of 18 days follows, in which subsequently all Kauravas and nearly all descendants of the Pandavas are annihilated. After restoring the world as the rightful king, son of dharma, Yudhishthira hands the kingdom to Parikshit, grandson of Arjuna and only surviving descendant of the Pandavas, and together with his brothers and their wife Draupadi depart toward Indra's heaven.

Perhaps the best known episode of the Mahabharata is the Bhagavad Gita, a text that has acquired a life of its own independent of its epic context because it encapsulates many of the central religious concepts of the Hindu tradition. It consists of a dialogue between Arjuna and Krishna, his charioteer, best friend, and the incarnation (*avatara*) of god about dharma, the nature of action (karma), and the transformation and the liberation of the self (atman) from the cycle of birth, death, and rebirth (samsara). In its epic context, the Bhagavad Gita addresses Arjuna's paralyzing despair at the thought of engaging in a dharmically justified battle, in which he will have to kill his kinsmen and thus destroy the family, which according to dharma must be protected. From Arjuna's perspective, he is caught in a no win situation: if he does not engage in battle, he is neglecting dharma as a warrior, and if he engages in battle, he must kill his kinsmen, which goes against family dharma. The 18 chapters of the Bhagavad Gita are Krishna's attempts to persuade Arjuna to engage his sacred duty as a warrior by contextualizing the actions (karma) that Arjuna must undertake within the larger religious context. Krishna expounds the nature of karma (actions and their consequences) in terms of not only duty but also in terms of Vedic sacrifice and the cosmic necessity to act. He simultaneously situates karma within the Upanishadic context of discriminating knowledge of the nature of the body, the self (atman) and brahman, and renunciation.

Illustration from the 17th century, depicting a scene from the epic Hindu poem "Mahabharata" with the hero Arjuna in a carriage behind Krishna, who is mounted on a horse. (The British Museum/Jupiterimages)

Krishna tells Arjuna that the self is eternal and indestructible. He advises Arjuna that the way to overcome his paralyzing despair is by engaging in action through disciplined devotion (*bhakti*), by performing all necessary acts as a sacrifice to Krishna. Throughout the often repetitive dialogue, Krishna integrates the moksha-perspective of the Upanishads, with its focus on knowledge and liberation, to the world-affirming orientation of dharma-based duties with its focus on society, family, and responsibility of daily life, which is the inherited perspective of the Vedic ritualists. The Bhagavad Gita presents its teachings in terms of three seemingly distinct paths (*marga*) or disciplines (*yoga*): the path of action (*karma yoga*), the path of discriminating knowledge (*jñana yoga*), and the path of devotion (*bhakti yoga*). In addition, these paths are integrated with the growing importance in Vedic thought of devotion (bhakti) to a transcendent, personal deity as a way to transcend the effects of action (karma) and attain salvation (moksha).

Dharma became a topic of specialization among scholar-Brahmans and led to the production of a body of literature elaborating the content of dharma—such as religious duties according to social class (*varna*) and caste (*jati*), stages of life (*ashrama*), dietary rules, expiations for transgressions, and the duties of the king —in a more systematic manner. In the discourse of dharma, duty according to social class (*varnadharma*) is understood as an expression of the cosmic order in the human, social sphere. Society, as depicted in the Dharma sutras and Dharma shastras, is one that is hierarchically stratified and understood to be linked to the creation of the cosmos. The nature of human society is found in Rig Veda 10.90, the famous Purusha

Sukta, where the four classes of human beings—but also the cosmic elements, gods, animals, and plants—are understood to emerge from the various parts of the body of *purusha*, the cosmic person. The origin of each social class from a distinct part of the body of purusha establishes the hierarchic distinction of the members of the four classes. Brahmans, who originate first from the mouth, the highest part of the body of Purusha, are invested with brahman (power of poetic formulation) and are the keepers of the Veda, who as scholar-teachers preserve and transmit the eternal truth of dharma. The warriors (Kshatriya) are the protectors of the people and overseers of government, who by the exercise of military and political power establish the conditions in which dharma operates by virtue of being identical with the power and might derived from the arms of Purusha. Originating from the thighs of Purusha, the merchants and agriculturalists (Vaishyas) represent the power of creativity, fertility, and productivity that they carry out as agriculturalists, merchants, and artisans. Being identical with the lowest part of the body of Purusha—the dharmic duty of the Shudras—the fourth and lowest class is to serve and support the upper three varnas.

In addition to the hierarchy of varna, which is understood in the Veda to be part of the very fabric of the cosmos, the Dharma sutras and Dharma shastras expound dharma in terms of another important system of social hierarchy known as jati, or caste. Jatis cannot be historically found in the Vedic texts, but Manava Dharma Shastra (ca. first century BCE to second century BCE), the oldest Dharma Shastra, popularly known as Manu, attributes the origin of various jatis to intermarriage between various varnas. The term "jati," literally meaning "birth," is usually translated as caste, which reflects Portuguese 14th-century travelers' understanding of the social hierarchy in India as being similar to the Portuguese and Spanish *castas*, meaning chaste, which referred to the system of social stratification along racial groups in Spanish colonies. The use of the English term "caste" with a racial tone is present from 1555 on. Hindus are born into a caste and remain a member of the group until death. As such caste groups are ascriptive in nature and endogamy tends to be a feature of caste, although hypergamous marriage is also quite normal. In part, caste reflects a traditional division of labor, especially along religious lines, such as barbers and potters. However, in the context of the modern society, all occupations are theoretically caste-free. Caste grouping are found everywhere in India, although ranking will vary from region to region. In both varna and caste systems, Brahmans are at the top of the hierarchy, while *dalits*, or untouchables, who perform the most polluting tasks, are excluded from the varna system.

The opposition between purity and pollution is an operative principle in the hierarchy of castes. Pollution is understood to be a quality of the body that is transferable, especially through bodily substance, which must be controlled and kept at bay in order to maintain one's relative purity in relation to another group. Purity and pollution can be most vividly observed in the commensal interaction among different caste groups in which the relatively superior rank of groups is expressed in terms of the distribution and acceptance of food. By accepting food and the inherent pollution that is absorbed by the food, a group concedes its relatively inferior status. Superior status is established in relation to the caste groups that will accept one's food, which implies one's relative high status in relation to them.

In addition to varna, dharma is elaborated in terms of system of stages (*ashrama*) of an individual's life, traditionally counted as student (*Brahmacarin*), householder (*Grihastha*), forest-dweller (*Vanapratha*), and renunciant. The system of ashramas as alternative ways of life for a twice-born man, a male of the upper three varnas, has its foundation in the Veda, where originally each ashrama was an independent, alternative life way. After completing his period of Vedic study under the tutelage of a qualified teacher, a man could enter any of the three subsequent ashramas or could optionally choose to remain a lifelong celibate student. The earliest formulation of the ashrama system as a theological construct in which the four ashramas are conceived in a sequential manner to be undertaken in succession over the course of a lifetime is found in Manu. In this model, each quarter of a man's life is identified with each of the successive ashramas. It is the duty of a father to make arrangement for his son to study the Veda and rite of initiation (*upanayana*), at which time he goes to live in the home of his teacher.

During his period of study, the student remained celibate and undertook the daily recitation of the Veda, daily ritual oblations to the gods, *rishis*, and ancestors, daily rounds of begging for alms, and various ritual vows. Upon the completion of his Vedic education, the young man enters the second stage, the householder, which is marked by marriage, the establishment of the ritual fire, and performance of the five great sacrifices (*mahayajñas*)—the recitation of the Veda to Brahman, offerings of food and water to the ancestors, offerings in the sacred fire to the gods, hospitality rituals for human guests, and *bali* offerings of food to *bhutas* (semi-divine beings). According to Manu, when his skin has become wrinkled and his hair has turned gray, and when he has fulfilled his obligations as a householder, he may retire with his wife to the wilderness outside the village to continue his ritual obligations to the sacred fires. The forest-dweller continues to maintain the ritual fires, performs the five daily sacrifices, and in addition undertakes increasingly severe ascetic practices that include wearing wet clothes during winter, sitting around five fires in the summer, and eating only flowers, roots, and vegetables. Through his performance of dharma and engagement in new ascetic practices, he prepares for the attainment of moksha, while still connected to the social world.

The final ashrama, the renunciant stage, is referred to by various terms in smriti literature, including *parivrajika* (wanderer) and *sannyasa* (renouncer). Only after having fulfilled his three primordial debts to the gods, rishis, and ancestors, may he divest himself of the vestiges that connected him to dharma—hut, wife, food, and ritual fires. Giving up these, the renunciant is now beyond all social responsibilities, beyond dharma, and his only obligation is the pursuit of moksha. As a renunciant or wandering acetic, he never settles in one place and subsists by begging for alms. According to Manu, the renunciant channels all his energy on controlling his body and mind through the practice of breath control and the restraint and eventual withdrawal of the senses. By achieving complete awareness of body and mind, the renunciant aims to realize the identity of the individual self (atman) and brahman and achieve liberation from samsara.

Sex and gender is implicit in the discourse on dharma. Like Shudras, women are made into a social "other" by their exclusion from upanayana and the study of the Veda; as such they are not really *dvijas*, since they are not reborn in the Veda. Although it is clear from the earliest Vedic texts on that a sacrificer must be married in order to carry out any ritual duties, women do not have the qualifications to independently sponsor any *shrauta* ritual. This ambivalence is reflected in Manu's well-known dictum that women must never be independent and must always be guarded by a man: her father guards her in childhood, her husband guards her in youth, and her son guards her in old age. These texts, which regard women as the source of all auspiciousness, express the concern for guarding a woman's inherent power from misuse or abuse. Her highest duty is to serve her husband as lord, which will lead her to heaven. However, smriti literature, although agreeing on the generally subservient status of women, also present different points of view regarding women's independence at it relates to women's property.

Carlos Lopez

See also: Hinduism; India, Contemporary Religion in: Asian Religions; India, Contemporary Religion in: Middle Eastern Religions; India, Hinduism in, Ancient Vedic Expressions; India, Hinduism in: Medieval Period; India, Hinduism in: Modern Period; Jainism; Meditation; Pilgrimage; Temples—Hindu; Women, Status and Role of; Yoga.

References

General

Doniger, Wendy. *The Hindus: An Alternative History*. New York: Penguin Press, 2009.

Flood, Gavin, ed. *The Blackwell Companion to Hinduism*. Oxford: Blackwell, 2003.

Lorenzen, David N. *Who Invented Hinduism?: Essays in Religion in History*. Delhi. Yoda Press, 2006.

Michaels, Axel. *Hinduism: Past and Present*. Princeton: Princeton University Press, 2004.

Mittal, Sushil, and Gene Thursby, eds. *The Hindu World*. New York: Routledge, 2004.

Mittal, Sushil, and Gene Thursby, eds. *Studying Hinduism: Key Concepts and Methods*. London and New York: Routledge, 2008.

Sharma, Arvind, ed. *The Study of Hinduism*. Columbia: University of South Carolina Press, 2003.

Wolpert, Stanley A. *A New History of India*. 8th ed. New York: Oxford University Press, 2009.

Classical Period

Hiltebeitel, Alf. *Rethinking the Mahabharata: A Reader's Guide to the Education of the Dharma King*. Chicago: University of Chicago Press, 2001.

Leslie, Julia. *Authority and Meaning in Indian Religions: Hinduism and the Case of Valmiki*. Aldershot, Hants, England, and Burlington, VT: Ashgate, 2003.

Olivelle, Patrick. *The Ashrama System: The History and Hermeneutics of a Religious Institution*. Oxford: Oxford University Press, 1993.

Phillips, Stephen H. *Yoga, Karma, and Rebirth: A Brief History and Philosophy*. New York: Columbia University Press, 2009.

Richman, Paula, ed. *Ramayana Stories in Modern South India: An Anthology*. Bloomington: Indiana University Press, 2008.

■ India, Hinduism in: Medieval Period

From the third through the sixth centuries CE, most of India was united in the Gupta Empire, a regime marked by the supportive environment given to art, culture, and intellectual endeavors. With the disintegration of the empire through the sixth century, India was divided into a variety of smaller kingdoms. The subcontinent then faced a significant discontinuity with the invasions of the Muslims, especially in the 11th through the 13th centuries. With the establishment of the first Delhi Sultanate by the Mamluk dynasty (1206–1290), Muslim regimes would come to rule the largely Hindu population, especially in northern India. In 1526, the Sultanate would be succeeded by the Mughal Empire, which remained in place until the arrival of the British. The Mughal came to rule most of the Indian subcontinent by the early 18th century, but would be brought to an end in the mid-19th century.

The emergence of the Muslims to power would have significant consequences religiously, including the disappearance of Buddhism, the founding of Sikhism (and the later Sant mat movement), and in the 20th

A section of the Sri Bhagavata Purana. (The British Museum/StockphotoPro)

century, the opting out of independent India by many Muslims who would found the modern states of Pakistan and Bangladesh. Beginning in the 18th century, Hinduism's forward trajectory was greatly affected by India's being targeted by Christian missionary activity, the Christian missionary movement receiving significant support by the British colonial establishment in the 19th century.

The massive political, economic, and social changes in Hinduism in India through the medieval period (ca. 600–1600) are reflected in the complex body of narrative literature produced during this period, which contain law codes, prescriptions for worship and pilgrimage, cosmogonic narratives, and stories and genealogies about gods and kings. This highly heterogeneous body of *smriti* are known as *Puranas*, literally "ancient stories." The Puranas' self-understanding and authority in the tradition is derived from the Veda, with the latter understood as *shabdhapradhan* (that whose chief concern is sound), while the Puranas are *arthashabda* (that whose chief concern is meaning). The authorship of the Puranas is attributed to the sage Vyasa.

As a genre, purana encompasses everything from the Veda to the epics, including old stories that were told but not collected in the Veda. Indeed, some Puranas claim that they were created earlier than the Vedas, while the Bhagavata Purana (ninth to 13th centuries) clearly states that the Brahma, the creator, spoke the Veda first and the Puranas followed. The Puranas usually list 18 great puranas (*mahapuranas*) and another list of 18 minor puranas (*upapuranas*). The mahapuranas include Agni, Bhagavata, Bhavishya, Brahma, Brahmanda, Brahmavaivarta, Garuda, Kurma, Linga, Matsya, Markandeya, Narada, Padma, Vishnu, Varaha, Vamana, Vayu, Shiva and Skanda. The heterogeneity of the material contained in these texts, some of which was collected during the Gupta period (ca. 320–500 CE), but which includes much older material, makes the dating of these texts nearly impossible. Although in some sense the Puranas are a type of catch-all, the narratives present a set of themes and concepts that are central to the understanding of the Hindu tradition, in particular, the narratives about the nature of the cosmos and the various *devas* of the Hindu tradition.

The various narratives about the gods and goddesses and their deeds are presented in the Puranas within an established cosmogonic and cosmological framework. The universe is conceived as uncreated, beginningless, and eternal, but undergoes periodic cycles of dissolution and re-constitution or secondary creation. The cosmic cycle of dissolution and re-creation underpins the texts' understanding of time as simultaneously cyclical and linear. One system of time in the Puranas is the *yuga* system. The cyclical cosmic process is understood to consist of four ages or yugas, each cycle's duration being progressively shorter than the previous one. The yugas are named for the throws of dice: Krita (1,728,000 human years), Dvapara (1,296,000), Treta (864,000), and Kali (432,000). A *mahayuga*—a cycle of four yugas—ends in cosmic dissolution (*pralaya*), which is followed by another

mahayuga cycle. The cosmic process and time are also intimately connected to *dharma*. The progressive decline of the virtue of human beings and the well being of the world is a feature of each subsequent yuga. Thus, each yuga is understood in moral terms, with Krta Yuga representing the height of ideal time when dharma is universally upheld. The Kali Yuga, the present age of the world, is conceived as the lowest point of dharma, in which society is turned upside down, where Brahmans act like Shudras and Shudras attain kingship.

The cosmic framework of the Puranas is also conceived in terms of the activity of the three great deities, the *trimurti*, Brahma, Vishnu, and Shiva. Brahma, the grandfather, creates the universe at the beginning of each yuga, which is then maintained by Vishnu's activity, and is destroyed at the end of the yuga by Shiva. The classic images depicting the cosmic process show Vishnu lying on the giant serpent Shesha, literally "the remnant," floating on the cosmic ocean. From Vishnu's navel grows a lotus flower upon which Brahma sits, distinguished by his four faces and often holding the Vedas, the first product of creation. In the famous relief at the Durga Temple at Deoghar (ca. 425 CE), Shiva, mounted on his animal vehicle (*vahana*), the bull Nandi, is depicted next to Brahma.

In addition to the influence of Sanskrit-based tradition, Hinduism in the medieval period was shaped through the religious sentiments expressed in vernacular religious literatures from other parts of the subcontinent, especially from South India. The songs and poems especially of Tamil poet-saints—the Vaishnava Alvars, the Shaivite Nayanars, and the yoga-centered Siddhas—have influenced the flavor of devotionalism (*bhakti*) in Hinduism. These bhakti poets not only composed stressing the centrality of god's grace for salvation, but also criticized the privileged position of orthodox Brahmans. This criticism often extended to both Brahmanic ritual practices as well as attacks on traditional social ideology of *varnashramadharma*.

The Puranas also contain the narratives that form the core of the religions of Vishnu (Vaishnavism), Shiva (Shaivism), and the Goddess (Shaktiism), as well as other prominent deities of the pan-India Hindu pantheon including Ganesha, Skanda, and Hanuman. As such, the Puranas reflect the crystallization of a long period in the rise in popularity of these gods and their respective cults.

The systematic development of Hindu thought can be traced to the metaphysical speculation of the Rig Veda, which asks about the source of the cosmos, as well as the systematic inquiry into the meaning of sacrifice found in the Brahmanas and Upanishads. Over several hundred years, *darshanas*, or "ways of seeing," emerged out of the speculative context of the Vedic tradition through exegesis of various foundational texts. Darshanas are systems of metaphysical speculation that address many of the same questions that Western philosophy undertake, but they are also concerned with systematic understanding of the nature of the divine. Thus, each darshana represents the history of speculation that encompasses epistemology, metaphysics, ethics, social customs, aesthetics, psychology, cosmology, grammar, logic, and speculation about language, which include both the orthodox (*astika*) Hindu darshanas as well as the heterodox (*nastika*) system of Jainism, Buddhism, and the Lokayata (materialists). All schools of philosophical/theological thought in South Asia are primarily exegetical traditions that systematically develop through commentaries and sub-commentaries that elucidate the school's founding text and subsequent explanations. The founding text is generally a *sutra* text, which is the first systematic presentation of key concepts usually found in the Veda. Sutras are short, pithy, terse formulations that attempt to express the essence of the system and generally are difficult to decipher without the additional explanations provided by commentaries. Historically, the various systems of Hindu thought started around the same time and developed in constant engagement and criticism of one another. This can be seen in the common technique of argumentation that all schools use to elaborate their arguments. At the outset of the argument, the opponent's view (*purvapaksha*) is stated, followed by critical assessment of the opponent's view (*khandana*), and after providing a digest of the objections to the purvapaksha by rival darshanas, the demonstrated conclusion (*siddhanta*) against the purvapaksha is presented.

There are five basic religious presuppositions that underpin Hindu darshanas: the reality of the self (*atman*), dharma, *karma*, liberation (*moksha*), and the means to achieve it (*sadhana*). Beyond these presuppositions, there is a common epistemological framework shared by all schools: the knowing subject (*pramata*), the object which is to be known (*prameya*), and the process of knowing (*pramiti*). There are six means of valid knowledge (*pramana*): perception (*pratyaksha*); inference (*anumana*); authoritative testimony (*shabda*); analogy (*upamana*); presumption (*arthapatiti*); and proof of non-existence (*abhava*). The means of valid knowledge accepted by any of the six orthodox schools of Hindu thought will depend on the types of knowledge that they recognize.

The term *nyaya* is derived from the Sanskrit verb meaning "to go" and the verbal prefix *ni-*, "back, into," meaning that by which one is led back (to a conclusion). Thus, the focus of the Nyaya School is primarily epistemological: how do we know something based on a valid means of knowledge—perception, inference, and authoritative testimony. Like the Vaisheshika School, Nyaya's ontological standpoint is one of pluralistic realism, which is grounded in its procedures for establishing correct inference. In Indian philosophical debates, there are two types of inference: *svarthanuma* (inference aimed at convincing oneself) and *pararthanumana* (inference aimed at convincing another). It is the latter type that plays a crucial role in a debate that aims at discerning the real nature of what is being investigated and imparting that truth to another party. The aim of debate is to establish the correct application of inference that is required to help the listener in redirecting the thought process in the proper manner. The standard Nyaya five-pronged proof is the method that all Hindu and non-Hindu schools of thought employ. Inferential proof requires: (1) premise; (2) cause or reason (*hetu*); (3) example; (4) application of the example; and (5) conclusion. Within this framework, there is a constant burden of establishing another particular example and application. The emphasis on particularity leads to an argument that moves from one particular case to another particular case through a generalized, universal statement. Nyaya arguments were concerned with the soundness of the argument based on its relevance to the lived experience. The founding text of the Nyaya School is the Nyaya Sutra of Gautama (ca. 400–100

BCE), which seems to have undergone several redactions, since in its present form it incorporates material from earlier manuals and an awareness of Buddhist philosophy of Emptiness (*shunyata*), as well as Nagarjuna's (ca. 150–250 CE) critique of pramana-theory.

Vaisheshika gets its name from the term *vishesha*, "particularity," a characteristic that distinguishes one thing from all other things. The main concern of this school of thought is to categorize nature in terms of fundamental categories. The ontological perspective of the Vaisheshika School is essentially pluralistic and atomistic; there is a plurality of real existents that are eternally related but not identical. There are nine fundamental substances: five material substances (earth, water, fire, air, and ether/space) and four non-material substances (time, space/direction, self, and mind). All material objects are made up of atoms (*paramanu*). There are many distinct selves (atman), which are distinguished only by their relative and specific visheshas, but each atman is eternal and unbound, even to space and time. The self is the substance of the quality of consciousness, which as witness and knower to experience must be different from matter, consciousness, sensations, and mind. Liberation is achieved when atman attains a state of complete qualitylessness. Vaisheshika accepts only two valid means of knowledge: perception and inference. The Veda is a valid source of knowledge, which is understood to be based on perception, and ritual injunctions contained therein are equally valid because they are based on inference. The founding text of the tradition is the Vaisheshika Sutra of Kanada (ca. 500–300 BCE) and its earliest commentary is the Padarthadharmasamgraha ("The compendium of the nature of fundamental categories") by Prashastapada (ca. 400 CE).

Samkhya is the oldest systematic school of thought in the Hindu tradition, whose key ideas are found in the Rig Veda and the Upanishads. The term *samkhya*, "enumeration," informs us about the central focus of this school: the enumeration and classification for the purpose of discriminating between spirit (*purusha*) and primal matter (*prakriti*) in order to attain liberation (*kaivalya*). Samkhya is a radically dualistic school that distinguishes between two distinct ontologically real entities, purusha and prakriti, which are understood to be distinct and eternally entangled. Purusha is pure consciousness, unmediated and unlimited, whose presence is the effective cause of the evolutionary process that gives rise to *budhi* or *mahat* (mind) and subsequently to *ahankara*, literally the "I-maker" or ego-consciousness. Prakriti is non-conscious and everchanging. In the presence of purusha, it transforms and evolves into a manifested state through a series of 25 categories of reality, which comprise the world of experience. Prakriti is understood to consist of three qualities (*gunas*)—*sattva* (luminosity and intelligence), *rajas* (energy and activity), and *tamas* (darkness and inertia). It is through the discrimination of these individual psycho-philosophical categories and cosmological categories from the eternally free and unbound purusha that liberation is attained. The non-discriminating identification of purusha with prakriti, as ahankara, is bondage, which can only be shattered through discriminating knowledge. The foundational text of the Samkhya School is the Samkhyakarika of Ishvarakarna (350–500 CE).

Yoga refers both to the practical method for unifying consciousness and to a systematic exposition of the basic principles presented within a framework that adopts the dualistic metaphysical system of Samkhya and frames liberation in terms of the fluctuations, modification, and modulations of the mind (*citta*) that interrupt pure consciousness. In the Yoga Sutra of Patañjali (third century BCE), the basic principles of yoga were first systematically presented. Citta is identical with Samkhya's *manas*, the first manifestation of prakriti, which is the cause of differentiation. The cessation of all change means that citta is merged back into prakriti, which is termination of the false connection and identity of purusha as seer and prakriti as the seen. The five fluctuations of the mind—valid knowledge, misconception, conceptualization, sleep, and memory—may be inhibited through the cultivation of detachment. In Yoga, citta encompasses Samkhya's buddhi, manas, and ahankara and is both the cause and means of escape from bondage. Citta is understood to arise from *asmita* (i-am-ness), the self-consciousness that experiences and as such its eradication is necessary for liberation. Yoga stresses the radical disconnect between the self that experiences and the true self (purusha), which is in every sense other than asmita but is the point where purusha and prakriti become entangled.

The school of Mimamsa or Purva Mimamsa (earlier investigation) is primarily a tradition of exegesis concerned with the understanding of Vedic ritual injunctions. For Jaimini (ca. 200 BCE), author of the Purva Mimamsa Sutra, the founding text of the school, Vedic injunctions reveal dharma, the proper order of the cosmos. The correct performance of sacrifices produces a transcendent unseen result (apurva), which leads to the particular result of sacrifice. Apurva is the metaphysical link between the ritual act and its result and is inherently connected to the verbal force of the ritual command (vidhi), rather than to the actor, the action, or the result. The particular goal of performing sacrifices is heaven (svarga) rather than moksha. For Mimamsikas, dharma is unknowable outside of Vedic injunctions, which states what is to be done and what is not to be done. The efficacy of the injunction is not located in the intention of an actor but resides in the imperative verbal form of the injunction, which is manifested as an attitude (bhavana) of the actor. Jaimini accepts authoritative testimony (shabda) as the only means of knowledge that is infallible in relation to the unseen effect (apurva). There are two branches of Purva Mimamsa named after their respective founders, Kumarila Bhatta (seventh century) and his contemporary, Prabhakara.

Perhaps the best known school of Hindu thought by Westerners is Vedanta, which has had significant influence on the various ritual and theological tradition, sampradayas, and late 19th-century Hindu movements that re-imagined and aimed to re-model society based on a purified form of Hinduism. Vedanta literally means the "end of the Veda" and refers in particular to the Upanishads, which stand as the last section of each Vedic collection. The school of Vedanta understands the Upanishads to contain the essential truth of the Veda. The foundational text of the school is the Vedanta Sutra or Brahma Sutra of Badarayana (ca. 400 BCE). Like Jaimini, Badarayana understood the Veda as the primary means of knowledge. However, unlike Jaimini, whose sutra opens with an inquiry into dharma (atho dharmajijñasa), Badarayana's main focus is the nature of brahman as the essential human pursuit (athato brahmajijñasa). The two schools together focus on the two major themes in the Veda: dharma, the realm of sacrificial performance that leads the qualified sacrifice to the ultimate goal (heaven) and brahman, the object of ultimate transformative knowledge that leads to liberation (moksha) from the cycle of birth and rebirth (samsara), which is the primary concern of the qualified renouncer. In both cases, qualifications are determined by the orthopraxic tradition of the Veda, which takes into account the centrality of the study of the Veda. There are several sub-schools of Vedanta that are unified by the acceptance of the primacy of the Veda (especially the Upanishads), Badarayana's sutras and the Bhagavad Gita, although there are some disagreements as to the number of authoritative Upanishads. The three most important traditions are Advaita (non-dualism) founded by Shankara (ca. 788–820), Dvaita (dualism) by Madhva (1199–1531), and Vishishtadvaita (qualified non-dualism) by Ramanuja (ca. 1027–1147).

The foundational text of the Advaita sub-school of Vedanta is the earliest surviving commentary of the Vedanta Sutra, Shankara's Brahma Sutra Bhashya. Shankara takes an epistemological stance by which he critiques human knowledge as inherently faulty. All knowledge is distorted by superimposition (adhyasa), thus making it impossible for human beings to see things-in-themselves as identical with self's pure subjectivity, which is identical with brahman, the absolute. Superimposition of the self on what is not self and of what is not self on the self is the inherent way in which consciousness operates. It is only through the removal of ignorance (avidya), which Shankara understands to be identical with illusion (maya), that the self can be revealed as the witnessing subject (rather than the knowing self), which is identical with brahman. Thus, for Shankara, the world is epistemologically indeterminate (anirvacaniya); it neither exists nor does not exist. Avidya is inherent to human nature, but not to the self. It is this ignorance that entangles the person in samsara, but the realization of the identity of self and brahman shatters the veil of ignorance and maya and leads to moksha. Shankara's primary effort is to clarify the epistemic problem of superimposition, which can only be overcome through correct understanding and interpretation of Veda and the refutation of false views. Knowledge of the self can only be achieved through the Veda, which also includes the ritual portion of the text and devotion to a personal deity. Thus, Shankara's system of thought is necessarily orthodox and orthopraxic, as both ritual (dharma) and devotion are understood to be necessary for the attainment of knowledge that leads to the effacement of superimposition and ignorance.

In contrast to Shakara's interpretation of the absolutely non-dualistic interpretation, Madhva holds that scriptures maintain a complete distinction (bheda) and dualism (dvatia) between the self and brahman as a personal deity. Whereas for Shankara, brahman is ultimately without qualities or attributes (nirguna), for Madhva as well as Ramanuja, the highest manifestation of brahman has attributes (saguna). The individual self (jiva) consist of spiritual self-consciousness, whose nature is pure consciousness. The self is a mirror image of brahman as god and such is dependent on brahman. Madhva establishes five categories of differences: between the Lord and self (jivatman), between infinite number of selves, between the Lord and matter (prakriti), between the self and matter, and between phenomena and matter. All things, which are distinguished by particularity (vishesha), depend on the Lord. Liberation is identical with the self's innate state of pure consciousness and bliss, which necessarily participates in the bliss of the Lord. Madhva rejects karma as duty and rejects bhakti in the sense of meditation (dhyana) as leading to libration. Only the continuous inquiry into the Lord (brahmajijñasa), which is free from all preconceptions and the realization that all things in the world are non-enduring and without essence can affect liberation through total devotion to Vishnu. Continuous inquiry into the Lord is understood to be possible only through grace (prasada) of the Lord. Unlike Shankara and Ramanuja, Madhva's exegetical method extends beyond the Veda, the Vendanta Sutras and the Bhagavad Gita and includes puranic sources such as the Vishnu Purana and Bhagavata Purana.

Ramanuja's qualified non-dualism (vishishtadvaita) may be understood to stand somewhere between the extreme non-dualism of Shankara and absolute dualism of Madhva. Like Madhva, Ramanuja writes from a theistic perspective and argues that Shankara's absolute non-dualistic reading of the texts is against reason, against the common understanding of language, and against the texts themselves. Ramanuja rejects Shankara's epistemic position that there are two levels of truth, a higher truth of the brahman and a lower truth that only represents brahman as a personal deity. Ramanuja understand the texts to make the single claim that brahman is the essence of the universe and the individual self and is also a personal being. Ramanuja expounds a view of non-qualified dualism in which Brahman, the individual soul, and the world are understood as identical in essence but distinct manifestations of the same essence. Both the self and the world are completely dependent on brahman but are yet distinct from Brahman. Ramanuja develops the image of the world of sentient and insentient matter as the body of Brahman, which is real rather than ontologically and epistemologically indeterminate. Liberation from samsara consists of the complete apprehension of the glory and nature of brahman; it is not an experience of identity with Brahman who is eternal distinct from the individual soul. Ramanuja develops the notion of quailed dualism in his Sri Bhashya, a commentary on the Vedanta Sutras, as well as his commentary on the Bhagavad Gita.

Carlos Lopez

See also: Benares; Buddhism; Christianity; Devotion/ Devotional Traditions; Divine Life Society; Diwali; Hinduism; Holi; India, Contemporary Religion in: Asian Religions; India, Contemporary Religion in: Middle Eastern Religions; India, Hinduism in: Ancient Vedic Expressions; India, Hinduism in: Modern Period; International Society for Krishna Consciousness; Jainism; Janmashtami; Meditation; Muhammad; Nagarjuna; Patanjali; Pilgrimage; Shaivism; Shaktism; Sikhism; Temples—Hindu; Vaishnavism; Women, Status and Role of; Yoga.

References

General

Doniger, Wendy. *The Hindus: An Alternative History*. New York: Penguin Press, 2009.

Flood, Gavin, ed. *The Blackwell Companion to Hinduism*. Oxford: Blackwell, 2003.

Lorenzen, David N. *Who Invented Hinduism?: Essays in Religion in History.* Delhi: Yoda Press, 2006.

Michaels, Axel. *Hinduism: Past and Present.* Princeton, NJ: Princeton University Press, 2004.

Mittal, Sushil, and Gene Thursby, eds. *The Hindu World.* New York: Routledge, 2004.

Mittal, Sushil, and Gene Thursby, eds. *Studying Hinduism: Key Concepts and Methods.* London and New York: Routledge, 2008.

Sharma, Arvind, ed. *The Study of Hinduism.* Columbia: University of South Carolina Press, 2003.

Wolpert, Stanley A. *A New History of India.* 8th ed. New York: Oxford University Press, 2009.

Medieval Period

Dimmitt, Cornelia, and J. A. B. van Buitenen, eds. *Classical Hindu Mythology: A Reader in the Sanskrit Puranas.* Philadelphia: Temple University Press, 1978.

Eino, Shingoo. *The Genesis and Development of Tantrism.* Tokyo: University of Tokyo, Institute of Oriental Culture, 2009.

Kinsley, David. *Hindu Goddesses: Visions of the Divine Feminine in the Hindu Religious Tradition.* Berkeley: University of California Press, 1986.

Pintchman, Tracy, ed. *Women's Lives, Women's Rituals in the Hindu Tradition.* Oxford: Oxford University Press, 2007.

Rocher, Ludo. *The Puranas.* Wiesbaden: O. Harrassowitz, 1986.

Hindu Practice and Ritual

Carman, John B., and Frederique Apfell Marglin, eds. *Purity and Auspiciousness in Indian Society.* Leiden: Brill, 1985.

Dumont, Louis. *Homo hierarchicus: The Caste System and Its Implications.* Chicago: University of Chicago Press, 1980.

Eck, Diana. *Darshan: Seeing the Divine Image in India.* 3rd ed. New York: Columbia University Press, 1998.

Feldhaus, Anne. *Connected Places: Region, Pilgrimage, and Geographical Imagination in India.* New York: Palgrave Macmillan, 2003.

Fuller, C. J. *The Camphor Flame: Popular Hinduism and Society in India.* Princeton, NJ: Princeton University Press, 2004.

Tachikawa, M., S. Hino, and L. Deoadhar. *Puja and Samskara.* Delhi: Motilal Banarsidass, 2001.

Willis, Michael D. *The Archaeology of Hindu Ritual: Temples and the Establishment of the Gods.* Cambridge: Cambridge University Press, 2009.

■ India, Hinduism in: Modern Period

Hindu thought and practice in the modern world (1700–present) has been shaped by several historical factors, none more significant than the European encounter with India that was inaugurated by Vasco de Gama in 1498. As the power and influence of the Muslim Mughal rulers faded after the death of Aurangzeb (r. 1658–1707), the influence of French and British colonial power grew especially through the economic influence of the British East India Company (1600–1858) and the eventual takeover of all its rights and interests by the British Crown (1858–1947). British colonial authorities attempted to govern Hindus according to their traditions, values, and laws, as long as they did not challenge Western standards. These efforts led to the production of knowledge about the East, Hindus, and their traditions for the practical purpose of empire-building and the civilizing Christian mission that spread alongside British political and economic domination. At the same time, European style mass-education conducted in English and reform-minded Western intellectual traditions were introduced to the colonial territory.

The colonial enterprise of empire-building and the Orientalist project, which aimed to construct Hinduism as "other," produced several responses from Hindus that re-conceived their native tradition by adopting Western intellectual traditions. Many of the English-educated Hindu reformers came to look upon many aspects of their tradition as corrupt and degraded, such as the caste system, image worship, and social practices like child-marriage and *sati* (widow-burning). In many ways, these reformist movements were attempting to wrest the discourse on Hinduism away from European Orientalists by redefining and sanitizing

Hinduism in terms of the Western Romantic notions of Eastern religions and Hinduism in particular.

One of the earliest Hindu reform movements was led by Ram Mohan Roy (1772–1833), often called the father of modern India and the founder of the Brahmo Samaj. Educated at the Muslim University in Patna and having studied Sanskrit in Varanasi, Roy developed much of his understanding of Hinduism while employed by the East India Company. His studies and experiences led Roy to understand true Hinduism to be found in the Upanishads. The true god was transcendent, unchanging but knowable through reason and from the laws of nature. He rejected polytheism, image worship, rituals and sacrifices, and concepts such as karma and rebirth. Roy maintained that all religions were one and that Hinduism was a universal religion of tolerance. Hinduism was in need of being purged of superstitions that had no foundation on texts or reason. Members of the Brahmo Samaj met regularly in Calcutta to read and discuss the sacred texts, the Upanishads, to sing hymns, and to listen to sermons on the single principle that underlies true religion. Roy's vision of Hinduism as implemented in the Brahmo Samaj found a receptive audience, especially among lower-class Brahmans and the growing urban middle classes of merchants and traders.

Dayananda Saraswati's (1824–1883) movement for reform crystallized into the Arya Samaj, which like Roy's movement aimed at a return to a purer form of Hinduism. However, unlike Roy, Dayananda saw the core of Hinduism to be found in the Veda and called for a revival of *sanatana dharma* (eternal law), which included the elimination of superstitions such as image worship and pilgrimage to sacred places, and social reforms including support for widow remarriage and eradication of child marriage; all which he claimed had no foundation in the Veda. He viewed the Veda as eternal, true, and binding; all other texts were later accretions that diluted the truth of the Veda. The Arya Samaj spread its message of a return to Vedic culture through its network of schools, which stressed the teaching of Sanskrit, the ancient language of the Vedas, as well as Hindi. The Arya Samaj was successful in reconverting low-caste converts to Islam and Christianity. Dayananda and the Arya Samaj teachings advocated an aggressive form of Hindu nationalism based

on the return to the Veda that continues to shape strands of Hindu national politics and cultural life.

Ramakrishna Paramahamsa (1836–1886) and his chief disciple, Swami Vivekananda (1863–1902), were seminal figures in 19th-century Hindu reform and in the promotion of Hinduism as a world religion. Unlike Roy and Dayananda, their concern was the articulation of Hinduism's universality and the pluralistic acceptance of all religions as aspects of one truth, rather than a concern with purifying Hinduism of idolatrous aspects that were objectionable to Westerners. Raised as a rural Brahman with no formal education, Ramakrishna served as the priest of a Kali temple at Dakshinesvar, just north of Calcutta. He is said to have frequently experienced religious ecstasy (*samadhi*) as a result of devotional practices focused on Hindu deities, including Kali, Sita, Rama, and Krishna, as well as religious figures from other religions, including Muhammad and Jesus. He came to believe that a single transcendent Reality was the common core of all of the world's great religions. Ramakrishna interpreted his various experiences through the Advaita Vedanta view of different levels of religious truth, broadening this viewpoint to include the theistic and monistic stands of other religions. Ramakrishna became an object of devotion and influenced both uneducated villagers and middle-class intellectuals from Calcutta. By the time of his death in 1886, he was already widely regarded as a great saint.

Narendranath Datta, later known as Swami Vivekananda, is the most well known and influential follower of Ramakrishna. After becoming a disciple of Ramakrishna and eventually becoming a renunciant, Vivekananda became one of the authoritative voices that shaped the West's view and understanding of Hinduism. At the Parliament of World Religions of 1893, he successfully gave voice to Ramakrishna's vision of the unity of all religions while stressing the value of diversity. During a four-year lecture tour in the United States, Vivekananda founded the Vedanta Society. Upon his return to India in 1895, he founded the Ramakrishna Mission, the aim of which was the promotion of educational and medical relief programs.

It is impossible to detangle the efforts of Hindu reform leaders of the late 19th and early 20th centuries from the social and political context of the times. The vision of Hinduism preached by Roy, Saraswati, and Ramakrishna were not limited to the personal experiential and theological dimensions but were implicitly political and aimed at revitalizing society. Mohandas K. Gandhi (1869–1948) perhaps stands as the reformer who most successfully integrated the language of religion and Hinduism into Indian nationalistic aspirations for independence from British imperialism. As a young man, he studied law at University College, London, where he was profoundly influenced by the Western intellectual ideals of democracy, equality, and individual autonomy. He also was influenced by the writings of Russian writer Leo Tolstoy (1828–1910) on voluntary simplicity and of American philosopher Henry David Thoreau (1817–1862) on passive resistance to governmental injustice. After completing his education, Gandhi took a position with a firm in South Africa to fight to remedy the grievances of Indians in South Africa. While in South Africa, Gandhi implemented and perfected many of his political tactics in the struggle against racial discrimination and hatred of indentured workers from South Asia. His personal and professional experience defending the rights of indentured workers through the work of the Natal Indian Congress radically changed Gandhi's perspective on the nature of freedom under the rule of empire. After returning to India in 1915, Gandhi espoused the lifestyle and life ways of the average Indian, discarding the business suit in favor of the traditional Indian *dhoti* and adopting many of the traditional dietary habits of poor Indians.

Gandhi transformed the political debate in India by his appeal to religious language, primarily Hindu, to mobilize the masses in nonviolent efforts to protest and eventually drive out British power from India. Like Roy and Dayananda, Gandhi accessed the language of the Upanishads, the language of truth (*satya*) as the central pursuit of humanity. Like Roy and Vivekananda, Gandhi espoused the belief in the essential unity of all as a central political and social ideology of harmony and non-violence (*ahimsa*). For Gandhi, oneness and nonviolence are manifestations of truth. Gandhi's notion of grasping the truth (*satyagraha*) was both religious and political, aiming to create welfare for all through the individual practice of self-control over anger and violence, sexuality, and dedication to justice

and truth. In making chastity a key political value, Gandhi rearticulated the important Vedic ideal of the *brahmacarin*, the celibate student of the Veda, in the service of a political outlook that would lead to the welfare of all.

Gandhi's vision of truth as a moral and ethical code also included a call to end the plight of untouchables, or *dalits*. Gandhi referred to untouchables, persons who were considered to be outside the traditional system of *varnashradharma*, as children of god (*harijans*). Like Roy, he saw the caste system and untouchability to have no foundation in tradition and to be a corrupting force on society, the eradication of which would transform it. Gandhi's vision of Hinduism was influenced by many of the central Hindu concepts found throughout the Vedas, Upanishads, and Hindu epics, especially the Bhagavad Gita, such as nonviolence, celibacy, and the renouncer ideal, as well as by Christian notions of pacifism. His notion of an ethical Hinduism pays little attention to Hindu practice and rituals, gods and goddesses, or sacred stories beyond the ascetic lifestyle and their ethical bearing on the aesthetic or sensual dimension of the Hindu tradition.

Like Gandhi, Sri Aurobindo Ghose (1872–1950) was educated in England and attempted to apply a synthesis of Hindu religious and Western democratic ideals in the fight for Indian independence. After being arrested for anti-government activity, Aurobindo is said to have experienced the state of samadhi while in prison. After his release, he left for Pondicherry, where in 1910 he founded the Sri Aurobindo Ashram, which continues to flourish today. Aurobindo translated his intense spiritual experiences, including that of brahman as the one all-pervading reality and the world of appearances being totally illusory, into a system of "integral yoga," which aimed both at the union with the divine but also at the transformation of the outer and inner self. According to Aurobindo, both individual and social life are in the process of evolving from the illusion of distinct individualism through various stages of consciousness, until a state of superconsciousness is reached in which it is realized that brahman is the only reality that pervades all. He published several theological studies in English that provide a synthesis of Hindu and evolutionary ideas, including his *Essays on the Gita* and *The Life Divine*.

Portrait of Ramana Maharshi, a prominent 20th-century Indian spiritual teacher who lived and taught at Arunachala. (J. Gordon Melton)

Aurobindo's vision of Hinduism affirms the Vedic vision of worldly activity as the arena for individual and social transformation. The resulting synthesis of Hinduism with Western values has been widely influential in both the West and the East and has substantially influenced the development of transpersonal and humanistic psychology, as well as the New Age and Human Potential movements both in the United States and in Europe.

Contemporary Hinduism is not limited to these pioneering religious figures and their movements but co-exist alongside what one might call "traditional forms of Hinduism" both within and outside of theistic traditions, in temple rituals and festivals, in the renunciant orders of sannyasi and itinerant sadhus, in pilgrimages to holy sites, in music and art, in the various forms of Tantra and Yoga, and the observances that structure family life. A host of other contemporary Indian religious figures, such as A. C. Bhaktivedanta (1896–1977), founder of the International Society for Krishna Consciousness (ISKCON); Maharishi Mahesh Yogi (1918–2008); Swami Sivananda (1887–1963), founder of the Divine Life Society; and Meher Baba (1894–1969) have continued to articulate forms of revitalized Hinduism in both India and the West. Hinduism has also been marked by the emergence of a number of notable female charismatic saints around whom movements have gathered. The most notable may be Anandamayi Ma (1896–1982) and her contemporaries, such as Mira Richard (1878–1973), the Mother, Sri Aurobindo's companion. They created space for living female gurus, such as Mata Amritanandamayi (b. 1953) of the Ma Amritanandamayi Centres; Mother Meera (b. 1960), founder of the Mother Meera Society; Shri Mataji Nirmala Devi (b. 1923), founder of the Sahaja Yoga movement; Ma Yoga Shakti Saraswati (b. 1927), founder of the Yoga Shakti International Missions; and the collective female leadership of the Brahma Kumaris.

Living Hinduism in Practice Hinduism cannot be reduced to textual and intellectual tradition or to a set of concepts, which although important do not capture the complexity of the traditions. The history of concepts and ritual practices as seen in the various Hindu texts from the Veda to the Puranas as well as *smriti* and philosophical/theological traditions have always existed alongside a myriad of religious practices that have been equally important in shaping the religious life of Hindus. Ritual and sacrifice have been at the heart of Hinduism since the Veda and have been continually re-imagined, re-interpreted, and transformed for the last two and a half millennia. Indeed, it may be said that orthopraxy has been the unchanging feature of Hinduism, even as various lines of contradictory orthodox viewpoints have developed in the Hindu tradition.

It may be said that the spiritual core of Hinduism revolves around the human encounter and experience of the divine as mediated through ritual practice. The earliest such mediation was the Vedic sacrifice, personified as Agni, who as the priest of the gods was the link between the divine sphere and the human sphere. The centrality of the sacred, consecrated image of the deity (*murti*) both in the home and in the temple as an intersection between the two worlds comes to the fore in the ubiquitous Hindu ritual of worship, the *puja*. A puja consists of a series of ritual actions whose aim is to express devotion to the deity through a paradigm of hospitality. Hospitality is expressed through a series of offerings of food, water, flowers, incense, and cloth. During puja, especially in the home, the deity is asked to enter the icon, which is constructed by artisans according to traditional features described in the sacred stories of the deity. Only after the deity has been bid to enter the image (*avahana*) may the puja commence, since the image is now infused with the sacred. At the end of the ritual, the deity is dismissed (*visarjana*). However, images in temples are understood to be permanently consecrate and puja must be regularly offered by the temple priest (*pujari*), whose primary responsibility is to regularly perform puja for the deity, regardless of whether devotees are present or not. During the ritual, the consecrated image of the deity is bathed in various sacred substances, dressed in new clothes, and adorned with jewels and perfumes, including traditional marks with *kumkum* paste on the forehead or bridge of the nose (*tilaka*). The dressing and the offering of food to the deity is made behind a curtain in the temple. Upon being regally dressed, the deity reappears to the worshippers, who receive the sacred sight (*darshan*) of the deity. The act of seeing the deity and being seen by the deity is considered by most Hindus to be the central element of puja, many of whom will state that their visit to a temple is for the explicit purpose of "getting darshan." Another element of puja is the offering of light, called *arati*. During arati, the pujari moves a five-wicked oil lamp or camphor flame in a circular pattern in front of the deity, while ringing bells and reciting hymns of praise. After offering of light, the lamp is passed among devotees, who take in the light and warmth of the god's light by cupping their hands over the flame and then touching their faces and eyes, symbolically transferring the light into themselves. Finally, devotees also receive *prasad*, the grade of the deity in the form of the remnants of the food that had been offered to the deity, which becomes sanctified through contact with

the deity. Puja is practiced by the majority of Hindus in home shrines, which are often located in a separate room or area that is ritually cleansed where murti of the deity are kept. In the home, puja is generally performed daily or weekly primarily by women of the family.

As a locale of puja, the Hindu temple (*mandir*) is conceived as the encapsulation of the universe, which is mapped out in the Vastu Purusha Mandala, the geometric blueprint of the temple. Like the Vedic ritual, the temple *mandala* systematically identifies the parts of the body of the cosmic man (*purusha*), who is the source of the ordered universe with the various parts of the temple. As such, the Hindu temple is conceived as identical with the cosmos itself. The mandir is considered the abode of the gods and as such it is the permanent residence of the deity. The architectural plan of the Hindu temple reflects a transition from profane space to the sacred space, the core of which is the womb chamber (*garbhagriha*), where the deity of the temple resides. As the devotee progressively moves toward the inner sanctum, the experience of transition is highlighted by the myriad of images carved in the exterior and interior walls of the temple. The temple functions as a connecting point, a crossing place, a *tirtha* to the divine and from the divine where the proximal separation between the two spheres is closest.

The immanence of the divine is also understood by Hindus to be accessible through the very land of India. The land becomes a tirtha, a sacred ford where the divine has crossed down to Earth and therefore created a spiritual bridge to the other side. Many of these sacred sites are intimately connected with the events in the lives of great religious figures and gods related in the sacred stories of the tradition. Braj, the sacred land of Krishna, which is located within the triangle formed by Delhi, Jaipur, and Agra, is a living museum of the places where Krishna engaged in his divine play (*lila*). To enter the circle of Braj and engage in play which imitates Krishna's lila is to participate in the presence of Krishna. Similarly, Varanasi (aka Benares), the eternal city of Shiva, perhaps the best-known tirtha outside India, is the place where many Hindus hope to die. It is simultaneously the city of death, liberation, and eternal life because it is Shiva's most beloved place on Earth, which he vowed to hold above the cycle of creation and destruction for all time. Pilgrimage (*tirthayatra*) to sacred rivers such as the Ganga, Yamuna, or Narmada or to the sacred places of the goddess (*pitha*) is an important part of the religious life of Hindus through which they experience the India of the religious imagination. According to the texts that glorify (*mahatmyas*) individual tirthas, the simple act of going to such places destroys sins and evil and may even lead to liberation.

The yearly religious calendar is punctuated by a number of festivals (*utsava*), many which are Pan-Indian and others that are local or regional in character. Festivals are often connected to the agricultural cycle, the harvest and sowing season, or celebrate events in the life of the gods, events in the sacred narratives, or astrologically significant events such as solstice, equinoxes, or eclipses. During festivals connected with specific temples and their residing deities, devotees come to have darshan of the temple murti, which is brought out of the temple and taken in a procession around the village or town. Pan-Indian festivals including Krishna's birthday (Krishna Janmashthami), Ganesha Caturthi, Diwali (festival of lights), and Holi are some of the most important festivals in the Hindu religious calendar.

Religious rituals have both a communal and a personal dimension and the intersection of these two dimensions is important in the Hindu tradition. Rituals know as *samskaras*, lifecycle rites or rites of passage, have been a central feature of Hindu identity and religiosity since the Vedic period. These rites mark the crucial moments in the life of an individual member of society, beginning at conception through the funerary rituals (*shraddha*). They ritually fashion the social, religious, and spiritual identity of the individual and simultaneously legitimize the social institutions that uphold traditional Hindu society. The Veda and the later smriti texts present samskaras primarily as they apply to male Brahmans and by extension to males of the upper three varnas (Brahmans, Kshatriyas, and Vaishyas) within the fourfold *ashrama* system. According to the traditional domestic ritual texts of each Vedic school, the numbers of samskaras varies from 12 to 18, while later texts such as Manava Dharma Shastra mention 13. Although all samskaras are con-

sidered essential, *upanayana* (rite of initiation), *vivaha* (marriage) and *anyeshti*, shraddha (funerary rites) continue to be considered among contemporary Hindus to be essential to Hindu identity.

The upanayana is the rite of initiation of a young boy who belongs to the upper three varnas into study of the Veda under the guidance of a qualified teacher (*guru*). During the period of studentship, the young student remains celibate, studies the Veda, serves his guru, and offers oblations. The ceremony is marked by the bestowal of the sacred thread, which is worn by the young man and distinguishes him as a twice born man (*dvija*), and reciting the sacred *gayatri* mantra. After the period of Vedic education (brahmacarin), the young man moves to the householder ashrama, which requires that he find a suitable bride. In contemporary Hindu society, the upanayana ceremony is still considered essential and has been generally included in the long sequence of events of marriage ceremony, often performed the day preceding the marriage. According to Manava Dharma Shastra, for women, marriage is equal to upanayana and the duty of serving her husband is identified with the study of the Veda. Although Sanskrit texts have not preserved a set of rites of passage for women that parallel those for men of the upper three varnas, several ethnographic studies have shown that alternative ritual traditions for women have been part of the religious landscape of India at various local levels, which give expression to women's voices and religious hopes outside the brahmanic orthopraxic framework.

The rites that come at the end of life (anyesthi)—funerary rites generally known as shraddha—focus on reintegration of the family, whose social intercourse with the larger community has been interrupted by the pollution associated with death, and on transition of the departed family member from this world to heaven. Traditionally, there have been various methods of disposing of the bodies of the dead, including cremation, inhumation, and burial, depending on social status, caste, and gender. Normally, cremation takes place immediately after death, at which time the body is prepared by being shaved (if male), anointed with sandalwood paste, and wrapped in cloth. According to the Vedic and smriti texts, the cremation fire of the deceased should be lit from his domestic ritual fire. The shraddha rites, which last for 12 days following cremation, include the preparation and offering of rice balls (*pindas*) to the deceased, which ritually constructs his new heavenly body. The rites continue for 10 days and conclude with the *sapindakarana* ceremony, in which the recently deceased ritually transitions from the liminal ghostly world (*preta loka*) to the world of the departed ancestors (*pitr loka*). The belief in the heavenly afterlife, which is found as early as the Rig Veda, co-exists side by side with the belief in karma, rebirth, reincarnation, and moksha.

There has always been a wide range of beliefs, ritual practices, and theological perspectives woven into the tapestry that is called Hinduism that historically have been inherently understood by their practitioners as a unity in diversity. As one can see from the earliest Hindu texts, the Vedas, it is diversity of points of view, of textual transmission, of ritual thought and practice, of deities, and of understandings about the nature and purpose of human beings that produce the ever meaningful matrix which we call Hinduism.

Carlos Lopez

See also: Arya Samaj; Brahma Kumaris; Brahmo Samaj; Buddhism; Christianity; Devotion/Devotional Traditions; Divine Life Society; Global Country of World Peace; Hinduism; Holi; India, Contemporary Religion in: Asian Religions; India, Contemporary Religion in: Middle Eastern Religions; India, Hinduism in: Ancient Vedic Expressions; India, Hinduism in: Medieval Period; International Society for Krishna Consciousness; Jainism; Janmashtami; Meditation; Mother Meera, Disciples of; Muhammad; New Age Movement; Pilgrimage; Shaivism; Shaktism; Sikhism; Sivananda Saraswati, Swami; Sri Aurobindo Ashram; Temples—Hindu; Vaishnavism; Vedanta Societies; Women, Status and Role of; Yoga.

References

General

Doniger, Wendy. *The Hindus: An Alternative History.* New York: Penguin Press, 2009.

Flood, Gavin, ed. *The Blackwell Companion to Hinduism.* Oxford: Blackwell, 2003.

Lorenzen, David N. *Who Invented Hinduism?: Essays in Religion in History.* Delhi. Yoda Press, 2006.

Michaels, Axel. *Hinduism: Past and Present.* Princeton, NJ: Princeton University Press, 2004.

Mittal, Sushil, and Gene Thursby, eds. *The Hindu World.* New York: Routledge, 2004.

Mittal, Sushil, and Gene Thursby, eds. *Studying Hinduism: Key Concepts and Methods.* London and New York: Routledge, 2008.

Sharma, Arvind, ed. *The Study of Hinduism.* Columbia: University of South Carolina Press, 2003.

Wolpert, Stanley A. *A New History of India.* 8th ed. New York: Oxford University Press, 2009.

Modern Period

Dalmia, Vasudha, and Heinrich von Stietencron, eds. *The Oxford India Hinduism Reader.* Oxford: Oxford University Press, 2009.

Smith, David. *Hinduism and Modernity.* Oxford: Blackwell, 2003.

Van der Veer, Peter, ed. *Religious Nationalism: Hindus and Muslims in India.* Berkeley: University of California Press, 1994.

Williams, Raymond Brady. *An Introduction to Swaminarayan Hinduism.* Cambridge: Cambridge University Press, 2001.

Hindu Practice and Ritual

Carman, John B., and Frederique Apfell Marglin, eds. *Purity and Auspiciousness in Indian Society.* Leiden: Brill, 1985.

Dumont, Louis. *Homo hierarchicus: The Caste System and Its Implications.* Chicago: University of Chicago Press, 1980.

Eck, Diana. *Darshan: Seeing the Divine Image in India.* 3rd ed. New York: Columbia University Press, 1998.

Feldhaus, Anne. *Connected Places: Region, Pilgrimage, and Geographical Imagination in India.* New York: Palgrave Macmillan, 2003.

Fuller, C. J. *The Camphor Flame: Popular Hinduism and Society in India.* Princeton, NJ: Princeton University Press, 2004.

Tachikawa, M., S. Hino, and L. Deoadhar. *Puja and Samskara.* Delhi: Motilal Banarsidass, 2001.

Willis, Michael D. *The Archaeology of Hindu Ritual: Temples and the Establishment of the Gods.* Cambridge: Cambridge University Press, 2009.

India in Western Religious Imagination

Orientalism comes in two flavors: negative and positive. Representations of India in Western sources from antiquity to the contemporary period range from disparaging stereotypes that focus on the caste system and the purported evils of "idolatry," to depictions of India as a source of the most profound spiritual wisdom. Whereas older sources, beginning with Herodotus, generally present India as the negative "other," the Romantic period in particular saw the beginnings of a wave of fascination with all things Indian, spreading among the learned classes in Europe and North America. In their attempts to depict the spiritual wisdom of India, individual authors could focus on very diverse ideas and customs: yoga, mysticism, philosophy, Tantra, reincarnation, and much else beside. Western audiences were inspired to adopt some of these religious elements, or to see parts of their own heritage as being originally of Asian origin. India, in short, became both a source of various religious ideas and a screen for the projection of many others.

Gradually, and especially from the turn of the 20th century, the fascination with India, which originally was a literary and philosophical phenomenon, became the point of departure for a more diverse variety of social formations. For large audiences, elements of Hinduism and Buddhism continue to be treated as mysteries to be sampled on the printed page. Smaller numbers of people participate in practices inspired by India, either on a more sporadic basis (for example, as customers paying to participate in yoga classes) or with much greater levels of commitment (for example, as converts to Indian-inspired new religious movements). A brief survey such as this can only attempt to present thumbnail sketches of a few prominent themes in a topic of vast dimensions.

The belief in reincarnation has deep historical roots in Western religious history. Although rejected by the church, classical sources mentioning reincarnation were well known in the Middle Ages and beyond and made it possible for the intrepid few (Guillaume Postel [1510–1581], Giordano Bruno [1548–1600], Franciscus Mercurius van Helmont [1614–1699], and others) in the early modern age to profess sympathy for reincarnationist claims. As references to reincarnation became more widespread in 18th- and especially 19th-century writings, India increasingly became a source of legitimacy as well as a source of inspiration for authors promoting this concept. Theosophy, the movement and religious milieu that since the late 19th century has become particularly associated with belief in the rebirth of the human soul in a new body, presented its sympathizers with a view of reincarnation that differed quite radically from most of the versions of this belief that were widespread in India. Classical Hindu traditions usually suggest that the sum of good and evil deeds accumulated over this as well as past lives can lead to a rebirth in one of many different shapes, for instance, as an animal. Rebirth is thus a hierarchical process, by which auspicious incarnations (as a high-caste human) may well be followed by rebirth as an animal. Theosophical conceptions of reincarnation, on the contrary, see rebirth as a didactic process by which experience is accumulated and spiritual progress can be made in life after life. Theosophically inspired versions of reincarnation belief are widespread in the contemporary West, whereas versions more reminiscent of classical Hinduism are generally restricted to specific new religious movements.

Yoga and *meditation* in the West are also essentially phenomena with roots in the mid- to late 19th century. The transfer of these practices from India to contemporary Europe and North America has, again, entailed significant changes. Whereas these religious practices were in India often reserved for religious elites, yoga and meditation is in modern Western countries usually accessible to all. Yogic practice is in Hindu traditions typically embedded in specific soteriological contexts, for example, in a conception of human life as one stage in a vast cycle of incarnations, where the accumulation of religious merit according to specific methods can aid in improving one's prospects for a positive rebirth, or eventually for liberation from the cycles of rebirth. Western understandings of yoga and meditation are quite diverse and are influenced by prevalent secularized discourses on the benefits of yoga as a form of exercise or a way to maintain good health, by conceptions of meditation as a means of reducing stress, and by individual reflection on the place of yoga in one's life.

Besides such rather secularized practices, Western audiences have also become acquainted with consid-

The Beatles join the Maharishi Mahesh Yogi, center, as they arrive by train at Bangor, Wales, to participate in a weekend of meditation, on August 26, 1967. The Maharishi is the founder of the International Meditation Society. (AP/Wide World Photos)

erably more mystical strains of yoga and meditation. The existence of *Tantrism* may have been known to select Western audiences in the 18th century and became more widely spread via late 19th-century texts such as those by Arthur Avalon, pseudonym of Sir John Woodroffe (1865–1936). To judge from the titles published and the number of Western interpretations available, the most widely incorporated element of Tantric yoga is the understanding that the human body comprises an occult physiology, with invisible channels serving as conduits of vital force, *prana*, and particular nodes where this energy manifests in especially potent form, the *chakras*.

A widespread idea among Westerners who sympathize with religious ideas and practices of Indian origin is that these are supported by scientific evidence. It is commonly suggested that the stress-reducing effects of meditation can be investigated and corroborated by the latest scientific means and that the chakras have an objective existence and could potentially be registered and measured as objectively as the elements of more conventional physiology. Two particularly influential attempts to draw parallels between Indian religious philosophies and contemporary Western science can be mentioned here. Transcendental Meditation, a movement founded by Maharishi Mahesh Yogi (1918–2008), is indebted to Vedantist forms of Hinduism, but insists on its secular and scientific nature to the extent that its spokespersons will typically deny having anything to do with religion. What from one perspective could be seen as a classical religious claim, namely, that intense spiritual practice (that is, particular forms of meditation) can lead to seemingly miraculous examples of mind dominating matter (levitation), is within the context of Transcendental Meditation seen as objective fact resting on scientific foundations. The other example concerns the writings of Fritjof Capra (b. 1939), known for his suggestion (in his bestselling book *The Tao of Physics*, published in 1975) that there are highly significant parallels between the metaphysical statements of Indian mystics and the worldview of contemporary particle physics and quantum mechanics.

As these examples illustrate, the influence of India manifests itself in very diverse and partly incommensurable ways in various widely divergent new religious movements, and in what has been characterized as the cultic milieu where one can believe and practice without belonging to any organization, and where religious "practice" can typically consist in the reading of books.

Olav Hammer

See also: Global Country of World Peace; Meditation; Reincarnation; Tantrism; Yoga.

References

Clarke, J. J. *Oriental Enlightenment: The Encounter between Asian and Western Thought.* London and New York: Routledge, 1997.

De Michelis, Elizabeth. *A History of Modern Yoga.* London and New York: Continuum, 2004.

Halbfass, Wilhelm. *India and Europe: An Essay in Understanding.* Albany: State University of New York Press, 1988.

Schwab, Raymond. *Oriental Renaissance: Europe's Rediscovery of India and the East 1680–1880.* New York: Columbia University Press, 1984.

Indian Pentecostal Church of God

The Indian Pentecostal Church of God, also known as India Pentecostal Church of God (IPC), is the largest Pentecostal denomination in India. It now has 2,000 local congregations spread all over India, Australia, North America, and the Gulf countries and claims a membership of 700,000. Sixty of the congregations are in the United States among the Malayalam-speaking Asian Indians. In India, the majority of its members are in the states of Kerala, Andhra Pradesh, and Tamil Nadu, with the headquarters in the state of Kerala.

The Indian Pentecostal Church is one of the indigenous movements that emerged out of the revivals that took place in South India in the early part of the 20th century. There were three significant revivals in the state of Kerala in the years 1873, 1895, and 1908, accompanied by manifestations of the outpouring of the Holy Spirit. Unlike the first two revivals, the third one was sustained by the arrival in 1909 of George Berg, fresh from the Pentecostal revival that was then occurring at Azusa Street in Los Angeles. Berg was not associated with any of the Pentecostal denominations then in their initial formative stages. Thus he led in the formation of various Pentecostal house churches long before the arrival of missionaries representing the various different Pentecostal groups. These house churches organized themselves to come together to worship once a month and later adopted the name South India Church of God in 1924.

In 1926 the South India Church of God and the South India Full Gospel Church, led by Pastor Robert F. Cook, an American Pentecostal missionary, merged to form the Malankara Pentecostal Church of God. However, in 1930 the South India Pentecostal Church of God, which was led by Native peoples, came out of this union in order to assert their independence and autonomy. As the remaining denomination began to spread to different parts of India from the state of Kerala, in 1934 it assumed its present name, Indian Pentecostal Church of God.

The revivals that took place in Kerala affected churches that belonged to the Syrian Orthodox tradition, and a significant section of the IPC's membership is of a Syrian Orthodox background. Because of its origin, IPC, along with other Pentecostal churches of Syrian Orthodox background, developed an apologetic against Syrian Orthodox Church beliefs and practices in addition to classical Pentecostal doctrines. A somewhat unique aspect of the IPC, this particular part of their theology was insignificant outside the state of Kerala, since the Syrian Orthodox in India is limited to this state.

Otherwise, the IPC shares broadly the doctrinal basis of the Church of God (Cleveland, Tennessee) and the Assemblies of God, and thus fits into the classical Pentecostal tradition.

The most remarkable distinctive feature of the denomination is its polity, which is characterized by independence and autonomy. A General Council elected by the members of the various regions is the highest legislative body. However, the General Council does not exercise any administrative powers. The State Councils or Regional Councils are comprised of various ecclesiastical districts. Each of these districts or centers, as they are variously called, is presided over by a center pastor who is appointed by the State Presbytery. The control of the State Presbytery over the local congregation is minimal, limited to the appointment and transfer of pastors. Otherwise, the local congregations are autonomous, though a sense of corporate identity is maintained.

The IPC from its very beginning refused to be affiliated with any foreign mission organization at the cost of the independence and autonomy of the local congregations. This lack of foreign control and the freedom that ensued is considered to be the reason IPC has a better growth rate than other classical Pentecostal denominations in India.

Peniel Hall
Pallipad Post
Alleppey District
Kerala 690 512
India
http://www.angelfire.com/al3/ipcpallipad/ipc.html
Paulson Pulikottil

See also: Assemblies of God; Church of God (Cleveland, Tennessee); Pentecostalism.

References

Abraham, K. E. *IPC, the Early Years.* Kumbanad, Kerala: K. E. Abraham Foundation, 1955.

Pulikottil, Paulson. "Pentecostalisms in Independent India." In *Theological Symposium for Asian Church Leaders.* Seoul: 18th Pentecostal World Conference, Seoul Host Committee, 1998.

Varghese, Habel G. *K. E. Abraham: An Apostle from Modern India.* Kadambanad, Kerala: Christian Literature Service of India, 1974.

■ Indonesia

The modern island nation of Indonesia is the fourth most populous country in the world with 240,000,000 people (behind China, India, and the United States). They reside on some 17,500 islands, of which 1,000 are permanently inhabited. The 736,000 square miles of land territory is surrounded by 4 times that amount of navigable waters. The total area of the country is analogous to that of the United States. Immediately to the north are Malaysia, Singapore, and the Philippines, with Australia to the south. The Equator slices through the center of Indonesia.

The larger islands include Sumatra, whose western shore line faces the Indian Ocean; Java; Bali; Sulawesi, Timor; the Moluccas; and the eastern half of the island of New Guinea, known as Irian Jaya. Indonesia also includes the southeastern half of the island of Borneo, known as Kalimantan.

The islands are geologically unstable, and life is frequently affected by earthquakes, volcanic activity, and tsunamis. A line of volcanoes stretches along the southwestern coast of Sumatra, the southern coast of Java, through Bali to Timor. Included in that line are some of the Earth's most active volcanoes, including the legendary Krakatoa, located in the Sunda Strait between Java and Sumatra, whose famous eruption in 1883 created global effects. Indonesia has the largest number of historically active volcanoes (76), and has suffered the highest numbers of eruptions producing fatalities and the related destructive effects such as earthquakes, tsunamis, and pyroclastic flows. Banda Aceh, a city at the northern tip of Sumatra, was hit in 2004 by the devastating Sumatra-Andaman earthquake and tsunami, which took its place as one of the five largest earthquakes in recorded history. More than 100,000 Indonesians died.

Human habitation of Indonesia was quite early. Java was the site of one of the first finds of the bones of *Homo erectus*, a direct ancestor of modern man, the remains of which are popularly known as Java Man. It is assumed that during the last glacial cycle, land bridges connected what is now Indonesia with the rest of Asia and that humans moved into these warmer areas as the Earth's temperature cooled. When the

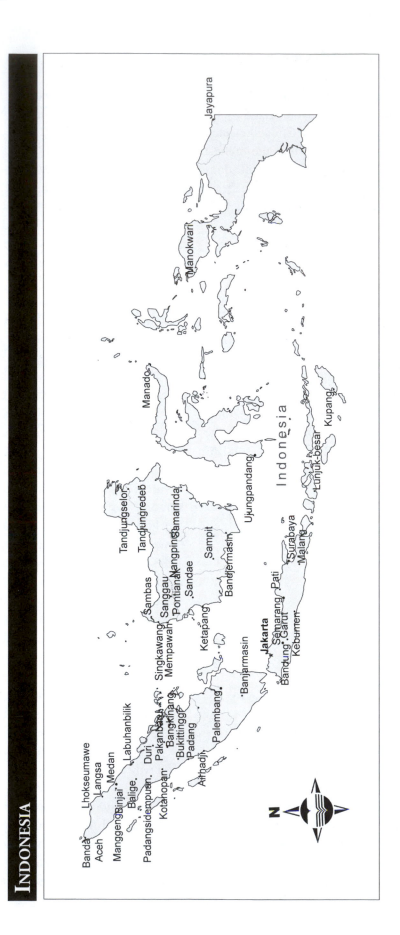

Ninth-century Buddhist temple at Borobudur in present-day Indonesia. (Corel)

glaciers melted, these land bridges were submerged and contact with the lands to the north was cut. Sumatra is currently separated from the Asian mainland (Malaysia) by a relatively narrow strait.

The Indonesian population is divided into hundreds of ethnic groups, the majority of whom speak one of the Malay or Austronesian languages. Most Indonesians trace their heritage to the southern part of China. The early inhabitants of the many islands followed a variety of indigenous ethnoreligions, though there were some commonalities such as a belief that all objects had their own life force, with some people such as the religious functionaries and the tribal leaders having relatively more of this life force. They also believed in life after death and most venerated their ancestors. The religious life was based in a variety of functionaries, including shamans and healers, with tribal leaders sharing religious and secular duties in complex ways.

By the beginning of the Common Era, Indonesians were trading with neighbors as far away as India and China. Growth of trade with India led to the influx

of Hinduism and then of Buddhism. Hinduism came to dominate the coastal regions of Sumatra, Java, and Borneo. While knowledge remains sketchy, various kingdoms are known to have existed, as evidenced by the stone buildings they left and the accounts in Chinese records left by ambassadors who visited them. In the fourth century, the Taruma Kingdom emerged in western Java, and a century later, Srivijaya, a Malay kingdom, was established on Sumatra. The Chinese Buddhist monk Fa Xian visited Java at the end of 412 CE and noted that both Hinduism and indigenous religions were widespread. Christianity had a miniscule beginning on Sumatra in the seventh century.

In the seventh century, an Indian-based kingdom, Sailendra, began its emergence as the main power in central Java and for several centuries was a dominant force. The rulers were followers of Vajrayana Buddhism, which they promoted throughout their regime. About 770, the Sailendra King Vishnu (or Dharmatunga) began building Borobudur, the massive Buddhist stupa located not far from present-day Yogyakarta. The largest Buddhist monument in the world, it took a generation to complete, the task being finished by King Samaratunga around 825.

Samaratunga's reign also constituted the zenith of his dynasty's power. His successor Balaputra lost his throne to a rival, Patapan, of the Sanjaya dynasty. The Sanjaya dynasty had emerged on Java in the eighth century and had existed beside the Sailendra. In taking control of central Java it pushed the Sailendra regime eastward to Bali and replaced Buddhism as the dominant religion with Hinduism on Java. Thus Borobudar was largely abandoned. Around 910 CE, Sanjaya King Daksa succeeded to the throne and began the erection of the Hindu temple complex at Prambanan. When completed it included three major temples, one to Shiva, one to Vishnu and Brahma, and one to the mythical animals upon which they rode—Shiva's bull Nandi, Brahma's sacred swan Hamsa, and Vishnu's eagle Garuda. Over the centuries, the Garuda emerged as a symbol of Indonesia and now also appears on the planes of the airline Garuda Indonesia. By the end of the 10th century, the Sanjaya Empire covered Java, had conquered Bali and parts of Kalimantan, and threatened the Srivijaya kingdom of Sumatra.

At the end of the 10th century (911–1007 CE), a new, powerful kingdom of Singasari emerged in East Java. Its king, Dharmawangsa, a Hindu, saw to the translation of both the Mahabharata epic and the Bhagavad Gita into Javanese. After he was killed in an attack upon his capital, a new kingdom would arise led by Airlangga (d.1049), who subsequently made peace with the Srivijaya on Sumatra and then extended his rule over all Java and Bali. He is known for his tolerant policies toward both Hindus and Buddhists, and after many years of rule, retired to live his last years as an ascetic. One of Airlangga's descendants, King Jayabaya of Kediri (1135–1157), is remembered for his prophetic vision for the land. He saw the loss of self-rule in Indonesia and predicted that it would subsequently be ruled by a white race and then a yellow race. Today, many see the years of Dutch and Japanese rule to be a fulfillment of his prediction.

The year 1292 was an eventful one in Indonesian history as the Chinese emperor Kublai Khan (1215–1294) directed an attempted invasion of Java. About that same time, a rebellion in the court of the king of Sumatra led to the king's death and to his son-in-law

Wijaya founding a new court at Majapahit. When the Mongol forces arrived, he made an alliance with them and established his rule on the island. He then turned on the Mongols and drove them back home. The kingdom he founded would soon become the most powerful kingdom in the history of Indonesia. Under King Hayam Wuruk, not only were the islands of the present national state brought under its uniting rule, but territory was added from what today are Vietnam, Cambodia, and the Philippines. The kingdom was not as stable as it might appear, as much of its territory continued to be ruled by local princes who paid tribute. These local rulers would eventually become the source of the Majapahit kingdom's subversion.

The Coming of Islam   Islam began to spread to Indonesia in the 13th century, brought by visiting merchants from Gujarat (India) and Persia (Iran), and even as the Majapahit kingdom was developing, in 1297, Sultan Malek Saleh (d. 1297) became the first ruler in Indonesia to convert. As Islam continued slowly to spread, especially in the coastal towns in Sumatra and Java, formerly Hindu rulers accepted the new faith. Crucial in the process was the conversion of Raden Patah, a prince of the royal family that ruled Majapahit, who in 1478 established an Islamic sultanate at Demak in central Java in 1478. Malek Saleh was reputedly taught by Sunan Ampel (1401–1481), one of the Islamic mystics/holy men known as the Wali Sanga. Sunan Ampel also seems to have inspired the original construction of the large mosque that still exists in the center of Demak.

The men who later came to be called the Wali Sanga had been coming to Java since the beginning of the 15th century. They are given the bulk of the credit for the spread of Islam and have thus come to have a hallowed place in the tradition, while their tombs have become places of pilgrimage. Traditionally, the number of Wali Sanga is set at nine, though putting together the diverse lists of the individuals indicates that there were more.

Where Islam was established, it was passed on from generation to generation by local teaching complexes called *pesantrens*. These pesantrens included the home of a resident Muslim scholar who knew theology, classical legal interpretations, and some devotional knowledge derived from Sufism; a mosque; and some residential facilities for the more dedicated students.

The Demak Sultanate spread both westward and eastward in Java and early in the 16th century had become the dominant power on the island. In 1527, Demak conquered what was left of the Hindu Majapahit kingdom. From that point, the sultans of Demak presented themselves as the successors to the former Majapahit state. Through the rest of the century, both Islam and the state of Demak spread through what is now Indonesia, though the spread of one was not necessarily contingent on the other.

As the Demak Sultanate emerged, the Portuguese widened their exploration of the costal lands around the Indian Ocean to Malaysia and Indonesia. In 1511, they took Melaka on the northern coast of Malaysia and forced the sultan to flee. Within two years, the last remnant of the Majapahit state was destroyed, and the Portuguese founded the town of Sunda Kelapa, which would later become the modern city of Jakarta. (In 1527, Demak took control of Sunda Kelapa and renamed it Jayakarta.) As the Portuguese expanded their territory, many Muslims chose to move. The arrival of significant numbers of Muslims in northern Sumatra led to the development of Aech as a Muslim state. By 1515, the Portuguese stretched their exploration eastward to the island of Timor.

Even as sultans of Demak and of Aech and the Portuguese sought allies on the other Indonesian islands, in 1521 the Spanish made their first appearance in the area as the remnant of Ferdinand Magellan's (1480–1521) crew sailed south from the Philippines (where Magellan had been killed) through Indonesia to Timor on what became the first round-the-world voyage. Magellan, a Portuguese, sailed with a Spanish crew. The Spanish returned in force before the decade was out. Unable to take Melaka, they took control of the Philippines.

The spread of the Portuguese opened opportunity for the arrival of Christianity in Indonesia. Pioneering that work was the Jesuit priest Francis Xavier (1506–1552), who arrived in Melaka in 1545 and spent the first half of the next year opening work in the Moluccas—most notably Ambon, Ternate, and More. As the Roman Catholic mission spread, Dominicans arrived to support the evangelistic work. Now popularly referred to as the Spice Islands, the Moluccas became the most valued prize among the competing European powers for the various agricultural products, like nutmeg and cloves, which grew in great quantities.

In 1579 another new player in the game arrived, the British, in the person of Sir Francis Drake (1540–1596), who having harassed the Spanish in the Americas, sailed across the Pacific to land at Ternate, recently wrested from Portuguese control by the local residents. Sultan Babullah, who opposed both the Spanish and the Portuguese, welcomed Drake and offered his friendship to England. Drake's activity would have significant consequences for Indonesia. He exposed to the whole of Europe that the Spanish were active in the Far East in spite of the fact that the pope had assigned the Portuguese hegemony in the region (as he had assigned hegemony in the Americas to the Spanish). In a bind, the Spanish King Philip II solved his problem by invading Portugal, assuming the Portuguese crown for himself, and taking control of its colonies. The gain was short lived, however, as eight years later, in 1588, the Spanish were crushed when its fabled Armada was destroyed by the British.

The Dutch Era   With the defeat of the Armada, Indonesia was opened to still another European power, the Dutch. At about the same time that Spain moved to take over Portugal, it lost the Netherlands when its citizenry revolted. England supported the Dutch, and all hope of regaining control of its lost territory was destroyed along with the Armada.

The Dutch almost immediately took advantage of their new status. They sent an initial expedition designed to test the feasibility of opening trade, which arrived in the Indonesian islands in 1596. The voyage had limited success but set the stage for a much larger effort several years later. The Dutch founded the Dutch East India Company with the goal of taking charge of the trade in spices from the islands. Almost simultaneously, the Dutch Reformed Church began recruiting missionaries to spread Protestant Christianity wherever the Company established its hegemony. Their gaining hegemony in the Indies would not go entirely uncontested, as the Portuguese fought to hold on to their territory and the British chartered their East India

Company and opened their first trading center at Banda on the north tip of Sumatra.

Neither the Dutch nor British traders were enthusiastic about religion and did little to support the Protestant missionaries, with the exception of the Dutch suppressing the Roman Catholic Church in the areas under its control. The first Protestant (Dutch) church was formed at Ambon, in the Moluccas, in 1615. By the end of the 1620s, the Dutch were in firm control of the spice-rich Moluccas.

Both the British and the Dutch established forts adjacent to Jayakarta. In 1619, the city became a battleground, changing hands several times before being burned to the ground. The Dutch emerged in control and from their fort began building a new city, which they named Batavia. The head of the Dutch East India Company, Jan Pieterszoon Coen (1587–1629), attempted to turn the Company into a political entity and made the first steps toward turning the island into a Dutch colony.

The Dutch East Indies Company was primarily interested in trade and profit and controlled the region economically. Numerous small Indonesian kingdoms rose, existed for longer and shorter periods, and fell. Rather than attempt to replacing local rulers with Dutch administrators, the Company tended to be satisfied with keeping a stranglehold on trade and moving against any open revolts.

To assist their control of the islands, the Company invited many Chinese to take up residence in the islands. The Chinese had been there for centuries, operating way stations for trade between China and India and the Middle East. The Dutch encouraged further settlement of the Chinese and used them as go betweens with the local populations that produced the products the Dutch so valued. The arriving Chinese brought Chinese indigenous religion to the island as well as introducing Chinese Buddhism. Two temples now located in Jakarta date to the 1660s. At the same time, many of the leading Chinese who had been able to ingratiate themselves with local rulers converted to Islam.

Through the 18th century, the growth of Protestantism was slow, but it slowly emerged in those areas controlled by the Dutch East India Company. A New Testament appeared in 1668 and the complete Bible in 1733, but many congregations were without regular pastoral care. Also, due to the difficulties of transportation and communication, no regional synods emerged. By default, the church council in Batavia provided overall leadership. Indonesians served as preachers and teachers but were not admitted to ordination and could not serve the sacraments. By the time that the Company went bankrupt in 1799, there were some 50,000 Christians throughout the islands.

The failure of the Company and the assumption of direct control of the islands had significant implications for the Christian community. A new colony, the Dutch East Indies, emerged as a political entity. The government professed to be religiously neutral and made no direct efforts to suppress Islam or the remnants of Hinduism (especially on Bali) and Buddhism. It did reverse the Company's policy relative to Roman Catholicism, and priest-missionaries began to arrive in force. It organized all the Protestant work into the Protestant Church of the Netherlands Indies and tied it to the state church in Holland. As a part of the officially neutral state church, it developed no further missions. That peculiar policy opened the door for a spectrum of new missionary agencies, both those based in Holland and others based in various European and North American countries. The first missionaries to arrive were sent to tend the small communities of Christians beyond the care of the Protestant Church of the Netherlands Indies. Then as the number of missionaries multiplied, numerous entirely new missions were opened, especially among the people groups that still followed one of the indigenous religions.

Various Reformed and Lutheran missionary agencies (such as the Basel and Rhenish Missions), especially some influenced by the European Pietist movement, took the lead in evangelizing the Indies through the 19th century, but by the end of the century they were joined by Baptists, the Salvation Army, and the Seventh-day Adventists. Additional churches arrived through the 20th century, including the Christian and Missionary Alliance and the Jehovah's Witnesses.

The newer missionaries tended to focus their effort locally, in the language of the people among whom they worked. While some Christian activity produced sizable churches, language, ethnic divisions, and the difficulty of traveling between the islands became bar-

Indonesia

Religion	Followers in 1970	Followers in 2010	% of Population	Annual % growth 2000–2010	Followers in 2025	Followers in 2050
Muslims	91,060,000	188,164,000	78.5	1.33	210,973,000	227,738,000
Christians	11,339,000	28,992,000	12.1	1.41	35,796,000	42,008,000
Protestants	6,268,000	17,100,000	7.1	1.64	21,000,000	21,000,000
Roman Catholics	2,620,000	6,650,000	2.8	0.49	8,200,000	11,000,000
Independents	2,424,000	6,800,000	2.8	1.92	8,500,000	12,000,000
Ethnoreligionists	6,570,000	5,900,000	2.5	1.32	5,000,000	5,000,000
New religionists	6,000,000	4,350,000	1.8	0.29	4,300,000	4,000,000
Hindus	2,318,000	4,550,000	1.9	1.32	5,100,000	5,500,000
Agnostics	950,000	3,250,000	1.4	1.84	5,000,000	7,000,000
Chinese folk	980,000	2,100,000	0.9	1.32	2,400,000	2,550,000
Buddhists	1,099,000	1,970,000	0.8	1.32	2,200,000	2,400,000
Atheists	200,000	288,000	0.1	1.32	400,000	600,000
Baha'is	10,700	30,000	0.0	1.32	50,000	80,000
Sikhs	5,000	5,900	0.0	1.32	7,500	9,000
Jews	100	200	0.0	1.39	300	300
Total population	**120,532,000**	**239,600,000**	**100.0**	**1.32**	**271,227,000**	**296,885,000**

riers to the development of national organizations. Thus, a number of Protestant denominations developed, a few developing into memberships in the hundreds of thousands, including the Batak Christian Protestant Church, the Christian Churches of Java, the Evangelical Church of Indonesia, the Evangelical Christian Church of Irian Jaya, the Indonesia Protestant Christian Church, the Karo Batak Protestant Church, the Pentecostal Church of Indonesia, and the Toraja Christian Church.

As of 2009, 27 Protestant churches were members of the World Council of Churches. The World Evangelical Alliance is also active in Indonesia through The Fellowship of Indonesia Evangelical Churches and Institutions. As of 2008, Christianity made up approximately 13 percent of the population, of which 7 million are Roman Catholics, 14 million Protestants, and 7 million post-Protestant and evangelical Christians.

Modern Indonesia In the middle of the 20th century, the Dutch East Indies went through a significant trauma. Dutch control was ended by the invasion and occupation of the islands by the Japanese. After the war and the Japanese, before the Dutch could reassert control, suppressed independence efforts from before the war were invigorated. Immediately after the war, indigenous forces rose up and asserted the establish-

ment of the new state of Indonesia, and appointed Sukarno (b. Kusno Sosrodihardjo, 1901–1970) as the first president. The Dutch instituted hostilities to try to regain their hegemony but admitted defeat in 1949.

The new Republic of Indonesia was founded on a rather unique set of principles termed the Panca Sila, through which the government recognizes the role of religion in the life of the nation and the daily life of the citizenry. Religion is also seen as a factor in maintaining the unity of the nation. The five principles in the Panca Sila include belief in God, humanity, national unity, consultative democracy, and social justice. Indonesia thinks of itself as a democracy in which a variety of religions and beliefs are recognized. It considers itself a religious state, meaning it is neither an Islamic nor a secular state, but a country with a religious foundation.

Since independence, Indonesia has experienced a variety of upheavals as attempts to unify the multi-ethnic, multi-linguistic, and multi-religious country have been met with various separatist movements. The 1945 Constitution rejected the extremes of Western individualism and Marxist Communism, choosing instead to emphasize the Panca Sila and institutionalize a strong presidency. In 1959, President Sukarno, who had acquired additional powers year by year, attempted to respond to the various tensions in the country by disbanding the Constituent Assembly, whose members had been unable to operate effectively due to allegiances to the various ethnic, linguistic, and regional constituencies they represented. He also invited the Communists into the political community and reverted to the unrevised Constitution of 1945. In 1963, Sukarno was named president for life.

In 1965, with Sukarno ill from kidney disease, a coup attempt led to the death of six senior army generals (the army having been strong supporters). A surviving General Suharto (1921–2008) became the new president. He continued to emphasize the importance of the Panca Sila ideal. At the same time he moved to create a more uniform Indonesia and build a strong autocratic centralized government, while using the army to assist his rule.

Among those who suffered the most from his policies were the Chinese. Wishing to integrate them more completely into mainstream Indonesian society, in 1967 he instituted a set of policies that led to the closing of the Chinese-language publishing centers and Chinese schools, and a ban on the public display of Chinese script. All non-Islamic Chinese religious expressions were confined to households. Individual Chinese citizens were "encouraged" to take an Indonesian name. These policies remained in effect until the end of Suharto's presidency (1998).

His Timor policy proved one of the most visible failures of the Suharto years. The eastern half of the island came out of World War II as a surviving remnant of the former Portuguese presence in region. The western part of the island had been part of the Dutch East Indies and was incorporated into independent Indonesia in 1949. The two parts of the island were divided ethnically and religiously (with East Timor predominantly Roman Catholic). Following the withdrawal of the Portuguese in 1975, Indonesian forces invaded East Timor and attempted to integrate it into the country. Resistance was encountered on all levels. In 1996, two men, one being Roman Catholic Bishop Carlos Filipe Ximenes Belo, were awarded the Nobel Peace Prize for their efforts to end the conflict. In 1999 a public referendum rejected Indonesian rule and shortly thereafter the Indonesian occupying force withdrew. East Timor attained full independence in 2002 as the new nation of Timor Leste.

Meanwhile, Islam remains the dominant religion of Indonesia, and today it is the most populous Muslim country in the world. More than 80 percent of the citizenry consider themselves Muslims, most of the Shafiite School of Islam. At the same time, Indonesia recognizes five major world religions: Islam, Hinduism, Buddhism, Catholicism, and Protestantism. As in China, Indonesia views Catholicism and Protestantism as separate religions, though their relationship as two branches of Christianity is also understood. Chinese indigenous religions are generally grouped together under Buddhism. A variety of local religious traditions have come to be officially classified as forms of Hinduism. Hinduism has special status on Bali, where the great majority of residents follow the faith.

One sign of its religious foundation is the large national mosque that was erected soon after independence. Today, the Istiqlal Mosque (Independence Mosque), located in the center of Jakarta, is the largest mosque in Southeast Asia whether measured in terms of the number of worshippers it can accommodate, the size of the building, or the land it covers.

The Indonesian Muslim community includes a number of Sufi groups, Sufism having a long and honored presence on the islands that goes back to the Wali Sango. Sufism permeated Indonesian Islam and accounts for much of the country's relatively irenic religious atmosphere. Today there are numerous Sufi communities in Indonesia including local representatives of the Chistiniyya, Naqshbandriyya, Qadiriyya, Shadhiliyya, and the Tijaniyya Sufi orders. By the early 20th century, Sufism was largely viewed as being on the wane, its primary visible adherents being elderly men residing in the smaller villages. In the 19th century, it had been challenged by Wahhabism and the Islamic modernist movement. Though from the opposite ends of the Islamic spectrum, the two movements agreed on stripping Islam of a variety of older folk elements to which Sufis seemed the most attached. Through the 20th century, however, Sufi spirituality enjoyed a marked revival in urban areas and now has found the allegiance of the young and old of both sexes.

On one edge of Indonesian Sufism are a variety of Islamic-influenced spiritual movements such as Subud, Sapta Dharma, and Sumarah that also exist as part of the larger religious world of Indonesia. Generally known as Kebatinan or Kejawen, these groups represent a modern spirituality that draws on indigenous beliefs and practices, especially those of Java, as well as elements from Hinduism and Buddhism. Since independence, neo-Confucianism has also asserted itself as a religious community.

To deal with this multi-religious community, the Indonesian government established a Department of Religion in 1946. The Department of Religion subsequently grew into one of the largest government departments, among its other duties being the promotion of religious harmony and the management of conflicts that might arise among the varied religious communities, and cooperation with other countries in the field of higher education (including scholarly exchange programs). The department also regulates marriage and divorce among Muslims and facilitates Indonesian participation in the Islamic pilgrimages (the hajj).

J. Gordon Melton

See also: Ancestors; Baptists; Basel Mission; Batak Christian Community Church; Borobudar; Chinese Religions; Chistiñiyya Sufi Order; Christian and Missionary Alliance; Christian Churches of Java; Ethnoreligions; Evangelical Christian Church of Irian Jaya; Indonesia, Buddhism in; Indonesia, Confucianism in; Indonesia, Hinduism in; Jehovah's Witnesses; Karo Batak Protestant Church; Mosques; Prambanan; Qadiriyya Sufi Order; Rhenesh Mission; Roman Catholic Church; Salvation Army; Seventh-day Adventist Church; Shadhiliyya Sufi Order; Subud; Sumarah; Tijaniyya Sufi Orders; Timor Leste; Toraja Church; Wahhabi Islam; World Council of Churches; World Evangelical Alliance.

References

Abdullah, Taufik, and Sharon Siddique, eds. *Islam and Society in Southeast Asia.* Singapore: Institute of Southeast Asian Studies, 1986.

Bauswein, Jean-Jacques, and Lukas Vischer, eds. *The Reformed Family Worldwide: A Survey of Reformed Churches, Theological Schools, and International Organizations.* Grand Rapids, MI: William B. Eerdmans Publishing Company, 1999.

Boland, B. J. *The Struggle of Islam in Modern Indonesia.* The Hague, Netherlands: H. H. L. Smith, 1970.

Geels, Antoon. *Subud and the Javanese Mystical Tradition.* Richmond, Surrey, UK: Curzon, 1997.

Geertz, Clifford. *The Religion of Java.* Glencoe, IL: Free Press, 1958.

The Growing Seed: The Christian Church in Indonesia. 20 vols. Jakarta: DGI Institute, 1976–.

Howell, Julia Day. "Sufism and the Indonesian Islamic Revival." *Journal of Asian Studies* 60, no. 3 (August 2001):701–729. http://www.indopubs.com/indosufism.pdf. Accessed September 15, 2009.

Howell, Julia Day, Subandi, and Peter L. Nelson. "Indonesian Sufism, Signs of Resurgence." In *New Trends and Developments in the World of Islam*, edited by Peter B. Clarke. London: Luzac Oriental, 1998.

"Indonesia's History and Background." *AsianInfo.Org.* http://www.asianinfo.org/asianinfo/indonesia/pro-history.htm. Accessed September 15, 2009.

Kipp, R. S., and S. Rogers. *Indonesian Religions in Transition.* Tucson: University of Arizona Press, 1987.

McVey, Ruth, ed. *Indonesia.* New Haven, CT: Yale University Press, 1963.

Munoz, Paul Michel. *Early Kingdoms of the Indonesian Archipelago and the Malay Peninsula.* Paris: Editions Didier Millet, 2006.

Noer, Deliar. *The Modernist Muslim Movement in Indonesia, 1900–1942.* Singapore: Oxford University Press, 1973.

"An Online Timeline of Indonesian History." *Serajah Indonesia.* http://www.gimonca.com/sejarah/sejarah01.shtml. Accessed September 15, 2009.

Woodard, M. R. *Islam in Java: Normative Piety and Mysticism in the Sultanate of Yogyakarta.* Tucson: University of Arizona Press, 1989.

Indonesia, Buddhism in

When Indonesia became independent in 1950, almost nothing from the Buddhist cultures that had thrived in

A Buddhist temple in Sumatra, Indonesia. (Corel)

Sumatra, Java, Bali, and East-Kalimantan between approximately the fourth and the 16th centuries CE had survived the Islamization of the archipelago. Today, only some stone inscriptions; Buddhist statues and seals; remnants of ancient temples, such as the eighth-century Central Javanese Borobudur; ancient Chinese reports; and a few survivals in some of the local traditions bear witness to the expansion of different Buddhist schools throughout the western part of maritime Southeast Asia.

The first more comprehensive historical account of Buddhist influence in the archipelago was written by I-Ching, a Chinese Buddhist pilgrim who, in 671, embarked on a journey from Canton to India. In order to await favorable monsoon winds, he stopped over in Palembang, the center of an emerging Buddhist empire in Sumatra called Srivijaya. I Ching recommended the local religious schools to Chinese students of Buddhism, after he himself had studied Sanskrit grammar in Srivijaya for six months. In 672, he departed to

India, returning to Srivijaya on his way back to China. I-Ching observed that Mahayana had only recently been introduced to Sumatra, whereas the Mulasarvastivadanikaya—the Theravada canon in Sanskrit—had been followed for a long time. This tallies with the finds of Amaravati-style Buddha statues in Sumatra, West-Kalimantan, and Java, pointing to the dissemination of early Buddhist schools, often classified as Theravada, since the second century. In the late seventh century, however, Mahayana schools of Buddhism began to acquire ideological dominance over the regional courts. Renowned Mahayana teachers from India traveled to Srivijaya, among them Vajrabodhi, the first teacher of the Yogacara school and abbot of Nalanda, as well as Atisa, the reformer of Buddhism in Tibet. The former visited Sumatra in 741, and the latter studied for 12 years (1011–1023) under the local high priest, Dharmakirti.

Between 750 and 850, a Mahayana Buddhist dynasty also reigned in Central Java: the Sailendra, who erected the famous terraced temple-monument Borobudur. Their influence ended inexplicably in the mid-ninth century, while an older dynasty attached to the worship of Siva re-emerged to rule the island. Nevertheless, Buddhism continued to coexist with Hinduism, both gradually blending into a distinctly Old Javanese creed called Siva-Buddha religion. The last regime to follow it, the East Javanese Empire of Majapahit, was eventually conquered by Muslim forces around 1530. By then, North India, the Malay Peninsula, and Sumatra had already undergone a thorough Islamization process, which had severed large-scale communication between Java and the Buddhist countries of South and Southeast Asia. Majapahitan culture survived in Bali, though, transforming into a distinctly Balinese blend of Buddhism, Saivism, and ancestor worship.

Buddhism was reintroduced to Indonesia in a totally different form in the first decades of the 20th century. It was, in fact, the increasingly popular Theosophical Society that sparked growing interest in Buddhism among Dutch colonials, Chinese immigrants, and Native noblemen. Offering the Dutch a more rational version of Asian spirituality, Chinese immigrants a way of reinvigorating their Chineseness, and subjugated Javanese as well as Balinese noblemen a medium through which to reconnect to their glorious ancient past, Buddhism was disseminated in a Theravada and a Chinese Mahayana guise. In 1934, the Sri Lankan monk Narada Mahathera visited Java, planting a Bodhi tree at the recently restored Borobudur. It was actually a seedling from a Bodhi tree in Sri Lanka, which had itself been grown from a seed of the original Bodhi tree in Bodh Gaya. The latter had been brought to Sri Lanka in the late 19th century by the Theosophist Ir. Meertens. Narada Mahathera's gift thus reflected one of the trajectories of Buddhist revival in modern Indonesia. As Theravada followers forged closer contacts with Buddhist monasteries in Sri Lanka, Burma, and Thailand, Chinese Mahayana priests were invited to some of the Indonesian-Chinese Buddhist communities. Still, there were no clear-cut boundaries between the two groups.

In 1953, an Indonesian-born Chinese, Tee Boan-An, a former Theosophist and student of the Chinese Mahayana priest Chen Ping Lau He Sang, departed to Burma, where he was ordained as the first Theravada monk from Indonesia in 1954. Under his new name, Ashin Jinarakkhita, he returned to Indonesia the same year. In 1955, he formed the first Buddhist lay association, Persaudaraan Upasaka Upasika Indonesia (PUUI), in independent Indonesia, which he integrated two years later into the Indonesian Buddhist Association (Perhimpunan Buddhis Indonesia, Perbudi), comprising both the Theravada and Mahayana priesthood and their following. In order to acquire official recognition of Buddhism from the Indonesian Ministry of Religion, Jinarakkhita had from early on tried to adapt Indonesian Buddhism (Buddhayana) to universal monotheism (Ketuhanan Yang Maha Esa) as professed in the Indonesian Constitution. By equating the primordial Buddha (Adi-Buddha) with God, however, he eventually provoked the split-up of the national Buddhist community. There were those who could not endorse even the faintest allusion to theism, and there were others who increasingly rejected the spiritual guidance of Buddhists specially approved of by the Indonesian government. This has applied in particular to the strict followers of Theravada as well as to Nichiren Shosho International, which became popular in Indonesia in the 1970s. Members of the Chinese-Indonesian community, on the other hand, preferred a kind of folk Buddhism that also incorporated Daoist and Confucian tenets and customs (Tridharma).

In the last generation, the True Buddha School, a Chinese Vajrayana Buddhist group that originated in Taiwan, has built an impressive presence across Indonesia. In the process, the leaders discovered many Vajrayana Buddhists already present in central rural Java who trace their religion to the days of the building of Borobudar. Recognizing their beliefs as being reproduced by the true Buddha School, many have affiliated, and in return their leaders have been given special status in the school.

After the fall of the Sukarno government in May 1998, religious liberalization encouraged a part of the Chinese-Indonesian community to drop out of Tridharma Buddhism and to fight for the recognition of neo-Confucianism as a religion. This recognition was granted by former president Abdurrahman Wahid in 2000. Today, Indonesia's 2 to 3 percent Buddhists are a heterogeneous minority supporting monotheistic

Buddhayana, Theravada, various Mahayana traditions (Chinese, Tibetan, Japanese, reinvented Javanese), Tridharma, and Nichiren.

Martin Ramstedt

See also: Borobudur; Mahayana Buddhism; Nichiren Shoshu; Theravada Buddhism; True Buddha School.

References

Brown, Iem. "The Revival of Buddhism in Modern Indonesia." In *"Hinduism" in Modern Indonesia: Hindu Dharma Indonesia between Local, National, and Global Interests,* edited by Martin Ramstedt. Richmond, Surrey, UK: Curzon, 2002.

Coedès, Georges. *The Indianized States of Southeast Asia.* Honolulu: East-West Center, 1968.

Ishii, Yoneo. "Modern Buddhism in Indonesia." In *Buddhist Studies in Honour of Hammalava Saddhatissa,* edited by Gatare Dhammapala, Richard Gombrich, and K. R. Norman. Nugegoda, Sri Lanka: University of Sri Jayewardenepura, 1984.

Soekmono, J. G. Casparis, and Jacques Dumarçay. *Borobudur: Prayer in Stone.* Singapore: Archipelago Press, 1990.

Indonesia, Confucianism in

Chinese travelers were journeying in maritime Southeast Asia as early as the beginning of the Christian era. They acquired a dominant position as interlocal traders and merchants in the populous areas of the western part of what is now Indonesia, before the arrival of the Dutch at the end of the 16th century. The Dutch East India Company, formed in 1602, succeeded in ousting the Chinese from their dominant position in Southeast Asian commerce. By creating an apartheid society, consisting of "Europeans," "Natives," and "alien Orientals," the Dutch also obstructed the blending of Chinese immigrants with the indigenous peoples. Furthermore, from 1900 on, colonial policy began to expressly favor the interests of the Natives to the detriment of the Chinese, who were pictured as amoral and unscrupulous exploiters impeding the progress of the Native race.

The Chinese community reacted by revitalizing its Chinese identity. In 1900 the Chinese Association (Tiong Hoa Hwee Koan [THHK]) was established in Batavia, with branches founded in all major cities of the Dutch East Indies. The THHK set out to promote Confucianism as the spiritual power of all Chinese, taking up efforts similar to those of the leader of the Confucian reform movement in China, K'ang Yu-wei (1858–1927), who had been trying to establish neo-Confucianism as a national religion in the motherland. Countering the increasing inability of Chinese people in Indonesia to understand *guo-yu* (the national language, or Mandarin), the THHK established more than 250 Chinese schools where students received lessons in both Confucianism and Mandarin, alongside a modern education. Already in 1906, the first Confucian shrine, Boen Bio, was built in Surabaya, in northeast Java. In 1918 the Confucian Religion Council was founded in Surakarta, central Java, and in 1923 a congress was held at nearby Yogyakarta, during which the Center for the Confucian Religion Assembly (Khong Kauw Tjong Hwee) was established. The first book on Confucianism in the Malay language, *Bahasa Melayu Betawi*, had already been published in 1897. By 1936 a translation of four Confucian texts (the *Ta Hsueh* [*Great Learning*], *Chung Yung* [*Doctrine of the Mean*], *Lun Yu* [*Analects*], and *Mencius*) had followed. In addition, several weeklies in the Malay language were published to effectively promote Confucianism.

During the Indonesian struggle for independence, the Indonesian Chinese asserted their anti-colonial attitude. In 1946 Sukarno (1901–1970), the leader of the Indonesian independence movement, granted Confucianism the status of "religion" (Agama Khonghucu). Ruling as Indonesia's first president from 1945 on, Sukarno reconfirmed his decision in 1961. He thereby supported the claims of the Khong Kauw Tjong Hwee Indonesia—as it was now called—that the Confucian concept of heaven (*thian*) is equivalent to Christian and Muslim monotheism, that Confucius was a prophet, and that the Confucian ethic is "religious law" to be observed by all Confucianists. Consequently, the Su Si, a compilation of the above-mentioned four classical texts, was instituted as a "holy book," and Confucius's birthday (August 27) and the day of his death (February 18) were made official holidays for his followers.

Affirming the necessity to assimilate, the Khong Kauw Tjong Hwee Indonesia dropped its Chinese name in 1964 and took the Indonesian designation Gabungan Perhimpunan Agama Khonghucu Seluruh Indonesia (Federation of Associations of the Confucian Religion in the whole of Indonesia). At the same time, the Youth Association of the Confucian Religion (Gabungan Pemuda Agama Khonghucu) was established, paralleling the youth organizations of all the other recognized religious communities in Indonesia.

When General Suharto (b. 1921–2008) emerged as the most powerful man in Indonesia after quelling an abortive coup in 1965 and eventually deposing Sukarno as president, he was at first also prepared to accept Confucianism as an officially recognized religion. Pursuing a rigorous purge of atheism and Communism, his regime made religious affiliation obligatory for every citizen. Hence, Confucianism needed to adapt to the rigid standards of the Ministry of Religion to counter the increasingly voiced accusation that it was nothing but an alien philosophy of ethics and not a universal religion.

In 1967 the Supreme Council for Confucian Religion in Indonesia (Majelis Tinggi Agama Khonghucu Indonesia [MATAKIN]) was established. Regional branches were also formed, the so-called Councils for Confucian Religion in Indonesia (Majelis Khonghucu Indonesia [MAKIN]). More than one hundred places of worship (lithang) were built. Following the model of the Christian churches, a Confucian clergy was formed that includes haksu (high priests), bunsu (Confucian teachers), and kausing (missionaries). Alongside the youth organization, a Women's Association (Wanita Agama Khonghucu Indonesia) was founded. Confucian rites were celebrated with deep religiosity. Chinese New Year (Imlek) has become the best-known festivity of the Confucian yearly cycle. There are also monthly services, Sunday services, funerals, and weddings, at which altar boys and girls assist the officiating priest and a choir sings Confucian hymns.

Yet, all these measures could not abate the growing doubts about the religious status of Confucianism. In 1969, one year after his official appointment as president, Suharto interdicted all public manifestations of Chinese culture, demanding "full assimilation." Consequently, Confucian weddings were not acknowledged anymore. Children resulting from such unions were denied birth certificates and thus normal civic rights. Confucianism and Mandarin could no longer be taught at public schools. From 1977 on, Confucianists were forced to have their children educated in one of the recognized religions. Nevertheless, private practice of Confucianism was not forbidden, and the MATAKIN was still allowed to exist under the supervision of the Directorate General for the Guidance of the Hindu and Buddhist Communities (Direktorat Jenderal Bimbingan Masyarakat Agama Hindu dan Budha). Nonetheless, many ethnic Chinese chose to convert to Buddhism and even to Christianity and Islam, while secretly continuing to perform Confucian rites, including Imlek.

As a result, official Confucian membership numbers became obscure. In 1974 the MATAKIN counted 3 million followers, while the official census registered only 99,920 people (0.8 percent of the total Indonesian population). In order to counter anti-Chinese policies, the Indonesian Chinese Eternal Cultural Foundation (Yayasan Lestari Kebudayaan Tionghoa Indonesia) was formed. One of its major goals was to achieve the official recognition of Confucianism as a religion and of Imlek as a national holiday. Although this effort gained significant support from representatives of other denominations, anti-Chinese sentiments continued to smolder among the Muslim majority, impeding official recognition of Agama Khonghucu. In the wake of the Asian economic crisis and the ensuing demise of the Suharto regime, Indonesian Chinese were blamed for the destitute Indonesian economy and suffered severe pogroms. Their situation improved notably when Abdurrahman Wahid (b. 1940) was elected president in October 1999. Wahid instantly lifted the ban on the public celebration of Chinese festivities, making Imlek an optional state holiday and eventually recognizing Agama Khonghucu as one of the religions adhered to by the Indonesian people. This helped to restore a sense of pride and recognition among the Indonesian Chinese, who today are estimated at 16 to 17 million people (7 to 8 percent of the total Indonesian population). Confucianists are numbered at around one million people.

However, the performance of the classical Confucian rites has become a thing of the past, since most of them require the participation of large, extended families. Most of the Indonesian Chinese today have small, nuclear families consisting of four to five people. Moreover, modernization has led people to concentrate more on the future than on their filial duty toward their ancestors. Just like Christmas in the West, Imlek has become, above all, a good opportunity for social gatherings as well as commercial pursuit.

Martin Ramstedt

See also: Atheism; Confucianism; Confucius.

References

Coppel, Charles A. "The Origin of Confucianism as an Organized Religion in Java, 1900–1923." *Journal of Southeast Asian Studies* 7, no. 1 (1981): 179–196.

Coppel, Charles A. "Is Confucianism a Religion? A 1923 Debate in Java." *Archipel* 38 (1989): 125–135.

Kwee Tek Hoay. *Origins of the Modern Chinese Movement in Indonesia*. Ithaca, NY: Cornell University Press, 1962.

Lasiyo. "Agama Khonghucu: An Emerging Form of Religious Life Among the Indonesian Chinese." Ph.D. diss., University of London, School of Oriental and African Studies, Centre of Religion and Philosophy, 1992.

Suryadinata, Leo. "Confucianism in Indonesia. Past and Present." *Southeast Asia: An International Quarterly* 3, no. 3 (1974): 881–903.

Indonesia, Hinduism in

During the period when Bali was coming under Dutch control between 1846 and 1908, the island was recognized as the last Hindu enclave by European Orientalists and soon became famous as such in the international jet set. The Balinese on their part, however, had not hitherto considered themselves as Hindus. Instead, the elite of traditional Balinese caste society, that is, the *satria* and *wesia* kings (*raja*) as well as the *brahmana* priests (*pedanda*), had seen themselves as descendants of the last Hindu-Javanese kingdom of Majapahit, which had fallen to Muslim forces around 1530. The Majapahitan culture and religion itself had been a blending of elements of different Buddhist schools, Vaishnavism, Saivism, and autochthonous traditions involving ancestor worship.

Ancient Indian culture had influenced the western part of the archipelago since approximately the second century CE. Among the earliest archaeological finds pointing to the dissemination of various strands of classical Hinduism in West Kalimantan as well as West and East Java from at least the fifth century on were the names of kings inscribed in stone, along with statues of Siva, Vishnu, and Brahma as well as those of their respective vehicles and family. The construction of the various Shaivite temples (*candi*) in Central Java from the late eighth century on culminated in the famous Candi Prambanan that was built in the mid-ninth century. Here, we also encounter the earliest proof of the dissemination of the Ramayana in the archipelago: a detailed relief recounting the story of Rama and Sita according to the Valmiki version. From the 10th century until the fall of Majapahit, a rich literature in the Old Javanese language developed in East Java, recreating both the Ramayana and Mahabharata in the local vernacular as well as addressing topics of other Indian works in an idiosyncratic manner. The Indian epics had a great impact on aesthetic development at the Hindu-Javanese courts, whereas the study of the Indian philosophical systems, Mimamsa, Samkhya, and Yoga, as well as the texts and practices of the Saiva Siddhanta, were the domain of the Shaivite priesthood. At the royal rituals, geared to reaffirm and reinforce the sacrality of local kings and their realms, the latter practiced side by side with Vaishnava and Buddhist clerics.

The practice of deifying dead local rulers continued to thrive in Bali, the heir of Hindu-Javanese culture after the downfall of Majapahit at the beginning of the 16th century. The three upper castes (*triwangsa*), tracing their descent back to noblemen and priests from Majapahit, actually sponsored a plethora of local rituals that revolved around commemorating their Javanese ancestors (*bhatara*). The Sudra majority were obliged to join in the veneration of the progenitors of their patrons and rulers. These rituals—in fact, all traditional rituals—were ultimately designed to reestablish or maintain the correspondence between the visible world (*sakala*) and the universal principles of the cosmic order that had emanated from Siva and

Prambanan ruins in East Java, Indonesia. (Dreamstime)

were believed to be hidden in the invisible world (*nis-kala*). Successful performance of the rituals (*yadnya*) would activate the life-giving aspects (*kerta*) of the transcendent yet immanent cosmic principles, and important agents in this process were the ancestors of the noble families.

Although the various categories of Balinese priests practiced yoga and meditation (*semadi*), the majority of Balinese were thus immersed in a ritual system that largely consisted of details resembling other so-called animistic traditions in the archipelago. As soon as Bali was integrated into the Dutch East Indies, both Christian and Muslim missionaries were referring to this majority when claiming that the Balinese were not really Hindu but rather "animistic heathens" strongly in need of "religion." At the same time, the socio-political innovations introduced by the Dutch colonial administration began to threaten traditional beliefs and lifestyles. In order to protect their religion against destructive outside influence, while also proposing to

abolish customs that were not in accordance with the new times, several religious reform organizations were formed between 1917 and 1942 (the beginning of the Japanese occupation). Influenced by European Orientalists, who confirmed the link between Balinese culture and ancient Indian religion, as well as the Theosophical Society, who considered the Hindu-Javanese and Balinese nobility as descendants of the "Aryan race," these reform organizations looked to India for orientation. The more progressive ones embraced key issues of Indian reformed Hinduism, as seen in such groups as the Brahmo Samaj, professed by Rabindranath Tagore (1861–1941), who visited both Java and Bali in 1927. The more conservative ones, however, had stronger leanings toward (Balinese) orthodoxy and endorsed the (local) caste system.

After World War II and the ensuing independence of the unitary Indonesian nation-state, the Balinese experienced unexpected discrimination against their religion on the part of the Muslim-dominated Indonesian

Ministry of Religion. In order to comply with the Indonesian Constitution, which made belief in universal monotheism mandatory for every citizen, and to avoid forced conversion to either Islam or Christianity, the Balinese again resorted to Indian reformed Hinduism to reformulate the tenets of their belief. In 1961, the monotheistic Hindu Dharma was officially recognized by the Indonesian government. When adherence to a recognized religion became a matter of survival during the purge of Communism in late 1965, members of other ethnic groups in Java, South Sulawesi, North Sumatra, and Central Kalimantan with no inclination to convert to Islam or Christianity began to embrace Hinduism as an umbrella under which to continue their various local traditions. Although it is true that Indonesian Hinduism has been lenient toward the practice of local customs, the increasing influence of more discriminate Indian sects and movements, especially since the beginning of the 1990s, has widened the rift between the various factions within the Indonesian Hindu community. Today, the approximately 6 million Indonesian Hindus (2.9 percent of the total population) are not only divided along ethnic lines, but also on the basis of different attitudes toward issues such as vegetarianism, hegemony of priests trained in Indian philosophy rather than local concepts and practices, ritualism rather than greater emphasis on spiritual practices like prayer and meditation, and caste privileges.

When Hindu rule on Java was replaced by Muslim rule, the royal temple complex Prambanan was abandoned and later lost to the jungle and then to the memory. It was rediscovered in the 18th century, though refurbishment waited until the 20th century. In the last generation it has become both a major tourist site in the country and a renewed focus for the Hindu community.

Martin Ramstedt

See also: Ancestors; Brahmo Samaj; Meditation; Prambanan; Shaivism; Vaishnavism; Vegetarianism; Yoga.

References

Bakker, F. L. *The Struggle of the Hindu Balinese Intellectuals: Developments in Modern Hindu Thinking in Independent Indonesia*. Amsterdam: VU University Press, 1993.

Coedès, Georges. *The Indianized States of Southeast Asia*. Honolulu: East-West Center Press, 1968.

Iyer, Alessandra. *Prambanan: Sculpture and Dance in Ancient Java. A Study in Dance Iconography*. Bangkok: White Lotus Press, 1998.

Lyon, Margaret L. "Politics and Religious Identity: Genesis of a Javanese-Hindu Movement in Rural Central Java." Ph.D. diss., University of California, 1977.

Ramstedt, Martin, ed. *Hinduism in Modern Indonesia: Hindu Dharma Indonesia Between Local, National, and Global Interests*. Richmond, Surrey, UK: Curzon, 2002.

Indonesian Christian Church

The Indonesian Christian Church (Huria Kristen Indonesia [HKI]) originated as a split in the Rhenish Mission work (now the Protestant Christian Batak Church) on Sumatra. Some of the Indonesian leaders were seeking the ordination of Batak ministers and the elevation of more Batak people into other leadership positions. All of the ordained ministers were German, and they controlled the affairs of the church. Those who left were in northern Sumatra and spoke the Toba Batak language. The strength of the church remains in rural areas of Sumatra, but the church has spread as its members moved around the country in the latter part of the 20th century.

The new church adopted the organization of the parent body, with a synod headed by a president as the highest legislative body. Most pastors receive their training with the Theological Faculty at Nonmensen University. The church operates among some of the poorer people of Sumatra and has a rather limited institutional program. It has managed to develop a set of primary and secondary schools. It has also nurtured a project to bring clean drinking water to some of the more remote villages.

The ministerium of the church have worked on the problem, so crucial to Indonesian Christian life, of the relationship of Christian precept to *adat*, the rules and customs that have traditionally been passed down through the culture.

In the 1970s, with assistance from the Evangelical Lutheran Church in America and in cooperation with the Simalungun Protestant Christian Church, the HKI developed an innovative program for educating the church's large group of teacher-preachers who did not have the opportunity for seminary training. The program dealt with many immediate situations these leaders encountered but also included instructions in traditional theological topics. Integral to the program was the willingness of some older pastors to become mentors to the younger workers.

In 2005, the church reported 220,000 members. It is a member of the Lutheran World Federation and since 1965 of the World Council of Churches.

Indonesian Christian Church
Jalan Melanchton Siregar No. 111
Pematangsiantar 21128, North Sumatra
Indonesia

J. Gordon Melton

See also: Lutheran World Federation; Protestant Christian Batak Church; Rhenish Mission; World Council of Churches.

References

Bachmann, E. Theodore, and Mercia Brenne Bachmann. *Lutheran Churches in the World: A Handbook.* Minneapolis, MN: Augsburg Press, 1989.
Van Beek, Huibert. *A Handbook of the Churches and Councils: Profiles of Ecumenical Relationships.* Geneva: World Council of Churches, 2006.

Indonesian Gospel Tabernacle Church

The Indonesian Gospel Tabernacle Church (Gereja Kemah Injil Indonesia [GKII]) originated with a decision by the Christian and Missionary Alliance (CMA) to launch missionary work in the Netherlands Indies (now Indonesia). The decision was implemented by Robert A. Jaffray (1873–1945), who had worked in China for the previous 30 years. In 1927 he and Leland Wang founded the Chinese Foreign Mission Union and began work among Chinese migrants in several Indonesian urban areas. They also responded to an opening among the Mahakam people on Kalimantan and soon had a church of more than 2,000 members. Jeffray settled in Makassar, which became the early center of the work. In 1930 he opened a publishing house and two years later a Bible school.

One by one, the CMA selected areas neglected by both the Dutch Reformed missionaries and the German missionaries (primarily from the Rhenish Mission) and opened work in East Kalimantan, Lombok (1929), Bali (1931), Southern Sumatra (1933), and West Kalimantan (1935). Additional missions appeared over the next seven years. The greatest response came in East Kalimantan and Irian (opened in 1939). A second Bible school was opened in East Kalimantan in 1938. The use of Bible school graduates allowed the mission to spread rapidly and prepared it for independence. The mission also pioneered the use of an airplane to overcome the problems of travel through jungle terrain.

As the mission spread, it encountered people who had moved around the islands. Upon their conversion many of them returned to their homes and began churches in regions where there was an already existing Reformed church. Reformed church leaders rose to oppose the CMA. It was condemned for its relative lack of theological education and its introduction of American methods of missionary work. Working with the government, the Reformed church had the CMA expelled from several locations, including Bali. However, the mission had already become a large organization and by 1941 had 139 mission stations and had placed more than 100 Indonesian workers into the field.

The loss of the relatively small number of missionaries (20) during the war did not affect the CMA work as badly as that of the Reformed churches; however, the pain was real. Four American missionaries and 10 Indonesian workers were killed. Jeffray was one of two missionaries who died while interned. The Japanese forced the CMA church to join the regional councils of churches that it imposed upon the Protestant community (following a pattern already in place in Japan).

After the war, an expansive program to take the church to all of Indonesia had spectacular results. In 1951, the work was organized into three regional churches. Five years later these churches were given independence, and the missionaries became subordinate to the new church authorities. A new relationship between the now independent churches and the parent body was negotiated. In 1965, the three churches entered into a fellowship, Kemah Injil Gereja Masehi Indonesia. This fellowship grew to include three additional independent churches that matured from the CMA missionary efforts. In 1983 the fellowship was transformed into the new united Indonesian Gospel Tabernacle Church.

One sign of the growth of the new church during the 1970s and 1980s was the founding of additional Bible schools and the maturing of the original Bible school into the Jaffray Bible College (1958) and the Sekolah Tinggi Theologia Jeffray (1966). In 1990 the church reported 323,000 members. The church is a member of the Evangelical Fellowship of Asia, through which it is related to the World Evangelical Alliance and to the Alliance World Fellowship.

In the last generation, one member of the Indonesian Gospel Tabernacle church, Benny Giay (b. 1955), a theologian at the Walter Post Theological College in Western Papua, has gained notoriety for his activism on behalf of the rights of Papua people who reside in the western, Indonesian half of the island of New Guinea. In his various writings he has argued for a high degree of Papuan autonomy within the Indonesian state and system.

J. Gordon Melton

See also: Alliance World Fellowship; Christian and Missionary Alliance; Rhenish Mission; World Evangelical Alliance.

Reference

Bauswein, Jean-Jacques, and Lukas Vischner, eds. *The Reformed Family Worldwide: A Survey of Reformed Churches, Theological Schools, and International Organizations*. Grand Rapids, MI: William B. Eerdmans Publishing Company, 1999.

Initiatives for Change/Moral Rearmament

See CAUX-Initiatives for Change.

Insight Meditation Society

The Insight Meditation Society (IMS) was founded in 1975 on the 80-acre site of a former Catholic seminary and boys' school just north of Barre, Massachusetts, as a nonprofit organization for the intensive practice of insight meditation (*vipassana*), a system largely developed by the Burmese monk Mahasi Sayadaw (1904–1982). Part of what some individuals refer to as a 20th-century modernization movement in Theravada, vipassana is an intensive form of meditation aimed primarily at a lay-oriented audience and designed to promote the attainment of the first of the four traditional levels of sainthood.

The site was purchased collectively by Joseph Goldstein, Jack Kornfield, Sharon Salzberg, and Jacqueline Schwartz, each of whom had studied with Asian vipassana teachers. Goldstein (b. 1944) studied with Mahasi Sayadaw (1904–1982) and his students Anagarika Munindra (1914–2003) and U Pandita (b. 1921); Salzberg (b. 1952) studied with S. N. Goenka, Mahasi Sayadaw, Munindra, and U Pandita; Kornfield (b. 1945) studied with Achaan Cha (also Ajahn Chah, 1918–1992) and Mahasi Sayadaw. Each returned to the United States to begin teaching various retreats, and although these initial retreats were what Gil Fronsdal calls "a hybrid of Asian forms," their collective style was eventually geared for a Western audience of convert Buddhists, and thus virtually stripped of the religious trappings of Theravada, such as rituals, chanting, and the like. A forest refuge opened in 2003. Jack Kornfield moved to California in 1981, eventually founding Spirit Rock Meditation Center in western Marin County.

There are a number categories of teacher at IMS, as the center is called. These include senior Dharma teachers, comprised of a 16-person group of "core" faculty and a larger list of visiting teachers. In addition, there is always a "resident teacher" at the center. IMS sponsors various retreats for beginning and experienced meditators, consisting of daily meditation and nightly Dharma talks, interspersed with individual and group interviews with the teachers. The retreats are profoundly rigorous in nature, generally beginning as early as 5:00 a.m. and maintaining a routine of alternating periods of silent sitting and walking meditation, culminating around 10:00 p.m. Participants live in austere single quarters, segregated by gender, and all meals are vegetarian. In addition to the group retreats, experienced meditators may engage in self-retreats, work retreats, and long-term practice retreats. There is also a youth outreach program. In the quarter-century since its founding IMS has grown enormously and now accommodates more than 2,500 retreatants annually, ranging from 2-day weekend retreats to one 84-day retreat. Most retreats are 7 to 9 days in length.

Although Asian vipassana teachers focus on the attainment of freedom, negatively defined as the freedom from certain characteristics such as greed, hatred, and delusion (the traditional "three poisons" of Buddhism) and positively defined as the attainment of *nibbana* (*nirvana*), Western teachers like those at IMS stress the positive aspects of freedom, such as stress reduction, a happy life, and compassionate living. Although many traditional Theravada practices, such as merit-making, and taking monastic vows, are not emphasized, four concomitant practices of vipassana are stressed: mindfulness (Pali: *sati*), loving-kindness (*metta*), ethics (*sila*), and generosity (*dana*).

Like many American Buddhist communities, IMS has developed an academic component in order to help its practitioners to combine practice and study in a mutually reinforcing environment. To that end, the Barre Center for Buddhist Studies (BCBS) was founded in 1989 on 90 acres of wooded land, a half mile from IMS. The center's executive director is Andrew Olendzki, and the resident scholar and programming director is Mu Soeng, a former Zen monk. In addition to Spirit Rock Meditation Center, the Cambridge Insight Meditation Center near Boston, the Vipassana Foundation of Maui, and Gaia House in the United Kingdom are associated with IMS. Although IMS generally maintains a low-profile, it has also been a leader in developing practices based on compassion and ethics for members and teachers alike. It has even developed an "Insight Meditation Teacher's Code of Ethics," which has enabled IMS to remain remarkably free of the scandals that have been documented in other American Buddhist communities. IMS also offers a rich series of online resources via their website at www.dharma.org. These include audios of guided medita-

tions, a glossary of terms, URLs for related websites, and a strong list of suggested readings.

The Insight Meditation Society is headquartered in Barre. The associated periodical, *Inquiring Mind*, is the national journal of the vipassana meditation movement. It can be accessed online at www.dharma.org/ij/index.htm.

Insight Meditation Society
1230 Pleasant Street
Barre, MA 01005
http://www.dharma.org

Charles S. Prebish

See also: Meditation.

References

Fronsdal, Gil. "Insight Meditation in the United States: Life, Liberty and the Pursuit of Happiness." In *The Faces of Buddhism in America*, edited by Charles S. Prebish and Kenneth K. Tanaka. Berkeley: University of California Press, 1998.

Fronsdal, Gil. "Virtues Without Rules: Ethics in the Insight Meditation Movement." In *Westward Dharma: Buddhism Beyond Asia*, edited by Charles S. Prebish and Martin Baumann. Berkeley: University of California Press, 2002.

Prebish, Charles S. *Luminous Passage: The Practice and Study of Buddhism in America*. Berkeley: University of California Press, 1999.

Seager, Richard Hughes. *Buddhism in America*. New York: Columbia University Press, 1999.

Integral Yoga International

"Integral yoga" refers both to the synchronization of the several forms of yoga teachings and to a specific group founded by Sri Swami Satchidananda (1914–2002), an Indian Hindu teacher who settled in the United States in the 1960s. Sri Swami Sivananda Saraswatiji Maharaj (1887–1963), a renowned Hindu teacher and revered holy man of the 20th century, is credited with first using the concept "integral yoga." Integral yoga basically means a practice that synthesizes the major yoga traditions—*hatha*, *raja*, *bhakti*, *jnana*, and *karma*. Sivananda also added a sixth, *japa yoga*, a practice based on the repetition of a mantra.

Sri Swami Satchidananda was one of several Sivananda disciples who carried his teachings beyond the traditional boundaries of Hinduism in India. Other disciples of Sivananda used the concept "integral yoga," but it is Satchidananda who is credited with both popularizing the concept and developing a synthesis of yoga teachings. (Sri Aurobindo, operating from a complexly different tradition, also used the term "integral yoga.") Satchidananda's organization has trademarked the term.

Satchidananda was born in 1914 in a small village of South India. After studying agriculture and science, he worked at several commercial and technical positions. Dissatisfied with these endeavors, he determined at age 28 to pursue a spiritual quest. He isolated himself and explored yoga through texts; later Satchidananda sat at the feet of several of India's great religious teachers.

In 1947 Satchidananda's spiritual quest led him to Swami Sivananda. He was initiated as a *sannyasin* (monk) in 1949 and, because of his mastery of the various forms of yoga, was given the title *yogiraj*, meaning "master of yoga." Satchidananda's affiliation with Sivananda and the latter's Divine Life Society extended over almost two decades. In addition to extensive lectures throughout India, Satchidananda taught yoga and established centers in Sri Lanka (then Ceylon), Hong Kong, Japan, Malaysia, Singapore, and the Philippines.

A two-day trip to New York in 1966 was extended to five months and eventually led to the establishment of the United States as Satchidananda's base for worldwide operations.

In October 1966, the first Integral Yoga Institute was founded in New York City. In 1972 Yogaville-West, a community for those who practiced integral yoga, was created in Seigler Springs, California. A year later Yogaville-East was founded in northeast Connecticut and served as the American headquarters for integral yoga for almost 10 years.

Swamiji, as Satchidananda is known to his disciples, has also been instrumental in advocating and sponsoring ecumenical, or interfaith, programs. For more than 50 years he has initiated and participated in many interfaith gatherings around the world. The goal of integral yoga, writes Swami Satchidananda, "is to realize the spiritual unity behind all the diversities in the entire creation and to live harmoniously as members of one universal family." Through the years he has helped popularize the teaching that "Truth is One, Paths are Many."

Through a gift from folksinger Carole King, Integral Yoga International acquired 600 acres of woodlands in Buckingham County, Virginia, in late 1979, which became the movement's world headquarters. Here, on the banks of the James River, Sri Satchidananda constructed the Light of Truth Universal Shrine (LOTUS), a shrine to all the world's religions. Dedicated in July 1986, the LOTUS shrine is intended as a place where all faith traditions can come to worship and pray and find the One Spirit that unites all.

The Satchidananda Ashram-Yogaville is both a monastic order and a teaching center. Currently, approximately 80 persons live on the property, and an additional 200 affiliates reside near the ashram. More than 50 instructional programs and retreats are offered annually, most lasting for 1 to 2 weeks. Integral Yoga International has four institutes in the United States and one each in Canada and India. Integral Yoga International maintains 37 centers in 28 countries, almost half of which are in the United States. It also maintains a set of interrelated Internet sites, including web pages for the Satchidananda Ashram Yogaville (http://yogaville.org/), Integral Yoga Institute (www.integralyogaofnewyork.org), and the Integral Yoga Teachers Association (www.iyta.org). More than 400 persons in 23 countries are certified to offer instruction in integral yoga.

Integral Yoga International
Route 1 Box 1720
Buckingham, VA 23921
http://www.iyiva.org/
Sarah Meadows and Jeffrey K. Hadden

See also: Divine Life Society; Meditation; Sivananda Saraswati, Swami; Sri Aurobindo Ashram; Yoga.

References

Bordow, Sita, et al. *Sri Swami Satchidananda: Apostle of Peace.* Yogaville, VA: Integral Yoga Publications, 1986.

Mendelkorn, Phillip, ed. *To Know Your Self: The Essential Teachings of Swami Satchidananda*. Garden City, NY: Anchor Books, 1978.

Satchidananda, Sri Swami. *The Yoga Sutras of Patanjali*. Yogaville, VA: Integral Yoga Publications, 1978.

Satchidananda, Sri Swami, and Phillip Mandelkorn. *To Know Your Self: The Essential Teachings of Swami Satchidananda*. Rev. ed. Yogaville, VA: Integral Yoga Publications, 2008.

Weiner, Sita. *Swami Satchidananda*. New York: Bantam Books, 1972.

Intercontinental Church of God

See Church of God, International; Churches of God Outreach Ministries, Intercontinental Church of God.

International Association for Religious Freedom

The oldest interfaith organization operating on the international scene, the International Association for Religious Freedom was founded in Boston, Massachusetts, by liberal religious leaders in 1900. That year people from various countries had gathered to attend the 75th anniversary gathering of the American Unitarian Association. In the United States that year was Protap Chundar Mozoomdar (1840–1905), a spiritual teacher from India and representative of the Brahmo Samaj, with which the Unitarians had developed a close relationship. The president of the Unitarians, Samuel A. Elliott (1862–1950), also played a prominent role in the founding of the new Association.

Founded as the International Council of Unitarian and Other Religious Liberals, but soon changed to International Council of Religious Liberals, the Association met annually until World War I prevented its gatherings. After the war it continued to meet but seemed to have lost its purpose. However, in the post–World War II climate of urgency, it was reorganized as the International Association for Liberal Christianity and Religious Freedom. Its headquarters were established in the United States but soon moved to Germany. As religious liberty was the motivating force, it soon adopted the name by which it is currently known. It has subsequently attracted an interfaith coalition of leaders from around the world, though in the West it retains a primary contact with Unitarians. The North American chapter still gathers with the annual meeting of the Unitarian Universalist Association general assembly.

The International Association sponsors a congress of its members that meets every four years, with the venue moving among its four major regions (East Asia, South Asia, North America, and Europe/Middle East). It deals with particular pressing issues, among the many issues in religious freedom at any moment, as they are brought before it. In 2008, it reported 90 affiliated local groups in 25 countries.

International Association for Religious Freedom
c/o Konko Church of Izuo
3-8-21 Sangenya-Nishi
Taisho-ku, Osaka
551-0001, Japan
http://www.iarf.net/

J. Gordon Melton

See also: Brahmo Samaj.

References

Bowie, W. Copeland. *Liberal Religious Thought at the Beginning of the Twentieth Century: Addresses and Papers at the International Council of Unitarian and Other Religious Thinkers and Workers, Held at London, May 1901*. London: Philip Green, 1901.

Miller, Russell E. *The Larger Hope: The Second Century of the Universalist Church in America, 1870–1970*. Boston: Unitarian Universalist Association, 1985.

International Association of Reformed and Presbyterian Churches

The International Association of Reformed and Presbyterian Churches was founded in 1962 by delegates attending the meeting of the International Council of Christian Churches (ICCC) meeting in Amsterdam, the Netherlands. The ICCC represents the most conservative wing of Protestantism, usually referred to as Fundamentalist. It is militantly opposed to the most liberal wing of the Protestant community, as represented by the World Council of Churches (WCC) and the World Alliance of Reformed Churches (WARC). The immediate inspiration for the formation of the International Association was the trip of the moderator of the Church of Scotland (a prominent member of both the WCC and WARC) to the Vatican.

The ICCC and the International Association both strongly affirm the infallibility and inerrancy of the Bible and demand the separation of Christians from all apostasy and heresy (which they believe have permeated the more liberal churches). Reverend Carl McIntire (1906–2002), a Presbyterian who spearheaded the formation of the ICCC and also took the lead in forming the International Association. Dr. A. B. Dodd of Taiwan and Dr. J. C. Maris of the Netherlands were the first moderator and secretary, respectively.

The churches of the ICCC from the Reformed Presbyterian tradition constituted the first members of the Association. The International Association has its headquarters at the same location in Collingswood, New Jersey, as the headquarters of the ICCC in America and the Bible Presbyterian Church founded by Carl McIntire.

International Association of Reformed and
  Presbyterian Churches
PO Box 190
Hadden Ave. and Cuthbert Blvd.
Collingswood, NJ 08108

J. Gordon Melton

See also: Church of Scotland; World Alliance of Reformed Churches; World Council of Churches.

Reference

Harden, Margaret C., comp. *A Brief History of the Bible Presbyterian Church and Its Agencies.* Privately published, 1968.

International Church of the Foursquare Gospel

The International Church of the Foursquare Gospel was founded by Aimee Semple McPherson (1890–1944),

Portrait of early-20th-century evangelist Aimee Semple McPherson, founder of the International Church of the Foursquare Gospel. (Hulton Archive/Getty Images)

one of a small group of prominent female Christian ministers in the United States in the first half of the 20th century. McPherson was born in Canada. Her mother had been a member of the Salvation Army, a Holiness church, but as a teenager Aimee experienced the baptism of the Holy Spirit as evidenced by speaking in tongues. A short time later she married Robert Semple. In 1910 they moved to China as missionaries. He became a victim of the climate, and Aimee returned to the United States with her baby daughter, also named Aimee. Aimee subsequently married Harold S. McPherson and the pair toured the country as independent Pentecostal evangelists, though their marriage finally ended in divorce.

Following World War I, McPherson emerged as a popular evangelist in spite of derision because of her gender, winning an audience through her oratorical abilities. In 1918 she settled in Los Angeles and led in the construction of Angelus Temple. At the same time she opened an evangelistic and training institute to educate leadership for what was quickly to become the Pentecostal denomination. By 1921 there were already 32 congregations, and McPherson formed the Echo Park Evangelistic Association. The International Church of the Foursquare Gospel was formed four years later. Work was concentrated along the West Coast but soon spread to Canada.

McPherson developed a unique presentation of the Pentecostal message, which she called the foursquare gospel (a variation of the fourfold gospel of Benjamin Albert Simpson [1843–1919], founder of the Christian and Missionary Alliance). The name Church of the Foursquare Gospel derived from the church's emphasis on the fourfold role of Jesus Christ, as Savior, Baptizer with the Holy Spirit, Healer, and Coming King. Otherwise the church is theologically at one with other trinitarian Pentecostals.

The Church of the Foursquare Gospel moved easily into the global missionary thrust that had been inherent in the Pentecostal movement ever since the 1906 revival in Los Angeles that founded it. Through the last half of the 20th century, the great majority of the membership was found outside of the United States. As of 2008, the church reported 8,439,618 members in 59,620 churches and meeting places in 144 countries. Less than 5 percent of the membership (255,773) is now (2006) in the United States.

The headquarters of the International Church of the Foursquare Gospel is in Los Angeles. It is a member of the Pentecostal/Charismatic Churches of North America and participates in the Pentecostal World Fellowship. The church is led by its president. After her death in 1944, Aimee McPherson was succeeded as president by her son Rolf McPherson (b. 1913), who led the church until 1988. He was followed by John R. Holland, who held the office from 1988 to 1997 and was succeeded by Paul C. Risser. The current president is former mega-church pastor Jack W. Hayford. The highest legislative authority in the church is the delegated general convention.

International Church of the Foursquare Gospel
1910 W. Sunset Blvd., Ste. 300

Los Angeles, CA 90026
http://www.foursquare.org/

J. Gordon Melton

See also: Christian and Missionary Alliance; Pentecostal World Fellowship; Pentecostalism.

References

Blumhofer, Edith L. *Aimee Semple McPherson: Everybody's Sister.* Grand Rapids, MI: William B. Eerdmans Publishing Company, 1993.

Duffield, Guy P., and Nathaniel M. Van Cleve. *Foundations of Pentecostal Theology.* Los Angeles: L.I.F.E. Bible College, 1983.

Epstein, Daniel Mark. *Sister Aimee: The Life of Aimee Semple McPherson.* New York: Harcourt Brace Jovanovich, 1993.

Hadden, Jeffrey K., and Charles E. Swann. *Prime Time Preachers: The Rising Power of Televangelism.* Reading, MA: Addison-Wesley, 1981.

McPherson, Aimee Semple. *This Is That.* New York: Garland Publishing, 1985.

International Churches of Christ

The International Churches of Christ (ICC) began as a renewal movement within the Churches of Christ (non-instrumental), a conservative American Free Church body. The Church of Christ shared a Protestant/Free Church theological tradition but adopted an ultra-congregational organization that placed all authority in the local congregation and rejected any effort to create denominational structures that served all of the congregations. Many leaders in the Churches of Christ identified it with the true church and suggested that only people who were baptized after understanding the nature of baptism for the remission of sins were truly baptized. They generally demanded rebaptism of any person joining with them who had been baptized in another denomination.

In the 1960s, what was called the discipling movement spread through American evangelical churches. The movement had as its goal the changing of nominal churchgoers into active Christian disciples. The movement took its name from the assignment of a new Christian to an older, more mature Christian who became the younger person's mentor in the faith. The mentoring relationship meant regular contact above and beyond contacts at congregational gatherings. There was an expectation that the disciple would accept the guidance of the mentor. During the height of the discipling movement, it was widely criticized for the often invasive and controlling guidance imposed upon young Christians.

The discipling movement entered the Churches of Christ through the Crossroads Church of Christ in Gainesville, Florida (adjacent to the University of Florida). Using the discipling program in its campus ministry at the University of Florida, it experienced spectacular success. It also became quite controversial. Eventually the Crossroads congregation withdrew their support for the program.

Among the people influenced by the Crossroads congregation during the heyday of the discipling movement was Kip McKean (b. 1954). He went on to become the pastor of a small congregation of the Churches of Christ in Lexington (suburban Boston), Massachusetts. In 1979 he challenged the members of the congregation to make a new commitment to restore the Christianity of the Bible. Starting with only 30 members, he asked them to commit their lives totally to Christ and, most important, to hold that as a standard for all of the people they converted to Christ. The Church of Christ, they believed, consisted totally of disciples.

Integral to the program was discipling. Every person in the church assumed a discipling relationship with an older member and discipled one or more newer members. McKean also wrote a set of Bible lessons called the First Principles, which the church members were to master and use in teaching those whom they were discipling. It was assumed that disciples would spend part of their time each week engaged in evangelistic activity, and that they would spend time each week discussing their progress in the Christian life and any personal issues of importance with their mentor.

The church grew, moved into Boston proper, and took the name Boston Church of Christ. It grew spectacularly through the 1980s. In 1981, McKean announced a plan for the evangelization of the world in the next generation. He would send a small group of disciples to key urban centers. As they gathered disciples, they would in turn send teams out until all the world's capital cities had congregations. The movement would then go to the smaller cities until all the world was covered. The first congregations were seeded by the Boston Congregation in Chicago and London. New York, Toronto, Johannesburg, Paris, and Stockholm followed. Eventually the church reached out to Asia—Tokyo, Manila, Singapore, and Bangkok. It continued to expand through the 1990s.

The implementation of the plan involved a dramatic change from the more traditional organizational structure of the Churches of Christ. Instead of the congregational autonomy so prized within the Churches of Christ, the movement that was growing from the Boston Church had a strong centralized organizational structure put in place to carry out the discipling program and the plan for world evangelism. As the movement spread, World Sector leaders were appointed and given responsibility for evangelizing their part of the globe. In 1990, McKean moved to Los Angeles, and the movement has been centered there ever since. As criticism of the movement by the Churches of Christ mounted, the movement formally defined itself as no longer a part of the Churches of Christ and took the name International Churches of Christ.

In 1994, McKean, his wife, and all of the World Sector leaders and their wives signed an "Evangelism Proclamation" declaring their intent to plant a church in every nation with a city of at least 100,000 people by the year 2000. At that time they had started 146 churches in 53 nations. As of July 2000, the ICC reported 393 churches worldwide.

The International Churches of Christ distinguished itself from its parent body on several issues above and beyond the church organization. The ICC believes that it is the movement of God in this generation and thus has a unique role in evangelizing the world. It is this belief that underlies the strong commitment that is so characteristic of members. It has introduced instrumental music, in a limited manner, to the church and has given an unprecedented role to women in the leadership (though it has not admitted them to the ordained ministry).

The church has organized HOPE Worldwide, a volunteer program that conducts numerous social service projects around the world. It also now has special consultative status with the Economic and Social Council of the United Nations.

Although the church has pursued its program of growth and expansion, a number of former members who had bad experiences in the church and subsequently dropped away from the church and its discipling program have complained about the church. Some have suggested that the disciplined life demanded of members is inherently manipulative and destructive of personal freedom and choice. Some have denounced it as a cult. In the face of criticisms the ICC has modified but not discarded the discipling program and provided more formal guidance for those serving as mentors. Criticism of the church peaked in the early 1990s, when those who opposed the church for the changes it had introduced in the original ideas and organization of the Churches of Christ joined forces with those who saw it as engaged in brainwashing. With the demise of the brainwashing theory in the 1990s, criticism has significantly decreased.

External criticism of the ICC had significantly diminished by the beginning of the new century, but it would soon be replaced by significant internal turmoil beginning in 2001. Toward the end of that year, concerned with the perceived instability within the McKean family, the leadership announced that Kip and Elena McKean would begin a sabbatical leave from their leadership role. It was noted that their daughter Olivia McKean had recently left the movement. A year later, Kip McKean tendered his resignation as world evangelist, Elena surrendered her position as world women's leader, and the leadership in general abandoned the organization around World Sectors.

Several months after the McKeans' resignations, in February 2003, Henry Kriete, a prominent British church leader, circulated a paper, "Honest to God," in which he offered a stinging critique of the state of the movement. Several months passed, and in the summer, the McKeans moved to Portland, Oregon, from where Kip McKean released a response to Kriete in the form of an open circular letter to the movement that he entitled "From Babylon to Zion." The letter included his assertion that he was ready to return to his earlier role leading the movement.

By the time McKean expressed his desire to reassume leadership, a significant number of the other leaders had lost confidence in him. As discussions and negotiations on the direction of the movement proceeded, in 2005, 84 leaders formally withdrew fellowship from him. At that point, McKean abandoned any attempt to return to leadership of the ICC and in 2006 formed a new movement that he called the Sold-Out Discipling Movement Churches. He and his wife subsequently founded the City of Angels International Christian Church in Los Angeles as the flagship congregation of the new movement.

The break with McKean (and the rancor that immediately preceded it) cost the ICC. There were major membership losses in 2003 and 2004. The ICC leadership estimated membership at the end of 2007 at 90,130, representing a 33 percent decline from the peak membership in 2002 of 135,046. At present (2007), there are still 562 congregations worldwide.

International Churches of Christ
3530 Wilshire Blvd., Ste. 1750
Los Angeles, CA 90010
www.icocco-op.org
www.disciplestoday.org

J. Gordon Melton

See also: Churches of Christ (Non-Instrumental); Free Churches; Women, Status and Role of.

References

The Disciple's Handbook. Los Angeles: Discipleship Publications International, 1997.

Ferguson, Gordon. *Discipleship: God's Plan to Train and Transform His People*. Los Angeles: Discipleship Publications International, 1997.

Ferguson, Gordon. *Prepared to Answer*. Los Angeles: Discipleship Publications International, 1995.

Nelson, Robert. *Understanding the Crossroads Controversy*. Fort Worth, TX: Star Bible Publications, 1981.

Paden, Russell. *"From the Churches of Christ to the Boston Movement: A Comparative Study."* M.A. thesis, University of Kansas, 1994.

International Coalition for Religious Freedom

The International Coalition for Religious Freedom is one of several interfaith organizations inspired by and receiving the majority of its support from the Unification movement, headed by Korean minister Sun

Myung Moon (b. 1920). In spite of its significant relationship to a single group, the Coalition strives to be completely nonsectarian in its program and work. It is based on a commitment to religious freedom for all and a belief that every religious entity has a right to freedom of religious belief and expression as conscience leads, a right that is balanced by the requirements of generally acceptable laws against criminal behavior.

The Coalition, founded in 1997, builds on and supersedes the work of the Coalition for Religious Freedom founded in 1983. It first major activity was the holding of a set of conferences in 1998 under the general theme, "Religious Freedom and the New Millennium." Sessions were held in Washington, D.C., Tokyo, Berlin, and São Paulo. Each session brought together religious leaders, scholars, and human rights activists to discuss the main points of religious suppression in the world and to highlight the issues faced in the creation of a more religiously free society.

The coalition in its short history has focused upon some peculiar problems faced by the Unification movement, including the deprogrammings against its adherents in Japan and the denial of entry to Rev. Moon in some European countries, but has been broadly attentive to problems of other minority religious bodies as well.

International Coalition for Religious Freedom
7777 Leesburg Pike, Suite 309N
Falls Church, VA 22043
http://www.religiousfreedom.com

J. Gordon Melton

See also: Unification Movement.

Reference

Religious Freedom and the New Millennium. Falls Church, VA: International Coalition for Religious Freedom, 2000.

International Conference of Reformed Churches

The International Conference of Reformed Churches (ICRC) was founded in 1982 as an ecumenical fellowship of conservative Reformed churches. The original gathering included representatives of nine Reformed and Presbyterian denominations who assembled at Groningen, Netherlands, at the invitation of the Reformed Churches (Liberated). The Reformed Churches (Liberated) was formed during World War II in the midst of a controversy within the Netherlands Reformed Church. As theological debate took place on a variety of issues around the grace of God, the church's synod issued several doctrinal statements. The issuance of the new doctrinal statements aroused a secondary issue when a protest was generated over the new statements, which were binding on the teaching elders in the church.

Leading the protest was Professor K. Schilder (1890–1952), who argued that pressing new theological positions on the church was not the way to end the controversy. He was excluded from the church's ministry and with his supporters, including a number of congregations, he led in the formation of the Reformed Churches (Liberated). The church grew into a substantial denomination with more than 100,000 members. It was conservative in orientation and soon developed a close relationship with the Christian Reformed Churches in the Netherlands.

Those who formed the ICRC felt that there was an attack within the large Reformed world on both the authority of the Bible and the Reformed creeds that had been promulgated in the 16th century. The ICRC adopted the Bible, the "Three Forms of Unity" (Belgic Confession, Heidelberg Catechism, Canons of Dort), and the Westminster documents (Westminster Confession, Westminster Larger and Shorter Catechisms) as the basis of their fellowship. Member churches are expected to be loyal to the confessional standards of the Reformed tradition.

The first assembly of the ICRC was held in Edinburgh in 1985 and hosted by the Free Church of Scotland. Subsequent meetings were held in Langley, British Columbia, Canada (1989); Zwolle, Netherlands; and Seoul, Korea. The 2009 conference was in Christchurch, New Zealand, with the Reformed Churches of New Zealand serving as the host. Prominent members of the Conference included the Orthodox Presbyterian Church, Canadian Reformed Churches, and the Presbyterian Church of Korea (KoShin). In 1995, the Christian Reformed Churches in the Netherlands, formerly associated with the International Council of Christian Churches and the Reformed Ecumenical Council, joined the ICRC.

The ICRC promotes cooperation in missions and the presentation of a united front on the Reformed faith and related issues by its member churches. Some 25 Reformed churches worldwide are now (2009) members of the Conference.

International Conference of Reformed Churches
c/o Reverend C. Van Spronsen
8586 Harbour Heights Road
Vernon, BC
V1H 1J8. Canada
http://www.icrconline.com/

J. Gordon Melton

See also: International Council of Christian Churches; Orthodox Presbyterian Church; Reformed Ecumenical Council.

Reference

Bauswein, Jean-Jacques, and Lukas Vischner, eds. *The Reformed Family Worldwide: A Survey of Reformed Churches, Theological Schools, and International Organizations.* Grand Rapids, MI: William B. Eerdmans Publishing Company, 1999.

International Congregational Fellowship

The International Congregational Fellowship arose to meet the need for greater expression among those Christian churches that believed that the Congregational form of church life was the best form in the contemporary democratic world. Much of that thrust was lost in the merger of the General Council of Congregational Christian Churches into the United Church of Christ (1957), the merger of the International Congregational Council into the World Alliance of Reformed Churches (1966), and the merger of the Congregational Church in England and Wales into the United Reformed Church (1972). In the meantime, churches that stayed out of the mergers that created the United Church of Christ and the United Reformed Church formed the National Association of Congregational

Christian Churches and the Congregational Federation of England.

The continuing Congregational churches made common cause in 1975, largely prompted by David Watson in England and John Alexander in the United States. People from six countries met to form the International Congregational Fellowship. They announced the first conference for 1977, at which time they signed a document called "The Chiselhurst Thanksgiving," affirming their allegiance to the Congregational Way.

The Fellowship has organized as a gathering of individuals concerned with the promotion of the congregational form of church life rather than an association or council of denominations. Most Congregational churches are already members of either the World Council of Churches or the World Alliance of Reformed Churches or both. The Fellowship's primary program is its quadrennial conference to advocate for Congregationalism.

The Fellowship holds international conferences quadrennially. Aside from the contacts given below, regional secretaries also now (2009) exist for Central Europe, Africa, Asia, Central and South America, North America, the Pacific and Australia, The United Kingdom, and Wales. The fellowship stays in touch with Congregationalists in more than 50 countries. The first issue of the biennial *International Congregationalist Journal* appeared in 2001.

International Congregational Fellowship
Co-Moderators Elect
Reverend Dr. Patrick Shelley
c/o Lake Country Congregational Church
400 West Capitol Drive
Hartland, WI 53029-1921

Reverend Dr. Harding Stricker
Asociaciòn Civil Cristuana Congregacional
Suriname 156, C C 24
3328 Jardin America
Misiones, Argentina
http://www.intercong.org/

J. Gordon Melton

See also: Congregationalism; United Church of Christ; United Reformed Church (of the United

Kingdom); World Alliance of Reformed Churches; World Council of Churches.

Reference

Bauswein, Jean-Jacques, and Lukas Vischner, eds. *The Reformed Family Worldwide: A Survey of Reformed Churches, Theological Schools, and International Organizations*. Grand Rapids, MI: William B. Eerdmans Publishing Company, 1999.

International Council of Christian Churches

The International Council of Christian Churches (ICCC) was founded in 1948 at the instigation of the American Council of Christian Churches (ACCC). The ACCC had in turn resulted from a split within the Protestant Fundamentalist movement in the 1940s. Fundamentalism had arisen in American Protestantism as a protest against what was seen as a departure from essential Christian beliefs by liberal Protestants in the early decades of the 20th century. The battle between Fundamentalists and Modernists (as the liberals were called) came to a head in the 1930s, when many Fundamentalists left the major Protestant denominations in the United States. Other Fundamentalists remained within the larger denominations as conservative voices.

In the late 1930s, some Fundamentalist leaders demanded that a complete separation from the liberal denominations should occur, and that ties should be broken with conservative leaders who remained in these older groups. Those conservative leaders who were willing to keep fellowship with conservatives within the older churches became known as evangelicals and later organized the National Association of Evangelicals.

Those demanding complete separation found a leader in Dr. Carl McIntire, a Presbyterian minister and founder of the Bible Presbyterian Church. He led in the formation of the American Council of Christian Churches in opposition to the Federal Council of Churches (now the National Council of Churches of Christ in the U.S.A.). The ACCC also opposed the World Council of Churches (WCC), whose organization gained momentum in the years immediately after World War II. As the organizational conference of the WCC was announced for Amsterdam in 1984, McIntire called together his associates from around the world to gather in Amsterdam just a few days prior to the initial assembly of the WCC. In succeeding years, the much smaller ICCC often held its meeting to coincide with the WCC meeting.

The ICCC is a Fundamentalist Protestant body that affirms the infallibility and inerrancy of the Bible and the need for a complete separation from heresy and apostasy, especially as these are embodied in the WCC or the WEA or any of their affiliates. The ICCC faced a severe crisis in 1970 when the 30 years of leadership by McIntire was challenged. In 1969 the ACCC removed McIntire from his role as the leader of the organization. The ICCC chose to affirm McIntire, and the ICCC and the ACCC dropped their relationship. McIntire moved to create a new American affiliate of the ICCC, now known as the ICCC in America.

At its meeting in Amsterdam in 1998, the ICCC reported 700 denominations from more than 100 countries represented in its membership. The 17th World Congress of the ICCC met in Korea in 2005. The Congress meets every five years.

International Council of Christian Churches
General Secretariat
3 & 5 Tavistock Avenue
Singapore 555108
http://www.iccc.org.sg/

J. Gordon Melton

See also: World Council of Churches; World Evangelical Alliance.

Reference

Harden, Margaret C., comp. *A Brief History of the Bible Presbyterian Church and Its Agencies*. Privately published, 1968.

International Council of Christians and Jews

The International Council of Christians and Jews (ICCJ) is an association of national organizations from more than 30 countries dedicated to the dialogue between Christians and Jews at all levels and increas-

Martin Buber House in Heppenheim, Germany, is the headquarters of the International Council of Christians and Jews. (ICCJ)

ingly the wider encounter between Jews, Christians, and Muslims. The ICCJ was founded in 1946 as awareness of the extent of the Holocaust spread across Europe and North America. W. W. (Bill) Simpson, the leader of the British Council of Christians and Jews, was named the first executive secretary.

At the original gathering of the Council, at Seelisberg, Switzerland, in 1947, a 10-point statement was issued that called Christians, among other things, to avoid distorting Judaism with the object of extolling Christianity; identifying Jews as the enemies of Jesus; associating Jews with the killing of Jesus; and promoting the notion that the Jewish people are reprobate, accursed, or reserved for a destiny of suffering. The work of the ICCJ contributed to the changing views of the Roman Catholic Church toward the Jewish community that were proclaimed during the Second Vatican Council and a host of statements renouncing anti-Semitism and anti-Jewish theological perspectives and biblical interpretations by major Protestant bodies. As a result, most Protestant bodies, especially those associated with the World Council of Churches, withdrew support from efforts to convert Jews to Christianity.

Among the oldest affiliated member organizations was the National Council of Christians and Jews (now the National Conference for Community and Justice), which had been founded in the United States in 1927. A pioneer in Jewish-Christian dialogue, in the post–World War II context it expanded its role to include a broad program of activities aimed at ending religious, racial, and other forms of bigotry.

Knowledge of the Holocaust provided fuel for the Jewish-Christian dialogue through the 1970s, and the continued tension in the Middle East has spurred the broadening of dialogue to include Muslims. Beginning in Europe, the dialogue has spread worldwide into most countries with a significant Jewish presence, from Argentina to Australia and New Zealand. In 2009, it reported local chapters in 32 countries.

The ICCJ has its headquarters at the Martin Buber House, the home of the Jewish mystic and theologian prior to his having to leave Germany due to the rise of Nazism. The ICCJ has made a special effort to bring women and youth into the work of dialogue and sponsors the Abrahamic Faith Council to focus its efforts with Muslim dialogue. It maintains an extensive Internet site dealing with Jewish-Christian relations at http://www.jcrelations.net.

International Council of Christians and Jews
Martin Buber House
Werlestrasse 2
Postfach 1129
D-64628 Heppenheim
Germany
http://www.iccj.org

J. Gordon Melton

See also: Roman Catholic Church; World Council of Churches.

Reference
Rosen, David. "The Impact of the Jewish-Christian Dialogue Upon Theological Thought." 1997. http://rabbidavidrosen.net/articles.htm. Accessed June 15, 2009.

International Council of Community Churches

Community churches first appeared late in the 19th century in the United States as one response to the increasing religious pluralism, especially the many sects into which Protestantism had split. Nonsectarian community churches were an alternative to the establishment of multiple congregations of denominationally affiliated congregations. Such congregations were logical in smaller communities that could not support the array of denominational institutions. Then, in the early 20th century, in response to the ecumenical movement, a variety of united congregations (formed by the merger of congregations of different denominational affiliations) also appeared on the scene. In the 1920s, the initial attempts to network such nondenominational congregations began.

Reverend Orvis F. Jordan of the Park Ridge Community Church in Illinois became the center of one such network, the Community Church Workers, founded in 1923. The organization lasted into the 1930s. Community Church Workers operated primarily among churches serving the Anglo community, and a similar structure emerged that served African American churches, the National Council of the People's Church of Christ and Community Centers of the United States and Elsewhere.

Through the 1930s, various approaches to the Federal Council of Churches were made, but the Council failed to act on petitions to recognize the community church ideal. Then, after World War II, a new attempt at organization led in 1946 to the formation of the National Council of Community Churches. This group merged with the predominantly African American Council in 1950 to create the International Council of Community Churches. This Council underwent several name changes due to the loss of several foreign congregations, but in 1983, following the affiliation of congregations in Canada and Nigeria, the original name was again adopted.

By the very nature of its stance as nonsectarian, the Council has proposed no doctrinal statement, but member ministers and churches generally operate out of a liberal-Protestant, ecumenically minded stance. The Council describes itself as committed to Christian unity and working "toward a fellowship as comprehensive as the spirit and teachings of Christ and as inclusive as the love of God."

The Council is organized as a loose association of autonomous congregations, with the different Council offices primarily facilitating communication between congregations. The officers also represent the congregations in various official capacities with the government and the larger religious world. At the end of the 1990s the council joined the World Council of Churches and more recently joined in the new ecumenical Churches Uniting in Christ.

In 2006, the Council reported 157 member churches with a combined membership of 73,174. Approximately 1,000 additional congregations are affiliated with the Council and participate in various levels of its fellowship. Some 5 percent of the congregations have a dual membership in a denomination.

International Council of Community Churches
7808 College Dr., No. 25E
Palos Heights, IL 60463
http://www.icccusa.com/

J. Gordon Melton

See also: World Council of Churches.

References

Shotwell, J. Ralph. *Unity without Uniformity.* Homewood, IL: Community Church Press, 1984.

Smith, J. Philip. *Faith and Fellowship in the Community Church Movement: A Theological Perspective.* Homewood, IL: Community Church Press, 1986.

International Council of Unitarians and Universalists

The International Council of Unitarians and Universalists (ICUU) was founded in 1995 as an effort to further contact between Unitarians and Universalists across national boundaries. Its formation evolved from the new level of international contact that had followed the formation of the Unitarian Universalist Association by the merger of Unitarians and Universalists of North America in 1961. Previously, international contacts had been focused within the International Association for Religious Freedom. Then, in 1987, the General Assembly of Unitarian and Free Christian Churches of the United Kingdom passed a resolution favoring the organization of a new international cooperative structure. The ICUU is specifically mandated to nourish Unitarian and Universalist communities around the world. The founding meeting was held in

Essex, Massachusetts, at which Reverend David Usher was elected president.

Although there is no creed, the ICUU adopted a brief affirmation: "We affirm our belief in religious community based upon liberty of conscience and of individual thought in matters of faith, the inherent worth and dignity of every person, justice and compassion in human relations, responsible stewardship of earth's living system, and our commitment to democratic principles." Unitarian Universalism is a religion of Oneness, and members heartily affirm the "interdependent web of all existence of which we are a part." Often oppressed as heresy, for centuries Unitarians and Universalists were scattered. Today, its churches and temples include Christians, Buddhists, Pagans, and many others. They welcome "All Souls," and are known for their witness for social justice and freedom of thought.

Members of the ICUU believe that Unitarian and Universalist teachings go back to the first Christians. Some early Christians spoke of Jesus as a "son of God by adoption" (the oldest Gospel, Mark, has no birth story). They saw only the Father as God, denying the Trinity. Others said that if God is Love, all will be saved. During the 16th-century Reformation both teachings resurfaced after years of marginalization. In 1531, a Spanish theologian and physician, usually known by his Latin name, Michael Servetus (1511–1553), wrote *De Trinitatis Erroribus* (*On the Errors of the Trinity*). Arrested during a visit to Geneva, he was burned at the stake on October 27, 1553, with the "blessings" of Reformed leader and theologian John Calvin. Subsequently, Unitarian churches developed in Poland under the leadership of an Italian theologian, usually known by his Latin name, Laelius Socinus (1525–1562), and in Transylvania under the leadership of a Hungarian cleric and theologian, usually known as Francis David (1510–1579). The Polish Church was suppressed for centuries, but there is now a Unitarian presence in Warsaw. Since 1568, Hungarian Unitarians have continued in hundreds of villages and cities in Romania and Hungary. Composer Bela Bartok (1881–1945) was a member of Second Unitarian Church, Budapest.

Unitarians and Universalists were common in many dissenting chapels in Britain. Many fled to North America, including Reverend Joseph Priestley (1733–1834; discoverer of oxygen), who established the first Unitarian Church in Philadelphia. Five U.S. presidents were Unitarian, including John Adams, Thomas Jefferson, and William Howard Taft. Well-known Universalists include Clara Barton, who founded the American Red Cross, and P. T. Barnum, of circus fame. UUs, as they are often called, have made major contributions to science with Nobel Prize winners such as Linus Pauling and George Wald. Of special note are Unitarian contributions to literature. American writers Louisa May Alcott, Nathaniel Hawthorne, Henry Wadsworth Longfellow, Herman Melville, Ralph Waldo Emerson, and Kurt Vonnegut were Unitarians, as were British authors Elizabeth Gaskell and Charles Dickens. Dickens wrote *A Christmas Carol*, in 1843, the same year he joined a Unitarian Church in London. Late 20th-century Unitarians include Lord Alan Bullock, first Unitarian vice chancellor of Oxford; Sir Tim Berners Lee, creator of the World Wide Web; and Dr. Dana M. Greeley, co-founder of Religions for Peace.

Hundreds of UUs have suffered imprisonment and death for their faith. It was only in 1813 that English law accepted Unitarians. In the Czech Republic, before World War II, Dr. Norbert Capek was minister to the largest Unitarian Congregation in the world in Prague, with 3,500 members. Capek wrote beautiful hymns, some of which are translated in modern hymnbooks. But with the Nazi occupation, Capek died in a gas chamber. Dozens of other Unitarians were taken to concentration camps. After almost 50 years of oppression under the Communists, the Czech congregations are reviving. In cooperation with the ICUU, two Czech ministers have trained at seminaries in the United States.

The seven-member ICUU Executive Committee is elected by the ICUU Council. One hundred UUs from around the world come as delegates to ICUU council meetings in odd-numbered years. At the 2007 ICUU council meeting in Germany, there were delegates from more than 25 countries, including the Philippines, India, Indonesia, Nigeria, Kenya, Burundi, South Africa, New Zealand, Bolivia, Argentina, Britain, Denmark, Germany, Spain, France, The Czech Republic, the United States, Mexico, and Canada. There are 165,000 UUs in North America, 90,000 in Hungary and Romania, 10,000 in India, 6,000 in Great Britain,

2,000 in Germany, and about 15,000 scattered in small congregations from Nigeria to Japan.

ICUU Officers 2007–2009 are Reverend Brian Kiely, president, Canada; Reverend Gordon Oliver, South Africa, vice president; Jaume de Marcos, Spain, secretary; Reverend David Shaw, treasurer, United Kingdom. The executive secretary, Reverend John Clifford, Scotland, retired in 2009, and Steve Dick was appointed to replace him at the Council Meeting in Cluj-Napoca, Romania, September 1–5, 2009. The ICUU conducts programs for training in worship and ministry. Recent programs have held in Kenya and in the Khasi Hills of India. The ICUU has also hosted a Conference on Michael Servetus, and Symposiums at Oxford and Cluj-Napoca (Koloszvar) Romania.

International Council of Unitarians and Universalists
Essex Hall
1-6 Essex St.
London WC2R 3 HY
United Kingdom
www.icuu..net: current ICUU programs.
http://www.unitarian.org.uk: has published several
    recent Unitarian books.
http://www.uua.org: 100s of UU books available at
    this website (Beacon Press & Skinner House)

Richard Boeke

See also: International Association for Religious Freedom; Unitarian Universalist Association.

References

Boeke, Richard. *God Is No-Thing.* London: Unitarian Information Service, 2007.
Buehrens, John A. *A Chosen Faith: An Introduction to Unitarian Universalism.* Boston: Beacon Press, 1998.
Henry, Richard. *Norbert Fabian Capek.* Boston: Skinner House Books, 1999.
Williams, George H. *The Radical Reformation.* 3rd ed. Kirksville, MO: Thomas Jefferson University Press, 1992.

International Evangelical Church

The International Evangelical Church and Missionary Association (IEC) is a fellowship of Pentecostal churches that was formed in 1964 primarily to provide a legal cover for the Italian missionary activity of independent Pentecostal missionary John McTernan. The IEC expanded to the United States in the early 1980s to include the ministry of John Levin Meares (1920–), founder of Evangel Temple in Washington, D.C. The nephew of a former general overseer of the Church of God (Cleveland, Tennessee), Meares became a minister as a young man and served several Church of God congregations in Tennessee.

In 1955 Meares decided to resign his pastorship in Memphis in order to assist independent evangelist Jack Coe in a series of revival meetings in Washington, D.C. Meares decided to stay in Washington to build a Church of God congregation there, which he called the Washington Revival Center. He also started a radio show called *Miracle Time.* Although Meares was white, the major response to his ministry was from African Americans. The Church of God (Cleveland, Tennessee) was a white-controlled denomination with very intolerant attitudes about race at the time. In May 1956, Meares was disfellowshipped by the Church of God for starting an unlicensed ministry. He continued as an independent minister, and in 1957 his congregation settled in an abandoned theater, which was named the National Evangelistic Center.

John McTernan became associated with Meares soon after the latter arrived in Washington. The IEC, beginning with a few Italian churches, had reached out to include a group of Brazilian churches under Bishop Robert McAleister, as well as some churches in Nigeria led by Bishop Benson Idahosa (1938–1998). Meares became the new vice president of the IEC.

In the 1960s, Meares's ministry shifted from an emphasis on miracles to an emphasis on praise and the gift of prophecy. After the assassination of Martin Luther King Jr. in 1968 and the riots that followed, almost all of the remaining white members left the National Evangelistic Center. Membership dropped to several hundred black members and then slowly began to increase again. In the early 1970s, the 300 remaining members of Meares's Washington congregation reorganized and decided to build a $3 million facility. The result was the Evangel Temple, which opened in 1975.

The IEC joined the World Council of Churches in 1972. In 1974, McTernan died and Meares found himself at the head of the IEC. In 1982 IEC founded a new Pentecostal ecumenical organization, the International Communion of Charismatic Churches, which includes the branches of the International Evangelical Church, the Gospel Harvesters Church founded by Earl P. Paulk Jr. (1927–2009), and others. The bishops of the International Communion of Charismatic Churches—McAleister, Paulk, and Idahosa—consecrated Meares as a bishop in 1982.

The International Evangelical Churches and Missionary Association emerged out of Meares's capacity as mediator between black and white Pentecostal communities, which had diverged over a period of many years. In 1984 Meares began the annual Inner-City Pastor's Conference, which draws together the pastors (primarily African American) of the many churches of the association from around the United States and Canada. More than 1,000 pastors attended the Inner-City Pastor's Conference in 1987.

The IEC has its headquarters at Evangel Temple, which in 1991 relocated to suburban Maryland. At that time, led by Don Meares, John Meares's son, Evangel Temple had more than 1,000 members. It remains a strong suburban Washington, D.C., congregation. The IEC had approximately 500 congregations worldwide, more than 400 of which were in Africa. There were approximately 40 member churches in South America, 20 in Italy, 20 in the United States, and 1 in Jamaica. Current statistics are not available. The IEC is no longer a member of the World Council of Churches.

International Evangelical Churches and Missionary
　　Association
Evangel Temple
13901 Central Ave.
Upper Marlboro, MD 20772–8636

James R. Lewis

See also: Church of God (Cleveland, Tennessee); Pentecostalism; World Council of Churches.

References

Evangel Temple's 30th Anniversary Historical Journal. Washington, DC: Evangel Temple, 1985.

Meares, John L. *Bind Us Together.* Old Tappan, NJ: Chosen Books, 1987.

International Evangelical Church, Soldiers of the Cross

The International Evangelical Church, Soldiers of the Cross, was founded in Havana, Cuba, as the Gideon Mission in the 1920s. The founder, Ernest William Sellers (d. 1953), affectionately known as "Daddy John," was assisted in his work by three women—Sister Sarah, Mable G. Ferguson, and Muriel C. Atwood. Sellers became the bishop of the church, a post he held until 1947, when he was named the church's Apostle, and three other bishops were designated.

The church began to expand beyond Cuba in 1950, when two missionaries were commissioned. Arnaldo Socarras pioneered the church in Mexico, and Arturo Rangel Sosa opened work in Panama. Daddy John's successor, Angel Maria Hernandez y Esperon, placed special emphasis on the expansion of the church and started work in eight additional countries around the Caribbean.

Bishop Arturo Rangel succeeded Hernandez as the third Apostle. He continued the expansion of the church internationally, commissioning the first missionaries to the United States. However, that same year (1966), Rangel, one of the church's bishops, and an evangelist disappeared. The three have not been heard of since. Eventually, the remaining bishops, Florentino Almeida and Samuel Mendiondo, took control of the church, and in 1969 they moved its headquarters to Miami, Florida.

The Soldiers of the Cross is a Sabbath-keeping Pentecostal church. The Law of God as presented in the Ten Commandments is revered, and the dietary restrictions mentioned in Genesis 7:2 and Leviticus 11 are seen as proper for today. Although their beliefs are largely in line with Pentecostalism, they practice baptism as a first step to salvation, the Lord's Supper as a commemoration of Christ's death (as opposed to his resurrection), and foot washing as a sign of humility. They have adopted an apolitical stance in regard to the social order.

The church is led by Archbishops Florentino Almeida and Samuel Mendiondo. The church adopted its present name in 1974 to avoid any confusion between it and Gideons International, the older Bible-distribution ministry. In the 1980s the church had some

1,500 members in the United States, with some 100,000 in 20 countries throughout Latin America, as well as Spain and Germany.

International Evangelical Church, Soldiers of the
    Cross
636 NW 2d St.
Miami, FL 33128

J. Gordon Melton

See also: Pentecostalism; Sabbatarianism.

Reference
Melton, J. Gordon. *Encyclopedia of American Religions*. 8th ed. Detroit, MI: Cengate, 2009.

International Federation of Free Evangelical Churches

The International Federation of Free Evangelical Churches is an ecumenical association of churches that trace their beginnings to a Pietist Free church impulse in continental Europe in the 19th century. The earliest phase of this revival can be seen in Switzerland, where Free churches (that is, Protestant but separated from the state church) were formed in Berne, Basel, and Zurich. Progress was slow, as authorities discouraged the movement. However, as early as 1834, there was an attempt to associate with similar churches in France and Northern Italy. In 1910, the Swiss congregations came together as the Union of Free Evangelical Churches in Switzerland. A similar revivalist impulse in Sweden gave birth to the Mission Covenant Church, which, due to the steady immigration of members to the United States, developed a strong branch in North America. Branches also developed in Denmark and Norway.

Throughout Europe, churches that shared the same Pietist approach to the faith and accepted the Bible as their only creed also emerged. During the 20th century, the Mission Covenant Church developed a strong mission program, which included Africa and Latin America. Through the mid-20th century, these mission efforts matured into autonomous churches that retained a close association with their parent body.

Leaders from the various European Free churches began to meet in the 1920s and were in the 1930s joined by Covenant leaders from the United States. Interrupted by World War II, the meetings were picked up after the war, and in 1948, the International Federation of Free Evangelical Churches emerged. The federation has held international gatherings as irregular intervals since that time. The Federation now (2009) includes some 33 member churches based in 23 countries around the world.

General Secretary
International Federation of Free Evangelical
    Churches
c/o Mission Covenant Church of Sweden
Box 6302
SE-113 81 Stockholm
Sweden
http://www.iffec.com/

J. Gordon Melton

See also: Free Churches; Mission Covenant Church of Sweden.

References
Bauswein, Jean-Jacques, and Lukas Vischner, eds. *The Reformed Family Worldwide: A Survey of Reformed Churches, Theological Schools, and International Organizations*. Grand Rapids, MI: William B. Eerdmans Publishing Company, 1999.

Westin, Gunar. *The Free Church through the Ages*. Nashville: Broadman Press, 1958.

International Federation of Secular Humanistic Jews

For more than a century, Jewish scholars and writers have attempted to articulate a secular ideology compatible with Jewish tradition, but only in the late 20th century did such a perspective give rise to organized structures like those of the various religious groups. In the 1960s, Rabbi Sherwin T. Wine (1928–2007) founded a synagogue in Birmingham (suburban Detroit), Michigan, which affirmed both the congregation's Jewish heritage and the Humanistic philosophy articulated by Wine. He was soon joined by Rabbi

Daniel Friedman of suburban Chicago. They led in the founding of the Society for Humanistic Judaism, which espoused a nontheistic form of Jewish theology.

Wine began a periodical and started to make his case in both Jewish circles and the larger world of Rationalists, atheists, and Humanists. Many ethnic Jews had shed their tradition and identified themselves as atheists and Humanists, and some welcomed the perspective and community offered by the idea of Humanistic Judaism. By 1986, enough international support had manifested that the International Federation of Secular Humanistic Jews could be organized. The first president of the new association was Yehuda Bauer, a distinguished scholar at Hebrew University in Jerusalem, and Albert Memmi of the University of Paris (Sorbonne) was named the honorary president.

The Federation supports a perspective that sees Jewish tradition as a human-centered history, culture, civilization, ethical values, and the shared fate of the Jewish people. The secular approach indicates that the Jewish community has both the ability and the responsibility to assume control of Jewish destiny. Affiliated national organizations are found in Israel, the United States, Canada, France, Belgium, Australia, Mexico, Argentina, Uruguay, and the countries of the former Soviet Union.

The International Federation of Secular Humanistic
    Jews
224 West 35th St., Ste. 410
New York, NY 10001
http://www.ifshj.org

J. Gordon Melton

See also: Humanism; Unbelief.

References

Cohn-Sherbok, Dan, Harry T. Cook, and Marilyn Rowens, comps. *A Life of Courage: Sherwin Wine and Humanistic Judaism.* Farmington, MI: International Institute for Secular Judaism, 2003.

Goodman, Saul N. *The Faith of Secular Jews.* New York: KTAV Publishing House, 1976.

Ibry, David. *Exodus to Humanism: Jewish Identity without Religion.* Buffalo, NY: Prometheus Books, 1999.

Wine, Sherwin T. *Humanistic Judaism.* Buffalo, NY: Prometheus Books, 1978.

International Fellowship for Impersonal Enlightenment

See Evolutionary Enlightenment.

International Humanist and Ethical Union

The International Humanist and Ethical Union (IHEU) is a global organization uniting Humanists, Rationalists, atheists, secularists, and various nontheistic religionists. It was founded in Amsterdam, Netherlands, in 1952 by representatives from seven organizations. It has grown to include a wide variety of liberal religionists (such as the Unitarian Universalists) as well as both secular and religious Humanists.

The Union was created to offer the public an alternative to religion and to totalitarian political systems. Humanism was seen as a philosophy that centered on respect for human beings as moral and spiritual beings. Its original 1952 statement defined Humanism as a way that was democratic, ethical, and aimed at the maximum possible fulfillment through creative and ethical living. A more considered statement in 1966 spoke of what was termed Ethical Humanism. It projected a primal need to take responsibility for human life in the world. It acknowledged human interdependency and the need for humans to respect one another. Human progress will come as freedom of choice is extended, and justice will come from the acknowledgment of human equality. Their position has been spelled out in the 1988 "Declaration of Interdependence: A Global Ethics."

To accomplish their goals, Humanists have been involved in numerous activities and take advantage of a variety of means of disseminating their views. They have been particularly active in defending democracy, promoting civil rights, assisting victims of sexual violence, and advocating for those negatively affected by religious intolerance (including opposing female circumcision in some Muslim countries). In different countries, IHEU member organizations have fought for contraception and abortion rights; supported gay/lesbian concerns; provided nonreligious rites of passage for youth; and sponsored alternative counselors for hospitals, prisons, and the armed forces.

The IHEU represents its member organizations at the United Nations (including UNESCO and UNICEF) and the Council of Europe. It was a founding member of the UNESCO NGO Working Group on Science and Ethics. The Union is organized democratically and includes full member and associate member organizations. It also has a place for individuals as member supporters. Its international periodical, the *International Humanist*, is published in Canada. There are secretariats for Latin America and South Asia and several associated networks built around various issues and concerns. In 2009 the Union reported more than 100 organizations in more than 40 countries as members.

International Humanist and Ethical Union
IHEU Secretariat
47 Theobold Rd.
London WC1X 8SF
UK
http://www.iheu.org/

J. Gordon Melton

See also: Atheism; Council for Secular Humanism; Humanism; Unbelief; Unitarian Universalist Association.

References

Flynn, Tom, ed. *The New Encyclopedia of Unbelief*. Amherst, NY: Prometheus Press, 2007.

Gasenbeck, Bert, and Babu Gogimeni, eds. *International Humanist and Ethical Union, 1952–2002: Past, Present and Future*. Utrecht: De Tijdstroom, 2002.

Stein, Gordon, ed. *The Encyclopedia of Unbelief*. 2 vols. Buffalo, NY: Prometheus Books, 1985.

International Lutheran Council

The International Lutheran Council (ILC) is a global association of conservative (confession-oriented) Lutheran bodies that emerged in stages in the years after World War II. Among the factors undergirding the Council was the changed status of many missions founded by the Lutheran Church–Missouri Synod that had matured into independent national churches. Moreover, in Europe especially, during the 20th century a variety of churches had come into being that assumed a theological stance similar to that of the Missouri Synod.

The ILC dates its beginning from a meeting of leaders from several confessional Lutheran churches in Uelzen, Germany, in July 1952. Seven years later, a second meeting was held in Oakland, California, specifically around the topic, "The Fellowship between Our Churches." At the third meeting, in Cambridge, England, the name International Lutheran Theological Conference was adopted for what became a series of similar gatherings that were held through the next three decades. Eventually, attention turned toward working out a formal agreement for communion between the different churches, which was embodied in a constitution that was accepted in 1993. With the adoption of the constitution at a gathering in Antigua, Guatemala, the ILC came into existence. By this time, churches from around the world had joined in the negotiations. The doctrinal basis of their fellowship is the common acceptance of the holy scriptures as the inspired and infallible Word of God and of the Lutheran Confessions contained in the *Book of Concord* (originally published in 1580) as the true and faithful exposition of the Word of God.

The ILC now functions for communication, fellowship, mutual encouragement, and mutual assistance between the member churches. Although many of the ILC churches began with missionary efforts of the Lutheran Church–Missouri Synod, some, such as the Evangelical Lutheran Free Church in Denmark and the Confessional Lutheran Church of Finland, arrived at their position independently.

In 2001, the ILC included 30 member churches drawn from 5 continents.

International Lutheran Council
1333 South Kirkwood Rd.
St. Louis, MO 63122-7295
http://www.ilc-online.org/

J. Gordon Melton

See also: Lutheran Church–Missouri Synod; Lutheranism.

Reference

Nafzger, Samuel H. "The Book of Concord: A Source of Harmony." http://www.ilc-online.org/pages/default.asp?NavID=82. Accessed June 15, 2009.

International Meditation Centres

The history of International Meditation Centres begins with the life of the founder, Sayagyi U Ba Khin (1899–1971). He was born in Burma (later Myanmar) in 1899, and he served in the colonial administration of British Burma in the Accountant General's Office. After independence in 1948 he was made the accountant general. Under Prime Minister U Nu, all government departments were encouraged to form Buddhist associations, and Sayagyi U Ba Khin decided to teach meditation to his office staff.

He had been authorized by two eminent meditation teachers of Myanmar to teach meditation: by his own meditation teacher, Saya Thet Gyi (1873–1945), a disciple of the Ledi Sayadaw (1846–1923) and the Webu Sayadaw (1896–1977), the reputed arhat of Myanmar. After talking to Sayagyi U Ba Khin at length, the Webu Sayadaw told him in 1941, "Great Disciple, you have to share your Dhamma. Give the Dhamma you have to everyone."

Sayagyi U Ba Khin's aim was to teach meditation to the staff of his office and to foreigners, as very few monks spoke English then. Being aware of the pressures of urban modern life, he knew that he would have to be able to give students a lasting taste of the *dhamma* (Buddhist teaching) in a relatively short time. In the Vipassana Research Association, together with his disciples, he developed a technique to teach insight (*vipassana*) very effectively in 10 days, 2 weekends and the week in between. He taught in the Dhamma Yaung Chi Pagoda, a pagoda specifically designed by him for meditation.

The first International Meditation Centre (IMC) was established in 1952 in Yangon (Rangoon). It is operated by the Vipassana Association of the Accountant General's Office. Sayagyi U Ba Khin held the office of president of the Association and taught meditation at the IMC until his death in 1971, always assisted by Sayamagyi Daw Mya Thwin (b. 1925). Being his senior disciple, she continued teaching at the IMC Yangon after U Ba Khin's demise, until she and her husband, Sayagyi U Chit Tin, came out of Myanmar in 1978 to teach in other countries. Since then they have established five other International Meditation Centres: United Kingdom in 1979, Western Australia in 1981, the United States (Maryland) in 1988, New South Wales (near Sydney) in 1989, and Austria (in Carinthia) in 1990. All the centers outside Myanmar have regional teachers who conduct courses or assist the senior teachers when they are present. All five centers have Dhamma Yaung Chi Pagodas, which are replicas of the pagoda at the IMC Yangon. At the IMC Yangon, Sayagyi U Tint Yee (b. 1921), a disciple of U Ba Khin and the present president of the Vipassana Association of the Accountant General's Office, leads the courses.

All the IMCs in the tradition of Sayagyi U Ba Khin hold regular 10-day retreats that are frequented by people of all religions. The courses are still taught according to the system established by Sayagyi U Ba Khin. The first five days are dedicated to *anapana* meditation to develop *samadhi* (one-pointedness of mind). The remaining time is dedicated to vipassana, or insight.

Sayamagyi Daw Mya Thwin and Sayagyi U Chit Tin regularly organize 10-day ordination courses for their disciples in order to give them the opportunity to ordain as Buddhist *bhikkhus* (monks) and meditate in robes. They have also led pilgrimages to the sacred Buddhist sites in India, Sri Lanka, and Myanmar.

International Meditation Centres
31a Inya Myaing Rd.
Bahan PO
Yangon
Myanmar

Splatts House
Heddington
Wiltshire SN11 0PE
UK
http://www.internationalmeditationcentre.org/
Roger Bischoff

See also: Buddhism; Meditation; Vipassana International Academy.

References

Coleman, John E. *The Quiet Mind.* London: Harper and Row, 1971.

King, Winston L. *Theravada Meditation.* University Park: Pennsylvania State University Press, 1980.

Sayagyi U Ba Khin. *Dhamma Texts.* Rev. ed. Heddington, UK: Sayagyi U Ba Khin Memorial Trust, 1999.

Sayagyi U Chit Tin. *Knowing Anicca and the Way to Nibbana.* 2nd rev. ed. Heddington, UK: Sayagyi U Ba Khin Memorial Trust, 1997.

Vipassana Research Institute Staff. *Sayagyi U Ba Khin Journal: An Anthology of Articles from the Vipassana Research Institute.* Onalaska, WA: Pariyatti Publishing, 2002.

International New Thought Alliance

The International New Thought Alliance (INTA) is a loosely structured association of New Thought churches, religious institutions, and individuals, which seeks to promote harmony and cooperation within the movement while also increasing awareness of New Thought throughout the world. It publishes a quarterly magazine, *New Thought*, operates the Addington/INTA Archives and Research Center, and hosts annual congresses in large urban centers in North America, chiefly in the United States. The Alliance's 10-point "Declaration of Principles" is a generic New Thought creed, which stresses traditional themes such as the goodness of God, the divinity of humanity, and the causative nature of consciousness. INTA is organized by districts, of which there are more than 100 worldwide, with slightly more than half being in the United States.

Fully vested membership is open to laypersons as well as clergy. INTA is led by a president and managed by a chief executive officer, in cooperation with an executive board. The president and members of the executive board are elected at annual congresses. Organizationally, INTA is the most open and democrati-

cally structured of all major New Thought groups, and its broad and inclusive membership requirements allow for significant diversity among individual participants, all of whom have voting privileges. Institutional membership has stricter guidelines than individual membership, but only slightly so.

INTA traces its origin to a 1914 New Thought conference in London, England. It held its first annual congress in 1915 in San Francisco and was incorporated in 1917 in Washington, D.C. The Alliance's organizational roots can be traced back to the National New Thought Alliance (1907), the New Thought Federation (1904), the first "New Thought Convention" (1899), and perhaps even the International Divine Science Association (1892). Although each of these predecessor organizations sought to unify the disparate groups in the mental healing movement, some with limited success, it was not until the formation of INTA that this goal was realized in such a way as to assure stability and longevity.

Unlike the various sects of New Thought, INTA has no easily identifiable founder. Its emergence as a coherent organization and successful overcoming of early institutional struggles were the result of the efforts of a number of talented leaders, all of whom committed themselves and in some cases the religious communities they had founded to the INTA mission. The list of early supporters reads like a New Thought who's who of the period: Annie Rix Militz (1856–1924), Myrtle (1845–1931) and Charles (1854–1948) Fillmore, Nona Brooks (1861–1945), Albert C. Grier (1864–1941), Thomas Troward (1847–1916), Horatio Dresser (1866–1854), Christian D. Larson (b. 1874), Orison Swett Marden (1850–1924), Elizabeth Towne (1865–1960), and Ella Wheeler Wilcox (1850–1919).

Although these high-profile celebrities were instrumental in giving the fledgling INTA valuable publicity and significant legitimacy as an umbrella organization for the entire New Thought movement, the real key to the Alliance's early success was a layperson and former employee of the U.S. Post Office, James A. Edgerton (1869–1938). Edgerton was the first president of the organization, a post he held from 1915 to 1923 and then again from 1934 to 1937. A skillful executive, diplomat, and bureaucrat, Edgerton left his stamp on the Alliance, which to this day follows the same basic organizational structures he put in place. No other person is as responsible for the establishment and development of INTA. Under his leadership, by 1920, the Alliance counted among its members Militz's Homes of Truth, Brooks's Divine Science, the Fillmores' Unity, Grier's Church of Truth, and countless numbers of their followers.

Over the years INTA has been largely successful in its role as an umbrella organization for the New Thought movement. It has been particularly fortunate to have had a number of talented presidents, of whom the most important are Raymond Charles Barker (1911–1988), Ervin Seal, Robert H. Bitzer (1896–1994), and Blaine C. Mays. Bitzer and Mays are especially notable for their success in expanding the international outreach of INTA. Together with Edgerton, they are the longest serving presidents of the Alliance, with Mays having served the longest of all: 1974–1996, 1997–2007, and 2008–present.

As with any broad-based ecumenical organization, comprised of diverse and often competing groups, INTA has seen a fair number of controversies. Perhaps the most notable ones occurred in 1922 and 1996. Precipitating causes are difficult to specify in any detail, but both events appear to have been the result of disagreements pertaining to the Alliance's leadership and some of its programs. By comparison, the removal of references to Jesus, Christ, and Jesus Christ, from the group's "Declaration of Principles" in 1954 appears to have caused no adverse reaction. The 1922 event led to the withdrawal of Unity School from the Alliance and the end of Edgerton's long tenure as president the following year. Edgerton returned to the presidency in 1934. The 1996 controversy led to the withdrawal of the leaders of a number of large churches and Mays's defeat in an election by Marguerite Goodall. Mays returned to the presidency in 1997. It is noteworthy that the year following Unity School's withdrawal, it began holding its own annual conventions, and in 1996 a number of the leaders who had withdrawn joined with others to establish what could be seen as a rival organization, the Association for Global New Thought (AGNT).

In the late 1990s INTA membership declined slightly. This may have been the result of several factors: fallout from the 1996 controversy, the rise of AGNT, the growth of another independent organization (Affiliated New Thought Network, established in 1993), as well as further institutional development of the major New Thought churches. As of 2008 membership currently stands at about 1,200, of which 168 are institutional members, representing all branches of the New Thought movement. Notable institutional members include the Association of Unity Churches, Religious Science International, Divine Science Federation International, and United Divine Science Ministries, International. INTA has districts in 51 countries and institutional members in 23. As is typical of New Thought groups (aside from Unity's Unity Village complex) there are no shrine centers in INTA, although trips to annual congresses may function as pilgrimages for highly committed members.

International New Thought Alliance
5013 E. Broadway Rd.
Mesa, AZ 85206
http://www.newthoughtalliance.org/
Dell deChant and Natalie Hobbs

See also: Divine Science Federation International/ United Divine Science Ministries International; Religious Science; Unity School of Christianity.

References
Albanese, Catherine L. *A Republic of Mind and Spirit*. New Haven, CT: Yale University Press, 2007.
Braden, Charles. *Spirits in Rebellion: The Rise and Development of New Thought*. Dallas: SMU Press, 1963.
deChant, Dell. "New Thought." In *World Religions in America*. 4th ed. Ed. by Jacob Neusner. Louisville: Westminster John Knox. 2009.

International Old Catholic Bishops' Conference

The Old Catholic movement developed in response to changes made in the belief structure of the Roman Catholic Church at the First Vatican Council (1870–1871), the most significant change being the declaration of papal infallibility and the elevation of papal authority it implied. In Munich in 1871, 44 dissenting

Roman Catholic professors, under the leadership of the German Catholic scholars Johann Joseph Ignaz von Döllinger (1799–1890) and Johannes Friedrich, signed a protest against the First Vatican Council's action. Congregations that rejected the pronouncement of the Council began to form, and they, in 1873, organized the Catholic Diocese of the Old Catholics in Germany with the consecration of Joseph Hubert Reinkens as bishop. He was consecrated at Rotterdam by the bishops of Deventer of the dissenting diocese in Holland, which re-formed as the Old Catholic Church of the Netherlands. Subsequent consecrations were held for the Old Catholic Church of Austria and the Old Catholic Church of Switzerland.

In 1889, the Old Catholic bishops created the Union of Utrecht, and in their initial declaration they complained of a variety of matters in which they felt that Rome had departed from the faith of the primitive church, including the doctrine of the Immaculate Conception of Mary and the universal authority of the bishop of Rome. At the same time that they organized the Union, the bishops decided to meet annually in conference to discuss any ongoing issues of importance. That annual conference evolved into the more formally organized International Old Catholic Bishops' Conference. The Conference has been extended to include bishops from the Old Catholic churches in other countries, including France, Yugoslavia, the Czech Republic, Sweden, Slovakia, the United States, and Poland.

The Conference is cooperative with the World Council of Churches, which most Old Catholic churches have joined, and its representatives meet annually with representatives of the other world Christian communions.

International Old Catholic Bishops' Conference
Kon. Wilhelminalaan 3
NL-3818 HN Amersfoort
Netherlands

J. Gordon Melton

See also: Catholic Diocese of the Old Catholics in Germany; Old Catholic Church of Austria; Old Catholic Church of Switzerland; Old Catholic Church of the Netherlands; Roman Catholic Church; World Council of Churches.

References
Moss, C. B. *The Old Catholic Movement*. Eureka Springs, AK: Episcopal Book Club, 1977.
Schnitker, Thaddeus A. "The Old Catholic Churches of the Union of Utrecht." http://www.tec-europe.org/partners/Utrecht_partners.htm. Accessed June 15, 2009.

International Pentecostal Church of Christ

The International Pentecostal Church of Christ traces its beginning to an early Pentecostal periodical, *The Bridegroom's Messenger*, started by Gaston B. Cashwell (1860–1916) in 1907 in North Carolina. Cashwell became a singular force in spreading the Pentecostal message throughout the South. Among the people influenced by Cashwell were Hattie Barth and Paul Barth, who in 1907 founded a church in Atlanta. They later opened a Bible school, and their ministry led to the formation of a new association of churches and ministers, the International Pentecostal Assemblies.

At the same time, in 1908, John Stroup, a minister with the Methodist Protestant Church (now a constituent part of the United Methodist Church), received the baptism of the Holy Spirit and began to spread the Pentecostal message through Kentucky and Ohio. His work led to the founding of the Pentecostal Church of Christ in 1917, with Stroup as its first bishop. In 1976, the Pentecostal Church of Christ merged with the International Pentecostal Assemblies to create the International Pentecostal Church of Christ.

Although the church has only some 5,000 members in the United States (2009), beginning in the 1930s in Brazil it built an extensive missionary program and has more than 150,000 members in sister churches in Brazil, India, Mexico, French Guinea, Kenya, the Philippines, Vietnam, and Uruguay. These national churches are indigenous and self-governing churches but considered a part of the International Pentecostal Church of Christ. The church maintains Beulah Heights Bible College in Atlanta.

International Pentecostal Church of Christ
PO Box 439

2245 U.S. 42, SW
London, OH 43140
http://www.ipcc.cc/

J. Gordon Melton

See also: Pentecostalism; United Methodist Church.

Reference

Burgess, Stanley M., and Eduard M. Van der Maas, eds. *The New International Dictionary of Pentecostal and Charismatic Movements*. Grand Rapids, MI: Zondervan, 2002.

International Pentecostal Holiness Church

One must step back into the 19th century to start the pilgrimage of the denomination known as the International Pentecostal Holiness Church. The story of this church takes in both the Fire-Baptized Holiness Church (FBHC), with origins in Iowa in 1895, and the Pentecostal Holiness Church (PHC) of North Carolina, launched by Ambros Blackman Crumpler (1863–1952).

A call was issued by Benjamin Hardin Irwin (b. 1854) for a general council of his organization to meet July 28 to August 8, 1898, in Anderson, South Carolina. Irwin designated the Anderson meeting the First General Council of the Fire-Baptized Holiness Association. The government was a totally centralized autocracy, with the general overseer chosen for life.

In 1900 the news broke that Irwin had been leading a double life. J. H. King (1869–1946), then ruling elder of Ontario, came to Lincoln for the purpose of assuming the editorship of *Live Coals of Fire*, Irwin's periodical. King called for a meeting of the general council, which convened in Olmitz, Iowa, June 30 through July 2, 1900. King, at age 31, was chosen as general overseer.

Meanwhile, A. B. Crumpler's desire to preach his view of Holiness again outweighed his desire to stay with the Methodist Episcopal Church (now an integral part of the United Methodist Church), so after a successful evangelistic campaign, he issued a call in the early part of 1900 for a meeting in Fayetteville, North Carolina, to organize a new denomination.

Crumpler had learned of the original Pentecostal movement at Azusa Street in Los Angeles from reports by Frank Bartleman in 1906 in James M. Pike's *Way of Faith* periodical. A North Carolina Holiness preacher in Crumpler's church, Gaston Barnabas Cashwell (1862–1916), traveled to Los Angeles and obtained the Pentecostal experience first hand. The North Carolina revival, which Cashwell initiated upon his return in the first days of 1907, quickly spread in the Southeast, while several holiness leaders and many of their members soon entered the Pentecostal fold.

A climactic battle for the Pentecostal Holiness Church occurred at the 1908 convention, which met in Dunn, North Carolina, on November 26. Crumpler, who had been unanimously re-elected there, finally brought the matter to a head by walking out of the convention. The convention ended with A. H. Butler as the president and the church totally in the hands of the Pentecostal preacher.

On January 30, 1911, in the octagon-shaped Pentecostal Holiness Church building at Falcon, North Carolina, duly elected delegates met for the purpose of effecting a consolidation between the Pentecostal Holiness Church and the Fire-Baptized Holiness Church. Such was accomplished by the close of the following day.

In 1999, the church reported 1,040,400 members and 8,383 churches worldwide of which 184,431 members and 1,771 churches were in the United States. By 2006, U.S. membership had grown to 248,398.

One of its most famous preachers was Oral Roberts (who left to join the United Methodist Church). Another, Bailey Smith, later became head of the Southern Baptist Convention, as did Charles Stanley, who also ranks among the most popular of electronic preachers.

International Pentecostal Holiness Church
PO Box 12609
Oklahoma City, OK 73157-2609
http://www.iphc.org/

Harold D. Hunter

See also: Pentecostalism; Southern Baptist Convention; United Methodist Church.

References

Campbell, Joseph E. *The Pentecostal Holiness Church: 1898–1948*. Franklin Springs, GA:

Publishing House of the Pentecostal Holiness Church, 1951.

Synan, Vinson. *Old Time Power: A Centennial History of the International Pentecostal Holiness Church.* Franklin Springs, GA: LifeSprings Resources, 1998.

International Society for Krishna Consciousness

The International Society for Krishna Consciousness (ISKCON) is known popularly as the Hare Krishna movement in America and around the world. Essentially a Hindu missionary movement from India centered on the devotional worship of the dark-skinned god Krishna, ISKCON as a religious institution is entering its fifth decade in America. The Krishna devotional community in India is not only the largest sectarian religious community in India, but also one of its oldest.

The worship of the god Krishna, "the All Attractive Lord" (whose name literally means "black" in Sanskrit), dates back to at least the second century BCE in India, as recorded in the famous scripture the Bhagavad Gita (Song to the Lord). A 10th-century text, the Bhagavata Purana (The Tales of the Lord) established the playful, cowherd god Krishna as one of the most popular divinities in India. The Bengali sage Caitanya (1486–1534), a contemporary of Martin Luther, led a reformation of Krishna worship that included translating scriptures into vernacular languages, instituting public forms of dancing and singing (*sankirtana*), and inviting women and outcastes into the predominantly male worship circle. It was Caitanya's evangelical Krishna tradition into which Abhay Charan De (1896–1977) was initiated as the spiritual master (*acarya* or *acharya*) called A. C. Bhaktivedanta Swami Prabhupada in 1932 in Bengal. Prabhupada brought his deep devotion to Krishna to America on September 17, 1965, when he arrived in New York City penniless and with a suitcase full of his translations of Krishna scriptures.

Prabhupada began his preaching ministry on the Lower East Side of New York City and attracted youth who were drawn to his piety and deep faith and to the intricate philosophy and exuberant rituals of the Hare Krishna tradition. In 1966, he incorporated his new society in New York and named it the International Society for Krishna Consciousness (ISKCON). As in Bengal, the worship Prabhupada taught to his American devotees was focused on devotion to Krishna through repetitive reciting of the names of Krishna (*nama japa*), worship in songs and prayers before the images of Krishna and his divine consort Radha (*puja*), and public dancing and singing to invite others to worship Krishna (*sankirtana*). Prabhupada's translations of and commentary on the key Krishna scriptures were distributed as a means of preaching and soliciting for money.

The Hare Krishnas' saffron robes and colorful saris, Indian chanting, and active proselytizing drew public attention to the group, made them quite visible, and invited criticism and even hostile opposition. Even during Prabhupada's lifetime, overenthusiastic devotees sometimes engaged in questionable behavior in their fundraising, exuberant proselytizing, and personal lifestyles. Prabhupada died on November 14, 1977. In that same year two Southern California devotees were charged with drug trafficking and a former devotee, Robin George, sued ISKCON after charging it with kidnapping and brainwashing. The California Krishna temples that were involved and ISKCON as an organization were ultimately exonerated from both the drug dealing and kidnapping and brainwashing charges. Nonetheless, certain devotees, including several gurus among the 11 appointed successors to Prabhupada, did act unlawfully or immorally, which fueled public opposition to ISKCON. In the early years after Prabhupada's death, guru scandals included the ouster of a controversial guru named Hansadutta from the Berkeley Krishna temple and the indictment of a Moundsville, West Virginia, guru named Kirtanananda for trademark infringements and conspiracy to commit murder. Though both of these gurus had been excommunicated from ISKCON before they ran into trouble with the law, the Hare Krishnas were embarrassed by these and other such public exposés of supposed spiritual leaders of the movement. Perhaps the most serious charges leveled at ISKCON had to do with child abuse. Even today, ISKCON is learning more from its adult "children" about why it was not wise for ascetic

The primary center for the Krishna Consciousness movement in the United States is their temple in Los Angeles, California. (J. Gordon Melton)

men and untrained teachers to run crowded Krishna boarding schools.

In spite of the imagined and real scandals that ISKCON endured, the positive dimension of the devotional movement centering on Krishna that Prabhupada preached has allowed ISKCON to persist and mature, not only in the United States but in nations throughout the world. During Praphupada's lifetime, his movement spread to Canada, England, Europe, Africa, and parts of Asia. By the late 1970s, ISKCON had more than 10,000 devotees living in more than 50 communities in the United States and 60 communities in 45 countries around the world. In addition, there were literally tens of thousands of devotees living beyond the temples themselves as lay adherents. By the turn of the millennium, ISKCON was less temple- and less America-centered. By the year 2000, only 45 temple and farm communities were active in the United States, with approximately 900 devotees living in them, yet these same communities attracted many householder families (*grihasthas*) and large numbers of Indian immigrants who embraced the Hare Krishna faith that Prabhupada had brought to America 35 years earlier.

Also by the year 2000, ISKCON had 325 communities in 75 countries on every continent. In 2002, ISKCON opened its first accredited center of higher learning, Bhaktivedanta College, which, in partnership with the University of Wales Lampeter, now offers degrees in theology. ISKCON's international Food for Life project distributes millions of free vegetarian meals each year to those in need, especially at their

Indian temples. Primary Hare Krishna devotional sites include Bhaktivedanta Manor outside London, the Palace at New Vrindavana in America, an international guesthouse and Vedic-style temple in Vrindavana, India, and a large devotional center in Mayapura, India. In 1998, while inaugurating a large new Krishna temple in New Delhi, India's prime minister, Atal Bihari Vajpayee, praised ISKCON for its success in the "globalization of the message of the Bhagavad Gita." Although some view ISKCON as simply an American religious cult, it can better be understood as a Hindu missionary movement promoting devotion to the Indian god Krishna, a movement that continues to gain popularity around the world even as its American membership base remains vital and stable.

Following Prabhupada's death, authority in ISKCON passed to the Governing Body Commission (GBC), composed of several initiating gurus and other senior devotees. Over the years the authority structure has become ever more decentralized, but the GBC stills provides guidance internationally. The GBC may be contacted through the GBC Journal, PO Box 1119, Alachua, FL 32616, or through Secretary, Governing Body Commission, PO Box 16146, Circus Avenue office, Calcutta 700 017, India. Information is available from the ISKCON Communication Office, 10310 Oaklyn Dr., Potomac, MD 20854, and at ic@pamho .net, or through the society's publishing house, the Bhaktivedanta Book Trust at www.krishna.com.

http://www.iskcon.com

Larry Dwight Shinn

See also: Devotion/Devotional Traditions.

References

Prabhupada, A. C. Bhaktivedanta Swami. *The Bhagavad Gita As It Is.* New York: Collier Books, 1968.

Rochford, E. Burke. *Hare Krishnas in America.* New Brunswick, NJ: Rutgers University Press, 1985.

Shinn, Larry D. *The Dark Lord: Cult Images and the Hare Krishnas in America.* Philadelphia: Westminster Press, 1987.

Rochford, E. Burke. *Hare Krishna Transformed.* New York: New York University Press, 2007.

International Sufi Movement, The

The International Sufi movement, a representative of Chisti Sufism, emerged following the death of India-born Hazrat Inayat Khan (1892–1927), who had founded the Sufi Order in the United States in 1910. Khan initiated a woman, Rabia Martin, and designated her as his successor. His choice was, however, rejected by Khan's family and his growing European following. Khan died at a relatively young age and had not written a will. Seizing upon this circumstance (and the fact that his son/successor was still a minor), the European members rejected Martin's leadership and organized the Sufi movement. They chose Maheboob Khan (1887–1948), Inayat's brother, as their new leader. He would be succeeded in 1948 by a cousin, Mohammad Ali Khan (1881–1958), Musharaff Khan (1895–1967), and Fazal Inayat Khan (1942–1990). Fazal resigned leadership in 1982.

After Fazal Khan's resignation, a collective leadership tried to assume control, but it soon met with dissent so deep as to split the movement. Hidayat Inayat Khan (b. 1917) soon emerged as the leader of the largest part of the Sufi movement. He shared leadership with Murshida Shahzadi. Hidayat, one of the sons of Hazrat Inayat, finally became the sole leader of the movement in 1993.

Hidayat Inayat Khan was only 10 years old when his father passed away in 1927. From his father he inherited a love of music. He studied at L'Ecole Normale de Musique and eventually became a professor in the Music School of Dieulefit, Drome, France, and conducted an orchestra in Haarlem, Holland. He wrote numerous compositions, including both secular music and a collection of Sufi hymns, and was a founding member of the European Composers' Union.

The Sufi movement resembles the Sufi Order International, headed for many years by Hazrat Inayat's elder son, Vilayat Inayat Khan (1916–2004), and is organized in five divisions to focus on universal worship, community, healing, symbology, and esoteric activity. The movement has spread across Europe to Canada and the United States. Members meet weekly for *dhikr* (worship) and classes.

The International Sufi Movement
11 rue John Rehfous
1208 Geneva
Switzerland
http://guess.workweb.net/sufi/

J. Gordon Melton

See also: Devotion/Devotional Traditions; Sufism.

References

The Gathas. Katwijk, The Netherlands: Servire, 1982.

Khan, Fazal Inayat. *Old Thinking: New Thinking.* New York: Harper and Row, 1979.

Khan, Hidayat Inayat. *Sufi Teachings.* Ecstasis, 1994.

International Yoga Fellowship Movement

The International Yoga Fellowship movement continues the work of Swami Satyananda Saraswati (b. 1923), one of the many disciples of Swami Sivananda Saraswati (1887–1863), the founder of the Divine Life Society. He lived with Sivananda at Rishikesh for 12 years beginning in 1943, but then, like other disciples, he left the Society to found his own independent work, the International Yoga Fellowship in 1956 and the Bihar School of Yoga, which opened in 1964.

Satyananda continued Sivananda's integral yoga format, based on the practice of *hatha* yoga exercises, but also integrating the additional approaches of *karma, jnana, bhakti,* and *raja* yoga. In 1968 he made a world tour, which first introduced his teachings to the world outside of India, and in the 1980s he wrote a number of popular books. Through these books, he became known as not only a teacher of integral yoga but an exponent of Tantric yoga. Tantra proposes the existence of a subtle human energy body that parallels the physical body. The subtle body explains the existence of psychic and spiritual experiences, and its cultivation and training is essential to the development of an enlightened state. Part of that process is the practice of *kundalini* yoga that activates the latent power believed by Tantric practitioners to reside at the base of the spine.

In the case of left-hand Tantra, as taught by Swami Satyananda, it also includes the use of sex to blend male and female energies and consciousness.

The International Yoga Fellowship movement spread in the 1960s by two routes. First, Indian disciples of Satyananda were among the many Indian nationals who migrated to Australia, North America, and Europe, and they have established centers primarily attended by Indian expatriates residing in the West. Many national organizations affiliated to the movement were formed by Swami Niranjannan Saraswati (b. 1960) including Satyananda Ashrams, U.S.A., in 1980.

Also, many Westerners have been attracted to the teachings of Satyananda, and they have been active in spreading his teachings among Western disciples. Australian yoga teacher John Mumford was initiated by Satyananda in 1973 and two years later authored *Sexual Occultism,* one of the first books offering details of the heretofore secret Tantric practices to the general public. Meanwhile, a Danish student who met Satyananda on his 1968 world tour moved to India with him and in 1970 returned to Denmark as Swami Janakananda Saraswati (b. 1939). He founded the Scandinavian Yoga and Meditation School in Copenhagen and in 1975 authored a second book detailing Satyananda's Tantric teachings.

The International Yoga Fellowship Movement has an Internet site at the address given below that includes links to its many centers around the world. In the 1990s, one of Satyananda's disciples, Paramahamsa Niranjanananda, founded Bihar Yoga Bharati as an academic center to supply the higher educational needs of the movement. Movement centers are now found on every continent, and in Europe the centers have organized the European Yoga Fellowship.

International Yoga Fellowship Movement
Bihar School of Yoga
Ganga Darshan
Fort Munger, Bihar 811201
India
http://www.yogavision.net/main_set.htm

J. Gordon Melton

See also: Divine Life Society; Tantrism; Yoga.

References

Janakananda Saraswati, Swami. *Yoga, Tantra and Meditation*. New York: Ballantine Books, 1975.

Mumford, John [Swami Anandakapila]. *Sexual Occultism*. St. Paul, MN: Llewellyn Publications, 1975.

Satyananda Saraswati, Swami. *Asana Pranayama Mudra Bandha*. 4th ed. Mongyar, Bihar, India: Bihar School of Yoga, 2008.

Satyananda Saraswati, Swami. *Sure Ways to Self-Realization*. Mongyar, Bihar, India: Bihar School of Yoga, 1983.

Satyananda Saraswati, Swami. *Taming the Kundalini*. Mongyar, Bihar, India: Bihar School of Yoga, 1982.

Satyananda Saraswati, Swami. *A Systematic Course in the Ancient Tantric Techniques of Yoga and Kriya*. Mongyar, Bihar, India: Bihar School of Yoga, 2004.

Teachings of Swami Satyananda Saraswati. Mongyar, Bihar, India: Bihar School of Yoga, 1981.

International Zen Association

The International Zen Association (IZA, also known as the Association Zen Internationale [AZI]) was founded by the Japanese Zen Buddhist priest Taisen Deshimaru (1914–1982) in 1970 as an organization to support his mission in Europe. It is now an umbrella organization of nonprofit associations that links 8 temples (residences of a teacher sanctioned by the Japanese *soto* school) and 65 urban centers (called *dojo* in the group) devoted to the practice of seated meditation (*zazen*) that all belong to the Deshimaru's lineage in the Japanese soto tradition. When including smaller or more recent centers (designated as "groups"), the IZA claims a presence in 13 countries and more than 200 practice centers worldwide. Few of those are located outside Europe and the headquarters are in Paris, which makes it a strongly European organization, as was once indicated by its former name, the Association Zen d'Europe. The oldest and biggest centers are in France, Germany, Switzerland, United Kingdom, Belgium, and Spain. Although the active membership in the IZA is around 2,000 individuals, the audience and network of sympathizers of the movement is much larger. Accord-ing to some members of the group, more than 15,000 persons have participated over time in its conferences, daily meditations, day-long intensive practice periods, or retreats.

Taisen Deshimaru arrived in France in 1967, shortly after receiving the priest ordination from one of the most respected Soto Zen priests in Japan, Kodo Sawaki (1880–1965). A former business executive, he came at the invitation of a visiting group of French members of the macrobiotic movement. As baby boomers started seeking Eastern masters in the late 1960s, Deshimaru Roshi's Parisian dojo became the basis of a rapidly expanding organization. The master's emphasis on practice rather than rituals or intellectual conceptions, his direct personality, and his provocative teachings (for example, urging his students to reconcile Eastern and Western philosophies through zazen) attracted many European disciples. The IZA claimed 25 centers in 1972, and by 1982, more than 53. A property was acquired in 1979, becoming the organization's temple of La Gendronnière (Loire-et-Cher, France). As confirmed by the 40th anniversary of his mission in the temple of La Gendronniere in 2007 and stated by the international website of the soto school, Sawaki's "last disciple"—as Deshimaru called himself in a book of tributes to his master—initiated the presence of that school in Europe, becoming in that process the patriarch of European soto Zen.

In *his Autobiography of a Zen Monk*, Deshimaru Roshi explained that his master's last instructions were to bring "the seed of Zen" to the West, since Zen was weakening in Japan and Asia in general. Deshimaru Roshi's agenda was to first transplant the Zen teachings in the West, then use those missions as a basis for reforming the institutions at home. Himself a lay practitioner for most of his training years, he gave priest ordinations (called "monks" and "nuns" in the group), interpreted as commitment to practice zazen in an otherwise lay life. In this regard, both his critical stance toward Buddhism in Japan and the lay practice pattern are very much in line with what can be observed among American Zen teachers. In the IZA groups, some rituals of Japanese Soto Zen were simplified by Taisen Deshimaru Roshi. In recent years, some of his former disciples have established non-urban dwellings with a small number of full time residents, a development that has been parallel to renewed ties with Japan, the re-establishment of the Soto Zen Buddhism Europe Office in June 2002 and the adoption by some members of the group of rituals closer to the Japanese forms.

Deshimaru introduced to his students the Soto Zen teaching of "just sitting" (*shikantaza*) and insisted that Zen is simply the practice of zazen, sitting cross-legged and observing one's mind and breathing, without trying to gain anything. He emphasized the practice of zazen and retreat periods where one could live, work, and practice with others. He tirelessly taught this practice, stating that his disciples would contribute to resolving what he saw as civilization's crisis, born of contradictions between intuition and rationality, science and religion.

The unexpected death of the charismatic founder sparked a crisis of succession. Some of his disciples left the organization, later receiving authorization to teach from other masters and founding their own organizations. Others stayed on, vowing to "carry on together the mission of their late teacher." They have been establishing their own temples and centers in recent years and some of them received transmission certificates from Japanese masters after the death of their master. Thus, for example, one of the closest disciples of Deshimaru, Stephane Kosen Thibault, has founded a network of groups that does not belong to the IZA, but clearly relates itself to Deshimaru's teachings (http://www.zen-deshimaru.com).

As the teachers of IZA now come of age as leaders and define their own teaching styles, reaching out to a new generation, it seems likely that they will also have to define, both collectively and individually, the future of their "Japanese connection." This is currently debated within the group. Some members hold cautious, if not somewhat negative views of maintaining close ties with Japan, while others believe that a dialogue with Japan is to be encouraged and will prove beneficial to the organization.

International Zen Association
175 Rue de Tolbiac
75013 Paris
France
http://www.zen-azi.org

Alioune Koné

See also: Soto Zen Buddhism; Zen Buddhism.

References

Deshimaru, Taisen. *Autobiographie d'un moine Zen.* 1977; re-edited by Taiko de Swarte and Nan Futsu. Lyon: Terre du Ciel, 1995.

Deshimaru, Taisen. *Sit.* Ed. by Philippe Coupey. Prescott, AZ: Hohm Press, 1996.

Finney, Henry C. "American Zen's 'Japan Connection': A Critical Case Study of Zen Buddhism's Diffusion to the West." *Sociological Analysis* 52, no. 4 (1991): 379–396.

Koné, Alioune. "L'ouverture de la montagne." Ph.D. diss., Ecole des Hautes Etudes en Sciences Sociales, 2009.

Koné, Alioune. "Zen in Europe: A survey of the territory." *Journal of Global Buddhism* 2 (2001). http://www.globalbuddhism.org.

Lenoir, Frédéric. *Le Bouddhisme en France.* Paris: Fayard, 1999.

Internet and Religion

For most people in the developed (and increasingly in the developing) world, the Internet is virtually unavoidable. In less than two decades the World Wide Web has gone from a technological curiosity to an inescapable fact of life for hundreds of millions of people. As the technology of computer-mediated communication continues to miniaturize, loading more and more features into smaller and smaller packages, as its social penetration deepens and more people have more and easier Internet access, and as social institutions seek to go "paperless" and administer an increasing variety of tasks electronically, the Internet will only increase in importance even as it increases in social transparency. That is, as more and more our lives are connected to the Net, those connections will seem to us less and less remarkable. Like telephones and toasters, computers and the world of electronic communication have become part of the furniture that structures daily life. Smartphone technology such as the Apple Iphone or RIM's Blackberry packs far more computing power in the palm of one's hand than was offered by all but the most powerful consumer desktops

Robert Thibadeau shows an image of the "Houses of Worship" website on his laptop computer while standing in front of St. Paul's Cathedral in Pittsburgh, October 10, 1997. Thibadeau hopes to connect as many of the world's Christian churches as he can through this project. (AP/Wide world Photos)

just a few years ago. In many social and professional situations devices such as these are ubiquitous and *not* having an Iphone or a Blackberry is more noteworthy than having one. Indeed, talking on, texting, or emailing on handheld devices has become so common (and dangerous) in recent years that many jurisdictions have passed laws prohibiting their use in motor vehicles.

As it has with most (arguably all) advances in communications technology, from cave painting and campfire stories to television broadcasting and wireless communication, religion occupies a significant

place in cyberspace. Just 20 years ago, when popularly available computer-mediated communication was in its technological infancy, computer literate religious believers discussed their faith, shared their concerns, and laid the foundation for an online community largely through dedicated bulletin board services. Primitive and painfully slow by comparison with even the most basic Internet service package today, these systems transmitted text only, perhaps with the occasional picture (which took a long time to download and even then required a special program to view). These are, however, the computer-mediated antecedents of dedicated discussion platforms such as Yahoo! and MSN Groups, social networking programs such as Facebook, MySpace, and Twitter, and visual media sharing sites such as YouTube, Flickr, and Photobucket. Now, in addition to a website, for many religious congregations around the world online information sharing—a Facebook group for the annual youth rally or dedicated to a special campaign, for example—is becoming more and more common. Religious leaders regularly post their messages online, in both text and video format, while congregants Twitter each other about the sermon—often while the pastor is actually speaking from the pulpit. In an effort to attract members of a younger, more technologically confident generation, religious organizations ranging from the United Church of Canada to the Church of Scientology have spent millions of dollars developing sophisticated websites that allow for services ranging from email hosting to chatrooms, and from online religious discussion and video teaching to computer-mediated prayer and meditation. From succinct "prayerful thoughts for the day" to rambling rants about current events and biblical prophecy, video clips recorded through onboard cameras are regularly uploaded to YouTube accounts by a wide range of Internet users. Often generating both text and video responses, these kinds of interaction are evolving into a new order of religious discourse unimaginable only a generation ago.

Contrary to much of the commercial and enthusiast hyperbole about the social prominence of the World Wide Web, however, it is unlikely that online versions of religious practice will significantly displace their offline counterparts, or that they will remain anything other than adjuncts of convenience for those with access to the technology. That is, they add to the experience of offline religious belief and practice, but do not (at least so far as we can determine at this point) replace it. That said, though, computer mediation is affecting religious belief and practice in some significant ways, if for no other reason than that *how* we do something inevitably impacts *what* we are doing. Many people, for example, use the Internet as a relatively risk-free means of exploring, or "trying on," different religious identities, especially identities that are unavailable to them offline, either through geographical isolation or social opprobrium. Young people interested in aspects of modern Paganism, for example, often turn to the World Wide Web in search of initial contact and basic information. Although those who choose to explore a Pagan path more intentionally rarely limit their practice to the online environment, it is not insignificant that the Web provides them a starting point that was unavailable a relatively few years ago. On the other hand, the essential anonymity of Web-based interaction also allows for the online performance of virtuosity, with a wide variety of men and women claiming religious status in the so-called virtual world that, in many cases, would hardly be accorded them in real life.

When discussing religion and computer-mediated communication, two preliminary conceptual distinctions are necessary: the categories of online activity and the relationships that exist between human religious belief and practice, and the Internet as a social technology.

First, there is the basic spectrum of online activity. Originally proposed as a dyad between religion online and online religion, but quickly recognized as a continuum of computer-mediated activity, this is the preliminary distinction between use of the Internet to communicate *information* about one's religion (that is, religion online) and as a vehicle to *practice* aspects of one's religion (that is, online religion). Posting information about a prayer meeting on one's church website or uploading the price list for various *puja* constitute the former, while convening a Facebook group or chatroom session to which members contribute prayers online or designing an interactive puja website are examples of the latter. Obviously, these are not discrete categories and there is often signifi-

cant crossover between them. In many cases, believers regard religious education, for example, as part of their religious practice. Taking an online course in the letters of Paul can be seen as a kind of devotional activity, something that informs and influences who they are as religious believers. Posting inspirational messages to a variety of discussion forums can be understood as contributing to the spiritual activities of one's co-religionists. This is not to say that all believers agree on the content or purpose of a particular online activity any more than they agree about all aspects of offline practice. They don't. Although many Roman Catholics, for example, suggest that online adoration of the Blessed Host carries the same spiritual value as ritual adoration in person, others vehemently disagree, arguing that only in the actual presence of the Host is the grace of God mediated and anything else is tantamount to heresy. It is important to remember that in the vast majority of cases online religious activity is a reflection (or refraction) of offline behavior and practice; it is not sui generis. Although some groups claim to be purely online religion, none (to this point, at least) has lived up to this contention.

Second, there are the practical and analytic relationships inherent in the words "on" and "and." That is, what is the difference between "religion on the Internet" and "religion and the Internet"? While this may seem a trivial distinction, it raises important issues for the scholarly study of religion in the context of computer-mediated communication. "Religion on the Internet" is that spectrum of online activity just discussed. That is, how are religious people using the World Wide Web to further their religious agendas, deepen their spiritual lives, and attract fellow travelers either on or to their particular path? Religion and the Internet, on the other hand, implicates both the ways in which the World Wide Web can be used to research religion and the manner in which computer-mediated communication is affecting religious belief and practice.

Few researchers would deny the convenience of electronic access to library catalogues, full-text runs of academic journals, popular magazines, newspapers, and religious publications, or the opportunity to view YouTube clips of research subjects. In this sense, the World Wide Web is an incredible boon to religious studies. There is also no doubt that the Internet dramatically increases the ability of scholars from around the world to collaborate on common research problems and electronic communication has in many ways streamlined the scholarly publication process. The vast amount of material vying for an Internet user's attention, however, along with the drastic difference in quality of information and the increasing popularity of online reference sources such as Wikipedia and its many versions and imitators, creates a data pool that is outside the normal scholarly review process and requires careful attention on the part of researchers. Put simply, there is a tremendous amount of erroneous information available online. Similarly, many scholars regard the advent of online peer-reviewed academic journals as a threat to the intellectual rigor of scholarly debate and discussion. With so many more venues for publication, they argue, how can the common denominator of peer-reviewed publication not decrease?

Religious studies research carried out online has its own benefits and problems. Although the ability to upload a survey and then access the data through a dedicated website undoubtedly makes the research process easier, it is limited to that portion of the population who use the Internet. Thus, given the various "digital divides"—regional, economic, racial, and age-based—unless they are specifically intended to research questions related to computer-mediated communication, online surveys provide a very narrow window into religious belief and practice. Industry and enthusiast hyperbole notwithstanding, and despite the increase of social penetration in developing areas of the world, far more people around the world go through their lives without regular Internet access than with it. Although computer-mediated communication can bring researchers in contact with a far broader range of believers than was possible through other means, the potential for conversion in online research raises the obvious ethical question of disclosure and the protection of research subjects. Since it is possible to hide one's identity as a researcher and join any number of online groups either by pretending to be something one is not (a member of that religion, for example) or simply by failing to disclose one's research agenda, the ability of research subjects to participate with full and informed consent is compromised.

One of the most interesting problems facing researchers of religion and cyberspace is the issue of social transparency. That is, as this technology becomes less socially remarkable, questions related to Internet effect on religious belief and practice become more difficult both to frame and to investigate. For many of those who first researched religion on the Internet, computer-mediated communication was a novelty. There was an obvious difference in the manner and content of communication. Written correspondence, for example, has a very different character and social life than email. The latter is often considerably shorter, occurs at a much higher turn-taking speed, employs an entirely different set of communicative conventions, and is ephemeral in the extreme—once read, the email is often deleted. Twenty years later, however, an entire generation of young people has had Internet access since grade school (if not kindergarten) and may never have handwritten a letter in their lives. Communicating by email, text or instant messaging, and social networking platforms such as Facebook and Twitter are as natural to them as using an ordinary telephone—in some cases moreso. For them, this is not a "different" technology. Investigating these advances in technology, usage, and social transparency will require a more longitudinal research approach, one that considers not just how a particular group is using computer-mediated communication, but how that usage has evolved over time and in response to technological change.

Douglas E. Cowan

See also: Church of Scientology; United Church of Canada; Wiccan Religion.

References

Apolito, Paulo. *The Internet and the Madonna: Religious Visionary Experience on the Web.* Chicago: University of Chicago Press, 2005.

Brasher, Brenda E. *Give Me That Online Religion.* San Francisco: Jossey-Bass, 2001.

Bunt, Gary R. *Islam in the Digital Age: E-Jihad, Online Fatwas, and Cyber Islam Environments.* London: Pluto Press, 2003.

Bunt, Gary R. *Virtually Islamic: Computer-mediated Communication and Cyber Islamic Environments.* Cardiff: University of Wales Press, 2000.

Campbell, Heidi. *Exploring Religious Community Online: We Are One In the Network*. New York: Peter Lang, 2005.

Cowan, Douglas E. *Cyberhenge: Modern Pagans on the Internet*. New York: Routledge, 2005.

Dawson, Lorne L., and Douglas E. Cowan, eds. *Religion Online: Finding Faith on the Internet*. New York: Routledge, 2004.

Hadden, Jeffrey K., and Douglas E. Cowan, eds. *Religion on the Internet: Research Prospects and Promises*. London and Amsterdam: JAI Press/ Elsevier Science, 2000.

Højsgaard, Morton T., and Margit Warburg, eds. *Religion and Cyberspace*. London: Routledge, 2005.

Ignacio, Emily Noelle. *Building Diaspora: Filipino Cultural Community Formation on the Internet*. New Brunswick: Rutgers University Press, 2005.

Inter-Religious Federation for World Peace

The Inter-Religious Federation for World Peace (IRFWP) is one of several international interfaith organizations that has been inspired by and is largely supported by the Unification movement, headed by Korean teacher Reverend Sun Myung Moon. The roots of the organization can be traced to a proposal put forth in the mid-1970s by Warren Lewis, a professor at the Unification Theological Seminary, that a centennial celebration of the 1893 World's Parliament of Religions be held in 1993. He received some initial backing and organized several exploratory conferences in the late 1970s that led to the founding of the Global Congress of the World's Religions in 1980.

The Global Congress held several meetings in the early 1980s that gave rise to two structures, the Council of the World's Religions, which sponsored interfaith meetings in locations around the world, and the Assembly of the World's Religions, a large interfaith gathering that convened every few years. Assembly meetings were held in New Jersey in 1985 and San Francisco in 1990. At the 1990 meeting, Rev. Moon announced the organization of the Inter-Religious Federation, which would supersede the Global Congress. This move was in line with other changes in the Unification movement, which was being reorganized into a set of peace federations.

The Inter-Religious Federation was formally created in 1991. While continuing the Global Congress, it also assumed the role of several other Unification structures, including the International Religious Foundation and the New Ecumenical Research Association. IRFWP seeks to bring the resources of the world's religions to bear on the primary goal of world peace. Peace is understood in all its facets as peace within the self and family units, peace within societies and between nations, peace within religions and between religious traditions, peace within and between cultures, and peace between the human and natural worlds.

The Federation is headed by a presiding council, which is assisted by a large board of advisors made up of a spectrum of religious leaders and scholars. There is an administrative staff who manages the IRFWP's programs on a day-to-day basis.

As of 2009, IRFWP reported active representatives in 192 countries. Among its major projects is Religious Youth Service, which brings youth of different faith backgrounds together to work on social service projects. The Federation also publishes a scholarly journal, *Dialogue to Alliance*.

Inter-Religious Federation for World Peace
4 W. 43d St.
New York, NY 10036
http://www.irfwp.org

J. Gordon Melton

See also: Moon, Sun Myung; Unification Movement.

References

Bryant, M. Darrol, John Maniatus, and Tyler Hendricks, eds. *Assembly of the World's Religions, 1985. Spiritual Unity and the Future of the Earth*. New York: International Religious Foundation, 1985.

Cenkner, William, ed. *Evil and the Response of the World's Religions*. New York: Paragon House, 1997.

Lewis, Warren. *Toward a Global Congress of the World's Religions*. Barrytown, NY: Unification Theological Seminary, 1978.

Walsh, Thomas G. *Assembly of the World's Religions, 1990: Transmitting Our Heritage to Youth and Society*. New York: Interreligious Foundation, 1992.

Wilson, Andrew, ed. *World Scripture: A Comparative Anthology of Sacred Texts*. New York: Paragon House, 1995.

■ Iran

Iran is the largest nation in central Eurasia and among the largest in southwestern Asia (aka Middle East) with a population just over 70 million and a physical size about the same as the state of Alaska. It is sandwiched between the Caspian Sea to the north and the Persian Gulf to the south with Iraq and Afghanistan dominating its western and eastern borders, respectively. The capital of Teheran is central to Iran's identity as a Persian state. Skirting the high and dry plateau of Iran are many of the other cities that gave birth to ancient Persian civilization, as well as becoming historic centers of religious thought and innovation. Moreover, numerous expansions and contractions of Persian political control in the region have resulted in a contemporary modern nation dominated by Islam (98 percent) but with an unexpected degree of ethno-religious diversity in the remaining, albeit tiny, section of the population. Religious minorities in Iran include Zoroastrians, Jews, Christians, and Baha'i adherents.

Zoroastrianism   The first documented religious tradition in Iran rose in conjunction with its earliest civilization about 3,500 years ago, and it flourished as the state religion of three pre-Islamic empires. Zoroastrianism is named for its founding prophet, Zarathustra (often known as Zoroaster), who probably lived in what is now eastern or northeastern Iran between the 15th and 17th centuries BCE. Poised midway between the great Mesopotamian civilizations to the west and the magnificent Indus Valley civilization to the east, Persia's early civilization and the religion created by its prophet shared with them similar ceremonial practices and conceptions of the divine and the nature of the universe, while simultaneously producing a particularly Persian point of view.

Although ritual practice (with an official priesthood called *magi*) and philosophical interpretations changed over the course of three millennia, and pre-Zoroastrian elements were incorporated into its canon, Zoroastrianism continues to depend on the teachings of Zarathustra for inspiration—particularly through the Avesta, or holy book, of which only a quarter is extant. An emphasis on personal responsibility and growth as a spiritual being, and a reverence for the good will of the divine in our material existence characterize the Zoroastrian perspective.

The Zoroastrian worshipping community has faced dramatic changes in its political position over the centuries. Receiving the patronage of kings previous to the introduction of Islam in the seventh century, Zoroastrians periodically wielded much influence in a region extending from Greece to northern India (an influence seen, for example, in concepts of resurrection, the heaven/hell dichotomy, and savior imagery). Eventually, Zoroastrianism became a minority religion in the land of its birth, and those who persistently practiced it left the great cities for the southern provinces of Kerman and Yazd. By the 10th century some Zoroastrians found it too difficult to remain in Persia and migrated to the region of Gujarat in western India, where they became known as Parsis (meaning people from Pars, or Persia). Today, Parsis are a small but economically important religious minority found in India's western cities. Back in Persia, a dwindling Zoroastrian community courageously survived invasions by the Seljuk Turks and Mongols (who were eventually converted to Islam), punishing taxes (*jizya*), and humiliating rules of public social interaction with the dominant group (*najes,* or ritual uncleanliness) by insulating themselves in rural and small-town settlements away from centers of political and economic power.

As the 20th century approached, the plight of Zoroastrians eased, as the jizya was revoked and educational opportunities improved. Eventually, during Pahlavi rule in the 20th century, Zoroastrians were recognized as descendants of an original, glorious Persian civilization, and iconic elements of their faith were made into nationalist symbols, including the new name of the

trians, though this number may be low, as intermarriage with Muslims is common.

Islam The seventh century CE proved to be a momentous time in Iranian history. The great Sassanid dynasty faced a major defeat in the Battle of Nihavend in 642 against Arab invaders, and their empire collapsed with the flight and murder of their last king, Yazdegird III, in 652. Incipient application of Islamic law and conversion to the faith was gradual in the first few centuries, but Islam eventually became the dominant and even imposed faith system for the majority of people by the time of invasions by Seljuk Turks and Mongols (who came to be known as the Mughals) in the 11th and 12th centuries. Through this period, and until the Safavid dynasty rose to power at the beginning of the 16th century, Sunni traditions prevailed in Persia.

Unorthodox movements arising out of Shia predispositions, held by groups such as the Ismailis and the Sufis, were flourishing in Iran as early as the 10th and 11th centuries. The Ismailis, some of whom continue to live in northeastern Iran, trace their origins to the lineage of Ismail (d. 760), the son of the sixth imam (revered as descended from Ali, son-in-law of the Prophet Muhammad). Ismail, who predeceased his father, is considered the seventh imam (hence the designation of Ismailis as Seveners) and the originator of a new lineage of imams (which later passed through another contested imam named Nizar). The Mongol invaders destroyed their religious center in the Alborz Mountains, causing Ismailis to flee the region. In 1840, the Nizari Ismaili leader, the Aga Khan, fled to British India, where he was successful in expanding the worshipping community. Today the majority of Nizari Ismailis, numbering several million, live outside of Iran.

Persia was the site where some of the first of the mystically oriented Sufi brotherhoods formed, several of which, such as the Qadiriyya, the Suhrawardi, and the Rifaiyya, not only spread through the region but over the centuries developed followings throughout the larger Muslim world. At the same time, the Sufi tradition contributed to the rise of a particularly Persian form of Shia Islam. The Sufis have historically been a brotherhood (and sisterhood) of mystical Shiite Muslims who eschew materialism and focus upon an ascetic and ecstatic form of spiritual expression and growth. Shah

Women gather at the tomb of 13th-century Shiite leader Imam Reza in Mashhad, Iran. The site is holy to the Shia Muslims of Iran. (Corel)

modern nation, Iran, which was taken from a passage in the Avesta. Zoroastrians began to move back to the cities and are now protected under Iran's Constitution with guaranteed parliamentary representation. In the aftermath of Iran's revolution in 1979, many Zoroastrians feared a return to oppressive conditions, and some migrated to Western nations in the early 1980s. When religious oppression did not materialize as expected, emigration eased, and the community experienced numerical growth, despite a rapid decline in the overall numbers of minority religious adherents between 1976 and 1996. Today, although Zoroastrians do not enjoy the patronage of the Iranian government and are subject to laws that restrict control over education and other social institutions, they have not suffered political or economic oppression beyond that experienced by citizens in general. Approximately 150,000 Zoroastrian adherents exist worldwide, with the largest concentrations in India, Pakistan, and Iran. The 2006 census of Iran reported 35,000 self-identified Zoroas-

Ismail, the founder of the Safavid dynasty, was a Sufi master who established a Sufi-inspired form of Shia as the state religion of Iran when he became king in 1501. More important, though, Shah Ismail conflated his political leadership with spiritual leadership. His followers, who were predominantly Turkic in origin, venerated him as both the *murshid-kamil* (the perfect guide) as well as an emanation of Allah himself. Eventually the majority of the Turkic and Persian populations were integrated through the persistent and forceful application of Safavid rule and religious leadership.

During the two and a half centuries of Safavid rule, Sufi groups were targeted as heretical, despite their role in the creation of the state religion. The Shiite leadership (called Ithna Ashariyya, or the Twelvers) have a special devotion to the 12 imams (Ali and his 11 successors) as intercessors between the believers and Allah. The 12 imams are Ali, al-Hasan, al-Husain, Ali Zayn, al-Abidin, Muhammad al-Baqir, Ja'far al-Sadiq, Musa al-Kazim, Ali al-Rida, Muhammad al-Taqi, Ali al-Naqi, al-Hasan al-Askari, and Ali ibn Muhammad Simmari. The imams are believed to have been chosen by Allah to direct destiny and guide believers in their earthly existence; thus, special prayers are offered to them and pilgrimage is made to their tombs.

The last, or 12th, imam is especially important (hence the designation as Twelvers) as he acquired the imamate at the age of five, and his caregivers kept him in perpetual hiding (well into adulthood) due to the fear of an assassination. This seclusion became institutionalized as the *ghaiba*, or lesser occultation. Twelvers believe he never died but simply disappeared from Earth around 939. Popularly known as al-Mahdi (the Guided One or the Hidden Imam), he will, it is believed, return to a debilitated Earth heralding justice and peace and preside over the Day of Judgment.

This state-sponsored form of Shia Islam continues to be the dominant sect of Islam in Iran today. An attempt was made to separate political and clerical leadership in the 20th century, but the effort came to an end in the 1979 Iranian Revolution. The Ayatollah Khomeini (1902–1989), leader of that revolution, promoted the doctrine of *velayat-e faqih*, or political guardianship of the community of believers by religious and legal scholars. This created a theocracy in contemporary Iran not even achieved by the Safavids.

Besides the Ismailis and Sufis, other groups of questionable orthodoxy—from the contemporary perspective of Sunni and Shia leadership—include the Ahl-e Haqq, who are concentrated around Lorestan and whose practices also have origins in a medieval Sufi order. Innovation of interpretation and praxis continues to this day.

Iranian innovation in religious philosophy has also produced one of the world's newest global faiths. The Baha'i Faith is a religion that enjoins its followers to recognize a transcendent and unknowable God through that God's multiple manifestations over the millennia (Zarathustra, Abraham, Moses, Gautama Buddha, Jesus, Muhammad, the Bab, and Baha'u'llah). Baha'u'llah (1817–1892), the name taken by Mirza Husayn Ali Nuri, which means "the Glory of God," came from a wealthy family in northern Iran and is the founder of this faith (1860s). He was originally a Babi, or one who followed the Bab, and he based his teachings on his own revelations as well as those of the Bab. The Bab (the Gate) was originally a merchant from southern Iran named Sayyid Ali Muhammad Shirazi (1819–1850), who claimed to have had visions in 1844 of the al-Mahdi (Hidden Imam). Later he claimed to be the 12th imam himself, with new revelations from Allah. His teachings were well received among the common folk across Iran, thus drawing the attention of orthodox religious leaders. Becoming more militant as a result of increasing persecution, Babis (his followers) took on the role of martyrs, as the Bab himself was imprisoned and fighting broke out in 1848. Eventually the Bab was executed by the government in 1850.

As a Babi, Baha'u'llah was imprisoned in Teheran in 1852, and in prison he claimed he had had his own revelatory visions. He was then exiled to Ottoman Iraq, where he lived the life of an ascetic in Kurdistan. By 1856 he returned to Iran, where he led a revival of Babism that morphed into the foundational philosophy of the Baha'i Faith. At first there was contention within the community concerning Baha'u'llah's claims and teachings, but by the 1870s most Babis became Baha'i.

The revival of what orthodox religious leaders saw as a heretical sect (whether in its original or new form) caused a renewal of persecutions, an increased militancy among Baha'is in their resistance and proselytizing activities, and their dispersal to other countries as early as the 1890s. Baha'u'llah himself lived in exile in Ottoman Turkey (Edirne, or Adrianople) and Syria (Akka, or Acre), where he wrote many of the treatises associated with Baha'i philosophical and ethical doctrine, while his son and grandson took over organizational duties.

Baha'i adherents in Iran have faced official persecution since the inception of their movement, with only a brief respite during the second Pahlavi regime (1941–1979). Currently about 6 million Baha'i followers can be found in more than 200 nations, while approximately 350,000 (this is a rough estimate) live in the land of its birth. Baha'i do not have constitutional protection, nor are they enumerated separately in the census. Some Baha'i in Iran are not likely to claim membership due to official discrimination in education and employment. The majority of Baha'i in Iran are ethnic Persians; thus, they are assimilated into all other social and cultural aspects of the dominant group.

According to the 2006 census of Iran, approximately 89 percent of Iran's people adhere to Shiite beliefs and practices in one form or another, while another 9 percent adhere to Sunni beliefs and practices. Sunni groups are primarily associated with a number of ethnic minorities that live in peripheral regions of Iran (for example, Azari Turks, Arabs, Kurds, Turkomen, Baluchis, Qashqais, Bakhtiaris). In addition to ethnic Sunni communities, Iran is home to a number of other religious minorities, which include Jewish and Christian communities.

Judaism   The Jewish community has been a part of Persian society for at least 2,500 years. When Babylonia fell to Cyrus the Great, he freed the Jews who had been in captivity there and allowed their return to Jerusalem. Some Jews remained in the Persian Empire, slowly moving eastward over the centuries, and gradually becoming culturally assimilated until they became ethnically indistinguishable from the Persian majority. Since the advent of Islam in Iran their circumstances have risen and fallen with the whims and attitudes of specific rulers. Despite their status as *dhimmi*, or people of the book (that is, people who follow what is regarded as holy scripture), Persian Jews in particular suffered harshly under the practice of *najes* (ritual uncleanliness) and were often relegated to occupations already considered lowly (for example, peddlers, dyers, weavers, entertainers) by the dominant political group. By the middle of the 19th century, Jews in Iran often lived in poverty in separate quarters (ghettoes) of the larger cities, they were subject to a poll tax, and they have most recently suffered a series of expulsions, forced conversions, and pogroms. When the Persian king, Naser al-Din Shah Qajar, visited Europe in 1848, European Jews brought to his attention the dire poverty and oppression Persian Jews suffered. The result of their entreaties was permission to provide financial help and lobbying for better treatment. This then led to the opening of the first modern Jewish schools.

Due in part to their new contact with Western Jews, Persian Jews began to migrate to Palestine by the late 19th century—a steady migration that has continued ever since. Under the second Pahlavi regime (1941–1979), they gained official political representation for the first time. The 1979 Revolution ended official Iran-Israeli cooperation, thus placing Persian Jews in a precarious political position. However, many Persian Jews had supported the Revolution, and the Islamic Republic Constitution recognized them as members of the Iranian nation with equal rights and responsibilities. Despite Jews being entitled to elect a deputy to represent them in Parliament, fears related to their perceived or real political relationship with Israel caused some Jews to suffer harassment, imprisonment, loss of property, and even death. Some individuals continue to be charged with being Zionist spies, although a recent (2000) court decision in Shiraz, in response to international pressure, reduced the sentences of 10 Jewish men convicted of spying for Israel.

The Israeli government was concerned and frustrated about the fate of Iran's Jews until Iraq invaded Iran in 1980. Iran felt vulnerable because of Western sanctions against it, which meant that it was forced to fight an international war without access to military hardware and badly needed parts. Under these circumstances an implicit agreement was made between Israel and the Islamic Republic: in exchange for spare parts, Persian Jews would be allowed to leave Iran. As many as 55,000 Jews have been allowed to leave since the Revolution.

As the new century begins, and although the Jewish population has declined significantly, Iran continues to

IRAN

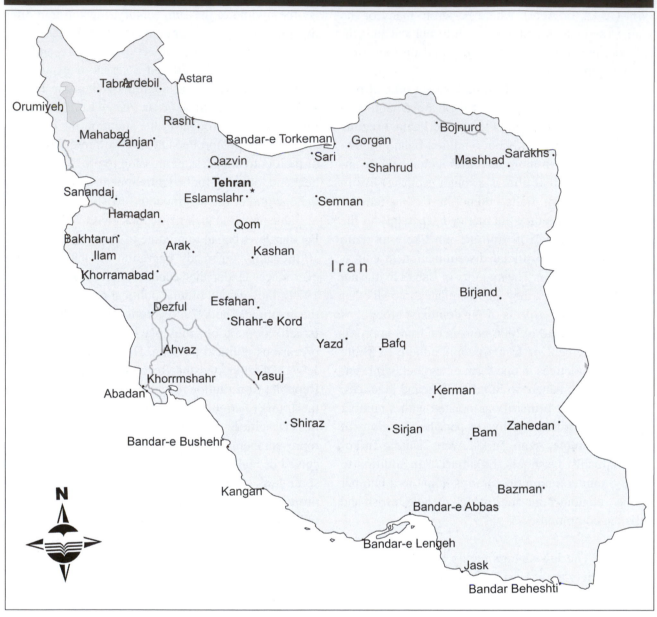

be a home to more Jews than any other Muslim state. Many who left the country did so as much for economic reasons, such as high unemployment, high inflation, and social limitations, as they did for political reasons—all of which were causes of the emigration of Muslim Iranians as well. North America and Israel are major destinations for most of Iran's Jewish emigrants. According to human rights activists, Iranian Jews are no longer persecuted because of their religion, and attendance at synagogues and Jewish functions has been higher than at any time before the Revolution. The Jew-

ish community itself sees its problems as stemming more from their political and economic relationship to the state. They hope that the new elections in 2009 will improve the overall national social and economic situations and help them to resolve specific problems, such as having school on Saturdays, the Jewish Sabbath. Primarily living in large urban areas, Jews now number only half as many as before the Revolution.

Christianity Christian communities in Iran also have a long history and tend to be associated with specific

Iran

Religion	Followers in 1970	Followers in 2010	% of Population	Annual % growth 2000–2010	Followers in 2025	Followers in 2050
Muslims	28,136,000	73,276,000	98.7	0.99	86,745,000	98,589,000
Christians	277,000	393,000	0.5	0.98	499,000	598,000
Orthodox	223,000	275,000	0.4	0.77	320,000	350,000
Independents	9,800	58,700	0.1	2.24	100,000	150,000
Roman Catholics	24,000	25,000	0.0	−0.34	30,000	35,000
Baha'is	250,000	200,000	0.3	−1.81	200,000	200,000
Agnostics	10,000	256,000	0.3	0.97	400,000	550,000
Zoroastrians	22,500	63,000	0.1	0.98	70,000	80,000
Hindus	8,000	34,100	0.0	0.98	50,000	80,000
Jews	88,900	18,000	0.0	0.25	18,000	18,000
New religionists	8,000	12,600	0.0	0.98	16,000	21,800
Sikhs	3,000	9,000	0.0	0.98	11,000	13,500
Atheists	2,000	9,400	0.0	0.98	12,000	16,000
Ethnoreligionists	0	4,300	0.0	0.97	6,000	8,000
Total population	**28,805,000**	**74,276,000**	**100.0**	**0.98**	**88,027,000**	**100,174,000**

ethnic groups. Armenians, Assyrians, and Chaldeans are officially recognized as religious minorities by the revolutionary Constitution, and they have had a Christian presence in Iran for nearly two millennia. On the other hand, Protestant communities (Congregationalists, Anglicans) emerged as missionary work began in the late 19th century. The original Protestant work, begun by the American Board of Commissioners for Foreign Missions, led to the formation of the Evangelical Church of Iran, the largest of the Protestant groups. The Assemblies of God brought Pentecostalism to Iran at the beginning of the 20th century.

Armenians represent the largest group, whose numbers were estimated to be 500,000 in the 2006 census. Their origins in Iran are traced to the efforts of a Safavid king. Shah Abbas Safavid (1587–1629) led the Armenians from Julfa in the contemporary nation of Azerbaijan to a town designed for their settlement and with the same name near Esfahan in 1605, in order to take advantage of their artisan and business skills. Since then, most have been educated professionals, skilled artisans, or trusted businesspeople, who have preserved their traditions, religion, language, and cultural festivities amid the dominant Muslim population. Today Armenian communities in Esfahan, Tehran, and Tabriz, affiliated with the Armenian Apostolic Church, are the largest Christian congregations in Iran. In recent decades they have become the favorite place to

live for those Armenians remaining in Iran, in large part because they have had better business opportunities there, and because they have been able to sustain their schools and social institutions in these cities.

The long-standing tolerant relationship between the Julfa Armenians and Shiite Iranians, as well as the contemporary diplomatic skills of Archbishop Korioun Papian (who presented Armenian cultural and festival traditions as religious in order to bring them under the protection of the Constitution), assisted the Armenian community during the most difficult period just after the revolutionary government came to power. Archbishop A. Manukian has suggested Islamic countries of the Middle East as the best place for Armenians to preserve their language and culture. Muslim majority nations rarely proselytize, and they promote traditional values. The return to traditionalism after the Revolution and the Iran-Iraq War were major factors influencing the migration of young Armenians, thus leaving a more elderly and urbanized population back in Iran. It appears that the revolutionary government's threat to a more secular lifestyle was a primary motivation for these individuals, while the threat of a more secular society was of concern to both Armenian bishops and Shiite clergy.

Assyrians and Chaldeans, religiously organized through the Apostolic Catholic Assyrian Church (also known as the Church of the East), are smaller numerically (10,000 in 2006) but have a much longer tradition of settlement in Iran than Armenians. Historically the Assyrians have been associated with the city of Urumiyeh (Rezayeh) in the northwest, and the Chaldeans with the Khuzistan region, especially Ahwaz. Their recent migration out of Iran (as well as to Tehran) was, to a large degree, caused by the Iran-Iraq War and their previous strong support for the Pahlavi regime. Before the development of university education among Muslims, the Assyrian and Chaldean communities were disproportionately represented in specialized technical and professional services, thus providing them the contradictory position of greater economic stability during hard economic times, but also creating the danger of becoming official or unofficial political targets because of some of the services they provided. Today more than 140,000 people of Assyrian and Chaldean heritage, hailing from the entire Middle Eastern region, live in the United States (mainly around Chicago and Detroit), where they have successfully established themselves.

Traditionally, Iranians have not perceived Armenians or Assyrians as proselytizers, even though they are Christian. On the other hand, Christian missionaries, particularly since the 19th century, have been seen as a threat to Muslim society, despite the fact that they have been involved in bringing education and health care services to all Iranians. American and European Christian missionaries opened schools in Tehran and other cities as early as 1881, almost two decades before the Jewish community. Establishing most of the earliest modern schools and colleges, such as Elburz College in Tehran, and hospitals with scientifically trained medical doctors, these philanthropic organizations served both Muslims and non-Muslims. Historically, European missionary activists in Iran had a higher rate of success in converting Armenians, Assyrians, and Jews than Muslims, sometimes causing deep resentments toward missionaries in these minority communities.

In Iran, both before the Revolution and since, apostasy (the conversion from Islam to any other faith) is a crime punishable by death. The degree to which people have actually been punished for apostasy varies from region to region and under specific rulers. On the other hand, historically, anyone who converts to Islam has the right to claim the property of his non-Muslim relatives. Thus, any religious group that actively seeks to convert others in Iran is regarded suspiciously, and this attitude has intensified since the Revolution. Both the Baha'i and Protestant Christian missionaries have been persecuted for their proselytizing activities, as well as their Muslim converts. Since 1979 several Muslim converts to Christianity, who were leaders of their churches, have been mysteriously killed. As Protestant Christian numbers have always been small, and they have not been enumerated separately, it is difficult to assess the effect of the Revolution on their migration and demographic experience, particularly in terms of different denominations.

Carolyn V. Prorok

See also: Abraham/Abram; American Board of Commissioners for Foreign Missions; Apostolic Catholic Assyrian Church of the East; Assemblies of God; Baha'i Faith; Bahá'u'lláh; Ismaili Islam; Moses; Muhammad; Pentecostalism; Qadiriya Rifa'i Sufi Order; Qadiriyya Sufi Order; Shia Islam; Suhrawardiyya Sufi Order; Sufism; Zionism; Zoroastrianism.

References

Bausani, Alessandro. *Religion in Iran: From Zoroaster to Baha'u'llah.* New York: Bibliotheca Persica, 2000.

Hemmasi, Mohammad, and Carolyn V. Prorok. "Demographic Changes in Iran's Recognized Religious Minority Populations since the Islamic Revolution." *African and Asian Studies* 1, no. 2 (2002): 63–86.

Mottahedeh, Roy. *The Mantle of the Prophet: Religion and Politics in Iran.* Oxford: OneWorld Books, 2008.

Ridgeon, Lloyd, ed. *Religion and Politics in Modern Iran: A Reader.* New York: I. B. Tauris, 2005.

Sanasarian, Eliz. *Religious Minorities in Iran.* Cambridge: Cambridge University Press, 2000.

■ Iraq

The land popularly known until World War II as Mesopotamia was carved out of the Ottoman Empire in

Shiite shrine in Samarra, Iraq, a city that hosted the Muslim caliphate after it was driven from Baghdad in 836 CE. The 10th and 11th imams of the Shiite sect are buried under the golden-domed building. (Corel)

several stages, beginning with the occupation of the British during World War I, its designation as a British Mandate in 1920, and its independence in 1932. Having been a part of the Ottoman Empire for many centuries, the national identity of the new country was not readily apparent to all and its subsequent life to the present has been challenged by the tensions between Shia and Sunni Muslim factions and the Arab/Kurdish ethnic division.

Geographically, Iraq lies in the Tigris-Euphrates River Valley and has two long borders with Iran to the northeast and Saudi Arabia to the southwest. The Persian Gulf lies to its southeast, but Iraq's access is highly limited by the placement of Kuwait. To the northwest lies Syria. And finally to the north, Iraq shares a border with Turkey, also home to a Kurdish minority. An estimated 28,200,000 people now reside in the 167,000 square miles of modern Iraq.

Through the millennia, Iraq has been the home of successive civilizations. Its most ancient history, however, is beyond the scope of this work, and this entry begins with the brief reign of Alexander the Great (334–327 BCE) and the Seleucid Empire, which followed. For several centuries, Mesopotamia functioned as a Seleucid desert outpost against the might of Roman conquest. However, between 133 and 117 BCE, the Roman Empire conquered much of Iraq. Frontier wars and political intrigues ensued that left Roman rule (now directed from Constantinople) in shambles and the

region vulnerable to onslaught from other would-be conquerors.

During the seventh century CE, Islam, a new monotheistic religion founded on the teachings of the prophet Muhammad (569–632) rapidly spread from the Arabian Peninsula to the neighboring regions. Following Muhammad's death, internal disputes quickly occurred over who would serve as the caliph, the title assumed by the leader of the Muslim community. When Ali ibn Abi Talib (ca. 602–661), the son-law of Muhammad, was killed in battle in 661 the Umayyad dynasty ruled until 750. Most followers of Ali, who believed the rule of Islam should be established under those of the same bloodline as Muhammad, became known as the Shia, while others who believed that rule by consensus was called for became known as Sunni. The Sunnite Umayyads allowed a degree of religious tolerance that included both Shia as well as Christians.

The Abbasid dynasty supplanted the Umayyads in 750. After using the Shiites to help topple their predecessors, the Abbasids turned on them and destroyed their holy sites. In the meantime, Iraq had become the most prosperous part of the empire. The Shiite Buwailids ruled briefly from the mid-10th century until the 11th, when the reins of power passed to Turkey and the Ottoman Empire, although the Abbasid caliph remained the titular head of state, reporting at times to the Ottoman emperor. In 1253, Hulaga or Hulegu, (ca. 1217–1265), a grandson of Genghis Khan (ca. 1167–1227), captured Baghdad, and by 1258 Abbasid rule faded away. Iraq was ruled by Mongols under the khan of Persia until 1335, when the Jalai'rids seized power and governed until the early 15th century. The Ottomans ruling from afar watched the rise and fall of these military and religious groups within their empire. They considered them to be a major threat to both the empire and to the Sunni tradition represented in the Hanafite School. Consequently, in 1534 Sultan Suleiman the Magnificent (1494–1566) conquered Baghdad, settling the question for the time being of who would rule.

Partially due to its location, Iraq only slowly absorbed Western influences. By 1800 there was a British resident at Basra, followed by a British consulate in 1802. France sent agents during the same period (and Catholicism was introduced by French and Italian religious orders). By 1914, the British were at war with the crumbling Ottoman Empire, leading to Britain being named the governing power. The British established a Christian regime that was politically foreign and religiously alien to the inhabitants. Immediate Arab nationalist sentiment, demonstrated in several insurrections, led the British to discontinue their new order, and an Arab Council of State was instituted, with Britain serving in an advisory capacity.

In 1921 Amir Faisal ibn Hussuan (1889–1933) assumed rulership of Iraq. After a decade of transition, Iraq was accepted into the League of Nations, in October 1932, as a sovereign state free from the British mandate. Unfortunately, freedom from foreign rule did not stabilize religious and national sentiments. Warfare soon broke out between Sunnis and the powerful Shia tribes of the Euphrates valley, while the Kurdish minority agitated for a separate state. Then in 1933, the Iraqi army massacred a number of the Assyrian minority, and the country experienced seven military coups between 1936 and 1941. After World War II, sentiment ran high against European intervention; Iraqis participated in the Arab-Israeli War of 1948 until a peace agreement was arranged. Most Jews, who traced their Iraqi heritage to ancient times, emigrated between 1948 and 1952. Today, there are fewer than 100 Jews left of that indigenous population, a record of which goes back to the dawn of history.

The Suez crisis between Egypt and Israel that began on October 29, 1956, and subsequent intervention of British and French forces affected Iraq deeply. Iraq severed diplomatic relations with France over French participation against Egypt. The students of Iraq rallied so stridently that colleges and schools were closed for a year and a half after disturbances in Mosul and Majaf caused deaths among the rioters. Martial law was imposed for one and a half years.

In 1958, King Faisal II (1935–1958), along with the Iraqi crown prince, was assassinated to make way for an independent republic. The power brokers of the coup were members of the socialist Ba'ath Party (founded in Syria in 1941). The leadership of General Abd al Karem Kassem (1914–1963), who headed the new government, was disturbed by further efforts of the Kurds to establish their independence. Kassem was assassinated in 1963, and the Ba'ath Party, dedicated to Socialism, Arab unity, and freedom from for-

eign intervention, took full and exclusive control of the country. However, fighting involving the Kurds continued. Attempts to solve the Kurdish problem were undermined by Iran, who tended to supported Kurdish aspirations out of their shared Shiite faith. Consequently, Iraq severed diplomatic relations with Iran. In August 1974, the hostile situation between the Kurds and the government led to 130,000 Kurds fleeing to Iran. A new peaceful solution fell apart when Iraq devastated parts of Kurdistan in 1975, leading to Kurds becoming displaced refugees, their homes and towns razed to the ground. (Of note, the initial reports of the use of chemical warfare by Iraq came from this military venture, which targeted both Iranians and Kurds.)

A new leader emerged in Iraq in 1979, when Saddam Hussein (1937–2006) became the president of the Revolutionary Party. He would emerge as both the prime minister and president of Iraq, posts he maintained until 2003. Under his leadership, a new Constitution, liberal by Iraqi standards, was approved in July 1990. Though offering the appearance of granting various liberties, the real power rested with Hussein. Hussein addressed the issue of an independent Kurdish territory but never acted, as numerous oilfields were located in the proposed territory. He also feared that the Shias would turn against his largely Sunni administration; the Kurds, however, manifested more aversion to the harsh government of Iran following the fall of the shah and the rise of the Ayatollah Khomeini (1902–1989) than rule from Baghdad.

At the end of the 1980s, Hussein developed a heightened displeasure with neighboring Kuwait, which had increased its demands for the repayment of loans made to Iraq to buttress the financial infrastructure of a failing economy. In return, Hussein accused Kuwait of stealing large oil reserves from the borders of the two countries. Then in 1990 he moved troops into Kuwait. U.S. President George H. W. Bush reacted quickly and in January 1991 launched a war against the occupation. The war ended after only a few weeks with heavy losses by the Iraqis. The real damage to Kuwait came when Hussein ordered his retreating army to set oil rigs on fire, turning much of Kuwait into a roaring mass of fire and smoke.

After the war, Iraq was alienated and isolated from most global political and economic structures. Its postwar relations were hampered by United Nations Security Council Resolution 687, which imposed economic sanctions. Iraq could have the sanctions lifted only by accounting for all weapons of mass destruction, including biological warfare equipment. Hussein refused, arguing the need for such weapons—in case Israel attacked his country.

Surviving foiled assassination attempts and failed coups, Hussein remained in power through 2002. During this time, he was repeatedly associated with the conspiracy that led to the attacks on the World Trade Center in New York and the Pentagon in Washington, D.C., on September 11, 2001. The assertion of such associations were used by President George W. Bush as justification for invading Iraq in 2003. A short time after the initiation of military action, Saddam Hussein was removed from power and executed, and a new government was installed in Bagdad. As this volume goes to press, Iraq has yet to be fully pacified. Though an elected government was installed in 2006, the country remains unstable, and U.S. forces continue hostilities against significant pockets of opposition.

Since the eighth century, Islam has remained the majority religion in Iraq. Shias claim the allegiance of 62 percent of the population, including the Kurdish minority, although their reflection in government offices has been relatively small as the government under Hussein privileged Sunnis, who exercised most of the leadership in the country. Most Sunnis follow either the Hanafite or Shafaiite schools of Islam, the latter strong among Kurdish Sunnis.

Within Shia Islam there are two major schools, the Usuli and the Akhbari. The smaller group, the Akhbaris are found primarily in southern Iraq (and parts of neighboring Iran). The larger Usuli school has the more liberal legal perspective and uses a degree of interpretation in reaching legal decisions. Iraq has several sanctuaries for the Shiite population, including Samarra and Al Khadimain. There is an Institute of Islamic Studies at Baghdad.

Although a very small minority of the Kurds are Christian, there are also Yazidi among the Kurds. The Yazidi follow a religion that blends Manichean, Jewish, Zoroastrian, Nestorian, and Christian elements. They worship with two sacred books: the Black Book and the Book of Revelation. Yazidis live mostly west of Mosul, but some are scattered in other regions. The Mandeans who dwell in Iraq are known as Sabeans to the Arabs. Gnosticism synthesized with Christian, Jewish, and Iranian elements, along with a taste of fertility worship, forms the infrastructure of their faith. Their principal books are the Treasure, the Book of John, and a book of hymns. Most of them live in lower Iraq at Basra and Kut, as well as southwest Iran. The Baha'i Faith, which originated in neighboring Iran, has found Iraq an equally hostile environment. Despite maintaining a presence in Iraq for 120 years, it numbers fewer than 2,660.

Christian communities in Iraq trace their history to the first century and the mission of the Apostle Thomas in the Jewish colonies. Church hierarchies developed under the patriarch of Antioch in the fourth century. In the next century, Nestorians sent missionaries to the region and declared a separation from Antioch. The Ancient Church of the East, or Assyrian Church, survived as the oldest Christian church in Iraq. It is aligned theologically with the Nestorians, who dissented from Roman Catholic and Eastern Orthodoxy on the nature of Christ's divinity. Seleucia-Ctesiphon, near Baghdad, was at one juncture in time the most important Patriarchate beyond the Roman Empire. From there, from the fifth through the 10th centuries, Nestorian missionary efforts spread Christian doctrine throughout the Middle East.

Twentieth-century schisms splintered the church. Its ancient headquarters, located in Kurdish territory, fell victim to Turkish expansion in the 1890s. In 1940, the patriarch relocated to America, from which he now leads the Apostolic Catholic Assyrian Church of the East. However, since the 1970s, a faction led by Mar Addai II (b. 1950), known as the Ancient Church of the East, has claimed to be the authentic Patriarchate. The Apostolic Catholic Assyrian Church, which supports Mar Dinka IV (b. 1935) as patriarch of the East, is acknowledged by the Vatican to be legitimate. The Iraqi government under Hussein supported the claims of the Ancient Church of the East.

Armenians have lived in Iraq for many centuries. The Armenian Apostolic Church, Diocese of Baghdad, is related to the Catholicate of Echmiadzin in Armenia. Primary schools exist in cities where there are priests to teach them. The Greek Orthodox have one

IRAQ

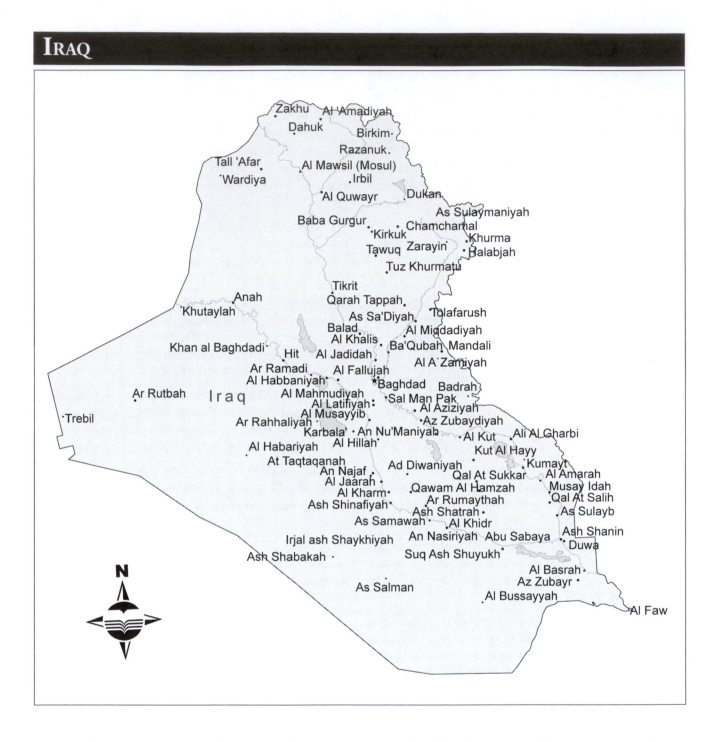

church in Baghdad, under the jurisdiction of the Greek Orthodox Patriarchate of Antioch and all the East. Its bishop resides in Kuwait.

The Roman Catholic Church dates its existence in Iraq to 1553, when the Eastern-rite Chaldean Catholic Church was recognized. Most Catholics are Chaldeans and now number about 242,000 adherents in 10 dioceses. The church's patriarch resides in Baghdad.

Iraq's Pontifical Seminary at Mosul is a joint effort of the Syrian and Chaldean communities. The Syrian Catholic Church numbers about 50,000 people in 2 dioceses. The first congregations started in 1790. The Armenian Catholic Church congregations, with some 2,150 members, were organized into the Diocese of Baghdad in 1954, led by an archbishop and 4 priests. The Greek Catholic Church's 300 members are served

Iraq

Religion	Followers in 1970	Followers in 2010	% of Population	Annual % growth 2000–2010	Followers in 2025	Followers in 2050
Muslims	9,656,000	29,905,000	97.4	2.42	42,226,000	60,473,000
Christians	386,000	508,000	1.7	−4.26	641,000	816,000
Roman Catholics	280,000	230,000	0.7	−3.78	300,000	350,000
Orthodox	85,600	130,000	0.4	−7.14	130,000	160,000
Independents	18,900	120,000	0.4	−2.20	170,000	250,000
Agnostics	30,000	153,000	0.5	1.20	250,000	400,000
New religionists	25,000	58,800	0.2	2.45	77,000	102,000
Atheists	10,000	49,000	0.2	2.53	80,000	120,000
Sikhs	3,000	6,000	0.0	2.25	8,000	10,000
Hindus	500	3,600	0.0	2.25	4,500	5,500
Baha'is	500	3,400	0.0	2.25	4,000	9,000
Buddhists	500	1,700	0.0	2.25	2,500	6,000
Jews	500	20	0.0	2.13	20	20
Total population	**10,112,000**	**30,688,000**	**100.0**	**2.25**	**43,293,000**	**61,942,000**

by a priest residing in Baghdad. A Latin diocese for Catholics was formed in 1632; however, there was no resident bishop until 1920. Latin Catholics number about 3,200 today. There are 200 Dominican and Presentation sisters, most of them Iraqi, who teach and do medical work.

Christians who today use Syriac liturgy are divided into Chaldeans, Nestorians (Assyrian Churches of the East), Syrian Catholics, and Syrian Orthodox, who are sometimes referred to as Jacobites. This group entered Iraq in the sixth century, and they still feel that they are original Iraqis and the oldest Christian group in Iraq. Mar Matta near Mosul has the oldest Christian monastery, with six resident monks. During the demise of the Ottoman Empire in 1917, Armenian Orthodox (Gregorians) and Armenian Catholics fled Turkey and settled in Iraq. Greek Orthodox and Greek Catholics are immigrant communities in Iraq and are small in number.

Protestantism made a late appearance in the 19th century. The first British missionary attempt in Iraq was through the London Jews Society in 1820. Americans started activity in Mosul in 1850 through the American Board of Commissioners for Foreign Missions. The Church Missionary Society started its mission in 1882 and persevered until World War I. The Arabian Mission of the Reformed Church in America started its program in Basra in 1889. They were as-

sisted by the Evangelical and Reformed Church (now a constituent part of the United Church of Christ) and the United Presbyterian Church in the U.S. (now a constituent part of the Presbyterian Church [U.S.A.]). In 1957 another group, the Presbyterian Church in the U.S.A., joined the efforts. However, no presently existing Iraqi church can be traced to these roots, converts having primarily been made from Nestorian or Assyrian congregations.

Today, Arab evangelical churches number about 10 church groups in Baghdad, Kirkuk, and Basra. All of these congregations are served by Egyptian ministers. Two Assyrian evangelical churches in Baghdad and Mosul are not affiliated administratively. The Armenian Evangelical Church claims one small congregation in Baghdad. A single Anglican congregation, serving expatriate British and Arabs, belongs to the Diocese of Cyprus and the Gulf of the Episcopal Church in Jerusalem and the Middle East. The Lutheran Orient Mission has attempted to convert Kurds since 1911 with little success. Other small religious groups that have worked in Iraq, such as the Assemblies of God, Basra Assembly, Evangelical Alliance Mission, and the Seventh-day Adventist Church are no longer active. In 1969 all American missionaries were ordered out of the country, though some of the missions they created continue under national leadership. In the 1990s, Pentecostal and Charismatic movements were popular, and now number some 265,000 adherents. Christians now constitute about 3 percent of the population.

Islam has been the state religion of Iraq, but all citizens were deemed equal before the law. The cultural rights of the Syrian-speaking groups were decreed in article 25 of the Constitution dated April 22, 1972, which protected the Assyrian and Chaldean Christians. Technically, the Revolutionary Council recognized three religious holidays for Christians—Christmas and two days for Easter—along with five stated holidays for Jews. Religious judges (*qadi*) presided over Muslim jurisprudence. The General Bureau of Waqf (law) based in Baghdad was the official agency for Muslim law courts. There were no religious courts for non-Muslims, who settle their issues in civil courts.

The end of the Saddam Hussein regime placed the Christian and other minority religious groups in a precarious position. Constituting less than 3 percent of the population, they were somewhat lost amid the chaos of the efforts of the larger Muslim factions to gain and maintain their position in the new government. Amid the general chaos of the continuing Iraqi War, they have been subject to murders, the burning of worship centers, the abduction of leaders, and disenfranchisement from participation in the new government. Attacks on the Christian community reached a new level in February 2008 with the abduction and murder of Archbishop Paulos Faraj Rahho (1942–2008), the Chaldean Catholic archbishop of Mosul. Responding to the attacks, some Christians migrated internally while many thousands left the country. The status of all the minority groups have been called into question, and their future remains uncertain.

Gail M. Harley and J. Gordon Melton

See also: American Board of Commissioners for Foreign Missions; Ancient Church of the East; Apostolic Catholic Assyrian Church of the East; Armenian Catholic Church; Assemblies of God; Baha'i Faith; Chaldean Catholic Church; Church Missionary Society; Dominicans; Episcopal Church in Jerusalem and the Middle East; Greek Catholic Church; Hanafite School of Islam; Muhammad; Presbyterian Church (USA); Reformed Church in America; Roman Catholic Church; Seventh-day Adventist Church; Shafiite School of Islam; Syrian Catholic Church; United Church of Christ.

References

Bailey, Betty Jane, and J. Martin Bailey. *Who Are the Christians in the Middle East?* Grand Rapids, MI: William B. Eerdmans Publishing Company, 2003.

Gonzalez, Nathan. *The Sunni-Shia Conflict and the Iraq War: Understanding Sectarian Violence in the Middle East*. Herndon, VA: Potomac Books, 2009.

Jabar, Faleh A. *The Shi'ite Movement in Iraq*. London: Saqi Books, 2003.

Little, David, and Donald K. Swearer, eds. *Religion and Nationalism in Iraq: A Comparative Perspective*. Cambridge, MA: Center for the Study of World Religions, 2007.

Moffett, Samuel Hugh. *A History of Christianity in Asia: Beginnings to 1500*. Vol. 1. New York: HarperCollins, 1992.

Nakash, Y. *The Shi'as of Iraq*. Princeton, NJ: Princeton University Press, 1994.

Rejwan, N. *The Jews of Iraq: 3000 Years of History and Culture*. Boulder, CO: Westview Press, 1985.

Wiley, J. N. *The Islamic Movement of Iraqi Shi'as*. Boulder, CO: Lynne Rienner Publishers, 1992.

Yildiz, Kerim. *The Kurds in Iraq: The Past, Present and Future*. London: Pluto Press, 2007.

■ Ireland

Ireland is the third largest island in Europe and is located northwest of the continent. It is divided into two political units: the Republic of Ireland, with its capital of Dublin, covers just over 80 percent of the island while Northern Ireland, with its capital of Belfast, remains a part of the United Kingdom. The republic has nearly 6 million people and the north about 1.7 million people. The majority of people are ethnic Irish with a strong minority population of Ulster Scots who mainly speak English. Irish is still spoken in some regions of western Ireland. Catholicism remains the dominant faith of the republic while the north is nearly evenly divided between Catholics and Protestants.

The division of Ireland's population into Catholic and Protestant Christianity is a legacy of English colonization of the island over several centuries. This legacy is simultaneously linked to the transformation of Irish Celtic traditions into Christian ones during the medieval period as well as more recent politicization of religious identities on the island. A brief overview of Ireland's religious history reveals these relationships.

Ireland's historical geography is a complex one that thoroughly intertwines earthy Celtic sensibilities with historic Roman and Anglo penetrations. An early, pre-Celtic tradition is difficult to ascertain at this time. Celtic ritual traditions were practiced over a wide area of western and northern Europe and included Ireland —possibly as early as the first millennium BCE. The Irish Celtic tradition shared with its continental counterparts a belief in the immortality of the soul, and a reverence for the natural forces and life forms of Earth (for example, wind, water, trees, eels) and its planetary connections (for example, sun, sky, moon). Moreover, its priests (known as druids) played a powerful role in the social and political life of the people; for example, they ceremonially validated the power of local and regional kings (or chieftains), inasmuch as they were literally married to the land they ruled (known as a *tuath*).

The fecundity and the health of the tuath was essentially reflected through the virility and sound mind of the ruler. In this context, certain groves of trees and natural springs were singled out for ritual observances that guaranteed the health of the land, the king, and individual petitioners. Ancient Irish Celts believed that subterranean, parallel energy lines, now called ley lines, intersected with rising and falling subterranean streams. If such a stream erupted as a spring at Earth's surface, then it was deemed a power point to be ritually utilized. Not all springs were so blessed, and not all springs maintained their power. Yet, over the years the power of some springs has been amazingly long-lived, while new ones continue to be found. Eels could often be found in the pools that formed around springs. Those eels fortunate enough to live in powerful springs were believed to live far longer than a normal life span.

Early in the fourth century of the Common Era, an adolescent boy of British Roman origin was captured and taken to Ireland as a slave for a local king (probably in Antrim). He became fluent in Irish and familiar with Celtic beliefs over a period of about six years before he escaped. This young man eventually returned to Ireland to evangelize for the church in Rome, and he later became known as Saint Patrick (the patron saint of modern Ireland). Most of the details of Patrick's life are open to debate, as is the original spelling of his name. The current scholarly consensus is that he returned to Ireland around 461, and he himself says in his Confession that he was not sent by any human authority but impelled by divine inspiration. Other sources suggest he returned to carry out a mission assigned to him by Pope Celestinus I (r. 422–432) in the year 431. Early in the mission Patrick met resistance to his evangelizing, particularly from the druids, who had much to lose if their ceremonies were no longer needed. He is said to have found success by challenging Celtic beliefs at important ceremonies by subverting key elements of these events (for example, ignoring a royal edict against lighting fires in the days before an important spring ritual, Patrick lit a Paschal—Easter Eve—fire that the druids could not extinguish) or killing eels at powerful springs with no apparent negative effects to his own person. He also established Christian worship sites on or around those places deemed powerful by the Celts (for example, springs, tree groves, mounds). Eventually he baptized kings, thus laying the groundwork for a future Christian Ireland.

The Irish did not become Christians magically overnight or even in a century's time, despite Patrick's successful mission. Instead, Christianity overlaid an essentially Celtic faith tradition like a veneer on a table. As an Irish monasticism took root and spread, elements of the Celtic tradition were drawn up into Christian orthodoxy, while simultaneously Celtic practices absorbed Christian explanations. What emerged was a Celtic Christian church that had only nominal ties to the church in Rome. Christian priests eventually supplanted kings as the center of politically charged spiritual power, and powerful springs became holy wells. This synergistic syncretism of two great ritual traditions can still be seen at tree groves, in cemeteries, and at the holy wells of Ireland today. Although some wells are associated with local saints (for example, St. Peakaun's Well at the Glen of Aherlow in County

St. Patrick's Well in Clonmel, Ireland. (Martin Mullen/Dreamstime.com)

Tipperary) and often reflect a strong Celtic sensibility through their accoutrements and local character, other wells (for example, St. Brigid's Well at Liscannor in County Clare) have national significance and blend Celtic and Christian meaning and use. Finally, some wells have been thoroughly Christianized in meaning and usage (for example, St. Brigid's Well at Killare in County Westmeath and near to the hill of Uisneach). Such syncretism has occurred over one and a half millennia, with dynamic processes of remythologizing and historicizing sacred sites. The more historicized a site, the more Christian it becomes. Folk piety continues to have strong Celtic elements.

Local control of church ritual and practice was shattered in 1171 with the culmination of an Anglo-Norman invasion that installed English control over the Irish church through the Synod of Cashel. *Culdees* (Christian monks of the Celtic tradition) carried on the rituals of the Celtic Church for at least four more centuries before they finally died out. In the meantime, the Church of Ireland was formally separated from the Roman Catholic Church and its papal administration and politically incorporated into the Church of England. Through the trials and tribulations of English expansion, the Elizabethan Wars of the 16th century, enslavement to Caribbean plantations, Cromwell's reign of terror in the 17th century, and the great famine in the 19th century, Irish identity with the Roman Catholic Church deepened and helped to maintain the Irish people's identity as Irish, despite the direct control of the official Church of Ireland by the English Crown. Eventually, through sustained events of resistance (for example, the Catholic-Gaelic Rebellion of 1641, the 1798 Rebellion) and changes in Britain's own political goals (during Queen Victoria's reign and Gladstone's rule as prime minister), the Catholic Church in Ireland was finally legalized in 1829, and the Church of Ireland was disestablished as the state church in 1869, at which point most Irish churches reverted to their Roman origins. Today the Church of Ireland still exists, but in an attenuated form. It shares its early history with the Roman Catholic Church of Ireland through its Celtic Christian period. It is now part of the worldwide Anglican Communion found in 164 nations. In Ireland it has approximately 400,000 members, of which 300,000 live in Northern Ireland and 100,000 in the Republic of Ireland. It is governed as a single church with 2 provinces (Armagh and Dublin) and 12 dioceses.

Contemporary Ireland is overwhelmingly Catholic. This arises from its early connection to the Roman Church as well as its anti-Catholic trial by fire under English rule. Political, ethnic, and religious identities have become fully and completely conflated with each other, given this colonial history. As a consequence, political tensions and violence continue to be articulated through people's identity as Catholic or Protestant. Protestant/Free Church Irish are now associated with a number of denominations, due to the resettlement of various Protestant groups by the English during colonial times as well as the conversion of some Catholic Irish. It is Protestant identity in general, though, that carries political significance and not the particular sectarian group as such. Not surprisingly, most Protestants live in Northern Ireland, and the counting of people's religious affiliation during each census cycle is loaded with political implications. In 2004, Northern Ireland had 690,000 Catholics (40.4 percent), 359,000 Presbyterians, 300,000 Church of Ireland members, 65,000 Methodists, 21,000 Baptists, 12,000 Brethren, 12,000 Free Presbyterians, 8,000 Congregational members, 12,000 Protestant (no denomination noted), and 11,000 Christians (no denomination noted); 200,000 do not identify themselves with a specific religion, and approximately 9,500 people identified themselves as non-Irish minorities (for example, Sikh, Muslim, Buddhist) or atheist. These numbers, particularly of those who do not name their faith association and those who claim only a general category (Protestant, Christian), reflect a context of deep division and pervasive politicization of religious identity.

An American news broadcast (ABC, September 6, 2001) noted that unpublished results from the 2001 census of Northern Ireland indicate that Catholics now comprise 47 percent of the population. This increase is likely due to the combined effects of increased self-identification by Catholics, the emigration of Protestants from Northern Ireland, and higher birthrates within the Catholic community. This increase in the Catholic proportion of the population will likely have significant political consequences. The Republic of Ireland continues to reflect a strong Catholic identity, suffused with Celtic influences. In 2004, 87 percent of the population identified themselves as Catholic, 2 percent were members of the Church of Ireland, and 11 percent belong to an "other" category such as those who identified as atheists.

The "other" category is mainly reflected in Dublin's religious scene and includes members of evangelical and Pentecostal churches, Western Esotericists, imported religions (often imported by immigrants) such as Islam, Buddhism, Hinduism, Sikhism, and various

IRELAND

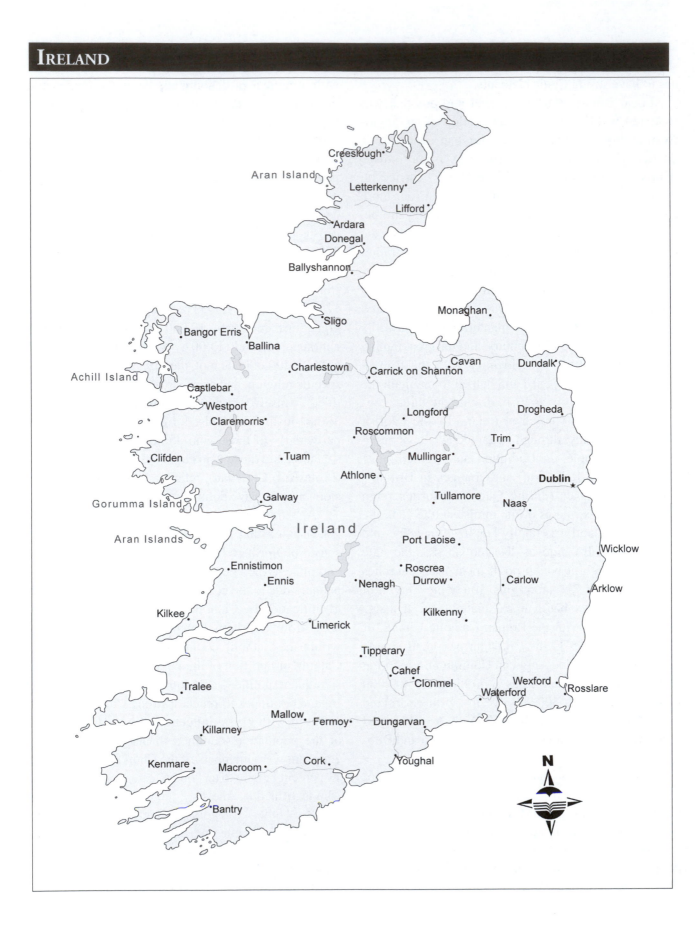

Ireland

Religion	Followers in 1970	Followers in 2010	% of Population	Annual % growth 2000–2010	Followers in 2025	Followers in 2050
Christians	2,938,000	4,310,000	95.2	1.57	4,916,000	5,644,000
Roman Catholics	2,682,000	3,566,000	78.8	0.68	4,000,000	4,555,000
Anglicans	97,500	91,000	2.0	–0.02	100,000	100,000
Protestants	26,800	50,000	1.1	0.98	65,000	85,000
Agnostics	10,200	156,000	3.4	5.92	275,000	420,000
Muslims	300	32,000	0.7	3.15	45,000	60,000
Atheists	1,200	13,000	0.3	8.62	18,500	25,000
Chinese folk	0	4,600	0.1	1.72	6,000	8,000
Hindus	0	4,300	0.1	1.72	6,000	10,000
Jews	4,000	1,800	0.0	1.72	1,800	1,800
Ethnoreligionists	0	1,900	0.0	1.72	2,500	2,600
Baha'is	600	1,800	0.0	1.08	3,000	5,000
Buddhists	0	550	0.0	1.75	800	1,300
Spiritists	0	450	0.0	1.73	600	800
Total population	**2,954,000**	**4,526,000**	**100.0**	**1.72**	**5,275,000**	**6,179,000**

new religions. Among the groups with centers in Ireland are the spectrum of Buddhists, the Universal White Brotherhood, the Baha'i Faith, the Church of Scientology, and the Unification Movement. It has also been a focus of the revivalist neo-Pagan movement based in the worldwide Fellowship of Isis headquartered at Huntington Castle in County Wexford.

The earliest reference to Irish Judaism was in the 11th century, and Jews are known to have come to Ireland following their expulsion from Portugal in 1496 and during the Napoleonic Wars early in the 19th century. As early as 1660, a prayer room was opened near Dublin Castle, and one Jewish seminary can be dated to the 1660s. The majority of the present-day Jewish community arrived between 1880 and 1910 from Eastern Europe. From a peak of 5,500, the community has dwindled to around 1,500, many having moved to Palestine after 1948. The several synagogues are Orthodox, except for one Reform synagogue.

Carolyn V. Prorok

See also: Anglican Communion/Anglican Consultative Council; Atheism; Baha'i Faith; Church of England; Church of Ireland; Church of Scientology; Druidism; Easter; Roman Catholic Church; Unification Movement; White Brotherhood.

References

Bitel, Lisa M. *Isle of the Saints: Monastic Settlement and Christian Community in Early Ireland.* Ithaca: Cornell University Press, 1990.

Brenneman, Walter L., Jr., and Mary G. Brenneman. *Crossing the Circle at the Holy Wells of Ireland,* Charlottesville: University of Virginia Press, 1995.

Gleeson, Tara. "The History of Judaism in Ireland." http://www.local.ie/content/14608.shtml/history/social_and_religious_history. Accessed September 15, 2001.

Jestice, Phyllis, ed. *Encyclopedia of Irish Spirituality.* Santa Barbara, CA: ABC-CLIO, 2000.

Tanner, M. *Ireland's Holy Wars: The Struggle for a Nation's Soul, 1500–2000.* New Haven, CT: Yale University Press, 2001.

Iroquois Confederacy

The Iroquois Confederacy (Haudenosaunee) consists of six Indian nations, comprising approximately 55,000 people, who live in the Finger Lakes region of New York, Wisconsin, and southern Ontario and Quebec. Originally the Haudenosaunee consisted of five Native

American tribes—from west to east, the Seneca, Cayuga, Onondaga, Oneida, and Mohawk. The Tuscarora, fleeing from skirmishes with the British, joined the Confederacy in the early part of the 18th century.

The origin of the Confederacy of these eastern woodlands tribes may have occurred on August 31, 1142. This precise date is surmised because a total solar eclipse of the Sun was prominently featured in the oral stories; an alternative date could be 1451. The core story of the founding of the Haudenosaunee as a Confederacy is probably a factual account that has become embellished with mythic details. In this myth, a mysterious, semi-divine figure was born in Huron territory on the northern shore of Lake Ontario. Achieving adulthood, he announced that he had a mission to bring peace to the warring tribes in his area. He constructed a canoe of stone, which his grandmother was sure would never float, in order to help convince the people that his message was of divine origin. Dekanawidah, as he was called, began an epic adventure and overcame many hurdles as he gradually convinced recalcitrant chiefs to forsake warfare, embrace peace, and forge an alliance with a strong moral sense of justice, consensus building, and compassion at its core, rather than greed and selfishness.

The prophetic journey of Dekanawidah had many twists and turns. The first was the conversion of Hiawatha, who had retreated to the margins of society and had become a cannibal because of the tragic deaths of his wife and daughter. When Hiawatha looked into his cooking pot he saw Dekanawidah staring up at him, but he thought it was his own reflection. The vision, reflected back to Hiawatha, put him into a meditative mode and he realized that life could be beautiful if he abandoned his evil ways of killing and eating people. Dekanawidah then taught Hiawatha about peace and explained the basic features of a government based on trust, checks and balances, and compromise. In this Confederacy, men would be chiefs, but they would be chosen by women and could be deposed by the clan mothers if they became corrupt. Each nation would still govern itself, but they would all cooperate for the common defense and promote peace. Both Dekanawidah and Hiawatha then journeyed together to convert other tribal chiefs.

Despite some resistance, chiefs of four of the Indian nations eagerly joined what is sometimes referred to as the Great Law of Peace, or more commonly just the Longhouse. The last person to be convinced was a physically deformed and mentally twisted wizard and chief of the Onondagas, named Atotarho. Through persuasion, singing songs of peace, and combing snakes from Atotarho's hair, Dekanawidah and Hiawatha removed the wizard's physical deformities and cured his mind. Atotarho became the first spiritual leader of the Longhouse. Atotarho's descendant, the keeper of the sacred fire, continues to live in Onondaga and is chosen for his moral and spiritual insight. After designating Atotarho as spiritual leader, Dekanawidah called the first council meeting, the Great Council of Sachems (chiefs), where he briefly uprooted the great tree of peace to bury the weapons of war in a cavern below and then replanted it as the symbol for the people's strength that comes from a political unity based on moral principles of law, justice, and peace.

The Longhouse, a rectangular wooden building that serves as a "church" for the Haudenosaunee, seems to have originated with the founding of the Confederacy at the time of Dekanawidah and Hiawatha. The roots of the indigenous spirituality of these Iroquoian-speaking groups, however, go much farther back to the original peoples who settled in the eastern woodlands of North America.

Probably the most ancient ritual practices still current among the Haudenosaunee are those of the medicine societies, the most famous of which is known today as the False Face Society. Men become members of this society when they dream of a mythic ancestor who has piercing eyes, and frequently a bent nose and crooked mouth. Such visions often occur after a person has been cured in a ritual where masked individuals have crept into the bedroom, shaking their rattles to drive away the illness. The dreamer describes the vision to a known carver, who then carves a chunk of wood out of a soft-wooded tree and then carves the details and paints the mask, usually red and black.

Although women don't wear the masks, they often initiate and mediate between the false faces and the sick individual. These masked figures are not only important in curing illness, but also in annual rituals of renewal, particularly in the autumn, spring, and winter, when they enter every house in a village to drive out potential illness and protect the people from severe storms. These agricultural rituals are very important to the people who respect the three "sisters"—beans, corn, and squash—and who early developed a hunting society that also depended on agriculture.

Numerous versions of a creation account (Fenton 1987, 95–114) describe the origin of the false faces. In most, the Creator is out walking, inspecting his creation, when he comes across a surly, huge, hunchbacked man who claims to have created the world. To settle the dispute they decide to have a contest of power where both figures would try to move a mountain. Impressively, the hunchback moves the mountain a few feet. But then the Creator moves the mountain a great distance behind him. The hunchback turns around so quickly that he breaks his nose and dents his face. The Creator, however, allows the old man, called the Thunderer, to live if he moves to the edge of the Earth and allows people to access his power to remove illness and keep them safe from severe winds and thunderstorms. The false faces are his representatives to the people.

A famous Seneca version of the creation myth (A. Wallace 1969, 85–93) has a divine woman fall from the heavens upon a Turtle Island. She gives birth to twins, one who creates order and beauty, the other who creates chaos. Eventually the twins engage in a contest to move the mountain. In this version that came from Cornplanter, Handsome Lake's brother, the Creator is called the "good twin," and the other the "evil twin." Even here, however, the pattern of transforming evil into good is more in line with the Dekanawidah myth than the probable Christian influence of using "good" and "evil" to describe the origin of the false face society.

A significant reform of the Haudenosaunee religion and culture occurred when the Seneca prophet, Handsome Lake (1735–1815), had a series of supernatural visions when he had nearly died of alcoholism. Engaging in conversations with Quaker (Society of Friends) reformers, who were attempting to help the Seneca escape from severe poverty, he first faced his own condition and gave up drinking. Through his visions he began to see the devastation of his people and created a moral code, centered on forswearing alcohol, wife beating, gambling, witchcraft, greed, quarreling, and the like. But, instead of converting to Christianity, he rooted this code in the traditional beliefs of his people, including the story of Dekanawidah. Although there was initially some tension between the old medicine societies and the religion of Handsome Lake, within a generation of his death, the Longhouse integrated both. Now at the Thanksgiving ceremonies in the fall, there is both a recitation of the Code of Handsome Lake and a purification ceremony by the false face society.

Two prominent religious traditions in the Haudenosaunee nations exist today—the Longhouse and Christianity. Conversion to Christianity originated in the 17th century; the most famous convert was Kateri Tekawitha (1656–1680), known as the Lilly of the Mohawks, who was recently beatified by the Catholic Church. Even though Christians today do not give the ancient rituals and myths much value or adopt the Code of Handsome Lake, they are comfortable at yearly agricultural festivals, where they see the dances as more a part of their culture than as religious truths. Others continue to follow the old ways of Handsome Lake and continue to tell the traditional creation accounts.

Thomas V. Peterson

See also: Christianity; Roman Catholic Church; Witchcraft.

References

Fenton, William N. *The False Faces of the Iroquois.* Norman: University of Oklahoma Press, 1987.

Hill, Loretta. "Iroquois Confederacy." http://www.everyculture.com/multi/Ha-La/Iroquois-Confederacy.html. Accessed September 15, 2009.

Parker, A. C. *The Code of Handsome Lake, the Seneca Prophet.* New York State Museum Bulletin 163. 1913; rpt.: Albany: University of the State of New York, 1983.

Wallace, Anthony F. C. *The Death and Rebirth of the Seneca.* New York: Random House, Vintage Books, 1969, 1972.

Wallace, Paul A. W. *The White Roots of Peace.* Philadelphia: University of Pennsylvania Press, 1946.

Ise Shrine, The

The Ise Shrine, located on Japan's eastern coast in Mie Prefecture, is an ancient site of traditional pre-Buddhist religion in Japan. Though at least a millennium old, none of the older structures remain at Ise due to the practice of the rite of *shikinen sengu*, by which the wooden buildings are burned and rebuilt every 20 years. This custom was first carried out in 690 CE. It is only during this ceremony that the general public is allowed to come close to the shrine.

There are two shrines in Ise. The Inner Shrine (Naiku) contains Amaterasuno Mikoto, the grandmother of Ninigi, who unified Japan, in Japanese traditional history; 3.7 miles distant from the Inner Shrine, the Outer Shrine (Geku) houses the Shinto deity, Toyouke, the goddess of agriculture.

Ise had a special status and from its beginning Buddhist rituals as well as terminology were prohibited. During the Kamakura period (1192–1333), when Japan was ruled by the shoguns based in Kamakura, Buddhism was privileged at the expense of traditional Shinto. One prominent family who favored more traditional beliefs, the Watarai family, who supplied the priests at the Outer Shrine at Ise, took the lead in developing a new revitalization of Shinto. Today, Ise remains the private shrine of the Japanese imperial household.

Essentially the Shinto religion as practiced at Ise stresses purity and honesty as ideals, with the goal of religious practice to perfect purity and honesty. The Ise Shinto priests have also attempted to reverse the previous Buddhist dominance in the land by speaking about the prominent Buddhas and bodhisattas as manifestations of Shinto *kami*, or deities.

People in traditional dress pull wood along the Isuzu River during the Okihiki-Gyoji ceremony on July 23, 2006, in Ise, Japan. The Okihiki-Gyoji ceremony is conducted every 20 years and involves the shrines of Ise Jingu being moved and reconstructed. (Getty Images)

The major text of Ise Shinto is the *Shinto gobusho* (*Five Books*), which dates from the Muromachi period (1334–1592).

Edward A. Irons

See also: Kamakura; Pilgrimage; Sacred Texts; Shinto.

References

Bocking, Brian. "Changing Images of Shinto: Sanja Takusen or the Three Oracles." In *Shinto in History: Ways of the Kami,* edited by John Breen and Mark Teeuwen. Richmond, Surrey: Curzon, 2000.

Itoh, Teiji. *The Roots of Japanese Architecture.* New York: Harper & Row, 1963.

Kasahara, Kazuo, ed. *A History of Japanese Religion.* Trans. by Paul McCarthy and Gaynor Sekimori. Tokyo: Dosei Publishing, 2001.

Tange, Kenzo, and Noboru Kawazoe. *Ise: Prototype of Japanese Architecture.* Cambridge: MIT Press, 1965.

Watanabe, Yasutada. *Shinto Art: Ise and Izumo Shrines.* New York: Weatherhill, 1974.

◆ Islam

Islam is a monotheistic faith that claims Allah (the term for God in Arabic) has revealed himself supremely through the Prophet Muhammad (570–632 CE) and in the Koran, the holy book of Islam given to the Prophet by the angel Gabriel. Muslims believe that Islam dates back to the creation of humanity and that Allah has spoken through a lineage of prophets that includes Adam, Noah, Abraham, Moses, and Jesus. Islam has traditionally taught that Muhammad was kept from sin by Allah (as were the prophets that that preceded him). His prophetic status secured the truth of the revelation he received and made him a model for future generations. Muslims look to the traditions about him (known as *hadith*) for guidance in belief and practice in all areas of life.

Islam is now the second largest religion in the world. As of 2005 there were 1.4 billion followers, almost one in 6 people on earth. The land in which Islam is now the majority faith stretches from the Middle East and across southern Asia to Indonesia, the latter with more than 170 million Muslims. India, Pakistan, and Bangladesh each have more than 35 million Muslims. Islam dominates northern Africa and its presence is growing in the sub-Sahara, where it is challenging both Christianity and nascent traditional religions for hegemony. Central Asia is also experiencing a resurgence of Islam while the immigration of millions of Muslims to Europe and North America is turning Islam into a truly global faith.

Some historians, like Michael H. Hart, believe that Muhammad may be the most significant person in history. Though Christianity claims more followers, Muhammad is viewed by some scholars as having had a greater impact on history, given the political depth of Islam, the range of Islamic law, and the breadth of Islamic political power, the depth and range of Islamic spirituality, and the all-encompassing ways in which Muhammad's teachings and example bear on every facet of life.

Muhammad the Prophet   Understanding Islam demands singular focus on the traditional version of Muhammad's life as accepted by most Muslims. Scholarly debate about this version is an important but secondary matter. What follows is the narrative that has been standard in Islamic life since the early centuries of Islam. It is generally accepted that Muhammad was born about 570 CE. Muhammad knew pain early in his life, since his father died before he was born and his mother shortly after his birth. He was raised by his grandfather for two years. After his grandfather's death Muhammad was cared for by an uncle until his teen years.

Muhammad went twice to Syria with his uncle. These trips provided the opportunity for an apologetic motif with assertion of Muhammad's early business prowess and external testimony to his spiritual potential. Muslims claim that Muhammad's prophetic status was foreseen by Christian monks, on the first trip by Bahira and on the second journey by a monk named Nastur.

A woman merchant named Khadijah entered into Muhammad's life and they were wed in 595, when Muhammad was about 25. Though she was considerably older, she bore him at least six children (the two boys died early). They had a loving marriage, and while Muhammad later took multiple wives, he did not do so until after Khadijah's death in 619.

Islam traces God's call to Muhammad to the 17th night of the month of Ramadan in the year 610 CE, when the angel Gabriel visited him on Mount Hira, near Mecca. According to Muslim sources, the prophet was profoundly shaken by the angelic encounter and turned to Khadijah and her cousin Waraqah for confirmation of his prophetic mandate. Most Muslims believe that sura 96 in the Koran is the first revelation given to Muhammad.

After a pause (*fatra*) of three years Muhammad carried Allah's message to his fellow Meccans. At first he was largely ignored though he gained a few converts, including Abu Bakr, a later caliph (leader). Then, as Muhammad spoke more forcefully against polytheism and idolatry, he earned the wrath of various tribal leaders, including those of his own tribe, the Quraysh. One uncle, Abu Labah, also resisted Muhammad and this earned both the uncle and his wife a place in hell, according to the commentators on sura 111. Some of the Prophet's enemies denounced Muhammad as possessed by *jinn* (evil spirits).

Muslims believe that in 620, one year after Khadijah's death, Gabriel brought the Prophet to Jerusalem on the back of a heavenly horse named Buraq. Sura 17:1 states: "Glory to (Allah) Who did take His servant for a Journey by night from the Sacred Mosque to the farthest Mosque, whose precincts We did bless." Muhammad was offered a drink of wine or milk and was commended by Gabriel for choosing the latter. After conversing with Jesus and other prophets, he ascended via a ladder (*miraj*) to the seventh heaven. Muslims claim that the Dome of the Rock, a Muslim shrine on the Temple Mount in Jerusalem, is built on the spot from where Muhammad ascended and descended. It is from this incident that Muslims believe that they have a stake in Jerusalem, and they consider the Temple Mount the third most holy spot in Islam.

Two years later in 622, in year one of the Muslim calendar, Muhammad and many of his followers fled to Medina, about 250 miles north of Mecca. This event, the Higra, marks the starting date of the Muslim calendar. For eight bitter years, the Prophet engaged in various military battles with his Meccan enemies. The most significant victory was one at Badr on March 15, 624, but there were losses as well, including one at Uhud in 625.

Muhammad's military life has always been used against him by critics. Focus has been made repeatedly on the death penalty he ordered on the Kurayza, the last major Jewish clan under his control. He accused them of treachery during a battle known as the "War of the Trench." According to traditional sources the Prophet ordered the beheading of more than 600 Jewish males. Sura 33:6 is said to refer to this episode. "And those of the People of the Book who aided them—Allah did take them down from their strongholds and cast terror into their hearts. (So that) some ye slew, and some ye made prisoners."

Another expedition, this time against the Mustalik clan, gained notoriety because of charges against Aisha, one of Muhammad's wives. She had been accidentally left behind on the return trip to Medina. When a lone Muslim soldier brought her back to camp, rumors started. Muhammad received a revelation exonerating his favorite wife. Sura 24:12 is said to address the gossip: "Why did not the believers—men and women—when ye heard of the affair,—put the best construction on it in their own minds and say, 'This (charge) is an obvious lie'?"

In 628 Muhammad negotiated a treaty at al-Hudaybiya with his leading Meccan enemies and in the next year he reached reconciliation with his own clan. In January 630 his army took control of Mecca and demolished the idols in and around the Kaaba, the main worship site. This site, traced by Muslims back to Abraham, would become the most holy in Islam. The Kaaba is now surrounded by the Al-Masjid al-Ḥarām mosque, now the largest in the world.

Medina continued to be the base for the prophet, but he made a final pilgrimage to Mecca in early 632. He was sick at the time and returned home. He died on June 8 of that year, in the embrace of Aisha. His burial place, and the mosque that has grown around it, is the second most important site for Muslim pilgrims.

Alfred North Whitehead is noted to have remarked that "philosophy is one long footnote to Plato." Likewise, Islamic history is one long footnote to Muhammad. Thus, Muhammad's journey—in all of its detail, from his military style, to his reaction to Jews and

Muslims bow their heads toward Mecca in prayer. Mecca, in present-day Saudi Arabia, is the birthplace of Muhammad, the prophet upon whose teachings Islam is based. (PhotoDisc/Getty Images)

Christians, to the way he brushed his teeth—becomes the paradigm for all Muslims. This includes Muhammad's beliefs and policies in all realms of life, whether religious, social, or political. His words, whether in the Koran or the hadith (traditions about the prophet) become the final authority since he is the Prophet of God.

Historical Accuracy and Muhammad As one might expect, Western scholars have expressed skepticism about the traditional biography of Muhammad. The doubts have been framed along three different lines. First, following David Hume, there is agnosticism in principle toward Muhammad's alleged miracles. They note the absence of such miracles in the Koran and argue that the miraculous accounts in the hadith are a later creation. Second, there is a more general suspicion of the hadith literature as a valid historical source. Ignaz Goldziher (1850–1921) provided a strong case that post-Muhammad Muslim communities read their

views and hearsay back into the life of the Prophet. John Wansbrough and Patricia Crone are the more modern advocates of the limited historical value of the hadith collections, whether those of Bukhari (810–870), Muslim (817–875), or the Shiite world. Of course, traditional Muslim scholars continue to evaluate the standard hadith as trustworthy.

It should be noted that some Western scholars are not totally skeptical of the Koran and hadith as sources for history. F. E. Peters argues in his *Muhammad and the Origins of Islam* that it is rational to expect that the Koran and hadith contain much that can be used for biography. The same logic applies to the earliest biographies (*sira*) of Muhammad, the most famous being Ibn Ishaq's *Life of the Apostle of God*.

A third line of Western skepticism has more to do with evaluation of the normative doctrinal and ethical claims in all traditional Muslim sources. To non-Muslim readers there is much that seems lacking. While

1514 | ◆ Islam

scrutiny along critical lines runs counter to dominant irenic approaches to Islam (Edward Said), one can make proper use of Said without capitulating to the kind of naïveté that sometimes appears in pluralist visions of Islam.

Questions can also be raised about the value and limits of Islamic jurisprudence. The Sufi tradition is based, in part, on some dismay over the increasing hold that jurists had on Islamic thought and practice. Likewise, modern discourse about Islam should allow freedom to confront what seem to be superstitious, anti-feminist, and rather undiplomatic elements in the hadith. Do angels really have wings? Did the Prophet teach that females make up the majority in hell? What did Muhammad believe about the *jinn*? Did Muhammad teach that Allah turned Jews into pigs and apes? Likewise, in the Koran itself, what is the proper reaction to the command in sura 4:34 about the beating of wives?

Debate over Muhammad's views mirror the three distinct views of him that have dominated discourse since his emergence as a prophet. Of first significance is the Muslim understanding. In all forms of Islam Muhammad is the ideal. The hadith material speaks of him in highest terms. One hadith states: "Allah's Apostle was the most handsome, most generous, and the bravest of all the people" (Bukhari 4:277).

The great philosophers of Islam cut their beards in accordance with Muhammad's example. Some Muslims refuse to eat watermelon because there was no evidence that Muhammad ever ate one. Female circumcision, a topic not covered in the Koran, is supported or abandoned based on speculation about whether Muhammad opposed it or not. As another example, the Muslim *hajj* is based on duplicating the prophet's journey.

No vision of Islam can proceed without appeal to Muhammad. This applies whether it is about advocating traditional values, feminism, gay rights, democracy, honor killings, or even acts of terrorism. Professed allegiance to Muhammad was used to justify the destruction of the famous Buddhist statues in Bamyam in 2001. The sale of heroin in Afghanistan is defended as a necessary tactic in line with the prophet's military actions.

The high view of Muhammad is also shown in Muslim offense toward any who question the Prophet. Muslim attacks on Salman Rushdie and the *fatwah*

against him by the Shiite cleric Ayatollah Khomeini in 1989 had to do with the novelist's perceived insults against Muhammad and his favorite wives. Ahmed Deedat, a popular Muslim apologist, attacked the novelist in a pamphlet called *How Rushdie Fooled the West*. His conclusion about Rushdie speaks for itself: "Mired in misery, may all his filthy lucre choke in his throat, and may he die a coward's death, a hundred times a day, and eventually when death catches up with him, many he simmer in hell for all eternity!"

Likewise, Muslims protested throughout 2006 over publication of cartoons of the prophet in the Danish newspaper *Jyllands-Posten*. The images were printed in September 2005 and reprinted worldwide. There was further anger in the fall of 2006 over a controversial reference about Muhammad made by Pope Benedict XVI in a speech at the University of Regensburg. The pope quoted the words of Manuel II Palaiologosa, a 14th-century Byzantine emperor: "Show me just what Muhammad brought that was new and there you will find things only evil and inhuman, such as his command to spread by the sword the faith he preached." The pope and the Vatican issued qualifying statements in the weeks following his lecture.

A second assessment of Muhammad has emerged in the last century or so. There are scholars who hold Muhammad in much esteem, without accepting that he is sinless or that he is *the* Prophet of God. Among Western Christian scholars, this new approach has been adopted by W. Montgomery Watt, Kenneth Cragg, Wilfred Cantwell Smith, and Hans Küng.

Küng, a Roman Catholic, first addressed the issue of Muhammad in *Christianity and the World Religions*. He presents seven parallels between Muhammad and the prophets of Israel, outlines the immense contribution of Muhammad, and concludes by citing a document from the Second Vatican Council (1962–1965) that states that the Catholic Church "also looks upon the Muslims with great respect: They worship the one true God who has spoken to man." Küng states: "In my opinion, that Church—and all the Christian Churches —must also 'look with great respect' upon the man whose name is omitted from the declaration out of embarrassment, although he alone led the Muslims to the worship of the one God, who spoke *through* him: Muhammad the Prophet."

In his 2007 opus *Islam: Past, Present and Future* Küng restated his high view, while offering some significant criticisms of Muhammad. Other scholars, such as John Hick, Paul Knitter, and Wendy Doniger, have argued for the basic truth of all of the great world religions and the integrity of each founder. Karen Armstrong, a former Catholic nun, offered a lofty view of Islam in her *Muhammad: A Biography of the Prophet*, a bestseller that received some serious critique for her apologetic tone.

According to a third view, that forms a strong theme in Christian writing, Muhammad is the embodiment of evil. This tradition of contempt began in the early medieval period, as Christian and Muslim armies fought for land control from North Africa, across the Middle East, and into Europe. The wars were viewed by many Christians as the necessary struggle against the Antichrist himself—Muhammad. Dante's *Inferno* puts the Islamic leader in the lower realms of hell. Similar diatribes against Muhammad continued after Dante and through the Reformation to the present.

Secular writers have also offered some harsh critiques of Muhammad. He has been pictured as ignorant, barbaric, and immoral. He was on occasion characterized as either a hypocrite or delusional, perhaps the victim of epileptic seizures, whose success with converts had more to do with promises of sexual reward, material gain, and the proverbial Islamic sword than with any truth in his teaching.

In the aftermath of the bombing of the Pentagon in Washington, D.C., and the World Trade Center in New York City on September 11, 2001, some editorials in the secular press hinted at Muhammad's dark side, with subtle accusations that the terror that had been visited on New York and Washington had its roots in the life and teaching of the Muslim prophet. They cite Muhammad's all-or-nothing mentality, his expansionist vision, his dictatorship, and, of course, his love for jihad. Both religious and secular critics have traced the Koran to less than divine inspiration.

The Origin of the Koran   Many Muslims believe that the Koran is eternal since its origin lies in Allah's eternal mind. Other believers argue that it is a created revelation. The vast majority of Muslims believe that the angel Gabriel dictated the revelations to Muhammad. He then recited the words to Khadijah, his first wife, and then to other followers. After Muhammad's death, a number of Muslim scholars formed the final edition of the Koran in the time of Uthman (d. 656), the third ruler (caliph) after the prophet.

Most Muslims are ignorant of skeptical attacks on the Koran. Most believe that the Prophet could not read or write, a point used to argue for the divine origin of the Koran. Western scholars have debated to what extent the Koran can be viewed as a trustworthy historical source. Recent skepticism takes its chief cue from the work of John Wansbrough, mentioned earlier, one of the major figures in modern study of the Koran.

The Koran contains 114 suras, or chapters, and more than 6,000 verses. The suras are arranged by size, with the shorter chapters near the end. Islamic tradition states that the shorter chapters came first in Muhammad's life while the longer chapters were revealed after the prophet conquered Mecca in 630 CE. In other words, the Koran should be read in reverse order if one wants a basic sense of unfolding revelation.

The titles of the various chapters relate to some word or idea in the chapter, though there is often no unifying theme in the various suras. Some Muslim writers attempt to argue for divine inspiration in the Koran by pointing to mathematic and scientific wonders in the text. Mention is made of the Koran's accuracy on medical matters as well.

Major Themes of the Koran   Anyone who reads the Koran for the first time finds it confusing. It is not orderly or systematic, as most Muslims acknowledge, and the text is not always clear. There is no grand narrative in the Koran and the material is not ordered thematically. This means that the best way to understand it is to get a sense of its major themes and those topics that appear constantly throughout.

Allah   The Koran is a text about Allah where the word itself appears more than 2,500 times. As in Judaism and Christianity, God is eternal, omnipotent, omniscient, and omnipresent, and is a spirit being. However, the Koran moves beyond these two other religions by placing greater stress on God's sovereignty and the notion of predestination.

Sura 59:23 is an example of a high view of God: "God is He, than Whom there is no other god; the Sovereign, the Holy One, the Source of Peace (and Perfection), the Guardian of Faith, the Preserver of Safety, the Exalted in Might, the Irresistible, the Supreme: Glory to God!"

The Koran puts more focus on the justice of God than his love but it is wrong to imply that the Koran has no sense of God's love. Rather, his love is to be understood through the lens of his holiness. His mercy, a major theme, is related to the willingness of people to turn from evil, though even that repentance is ultimately an outgrowth of God's ultimate will.

Muhammad   The Prophet is the key human person in the holy text though he is only mentioned by name four times. However, he is the recipient of the revelation and the subject of many passages. When Muhammad is quoted, Muslims contend that these words represent the words of Allah.

As is commonly known, Muhammad is "the Seal of the Prophets," (sura 33), a phrase interpreted to mean he is the last and greatest prophet. Muhammad is a judge to his followers (4:65), and is worthy of respect (2:104; 4:46). Muhammad's role was foreseen by Moses (46:10) and by Jesus in sura 61:6. "O Children of Israel! I am the apostle of God (sent) to you, confirming the Law (which came) before me, and giving Glad Tidings of an Apostle to come after me, whose name shall be Ahmad." Ahmad is a shortened form of Muhammad.

Muhammad's message is universal (34:28) and he is the sign of Allah's mercy to the world (9:61; 28:46–47; 76:24–26). The prophet is described as prayerful (74:3), gentle (3:159), concerned about his disciples (9:128), and anxious for unbelievers to repent (12:97; 25:30). He had an "exalted standard of character" (68:4). As noted earlier, he had his critics who accused him of craziness (7:184) and being under demonic influence (81:22).

His followers received instructions about proper social etiquette with the prophet. They could only visit his home with permission and they were to avoid arriving early or staying too long. The Koran says disciples are to avoid "familiar talk" with the Prophet. Such behavior "annoys the Prophet: he is ashamed to dismiss you, but God is not ashamed (to tell you) the truth" (33:53).

Biblical Material   The Koran gives significant attention to figures and stories drawn from the Hebrew Bible and the Christian New Testament. Jews and Christians are referred to as "the people of the book" (3:64; 29:46). Muslims believe that Allah revealed himself to Jews and Christians, though both groups altered their scriptures. Muslims use this to explain why both Jewish and Christian accounts often differ from the way they are reported in the Koran. Critics of the Koran argue that its biblical material is often presented through the lens of Jewish and Christian views that were popular in Muhammad's time.

In terms of biblical figures, Moses gets most mention in the Koran with more than 500 verses, or almost 10 percent of the text. Noah, Abraham, Joshua, David, Jesus, and Mary are also awarded major attention. Muslims often draw parallels between Muhammad and Moses, since both are lawgivers. As well, comparison is made between Muhammad and King David, since both led their citizens into warfare for God.

Jesus   The Koran holds Jesus in the highest regard. He is called a Sign from God. His miracles are noted and the claim that he was born of the Virgin Mary is accepted. The followers of Jesus were called Muslims, according to the Koran. Jesus can be called apostle and messenger of God, though he is not the Son of God. He is a prophet, which is the highest title one can be given under Islam's strict monotheism.

Muslims tell a somewhat different story of Jesus' life than that in the canonical Gospels. For example, Muslims do not believe that Jesus died on the cross. In sura 4:157, one of the famous verses of the Koran, it speaks about enemies of Allah who insulted the Virgin Mary and who brag: "We killed Christ Jesus the son of Mary, the Apostle of God." The text then reads: "but they killed him not, nor crucified him, but so it was made to appear to them, and those who differ therein are full of doubts, with no (certain) knowledge, but only conjecture to follow, for of a surety they killed him not." Muslims believe that Jesus ascended to heaven and will return to earth to battle the Antichrist.

True Believers Much of the Koran is devoted to description of the life of those who submit to Allah. The word "Muslim" actually has the meaning of submission behind it. Though Islam is a religion of law, the Koran is more preoccupied with larger principles than legal niceties. The Muslim follows Allah and trusts his will as absolute. Hence, Muslims often repeat the word *inshallah*, which is Arabic for "if God wills." The devout Muslim abandons all false gods since Allah alone is "lord of the east and the west" (73:9). Following Allah means, of course, following Prophet Muhammad, as noted earlier.

The Koran mandates prayer (2:238, 70:9, and 87:15, for example) and also fasting (2:185). The true believer should be forgiving, peaceful, and faithful. Charity is commanded and good works are a sign of true faith (3:114). Allah's disciple obeys divine instructions on marriage (4:23; 5:5) and on inheritance laws (4:11, 126).

The true Muslim avoids evil in all its forms. This means no gambling, drinking, usury, and unlawful food (*haram*). Skeptics are to be avoided. Sura 44:9 warns against those "who play about in doubt." Muslim males may have multiple wives, but cannot have more than four (3:3). Sexual lust is wrong. Given this, modesty is important, especially in females (24:31, for example), a principle much maligned in Western reaction to various forms of veiling among Islamic women.

Heaven, Hell, and Judgment Day The Koran gives enormous weight to issues about life after death. The rewards of heaven and the pains of hell are ever-present themes. In one popular English translation (Yusaf Ali) the word "hell" appears 94 times. There is a strong tradition in Islam, especially Shiite, that the battle against Satan at the end of time will be led by a messianic figure called the Mahdi who, in turn, will receive assistance from Jesus. Speculation about the soon appearance of the Mahdi has led to apocalyptic enthusiasm at different times and places in Islamic history.

Heaven is pictured as a garden paradise, with mansions, fountains, food and drink, and sexual pleasure (56:12–40, for example). The latter has become a matter of modern-day curiosity, given claims that Muslim martyrs will be rewarded with 72 virgins. This rather precise detail is from one of the lesser known hadith

collections (al-Tirmidhi 824–892) and not explicitly from the Koran. The general idea of sexual reward in paradise is, however, well established in Islamic thought and applies to all Muslims, male and female, whether martyrs or not. The Koran also states that the greatest bliss is "God's goodly acceptance," which is "the triumph supreme" (9:72).

The Koran's picture of hell is given with brevity and clarity. For example, the damned will wear garments of fire and drink boiling water (14:16; 47:15). There will be no escape from hell. Sura 13:18 notes: "But those who respond not to him—even if they had all that is in the heavens and on earth, and as much more, (in vain) would they offer it for ransom. For them will the reckoning be terrible: their abode will be Hell—what a bed of misery!" There is virtually nothing in the Koran that warrants any hope of deliverance from hell or any vision of universal redemption.

The Five Pillars of Islam The focus of Sunni Islam, submission to God, finds expression in five practices, popularly known as the five pillars. For Shia Muslims, a minority group, there is a different expression of basics. For Sunni believers, the first pillar is the well-known profession of faith known as the *shahadah*: "There is no God but Allah, and Muhammad is His messenger." These words seek to establish the supremacy of Allah as the one true God and the finality of Muhammad as Allah's ultimate prophet.

Second, faithful Muslims obey the call to prayer (*salat*), which is to happen five specific times every day. Muhammad first advised his followers to pray facing toward Jerusalem, but soon reoriented his followers toward Mecca. Kenneth Cragg, one of the great Christian scholars of Islam, writes: "Islam and prayer are in truth inseparable." Islamic law provides detailed instructions on proper washings related to *salat*. These can be partial washings (*wudu*) or full (*gushi*). As well, scholars of Islam give detailed guidance on obstructions to prayer, including whether various bodily functions negate proper prayer. Men and women usually pray in separate areas of the mosque, though some Muslim feminists argue that women should be allowed in the front on occasion.

The Muslim place for worship, the mosque, is called a house of prayer, as that is the primary activity that occurs there. Though some mosques are quite elaborate, dramatic works of architecture, even opulent, the requirements of a mosque are relatively simple—an open space for the faithful to gather and a *mihrab*, a niche in the wall indicating the *qibla*, or direction, toward which prayer is offered. The direction is always toward the Kaaba in Mecca. Muslims generally gather at the mosque on Fridays for prayer. Men and women are segregated during the prayer time.

Third, Muslims are supposed to give a percentage of their worth to the poor and needy. The tithe, or *zakat*, is collected by a few Muslim states, but most Muslims give through leaving money in the metal zakat box in their local mosque. The zakat involves giving 2.5 percent of the Muslim's assets, but it is not charity since it is an obligatory act, one that is usually to be done in private.

Fourth, unless prevented by bad health, all Muslims are to fast, that is, to abstain from all food, water, and sexual activity from sunrise to sunset during the entire month of Ramadan. The fast offers a time for spiritual reflection, repentance, and giving to the poor. The whole Koran is often recited in evening worship over the 30-day period. Ramadan ends with a celebratory feast day known as Eid ul-Fitr.

The last pillar is known as the *hajj* and concerns the duty of all able-bodied Muslims to make a pilgrimage to Mecca at least once in their lifetime. Only Muslims are allowed inside Mecca. Many Muslims regard their experience of the hajj to be the greatest spiritual moment of their lives.

Males are instructed to wear simple white garments while women can wear their traditional dress. The pilgrims enter Mecca while reciting "Here I am at your service, O God, here I am!" They circle seven times around the Kaaba, the temple Muslims believe was built by Abraham and Ishmael. The pilgrims engage in a ritual of running between two mountains outside of Mecca, in memory of the plight of Hagar looking for food and water. Muslims also throw stones at a pillar that symbolizes Satan, and sacrifice animals in duplication of the narrative involving Abraham's willingness to sacrifice his son. Muslims believe that Ismail rather than Isaac was the subject of this incident.

Jihad, Islam, and Terrorism The idea of *jihad* (literally, struggle) has emerged in the contemporary world as one of the most critical and controversial of Islamic beliefs. The modern Western controversies surrounding jihad have their epicenter in the events of September 11, 2001. Although many Muslims and some scholars contend that the word simply means spiritual struggle, jihad has often been interpreted in a more literal fashion as Holy War.

In February 1998, three and a half years before September 11, Osama bin Laden, the founder and leader of al-Qaeda, made his own views clear. Along with other groups representative of 20th-century Islamism from Egypt, Pakistan, and Bangladesh, he issued a *fatwa*, or legal ruling, that called on Muslims "to kill the Americans and their allies—civilian and military." He added that this struggle is an individual duty for every Muslim who can do it in any country in which it is possible to do it.

In contrast, the vast majority of Muslim countries have opposed Osama bin Laden since September 11. For example, the governments of Bahrain, Egypt, Iran, Lebanon, Oman, Pakistan, Palestine, Qatar, Saudi Arabia, Turkey, United Arab Emirates, and Yemen expressed their condemnation of the terrorist attacks almost immediately.

Terrorist attacks have brought to the surface intense disagreement within the Muslim community over the meaning of jihad and the nature of true Islam. The roots of these contemporary conflicts about Islam's real identity lie in ancient debates about the teaching of the Koran, the example of the Prophet, the legitimacy of non-Muslim governments, and the place of war in Islamic ideology.

Despite the debate, the following observations emerge from careful study:

The Koran uses the term "jihad" to describe both spiritual struggle and just war.
The Prophet engaged in warfare.
The Prophet taught that Islam must be spread to the whole world.
Islamic law justifies self-defense and certain acts of war.
Muslims often conquered non-Arab lands and peoples through war.
Most Muslims divide the world into two: Islam (the realm of peace) and non-Islam (the realm of no-peace).

Many Muslims believe that all countries should follow Islamic law.

Some Muslim countries (like many non-Muslim countries) are nondemocratic and crush dissent.

Most Muslims find the focusing of Western-Middle Eastern discussions around "jihad" and "terrorism" by non-Muslims as a talisman to avoid critical scrutiny of Western weaknesses and American failures. This critique includes a negative assessment of Western culture (with its emphases on material possessions and sexuality) while emphasizing Muslim objections generally with Western imperialist activity in Muslim lands and particularly recent military campaigns in Iraq and Afghanistan. More specifically, the abuses at Abu Ghraib prison riled Muslims (and non-Muslims) as have recent American legal sanctions to what is usually regarded as torture. Most Muslims regard support for Israel with contempt and view with considerable consternation Western complicity with repressive dictatorships in the Middle East and Central Asia. The latter has been reported on at length by the famous British journalist Robert Fisk.

There are some 70 major terrorist groups operating in the world as the 21st century begins. Of these, more than 30 have an Islamic orientation. Of the rest, a few are well known—the Irish Republican Army or Aum Shinrikyo (the group that spread poison gas in the Tokyo subway system). Among the Islamic groups, the most well known are the Abu Nidal Organization (also known as Black September), the Islamic Group, or IG (Al-Gama'a al-Islamiyya), the Armed Islamic Group (GIA), Hamas, Hizballah (Party of God, also known as Islamic Jihad), and al-Qaeda. Though relatively small in membership, these groups have some popular support throughout the Muslim world, and their actions are widely debated. Various governments have moved against groups accused of engaging in terrorism such as the Muslim Brotherhood (Egypt). Other militant groups, such as the Jamaat-e-Islam in Pakistan, have emphasized education and political action in order to attain their ends.

The Branches of Islam   Like all religions, Islam has not maintained its original unity. Within a generation of the Prophet's death, Muslims were at war with each other over political leadership and the proper interpre-

tation of Islamic spirituality. Generally, Muslims can be grouped under three major branches: Sunni Islam; Shia Islam, also known as Shiite; and Sufism.

Sunni Islam represents the largest grouping in Islam. Of the world's 1.2 billion Muslims, more than one billion are generally counted as Sunni, which is about 90 percent of all Muslims. This figure is somewhat deceptive, however, since Sufism is probably under-reported in many parts of Africa, the Middle East, and Asia.

Sunni Muslims trace themselves back to the prophet but separate from Shia Muslims over the question of proper authority in Islam. Differences here relate to competing claims about connection to Muhammad, the text of the hadith, the shape of Islamic law, and the nature of salvation. Sunni Muslims have themselves disagreed over the methodology of interpreting Muslim law and have divided into four main schools of jurisprudence: Hanafite, Malikite, Shafiite, and Hanbalite.

There are about 170 million Shia (or Shiite) Muslims globally. In spite of minority status, the Shia version of Islam received enormous attention because of the Islamic revolution in Iran in 1979. The shah of Iran was deposed, and the Ayatollah Khomeini (1902–1989), the well-known Shiite Muslim leader, returned from exile in France to run the country. The Iranian view of the West was and is shaped powerfully by anger over British and American plots to foment a coup in Iran in 1953–1954.

In Sunni Islam, the imam is the person who leads prayer in the mosque. In Shiite Islam the word "imam" is used most significantly of major leaders chosen by Allah to guide Shia Islam in its earliest and most important years. One Shia group believes there were 12 such leaders while the Ismaili Muslims argue that there were only 7. The Zaydiyya Shia, a minority group in Yemen, contends there were five imams. The Twelver group and the Ismaili Muslims place emphasis on the claim that the last imam is alive, but placed in a state of supernatural hiddenness by Allah. There are about 150 million Twelver Shi'ites in the world and about 15 million Ismailis. The most famous Ismaili is the Aga Khan, the hereditary leader of the Nazari branch.

Shia Muslims give enormous significance to the martyrdom of Husayn, whose father Ali (d. 661), was the son-in-law of the prophet. Husayn and fellow Muslims were killed by Sunni Muslims at Kerbala (in modern-day Iraq) on the 10th day of the Muslim month of Muharran in 680. Shia Muslims engage in elaborate rituals to honor his memory, and Shia pilgrims travel to his shrine in Karbala.

The Sufis are famous as the mystics of Islam. Some scholars estimate their numbers at 240 million throughout the world. Sufism emerged when Islam became legalistic and materialistic in the twilight years of the earliest Muslim dynasties. Al-Ghazali (1058–1111), the great Islamic devotional writer, turned to Sufism as an alternative to the speculative, uncertain paths of philosophy and reason. Sufism is most famously represented by the Whirling Dervishes (*darvishes*; literally, beggars), who practice a kind of mystical dance used to help the dancer resist outside stimuli and focus on the mind of Allah. Rumi (1207–1273), the great Persian poet and mystic, is probably the most famous Sufi.

Islam has often been shaped by local folk customs. Thus, scholars often speak of a folk Islam. Muslims in Pakistan or Nigeria use charms to ward off evil while in India strands of hair are hung at shrines to protect children. In many Muslim countries the Muslim shaman uses local tribal customs to keep Satan away. Muslims in many Islamic countries use magical objects to keep from being hurt by the evil eye. More orthodox Muslims dismiss these folk traditions as superstition.

The Progress of the Faith   The dominant motifs of the Prophet Muhammad's life become the pattern, in one form or another, in Islamic history from the seventh century to the present. His own defense of Islamic truth is duplicated through the centuries by given leaders and movements. His willingness to bear arms under particular circumstances becomes the standard for declarations of jihad. His concern for a united community of the faithful is replicated worldwide from his death to the present, as Muslims of all types unite in the annual hajj to Mecca.

Muhammad's expansionist vision gripped Islam in the earliest years following the death of the Prophet. The rapid spread of Islam is probably the most striking thing about the first century of Islamic life. Muslims conquered Damascus by 636, ruled Jerusalem by 638, and controlled Syria by 640. Egypt came under Islamic control by 646, and the Sassanid dynasty in Persia fell by 651. Muslims moved into Spain in the early eighth century, and King Roderick of Spain was defeated in 711. Though Charles Martel stopped the Muslim advance in southern France in 732, the extent of the Islamic empire by then is startling.

The incredibly rapid spread of Islam is especially noteworthy, given the hostilities that dogged Islam from its inception. It is as if the strife in Muhammad's own life, and his battles with fellow Arabs, became a deep psychic reality in the Islamic mindset, setting brother against brother. Thus, Uthman, the third caliph in Sunni Islam, was assassinated in 656. The Kharijites formed in 657 out of direct opposition to Ali, the fourth caliph in the Sunni tradition, because of his perceived weaknesses in responding to the emerging Umayyad dynasty.

These tensions between those faithful to Ali (the Shiites) and the early Umayyad leaders culminated in the killing of Husayn, Ali's son, in 680 CE. As noted earlier, this killing radically impacted the Shias, who trace their roots to Ali as the proper successor to Muhammad. The war between Iran and Iraq in the 20th century played out against the backdrop of these earliest days of hostility.

Divisions within Islam are reflected to some degree in the changing Islamic dynasties. Albert Hourani documents more than 30 dynasties in *A History of the Arab Peoples*. Some of these emerge as a result of victory over Christian, Hindu, or Buddhist opposition, but many are simply a reflection of one Muslim dynasty expanding its control base by conquering other Islamic rulers and peoples. Often a dynasty crumbled from within as a once trusted servant from outside the tribe or nation started his own kingdom. As often as not, the dynasty crumbled when an heir did not have the capacity to rule as a monarch and lost the support of the people and the court, or was unable to lead the defense of the land from outsiders. This was certainly the case in medieval Spain.

Such realities explain why many dynasties, like the Aglabids in eastern Algeria (800–909) or the Buyids in Iran/Iraq (932–1062) or the Almohads in the Maghreb (1130–1269), did not survive. Survival between various Muslim groups is a tribute to the political acumen displayed in dynasties that spanned over half a millennium. The Abbasids ruled the Middle East and North Africa from 749 through 1258. The Ottomans dominated the Muslim world from 1281 through to 1922, a staying power rarely found in the history of civilizations.

The story of unrest in Islamic history is to a great degree the story of political and military rivalries, sometimes rooted in nationalist, ethnic, and tribal realities, as in the conflicts between Arab and non-Arab Muslims. However, divisions are also a reflection of competing visions of what constitutes true Islam. This is most evident, of course, in ongoing tensions between Sunni and Shiite, but was also reflected in the treatment of those deemed to be unfaithful to basic Islamic doctrine, practice, and the dictates of Muslim law.

For example, there were a few leaders who denied that Muhammad ever taught that he was the final prophet, and they duplicated his call to a new revelation from Allah. Thus, in the mid-eighth century Al-Muqanna (aka Hashim ibn Hakim) declared himself to be a prophet and a god. The view that the Koran is eternal was resisted strongly by the Mutazalite movement of the early decades of the ninth century. Sufi Muslims have been the frequent targets of the wrath of orthodoxy. Al-Hallaj, a Sufi master, was tortured and beheaded in 922.

Internal tensions between Muslims pale somewhat in light of the animosities fueled in the early years of Muslim-Christian conflict. Toledo was recaptured by Christians in 1085, good news for Catholic and Orthodox leaders, who were stunned by the Seljuk defeat of the Byzantines at Manikert in 1071. Pope Urban II (r. 1088–1099) called for a crusade against the Turks in 1095, and Jerusalem was in Christian hands by the end of the century.

Muslim misfortunes were reversed under Saladin (Salah-ad-Din Yusuf ibn-Ayyub, 1138–1193) who served as a minister to the Islamic Fatimid rulers in Egypt. Saladin took control of Egypt in 1171 and went on to retake Jerusalem from the Christians in 1187, just five years before his death. In the next century the anti-Islamic focus of the Christian Crusades gave way to hostilities between Catholic and Orthodox Christians. Their doctrinal split of 1054 was sealed in blood when Catholic armies sacked Constantinople in 1204, in a spree of murder, rape, and theft.

Historians trace the rise of the Ottoman Empire to 1281 when Osman I (1258–1321) took over as *bey* (ruler) after his father's death. Osman is known chiefly for his exploits against the Byzantine lands. The 14th century witnessed radical shifts in power between competing Islamic dynasties and armies (Ottoman, Mongol, Hafsid, Mamluk, Ilkhanid, Timurid). Despite the shifting political and military scene, Muslims were free to travel through the whole Islamic world. Ibn Battutah (1304–1368), one famous explorer, traveled for almost 30 years.

Ottoman ruler Mehmed II conquered Constantinople in 1453. In the next century the Mughal leader Babur (Zahir-ud-Din Muhammad, 1483–1530) was victorious at a battle in Panipat in 1526. Suleiman I (1494–1566), the great Ottoman leader, ruled as far north as Budapest, as far west as Morocco, east to Iraq, and south to Yemen. His naval commander Khair ad-Din (aka Barbarossa) ruled the eastern Mediterranean for decades. During the same time period, Akbar (1542–1605), the third Mughal emperor, controlled a large part of northern India from 1556 through 1605. Songhai, the large African empire, was under Saadi Muslim rule by 1591.

Indonesia, now the most populous Muslim country, was under Islamic influence by the 16th century. Shah Jahan (d. 1666) started construction of the Taj Mahal in Agra in 1632, and Morocco came under Alawi control in 1668. However, Islamic expansionism received a severe blow with the draining of Ottoman powers in wars with Poland from 1682 through 1699. Further, in a dramatic turn, the Ottomans again failed to take Vienna in 1683. The Muslim threat to Christian Europe declined in face of the waning of Ottoman power and the rising military superiority of a revived Europe.

However, it is inconceivable that Islam could have been destroyed either by bullets or by competing beliefs. By the time Napoleon conquered Egypt in 1798, Islam had survived for almost 1,200 years. The famous French leader captured Muslim lands but was unable to win their hearts or minds, regardless of Muslim respect for his military prowess.

Islamic orthodoxy has dealt harshly with innovative movements in the modern era. Druze Muslims, based largely in Lebanon, faced steady persecution through the 20th century. As well, the Ahmadiyya Muslims have endured widespread harassment for their "heretical" view that their founder, Mirza Ghulam Hazrat Ahmad Qadiyani (1835–1908), is a prophet and the promised messiah (*madhi*) of Islam. The Nation of Islam has faced a cold reception in America for its assertion of unorthodox belief. The Baha'i Faith, a new religion born in Iran, has seen many of its members martyred since its inception. (One of the Baha'is problems was the perception that the Baha'is had aligned with the shah and many of the shah's secret police were Baha'is.)

On a global scale, modern Islam has been impacted most by the powerful ideologies that have swept the West since the Enlightenment. Skepticism and Rationalism has either eroded confidence in Islam or determined the nature of Islamic apologetic. As with Catholic monarchies, various notions of democracy have also threatened Muslim leaders and regimes. Muslim thinkers have been forced to articulate a reconstructed Islam to respond to emerging global ideologies.

The success of Islamist movements in the 20th century was based on the work of purists in the previous two centuries who were alarmed by the decline of Muslim power and stability, a reality that signaled to them that the ideals of the Prophet had been betrayed by his professed followers and leaders.

The revivalist impulse in Saudi Arabia goes back to the writings of Muhammad al-Wahhab (1703–1792). He was the ideological founder of the Wahhabi movement, which eventually gained control in the heartland of Islam. He also influenced Islamic reformers in the next century, most notably Jamal al-Din al-Afghani (1838–1897) and his student Muhammad Abduh (1849–1905).

In the 20th century anti-colonial, pro-Arabic, and pro-Islamic movements dominated the Muslim story. There was not simply a resistance to the West of the kind expressed in Ali Shariati's influential work *Westoxication* (1962), but also a strong revolt against Arab governments viewed as un-Islamic and corrupt. As noted earlier, Iran became the scene of Shiite radicalism that led to the toppling of the shah in 1979, leading to the present theocratic state.

The Muslim Brotherhood, founded by the youthful Hasan al-Banna (1906–1949), was formed in 1928. Iraq gained independence in 1932. Sayyid Abul A'la Mawdudi (1903–1979) championed Muslim ideals in both India and Pakistan through his Jamaat-e-Islam movement. Hasan al-Banna was assassinated in 1949 for his push for radical reform in Egypt. Sayyid Qutb (1906–1966), unimpressed by his student days in America, took up al-Banna's cause and became the new voice against secular trends in Egypt and throughout the Muslim world. He was executed by the Egyptian government in 1966.

Afghanistan gained freedom from Soviet oppression in 1989. Islamic radicalism gained a foothold in Indonesia (the most populous Muslim country) late in the 20th century, and similar forces arose in Nigeria, Sudan, Algeria, and Pakistan. Less volatile expressions of Islamic ascendancy are seen with the formation of the League of Arab States in 1945 and the Muslim World League in 1962. Even the Million Man March on October 6, 1995 (promoted by Nation of Islam leader Louis Farrakhan), was seen by many as an expression of Islam's growing potency.

The Palestinian question also fueled the growth of Islamic militancy. Tensions in Palestine between Muslims (and Arab Christians) and Jews date back to the first wave of Jewish immigrants in the late 1800s. The British government's 1917 Balfour Declaration heightened Arab unrest, as did Western support for a Jewish state 30 years later, both providing the context for the declaration of the state of Israel in May 1948.

Six wars between Arabs and Jews since Israel's formation have further heightened Muslim-Jewish hostilities. These tensions were also shown in the rise of the first intifadah (uprising) in 1987. A second intifadah in 2000 followed the breakdown of talks at Camp David between Yasser Arafat (1929–2004) and Israeli Prime Minister Ehud Barak. Islamic militant groups like Hamas and Hezbollah have called for an armed jihad against Israel. In 2009 U.S. President Barack Obama inherited the Israeli-Palestinian conflict as one of his most important foreign-policy issues.

American exposure to radical Islamism came with the arrest of Americans in Tehran in 1979, the bombing of the World Trade Center in 1993, the explosions at American embassies in Africa, the attack on the USS *Cole* in Yemen, and then the attacks of September 11. These events are an indication of the depth of Islamic mistrust and hatred of the West, but they also have illustrated the deep ideological divisions among Muslims over what constitutes ideal Islam and its proper defense.

The revivalist trends of the last two centuries, expressed in moderate and extreme Islamist movements, have created a dilemma for the Islamic world. On the one hand, the success of Islamism has led to a new pride about the faith proclaimed by Muhammad. Nevertheless, the fundamentalist impulse has created renewed conflict among Muslims, expressed in divisions over Islamist groups, including the Taliban in Afghanistan. As well, there are bitter internal disputes about the role of women, human rights, and the proper scope of Islamic law in both the Islamic world and the West.

James A. Beverley

See also: Abraham/Abram; Ahmad, Mirza Ghulam Hazrat; Angels; Baha'i Faith; Calendars, Religious; Companions of the Prophet; Druze; Hanafite School of Islam; Islamism; Ismaili Islam; Istanbul; Jamaat-e-Islam; Jerusalem; Malikite School of Islam; Mary, Blessed Virgin; Masjid al-Ḥaram Al; Mecca; Medina; Moses; Mosques; Muhammad; Muslim Brotherhood; Muslim World League; Nation of Islam; Pilgrimage; Relics; Shafiite School of Islam; Shiah Fatimi Ismaili Tayyabi Dawoodi Bohra; Wahhabi Islam; Women, Status and Role of.

References

General Sources

Cragg, Kenneth. *The Call of the Minaret.* Maryknoll, NY: Orbis, 1985.

Esposito, John. *Islam: The Straight Path.* Oxford: Oxford University Press, 1998.

Fisk, Robert. *The Great War for Civilization.* New York: Knopf, 2005.

Friedman, Thomas. *From Beirut to Jerusalem.* New York: Farrar Straus and Giroux, 1989.

Godlas, Alan. "Islamic Studies, Islam, Arabic, and Religion." Academic website: www.arches.uga.edu/~godlas.

Hourani, Albert. *A History of the Arab Peoples.* Cambridge: Harvard University Press, 1991.

Huntington, Samuel. *The Clash of Civilizations.* New York: Simon and Schuster, 1996.

Karsh, Efraim. *Islamic Imperialism.* New Haven: Yale, 2006.

Kramer, Martin. *Ivory Towers in the Sand.* Washington, DC: Washington Institute for Near East Policy, 2001.

Küng, Hans. *Islam: Past, Present, and Future.* London: Oneworld, 2007.

Lewis, Bernard. *Islam and the West.* Oxford: Oxford University Press, 1993.

Makiya, Kanan. *Cruelty and Silence.* New York: W. W. Norton, 1993.

Miller, Judith. *God Has Ninety-Nine Names.* New York: Simon and Schuster, 1996.

Morris, Benny. *Righteous Victims.* New York: Vintage, 2001.

Muhaddith. Al-Muhaddith: General Islamic web resource. www.muhaddith.org.

Rahman, Fazlur. *Islam.* Chicago: University of Chicago Press, 1979.

Ramadan, Tariq. *In the Footsteps of the Prophet.* New York: Oxford University Press, 2007.

Rippin, Andrew. *Muslims.* London: Routledge, 2000.

Roald, Anne Sofie. *Women in Islam.* London: Routledge, 2001.

Schulze, Reinhard. *A Modern History of the Islamic World.* New York: New York University Press, 2000.

Sedgwick, Mark. *Islam and Muslims.* Intercultural Press, 2006.

Van Ess, Josef. *The Flowering of Muslim Theology.* Cambridge: Harvard University Press, 2006.

Wansbrough, John. *Quranic Studies.* Oxford: Oxford University Press, 1977.

Warraq, Ibn, ed. *The Quest for the Historical Muhammad.* Buffalo: Prometheus Books, 2000.

Watt, W. Montgomery. *The Majesty That Was Islam.* New York: Praeger Publishers, 1974.

Muhammad

Cook, Michael. *Muhammad.* Oxford: Oxford University Press, 1983.

Lings, Martin Lings. *Muhammad*. Rochester: Inner Traditions, 1983.

Motzki, Harald, ed. *The Biography of Muhammad: The Issue of the Sources*. Leiden: E. J. Brill, 2000.

Peters, F. E. *Muhammad and the Origins of Islam*. Albany: State University of New York Press, 1994.

Ramadan, Tariq. *In the Footsteps of the Prophet: Lessons from the Life of Muhammad*. New York: Oxford University Press, 2007.

Rubin, Uri., ed. *The Life of Muhammad*. Aldershot: Ashgate, 1998.

Watt, W. Montgomery. *Muhammad: Prophet and Statesman*. London: Oxford University Press, 1961.

Shia Traditions

Daftary, Farhad. *A Short History of the Ismailis*. Princeton, NJ: Marcus Wiener, 1998.

Davoodbhoy, T. A. A. *Faith of the Dawoodi Bohras*. Bombay, Department of Statistics and Information, Dawat-e-Hadiyah, 1992.

Halm, Heinz. *Shiism*. Trans. by J. Watson. Edinburgh: Edinburgh University Press, 1991.

Khomeini, Ruhollah. *Islamic Government*. New York: Manor, 1979.

Roy, Shibani. *The Dawoodi Bohras: An Anthropological Perspective*. Delhi: B. R. Publishing, 1984.

Tabataba'i, Sayyid Muhammad Husayn. *Shi'ite Islam*. Trans. and ed. by S. H. Nasr. Albany: State University of New York Press, 1975.

Ul-Amine, Hasan. *Shorter Islamic Shi'ite Encyclopedia*. Beirut: n.p., 1969.

Yann, Richard. *Shi'ite Islam*. Oxford: Blackwell, 1995.

Sufism

Chittick, William T. *Sufism: A Beginner's Guide*. Oxford: Oneworld Publications, 2007.

Cornell, Vincent. *Realm of the Saint: Power and Authority in Moroccan Sufism*. Austin: University of Texas Press, 1998.

Ernst, Carl. *The Shambhala Guide to Sufism: An Essential Introduction to the Philosophy and Practice of the Mystical Tradition of Islam*. Boston: Shambhala, 1997.

Nasr, Seyyed Hossein. *The Garden of Truth: The Vision and Promise of Sufism, Islam's Mystical Tradition*. New York: HarperOne, 2008.

Nasr, Seyyed, ed. *Islamic Spirituality: Manifestations*. London: SCM, 1991.

Rizvi, Syed Athar Abbas. *A History of Sufism in India*. 2 vols. New Delhi: Manoharlal, 1978.

Schimmel, Annemarie. *Mystical Dimensions of Islam*. Chapel Hill: North Carolina Press, 1975.

Sedgwick, Mark. *Sufism: The Essentials*. Cairo: AUC Press, 2003.

Trimingham, Spencer. *The Sufi Orders in Islam*. Oxford: Clarendon Press, 1971.

Jihad and Islamism

Bergen, Peter L. *Holy War Inc.* New York: Free Press, 2001.

Bonner, Michael. *Jihad in Islamic History*. Princeton, NJ: Princeton University Press, 2006.

Cole, David. ed. *The Torture Memos*. New York: The New Press, 2009.

Coll, Steve. *Ghost Wars*. New York: Penguin, 2004.

Coll, Steve. *The Bin Ladens*. New York: Penguin, 2008.

Gartenstein-Ross, Daveed. *My Year Inside Radical Islam*. New York: Tarcher, 2007.

Mayer, Jane. *The Dark Side*. New York: Doubleday, 2008.

Pipes, Daniel. *Militant Islam Reaches America*. New York: Norton, 2003.

Rashid, Ahmed. *Descent into Chaos*. New York: Viking, 2008.

Ricks, Thomas. *Fiasco*. New York: Penguin, 2006.

Scheuer, Michael. *Marching toward Hell*. New York: Free Press, 2008.

Woodward, Bob. *State of Denial*. New York: Simon & Schuster, 2006.

Wright, Lawrence. *The Looming Tower*. New York: Knopf, 2006.

Islamism

Islamism (also known as Islamic revivalism or, popularly in the West, as Islamic fundamentalism) is the name given to a set of popular new religious move-

Mosque, London. (J. Gordon Melton)

ments that appeared in the Muslim world through the 20th century, though these newer movements have their roots in older groups that in the 18th and 19th centuries criticized the faltering Ottoman Empire and the intrusion of Western powers in the Middle East. The 1922 fall of the Ottoman caliphate, whose empire had once stretched from North Africa to Persia and from Yemen to the gates of Vienna, and the rise of national states in its place became the seminal event in the emergence of this movement, which has as a keynote the call to return to an Orthodox Islamic state in which Islamic law gives shape to the community's life. The Islamic tradition is strongly opposed to the modern Enlightenment ideal of separation of religion and government that now prevails in most of the non-Muslim world.

In the last generation the Islamist tradition, a relatively small movement in the Islamic world, has been wedded to a program of terrorism, here defined as activity that does not so much have as its end the destruc-

tion of any given designated target but of using a target as a means of spreading anxiety, destabilizing the social order, and provoking a reaction from the targeted enemy. A relatively small number of people can use terrorist tactics to mobilize reactions far more extensive and costly than the energy and resources expended by the terrorist group.

Among the first movements that took advantage of the weakening of the Ottoman Empire was the Wahhabi movement, named for Mohammad ibn Abd-al-Wahhab (ca. 1703–1791), who emerged in Arabia as a critic of the Ottoman Empire, the lax practice of Islam among the Sunnis (the largest group), and the tolerance of what he considered the heretical practices of the various Sufi brotherhoods. He adopted a literalistic approach to the interpretation of the Koran, the Muslim holy book, and the hadith, the sayings of and traditions concerning the Prophet Muhammad. He gained an initial following around Mecca, but found long-lasting support from the Saud family. Around 1763, the Saudi sheikh began a conquest of Arabia. The Ottoman sultan tried to halt the erosion of his territory, but only in 1818 was he able to drive the Sauds into the desert. They were gradually pushed back until 1889, when they fled into exile in Kuwait. The almost dead Wahhabi movement was reborn when the head of the Saud family recaptured the family's traditional capital, Riyadh, in 1902 and over the next generation took control of what in 1932 became Saudi Arabia.

After World War II, the wealth of the Saudis allowed them to become missionaries for Islam and for the strict interpretations of Islamic law demanded by the Wahhabi perspective. Their striving in the cause of Islam (*jihad*) was manifest in the creation of the Committee for Encouraging Virtue and Preventing Vice to enforce public conformity to Islamic law in Saudi Arabia, the founding of the World Muslim League, support for the building of mosques in the West, and the sending out of a significant number of Wahhabi teachers to Muslim countries to win Muslims to their way.

Another significant movement that presaged 20th-century Islamism was the Pan-Islamic Unity movement launched by Persian teacher Sayyid Jamal al-Din al-Afghani (1838–1897). While Wahhab concentrated his criticisms on the laxity of Sunni Muslims and the heretical practices of Sufi and Shia Muslims in Arabia, al-Afghani had traveled widely in the West and turned his critical pen against the Western nations, their immoral and degenerate culture, and their imperialist designs on the Middle East. He also picked up the Wahhabi critique of lax Muslims and called for the removal of some Muslim leaders of whom he disapproved.

Al-Afghani wrote at a time that Great Britain was making its presence felt in the Middle East, especially in Yemen, Egypt, and the Sudan. At the same time, the French were asserting themselves as the new colonial power over Islamic territories in northwest Africa, and they cooperated on the building of the Suez Canal in the 1860s. Throughout this period, the Ottomans were being slowly pushed out of the Balkans, a process that culminated in World War I and the choice of the sultan to side with the Austro-Hungarians. Following the war, a variety of national states arose in the former Ottoman lands, and in 1922 the sultan was deposed to make way for the modern state of Turkey. The final end of the Ottoman era, together with the disappearance of the caliphate, which had been in place in some form since the death of the Prophet Muhammad in 632 CE, set the stage for a new breed of revitalization movements.

Al-Imam Hassan al-Banna (1906–1949) grew up in an Egypt dominated by Great Britain. He became the disciple of al-Afghani through Muhammad Rashid Rida (1865–1935), who continued al-Afghani's message in a periodical, *al-Manar*, that called Muslims to seek inspiration from the example of virtuous early Muslims. Rida was still active when, just six years after the fall of the caliphate, al-Banna founded Al-Ikhwan Al-Moslemoon, the Muslim Brotherhood, which began as a movement calling Egyptian youth to put away non-Muslim aspects of their life (including folk magic) and living their life according to the Koran and hadith. As the movement spread, its program expanded and came to include an array of social programs, including the Muslim Mothers' Institute for the education of women.

In the mid-1930s, however, al-Banna and the Brotherhood members were especially affected by the volatile developments in Palestine that followed the pullout of British forces. And when the state of Israel was proclaimed in 1948, members of the Brotherhood joined the forces fighting the new government. Within Egypt, they had also become more radicalized, and several assassinations of government officials were attributed to them. Publicly, al-Banna emphasized the need to Islamize the government. He was himself assassinated in March 1949.

The movement continued in Egypt until suppressed by then Prime Minister Gamel Abdel Nasser (1918–1970) in 1954, by which time Sayyid Qutb (1906–1966) had become its new theoretician. Nasser did not totally destroy the Brotherhood, which continues to the present, but he did succeed in marginalizing it for many years, during which time its impulse passed to other groups. Among those newer movements was the Jamaat-e-Islam. Founded by Indian Muslim Sayyid Abul A'la Mawdudi (1903–1979), the Jamaat emerged in the context of the Indian independence movement and the separation of Pakistan as an independent state. As a young intellectual, Mawdudi began to ruminate on the conflict between Islam and Western culture. He also criticized Indian nationalism, the effect of which he concluded would be the destruction of Muslim identity. As he watched Muslim leaders toy with various strands of political and cultural ideologies, he saw a need to reconstruct Islamic thought. That need led to the founding of Jamaat-e-Islam in 1941. He moved to what is now Pakistan, where he worked for the formation of an Islamic state, and was often the object of negative government action for his criticisms of their un-Islamic nature.

During his long career, he authored more than 100 books and pamphlets, the most important of which were translated into various Middle Eastern and European languages. Beginning in 1956 he traveled widely, which served to further his influence. Although many were quite critical of his ideas, he found pockets of support throughout the Muslim world. His influence was expanded through the effort of the Egyptian Muslim Brotherhood leader Sayyid Qutb. Qutb was changed through his reading of Mawdudi in 1951 on the heels of his sojourn in America. He had seen the problem of American culture and was inspired by Mawdudi's idea of Islam as a complete way of life. The ideas of al-Banna and Mawdudi came together for him in a revised program to turn Egypt into an Islamic state. He suggested that a revolutionary vanguard should take over the government and then slowly reimpose Islam on Egyptian society. His mature thought appeared in

The Grand Mosque, Paris, is the largest mosque in France. (J. Gordon Melton)

his 1965 book, *Milestones* (*Ma'alim fi al-tariq*), the ideas of which led directly to his execution the next year. His writings, however, survived, and they now stand beside Mawdudi's as the major literary expression of the first generation of Islamism. They have provided the platform on which the later, more violent groups have built, their ideas being cited to support programs that have included assassinations, guerrilla warfare, and widespread terrorist activity, and in the case of both the Islamic Nationalist Front (Sudan) and the Taliban, successful revolutions.

Crucial to the development of the Islamist position was the assassination of Egyptian President Anwar Sadat (1918–1981), a reaction to the Camp David Accords, by which Egypt recognized the state of Israel. A booklet was left at the site of his death, roughly translated as *The Neglected Duty*. Building on Qutb's idea, this pamphlet blamed the West for Islam's problems. Its content suggested that all of the citizens of those

Western countries that were attempting culturally to undermine Islamic society were guilty of attacking Islam, and hence were viable targets for death. This position spread among Islamist groups and has become basic to the terrorist program.

The opposition to the influx of Western political influence and culture, as well as to the leadership of secularized Muslims ruling countries apart from Islamic law, was strongest in Sunni countries, and prior to 1979 had its only major success in Saudi Arabia. However, Islamic revivalism also developed a presence in Shiite countries. In Persia, it appeared in the person of a young student, Navvab Safavi (1923–1956). He headed a secretive group known as the Devotees of Islam. The small group developed a program opposed to foreign influence in Persia (Iran) and is credited with the assassinations of government officials (including a prime minister and several intellectuals). In the mid-1950s the Devotees were suppressed and Safavi executed (1956). The thrust of the group, however, was not lost. It survived in the thoughts of the Ayatollah Khomeini (1902–1989), who as a relatively unknown cleric protested Safavi's being put to death. It then came to the forefront in the Iranian Revolution, as a result of which the secularized government of the shah was replaced by a new government that reunited clerical and political power in Iran and inspired a variety of Safavi groups in other countries with a significant Shiite presence.

In the 1980s and 1990s, the Islamist movement emerged in every Muslim country with more or less approval from the government's leaders. Among the more famous groups are Hizballah (the Party of God, also known as Islamic Jihad, Lebanon); Hamas (the Islamic Resistance Movement, Lebanon), an outgrowth of the Palestinian branch of the Muslim Brotherhood; the Islamic Salvation Front (Algeria); the National Islamic Front (Sudan); and al-Jama'a al Islamiiya (Egypt). The Russian incursion into Afghanistan occasioned the rise of a new group inspired by the Wahhabis, the Taliban, which emerged as the power in the land after the Russians were driven out. In 1995, Egyptian Sheikh Omar Abdel Rahman and nine other Islamists from various countries were convicted on charges related to the bombing of the World Trade Center in 1993. Out of the battle to overthrow the Russians, the Iraqi invasion

A 14th-century Turkish painting of angels, by Ahmet Musa, Topkapi Museum, Istanbul. The concepts of a final judgment and life in the hereafter were tenets of Islam from the beginning of Muhammad's teaching. The Koran describes heaven as a shaded garden with fountains, abundant food and drink, and beautiful maidens. (Instructional Resources Corporation)

of Kuwait, and the success of the coup in Sudan in 1989, Saudi Arabian Osama bin Laden (b. 1957) developed one of the most radical of Islamist groups, al-Qaeda, accused by Western political leaders of masterminding the attacks on the World Trade Center in New York City and the Pentagon in suburban Washington, D.C., on September 11, 2001. Bin Laden apparently was introduced to the spectrum of Islamist thought by Muhammad Qutb, the brother of Sayyid Qutb, and Abdullah Azzam (1941–1989), a Jordanian who worked with Hamas prior to taking a post at King Abdul Aziz University in Jeddah, Saudi Arabia. While sharing a common heritage in the earlier movements, each organization has been particularly involved in local issues and at times (especially after the events of September 11, 2001) often eager to identify with or distance itself from particular actions believed to have been taken by another group.

During the last quarter of the 20th century, the question of Palestinian rights, the leadership of Afghanistan, the Gulf War, and the interaction of the Middle East and Western countries over oil were but a few of the issues focusing the attention of the different Islamist groups. In this context the distinctions between a new religious movement, a political activist group, and even a terrorist group become quite blurred. In the wake of some of the horrendous events that have been ascribed to various groups, it is often forgotten and/or seen as irrelevant that the actions can be traced to religious motivations. Given the nature of the more positive central teachings of the major religions, the violence that has punctuated religious history can easily be ignored, No religion of any size or length of time on Earth has been able to separate itself completely from identifications with governments and the wars they have waged.

Following the attacks on the Pentagon and World Trade Center, the United States initiated a military operation in Afghanistan under a policy enunciated by President George W. Bush that it would treat governments that gave haven to terrorist groups the same as the groups. The stated aims of the operation were to find Osama bin Laden and those other al-Qaeda officials deemed directly responsible for the attacks on America, to destroy al-Qaeda as a viable organization, and to replace the Taliban rule in Afghanistan. Of the three objectives, the first two were not accomplished and the third only partially accomplished. Both al-Qaeda and the Taliban leadership retreated into the mountains along the Afghanistan-Pakistan border and have survived, the latter still in control of part of the country.

In 2003, claiming that Iraq possessed weapons of mass destruction and had supported al-Qaeda, the United States invaded the country with the goal of removing dictator Saddam Hussein (1937–2006). In this case, the regime was quickly toppled and Hussein eventually captured. A new government was installed and it executed Hussein in 2006. However, as in Afghanistan, the military operation proved unable to subdue the countryside and, as of 2009, operations continue.

In January 2009, Barack Obama assumed the presidency of the United States with a pledge of ending the war in Iraq as soon as possible and completing the war in Afghanistan. Meanwhile, since the beginning of the Afghanistan war, al-Qaeda has been active but has no spectacular success to report. Its leader has periodically issued statements, but they reflect on new theoretical developments. Groups allied to al-Qaeda also continue activities, and bombings and bombing attempts traced to Islamist groups have become an almost daily occurrence, most being suicide bombings. However, there has been the occasional spectacular event such as the 2004 bombing in Madrid and the 2009 hotel-takeover in Mumbai.

Since the end of the 1940s, the ideology of the Islamists has placed them in conflict with the authorities in a host of countries whose laws they have violated in pursuing their ends. While many Islamists have died in violent incidents, many have also landed in jail. In recent years, efforts to counter what are seen as extremist and anti-Muslim ideology, especially the justification of targeting innocent people even in the pursuit of a high ideal, have been stepped up, and Muslim clerics have made repeated efforts to convert Islamists to a more traditional Muslim position. The withdrawal of the belief that Allah condoned the killing of non-combatants who did not support the Islamist position would undermine the Islamist program.

J. Gordon Melton

See also: Islam; Jamaat-e-Islam, Muhammad; Muslim Brotherhood; Taliban; World Muslim Congress.

References

Bergen, Peter L. *Holy War, Inc.: Inside the Secret World of Osama bin Laden*. New York: Free Press, 2001.

Esposito, John, ed. *Voice of the Resurgent Islam*. New York: Oxford University Press, 1983.

Faridi, Fazlur Rahman. *Fundamentalism vis-a-vis Islamic Movement*. Delhi: Markazi Makatba Islami, 1994.

Gwynne, Rosalind. "Al-Qa'ida and al-Qur'an: The 'Tafsir' of Usamah bin Ladin." http://web.utk.edu/~warda/bin_ladin_and_quran.htm. Accessed June 15, 2009.

Hamud, Randall B., ed. *Osama Bin Laden: America's Enemy in His Own Words*. San Diego: Nadeem Publishing, 2005.

Jacquard, Roland. *In the Name of Osama Bin Laden: Global Terrorism and the Bin Laden Brotherhood*. Durham, NC: Duke University Press, 2002.

Jansen, Johannes J. *The Dual Nature of Islamic Fundamentalism*. Ithaca, NY: Cornell University Press, 1996.

Jansen, Johannes J. *The Neglected Duty: The Creed of Sadat's Assassins and Islamic Resurgence in the Middle East*. New York: Macmillan Company, 1986.

Juergenmeyer, Mark. *Terror in the Mind of God: The Global Rise of Religious Violence*. Berkeley: University of California Press, 2001.

Kramer, Martin. "Fundamentalist Islam at Large: The Drive for Power." *Middle East Quarterly* (June 1996). http://www.meforum.org/meq/june96/kramer.shtml. Accessed November 1, 2001.

Lia, Brtynjar. *The Society of Muslim Brothers in Egypt: The Rise of an Islamic Mass Movement, 1928–1942*. Reading, UK: Ithaca Press, 1998.

Mawdudi, Sayyid Abul al-Mawdudi. *A Short History of the Revivalist Movement in Islam*. Delhi: Markazi Maktaba Islami, 1972.

Melman, Yossi. "Is it possible to 'de-radicalize' terrorists?" *Haaretz.com* (May 21, 2009). http://www.haaretz.com/hasen/spages/1087126.html. Accessed June 15, 2009.

Milton-Edwards, Beverly. *Islamic Fundamentalism since 1945*. New York: Routledge, 2005.

Moussalli, Ahmad S. *Radical Islamic Fundamentalism: The Ideological and Political Discourse of Sayyid Qutb*. Syracuse, NY: University of Syracuse Press, 1994.

Qutb, Sayyid. *Milestones*. Beirut, Lebanon: Holy Koran Publishing House, 1978.

Rashid, Ahmed. *Taliban: Militant Islam, Oil and Fundamentalism in Central Asia*. New Haven, CT: Yale University Press, 2001.

Sivan, Emmanuel. *Radical Islam: Medieval Theology and Modern Politics*. New Haven, CT: Yale University Press, 1985.

Ushama, Thameem. *Hasan Al-Banna: Vision & Mission*. Kuala Lumpur: A. S. Noordeen, 1994.

■ Isle of Man

The Isle of Man, located in the Irish Sea northwest of the city of Liverpool, is a British Crown dependency, though officially not included in the United Kingdom. A mere 220 square miles, the island is home to 72,000 people, the majority of whom are Norse Gaelic. Many speak English, but a minority hang on to their dialect of Gaelic.

The island was inhabited during the first millennium BCE by Celts. Irish Catholic monks arrived on the island around year 400 of the Common Era and began the process of converting the population, a process that

St. Germain's Cathedral on the Isle of Man, England, ca. 1890s to early 1900s. (Historic Print & Map Company)

ISLE OF MAN

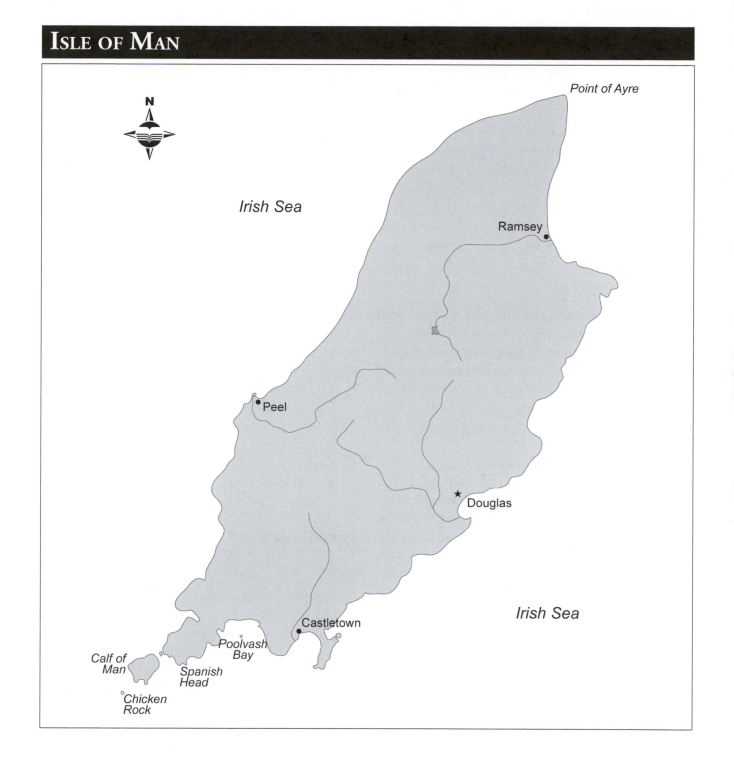

appears to have been completed over the next two centuries. The island was invaded by Vikings in the ninth century and annexed to Norway. The Vikings introduced a system of government, the Tynwalt, which remains the governing system to the present. The island remained a Norwegian possession until sold to Scotland in 1266. It came into British hands a century later.

The island existed as a semi-autonomous possession for the next 500 years, but in the 18th century it became a haven for smuggling to the point that the British acted and turned the Isle into a dependency. It still operates as a self-governing dependency of the United Kingdom, which is responsible for any foreign relations.

Isle of Man

Religion	Followers in 1970	Followers in 2010	% of Population	Annual % growth 2000–2010	Followers in 2025	Followers in 2050
Christians	52,800	65,800	83.8	0.25	63,100	54,700
Anglicans	28,000	34,300	43.7	−0.17	32,100	27,500
Protestants	10,800	9,600	12.2	0.09	9,300	8,500
Roman Catholics	5,000	7,400	9.4	0.72	8,000	8,500
Agnostics	3,800	10,500	13.4	1.14	12,000	14,000
Atheists	0	1,800	2.3	5.04	2,600	3,500
Hindus	0	170	0.2	0.49	200	300
Muslims	0	170	0.2	0.49	200	300
Jews	50	60	0.1	0.36	80	100
Total population	**56,600**	**78,500**	**100.0**	**0.46**	**78,200**	**72,900**

The Isle of Man remained Roman Catholic until the Reformation of the 16th century, when its churches were incorporated into the Church of England. The Diocese of Sodo and Man retains the religious allegiance of the largest percentage of the island's residents. It also has a special relationship with the state and retains its own canon law, which differs somewhat from the rest of the Anglican Church.

The Roman Catholic Church has revived on the Isle of Man, as it has in the rest of the United Kingdom after several centuries of repression following the Reformation. It is currently the second largest church on the island, the congregations being included within the Diocese of Liverpool.

John Wesley, the founder of Methodism, first visited the Isle of Man in 1777, and the Methodist Church (UK) remains the third largest faith on the island. It now competes, however, with a spectrum of more than 20 Protestant and Free Church denominations. With the exception of the United Reformed Church of the United Kingdom and the Baptist Union of Great Britain, whose work began in the 19th century, the remaining churches have relatively small memberships.

J. Gordon Melton

See also: Baptist Union of Great Britain; Church of England; Methodist Church; Roman Catholic Church; Wesley, John.

References

Ashley, A. *The Church in the Isle of Man.* London: St. Anthony's Press, 1958.

Barrett, David, ed. *The Encyclopedia of World Christianity.* 2nd ed. New York: Oxford University Press, 2001.

Moore, David W. *The Other British Isles: A History Of Shetland, Orkney, The Hebrides, Isle Of Man, Angelsey, Scilly, Isle Of Wight And The Channel Islands.* Jeffersonville, NC: McFarland & Company, 2005.

Randles, Jenny. *Supernatural Isle of Man.* London: Robert Hale, 2006.

Ismaili Islam

Following the death of Ja'far al-Sadiq (d. 765 CE), the imam around whom much of the Shiite Muslim community had gathered, a crisis of leadership emerged. The Shia community had invested authority in the physical family of the Prophet Muhammad (ca. 570–632) and in the descendants of his son-in-law, Ali ibn Abi Talib (d. 661). During the eighth century, that lineage had passed to the eldest sons in the family of Ali's son al-Husyan. However, the eldest son of al-Sadiq, designated the sixth imam, Ismail al-Mubarakhad (d. 760), died prior to his father. The main body of Shiites turned their attention to the younger brother, Musa al-Kazim (d. 796/797), and continued their leadership through his descendants.

One group of Shiites clung to Ismail as the seventh imam (ruling authority) of their community (hence their popular designation as Seveners), and chose his son Muhammad al-Matymum (d. 813) to lead them. Through Muhammad, a new line of caliphs developed. The movement spread through the next century and became particularly strong in North Africa. In 945, the Ismailis established control in Tunisia, from which they spread westward to the Atlantic. In 969 the Ismailis unseated the ruler of Egypt, and in 973 established their imam as the new caliph with his throne in the new city of Cairo. The Fatimid Empire (named after Fatimah, the daughter of Muhammad and wife of Ali) soon moved into the older territories controlled by the Sunni caliph now headquartered in Baghdad. Syria briefly fell under its control.

The Fatimid dynasty lasted for two centuries. Egypt prospered, and a relatively tolerant attitude toward other religions was evident. Among the Fatimids' cultural accomplishments was the founding of Al-Azhar University. The beginning of the end of the Fatimid dynasty came with the split of the Fatimid community into two factions in 1094. The ruler, Abu Tamim Ma'add al-Mustansir bi'llah (d. 1094), had intended that his son Abu Mansur Nizar (1045–1095) should become his successor. However, forces within the community that favored his younger brother Abu'l-Qasim Ahmad (1074–1101) declared him the new caliph. In the civil war that resulted, Nizar was defeated and subsequently executed; however, his line of succession was recognized by the important Ismaili community in Persia and Iraq. Ismailis in Syria, Yemen, and India recognized the lineage through Abu'l-Qasim Ahmad, known as al Mustali. They were later known as Mustali Ismailis.

The remaining Mustali Ismaili rulers of the Fatimid regime were beset with problems, including the Christian Crusades. Originally, the Fatimids had aligned with the Crusaders against their mutual enemy, the Abbasid caliph. However, in the 12th century, the Crusaders turned on the Fatimids and were able to inflict several defeats that left them in a greatly weakened condition. They were thus unable to withstand the onslaught of the Abbasid leader, Saladin the Magnificent (1138–1193), who took Cairo in 1171. They were also afflicted with internal dissension, which included several important splits over succession to the imamate.

One important faction of the Mustali Ismailis supported the cause of al-Tayyib, the infant son reportedly born to the assassinated Caliph al-Amir in 1130. An elder member of the family assumed the role of regent; the infant al-Tayyib was never seen, and his fate remains unknown. In the years after the fall of the Fatimid dynasty, most of the Ismaili factions were suppressed. However, the Ismaili leader in Yemen, Queen al-Sayyida, came to believe in the imamate of al-Tayyib. Because of her efforts, the followers of al-Tayyib alone survived among the several Mustali factions. Because her powers extended to Gujarat, this group also survived in India, where the Mustali Tayyib Ismailis became known as Bohras.

Meanwhile, the Ismailis who had favored Nizar came to believe that he was the reincarnation of Ismail returned to earth to rule. They also saw Nizar as the initiator of a new lineage of imams. Withdrawing from Egypt, his descendants moved to the new center of their support in Persia. A new headquarters arose at Alamut, a mountain outpost in northern Persia (Iran).

The Alamut era began one of the more infamous eras in Islamic history, as Nizari Ismaili leaders perpetuated their dream of continuing the Fatimid dynasty and ultimately replacing the Sunnite caliph in Baghdad. Alamut became a center of guerrilla warfare carried out through a network of Ismaili communities, now largely working underground, throughout the Abbasid-controlled lands. To undergird their new life, the Ismaili leadership proposed a doctrine of repudiation, the right to break the laws of Islam as a preparation for the arrival of al-Mahdi (the retuning seventh Imam), who would upon his appearance restore them. The Nizari offered followers wine and hashish and called for jihad (holy war) against the Sunni majority. From their use of hashish they became known as the Assassins—a word that later became attached to their practice of sending agents skilled in the arts of poisoning, killing, and disguise to murder targeted leaders. They were accredited with the murder of several caliphs.

The Assassins existed for the next two centuries as a cancer in the empire, operating from Alamut and other mountain fortresses in Syria and Palestine. The beginning of the end of the Assassins came with the fall of Alamut to the Mongols in 1256, though some of the Syrian fortresses held out until the 16th century, by which time the Ottoman Empire had arisen. Though no longer a military force, the Nizari Ismailis did not disappear. The lineage of imams continued, and in the

1830s the imam was given the title Aga Khan. The Alamut era also gave birth to several additional new variations on Shiite perspectives, most important, Alevism. The Alevis continue as a minority religious community in Turkey, Lebanon, and Syria. There are a number of separate Ismaili groups holding dissenting opinions on issues concerning the predicted al-Mahdi, though each is quite small, with membership numbering in the hundreds.

Very early in their history, the Ismailis began to engage in some mystical and even occult speculations. From their beginning with the seventh Shia imam, numerology began to play a role in their thought. Other events prompted the development of various secret rituals, some of which took on special importance when combined with speculation over the end of the age and the reappearance of al-Mahdi. These speculations, although done in the context of Orthodox Islam, on occasion challenged the tradition, especially when the Ismailis critiqued Muslim law.

Today, the great majority of Ismailis are Nizari associated with the Aga Khan, now operating through the His Highness Prince Aga Khan Shia Imani Ismaili Council, which in turn works through a variety of national and local branches around the world. The majority reside in India, though during the 20th century they became dispersed worldwide. During the late Alamut era, a number of missionaries were sent to India from Persia, and a thriving Ismaili community developed in Gujarat and the Sind (now part of Pakistan). When in 1840, the then Aga Khan was forced out of Persia, he settled among the larger concentration of his followers in India, where they are locally referred to as Khojas, a term of respect meaning "honorable person."

Those Ismailis who trace their lineage back to al-Tayyib and al-Mustali also survived primarily in western India, in the area around Mumbai (Bombay). Here they have split into several groups and are now dispersed around the world. The largest group is organized as the Shiah Fatimi Ismaili Tayyabi Dawoodi Bohra.

J. Gordon Melton

See also: Alevism; Ali ibn Abi Talib; Bohras; His Highness Prince Aga Khan Shia Imami Ismaili Council; Muhammad; Shia Islam; Shiah Fatimi Ismaili Tayyabi Dawoodi Bohra.

References

Corbin, Henry. *Cyclical Time and Ismaili Gnosis.* London: Kegan Paul International, 1983.

Daftary, Farhad. *A Short History of the Ismailis.* Princeton, NJ: Marcus Wiener Publishers, 1998.

Frischauer, Willi. *The Aga Khans.* New York: Hawthorn Publishers, 1971.

Jackson, Stanley. *The Aga Khan.* London: Odhams Press, 1952.

Lewis, Bernard. *The Assassins: A Radical Sect of Islam.* New York: Basic Books, 1968.

Nanji, A. *The Nizari Isma'ili Tradition in the Indo-Pakistani Subcontinent.* Delmar, NY: Caravan Books, 1978.

▪ Israel

The modern state of Israel is located on land with a rich religious history, much of which is recorded in the Hebrew Bible (the Christian Old Testament). That history includes a variety of Pagan faiths (whose presence dates to at least 7000 BCE) and preeminently Judaism. Much of this ancient history lies beyond the reach of this encyclopedia, which picks up the story with the entrance of Alexander the Great (356–323 BCE).

Over the centuries, the borders of the political entities that were Israel/Palestine changed with relative frequency as different invading forces found more or less success. The malleability of the borders has remained the case over the decades since the founding of the modern state of Israel in 1949. In 1967, Israel occupied land that had been designated by the United Nations for a Palestinian state. Since that time, the Gaza Strip and West Bank have been under variant levels of Israeli oversight, though there is widespread agreement that they will eventually become the core of an independent state.

As of 2008, Israel proper consists of 8,020 square miles of territory on the Mediterranean Sea. It is bounded on the south by Egypt, the north by Lebanon, and the east by Jordan and Syria. The West Bank consists of 2,263 square miles of territory sandwiched

Orthodox Jews pray at the Western Wall, Jerusalem, Israel. The sacred Jewish site is also known as the Wailing Wall and is considered both a monument to the destruction of the Second Jerusalem Temple in 70 CE and a national symbol of Israeli honor. (Corel)

between Israel and Jordan and north and west of the Dead Sea. The Gaza Strip includes some 139 square miles on the Mediterranean Sea immediately north of the Egyptian border. There are 11 million people (2008) in Israel and the Occupied Territories, of which 2.4 million reside in the West Bank and 1.5 in the Gaza Strip.

Israel was incorporated into Alexander's kingdom, and during the succeeding Ptolemaic Empire, Greek culture was imposed on the region. The predominantly Jewish residents revolted in 165 BCE under Judas Maccabaeus, and the land remained independent until overrun by Rome in 53 BCE. A revolt in 66 CE led to the destruction of Jerusalem (including the Jewish temple in 70 CE), and a later revolt in 131 led to Jews being forbidden to enter Jerusalem and the land being renamed Syria Palestina. The Roman occupation and suppression of independence movements led to widespread Jewish migration around the Mediterranean Basin and then throughout Europe.

Israel remained under Roman control, part of the Eastern Roman Empire, known after the fall of the empire in the West as the Byzantine Empire. The land was overrun by Muslim Arabs in the 630s and became a center of Islamic culture. It also became the focus of Christian Crusades during the Middle Ages, resulting in the periodic occupation of Jerusalem and portions of Palestine by European Christian forces. However,

the rise of the Ottoman Empire re-established Islamic hegemony until the empire's collapse in 1918, at the end of World War I.

Great Britain took control of Palestine in 1918. A year earlier, in the famous Balfour Declaration, the British government had promised the world's Jewish community a homeland in Palestine; however, little progress was made on that promise through the next decades. In the meantime, Jews flocked to the cause of Zionism, the crusade to establish a modern counterpart of the ancient Jewish state, and Zionist organizations assisted Jewish migration to Palestine. Then, following the Jewish Holocaust of World War II, many survivors found their way to Palestine, and in 1948 they declared the formation of Israel. Those countries that had been victorious in the war gave more or less tacit approval to the new country. The creation of Israel caused the displacement of many Palestinians (mostly Muslims) and has led to more than a half century of conflict between Israel and its neighbors (all predominantly Muslim), a conflict that shows little sign of any final resolution.

Israel's original borders were enlarged in the war that followed immediately upon its formation and the Six-Day War (1967). Land taken from Egypt in 1967 was returned as part of the Camp David Accords (1977). The Accords vividly manifested the complicated support system that maintains Israel, which has continued to receive significant financial and military resources from the United States. That support is, in turn, maintained by a coalition of Jewish and conservative Protestant Christian organizations. In the meantime, the liberal Protestant community has tended to support the cause of the Palestinians and their demands for some justice in the light of their claims to Palestine as their homeland.

As the new century begins, Israel is the home to one of the most diverse religious communities in the world. The ancient site of the emergence of Judaism, Israel has had a continuous Jewish presence throughout history, though the size of that community has varied considerably from century to century. As Jews dispersed around the world, numerous variations of Jewish religious life developed, and many who were ethnically Jews secularized and developed a nonreligious ideology.

In 1950, the Israeli government passed what was referred to as the "Law of Return." It gave every Jew in the world the right to migrate to Israel and settle there. As a result, as the new century begins, approximately 75 percent of the population are Jews. By 1995, 53 percent of the Jewish population had been born in Israel, 42 percent were first-generation immigrants from Europe or the Americas, and 5 percent came from Africa and Asia. The government includes a Ministry of Religion assigned to deal with the needs and problems of the Jewish community. It is active through a number of local councils and committees that operate in towns across the country. Religious matters are also referred to the Chief Rabbinate of Israel, consisting of two chief rabbis, one Ashkenazi (of European heritage) and one Sephardic (of Spanish/Portuguese heritage).

The Jewish community is divided both ethnically and theologically. The primary division is between those Jews who had a background on the Iberian Peninsula (where Jewish life flourished in the Middle Ages, prior to the expulsion of the Jews at the end of the 15th century), and those from Northern and Eastern Europe (including Germany, Poland, and Russia). However, Jews from India (Bene Israel), Ethiopia (Beta Israel), and Yemen have significantly extended the definition of who are Jews for purposes of the Law of Return. The refinement of that definition has been assisted by the denial to African American converts to Judaism and Jewish converts to Christianity from North America and Europe the rights and privileges under the Law of Return.

During the 19th and 20th centuries, Jews in Europe and North America divided first into Orthodox and Reform factions, each with their own rabbinical and congregational organizations, and then developed a spectrum of communities divided by differences over theology and adherence to traditional Jewish religious practices related to dress codes, the consumption of kosher food, the role of women, and activity on the Sabbath. Large communities that adhered to a Conservative Judaism (between the Orthodox and Reform perspective) and a Reconstructionist Judaism (that developed from the Conservative perspective) also emerged. On the far ends of the spectrum are ultra-Orthodox groups and several secularized groups rep-resented by the International Federation of Secular Humanistic Jews.

The mystical and esoteric tendency within the Jewish community came together in the modern world in Hasidism, which spread especially through Eastern Europe in the 18th and 19th centuries. Though severely weakened by the Holocaust, Hasidism has survived in a spectrum of older groups (the largest being the Lubavitch movement) and several newer neo-Hasidic groups such as the Kabbalah Learning Centre, founded in Palestine in 1922.

Orthodox Judaism is the only form of Judaism recognized in Israel. In 1948, the government recognized the Chief Rabbinate as the ruling authority for Judaism. Among the powers assigned to the Chief Rabbinate are matters concerning Jewish marriage, divorce, and burial; decisions concerning the status of any immigrants whose Jewish identity is questioned; and designation of restaurants as kosher. Reform Judaism as the "Movement for Progressive Judaism" and Conservative (or Masorti) Judaism have secular corporate status but have not been recognized by the Chief Rabbinate. There are no provisions in Israeli law for secular marriage or divorce; both non-Orthodox religious Jews and secular Jews continually confront the authority of Orthodox Jewish leadership.

Christianity was born in Israel, developing from the ministry of a Jewish teacher, Jesus bar Joseph, a Nazarite executed by Roman authorities around 30 CE. The early Christian community was centered on Jerusalem, and it was at the famous Council of Jerusalem (Acts 15) that the decision to redirect Christianity toward the non-Jewish world was made. Following the acceptance of Christianity by the Roman Empire, and especially with the rise of Byzantium as the new capital of the empire, Constantinople, Palestine was dominated by Christianity. This hegemony ended with the rise of Islam as the great power in the eastern Mediterranean in the seventh century. Although Islam came to dominate the religious community, Christianity remained alive as, like Judaism, a tolerated religion of the book, and a Christian presence continued through the centuries. Christianity briefly returned to power during the Crusades but has remained a minority since the rise of the Ottoman Empire in the 16th century.

ISRAEL

Today, the entire spectrum of Christianity has appeared in Israel, with many Christian groups supporting at least a token presence in what is considered the Christian Holy Land. Traditionally, the land has been the territory of the Greek Orthodox Patriarchate of Jerusalem, which has an honored place as the oldest Christian community in the area. In 451, at the Council of Chalcedon, Jerusalem was formally recognized as one of the four major Orthodox patriarchates. The Roman Catholic Church entered Palestine at the time of the Crusades and is now represented by bishops over both Latin-rite and Eastern-rite dioceses. Roman Ca-

tholicism has replaced Eastern Orthodoxy as the largest Christian community in Israel. The Church of England launched a mission in the Eastern Mediterranean in the 19th century, which has resulted in the present Episcopal Church in Jerusalem and the Middle East.

Protestantism began to develop a life in Palestine in 1839 with the entrance of representatives of the Church of Scotland. Lutherans and Anglicans began a cooperative work in the 1840s, and the Free Church of Scotland came in 1885. The older Scottish work continues today as the St. Andrew's Scots Memorial Church in Jerusalem. Through the 20th century, a number of American and British groups began work, especially after the foundation of the state of Israel. Many conservative evangelical and Pentecostal Christians have seen the emergence of Israel as a prophetic event indicating the beginning of the end-time events described in the book of Revelation in the Christian Bible. The spread of different prophecies regarding the nature of those events have led different groups to launch missionary activities directed toward the Jews both in Israel and elsewhere, and/or to develop a presence in Jerusalem to await the end time, which will include the Second Coming of Jesus.

Although the great majority of Christians in Israel are Palestinians or expatriates, among them is a late-20th-century movement, Messianic Judaism, built around Jewish converts to Christianity who wish to retain their Jewish culture and who emphasize the Jewish element in Christianity (which adopted the Jewish scriptures as part of its Bible). Messianic Jews meet in synagogues (rather than churches) and have been especially condemned by the rest of the Jewish community as dishonest and subversive. Messianic Jews have been denied citizenship in Israel under the Law of Return.

Islam emerged suddenly in the seventh century and spread quickly from its point of origin in Arabia. An Arab army conquered Palestine in the 630s, and Muslims were the dominant religious force in the area until 1948. Most Muslims are Sunnis of the Hanafite School, though some Shafaiites and Hanbalites are also present. Since the rise of the state of Israel, a variety of groups who follow a conservative form of Islam

Israel

Religion	Followers in 1970	Followers in 2010	% of Population	Annual % growth 2000–2010	Followers in 2025	Followers in 2050
Jews	2,475,000	5,295,000	72.8	1.93	6,268,000	7,512,000
Muslims	322,000	1,395,000	19.2	2.02	1,640,000	1,970,000
Agnostics	20,000	315,000	4.3	1.92	500,000	650,000
Christians	79,000	162,000	2.2	1.03	159,000	159,000
Roman Catholics	47,100	120,000	1.7	2.27	130,000	130,000
Orthodox	18,400	40,000	0.6	−1.99	35,000	30,000
Independents	2,900	21,000	0.3	0.97	25,000	30,000
Atheists	1,000	36,700	0.5	1.91	50,000	65,000
Buddhists	0	27,500	0.4	1.92	40,000	70,000
Chinese folk	0	27,000	0.4	1.92	42,000	65,000
Baha'is	400	12,000	0.2	1.95	20,000	30,000
New religionists	950	1,900	0.0	1.93	2,500	4,000
Hindus	0	300	0.0	1.98	1,000	2,000
Total population	**2,898,000**	**7,272,000**	**100.0**	**1.92**	**8,722,000**	**10,527,000**

(Wahhabi) and/or identify with the political struggle of Palestinians have emerged.

The larger Muslim community in Israel is directed by a number of religious councils. Disputes are sent to one of four religious courts, which are assisted by a court of appeals in Jerusalem. Islam is recognized by the state, and most imams are paid out of the state treasury. This status continues a practice still in effect under Islamic rule, in which a spectrum of Jewish and Christian communities were recognized by the state, assigned responsibility for marriage and burial, and supported financially by the state. One implication of this system is that marriages by unrecognized groups are not recognized by the state.

Although Jews and Muslims lived together for many centuries in relative peace, since the formation of the state of Israel, tension has existed between the Jewish authorities and especially those Muslims in Israel (some 12 percent of the population) who have been displaced from their traditional home by the developing state.

Besides the main bodies of Judaism, Islam, and Christianity, there is a spectrum of distinctive groups that have a lengthy history in the region and a relation with one or more of the larger groups. Included are the Druze (which emerged out of Islam in the 11th century); the Baha'i Faith (which emerged out of Shia Islam in Iran but now has its international headquarters

in Haifa, Israel); the Kairites (a Babylonian Jewish group); and the Samaritans (a Jewish group that resulted from the intermarriage of Jews and Assyrians in the eighth century BCE). The latter, now a small group of only a few hundred, have become internationally known because of the story of the Good Samaritan included in the Christian New Testament (Luke 10:30–37).

A variety of new religions have arisen in Israel. Among the first of the new youth-oriented religions to manifest were the International Society for Krishna Consciousness and the Transcendental Meditation movement. In the 1980s, an anti-cult movement developed and targeted any groups that it saw as tending to alienate young adults from Orthodox Judaism. It has been especially concerned with Messianic Judaism and other Christian groups that have a history of targeting Jews for conversion. Given the symbolic power of Jerusalem and other holy sites in Israel, a great deal of concern arose at the end of 1999 over possible violent reactions from both Jewish and Christian movements to the end of the century, though no such violence manifested.

Israel, while favoring Orthodox Judaism, and offering special recognition and support to a small number of the larger religious communities, also proclaims religious freedom. That policy has allowed the pluralism so evident in the urban centers. Most Christian groups, especially the Protestant groups, are not recognized, and the registration of marriages performed by Protestant ministers remains a problem. Many Protestant groups are members of the United Christian Council in Israel and are working for some level of recognition for their members. The Council is affiliated with the World Council of Churches. Most of the older Catholic and Orthodox groups are members of the Middle East Council of Churches, which is also affiliated with the World Council.

Government policy has, in the main, been directed toward the larger communities, and to that end a Department of Muslim Affairs and a Department of Christian Affairs are included within the Ministry of Religions. Much of the energy of the ministry is spent, not so much in supporting Muslim and Christian religious activity, as in isolating non-Jewish religious groups from young Israelis who might be tempted to reject Judaism. A variety of organizations are dedicated to interfaith dialogue, both in an effort to improve relationships between the different religions and to apply religious insights to Israel's ongoing problems.

J. Gordon Melton

See also: Baha'i Faith; Bene Israel; Beta Israel; Church of England; Church of Scotland; Conservative Judaism; Druze; Eastern Orthodoxy; Episcopal Church in Jerusalem and the Middle East; Greek Orthodox Patriarchate of Jerusalem; Hanafite School of Islam; Hanbalite School of Islam; Hasidism; International Federation of Secular Humanistic Jews; International Society for Krishna Consciousness; Judaism; Kabbalah Learning Centre; Karaites; Lubavitch Hasidism; Messianic Judaism; Middle East Council of Churches; Orthodox Judaism; Reconstructionist Judaism; Reform Judaism; Roman Catholic Church; Shafiite School of Islam; Wahhabi Islam; World Council of Churches.

References

Aviad, J. *Return to Judaism: Religious Renewal in Israel.* Chicago: University of Chicago Press, 1983.

Colbi, S. P. *A History of Christian Presence in the Holy Land.* Lanham, MD: University Press of America, 1988.

Idinopoulos, T. A. *Jerusalem Blessed, Jerusalem Cursed: Jews, Christians, and Muslims in the Holy City from David's Time to Our Own.* Chicago: Ivan R. Dee, 1991.

Israeli, R. *Muslim Fundamentalism in Israel.* London: Brassey's, 1993.

Mazie, Steven V. *Israel's Higher Law: Religion and Liberal Democracy in the Jewish State.* New York: Lexington Books, 2006.

Peled, Alisa Rubin. *Debating Islam in the Jewish State: The Development of Policy Toward Islamic Institutions in Israel.* Albany: State University of New York Press, 2001.

Rebiai, Marcel. *Islam, Israel, and the Church.* Fort Mill, SC: Morningstar Publications, 2007.

Shahak, Israel, and Norton Mezvinsky. *Jewish Fundamentalism in Israel.* London: Pluto Press, 2004.

Wigoder, G. *New Encyclopedia of Zionism and Israel.* London: Associated University Presses, 1994.

Istanbul

Istanbul is the Turkish name for Constantinople, the former capital of the Byzantine Empire that fell to the Muslims in 1453. It remains the center of Eastern Orthodoxy and there are many churches still in the city, but they are vastly outnumbered now by mosques, some of which are actually in or on former churches. The city became the capital of the Ottoman Empire, and from here a huge territory was ruled, and its ruler was the official caliph of the Sunni Islamic world. Some remarkable architects such as Sinan worked in the city and an extraordinary number and variety of beautiful mosques, some of a monumental scale, were constructed. A number of synagogues also exist for the small local Jewish population.

Istanbul was a significant Christian city, the capital of the Eastern Roman Empire under Constantine I and later emperors, and the place of three church council meetings to settle doctrine in 381, 553, and 680–681. Kadıköy (Chalcedon) was the host of a council in 451 and is in the wider Istanbul area today. About 500 churches existed in the city in the Middle Ages while it was the Byzantine capital, some transformed into mosques after the Muslim conquest. Many survive, however, and there are Byzantine, Greek Orthodox,

The Sultan Ahmet Mosque in Istanbul. (Corel)

Armenian, Syrian Orthodox, Catholic, and Protestant churches in the city today. Most important, the Ecumenical Patriarchate, the spiritual center of the Orthodox Church, is located in the city.

In the old city the most famous churches include Hagia Sophia (now a museum), Hagia Eirene and the Church of Saint Sergios and Bacchus (Küçük Aya Sofya), the Rose Mosque (Theodosia Church), and by the Golden Horn the Surp Hreşdagabet Church and the Zeyrek Mosque (Pantokrator Monastery Church). Across the Golden Horn is the Church of England Crimean Memorial Church (Christ Church) and the Virgin Mary Syrian Orthodox Kadim Church along İstiklal Caddesi. Farther north are the Asdvadzadzin Church in Beşiktaş, Fokas Church in Ortaköy and Surp Haç Armenian Church in Kuruçeşme. On the Asian side of the city are the Nigoğayos Church in Beykoz, and the Eufemia and Takavor churches in Kadıköy. Even the Princes' Islands contain churches. The building of churches in Istanbul did not cease with the Muslim conquest of Fatih Sultan Mehmet. Many of the churches of Beyoğlu, Şişli, and the Asian side of the city date from after the 16th century. Like all of Istanbul's buildings, its churches frequently suffered from earthquake and fire. The periodic hostilities between the Muslim majority and the Christian minorities in the 20th century often led to attacks on churches and the expulsion of Christians.

There are several synagogues in Istanbul, ranging from Neve Shalom, quite recently built and with a magnificent chandelier, and other synagogues built for distinct Jewish communities, some like Ahrida being quite old. Recent terrorist attacks on Istanbul synagogues have restricted access to them.

Accounts of Istanbul invariably refer to its multicultural status, but in fact today the city is overwhelmingly Muslim, and in the 20th century waves of persecution against its Christian, in particular Greek and Armenian, communities thoroughly reduced the size of non-Muslims in Istanbul. Many of the buildings remain, however, so there is certainly in architectural terms some religious variety. The capturing of the Byzantine Empire resulted in a huge amount of mosque and *madrasa* building in Istanbul, and the Ottoman Empire had the services of a brilliant architect, Sinan, who is responsible for some of the most remarkable structures, including the Şezade, Selimiye, Suleymaniye, Rüstem Paşa, and many more, which often include far more than just mosques, but associated buildings such as hospitals, tombs, schools, domestic sections, and so on, all employing Sinan's skill at combining simplicity of form and ornamentation in what often turn out to be huge structures. Since the 16th century mosque building has continued to flourish in Istanbul, and there has been some considerable variation in style. The rapid expansion of the city into the suburbs and countryside, and the growing religiosity of Turkey has led to a steady building program of Islamic structures all through the city.

One of the most impressive mosques is the Sultan Ahmet mosque in the heart of the city, with six unusually slim minarets rather than two or four; it is sometimes called the Blue mosque because of the blue tile work on its exterior. Slightly outside the city is the first mosque built after the taking of the city, the mosque of Eyüp, the standard bearer of the Prophet Muhammad, who is supposed to have died at that spot in an assault on the city.

The Fatih mosque commemorates Fatih Sultan Mehmet, the conqueror of Istanbul and is the site of his mausoleum, and also has a hospital, library, school, and baths, and covers a considerable amount of space. Like several mosques in Istanbul, it is built on the remains of a church. The Beyazit Mosque also comprises of a wide range of buildings along with the mosque itself, but possesses little of the coherence of the Fatih mosque complex.

The 17th-century Yeni Cami, or new mosque, is in Eminönü and has a very impressive tiled interior, while the 19th-century Ortakoy Mosque is in the baroque style, and has elaborate interiors.

Another baroque mosque is the Dolmabahçe, in the palace of the same name, and this contains a wide assortment of styles, and was designed like many of the big mosques—to impress. Here the royal family could pray and receive visitors, and its dramatic position on the Bosphorus makes it a very theatrical building. One of the most melancholy mosques is the Zeyrek Mosque. It was called the Pantocrator in the 12th century, a complex of three churches, in which the royal family was buried, and after the Ottoman conquest in 1453 the buildings became first a madrasa and then a mosque. It is in poor condition and brings to the fore the issue of how to renovate so many old and crumbling religious buildings.

Oliver Leaman

See also: Church of England; Constantine the Great; Ecumenical Patriarchate/Patriarchate of Constantinople; Hagia Sophia; Mosques; Synagogues.

References

Freely, John. *Istanbul: The Imperial City.* New York: Penguin, 1998.

Gül, Murat. *The Emergence of Modern Istanbul.* London: I. B. Tauris, 2009.

Necipoğlu, Gulru. *The Age of Sinan: Architectural Culture in the Ottoman Empire.* London: Reaktion Books, 2005.

Italian Assemblies of God

The Italian Assemblies of God (Assemblee di Dio in Italia [ADI]) is the largest Pentecostal body in Italy, and Italy's third largest organized religious group after the Roman Catholic Church and the Jehovah's Witnesses. The denomination adopted its name in 1947, when the majority of Italian Pentecostal Churches (most of them established after World War I by immigrants returning from the United States) entered into a treaty with the Assemblies of God (based in the United States). ADI, however, is an independent institution, with its own Italian peculiarities; it did not originate

from missionaries sent by the Assemblies of God missions, but from separate Italian American Pentecostal congregations established in America at the beginning of the 20th century, which developed their own independent missions in Italy. Thus, the Italian Assemblies of God cannot be regarded as simply a branch of the U.S. Assemblies of God.

Italian Pentecostals suffered severe persecution under the Fascist regime in the late 1930s and early 1940s. In December 1945, Swiss pastor Hermann Parli (1916–1998) was dispatched to Italy by the Assemblies of God in Great Britain to check how much had survived of Italian Pentecostalism. Through him, contacts with the Assemblies of God in the United States were also established. ADI was formally established on May 22, 1948, with Umberto Gorietti (1904–1982) as the first president and Roberto Bracco (1915–1983) as first secretary. By 1955, member churches had already exceeded 300, with more than 20,000 members (although a part of Italian Pentecostalism resisted institutionalization and, to this date, remains independent of the ADI).

In 1951, the U.S. Assemblies of God sent pastor Antonio Piraino (1915–1992) to Italy in order to help the ADI to expand. ADI also maintained relationships with the Christian Church in North America, an independent Italian American Pentecostal body connected with the origins of Italian Pentecostalism, which in turn sent to Italy pastor Antonio di Biase (1897–1974). With the help of these American churches, ADI was able to establish its own academic institution in 1954, the Istituto Biblico Italiano, under the leadership of Vincenzo Burchieri (1893–1962), sustained by an Italian Christian Educational Foundation. In 1956, ADI launched a Christian radio channel and opened the Orfanotrofio Betania, an orphanage founded by Eliana Rustici (1912–1966); it was the first of several charitable institutions. On December 5, 1959, ADI was officially recognized by the Italian government, and in 1960 financial help from America was discontinued. In 1976, ADI entered into a "spiritual affiliation" agreement with both the Christian Church in North America and its European counterpart, the Italian Christian Churches in North Europe, in order to emphasize that its relationship with the Assemblies of God was not an exclusive one. In 1983, the Missione Evangelica

Zigana (Gypsy Evangelical Mission), with some 700 Italian Gypsy members, merged within the ADI. In 2006 several churches of the Bari region separated themselves from the ADI over a dispute on the financial autonomy of local churches and established the independent Chiesa Cristiana Evangelica Assemblee di Dio with a Web site www.assembleedidio.it (while ADI's site is at www.assembleedidio.org). Both the name and the domain name of the newly established splinter group are the subject matter of a legal challenge by ADI, which remains unresolved at the time of this writing.

In 1986, ADI president Francesco Toppi entered into a Concordat with the Italian government, thus enabling inter alia ADI to receive its share of the national religious tax. Member churches currently number more than 1,000, with some 140,000 members. ADI publishes three official periodicals and supports several local radio stations. ADI emphasizes the need for a solid, conservative biblical formation for its pastors, and criticizes the Charismatic churches of second-generation Italian Pentecostalism for putting experience over theological formation and doctrine. In that same light, ADI pastors do not participate in the ecumenical enterprises some of those churches have promoted with non-Pentecostal Protestants and with the Roman Catholic Charismatic Renewal movement.

Assemblee di Dio in Italia
Via dei Bruzzi 11
00185 Rome
Italy
http://www.assembleedidio.org
        Massimo Introvigne and PierLuigi Zoccatelli

See also: Assemblies of God; Jehovah's Witnesses; Pentecostalism; Roman Catholic Church.

References

Stretti, Eugenio. *Il movimento pentecostale. Le Assemblee di Dio in Italia.* Turin: Claudiana, 1998.

Toppi F. *E mi sarete testimoni. Il Movimento Pentecostale e le Assemblee di Dio in Italia.* Rome: ADI Media, 1999.

Womack, David A., and Francesco Toppi. *Le radici del Movimento pentecostale in Italia.* Rome: ADI Media, 1989.

Italo-Albanian Catholic Church

The Italo-Albanian Catholic Church (aka the Italo Greek Catholic Church) is a small body in full communion with the Roman Catholic Church that exists among people of Greek heritage in southern Italy and Sicily. Christianity in this area developed using the Greek language and following the customs of the Eastern Church rather than the Latin Church, even though it was included in the area under the developing authority of the bishop of Rome. Through the centuries the process of Latinization began, but before it was completed, in the eighth century, the region was shifted from the jurisdiction of Rome to that of Greek Byzantium. Subsequently, a revival of Greek Christianity ensued. In the 11th century, the region was conquered by the Normans. Though returned to the Roman jurisdiction, the Byzantine church was strongly entrenched, and it was only slowly re-Latinized.

The progress that seemed to be leading to the eventual disappearance of the Byzantine rite in southern Italy was reversed in the 1400s when a number of Albanians moved into the area. Those from southern Albania followed the Byzantine rite. Their persistence was rewarded in 1595 when a bishop was appointed for them. Although it remained relatively small and even continued to decline, the Vatican looked with favor on the community and began a slow process of recognition of the group; eventually, in the 19th century, it was given full recognition within the church. In 1732 a seminary was founded in Calabria, and a second opened two years later in Palermo.

Today there are two dioceses serving the church, the Diocese of Lungro, erected in 1919, and the Diocese of Piana degli Albanesi, created in 1937. A third bishop resides at the monastery of Santa Maria de Grottaferrata and serves as its abbot. The monastery was founded in the 11th century and is the oldest structure representative of the continuing Greek tradition in Italy. There is one parish in the United States, the Italian Byzantine Rite Catholic Mission of Our Lady of Grace on Staten Island, New York.

The Italo-Albanian Catholic Church may be contacted through the bishop of Lungro, Vescovado, Corso Skanderberg 54, 87010 Lungro, Italy, or the bishop of Piana degli Albanesi, Piazza S. Nicola 1, 90037 Piana degli Albanesi (Palermo), Italy. In 2009, there were some 64,000 members.

Italian Byzantine Rite Catholic Mission of Our Lady
    of Grace
51 Redgrave Avenue
Staten Island
NY 10306-3620
http://www.byzantines.net/OurLadyofGrace/index
    .htm

J. Gordon Melton

See also: Roman Catholic Church.

Reference

Roberson, Ronald G. *The Eastern Christian Churches—A Brief Survey.* 5th ed. Rome: Edizioni Orientalia Christiana, Pontificio Istituto Orientale, 1995.

■ Italy

Located in Southern Europe and one of the original founding members of the European Union, Italy, whose capital city is Rome, has a population of 59.6 million according to the last census (2008).

Italy, as a political entity, only came into existence in 1861, when the "artichoke policy" pursued by the Kingdom of Sardinia, which had successively conquered all the Italian *staterelli* (small states), led ultimately to the establishment of the Kingdom of Italy, with Turin as its first capital. The capital was moved to Florence in 1866, and in 1870 to Rome, after Italian troops had entered the holy city (which had previously been the capital of an independent state ruled by the pope). Within the territory of the Kingdom of Italy, Roman Catholics constituted a large majority (although hypotheses about the percentage of religious practice vary), with Jews forming the largest minority and Protestants confined to the Waldensian valleys in Piedmont.

The Roman Catholic Church had been largely hostile to the unification of Italy, achieved by the Kingdom of Sardinia ruled by an anticlerical elite, and became even more hostile after the seizure of Rome in 1870. Popes not only routinely excommunicated kings of

Italy, but also prevented Italian Catholics, under threat of excommunication, from participating in political life either as candidates or voters, under the *non expedit* (Latin: it is not appropriate) policy. As a consequence, Italy became a strange democracy in which the papal veto, together with limitations connected with wealth and the exclusion of women, encouraged fewer than 3 percent of Italian adults to vote in most elections. Only in the period immediately preceding World War I were some limited exceptions to the *non expedit* policy allowed.

In the meantime, Protestants (both Italian Waldensians and all sorts of missionaries from the United States and United Kingdom) saw themselves as obvious supporters of the kingdom's ruling elite and tried to capitalize on Catholic hostility to the unification in order to establish themselves as the natural allies of the newly established government. Quarrels between the various Protestant denominations prevented the establishment of a national Protestant church, however, and political sympathies did not easily translate into religious conversions, although various Protestant groups (Waldensian Church, Evangelical Baptist Union of Italy, Evangelical Methodist Church of Italy, Christian Brethren, and different independents, followed later by the Churches of Christ and the Salvation Army) were established in all Italian regions, including in the South, where the only Protestant presence had been virtually wiped out in the 16th and the 17th centuries.

In 1922 Benito Mussolini (1883–1945) seized power, having staged a successful coup (the so-called March to Rome), thereby leaving him free to establish his Fascist regime. Although Mussolini was originally an anticlerical freethinker, he later declared himself a Roman Catholic and tried to ingratiate himself with the Roman Catholic Church. Within the framework of this policy, he entered, on February 11, 1929, into a Concordat with the Holy See. The Italian state officially recognized the tiny independent "State of the Vatican" ruled by the pope and granted a number of privileges to the Catholic Church, including state salaries for parish priests and the teaching of the Catholic religion, controlled by local bishops, in public schools. After 1929, the initial Fascist tolerance of religious minorities turned into discrimination and persecution, particularly of those groups recently established

The Chapel of the Holy Shroud, Turin, Italy. (J. Gordon Melton)

by immigrants who had converted in the United States and returned to Italy (Pentecostals, Seventh-day Adventists, Jehovah's Witnesses).

After World War II, Italy became a democracy and a republic, with a new Constitution theoretically guaranteeing full religious liberty to all. Fascist laws that discriminated against most minorities, however, took time to dismantle. Restrictions governing Pentecostals, for instance, were abrogated only in 1955. The Constitutional Court played a pivotal role, however, and by the 1960s most restrictions had been abolished. This allowed several dozen denominations to establish themselves in Italy, some of them continuing a presence started in the early 20th century. Only two groups, however, were really successful: Jehovah's Witnesses, which firmly established themselves as the second larg-

est religion among Italian citizens, and the Pentecostal movement, a good half of which had been unified between 1947 and 1948 into the Italian Assemblies of God. Today among the current 409,000 Italian Protestants, only 60,000 belong to "historical" churches (such as Lutheran, Reformed, Waldensian, Methodist, Baptist), while the majority attends Pentecostal and other "non-historical" evangelical churches.

The 1980s saw dramatic changes in the Italian religious scene, with Prime Minister Bettino Craxi (1934–2000) in 1984 renegotiating the Concordat with the Roman Catholic Church. It was formally declared that Roman Catholicism was no longer Italy's official religion (a largely symbolic move, since for all practical purposes this was already the case, thanks to a number of Constitutional Court decisions), and the church financing system was restructured. The salary paid by the state to parish priests was thus replaced by a national cultural and religious tax. Taxpayers were invited to specify, by indicating it on their tax return forms, their option for a participating church or state charity. (Later, national corruption scandals resulted in the state charity being selected by a very small number of taxpayers, thus in practice largely making the tax a purely religious one.)

The uniqueness of the Italian system (compared, for example, with Germany) is that there is no way for taxpayers to escape the payment of the religious tax (0.8 percent of their total taxes). Should a taxpayer fail to mark any of the options given, then 0.8 percent of his or her total taxes is divided among the participating churches in proportion to the national percentage attributed to each church, based on those who actually marked a particular option. Let's say, for instance, that the Lutheran Church has been selected in a given year by 2 percent of those who have marked one of the options; this means that the Lutheran Church will also receive a corresponding 2 percent percentage of the total amount of the religious tax paid by those taxpayers who have not marked any option.

The new system allowed the implementation of the Constitutional provision calling for Concordats (known as *Intese*, with the name *Concordato* being exclusively reserved for the treaty with the Holy See) to be signed between the government and religious bodies other than the Roman Catholic Church. As a result, new Concordats have been entered into with the Waldensian and Methodist churches (1984), the Seventh-day Adventist Church (1988), the Italian Assemblies of God (1988), the Union of Italian Jewish Communities (1989), the Italian Lutheran Church (1995), and the Italian Baptist Union (1995). Adventists and Assemblies of God Pentecostals, however, have elected to receive only the money of those taxpayers who, on their tax forms, opt explicitly for them, thus waiving their rightful participation in the division of the taxes paid by those who fail to mark a specific option. Baptists have so far elected not to receive any part of their share of the religious tax.

In 1999, the then prime minister Massimo D'Alema signed Concordats with the Italian Buddhist Union and the Jehovah's Witnesses. In 2007, D'Alema's suc-cessor Silvio Berlusconi signed new Concordats with the Greek Orthodox Church, the Church of Jesus Christ of Latter-day Saints, and the Italian Hindu Union (which includes a number of "traditionalist" Hindu temples and organizations. In order to become effective, however, such Concordats have to be ratified by Parliament, and this has not yet occurred at the date of this writing. In the meantime, in 1998, the government opened negotiations with the Greek Orthodox Church, the Church of Jesus Christ of Latter-day Saints, and the Alliance of Evangelical Christian Churches in Italy (which includes a number of Evangelical Pentecostal and non-Pentecostal churches), and in 2001 with Soka Gakkai International (the largest Italian Buddhist body that is not a member of the Italian Buddhist Union) and the Italian Hindu Union (which includes a number of "traditionalist" Hindu temples and organizations).

The Italian system has proved remarkably effective in assuring religious harmony and in preventing national religious controversies in Italy. Tax exemption and freedom to operate are largely granted to all sorts of religious bodies, unlike in France and Germany; for example, the founding fathers of the Italian Republic explicitly repudiated any attempt to limit religious liberty in the name of "public order" (as Fascism had) or allegiance to the Constitution, thereby granting full freedom of operation and proselytization to groups whose values are different from those shared by the Italian majority. More than 100 religious groups also enjoy official government recognition and are granted additional advantages (while tax exemption and freedom of proselytization do not require statutory recognition).

The eight churches that have, so far, entered into Concordats with the Italian government constitute an elite group of religious bodies whose national relevance is thus explicitly recognized. No church or religion is "entitled," by right, to a Concordat; entering into it is a purely political decision, fully discretionary, and requiring the approval of both government and parliament. Groups without a Concordat, however, are deprived neither of basic liberties and tax exemption, nor of "recognition"; they are simply not (or not yet) officially recognized as "partners" of the government, and are not financed by taxpayers' money. Under the post-1984 system, the Roman Catholic Church receives

ITALY

more money than ever before, and most participating minorities also receive enough funds to not only take care of their activities in Italy, but also finance some of their activities abroad.

The 1980s also saw a change in Italy's religious map following a massive influx of foreign immigrants, mostly from Africa and Asia, and later from Eastern Europe, both for economic reasons and because of new legal developments making it easier to leave post-Communist European countries and to enter Italy. As a result, what had been quite small minorities grew into substantial religious bodies. The Sunni Muslims (fewer than 1,000 in the 1960s), for instance, had reached 1,300,000 by the year 2008, while the number of Eastern Orthodox Christians rose from 15,000 to 1,140,000, as a result of the increased number of Eastern European immigrants (particularly Romanian) entering Italy after 1989. Buddhism also grew, although there are more Italian (107,000) than immigrant (55,000) Buddhists, due primarily to the quite remarkable development of Soka Gakkai (which numbers at present some 50,000 members). Some groups of Indian origin, particularly those connected with the Sathya Sai Baba Movement and the Osho Commune International founded by Osho Rajneesh (1931–1990), have also been quite successful in Italy. Although statistics about the Church of Scientology are notoriously intractable and controversial, it is quite likely that more people attend Scientology courses in Italy than anywhere else in Europe. There are also some 13,500 members of esoteric and occult groups, with Damanhur (in Piedmont) being probably the largest residential esoteric community in the world, comprising some 600 "citizens" living communally in its main center.

Among Italian citizens, active Roman Catholics represent roughly one-third of the population, with some 20,000 "fringe Catholics," members of movements not recognized by the bishops as part of the Catholic fold (half of them members of Luigia Paparelli's Divine Mission). Non-Catholics represent 2.12 percent of Italian passport holders residing in Italy, as follows:

Fringe Catholics	20,000
Eastern Orthodox Christians	57,500
Protestants	409,000
Jews	29,000

Jehovah's Witnesses (and splinter groups)	400,000
Other Christian Groups	26,000
Muslims	40,000
Baha'is and Other Middle Eastern Groups	3,000
Hindus and Neo-Hindus	18,000
Buddhists	107,000
Osho-related Groups	4,000
Sikhs, Radhasoamis, and Derivations	2,500
Other Far Eastern Groups	1,000
Non-Buddhist Japanese New Religions	2,500
Ancient Wisdom and Esoteric Groups	13,500
Human Potential Movements	20,000
New Age Movements	20,000
Others	5,000
Total	1,178,000

On the other hand, in addition to some 775,000 Catholic immigrants, there are also currently more than 2,321,900 non-Catholic immigrants on Italian soil, namely:

Muslims	1,153,400
Eastern Orthodox Christians	836,000
Protestants	180,000
Buddhists	37,000
Hindus	45,000
Sikhs, Radhasoamis	15,000
Other Far Eastern and African Religions and Groups	30,000
Jews	7,000
Jehovah's Witnesses	15,000
Others	3,500

As a consequence, non-Catholic minorities constitute roughly 5 percent of the entire population present on the Italian territory. Catholic church attendance in Italy is among the highest in Europe. After a decline in the 1960s and 1970s, the trend was reversed, and Sunday attendance started growing again from the late 1980s on, reaching 35 percent of Italians who report to attend at least monthly by the year 2000, although

Italy

Religion	Followers in 1970	Followers in 2010	% of Population	Annual % growth 2000–2010	Followers in 2025	Followers in 2050
Christians	47,597,000	47,502,000	80.5	0.22	44,551,000	40,050,000
Roman Catholics	50,697,000	55,652,000	94.3	−0.02	52,400,000	46,685,000
Independents	61,000	548,000	0.9	2.54	750,000	810,000
Marginals	85,400	450,000	0.8	0.61	600,000	700,000
Agnostics	4,950,000	7,680,000	13.0	0.59	9,000,000	9,500,000
Atheists	1,179,000	2,200,000	3.7	0.64	2,500,000	2,750,000
Muslims	43,000	1,500,000	2.5	2.36	1,850,000	2,100,000
Chinese folk	0	45,000	0.1	0.33	50,000	55,000
Jews	37,000	38,000	0.1	0.33	35,000	35,000
Sikhs	0	24,000	0.0	0.33	28,000	30,000
New religionists	10,000	19,000	0.0	0.17	27,000	33,000
Buddhists	2,000	8,800	0.0	0.33	12,000	18,000
Hindus	0	8,000	0.0	0.29	15,000	25,000
Baha'is	4,200	5,000	0.0	0.20	8,000	10,000
Ethnoreligionists	0	2,100	0.0	0.33	3,000	3,500
Total population	**53,822,000**	**59,032,000**	**100.0**	**0.33**	**58,079,000**	**54,610,000**

figures are controversial and recent years have witnessed a debate among sociologists about possible over-reporting. For those accepting the figures at face value, Italy seems to represent a solid confirmation of rational choice theories. Legal limitation of pluralism from the 1950s to the 1980s corresponded to a decline in general church attendance and to a greater increase in membership figures for groups in fringe niches (particularly Jehovah's Witnesses). The legal and practical establishment of an effective religious pluralism in the 1980s, on the other hand, led to a renewed interest in religion and church attendance in general, while groups such as the Jehovah's Witnesses experienced a slower growth rate.

As everywhere else in Europe, the tragic events of 2001 have worsened the already prevailing tensions between sections of the Italian population who are suspicious of Islam in general and the Muslim minority, as well as making the prospects of a Concordat with one or more of the largest Italian Islamic organizations even more difficult. On the other hand, both the Italian legal system (plus reminiscences of the Fascist persecution of minorities, which created in 1930 under the name of *plagio* a criminal offense very similar to what would later be called brainwashing; in 1981, the existence of such provision in Italian law was declared contrary to the democratic constitution

by the Constitutional Court), and the visible presence in the media of a number of scholars of new religious movements who are critical of the anti-cult movement (most of them associated with CESNUR, the Center for Studies of New Religions, established in Turin in 1988), have so far prevented in Italy any significant anticult scare of the kind prevalent in other European countries, such as neighboring France. Although both secular and Catholic opposition to such groups as the Jehovah's Witnesses and the Church of Scientology does exist in Italy, its institutional influence has so far been comparatively limited.

Massimo Introvigne

See also: Christian Brethren; Church of Jesus Christ of Latter-day Saints; Church of Scientology; Churches of Christ; Evangelical Baptist Union of Italy; Evangelical Methodist Church of Italy; Italian Assemblies of God; Jehovah's Witnesses; Roman Catholic Church; Salvation Army; Sathya Sai Baba Movement; Seventh-day Adventist Church; Soka Gakkai International; Unification Movement; Waldensian Church.

References

Center for Studies on New Religions, Torino, Italy. http://www.cesnur.org Accessed September 25, 2001.

Introvigne, Massimo, PierLuigi Zoccatelli, Nelly Ippolito Macrina, and Verónica Roldán, *Enciclopedia delle Religioni in Italia*. Leumann (Torino): Elledici, 2001.

Ivory Coast

See Cote d'Ivoire.

Izumo Ôyashirokyô

Izumo Ôyashirokyô, formally known as Izumo Tai-shakyõ, one of the oldest of Japanese new religions, was founded by Senge Takatomi (1845–1917). In 1873 Senge, a Shinto priest of Izumo Taisha (the Grand Shrine of Izumo), gathered like-minded shrine adherents into a voluntary religious association, meeting at the shrine but organizationally distinct from it. This association was finally authorized by the government in 1882. The main deity of this sect is Ôkuninushi no Kami, the mystical ruler of the nether world. Prayer to unite with kami though reciting Shingo (words of Kami) and Okunigaeri (a religious pilgrimage to Izumo Taisha) are of importance in its practices. Its main scriptures are Kyôshi Taiyô, Daidô Yôgi, Daidô Mondô, Izumo Mondô, and Sôsaisiki.

The current leader of Izumo Ôyashirokyô is Senge Michihiko. As the new century began it reported 1,236,771 members.

Izumo Ôyashirokyô
Taish-machi
Hikawa-gun, Shimane prefecture
699-07
Japan

Keishin Inaba

See also: Shinto.

References

Hori, Ichiro, et al., eds. *Japanese Religion: A Survey by the Agency for Cultural Affairs*. Tokyo: Kodansha International, 1972.

Nobutaka, Inoue. "The Formation of Sect Shinto in Modernizing Japan." *Japanese Journal of Religious Studies* 29, nos. 3–4 (2002): 405–426.

J

◆ Jainism

Jainism is generally seen as a reaction to the leadership of the Hindu community by the elite Brahman caste in the sixth century BCE. The name, Jain, derives from *jina* (victory), a reference to their founder, Mahavira, who was called the Victor. Jains are disciples of the Victor.

Many Jains reject the contemporary scholarship on their religion's origins and point instead to a lineage of 24 saints, the Tirthanikaras, among whom one female is included, Mallinatha. The 22nd in the lineage, Nemi, is reputed to have lived for 1,000 years, just one of the attributions ascribed to the saints that have caused many to see them as mythological rather than historical beings. History begins with Parsva (b. ca. 872 BCE), the son of the ruler of Benares, India. As a young man he became a notable soldier and the husband of a princess. However, during his 30th year he renounced his royal life and became an ascetic. He wandered India and as disciples came to him he laid out a life based on four vows—do not take life, do not lie, do not steal, and do not own property. He died in Bengal, and the place of his death, Mount Sammeda, remains a site of pilgrimage and reverence for the Jain community.

Parsva was succeeded by Vardhamana (b. ca. 599–ca. 527), later known as Mahavira, a member of the warrior caste. During most his life as a Jain, he lived without clothes, seen as a visible sign of his renunciation of worldly possessions. Spending some 12 years as an ascetic, he is said to have become the Victor over his worldly passions. The state of realization he attained is known as *keval-jnana*, considered to be perfect perception, knowledge, power, and bliss. He spent the next 30 years traveling on bare feet around India preaching to the people the eternal truth he had realized. He attracted people from all walks of life, both rich and poor, from royalty to untouchables. During his time, the largely monastic community assembled by Parsva was increased by the development of a lay community. Mahavira organized his followers into a fourfold order of monks (*sadhu*), nuns (*sadhvi*), laymen (*shravak*), and laywomen (*shravika*).

He also added a fifth vow—poverty—to the original four vows for the monks and nuns. These would form the basis of the main values of Jain life today: non-violence (*ahimsa*), or the refusal to cause harm to any living things; truthfulness (*satya*), or the speaking only of harmless truth; non-stealing (*asteya*), not to take anything not properly given; chastity (*brahmacharya*), or refusal to indulge in sensual pleasures; and non-possession (*aparigraha*), or detachment from people, places, and material things. Laypeople were to value the vows but lead a somewhat less austere existence.

Jain teachings remained as oral teachings for several centuries following Mahavira's death. They were finally given written form around 300 BCE and these texts exist today as the Jain sacred writings.

The Jain community experienced growth for its first decade. Around 300 BCE, it split into two basic communities—the Svetambaras (who wore white cloths) and the Digambaras (air-clothed or unclothed)—and over the centuries each divided into a number of sub-sects. The community reached its peak in the 12th century, when the ruler of Gujarat was converted to Jainism by Hemecandra (1088–1172) and turned Gujarat into a Jain state. In the next century, however, the Muslim conquest of India began and further growth was largely blunted. Periodically, both Hindus and Muslims turned on the Jains.

Jain Beliefs The Jain teachings picture a three-story universe, the middle level being the realm of human existence. The goal of human life is to allow the soul to reach nirvana, or the state of *moska* (liberation), pictured spatially as the top of the universe, where it can remain in a state of eternal bliss and peace. Commonly at the end of life one goes to the lower realm, a dark place where people are punished for various misdeeds. There is also a heavenly realm of the gods and saints, but it is not one's goal.

The earthly realm is the realm of human action. The human soul is seen as consisting of a set of *jivas*, or immaterial monads. These monads are intermixed with *karma* (consequences of one actions), which are pictured as particles. Karmic matter (*ajiva*) gives color to the monads. Colors (*leysas*) range from the worst (black) to blue, gray, red, yellow, rose, and white. Each color is associated with characteristics. A black color to one's jivas is indicative of cruelty, while a person of a dispassionate and impartial nature is seen as having yellow as the predominant color. All actions produce karma, even good ones, thus the ideal is non-action and detachment.

The Jain understanding of the goal of life has ensured that ethics is of primary importance in the individual's life. The person ready to become a full member of the community must first profess faith in the teachings of the Jain saints and then renounce all attachments to other religions. That having been done, they are ready to take the 12 vows. They vow: (1) not intentionally to take life, especially of a jiva (*ahimsa*); (2) not to lie or exaggerate (*satya*); (3) not to steal (*achaurya*); (4) to refrain from marital unfaithfulness and unchaste thoughts (*bhramacharya*); (5) to limit accumulation of possessions and give away extras (*aparigraha*); (6) to consciously limit oneself so as to decrease the possibility of committing transgressions (*dik*); (7) to limit the number of both consumable and non-consumable items in one's possession (*bhoga-upbhoga*); (8) to avoid unnecessary evil (*anartha-danda*); (9) to observe periods of meditation (*samayik*); (10) to observe periods of self-imposed limitations (*desavakasika*); (11) to live for a period as an ascetic or monk (*pausadha*); and (12) to support the monastic community (*atithi samvibhaga*).

The Jain vows carry some general implications for living one's life. Jains are vegetarians and do not even consume eggs. They refrain from any occupations that involve the destruction of living creatures; even farming, which may harm living creatures in the process of plowing and planting, is avoided. Business and scholarship are more acceptable. The monastic life is most preferred.

Monks, recognized by their shaved heads, are organized into communities each headed by an *acarya*, or superior, who possesses the authority for structuring the community and overseeing instruction. Monks and nuns tend to itinerate around the countryside. However, during the rainy season they will congregate for periods of concentrated study, practicing austerities, and meditation. Part of the rationale for staying inside at this time is protection of the many life forms brought out by the wet weather.

Following the Jain path ideally leads to heightened levels of self-realization. The five steps along the path to liberation are recognized as right perceptions (*mati*); clear scriptural knowledge (*sruta*); supernatural knowledge (*avadhi*); clear knowledge of the thought of others (*manahparyaya*); and omniscience (*kevala*). Those who attain kevala are also identified as perfected ones (*siddhas*). Jains accept the idea of reincarnation and believe that the upward path may take many lifetimes. In the end, the fully realized soul will fly to the top of the universe and there reside in a karma-free condition.

To assist the process of life, the Jain life, and attaining heightened levels of realization, the Jain community has built numerous temples, which are identified with the Jain symbol, a swastika above which are three dots and a half moon. The swastika is an ancient symbol in Asia and has no relation to its modern adoption in the 1930s by the German Nazis. Temples may be the abode of statues of the saints, and veneration of the saints easily transforms into worship. In Digambara temples, the figures are depicted as nudes, standing with their eyes cast downward. In the Svetambara temples, the figures tend to be seated with their legs crossed. Both types of temples follow a cycle of ceremonies and rites.

Divisions within the Jain Community The major division in the Jain community between the clothed and unclothed monks may go back even to the time of Mahavira and his living for so many years in a naked

A Jain ceremony taking place at a Ranakpur temple, India, 2006. Founded by Lord Mahavira, the 24th Tirthankara (Prophet), around 500 BC, the Jain religion is one of the famous religions in Rajasthan. (Rene Drouyer/Dreamstime .com)

state. However, the formalization of the division became intertwined with a second problem—the writing down of the Jain scriptures. As generations came and went, Jain leaders pondered the problem created by having to memorize and pass on the scriptures and came to realize that material was continually being lost. Thus, around 300 BCE, they began the process of writing down and compiling what was remembered.

The decision to write down the scriptures was, in part, occasioned by events growing out of a great famine that spread through northern India. During this time, an important chief leader Bhadrabahu led a segment of the community to the south. While there, in the hills of Shravana Belgola, Bhadrabahu committed ritual suicide by starvation, a practice that was quite acceptable among the Jains for one already approaching the end of his life. After the famine ended, the group returned to the north only to discover that the monks had abandoned their life without clothes. They also realized that

they had lost a segment of the Jain scripture, which Bhadrabahu had failed to teach to his successor.

Over the next centuries the division of the community around those monks who wore clothes and those who did not formally resulted in the separation of the Digambaras from the Svetambaras.

The Digambaras teach that nudity was integral to the teachings of Mahavira, and that it is completely in line with the observation argument that a monk should be devoid of any possessions (such as clothes) and devoid of the desire to protect his body from the elements. They depict Mahavira in complete nudity, without any ornamentation, with downcast eyes. They also teach that Mahavira never married and was celibate throughout his earthly existence.

Regarding the scriptures, the Digambaras teach that the words of Mahavira, reputedly contained in the eleven *angas* of the Jain canon, were lost forever during the famine as Bhadrabahu did not pass them on.

Hence they refuse to accept the 11 angas of the Jain canon as owned by the Svetambaras and now form part of the 41 Sutras.

Finally, the digambaras hold that women cannot join the order of those in the renounced life as they were not qualified for the austere life the order demanded from each of the adherents. Today the Digambaras are found mostly in the southern part of India, especially in Mysore state, where the group led by Bhadrabahu had journeyed some 2,000 years ago. The modern Indian state has moved to limit the public nudity of the Digambara monks.

In contrast, the Svetambaras teach that some of the Tirthankaras (those of the lineage of saints) did not live life in the nude. Most important, Parsva, the saint immediately prior to Mahavira, wore white robes. They note that prior to his becoming an ascetic, Mahavira had lived a householder's life, that he had married and fathered a daughter, and that he did not become an ascetic until his parents had died and he had fulfilled his necessary family duties. They also make note of an incident in his life. He began his renounced life as a clothed monk until one day the white robe he wore was caught in a thorny bush, and as he moved on the robe was pulled off. Never holding on to worldly things, Mahavira simply left it and continued on his way naked. Thus, they argue, Mahavira's nudity was not consciously adopted but was an accident of the moment.

Regarding the scriptures, the Svetambara believe that the words of Mahavira were not lost during the great famine and accept the authority of the 11 angas of the Jain canon. They also believe that women can attain sainthood, calling to their cause the case of the 19th Tirthankara Malli, who was a female. Today the Svetambaras are located primarily in Gujarat and Rajashan.

In modern times, both the Digambaras and the Sevtambaras have divided into a number of sub-sects that go under such names as Sthanakavasi, Terapanthi, Beespanthi, Japneeya, and Murtipujak. Typically, a distinguishable sub-group within the Jain community consists of a group of monks, the temples and monasteries they operate, and the laypeople who support them.

The Sthanakavasi Jain tradition, for example, can be traced to the Gujarati Jain reformer Lumpaka (ca. 1415–1489), who protested the lax practice of the Murtipujak Svetambara monks. Lumpaka worked as a scribe copying manuscripts for Jain monks. In his work he discovered that Jain scriptures do not mention any practice of giving money (for temple construction, for example) as a means to merit, the performance of worship before images, or rituals involving acts of violence such as the breaking of flowers. He rejected image-worship as well as the authority of several texts within the canonical texts that contain references to such worship. He began to live as an ascetic, following the oldest textual prescriptions. Lumpaka gained a following in Gujarat, which was continued by his first disciple, Bhana, who seems to have initiated some 45 followers during the 1470s.

Early in the 16th century, the Sthanakavasi split into several groups, which by mid-century had become some 13 independent branches, which further divided into additional distinct sub-groups, however, by the 20th century, only 4 branches remained in existence.

The Terapanth Svetambara Jain tradition was founded by Acarya Bhiksu (1726–1803), who had become attached to an acarya of the sub-sects of the Sthanakavasi tradition in the 1750s. Then, in 1760, complaining of the laxity of the Sthanakavasis, he founded his own order at Kelva near Rajsamand. In its early years, the new order attracted only 13 male members (including Bhiksu), and his critics labeled his group the path of the 13, or *terah panth.* Bhiksu turned the label to his favor by slightly changing it to *tera panth,* or your path.

Underlying the original break was a disagreement over the understanding of the Jain teaching on karma. Jains believe that the soul must renounce all violence (and ultimately all action) to achieve liberation from karma. The Sthanakavasis also emphasize the role of compassion as a religious virtue and suggest that, for example, charitable actions have a positive karmic result. In contrast, Bhiksu assumed a more narrow interpretation based upon the understanding that bad karma and good karma equally obstructed the process of liberation and hence both must be avoided. Thus, he reasoned, acts of compassion were sinful.

Contemporary Jain Communities   Today, in India, the followers of Jainism engage primarily in business and trade. The committed are known for their fasting, nonviolence, vegetarianism, philanthropy, and simple lifestyle. They do not make the sharp break with the Hindu community (as for example the Buddhists and Sikhs do), and in turn the Hindu majority see them as a sister community.

Through the 20th century, Jain communities were established around the world. Among the earliest appearances of Jains outside of India, one occurred in 1893 when Virchand Gandhi made a presentation at the Parliament of the World Religions in Chicago. His travel to Chicago was opposed by many of his colleagues, who believed that travel by any means other than on foot was immoral. He would be followed by a few others, such as Champat Rai Jain, who traveled to England in the 1930s, but no communities emerged until after World War II. Migration to England began in the 1950s, and by the 1990s there were some 30,000 in the United Kingdom, most from Gujarat. They have been organized into the Federation of Jain Organisations (11 Lindsay Dr., Kenton, Middlesex HA3 0TA, UK).

Significant migration to North America began in the 1970s and centers have been opened in most states in the eastern half of the nation as well as Texas and California. These now cooperate (along with Canadian centers) in the Federation of Jain Associations in North America (1902 Chestnut St., Philadelphia, PA). Several Jain teachers have also come to the United States and founded organizations that reach out to the larger non-Indian population: the International Nahavir Jain Mission and the Jain Meditation International Center.

Jain centers and temples may also now be found in Australia, Singapore, Hong Kong, and Japan.

J. Gordon Melton

See also: Asceticism; Benares; Mahavira; Meditation; Monasticism; Pilgrimage; Reincarnation; Sthanakavasi Jain Tradition; Terapanth Svetambara Jain Tradition; Vegetarianism; Women, Status and Roles of.

References

Babb, Lawrence A. *Absent Lord: Ascetics and Kings in a Jain Ritual Culture.* Berkeley: University of California Press, 1996.

Banks, M. *Organizing Jainism in India and England.* Oxford: Clarendon Press, 1992.

Cort, John E. *Jains in the World: Religious Values and Ideology in India.* Oxford: Oxford University Press, 2000.

Cort, John E. *Open Boundaries: Jain Communities and Cultures in Indian History.* Albany: State University of New York Press, 1998.

Dundas, Paul. *The Jains.* New York: Routledge, 2002.

Jain, Muni. *Jaina Sects and Schools.* Delhi: Concept Publishing, 1975.

Jain, Prem Suman. *Essentials of Jainism.* Boston: Jain Center of Greater Boston, 1984.

Jaini, Padmanabh S. *The Jaina Path of Purification.* Berkeley: University of California Press, 1979.

"Jainism: Jain Principles, Tradition and Practices." http://www.cs.colostate.edu/~malaiya/jainhlinks .html.

Long, Jeffrey D. *Jainism: An Introduction.* London: I. B. Tauris, 2009.

Rankin, Adrian. *The Jain Path: Ancient Wisdom for the West.* Berkeley, CA: O Books, 2005.

Roy, A. K. *History of the Jainas.* Colombia, MO: South Asia Books, 1984.

Sangave, Vilas. *Jaina Religion and Community.* Long Beach, CA: Long Beach Publications, 1996.

Satyaprakash. *Jainism: A Select Bibliography.* Subject Bibliography Series, vol. 6. Gurgaon, Haryana: Indian Documentation Service, 1984.

Shah, Natubhai. *Jainism: The World of Conquerors.* Portland: Sussex Academic Press, 1998.

Tobias, Michael. *Life Force: The World of Jainism.* Berkeley, CA: Asian Humanities Press, 1991.

Williams, Raymond. *Religions of Immigrants from India and Pakistan: New Threads in the American Tapestry.* Cambridge: Cambridge University Press, 1988.

Jamaat-e-Islam

The Jamaat-e-Islam, a major organizational component of the international movement variously called Islamism or, in the West, Islamic fundamentalism, was founded in 1941 by Sayyid Abul A'la Mawdudi (1903–1979). He was raised in a family that had for many years supplied leadership to the Chistiniyya Sufi Order in India. In his teen years he became a newspaper editor and began to participate in various Islamic movements that had emerged in the context of the British rule of India. Among these was the Khilafat movement (1918–1924), whose aim was to save the then dying Ottoman Empire after the disasters of World War I. At the same time, it also promoted Muslim political interests in India.

Toward the end of the 1920s Mawdudi wrote his first book, a study of war and peace in Islamic law. During the 1930s he began to concentrate on the issue of Islam's conflict with the West and the modern age. He offered a perspective based directly upon his study of the Koran, the Muslim holy book, and the *hadith*, the sayings of and traditions concerning the Prophet Muhammad. The more he looked at Western culture, the more he criticized fellow Muslims who were becoming Westernized. Then toward the end of the decade he moved to the Punjab to establish a research center, Darul-Islam, to train scholars and to launch a reconstruction of Islamic thought.

The plan to reconstruct the Muslim perspective led to Mawdudi's founding of the Jamaat-e-Islam, a religious organization that could also operate as a political organization in the context of the changes about to overtake India. He moved to Pakistan in 1947 to work for the development of an Islamic state (in which Islamic law would be the law of the land). When his goals were not realized, he became an ongoing critic of the government and was often arrested and imprisoned for expressing his antigovernment ideas. A prolific writer, he authored more than 100 books and pamphlets during the next quarter of a century. With the partition of India into India and Pakistan in 1947, the Jamaat split into Indian and Pakistani sections. Other related groups (but organizationally independent) were later founded in Kashmir, Bangladesh, Sri Lanka, and Afghanistan.

Around 1940, Mawdudi completed a brief work, *A Short History of the Revivalist Movement in Islam*, which, in perspective, can be seen as an early manifesto of Islamism. He presents Islam, the teachings delivered by the prophets from Adam to Muhammad, as focused upon the establishment of the kingdom of God on Earth and the enforcement of the system of life Allah gave to humanity. The prophets sought to revolutionize the intellectual and mental outlook of the population, to regiment those peoples who had accepted Islam in the Islamic pattern, and to organize the various segments of social life on an Islamic basis.

The time of the establishment of the Muslim community by Muhammad (ca. 570–632) was followed by the period of the "rightly guided caliphs." However, "ignorance" crept into the rule of successive caliphs (as early as the 650s under the third caliph, Uthman) and hence in every age there has been a need for successive *mujaddids*, revivers of Islam, people who accomplish an extraordinary work in rejuvenating true Islam. A mujaddid must accomplish several tasks: diagnose his contemporary situation; define the place to strike the blow to break the power of un-Islam and allow Islam to again take hold; encounter the political forces attempting to suppress Islam; and take authority from un-Islam and in a practical manner re-establish government on the pattern of those initial "rightly guided caliphs." This program is not just for one country; it aims for the establishment of Islam as the predominant force for all humankind. Ultimately, the instrument for carrying out this program would be the person known in Islamic theology as al-Mahdi, the coming one, whom Mawdudi saw as a modern revolutionary who would draw people to him by the quality of his life and his leadership ability. He will overcome ignorance and establish the Islamic state, not by any supernatural acts, but by statesmanship, political sagacity, and strategic skill.

The Jamaat developed an organization and program to embody the vision outlined by Mawdudi. It has been headed by an *amir*, the first being Mawdudi (1941–1972), and the Majlis-e Shura, a consultation council, a representative body drawn from the various segments of the membership. The amir is the supreme authority. Mawdudi was succeeded by Main Tufail Muhammad (1972–1989) and the present amir, Qazi Hussain Ahmad. The shura has control over all doctrinal issues and may by two-thirds vote veto the ruling of an amir. One of the senior members of the shura occupies the seat of the amir if it becomes vacant.

The Jamaat has a four-point program for the transformation of Islamic society. It begins in an appeal to reason, showing listeners how Islam can be effectively applied to the contemporary situation. The appeal to virtue reaches out to those people already predisposed to the erecting of a just and upright society. The educational efforts give birth to a program of social reform. To this end, the Jamaat has created a variety of agencies, including educational institutions, programs for moral uplift, and charities to help the weaker members of society.

The fourth aspect of the program looks for the actual change of leadership in society, beginning with intellectual, social, and cultural leaders and culminating in political leaders. Looking for long-term transformation, the Jamaat trains the more capable among its members in its conservative view of Islam so that they can then assume the leadership roles in society. In this manner, the Jamaat attempts to affect all dimensions of human life.

The work of the Jamaat-e-Islam has been significantly extended by the formation of a set of autonomous but ideologically aligned institutions. One group of organizations deals with publication of Islamic material. Among several such organizations is Islamic Publications Ltd. Lahore. The Jamaat also seeks to found organizations dedicated to bringing Islam into various specialized groups (including different occupations). Among the first Jamaat-affiliated groups was the Islami Jamiat-e Talaba, the student organization, founded in 1947.

The Jamaat has come to include a broad range of conservative Muslims in Pakistan. Following the bombing of the World Trade Center in New York City and the Pentagon in suburban Washington, D.C., on September 11, 2001, members of the Jamaat have been generally supportive of the Taliban and al-Qaeda. Following the threat of the United States launching military operations in Afghanistan, the current leader of Jamaat-e-Islam, Qazi Hussain Ahmad, was quoted as saying, "Any attack on Afghanistan is an attack on Pakistan, and we will resist it."

Internationally, the Jamaat has been active in supporting like-minded groups around the world, from Kashmir and Afghanistan to Bosnia and the Philippines. These groups include those that bear its name in different countries and other groups of the Islamist movement, such as Hamas (Palestine), Ma'Shoomi (Indonesia), the Islamic Party of Malaysia, and al To'iah-al Islamia (Kuwait). Specific outreach efforts of the Jamaat include the UK Islamic Mission, the Islamic Foundation in Europe, and the Muslim Student's Association of the U.S. and Canada (MSA). In 1983 MSA created the Islamic Society of North America as an umbrella structure to coordinate the many Islamic organizations that had been founded by MSA in North America. The latter has become well known for its nurturing of a variety of associations of Islamic scholars and professionals. The Jamaat has associated groups in France, Spain, and Japan, and throughout Latin America.

The Jamaat-e-Islam is to be distinguished from another Pakistani group, the Jamiat-ul-Ulema-e-Pakistan, a more extreme group that is known for signing the *fatwa* (literally, declaration on a legal matter) against the United States issued by Osama bin Laden in 1998.

Jamaat-e-Islam
c/o The General Secretary, Mansura
Multan Rd.
Lahore 54570
Pakistan
http://www.jamaat.org/new/english

J. Gordon Melton

See also: Chistiñiyya Sufi Order; Islam; Islamism; Muhammad.

References

Ahmad, Khurshid, and Zafar Ishaq Ansari. *Mawdudi: An Introduction to His Life and Thought.* Leicester, UK: The Islamic Foundation, 1979.

Al-Mawdudi, Sayyid Abul. *Fundamentals of Islam.* Lahore: Islamic Publications, 1975.

Al-Mawdudi, Sayyid Abul. *The Islamic Movement: Dynamics of Values, Power, and Change.* Leicester, UK: The Islamic Foundation, 1984.

Al-Mawdudi, Sayyid Abul. *A Short History of the Revivalist Movement in Islam.* Delhi: Markazi Maktaba Islami, 1972.

Esposito, John, ed. *Voice of the Resurgent Islam.* New York: Oxford University Press, 1983.

Jansen, Johannes J. *The Dual Nature of Islamic Fundamentalism.* Ithaca, NY: Cornell University Press, 1996.

Kramer, Martin. "Fundamentalist Islam at Large: The Drive for Power." *Middle East Quarterly* (June

1996). http://www.meforum.org/meq/june96/kramer.shtml. Accessed November 1, 2001.

Nasr, Seyyed Vali Reza. *The Vanguard of the Islamic Revolution: The Jama'at-i Islami of Pakistan.* Berkeley: University of California Press, 1994.

■ Jamaica

Jamaica is an island in the Caribbean Sea south of Cuba and west of Haiti. Its population of 2.8 million (2008), the great majority of whom are of African descent, is spread across the 4,244 square miles of the popular tourist destination. When Christopher Columbus first traveled along the Jamaican coast in the 1490s, he found the island inhabited by the Arawaks, who had taken it over from its earlier inhabitants, the Guanahatabeys. Diego Colon (Columbus's son) conquered Jamaica for Spain, an event that proved disastrous for the Arawaks, who over the next two centuries were largely eliminated. Spain began the development of a plantation culture, but by the 1590s it was under constant threat from the British. The British took control in 1655, and in subsequent years the island became the headquarters of British privateers (licensed pirates).

During the 18th century, the British fought the Maroons, those Africans who escaped slavery and formed free black communities in the central highlands. Some 200,000 Africans came to live on the island, most working in the sugar mills. Slavery was ended in 1838, but the end of slavery was followed by widespread poverty and sporadic periods of unrest. Jamaica was given internal autonomy in 1959 and full independence in 1962.

Christianity was brought to Jamaica by the Spanish at the beginning of the 16th century, and almost all of the residents were members of the Roman Catholic Church at the time of the British takeover. Prohibited for many years, the church was re-established in 1837, when a contingent of Jesuits arrived just prior to slav-

Rastafarian priests worship, July 16, 2003, in Kingston, Jamaica. (AP/Wide World Photos)

Jamaica

Religion	Followers in 1970	Followers in 2010	% of Population	Annual % growth 2000–2010	Followers in 2025	Followers in 2050
Christians	1,708,000	2,328,000	84.5	0.69	2,409,000	2,238,000
Protestants	503,000	1,030,000	37.4	1.91	1,100,000	1,050,000
Independents	172,000	260,000	9.4	0.95	310,000	330,000
Roman Catholics	161,000	110,000	4.0	−0.62	150,000	175,000
Spiritists	128,000	280,000	10.2	0.71	296,000	281,000
Agnostics	17,000	115,000	4.2	1.10	160,000	190,000
Hindus	5,600	16,500	0.6	0.71	18,000	19,000
Baha'is	3,100	5,300	0.2	0.71	9,000	14,000
Chinese folk	1,000	3,700	0.1	0.71	5,000	7,000
New religionists	1,000	2,800	0.1	0.71	4,000	5,000
Muslims	3,000	2,500	0.1	0.72	3,500	4,500
Atheists	0	1,500	0.1	0.71	2,500	3,600
Jews	1,800	550	0.0	0.69	600	600
Buddhists	300	330	0.0	0.70	400	500
Total population	**1,869,000**	**2,756,000**	**100.0**	**0.71**	**2,908,000**	**2,763,000**

ery being abolished. There is now an archbishop in Kingston and a bishop in Montego Bay.

The Church of England was brought to the island by the British forces in the 17th century, though a bishop was not appointed for the land until 1824. Today, Anglican work has been incorporated in the Church in the Province of the West Indies. Interestingly enough, the next group to begin work on Jamaica were the Friends (Quakers), though their work remained small until the Iowa Yearly Meeting (United States) began a mission in 1881. The Jamaica Yearly Meeting was organized in 1941.

Jamaica benefited from the beginning of the world Protestant missionary movement, whose initial phase (carried out by the Moravians and Methodists) was directed toward the Caribbean region. Moravians arrived in Jamaica in 1754 and the Methodists in 1789. Moravian work began at the request of two British members who owned land in Jamaica. The first missionary was to instruct the Africans residing on the two plantations. The work soon spread to neighboring plantations, and from there the Moravian Church in Jamaica emerged. Methodist bishop Thomas Coke (1747–1814) visited Kingston early in 1789, and before the year was out William Hammett arrived from the United States to launch the Methodist mission (which remained under the authority of the British Conference). That church

is now a part of the larger Methodist Church in the Caribbean and the Americas. Both churches benefited from their opposition to slavery.

In the meantime, in 1782, George Lisle (ca. 1750–1828), a former slave in the American colonies, left the territory of the emerging United States with the British who had been driven out by the Revolution. He had been a Baptist preacher, and in Jamaica he founded the Baptist Church, which has become the source of two of the largest religious bodies in the country—the more staid Jamaica Baptist Union and the charismatic Revival Zion, which came to the fore in 1860 as the center of a nationwide revival movement.

Toward the end of the 19th century, the Seventh-day Adventist Church began work, which enjoyed great success in the 20th century. Presbyterians, Congregationalists, and the Christian Church (Disciples of Christ) merged in 1956 to form the United Church in Jamaica and the Cayman Islands.

Jamaica was close enough to the United States that a spectrum of Protestant churches began work and now contributes to the pluralistic atmosphere that pervades the land. There are a number of Pentecostal churches that compete for members, though no one has emerged as a significantly larger group. There are several churches that were founded in Jamaica, though fewer than in other countries, perhaps because

indigenous leadership developed in the older churches through the 19th century.

Many of the older churches relate to each other through the Jamaica Council of Churches (which also includes the Roman Catholics). It is affiliated with the World Council of Churches. Many of the newer, more conservative churches are affiliated to the Jamaica Association of Evangelicals, which is associated with the World Evangelical Alliance.

Jamaica is home to a variety of groups that are part of its unique history. Early in the 20th century, Marcus Garvey (1887–1940) organized a movement, the Universal Negro Improvement Association, to end discrimination against African people throughout the Western world. His effort led to a new emphasis on Jamaicans' African heritage, and an interest developed in Ethiopia (the term often referring to the nation of Abyssinia and at times to Africa in general). One result of the Garvey movement was the founding of several groups with claims to an Ethiopian heritage, including the Ethiopian Orthodox Tewahedo Church (with headquarters in Addis Ababa) and the Ethiopian Zion Coptic Church, with more dubious connections to Africa.

The most famous Ethiopian movement was Rastafarianism. In 1927, Garvey predicted the crowning of a black king in Africa whose emergence would be a sign of the coming redemption of Africans in the Western world from their situation. Eight years later, the coronation of Haile Selassie appeared to many to be confirmation of the prophecy. In addition, several ministers in Jamaica saw the new emperor as the fulfillment of several biblical prophecies. The members of the movement soon ran into trouble with officials when Leonard Howell was arrested for circulating pictures of Haile Selassie and telling people that they were passports back to Africa.

Through the next decades, the Rastafarians became known for their dreadlocks (hair styled to resemble a lion's mane), their use of marijuana (or *ganja*, as they called it), and their liberation-oriented music (reggae), which has transcended their movement to become popular internationally. Some of the early Rastafarians had been members of the Bedwardian movement, started by the prophet Alexander Bedward in August Town. Bedward offered miraculous cures to people, whom he dipped in the nearby Hope River. In the early 1900s, he had a huge island-wide following and was later immortalized in the folksong "Slide Mongoose."

Jamaica has become home to a variety of West African religions that have survived with a Roman Catholic overlay and are today known as Santeria or the Obeah movement, distinguished by the experience of possession by the deities, shared by both leaders and lay members. Equally interesting are the Spiritual Baptists, a group that mixes African and Protestant Christian elements. Those religions that have incorporated African elements appear to have a bright future in Jamaica.

There is a small community of Jews (Sephardic), one mosque serving some East Indian and Syrian residents, and a growing number of spiritual assemblies of the Baha'i Faith. Many of the East Indians are Hindus, who gather at the Prema Satsangh in Kingston. Other Hindu groups include the Ananda Marga Yoga Society, the Brahma Kumaris, and the International Society for Krishna Consciousness. Among the new religions, the Church of Scientology and the Unification movement have centers.

J. Gordon Melton

See also: Ananda Marga Yoga Society; Baha'i Faith; Brahma Kumaris; Christian Church (Disciples of Christ); Church in the Province of the West Indies; Church of England; Church of Scientology; Ethiopian Orthodox Tewahedo Church; Ethiopian Zion Coptic Church; Friends/Quakers; Methodist Church in the Caribbean and the Americas; Moravian Church in Jamaica; Rastafarians; Roman Catholic Church; Santeria; Seventh-day Adventist Church; Spiritual Baptists; Unification Movement; United Church in Jamaica and the Cayman Islands; World Council of Churches; World Evangelical Alliance.

References

Arbell, Mordechai. *The Portuguese Jews of Jamaica.* Kingston: University of the West Indies Press, 2000.

Gordon, S. C. *God Almighty Make Me Free: Christianity in Preemancipation Jamaica.* Bloomington: Indiana University Press, 1996.

McGasvran, D. A. *Church Growth in Jamaica.* Lucknow, India: Lucknow Publishing House, 1961.

Moorish, I. *Obeah, Christ, and Rastaman: Jamaica and Its Religion.* Cambridge: J. Clark, 1982.

Simpson, G. E. *Black Religions in the New World.* New York: Columbia University Press, 1978.

Stewart, Diane. *Three Eyes for the Journey: African Dimensions of the Jamaican Religious Experience.* New York: Oxford University Press, 2005.

Stewart, R. J. *Religion and Society in Post-Emancipation Jamaica.* Knoxville: University of Tennessee Press, 1992.

Jamaica Baptist Union

At the end of the American Revolution, in 1782, George Lisle (ca. 1750–1828), an ex-slave who had formed the first African American Baptist congregation in the American colonies, left Savannah, Georgia. Traveling with the retreating British troops he arrived in Kingston, Jamaica. His letter of recommendation secured him a job in Spanish Town, and in his spare time he began preaching. Within a year he had formed the first Baptist congregation in Jamaica. Over the next 20 years, in spite of the difficulties imposed by the slavery system, he had led in the founding of churches across the island. Early in the new century, several of the preachers he had recruited began to correspond with the Baptist Missionary Society (BMS) in England.

In 1814, John Rowe arrived from England to establish formal contact between the British and their Jamaican counterpart. The BMS began to send missionaries, whose work further spread the movement. A major obstacle developed in 1831 when a slave insurrection was identified with the Baptist church members, most of whom were slaves. The plantation owners reacted by burning many Baptist (and Methodist) chapels. The insurrection became a factor in ending slavery throughout the British Empire, and former missionaries from Jamaica became effective advocates of abolition in their homeland. The resulting abolition of slavery in 1833 and full emancipation for African residents in Jamaica allowed the Baptists a new beginning. Missionaries William Knibb (1803–1845), Thomas Burchell (1799–1846), and James Philippo (1798–1879) led in the founding of communities of freedmen, in which former slaves were given plots of land to farm. Also, by owning land they became able to vote.

In 1842, Jamaican Baptists, then organized into an Eastern and a Western Union, declared their independence from the BMS. They founded the Jamaica Baptist Missionary Society, and the following year, the Society sent its first missionaries to Africa. It later supplied missionaries for various locations around the Caribbean. In 1843, the Jamaican Baptists also established Calabar Theological College, the fountainhead of an education system that eventually crisscrossed the island. Finally, in 1849, the Eastern and Western Unions united to form the Jamaica Baptist Union.

Through the 19th century, missionaries from England continued to assist the Jamaican Baptists. In 1892, the salaries for these missionaries were finally withdrawn by the BMS. The loss of funds from England began an era of painful transition that resulted in a net membership loss over the first half of the 20th century, not an unimportant part due to the migration of large numbers of Jamaicans to Central America. Some turnaround occurred after World War II.

The Jamaica Baptist Union is an ecumenically oriented body. It joined the Baptist World Alliance at the time of its founding and is today a member of the World Council of Churches. In 1910, it formed an Evangelical Council with the Methodists, Presbyterians, and Anglicans. In 1966, Calabar College merged into the newly formed cooperative United Theological College of the West Indies, whose campus is adjacent to the University of the West Indies in Kingston.

The union is organized congregationally. Many churches, unable to support a full-time pastor, are organized into circuits that share ministerial leadership. A president and other executive officers are elected at the annual meetings of the Union. In 2005, the Union reported 43,000 members and 314 congregations.

Jamaica Baptist Union
6 Hope Road
Kingston 10
Jamaica

J. Gordon Melton

See also: Baptist World Alliance; World Council of Churches.

References

Russell, Horace O. *The Baptist Witness.* El Paso, TX: Carib Baptist Publications, 1983.

Russell, Horace O. *Foundations and Anticipations: The Jamaica Baptist Story, 1783–1892.* Columbus, GA: Brentwood Christian Press, 1993.

Sibley, Inez Knibb. *The Baptists of Jamaica.* Kingston: Jamaica Baptist Union, 1965.

Van Beek, Huibert. *A Handbook of the Churches and Councils: Profiles of Ecumenical Relationships.* Geneva: World Council of Churches, 2006.

Janmashtami

Janmashtami is a Hindu holiday that celebrates the birth of Lord Krishna, an incarnation of the deity Vishnu. It is celebrated on the eighth day of the dark half of the lunar month of Shraavana (mid August to mid-September on the Common Era calendar). While celebrations of Janmashtami can be found among Hindus around the world, the most intense celebrations occur in the Braj region, Uttar Pradesh, the land of Krishna. The largest city in the region is Mathura, the traditional birthplace of Krishna, and nearby is Vrindavan, where Krishna spent his happy childhood days.

The celebration of Janmashtani begins the day before with a fast that continues into a vigil through the evening, a remembrance that Krishna was born in the evening hours. At midnight, the statue of the infant Krishna is bathed and placed in a cradle. Prayers (*aarti*) are said and the fast is broken. According to Krishna's biography, soon after his birth, his father whisked him away to a foster home for his own safety. Women draw prints of baby feet walking toward the house symbolic of the infant entering its foster home. During the day, people will perform Rasa lila, dramatic enactments of the life or play of Krishna.

In Mahashastra, whose capital is Mumbai, Janmashtami is known as Dahi Handi (*handi* being a clay pot filled with buttermilk). Prior to the festival, the handis will be positioned at a significant height (as much as two to three stories). Young men will form human pyramids, while the person on top attempts to break the handi. If successful, the contents will spill over the entire group, which is now able to celebrate their accomplishment by a united effort. In contemporary Mumbai, different organizations offer substantial prizes to groups able to crack their handi, and groups called *govindas* (another name for Krishna) will travel around the city trying to crack as many handis as possible.

Janmashtami is a celebration of great joy and an affirmation of social oneness.

Constance A. Jones

See also: Hinduism.

References

Harshananda, Swami. *Hindu Festivals and Sacred Days.* Bangalore: Ramakrishna Math, 1994.

Mukuncharandas, Sadhu. *Hindu Festivals (Origin Sentiments & Rituals).* Amdavad, India: Swaminarayan Aksharpith, 2005.

Sharma, Nath. *Festivals of India.* New Delhi: Abhinav Publications, 1978.

Shekar, H. V. *Festivals of India: Significance of the Celebrations.* Louisville, KY: Insight Books, 2000.

Welbon, Guy, and Glenn Yocum, eds., *Religious Festivals in South India and Sri Lanka.* Delhi: Manohar, 1982.

■ Japan

Japan consists of an extensive archipelago off the far eastern coast of the Asian continent. One of the world's most homogeneous nations (a factor in the shaping of its cultural and religious histories), its population is around 125 million, with barely one percent of that population consisting of non-Japanese inhabitants. Its capital since the mid-19th century, Tokyo, is one of the world's most populous cities, while Japan is now one of the world's most technologically advanced societies and one of its leading economic powers. Japan has developed from a feudal imperial society in the mid-19th century, in which state, political power, and religion were closely aligned, into a modern liberal democracy in the present day that constitutionally separates religion and the state, and places religion solely in the

Children in traditional kimonos play with pigeons at Nagano's Zenkoji Temple; three-, five-, and seven-year-old children of Buddhist families visit temples or shrines on November 15 (Shichi-go-san) to give thanks for their healthy growth. (AP/Wide World Photos)

private sphere. Such modernization has been accomplished while retaining many aspects of the past, notably the continuation of the imperial lineage and of the emperor as titular head of state.

Japan has had a complex religious history in which religious forces from outside Japan (notably from continental Asia) have fused with indigenous forces to produce a variegated religious structure comprising a number of organized religions, including Shinto, a tradition that developed in Japan with a specific focus on the Japanese situation, and Buddhism, which came to Japan from continental Asia in the sixth century CE. It also has a continuing folk religious tradition centered on customs, beliefs, and practices that extend back thousands of years. The modern age has seen the emergence of a large number of new religious movements in response to the issues of modernization and cultural change, movements that speak to the needs of individuals in the modern day. Besides these religious influences, mention also should be made of Confucianism and Daoism, two Chinese traditions that entered Japan along with Buddhism and that, while not operating as separate traditions in Japan, have deeply influenced Japanese Buddhism and made their impression on the religious culture of Japan, and Christianity, which has been active in Japan since the mid-19th century.

Although this complex array of traditions has produced immense variety in Japanese religious life, it has also produced many areas of unity and areas of interaction between the various traditions in the ordinary lives of people. This is especially evident in the two main historical traditions of Shinto and Buddhism, which have complemented each other ritually in the individual lifecycle, Shinto being the most common operative religious system for commemorating births and for providing spiritual protection in the formative years of life, and Buddhism the commonly used religious framework for dealing with death, funerals, and the afterlife. Thus people may have affiliations to more than one tradition without feeling any sense of contradiction, while there is much shared ground within the traditions and the ways they function and serve people.

The indigenous prehistoric religion of Japan was based around the veneration of *kami*, a term that means god or deity, and may be either singular or plural. There were infinite numbers of kami, ranging from nature deities to the spirits of clan ancestors. The relationship between humans and kami was a reciprocal one, with humans venerating, praying to, and making offerings to the kami, whose role was to reciprocate by providing benefits, such as good harvests, and by overseeing the fortunes of the living. This indigenous tradition coalesced into a folk tradition centered around calendrical rituals, and eventually also into Shinto. The word "Shinto" means "the way of the gods" and indicates a tradition centered on myths that tell of the land and people of Japan being given life by the kami, who are considered as the protectors of Japan and as the ancestors of the Japanese imperial family. Such myths have, over the centuries, bound Shinto, the emperor, and the nation together and given Shinto a particularly nationalist orientation.

Buddhism entered Japan in the sixth century of the Common Era, along with various influences it had absorbed in China, including Daoist divination practices and Confucian ethical concepts affirming the importance of venerating one's elders and parents and placing great emphasis on caring for the spirits of the dead, who were worshipped as ancestors. Buddhism also brought with it a variety of practices and rituals that have influenced Japanese religion ever since, ranging from the study of scriptures to meditation, pilgrimage, and mortuary rituals. Buddhism received support from the imperial court and became a central element within the Japanese political system through much of Japanese history until the 19th century.

Japanese Buddhism is striking for the variety of sectarian developments and innovative leaders it has produced. In the early ninth century the monks Saicho (767–822) and Kukai (774–835), respectively, established the Tendai and Shingon Buddhist sects, the former combining esoteric and exoteric elements and based on the teachings of the Lotus Sutra, and the latter centered on esotericism. Both introduced a reverence for mountains along with ascetic elements into their Buddhism. In the Kamakura period, between the late 12th and the 14th centuries, a number of new Buddhist leaders emerged to establish new forms of Buddhism, including the Rinzai and Soto Zen traditions based on meditation practices and founded in Japan by Eisai (1141–1215) and Dogen (1200–1253), respectively; the Pure Land sect founded by Honen (1133–1212) and the

True Pure Land sect founded by Shinran (1173–1262), both sects based in faith in the Buddha Amida; and the Nichiren sect established by the charismatic prophet Nichiren (1222–1282), who espoused a nationalistic form of Buddhism based on the Lotus Sutra.

In the 16th century Japan also encountered Christianity through the activities of Catholic missionaries who were briefly successful in attracting converts there. However, in the early 17th century Japan's political rulers, fearing that Christianity would become a Trojan horse leading to the subversion of their power and the development of colonialism, banned the religion completely. Between the 17th and 19th centuries the country was virtually closed to the outside world, while all Japanese people were forced to take an oath of allegiance to Buddhism and to conduct the funerals and memorial services of their ancestors at their local Buddhist temples. These rules transformed Buddhism into a de facto pillar of the state, gave it a monopoly on the performance of death rituals, and helped build a close bond between the Buddhist temple and the household and family structures, through which the ancestors were memorialized, a bond that has largely endured, although becoming weaker in very recent times, especially among younger urban Japanese. In addition, both Buddhism and Shinto, which have traditionally drawn their strongest support in rural Japan, face severe problems because of declining populations outside the main city areas; many rural temples and shrines have closed because of a lack of local populations to support them. In the cities, growing interest in secular alternatives to the traditional Buddhist funeral and memorialization process has begun to erode support structures there.

In the mid-19th century, Japan, forced to open up to the outside world, engaged in a process of modernization. The Meiji Restoration of 1868, which paved the way for the development of the modern Japanese state, led to sweeping changes in the socio-religious structure. Buddhism lost its privileged position, although its central role in dealing with death and the ancestors enabled it to retain substantial support from the populace, while Shinto was elevated to the status of a national religion, and the emperor was portrayed as a sacred figure. In the latter 19th and first half of the 20th centuries, Shinto became part of the Japanese na-

tionalist project, which led to the repression of dissident groups inside Japan (including religious movements) and to Japan's aggressive expansion beyond its own territory, and eventually to its engagement in World War II. After Japan's defeat and occupation by Allied forces, the links between the state and religion were broken, the emperor was no longer considered a divine entity, and a new Constitution was enacted in 1946, which, for the first time in Japanese religious history, guaranteed religious freedom and allowed religions to operate free from state interference, but also without state support.

This change especially benefited the new religions, movements that began to emerge in Japan from the first half of the 19th century on, when rapid social and economic change and modernization led to much unease throughout society. A number of such movements arose, including Kurozumikyo, founded by the divinely inspired Shinto priest Kurozumi Munetada (1780–1850) in 1814; Tenrikyo, founded by the female Nakayama Miki (1798–1887) in 1837; and Omoto, founded by Deguchi Nao (1836–1918) in 1892. They were usually led by charismatic individuals claiming that they had received new truths for a new age from newly revealed deities, and often promising to bring about spiritual transformation in, and the eradication of injustice from, society. Often, too, these movements offered their followers readily accessible spiritual techniques of problem solving and healing, and thus managed to build large followings, especially in Japan's rapidly developing cities. The continuing emergence and development of new religions was a dominant feature of 20th-century Japanese religion, with a variety of Buddhist-oriented movements such as Soka Gakkai (known outside Japan as Soka Gakkai International), Reiyukai, and Rissho Kosei Kai developing in the 1920s and 1930s.

In postwar Japan, the continuing development of, and high levels of membership in new religions has been one of the most prominent features of religious life. Many of the movements established in the prewar period developed mass followings, most notably Soka Gakkai, which built a membership running into several millions while also establishing a national newspaper, a university, and a political party, the Komeito, which is now independent of its religious parent but

JAPAN

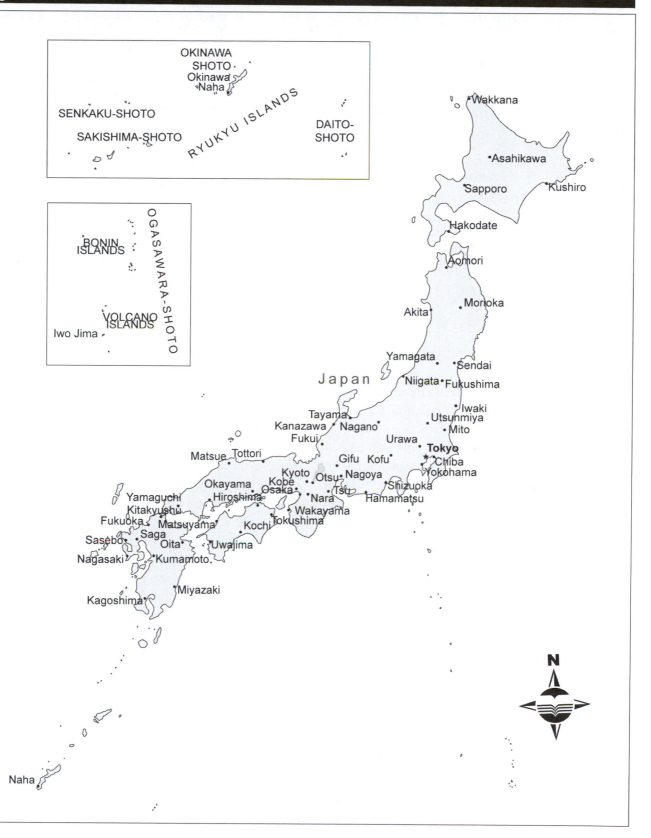

Japan

Religion	Followers in 1970	Followers in 2010	% of Population	Annual % growth 2000–2010	Followers in 2025	Followers in 2050
Buddhists	64,685,000	71,562,000	56.0	0.15	65,101,000	51,314,000
New religionists	21,300,000	33,150,000	25.9	0.13	31,500,000	26,500,000
Agnostics	9,737,000	13,100,000	10.3	0.13	14,150,000	13,750,000
Atheists	1,280,000	3,700,000	2.9	0.13	4,500,000	5,000,000
Christians	3,100,000	2,903,000	2.3	−0.18	3,147,000	3,071,000
Marginals	171,000	770,000	0.6	0.16	850,000	900,000
Independents	460,000	633,000	0.5	0.70	800,000	850,000
Protestants	435,000	544,000	0.4	0.94	580,000	570,000
Shintoists	4,173,000	2,680,000	2.1	0.13	2,550,000	2,200,000
Chinese folk	40,000	294,000	0.2	1.81	260,000	240,000
Muslims	0	185,000	0.1	0.14	200,000	200,000
Confucianists	0	127,000	0.1	−0.68	130,000	130,000
Hindus	5,000	25,700	0.0	0.14	30,000	40,000
Baha'is	9,800	16,000	0.0	0.13	25,000	38,000
Ethnoreligionists	0	10,200	0.0	0.13	15,000	20,000
Sikhs	0	2,000	0.0	0.13	3,000	4,000
Jews	1,000	1,500	0.0	0.13	1,500	1,500
Jains	0	1,600	0.0	0.14	1,800	2,000
Total population	**104,331,000**	**127,758,000**	**100.0**	**0.14**	**121,614,000**	**102,511,000**

retains close links with it. The latter part of the 20th century saw the rise of a new wave of new religions (sometimes referred to by scholars as "new" new religions), including Agonshu, a movement based on esoteric Buddhism and founded by Kiriyama Seiyu (b. 1921), and Kofuku no Kagaku, founded in 1986 by Okawa Ryuho (b. 1956), who claims to be the incarnation of the Eternal Buddha who has come to transform the world spiritually. These movements have millennial orientations, attracting a following especially among young, well-educated urban Japanese who are deeply worried about the challenges to their cultural identity through the growth of Western influences in Japan and who are deeply concerned about threats posed to the planet by environmental problems and the threat of nuclear war.

In contemporary Japan the majority of Japanese describe themselves as being associated with both Shinto and Buddhism. Their primary association with Shinto is through festivals and community, lifecycle, and calendar rituals, including the New Year's festival, in which well over 80 million Japanese (the number has risen regularly over the past two decades) visit shrines (and some popular Buddhist temples) at the start of the

year to pay their respects to the kami and to pray for good luck in the coming year. With Buddhism the primary link is through funerals, and household-based memorial rites for the ancestors. Yet at the same time, because these activities are predominantly social in orientation, many people who participate in them also describe themselves as not religious and have little other association with these traditions. Thus, although close to 90 percent of the population, according to surveys, have participated in various cyclical rites at Buddhist temples connected with the ancestors, the numbers who are devotional adherents of the Buddhist sects is considerably lower. At the same time, however, many Shinto shrines and Buddhist temples have extensive clienteles who visit them regularly to pray for good luck, while pilgrimages, especially to Buddhist temples such as the 88 pilgrimage temples on the island of Shikoku, are a popular form of devotionalism that attracts large numbers of practitioners each year.

Although the traditional religions have struggled to retain a following in the modern era, the new religions continued to attract support at least until the mid-1990s; in the period from the early 1980s into the 1990s, for example, groups such as Agonshu and Kofuku no

A Shinto priest blesses climbers at the Fuji Sengen shrine at the base of Mount Fuji. The shrine was built in the ninth century to appease the Fuji volcano. The Shinto goddess and main deity of Mount Fuji, Konohana Sakuya Hime, is believed to reside within the shrine. (Kazuhiro Nogi/AFP/Getty Images)

Kagaku attracted hundreds of thousands of followers. In all it is estimated that perhaps 20 percent of the population (around 20 million people) may belong (or may have belonged to) to a new religion. However, since the mid-1990s, such growth has largely petered out, and many, especially older, new religions have entered periods of retrenchment. Partly this has been due to a new wave of religious options that have, especially among younger Japanese, provided new alternatives to organized religious groups in very recent times. The rise of what have been called new spirituality movements with New Age religious orientations, which offer the opportunity to engage in a variety of practices and religious techniques, without making demands in terms of formal religious belonging and commitment, has been an especially prominent modern development that is proving attractive to growing numbers of people. Bookshops in cities such as

Tokyo and Osaka often have "spiritual corners" full of self-help manuals and books about spirituality, meditation, channeling, and the like, and books of this sort sell in large quantities. There is also a growing interest in a variety of spiritual techniques and practices, ranging from divination and numerology to yoga and meditation. Although it is unclear how many people actively follow such practices, it is evident that this is a growing trend and that many people now eschew formal religious affiliations, constructing for themselves a self-help religious path through which to live their lives in the frenetic urban environment of modern Japan.

In addition, a small number (generally considered to be under two percent of the population) of Japanese have turned to Christianity in one form or another since it was allowed back when Japan opened to outside influences in the mid-19th century. Christians of all denominations have since been active in establishing churches and educational institutions throughout the country, and many Japanese have expressed some degree of affinity with Christian ideas. However, Christianity has never managed to translate this affinity into a sizable following, largely, it would appear, because its teachings fail to fit with the Japanese emphases on venerating the ancestors and on engaging in religious traditions that affirm a sense of identity, social integration, and belonging. Prominent in the Christian establishment are the Roman Catholic Church, the Holy Catholic Church in Japan (Anglican), the Holy Orthodox Church in Japan, the Japan Baptist Convention, and the United Church of Christ in Japan. The latter was formed as World War II began, when the government forced all of the Protestant missionary churches to unite into one body. Other religious groups from outside Japan that have established a small but notable presence in the country include the Jehovah's Witnesses and the Unification Church.

One of the "new" new religions, Aum Shinrikyo, has created a new challenge to religion in Japan. In 1995 devotees of Asahara Shoko (b. 1955), founder and leader of Aum Shinrikyo (which renamed itself as Aleph in 1999), carried out a nerve gas attack on the Tokyo subway. Although Aum acted alone, and was radically different in its world-negating pessimism and its communal structure from other religions in Japan, the Aum affair has had major repercussions for all religious movements in Japan. It has led to the laws governing the administration and regulation of religious organizations being strengthened, while there have been numerous calls from politicians of all persuasions for greater state control of religious movements. Beyond precipitating such legal changes, the Aum affair has given added influence to a variety of critics, ranging from those on the political left, who regard religion as an outmoded and corrupting influence on society, and who have used Aum as a way of attacking religious movements in general, to mainstream supporters of the traditional religions, who have used Aum as a way of claiming that all new religions are potentially dangerous. In particular, the affair has damaged the general image of religion, and has contributed to a widespread antipathy to, and reluctance to engage in, organized religion—a tendency that has,

if anything, added to the above-mentioned turn toward a more informal, self-directed approach to religious behavior and has weakened the support structures of organized religions.

Given that the religious traditions that have flourished in Japan have been especially concerned with the particular nature of the Japanese situation, it is unsurprising that they have had comparatively little impact beyond Japanese shores. When Japanese religions have spread abroad, it has mainly been along ethnic lines, among the Japanese immigrant communities that settled in Latin America, Hawaii, and North America from the late 19th century on. These communities carried their local religious customs with them, so that, for example, Buddhism continued to be the main vehicle for dealing with death. Thus, in Hawaii Buddhist temples and festivals such as o-Bon (the summer festival commemorating the spirits of the dead) continue to attract the support of many in the Japanese American community. Shinto has endured less well, probably because of its close associations with the land of Japan, and although its shrines may be found in areas where Japanese immigrants have settled (for example, Hawaii), they are less well supported than the Buddhist temples. Many Japanese new religions have gained a footing among overseas Japanese communities. Several of the older new religions, for example, have developed extensive support networks overseas, including Soka Gakkai (which is the largest Japanese religious movement both in and outside Japan) and Tenrikyo, which have put down roots in the Japanese communities of South America and elsewhere.

Outside the Japanese overseas communities, Japanese religions have met with limited success. Zen Buddhism has achieved some recognition in the West, initially through the writings of D. T. Suzuki (1870–1966) and later because of the activities of Zen priests such as Suzuki Shunryu (1904–1971) and Deshimaru Taisen (1914–1982), who established Zen meditation centers in Europe and North America. Nowadays Zen is one of the most highly visible forms of Buddhism operative in the West, attracting numerous practitioners and giving rise also to many centers now run or established by Westerners, some of whom have become Zen monks and nuns, and has more recently begun to develop a following among young urban elites in Latin

America (notably Brazil) as well. Other Japanese Buddhist sects such as Shingon and Pure Land have been less well known or successful beyond Japan, although they, too, have established temples and developed small followings in Europe and the United States.

Some Japanese new religions have expanded beyond Japan and the Japanese immigrant community. The most successful has been Soka Gakkai, whose combination of Buddhist principles with affirmative teachings that emphasize personal success and development, has attracted many, especially upwardly mobile, followers in the United States and Europe. Another that has had some success has been Mahikari, whose emphasis on spiritual healing has helped it develop a small following in Europe, Australia, the Caribbean, and parts of Africa. Few other movements have developed more than a small number of non-Japanese followers. Overall, Japanese new religions have not traveled particularly well overseas, probably because their teachings and practices are so closely associated with the Japanese situation and Japanese religious worldview that their messages do not always appear capable of the universalism that is necessary for expansion beyond the confines of their own cultural milieu.

Ian Reader

See also: Agonshu; Aum Shinrikyô/Aleph; Dogen; Eisai; Fuji, Mount; Holy Orthodox Church in Japan; Ise Shrine, The; Japan Baptist Convention; Kamakura; Kofuku no Kagaku; Kurozumikyô; Nara; Nichiren; Omoto; Pure Land Buddhism; Reiyukai; Rissho Kosei-kai; Roman Catholic Church; Saicho; Shingon Buddhism; Shinto; Soka Gakkai International; Soto Zen Buddhism; Sukyo Mahikari; Tenrikyo; Tian Tai/Tendai Buddhism; United Church of Christ in Japan; Zen Buddhism.

References

Earhart, H. Byron. *Japanese Religion: Unity and Diversity.* Belmont, CA: Wadsworth, 1982.
Hardacre, Helen. *Kurozumikyô and the New Religions of Japan.* Princeton, NJ: Princeton University Press, 1986.
Mullins, Mark R., and Richard Fox Young, eds. "Japanese Religions Abroad." *Japanese Journal of Religious Studies* 18, nos. 2–3 (1991).
Nelson, John. *The Guise of Shinto in Contemporary Japan.* Honolulu: University of Hawaii Press, 1999.
Reader, Ian. *Religion in Contemporary Japan.* Basingstoke, UK, and Honolulu: Macmillan and University of Hawaii Press, 1991.
Rocha, Cristina. *Zen in Brazil: The Quest for Cosmopolitan Modernity.* Honolulu: University of Hawaii Press, 2006.
Shimazono, Susumu. *From Salvation to Spirituality: Popular Religious Movements in Japan.* Melbourne: Trans Pacific Press, Australia, 2004.

Japan Baptist Convention

The Japan Baptist Convention (Nippon Baputesuto) can be traced to the opening of Japan to the West by U.S. admiral Matthew C. Perry (1794–1858) in 1853. Among the men aboard Perry's flagship was a marine, Jonathan Goble (1827–1896), who also happened to be a Baptist. He was eager to gather information on the possibility of a Christian missionary enterprise in the land. To that end, he made the acquaintance of a Japanese castaway, who returned to the United States with Goble. After the U.S.-Japanese treaty of 1859, Goble obtained the support of the American Baptist Free Mission Society (a slavery abolitionist group), and in 1860 he and his wife, Eliza Goble, settled in Japan.

In 1872, with the American Civil War past and the country beginning to recover, the American Baptist Missionary Union (ABMU) assumed the responsibility for the American Baptist Free Mission Society. The Gobles were joined by Nathan Brown (1807–1886) and Charlotte "Lottie" Brown (d. 1923), his wife. The four organized the First Baptist Church of Yokohama in 1873. Brown soon took the lead in the mission and translated the Bible into Japanese. The mission was slow in forming schools and opening a theological seminary but in 1898 received a ship from a donor in Scotland and used it to travel around the Japanese islands. Then, in 1908, William Axling (1873–1963) and Lucinda Axling established an institutional (multiservice) church in Tokyo. Before Axling left for the United States almost 50 years later, the government of Japan made him an honorary citizen.

Missionaries from the Southern Baptist Convention, under a comity agreement with the ABMU, began work in southwestern Japan in 1889. The work was centered on Kyushu, the southernmost of Japan's major islands. Schools were opened (two of which developed into colleges), and in 1918 the West Japan Baptist Convention was organized. That same year the American Baptists organized the East Japan Baptist Convention. With World War II on the horizon, these two groups merged.

In 1941, the government forced the formation of the United Church of Christ in Japan and made all of the Protestant bodies join it. Following the outbreak of war with the United States following Pearl Harbor, all the remaining missionaries were interned and repatriated. After the war, William Axling was the leading voice in advocating that the Baptists remain with the United Church. Some did. However, some American Baptist congregations left in 1952 and in 1958 formed the Japan Baptist Union.

In 1947, 16 churches related to the Southern Baptist Convention withdrew from the United Church and founded the Japan Baptist Convention. It launched an aggressive evangelism program. In the next generation more than 225 new congregations were founded. It established Jordan Press and a hospital in Kyoto. In 2009, it reported 329 churches and 34,077 members, approximately two-thirds of all the Baptists in Japan.

The Japan Baptist Convention is a member of the National Christian Council of Japan and the Baptist World Alliance. The convention also has a working relationship with the Okinawa Baptist Convention, a cooperative venture of the American Baptists and Southern Baptists.

Japan Baptist Convention
4762-11 Takanoo-cho
Tsu-shi, Mie-ken 514-22
Japan

J. Gordon Melton

See also: Baptist World Alliance; Southern Baptist Convention; United Church of Christ in Japan.

References

Garrott, W. Maxfield. *Japan Advances.* Nashville: Convention Press, 1956.

Parker, F. Calvin. "Jonathan Goble: Missionary Extraordinary." *Transactions of the Asiatic Society of Japan* (third series) 16 (1981): 77–107.

Parker, F. Calvin. *The Southern Baptist Mission in Japan, 1889–1989.* Lanham, MD: University Press of America, 1991.

Japan Buddhist Federation

The Japan Buddhist Federation (JBF; Zen Nihon Bukkyokai) is an umbrella organization of more than 100 groups that encompasses all of the traditional Japanese Buddhist schools. Its member groups account for more than 90 percent of all temples and are located throughout Japan's provinces. It is the only such federation of Japanese Buddhist organizations.

The organization has its origins in the Bukkyo Konwakai (Buddhist Discussion Group) formed in 1900 to oppose state control of religion. It went through incarnations as the Dai Nippon Bukkyokai (Greater Japan Buddhist Association) and the Nihon Bukkyo Rengokai (Japanese Buddhist Union) before assuming its present name and becoming incorporated as a religious juridical body in 1957.

The JBF is engaged in a wide range of activities involving the entirety of the Japanese Buddhist world. Its primary activities strive to advance communication, the exchange of information, and the promotion of friendship among its member organizations. It also provides legal advice for its members. In addition, the JBF is a member of the Nihon Shukyo Renmei (Confederation of Japanese Religions), which includes representatives from Shinto, Christian, and new religious organizations. As a representative of the Buddhist world, it serves as a vehicle for communication with other religions, as well as for negotiation with political and bureaucratic authorities. It also functions as the Japanese branch of the World Fellowship of Buddhists (WFB), serving to promote exchange between Buddhists throughout the world.

At present, the JBF is engaged in educational activities intended to increase awareness concerning the protection of human rights within Japan, especially in regard to the elimination of discrimination toward

Japan's *buraku* class (underclass). It has also undertaken a research project to investigate the relationship between discrimination and the Buddhist scriptures.

The organization actively opposes recent amendments to the law governing religious bodies allowing for greater taxation and increased state monitoring of the finances of religious institutions. It also seeks to provide information about controversial issues, such as euthanasia in cases of brain death and the debate over organ transplants, both by organizing seminars and through its journal *Zenbutsu*, published in Japanese. The journal, with a circulation of 9,000, has been published since 1953, three times a year.

The offices of the Japan Buddhist Federation are located on the grounds of the Jodo (Pure Land) temple in Tokyo. The Federation is composed of a number of administrative organs, including a Board of Directors, a Board of Directors for Everyday Affairs, a Board of Trustees, an Office of General Affairs, and specialized committees for the examination of particular topics.

Japan Buddhist Federation
Zojo-ji
4-7-4 Shiba koen
Minato-ku, Tokyo 105-0011
Japan
http://www.jbf.ne.jp/n02/

John LoBreglio

See also: Buddhism; Jodo-shu; World Fellowship of Buddhists.

Reference

Zenbutsu. Tokyo: Japan Buddhist Federation, 1953–present.

Javanism

"Javanism" (*kejawen*) is a term for diverse spiritual practices of Javanese speakers who place their syncretic ancestral culture above specific religious affiliations. It is almost synonymous with *kebatinan*, which refers to Javanese mystical movements. Most Javanists stress that their practices are rooted in perennial indigenous traditions of wisdom, arguing that these predate even Indian influences.

There are several dozen major movements with Java-wide and, in a few cases, genuinely Indonesian membership. These include organizations such as *Pangestu*, *Sapta Darma*, *Subud*, *Sumarah*, Ilmu Sejati, and Hardopusoro. It has been estimated that 3 to 5 percent of the Javanese population are actively engaged in kebatinan practices, but perhaps a quarter of Javanese speakers (of whom there are over 60 million) empathize with the spiritual style of these movements.

Kebatinan groups existed within the colonial framework but were usually secretive. Arguably they began to adopt modern form in reaction to the crystallization of modernist Islamic organizations. Among those the Mohammadiyah (founded in 1911) was especially anti-mystical in its early years. Most movements only came into public view during the revolution of the late 1940s, while Indonesia was attaining independence. Then, paralleling the organizing process in the 1950s through all sectors of Indonesian society, major movements became formally organized. During the early 1950s a number of movements argued that they deserved recognition as separate religions, suggesting that in the context of national independence it would be an anomaly if only imported religions received government approval. Some movements maintained that argument into the 1970s; most accepted they were unlikely to get formal recognition.

Within Indonesia these movements are now termed *kepercayaan*, simply meaning "beliefs." Other designations have included *kejiwaan* or *kerohanian*, the first from a Sanskrit root, the second from Arabic, and both meaning "spiritual," and *kawruh kasunyataan*, roughly, "knowledge of Truth." Whatever the preference (which varies among movements), there is always a disavowal of the association with *klenik*, black magic and occultism, as that is the charge most often leveled against them by Muslim critics.

In opting for the designation kepercayaan, Javanist movements were self-consciously staking a claim to legitimacy within the provisions of the 1945 Constitution. That Constitution was readopted by Sukarno (1901–1970; r. 1949–1967) in 1959 and has remained sacred under Suharto (b. 1921) and even his recent successors. Inclusion of the term kepercayaan in the Constitution was credited to Wongsonegoro, who became the patron of umbrella movements on behalf of mysticism during the 1950s. The first of these, the BKKI (Badan Kongres Kebatinan Indonesia, or Congress of Indonesian Mystical Movements), was founded in 1955 by him. In Yogyakarta in December 1970 a successor organization was named the SKK (Sekretariat Kerjasama Kepercayaan) and subsequently renamed HPK (Himpunan Penghayat Kepercayaan).

Paul Stange

See also: Pangestu; Sapta Darma; Subud; Sumarah.

References

Beatty, Andrew. *Varieties of Javanese Religion: An Anthropological Account.* Cambridge: Cambridge University Press, 1999.

Geels, Antoon. *Subud and the Javanese Mystical Tradition.* Richmond, Surrey, UK: Curzon, 1997.

Geertz, Clifford. *The Religion of Java.* Chicago: University of Chicago Press, 1976.

Kartodirdjo, Sartono. *Protest Movements in Rural Java.* Singapore: ISEAS/Oxford University Press, 1973.

Mulder, Niels. *Mysticism in Java: Ideology in Indonesia.* Amsterdam and Singapore: Pepin Press, 1998.

Stange, Paul. *The Sumarah Movement in Javanese Mysticism.* Ph.D. diss., University of Wisconsin, 1980.

Jehovah's Witnesses

The Jehovah's Witnesses are an organization within the group of Christian sects and denominations sometimes referred to as the "Adventist Family." While the organization began in the United States, it has spread throughout the world, although its growth is believed to have slowed somewhat in recent years. Witnesses believe the world is now in its last days. They hold that Christ began his invisible presence on Earth in 1914 and that Armageddon will occur in the very near future.

The American Charles Taze Russell (1852–1916) is generally regarded as the founder of the movement and is the originator of the group's basic system of beliefs. In 1879, Russell began publishing *Zion's Watch Tower and Herald of Christ's Presence*, in which he argued that the millennium was imminent and that Christ's invisible presence on Earth had begun in 1874. Russell began attracting followers, known as Bible Students, and in 1884 the Zion's Watch Tower Tract Society was incorporated. Russell's successor, Joseph Franklin Rutherford (1852–1942), can be credited with the development of the present-day hierarchical, or "theocratic," organizational structure as well as with the coining of the name "Jehovah's Witnesses." A period of concerted efforts at growth and global expansion began under third President Nathan Knorr (1915–1975) and has continued under the succeeding two presidents. In October 2000, the Witnesses announced a plan for reorganization in which theological and administrative responsibilities would be divided for the first time.

While the organization has been consistent in its belief in the imminent coming of the millennium, several different dates have been put forward for the end of the present era, the most recent being 1975. As a result of their interpretation of Revelation 7:4–9, Witnesses believe that 144,000 "chosen" people will rule the world from heaven with Jesus after Armageddon. Others, members of the "Great Crowd," will be resurrected during the millennium and given the opportunity to earn eternal life on Earth through obedience to God.

Jehovah's Witnesses believe that they embody the true church, the "faithful and discrete slave" responsible for acting according to the divine plan. Although they consider themselves Christian, they reject a number of ideas put forward by most Christian groups. Witnesses reject the doctrine of the Trinity and emphasize the oneness of God, to whom they refer as Jehovah. They regard Jesus as a perfect, but fully human, being who sacrificed his life as a ransom for sinful humanity. Witnesses reject the notion of hell as contrary to God's loving nature, and they reject the notion of the immortality of the soul.

Witnesses regard Christmas, Easter, birthdays, and other holidays as Pagan in origin and do not celebrate them. Their only sacred observance is the commemoration of Christ's death during Passover. Weekly observances emphasize public talks, training for witnessing work, and study of the *Watch Tower* and other Witness publications rather than the kinds of prayer or ritual usually associated with Christian worship. Because the last days are at hand, the most important work for Jehovah's Witnesses is door-to door "preaching," or "publishing," in order to separate the saved from the damned.

The practice of "publishing" has brought Jehovah's Witnesses some notoriety in a variety of nations. Also controversial is their refusal to accept blood transfusions as a result of their interpretation of the biblical injunction against eating blood. But perhaps the source of the most tension between Witnesses and "the world" has been their refusal to serve in the military, to participate in patriotic exercises, and to join political parties. These positions have led political officials in many states to brand Witnesses as unpatriotic or enemies of the state and to subject them to persecution.

As of 2008, approximately 7.2 million Witnesses were active in 236 countries and territories. A total of 17,790,631were in attendance at the memorial of Christ's death in 1999, and 289,678 were baptized. Growth in recent years has slowed, but the number of publishers worldwide continues to grow by a rate of about 2 percent. As a result of global expansion, less than 20 percent of all Witnesses live in the United States, the group's country of origin, while more than 25 percent live in Latin America.

Jehovah's Witnesses
25 Columbia Heights
Brooklyn, NY 11201-2483

Arthur L. Greil

See also: Russell, Charles Taze.

References

Holden, Andrew. *Jehovah's Witnesses: Portrait of a Contemporary Religious Movement*. London: Routledge, 2002.

Jehovah's Witnesses in the Divine Purpose. Brooklyn, NY: Watchtower and Bible Tract Society of New York, 1959.

Penton, M. James. *Apocalypse Delayed: The True Story of Jehovah's Witnesses*. 2nd ed. Toronto: University of Toronto Press, 1997.

Jerusalem

Jerusalem is a very old city that contains many sites of religious significance, and it continues today to be a source of considerable disagreement between the different Abrahamic religions and within each one also. For Jews it is the site of the temple, of which only a wall now remains (though probably not even a wall of the temple itself but probably just a wall close to it and once enclosing it). For Muslims it is the site of the Prophet's miraculous night journey from the Hejaz on Buraq, and his ascension through the heavens, and for Christians it is where Jesus was crucified and spent much of his life. The city is now the capital of the state of Israel, but its final status is still very much in question.

Jerusalem is replete with sites of sacred significance. King David, its founder, is said to be buried on Mount Zion, and this is also the site of the Last Supper, according to many Christians. It is also the place where Jesus reappeared after being dead for three days. This event is represented by the coenaculum, or the cenacle, a small, two-story structure within a larger complex of buildings on the summit of Mount Zion. The Franciscans built the upper storey in the 14th century to commemorate the Last Supper. It is also identified as the "upper room" in which the Holy Spirit descended upon the Apostles at Pentecost (Acts 2:2–3). The ground-floor room beneath the coenaculum contains a cenotaph that since the 12th century has been known as the "Tomb of King David"—even though the recorded burial place of the king was in the "City of David" on the Ofel Ridge (1 Kings 2:10). Beneath the level of the present floor are earlier Crusader, Byzantine, and Roman foundations. An apse behind the cenotaph is aligned with the Temple Mount, leading to speculation that this part of the building may have been a synagogue. Christian traditions also point to Mount Zion as the place where the Virgin Mary had fallen asleep for the last time. On that spot, a massive Benedictine basilica, named the Dormition Abbey, was erected. The Franciscans, on their return to Jerusalem, built the present Chapel of the Coenaculum in 1335. The *mihrab*, a Muslim prayer niche, was added in 1523, when the Franciscans were evicted from the building and the chapel was converted into a mosque.

The Via Dolorosa commemorates the Passion of Jesus and allows visitors to relive that experience, to a degree, while the site of the ascension on the Mount of Olives is also available. At the Garden of Gethsemane Jesus had prayed for the cup to be taken from him, and the Church of the Holy Sepulcher is yet another site of the resurrection, a very old church indeed that is possibly built on a Roman temple. It is sometimes identified with Golgotha, the place of the crucifixion, although this is probably some way outside the old walls of the city. The significance of this church means that it is shared by many denominations who do not always agree entirely on who controls what area and disputes that can become violent do arise.

The state of Israel came into the full possession of Jerusalem after the 1967 war and regards it as its indivisible capital, although no one else does. This means that Israel is in control of the religious sites of the three religions, and it has dealt with this by generally maintaining an Ottoman-like policy of leaving each community to regulate its own buildings, except where conflicts arise. So the two mosques on Temple Mount along with the other mosques in Jerusalem come under the authority of the Islamic *waqf*, or foundation, which looks after religious buildings, and Jews are not allowed onto the Temple Mount. There is great suspicion on both sides as to the intentions of the other, and some Muslims have denied that Jerusalem has any connection at all with Judaism and the temple, while some Jews and Christians see it as desirable for a third temple to be built on the Temple Mount, presumably after the removal of the mosques. The different Christian denominations are allowed to look after their own property in Jerusalem, but when a dispute arises, as it often does, the state steps in and tries to establish peace. Israel claims with some plausibility that there is now more freedom for the three religions than during the Jordanian occupation of Jerusalem from 1948 to 1967 since Jews can freely visit the city and its religious sites, which they could not do then. On the other hand, there are restrictions on Muslim worshippers, especially during times of tension, which did not exist when Jerusalem was controlled by a Muslim country.

The significance of Jerusalem for Jews cannot be overemphasized. It is mentioned more than 600 times in the Bible (but never in the Five Books of Moses) and three times a day in the prayers of traditional Jews, including a wish for the temple to be rebuilt. Synagogues are aligned so that the direction of prayer is toward Jerusalem and in particular the temple, and individuals praying anywhere are supposed to pray in that direction. For Muslims it is the third holiest city (hence its name, al-Quds) and the site of the first *qiblah*, direction of prayer, but is now largely significant because of the Prophet's night journey. He rode at night on the horse Buraq to Jerusalem, to the top of Mount Moriah and from there to the heavens to meet the prophets. In fact, the only reference in the Koran to Jerusalem is not that direct, but is only to the distant place of worship (*al-aqsa*) (17:1). For Christians, Jerusalem's significance rests on the life and death of Jesus there, and for some Christians the rebuilding of the temple plays an eschatological role without which Jesus will not return.

Mount Moriah is according to Jewish tradition the site of a number of key events in the Jewish Bible, including the temples, the sacrifice of Isaac, and Jacob's dream. It lies between Mount Zion to the west and the Mount of Olives to the east. It is regarded as the navel of the world, as the physical link between God and the Jews. Some early Christians believed that the navel stone of the universe lay in the Church of the Holy Sepulcher, where the True Cross had reposed, and the idea of Jerusalem as a particularly close place to heaven persisted in several metaphysical systems, including that of the Freemasons and their interest in the temple of Solomon and architectural symbols is based on it.

The idea of Jerusalem as an especially religious city has become very much part of the ideology of modern Israel, where it is contrasted with the largely secular and modern city of Tel Aviv, which resembles modern Western cities anywhere. Jerusalem remains a city where religious people tend to wish to live, and seek to preserve the religious character of their own areas. So the ultra-orthodox Jews who live in particular parts of the city may try to impose dress and behavior codes even on those just passing through their neighborhood, and restrict what can take place on the Sabbath, encouraging secular Jews to live in different parts of Israel. In Jerusalem the disputed nature of the city between Jews and Arabs has made it a natural focus of violence, which hardly encourages people to want to live there, unless they have strong religious reasons to do so.

According to the 2000 Israel Statistical Yearbook, there were at that time 1,204 synagogues, 158 churches, and 73 mosques in the city. Many of the synagogues are very small and belong to ultra-orthodox (*haredi*) communities who live in the city and spend much of their time involved in religious activities based in particular neighborhoods and minimizing their links with the state. The churches are made up of a wide variety of different denominations with foreign congregations and some with a local clientele among the Palestinian Christian population.

Oliver Leaman

See also: Franciscans; Moses; Pentecost; Synagogues.

References

Grabar, Oleg. *The Shape of the Holy: Early Islamic Jerusalem*. Princeton, NJ: Princeton University Press, 1996.

Hillenbrand, Robert. *The Architecture of Ottoman Jerusalem*. Louisville: Fons Vitae, 2002.

Mayer, Tamar, and Suleiman Mourad, eds. *Jerusalem: Idea and Reality*. London: Routledge, 2008.

Wasserstein, Bernard. *Divided Jerusalem: The Struggle for the Holy City*. New Haven: Yale University Press, 2001.

Jesuits

The Jesuits, officially the Society of Jesus, is one of the largest and more important religious orders that contributed to the worldwide spread of the Roman Catholic Church in the modern world. The order was founded by Saint Ignatius of Loyola (1491–1556) on August 15, 1534. At the founding, Loyola and six others took a vow of poverty and chastity and dedication to apostolic labor as enjoined by the pope. The Order was approved by the pope in 1540. As the Order evolved, it was divided into geographical provinces. Leadership is placed in a general congregation, a body that includes the superior general, the vicar general, all assistants and provincials, and two electors from each congregation. The meetings of the congregations are infrequent, usually called following the death of the superior general in order to elect his successor. The superior general serves for life and is the real leader of the Society, apart from the adopting of broad policies and legislation by the congregation.

The Order expanded rapidly and had gained almost 1,000 members by the time Loyola died. Its first major task was stemming the tide of Protestant advance. It is credited with turning back Protestant successes in France, Belgium, and parts of Central and Eastern Europe. Jesuits operated under cover in some Protestant countries where their detection meant arrest, torture, and possible execution. Higher education became the Order's primary tool, and the Order opened a number of colleges—46 before Loyola died and almost 100 more in the next generation. It also developed the modern seminary for the training of clergy, the most outstanding of which was the Roman College, now known as the Gregorian University, in Rome. These seminaries became important centers of learning that assumed the burden of countering the Protestant and other heresies.

Second only to education has been the Society's work in missions. The first missionary, commissioned within months of the Society's founding, was Saint Francis Xavier, who traveled to the East as a representative of the Jesuits. The Society grew as the exploration and colonization of the Western Hemisphere was beginning. Though several other orders, especially the Franciscans and Dominicans, were already on the scene in the French, Spanish, and Portuguese colonies, in the 1700s the Jesuits surpassed them in number of personnel. They were especially effective in the settlement of South America. The Society also opened work in Portuguese colonies on the coast of Africa, but Jesuits were frustrated in their efforts to slow the work of the slave merchants. Efforts in Asia centered on India, China, Japan, and the Philippines.

In 1773 the Society fell victim to its own success. Its educational attainments had placed members at the center of a number of controversies and led to the creation of numerous enemies. Others resented the work of missions that blocked the exploitation of people and land in the colonies. By the mid-18th century, proposals to suppress the Society began to be debated in Rome. Beginning in 1759, the Jesuits were expelled

A Jesuit-led Roman Catholic Church, Tokyo, Japan. (J. Gordon Melton)

from various South American countries, beginning with the confiscation of the Order's properties and possessions in Portugal. France acted against the Order in 1764, and Spain followed three years later. Under pressure, Pope Clement XIV dissolved the Society. Many became secular priests, and a few rose to power, among them John Carroll (1735–1815), the first archbishop in the United States.

Action on the suppression of the Order was not carried out in many places, and a remnant of the Order continued, possibly the most important group being the one in Russian-controlled Poland. Other pockets continued with tacit papal approval until 1814, when the suppression of the Order was repealed. The restored Order began with approximately 600 members. It grew steadily, and by the middle of the 20th century

had 35,000 members. The Order returned to its emphasis on higher education and scholarship, and the Society founded a number of outstanding colleges and universities. It also produced many Catholic scholars of note. At the same time the missionary emphasis also re-emerged, and thousands of members were sent to work in Africa and Asia. The expansion of the restored Society has not gone unchallenged; it has continually faced opposition from secular governments (especially France and Spain) and was totally suppressed by Communist rulers.

The Jesuits found an especially welcoming environment in the United States, though the Order was on occasion targeted by popular waves of anti-Catholicism. It has built a system of top-rated colleges and universities, among the most famous being Boston College;

Over the years, more than 25 Jesuits have been canonized.

The religious life, regulations, and directions for ministry are laid out in a set of writings known collectively as the Institutes. It includes a variety of papal documents; the Society's constitution; and the *Spiritual Exercises,* a book by Loyola outlining a special program of self-reflection and spiritual practice that each Jesuit utilizes as part of his own program of spiritual progress.

Society of Jesus
 CP 6139
00195 Roma
Italy
http://www.jesuit.org
http://www.sjweb.info/

J. Gordon Melton

See also: Francis Xavier; Ignatius of Loyola; Roman Catholic Church.

References

Barry, William A., and Robert E. Doherty. *Contemplatives in Action: The Jesuit Way.* Mahwah, NJ: Paulist Press, 2002.

Barthel, Manfred. *Jesuits: History and Legend of the Society of Jesus.* New York: Morrow, 1984.

Hollis, Christopher. *The Jesuits: A History.* New York: Macmillan, 1968.

Mitchell, David. *The Jesuits: A History.* New York: Franklin Watts, 1981.

Worcester, Thomas. *The Cambridge Companion to the Jesuits.* Cambridge: Cambridge University Press, 2008.

Portrait of Ignatius Loyola, who founded the Society of Jesus, also known as the Jesuits, in the 16th century. (Library of Congress)

Fordham, Georgetown, and Marquette universities; and the several Loyola Universities (Detroit, Chicago, New Orleans, Los Angeles).

In 2008, the Society of Jesus reported a total of 18,815 members of which 13,305 were priests, 2,295 were scholastic students, 1,758 were brothers, and 827 were novices. They were scattered around the world in 112 countries. Local residences/monasteries are organized into provinces, which in turn are divided among 10 regions called assistances. On January 19, 2008, Father Adolfo Nicolás was elected 30th superior general of the Society of Jesus. Headquarters of the Society is in Rome, as is its mother church, the Chiesa del Santissimo Nome di Gesù all'Argentina (the Church of the Most Holy Name of Jesus, or simply the Chiesa del Gesu).

JeungSanDo

JeungSanDo (also spelled Jeung Sanh Doh) is a new Korean religious movement, a Dao or Way, which grew out of the life and work of Kang Il-sun Sah-ok (1871–1909), better known as SangJeNim. He is believed by his followers to be the incarnation of the Lord God who ruled with the Triune God. The Lord God came from heaven to fulfill a set of prophecies, including the Buddhist prophecy of the coming Maitreya and the

Second Coming of Jesus expected by Christians. In JeungSanDo teachings, Shang-ti (Confucianism), the Jade Emperor (Daoism), Maitreya (Buddhism), and God (Western traditions) are the same. SangJeNim was the embodiment of this entity.

Kang grew up in poverty. In 1877 he reportedly experienced sudden enlightenment and in 1894 made the decision to save and enlighten the world. In 1901 he is believed to have defeated all evils and opened the Great Gate of Spirituality and to have begun the work of Reconstructing Heaven and Earth. He also began to gather disciples, the first of which was Kim Hyong-yol, designated the keeper of the Way of JeungSanDo. Kang predicted that within a relatively short time a good world would arise.

In 1907 he named Ko Pam-lye (1880–1935) as Sabu, the Head of all Women. He had already proclaimed that men and women were equal, and following his death in 1909, Lady Ko, better known as Tae-mo-nim (Holy Mother), became the leader of the movement. She assumed the task of propagating the new T'aeulju mantra, the chanting of which is believed to provide a lifeline to the enlightening and healing energy of T'aeul Heaven, the womb of the universe. Accompanying the mantra is a set of 16 tai chi movements corresponding to the sound symbols of the mantra, believed capable of activating the healing energy (*chi*) from the universe and pushing out the toxic energy from the body. Each movement is seen as related directly to the function of one or more internal organs. The movements are slow, controlled, and synchronized with the breath.

In the post–Korean War period, JeungSanDo experienced new life and began to spread throughout South Korea and then internationally. The publication of an English edition of the account of the founder's supernatural work, *JeungSanDo DoJeon*, in 1995 facilitated its movement into English-speaking lands.

As of 2009, JeungSanDo has centers in Japan, the Philippines, New Zealand, United Arab Emirates, Taiwan, Indonesia, Germany, the United States, Canada, and the United Kingdom.

JeungSanDo
c/o Jeung San Do Culture & Education Center
409-1 Jungri-don

Daedeok-gu, Daejeon
306-824, Republic of Korea
http://www.jsd.or.kr/jsd.net/ (in Korean)
http://www.jeungsando.org/ (in English)

J. Gordon Melton

See also: Buddhism; Confucianism; Daoism; Energy.

References

Flaherty, Robert Pearson. "JeungSanDo and the Great Opening of the Later Heaven: Millenarianism, Syncretism, and the Religion of Gang Il-sun." *Nova Religio* 7, no. 3 (March 2004): 26–44.

Gyeong-cheon, An. *The Holy Grand Master Sabunim's Lectures: The Way of Perfection.* Daejon, Republic of Korea: JeungSanDo Press, 1981.

JeungSanDo DoJeon. Seoul, Korea: Daewon Publishing Company, 1995.

JeungSanDo Publication Association, ed. *The Teachings of JeungSanDo.* Daejon, Republic of Korea: Daewon Press, 1997.

Jiu-Hua Shan

Jiu-Hua Shan is one of the four Buddhist sacred mountains of China. Located in Anhui Province, southwest of Nanjing, it is the mountain of the east. It is also considered especially sacred to Ksitigarbha (or Dizang) Bodhisattva.

The Buddhist history at Jiu Hua is usually dated from the arrival of Fu Hu, a monk who settled there in 503 CE and built a temple, called Fu-Hu-Cell. The middle of the eighth century became a time of significant Buddhist expansion. In 719, during the Tang dynasty (618–907), the Korean Prince Kim Gio Gak (aka Jin-Qiao-Jue, d. 793) came to live on Mount Jiuhua. He meditated for 75 years at Mount Jiu Hua and passed away at the age of 99. To the people, he closely resembled Bodhisattva Ksitigarbha and after his death, many came to believe that he was an emanation of the bodhisattva. He came to be called Gold Bodhisattva Dizang and a pagoda was built for his veneration. The building that came to house the seven-story pagoda was called the Hall of the Incarnation. From Kim Gio

Gak's stay, the mountain began to be identified with Ksitigarbha Bodhisattva.

As occurred at Wu Tai Shan in the north, the suppression of Buddhism under the reign of Tang Emperor Wuzong in 845 CE led to the closing and/or destruction of the Buddhist temples at Jiu Hua Shan and forced most of the monks and nuns who had resided there to return to secular life.

Buddhism was revived at Jiu Hua during the Five Dynasties period (907–960) but did not really expand until the Ming dynasty (1368–1661). The first Ming emperor, Chu-Yuan-Chang, had been a monk in An-Hui before assuming the throne. He and his successors provided funds to restore Hua-Cheng Temple, the oldest temple on the Mountain. Each year, the emperor came to Jiu-Hua Mountain on the 30th day of the 7th lunar month to worship Ksitigarbha Bodhisattva, each year. The emperors of the Qing dynasty (1662–1911) favored Vajrayana Buddhism and continued the annual attention to the mountain, though most favoring Wu Tai Shan. During this time, as many as 5,000 monks and nuns resided in more than 300 monasteries on Jiu Hua Mountain.

The policies imposed on Buddhism by the secular government of the Republic of China worked against the survival of Buddhist temples and monasteries. Some were abandoned and closed, others appropriated for secular use. All the temples were closed during the Cultural Revolution in the 1960s. Beginning in the 1980s, the temples were allowed to reopen, and, since that time, the government has donated funds to restore many of them. New ones have also been opened. Today, approximately 100 temples and monasteries can be found on or at Jiu-Hua Mountain. Almost all are dedicated to the worship of Ksitigarbha Bodhisattva, who is represented in a variety of unique pictures and statuary.

Among the many temples on Jiu Hua is the Hua-Cheng Temple, the oldest temple on the mountain, which also houses the Historical Relics Museum of Jiu-Hua Mountain. On display there are the Buddhist sutras from the Tang and Ming dynasties and the handwritten documents of the Emperor K'ang-His/Kang-Xi and Emperor Qian-Lung's of the Qing dynasty. In the Corporeal Body Hall of Bai-Sui Temple is the 350-year-old mummy of Monk Wu-Xia, still in good condition.

In 2001, plans were announced to create a mega-statue of Ksitigarbha at 155 meters (509 feet) to be completed around 2004. Several years later the date was changed to around 2008 and the size revised downward to 99 meters (325 feet), in honor of Kim Gio Gak, the emanation of Ksitigarbha, who reputedly ended his life when he was 99 years old.

The greatest time for pilgrims and tourists at Jiu Hua Mountain today is on Ksitigarbha's birthday, the 30th day of the 7th lunar month or the next day, the first day of the 8th lunar month.

Edward A. Irons

See also: Emei Shan; Ksitigarbha's/Jizo's Birthday; Mountains; Putuo Shan; Wu Tai Shan.

References

Le Bich Son. "Jiu-Hua Mountain: The Sacred Site of Ksitigarbha Bodhisattva." http://www.lebichson.org/Eng/00Jiuhua.htm. Accessed May 15, 2009.

Nanquin, Susan, and Chün-Fang Yü, eds. *Pilgrims and Sacred Sites in China.* Berkeley: University of California Press, 1992.

Shunxun, Nan, and Beverly Foit-Albert. *China's Sacred Sites.* Honesdale, PA: Himalayan Institute Press, 2007.

Jodo-shinshu

Jodo-shinshu (True Pure Land School) belongs to the so-called Pure Land tradition, the largest current of traditional Japanese Buddhism of which Jodo-shinshu constitutes the largest denominational family. The 10 existing Jodo-shinshu denominations count approximately 15 million adherents, more than 20,000 temples, and 30,000 priests (more than 90 percent male) in Japan.

The denomination traces its origin to Shinran (1173–1262), a disciple of Honen (1133–1212), the founder of Jodo-shu. Shinran was an adherent of the powerful "movement of the exclusive and single-minded *nembutsu*," which was deemed heretical by the established Buddhist orders. When the movement was prohibited in 1207, Honen and some of his followers, including Shinran, were excommunicated and exiled. Shinran's exile to Echigo, where he started to propagate his own interpretation of Honen's Pure Land teachings, is traditionally regarded as the starting point of the Jodo-shinshu. Being expelled from the Buddhist order, Shinran regarded himself as neither priest nor lay, married, and had children, thus paving the way for the eventual abolishment of celibacy in Japanese Buddhism as well as for hereditary priesthood. After his death, his youngest daughter Kakushin functioned as the first caretaker of her father's mausoleum at Otani, east of Kyoto. She was supported by followers of Shinran, and out of this group of caretakers evolved what is now known as the Jodo-shinshu. In 1321 Shinran's grandson Kakunyo turned the mausoleum into a temple and called it Hongan-ji, which eventually became one of Japan's most powerful religious institutions.

The group of Shinran's descendants did not gain any notable influence, however, until Rennyo (1415–1499), the so-called Eighth Chief Priest of Hongan-ji. The expansion of the sect, being involved in a number of peasants' uprisings known as *ikko-ikki*—referring to the then customary designation "Ikkoshu" for the sect—engendered suspicion among the established orders. The army of Tendai monks attacked Hongan-ji several times, and the temple was moved to other places more than once. Still, the influence of the Jodo-shinshu in the provinces grew and its temples took the shape of fortresses, while its chief priests (*monshu*) became as powerful as secular lords. In the late 16th century the sect's headquarters, Ishiyama Hongan-ji—a temple-fortress located in present-day Osaka—was destroyed by the troops of Oda Nobunaga, who regarded the powerful Buddhist temples as major obstacles to the unification of Japan. In 1592 the Hongan-ji was rebuilt in Kyoto. Ten years later, due to disputes over the leadership of the Hongan-ji, a new temple was founded east of the original Hongan-ji. The sect's headquarters was thus divided into the Eastern Hongan-ji and the Western Hongan-ji. The former is the headquarters of the Otani branch, the latter that of the Hongan-ji branch of Jodo-shinshu. The Otani-ha counts approximately 5.5 million members and 8,698 temples. The Hongan-ji branch, which is known in the United States as the Buddhist Churches of America, has approximately 7 million members, more than 32,000 priests, and 10,281 temples. Both groups are members of the Japan Buddhist Federation through which they relate to the World Fellowship of Buddhists.

Besides these two, there exist today eight more branches of comparatively minor significance. The lay-oriented Jodo-shinshu has abolished all monastic elements, and training of priests has been reduced to the extreme. The major branches of Jodo-shinshu run universities and other educational institutions, and actively promote scholarly and social activities.

Doctrinally, the Jodo-shinshu differs considerably from the Jodo-shu, which derives its teachings from Shinran's master Honen. Among the so-called Three Pure Land Sutras the *Muryoju-kyo* (Sutra on the [Buddha of] Immeasurable Life) holds the central position. Shinran stressed faith in the "Other Power of Amida Buddha's Vow" rather than the practice of calling upon this Buddha's name (*nembutsu*). According to his interpretation, the *nembutsu* is merely a thankful reaction to the experience of absolute faith in the fact of being saved by Amida, which, again, is conferred to men by the Buddha. Shinran emphasized the sinful beings' utter dependence on Amida's grace, which is particularly directed toward those who are unable to do any religious or secular good.

Jodo-shinshu has been remarkably active and successful in overseas missions, also among non-Japanese, especially in Canada, the United States, Brazil, and Western Europe. In recent years, however, membership in the United States has been shrinking significantly.

Honganji-ha
600-8501 Kyoto-shi
Shimogyo-ku
Horikawa-dori
Hanaya-machi sagari
Official website in Japanese: http://www.hongwanji .or.jp/
Official website in English: http://www2.hongwanji .or.jp/english/

Otani-ha
600-8308 Kyoto-shi
Shimogyo-ku
Karasuma-dori
Shichijo-agaru

Tokiwa-chō
Official website: http://www.tomo-net.or.jp

Christoph Kleine

See also: Honen; Japan Buddhist Federation; Jodo-shu; Pure Land Buddhism; Shinran; World Fellowship of Buddhists.

References

Buddhist Handbook for Shinshu Followers. Tokyo: Hokuseido Press, 1969.

Dobbins, James C. *Jōdo Shinshū: Shin Buddhism in Medieval Japan.* Bloomington: Indiana University Press, 1989.

Jodo Shinshu. A Guide. Kyoto: Hongwanji International Center, 2002.

Porcu, Elisabetta. *Pure Land Buddhism in Modern Japanese Culture, Numen Book Series; 121.* Leiden: Brill, 2008.

Pure Land Buddhism WWW Virtual Library by Jérôme Ducor. www.pitaka.ch/indxshin.htm.

The Collected Works of Shinran. Kyoto, Jodo Shinshu Hongwanji-ha (Honganji International Center) 1997. 2 vols. Shin Buddhism Translation Series. Vol. 1: The Writings; vol. 2: Introductions, Glossaries, and Reading Aids. http://www .shinranworks.com/.

Jodo-shu

Jodo-shu (Pure Land School) belongs to the so-called Pure Land tradition of Japanese Buddhism, to which almost 20 million Japanese adhere. The major branch of the denominational family called Jodo-shu counts approximately 6 million adherents, 6,932 temples, and 8,000 clerics (more than 90 percent male) in Japan and thus constitutes one of the major Japanese Buddhist denominations.

Tradition claims that Jodo-shu was founded in 1175 by the Tendai monk Honen (1133–1212) when he decided to leave the Enryaku-ji Monastery on Mount Hiei in order to propagate his Pure Land teaching among the populace. Honen maintained that the then already popular practice of invoking Amida Buddha's name (a practice called in Japanese *nembutsu*) with the intention of being born in his Pure Land of Bliss was the only appropriate practice in the "latter days of the dharma" (Buddhist law). Honen chose the so-called Three Pure Land Sutras as the scriptural basis of his Jodo-shu and claimed to follow the interpretation of these scriptures by the Chinese monk Shandao (613–681). According to Shandao, Amida Buddha himself, in his vow to save all sentient beings, had selected the act of calling upon his name as the practice that would inevitably lead to birth in his paradise, and thus liberate from the circle of birth and death. Honen also adopted Daochuo's (562–645) distinction between the Gateway of the Holy Path, under which he subsumed all the teachings and practices of Mahayana as well as so-called Hinayana Buddhism, and the Gateway of the Pure Land. Honen's major ideas are developed in his *Collection of Passages on the Selection of the Nembutsu in [Amida's] Original Vow (Senchaku-hongan-nembutsu-shu)*, written, according to tradition, upon the request of regent Fujiwara Kanezane in 1198. Jodo-shu places itself in the tradition of the Chinese monks Tanluan, Daochuo, Shandao, Huaigan, and Shaokang, but lacks any incessant lineage of personal transmission up to Honen, a fact that weakened the movement's claims of orthodoxy.

Under the doctrinal guidance of Honen the movement of the "single-minded and exclusive nembutsu" grew rapidly. Many clerics and laymen appreciated Honen's simple but persuasive message. However, the established Buddhist orders and schools harshly criticized the movement for being intolerant, exclusionist, one-sided, and heretical. After a number of scandals had raised fears that Honen's followers might bring about social disturbance, the secular authorities yielded to the demands of the Buddhist establishment and prohibited the movement's activities in 1207. As a consequence, Honen and a couple of his close disciples were excommunicated and exiled. The popularity of his doctrine, however, remained unbroken. After Honen's death in 1212 the movement split into several branches, among which the so-called Chinzei branch eventually became dominant. Until the early 17th century, however, Jodo-shu failed to gain official recognition as an independent denomination. After World War II several factions seceded, but in 1962 they merged again, and

Pure Land Buddhist temple, Taichung, Taiwan. (J. Gordon Melton)

the Chion-in in Kyoto, founded in 1234 by Honen's disciple Genchi at the site where his master had resided, was accepted as Jodo-shu's headquarters, or Grand Head Temple. A second, much smaller denominational family of Jodo-shu is called Seizan-ha. The three denominations belonging to the Seizan group count less than 500,000 adherents.

A monastic way of life is mainly upheld by nuns, whereas the temples are run by married male priests; a priest will, as a rule, bequeath his temple to his eldest son. Jodo-shu runs universities, colleges, schools, and kindergartens, and promotes various scholarly and social activities. It is a member of the Japan Buddhist Federation, through which it relates to the World Fellowship of Buddhists. Major strongholds of Jodo-shu outside Japan are regions with a large Japanese population such as Hawaii (14 institutions), the United States

(2 temples), and Brazil (2 temples). Hitherto, the denomination has developed no notable missionary activities among non-Japanese.

Jodo-shu Headquarters
605-0062 Kyoto-shi
Higashiyama-ku, Hayashi Shita-machi 400-8
Japan
Official website in Japanese: http://www.jodo.or.jp
Official website in English: http://www.jodo.org/
Jodo Shu Research Institute: http://www.jsri.jp/

Christoph Kleine

See also: Honen; Japan Buddhist Federation; Pure Land Buddhism; World Fellowship of Buddhists.

References

Coates, Harper H., and Ishizuka Ryūgaku. *Honen the Buddhist Saint: His Life and Teaching.* Kyoto:

The Society for the Publication of Sacred Books of the World, 1925.

Kleine, Christoph. *Hōnens Buddhismus des Reinen Landes: Reform, Reformation oder Häresie.* Frankfurt/Main: Peter Lang, 1996.

Machida, Soho. *Renegade Monk: Hōnen and Japanese Pure Land Buddhism.* Berkeley: University of California Press, 1999.

Senchakushū English Translation Project, ed. *Hōnen's Senchakushō: Passages on the Selection of the Nembutsu in the Original Vow (Senchaku Hongan Nembutsu Shō).* Classics in East Asian Buddhism. Honolulu and Tokyo: The Kuroda Institute, 1998.

Pure Land Buddhism WWW Virtual Library by Jérôme Ducor. http://www.pitaka.ch/indxshin .htm. Accessed March 21, 2009.

John of God Movement, The

While John of God has been working as a medium-healer in Brazil for four decades, only in the past decade has he become well known overseas. In 2006 alone he was invited to conduct healing events in Germany, the United States, and New Zealand. He returned to the United States and New Zealand in 2007, and in 2008 and 2009 he was once again in the United States. A large number of people attended each of these events, and many more have been to his healing center in the town of Abadiânia, central Brazil. Among the visitors are guides, healers, and the ill, who wish either to improve their healing powers or to obtain treatment. Several of them are building homes and establishing businesses (guest houses, restaurants, and Internet cafes) around the Casa de Dom Inácio, the healing center.

João Teixeira de Farias—aka João de Deus in Brazil and John of God overseas—was born in Cachoeira da Fumaça, a small town in the state of Goiás in 1942. He grew up in poverty and had very little schooling. João started prophesying at an early age and recalls having his first vision at 16. He tells of how while bathing in a river, Santa Rita de Cássia, an important saint in the Brazilian Catholic pantheon, appeared. Attesting to the highly syncretic nature of the Brazilian religious arena, it is alleged that the Catholic saint told him to go to a Kardecist Spiritist center in Campo Grande (the present capital of Mato Grosso do Sul state). There, for the first time, he maintains that he took on the entity of King Solomon and healed many people while oblivious to what he was doing. This was the first of the more than 30 entities he now channels.

After this incident, he traveled around central and northern Brazil healing people and doing odd jobs. Following the instruction of his spiritual guides, he finally settled in a small building near the highway in Abadiânia, a village 62 miles southwest of Brasília (Cumming and Leffler 2007, 1–5; Pellegrino-Estrich 2001, 42–43; Póvoa 1994, 45–47). John of God asserts that he is the medium of the spirits of deceased doctors, surgeons, healers, saints, and people who were remarkable in their lifetimes. He says he takes on these entities in a trance and does not remember his acts when he becomes conscious again. John of God is part of a small but significant group of medium healers who use kitchen knives, scissors, and scalpels to operate on people while in trance.

Although he declares himself Catholic, his is a highly syncretic Catholicism combining Kardecist Spiritism, Umbanda, and Freemasonry. Kardecist Spiritism is the religion that is flagged whenever people inquire about John of God's healing practices. Spiritist books are sold at the Casa shop; books and documentaries by foreign guides all call John of God's cosmology Spiritism.

Casa de Dom Inácio opens only three days a week. There are two healing sessions a day with approximately 500 people at each. Several healing methods are used by John of God in trance. He may prescribe herbs (sold at the Casa pharmacy), crystal beds (where the patient lies under a stand with seven fingers where crystals are placed, one for each chakra), sacred waterfall baths, meditation (or "current"), and invisible or visible (with cut) operations. Operations are conducted "to resolve a current physical ailment . . . to resolve a future health problem or . . . to clear some spiritual issue that is affecting your life and your mission" (Casa Guide for English Speaking Visitors 2006, 18). Patients undergoing invisible operations are told to close their eyes and place their hands on the sick part of the body while a volunteer prays aloud. Operations are concluded when John of God comes to the room and announces: "In the name of God you are all operated on." People are then to go back to the *pousadas* (guest houses) and rest for 24 hours before they can return to the Casa. Those who have visible operations may have their skin cut with a scalpel, have their eyes scraped with a kitchen knife, or have surgical scissors inserted into their nostrils. An operation in one area of the body may be for another area. There is no asepsis or anesthetic, but people say they do not experience pain or develop infections.

If people cannot come to the Casa, they can send their picture through a friend or the guides. John of God in trance may draw a cross on the picture (meaning the person will need to come to the Casa eventually) and prescribe herbs. Another means of keeping the transnational connection and hence continuing the healing process is through crystal beds. While crystal beds were only found at the Casa, recently it has started selling them to foreigners. The sacred objects bought at the Casa shop, the DVDs, books on Spiritism and John of God, and crystal beds create a growing global network of healers, tour guides, and people who are ill or are seeking spiritual growth. They carry flows of ideas on French-Brazilian Spiritism, mediumship, and particular methods of healing to their home countries. In many parts of the world followers have started to meet to "sit in current" (meditate) as they would in the Casa. Accordingly, they believe the entities are present and may heal them. Some people are learning Portuguese to communicate with the healer.

This traffic of people, commodities, and ideas has created a snowball phenomenon: the more intense the traffic, the more people go to Brazil. The Internet has certainly had a role in this intensification: sites selling tours and books and films of visible surgeries on You Tube have facilitated the spread of information about the center.

Cristina Rocha

See also: Freemasonry; Meditation; Pilgrimage; Possession; Roman Catholic Church; Spiritism; Umbanda.

References

Cumming, Heather, Karen Leffler, and Amri Goswami. *John of God: The Brazilian Healer Who's Touched the Lives of Millions*. New York: Atria Books/Beyond Words, 2006.

Pellegrino-Estrich, Robert. *The Miracle Man: The Life Story of Joao de Deus*. Goiania: Grafica Terra, 2002.

Rocha, Cristina. "Global Power Relations at Play in Fieldwork: Researching Spiritism in Brazil." In Fieldwork in Religion special issue, *Religion and Fieldwork in Latin America* 3, no. 2 (2009).

Rocha, Cristina. "Seeking Healing Transnationally: Australians, John of God and Brazilian Spiritism." *TAJA (The Anthropology Journal of Australia)* 20, no. 2 (2009): 229–246.

Rocha, Cristina. "Quêtes transnationales de médecines 'traditionnelles': la guérison spirituelle brésilienne en Océanie." *Socio-Anthropologie* 21 (2007): 37–50.

Rocha, Cristina. "Spiritual Tourism: Brazilian Faith Healing Goes Global." In *On the Road to Being There: Studies in Pilgrimage and Tourism*, edited by William H. Swatos, 105–123. Leiden: Brill, 2006.

John XXIII, Pope

1881–1963; r. 1958–1963

Pope John XXIII, an obscure elderly cardinal elected as pope in 1958 as a compromise candidate by a conflicted college of cardinals, became the most influential pope of the 20th century. He called the Second Vatican Council, which worked to reform the church and which altered longstanding relations with other Christian communities, Judaism, and the other major world religions.

John XXIII was born Angelo Guiuseppe Roncalli to a peasant family in Sotto il Monte, Lombardy, in northern Italy, on November 25, 1881. He was directed toward the priesthood from early in his life and as a youth was sent to Rome to study. He was ordained as a priest in 1904 and the following year became the secretary to the bishop of Bergamo. During his decade in that position, he also taught church history in the diocesan seminary. His priestly career was interrupted in 1914 by World War I. He was drafted into the army

Most noted for convening the Second Vatican Council, Pope John XXIII ushered in a period of reform in the Catholic Church, seeking to promote Christian unity and to reach the poor of the world. (Library of Congress)

and served in the medical corps as a stretcher bearer. The vicious nature of the war deeply affected him and led to a lifetime of peacemaking activity.

As a student, the young Roncalli developed a positive attitude toward the modern world and privately criticized Pope Pius X (r. 1903–1914) for a seeming fear of modernity. After the war, he was called to Rome, where he held a minor office in the congregation for the missions. He showed a degree of independence by opposing Vatican policy with his support of the Popular Party headed by Luigi Sturzo, a popular political leader who opposed the rise of Mussolini. At this time he developed a relationship with future cardinal and pope Giovanni Battista Montini (1897–1978).

Roncalli's career moved upward through the 1920s. In 1921, Pope Benedict XV (r. 1914–1922) named him the Italian president of the Society for the Propagation of the Faith. In 1925, Pope Pius XI (r. 1922–1939) appointed Roncalli as apostolic nuncio to Bulgaria. The office carried the rank of archbishop. At the time of his consecration, he announced his motto *obedientia et pax* (obedience and peace), which some saw as a rebuke of the Fascist motto, *credire, obedire, combattere* (believe, obey, fight). His task also took him from Italy and the Vatican and placed him in direct contact with Eastern Orthodox Christians and Muslims, as well as making him an advocate for a Roman Catholic community (both Latin rite and Eastern Catholic) that existed as minorities.

In 1934 Roncalli received a further appointment as apostolic delegate to Greece and Turkey, which led to his move to Istanbul. Here he came in direct contact with Photius II (r. 1929–1935) and his successor Benjamin I (r. 1936–1946), who as ecumenical patriarchs were the spiritual leaders of the Eastern Orthodox community. Remaining in Istanbul through World War II, he used his diplomatic position to assist the network that facilitated the movement of many Jews from Eastern Europe to Palestine.

Roncalli's efforts were rewarded after the war with is assignment to France as the papal nuncio. However, he again found himself in a very different war, a war of words between the Vatican, which revived older antimodernist themes, and a growing relationship with some of the leading French Catholic thinkers, all working on the intellectual horizons—Ives Congar (1904–1995), Jacques Maritain (1882–1973), Henri de Lubac (1896–1991), and Emmanule Cardinad Suhard (1874–1949). He proved a skillful diplomat.

Now in his senior years, in 1953 the Vatican named Roncalli the cardinal archbishop of Venice, a post seemingly designed to allow the aging cleric a comfortable retirement. Instead, he became a hardworking archdiocesan leader. He made it his task to visit every parish and join in the effort of finding jobs for the unemployed. He worked openly with Socialist and Communist leaders on common goals.

Then, in 1958, he attended the conclave of cardinals called to elect the new pope. Unable to reach a decision, the conclave turned to the aging cardinal Roncalli to hold the office for a few years. He took the name John XXIII, an interesting choice given his background in church history, as it asserted a lineage of Pope Gregory XII (r. 1406–1415) over against the claim of anti-pope John XXIII (r. 1410–1415), whose resignation of the papacy cleared the way for healing one of the major schisms in church leadership.

Quickly, Roncalli startled the people who had placed him in office. He held informal and lighthearted meetings with laypeople; he traveled outside the Vatican; and, a prelude of things to come, he removed a phrase referring to "perfidious Jews" from the prayers for Holy Week. Then, in an even more startling act, the new pope culminated his first year in office by announcing his call for a new all-church Council, choosing as his podium the church of St. Paul's Outside the Walls, whose very name conveys its location outside the original precincts of Rome. He then used his diplomatic skills to prevent the attempts of curial conservatives to first delay the Council and then limit the subjects to be considered.

Pope John freed the Council to discuss a broad spectrum of issues, and the bishops passed a number of statements on the church. Major decisions included the promotion of worship in the language of the worshipping community instead of ecclesial Latin; a denunciation of anti-Semitism and a new openness toward the Jewish community; a call for more positive relations with Protestant and Eastern Orthodox churches; further recognition of Eastern Catholics; and building a dialogical relationship with the major world religions.

Pope John XXIII died June 3, 1963, before the Council could complete its work. His old friend Giovanni Battista Montini was elected to succeed him. Much more conservative than his predecessor, Pope Paul VI (r. 1963–1978) acted quickly to first remove the issues of priestly celibacy and artificial birth control from the Council's agenda and then to end the Council's work in 1965. However, by this time, most of the Council's business had been finished.

In the wake of Vatican II, the Roman Catholic Church entered a generation of adaptation to the changes wrought by the Council, which became most visible in the institution of the new Mass and the discipline (and schism) of the pockets of the most conservative elements of the church. A new era of dialogue with Protestants, Eastern Orthodox, and the various communities of the non-Christian religions was launched

(and still continues) at all levels of the church's life, and significant steps were made to rid the church of all remnants of anti-Semitism.

J. Gordon Melton

See also: Eastern Orthodoxy; Roman Catholic Church.

References

Calvez, Jean-Yves. *The Social Thought of John XXIII: Mater et Magistra.* Chicago: Regnery, 1965.

Hales, E. E. Y. *Pope John and His Revolution.* Garden City, NY: Doubleday & Company, 1965.

Hebblethwaite, Peter. *Pope John XXIII: Shepherd of the Modern World.* Garden City, NY: Doubleday, 1985.

John XXIII, Pope. *Journal of a Soul.* New York: McGraw-Hill, 1965.

Riga, Peter J. *John XXIII and the City of Man.* Westminster, MD: Newman Press, 1966.

Johnston Island

Johnston Island, a coral atoll in the central Pacific Ocean, is a small island dominated by an airfield. With it is another island, Sand Island, and two islands created by human effort. The two original islands have been greatly enlarged by a process known as coral dredging, the same process used to create the two additional islands. The total land mass of the four islands is about one square mile. The population is currently around 1,300 military and related civilian personnel.

Johnston Island was uninhabited when it was discovered in 1807 by the British sea captain for whom the island is named. The nearby Sand, East, and North islets are now combined in a U.S. dependency. Since 1934 the islands have been under the administration of the United States Navy, and unauthorized civilian visitors are not allowed.

There are no permanent religious buildings or congregations on the islands, and all services are organized by navy chaplains, primarily for those members of the Roman Catholic Church or of Protestant profession (interdenominational services without any attempt to deal with particular Protestant denominations).

J. Gordon Melton

See also: Roman Catholic Church.

References

Barrett, David, ed. *The Encyclopedia of World Christianity.* 2nd ed. New York: Oxford University Press, 2001.

Bissio, Roberto Remo, et al. *Third World Guide 93/94.* Montevideo, Uruguay: Instituto del Tercer Mundo, 1992.

■ Jordan

The modern country of Jordan is noted as a major site of civilization going back to the Paleolithic Age. As presently constituted, the country includes some 35,637 square miles of territory west of the state of Israel. It additionally shares borders with Syria, Iraq, and Saudi Arabia. The population is currently 6.2 million (2008).

Archaeological evidence indicates that the area has been occupied since ancient times. In the biblical era, it was occupied by the nations of Gilead, Moab, and Edom. In 331 BCE, Alexander the Great (356–323) conquered the area today known as the Near East, including this area, bringing Hellenic culture along with his conquering army.

Between 400 BCE and 106 BCE, the Nabataean civilization flourished in what is now southern Jordan. Its ancient capital, Petra, now a popular tourist attraction, was in its time one of the desert outposts of the Roman Empire. During the rule of the Roman Empire between 63 BCE and 324 CE, the Decapolis, a league of 10 cities (of which Jeresh, Philadelphia [now Amman], Umm, Qais, and Pella were in Jordan) was formed to facilitate commercial enterprise. Later during the Byzantine period (324–632), Jordan provided commercial wares and foodstuffs to travelers on caravan routes linking the Mediterranean to China.

Of interest to Jews and Christians are the numerous holy sites located in Jordan, recorded in both Hebrew scripture and New Testament writings. John the Baptist is supposed to have lived in the area around Bethany beyond the Jordan River, the river where John baptized Jesus. There are reports that Jesus also traveled to Bethany seeking a safe haven from hostile groups. It is thought that the cities of Sodom and Go-

The Petra Great Temple, Jordan. (Corel)

morrah, whose destruction is described in Genesis, were near the Dead Sea. Another location near Mukawer is supposed to be the site where John the Baptist was imprisoned by Herod Antipas, who later beheaded John to please his wife, Salome. Mount Nebo, 3,281 feet above the Dead Sea, is noted as the area where Moses first saw the Holy Land and where he subsequently died and was buried.

The Arab-Islamic era began in 630 and during that era the region was ruled by the Umayyad and Abbasid dynasties, of Damascus and Baghdad, respectively. In the seventh century, this region was the site of the Battle of Yarmuk, in which the Arabs fought Heraclius (ca. 575–641), the Byzantine emperor, and won access to the Fertile Crescent, now in Iraq. During the Crusades, the western region of the territory served as the operational base for the military. In 1099, the Crusaders occupied Jerusalem. By 1187 Saladin (Salah

JORDAN

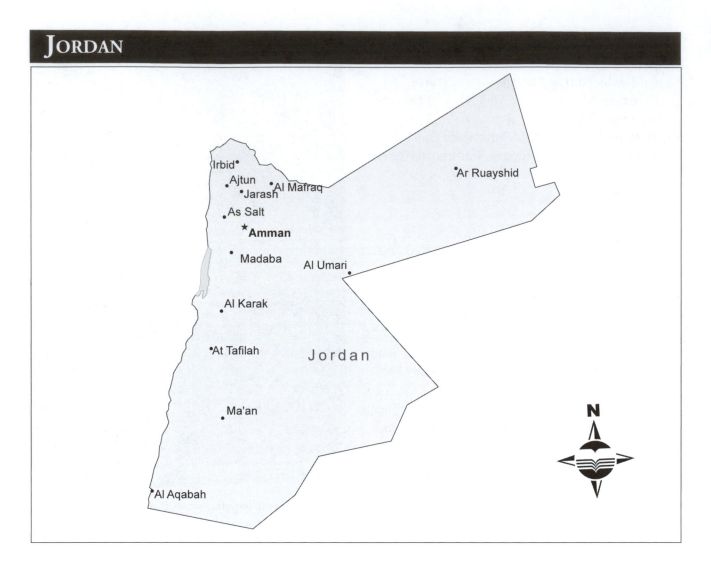

ad Din; 1137–1193) had fought, conquered, and driven back the Crusaders at Kerek, resulting in their withdrawal from the Near East.

A 300-year rule by the Mamelukes, a military and political force made up of former slaves from Egypt, followed, and then Jordan fell to the Ottoman Empire, which made the territory a district administered from Damascus until World War I. The clandestine Sykes-Picot Treaty between France and England in 1916 gave the French control over Lebanon and Syria, while England gained a mandate over Iraq and Palestine (Palestine then included modern Jordan).

From 1920 until May 1946, the conflict and warfare over boundary lines and rulership continued. In 1920, Prince Abdullah (1882–1951) seized power and organized the nomadic Jordanian Bedouins, who were loyal to him. Fearing a hostile outbreak, the English offered Abdullah the Emirate of Transjordan (under their protection), while his opponent, Faisal, received control of Mesopotamia, now known as Iraq.

After taking part in the Arab-Israeli war of 1948–1949, Transjordan took the name of Jordan and annexed Arab Palestine, including the West Bank of the Jordan River, along with Palestinian refugees who had left Israel and Jerusalem. Palestinians make up two-thirds of the population of Jordan. King Hussein (1953–1999), who assumed the throne in 1953, supported the Palestine Liberation Organization (PLO). An incident known as Black September occurred in September 1970, when a number of Palestinians were killed by the army of Jordan for political reasons. Despite internal problems caused by a refugee situation, it is the money that Palestinian migrant workers send home to Jordan that underwrites the economy. In July 1989,

Jordan

Religion	Followers in 1970	Followers in 2010	% of Population	Annual % growth 2000–2010	Followers in 2025	Followers in 2050
Muslims	1,512,000	6,040,000	93.6	3.07	7,494,000	9,424,000
Christians	83,400	197,000	3.1	−0.63	200,000	216,000
Orthodox	38,600	135,000	2.1	0.01	130,000	130,000
Roman Catholics	30,400	32,700	0.5	−3.73	30,000	32,000
Protestants	5,900	11,500	0.2	1.10	18,000	25,000
Agnostics	22,000	164,000	2.5	2.78	250,000	350,000
Atheists	3,500	31,900	0.5	2.85	44,000	65,000
Baha'is	700	16,500	0.3	2.99	35,000	60,000
New religionists	1,200	3,500	0.1	2.93	5,000	6,000
Total population	**1,623,000**	**6,453,000**	**100.0**	**2.93**	**8,029,000**	**10,121,000**

Hussein relinquished his claim to the West Bank, which had been lost to Israel in the 1967 war. Problems with the cabinet led to some political reforms, and voting was allowed in 1989. In 1991, Hussein joined the leadership of the several political parties in signing a new Constitution, which included political rights for women and removed the restrictions that had disallowed a free press. In 1999, Hussein was succeeded by his son, King Abdullah, the present ruler of Jordan.

Folk culture has left an indelible imprint on Jordan from the pre-Islamic era. Of the folk beliefs, belief in the evil eye is the most common (as it is in a number of Mediterranean countries). Other practices, although done in the name of Islam, are antithetical to Islamic orthodoxy. For example, amulets made of paper containing verses from the Koran are worn, prepared by heterodox shaykhs for spiritual empowerment and protection, and people frequent "saints," who are believed to have holiness (*baraka*). Visits to shrines are typical for people who wish to have children, a practice frowned upon by orthodox Islam. Jordanian Muslims generally have a strong work ethic, and pious expressions such as *inshallah* (God willing) and *bismallah* (in the name of God) accompany most important everyday activities.

In 1948, the population of the East Bank was about 340,000. The 1950 annexation of the West Bank swelled the population to about 900,000. After the 1957–1958 civil uprising an additional 250,000 to 300,000 West Bank Palestinians entered Jordan as refugees. Most refugees live in camps of hasty construction with poor sanitation facilities around Amman and the northern areas. Palestinians of the East Bank are caught in the throes of a national identity crisis.

During the 1950s pan-Arabism emerged, and Jordan's leaders strongly recommended Jordanian sovereignty over the contested areas. The loss of the West Bank in 1967 and subsequent Israeli occupation furthered a nationalist climate that promoted the PLO, which offered an alternative identity for the displaced Palestinians. Today the Palestine Authority led by Mahmoud Abbas (b. 1935) attempts to provide a sort of government protection agency for the Palestinians who through warfare and border disputes are dispersed in several countries that are not their original homeland. King Hussein of Jordan (1935–1999) attempted to modernize Jordan. His oldest son Abdullah (b. 1962) has assumed the throne and seems to be following the policies his father had put in place. Noteworthy is that Abdullah's wife is a Palestinian. The government has moved from an absolute monarchy in 1946 to a constitutional monarchy in 1991. There is a Senate with 40 members and a House of Representatives with 60 members.

More than 90 percent of the Jordanians are Muslims, with approximately 8 percent Arab Christians. The majority of Christians are Orthodox, the area being traditionally assigned to the Greek Orthodox Patriarchate of Jerusalem. Those affiliated with that Patriarchate make it currently the largest Christian body in the country, with more than 80,000 members.

There is a small group of Greek Catholics (30,000), attached to the patriarch of Jerusalem of the Melkite Catholic Church, and a Latin Rite Roman

Catholic Church community of about 12,000. There are a few congregations of Orthodox churches headquartered in neighboring countries, including the Syriac Orthodox Patriarchate of Antioch and All the East, the Coptic Orthodox Church, and the Armenian Apostolic Church (See of the Great House of Cilicia).

The Church of England has had mission stations in Jordan for more than a century. The Church Missionary Society, along with the Jerusalem and the East Mission, had to cut back services after the war of 1948, but work continues as part of the Episcopal Church in Jerusalem and the Middle East. The Old Hospital at Nablus is now maintained by the Arab Episcopal Community. There is a Bishop's School for Boys in Amman and St. George's School in Jerusalem.

The Christian and Missionary Alliance has been working in Jordan for more than 50 years and wishes to turn its property over to the Evangelical Church of the Christian Alliance, who have no missionaries but several pastored congregations. The Southern Baptist Convention began work in 1952, but political instability caused their work to languish. They have a bookstore and five churches affiliated with the Jordanian Baptist Convention, now possibly the largest Protestant Free church group, with more than 1,500 members. (The larger Evangelical Lutheran Church in Jordan had its work on the West Bank, and so is now in Israeli territory.) The very conservative Independent Board for Presbyterian Foreign Missions has worked in occupied Jordan south of Jerusalem. The Baraka Bible College opened in 1970, offering a bachelor in theology degree. World Presbyterian Missions has worked in Aqaba and Ma'an, in the extreme southern portion of Jordan. American Friends (Quakers) have had two excellent schools at Ramallah on the West Bank (now Israeli territory).

Church World Service and Lutheran Relief, as well as the Mennonite Central Committee, have been engaged in relief work in Jordan for a number of years. These groups provide resources to Palestinian refugees and have distributed food, clothes, and medicines in Jordan proper and in the West Bank. The Conservative Baptist Foreign Mission Association arrived in Jordan in 1956 and, except for a brief period during the 1967 war, has had a small presence in Amman, with 3 churches totaling about 170 people. Also present in the country are the Seventh-day Adventist Church, the United Pentecostal Church, and the Church of the Nazarene.

Islam continues to be by far the largest religious group, with 93.5 percent of the population. Most are Sunnis who follow the Shafaiite School of jurisprudence. There is a small group of Chechens of Caucasian extraction who are Shias, and some 3,000 Alevis. Nomadic Bedouins follow their ancient customs first before the teachings from Islam.

There are some adherents of the Baha'i Faith near Adasiya in the Jordan Valley, and members of the Druze tradition are generally found near the Syrian border. Among the more interesting groups in the country is the Essene Church in the Hashemite Kingdom of Jordan, a Gnostic group.

The government has accorded official government recognition to the Greek Orthodox, Roman Catholic, Greek Catholic (Melkite), Armenian Orthodox, Maronite Catholic, Assyrian, Anglican, Lutheran, Seventh-day Adventist, United Pentecostal Church International, and Presbyterian churches. Several other churches are registered with the Ministry of Justice as societies rather than churches. The government does not recognize Jehovah's Witnesses, the United Pentecostal Church International, the Churches of Christ, or the Church of Jesus Christ of Latter-day Saints, though all are holding religious services without interference. Although they can practice their faith rather freely, Christians are discouraged from encouraging conversion to the Christian faith, since conversion attempts are considered legally incompatible with Islam and hence officially prohibited.

Members of the Baha'i Faith face official discrimination. Rather than viewing them as a separate religion, authorities define them as Muslims, thus their personal and family matters are referred to the Muslim law courts for adjudication. The government also refuses to register property belonging to the Baha'i community. In spite of these regulations, however, Jordan offers its minority religions more freedom than many of its neighboring countries.

Gail M. Harley and J. Gordon Melton

See also: Alevism; Armenian Apostolic Church (See of the Great House of Cilicia); Baha'i Faith; Christian and Missionary Alliance; Church of England; Church of Jesus Christ of Latter-day Saints; Church of the Nazarene; Coptic Orthodox Church; Druze; Episcopal Church in Jerusalem and the Middle East; Greek Orthodox Patriarchate of Jerusalem; Jehovah's Witnesses; Melkite Catholic Church; Roman Catholic Church; Seventh-day Adventist Church; Shafiite School of Islam; Southern Baptist Convention; Syriac Orthodox Patriarchate of Antioch and All the East; United Pentecostal Church International.

References

Moaddel, Mansoor. *Jordanian Exceptionalism: A Comparative Analysis of State-Religion Relationships in Egypt, Iran, Jordan, and Syria.* New York: Palgrave Macmillan, 2002.

Salibi, Kamal S. *A Modern History of Jordan.* London: I. B. Tauris, 1993.

Tal, Nachman. *Radical Islam: In Egypt and Jordan.* Eastbourne, East Sussex, UK: Sussex Academic Press, 2005.

Judaism

Jewish synagogue, London. (J. Gordon Melton)

Judaism refers to the religious traditions of the Jewish people, a people dispersed since antiquity, whose major contemporary centers, in the United States and Israel, reveal a startling diversity of beliefs, praxis, and even ethnicities. Nevertheless, these varying interpretations of Judaism share the historic concepts of Torah, as both a record of the early history of the Jewish people and as a body of precepts and laws guiding its behavior; Israel, meaning the ancient homeland and the nation; and God and the unique covenant the Holy One made with the chosen people to give to them the land of Israel and the Torah in return for their obedience to sacred laws. The Jewish people today believe themselves to be the direct descendants of ancient Israel as described in the Torah. However, at various times and places other individuals and groups entered into this nation.

Because Jewish heritage reaches back almost to the beginnings of recorded history in the Middle East, the 4,000-year-old history of Judaism and the Jewish people rests on an ongoing process of interpretation of scripture and adaptation of traditions to new and changing historic and geographic contexts. Yet, across time and space, certain concepts have remained constant, even as they have undergone adaptation. Therefore, the Jews, as a nation, live bounded within a cycle of time that mandates the observance of Sabbaths and sacred occasions—the New Year (Rosh Hashanah) in the early fall, Yom Kippur (the Day of Atonement), the Feast of Tabernacles (Sukkoth), Passover (Pesach), and Pentecost (Shavuot). Another cycle of rituals and rites governs the great occasions of life from birth to death and even such quotidian experiences as diet and dress.

Ancient Origins The ancient origins of the Jewish people are recounted in the Hebrew Bible, the first great work of what would become an extensive body of sacred literature. The Hebrew Bible, which Christians hold sacred as the Old Testament, consists of three large sections: the Torah, also known as the Five Books of Moses (Genesis, Exodus, Leviticus, Numbers,

Deuteronomy), which is read as the centerpiece of the Sabbath worship service; the Prophets, which follow the history of this people after the death of Moses and into the monarchy of the great kings David and Solomon and their heirs, and which also contain books of sacred prophecies; and the Writings, a collection of books diverse in style, including Psalms and Proverbs, and written at varying times.

According to the Torah, after the creation of the Earth and humanity, a clan emerged headed by the patriarch Abraham. Genesis relates the story of Abraham's covenant with God, or Yahweh (spelled in Hebrew as YHWH), and God's promise to make of Abraham's descendants through his wife Sarah a nation and to give them the land of Canaan. One sign of that covenant was the circumcision of all of the males among Abraham's people. God repeated the promises of the covenant to Abraham's son Isaac and to his grandson Jacob. Jacob had 12 sons. At a time of famine in Canaan, Jacob's descendants relocated to Egypt, where one of Jacob's sons, Joseph, who had been sold into slavery by his jealous brothers, had risen to a position of prominence. Thus, by the end of Genesis, the children of Abraham resided in Egypt.

The book of Exodus opens several generations later when a Pharaoh, who did not know Joseph, feared that the expanding population of the Hebrews—now called the Children of Israel or the Israelites, after Jacob who was also called Israel—would unite with his enemies. Pharaoh enslaved the Children of Israel, and then ordered the death of all male newborns. But the infant Moses survived and, as the text relates, was found by Pharaoh's daughter and raised as an Egyptian in the palace court.

As an adult, Moses fled to Midian after killing an Egyptian who was beating an Israelite slave. While tending his flock, he had an encounter with God who spoke from a burning bush that would not be consumed. God told him to return to Egypt and free his people. God identified himself as "I am that I am" and told Moses to tell the Israelites that "The Lord God of your fathers, the God of Abraham, the God of Isaac, and the God of Jacob, hath sent me unto you" (Exodus 3:14–15). God also called Aaron, Moses' brother, to assist him.

After this encounter Moses returned to Egypt to negotiate the release of the Israelites, initially asking that they be permitted to go into the wilderness for three days to worship their God and then demanding their exodus from Egypt. According to the story recounted in Exodus, God sent 10 plagues to afflict the Egyptians, but Pharaoh only relented at the last of the plagues, the death of the first-born. Nevertheless, even as the people departed, Pharaoh's army pursued, and the miracle of the parting of the Reed Sea (as modern scholars have correctly translated this) allowed the Israelites to cross out of Egypt into the Sinai, but the waters returned to engulf Pharaoh and his chariots.

It is imperative to emphasize that, while the early books of the Hebrew Bible describe the origins of the ancient Israelites, no extra-biblical evidence confirms or denies this ancient story of Abraham's wanderings in Canaan or the exodus from Egypt. The first extra-biblical reference to the people Israel appears on the stele of Pharaoh Merneptah (1213–1203 BCE), which reports inaccurately that this Pharaoh had utterly destroyed the people Israel. Nevertheless, scholars and scientists continue to seek evidence for the possibility of the events described, which remain sacred to the Abrahamic religions, while skeptics assert that the stories of the Bible have no basis in history and their miracles are irrational myths.

Having successfully escaped, the Hebrews journeyed to Mount Sinai. There Moses received a new revelation, a new covenant between God and the people—they agreed to worship God, and God gave them the laws, including the Ten Commandments, by which they were to live. The people accepted the covenant, but soon afterward turned their backs on it by violating one of its essential laws prohibiting graven images. It would be a generation before the people moved from the Sinai wilderness into their promised land, Canaan.

Joshua succeeded Moses as head of the community and led the Israelite conquest of Canaan. At this point the ancient nation came into existence in the land of Israel. The story of the next centuries is told in terms of the struggle to remain loyal to the One God, in contrast to the surrounding polytheistic cultures, the struggle to fend off conquest by various neighbors,

View of the Temple Mount in Jerusalem, from a 19th-century engraving. The temple at Jerusalem was built and destroyed three times between the 10th century BCE and the first century CE; control of this holy city continues to be a source of strife to the present day. (John Clark, Ridpath, *Ridpath's History of the World,* 1901)

and the development of leadership. Israel was divided into the 12 tribes named for Jacob's sons. Joshua assigned land to each tribe, and a series of seers, judges, priests, and prophets emerged to guide the people according to God's will. These divinely inspired leaders dealt with a range of problems and provided some overall guidance to the confederation of tribes. (As with the books of the Torah, scholars debate the historicity of the biblical books of Joshua and Judges.)

During this time, worship was centered at Shiloh, where the symbol of the Israelites' covenant with God, the ark of the covenant, and worship of God, through the animal sacrificial cult, was maintained by the priests. The site was overrun ca. 1050 by the Philistines, who captured the ark. The Philistine victory led directly to the Israelite decision to create a stronger central government, the monarchy. Around 1000 the kingdom of Israel emerged, with Saul as its first king

(r. ca. 1020–1000). Saul's troubled reign was followed by that of David (ca. 1000–962), Israel's greatest king. He defeated the Philistines and, after capturing the hill city of Jerusalem from the Jebusites, made it the religious and political center of his empire. David's son and successor, Solomon, went on to build the first temple there. From this time forward Jerusalem would remain the Jews' holy city, a tenet eventually shared by Christianity and Islam, the other Abrahamic religions.

Solomon's successor, Rehoboam (r. ca. 934–917), could not hold the kingdom together, and in 931 it split into two: the northern kingdom, which was called Israel, and the southern kingdom known as Judah, named for the largest of its two tribes. Both kingdoms prospered for the next two centuries. But in 721 the rising empire of Assyria conquered Israel, scattering its people—the legendary Ten Lost Tribes of Israel. A century later, when Assyria was eclipsed by the rise of Babylonia, the Babylonians overran Judah, and, in 586, conquered Jerusalem, destroyed the temple, and exiled its inhabitants to the city of Babylon.

How the stories of Israelite origins and history came to be recorded in the Hebrew Bible remains a matter of conjecture. Scholars hypothesize that, during the time of the two kingdoms, differing accounts were recorded that were later, during the Babylonian exile, redacted into what became the Torah. One hypothesis argues that the original sources used different names for God—one preferring the name *Elohim* in the account of events prior to the revelation to Moses at Sinai, the other calling the Israelite God YHWH, translated into English as Lord.

The time from the emergence of David and Solomon through the two kingdoms was also the era in which independent religious voices, those of the prophets, would arise to challenge the rulers and the priests wherever they saw corruption or false worship. Among the prophets, the voices of the two collected in the book of Isaiah (First Isaiah, eighth century, chapters 1–39; Second Isaiah, sixth century, chapters 40–66; scholars conjecture that these latter chapters may contain a third voice) stand out for their emphasis upon monotheism, worship of Yahweh as the God of history, and the vision that in the future all nations would come to worship the One God.

Prophets would continue to arise among the ancient Israelites even after Babylonia fell in 539 to Persia. The Persian king Cyrus (ca. 585–529) permitted the Jews—who so desired—to return to Jerusalem where they resumed worshipping God and, in 515 dedicated the second temple. Those who remained behind in the Persian Empire formed the origins of what the Jews, as this people would now be called, have named the diaspora, or dispersion. From then until today, the history of the Jewish people must trace the various civilizations of the Jews who have lived both within the land of Israel and in the diaspora communities that have flourished and disappeared over the ages.

The Greek and Roman Eras   In 332, Alexander the Great (356–323) captured Jerusalem. Following Alexander's death, his empire split among his generals. Judea first became part of the Ptolemaic kingdom based in Egypt, and then around the year 200 it came within the orbit of the Seleucid kingdom, centered in Syria. After several decades, the Seleucids clashed with traditionalists in Jerusalem and Judea. The issue came to a head during the reign of the Seleucid king Antiochus IV (r. 175–163). In his attempt to suppress Jewish dissent, Antiochus IV desecrated the temple and forbade the observance of the Sabbath (the weekly day of rest commanded in the Mosaic covenant), the study of the Torah, and the practice of circumcision. His actions sparked a revolt led by a family known as the Maccabees. Their capture of the temple and its rededication are commemorated annually in the Jewish winter festival of Hanukkah. Eventually, the Maccabees and their heirs threw off Seleucid rule and established an independent Jewish state in 142, known as the Hasmonean kingdom. The state would remain independent until the Roman conquest in 63 CE.

During the centuries of an independent Judea, a variety of groups emerged within the Jewish community. Prominent among them were the Sadducees and the Pharisees. The former argued against the authority of much of the oral tradition of interpreting the Torah, opting to keep control of interpretation in the hands of the priesthood. The Pharisees argued for a broader interpretation of the Torah, using the oral tradition and placing the authority in the hands of a learned elite.

The Pharisaic party would come to dominate, eventually giving rise to the era of classical Judaism, led by the rabbis or great sages of the Jewish people.

Judea's independence ended with the arrival of the Romans. It appears that the turmoil of Roman occupation and the establishment of a local puppet government created an environment in which a wide spectrum of Jewish groups emerged. Among these was the Qumran community (Dead Sea sect), which was forgotten until a library of their material was uncovered in the 1940s on the edge of the Dead Sea, where they had retreated to create their communal society. The Qumran community lived a separated life marked by discipline and hope for the arrival of a messianic figure. Scholars have argued for a half century over the possible influence of the Qumran community on the founding of another group, the Jesus movement that would eventually grow into Christianity.

Both the Qumran community and the Jesus movement were symbolic of unrest in the land, caused not only by Roman rule but by offensive Roman policies that were contrary to Jewish law and practice. A revolt against Rome broke out in 66, and an army was dispatched to quell it. Jerusalem fell in 70 and the second temple was razed. Resistance would continue for a few more years, most notably at the mountain fortress Masada, where, in 73, defenders committed suicide prior to its fall.

Even prior to the Roman era, diaspora Jewish communities thrived around the Mediterranean Basin. Possibly hundreds of thousands resided in Alexandria during the first century.

In direct response to the loss of the temple, Jochanan ben Zakkai, a Pharisee, created a new school to continue the Pharisaic tradition of Torah interpretation. The learned Pharisees, or rabbis (teachers), as they were now called, fixed the canon of books, now assembled as the Hebrew Bible. With the sacrificial cult in the temple destroyed and with the concomitant loss of the centrality of the priesthood, the rabbis emphasized worship in the synagogue, a well-established institution and the local center for the gathering of the community for prayer and for the study and teaching of the Torah. As the settings for communal prayer three times a day, the synagogues now became the center of public Jewish religious life. The rabbis fixed the liturgies for the various synagogue services. They acknowledged God's covenant and hoped for the coming of Israel's messiah and the rebuilding of the destroyed temple.

Equally important, the rabbis carried on discussions concerning the oral law, commentary and interpretation of the Torah to apply its teachings to daily living. Rabbis began to write down these commentaries, and, at the beginning of the third century, an initial authoritative edition appeared as the Mishnah (literally, repetition). The Mishnah contains the opinions of more than 100 Jewish scholars. Its laws guide Jewish behavior, establishing such customs as the order of the blessings and the kinds of work prohibited on the Sabbath. Its regulations continue to guide Jewish religious praxis today.

In the next centuries the process of interpretation of the Torah continued with the Mishnah as its basis. In Palestinian academies in Tiberias and Caesarea, rabbis produced the commentary called the Gemara (completion). By the year 400 their commentaries with the relevant parts of the Mishnah were redacted into the text known as the Jerusalem Talmud. However, the writing down of the Mishnah also allowed the old Jewish community at Babylon, which had continued from the sixth century BCE, to establish rival academies. These emerged, in time—especially after Palestinian Jewry was affected by the division of the Roman Empire and then its decline—as authoritative centers for the Jewish world. Their commentaries, also called Gemara, were redacted, with the relevant sections of the Mishnah, into the Babylonian Talmud by 500. The two Talmuds, which do differ from one another, recorded comments from more than 2,000 teachers and covered numerous topics not mentioned in the Mishnah. (The attempt to establish the authority of the Talmud would lead to the emergence of one group that rejected the idea of the oral law and many of the rules and rituals derived from it. Through the centuries the Kararites have survived as a tiny minority tradition in the Jewish world.)

The legislation contained in the Torah, Mishnah, and Gemara, and all subsequent commentaries and texts of Jewish law constitute *halacha*, the law (literally, "the way a faithful Jew walks"). To be a faithful Jew was to acknowledge God's covenant with the community and to order one's life in conformity to God's law, which covered every imaginable aspect of life. In fulfilling the law, an individual sanctified life from moment to moment. Concern with proper behavior took center stage, although theological speculation still had its place.

While the rabbis were debating the laws of the Mishnah and Talmud, they also adapted the Jewish calendar and its holidays. The seder, a ritual and meal celebrating the Israelites' deliverance from Egypt, was developed for the celebration of Passover. The rabbis fixed the future calculation of the Jewish calendar, which had once required witnesses to the new moon in Jerusalem. This guaranteed that Jews wherever they lived would celebrate holy days at the same time and in the proper season. It should also be noted that in antiquity Jews in the diaspora had added a second day to their celebration of festivals, a custom that developed out of concern that word of the new moon's appearance might not reach diaspora Jewish communities in time for the celebration of Rosh Hashanah. This explains why some Jews today celebrate a single day of many festivals, as is done in the modern state of Israel and among some diaspora Jewish communities, and why others celebrate two.

With liturgies of Sabbaths, festivals, and weekdays, rituals for holidays and life's passages, an ever-growing corpus of halacha, a fixed calendar, and a synagogue for every Jewish community, Judaism appeared ready to survive until God would send the messiah and return the nation to the land of Israel. Indeed, from a presentist perspective, the first generations of rabbis built the platform upon which Jewish history would henceforth develop.

Judaism in the Diaspora   Through the dispersion of the Jewish community (even prior to the Roman era), Jewish ideas found their way to new Jewish communities that emerged in unexpected places. Jews traveled westward around the Mediterranean Basin, and a flourishing community emerged on the Iberian Peninsula. Very distinctive Jewish communities, including the Beta Israel and the Lemba, developed south of Judea in Yemen, Ethiopia, and even in far-off Zimbabwe. Jew-

The Paradesi Synagogue is the oldest synagogue in the Commonwealth of Nations, located in Kochi, South India. It was built in 1568 by the Malabar Yehudan people or Cochin Jewish community in the Kingdom of Cochin. (Yuliya Kryzhevska/iStockPhoto)

ish communities also sprang up in the East, in Mesopotamia, Afghanistan, and even India, where the Bene Israel and Jews of Cochin would become integrated into the society.

The dispersion of the Jews would at times be encouraged by economics, but all too frequently it was caused by persecution or the threat thereof. Jews encountered difficulties from the Romans, who did not understand their monotheism. Then, they found themselves under attack from the Christians, especially as Christianity developed as a separate religion followed primarily by Gentiles (that is, non-Jews) and one that saw itself as superseding Judaism. In the seventh and eighth centuries, Islam emerged as a new force sweeping out of the Arabian desert and across North Africa, into Spain, and throughout the Middle East to Mesopotamia, Persia, and Central Asia. By the eighth century, the majority of the world's Jews resided in the lands of the Muslim Caliphate, where they were mostly tolerated as a protected people. In many places in the Muslim world Jewish culture and intellectual life flowered.

Spain was an important center of Jewish life. Jews flourished under the Muslim caliphate in the eighth through the 11th centuries but were persecuted when, at the end of the 11th century, the Almoravid dynasty from Morocco extended its control into Spain, and these Islamic rulers took actions against the Jews, including the closing of the synagogues. During the next centuries the region would be dominated by the interests of competing Muslim factions and the reassertion of Christian hegemony. The re-establishment of Christian rule in Spain and Portugal eventually proved disastrous for the Jews, who were banished from their homes in 1492 and 1497, respectively.

Spain was also the birthplace of Moses ben Maimon (1135–1204), better known as Maimonides, who fled his homeland during the later Almohades persecution and eventually settled in Egypt. He became the author of a large code of Jewish law, the Mishnah Torah. He also articulated the 13 principles of Jewish belief. They require that Jews affirm the oneness of God, the revelation of Torah, and belief in the coming of the messiah. In the contemporary world traditional Jews continue to affirm these principles.

With his love of Greek philosophy, especially Aristotle, Maimonides, the author of the *Guide for the Perplexed*, stood in contrast to another Spanish teacher, Moses de Leon (1250–1305), who lived and worked in Granada. De Leon lifted Jewish mysticism to a new level with his compilation, the *Zohar*—a mystical commentary on the Torah. Judaism, of course, has a long mystical tradition. Kabbalah, the Jewish mystical tradition which emerged in medieval Spain, pictures the cosmos as the emanation of God through 10 realms called *sephirot*. The last of these emanations, *malkuth*, is roughly equivalent to the mundane world. For the Kabbalist, the Torah, properly interpreted, is a doorway into the invisible mystical realm. De Leon's work would find a capable interpreter in the post-expulsion era in

Isaac Luria (1534–1572). Later, in the 18th century, a separate branch of traditional Judaism—Hasidism—would also emphasize Judaism's mystical dimension.

In the Middle Ages Jews also spread north from Palestine into Europe, establishing communities in England, France, Italy, Germany, and Eastern Europe. Although these communities sometimes attained a stable life as minority groups in Christian lands, their history was punctuated by discrimination, persecution, massacres, and expulsions. Christian theology, which blamed the Jews for the death of Jesus, justified the denigration of this people. Over time, Christian anti-Jewish animus extended beyond restrictive legislation, such as the identifying Jewish badge, to imagine that Jews were inimical to Western Christendom, and that Jews even kidnapped Christian children for secret rituals. In this atmosphere of mistrust and misunderstanding, Jews faced the continual threat of sudden outbreaks of violence.

Jews were expelled from England in 1290 and from France early in the next century. The expulsion from Spain in 1492 led to further expulsions from Sicily (1492–1493), Lithuania (1495), Brandenburg, Germany (1510), Tunisia (1535), and Naples (1641). At around this same time urban governments established the first of the ghettos, closed communities that segregated the Jews from the larger society, the first one being created in Venice in 1516. As a result of expulsion and persecution, many Jews moved to Poland, which became a major center of European Jewish life. A vital community also developed in Holland in the 16th century, the most religiously tolerant land in Western Europe. Though segregated from the larger community, the Jewish communities developed a rich culture.

The expulsion of the Jews from Spain led many to find haven in the lands of the Ottoman Empire, which at the time stretched from the Balkans across the Middle East and into North Africa as far as Algeria. Many Jews also moved into the newly discovered Americas. They first became visible at Recife, Brazil, during the brief occupation by the Dutch (1630–1654). After the loss of Recife, the Jews dispersed throughout the Americas to such places as the Dutch settlement on the island of Curaçao and to the North American colonies of New Amsterdam (soon to become New York) and later to Newport, Rhode Island.

There were only six synagogues in the United States at the time of its founding, but through the 19th century the Jewish community was increased many-fold by immigration, first by tens of thousands of German and central European Jews and then by hundreds of thousands of eastern European Jews. These Jews from northern, central, and eastern Europe, known collectively as Ashkenazim, completely overwhelmed the original community of American Sephardic Jews, who traced their heritage through Spain and Portugal.

Development of the Modern Jewish Community
Through the 18th century, Jewish religion remained largely rooted in the teachings and traditions based on the texts that had developed in Palestine and Babylonia in the early centuries of the first millennium CE. However, during the late 18th and 19th centuries, Jewish life underwent a remarkable change, the result of the liberal policies toward Jews that grew out of the Age of Enlightenment and its demand for separation of church and state. The French Revolution had emancipated the Jews, granting Jewish men civil rights as individuals and annulling all anti-Jewish legislation, but demanding that Jews adapt to Western civilization in return. The Napoleonic wars carried these ideas to Jewish communities across Europe.

Now Jews, seeking to respond to modernity, consciously sought ways to integrate and assimilate into the larger Gentile society. One response was the creation of Reform Judaism, a new way of being Jewish that emphasized what were seen as the eternal truths of the faith, as opposed to irrelevant ancient practices. Arguing that God's revelation was progressive, German Rabbi Abraham Geiger (1810–1874) began to introduce changes into his synagogue in Breslau. Many traditional practices were discarded, including a variety of dietary restrictions, traditional beliefs were modified in favor of emphasis on an "ethical monotheism." Reform Judaism caught on quickly in the United States, where Rabbi Isaac Mayer Wise (1819–1900) championed the cause.

Geiger found strong opposition among the traditionalists in the Jewish world. Rabbi Samson Raphael Hirsch (1808–1888) of Frankfurt am Main led the forces that would affirm traditional, or as it would come eventually to be called, Orthodox Judaism. In the United States Isaac Leeser (1806–1868) championed the traditionalist position in opposition to Rabbi Wise.

Between Orthodoxy and Reform, a third alternative was proposed by Zacharias Frankel (1801–1875). He recognized both the need to respond to the new consciousness of history and the Reform idea of Judaism as constantly changing with the times. However, he rejected the radical stripping of "outdated" ritual from the synagogue, especially Reform's willingness to jettison Hebrew as the language of prayer. He appreciated ritual as an expression of deeply felt realities. He therefore proposed a third way that has subsequently come to be known as Conservative Judaism, or in contemporary Israel, the Masorti movement.

In the meantime, Hasidism had been born in Poland, the product of both the Kabbalistic writing of de Leon and Luria and the experiences of men like Israel ben Eliezer (1700–1760), known as the Baal Shem Tov, the Master of the Good Name (of God). Reportedly an unlearned man, the Baal Shem Tov became known as a healer, and as a teacher he called into being a community whose centers were built around men known for one or more charismatic traits, often as wonder-workers. Although perfectly observant in belief and practice, the Hassidim and their courts were often seen as competitors to rabbinical Judaism and the synagogue. Many branches of Hasidism developed as different leaders established their work in the various cities and countries of Eastern Europe.

Zion, Holocaust, Israel In the second half of the 19th century, Jews continued to win emancipation in various countries in Europe. For example, several German states emancipated their Jews, and, in 1871, when Germany became unified, German Jews achieved full emancipation. But, even as Jewish integration into European civilization proceeded apace, reaction against new patterns of Jewish life and culture set in. Now what had once been a religiously based animus against the Jews evolved into racial anti-Semitism, hatred of the Jews rooted in the idea that they were a distinctive race that bore immutable, degenerate characteristics and whose members sought to undermine the foundations of Western civilization.

The culmination of 19th-century anti-Semitism was the infamous Dreyfus affair in France. Meanwhile

Jewish father and son with a shofar, a ram's horn used in Rosh Hashanah holiday celebrations; the horn is sounded in temple, marking the beginning of the High Holy Days. (Geoff Manasse/Photodisc/PictureQuest)

in tsarist Russia, a new wave of violence had broken out against Jewish communities following the assassination of Tsar Alexander II in 1881. Waves of violence, known as pogroms, would continue there for the next decades.

Renewed violence and new forms of Jewish hatred in the 19th century provided the environment in which Zionism developed. In 1896, Hungarian-born Theodore Herzl (1860–1904) published his call for a Jewish nation, and the next year he founded the World Zionist Congress to plan for the future state. The rise of Zionism also called attention to the growing secularization of the Jewish community, for many of the early Zionists rejected religious praxis and belief, even as they saw Zion as the historic homeland of the Jewish people and planned to create a Jewish state there.

The idea of creating a Jewish state in Palestine, at the time still part of the Ottoman Empire, divided Jewish leaders. However, early supporters began to purchase land and to move there. Zionism as a national political movement gained greatly when, in 1917, Lord Arthur James Balfour (1848–1930), the British foreign secretary, wrote a letter to Lord Rothschild confirming the sympathy of His Majesty's Government for Zionist aspirations. Between 1900 and 1930, a quarter of a million Jews migrated to Palestine, which had fallen to the British when the Ottoman Empire was dismantled at the end of World War I. Migration increased during the next decade in response to persecution by the Nazis.

The history of the Middle East would likely have been very different had it not been for the Nazi Holocaust, the apogee of modern racial anti-Semitism. The Nazis murdered six million Jewish men, women, and children. Even before the full extent of the tragedy was known, much sympathy flowed to the survivors, and the Soviet Union favored the creation of a Jewish state over the continued presence of Great Britain in

Palestine. Following a 1947 United Nations vote to partition Palestine into a Jewish state and an Arab state, events moved rapidly. In May 1948 the British ended their mandate over Palestine, and Jewish leaders proclaimed the new state of Israel. The concomitant Arab Palestinian state did not emerge.

Crucial to the development of Israel since its establishment has been the Law of Return. Originally passed in 1950, the law sought to solve the problem of Jewish persecution by granting every Jew residing anywhere in the world the right to migrate to Israel. As a result of this law, millions of Jews from communities around the world have moved to Israel during its brief history. They include Jews from historic communities in Arab countries, like Egypt and Yemen, who fled renewed anti-Jewish persecution following the establishment of the state of Israel, and approximately a million Jews from the countries of the former Soviet Union. Though a small minority of Orthodox Jews (Neturei Karta, Satmar Hasidism) continue to lobby against Israel, believing the state should not exist until the messiah comes, the world's Jews overwhelmingly support the existence of the Jewish state.

Modern Jewish religious life remains centered around the synagogue, each usually led by a rabbi. In turn, the synagogues are organized into national associations of synagogues and rabbis. Each of the major Jewish groups, Reform, Orthodox, Conservative, and the most recently formed Reconstructionist community, has national organizations in each country where they have multiple synagogues. Orthodoxy is divided by cultural traditions; German, eastern European, and Sephardic Jews retain a level of separation (World Sephardic Federation), and new forms of Orthodoxy have arisen around 20th-century issues (Young Israel and Gush Emumim). The national associations also participate in umbrella organizations serving the whole Jewish community, such as the World Jewish Congress, and some have formed international cooperative fellowships that serve their own constituency worldwide, such as the World Union for Progressive Judaism.

Today (2009), the world's two largest Jewish communities are in Israel and in the United States. Together they comprise more than 80 percent of world Jewry. Of the 5.2 million U.S. Jews, only around half are formally affiliated to a synagogue. Some 5.3 million Jews reside in Israel, where they make up more than three-fourths of the population. Large communities also continue in France (491,000), Argentina (185,000), Canada (374,000), and the United Kingdom (300,000).

Pamela S. Nadell and J. Gordon Melton

See also: Bene Israel; Beta Israel; Cochin Jews; Conservative Judaism; Gush Emumin; Hasidism; Karaites; Lemba; Moses; Neturei Karta; Orthodox Judaism; Reform Judaism; Satmar Hasidism; World Sephardic Federation; Young Israel.

References

Bridger, David, ed. *The New Jewish Encyclopedia.* New York: Behrman House, 1976.

De Lange, Nicolas. *Atlas of the Jewish World.* New York: Facts on File, 1984.

Eckstein, Yechiel. *What You Should Know about Jews and Judaism.* Waco, TX: Word Books, 1984.

Efron, John. Steven Weitzman, Matthias Lehman, and Joshua Holo. *The Jews: A History.* Upper Saddle River, NJ: Pearson Prentice Hall, 2009.

Flannery, Edward H. *The Anguish of the Jews: Twenty-Three Centuries of Antisemitism.* Ramsey, NJ: Paulist Press, 1885.

Johnson, Paul. *A History of the Jews.* New York: HarperCollins, 1988.

Karesh, Sara E., and Mitchell M. Hurvitz. *Encyclopedia of Judaism.* New York: Facts on File, 2006.

Mendes-Flohr, Paul, and Jehuda Reinharz. *The Jew in the Modern World: A Documentary History.* New York: Oxford University Press, 1995.

Mintz, Jerome R. *Hasidic People: A Place in the New World.* Cambridge: Harvard University Press, 1992.

Neusner, Jacob. *Signposts on the Way of Torah.* Belmont, CA: Wadsworth Publishing, 1998.

Raphael, Marc Lee. *Judaism in America.* New York: Columbia University Press, 2003.

Rosenberg, Roy A. *The Concise Guide to Judaism: History, Practice, Faith.* Denver, CO: Mentor Books, 1991.

Rudavsky, David. *Modern Jewish Religious Movements: A History of Emancipation and Adjustment.* 3rd ed. New York: Behrman, 1979.

Sachar, Howard M. *The Course of Modern Jewish History.* New York: Dell, 1977.

Sarna, Jonathan. *American Judaism.* New Haven: Yale University Press, 2004.

Scheindlin, Raymond. *A Short History of the Jewish People.* New York: Oxford University Press, 2000.

Scholem, Gershom. *Major Trends in Jewish Mysticism.* New York: Schocken Books, 1954.

Seltzer, Robert M. *Judaism: A People and Its History (Religion, History, and Culture).* New York: Macmillan, 1989.

Shanks, Hershel. *Ancient Israel: From Abraham to the Roman Destruction of the Temple.* Englewood Cliffs, NJ: Prentice-Hall, 1999.

Silver, David J., and Bernard Martin. *History of Judaism from Abraham to Maimonides.* New York: Basic Books, 1974.

Uterman, A. *Jews: Their Religious Beliefs and Practices.* London: Routledge, 1981.

Wigoder, Geoffrey, ed. *The New Standard Jewish Encyclopedia.* New York: Facts on File, 1992.

K

Kabbalah Learning Centre

The Kabbalah Learning Centre is a relatively new effort to make the mystical wisdom of the Jewish Kabbalah—traditionally identified with the Hasidic movement and long the exclusive possession of an elite group of advanced students of a small number of rabbis—available to the Jewish community as a whole and even beyond, to seekers who are not Jewish. Rabbi Yehuda Ashlag (1886–1955) began this process by translating the Zohar, the basic text presenting the Kabbalistic wisdom, from Aramaic into modern Hebrew. He organized the text and wrote an introduction, later translated into English and published as the Ten Illuminations. In 1922 he founded the Kabbalah Learning Centre (also known as the Research Centre of Kabbalah) in Palestine. The Centre became the vehicle for Ashlag's continued work of translating and publishing the Zohar, which was completed in the 1950s.

Ashlag was succeeded by Rabbi Judah Brandwein (d. 1969), among whose major accomplishments was the republishing of the works of 16th-century Kabbalist, Rabbi Isaac ben Solomon Luria (1534–1572), thus making available these previously difficult-to-find works. Brandwein also added a set of notes and cross-references to the texts. He was in turn succeeded by Rabbi Philip S. Berg (formerly Philip S. Gruberger, b. 1929) the present leader of the Centre. Berg had grown up in the United States and met Brandwein in 1962. Berg has been a prolific author and has also worked on the production of an English translation of the complete Zohar.

Berg sees his task as presenting the Kabbalah to the whole world. He greatly expanded the operation of the Centre, opening teaching sites across Israel and in many European and North American cities. His basic text, *Kabbalah for the Layman*, was translated into Spanish, French, German, Persian, and Russian. He has also written books on reincarnation and astrology, which have appealed to people previously attracted to the New Age movement. One of the Centre's self-assigned tasks is to reach out to Jews in the New Age and bring them back to Judaism from popular Esoteric teachings.

As of 2009, The Kabbalah Centre reported 32 centers and study groups across the United States and 66 in other countries around the world. Its primary World Centres are found in Brazil, Argentina, Venezuela, Mexico, Israel, Cote d'Ivoire, Germany, United Kingdom, Poland, Russia, and Canada.

Israeli critics of Berg and the Centre have decried his attempts to teach the Kabbalah to a popular audience, pointing out that instruction was previously limited to males who were at least 40 years of age. More important, they have questioned his credentials; the yeshiva that Rabbi Brandwein headed denies any relationship with Berg. Berg has countered by publishing several volumes of his correspondence with Brandwein as evidence of their close relationship.

Kabbalah Learning Centre
c/o The Kabbalah Centre
1054 S. Roberson Blvd.
Los Angeles, CA 90035
http://www.kabbalah.com/

J. Gordon Melton

See also: Hasidism; New Age Movement.

References

Ashlag, Yehuda. *Kabbalah: A Gift of the Bible.* Jerusalem, Israel: Research Centre of the Kabbalah, 1994.

Berg, Philip S. *Kabbalah for the Layman*. 3 vols. New York: Research Center of Kabbalah Press, 1988, 1991, 1993.

Berg, Philip S. *Miracles, Mysteries, and Prayer*. 2 vols. New York: Research Center of Kabbalah Press, 1993.

Levine, Art. "The Accidental Kabbalist." http://art levine.blogspot.com/articles/The%20Accidental %20Kabbalist.htm. Accessed May 15, 2009.

Kagyupa Tibetan Buddhism

The Kagyu tradition (literally "transmitted command"), one of the four major schools of Tibetan Buddhism, is the result of a fusion of late Mahayana and Tantric teachings, both introduced by a lineage of Indian and Tibetan masters: Tilopa (988–1069), Naropa (1016–1100), Marpa (1012–1096), Milarepa (1040–1123), and Gampopa (1079–1153). The Kagyupa trace their origin to the Buddha Varjadhara. Traditionally, Marpa is considered to be the founder of the Kagyupa. Historically, however, the credit goes to the disciples of Gampopa. They established a number of sub-schools, including Karma-Kagyupa Tibetan Buddhism, as a well as the Padmodrupa (named for its founder, 1110–1170), which developed into a tree of lineages of which Drigung, Taklung, and Druk have persisted through the centuries along with the Karma. Although only minor differences in practice and ritual are discernible among these branches, each one underwent its own specific historical and geographical developments.

Originally, religious leadership was transmitted from uncle to nephew, but later branches adopted the reincarnation system of *tulku* (an incantation of a saintly person or deity). Neither strict celibacy nor exclusive membership to the institution was demanded by the early orders. Rather than a unified religious branch, the Kagyu order can be seen as a complex combination of organized monasticism and master-to-disciple tantric transmission.

Despite its emphasis upon oral transmission, the Kagyu tradition constitutes a matrix of teachings embodied in three basic texts. The first of these is the *Mahamudra* (Great Seal), a body of doctrine emphasizing meditation (Sanskrit: *sadhana*) and the consciousness of emptiness (Sanskrit: *shunyata*). Second, the *Six Yogas of Naropa* exposes the "extraordinary practices" (Tibetan: *naro chodrug*): "heat yoga" (Tibetan: *tumo*), "illusory body" (Tibetan: *gyulu*), "dream" yoga (Tibetan: *milam*), "clear light" perception (Tibetan: *osel*), "consciousness transmission" (Tibetan: *phowa*), and the yoga of the "intermediate states" between death and rebirth (Tibetan: *bardo*). Third, in his *Precious Ornament of the Liberation*, Gampopa offers a synthesis of the Kagyu and Kadam teachings in which he reaffirms the universal nature of Buddha. The realization of Buddhahood is possible by means of specific techniques: training of the mind (Tibetan: *lodjong*), "mindful awareness" (Tibetan: *chine*), and "penetrative seeing" (Tibetan: *lakhtong*), in addition to the "spirit of enlightenment" (Sanskrit: *bodhicitta*), the achievement of the "perfections" (Sanskrit: *paramita*), and merit-making performance (Sanskrit: *puja*), which are basic Mahayana practices. Of primary importance to the Kagyupa are faith and devotion to a qualified master (Sanskrit: *guru*; Tibetan: *blama*) considered as a "spiritual friend." Thus, Kagyu practice consists, on the one hand, of ascetic experiences of yoga and meditation as well as subtle Tantric techniques (that is, the visualization of deities), and, on the other hand, of ritual and collective performances (chants, pilgrimages) and expressions of devotion to the master and the lineage.

Many of the Kagyu dignitaries, especially those of the Karma school, played an important role in the political and religious history of Tibet. Exercising local power in their areas of settlement, the Kagyupa never fully achieved headship of the Tibetan nation. Their influence, however, extended to the borderlands of Tibet: the Drigung in Nepal and Ladakh (northern India), the Drukpa in Ladakh and in Buthan, and the Karma in Sikkim (India). Since the early 1970s, the Kagyupa have found new host countries in the West (Europe and North America).

Lionel Obadia

See also: Karma-Kagyupa, Tibetan Buddhism; Milarepa; Naropa; Tibetan Buddhism; Yoga.

References

Snellgrove, David. *Indo-Tibetan Buddhism: Indian Buddhists and Their Tibetan Successors*. London: Serindia, 1987.

The west face of Mount Kailas, the holiest mountain in Buddhism, Hinduism, and Bon faith, believed to be the center of the world. (Dreamstime)

Snellgrove, David, and Hugh Richardson. *A Cultural History of Tibet*. London: Weidenfeld and Nicolson, 1968.

Stein, Rolf. *Tibetan Civilization*. Stanford: Stanford University Press, 1972.

Tucci, Guiseppe. *The Religions of Tibet*. Berkeley and Los Angeles: University of California Press, 1980.

Kailas, Mount/Lake Manasarovar

Mount Kailas, a spectacular peak in the Himalayan Mountains of western Tibet and the equally beautiful Lake Manasarovar, which lies at its base, are sacred to Tibetan Buddhists, followers of Tibet's Bon religion, and both the Jains and Hindus of India. The mountain is located north of the western border of Nepal and northeast of New Delhi. The mountain's peak reaches a height of 22,028 feet and sticks prominently above the surrounding landscape. The peak itself has a distinctive pyramidal shape with four steep triangular façades. On the southern façade, a vertical crease across the horizontal layers of rock presents a swastika design, which Hindus view as a symbol of the god Vishnu and Buddhists as an auspicious symbol, which will often be seen on the chest of statues of Gautama Buddha, the sides of Buddhist temples, and the covers of Buddhist books. The melting waters from the mountain's glaciers feed Lake Manasarovar (the highest freshwater lake of any size in the world) and ultimately four of the world's longest rivers: the Indus, the Brahmaputra, the Sutlej, and, most important, the Ganges.

Hindus identify the mountain with Shiva and consider it the axis of the world. It and the rivers it feeds form an immense sacred landscape that includes southwestern Tibet, northern India, Pakistan, and Bangladesh. Saivite Hindus point to the mountain as the home of Shiva, where he sits aloof in the practice of the highest yoga and also engages in Tantric practices with his several consorts. It is the place that Shiva met one of his consorts, Meenakshi. The daughter of a king, Meenakshi was born with three breasts. According to the legend, she was told that she would lose one of them when she met her future husband, which occurred when she first encountered Shiva. Thus Hindu pilgrims come to identify the mountain as Shiva's *linga* and the lake as Meenakshi's *yoni*.

Their wedding was said to have occurred at Madurai, Tamil Nada, where a temple was erected in 1560 in Meenakshi's honor. At the end of each day, the temple doors are shut, and, as music is played, temple priests take the statue of Shiva from its daytime resting spot into a room set aside as Meenakshi's bedroom. There Shiva remains until six o'clock the next morning, when he is brought out again for public viewing. Three annual festivals at the temple mark Shiva and Meenakshi's life together.

Tibetan Buddhists identify Mount Kailas with Mount Meru, the mythological center of the universe and symbolic of the single-pointedness of mind sought by practitioners. Pilgrims circumambulate Lake Manasarovar, occasionally stopping to bathe in its waters and quench their thirst. Bathing in the lake is said to

Lake Manasarovar is the largest lake in Tibet and a holy lake in Tibetan culture. (Bayon/Dreamstime.com)

assist one's entrance into paradise, and drinking the water can lead to healing. The mountain embodies the father principle and the lake embodies the mother principle. To complete the trek around the lake, which may consume three days or more, holds the promise of instant Buddhahood.

Local legends tell of an encounter between Tibetan Buddhist pioneer Milarepa (1040–1123) and a representative of Tibet's traditional Bon religion, the shaman Naro Bon-chung. They engaged in a contest of spiritual powers. As the contest proceeded, the Bon leader flew to the top of Mount Kailas on his drum. He arrived only to find Milarepa already waiting for him. Buddhists claim that the triumph of Buddhism and its displacement of Bon as the chief religion of Tibet can be dated to this encounter. In circumambulating the mountain, pilgrims will pass by a set of footprints that Buddhists believe to be Milarepa's. There is also a shrine that houses his silver-covered conch shell.

The predominance of Buddhism in Tibet has meant that Buddhists have tended to have the greatest access to the mountain over the centuries and they have used their proximity to erect some 13 monasteries adjacent to the mountain and the lake, and dotting the path the pilgrims follow to each. These monasteries were un-

fortunately targeted by the Red Guards during the Cultural Revolution (1966–1976). The Chinese took the artwork, destroyed the buildings, and scattered the monks. It was not until 1981 that pilgrimages were again allowed to resume and the process of rebuilding the monasteries begun. To date only a small percentage of the monastic community has returned to assist pilgrims.

Not to be denied their role at the mountain, Jains believe that Rishaba, the first of their 24 *tirthankaras* (teachers), is said to have received his enlightenment at Mount Kailas.

J. Gordon Melton

See also: Bon Religion; Milarepa; Pilgrimage; Tibetan Buddhism.

References

Johnson, Russell, and Kerry Moran. *The Sacred Mountain of Tibet: On Pilgrimage to Kailas.* Rochester, VT: Park Street Press, 1989.

Pranavananda, Swami. *Kailas-Manasarovar.* Calcutta: S. P. League, 1949.

Thurman, Robert A. F. *Circling the Sacred Mountain: A Spiritual Adventure through the Himalayas.* New York: Bantam, 1999.

Kamakura

Kamakura, today a small town south of modern Tokyo, was, following the shogun's wrestling the power from the emperor at the end of the 12th century, briefly the capital of Japan. The time of the shogun's residency in Kamakura subsequently became a time of intense religious ferment and creativity, especially for Buddhism, which the shogun privileged. Kamakura is home to some 65 Buddhist temples, 19 Shinto shrines, and one of the most famous Buddha mega-statues in the world.

Kamakura's significance begins to emerge as one visits its many temples and shrines. It suddenly jumped out of historic obscurity at the end of the 12th century when the Minamoto family took control of Japan from the emperor and established their government in the city. Though the emperor continued formally on his throne in Kyoto, the power now resided in Kamakura even as the Minamoto shogun paid the emperor outward respect. The Kyoto drama ended in 1221, when the shogun's army defeated the belligerent imperial forces, but again, the emperor and his court remained in place. The Shogunate continued to rule until 1333, when the imperial rule was reestablished.

The 13th century saw the activity of many of the most famous Japanese Buddhist leaders, including Honen (1133–1212), Shinran (1173–1262), Eisai (1141–1215), Dogen (1200–1253), Ippen (1239–1289), and Nichiren (1222–1282). Honen founded, and Shinran and Ippen expounded upon, Japanese Pure Land Buddhism. In an age in which Buddhism was seemingly in decline, the trio approached the public with the offer to end their cycle of rebirth by entry into a new home in the Pure Land (heaven) through the regular recitation of the *nimbutsu*, the name of Amida Buddha. The simple piety built around the nimbutsu would project Pure Land Buddhism into its role as Japan's largest Buddhist community.

Zen arrived in Japan early in the seventh century, but not until the early Kamakura period (1185–1333) did it gain a real foothold throughout the country. Eisai became the instrument of introducing Zen Buddhism into Japan and is today thought of as its founder. Initially turned away by the Buddhist establishment in Kyoto, Eisai seized the opportunity provided by the emergence of the Kamakura shogunate. In 1200 he es-

tablished Jufuju-ki, the first Zen center in Kamakura, and discovered strong support among the warriors (the samurai) that were the basis of the shogunate's power.

Eisai followed a form of Zen called Rinzai, whose practitioners believed they would find enlightenment through spontaneous flashes. They became best known for their use of the *koan*, questions whose answers seem to defy logic. In the realization of the answer one is pushed toward enlightenment. In 1214, Eisai also wrote a treatise on tea and its healthful qualities that would become the source of later Japanese adoption of the beverage and its practice of the tea ceremony.

Dogen, Eisai's later contemporary, established the Soto School of Zen in Japan. Soto placed more faith in long periods of meditation and is best known for its practice of *zazen*, or sitting meditation. Dogen's stay at Kamakura was very brief. He moved there in 1247, but found Rinzai practice so firmly established that he moved on to more fertile territory.

Today, Engaku-ji and the four other Rinzai temples in Kamakura maintain the Zen base in the region. Engaku-ji later attained even greater significance for the role it was to play in the spread of Zen to the West. Soyen Shaku (1859–1919), the Zen teacher who attended the World Parliament of Religions in 1893, was from Engaku-ji, and this center would be among the first Zen centers to open its doors to Westerners.

Kamakura Pure Land Buddhism would become most visible in Kamakura by way of Daibutsu, the giant statue of the Buddha that has become one of the most recognizable images of Japan. Weighing approximately 121 tons, it is 43 feet in height and about 30 feet wide, from knee to knee. Originally constructed of wood, it was significantly damaged in a storm and in 1252 it was reconstructed in bronze. It was cast in several pieces and assembled in its present resting place. Several structures built over the statue at various times have been destroyed, and since 1495 it has remained in the open. Though a statue of an enlightened one, it is not of Gautama Buddha (the founder of Buddhism) but of the bodhisattva Amida Buddha, around which Pure Land Buddhism is focused. It was originally constructed after the shogun had seen the giant statue of Vairocana Buddha (called Birushana in Japan) at Nara.

A youthful Nichiren (he was ordained as a priest at age 15) began his quest for spiritual truth just as Pure

Land Buddhism spread across Japan. He asked why people who put their faith in the nimbutsu still experienced the spectrum of painful conditions. This and other equally puzzling problems motivated his studies after he settled in Kamakura in 1238. Four years in Kamakura and 11 years roaming the countryside visiting the spectrum of Buddhist groups then operating in the country led him to one firm conclusion, that the writing known as the Lotus Sutra, somewhat promoted by the Tendai Buddhists, summarized the essential teachings of the Buddha.

When, in 1253, Nichiren announced his new Buddhist practice, he did so by attacking faith in the nimbutsu, which was to be replaced with the chanting of the "Great Title" of the Lotus Sutra, that is, "Namu Myoho Renge Kyo." He offered this new practice as the practical way for everyone to realize the deepest truths of Buddhism. Pure Land leadership reacted immediately, intensely, and negatively. Feeling his life threatened, Nichiren sought refuge in Kamakura. From his small hut, he worked the streets preaching to whoever would listen. His anti-elitist message took hold among common people.

Nichiren's efforts aroused active opposition from both Buddhist leaders and government authorities. His house was burned down in 1260, and the following year he was arrested and exiled. He returned to Kamakura in 1263. The government more or less tolerated him until 1271, when he was again formally exiled. In 1274, he returned to Kamakura, again approaching the government to gain its backing. Again he failed, and reconciling himself to the role of outcast, he settled permanently at Mount Minobu, the center from which Nichiren Buddhism would spread throughout Japan. Contemporary Nichiren Buddhists revere the several Nichiren-shu temples at Kamakura as they recall their founder's adventures there.

Apart from the spread of the new forms of Buddhism during the Kamakura period, several of the temples have some individual characteristics that continue to attract special constituencies. Tokeiji, for example, is famous as a haven for females. Since the 13th century it has served as a refuge for battered wives who could get a divorce by serving as nuns at the temple for a few years. The Hase Kannon Temple boasts the tallest wooden statue in Japan, an 11-headed carving of the bodhisattva Kannon (aka Kwan Yin), the bodhisattva of mercy.

Buddhism dominated the Kamakura period, though Shinto was not neglected. Among the oldest temples in Kamakura is the Amanawa Jinja, dating to the eighth century. This shrine was protected by the shogun, though otherwise distinctly favoring Buddhism, as one of his relatives' wives believed that she received help in bearing a son from her activity at the *jinja*.

When the shogunate fell in 1333, the power once again shifted to Kyoto, and Kamakura lost its place on history's stage. The once bustling city again assumed the role of a small, quiet town. Rediscovered in the post–World War II world, today Kamakura draws visitors from around the world—pilgrims and tourists, believers, students of religion, and those who merely appreciate the artistry of the buildings and gardens.

Edward A. Irons

See also: Dogen; Eisai; Honen; Nichiren; Nichiren Shoshu; Nichirenshu; Pure Land Buddhism; Shinran; Statues—Buddhist; Shinto; Temples—Buddhist; Zen Buddhism.

References

Kasahara, Zazuo, ed. *A History of Japanese Religion.* Tokyo: Kosei Publishing Co., 2001.

Mutsu, Iso. *Kamakura: Fact and Legend.* Tokyo: Tuttle Publishing, 1995.

Saunders, E. Dale. *Buddhism in Japan with an Outline of Its Origins in India.* Philadelphia: University of Pennsylvania Press, 1964.

■ Kanaky

Kanaky, or New Caledonia, officially the Territoire d'Outre-Mer de la Nouvelle-Calédonie, is a French overseas department consisting of the large island of New Caledonia and several sets of smaller islands in the South Pacific west of Australia. The islands include 7,171 square miles of land. The largest group, though not a majority, of the 225,000 residents (2008), is Melanesian. Approximately a third of the inhabitants are European.

European discovery and naming was made by Captain James Cook (1728–1779) in 1774. The is-

KANAKY

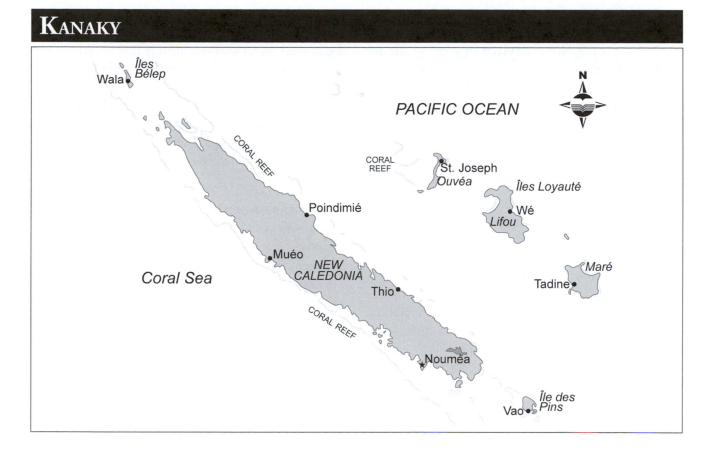

Kanaky

Religion	Followers in 1970	Followers in 2010	% of Population	Annual % growth 2000–2010	Followers in 2025	Followers in 2050
Christians	96,000	214,000	84.6	1.57	247,000	285,000
Roman Catholics	73,500	128,000	50.8	1.60	157,000	187,000
Protestants	17,900	37,500	14.8	1.04	43,000	52,000
Independents	3,000	15,500	6.1	2.99	18,000	21,000
Agnostics	3,300	24,800	9.8	3.17	38,000	52,000
Muslims	4,400	7,200	2.8	1.73	8,400	9,900
Atheists	0	2,800	1.1	1.72	3,500	4,500
Buddhists	400	1,700	0.7	1.73	2,500	3,500
New religionists	100	1,000	0.4	1.72	1,500	2,000
Baha'is	400	950	0.4	1.72	1,600	2,400
Ethnoreligionists	300	450	0.2	1.74	500	500
Jews	100	100	0.0	0.00	100	100
Total population	**105,000**	**253,000**	**100.0**	**1.72**	**303,000**	**360,000**

lands had been home to Melanesians, primarily of the Kanaka group, for more than 3,000 years. The French occupied New Caledonia in 1853 and developed a harsh, repressive culture. French settlement was spurred by the discovery of nickel and chromium deposits. In 1998, the French signed the Noumea Accord designed to transfer governing autonomy to local leadership over several decades. The agreement also includes the holding of several plebiscites on complete independence.

The indigenous religions of the New Caledonians were largely destroyed and replaced by Roman Catholicism, but they have survived in some of the remote mountainous areas. Indigenous religious practice was given some new life by the introduction of the so-called cargo cults after World War II, primarily from the New Hebrides.

The first Christian missionary, a Methodist from Tonga, arrived in New Caledonia in 1834. He was joined in 1843 by two Samoans, who arrived as representatives of the London Missionary Society (LMS), a Congregationalist-based organization. European LMS missionaries came in the 1850s. Their combined efforts led to the formation of the Evangelical Church in New Caledonia and the Loyalty Islands, the largest Protestant body in Kanaky. It now commands the allegiance of around 15 percent of the population of 165,000 people. It experienced a schism in 1960, leading to the formation of the Free church.

The first priests of the Roman Catholic Church arrived in 1843, and following the French occupation the church enjoyed official support. In its second generation, it moved to develop indigenous leadership, and the first priests from New Caledonian members were ordained in 1884. The capital, Noumea, became the center of French Catholic life throughout the south Pacific, and in 1966 it became the home of the archbishop of Noumea, whose territory also includes the Wallis and Futuna Islands. Through the 20th century, the population of Kanaky became quite diverse, with measurable numbers of Anglos of British heritage, Eastern Europeans, Chinese, and representatives of many people from various other South Pacific islands. The present spectrum of religions now present in the islands can be traced to the mid-1880s, with the arrival of missionaries from the Reorganized Church of Jesus Christ of Latter-day Saints (now the Community of Christ). Its sister, the Church of Jesus Christ of Latter-day Saints, began work in the 1950s after some members from Tahiti moved to New Caledonia to work in the nickel mines. The work is part of the Fiji Suiva Mission.

Through the 1900s, other Christian groups established work on the islands, including the Seventh-day Adventist Church (1925), the Jehovah's Witnesses (1950), the Assemblies of God (1969), and Baptists International Missions, an American-based fundamentalist Baptist organization (1995). The Baha'i Faith began work in 1952. Buddhism is practiced by a segment of the Vietnamese community, though the majority is Roman Catholic. There is a small community of Muslims, mostly Sunnis of the Shafaiite School of Islam from Indonesia. There is also a long-standing community of Rosicrucians affiliated with the Ancient and Mystical Order Rosae Crucis.

J. Gordon Melton

See also: Ancient and Mystical Order Rosae Crucis; Assemblies of God; Baha'i Faith; Church of Jesus Christ of Latter-day Saints; Community of Christ; Evangelical Church in New Caledonia and the Loyalty Islands; Free Churches; Jehovah's Witnesses; London Missionary Society; Roman Catholic Church; Seventh-day Adventist Church; Shafiite School of Islam.

References

Forman, Charles H. *The Island Churches of the South Pacific: Emergence in the Twentieth Century.* Maryknoll, NY: Orbis, 1982.

Kohler, J. M. *Christianity in New Caledonia and the Loyalty Islands: Sociological Profile.* Noumea, New Caledonia: Office de la Recherche Scientifique et Technique Outre-Mer, 1981.

Sectes et denominations en Nouvelle-Calédonie. Noumea, New Caledonia: Eglise évangélique en Nouvelle Calédonie et aux Iles Loyauté, Commission d'education chrétienne, 1973.

Trompf, G. W. *Payback: The Logic of Retribution in Melanesian Religions.* Cambridge: Cambridge University Press, 1994.

Kaplan, Mordecai Menahem

1881–1983

Mordecai Menahem Kaplan, a Conservative Jewish rabbi and seminary professor, was the founder of Reconstructionism, a new school of Jewish life and faith that has emerged as a major new community of American Judaism in the 20th century.

Kaplan was born June 11, 1881, in the town of Svencionys, Lithuania. Toward the end of the decade

Meeting at the Jewish Theological Seminary in 1952 between (from left to right): Chancellor Louis Finkelstein, Professor Mordecai M. Kaplan and librarian Alexander Marx. (Time & Life Pictures/Getty Images)

when he was only eight years old, his family immigrated to America. He attended public school but received a traditional Jewish supplementary education. After high school, he entered Columbia University, where he encountered the modern critical study of the Bible and religion in general. He subsequently attended the Jewish Theological Seminary (JTS), in New York City, and was ordained as an Orthodox rabbi there in 1902. Shortly thereafter, he began his professional career as a rabbi at Congregation Kehilath Jeshurun, an Orthodox synagogue in New York City.

In 1909, Kaplan returned to his seminary alma mater where he served as dean for the seminary's Teachers Institute. He was soon named professor of homiletics, Midrash, and philosophy. He would remain at JTS for the next half century, during which time he would become best known for his many extra-curricular activities.

In 1912, he joined with colleague Rabbi Israel Freidlander in forming Young Israel, an Orthodox movement designed to reach out to the continuing waves of new Jewish immigrants coming into the United States from Eastern Europe and facilitate their assimilation into American life in such a way as not to destroy their Jewish life and culture. The first Young Israel congregation was founded in 1913.

In 1917, in addition to his teaching chores, Kaplan resumed his life as a synagogue leader. At the synagogue, he began the development of new approaches to Judaism that would lead him farther and farther from the Orthodoxy with which he began. He began to transform the synagogue by seeing it more as a community center than primarily a Sabbath worship center. His effort led to his being fired from his position. As a result, with his supporters, Kaplan founded a new synagogue center, the Society for the Advancement of Judaism, which went on to become one of the more important Jewish congregations in New York City. As it grew, it became a model for additional congregations around North America. It also moved Kaplan from a position within Orthodox Judaism to Conservative Judaism.

In 1934, Kaplan published his most well-known book, *Judaism as a Civilization*, in which he called for a "reconstruction" of Jewish life around the image of Judaism as a civilization rather than simply a religion. Subsequently, he began the journal, *The Reconstructionist*, to expand and elaborate upon the idea in the book. As a result, a movement—Reconstructionist Judaism—developed in the space between Conservative and Reform Judaism.

Reconstructionism was intended to facilitate the strengthening of Conservative Judaism's commitment to Jewish law, the study of Jewish literature, the ideal of Israel, while appropriating the critical study of ancient holy books and responding to the needs of life in the 20th century. Kaplan saw Judaism as an evolving (hence changing) religious civilization with its center in the community's life. His emphasis would lead to an empowering of the lay community in Reconstructionist synagogues. The formalization of the movement proceeded in stages, the first step being the organization of the Jewish Reconstructionist Foundation in 1940. The Foundation assumed responsibility for the journal, with Kaplan remaining as head of the editorial board through the 1950s.

As the Reconstructionist movement became more visible, it drew criticism, and even Kaplan's fellow faculty members began to reject the direction his thought was taking him. As early as 1941, the JTS faculty sent Kaplan a letter rejecting his views, though no steps were taken to fire him. The publication of the *Sabbath Prayer Book* in 1945 became crucial in his relationship with the larger orthodox community. Three leading JTS professors—Alexander Marx, Louis Ginzberg, and Saul Lieberman—wrote an open letter condemning Kaplan's new prayer book and the direction of his rabbinic career. Further, Kaplan's prayer book led the Union of Orthodox Rabbis of the United States and Canada to excommunicate him and declare his work unacceptable. Eventually, Young Israel would condemn his approach as heretical and delete any reference to the role he played in its founding.

In spite of the criticism, Kaplan continued to write and gained a level of respect for his intellectual acumen. Among his many books are *The Future of the American Jew* (1948); *Questions Jews Ask: Reconstructionist Answers* (1956); *Judaism without Supernaturalism: The Only Alternative to Orthodoxy and Secularism* (1958); *The Greater Judaism in the Making: A Study of the Modern Evolution of Judaism* (1960); *The Purpose and Meaning of Jewish Existence: A People in the Image of God* (1964); and *The Religion of Ethical Nationhood: Judaism's Contribution to World Peace* (1970). He retired from JTS in 1963. Five years later, his son-in-law Ira Eisenstein led in the creation of the Reconstructionist College, a major step in Reconstructionism transformation from a movement within Conservative Judaism into a new Jewish denomination.

As the 21st century begins, Reconstructionism has been largely accepted in North America as a separate Jewish way beside that of Orthodox, Conservative, Reform, and Hasidic Judaism. Though almost all Orthodox and many Conservative Jews distanced themselves from Kaplan, many Reform and more liberal Conservative rabbis, without formally affiliating with Reconstructionism, have shown an affinity for Kaplan's worldview. The Reconstructionist movement remains small beside that of the other branches of Judaism and is largely confined to North America.

J. Gordon Melton

See also: Conservative Judaism; Reconstructionist Judaism; Young Israel.

References

Alpert, Rebecca T., and Jacob J. Staub. *Exploring Judaism: A Reconstructionist Approach.* Wyncote, PA: Reconstructionist Press, 1985.

Gilman, Neil. *Conservative Judaism: The New Century.* West Orange, NJ: Behrman House Publishing, 1993.

Gilman, Neil. *Sacred Fragments: Recovering Theology for the Modern Jew.* Philadelphia: Jewish Publication Society, 1992.

Gurock, Jeffrey, and Jacob J. Schacter. *A Modern Heretic and a Traditional Community: Mordecai M. Kaplan, Orthodoxy, and American Judaism.* New York: Columbia University Press, 1997.

Kaplan, Mordecai M. *Judaism as a Civilization: Toward a Reconstruction of American Jewish Life.* Philadelphia: Jewish Publication Society, 1994.

Karaites

Karaites are Jews who do not accept the authority of the Talmud—the commentary on Jewish law (the Torah)—as the authoritative interpretation of Jewish practice. The Karaites consider themselves the original Jews who follow only the Torah, from which later rabbinical Judaism has separated. A separate Karaite community could be distinguished as early as the eighth century CE in Babylonia (Iraq), where Anan ben David is said to have revitalized a lineage that had passed through a variety of earlier groups, including the community at Qumran known from the Dead Sea Scrolls. Many modern historians have questioned the association of Anan with Karaism and suggest that the first Karaites were a medieval group that appropriated the account of Anan to give themselves a longer history.

In any case, late in the ninth century the Karaite movement spread through the Jewish community then residing in the larger Islamic Empire and eventually became established in Palestine. After its Palestinian centers were destroyed by the First Christian Crusade in 1099, the leadership of the Karaite community relocated to Byzantium. After the fall of Constantinople to the Ottomans, Karaites migrated northward toward Poland and Lithuania and eastward to the Crimea. Much of the Eastern European Karaite community was destroyed during World War II.

The strongest Karaite community to survive into the mid-20th century was in Egypt, but in the late 1950s most relocated to Israel. As the 21st century begins, there are some 30,000 Karaites in Israel, with smaller communities in Egypt, France, and the San Francisco Bay Area of California. Major Israeli centers are found in Ramla and Ashdod. The American community is focused on the Karaite synagogue in Daly City, California.

Karaites reject the idea that rabbis are the main authority for interpreting the Torah. Instead, they believe that individuals are responsible for studying the Bible and for reaching the best interpretation for their situation, since in the end, it is the individual who will face judgment. This individual approach regularly introduces various interpretations into the community and ensures a level of diversity. Karaites do accept the authority of the Tenach (or Tanakh)—the Hebrew Bible (called the Old Testament by Christians)—but they reject other writings such as the Apocrypha, the Pseudepigrapha, the Christian New Testament, and the Muslim Koran. They believe in the future arrival of a Davidic Messiah (Isaiah 11:1), a human king filled with God's prophetic spirit. The Messiah will not be a divine or semidivine creature.

Over the centuries, Karaites have developed several practices that differ from those of the larger Jewish community, and their variant interpretations of Jewish law make intermarriage between Karaites and other Jews difficult. Karaites also calculate their calendar from actual observation of the new moon, and thus it varies slightly from that now common in Judaism. Karaites prohibit sexual relations on the Sabbath, whereas Orthodox Jews have seen the Sabbath as a particularly good time for sexual activity. Karaite synagogues do not have chairs, and the liturgy is very different from that in other Jewish traditions. They do not recognize the post-biblical holiday, Hanukkah.

The Karaite Jewish community is most easily contacted through their American adherents. Most recently, American Karaites have founded the Karaite Jewish University (PO Box 1971, Hedgesville, WV 25427).

Karaite Jews of America
    Congregation B'nai Israel
1575 Annie St.
Daly City, CA 94915
http://www.karaites.org/

J. Gordon Melton

See also: Calendars, Religious; Hanukkah; Judaism.

References
Birmbaum, Philip, ed. *Karaite Studies*. New York: Sepher-Hermon Press, 1971.
Liccha, Shawn, Nehemia Gordon, and Meir Rekhavi. *As It Is Written: A Brief Case for Karaism*. Arlington, TX: Hilkiah Press, 2006.
Nemoy, L. Leon. *Karaite Anthology*. New Haven, CT: Yale University Press, 1952.
Qanai, Avraham, ed. *An Introduction to Karaite Judaism: History, Theology, Practice, and Culture*. Albany, NY: Qirqisani Center, 2003.
Schur, Nathan. *History of the Karaites*. Frankfurt am Main and New York: Peter Lang, 1992.

Karbala

The town of Karbala in present-day Iraq, south of Baghdad, joins the nearby community of An Najaf as one of the most holy sites of Shia Muslims. The Shias form the second largest Muslim community, though the main Sunni community is almost 10 times larger in size. The Shia minority traces their origin to the squabbles over control of the emergent Islamic Empire in the decades after the Prophet Muhammad's death in 632 CE. After Muhammad, leadership of the Islamic community passed successively to the four caliphs. Following the assassination of the Caliph Uthman in 656, Ali ibn-Abi-Talib (ca. 600–661), Muhammad's son-in-law

Thousands of Iraqi Muslim Shiite pilgrims crowd around the shrine to Imam Hussein in Karbala on April 21, 2003, in a ritual known as the festival of Arbaiin, where the faithful came to the city to honor the first Shiite martyr, Imam Hussein (grandson of the prophet Muhammad). (AFP/Getty Images)

(the husband of Fatima) was chosen to succeed him by the powers that existed in Medina, Arabia. Ali was challenged by Mu'awiya (r. 661–680), and when Ali was assassinated in 661, most Muslims, including Ali's supporters, acknowledged him as the new caliph. Thus began the Umayyad dynasty that would rule Islam for the next century.

The year 680 became a watershed. Ali's two sons, Hasan (d. 669) and Husayn (626–680), had accepted Mu'awiya, but following Mu'awiya's death in 680, Husayn refused allegiance to his son Yazid (d. 683) as the new caliph and made plans to move to Mesopotamia (Iraq), where he believed he had strong support. However, as he journeyed to his goal, the caliph's forces blocked his progress at Karbala. When Husayn refused to surrender, he and all 86 of his companions were killed. He was seen as a martyr by his supporters,

who turned the site of the deaths and the burial site of Husayn into a pilgrimage site. As the Shia Muslims emerged as a distinctive group, disagreeing with the Sunni on a variety of lesser points of belief and practice, they came to view Karbala as a most holy site. A key of divergence between the two groups is the acknowledgment that Islamic leadership properly passed to Ali and Husayn rather than the caliphs of the Umayyad dynasty.

The mosque-shrine, Masjid al-Hysayn, built at his burial site, memorializes the martyrdom of Husayn, which is additionally commemorated in an annual pageant that symbolically re-enacts his death. Over the centuries, the shrine has been targeted by the Shias' enemies. It has been destroyed and rebuilt on a number of occasions. In 850, for example, Sunni ruler al-Mutawakil (r. 847–861), hoping to stop Shia pilgrimages, destroyed the shrine. Most recently, in 1801, the ultra-conservative Wahhabis, who would eventually come to dominate neighboring Saudi Arabia, targeted it. When rebuilt, the walls of the new courtyard were decorated with the entire text of the Koran. It was again damaged in the 1991 Gulf War only to be restored. During the second Gulf War, American forces made a self-conscious effort to spare it further damage.

Shia Muslims make pilgrimages to Karbala throughout the year, but two dates draw the greatest number. Ashura, the 10th day of the month of Muharram on the Muslim calendar, marks the day of Husayn's death. They also show up 40 days later, the 12th day of the month of Safar. At these times, pilgrims participate in various activities re-enacting the battle and deaths. Men will march through the street flagellating themselves and will allow cuts to be made on their heads. Press coverage often pictures young males with blood freely flowing from their various wounds. The majority, less demonstrative in their commemoration of the battle and deaths, purchase objects made from the clay of the battlefield.

Among the martyrs of 680 was Abbas, Husayn's half-brother. His tomb is located a mere 1,500 feet from Masjid al-Husayn and has become the second site most visited by pilgrims. Abbas is seen as a source of miraculous healings, and healing powers have also been ascribed to the small clay tablets that may be purchased and consumed by those seeking a restoration of health.

Iraqi ruler Saddam Hussein (r. 1979–2003) operated from a power base in the Sunni-dominated areas of Iraq and, during most of his regime, forbade public celebrations at Karbala by the Shia majority in his country. Such celebrations were held for the first time in more than a quarter of a century in 2003 following his being driven from power.

J. Gordon Melton

See also: An Najaf; Martyrdom; Muhammad; Shia Islam; Wahhabi Islam.

References

Aghaie, Kamran Scot. *The Martyrs of Karbala: Shi'a Symbols and Rituals in Modern Iran.* Seattle: University of Washington Press, 2004.

Hyder, Syed Akbar. *Reliving Karbala: Martyrdom in South Asian Memory.* Oxford: Oxford University Press, 2008.

Nakash, Yitzhak. *The Shi'is of Iraq.* Princeton, NJ: Princeton University Press, 2003.

Karma-Kagyupa, Tibetan Buddhism

The Karma-Kagyu branch is one of the many sub-schools of Kagyupa Tibetan Buddhism. It was founded by Düsum Khyenpa (1110–1193), a disciple of Gampopa (1079–1153), who established several temples during his lifetime, as well as the headquarters of the Karma-Kagyupa in the monastery of Tsurphu (1185). Because of their Kagyu heritage, the Karma-Kagyupa emphasize yoga and Tantric practices. The Karma-Kagyu path to enlightenment follows a succession of steps leading to mental quietness (Sanskrit: *shamata*). Preliminary practices of purification (Tibetan: *ngondro*) such as prostration, mandala offerings, recitation of the mantra of Vajrasattva, and guru yoga precede higher meditations and the visualization of deities (such as Tchenrezig, Tara, and Mahakala), considered to be mediums through which wisdom is expressed.

From the 12th century on, the Karma-Kagyu order flourished in the central and eastern provinces of Tibet and later acquired political support within the imperial courts of Mongolia and China. By the 13th century the Karma-Kagyupa were competing with the Sakyapa for Mongol patronage, and during the 15th and 16th centuries they faced sporadic and localized conflicts against the Gelugpa. In the 17th century, the Dalai Lamas' dominance weakened the political power of the Karma-Kagyupa in Tibet.

The Karma-Kagyu order claims to have pioneered the Tibetan system of voluntary reincarnation (*tulku*) of religious authority. Under this system, Karma-Kagyu leadership was passed on for eight centuries in an unbroken succession of reincarnated masters, or *karmapa* (literally, "black hat"). A second tulku lineage was added to the first: Khaydrup Drakpa Senge (1283–1349) became the first *sharmapa* ("red hat"), the second highest Karma-Kagyu spiritual leader. As a consequence, the doctrinal and hierarchical structure of the Karma-Kagyu branch became inextricably linked to these two figures.

In 1950, Tibet was annexed by China. The 16th karmapa, Rangjung Rigpe Dorje (1924–1981), escaped from Tibet just before the open repression by China started in 1959. He established new headquarters in Rumtek, near Gangtok, Sikkim (now an Indian state), in 1966. In an effort to preserve the Karma-Kagyu tradition, he participated actively in the Western dissemination of Buddhism during the late 1960s and the 1970s.

The very first Tibetan temple in the West, Samyé Ling, was founded in Scotland in 1967 by two Karma-Kagyu lamas, Chogyam Trungpa Rinpoche (1939–1987) and Chuje Akong Rinpoche. In 1973, Trungpa established the Vajradhatu Organisation (now known as Shambhala International), thus initiating the creation of Western Kagyu orders. The Karma-Kagyu quickly developed into one of the largest Tibetan branches to spread and settle outside Asia. As of the late 1990s, hundreds of temples and thousands of followers were estimated to be scattered throughout the world, principally in the West. Following new routes, the old Tibetan tradition has now established new roots outside the Land of Snow.

The late karmapa died in 1981, and the recent and controversial recognition of two candidates for the succession—Trinley Thaye Dorje (b. 1983) and Urgyen Trinley Dorje (b. 1985)—is a major source of division among the Karma-Kagyupa. Urgyen Trinley Dorje and his followers have their headquarters in Rumtek, Sikkim, India. They are represented in the Americas by the Karma Triyana Dharmachakra. Many Western Karma-oriented groups, especially the Diamond Way organization led by the Danish-born master Ole Nydahl, support Thaye Dorje. Nydahl has founded more than 590 affiliated groups in North and South America, Western Europe, and most significant, in many countries of the former Soviet Union. Thaye Dorje and his followers had their headquarters in New Delhi, but nowadays expand worldwide, and in the late 2000s, approximately 650 groups worldwide were under his guidance.

Lionel Obadia

See also: Diamond Way Buddhism; Gelugpa; Kagyupa Tibetan Buddhism; Meditation; Sakyapa; Shambhala International; Tibetan Buddhism.

References

Batchelor, Stephen. *The Awakening of the West: The Encounter of Buddhism and Western Culture.* London and San Francisco: Thorsons, 1994.

Karma Trinley. *The History of the Sixteen Karmapas of Tibet.* Boulder, CO: Prajna Press, 1980.

The Karmapa Conflict. http://www.karmapa-issue.org/. Accessed June 15, 2009.

Stein, Rolf. *Tibetan Civilization.* Stanford: Stanford University Press, 1972.

Karo Batak Protestant Church

The Karo people, one division of the larger Batak cultural group, reside in northern Sumatra. They were the last of the Batak people toward whom the Dutch Reformed missionaries directed their attention; however, in 1890 a missionary from the independent Nederlandsch Zendelinggenootchap started evangelizing in the area. He ran into immediate opposition, as the Karonese interpreted his presence as part of an effort by the Dutch to steal their lands. There were only 5,000 converts in the first half century.

During the 1930s, an effort was made to build indigenous leadership within the relatively small Karonese Christian group, and in 1941 the first Karonese pastors were ordained and the Karo Batak Protestant Church was created and granted autonomy. Almost immediately the church confronted challenges, with the beginning of the war with Japan and then the formation of Indonesia as a new nation. However, the many years of work began to reap rewards in the 1950s, when mass movements led many into the church, even as Islam also began to grow in the same region. During the last half of the 20th century more than 220,000 people joined the church. This growth is partly accounted for by a reformulation of church life, as the leadership has rid itself of attitudes hostile to Indonesian culture inherited from the Dutch missionaries.

In 2006, the Karo Batak Protestant Church reported 276,912 members. The church has a presbyterian polity, and its synod is the highest legislative body. At its inception the church adopted traditional Reformed statements of faith, but in 1979 it also adopted a new confession (revised in 1984), which its members had written. In 1987 it began to ordain women to the ministry, though female elders had been present from the beginning of the century.

During the early part of the century the church began to develop a school system and opened its first medical facilities. These have now been extended, and an orphanage, a home for seniors, and a credit bank have been added. The church is a member of the World Council of Churches and the World Alliance of Reformed Churches.

Karo Batak Protestant Church
Jalan Kapten Pala Bangun no. 66
Kabanjahe 22115
Sumatra Utara
Indonesia

J. Gordon Melton

See also: World Alliance of Reformed Churches; World Council of Churches.

References

Bauswein, Jean-Jacques, and Lukas Vischner, eds. *The Reformed Family Worldwide: A Survey of Reformed Churches, Theological Schools, and International Organizations.* Grand Rapids, MI: William B. Eerdmans Publishing Company, 1999.

Van Beek, Huibert. *A Handbook of the Churches and Councils: Profiles of Ecumenical Relationships.* Geneva: World Council of Churches, 2006.

Kashmir Saivism

The Tantric Saivism or Shaivism of Kashmir is based on a canon of scriptures, called Agamas or Tantras, which are held to be revealed by the highest deity, Shiva (or Siva), and in which Shiva himself teaches the foundations of the Saiva religion. These scriptures were produced several centuries before the culmination of exegetical activity between the ninth and 11th centuries, when dualistic and monistic schools competed for their correct interpretation. Kashmir Saivism found its origin in one of these monistic schools.

The Kashmirian dualist school, called Saiva Siddhanta, considered Shiva, the soul, and the world as ontologically separate and ultimately real entities. According to the dualists, the soul is bound to transmigration by a beginningless defilement. The soul is therefore born into this world in order to experience its *karma*, remove the defilement, and thus gain liberation. In order to reach this freedom from transmigration the soul has to be initiated into the Saiva religion: the rite of initiation and the subsequent practice removes the defilement, so that the soul can be released at death.

Apart from the Siddhanta and its ritual, which centered on the worship of Sadasiva (a form of Shiva usually pictured with 5 heads and 10 arms), there existed more heterodox cults of female deities, as for instance the Trika ("trinity"), in which three goddesses (Para, Parapara, and Apara) are worshipped, or the Krama ("sequence"), in which cycles of different manifestations of Kali are revered. Adherents of these cults upheld as valid the same canon of scriptures revealed by Shiva as did the Siddhanta, but based their views and practices on a different segment of the text. According to the cults' philosophical system, which is named after its main text, Recognition (Pratyabhijna), there is only one reality, namely, consciousness of Shiva, from which souls and the world appear spontaneously. According to this monistic tradition, defilement is merely the soul's ignorance of its true identity as Shiva. Once this identity is recognized, liberation occurs, even in this life.

Both the dualists and the monists had an impact in the rest of the Indian subcontinent. The southern Saiva-Siddhanta was heavily influenced and even dependent on the philosophical system their Kashmirian predecessors had developed, and the monist philosophy was integrated into other Tantric systems, most notably the Srividya. In Kashmir the monist system survived in a Gnostic form, which was termed Kashmir Saivism when its works were first published at the beginning of the 20th century.

Isolated in the Kashmir Valley, the followers of Kasmir Saivism have remained relatively few in number, a situation maintained by Muslim dominance in the region. In recent years, many Saivites have fled the war-torn valley of Kashmir and relocated to Jammu, New Delhi, and other sites throughout northern India. The Saivite philosophy attracted the attention of modern

Indian charismatic gurus like Bhagwan Shree Rajneesh, or Osho (1931–1990), who founded the Osho Commune International, and Swami Muktananda (SYDA). The last traditional Kashmirian guru who claimed to transmit the Kasmir Saivist system, Swami Lakshman Joo, has been the starting point of an American-based group, the Kashmir Saivism Fellowship, which may be contacted through its website.

http://www.kashmirshaivism.org/

Jürgen Hanneder

See also: Tantrism.

References

Hughes, John. *Self Realization in Kashmir Shaivism: The Oral Teachings of Swami Lakshmanjoo.* Albany: State University of New York Press, 1994.

Lakshman Joo Raina, Swami. *Kashmir Saivism: The Secret Supreme.* Albany: State University of New York Press, 1985.

Sanderson, Alexis. "The Doctrine of the Malinivijayottaratantra." In *Ritual and Speculation in Early Tantrism: Studies in Honour of André Padoux,* edited by Teun Goudriaan, 281–312. Albany: State University of New York Press, 1992.

Sanderson, Alexis. "Saivism and the Tantric Traditions." In *The World's Religions: The Religions of Asia,* edited by Friedhelm Hardy, 128–172. London: Routledge, 1990.

A Russian Orthodox church in Uralsk, Kazakhstan. (Peke/Dreamstime.com)

■ Kazakhstan

The relatively new country of Kazakhstan, named as the homeland of the Kazakh people, is a large central Asian country that stretches between China's western border and the Caspian Sea. It shares additional borders with Russia to the north and Turkmenistan, and Uzbekistan. It includes 1,030,815 square miles of territory. About half of its 15.3 million citizens (2008) are Kazakhs.

The area that now constitutes the modern nation of Kazakhstan was inhabited by various peoples as early as 2000 BCE. At a later date, it was overrun by Attila's Huns and then by the Turks. In the eighth century CE, a Turkish kingdom emerged that would create a high culture, especially in western sites along the shores of the Caspian Sea. At this time Islam was introduced. Over the following centuries, a sense of identity would slowly grow among the Kazakh peoples, tied together by their Turkish dialect and Hanafite Sunni Islam, though after the fall of the Turkish kingdom there was no uniting political entity.

Russians began to expand southward into Kazakhstan in the 18th century, and in the first half of the 19th century all of the country was annexed to Russia. The new authorities completely reorganized the ruling administration and moved to pacify still independent-minded local rulers. Russia exploited the region's min-

Kazakhstan

Religion	Followers in 1970	Followers in 2010	% of Population	Annual % growth 2000–2010	Followers in 2025	Followers in 2050
Muslims	3,516,000	8,174,000	51.9	0.90	10,831,000	12,410,000
Agnostics	4,118,000	4,032,000	25.6	–0.25	2,900,000	2,000,000
Christians	2,450,000	2,106,000	13.4	–0.30	2,180,000	2,215,000
Orthodox	2,067,000	1,660,000	10.5	–0.43	1,600,000	1,500,000
Roman Catholics	20,000	184,000	1.2	0.27	240,000	280,000
Independents	17,500	115,000	0.7	3.08	150,000	200,000
Atheists	3,000,000	1,380,000	8.8	0.01	1,000,000	600,000
Ethnoreligionists	0	25,000	0.2	0.34	25,000	25,000
Buddhists	10,000	18,000	0.1	0.34	20,000	25,000
New religionists	4,000	7,000	0.0	0.34	10,000	12,000
Jews	12,000	5,500	0.0	0.34	5,500	5,500
Baha'is	0	8,000	0.1	7.71	12,000	15,000
Zoroastrians	0	2,500	0.0	0.35	2,500	2,500
Sikhs	0	800	0.0	0.35	1,000	2,000
Total population	**13,110,000**	**15,759,000**	**100.0**	**0.34**	**16,987,000**	**17,312,000**

eral wealth while using the area as a place to banish political dissidents.

Kazakhs rebelled in 1916 in reaction to an order from the tsar for universal military mobilization. The rebellion was crushed and the nation was incorporated into the Soviet Union. Kazakhstan was one of the first of the Soviet Republics to push for independence during the Gorbachev era at the end of the 1980s, and it became an independent country in 1991.

By the 1990s, there were about as many Russians as Kazakhs in the country, but the Russian population dropped significantly during the 1990s. Russians were approximately 35 percent of the population as the 21st century began. Russian Cossacks have emerged as a conservative minority, demanding that Russia take back the section of Kazakhstan that they largely control. Russia has demanded that the new Kazakh rulers treat the Russian minority fairly.

Islam came to the area in 649 with the Arab caliph Uthman ibn Affan (644–656). In the 13th century, the Mongols captured Kazakhstan, but they too converted to Islam, and in 1360 the Mongol Khan Tamburlaine (1336–1405) established the famed city of Samarkand as his capital. His army stretched the Mongol Empire to Poland and overran the Russian cities of Moscow and Kiev. Following the Russian invasion and takeover in the 19th century, Muslim Kazakhs were marginalized. In this context, the Sufi Brotherhoods emerged

as the focus of a variety of independence movements. They were especially opposed to the secularization of the public schools by the Soviets. In the 1930s, Stalin instituted a harsh policy of repression that included the closing of the remaining Muslim schools, suppressing the Sufi organizations, and the further reduction of functioning mosques.

In 1943 the Russians created the Muslim Spiritual Board of Central Asia with headquarters at Tashkent, Uzbekistan. All imams had to register with the board, which controlled two seminaries for the training of religious leaders. Even as the board took more control, Kazakhstan took significant steps toward secularization, generally attributed to both the negative pressure of the long Soviet rule and the improved educational level of the general public. Today, most Muslims are content with the present government, although some younger, more conservative believers are pushing for the creation of an Islamic state.

Although most Kazakhs identify as Muslims, because of their isolation from the main centers of the Muslim world a form of popular folk Islam has established itself among the majority of religious practitioners. Their practice includes a number of activities generally denounced by more learned Muslims, including the visiting of the graves of Muslim "saints," to curry favor, the use of verses from the Koran on amulets, and ancestor veneration.

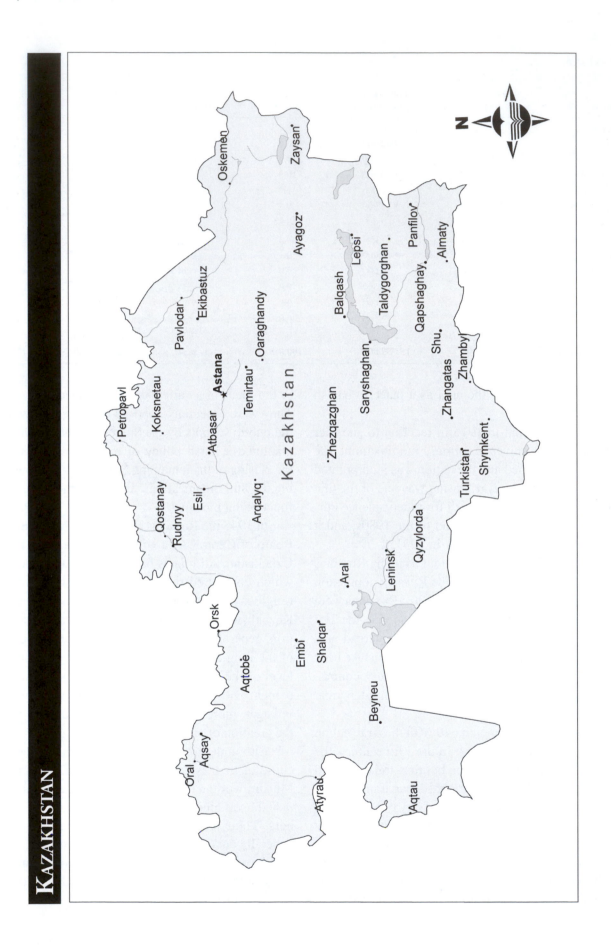

An amulet protecting from the evil eye; belief in the evil eye is found in Islamic doctrine, and attempts to ward off the curse typically revolve around the use of amulets. (Travel Pictures Gallery)

Christianity was established in Kazakhstan and a variety of sectarian religious expressions were introduced in the wake of Russian occupation and the encouragement of immigration to the region. The Russian Orthodox Church (Moscow Patriarchate) is now second in size only to Sunni Islam as a religious community. There are three dioceses, whose bishops reside at Almaty, Shymkent, and Oral.

The first Baptist church in Kazakhstan was established in 1908 after Gavriel I. Mazaev, the brother of the president of the Russian Baptist Union, moved to Petropavl near the Russian border. Other churches were formed as settlers from different parts of the

Soviet Union arrived over the next decades. Russian Baptist ranks were swelled by the arrival of displaced Germans during World War II. Unable to form separate congregations, the German-speaking believers attended the Russian Baptist churches that accommodated them with German services. They were able to grow slowly in the decades following the war and expanded greatly in the 1990s. By 1995 more than 170 congregations had come together in the Union of Evangelical Christians–Baptists, the largest of the several Protestant/Free church organizations in the country.

A number of competing groups ultimately derive from the Baptist Union. One group of Baptists who are not part of the Union and who have refused to register with the government have been the subject of government actions aimed at forcing them either to register or to dissolve.

Among the several groups to find their way into Kazakhstan in the 20th century was the Seventh-day Adventist Church. The work grew slowly during the Soviet era, but the Kazakhstan Conference was organized in 1879 and by the mid-1990s there were 36 congregations. Pentecostalism also has a small presence in the country. A fair number of immigrants moved into Kazakhstan during the 20th century, including a number of Koreans. The Korean community supports both Baptist churches and Buddhist centers.

Through the 1990s to the present, minority (mostly Christian) religious groups have complained that intolerance of religious freedoms has been institutionalized in Kazahkstan through the religious registration regulations that on the one hand require registration for a group to exist but on the other make registration a difficult process. Jehovah's Witnesses and Baptists have reported the most problems. Tensions with minority religions over issues of burial of church members, proselytization activities, and worship in unregistered facilities have kept Kazakhstan in the news.

J. Gordon Melton

See also: Russian Orthodox Church (Moscow Patriarchate); Seventh-day Adventist Church.

References

Cummings, Sally. *Kazakhstan: Power and the Elite.* London: I. B. Tauris, 2005.

Khalid, Adeeb. *Islam after Communism: Religion and Politics in Central Asia*. Berkeley: University of California Press, 2007.

Lewis, David C. *After Atheism: Religion and Ethnicity in Russia and Central Asia*. London: Macmillan Palgrave, 2000.

Muslims of the Soviet East (English ed.). Tashkent, Uzbekistan: Muslim Religious Board of Central Asia and Kazakhstan, 1968–. Various issues.

Kedarnath

Kedarnath is a remote Hindu sacred pilgrimage site located in the Himalaya Mountains at a height of 11,760 feet. Kedarnath, the name of both a temple and the small town in which the temple is located, is one of the four Char Dham pilgrimage sites. The four sites are considered the abodes of God in the four directions of India. Kedarnath is the site in the north.

The temple is traced to prehistoric times, and even to the mythological past when the deity Shiva meditated here. In the Indian epic, the Mahabharati, the Pandav brothers, the sons of Pandu—Yudhishtir, Bhim, Arjun, Nakul, and Sahadev—were all married to the same woman, Draupadi. And as one, they fought and won a war against their cousins the Kauravas and an alienated half-brother. Despondent over the war, they visited the sage Ved Vyas (to whom authorship of the Mahabharati is generally ascribed), who advised them to meet with Shiva. Shiva could forgive them for the deaths of their kin. Shiva did not wish to forgive the brothers, and he hid from them at several places and finally at Kedarnath. The brothers eventually tracked him to his hiding place. As they approached, he turned himself into a bull and hid in plain sight among the cattle on the hillside. Still toying with the brothers, as the brothers were about to find him, he began to sink into the ground, head first. He was halfway in when one of the brothers grabbed his tail. At that moment, Shiva appeared and granted the brothers forgiveness. He also told them to worship the hind portion of the bull that remained above ground. The brothers were said to have subsequently built the first temple.

The story does not end there, and later on portions of the bull (that was Shiva in disguise) reappeared in other locations in the area—the Pashupatinath Temple at Kathamndu, Nepal, and four locations near Kedarnath. The bull's hair is at Kalpeshwar, the face at Rudranath, the chest and arms at Tungnath and the navel area at Madh Maheshwar. Kedarnath and the five other Shiva temples are the only locations where the different parts of his body rather than the lingum of Shiva is worshipped. The five locations in India are collectively referred to as the Panch Kedar (Five Kedar). A visit to all five sites is said to wash away a lifetime of sins of the pilgrim.

The temple at Kedarnath is open six months of the year, from the late spring through the fall. Snow makes the town inaccessible through the winter, and worship is transferred to a more accessible site at this time. The temple is under the care of priests of the Lingayata sect. This is a monotheistic Hindu sect that worships Shiva and identifies Shiva with the true self.

J. Gordon Melton

See also: Pilgrimage; Temples—Hindu.

References

Gupta, Subhadra Sen. *Badrinath and Kedarnath: The Dhaams in the Himalayas*. Calcutta: Rupa & Co., 2002.

Harshananda, Swami. *Hindu Pilgrim Centres*. Bangalore: Ramakrishna Math, 2005.

Malhotra, S. S. L. *Pilgrimage: A Journey and a Trek to the Himalayan Shrines of Badrinath, Kedarnath and Hemkund Sahib*. London: Trafford Publishing, 2006.

■ Kenya

Kenya is an East African country on the Indian Ocean between Tanzania and Somalia. It shares additional borders with Ethiopia, Sudan, and Uganda. Included within its 225,000 square miles are a variety of noteworthy geographical features from Lake Victoria in the southwest to the Rift Valley in northwestern Kenya where some of the oldest humanoid remains known were found. Kenya's 40 million citizens come from a variety of African people groups. In relatively modern times, it became the home of the Bantu people, divided culturally into a number of groups. Additional

Islamic mosque in Nairobi. There are 42 ethnic groupings in Kenya, who speak a variety of languages and practice a variety of religions. (Corel)

African peoples reside in the north and east near the country's borders with Sudan, Ethiopia, and Somalia.

Beginning in the seventh century, various groups from the Arabian Peninsula formed settlements along the eastern coast of Africa. In 975 CE, Ali bin Sultan al-Hassan, a prince from Shiraz (Iran), was driven from his country and relocated to the coast of Kenya, where he built several cities including Manisa (now Mombasa). The Arabs mixed with the Bantus and built a trading culture that eventually extended as far south as Mozambique. These cities flourished through the 16th century, when the Portuguese arrived. The Portuguese were determined to monopolize trade with India and set about occupying and destroying the cities. The Portuguese were forced out in 1698, and the coastal culture did not recover.

In the 19th century, the Masai, a group of Nilotic people, established their authority through much of the interior. Their hegemony was short lived, however,

as their power was built upon their herding of domesticated cows, which were largely wiped out in a massive epidemic. At the end of the 19th century, a series of agreements among the European powers gave England hegemony in Kenya and neighboring Uganda. The British government moved to construct a railroad from Mombasa to Nairobi to Kampala, the capital of Uganda. As the railroad was constructed, Europeans moved in and settled on the land. These lands were primarily taken, without compensation, from the Kikuyu people.

In 1944 a movement was created to defend Kikuyu interests. Two important organizations were the Kenya Africa Union, headed by Jomo Kenyatta (ca. 1891–1978), and the secret group called Mau Mau, which operated as a terrorist organization attacking settlers' property and persons. Through the 1950s, a variety of repressive measures were instituted, but finally in 1960 Kenyatta's organization was recognized as the Kenya

Kenya

Religion	Followers in 1970	Followers in 2010	% of Population	Annual % growth 2000–2010	Followers in 2025	Followers in 2050
Christians	7,075,000	33,393,000	82.2	2.85	48,463,000	73,546,000
Protestants	1,646,000	12,000,000	29.5	2.46	17,750,000	27,600,000
Roman Catholics	1,936,000	9,200,000	22.6	1.51	12,820,000	18,000,000
Independents	1,666,000	6,720,000	16.5	2.29	10,000,000	16,000,000
Ethnoreligionists	3,228,000	3,606,000	8.9	0.91	3,500,000	3,385,000
Muslims	736,000	2,870,000	7.1	2.64	4,060,000	6,050,000
Baha'is	124,000	420,000	1.0	2.64	600,000	900,000
Hindus	63,000	200,000	0.5	2.64	300,000	450,000
Jains	31,000	76,000	0.2	2.64	115,000	190,000
Agnostics	2,000	40,000	0.1	2.64	80,000	150,000
Sikhs	13,000	35,000	0.1	2.64	50,000	75,000
Jews	700	2,400	0.0	2.64	3,500	5,000
Atheists	0	1,200	0.0	2.64	3,000	5,000
Zoroastrians	270	700	0.0	–1.19	600	500
Buddhists	0	350	0.0	2.63	600	1,000
Total population	**11,273,000**	**40,645,000**	**100.0**	**2.64**	**57,176,000**	**84,757,000**

African National Union. Kenya became an independent country in the British Commonwealth in 1963, and Kenyatta was elected president the following year. Following Kenyatta's death in 1978, Daniel arap Moi (b. 1924) succeeded him as president. Currently (2008), the country is led by President Mwai Kibaki (initially elected in 2002) and Prime Minister Raila Amolo Odinga (appointed in 2008) who represent the two largest political parties in the country.

Traditional religions remain strong in Kenya, although the number of practitioners dropped steadily through the last half of the 20th century. In the 1940s the percentage had dropped to around 60 percent, and by the 1970s an estimated 30 percent of the population was following traditional faiths. That percentage had further decreased to approximately 10 percent by the end of the century.

The first attack upon traditional religions came from Islam, which was brought by Arab settlers in the 10th century. Islam remained concentrated along the coast and the region adjacent to the border with Somalia. Sunni Islam of the Shafaiite School is strongest among the Somali people (who are almost all Muslim) and has a large following among the Digo, Boran, Pokomo, and Duruma peoples. In the years following independence, Islam suffered a loss in Kenya as Somali people moved to Somalia and as Muslims along the coast reverted to their traditional religion. However, Islam has since grown because of the migration of a number of Indians and Pakistanis. The largest group of immigrants follow the Shafiite School, but significant numbers follow the Hanafite School and there are also many Shia Muslims. Minority groups include the Shiah Fatimi Ismaili Tayyabi Dawoodi Bohras, Ismailis, and Ithna-Asharis. There is also a community of several thousand members of the Ahmadiyya Muslim movement. In the years since World War II, the Baha'i Faith has had rapid growth both among the Bantu groups and among the Asian Indians.

Christianity was introduced into Kenya by the Portuguese, and evangelistic activity coincided with the destruction of the coastal culture. Although a mission was established and a number of converts were received into the Roman Catholic Church, the work was lost when the Portuguese were driven away. Christianity did not return until 1844, with the arrival of Johann Ludwig Krapf (1810–1881), a Church of England missionary representing the Church Missionary Society. Krapf's work was confined to the coast until the arrival of John Rehmann two years later. Backed by the British government for many years, the Anglican community would become the largest in Kenya and finally emerge as the Church of the Province of Kenya.

KENYA

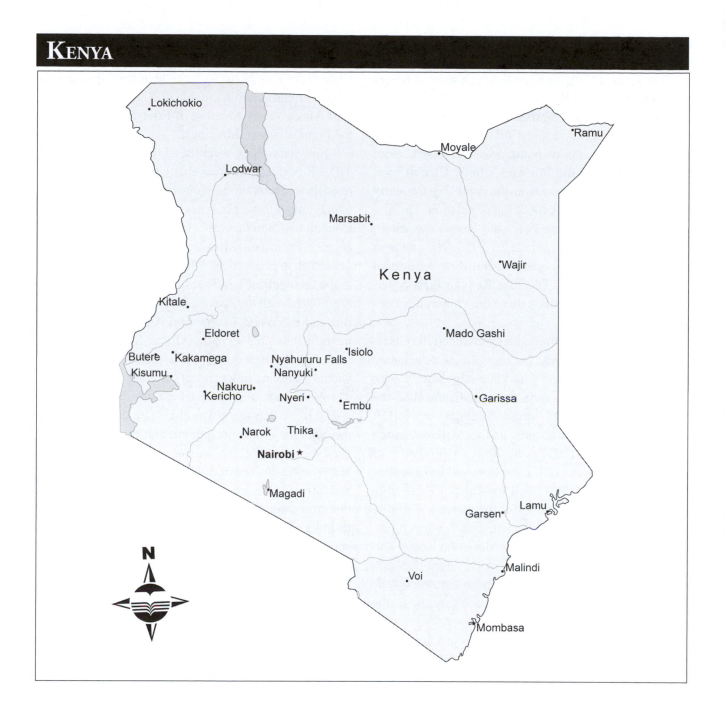

British Methodists, representatives of the United Methodist Free Churches (now a constituent part of the Methodist Church in the United Kingdom), came to Mombasa in 1862. They expanded their work along the Tana River and then into the area northeast of Mount Kenya. It is now known as the Methodist Church of Kenya. It would be the end of the century before other churches would discover Kenya; representatives of the Church of Scotland came in 1891, and of the Africa Inland Mission four years later. The African Inland Mission had spectacular success. Its founder, Peter Cameron Scott, led the first missionary team, which proved a disaster, but a second effort soon after the turn of the century opened work successively among the Nzawi, Masai, and Tugen peoples. The mission became independent as the African Inland Church in 1943, by which time it had eclipsed all other churches with the exception of the Catholic and Anglican churches.

Numerous additional missions were started after the opening of western Kenya by the railroad in 1902.

The Roman Catholic Church began work in Kenya anew in 1889, with the arrival of the White Fathers. The church supported a broad program in Kenya, and the White Fathers were soon joined by priests from a variety of orders. As response was significant, more priests arrived and the Roman Catholic Church soon became the largest church in the land. By the early 1960s it claimed 20 percent of the population. The first Kenyan was ordained in 1927, and Kenya was established as a separate province in 1953. Nairobi was erected as an archepiscopal see and three additional dioceses were named. The first Kenyan bishop was consecrated in 1957. Since then, the church has continued to expand.

Two factors have dramatically changed the Christian community in Kenya. The move to create what are termed African Initiated Churches is generally seen as beginning in Kenya with the establishment of the Momiya Luo Mission by former Anglicans in 1914. It was followed by such groups as the African Church of the Holy Spirit (1927), the Kenya Foundation of the Prophets Church (1927), the National Independent Church of Africa (1929), and the Gospel Furthering Bible Church (1936). In 1962 the Roman Catholic Church experienced a significant schism when members left to found the Legion of Mary, the largest single Roman Catholic schism in Africa. More than 200 independent denominations had been formed by the 1970s, and the number has continued to grow to the present.

The second factor to shape Kenyan Christianity has been Pentecostalism, which was brought to Kenya in 1910 by representatives of the Pentecostal Assemblies of Canada. Other North American and European Pentecostal churches began work over the course of the 20th century. The original work, now known as the Pentecostal Assemblies of God, and an African Initiated Church, the African Independent Pentecostal Church, are among the largest churches in the country. The African Independent Pentecostal Church was at one time the largest Protestant Free Church in the country, though it has now been eclipsed by the African Inland Church. Additional churches that grew out of

the work of the Church of God (Anderson, Indiana), the Salvation Army, and the Seventh-day Adventist Church are now home to large memberships, and the largest Friends church outside of North America is the East Africa Yearly Meeting of Friends (affiliated with the Friends United Meeting).

Kenya has been a center of ecumenism in Africa. The All Africa Conference of Churches is headquartered there. The National Council of Churches of Kenya, which unites those churches affiliated with the World Council of Churches, traces its beginning to the Alliance of Protestant Missions founded in 1918. More conservative evangelical churches are brought together in the Evangelical Fellowship of Kenya, which in turn is affiliated with the Association of Evangelicals of Africa and the World Evangelical Alliance. Several ecumenical structures serve the African Initiated Churches, including the East African Christian Alliance and the United Orthodox Independent Churches of East Africa.

With such a diverse Christian community, one would think that there would also be diversity among the other major religious communities, and such is indeed the case. For example, as early as 1886 the first Nams came to Kenya, along with Hindus and Sikhs who arrived to work on the railroad project. Although the great majority of Indians and Pakistanis returned to India after the completion of the railroad, enough stayed to create a significant community as the century progressed, and they numbered 100,000 by 1970. Members of both the Terapatha Svetambara and the Terapatha Digambara Jains are present, though the former are in the majority. A variety of Hindu groups are present, many having brought their religion from different parts of India. These older groups cooperate with the Hindu Council of Kenya. Among the newer movements, the Arya Samaj have a strong following, and the International Society for Krishna Consciousness has gathered members among the indigenous population. The Sikhs have established their main center in Nairobi, but members now live in other parts of the country as well. All three groups have declined since World War II as members have either returned to India or converted to the Baha'i Faith.

Among newer Indian groups, Sahaja Yoga and the Osho International Commune have small followings.

The Theosophical Society brought the Western Esoteric tradition from its international headquarters in India, and there is also a very small group of Zoroastrians (Parsis).

Buddhism was unknown in Kenya until 1993, when a Tibetan lama came to Nairobi to form a Buddhist society. He left after giving a basic course on meditation, but the next year, Maung Soe Myint, a native Kenyan, traveled to Myanmar to study Vipassana meditation. He returned with books, tapes, and videos and shared them with the members of the Buddhist Society in Nairobi. As a result, Chanmye Sayadaw was invited to visit Kenya and other African countries, and he came in 1995. As a result of that visit, the first *vihara* (monastery) in Africa was constructed by the Myanmar community in South Africa. Also in the 1990s, a center of Karma-Kagyupa Tibetan Buddhism has been opened, and a small Buddhist community has begun to take its place in Kenyan society.

In 1903 the British government offered the Zionist Organization land in what is now Kenya upon which to create a semiautonomous Jewish settlement. Although the organization officially turned down the offer, some individual Jews responded to it and settled in Kenya. Today the community consists of approximately 165 families who meet together for worship at the Nairobi Hebrew Congregation.

J. Gordon Melton

See also: African Inland Church; All Africa Conference of Churches; Arya Samaj; Baha'i Faith; Church Missionary Society; Church of England; Church of God (Anderson, Indiana); Church of Scotland; East Africa Yearly Meeting of Friends; Friends United Meeting; Friends/Quakers; Hanafite School of Islam; International Society for Krishna Consciousness; Ismaili Islam; Karma-Kagyupa, Tibetan Buddhism; Legion of Mary; Methodist Church; Methodist Church in Kenya; Pentecostal Assemblies of Canada; Roman Catholic Church; Sahaja Yoga; Salvation Army; Seventh-day Adventist Church; Shafiite School of Islam; Shiah Fatimi Ismaili Tayyabi Dawoodi Bohra; Terapanth Svetambara Jain Tradition; White Fathers; World Council of Churches; World Evangelical Alliance.

References

Barrett, David B., et al., eds. *Kenya Churches Handbook: The Development of Kenyan Christianity.* Kisumu, Kenya: Evangel Press, 1973.

"Bibliography of Christianity and Religion in Kenya." In *Kenya Churches Handbook*, 315–332. Kisumu, Kenya: Evangel Press, 1973.

Fedders, A. *Peoples and Cultures of Kenya.* Nairobi, Kenya: Transafrica, 1979.

"The First Myanmar Bikkhu Missionary to Step on African Soil." http://web.ukonline.co.uk/buddhism/kolay/01b.htm. Accessed December 1, 2001.

Githieya, F. K. *The Freedom of the Spirit: African Indigenous Churches in Kenya.* Atlanta: Scholars Press, 1997.

Hofer, Katherine. *Implications of a Global Religious Movement for Local Political Spheres: Evangelicalism in Kenya and Uganda.* Baden Baden, Germany: Nomos Publishers, 2006.

Nthamburi, Z. J., ed. *From Mission to Church: A Handbook of Christianity in East Africa.* Nairobi, Kenya: Uzima Press, 1991.

Rasmussen, Ane Marie Bak. *Modern African Spirituality: The Independent Holy Spirit Churches in East Africa.* London: I. B. Tauris, 1996.

Sabar, Galia. *Church, State and Society in Kenya: From Mediation to Opposition.* London: Routledge, 2001.

Sobonia, Neal. *Culture and Customs of Kenya.* Westport, CT: Greenwood Press, 2003.

Kenya Evangelical Lutheran Church

Kenya Evangelical Lutheran Church is one of two Lutheran denominations in Kenya. It should not be confused with the Evangelical Lutheran Church in Kenya. The Kenya Evangelical Lutheran Church has its origins in the several Lutheran missions in neighboring Tanzania begun in the 19th century by American and European missionaries. These missions led to the creation of seven separate Lutheran denominational bodies that affiliated with each other in 1938 as the Federation of Lutheran Churches. The churches of the

Federation formally merged in 1963 to become the Evangelical Lutheran Church in Tanzania. Work spread to Nairobi and Mombasa, Kenya, in the mid-1960s and in 1968 a Kenya Synod was registered. Through the 1970s, Lutheranism expanded across the country and in the 1980s efforts to reorganize as an independent body resulted in the formal establishment of the Kenya Evangelical Lutheran Church. Its beginning was celebrated in 1992.

The relatively new church maintains broad ecumenical and fraternal relationships. It partners with the Evangelical Lutheran Church in America, with German Lutherans in Bavaria and North Elbia, and with its parent Evangelical Lutheran Church in Tanzania. It is a member of the Lutheran World Federation and the World Council of Churches. In 2005, it reported 30,000 members.

Kenya Evangelical Lutheran Church
Nile Road, PO Box 54128
Nairobi
Kenya

J. Gordon Melton

See also: Evangelical Lutheran Church in America; Evangelical Lutheran Church in Kenya; Evangelical Lutheran Church in Tanzania; Lutheran World Federation; World Council of Churches.

Reference

Van Beek, Huibert. *A Handbook of the Churches and Councils: Profiles of Ecumenical Relationships.* Geneva: World Council of Churches, 2006.

Khilafat Movement

The Khilafat movement (also known as the Caliphate movement) was a post–World War I movement that emerged among Muslims in India (1919–1924) that lobbied for the sultan of the Ottoman Empire being maintained in office as the caliph acknowledged by all Muslims, symbolically if not politically. The movement arose in the wake of the Ottoman Empire having experienced a century of decline as Europeans, primarily the Austro-Hungarian Empire, had pushed the Ottomans from the Balkans, and the independent states of Greece, Romania, Serbia, and Bulgaria had emerged. In North Africa, the empire saw the loss of Algeria, Tunisia, Libya, and Egypt. The empire's fate was essentially sealed by its default on its international debt toward the end of the 19th century, but it survived for several decades as rival European powers vied for control in the Mediterranean. The Ottomans sided with the losers in World War I (1914–1918), which occasioned its final swift demise. The Ottoman Sultanate was abolished in November 1922, after which the last sultan left what became the new country of Turkey.

World War I ended with the sultan nominally still in power. In 1919, Muhammad Ali (d. 1931), his brother Shaukat Ali (d. 1938), Abul Kalam Azad (d. 1956), and Mukhtar Ahmad Ansari (d. 1936) launched an effort to mobilize the Muslim community across the Indian subcontinent, a community then divided by language, geography, and sectarianism. Though India had never been a part of the Caliphate through the centuries, the leaders advocated its preservation as the symbolic center of the Muslim world. They also wanted to keep Arab lands and especially its holy sites free of non-Muslim (especially British) control, however, when the Khilafatists sent delegations to Europe to press their demands, their representatives were, on occasion, charged with conspiracy and imprisoned by the British authorities.

The Caliphate had arisen in the wake of the Prophet Muhammad's death, the office initially held by four individuals who had been Companions of the Prophet. It was then held by a series of dynasties, but experienced a discontinuity when in 1258 the Mongol invaders captured Baghdad. The Ottoman Empire had emerged in stages at the end of the 13th century and soon incorporated all of the territory of the old Caliphate and beyond. It also claimed to be the continuing Caliphate.

This Indian pan-Islamic movement represented, in the first instance, an initial attempt to mobilize the elements of the Muslim community, using a singular moment in Muslim history, which had been brought together, despite older separating boundaries, under the single British Indian colonial administration. As World War II ended, the Muslim world faced the complete dismemberment of the Ottoman Empire, the part of it primarily falling under British colonial rule. The Indian Muslims had themselves seen the Mughal Empire, which had grown to rule much of India in the 16th century, displaced by British rule in India in the mid-19th century.

Soon after its founding, the Khilafat movement received a boost when Mohandas K. Gandhi (1869–1948), the leader of the Indian National Congress, aligned with it as part of his strategy of noncooperation with British rule. Gandhi advocated boycotting British products, abandoning offices in the Anglo-Indian government, and passively-aggressively challenging British rule. As Hindus dominated the Congress, his alignment with the Khilafat movement had the effect of improving Muslim-Hindu cooperation across the country and spread the belief among Indian Muslims that independence was in their self-interest.

The Khilafat movement appeared to be growing for several years, but in early 1922 Gandhi suspended his noncooperation policy and the coalition between the Khilafat leaders and the Congress came to a swift end. Then, in the fall of 1923, Mustafa Kemal Ataturk (1881–1938) proclaimed the existence of the secular nation of Turkey and early the next year officially abolished the Caliphate.

The Indian Khilafat movement, during its brief existence, tried to stop the overwhelming move of historical forces that saw first European colonial forces and then nationalist forces within Muslim countries reorganize the old empire along historical, ethnic, and linguistic lines. It would be succeeded by a variety of groups primarily refocused upon the Indian move toward independence, the role of Islam in an independent India, and ultimately, the formation of Pakistan and Bangladesh.

Outside of India, the Caliphate revival idea was inherited by the Muslim Brotherhood in Egypt and the many organizations it spawned.

J. Gordon Melton

See also: Companions of the Prophet; Muhammad; Muslim Brotherhood.

References

Ahmed, Aziz. *An Intellectual History of Islam in India.* Edinburgh: Edinburgh University Press, 1979.

Minault, Gail. *The Khilafat Movement: Religious Symbolism and Political Mobilization in India* New York: Columbia University Press, 1982.

Titus, Murray T. *Islam in India and Pakistan: A Religious History of Islam in India and Pakistan.* New Delhi: Musnhiram Manoharlal, 2005.

Khyentse Foundation, The

The Khyentse Foundation was established in 2001 by Dzongsar Khyentse Rinpoche (b. 1961), grandson of the great Tibetan Nyingma lama Dudjom Rinpoche (1904–1987), and head of a number of monasteries both inside and outside China. The Foundation was initially intended to provide support for Dzongsar Khyentse's monastic communities in India and Bhutan; however, its objectives soon expanded and now encompass the sponsorship of translation of Buddhist texts, the preservation of ancient manuscripts, the establishment of academic chairs in Western universities —the first being the Distinguished Professorship in Tibetan Buddhism at the University of California, Berkeley, in 2007—and the development and support of retreat environments.

Dzongsar Khyentse Rinpoche was trained in Buddhist studies from a very young age and is a prominent scholar of the Tibetan *ris-med* (non-sectarian) tradition, following the heritage of Jamyang Khyentse Wangpo (1820–1892) and other *ris-med* masters. He attended Sakya College in India and studied with some of the greatest contemporary masters, particularly H. H. Dilgo Khyentse Rinpoche and Khenpo Appey Rinpoche. He also studied at the School of Oriental and African Studies at the University of London in 1992, and is the author of *View and Practice in Buddhism* and the best-selling *What Makes You Not a Buddhist* (Shambhala, 2006). His *Commentary on Chandrakirti's Madhyamakavatara: Introduction to the Middle Way* is studied and appreciated by Buddhist students the world over. In addition to writing, Dzongsar Khyentse Rinpoche is also active in film: he served as an advisor to Bernardo Bertolucci on *Little Buddha* and went on to write and direct two of his own films: *The Cup* (Palm Pictures, 1999) and *Travellers & Magicians* (Prayer Flag Pictures, 2003).

Dzongsar Khyentse Rinpoche began teaching in the West in the mid-1980s and established retreat centers in Australia (Vajradhara Gonpa at Kyogle) and

Kadam stupa in Bodhgaya, India, built by Dilgo Khyentse Rinpoche. (Yuliya Kryzhevska/Dreamstime.com)

Canada (Sea to Sky retreat center near Vancouver). He inherited the position of abbot of Dzongsar Khamje College in Sichuan, China, from his predecessor, Jamyang Chokyi Lodro (1893–1959). In the 1980s he established the Dzongsar Institute in Bir, North India, which was expanded and renamed as the Chokyi Lodro Institute at Chaundra in 2004.

The Khyentse Foundation was established in order to provide lasting structures to support the study and practice of Buddhism. It contributes to the text preservation and conservation initiatives of like-minded organizations such as the Tibetan Buddhist Resource Center (TBRC) and the Fragile Palm Leaves Foundation. Under the direction of Gene Smith, TBRC has acquired more than 15,000 volumes of Tibetan texts, the largest collection in the world. These precious texts are scanned, formatted, and archived for future distri-

bution. Fragile Palm Leaves collects, preserves, and publishes Pali texts; translates previously untranslated Pali texts into English, Thai, and other languages; and coordinates information about the Buddhist literature of Southeast Asia, both regionally and internationally. These preservation initiatives benefit not only Buddhists, but also the world at large by making available highly developed traditions of scholarship and practice, including metaphysics, ethics, philosophy, psychology, medicine, poetry, and art.

In March 2009 the Khyentse Foundation sponsored the Translating the Words of the Buddha Conference in Bir. This attracted more than 50 translators of Tibetan texts, including 6 reincarnate lamas and famous Western scholars including Matthieu Ricard and Robert Thurman. The attendees agreed to long-term plans to translate the entire Buddhist literary heritage.

By taking a global outlook as a starting point, the Khyentse Foundation is modeling a unique approach to the promotion of Buddhism.

Khyentse Foundation
PO Box 156648
San Francisco, CA 94115
http://www.khyentsefoundation.org/

Diana Cousens

See also: Nyingma Tibetan Buddhism; Reincarnation; Tibetan Buddhism.

References

Fragile Palm Leaves Foundation. http://echo .mpiwg-berlin.mpg.de/content/buddhism/fplf. Accessed March 22, 2009.

Jones, Noa. "An Uncommon Lama." *Shambhala Sun,* November 2003.

Khyentse, Dzongsar Jamyang. *What Makes You Not a Buddhist.* Boulder, CO: Shambhala Publications, 2006.

Khyentse Foundation. http://www.khyentse foundation.org/communique.html/. Accessed March 21, 2009. http://www.khyentsefoundation .com/2009_02_translating_the_words_of_the _buddha_conference.html. Accessed March 22, 2009.

Patten, Lesley Anne, writer/director, documentary film. *Words of My Perfect Teacher,* 2003.

Tibetan Buddhist Resource Centre. http://www.tbrc .org/index.xq.

Kimbanguist Church

Claimed by some to be the largest church instituted in Africa with some 7 million members (actual figures are probably much lower), this church is most commonly known as the Kimbanguist Church. Simon Kimbangu (ca. 1887–1951) was born in the village of Nkamba in western Congo. On April 6, 1921, the founding date of the church, he was reported to have performed miraculous healings, the first of many reported miracles. His fame spread, and thousands flocked to Nkamba (later called Nkamba-Jerusalem) to be healed and to experience this revival for themselves. Kimbangu preached against fetishes and proclaimed trust in God, moral chastity and monogamy, love for one's enemies, and obedience to government authority.

In spite of his peaceful message, the local Belgian colonial administrator, Morel, was ordered to arrest Kimbangu and Nkamba was plundered by soldiers. Many of Kimbangu's supporters (including Baptist deacons) were imprisoned, but the prophet himself managed to escape. Less than two months after the beginning of the revival, Kimbangu was forced underground. The movement continued to grow, and in August 1921 a state of emergency in the region was declared and military occupation commenced.

Stories abounded about Kimbangu's miraculous escapes from arrest until he, following Christ's example, gave himself up voluntarily to the police in September. On October 3, 1921, after a trial before a three-man military tribunal without the opportunity to defend himself, Kimbangu was found guilty of sedition and hostility toward whites and was sentenced to 120 lashes and the death penalty. The sentence was commuted to life imprisonment after pleas for mercy were made to the Belgian king. Kimbangu was imprisoned in solitary confinement in Elisabethville (now Lubumbashi), 1,243 miles from his home. He was never released; his family was never allowed to visit him (nor was any Protestant minister). He died in prison 30 years later, on October 12, 1951.

Kimbangu's followers, forced underground, continued to increase. Kimbangu was now a national hero, and his wife, Muile Marie, became the leader of the underground Kimbanguist movement until her death in 1959. The colonial authorities, supported by European missions, persecuted Kimbanguists everywhere. They were imprisoned, exiled, and restricted; about 150,000 Kimbanguists were deported during the period 1921–1957. Deportations actually helped the movement spread across the entire Congo and become a multiethnic national movement.

In 1955 the Kimbanguists held a demonstration in Leopoldville against their persecution, and the following year they appealed to the United Nations. They did not organize themselves into a denomination until 1956, and the Kimbanguist Church (Église de Jésus Christ sur la terre par le prophète Simon Kimbangu, or EJCSK) was only formally constituted in 1961. In

December 1959, six months before the country's independence, the EJCSK was given official recognition. The youngest son of Kimbangu, Joseph Diangienda (1918–1993), became head of the church as legal representative, and his brother Salomon Dialungana Kiangani (1917–2001) became keeper of the holy city, Nkamba-Jerusalem. After independence in 1960, the church grew rapidly, but it failed in its attempt to unite all the disparate Kimbanguists into a single national church. In 1960 Simon Kimbangu's remains were reinterred at Nkamba-Jerusalem and a mausoleum was built in his honor, now a place of pilgrimage. The pool at Nkamba where Kimbangu used to send the sick to bathe, called Bethesda, is regarded as holy water and used in rituals all over central Africa; Kimbanguists sprinkle and drink it for healing, purification, and protection.

A multitude of 350,000 Kimbanguists held their first Communion service at Nkamba on April 6, 1971, 50 years after Kimbangu began his public ministry and, it was said, in obedience to his post-resurrection command. Two months before this occasion, Diangienda "sealed" thousands of members in the Lower Congo with a "special blessing," the sign of the cross. The Eucharist is now celebrated three times a year by the EJCSK, at Christmas and on April 6 and October 12 (the significant dates of Kimbangu's life).

Several secessions from the EJCSK occurred during the 1960s, but President Mobutu Sese Seko's severe repression and tougher laws regarding the registration of churches discouraged these. By 1968 there were 93,600 children in EJCSK schools, and church-sponsored clinics, agricultural settlements, brickyards, and many other successful enterprises were established.

In 1969 the EJCSK was admitted to the World Council of Churches (where its membership is now in question over its unorthodox beliefs) and was declared by President Mobutu to be one of three recognized churches in the Congo, the largest after the Roman Catholic Church. Diangienda died in 1993 and his elder brother Salomon Dialungana Kiangani became head of the church until his death in 2001, when he was succeeded by his son Simon Kimbangu Kiangani.

Kimbanguist Church
PO Box 9801

Kinshasa 1
Democratic Republic of Congo

Allan H. Anderson

See also: Roman Catholic Church; World Council of Churches.

References

Hastings, Adrian. *The Church in Africa, 1450–1930*. Oxford: Clarendon, 1994.

MacGaffey, Wyatt. *Modern Kongo Prophets: Religion in a Plural Society*. Bloomington: Indiana University Press, 1983.

Martin, Marie-Louise. *Kimbangu: An African Prophet and His Church*. Oxford: Basil Blackwell, 1975.

■ Kiribati

Kiribati is one of the more recently formed nations carved out of the scattered islands of the South Pacific. The widely scattered islands are found spread over 1,000 miles of ocean north of Tuvalu, Tokolau, the Cook Islands, and French Polynesia. The islands have a combined land area of 313 square miles and are home to an estimated 110,000 people (2008).

In the ancient past these islands were inhabited by Micronesian people, who had their initial contact with Europeans in 1764, when the British arrived. For the next two centuries the islands would be known as the Gilbert Islands. The islands were largely ignored for a century, but in 1856 they were settled by Hiram Bingham Jr. (1831–1908), from the American Board of Commissioners for Foreign Missions, which represented Congregationalists and Presbyterians. By the end of the decade a flourishing trade in copra and palm oil had developed. The work of the American Board expanded through the rest of the century. In 1892 the islands had been named as a British protectorate and in 1916 they became a crown colony. Following this last action, the American Board relinquished its backing of the missionary effort in favor of their British counterpart, the London Missionary Society. In 1916 the Gilbert Islands and the Ellice Islands to the south were grouped together as the Colony of the Gilbert and Ellice Islands. In 1975 the Ellice Islands were

KIRIBATI

Tarawa

Bairiki

Kiribati

Religion	Followers in 1970	Followers in 2010	% of Population	Annual % growth 2000–2010	Followers in 2025	Followers in 2050
Christians	42,700	96,500	97.0	1.81	118,000	144,000
Roman Catholics	23,900	54,900	55.2	1.78	66,000	80,000
Protestants	24,600	42,200	42.4	1.59	52,000	62,000
Marginals	90	13,300	13.4	3.19	18,000	25,000
Baha'is	1,100	2,500	2.5	1.83	4,000	5,000
Agnostics	100	550	0.6	6.24	1,000	1,500
Buddhists	0	20	0.0	1.76	30	50
Atheists	0	10	0.0	0.00	20	30
Total population	**43,900**	**99,500**	**100.0**	**1.83**	**123,000**	**151,000**

Father Cantorro, a Ponapean priest, standing in front of a destroyed church in Kiribati, 1949. (Time & Life Pictures/ Getty Images)

separated from the Gilbert Islands, and they are now known as the nation of Tuvalu.

In the meantime, Roman Catholicism was brought to the island by several Gilbertese who had converted while working in Tahiti. They began to share their faith with their neighbors on the island of Nonouti and had raised up a community of some 500 believers by 1888, when the first priests arrived. The work grew through the 20th century, and in 1966 a diocese was established at Bairiki on the main island of Tarawa. It now includes both Kiribati and Tuvalu. The Christians of Kiribati are almost evenly divided between Roman Catholics and Protestants.

The 19th-century Protestant work on the Gilbert and Ellice Islands led to the formation of a Protestant church serving the entire colony. Anticipating the separation of the two sets of islands, and reflecting the different ethnic backgrounds predominating in each, the church was divided into two independent churches (the Kiribati Protestant Church and the Church of Tuvalu). The Kiribati Protestant Church is the largest Protestant group in the country. It has, however, been joined by a number of other churches, including the Seventh-day Adventist Church (1947), the Church of God (Cleveland, Tennessee) (1955), the Elim Fellowship (1991), and the Anglican Church (part of the Anglican Church in Aotearoa, New Zealand, and Polynesia). The Baha'i Faith has also enjoyed some success in Kiribati since it emerged in 1955; assemblies may be found throughout the islands.

J. Gordon Melton

See also: American Board of Commissioners for Foreign Missions; Anglican Church in Aotearoa, New Zealand, and Polynesia; Baha'i Faith; Church of God (Cleveland, Tennessee); Church of Tuvalu; Kiribati Protestant Church; London Missionary Society; Seventh-day Adventist Church.

References

Forman, Charles H. *The Island Churches of the South Pacific: Emergence in the Twentieth Century.* Maryknoll, NY: Orbis, 1982.

Healey, N. *A Brief Introduction to the Kiribati Protestant Church.* Bairiki Tarawa, Kiribati: Kiribati Protestant Church, 1983.

Macdonald, Barrie. *Cinderellas of the Empire: Towards a History of Kiribati and Tuvalu.* Canberra: Australian National University Press, 1982.

Tlai, Sister Alaima. *Kiribati: Aspects of History.* Suva, Fiji: University of the South Pacific, 1979.

Toakai, T. "A Study of the Two Denominations in Tabiteuea, Kiribati: Kiribati Protestant Church and the Roman Catholic Church." B.D. thesis, Pacific Theological College, 1980.

Kiribati Protestant Church

Protestant Christian faith was introduced to the Gilbert Islands in 1852, when Hiram Bingham Jr. (1831–1908), the son of one of the pioneer Congregationalist missionaries in Hawaii, settled on the island of Abaiang. Bingham had previously worked on Hawaii and was dispatched by the Hawaiian Missionary Society, an organization that had developed out of the Hawaiian Mission, originally established by the American Board of Commissioners for Foreign Missions. He was assisted by Hawaiians who had come to Christianity through the Congregational Church. Their work spread through the northern Gilbert Islands.

In 1870 the British-based London Missionary Society (LMS), which also had a Reformed/Congregationalist background, began work in the southern Gilbert Islands, assisted by workers from its Samoan mission. Following World War I, the Hawaiians withdrew and turned their work over to the LMS and its successor bodies. The church became independent in 1969 as the Kiribati Protestant Church and the British Congregationalists withdrew their support. In 1970 the Gilbert Islands became independent as the new nation of Kiribati.

The Kiribati Protestant Church has a Reformed theological perspective and a Congregational polity. It is the largest Protestant religious organization in the country, with approximately 28,000 members out of a total population of 81,000. It sponsors the Tangintebu Theological College, founded in 1900, located on Tarawa.

The church is a member of the Kiribati National Council of Churches and the World Council of Churches, and it participates in the Pacific Conference of Churches. In the 1990s, after recognizing a need for assistance, the Christian Congregational Church in Canada launched efforts to support the church with literature and study materials and input on church renewal. In 2005, the church reported 130,000 members (slightly more than half the country's population) in 96 congregations.

Kiribati Protestant Church
PO Box 80
Antebuka, Tawara
Kiribati

J. Gordon Melton

See also: London Missionary Society; World Council of Churches.

References

Forman, Charles H. *The Island Churches of the South Pacific: Emergence in the Twentieth Century.* Maryknoll, NY: Orbis, 1982.

Healey, N. *A Brief Introduction to the Kiribati Protestant Church.* Bairiki Tarawa, Kiribati: Kiribati Protestant Church, 1983.

Toakai, T. "A Study of the Two Denominations in Tabiteuea, Kiribati: Kiribati Protestant Church and the Roman Catholic Church." B.D. thesis, Pacific Theological College, 1980.

Van Beek, Huibert. *A Handbook of the Churches and Councils: Profiles of Ecumenical Relationships.* Geneva: World Council of Churches, 2006.

Kôdô Kyôdan

Kôdô Kyôdan is a Japanese new religion founded by Okano Shodo (1900–1978), a Tendai Buddhist monk, along with his wife, Kimiko. They joined Reiyukai in 1934, and then in 1936 they established a branch organization in Yokohama named Kodokai, which became independent of Reiyukai in 1939 under its present name.

The main scripture of Kôdô Kyôdan is the Lotus Sutra, known as Jukueki Shobo among its members. Kôdô Kyôdan focuses on revealing the Lotus Sutra's original message in order to unite the study of the doctrine with its practice. *Kodo* means "the path of filial piety," which is very important in the teachings of Kôdô Kyôdan. Adherents conduct meetings for spiritual training, hold daily discussion meetings, and worship ancestors in the belief that honoring them brings protection and happiness to the family. Kôdô Kyôdan celebrates Hana Matsuri in April to commemorate the birth of Shakamuni Buddha and observes the Obon festival for the ancestors in the summer.

In 1975, three years before his death, Okano Shodo was succeeded by his son, Okano Shokan. As the 21st century began, Kôdô Kyôdan reported 327,701 members. It is a member of the Japan Buddhist Federation.

Kôdô Kyôdan
38 Torigoe, Knagawa-ku
Yokohama-shi, Kanagawa Prefecture 221-0044
Japan

Keishin Inaba

See also: Buddha, Gautama; Japan Buddhist Federation; Reiyukai.

References

Hori, Ichiro, et al., eds. *Japanese Religion: A Survey by the Agency for Cultural Affairs.* Tokyo: Kodansha International, 1972.

Shodo, Okano. *An Introduction to Kodo Kyodan Buddhism* (in Japanese). Yokohama: Kodo Kyodan, 1967.

Kofuku no Kagaku

Kofuku no Kagaku (the Science of Human Happiness), a Japanese "new, new religion" (*shin shin shukyo*), was started in Tokyo in 1986 by Okawa Ryuho (b. 1956), a former employee of Tomen, a Japanese trading house. During his days as a law student at Tokyo Imperial University, Okawa began to become aware gradually, through the consciousness of Shakyamuni the Buddha, that he was the incarnation of the supreme grand spirit known as El Cantare. Although the movement's teachings have come to take on a more Buddhist tone, Okawa continues to be addressed by this title in ceremonies.

The movement experienced phenomenal growth during the first 10 years of its existence, owing in large measure to the careful organization and planning of its strategy of expansion. As students concerned with the science of human happiness, members spent the first three years studying the teachings of Master Okawa, as the founder is known, and only later was stress placed on expansion. In 1990, called Sunrise 90, the declared aim of the movement was to raise the Sun of Truth, that is, to spread the name of the movement throughout Japan. An estimated 77,000 new recruits joined the movement in that year alone. The year 1991 saw the introduction of the "miracle three-year project," the aim of which was to make Kofuku no Kagaku the largest and most influential religion in Japan and to bring about a revolution there. In 1994 a full-scale program of missionary work was launched with the aim of establishing the movement in countries outside Japan. That year the movement's first overseas offices were opened in London and New York.

Although this missionary program has had some success in Brazil, where there were some 3,000 practitioners in 2001, results elsewhere have been disappointing. As is the case in other new, new religions, Kofuku no Kagaku has made and makes use of all of the most advanced forms of mass communication to spread its teachings. It has produced several feature films, the first of which, *The Terrifying Revelations of Nostradamus*, was released in 1994, with Okawa himself as the executive director. The movement's publications, moreover, run into the hundreds. *Hermes: The Winds of Love* was released in 1997.

Controversy came with growth in Japan. Forthright and decisive, Okawa is said to have written hundreds of books, the best known of which is *The Laws of the Sun* (1990), which provides an elaborate account of the movement's cosmology and has assumed the status of a sacred text. The key idea of this book in relation to Okawa's own role is that he is the one who reveals to the contemporary world the "rising of the Sun of God's Truth," which provides human beings with essential light and energy and which is often prevented from reaching them by "dark clouds." Other writings often used in seminars and cited by practitioners are *The Laws of Gold* (1991) and *The Laws of Eternity* (1991).

Until recently, Okawa spoke and wrote a great deal about the imminent advent of the Apocalypse and the subsequent coming of Utopia—that is, a world in which everyone can declare without any reservations that they are happy. Being happy means living with a mind and heart full of love and compassion. Thus, Utopia begins in the mind and heart of each individual, whose calling is then to transmit compassion to others.

The teachings of Kofuku no Kagaku speak of four Principles of Happiness: love, knowledge, development, and self-reflection. The practice of these principles is said to enable an individual to acquire the "right mind," indispensable to happiness. The most important principle is love, and the essence of real love is giving, and the practice of this kind of love is the beginning of happiness.

Over time, the movement has taken on a more Buddhist character, and the leadership itself is often at pains to stress its Buddhist credentials. The focus has shifted from broad cosmological concerns to the central concerns of Buddhism, such as the three treasures, the Buddha, the Dharma, and the Sangha.

The movement has built a number of meditation centers, including the Shoshin-Ken (House of the Right Mind) and the Mirai-kan (House of the Future), both at Utsunomiya, some 62 miles northeast of Tokyo in Tochigi Prefecture. Both of these centers are regarded as the Shoshin-Kan, or main temple.

Terms of membership have changed several times since the movement began in 1986, and each time they have become less demanding. Moreover, for some time now the term *kaiin* (member) has not been used to describe the ordinary practitioner, who is known instead as a *shinja* (believer). Although there are various types of believers, the term is generally applied to all those who attend seminars and read the founder's writings, the most important of which is *The Laws of the Sun* (1990).

Kofuku no Kagaku
1-2-38 Higashi Gotanda
Shinagawa-ku, Tokyo 141-0022
Japan
http://www.kofuku-no-kagaku.or.jp/en/

Peter B. Clarke

See also: Buddha, Gautama; Meditation.

References

Masaki Fukui. "Kofuku no Kagaku. The Institute for Research in Human Happiness (IRH)." In *A Bibliography of Japanese New Religions,* edited by Peter B. Clarke, 149–167. Eastbourne, England: Japan Library, 1999.

Okawa, Ryuhu. *The Laws of Eternity*. Tokyo: IHR Press, 1991.

Okawa, Ryuhu. *The Laws of Gold*. Tokyo: IHR Press, 1991.

Okawa, Ryuhu. *The Laws of the Sun. The Revelations of Buddha that Enlightens the New Age*. Tokyo: IRH Press, 1990.

Trevor, Astley. "The Transformation of a Recent Japanese New Religion. Okawa Ryuhu and Kofuku no Kagaku." *Japanese Journal of Religious Studies* 22, nos. 3–4 (1995): 343–380.

Kokuchu-Kai

Kokuchu-kai, literally translated as "National Pillar Association," was founded in Japan by Tanaka Chigaku (1861–1939) in 1914. Kokuchu-kai and the ideas of Tanaka Chigaku represent the nationalistic form of Nichiren Buddhism, and Tanaka and his followers tried to make the teachings of Nichiren, the founder of the Nichiren-shu of Buddhism in Japan, into the pillar of Japanese nationalism.

Tanaka Chigaku was born in 1861 at Nihonbashi in Tokyo. Tanaka was influenced by his father, who was a devoted follower of Nichiren Buddhism but critical of established Buddhist sects. After the death of his parents, Tanaka became a novice at a Nichiren Buddhist temple called Myokakuji in Tokyo. But he soon became disillusioned with the practices of traditional Buddhist temples and in 1879 renounced his priestly vows. In 1880 Tanaka started his own lay Buddhist movement, Renge-kai (Lotus Society), in Yokohama, for propogating "true" Nichiren Buddhism. In 1884 Tanaka shifted to Tokyo and renamed his organization Rissho Ankoku-kai. In 1914 he reorganized the movement, and at Miho village in Shizuoka Prefecture, where he had previously built the Saisho-kaku as an auxillary center, he established the Kokuchu-kai—its name derived from Nichiren's words "I am the pillar of the state." Kokuchu-kai was an amalgamation of all his followers as well as his activities, and it continues today as the principal organization devoted to Tanaka Chigaku and his work.

It was out of his conviction that the traditional Buddhist sects needed to be reformed that Tanaka launched his lay Buddhist movement with a call to "revive the way of the founder" (Nichiren). The importance that Tanaka attached to the lay practice of Buddhism is evident in his institution of a wedding ceremony according to Buddhist rites. However, Tanaka's call for reformation was not restricted to Buddhism; through *shakubuku* (forced proselytization), it aimed at the reformation of the Japanese state as well as of the whole world. One of Tanaka's major works, published in 1901, was *Shumon no Ishin* (*Reformation of the Sect*). In this monograph, he advocated the unification of Japanese Buddhism and its transformation into a great Nichiren organization that would serve as a kind of state religion.

The objective behind the founding of Kokuchu-kai as well as its predecessor organizations was to advocate Nichirenshugi, or Nichirenism. The term "Nichirenshugi," coined by Tanaka himself in 1901, was meant to express the fusion of Nichiren's teachings with the doctrine of Nihon Kokutai. Tanaka's nationalistic philosophy was an interpretation of Nichiren Buddhism in the light of state-Shinto ideology and the emperor system. The publications of Kokuchu-kai, such as *Myoshu*, *Nichirenshugi*, *Kokuchu Shimbun*, and *Tengyo Minpo*, reveal Tanaka's conception of Buddhism as being useful in the protection of the state.

In 1928 this organization built a stupa (dome-shaped shrine) memorial park in Tokyo called Myoshudaireibyo. Here the ashes of all the deceased are placed under one stupa, thus symbolically expressing the equality of humankind. After Tanaka's death in No-

vember 1939, his eldest son Tanaka Houkoku took over the leadership of Kokuchu-kai, and, in 1949, his son Tanaka Koho became the *kaicho* (president/chairman) of the organization. In 1996, Tanaka Kikyu took over as the kaicho of Kokuchu-kai. In the years since the end of World War II, Kokuchu-kai has mainly been involved in publications, symposiums, and the like. In the year 2000, it had a membership of about 20,000 people in 84 branches, including an overseas branch in Brazil.

Even in the postwar period, Kokuchu-kai has maintained a nationalistic emphasis in its activities. Kokuchu-kai is at present campaigning to rename April 28, which is now observed as "Greenery Day" in Japan, as "Showa Day" because it is the birthday of Showa Emperor Hirohito. The significance of this movement lies not so much in its size or activities but in its influence on important personalities of modern Japan. Japanese poet Miyazawa Kenji and army officer Ishiwara Kanji, who planned to spread the Imperial Way throughout the world, were members of Kokuchu-kai. Ultranationalists such as Inoue Nissho, Meiji period intellectuals such as Takayama Chogyu, and a major scholar of Japanese religion, Anezaki Masaharu (1873–1949), were also greatly influenced by Tanaka's teachings of Nichirenshugi.

Ranjana Mukhopadhyaya

See also: Nichiren; Nichirenshu.

References

Kokuchukai Hyakunen-shi. Editorial supervision by Tanaka Koho. Tokyo: Kokuchukai, 1984.

Lee, Edwin B. "Nichiren and Nationalism: The Religious Patriotism of Tanaka Chigaku." *Monumenta Nipponica* 30 (Spring 1975): 19–35.

Otani Eiichi. *Kindai Nihon no Nichirenshugi undo*. Kyoto: Hozokan, 2001.

Tanaka Koho. *Tanaka Chigaku*. Tokyo: Shinsekaisha, 1977.

Konkokyo

Konkokyo, Religion of Golden Light, was founded in 1859 by Kawate Bunjiro (1814–1883), a peasant farmer from Okayama prefecture who had received numerous divine messages from the malevolent golden *kami* Konjin, whom he had at one time offended. Kawate believed not only that from 1859 he had become possessed by Konjin, whom he referred to as the Golden Principle Parent, or Kami, of the Universe (Tenche Kane no Kami) and the Great Kami of Golden Light (Konko Daijin), but that he himself had actually become this same deity who had previously commanded him to leave farming and dedicate his life to the practice and teaching of *toritsugi* meditation.

Under the Meiji rulers who assumed power in 1868, Konkokyo aligned itself with state-sponsored Shinto, a decision it later reversed.

Konkokyo's principal sacred text is Tenchi Kakitsuke (Divine Reminder). Its primary focus of worship is Tenchi Kane No Kami, and its main teaching concerns the reciprocal relationship between this Principle Parent or God and humanity, which gives fulfillment tò both. Suffering results from the fact that human beings ignore this fundamental principle. The Principal Parent is the original source of all living beings and things, and so every individual life is linked to this source. The purpose of *toritsugi* meditation is to connect individuals with the Principal Parent and with all the kami. Konkokyo mediators have the power to convey messages from the kami to individuals. The converse is also the case. This is not strictly a Shinto practice, nor is the belief in Tenchi Kane No Kami a Shinto belief.

The movement celebrates several major and minor festivals throughout the year including the New Year, Spring and Autumn Festivals, the Church Foundation Festival, and the Founder's Birthday Festival.

Konkokyo's headquarters remain in Okayama, where it was founded, although it also has an international center in Tokyo. As in other Japanese religions, among them Tenrikyo, the spiritual leader, or *kyoshu*, is chosen from the founder's descendants. Administratively, Konkokyo is divided into districts under *kyokan*, or district heads, who are chosen from the leaders of the churches in the districts. The membership in Japan is around 400,000. By comparison, the membership overseas is small, totaling only around 2,000 for Canada, South Korea, the United States, Brazil, and Paraguay together.

Konkokyo Main Headquarters
Otani 320, Konko-cho, Asakuchi-gun
Okayama-ken 719-0111
Japan

Konkokyo International Center (for non-Japanese-speaking inquirers)
2-17-11 Hongo, Bunkyo-ku
Tokyo 113-0033
Japan
http://www.konkokyo.or.jp/eng/ (multilingual)

Peter B. Clarke

See also: Meditation; Shinto.

References

Hardacre, Helen. "Creating State Shinto: The Great Promulgation Campaign and the New Religions." *Japanese Journal of Religious Studies* 12, no. 4 (1986): 29–64.

McFarland, H. Neil. *The Rush Hour of the Gods: A Study of New Religious Movements in Japan.* New York: Macmillan, 1967.

Shimazono, Susumu. "The Living Kami Idea in the New Religions of Japan." *Japanese Journal of Religious Studies* 6, no. 3 (1979): 389–412.

Voice of the Universe: Selected Teachings of Konkokyo. Okayama-ken: Konkokyo Honbu, 1996.

■ Korea, Democratic People's Republic of (North Korea)

The Democratic People's Republic of Korea (DPRK; North Korea) occupies the northern half of the Korean Peninsula. It includes 46,540 square miles of territory with a population of 23.5 million citizens. The country shares a history with the Republic of Korea (South Korea) through World War II and the end of the Japanese invasion and occupation of the Korean Peninsula. At the war's end, Soviet troops moved into the northern half of the country and stopped at the 38th parallel, where they awaited the arrival of the U.S. forces moving in from the south. The United Nations called for an election and the establishment of an independent government, but the two superpowers could not

The Pohjon Temple was founded in 1024 and is the most important Buddhist sanctuary in North Korea. (Thomas Gutschker/dpa/Corbis)

agree on procedures. The south went ahead with elections, and Syngman Rhee (1875–1965) assumed the presidency. In the north, the Provisional People's Committee proclaimed the Democratic People's Republic of Korea, and Kim Il Sung (1912–1994) emerged as prime minister. The Soviet Union withdrew its forces in December 1948.

The two Koreas were unable to resolve their different visions for the future of the country, and war broke out in 1950. An armistice was arranged in 1953. No permanent peace treaty has been signed, and the border between the two countries is still regarded as something of a battle line.

Kim Il Sung and the Korean Workers' Party led the country in the decades after the war. In the 1990s, he began preparing the way for his son Kim Jong Il

(b. 1942) to succeed him. In 1992, Kim Il Sung was named the Grandfather of the Nation and his son the Father of the Nation. Kim Jong Il was also named the president of the People's Assembly (the legislature) and secretary general of the Korean Workers' Party. He succeeded his father in 1994.

From its inception, the government of North Korea has been officially Marxist and atheist. However, by the end of World War II a wide variety of Protestant groups had opened missions throughout the northern part of Korea, including the Presbyterians, the Anglicans, the Methodists, the Baptists, and the Seventh-day Adventist Church. Even the Swedenborgian movement had given birth to some 40 congregations. The Roman Catholic Church had a diocese at Pyongyang.

NORTH KOREA

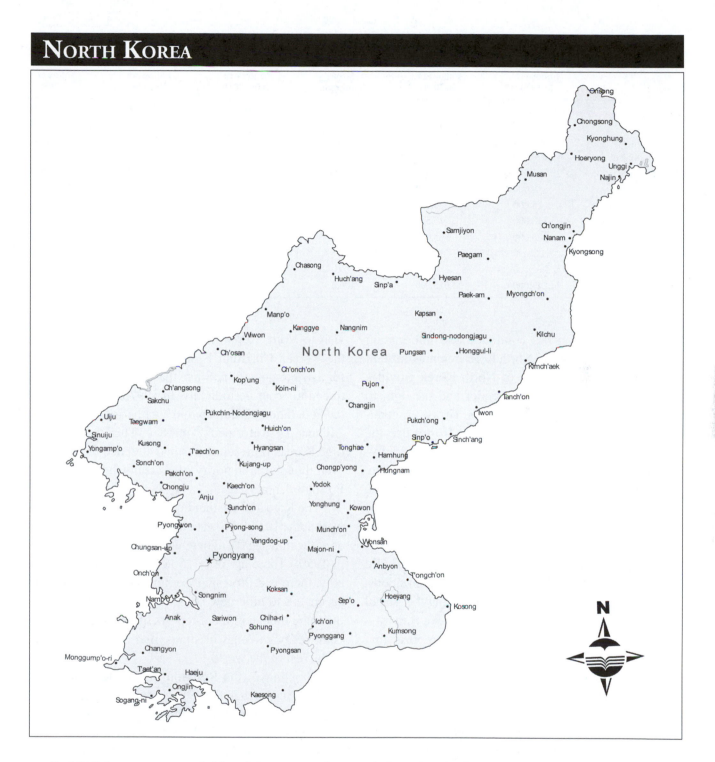

In 1946 the government initiated the suppression of religious organizations and arrested many religious leaders. Then the government organized the Ki Dok Kyo Kyo Do Yen Mange, or Christian League, to facilitate church support for the new government. In 1950 the Methodists and Presbyterians were forced to combine their seminaries. Through the 1950s, as it became obvious that the Christian League was being eschewed by the great majority of believers, a full-scale repression of Christianity began. At the height of the Korean War, the United States occupied much of North Korea. When U.S. forces withdrew, some 2 million people fled south. Priests and other church workers either fled the country, moved to the south, or were arrested.

Korea (Democratic Peoples Republic of, North)

Religion	Followers in 1970	Followers in 2010	% of Population	Annual % growth 2000–2010	Followers in 2025	Followers in 2050
Agnostics	6,466,000	13,377,000	55.7	0.59	13,736,000	11,969,000
Atheists	2,253,000	3,742,000	15.6	0.58	3,800,000	3,600,000
New religionists	1,800,000	3,094,000	12.9	0.58	3,250,000	3,176,000
Ethnoreligionists	3,298,000	2,935,000	12.2	0.58	2,600,000	2,400,000
Christians	142,000	484,000	2.0	0.28	1,415,000	3,027,000
Independents	8,000	425,000	1.8	0.30	900,000	2,000,000
Roman Catholics	15,000	40,000	0.2	0.00	300,000	600,000
Protestants	118,000	13,500	0.1	0.27	200,000	400,000
Buddhists	288,000	365,000	1.5	0.58	390,000	420,000
Chinese folk	0	15,400	0.1	0.58	32,000	64,000
Muslims	0	3,100	0.0	0.58	5,000	10,000
Total population	**14,247,000**	**24,015,000**	**100.0**	**0.58**	**25,228,000**	**24,666,000**

Harsh repression has continued and information about religious practice in North Korea remains difficult to obtain. The Constitution of North Korea provides for both freedom of religious belief and the right to use buildings for religious purposes. However, genuine religious freedom does not exist. In practice the government discourages all organized religious activity except that which serves the interests of the state. The Constitution also stipulates that "no one can use religion as a means to drag in foreign powers" or to disrupt the social order. Thus, religious belief is considered an affront to government authority, and religion is often seen as subversive in its attempts to build extra-government relations with foreign organizations. The government uses the cause of protecting the "social order" as a rationale for sporadic suppressive activity.

Nonetheless, there are continuing reports that Christian churches, Buddhist temples, and a few centers of Chondogyo have survived. Since 1988 the government has allowed and informally sponsored several religious organizations in Pyongyang. Leaders of these organizations, including two Protestant churches and a Catholic church, have some limited contact with non-Korean religious officials and organizations, especially those engaged in supplying relief aid within the country. Protestants are represented through the Korean Christian Federation, which in 1983 published an edition of the Bible and a new hymnbook. Representatives of the World Council of Churches made their first

visit to North Korea in 1985, and representatives for the Korean Christian Federation visited Switzerland for a meeting in 1986. Since that time contact has continued to occur periodically. In 1997 four members of the Federation participated in a gathering of the World Alliance of Reformed Churches. This was the first time Korean representatives had attended the meeting, even though the majority of Korean Christians are of Presbyterian heritage.

The Korean Christian Federation reports that there were some 10,000 Protestant Christians in North Korea as of the mid-1990s. (There were an estimated 120,000 in 1950.) There are only 25 active ministers. Reportedly, there is a Protestant seminary that is allowed to accept six to nine new students every three years. At the same time, continual reports of the arrest and execution of practicing Christians filter out of the country to the rest of the world.

Chondogyo (the Religion of the Heavenly Way) emerged in Korea in the 19th century as a popular new religion. At latest report, the government-sponsored Chondogyo Young Friends Party exists as a sanctioned vehicle for this religion, which is still popular among the people.

The United States Commission on International Religious Freedom is but one watchdog agency that cites North Korea as a country which, though formally acknowledging the ideal of religious freedom, severely suppresses all religion. It currently (2008) summarizes its findings thusly: "Religious freedom is essentially absent in North Korea, where the government severely represses public and private religious activities and enforces a policy of actively discriminating against religious believers. The Commission has received reports that DPRK officials have arrested, imprisoned, tortured, and sometimes executed North Korean citizens who were found to have ties with overseas Christian evangelical groups operating across the border in China, as well as those who engaged in unauthorized religious activities such as public religious expression and persuasion." The U.S. Department of State estimates North Korea to have 10,000 Protestants, 10,000 Buddhists, and 4,000 Catholics.

Korean Christian Federation
c/o Central Committee of the KCF
Konguk-Dong, Man Gyung Dae District
Pyongyang
Democratic People's Republic of Korea

J. Gordon Melton

See also: Chondogyo; Roman Catholic Church; Seventh-day Adventist Church; Swedenborgian Movement; World Council of Churches.

References

Belke, Thomas J. *Juche: A Christian Study of North Korea's State Religion*. Batesville, OK: Living Sacrifice Book Co., 1999.

Buswell, Robert E., Jr., ed. *Religions of Korea in Practice*. Princeton, NJ: Princeton University Press, 2007.

Clark, A. D. *A History of the Church in Korea.* Seoul: Christian Literature Society of Korea, 1971.

Grayson, James H. *Korea: A Religious History*. Oxford: Oxford University Press, 1989.

Kim, Duk-Whang. *A History of Religions in Korea*. Seoul: Daeji Moonhwa-sa, 1988.

"U.S. Department of State Annual Report on International Religious Freedom for 2008: Democratic People's Republic of Korea." Released by the Bureau for Democracy, Human Rights, and Labor. Washington, DC, 2008. http://www.state.gov/g/drl/rls/irf/2008/108410.htm.

■ Korea, Republic of (South Korea)

The Republic of Korea (South Korea) occupies the southern half of the Korean peninsula, with some 46,540 square miles of land. It has a population of 48.4 million people (2008).

The Korean Peninsula has been inhabited since Paleolithic times. As China emerged, it viewed the Koreans as a constant nuisance and in the second century BCE attempted to establish hegemony over the peninsula. The Chinese threat appears to have been a catalyst for the formation of the three Korean kingdoms —Koguryo, Silla, and Paekche—that for many centuries controlled the Korean Peninsula. The warrior-like Koguryo people, with their capital at Pyongyang, reigned in the north from the first century BCE through the sixth century BCE. Then in the seventh century, Korea was united by the Silla Kingdom, which pushed a remnant of the Koguryo people farther north into Manchuria, where they established the Kingdom of Parhae. The period of the unified Silla Kingdom (668–935) was one of great prosperity that helped define Korea as a nation.

In the 10th century, Shilla authority disintegrated and eventually gave way to a rebellion from the north. In 935 the Shilla Kingdom was replaced by the Koryo Kingdom, which would last into the medieval era. It finally fell into a decadent state in the 14th century, thus preparing the way for the 1388 takeover by General Yi Song-gye (1335–1408). Yi invaded the capital and began a thorough reform of the nobility, the army, and the system of land distribution. In 1392 he declared himself king and began the new Choson Kingdom. Underlying Yi's reforms was a shift of royal favor from Buddhism to Confucianism. Yi also built the new capital known today as Seoul.

In 1573 Japan was unified under a strong monarch, Toyotomi Hideyoshi (1537–1598). He invaded Korea in 1592 and quickly overran Seoul and headed north. Even as his army occupied the peninsula, China counterattacked and Korea's outstanding navy cut the Japanese supply lines. The Japanese were finally forced to retreat in 1593, but the conflict left Korea a devastated land. Korea remained independent, but its glory had passed. In the 19th century, Korea also faced the invasion of the West. In the middle of the century isolationist policies came to dominance, only to be reversed as Japan again became a threat. Korea was constantly having to balance the alternating claims of Japan and China, and as the century ended, a new threat appeared in the form of Russia.

The Russian threat became the excuse for Japan to invade and form a protectorate over Korea. That protectorate, which would last through World War II, would be remembered for its brutality. The atrocities committed continue to sour Japanese-Korean relations. After World War II, Korea was affected by secret agreements between the superpowers, by which the United States and the Soviet Union occupied the former Japanese territory. Their inability to reach an agreement on what they termed "the Korean problem" led to the Korean War and the division of the land into the two nations, the Republic of Korea in the south and the Democratic People's Republic of Korea in the north.

In 1947 the United Nations called for a nationwide election and the establishment of an independent government. The election was held in the south in 1948, and a new government was installed. The South Korean government had the support of the United States. The Soviet Union withdrew its troops from the north, but the United States remained in the south. The United States had the support of the United Nations, whereas the Soviet Union was temporarily boycotting the Security Council. Thus, when the North Koreans attacked in 1950, the United States came to the aid of South Korea. The bitter war was fought to a draw in 1953. A cease fire was arranged, but no permanent peace treaty was ever signed.

In the years since the war, South Korea has gone through a series of governments, including the dictatorship of Park Chung Hee (1917–1979), which began in 1961. Under Park, South Korea emerged as an Asian economic giant. He was assassinated in 1979. The country continues to struggle with creating a democratic government and solving the problem of unifying the Korean Peninsula.

While South Korea has moved toward democracy, it has allowed a relatively high degree of religious freedom, and the variant religious strains that have been introduced over the years have been allowed to persist and grow. Ancient Korean religion was a mystical faith built around a belief that material objects and the forces of nature possess spiritual entities. Included in this vast spirit world are the souls of ancestors. Intercourse with the spirits is carried out by the *mudang*, or shaman. Shamans remain popular religious figures who specialize in communication with the spirit world through ceremonies known as *kuts*, a colorful ritual performance that may take several days to complete. During this ceremony the shaman will become possessed of a spirit. Many who seek the services of the shamans otherwise identify themselves as Buddhists or Christians.

Buddhism entered Korea in the fourth century BCE from China, initially taking hold in the Koguryo Kingdom during the reign of Sosurim (371–381). At about the same time, in the 380s, an Indian missionary priest named Marananda introduced Buddhism in the Paekche Kingdom. The new faith enjoyed royal patronage and quickly gained a foothold. However, it was not until the sixth century that it was able to gain a following in the Shilla Kingdom, after the royal family accepted it in 527. By the 10th century and the emergence of the Koryo Kingdom, thousands of Buddhist temples dotted the Korean landscape.

The decline of the Koryo Kingdom was intimately connected with corruption among the leadership of Korean Buddhism. When General Yi took over in 1388, he banished Buddhism from his capital and disestablished it across the land. Without the government's support, the Buddhists suffered doubly from the Japanese invasion in 1592, as many temples were lost and never rebuilt. Buddhism experienced a revival in the 20th century and became somewhat identified with the struggle for independence from the Japanese, who were attempting to impose Shintoism. After the end of Japanese rule and the Korean War, a significant revival occurred with the Chogye Order, whose headquarters were established in Seoul during the Japanese occupation. Embracing emphases of both Zen and Pure Land Buddhism, this inclusivist Order now includes the majority of Korean Buddhists. However, other schools such as the relatively new Won Buddhism also have a measurable following. This developing community emphasizes the rejection of marriage by monks, a practice introduced by the Japanese.

SOUTH KOREA

Traditional Confucian ceremony in South Korea. (Korea Tourism Organization)

When Buddhism was disestablished by General Yi, it was replaced with the teachings of Confucius (551–479 BCE). Confucius had developed a philosophical-moral system that focused upon building ideal relationships in the family, the community, and the nation. Not really a religion, Confucianism nonetheless took on a ritual and religious cast. Even as Buddhism rose to power, Confucian thought provided the philosophical context for Korean society. Confucianism permeated the government and educational system and inspired General Yi's reforms. It also emphasized respect for one's ancestors and demanded that individuals refrain from any activity that might reflect badly upon their ancestry.

Centers of Confucian learning, such as the Confucian University in Seoul, maintain the teachings of the honored teacher and perform ceremonies that honor Korea's Confucian scholars. Associated with the university are numerous *sowon*, or study halls, which perpetuate Confucian ideals.

Christianity entered the country in the person of Father Gregorio de Cespedes, a Jesuit priest who accompanied the Japanese invasion force in 1592. As the chaplain to a Japanese general who had become a Christian, Cespedes made no impact on the Korean people. Two hundred years later, another Jesuit, Peter Grammont, began secretly working in Korea and converting the first Christians. Though initially outlawed, the Christian community has had a continuous presence since that time.

It would not be until 1836 that a permanent resident missionary, Pierre Maubant, began to gather the scattered Christian flock. Though Christianity was still outlawed and was subject to waves of official persecution, it spread through the country. In 1866 nine priests were arrested and beheaded. That same year, a Welsh Protestant missionary was killed along with 24 others aboard an American ship that ran aground near Pyongyang.

The Roman Catholic Church grew very slowly through the 19th and early 20th centuries, when it was largely overwhelmed by the Protestant movement. The first Catholic diocese was established in Taegu in 1911. There are now two archdioceses, Taegu and Seoul, and a number of dioceses. The church entered a growth phase after the Korean War and baptized more than half a million adults through the 1960s.

It would not be until the Amity Treaty between the United States and Korea was signed in 1882 that Christianity's outlaw status was lifted and Protestant missionaries were freely admitted to the country. The first to arrive was Horace N. Allen (1858–1922) of the Presbyterian Church in the U.S.A (now a constituent part of the Presbyterian Church [U.S.A.]). A physician, Allen saved the life of the nephew of the Korean queen, an act that radically improved the image of Christianity throughout the upper echelons of Korean society. He was followed in 1884 by the first ordained minister to come to Korea, Horace G. Underwood (1859–1916). Canadian and Australian Presbyterians also established missions, and in 1893 they came together to form the Council for Mission of the Presbyterian Churches, which evolved into the Presbyterian Church of Korea in 1907. Presbyterians were to enjoy great success in Korea, and today the majority of Protestant Christians belong to one of the many Presbyterian denominations that have been formed, though the majority are in one of the two larger groups, the Presbyterian Church of Korea (TongHap) or the Presbyterian Church of Korea (HapDong).

Robert F. Maclay (1824–1907), the Methodist superintendent in Japan, also visited Korea in 1884, during which time he received permission to open schools and hospitals. The first Methodist missionaries, representing the Methodist Episcopal Church, arrived in 1885. Dr. William B. Scranton (1856–1922) opened a medical center, and two other members of the party, Ella J. D. Appenzeller, the wife of Henry G. Appenzeller (1858–1902), and Mary F. Scranton, opened the first school for girls. Missionaries from the Methodist Episcopal Church, South, arrived in the 1890s. In 1930,

anticipating the 1939 union of the two Methodist churches (both now constituent parts of the United Methodist Church), the Korean missions merged to form the Korean Methodist Church.

The Anglicans were first represented in Korea by Bishop C. John Corfe of the Society for the Propagation of the Gospel, who settled in Seoul in 1890. The Anglican work had a growth phase through the 1930s and claimed some 10,000 members when World War II began. It lost half its members in the division of the country, but it recovered and has continued to grow into the 21st century. The church became independent in 1993 as the Anglican Church of Korea.

Baptists entered the country after the prominent Clarendon Baptist Church in Boston, Massachusetts, formed the Ella Thing Memorial Mission, which sponsored work in Korea beginning in 1895. That work was turned over to a Canadian, Malcolm C. Fenwick (1863–1935), who in 1905 organized the Baptists into the Church of Christ in Korea. This work grew and expanded into China, Manchuria, and Siberia. After World War II, the group made contact with the Southern Baptist Convention. It subsequently emerged as the Korean Baptist Convention and has enjoyed spectacular growth.

Pentecostalism appears to have entered the country in 1944 in the form of the True Jesus Church, a Oneness Pentecostal group founded in China. A host of American Pentecostal groups arrived in the 1960s, including the Church of God (Cleveland, Tennessee), the International Church of the Foursquare Gospel, and the United Pentecostal Church International. Pentecostalism took root quickly in Korea, and indigenous leadership appeared within a few years. The Yoido Full Gospel Church on Yoido Island in Seoul, founded in 1958 by Paul/David Yonghi Cho, has (b. 1936) become a denomination in itself. It is the largest Pentecostal congregation in the world, and its sanctuary was the site of the Pentecostal World Conference in 1973.

Since the end of the Korean War, numerous American denominations and evangelical missionary organizations have opened work in Korea, while tens of thousands of Koreans have come to the United States and created a host of new ethnic denominations. The more liberal Protestant churches are members of the National Council of Churches in Korea (founded in 1919 as the Federal Council of Churches and Missions),

Korea, Republic of (South)

Religion	Followers in 1970	Followers in 2010	% of Population	Annual % growth 2000–2010	Followers in 2025	Followers in 2050
Christians	5,750,000	20,150,000	41.4	0.65	20,652,000	18,397,000
Protestants	2,145,000	9,996,000	20.5	3.46	10,100,000	9,000,000
Independents	1,965,000	6,600,000	13.6	1.35	7,400,000	7,200,000
Roman Catholics	838,000	4,900,000	10.1	1.91	5,600,000	4,900,000
Ethnoreligionists	12,583,000	7,600,000	15.6	0.46	7,300,000	5,800,000
Buddhists	5,319,000	7,325,000	15.0	0.20	7,208,000	6,090,000
New religionists	3,380,000	7,390,000	15.2	0.46	7,420,000	6,400,000
Confucianists	4,758,000	5,250,000	10.8	0.11	5,250,000	4,400,000
Agnostics	100,000	730,000	1.5	0.46	900,000	900,000
Muslims	3,000	75,000	0.2	0.46	90,000	100,000
Atheists	5,000	50,000	0.1	0.46	70,000	90,000
Chinese folk	10,000	35,000	0.1	0.46	45,000	45,000
Baha'is	14,000	35,000	0.1	0.46	40,000	50,000
Shintoists	0	30,000	0.1	0.46	40,000	50,000
Hindus	0	2,200	0.0	0.46	2,500	3,000
Sikhs	0	1,200	0.0	0.46	1,800	2,000
Total population	**31,922,000**	**48,673,000**	**100.0**	**0.46**	**49,019,000**	**42,327,000**

affiliated with the World Council of Churches. Evangelical groups are united in the National Association of Evangelicals, affiliated with the World Evangelical Alliance. Several churches are aligned with the fundamentalist International Council of Christian Churches, including the Korean Presbyterian Church (HoHun).

Korea is also home to a wide variety of new religious movements. In the middle of the 19th century, amid a variety of new religious movements that began to emerge, one stood out. Tanghak, or so-called Eastern learning, arose in opposition to Christianity, or Western learning. Founder Ch'oe Che-u (1824–1864) saw his movement as a synthesis of Buddhism, Confucianism, and Daoism. However, his philosophy also became the basis of a political challenge to the central government. In 1864 the government forces defeated the main Tonghak army and executed Ch'oe Che-u, but his movement did not die. Instead, it reemerged as a purely religious movement called Chondogyo, which claimed several million followers at the time of the division of the country. It remains a potent force in Korean religion.

In more recent years, the U.S.-style religious freedom in South Korea has allowed the emergence of hundreds of new religions, which draw variously on the different older religious traditions that have been available in Korea through the centuries and also from neighboring China. Thus one finds new religions that draw concepts from shamanism, Christianity, Buddhism, and Confucianism. Prominent among the new religions is the Unification movement (Holy Spirit Association for the Unification of World Christianity), which has been exported from Korea to over 150 other countries. In the West it became the focus of the anticult movement of the 1970s. Other notable groups that are now having an impact beyond the land of their birth include JeungSanDo and the DahnHak movement founded by Seung-Heun Lee. The latter group draws heavily on Chinese *qigong* exercises.

J. Gordon Melton

See also: Anglican Church of Korea; Confucius; DahnHak; International Church of the Foursquare Gospel; International Council of Christian Churches; JeungSanDo; Korean Methodist Church; Pentecostal World Fellowship; Presbyterian Church (USA); Presbyterian Church of Korea (HapDong); Presbyterian Church of Korea (TongHap); Pure Land Buddhism; Southern Baptist Convention; True Jesus Church; Unification Movement; United Methodist Church; United Pentecostal Church International; World Council of Churches; World Evangelical Alliance; Yoido Full Gospel Church; Zen Buddhism.

References

Buswell, Robert E., Jr., *Religions of Korea in Practice*. Princeton, NJ: Princeton University Press, 2006.

Chongsuh, Kim, ed. *Reader in Korean Religion*. Songnam: The Academy of Korean Studies, 1993.

Clark, A. D. *A History of the Church in Korea*. Seoul: Christian Literature Society of Korea, 1971.

Clark, D. N. *Christianity in Modern Korea*. Lanham, MD: University Press of America, 1986.

Focus on Korea. 3 vols. Seoul: Seoul International Publishing House, 1988.

Grayson, James H. *Korea: A Religious History*. Oxford: Oxford University Press, 1989.

Hogarth, Hyun-key Kim. *Syncretism of Buddhism and Shamanism in Korea*. Seoul: Jimoondang International, 2002.

Kim, Duk-Whang. *A History of Religions in Korea*. Seoul: Daeji Moonhwa-sa, 1988.

Palmer, S. J., ed. *The New Religions of Korea*. Transactions of the Korea Branch of the Royal Asiatic Society, vol. 43. Seoul: Royal Asiatic Society, 1967.

Yum Chai-Shin. *Korea and Christianity*. Berkeley, CA: Asia Humanities Press, 2002.

Korean American Presbyterian Church

The Korean American Presbyterian Church is the largest of the several Presbyterian denominations to arise in the Korean American community. Since the end of the Korean War, thousands of Koreans have migrated to the United States, many of whom are members of the spectrum of Presbyterian bodies that exist in their homeland. They began to form congregations and presbyteries, often continuing ties to one of the denominations in Korea. In 1978 five presbyteries (California, the Midwest, New York, Pennsylvania, and Canada) of the more conservative churches united to form the Korean American Presbyterian Church. The meeting was held on the campus of Westminster Theological Seminary in Philadelphia, Pennsylvania, the school sponsored by the Orthodox Presbyterian Church.

The Korean American Presbyterian Church continues the tradition of the more conservative Presbyterian Church of Korea (HapDong), though the American church is administratively autonomous. After its establishment it moved immediately to found a seminary and to contact the many as yet unaffiliated Korean congregations known to exist in the United States and Latin America. The church adopted the Westminster Confession and catechism as its standards of faith.

By the mid-1990s the church reported 33,000 members in 19 presbyteries—including the Presbytery of Central South America, which united churches in Argentina, Brazil, Paraguay, and Chile. Member churches were also found in Canada and in several European countries. The church is a member of the National Association of Presbyterian and Reformed Churches, which includes the Presbyterian Church in America, the Orthodox Presbyterian Church, and several other conservative churches of the Reformed tradition.

The Korean American Presbyterian Church should not be confused with the Korean Presbyterian Church in America, created by congregations and ministers formerly affiliated with the Presbyterian Church of Korea (TongHap). Founded in 1976, the Korean Presbyterian Church in America is almost as big as its more conservative sister church, and it is a member of the World Alliance of Reformed Churches, cooperates with the Presbyterian Church (U.S.A.) on various programs, and is active in liberal Protestant ecumenism.

Korean American Presbyterian Church
125 S. Vermont Ave.
Los Angeles, CA 90004
http://www.kapc.org/

Korean Presbyterian Church in America
17200 Clark Ave.
Bellflower, CA 90706

J. Gordon Melton

See also: Orthodox Presbyterian Church; Presbyterian Church (USA); Presbyterian Church of Korea (HapDong); Presbyterian Church of Korea (TongHap).

Reference

Bauswein, Jean-Jacques, and Lukas Vischner, eds. *The Reformed Family Worldwide: A Survey of*

Reformed Churches, Theological Schools, and International Organizations. Grand Rapids, MI: William B. Eerdmans Publishing Company, 1999.

Korean Buddhism

Although Korea is often depicted as one of the most Confucian or Christian societies in modern East Asia, Buddhism has deep roots and a rich cultural heritage in this Northeast Asian country. Despite the unparalleled success of Christianity during the 20th century and the emergence of a Communist government in the north that persecutes religion, at the beginning of the 21st century, South Korea ranks as the 6th most Buddhist nation in the world by population figures and North Korea the 10th. Buddhists account for about half of the present population of South Korea, or 24,654,419 monks, nuns, and lay adherents, who belong to more than 50 different Buddhist sectarian organizations. Sixty percent of North Korea's population, or 13,747,306 people, are Buddhist.

Three Kingdoms Buddhism (ca. late fourth century–668 CE) According to Korean historical sources, Buddhism was transmitted from Chinese states to kingdoms on the Korean peninsula during the late fourth century. Although individual monks were active in these states perhaps as early as the early fourth century, the official introduction of Buddhism is presumed to have occurred in 372 CE when Fu Jian (r. 357–384), king of the Former Qin dynasty (351–394) in north China dispatched the monk-envoy Shundao (Korean: Sundo) to the northern state of Koguryo (37 BCE–668 CE) with scriptures and images. Because a few of the Chinese Northern dynasties, such as the Former Qin and Northern Wei (386–534), controlled vast empires stretching to Buddhist centers in eastern Turkestan, Chinese culture was brought into close contact with Indian, Persian, and Hellenistic civilizations. The Chinese interaction with Indian and Central Asian Mahayana Buddhism from the fourth through the eighth centuries engendered a new Sinitic form of Buddhism that spread to Korea. This Buddhism was characterized by a close relationship between the church and the state,

worship of Maitreya, the future buddha, and the study of scriptures and treatises of the Mahayana tradition.

In 384 the Serindian monk Maranant'a (Malananda; Kumaranandin) is said to have come to the southwestern state of Paekche (18 BCE–660 CE) view from the southern Chinese state of Eastern Jin (317–420). He was received well by the Paekche court, a monastery was prepared for him, and Native men ordained as monks. As a result of maritime relations, Paekche eventually disseminated Buddhism to the Yamato court in early Japan in the mid-sixth century (either 552 or 538). The Paekche court dispatched doctrinal specialists, artisans, and architects to Japan and helped lay the foundation for the rich Buddhist culture of the Asuka and Nara periods.

The southeastern state of Silla (57 BCE–935 CE) was the last to embrace Buddhism and consolidate power following Chinese bureaucratic models. In 535, six years after the martyrdom of the Buddhist adherent Ich'adon, the first monastery was commissioned by Silla king Pophung (r. 514–540). The Silla royalty utilized Buddhist symbolism to legitimize their rule, attempt to create and project autocratic power, and protect the state. Social institutions such as the *hwarang* (flower boy) organization instituted by Silla king Chinhung (r. 540–575) drew upon Maitreya symbolism as well as native religious elements.

Unified Silla Buddhism (668–935) Buddhism flourished to an even greater extent after the Silla Kingdom conquered the kingdoms of Paekche and Koguryo in 668. During this period, the major intellectual and practice traditions of the religion that had developed in China were introduced to Korea. Scholars suggest that doctrinal teachings that had been imported during the Three Kingdoms period coalesced into five scholastic traditions: the Kyeyulchong, focused on the study and training in monastic discipline; the Yolbanjong, which promoted the teachings of the Mahaparinirvana Sutra; the Popsongjong, a uniquely Korean school that emphasized an ecumenical outlook toward Buddhist doctrine; the Popsangjong, focused on the "consciousness-only" teachings of Yogacara; and the Wonyungjong, the Korean branch of the Flower Garland (Chinese: Huayan; Korean: Hwaom) tradition. The writings of important scholiasts, such as Wonhyo (617–686) and Uisang

Buddhist monk at the Haeinsa Temple in South Korea, which holds the Tripitaka Koreana, a set of Buddhist Scriptures carved onto 81,258 wooden printing blocks. (Courtesy of the Korea Tourism Organization)

(625–702), played an important role in developing Huayan thought in East Asia; and others, such as Wonch'uk (613–686), who was a close disciple of the famous Chinese pilgrim Xuanzang (d. 664), developed Sinitic Yogacara, and his writings exerted a profound influence on early Tibetan Buddhism.

Despite the importance of intellectual traditions, the cults of Maitreya; Avalokitesvara, the bodhisattva of compassion; Amitabha, the buddha of the Pure Land in the West; and Bhaisajyaguru, the Medicine Buddha; not only constituted a significant aspect of monastic practice but were actively promoted by monks and nuns, including the most intellectual exegetes. Devotional piety and patronage dominated lay expressions of worship among the royalty and nobility and influenced the patterns of piety among the populace. The Flower Garland tradition was most successful in synthesizing devotional practice with doctrine and de-

veloped a comprehensive system that made Buddhist beliefs intelligible to an increasing number of Koreans.

The introduction of Chan (Zen) Buddhist teachings, Son in Korean, one of the most important developments in Korean religious history, happened during the Unified Silla period. The monk Pomnang (fl. 632–646), who is believed to have trained with the fourth patriarch of the Chan school, Daoxin (580–646), appears to have attempted to synthesize the teachings of two early Chinese Chan lineages with the seminal doctrine of *tathagatagarbha* (womb of buddhahood) as described in the *Dasheng qixin lun* (*Awakening of Faith in the Mahayana*). One of Pomnang's successors eventually founded the Huiyangsan School, the oldest of Korea's Son traditions. During the eighth and ninth centuries many other Korean adepts in meditation founded other mountain traditions. These traditions are referred to as the Nine Mountain schools of

Son (Kusan Sonmun). Most of these lineages claimed descent from the Hongzhou School of the middle Chan period that eventually developed into the Linji School of the mature Chan tradition. The most prominent Korean Son monk was Kim Heshang (ca. 694–762), who was held as a patriarch in the Baotang School that flourished in the Sichuan region and who was the first Chan master known to the Tibetans.

Koryo Buddhism (918–1392) The Buddhist church enjoyed royal patronage to an unprecedented extent during the Koryo period. The state developed bureaucratic organs to administer the religion and the court and nobility sponsored many kinds of rituals regularly throughout the entire dynastic period to draw upon the power of the buddhas for symbolic legitimacy, protection, and wealth. Doctrinal schools (Kyo), Son sects, and ritual traditions increased to 13 during the Koryo period.

Reconciliation between the doctrinal schools and Son is the principal contribution of Koryo period Buddhists in the evolution of the Korean Buddhist tradition. The royal monk Uich'on (1055–1101) made a first attempt by seeking to combine the Son schools with significant doctrinal orientation in a revived Ch'ont'ae (Chinese: Tiantai) School. Although his attempt failed, the efforts of the charismatic Son proponent Chinul (1158–1210) have proved to be enduring. Instead of emphasizing scholasticism, Chinul synthesized a variety of Son and Kyo approaches to soteriological practice. The most enduring of these practices was the meditative investigation of the "critical phrase" (*hwadu*; Chinese: *huatou*), or *kongan* (Japanese: *koan*) practice, as it had been developed in China by Dahui Zonggao (1089–1163). Chinul's synthesis of Son and the teachings came to be regarded as a distinctively Korean school of Son called the Chogyejong. He and his disciples enjoyed patronage by the Koryo court and came to dominate the Buddhist church in the late Koryo period. Later, during the period of Mongol domination on the peninsula, the Son master T'aego Pou (1301–1392) labored to effect the merger between the remaining schools of Korean Son and the Chogyejong by introducing official transmission in the Chinese Linji (Korean: *Imje*; Japanese *Rinzai*) lineage. His efforts ensured that the Chogyejong would remain the dominant school of Korean Buddhism until the present.

Buddhism under the Choson (1392–1910) and the Modern Era Because the Choson court ultimately adopted Confucianism as its preferred ideology in the early 15th century, the Buddhist church came under increased scrutiny and the centralized supervision of the government. Schools and sects were forcibly combined and ultimately reduced to two traditions, Son and Kyo. Sosan Hyujong's (1520–1604) influential *Son'ga kwigam* (*Guide to the Son school*) exemplifies the practice orientation of the Son tradition during this difficult period for the religion in Korea.

Japanese influence in Korea in the late 19th century provided new opportunities and new pressures on the Korean Buddhist tradition. Japanese Nichiren sect missionaries forced the weak Choson court to lift a centuries-old ban on the presence of monks in the capital of Seoul. At the same time, Kyongho (1857–1912) revitalized Son practice in Korea and successors to his lineage continue to teach today. Some Buddhists were in favor of adopting policies followed in Japan as a means of strengthening the social position of Buddhism. Han Yongun (1879–1944) who studied in Japan, advocated that monks be allowed to marry if Buddhism were to play a practical role in modern society. Although the Korean Buddhist leaders were against the adoption of such a policy, the Japanese colonial government ultimately adopted it in 1926 by legalizing matrimony for monks. Most monks were married within 10 years, but after independence in 1945, Korean Buddhism was split between the T'aegojong, a liberal sect of married monks that had flourished under colonial rule, and the Chogyejong, a smaller faction of monks who maintained the practice of monastic celibacy. In 1954, after years of legal conflict, the Chogyejong won government support for its position of maintaining Korean traditions and was awarded possession of the 25 major monastic complexes and their subtemples on the Korean peninsula. Now in the early 21st century, the Chogyejong is the most dominant sect of Korean Buddhism and is attracting a new generation of lay believers and monastic postulants.

Richard D. McBride II

See also: Chinul; Chogye Order; Nichirenshu; T'aego Pou; Zen Buddhism.

References

Buswell, Robert E., Jr. "The Emergence of a 'Korean' Buddhism." In *Korean Buddhism in East Asian Perspectives*, compiled by the Geumgang Center for Buddhist Studies, Geumgang University, 23–44. Seoul: Jimoondang, 2007.

McBride, Richard D., II. *Domesticating the Dharma: Buddhist Cults and the Hwaŏm Synthesis in Silla Korea*. Honolulu: University of Hawaii Press, 2008.

Sørensen, Henrik H. "Buddhist Spirituality in Premodern and Modern Korea." In *Buddhist Spirituality II: Later China, Korea, Japan and the Modern World*, edited by Takeuchi Yoshinori, World Spirituality: An Encyclopedia History of the Religious Quest, no. 9, 109–133. New York: Crossroad Publishing Company, 1999.

Vermeersch, Sem. *The Power of the Buddhas: The Politics of Buddhism During the Koryŏ Dynasty (918–1392)*. Cambridge: Harvard University Asia Center, 2008.

Korean Christian Church in Japan

One source of Christianity in Japan has been Korea, where a vital Presbyterian mission operated through the last half of the 19th century. In 1909 the Presbyterian Church of Korea sent a minister, Han Sok-Po, to Tokyo to work primarily among Korean students at the university. This work continued during the years of Japanese occupation of Korea, beginning in 1910. The continued growth of the church in Korea allowed it to send additional evangelists. Over the next two decades congregations sprang up across the country, where many Korean expatriates resided.

The Japanese Presbyterian mission was forced into the United Church of Christ in Japan during World War II, but it separated from that organization soon after the war ended and continued as the Korean Christian Church in Japan. Organized according to a presbyterian church order, the church's congregations are divided into five regions, headed by a general assembly. The church accepts the Westminster Confession as its doctrinal standard.

In the later 1990s the Korean Christian Church in Japan reported 7,100 members in 100 congregations. It is a member of the World Council of Churches and the World Alliance of Reformed Churches.

Korean Christian Church in Japan
Japan Christian Center, Room 52
2-2-18 Nishi Waseda
Shinjuku-ku, Tokyo 191
Japan

J. Gordon Melton

See also: United Church of Christ in Japan; World Alliance of Reformed Churches; World Council of Churches.

References

Bauswein, Jean-Jacques, and Lukas Vischner, eds. *The Reformed Family Worldwide: A Survey of Reformed Churches, Theological Schools, and International Organizations*. Grand Rapids, MI: William B. Eerdmans Publishing Company, 1999.

Van Beek, Huibert. *A Handbook of the Churches and Councils: Profiles of Ecumenical Relationships*. Geneva: World Council of Churches, 2006.

Korean Methodist Church

In 1884, Robert F. Maclay (1824–1907), the superintendent of the mission of the Methodist Episcopal Church (MEC, now a constituent part of the United Methodist Church) in Japan, traveled to Korea and while there received permission to open schools and hospitals in the country. The following year the first missionaries arrived in the persons of the Reverend Harry G. Appenzeller (1858–1902) and his wife, Ella J. D. Appenzeller, and Dr. William B. Scranton (1856–1922) and his wife Mary F. Scranton and his mother. Their efforts launched modern, Western-style education on the Korean Peninsula. They were joined a decade later by C. F. Reid and Josephine P. Campbell, both representatives of the Methodist Episcopal Church, South (MECS, now a constituent part of the United Methodist Church). During the first decade of the new century, their work bore massive fruit, with a membership jumping from around 2,000 to more than 13,000 people. The MEC mission organized an annual conference (the basic organizational unit in Methodism) in 1908, and the MECS mission did so in 1918.

Through the first decades of the 20th century, the MEC and MECS pursued talks aimed at a merger, but Korean Methodists grew impatient. In 1928 and 1930, respectively, the conferences petitioned their respective general conferences for independence so that they could form one independent church in Korea. That permission was granted, and by the end of 1930 a new constitution had been written and the new Korean Methodist Church was organized. The new church also wrote a new creed for use in its teaching work that was translated and widely circulated through the U.S. churches, which finally merged in 1939. Though the Korean church was independent, it maintained close fraternal ties with its sister church in the United States.

The church was totally disrupted by World War II. The Japanese occupying forces isolated missionaries and made contact with overseas offices impossible. The Russians sealed the border between the northern and southern parts of the country, and Methodism lost half of its churches and many of its members. It had just reorganized when the Korean War began in 1950. However, in the decades immediately after the war and with the establishment of the cease-fire that kept Korea divided for the rest of the 20th century, the Korean Methodist Church enjoyed a growth period. Its membership doubled during the 1950s and again in the 1960s. The growth continued through the rest of the century, and by 2005 the church reported more than 1.5 million members worshipping in 5,489 churches. The church has also become a missionary body, sending evangelists to more than 54 countries, many working in close cooperation with the United Methodist Church and other Methodist bodies. It is a member of the World Methodist Council and was a founding member of the World Council of Churches.

Korean Methodist Church
KPO Box 285
Methodist Building 16F
64-B Taepyungro1-ga
Jung-gu, Seoul 110-101
Republic of Korea

J. Gordon Melton

See also: United Methodist Church, World Council of Churches; World Methodist Council.

References

Kim, Jinhung. *A Pictorial History of the Methodist Church in Korea*. Seoul: Archives of the Korean Methodist Church, 1995.

Park, I. G. *The History of Protestant Missions in Korea, 1832–1910*. Seoul: Yonsei University Press, 1970.

Stokes, Charles D. "History of the Methodist Missions in Korea, 1885–1930." Ph.D. diss., Yale University, 1947.

Yu, Chai-Shin. *Korea and Christianity*. Fremont, CA: Asian Humanities Press, 2004.

■ Kosovo

One of the newest countries on the world stage, Kosovo has existed since 1974 as an autonomous province of first Yugoslavia and more recently of Serbia. Beginning in the 1980s, Kosovoans, primarily of an Albanian ethnicity, began to call for complete independence. That call for independence increased through the 1990s and into the new century. It resulted in the declaration of autonomy in 2008.

Kosovo had been incorporated into Serbia in the 13th century. Toward the end of the next century, following the Battle of Kosovo in 1389, Serbia, including Kosovo, was incorporated into the Ottoman Empire. Over the next centuries, Turks and Albanians, both predominantly Muslims, moved into Kosovo and by the 19th century Serbians had become a minority segment of the population. The Ottoman Empire lost control of Serbia and Kosovo in 1912 and by the end of the decade no longer existed. Serbia existed in multiple national alignments through World War II when

The Old Stone Bridge, the 17th-century Sinan Pasha Mosque, and Saint Savior Orthodox Church in Prizren, Kosovo. (iStockPhoto)

Kosovo

in 1946 it was incorporated into the Federal Peoples Republic of Yugoslavia, the Socialist state headed by the dictator Marshal Tito (1892–1980). Yugoslavia disintegrated in 1991. In its last stages, it revoked the autonomous status for Kosovo

In 1991, as Yugoslavia fell apart, Albanian leaders in Kosovo held a referendum that favored independence. Serbia, then under strongman Slobodan Milo-

sevic (1941–2006), responded with repressive force. Armed intervention led to additional and more violent repressive measures that included displacement of ethnic Albanians and several massacres. Toward the end of the decade, NATO forces initiated a bombing campaign against the Serbian forces and forced their withdrawal. Deliberations as to Kosovo's future under United Nations hegemony began and continued for a number of

Kosovo

Religion	Followers in 1970	Followers in 2010	% of Population	Annual % growth 2000–2010	Followers in 2025	Followers in 2050
Muslims	1,020,000	1,874,000	89.9	1.02	1,900,000	1,841,000
Christians	133,000	178,000	8.6	1.08	166,000	161,000
Orthodox	86,000	100,000	4.8	0.81	90,000	85,000
Roman Catholics	40,000	68,000	3.3	1.61	63,000	59,000
Protestants	1,000	2,800	0.1	0.00	4,000	5,000
Agnostics	50,000	25,000	1.2	0.79	20,000	18,000
Atheists	10,000	6,500	0.3	0.19	4,000	3,000
Total population	**1,213,000**	**2,084,000**	**100.0**	**1.02**	**2,091,000**	**2,023,000**

years without a resolution to the situation. Milosevic was forced from office and in 2001 arrested and placed on trial for war crimes relative to the massacres in Kosovo. He died before his trial was concluded.

After negotiations in 2007 on the status of Kosovo failed to resolve the issue, the Kosovo Assembly declared independence on February 17, 2008. Over the next year, approximately 50 countries recognized the new country. Among the countries that have refused to recognize it is Serbia, which is pursuing several options in international law to have the province's independent status rejected.

Sunni Islam of the Hanafi School became the dominant religion in Kosovo through the 18th and 19th centuries. There is a small Sufi community, primarily of the Bektashi Order. Muslims are primarily found among those of the Turkish and Albanian ethnicity. The second largest group is the Serbian Orthodox Church. Eastern Orthodoxy had established itself in the 13th century and spread to every part of the country. Though the majority party for many centuries, it gradually moved to second place as ethnic Serbs reverted to minority status. Its churches and monasteries are still to be found in all parts of the new nation.

There is also a Roman Catholic minority, primarily of ethnic Albanians, in Kosovo. The church has enjoyed a spurt of growth in the post-Serbian era and now constitutes about 4 percent of the population (about 60,000 members). Catholics have welcomed the end of Serbian rule as, like the Muslims, they were often the targets of Serbian repression. The leader of the church is Bishop Marko Sopi. In 2000, the Vatican designated

Kosovo an apostolic administration and named Sopi as the apostolic administrator. Prior to that action, Kosovo's Roman Catholics had been part of the diocese of Skopje, based in neighboring Macedonia.

J. Gordon Melton

See also: Bektashi Order (Bektashiye); Hanafite School of Islam; Roman Catholic Church; Serbian Orthodox Church.

References

Duijzings, Ger. *Religion and the Politics of Identity in Kosovo*. New York: Columbia University Press, 2001.

Judah, Tim. *Kosovo: What Everyone Needs to Know*. Oxford: Oxford University Press, 2008.

Weller, Marc. *Contested Statehood: Kosovo's Struggle for Independence*. Oxford: Oxford University Press, 2009.

Koya, Mount

Mount Koya, the center of Shingon Buddhism in Japan, is both the name of a set of mountains located in Wakayama Prefecture (near Osaka) and the specific area on those mountains where a temple complex has been located. Much of the wooded area surrounding the temples has been appropriated as a vast cemetery. The particular site selected by Kukai was a mountain valley located amid eight peaks of the mountains. The valley offered the appearance of being in the middle of a lotus blossom. Over the years a town has emerged in the valley that is now home to a Buddhist university and some 120 temples.

In 816, Kukai (aka Kobo Daishi, 774–835), the founder of Shingon, resided in Kyoto. Wishing to escape the general chaos of city life and separate from the control of the established centers of the older Buddhist schools in Kyoto and nearby Nara, he requested a grant of land where he could construct a rural center for Shingon monks to concentrate on meditation and practice esotericism. When the emperor Saga (809–823) granted the mountain to him, Kukai moved quickly to construct a temple and associated buildings of his new monastic community. Unfortunately, due to his duties in Kyoto, he was himself unable to move to the new center until 832, but once there he would remain on Mount Koya for the rest of his life. He was eventually buried there, his tomb, Okuno-in, being one of the mountain's most sacred spots.

In the years after Kukai's death, a rivalry developed between the Shingon center in Kyoto (To-ji) and Mount Koya. To-ji had been granted to Kukai in 823 and it was the primary place for training students. Mount Koya became the site of their final examination and, most important, their ordination. The number of ordained priests was rigidly regulated by the state, and the privilege of examining and ordaining the monks purveyed considerable power. The power struggle between the two centers caused the emperor to intervene on several occasions. In 853, he ruled that the candidates for ordination would be examined at To-ji, while they were to be ordained at Mount Koya. In 862, he gave Mount Koya full jurisdiction over all Shingon ordinations. Finally, in 902, the emperor increased the number of ordinations, allowed an ordination platform to be erected at To-ji, and assigned a portion of the Shingon ordination to the Kyoto center.

Mount Koya took on more significance through the 10th century as Kukai increasingly became an object of veneration. The emperor contributed to the growing cult of Kukai by giving him the posthumous honorary title of "Kobo Daishi" (Great Teacher). Many Shingon followers now affirmed their belief that Kukai was not dead but at the end of his life had entered a deep trance state from which he now awaited the appearance of the coming Maitreya, the future Buddha. Some went so far as to elevate Kobo Daishi into an emanation or incarnation of Maitreya, which made Mount Koya part of Maitreya's heavenly realm.

The faithful erected a large stupa over Kukai's tomb, which took on added significance in 1107 when the emperor Horikawa (r. 1086–1107) was buried in front of it. Mount Koya immediately became a pilgrimage site of increasing importance as well as a very popular place to be buried.

Kukai had taught that women could not attain Buddhahood (not an unpopular opinion within the Buddhist community in the ninth century), and he did not allow women to come to Mount Koya or participate in any of its activities. Several centuries later, however, Bifukumon'in, one of the emperor's consorts, asked to be buried on Mount Koya. In 1160, her request was granted. She was an exception, and the only exception until 1872, when the anti-female policy was abandoned.

Today, To-ji is considered the administrative center of the main Shingon Buddhist sect in Japan. Mount Koya is the center for monastic practice and the main focus of pilgrimages.

J. Gordon Melton

See also: Kukai (Kobo Daishi); Meditation; Nara; Pilgrimage; Shingon Buddhism.

Reference

Izutsu, Shinryu, and Shoryu Omori. *Sacred Treasures of Mt. Koya: The Art of Japanese Shingon Buddhism.* Honolulu: Koyasan Reihokan Museum, 2002.

Kasahara, Kazou, ed. *A History of Japanese Religion.* Tokyo: Kosei Publishing, 2001.

Koyasan Reihokan Museum. *Sacred Treasures of Mount Koya: The Art of Japanese Shingon Buddhism.* Honolulu: University of Hawaii Press, 2002.

Nicoloff, Philip L. *Sacred Koyasan: A Pilgrimage to the Mountain Temple of Saint Kobo Daishi and the Great Sun Buddha.* Albany: State University of New York Press, 2007.

Saunders, E. Dale, *Buddhism in Japan.* Philadelphia: University of Pennsylvania Press, 1964.

Krishnamurti Foundations

Jiddu Krishnamurti (1895–1986) was a philosopher whose exploration of religion, psychology, and politics, as well as philosophy, addresses the great questions of human existence. His talks and publications, spanning six decades, influenced world leaders in politics, eminent scientists, and the general public, and continue to inspire many who seek a fresh understanding of the human condition. Born in 1895 in Madanapalle, near Madras in colonial India, Krishnamurti (literally, "the image of Krishna") grew up in an orthodox Brahmin family steeped in tradition, ritual, and a sacred view of the world. After the death of his mother when he was only 10 years old, he moved with his father and siblings to the headquarters in Madras of the Theosophical Society, a rapidly growing spiritual movement.

The Theosophical Society, founded in 1875 in New York City, began as an organization dedicated to a synthesis of science, religion, and philosophy with the credo "There is no religion higher than truth." Part of Theosophical teaching is the exploration of clairvoyant powers for discovering the hidden mysteries of nature and the esoteric powers of humanity. The Theosophists drew freely from their understanding of Western Esotericism and of Eastern thought, particularly Buddhist and Hindu cosmologies, to form a worldview that included a complex cosmology, an esoteric psychology, and an evolutionary scheme that encompassed eons. The synthesis of East and West, religion and science, and esoteric and exoteric understanding made Theosophy compelling to cosmopolitan, liberal people, regardless of nationality, who had been disappointed by the beliefs and practice of both religion and science and sought to unite the diverse peoples of the world in a peaceful brotherhood. It was to this milieu that the young Krishnamurti was exposed.

Drawing upon many religious traditions and prophecies, some leaders in the Theosophical Society at the time of Krishnamurti's youth were actively looking for a messiah, a World Teacher, who would destroy evil and restore righteousness. In his early teen years, Krishnamurti was adopted by the Theosophists as the World Teacher and appointed head of the Order of the Star in the East, an organization devoted to realizing the World Teacher's mission. For a number of years Krishnamurti traveled and addressed audiences in this role, maturing in his understanding of the Order, the Theosophical Society, and his role in each.

Over many months in 1922–1923, Krishnamurti experienced a profound transformation. Begun as meditation, Krishnamurti's transformation, called "the process," contained moments of great beauty and clarity offset by periods of physical pain, even agony. He often fell unconscious and appeared to converse with non-physical entities and to speak from several personas. Krishnamurti's report of his transformation of consciousness is consistent with other reports of mystical non-dualism—his personality dissolved into communion with the whole of life. In his words, "I was in everything, or rather everything was in me, inanimate and animate, the mountain, the work and all breathing things." Themes of his later teaching are found in his description of his transformation: "I have seen the Light. I have touched compassion which heals all sorrow and suffering; it is not for myself, but for the world."

From this time on, he experienced a growing dissatisfaction with the authority structure of the Theosophical Society and its emphasis on occultism. At the death of his brother, which the occultism of the Theosophical Society did not foresee, his dissatisfaction became overwhelming and he defined his stance relative to Theosophy as one of revolt. In his talks, dialogues, and writings, he began to stress the benefit of doubt and questioning, a direction antithetical to the Theosophical structure of that day. Rejecting all forms of spiritual authority, he disbanded the Order of the Star in the East in 1929, declaring, "Truth is a pathless land."

From then until his death in 1986, Krishnamurti ceaselessly taught his insights to a worldwide audience. He became a champion of freedom and inquiry and a relentless advocate of the discovery of truth without the aid of any organization, religion, or belief system. His teaching emphasized the necessity of developing awareness of one's conditioning and bondage to thought, fear, and time. His goal was to make humans "unconditionally free" and, to this end, he invited

Jiddu Krishnamurti lectures to a crowd of people in Pennsylvania in 1932. Krishnamurti was an Indian philosopher who believed that God must be experienced directly in order to be known. (Corbis)

those who listened to him to observe their inner selves, their motives and ways of thought, as well as events in the outside world. With each audience, Krishnamurti inquired into the basic nature of humanity and found that real self-transformation involves an instantaneous awareness of the psyche and its workings. Accompanied by simplicity and humility, this awareness could, he maintained, open a person to the "immensity" of life. Transformation is seen as "freedom from the known," escape from the conditioning, beliefs, and emotions inculcated since infancy. The "known," he says, includes time, sorrow, and bondage. To be free one must die to the "known" in order to meet truth, which is limitless, unconditioned, and unapproachable by any path whatsoever.

To Krishnamurti, living in thought ties one to the past. Freedom requires movement beyond the past,

beyond myth, tradition, and the products of thought. Knowledge, time, and thought are not a means to change, but are the psychological sources of sorrow, pain, and anxiety, because they are the mechanisms for bringing the past into the present. The unknown, the truth, cannot be grasped by thought, but must be apprehended in the immediate present. This apprehension or seeing is the force of change. No one can see for another, so external authority is of no use. Knowledge and time must be left behind, as must psychological dependence upon anyone. Krishnamurti quoted Shakyamuni Buddha often when he instructed, "Be a light unto yourselves."

Constantly warning of the dangers inherent in nationalism, political ideology, and religious belief, Krishnamurti maintained that the ending of human conflict can occur only with the cessation of misapplied thinking and its propensity for image-making of an inevitably harmful kind. Given the planetary interdependence of our times, each of us needs to see that, psychologically, "I am the world," and that to understand one's own consciousness is to understand human consciousness.

During his lifetime Krishnamurti created schools for children and young adults in India, the United States, England, and Switzerland. These alternative schools continue today in their mission to provide a new definition and practice of education, free from the conditioning and authority structures prevalent in modern educational institutions.

In his later years, Krishnamurti joined with the physicist David Bohm in exploring the human condition through a series of dialogues. Both men recognized the limitations of traditional didactic teaching and sought ways in which truth and insight can be discovered within individuals and small groups. All the Krishnamurti Foundations regularly hold dialogues that stress listening and exploring together in a relaxed, friendly environment, so that serious issues of common concern can emerge naturally—without didactic formalism or dogmatism. Krishnamurti and Bohm also predicted that the neuronal structure of the human brain could change fundamentally as the result of insight and inquiry.

Krishnamurti helped to establish Foundations in those countries where his teachings received the most response and which he visited regularly. The Foundations facilitated his travel, arranged for his public appearances, and published transcripts of his talks and dialogues. A large corpus of Krishnamurti's original writings and talks as well as his dialogues with Bohm have been made available in book and video form by the Krishnamurti Foundations in England (founded 1968), the United States (1969), and India (1971). These Foundations and the Krishnamurti committees in other countries sponsor regular dialogue groups and hold gatherings for study of the teachings. Consistent with the tenets of his thought, the Foundations have remained relatively non-institutionalized. A current directory reports that Krishnamurti organizations and schools are now found in 40 countries around the world.

Krishnamurti Foundation America
PO Box 1560

Ojai, California 93024-1560
www.kfa.org,

Krishnamurti Foundation Trust
Brockwood Park
Bramdean, Hampshire
SO24 0LQ
United Kingdom
www.kfoundation.org

Constance A. Jones

See also: Krishnamurti Foundations.

References

Holroyd, Stuart. *The Quest of the Quiet Mind: The Philosophy of Krishnamurti.* Wellingborough, Northamptonshire, England: Aquarian Press, 1980.

Jayakar, Pupul. *Krishnamurti: A Biography.* New York: Penguin, 1986.

Krishnamurti, Jiddu. *Commentaries on Living, from the Notebooks of J. Krishnamurti.* Ed. by D. Rajagopal. 3 vols. Wheaton, IL: Theosophical Publishing House, 1960.

Krishnamurti, Jiddu. *Freedom from the Known.* New York: Harper & Row, 1969.

Krishnamurti, Jiddu. *The Book of Life.* Madras: Krishnamurti Foundation India, 1975.

Krishnamurti, Jiddu, and David Bohm. *The Ending of Time.* San Francisco: Harper, 1985.

Lutyens, Mary. *Krishnamurti: The Years of Awakening. Krishnamurti: The Years of Fulfillment. Krishnamurti: The Open Door.* 3 vols. New York: Farrar Straus Giroux, 1973–1985.

Ksitigarbha's/Jizo's Birthday

Ksitigarbha (also known as Bodhisattva Earth Repository or Earth Womb, or in Japanese as Jizo), was a bodhisattva who had a special mission directed at saving those suffering in the various hell realms of Buddhist cosmology. As Jizo, he is especially revered in Japan for saving the souls of deceased children, including those who were lost due to abortion. He is known as an especially compassionate being, at times rivaling Guan Yin in that capacity.

Ksitigarbha is commonly represented seated or standing, with a pilgrim's staff in his right hand and a pearl in his left. He wears a monk's robe with his head shaved. His famous vow was, "I therefore vow never to become a Buddha before all the prisoners are released from the hell."

Ksitigarbha is most associated with Mount Jiuhua, in Anhui Province, one of the four sacred mountains of Chinese Buddhism. His main temple there is Hua Cheng Temple, which was founded in 401 CE, though the story that most ties him to the mountain dates from the eighth century. In 719, during the Tang dynasty (618–907), the Korean Prince Kim Gio Gak (d. 793) of what was then the Kingdom of Silla, took up residence at a hermitage on Mount Jiuhua. A charismatic soul, he gained a following that grew over the three-quarters of a century he remained on the mountain. By this time, people had come to believe him to be an emanation of Ksitigarbha Bodhisattva. And in the centuries afterward, they generalized their belief to thinking of the mountain as his domain. Beginning in the Song dynasty (960–1279) the number of temples began to multiply. More than 75 of the older temples remain in place.

The Huacheng Temple, the oldest of the temples of Mount Jiuhua, is believed to have been built as a residence for Kim Gio Gak. In 781, it was rededicated as the "bodhimandala" of Ksitigarbha. Today, it also contains a display of more than 6,000 texts of Buddhist scriptures that the temple received as a gift from the Ming Emperor Wanli (1563–1620).

Ksitigarbha's birthday is celebrated throughout East Asia on the first day of the eighth lunar month (some celebrate on the last day of the seventh month), around July 13, and at this time thousands flock to the mountain. As monks gather in the Pagoda of the Holy Body to stand vigil for the Ksitigarbha Bodhisattva, the mountain is filled with a generally festive atmosphere.

In 2001, plans were announced to create a mega-statue of Ksitigarbha 155 meters (509 feet) to be completed around 2004. Several years later the date was changed to around 2008 and the size revised downward to 99 meters (325 feet), dictated by the facts that there are 99 mountain apexes in the Jiuhua mountain area and that Kim Gio Gak considered the emanation of Ksitigarbha reputedly ended his life when he was 99 years old.

Veneration of the Ksitigarbha/Jizo figure is even greater in Japan than in China. As in China, Jizo serves his traditional roles as patron saint of expectant mothers, children, firemen, travelers, pilgrims, and the protector of all beings caught in the six realms of the Buddhist cosmic world that are subject to reincarnation. Jizo is also venerated as the guardian of unborn, aborted, miscarried, and stillborn babies, roles not assigned to him in mainland Asia. Thus here, his recognition is heightened and the celebrations both widespread and frequent. The 24th of every lunar month is Jizo's day, and the 24th day of the 7th lunar month is the Grand Assembly in his honor. Today the largest celebration is held on the 23rd and 24th days of the 8th month in Kyoto and greater Kansai, where events focus on prayers for the welfare of children.

J. Gordon Melton

See also: Jiu Hua Shan.

References

Bays, Jan Chozen. *Jizo Bodhisattva: Guardian of Children, Travelers, and Other Voyagers*. Boston: Shambhala, 2003.

Bays, Jan Chozen. *Jizo Bodhisattva: Modern Healing and Traditional Buddhist Practice*. Rutland, VT: Tuttle Publishing, 2001.

Boheng, Wu, and Cai Zhuozhi. *100 Buddhas in Chinese Buddhism*. Trans. by Mu Xin and Yan Zhi. Singapore: Asiapac Books, 1997.

Ksitigarbha Bodhisattva Sutra/ Ksitigarbha Bodhisattva Purva Prandhana Sutra. Also known as: Ksitigarbha's Fundamental Vows/Ksitigarbha's Fundamental Practices/Ksitigarbha's Fundamental Determination. Surabaya, Indonesia: Cetya True Buddha Surabaya, n.d.

Vessantara. *Meeting the Buddhas: A Guide to Buddhas, Bodhisattvas, and Tantric Deities*. Birmingham, UK: Windhorse Publications, 1998.

Kukai (Kobo Daishi)

774–835

Kukai was a famous and influential Japanese monk who founded Shingon, the Japanese version of esoteric

Buddhism. He was born into the gentry class and was well-versed in the Confucian classics. At the age of 14, he suddenly announced his desire to become a monk and after that day led a strictly ascetic lifestyle.

Kukai was one of the many monks to visit Tangera (618–907 CE) China. While there he studied under masters of both the Tian Tai and Vajrayana (Chinese esoteric) traditions. Upon his return to Japan he established his own monasteries and continued the Vajrayana (esoteric) initiations to new monks. He was appointed abbot of To-ji, a monastic center and temple near Kyoto, and this became the Shingon sect's center. He later moved to Mount Koya, where Shingon activities are centered to the present.

Kukai remains one of the best-known figures in Japanese Buddhism. His images can be seen in the grounds of many temples (not necessarily in the worship halls), and he is worshipped as an incarnation of the bodhisattva Maitreya. In the years after his death, as stories about him grew, he began to be called "Kobo Daishi" (or Kobo Great Teacher). Shingon altars will have a representation of him, an acknowledgment of his semi-deific status.

Edward A. Irons

See also: Confucianism; Koya, Mount; Shingon Buddhism; Tian Tai/Tendai Buddhism.

References

Abe, Ryuichi Abe. *The Weaving of Mangra: Kukai and the Construction of Esoteric Buddhist Discourse.* New York: Columbia University Press, 1999.

Hakeda, Yoshito S., trans. *Kukai: Major Works.* New York: Columbia University Press, 1972.

McGreal, Ian, ed. *Great Thinkers of the Eastern World.* New York: HarperCollins, 1995.

Payne, Richard K. "Ajikan: Ritual and Meditation in the Shingon Tradition." In *Re-Visioning "Kamakura" Buddhism,* edited by Richard K. Payne. Honolulu: University of Hawaii Press, 1998.

Tamura, Yoshiro. *Japanese Buddhism: A Cultural History.* Trans. by Jeffrey Hunter. Tokyo: Kosei, 2000.

Kumarajiva

344–413

Kumarajiva is considered one of the greatest translators of the Buddhist sutras. He played a vital role in the transference of Buddhism into China. Kumarajiva was perfectly suited to play this lynchpin role due to his unique background. He was born into royalty in Kucha, one of the oasis kingdoms along the north route of the Silk Road (in what is now the Xinjiang Province of China). Buddhism was strong in the land and his Buddhist mother encouraged Kumarajiva to study the sutras from the age of seven. He accompanied her on travels to visit learned monks in India and elsewhere. He was finally ordained as a Theravada monk in 364. His fame as an expert in Buddhism grew over time. It got to the point where the emperor of a Chinese dynasty, the Former Qin (351–394 CE), decided to attack

The Kumarajiva Sarira Pagoda, located in Caotang Temple in Huxian County, was built for keeping the remains of Kumarajiva. (Panorama Media [Beijing] Ltd./StockphotoPro)

Kucha in order to capture Kumarajiva and forcefully take him to his dynasty's capital. While this war raged the Former Qin itself was overthrown (383 CE). Kumarajiva then became a captive and a subject of negotiations. He was finally settled in Chang An, the capital of the new Chinese dynasty of the Later Qin (384–417), in 401.

Kumarajiva spent the remainder of his life translating Buddhist texts into Chinese. He was given all the resources needed by the current rulers, who seemed anxious to accrue merit by translation of the unexplored wisdom contained in Buddhist sutras. Kumarajiva recruited a large team of learned translators who spent years working on translations of 35 major texts. These translations were invariably done by teamwork and were not the work of any individual. Kumarajiva, knowing the essence of each text as well as the major languages, was able to review each prepared translation to ensure accuracy. The texts translated are often still used today. The Kumarajiva translation of the Flower Garland (Avatamsaka) Sutra, a massive work, which paved the way for the creation of the Hua Yan School of Chinese Buddhism.

Edward A. Irons

See also: Theravada Buddhism.

References

Mizuno, Kogen. *Buddhist Sutras: Origin, Development, Transmission.* Tokyo: Kosei Publishing, 1980, 1982.

Watson, Burton. *The Flower of Chinese Buddhism.* New York: Weatherhill, 1986.

Wright, Arthur F. *Buddhism in Chinese History.* Palo Alto, CA: Stanford University Press, 1959.

Kurozumikyô

One of the oldest of the Japanese new religions, Kurozumikyô was founded in 1814 by a Shinto priest, Kurozumi Munetada (1780–1850). Both his parents died as the result of an epidemic in 1812, and then he became critically ill and spent three years in bed. While praying to Amaterasu Omikami (the sun goddess), he awoke to his own healing and to the realization that the divine and human are essentially one and that con-

sequently there is neither birth nor death in this unity. This revelation, known as Tenmei Jikiju (direct reception of the will of heaven) occurred on November 11, 1814, and is commemorated as the beginning of Kurozumikyô.

After his revelation, Kurozumi began to preach this faith and is said to have healed people, attracting a considerable number of followers including a number of samurai and intellectuals. After his death in 1850, followers gathered together and formed religious associations in various provinces, and in 1876 they received official recognition as an independent Shinto sect from the government.

The followers of Kurozumikyô hold that the spirit that pervades the universe is that of Amaterasu Omikami and that people should seek, through communication with this spirit, to realize in experience the unity of the divine and human. Kurozumikyô reveres not only Amaterasu Omikami and the traditional *kami* pantheon but also the deified founder. Its primary unique practice is what is referred to as a "sun-swallowing rite," in which believers worship the Sun while inhaling the fresh air, thus appearing to swallow the Sun (a representation of the Spirit of God) and experiencing a oneness with Amaterassu Omikami. Kurozumikyô uses the founder's writings, Kurozumikyô Kyosho, as its sacred scripture. Its leadership is held by direct descendants of Kurozumi family; the current head is the sixth-generation successor, Kurozumi Muneharu.

Kurozumikyô's headquarters complex includes a shrine to the founder and a large preaching hall. Leaders are trained at the Omoto Gakuin (Omoto Institute). Kurozumikyô also sponsors an orphanage at Akasaka, Okayama Prefecture. As the 21st century began, it reported 280,620 members.

Kurozumikyô
2770 Ogami
Okayama-shi, Okayama Prefecture 701-1292
Japan

Keishin Inaba

See also: Shinto.

References

Hardacre, Helen. *Kurozumikyo and the New Religions of Japan.* Princeton, NJ: Princeton University Press, 1986.

Thomsen, Harry. *The New Religions of Japan.* Rutland, VT, and Tokyo: Charles E. Tuttle Company, 1963.

Kusinagara

Kusinagara, a town in eastern Uttar Pradesh, India, is one of the four key locations associated with the life of Gautama Buddha (ca. 563–ca. 483 BCE), the others being Lumbini, Sarnath, and Bodhgaya. It was the place chosen by the Buddha to live out his last days on Earth. During this time, he delivered a spectrum of important discourses, among the most important being the Mahaparinibbana Sutra centered on the ideal of diligence. Also, he would receive the last people who were personally admitted to the community (*sangha*) by him.

As important as were his final years, the events immediately following his death also attained a high level of significance. First, his body was cremated and some of his remains enshrined at Kusinagara. The other part of his remains, most notably the various bone fragments, were divided among eight Buddhist kings who then ruled various parts of India. These remains were late to become venerated as the Buddha's relics.

Kusinagara's importance greatly increased several centuries later when the Buddhist ruler, King Asoka (third century BCE), expanded his kingdom. He saw to the construction of a variety of religious structures in the town and essentially turned it into a vital Buddhist center that would remain such until the Muslim invasion in the ninth century. At that time, the residents were scattered, and Kushinagar was consumed by the jungles. Only in the 1880 was the town discovered by British explorers. Recent excavations have uncovered ruins of a large monastic community that appears to have survived into the 11th century.

To date, the earliest buildings unearthed at Kusinagara have been dated to the time of Ashoka. That being said, archaeologists have uncovered two very important ancient remains that have subsequently attracted the attention of Buddhist believers. The Chankhandi Stupa marks the spot, many believe, where Buddha was cremated. A large pillar originally erected by King Ashoka is located in the midst of the stupa, though none of the Buddha's relics that had been placed in the stupa have survived. Nearby, Mahaparinirvana Temple houses a large statue of a reclining Buddha, a type of statue particularly associated with Burmese Buddhists, some of whom paid to have the temple rebuilt in 1927.

Through the last half of the 20th century, Indian, Japanese, and Sri Lankan Buddhists contributed to the revival of Kusinagara as a Buddhist pilgrimage site. Initially, they pooled their resources and erected a modern Buddhist pilgrims' center. Then in 1994, King Bhumibhol Adulyadej of Thailand contributed a substantial sum to the project to reestablish Buddhism in India as part of the commemoration of the 50th anniversary of his assuming the Thai throne. In response, Thai Buddhists constructed Wat Thai Kusinara Chalermraj, a new contemporary Buddhist temple, one of several now serving pilgrims from all branches of Buddhism visiting Kusinagara.

Edward A. Irons

See also: Ashoka; Bodh-Gaya; Lumbini; Pilgrimage; Relics; Sarnath; Statues—Buddhist.

References

Majupuria, Trilok Chandra. *Holy Places of Buddhism in Nepal and India: A Guide to Sacred Places in Buddha's Lands.* Columbia, MO: South Asia Books, 1987.

Panabokke, Gunaratne. *History of the Buddhist Sangha in India and Sri Lanka.* Dalugama, Kelaniya, Sri Lanka: Postgraduate Institute of Pali and Buddhist Studies, University of Kelaniya, 1993.

Patil, D. R. *Kusinagara.* Delhi: Archaeological Survey of India, 1981.

Tulku, Tarthang, ed. *Holy Places of the Buddha.* Vol. 9: *Crystal Mirror.* Berkeley, CA: Dharma Publishing, 1994.

■ Kuwait

Kuwait is a small country at the western end of the Persian Gulf. Much of the land away from the shoreline is desert, primarily prized for the oil found beneath. Due to the inhospitable climate inland, the overwhelming majority of the 2,600,000 residents reside in cities and towns along the coast.

The Fatima Mosque in Abdullah Al Salim, Kuwait. (Kuwaitna/Dreamstime.com)

The West attained a heightened level of public awareness about Kuwait at the beginning of the 1990s, when it became the focus of a war between the United States and Iraq. The land now designated as Kuwait has been populated since ancient times, though its history is often forgotten amid the famous ancient centers of the neighboring countries such as Baghdad (Iraq), Persepolis (Iran), and Mecca (Saudi Arabia). However, its strategic location made Kuwait an important early port for trade between India and the Middle East.

In the seventh century CE the area was changed by the emergence of the Arab Muslims, and Kuwait was incorporated into an empire that centered on Baghdad. The glory of the empire was finally destroyed in

KUWAIT

Kuwait

Religion	Followers in 1970	Followers in 2010	% of Population	Annual % growth 2000–2010	Followers in 2025	Followers in 2050
Muslims	701,000	2,613,000	85.7	3.88	3,354,000	4,367,000
Christians	38,600	301,000	9.9	4.25	431,000	600,000
Roman Catholics	17,700	230,000	7.5	4.95	320,000	440,000
Independents	2,400	30,000	1.0	1.56	50,000	75,000
Orthodox	13,300	28,800	0.9	2.03	44,000	63,000
Hindus	3,800	100,000	3.3	3.91	140,000	180,000
Agnostics	0	22,000	0.7	3.91	40,000	60,000
Baha'is	1,000	10,000	0.3	3.85	15,000	22,000
Sikhs	0	4,500	0.1	3.91	7,000	10,000
Atheists	0	500	0.0	3.91	800	1,200
Total population	**744,000**	**3,051,000**	**100.0**	**3.91**	**3,988,000**	**5,240,000**

the 13th century by the Mongol conquests. Kuwait would again find some stability in the 16th century as part of the Ottoman Empire, though the desert that surrounds the populated areas along the coast gave the area some degree of isolation.

In the 18th century, the people of the region chose to designate a representative to handle their relationship with the Ottoman Empire. In 1756, Abdul Rahim al-Sabah, the leader of the Anaiza people, was chosen. Al-Sabah is the fountainhead of the present ruling family of Kuwait. To keep from being absorbed into what was emerging as Saudi Arabia as the Ottoman Empire weakened, the Kuwaitis sought British help. Beginning in 1779, a set of treaties were signed, and as a result Kuwait obtained British protection and finally became a British protectorate following World War I.

The protectorate denied Iraq's claim to Kuwait, a claim going back to earlier centuries when the area was subject to Baghdad. The country was given independence in 1961, although Iraq refused to acknowledge Kuwait's new status. The head of the al-Sabah family declared himself emir, and his descendants continue to rule.

Islam is the official religion of Kuwait and virtually all residents are practicing Muslims. The only non-Muslims are expatriates who have moved into the country for economic reasons (oil or trade). Most Kuwaitis are Sunnis of the Malikite School and are thus differentiated from the Saudis, who are primarily Sunnis of the Wahhabi School, and the Iraqis, who are primarily Shias. There are both Wahhabis and Shias in Kuwait.

Christianity is present in Kuwait primarily to serve the expatriate community. The Roman Catholic Church has a relatively strong presence, operating several schools and a hospital. The individual parishes represent different Eastern rites and the Latin rite, all united into a single vicariate. Non-Chalcedonian Eastern Orthodox traditions are represented by parishes of the Armenian Apostolic Church (Holy See of Echmiadzin), the Coptic Orthodox Church, the Ancient Church of the East (Iraq), and the Mar Thoma Strian Church of Malabar. There is also a community of Greek Orthodox believers.

Samuel Zwemer (1867–1952), who had introduced the Reformed Church in America into Bahrain, moved to Kuwait in 1903. The National Evangelical Church of Kuwait was organized that same year, though it did not have a building for worship until 1926. The Anglican Church in Kuwait was established during the height of the protectorate. The Christian Brethren and the assemblies associated with Bhakt Singh, an Indian leader with Plymouth Brethren roots, also have a small presence. Christians have a formal agreement not to attempt the conversion of Muslims. Also among the expatriates are some Hindus from southern India and some members of the Baha'i Faith.

J. Gordon Melton

See also: Ancient Church of the East; Armenian Apostolic Church (Holy See of Echmiadzin); Baha'i Faith; Christian Brethren; Coptic Orthodox Church; Malikite School of Islam; Mar Thoma Syrian Church of Malabar; Reformed Church in America; Roman Catholic Church; Wahhabi Islam; Zwemer, Samuel Marinus.

References

Ali, M. H. "Kuwait, Religion, and Politics." Ph.D. diss., Michigan State University, 1986.

Rizzo, Helen Mary. *Islam, Democracy and the Status of Women: The Case of Kuwait.* London: Routledge, 2004.

Sanmiguel, V. *Christians in Kuwait.* Beirut: Beirut Printing Press, 1970.

Kwan Um School of Zen

The Kwan Um School of Zen, officially founded in 1983, is an international association of Zen centers established by Seung Sahn (called Dae Soen Sa Nim, or "Great Honored Zen Teacher," by his disciples), who is regarded as the 78th patriarch in his lineage in the Chogye order of Korean Buddhism, and the first to live and teach in the West.

Born in 1927 in Seun Choen, North Korea, Seung Sahn (1927–2004) became a Buddhist monk in 1948. He studied with Zen Master Ko Bong Soen Sa Nim (1890–1962), and on January 25, 1949, he received Dharma transmission from his teacher. Seung Sahn arrived in the United States in May 1972, eventually establishing a small Zen center in an apartment in Providence, Rhode Island. The Providence Zen Center remains the head temple of Seung Sahn's international organization. As his English improved, Seung Sahn's teaching expanded, and he began giving precepts to his students as well. His first American disciple, Jacob Perl, was a former student of Shunryu Suzuki Roshi (1905–1971) at the San Francisco Zen Center, and of Tarthang Tulku (b. 1935) at the Tibetan Nyingma Meditation Center in Berkeley, California. Now known as Zen Master Wu Bong, in 1978, Perl helped establish the first Zen center in Poland, and is the Head Teacher in Europe. Another of his early disciples was Barbara Rhodes, a registered nurse who received *inka*, or teaching authority, in 1977 and Dharma transmission in 1992. She currently serves as School Zen Master and Guiding Dharma Teacher, after having helped found the Providence Zen Center. Zen Master Dae Kwang now serves as abbot of the Kwan Um Zen Center.

Seung Sahn eventually gave Dharma transmission to nearly a dozen individuals, including the deceased monk Su Bong, who had been designated as Seung Sahn's successor. He also authorized nearly 20 individuals as senior students, or Dharma masters (Ji Do Poep Sa Nims). Seung Sahn died on November 30, 2004. Seung Sahn's style of teaching was an eclectic combination of sitting meditation, Dharma lectures, *koan* study, prostrations, and chanting. He was sometimes said to teach the "Don't Know" style of Zen, tracing back to a tale about the Zen patriarch Bodhidharma. He was a prolific author, having written *Dropping Ashes on the Buddha*, *The Compass of Zen*, *Ten Gates*, *Only Don't Know*, and *The Whole World is a Single Flower—365 Kong-ans for Everyday Life*.

The Kwan Um School of Zen is headquartered in Cumberland, Rhode Island. It has nearly 100 affiliated centers in the United States, Canada, South Africa, Hong Kong, Israel, Korea, Malaysia, Singapore, and Australia, and throughout Europe and the Middle East. These centers generally have regular schedules for sitting meditation and Dharma talks, as well as longer, intensive retreats called *kyol che* (coming together) that generally run for one or two months. The school also publishes a journal known as *Primary Point*, begun in 1984. In addition, their own Primary Point Press offers a series of videos and books by and about Seung Sahn, as well as his teaching. In 1988 the school weathered a scandal involving sexual relationships between Seung Sahn and female members of his community.

Like many of the Western Buddhist groups today, Kwan Um School of Zen has an extremely well-developed website, which includes an online catalogue from which a variety of Dharma-related objects can be purchased. The site also offers an extensive archive of Kwan Um materials, and it provides links to the Internet sites of more than 50 other Kwan Um School affiliates and to a variety of other useful Buddhist websites, both scholarly and popular in nature.

Kwan Um School of Zen
Providence Zen Center
99 Pound Road
Cumberland, RI 02864
http://www.kwanumzen.com

Charles S. Prebish

See also: Bodhidharma; Meditation; Zen Buddhism.

References

Coleman, James. *The New Buddhism: The Western Transformation of an Ancient Tradition*. New York: Oxford University Press, 2001.

Prebish, Charles S. *Luminous Passage: The Practice and Study of Buddhism in America*. Berkeley and Los Angeles: University of California Press, 1999.

Seager, Richard. *Buddhism in America*. New York: Columbia University Press, 1999.

Soeng, Mu. "Korean Buddhism in America: A New Style of Zen." In *The Faces of Buddhism in America*, edited by Charles S. Prebish and Kenneth K. Tanaka. Berkeley: University of California Press, 1998.

■ Kyrgyzstan

Kyrgyzstan is a small Central Asian republic north of Tadzhikistan. It is also intimately connected with Uzbekistan to its west, as Uzbek and Kyrgyz peoples share a similar religious and linguistic background. It additionally shares a lengthy border with China to the east and Kazakhstan to the north. Kyrgyzstan's 73,861 square miles are home to 5,360,000 people (2008).

The antecedents of the Kyrgyz people moved into the region from the area north of the Caspian Sea. There they mixed with the local Turkish and Mongol peoples, creating the present-day Kyrgyz people. In the 18th century, Kyrgyzstan was brought under Chinese hegemony as a protectorate. In the 19th century, Russia moved into the region as part of its general expansion southward, and through the 1860s a Russian administration was in place in northern Kyrgyzstan. Russian immigrants flowed into the area, and in the 1870s the southern part of the country was annexed by Russia.

Russian authority was replaced by Soviet rule in 1917. As the Soviet Union developed, the region was transformed into the Federated Republic of Kyrgyzstan

A Russian Orthodox priest consecrates a bell as it is lifted into a cathedral in Leninskoye, Kyrgyzstan. (Vyacheslav Oseledko/AFP/Getty Images)

Kyrgyzstan

Religion	Followers in 1970	Followers in 2010	% of Population	Annual % growth 2000–2010	Followers in 2025	Followers in 2050
Muslims	1,004,000	3,951,000	71.9	1.79	4,944,000	5,508,000
Agnostics	862,000	950,000	17.3	−0.47	800,000	600,000
Christians	338,000	322,000	5.9	−0.35	304,000	309,000
Orthodox	275,000	251,000	4.6	−1.04	210,000	190,000
Protestants	43,400	21,000	0.4	1.67	30,000	40,000
Independents	19,500	24,000	0.4	4.66	35,000	40,000
Atheists	700,000	220,000	4.0	−1.81	100,000	75,000
Buddhists	5,000	25,800	0.5	1.19	32,000	45,000
Ethnoreligionists	50,000	22,000	0.4	1.21	18,000	16,600
New religionists	1,500	2,600	0.0	1.02	4,900	6,500
Jews	4,000	1,800	0.0	1.01	2,000	2,000
Baha'is	0	1,600	0.0	7.26	2,300	3,000
Zoroastrians	0	800	0.0	1.03	800	800
Total population	**2,964,000**	**5,497,000**	**100.0**	**1.02**	**6,208,000**	**6,566,000**

KYRGYZSTAN

in 1936. An independence movement developed in the 1980s that led to the establishment of an independent Kyrgyzstan in 1991.

The area carved out as the Kyrgyz homeland was among the last to be reached by Islam (ninth to 12th centuries), and only in the 19th century did Islam (of the Sunni Hanafite School) become the dominant religion of the country. Thus, the establishment of Islam was quite young when Russian forces invaded the country, bringing with them the Russian Orthodox Church. Christianity did not spread among the Muslim population. Like Christians, Muslims faced persecution under Soviet rule, but they clung tenaciously to their faith through the worst years of Soviet repression. In the years since independence was declared, a secular government has been established, and Islam has to some extent been revived. Subsequently, Islam has attained state recognition and its holy days are public holidays.

By the late 1990s it became clear that some Islamic conservatives, associated with Wahhabi Islam, were becoming active in the country, having found a base within the Uzbek minority. In 1998 a special de-

partment of the government was created to control Wahhabi activities.

Christianity entered the country with the Russians and through the 19th century was largely confined to the Russian communities. It has shrunk considerably since the 1990s, as Russians have returned to their homeland, many not wishing their children to attend schools dominated by the Kyrgyz language. Today, people of Russian heritage constitute approximately 12 percent of the population. Like Sunni Islam, however, the Russian Orthodox Church has gained state recognition, meaning that Orthodox Christian holy days are also state holidays. Today, the Russian Orthodox Church has one diocese that includes Uzbekistan, Turkmenistan, Tadzhikistan, and Kyrgyzstan.

As was the case in other Central Asian countries, the Baptists were the first Protestant/Free Church group to appear in Kyrgyzstan. In 1912, Rodion G. Bershadskii, his wife, and a family named Marafin moved from the Orenburg region of Russia to Bishkek. The congregation they formed became the first of several Baptist churches, and the movement primarily spread among German- and Russian-speaking residents. Since independence the church has been able to operate more openly, but it has also lost many members who have moved back to Russia or the West. During the last quarter of the 20th century, a German-based missionary agency, Licht im Osten, began working very quietly in Kyrgyzstan and neighboring countries. It has been able to operate more openly since independence, and in 1993 it opened a Bible school in Bishkek. In the 1990s, the Baptists, whose churches constitute the Union of Evangelical Christians-Baptists of Russia, began a significant post-Soviet outreach to Kyrgyz people.

Through the 20th century and into the 21st, the Seventh-day Adventist Church has had a small mission in the country, organizing the Kyrgyzstan Conference in 1978. By the mid-1990s, the Conference included 10 churches. There are also a few Pentecostal believers.

Following Kyrgyzstan's independence from the Soviet Union, it formed a State Agency on Religion and adopted a relatively liberal religious law that allowed the registration of a wide spectrum of religious groups. By 2008, over 2000 groups, most local congregations, had registered. Along the way, both the Unification movement and the Church of Scientology registered, but were subsequently denied status and banned in the country. Many among the governing authorities have felt the law was too liberal and have moved to pass new legislation that would greatly restrict registration for new, foreign-based, and small religious groups.

J. Gordon Melton

See also: Church of Scientology; Hanafite School of Islam; Russian Orthodox Church (Moscow Patriarchate); Seventh-day Adventist Church; Unification Movement; Union of Evangelical Christians–Baptists of Russia; Wahhabi Islam.

References

Anderson, John. *Kyrgyzstan: Central Asia's Island of Democracy?* London: Routledge, 1999.

Country Profile: Kyrgyzstan. London: International Institute for the Study of Islam and Christianity, 1994.

Khalid, Adeeb. *Islam after Communism: Religion and Politics in Central Asia.* Berkeley: University of California Press, 2007.

Rashid, Ahmad. *The Resurgence of Central Asia: Islam or Nationalism?* New York: St. Martin's Press, 1994.

L

Laba Festival

The Laba Festival is a Chinese celebration honoring ancestors that seems to have its roots in an ancient harvest festival, held to celebrate a bumper crop in hopes of having another the following year. Over time, however, it evolved into a celebration of one's ancestors. The contemporary festival remains as a building block in the Chinese veneration of ancestors. In the fifth century CE, the government decreed the 8th day of the 12th lunar month (January in the Western calendar) as the day for the Laba Festival.

As Buddhism was transmitted and grew in China, it identified the 8th day of the 12th lunar month as the day that Gautama Buddha gained enlightenment sitting under the Bodhi tree. The accompanying story told of how the Buddha had reached a point of discouragement and hunger in his practice. About to give up the pursuit, he encountered a shepherd girl who shared with him her porridge and rice. Revived and refreshed, he continued his meditation and eventually became enlightened.

Over succeeding centuries, the Buddhist and traditional Chinese celebration merged, and however an individual thought of it, all participated in the essential actions of preparing, sharing, and eating porridge. By the 11th century it became a national holiday. The Chinese ruler would give laba porridge to his underlings and send rice and fruits to the Buddhist monasteries. All families would make porridge, share it with their ancestors and neighbors, and then share it with their gathered family. It would be a good sign when all had eaten their fill and there were leftovers.

The Laba porridge is made with eight (for luck) main ingredients (including beans and grains) and eight supplementary ingredients (for sweetness and flavor). Preparation of the food begins the day before. The offering of the food to the ancestors and the distribution to neighbors (and of course the poor and needy) is done before noon on the eighth and then the family gathers to partake in what can be, depending on the importance placed on preparation, a most delicious meal.

J. Gordon Melton

See also: Ancestors.

References

Latsch, Marie-Luise. *Traditional Chinese Festivals.* Singapore: Greaham Brash, 1984.

Liming, Wei. *Chinese Festivals: Traditions, Customs, and Rituals.* Hong Kong: China International Press, 2005.

The Lady of All Nations

See Our Lady of All Nations.

Lakota, The

The Lakota people fled their homeland in the eastern woodlands of the present-day United States in the winter of 1776 under attack by the Ojibwa, who called them "Sioux," a derogatory name that suggested they were less than human. Learning to integrate horses into their new nomadic lifestyle, the Lakota soon became masters of the Midwestern plains and followed the plentiful buffalo herds for sustenance.

In a treaty at Fort Laramie in 1851, the U.S. government granted the Lakota 60 million acres of land in

Taos Indian man seated, holding peace pipe. (Library of Congress)

the Dakotas, but the westward expansion of European Americans, with its concomitant provocation and warfare, the discovery of gold, and the land-grabbing of the settlers soon whittled away this territory. Even the most sacred Black Hills were soon confiscated. Despite one decisive victory against General George Armstrong Custer (1839–1876), the Lakota could not stand against the brutal force of the U.S. Cavalry, whose most notorious act was the massacre of more than 300 Lakota people at Wounded Knee Creek in 1890.

Despite this tragic history and the loss of some knowledge of their sacred rites, the Lakota remarkably have continued most of their religious traditions. When they could no longer openly rebel against the prohibition of this practice, they hid boys who showed signs of being *wicasa wakan*, holy men or "medicine men," in remote areas of the reservation.

The center of Lakota religion is the sacred pipe, which is an essential part of every ceremony. According to the most fundamental of the Lakota sacred stories, the pipe was given to them generations ago by White Buffalo Woman. A sacred being, White Buffalo approached two young hunters in the form of an extraordinarily beautiful woman. When the older hunter reached out to possess her, he immediately dissolved into a pile of bones. Selfishness, manifested here as lust and greed, killed him. The younger hunter listened carefully as the sacred woman told him to return to his encampment, where his people were starving, and to tell them to prepare to receive her. The next day she presented the gift of the sacred pipe and instructed the people in its use.

Their "peace" pipe centers the Lakota people in the sacred. Lame Deer, an important 20th-century wicasa wakan, summarized the unifying symbols in the sacred pipe: "This pipe is us. The stem is our backbone, the bowl our head. The stone is our blood, red as our skin. The opening in the bowl is our mouth and the smoke rising from it our breath, the visible breath of our people" (Lame Deer 1972, 264). Through its ritual use, the Lakota create unity among themselves and put themselves in harmony with all living beings.

Although the pipe is smoked in many ritual situations, it is the predominant feature of the Inipi, a sweat bath, and the sweat bath is the first stage of almost every ritual undertaking. The sweat house is a small circular enclosure that represents the entire universe—every living creature is said to be somehow represented within. As the Lakota strip off their clothing and enter the Inipi, they strip away all bad thoughts and animosities. Before sitting down in the Inipi around a fire that is heating large rocks, they make a complete circle in a clockwise direction inside the structure—aligning themselves with the movement of the sun. The circle, like the sacred pipe, is a primary symbol for the Lakota people, representing not only the ideal of communal harmony but also the cycles of life.

The wicasa wakan then offers the pipe in the six cardinal directions (east, north, west, south, and toward both the sky and earth), which symbolically centers the people present in the circle. The fire is put out, water is poured on the heated rocks, the flap of the sweat house is closed, and worldly thoughts are driven out of the minds of the participants, who now enter into a spiritual harmony.

The Lakota culture is extremely rich in ritual. There are solitary rituals of initiation, where young men seek their spiritual identities by digging a vision pit on top of a hill, frequently somewhere in their sacred Black Hills. Yuwipi ceremonies allow the Lakota to get in touch with both the spirits of the earth and ancestral spirits, often for purposes of healing.

Sun dances are communal celebrations, lasting several days, which emphasize personal sacrifice for the communal good. The central moment occurs when a few dedicated men are pierced and have rawhide pulled through muscles in their backs or chests; they then hang from a pole in the center of the ritual grounds until the rawhide tears their skin apart. More important than this description, however, is the visionary and ecstatic experiences that occur during this time. And most important is the communal solidarity that occurs during this rite.

Although the ritual positions of men have often been highlighted in Lakota religion, there are corresponding ritual places for women in most rituals. Grandmothers cut their skin in solidarity with their grandsons who are undergoing a vision quest, young girls are the first to touch the tree that will become the center of the sun dance, and mothers frequently purify their homes by burning sage.

The 1990 census numbers the Lakotas (with the various sub-groupings) at 107,321 people, approximately one-third of whom live on reservations and trust lands in South Dakota. Although some Lakota combine their native heritage with Christianity, mostly Roman Catholicism, almost all of those who live on the reservation or in trust lands also participate in Lakota ritual activity, at least occasionally. Although not unanimously supported by the Lakota, the American Indian movement, cofounded in the early 1970s by Russell Means (b. 1939), an Oglala Lakota, did much to renew interest in all Native American spiritual traditions and helped expand awareness of these traditions beyond the boundaries of the reservations.

Thomas V. Peterson

See also: Native American Religion: Roman Catholicism.

References

Brown, Joseph Epes. *The Sacred Pipe: Black Elk's Account of the Seven Rites of the Oglala Sioux.* Norman: University of Oklahoma Press, 1953.

Lame Deer, John (Fire), and Richard Erdoes. *Lame Deer: Seeker of Visions.* New York: Washington Square Press, 1972, 1994.

Powers, William K. *Yuwipi: Vision and Experience in Oglala Ritual.* Lincoln: University of Nebraska Press, 1982.

"Tribute to the Oglala Lakota Sioux: Their History, Culture, and Leaders." http://www.geocities.com/Athens/Acropolis/3976/Hawk.html.

Lalibela

Lalibela is a small town of rural Ethiopia located in the Lasta Mountains some 250 miles north of Addis Ababa, the capital. The town, once the capital of the Zagwe dynasty of Ethiopia, arises from obscurity as the home of one of the most spectacular holy sites in the world—a group of 11 churches, each carved out of the granite bed rock of the area in such a way that their roof is at ground level. The origin of these buildings date to the reign of King Lalibela (r. ca. 1185–1225). Popular legends ascribe the origin of the rulers of Zagwe dynasty to the descendants of the handmaid of the queen of Sheba, though no independent evidence of the claim has come forth.

Legends aside, King Lalibela made a pilgrimage to Jerusalem, a trip that deeply affected his psyche. Immediately upon his return, he renamed the stream that flowed through his capital city, Roha (a name reflecting the red volcanic rock that underlies the town), after the Jordan River and a local hill after the Mount of Olives. He extended his efforts to create an Ethiopian Jerusalem by mandating the carving of the 11 churches. Sculptors carved seven of the churches straight into the cliffs of the mountainside. Their sanctuaries weave deep into the hillside. They then carved the four remaining churches from blocks of the volcanic rock isolated by excavating downward. They connected the churches to each with a number of small passages and tunnels. The entire project took 24 years.

While the trip to Jerusalem appears to have occasioned the church building, Lalibela's hagiography also speaks of a vision that the king had early in his life. According to the story, his older brother, the previous king, tried to poison Lalibela. Instead of dying, while recovering Lalibela was carried by an angel to heaven, during which time he was shown the work he would later accomplish.

Following the completion of the churches, Lalibela abdicated his throne. He became a hermit and spent the remaining years of his life in the holy space he had created. The Ethiopian Orthodox Tewahedo Church later canonized Lalibela and renamed the city in his honor. When the Zagwe dynasty came to an end in the 13th century, political power moved southward to Addis Ababa, but Lalibela remained the spiritual heart of Ethiopian Orthodoxy.

All the churches are still active centers of worship, and Lalibela receives pilgrims year round, with a significant concentration during the two weeks following Christmas. More than 10 percent of the town's residents are priests whose job is to serve the pilgrims and maintain the churches. Most of the churches remain in good condition and much of the original decorations of the interiors survive. Among the many pilgrims, many young women struggling with becoming pregnant make their way to the pool outside the Church of St. Mary, where they spend the night immersed in the pool in hopes of ending their barrenness.

The United Nations Educational, Scientific and Cultural Organization (UNESCO) has ranked the churches the eighth most unique historical site in the world, and the city was placed on the list of World Heritage Sites by the United Nations in 1978.

J. Gordon Melton

See also: Ethiopian Orthodox Tewahedo Church; Pilgrimage.

References

Bidder, Irmgard. *Lalibela: The Monolithic Churches of Ethiopia*. New York: Praeger, 1959.

Gerster, Georg. *Churches in Rock: Early Christian Art in Ethiopia*. London: Phaidon, 1970.

Hirsch, Bertrand. *Lalibela*. Madrid: UNESCO, 1997.

Kidane, Girma, and Elisabeth Dorothea Hecht. *Ethiopia's Rock Hewn Churches of Lalibela*. Stockholm: Royal Swedish Academy of Sciences/Pergamon Press, 1983.

Lambeth Palace

Lambeth Palace is the official London residence of the archbishop of Canterbury, the head cleric of the Church of England. It is located in Lambeth, on the south bank of the River Thames across the river from Westminster. Acquired by the archbishopric around 1200, the oldest remaining part of the palace is the Early English (13th century) chapel. Today the palace is the site of the decennial Lambeth Conferences held every 10 years, when all active Anglican bishops in the world gather for deliberations on the Anglican movement.

The palace played a significant role in a variety of historical events. In March 1378, proto-Reformer John Wycliffe appeared at the palace to defend himself from charges of heresy. During the hearing, a noisy mob gathered with the purpose of saving him; the bishops, divided over his teachings, dodged further confrontation by merely forbidding Wycliffe to speak further on the controversy. During the English peasants' revolt of 1381, rebels attacked the palace and captured Archbishop Simon of Sudbury, who was later executed by them.

In the 17th century, the so-called Lollard's Tower (built in the 15th century) was used as a prison. Reginald Cardinal Pole, who tried to return England to the Catholic fold during the reign of Mary I, lay in state in the palace following his death in 1558. Archbishop William Juxon rebuilt the palace's Great Hall in 1663 after it had been ransacked during the English Civil War.

The palace is also home to the Lambeth Palace Library, the official library of the archbishop of Canterbury and principal holder of records for the history of the Church of England. The library was founded by Archbishop Richard Bancroft in 1610, and now contains material dating as far back as the ninth century.

Around 1850 the adjacent parish church, medieval St. Mary-at-Lambeth, was rebuilt, only to be deconsecrated in 1972. It now serves as the Museum of Garden History.

See also: Church of England; Mary I.

References
Allen, Thomas. *The History and Antiquities of the Parish of Lambeth*. London: J. Allen, 1826.
Cryer, Mary. *A Short History of Lambeth Palace*. Worthing, UK: Churchman Publishing Limited, 1988.
Dodwell, C. R. *Lambeth Palace*. London: Country Life, 1958.
Ducarel, Andrew Coltee. *The History and Antiquities of the Archiepiscopal Palace of Lambeth, from its Foundation to the Present Time*. London, J. Nichols, 1785.

Lantern Festival

The Chinese Lantern Festival had its roots in the ancient past, possibly as early as the Shang dynasty, which came to an end around 1046 BCE. The festival occurs on the 15th day of the 1st lunar month. As the lunar months are calculated from new moon to new moon, the 15th day is coincidental with the full moon. Thus, the Lantern Festival celebrates the light of the first full moon after the New Year celebration heralding the coming spring. At times, the New Year's spring festival would be stretched out for two weeks, with the Lantern Festival bring it to a close. In the days before electricity, the festival celebrated the declining darkness of winter and the ability of the community to move about at night with human-made light. Lanterns were the popular mode of illumining the dark, and villagers used their artistic skills in the making of highly decorative lanterns. In recent times, temples and social groups would hold contests for the most beautiful and interesting lanterns.

The Lantern Festival took on religious connotations from the Daoist concept of three worlds (which was in turn rooted in Buddhist thought). The Lantern Festival celebrated the heavenly realm, while the later Double Seventh Festival celebrated the earthly realm and the Double Ninth Festival the human realm. Another account, from the Han dynasty (202 BCE–220 CE) tied the festival to the North Star. The Lantern Festival honored Ti Yin, the god of the North Star, who was seen as the balanced embodiment of the two opposing universal principles of yin and yang. He never changes his position in the sky.

Over time, as the meaning of the Lantern Festival changed, its essence remained as a way of asserting authority over darkness and a time for the general public to demonstrate its artistic creativity with unique, comical, and beautiful lanterns. The festival has lost much of its purpose with the coming of electricity and

A dragon boat floats down a river during the traditional lantern festival in China. (Everdancer/Dreamstime.com)

continues largely as a time for leisurely frivolity often expressed with fireworks and lion dancing.

One custom has survived, the posing and answering of riddles. This began when scholars amused their students and friends by hanging lanterns outside their homes on which they had written riddles. This action was later generalized into a popular custom of posing riddles as part of the broader celebration.

J. Gordon Melton

See also: Double Ninth Festival; Double Seventh Festival.

References

Kaulbach, B, and B. Proksch. *Arts and Culture in Taiwan.* Taipei: Southern Materials Center, 1984.

Latsch, Marie-Luise. *Traditional Chinese Festivals.* Singapore: Greaham Brash, 1984.

Liming, Wei. *Chinese Festivals: Traditions, Customs, and Rituals.* Hong Kong: China International Press, 2005.

Lao Buddhist Sangha

The Lao Buddhist Sangha is the community of monks that teaches Buddhism throughout the Lao People's Democratic Republic and administers all Buddhist temples. It is independent of similar national organizations in the other four Theravada Buddhist countries (Burma, Cambodia, Sri Lanka, and Thailand), and has been for more than six centuries.

From the time of its establishment during the reign of King Fa Ngum (1316–1373), founder of the Lao Kingdom of Lan Xang in the mid-14th century, the

Lao Buddhist Sangha has enjoyed both political patronage and social prestige. Its role in propagating social morality and respect for the throne gained it the support of Lao kings, who gave generously toward its upkeep.

The legitimation that the Sangha provided to the monarchy was strongest when the institution was unified. This was not always the case. Factions at court or opponents in succession struggles often had their monastic backers. Periodic "purification" of the Sangha was often thus an excuse to re-impose unity.

Little is known about sectarian division within the Sangha in the Kingdom of Lan Xang. We do know from the reports of the first Europeans to visit Viangchan (Vientiane) in the 17th century that much of the wealth of the kingdom was lavished on the monasteries of the capital. When Lan Xang split into rival kingdoms in 1707, the Sangha too was divided.

By the 19th century, when the Lao kingdoms had been reduced to tributary dependencies of Siam, the Lao Sangha reached its lowest point. Recovery was slow under French rule. The reform Thammanyut-nikay School founded by King Rama IV Mongut of Siam (1804–1868) gained a foothold in Laos alongside the dominant Maha-nikay, especially in the south. The sectarian antagonism that resulted divided the Sangha.

The establishment of Buddhism as the state religion by the independent Kingdom of Laos in 1953 greatly enhanced the status of the Sangha. At the same time, however, political and ideological conflict associated with the First and Second Indochina Wars led to increasing politicization, as both the royal Lao government and Communist Pathet Lao attempted to use the Sangha for their own political purposes.

Fearing Communist infiltration of the Sangha, the government attempted to bring it under closer administrative control. Monastic organization was made to parallel that of the civil administration. Officials at each level of the Sangha were appointed by officials at the next highest level—from village, to district, to province. At the apex stood the Sangharaja, elected by senior abbots from a short list acceptable to the Ministry of Religious Affairs.

In response, the Pathet Lao championed religious freedom while encouraging young monks to demonstrate against the government. Overt political activism lost the Sangha some respect, however, and weakened its cohesion. When the Pathet Lao seized power in 1975, the Sangha lost what little remaining independence of action it had retained. Hundreds of monks joined the approximately 300,000 ethnic Lao and tribal minorities who fled abroad (10 percent of the total population). Some established monasteries in their new countries of residence, notably in the United States, France, Australia, and Canada.

The Pathet Lao abolished the sectarian divide and formed instead the Lao United Buddhists Association (LUBA), a member organization of the party-dominated Lao Front for National Construction. The position of Sangharaja was replaced by the president of the LUBA, who required the endorsement of the Lao People's Revolutionary Party (LPRP).

The number of monks initially fell sharply after 1975, but numbers increased as Buddhism again became politically acceptable in the mid-1980s. In the form of the LUBA, the Sangha continues to perform its traditional role of providing education for disadvantaged youth and of providing advice on traditional medicine. As Communism lost its appeal in the 1990s, the LPRP increasingly turned to Lao nationalism for legitimation. Buddhism has been encouraged as central to Lao national culture, and even senior party officials now acknowledge the importance of the Sangha in the life of the nation.

Lao United Buddhists Association
Vat That Luang
Viang Chan (Vientiane)
Laos

Martin Stuart-Fox

See also: Theravada Buddhism.

References

Evans, Grant. *The Politics of Ritual and Remembrance: Laos since 1975*. Chiang Mai, Thailand: Silkworm Press, 1998.

Stuart-Fox, Martin. "Laos: From Buddhist Kingdom to Marxist State." In *Buddhism and Politics in Twentieth-Century Asia,* edited by Ian Harris, 153–172. London: Pinter, 1999.

■ Laos

Despite being a nominally Communist state, Laos, or the Lao People's Democratic Republic as it is officially known, is one of only five countries where the dominant religion is Theravada Buddhism. The other four are Sri Lanka, Burma, Cambodia, and Thailand, the last three of which share a common border with land-locked Laos, its other two neighbors being China and Vietnam. Laos has a population of 6.2 million (2008 estimate), while the capital, Viang Chan (Vientiane), has a little more than half a million inhabitants.

Lowland Lao make up only 55 percent of the country's ethnically mixed population, according to the 2005 census, with another 10 percent comprising closely related Tai minorities. As many as 50 other ethnic groups make up the rest, the largest of which are the Khmu and Hmong. While Lao and Tai are overwhelmingly Buddhist, other ethnic groups are animists of one kind or another. Only a few have been converted to Christianity.

Tradition has it that the Theravada form of Buddhism was introduced into Laos from Cambodia when the Lao Kingdom of Lan Xang was founded in the mid-14th century. In fact, Buddha images and inscriptions excavated near the Lao capital of Viang Chan (Vientiane) indicate that Mon monks propagated the religion there four centuries earlier.

Prior to their conversion to Buddhism, the Lao, like some of the upland Tai tribes in Laos today, worshipped a hierarchy of spirits, ranging from heavenly *thaen* to earthly *phi*. Some phi were territorial, protecting villages, districts, or principalities (*meuang*); others were malignant, causing sickness when they gained entry to a human body.

The ethnic, or lowland, Lao began moving into the middle Mekong basin as early as the ninth century. The Austroasiatic-speaking peoples who were there before

Pha That Luang in Vientiane, the capital of Laos. "The Golden Stupa" is the national symbol of Laos. (iStockPhoto)

LAOS

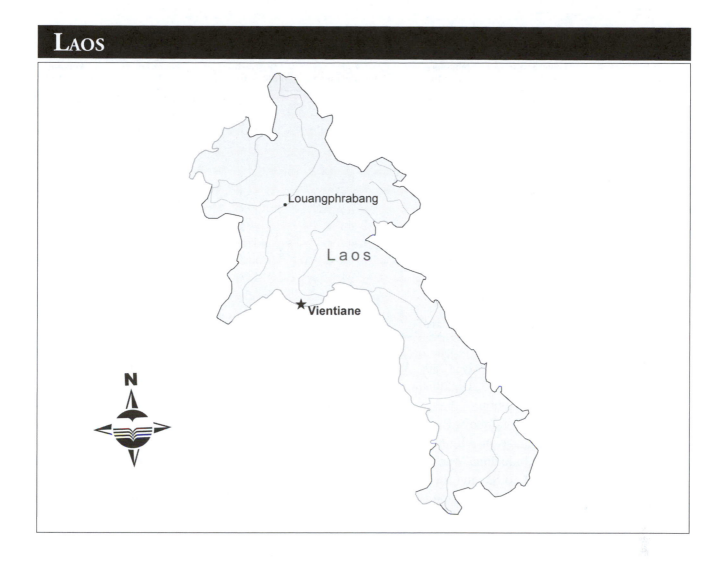

them, now known collectively as Lao Thoeng (Lao of the hill slopes, like the Khmu), worshipped their own array of spirits through a variety of rituals, including animal sacrifice. The most important collective ceremonies required ritual killing of a buffalo. Some Lao Thoeng tribes converted to Buddhism, but most have retained their traditional forms of animism.

Buddhism played a political role, as well as a social and spiritual role, in classical Lao society, for it legitimized the sociopolitical order. Conversely, the government favored Buddhism; the king ruled by right of superior merit (*kamma*), which he demonstrated by his beneficence toward the community of monks, the Lao Buddhist Sangha. By the early 17th century, when the first Europeans reached the Kingdom of Lan Xang, Viang Chan was a regional center for Buddhist

scholarship. After 1707, when Lan Xang was divided, decline set in, and Lao Buddhism reached its nadir after the Thai sack of Viang Chan in 1828.

About that time, new tribal minorities began entering northern Laos from China. Known collectively as the Lao Sung (Lao of the mountain heights), these include the Hmong and the Mien. All of these peoples worship a variety of celestial and terrestrial spirits. The Hmong practice a form of shamanism, while Mien religion has been influenced by Daoism.

Christianity was first taught in Laos by a Jesuit priest who arrived in Viang Chan in 1642. It was not until Laos became a French colony in 1893, however, that Catholicism gained a foothold in the country. Buddhism was then in decline, but few Lao were converted. Buddhism showed signs of recovery after a Buddhist

Laos

Religion	Followers in 1970	Followers in 2010	% of Population	Annual % growth 2000–2010	Followers in 2025	Followers in 2050
Buddhists	1,378,000	3,264,000	52.9	1.58	4,059,000	5,006,000
Ethnoreligionists	990,000	2,388,000	38.7	1.48	2,900,000	3,300,000
Agnostics	90,000	210,000	3.4	1.63	280,000	360,000
Christians	51,300	194,000	3.1	4.61	306,000	393,000
Protestants	9,200	125,000	2.0	4.55	200,000	250,000
Roman Catholics	41,500	52,000	0.8	3.83	75,000	90,000
Independents	300	16,500	0.3	7.80	30,000	50,000
Atheists	28,000	56,200	0.9	1.63	70,000	85,000
Chinese folk	9,000	22,100	0.4	1.63	35,000	50,000
Baha'is	100	14,500	0.2	3.60	25,000	40,000
New religionists	0	11,000	0.2	1.63	15,000	17,500
Muslims	5,000	7,500	0.1	1.62	12,000	20,000
Hindus	0	4,800	0.1	1.62	10,000	16,800
Daoists	0	300	0.0	1.65	1,000	1,500
Total population	**2,551,000**	**6,173,000**	**100.0**	**1.63**	**7,713,000**	**9,290,000**

Institute was established in the early 1930s. When Laos gained independence in 1953, Buddhism again assumed its role as the state religion.

Seizure of power by the Communist Pathet Lao in 1975 had an immediate impact on religion. For two decades during the Second Indochina War, both sides had attempted to enlist the Lao Sangha for their own political purposes. After seizing power, the Lao People's Revolutionary Party (LPRP) quickly reduced the Sangha to a pliant tool for the construction of Socialism. Attendance at Buddhist ceremonies continued, however, and more relaxed policies after the mid-1980s led to a moderate resurgence of Buddhism. Even Politburo members began attending important ceremonies.

According to the 2005 census, there were 84,750 Christians (about two-thirds are Catholic and one-third are Protestant), along with just over 1,800 Muslims and 1,000 Baha'i concentrated in urban centers. This compares with 3.75 million Buddhists and 1.74 million followers of various tribal religions. All religious affairs fall under the supervision of the Ministry of Culture, which serves as a regional center for the World Fellowship of Buddhists. The Sangha also has representation on the Lao Front for National Construction, along with other ethnic, social, and professional organizations.

Freedom of religion is guaranteed under the Lao Constitution, but there have been persistent claims of discrimination against Christians. The Lao government is suspicious of their loyalties abroad, Catholics to the Vatican, and evangelical Protestants to churches in the United States. By contrast, as Communism lost its ideological appeal in the 1990s, the LPRP began to turn to Lao nationalism as a source of legitimation, with Buddhism as its cultural core. Party leaders began attending Buddhist ceremonies, which encouraged greater popular attendance. And when Politburo members died, they were accorded elaborate Buddhist funerals. But though Buddhism has undergone something of a resurgence in Communist Laos, the Sangha still remains under the political control of the ruling party.

Martin Stuart-Fox

See also: Jesuits; Lao Buddhist Sangha; Roman Catholic Church.

References

Bunnag, J. "The Way of the Monk and the Way of the World: Buddhism in Thailand, Laos, and Cambodia." In *The World of Buddhism: Buddhist Monks and Nuns in Society and Culture,* edited by H. Bechert and R. Gombrich. London: Thames & Hudson, 1984.

Morev, Lev. "Religion in Laos Today." *Religion, State and Society* 30, no. 4 (2002): 395–407.

Stuart-Fox, Martin. *Historical Dictionary of Laos.* 3rd ed. Metuchen, NJ: Scarecrow Press, 2008.

Stuart-Fox, Martin. *The Lao Kingdom of Lan Xang: Rise and Decline*. Bangkok: White Lotus Press, 1998.

Stuart-Fox, Martin, and Rod Bucknell. "Politicization of the Buddhist Sangha in Laos." *Journal of Southeast Asian Studies* 13, no. 1 (1982): 60–80.

Laos Evangelical Church

In the 1870s, Daniel McGilvray (1828–1911), an American Presbyterian minister, settled in Chiang Mai, Thailand, from where he made regular trips into northern Laos during the years 1872–1898. As a result the first Protestant groups in Laos came into existence. A second effort to build a Christian presence was begun in the southern part of Laos in 1902 by Gabriel Contesse and Maurice Willy, two Swiss missionaries, who with their wives opened the first missionary station at Sing-Khone. As other missionaries moved into the territory, a few other Protestant churches were founded among a population that was dominantly Buddhist. By 1936 the Swiss missions had led to the formation of some 12 Christian communities. During this time, the first three Gospels were translated and published in Laotian (1908). A complete Bible appeared in 1932. In 1928 the Christian and Missionary Alliance added its strength to the small Christian work.

The two Christian communities, one in the north and one in the south, persisted in spite of the generally hostile environment, the ravages of World War II, and the rise of a secular Marxist government. In 1975 that government moved to curtail all religious activity, both Buddhist and Christian. This negative environment encouraged the two Christian groups to come together in 1982 and form the Laos Evangelical Church, which has subsequently received official recognition as a religious body. In 2008, the church reported some 100,000 members in 300 congregations. It is the second largest religious body in Laos. The church joined the World Council of Churches in 2008; it had previously been an active member of the Christian Conference of Asia.

The church is organized with a presbyterian church order, though it conceives of itself as interdenominational. It has accepted the Apostles' Creed as its doctrinal standard. Since 1965, a number of Laotians have moved to the United States. The Presbyterian Church (U.S.A.) has moved to provide an organization for Laotian Christians through its Lao Presbyterian Council.

Laos Evangelical Church
BP 4200
Vientiane
Laos P.D.R.

J. Gordon Melton

See also: Christian and Missionary Alliance; Presbyterian Church (USA); World Council of Churches.

Reference

Bauswein, Jean-Jacques, and Lukas Vischner, eds. *The Reformed Family Worldwide: A Survey of Reformed Churches, Theological Schools, and International Organizations*. Grand Rapids, MI: William B. Eerdmans Publishing Company, 1999.

Laozi

ca. 500 BCE

Laozi (literally, "Old Master") is a philosopher said to have lived as a contemporary of Confucius (the two met and debated), during the tumultuous Zhou dynasty (1122–256 BCE). The first account of his life was given in Sima Qian's *Shiji* (*Records of the Historian*). Sima states that Laozi was born in Chu, in today's central China, and worked in the Zhou ruler's court as an archivist. On a trip to the western regions (symbolic for being wild and untamed), Laozi met Yin Xi, the Guardian of the Pass. At Yin's request he wrote the *Daodejing*, the classic of the Way and its power, the first text of philosophical Daoism. The *Daodejing*'s pithy style and use of aphorisms makes it one of the most-read books today.

The name Laozi is an honorific title, and the given name of the man to whom it was applied is unknown. Some scholars believe that Laozi is actually a composite figure referring to several individuals. There are a variety of legendary stories about him, but very little grounded information.

Edward A. Irons

See also: Confucius; Daoism.

A huge statue of the ancestor of Taoism, Laozi, in Fujian, China. (Bbbar/Dreamstime.com)

References

Kaltenmark, Max. *Lao Tzu and Taoism.* Trans. by Roger Greaves. Stanford, CA: Stanford University Press, 1969.

Lao-Tse: Life and Work of the Forerunner in China. Gambier, OH: Grail Foundation Press, 1996.

McGreal, Ian, ed. *Great Thinkers of the Eastern World.* New York: HarperCollins, 1995.

Latin American Council of Churches

The Latin American Council of Churches (Concilio Latinoamericano de Iglesias [CLAI]) is an ecumenical organization composed of Protestant-derived churches and movements that was established to promote unity among Christians of the continent. CLAI was officially founded in November 1982 in Huampani, Peru. Today, its headquarters are in Quito, Ecuador.

The ecumenical movement among Protestants in Latin America took shape in the 1960s with the formation of many action groups, networks, and study centers dealing with issues like social justice, popular education, and human rights. These action-oriented structures were generally set up by individuals, not by the churches. Some of these were organized at the regional level. Liberation Theology became an important source of inspiration for ecumenical action. Popular ecumenism was also expressed in "base communities" formed by Christians from different churches who sought a spiritual basis for their social commitment.

However, it took churches in Latin America to decide to create their own regional ecumenical organization. The idea of creating a regional ecumenical body was discussed at a large meeting of Protestant-derived churches four years earlier, in September 1978, at Oaxtepec, Mexico. The emphasis was on a council that would not run programs and projects on behalf of its members, but would accompany the churches and provide space for participation and solidarity. It was also decided that the new council would not deal with project funding. From the beginning, a decentralized model was adopted with secretariats in five sub-regions, in order to be closer to the churches in their daily life and context. The churches and movements that compose CLAI confess Jesus Christ as Lord and Savior, according to the holy scriptures, and seek to fulfill their common calling and mission in unity, to the glory of God. Since 1978, CLAI has also become a focus point for the earlier ecumenical groups and networks.

Initially, CLAI attracted ecumenical Protestants from Spanish-speaking and Portuguese-speaking countries in Latin America whose denominations and service agencies were affiliated with the World Council of Churches (WCC). The specific purpose of CLAI was to promote evangelism as well as social change through its members, which initially included about 100 denominations and service agencies in Latin America. From its beginning, CLAI has depended financially on the WCC funding for its operations.

CLAI is a consultative and coordinating body that has no authority over its members in matters of doctrine, governance, practice, or worship. The main objectives of CLAI are to promote the unity of the people of God, to encourage and support its members in their task of announcing the gospel, and to promote theological and pastoral reflection and dialogue on the Christian mission and witness in the continent. Since 1978, the churches and groups that form CLAI have journeyed together with the intention to restore, in ways that are visible, and through concrete acts of witness and service, the unity they have found in Jesus Christ.

In the context of Latin America in the 1980s and 1990s, the churches affiliated with CLAI were inspired and motivated by the theme of hope and the building of a just and participatory society. CLAI has also focused on promoting peace in some of the conflict areas in the region, for example, in Colombia and Guatemala. The changes that came with the end of the Cold War prompted CLAI to reorganize and strengthen its institutional viability, to bring the organization closer to the member churches, and to widen its approach to churches that previously did not participate in the established ecumenical movement, in particular the Pentecostals.

In May 1980, approximately 650 worldwide "ecumenical Protestant" church leaders participated in a WCC-sponsored event in Melbourne, called the Tenth World Conference on Mission and Evangelism, which explored the place of the poor in the church's worldwide mission. Liberation Theology influenced conference discussions by focusing on questions of power, thus connecting the work of the church with the need to end political and economic oppression. The conference also highlighted the life and work of Jesus Christ as exemplifying Christian solidarity with the poor.

The Conference on Mission and Evangelism and other WCC-sponsored activities are highly regarded by CLAI members, who seek to put the agenda defined in those gatherings into practice in the Latin American context.

In order to achieve its objectives, CLAI maintains specialized programs dealing with the issues of women and gender justice, youth, health, faith, economy and society, global environmental citizenship, liturgy, and communications. Its five sub-regional secretariats are Andean (Bolivia, Chile, Ecuador, Peru); Brazil; Caribbean and Greater Colombia (Colombia, Cuba, Dominican Republic, Puerto Rico, Venezuela); Central America (Costa Rica, El Salvador, Guatemala, Honduras, Mexico, Nicaragua); and River Plate (Argentina, Paraguay, Uruguay).

In recent years, CLAI has given much attention to the Pentecostal churches in Latin America (several of which are now among its member churches) and to the involvement of evangelicals and Pentecostals in society and in politics. Exchanges have been organized between Pentecostal churches and other churches from different countries, for example, between Brazil and Chile.

Another priority of CLAI has been dialogue with confessional families of churches present in the continent, and with its partner churches and organizations in North America and Europe.

As of January 2006, CLAI had a total of 170 full, fraternal, and associate member churches and parachurch organizations in 19 countries, representing about 4.4 million Christians.

Consejo Latinoamericano de Iglesias (CLAI)
Inglaterra N32-113 y Mariana de Jesús
Quito, Ecuador
http://www.claiweb.org/

Clifton L. Holland

See also: Latin American Evangelical Pentecostal Commission; Pentecostalism; Women, Status and Role of; World Council of Churches.

References

Stoll, David. "The Evangelical Awakening in Latin America." Chapter 5 in *Is Latin America Turning Protestant? The Politics of Evangelical Growth.* Berkeley: University of California Press, 1990.

WCC-CLAI website. http://www.oikoumene.org/en/member-churches/regions/latin-america/latin-american-council-of-churches.html.

World Council of Churches (WCC) website. http://www.oikoumene.org/en/member-churches/regions/latin-america.html.

Latin American Evangelical Pentecostal Commission

The Latin American Evangelical Pentecostal Commission (Comisíon Evangélica Pentecostal Lationamericana) is a product of the rapid expansion of Pentecostal churches in South and Central America and the Caribbean since World War II and especially since the emergence of the Charismatic movement in the 1960s. The Charismatic movement introduced the Pentecostal experience into the older mainline churches, especially the Roman Catholic Church. As of 2006, the numbers of Pentecostal believers (many of whom remain active in the older non-Pentecostal churches) have reached as high as 20 percent in some Latin American countries while developing a visible presence in countries such as Peru and Ecuador where Protestantism has traditionally been less successful.

As early as the 1970s, the issue of unity and cooperation among the numerous Pentecostal denominations was raised, and in 1971, an initial meeting between Latin American and North American Pentecostal leaders took place in Buenos Aires. Over the next decades a series of gatherings, more or less formal, occurred. The idea of forming a more permanent structure for such meetings was proposed in 1978 at a gathering of Protestant church leaders at Oaxtepec, Mexico. The World Council of Churches sponsored meetings of Latin American Pentecostal leaders in 1988, 1989, and 1990 at various South American locations. At the meeting in Santiago, Chile, in 1990, the decision was made to constitute the Latin American Evangelical Pentecostal Commission.

The Pentecostal movement, in part due to its rapid growth, was motivated to cooperate in the search for answers to some widespread questions, including the need for better educated clergy, the best use of modern media (radio and television especially), the status and role of women, and the importance of cooperative activity. The development of Pentecostal ecumenism immediately raised issues of the limits of ecumenical endeavors, including contacts with the Roman Catholic Church, non-Pentecostal evangelicals, and the member churches of the World Council of Churches.

The Commission has sponsored meetings at both the national and regional levels and has expanded beyond South America to include member churches in Central America and from various Caribbean Islands, most notably Cuba and Puerto Rico. South America has also become the one area from which Pentecostal churches have joined the World Council of Churches. In most parts of the world, Pentecostal bodies have considered the member churches of the World Council to be too liberal in belief and practice to allow for ecumenical contact.

As of 2006, the Commission included some 70 member denominations representing most South American and Central American countries, plus Mexico, Cuba and Puerto Rico. Five of these denominations are also members of the World Council of Churches. To some extent the Commission sees itself as a temporary body and has called for an even more inclusive and more permanent Council of Pentecostal Churches of Latin America and the Caribbean.

J. Gordon Melton

See also: Pentecostalism; World Council of Churches.

Reference

Van Beek, Huibert. *A Handbook of the Churches and Councils: Profiles of Ecumenical Relationships.* Geneva: World Council of Churches, 2006.

■ Latvia

Latvia is located in northeastern Europe on the east coast of the Baltic Sea. Its area is 24,937 square miles. Total national border length is 1,157 miles. Latvia is bordered by Estonia to the north, Russia to the east, Lithuania to the south, and the Baltic Sea to the west. Its strategic location has made it an international crossroad for trade, commerce, and cultural exchange since ancient times. Vikings followed the "Amber Road" through Latvian territory along the Daugava River to reach Byzantium and the Mediterranean Sea.

Religious life in contemporary Latvia is characterized by the coexistence of several equally strong Christian confessions. The Latvian Evangelical Lutheran Church, the Roman Catholic Church in Latvia, the Orthodox Church in Latvia, the Union of Latvian Old Believer Congregations, the Union of Baptist Congre-

LATVIA

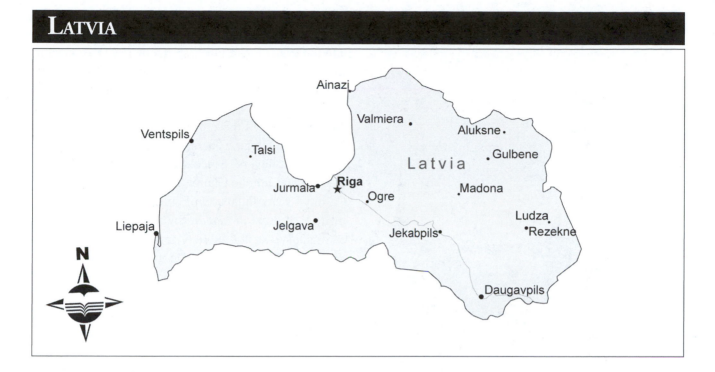

gations, and the Latvian Conference of Seventh-day Adventists have all endured for several centuries.

Although the Latvian government has not officially enumerated which religions it recognizes as "traditional," the Law on Religious Organizations prescribes that religion may be taught in public schools on a voluntary basis by representatives of the Evangelical Lutheran, Roman Catholic, Orthodox, Old Believer, Baptist, and Jewish religions only. Nontraditional denominations may provide religious education in private schools only.

The first information about Christianity in Latvia dates back to the 10th and 11th centuries, when Greek, Danish, and Slavonic missionaries tried to bring the Christian faith to the Baltic lands. In 1071 the first Christian church was built. German missionaries started their work in the 12th century, and around 1164 the monk Meinhard arrived in the land of the Livs. In 1186 Archbishop Hartwig of Bremen appointed Meinhard the first bishop of Livonia.

Nevertheless, progress in his mission was slow, and in 1198, two years after the death of Meinhard, Pope Celestine III (ca. 1106–1198) pronounced the First Crusade to Livonia. In 1199 Pope Innocent III (1161–1216) pronounced the Second Crusade to Livonia. Bishop Albert of Livonia and the Order of the Sword

Brethren conquered the land and baptized the people by the middle of the 13th century. The Roman Catholic Church prevailed from the 13th until the 16th century, when Evangelical Lutheranism entered the region. The beginning of the Reformation in Livonia dates to 1517, when the first advocate of Reformation ideas in Livonia, Andrea Knöpken (1468–1539), arrived in Riga and started to preach in the Church of Saint Peter. In 1554 the Landtag of Valmiera (Wolmar) proclaimed the principle of freedom of faith in all Livonia, and in 1555 the representative of the Master of the Livonian Order signed the Treaty of Augsburg. Since then, the Lutheran Church has been the most influential Christian church in Latvia. Over the next several centuries, the Evangelical Lutheran Church melded with German rule of Latvia. A popular church, however, was born after the proclamation of the independent Republic of Latvia in 1918. In September 1919, the Provisional Regulations for the Evangelical Lutheran Consistories were issued. At the Church Council of 1922 in Riga, Karlis Irbe was elected the first bishop of the Latvian Evangelical Lutheran Church. According to the census of 1935, there were 1,075,641 Evangelical Lutherans in Latvia, out of a total population of 1,950,502. The Soviet occupation of 1940, the German occupation during World War II, and the ensuing years of the

St. Peter's Church in Riga, Latvia, is one of the best samples of Gothic architecture in the Baltics. (Andrey Grinyov/Dreamstime.com)

Soviet regime dramatically changed the religious situation in the Latvian Evangelical Lutheran Church. As a result of decades of religious suppression, in 2008 only 435,000 Latvian Evangelical Lutheran believers remained.

The Roman Catholic Church began its recovery from the Reformation in the city of Latgale and in several congregations in Kurzeme during the period of the Counter-Reformation, late in the 16th century. Poland established its authority in Latgale in 1580, and the Roman Catholic Church dominated there from that time on. In 1918, the Diocese of Riga was renewed. In August 1920 the first Latvian bishop, Antonijs Springovičs, was ordained, and two years later, a Concordat with the Holy See was signed. The separate

province of the Roman Catholic Church consisted of two archdioceses, the Riga Archdiocese (from 1923) and the Liepaja Archdiocese (from 1937). According to the census of 1935, there were 476,963 Roman Catholics in Latvia. As of the beginning of 2008, the Roman Catholic Church in Latvia included the Riga Archdiocese and three dioceses—Liepaja, Rezekne-Aglona, and Jelgava. There were about 500,000 Roman Catholic believers. Since 1991 the highest office in the Roman Catholic Church of Latvia has been held by Cardinal Jānis Pujats. On February 21, 1998, he was made a cardinal *in pectore* by Pope John Paul II; his cardinalate was not publicly revealed until the consistory of February 21, 2001. He was one of the cardinal electors who participated in the 2005 papal conclave that selected Pope Benedict XVI.

The first information about the existence of Orthodox congregations in Latvia dates back to the 11th century. Until the Great Northern War (1700–1721), the Orthodox Church was repressed, but it grew measurably while the country was under the rule of the Russian Empire. In 1850 the Riga Diocese was established. In 1845, reacting to the difficult economic situation and responding to the appeal of Riga's Orthodox Bishop Filaret, the authorities began to force mass conversions of Latvian peasants from the Lutheran Church to the Orthodox Church. The effort culminated in 1846–1847, when the Lutheran Church lost around 113,000 participants. In 1935 there were 174,389 Orthodox believers. Today also in the Orthodox Church there are many converts from other religions and the number of Orthodox believers increased from 190,500 at the beginning of 2000 to 350,000 at the beginning of 2008.

The first groups of Old Believers appeared in Latvia in the second part of the 17th century. In 1659–1660, Old Believers emerged in Kurzeme (the Duchy of Kurland) and in Latgale near Daugavpils. The first Old Believers' church in Riga was built in 1760. Over the next decades, Daugavpils, Rezekne, Jekabpils, and Riga became the most significant centers for Old Believers, the majority of whom belong to the Pomorian, or the priestless, faction. There are around 2,287 Old Believers in Latvia today.

The Baptist movement appeared in Latvia at the end of the 19th century. In 1860–1861, the first congregations were established in Kurzeme, and in 1879

Latvia

Religion	Followers in 1970	Followers in 2010	% of Population	Annual % growth 2000–2010	Followers in 2025	Followers in 2050
Christians	1,200,000	1,567,000	69.9	−0.09	1,614,000	1,468,000
Orthodox	564,000	839,000	37.4	−0.61	880,000	770,000
Roman Catholics	340,000	430,000	19.2	1.01	435,000	410,000
Protestants	373,000	295,000	13.2	0.04	330,000	310,000
Agnostics	736,000	549,000	24.5	−1.96	390,000	250,000
Atheists	394,000	110,000	4.9	−1.16	50,000	30,000
Jews	24,000	9,000	0.4	−1.11	8,000	8,000
Muslims	5,000	6,000	0.3	−0.66	8,000	9,000
Hindus	0	1,000	0.0	1.63	1,500	2,000
Ethnoreligionists	0	300	0.0	−0.64	500	600
Buddhists	0	120	0.0	−0.68	200	400
Total population	**2,359,000**	**2,243,000**	**100.0**	**−0.66**	**2,072,000**	**1,768,000**

Latvian Baptists formed the Union of Baptist Churches. As of the beginning of 2008, there were about 7,089 Baptists in Latvia. In 1896 the first congregation of the Seventh-day Adventist Church was created in Riga. There are around 4,000 Seventh-day Adventists in Latvia now. The Latvian Conference, first organized in 1920, is part of the Baltic Union Conference.

Like the above-mentioned Christian confessions, the Jewish community has also been accepted as a traditional denomination in Latvia. This once large community was virtually destroyed in the Holocaust during the 1941–1944 German occupation of Latvia and now totals only 6,000 persons from which only about 247 persons are active Judaists.

On June 8, 2008, the Agreements between the State and the Latvian Evangelical Lutheran Church, the Orthodox Church in Latvia, the Union of Latvian Old Believer Congregations, the Union of Baptist Congregations, the Latvian Conference of Seventh-day Adventists, the United Methodist Church in Latvia, and Riga Jewish Parish were signed. In 1990–2000, many new religions appeared in Latvia. There are now 2,434 active Jehovah's Witnesses and about 800 active members of the Church of Jesus Christ of Latter-day Saints. Charismatic Christian congregations such as Jauna Paaudze (the New Generation) and Prieka Vests (Message of Joy) claim more than 20,000 members, although precise figures are not available. Pentecostals and Methodists number about 6,000 each, and the New Apostolic Church of North Rhine-Westphalia has about 1,000 members. Muslims number about 334 active members, the International Society for Krishna Consciousness numbers about 500 active members, and Buddhists have about 100 active participants.

Solveiga Krumina-Konkova and Nikandrs Gills

See also: Church of Jesus Christ of Latter-day Saints; International Society for Krishna Consciousness; Jehovah's Witnesses; Latvia, Paganism in; Latvian Evangelical Lutheran Church; Lutheranism; New Apostolic Church; Old Believers (Russia); Roman Catholic Church; Seventh-day Adventist Church.

References

Chernejs, Aleksandrs. *Latvijas Pareizticiga Baznica*. London: Community of St. John, 1996.

Krumina-Konkova, Solveiga, and Nikandrs Gills. "Die Lebendigkeit von Religion und Kirche im gegenwärtigen Lettland." In *Religiöser Wandel in den postkommunistischen Ländern Ost- und Mitteleuropas*, edited by Detlef Pollack, Irena Borowik, and Wolfgang Jagodzinski, 429–477. Würzburg: Ergon Verlag, 1998.

Krumina-Konkova, Solveiga. "New Religious Minorities in the Baltic States." In *New Religious Movements in the 21st Century,* edited by Phillip Charles Lucas and Thomas Robbins, 117–127. New York: Routledge, 2004.

Trups, Henrihs. *Katolu Baznicas vesture*. Riga: Avots, 1992.

Latvia, Paganism in

Ancient Latvian religious beliefs and practice were a regional expression of the ancient Baltic religion practiced throughout the Baltic-speaking world by people speaking Old Prussian, Latvian, and Lithuanian. The highest figure in the ancient Latvian religious system was Dievs, the creator of order in the world and the judge and guardian of moral law who actively took part in the everyday life of farmers. Dievs also was the personification of the sky, similar to the Indian Dyaus and the Greek Zeus. Perkons, the Thunderer, Saule, the Sun, and Meness, the Moon, also occupied important places in the pantheon of Latvian gods. In Latvian religion the Earth was personified and called Zemes mate, the Earth Mother. Latvians also worshipped the forest divinity, Mezha mate, as well as the goddess of human destiny, Laima. Under the influence of Christian-Pagan syncretism, the Virgin Mary has assumed some of the functions of Zemes mate and is worshipped as the goddess Mara.

The most important source for the study of Latvian paganism is folklore, including *dainas*, or short quatrains, of which there are around 2 million, and numerous folktales. Latvian folk religion was largely pushed aside by Christianity, but in the 1920s Ernests Brastins initiated a Latvian national revival movement. He systematized the Latvian way of looking at the world, called Dievturiba. Using the old Baltic form of the Latvian word *tureti*, Brastins coined the term "Dievturis" to name a person who keeps Dievs according to the ancient Latvian tradition. The Dievturi participate in three types of sacred events: rites of passage, seasonal feasts, and regular "praise meetings," or glorification.

The Dievturi have been joined by another form of Paganism, the folklore movement, which started in the 1970s. The ancient worldview and the feelings maintained in Latvian folklore found new expressions here. Adherents of this movement devote most of their attention to singing. Because the several elderly members of the movement are the direct heirs of the oral folk traditions, a larger body of singers rightly call themselves the true exponents of ancient folk wisdom.

Solveiga Krumina-Konkova and Nikandrs Gills

See also: Ethnoreligions; Wiccan Religion.

References

Biezais, Haralds. *Die Göttesgestalt der lettischen der Volksreligion*. Uppsala, Sweden: Acta Universitatis Upsaliensis, 1961.

Biezais, Haralds. *Die Hautgöttinnen der alten Letten*. Uppsala, Sweden: Acta Universitatis Upsaliensis, 1955.

Biezais, Haralds. *Die himmlische Götterfamilie der alten Letten*. Uppsala, Sweden: Acta Universitatis Upsaliensis, 1972.

Janis, Tupesu. "The Ancient Latvian Religion: Dievturiba." *Lituanus* 33, no. 3 (1987).

Latvian Evangelical Lutheran Church

In the beginning of the 16th century the cities of Livonia—Riga, Dorpat, and Revel—were among the first cities in the world to adhere to the teachings of the Protestant Reformation. The first Riga leader of the Reformation, accepting it in 1521, was Andreas Knöpken (1468–1539) from Treptova; he was joined the next year by Sylvester Tegetmeyer from Vittenberg.

Participation in the Reformation by Latvians, as opposed to German-speaking residents of Latvia, occurred primarily in Riga, where almost one-third of the inhabitants were non-Germans. The Reformation became the catalyst for the development of a Latvian written language and book printing. The Bible was translated into Latvian by pastor Ernest Glück, and his edition was published between 1685 and 1694.

In 1628 King Gustavus II Adolfus (1594–1632) of Sweden captured Riga and moved on in 1629 to take control of the southern part of modern Estonia and the Latvian Vidzeme. In Vidzeme the rules of the Church of Sweden (Lutheran) came into force in 1686. The territory of Livonia Latgallia was under the administration of Poland/Lithuania from 1561 to 1772 and given the name Inflantia. During this period Roman Catholicism prevailed in Inflantia. Russia incorporated Vidzeme in 1721, Inflantia in 1772, and the Duchy of Courland and Zemgallia in 1795. In the middle of the 19th century, conversions from Lutheranism to Orthodoxy on a mass scale were forced upon the people of

Vidzeme. There were 113,000 converts (12 percent of all Lutherans) in 1852 alone. A fresh wave of religious experience was brought to the country by the Herrhuterian Brothers, who established the Latvian Church of Brothers, also known as the Moravian Church. The church organized and adopted its rule of order in 1727.

During the period before World War I, the Lutheran Church was divided into the provincial consistories of Vidzeme, Courland, and Riga (until 1890) with a general consistory in St. Petersburg (1832). The German Lutheran nobility of the Baltic provinces obtained special privileges from the Russian czars. In 1914 approximately two-thirds of the 120 Latvian congregations were under noble patronage. With the foundation of the Latvian state in 1918, the patronage was abolished in 1920 and the nobility's rights were transferred to the elected representatives of congregations. In February 1922 a newly formed synod elected Karlis Irbe as the first bishop of the independent Latvian Evangelical Lutheran Church (LELC). He was succeeded by Teodors Grinbergs in 1932.

According to census data, the Lutheran Church embraced 55.15 percent of the Latvian population in 1935. However, at the end of World War II, 131 Lutheran pastors (55 percent) left Latvia to continue their religious mission elsewhere, even as the church in Latvia was being subjected to efforts by the Soviet regime to make it a loyal servant. In the late 1980s and early 1990s the church was one of the first institutions to enjoy spiritual and political freedom. Since 1993 the archbishop of Riga and Latvia has been Janis Vanags. Under his leadership, the LELC has again become an influential ecclesiastical body in the country. In June 2008, the new constitution (Satversme) of the LELC was passed and two new bishops, Einars Alpe and Pavils Brūvers, were elected to the dioceses of Daugavpils and Liepaja, respectively. The largest of the dioceses, Rigas Archdiocese, will be under the supervision of the LECL archbishop, Janis Vanags, who will also continue to be the church's overseeing bishop. In accordance with the new constitution of the LELC the Collegium of bishops was also established. In 1988 LELC had reported 206 congregations. By 1996 that number had increased to 294, with 324,280 members. In 1999 the church experienced a schism when some 400 members who adhered to a conservative interpretation of the Augsburg Confession established the Confessional Lutheran Church. There were about 435,000 Latvian Evangelical Lutheran believers at the beginning of 2008.

Solveiga Krumina-Konkova and Nikandrs Gills

See also: Lutheranism; Moravian Church, European Continental Province of the.

References

Adamovics, Ludvigs. *Dzimtenes baznicas vesture*. Riga, 1927.

Gills, Nikandrs, and Solveiga Krumina-Konkova. *The Latvian Evangelical Lutheran Church at the Threshold of Year 2000*. Religion, State & Society Series, vol. 27, no. 2. Oxford: Keston Institute, 1999.

Kiploks, Edgars. *Evangeliski-luteriskas baznicas sakumi un nostiprinasanas Latvija. Ticibas speka*. Lincoln, NB: LELBA, 1983.

Mesters Eriks. *Latvijas evangeliski luteriskas Baznicas vesture 1944–1990*. Riga: Klints, 2005.

Talonen, Jouko. *Church under the Pressure of Stalinism*. Rovaniemi, Finland: Historical Society of Northern Finland, 1997.

Lausanne Movement

The Lausanne movement (sometimes called simply Lausanne by participants) is a worldwide movement that mobilizes evangelical leaders to collaborate for world evangelization. It takes its name from Lausanne, Switzerland, the site of the first International Congress on World Evangelization in July 1974. Out of the Congress came both the Lausanne Covenant—a summary statement of evangelical beliefs, particularly those related to missions and evangelism—and the Lausanne Committee for World Evangelization, which provides leadership for the movement. The Lausanne movement, however, is one of voluntary cooperation and intentionally has avoided developing a large organizational structure.

Although the International Congress on World Evangelization (ICOWE, later Lausanne I) generally is considered the birthplace of the Lausanne movement, many within the movement also see it as the successor

Billy Graham is regarded as America's foremost modern-day evangelist, having devoted most of his life to spreading the Christian message throughout the United States and the rest of the world. (Shutterstock)

to the world missionary conferences of the late 19th century, and particularly to the 1910 World Missionary Conference held in Edinburgh, Scotland. There is, however, some irony in linking Lausanne and Edinburgh: the latter catalyzed not only a century of evangelistic and missionary activity, but also the modern ecumenical movement. Whether consciously or unconsciously, reaction against the ecumenical movement in general—and specifically against the World Council of Churches, successor to Edinburgh's Continuation Committee—played a role in the establishment of the Lausanne movement.

More directly, the Lausanne movement grew out of the social and political turmoil of the 1960s. In response, the American evangelist Billy Graham (b. 1918) wanted to encourage evangelicals from around the world to unite in global evangelism. Funded largely by the Billy Graham Evangelistic Association, and with the co-sponsorship of the American magazine *Christianity Today* and its editor Carl F. H. Henry (1913–2003), the World Congress on Evangelism (WCE) convened in Berlin, West Germany, in October 1966. Though led and funded largely by Americans, the WCE gathered more than 1,200 participants from 100 countries and offered attendees stories of how the Christian faith was spreading in the non-Western world.

Following the WCE, Graham began to sense a need for a larger conference that would go beyond encouraging global evangelization to actively strategizing about it. Nearly 200 evangelical leaders worldwide agreed when asked by Graham whether they saw a need for such a conference and would be willing to work toward it. The result was the ICOWE, which drew 2,700 delegates from 150 countries, the majority of them from the Global South. When guests, observers, and media representatives were included, the total attendance was around 4,000. *Time* magazine called it "possibly the widest-ranging meeting of Christians ever held."

The impacts of the ICOWE upon evangelical missions and evangelistic efforts, as well as upon evangelicalism in general, were many and far-reaching. Presentations by Ralph D. Winter (1924–2009) and Donald McGavran (1897–1990) of Fuller Theological Seminary's School of World Mission introduced many attendees to the idea of "unreached people groups" for the first time. As a result, over the following decades the missionary-sending strategies of most evangelical missions agencies, and countless churches, shifted from an emphasis on countries to a focus on people groups. The ICOWE also marked a shift by Western evangelicals from viewing those in the Global South as targets of evangelism to seeing them as full partners in evangelism.

Most significant, the ICOWE produced the Lausanne Covenant, a 15-point statement on evangelization affirming that salvation is found through Jesus Christ alone and that the Bible is divinely inspired, truthful, and authoritative. The Lausanne Covenant also acknowledged, among other things, that every culture has value (while repenting of the conflation of gospel and Western culture that often had characterized evangelical missions); that evangelism should be holistic, encompassing the pursuit of both social justice and spiritual transformation without confusing the two; that cooperation among Christians of many traditions, as well as between North and South, is imperative for the task of global evangelization; and that the power of the Holy Spirit is crucial for the work of evangelism, which involves engaging in spiritual warfare. Many churches and organizations subsequently adopted the Lausanne Covenant as a statement of belief.

Yet for all the successes of the ICOWE, the gathering also served to highlight, and even magnify, the differences in culture, theology, and worldview among evangelicals. The Lausanne Covenant's statement "Although reconciliation with man is not reconciliation with God, nor is social action evangelism, nor is political liberation salvation, nevertheless we affirm that evangelism and socio-political involvement are both part of our Christian duty" is particularly instructive here. One area of disagreement has been between those, frequently North Americans, who emphasize the "although" portion of the statement and those (often, but not exclusively, non-Western) who prioritize the "nevertheless" clause. Indeed, many attendees were so unhappy with the Lausanne Covenant that they did not sign it, and even some who did sign articulated criticisms of it, either immediately or over the following years.

For the most part, however, participants expressed a desire for ongoing communication even before the ICOWE had adjourned. The result was the Lausanne Continuation Committee, which met for the first time in January 1975 and renamed itself the Lausanne Committee for World Evangelization (LCWE). Not surprisingly, given the differences of opinion among ICOWE attendees on what constituted "world evangelization," one of the main issues facing the new LCWE was the extent of its mandate: was it limited to evangelism only, or did it extend to other areas addressed in the Lausanne Covenant? In response, the leaders ultimately chose both, stating that the LCWE's purpose was "to further the total biblical mission of the church, recognizing that in this mission of sacrificial service, evangelism is primary." Working groups—originally four, now expanded to eight—were formed the following year to address the various components of the LCWE's mandate. In addition, the Lausanne movement currently includes numerous special interest committees to aid in coordinating the efforts of denominations, ministries, and networks in specialized areas of evangelization (such as among Jews or international students), as well as senior associates who work to address specific issues of importance (such as diaspora populations and evangelism training).

From this desire to see the work begun in Lausanne continue has come a series of consultations, the first of which was held in 1977. Sponsored by one or more of the working groups, consultations convene to address specific issues raised by a Lausanne Congress or the Lausanne Covenant, with the resultant findings usually issued as a Lausanne Occasional Paper. The large Consultation on World Evangelization (COWE) held in Pattaya, Thailand, in 1980 was organized as a collection of 17 mini-consultations, each designed to address how to evangelize a specific religious, socioeconomic, or ideological group. The COWE produced both the Thailand Statement, issued by the consultation as a whole, and a series of occasional papers from each mini-consultation. Enthusiasm among participants in some mini-consultations was so high that they formed ongoing task forces, such as the Lausanne Consultation on Jewish Evangelism.

In the wake of the 1980 COWE, plans were begun for a second International Congress on World Evangelization (Lausanne II). Convened in Manila in July 1989, Lausanne II differed from the first ICOWE in several ways. It was sponsored not by the Billy Graham Evangelistic Association but by the LCWE, and was funded by a wide variety of churches, organizations, and individuals. It was larger and featured participants from more than 170 countries, including many with Communist or Socialist governments. More women, laypeople, and younger leaders were present than at Lausanne I.

In many ways, however, Lausanne II also marked a crisis point for the movement. It was criticized as having an over-representation of leaders from the Global North on the program platform, while many of the Southern leaders at Lausanne I were absent. There was tension over the presence and role of Pentecostal and charismatic evangelicals, who enjoyed a prominence, in presentations as well as attendance, that some saw as overshadowing "traditional" evangelicals. Still others objected that Roman Catholics had been invited to participate. The Manila Manifesto, issued as an elaboration upon the Lausanne Covenant, seemed to lack the impact that its predecessor had wielded. The Lausanne movement also experienced financial difficulties in the aftermath of the Manila Congress, adding to the strain. Finally, the AD2000 and Beyond movement, which received a large boost in Manila, seemed in the 1990s to flourish at the expense of the Lausanne movement.

Thus, the 30th anniversary of Lausanne I in 2004 brought not a third ICOWE, as might have been expected, but the Forum for World Evangelization. Like the 1980 COWE, it was held in Pattaya and consisted of mini-consultations, this time centered on the challenges facing the church in the 21st century. A third ICOWE is planned, however, for Cape Town in October 2010, to address evangelization in light of such challenges as postmodernism and pluralism; an increase in religious fundamentalism of all types; attacks on Christians and Christianity by secular intellectuals and the media; the shift of Christianity's center to the non-Western world; and globalization, particularly as it is manifested through increased urbanization and migration of populations.

The LCWE's stated goal is that Cape Town's expected 4,000 participants from 200 countries represent the church's current cultural, theological, and demographic diversity. Most (nearly 70 percent) are to come from outside Europe and North America. Half will be under age 50, and at least one-third will be women. Ten percent are to be from non-church vocations, including business, government, education, medicine, and the media. In addition, the LCWE is encouraging people worldwide to participate via electronic media such as online discussion groups, chat rooms, and streaming audio and video.

The Lausanne movement can be contacted through its Internet site, http://www.lausanne.org .

Albert W. Hickman

See also: Charismatic Movement; Evangelicalism; Fundamentalism; Globalization, Religion and; Pentecostalism; Roman Catholic Church; World Council of Churches.

References

Chapman, Alistair. "Evangelical International Relations in the Post-Colonial World: The Lausanne Movement and the Challenge of Diversity, 1974–89." *Missiology* 37, no. 3 (July 2009): 355–368.

Douglas, J. D. ed. *Let the Earth Hear His Voice.* Minneapolis, MN: World Wide Publications, 1975.

Douglas, J. D., ed. *Proclaim Christ Until He Comes: Calling the Whole Church to Take the Whole Gospel to the Whole World.* Minneapolis, MN: World Wide Publications, 1990.

Stott, John. "Twenty Years after Lausanne: Some Personal Reflections." *International Bulletin of Missionary Research* 19, no. 2 (April 1995): 51–56.

Stott, John, ed. *Making Christ Known: Historic Mission Documents from the Lausanne Movement, 1974–1989.* Grand Rapids, MI: William B. Eerdmans Publishing Company, 1997.

Leade, Jane

1624–1704

Jane Leade, a blind, elderly widow, became the leader of a Protestant non-Conformist group in London, known as the Philadelphian Society. Named after the sixth of the seven churches in Asia mentioned in Revelation (1:4; 3:7), they believed in the imminence of the millennium and the concept of universal salvation. Leade, a mystic and prophetess, drew on visions of Wisdom, or Sophia, and wrote at least 15 books and treatises, including a spiritual diary entitled *A Fountain of Gardens* that spans 16 years and is nearly 2,500 pages long. Remarkably, nearly all her works were translated into German and Dutch and published during her lifetime.

Jane Leade (nee Warde) was born in 1624 into a gentry family in Letheringsett, Norfolk, England. She wrote that during the family's Christmas celebrations in 1640, in her 16th year, and without any warning, she heard a voice saying, "CEASE FROM THIS, I HAVE ANOTHER DANCE TO LEAD THEE IN; FOR THIS IS VANITY." This sudden conversion experience plunged her into a spiritual turmoil and "nothing was able to give her any satisfaction or rest, or to ease her wounded spirit . . . which continued for the space of three years with very great anguish and trouble." It was then that she was determined to become a "Bride of Christ." She, however, married a cousin, William Leade, whom she described as "pious and godfearing," and they lived in London for 25 years and had 4 daughters (Lead, *Wars of David*, 16).

In April 1670, two months after the death of her husband, Leade started to receive a series of visions of Wisdom, or Sophia, whom she witnessed as "an overshadowing bright Cloud and in the midst of it a Woman." Three days later it gently commanded "Behold me as thy Mother," and six days after came the promise, "I shall now cease to appear in a Visible Figure unto thee, but I will not fail to transfigure my self in thy mind; and there open the Spring of Wisdom and Understanding" (Lead, *Fountain*, vol. 1, 18–21). The vision signaled the beginning of a spiritual relationship with Wisdom that lasted throughout Leade's life.

There was a significant turning point in 1674 when Leade met Dr. John Pordage (1607–1681), who introduced her to the writings of the German mystic Jacob Boehme (1575–1624). Influenced by Boehme's complex ideas, including alchemy, magic, Hermeticism, Gnosticism, and the Kabbalah, Leade believed in the Trinitarian model of the Godhead, though, unusually with Wisdom as an integral part—as a mirror of the Godhead. Leade moved into Pordage's household as his spiritual partner and "mate," where they shared Behmenist ideas and their mystical experiences. In the year of Pordage's death 1681, Leade published her first treatise entitled *A Heavenly Cloud Now Breaking* and she also took over Pordage's group of followers.

Leade's first publication aroused the curiosity of Dr. Francis Lee, a physician, who traveled from Leiden to meet her. He eventually married her widowed daughter, Barbara Walton. He regarded Leade as his "spiritual mother" and when Leade started to go blind, Lee acted as her amanuensis and editor. As she became known from her published writings, interest grew at home and additional Philadelphian groups were formed in Europe. Leade, however, eventually departed from the Behmenist tradition when she upheld the doctrine of apocatastasis, or universal salvation, and promoted the authority of her own revelations that she deemed were from God.

Leade was a millenarian who departed from a cataclysmic portrayal of the apocalypse, believing instead in spiritual regeneration, a quiet revolution that would occur inwardly. Through her emphasis on the spirit, Leade envisioned a future for all through God's love and through personal revelation. She influenced the 18th century cleric, William Law (1686–1761), who wrote *A Serious Call to a Devout and Holy Life* (1729) —one of the central spiritual texts of the 18th century. Leade's millenarian expectations were unusual in that she envisioned the future in a highly gendered way. In common with many people in the 17th century, Leade believed that the Second Coming of Christ was imminent, though her millenarian hopes unusually centered as much on Wisdom's, or Sophia's, return as on Christ's.

In 1704 Leade died. Her epitaph in the non-Conformist cemetery at Bunhill Fields in London reads, "Exuvias Carnis hic deposuit Venerabilis Ancilla Domini JANE LEAD, anno Peregrinationis suae lxxxi" (Here the Venerable Handmaid of the Lord, Jane Lead, has shed the outer garments of her flesh, in the year of her departure [from life], 80).

Julie Hirst

See also: Western Esoteric Traditions.

References

Gibbons, B. J. *Gender in Mystical and Occult Thought: Behmenism and its Development in England.* Cambridge: Cambridge University Press, 1996.

Hirst, Julie. *Jane Leade: A Biography of a Seventeenth-Century Mystic.* Hants: Ashgate, 2005.

Leade, Jane. *A Fountain of Gardens.* 3 vols. London: P. J. Loutherbourg, 1696.

Leade, Jane. *A Heavenly Cloud Now Breaking.* London: privately printed, 1681.

Leade, Jane. *Wars of David.* London: P. J. Loutherbourg, 1700.

■ Lebanon

Lebanon lies on the eastern edge of the Mediterranean Sea, between Israel and Syria, which bounds both its northern and eastern borders. Its 3.8 million people (2004) are overwhelmingly of Arab descent.

Lebanon's ancient and sometimes tumultuous history goes back to the beginnings of civilization. Phoenicians were among the earliest inhabitants of the land, migrating from the Arabian Peninsula about 3500 BCE. Major Phoenician hubs were Baalbek (named for the Canaanite storm god, Baal, who competed for devotees with the Israelite god, Yahweh), Beirut, Byblos, Tyre, and Sidon. The Phoenicians were noted for shipbuilding, and their alphabet also spread throughout the area.

Modern Lebanon was formerly a region that, like Israel, Jordan, and contemporary Syria, was once encompassed by greater Syria. Pompey the Great (106–48 BCE) assumed governorship of the region in 64 BCE and annexed it to the Syrian province, making it part of the Roman Empire. Aramaic replaced the Phoenician language, and Christianity became the primary religion by the fourth century CE.

Christianity spread in the region from Antioch, and the metropolitan of Antioch became one of the most revered leaders in the Eastern church, along with the metropolitans of Jerusalem, Alexandria, and Constantinople. The Council of Chalcedon (451) established Antioch's patriarchal status while delineating the bounds of its territory, sandwiched in between Constantinople and Jerusalem. The Council also issued a statement about the nature of Christ as fully God and fully man, which was considered the orthodox position on the subject by most Christians. However, in the territory of the Antiochean church there were dissenters, called Monophysites, who rejected the Chalcedonian position and formed the Syrian Orthodox Church of Malabar. The Greek Orthodox Patriarchate of Antioch and All the East remains the oldest of the Christian bodies in the region but has lost its position of hegemony in the Christian community, as it has been the major source from which each new movement in the region has gathered its members.

Islam took root in Lebanon in the seventh century. The two most important Islamic groups are the Sunnis and the Shiites. The Sunnis claim they are the only true followers of the faith, believing among other things that the leader of Islam should always be elected, rather than having the title conferred by heredity. Until 1959 they refused to accept the Shia as Muslims because they followed a hereditary caliphate. In the eighth century a minority group of Shiites, the Ismailis, created another division in the Islamic community. The split occurred over who should succeed Ja'far al-Sadiq (d. 165 CE) as the next imam, the leader of the Shia community. The new imam had to be an heir of Muhammad through his son-in-law. However, the next imam Ismail al-Mubarakhad (d. 760) had already passed away. The Ismailis chose to continue the lineage of imams through Ismail and selected one of his sons to lead them. In contrast, the majority of Shiites selected Musa al-Kazem, the younger brother of Ismail, as the legitimate heir. The Shiites continued the lineage until the 12th imam, a child, Muhammad al-Mahdi, disappeared mysteriously in 874.

Many Ismailis (called Fatimids after Ali's wife, and Muhammad's daughter, Fatima) settled in southern Lebanon around the Arameans. Their views influenced the Persians and Arabs of the desert, and their

Young Druze man with pistol and sheathed sword from Mont Liban, Lebanon, ca. 1889. (Library of Congress)

presence laid the groundwork for the rise of popular Islam in Lebanon. Shia and Ismaili leaders, who taught that Ali and his descendants were incarnations of God, contrasted sharply with Sunni perspective and its practices of consensus, by which religious leaders are appointed, not necessarily through blood kinship with the Prophet Muhammad.

Into this situation, another movement arose in the 11th century. A prophet named Muhammad ibn Isma'il ad-Darazi (d. ca. 1019) taught a new doctrine called Durzi, or Druze. He believed the Fatimid leader al-Hakim (996–1021), who suddenly disappeared in 1021, to be divine and awaited his return. Druzism emerged as an esoteric religion of secrecy. Those chosen to have access to the holy scripture abstain from wine, tobacco, and abusive language and observe monogamous marriages. The religion spread northward and

converted several significant nomadic Arab tribes and some of the Sabeans who practiced a Gnostic form of Christianity. Today, the Druzes number about 500,000. Their religious practice is simple, based on five commandments: sincerity, devotion to one another, decrying Paganism, never interacting with the devil, and belief in the unity of al-Hakim.

The Alawis, also called the Nusayris, have a small presence in Lebanon. It is highly probable they took their name from Muhammad ibn Nusayr (d. 868), a noted figure in Basra who in 859 declared himself the 10th imam. A Pagan and Christian substratum underlies this eclectic form of Islam. The Alawis have some religious characteristics that are similar to those of the Ismailis. Their festivals include Christmas and Epiphany, as well as the Muslim feasts of Adha and Ashura and the Persian Nawruz.

In 1516 Ottoman Turks took military control of the entire Mediterranean coast, including the area now called Lebanon. For the next 300 years local leaders operated in relative autonomy and developed religious and economic ties with Europe. In 1831 Muhammad 'Ali Pasha of Egypt (1769–1849) extended his domain northward, encroaching on the debilitated Turkish Ottoman Empire. The Turks, ruling from afar, were prompted to first set up a Christian-based government and then allowed France to step in to protect the Maronite Christians.

When the Ottoman Empire crumbled after World War I, the French declared Lebanon and Syria protectorates, dividing them into two provinces for administrative reasons. Today, the two countries remain separate. However, it was not until 1991 that Syria signed a formal agreement recognizing Lebanon as an independent country, and to this day Syria keeps 20,000 military troops garrisoned there because of the threat of invasion by Israel.

Lebanon became independent in 1943, by which time the groundwork for an unusual system of government had been laid. Lebanon practices a confessional form of government in which representation is based on religious affiliation. According to the National Pact, an unwritten agreement that reflects the country's confessionalism, the president must be a Maronite Christian, the prime minister a Sunni Muslim, the speaker of the Parliament a Shiite Muslim, and the armed forces

LEBANON

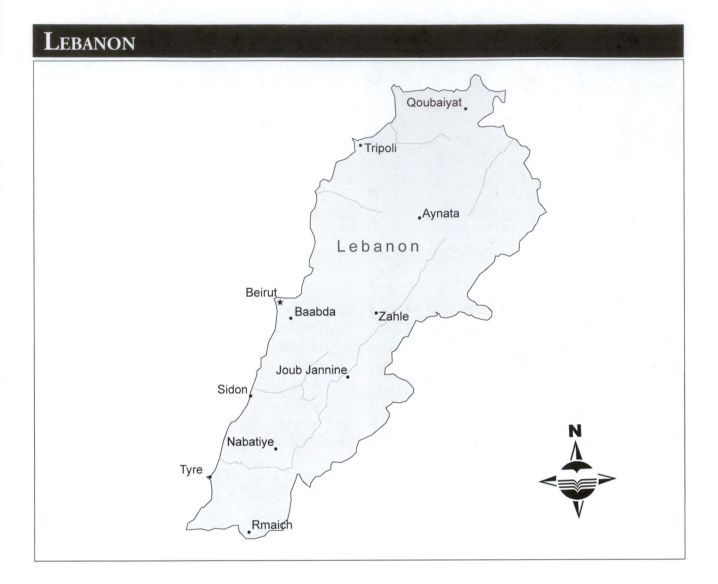

Qoubaiyat

• Tripoli

• Aynata

L e b a n o n

Beirut
★
• Baabda   • Zahle

Joub Jannine

Sidon

Nabatiye

Tyre

Rmaich

N

chief of staff a Druze. The census report from 1932 was used to establish the apportionment of government offices. At the time of Lebanon's independence, there were more Christians than Muslims. Today, 70 percent of Lebanese are Muslim and 30 percent are Christian. Under the 1991 Ta'if Accord, Muslims were given a more equitable representation in the legislature.

In Lebanon, all citizens carry a national identity card encoded with their religion. The government recognizes 5 Muslim sects (Shia, Sunni, Druze, Ismailite, and Alawite), 11 Christian traditions (4 Orthodox, 6 Catholic, and 1 Protestant), as well as Judaism. Religious affiliation defines how Lebanese citizens follow laws for marriage, divorce, adoption, and inheritance. While carrying certain benefits, this system has made

it difficult to establish a nationalist or secular unification. Today, Lebanon is a republic with a president, a cabinet, and a unicameral National Assembly.

Lebanon struggled through civil wars during the late 1970s and 1980s. Although it was once considered (along with Iran) to be among the most modern and Western-oriented countries in the region, this turmoil eroded Lebanon's stability. Problems began when a new census was not conducted even though the Muslim segment of the population had grown considerably. Then in the 1970s, a charismatic leader from Iran, Imam Musa Sadr (1928–ca. 1978), revitalized and mobilized the Lebanese Shiite community. He founded the Movement of the Disinherited in 1974, leading to the formation of AMAL (Afwaj al-Muqawamah al-

Lubnaniyyah), a socio-political network, and a militia force to protect Shiites.

Over the next decade, five events transformed Lebanon: the Lebanese Civil War of 1975, the disappearance of Musa Sadr in 1978 while visiting Muammar Qaddafi in Libya, the Iranian Revolution of 1978–1979, and the two Israeli invasions in 1978 and 1982. Some Shiites nurtured the idea that Musa Sadr was the "Imam of the Disinherited" and the occultation of the Hidden Twelfth Imam. The Israeli invasions impelled the Shiite community to protect itself.

In the 1980s Iran supported AMAL and two other groups, Hizbullah and the Islamic Jihad, all centered on Baalbek, a Shiite community in the Bezaa Valley. AMAL was rejected by some who saw it as too secular. Hizbullah, the Party of God, looked for an Islamic republic and felt empowered by the Koran (58:19–20) to fight against the party of Satan. Hizbullah argued that Western countries wished to banish the Koran, an idea that mobilized frightened Shiite clerics. Hizbullah emerged as an umbrella organization for a number of groups.

Although Lebanon remained neutral in the 1973 Arab-Israeli War, it did grant asylum to 300,000 Palestinians, mostly in the southern area. The refugee camps were makeshift and frequently the site of military action by both Israel and Lebanon. In June 1982, Israeli troops overran Lebanon and took over the Center for Palestinian Studies, administered by the Palestinian Liberation Organization (PLO). The PLO then agreed to leave Beirut under international supervision. On August 23, 1982, a wobbly Lebanese Congress selected Bashir Gemayel (1947–1982) to succeed President Elias Sarkis (1924–1982); however, the Maronite leader was assassinated in a dynamite attack before taking office. In 1988 pro-Israeli Maronite General Michel Aoun assumed the presidency, with Selim al-Hoss, a Muslim, as prime minister. On November 5, 1989, Rene Moawad (1925–1989), a Maronite Christian sympathetic to Muslim issues, was elected president, but like Gemayel he was assassinated before taking office. Aoun, lacking international support, entered self-exile in France.

In December 1990, the National Pact was nullified, and various government and military positions were parceled out to the various groupings (Sunni, Shia, Druze, AMAL, and so on) in accordance with a 6:5 ratio of Christians to Muslims. In April 1992, a new 24-member cabinet was formed, half of whom were Christian and the other half Muslim. Today, the population is about 75 percent Muslim, with the Sunni closely challenged by the Shiites, who are growing in numbers.

The Christian community is historically centered in the Greek Orthodox Patriarchate under the leadership of the patriarch of Antioch and the East, who is selected from the graduates of Maronite College in Rome. The Patriarchate is based in Damascus, Syria, with Lebanese dioceses in Aleppo, al-Hadath, Beirut, Marj Uyun, Tripoli, Tyre, Sidon, and Zahle. As the new century began, there were 300,000 Greek Orthodox in Lebanon (approximately 10 percent of the population).

As Muslims conquered the region in the seventh century, the Maronites, an indigenous Christian sect of uncertain origin, sought refuge in the Lebanese mountains. The words *maron* or *marun* in Syriac mean "small lord." Several theories trace them to John Maron, a fourth- or fifth-century monk, or to Maron of Antioch in the seventh century. In the seventh century, the Maronites separated themselves from the Patriarchate and elected their own bishop while remaining Orthodox in faith and practice. Although the Maronites had originally established ties with the Roman Catholic Church in 1182, they dissolved the relationship in the 16th century. When they re-established contact, it was with the understanding that they would retain the Aramaic, Arabic, and Karshuni (Old Syriac) script for their liturgy. During the Ottoman era (1516–1914), they remained isolated until 1857, when they revolted against the landed gentry, particularly the Druze, insisting on safe passage, political representation, and land ownership.

Today, the Maronite Catholic Church is the largest Christian group in Lebanon. Historically, Maronites have been country dwellers much like the Druze, but they are now scattered throughout the country, with the highest population in the Mount Lebanon area. The Maronites have traditionally dominated the upper socio-economic class. Prior to the civil war, they held 20 percent of the major political posts in Lebanon.

The Greek or Melkite Catholic Church forms the second largest Eastern rite community in Lebanon.

The Melkites split from the Greek Orthodox Patriarchate in the early 18th century and aligned with the Vatican, though continuing to use the Byzantine Greek rite and the Arabic language. The highest official of the church is the patriarch of Antioch, who lives near Beirut. He is elected by bishops in a synod and approved by the pope, who gives him a pallium. Greek Catholics permit icons in their churches but not statues. Most Greek Catholics in Lebanon live in Beirut and the central and eastern parts of the country. Their educational level is higher than that of most of the population, and they are proud of their Arab heritage. They make up approximately 3 percent of the population and as of 1986 numbered about 72,000 people.

The Syrian Catholic Church developed throughout the 17th century in response to successful missionary activity by the Roman Catholic Church among Syrian Orthodox faithful in Syria. Today it is based in Lebanon, and the patriarch resides in Beirut. There were times of conflict within the church over its closeness with the Syrian Orthodox Church of Antioch. The Syrian Orthodox did not accept the orthodox teachings concerning the nature of Christ. Instead, they were Monophysites (sometimes called Jacobites after their early leader, Jacobus Baradaeus [490–578]), who believed Jesus had only a divine nature. The Syrian Catholics, on the other hand, accepted the humanity of Jesus as described in the Catholic creeds.

The Syrian Catholic Church can be said to have begun in 1662, when those Syrians who accepted the Syrian-Antiochene Creed and were oriented to the papacy elected Andrew Akhidjan head of the Syrian Orthodox Church. After his death, the Orthodox and Catholic factions drew farther apart. During the 18th century, Syrian Catholics went underground because the Ottoman Empire favored the Orthodox. Then in 1782, the Syrian Orthodox patriarch declared his allegiance to Rome and fled to Lebanon. The Our Lady of Sharfeh Monastery was founded, and a new line of Syrian Catholic patriarchs was established. In 1885 the Ottoman Empire granted recognition to the Syrian Catholics, and in 1850 the church headquarters were moved to Mardin in southeast Turkey. The church expanded rapidly throughout the region, but due to the massacre of Syrians in World War I, many fled to Lebanon. The current patriarch, Ignasius Musa I Daud, is spiritual leader to 100,000 Syrian Catholics, mostly living in Lebanon, Syria, and Egypt. Worship is conducted in Syrian although most members speak Arabic. The Syrian Orthodox Church has dwindled today to less than 15,000 members.

The Episcopal Church in Jerusalem and the Middle East oversees a small number of Protestants in Lebanon. Their origins can be traced to the late 18th century, when Anglican missionaries traveled the Middle East and North Africa. Permanent work began with Joseph Wolff of the London Churches Ministry. In 1820 he began evangelizing among the Jewish people in the region, and an Anglican bishop was placed in Jerusalem in 1840, from which an Anglican presence throughout the Middle East developed. In 1957 the Diocese of Jerusalem was elevated to an archdiocese, and a separate diocese was created for Lebanon, Syria, and Jordan. That diocese merged into the Diocese of Jerusalem when the present Episcopal Church was formed in 1976.

The National Evangelical Synod of Syria and Lebanon is a Protestant organization now based in Anntelias, Lebanon, with about 4,000 members worldwide. Its history dates back to 1870, when the American Congregationalists turned over their missions to the American Presbyterians. Today it is autonomous. The Reformed Church in America has been working in former Ottoman territory since the 1840s; however, it does not have a large presence, choosing instead to work with other allied groups.

The first Protestant congregation to be recognized by the Ottoman authorities was founded by missionaries sent out by the American Board of Commissioners for Foreign Missions, which had been established in 1823 in Beirut. In 1886 Dr. Daniel Bliss, a Congregational missionary, founded the Syrian Protestant College, which in 1920 became the American University of Beirut. The university's charter reflects its ecumenical ideology, and its educational standards are benchmarks for other universities in the Middle East. (The United States, Great Britain, France, Denmark, and several other countries have dispatched missionaries to Lebanon. After World War I and the demise of the Ottoman Empire two churches were created. The National Evangelical Synod of Syria and Lebanon came together from several small congregations that unified.)

Lebanon

Religion	Followers in 1970	Followers in 2010	% of Population	Annual % growth 2000–2010	Followers in 2025	Followers in 2050
Muslims	874,000	2,542,000	60.1	1.50	2,982,000	3,258,000
Christians	1,516,000	1,414,000	33.5	0.76	1,434,000	1,501,000
Roman Catholics	1,089,000	1,150,000	27.2	0.06	1,200,000	1,250,000
Orthodox	357,000	340,000	8.0	−1.28	320,000	300,000
Independents	10,500	23,500	0.6	1.68	35,000	50,000
Agnostics	37,000	144,000	3.4	0.79	200,000	250,000
Buddhists	0	88,000	2.1	2.14	100,000	120,000
Atheists	12,000	33,000	0.8	1.47	60,000	80,000
Baha'is	1,000	3,700	0.1	1.53	6,000	10,000
Jews	3,000	100	0.1	1.23	2,000	2,000
Total population	**2,443,000**	**4,227,000**	**100.0**	**1.23**	**4,784,000**	**5,221,000**

The Southern Baptist Convention began work in Lebanon in 1921 but did not send missionaries as permanent residents until 1948. The Lebanese Baptist Convention has approximately 450 members. The Near East School of Theology, an ecumenical institution near the American University in Beirut, is supported by the United Church of Christ and the Presbyterian Church (U.S.A.).

The Near East Council is an ecumenical group of churches that dates from 1928. It has two regional councils, the Egypt Intermission Council and United Christian Council of Southeast Asia (Lebanon, Jordan, and Syria). Since 1948 this group has been engaged in helping the Palestinian refugees while serving parishioners throughout the Mediterranean area. Their finances generally come through the World Council of Churches and Church World Service.

Armenians have had a presence in Lebanon for centuries. The main group is a part of the Armenian Apostolic Church, attached to the Catholics of the House of Cilicia, established in 1441. Their number in Lebanon was significantly swelled by refugees from the massacres of Armenians that occurred in Turkey in 1915–1920 (after which many Armenians fled the region altogether), and now Lebanese Armenians number some 175,000. Beginning with the Crusades, Catholic missionaries began to proselytize Armenians, and a few congregations emerged from this work. In 1742 Abraham Ardzivian (1679–1749), an Armenian bishop, converted to Roman Catholicism and organized the Armenian Catholic Church. Pope Benedict XIV (1675–1758) named Ardzivian as the Armenian patriarch. He renamed himself Abraham Pierre I, and Pierre has become a traditional name for the Armenian patriarchs to choose. Under Ottoman rule, Armenian Catholics were subject to persecution because the Ottoman Caliphate wished to relate only to the Armenian Apostolic Church, whose patriarch was headquartered under their control in Constantinople. In 1829 the Armenian Catholic Church was finally recognized officially, and their patriarch moved to Constantinople. In 1928, the patriarch relocated to Beirut, Lebanon, where the church is still based. Today, the Armenian Catholic Church remains in full communion with the Roman Catholic Church.

The Jewish community in Lebanon dates to ancient times, much of its history being recorded in the Jewish Bible, known to Christians as the Old Testament. In the mid-1950s, some 7,000 Jews resided in Beirut, but the majority left during the fighting of 1967. Then the 1975–1976 civil war was conducted around the remaining Jewish neighborhoods, and about 1,800 people left at that time. Today fewer than 100 Jews remain in Lebanon.

Among the Arab population in Lebanon, about 12 to 15 percent are Palestinians who abide in makeshift refugee camps. Their plight is uncertain because they are stateless.

Gail M. Harley and J. Gordon Melton

See also: American Board of Commissioners for Foreign Missions; Armenian Apostolic Church (See of the Great House of Cilicia); Armenian Catholic Church; Episcopal Church in Jerusalem and the Middle East; Greek Orthodox Patriarchate of Antioch and All the East; Ismaili Islam; Maronite Catholic Church; Melkite Catholic Church; National Evangelical Synod of Syria and Lebanon; Presbyterian Church (USA); Reformed Church in America; Roman Catholic Church; Southern Baptist Convention; Syrian Catholic Church; Syrian Orthodox Church of Malabar; United Church of Christ; World Council of Churches.

References

Chamie, J. "Religious Groups in Lebanon: A Descriptive Investigation." *International Journal of Middle East Studies* 11 (1980): 175–187.

Deeb, Laura. *An Enchanted Modern: Gender and Public Piety in Shi'i Lebanon.* Princeton, NJ: Princeton University Press, 2006.

Deeb, M. "Shi'a Movements in Lebanon: Their Formation, Ideology, Social Basis, and Links with Iran and Syria." *Third World Quarterly* 10, no. 2 (1988): 683–698.

Esposito, John L. *The Straight Path.* Oxford: Oxford University Press, 1998.

Grafton, David. *The Christians of Lebanon: Political Rights in Islamic Law.* London: Tauris Academic Studies, 2004.

Khairallah, I. A. *The Legal Status of Non-Moslem Communities in the Near East, and Especially Syria and Lebanon.* Beirut: American University of Beirut, 1965.

Mackey, Sandra. *Lebanon: A House Divided.* New York: W. W. Norton, 2006.

Roberson, Ronald G. *The Eastern Christian Churches—A Brief Survey.* 5th ed. Rome: Edizioni Orientalia Christiana, Pontificio Istituto Orientale, 1995.

Saad-Ghorayab, Aaal. *Hizbu'llah: Politics and Religion.* London: Pluto Press, 2002.

Salam, Nawaf A., *Options for Lebanon.* London: I. B. Tauris, 2005.

Shaery-Eisenlohr, Roshanack. *Shi'ite Lebanon: Transnational Religion and the Making of National Identities.* New York: Columbia University Press, 2008.

Lectorium Rosicrucianum

Lectorium Rosicrucianum is one of the main international Rosicrucian bodies. In the 1920s Jan Leene (1896–1968) and his brother Zwier Wilhelm Leene (1892–1938) became the most important Dutch leaders of the California-based Rosicrucian Fellowship of Max Heindel (Carl Louis von Grasshoff, 1865–1919). On August 24, 1924, the Leenes had a spiritual experience that today is regarded as foundational for the Lectorium Rosicrucianum. The Leenes, however, who were joined in 1930 by Henny Stok-Huyser (1902–1990), only declared their independence from the Rosicrucian Fellowship in 1935, when they established the Rozekruisers Genootschap. After the premature death of Zwier Wilhelm in 1938, Jan Leene (using the pen name Jan van Rijckenborgh) and Mrs. Stok-Huyser (who signed herself as Catharose de Petri) began to put in writing their version of Christian Gnosticism, derived from Hermeticism, the 17th-century Rosicrucian movement, and the mystical Christianity of Jacob Boehme (Jakob Böhme) (1575–1624). Jan van Rijckenborgh translated Boehme's *Aurora* into Dutch, and in 1941 he was instrumental in founding a Jacob Boehme Society.

When the Nazis entered Holland, the movement was banned, its possessions confiscated, and its temples razed. Several members, including Jews, died in the concentration camps. In 1945, after the difficulties of the war period, the movement adopted the name Lectorium Rosicrucianum. Interested in Catharism, the two founders met Antonin Gadal (1871–1962) in France in 1948, Gadal being one of the key figures of the Cathar revival in the 20th century. At the same time, the Lectorium Rosicrucianum began to spread, first to Germany, where the Rosicrucian myth was as important as the Cathar tragedy was in southern France, and then to a number of other countries. The most notable success came, however, after the death of Van Rijckenborgh (1968) and Catharose de Petri (1990), who were replaced by an International Spiritual Directorate.

There are currently approximately 15,000 adherents of the Lectorium Rosicrucianum, who are divided into 14,000 "pupils" and about 1,000 "members," who await admission as pupils. After a waiting period of one or two years, the new pupils engage in a way of life in which a "balance of the consciousness" is regarded as essential. From this engagement stems a quest for mental, emotional, and physical purification, supported by vegetarianism and abstinence from alcohol, tobacco, and drugs. There is also a clear disapproval of other "unhealthy influences," in particular those allegedly transmitted by television, as well as the more subtle influences coming from the world of the dead (the "reflective sphere").

In order to understand the Lectorium, it is crucial to look at it in the light of Gnosticism and the Cathar tradition. The Lectorium proposes a classical Gnostic dualism between the divine, or static, world and the natural, or dialectic, world, which the true God did not create. As French historian Antoine Faivre has pointed out, it is difficult to reconcile this dualism with the Rosicrucian tradition, since the latter, at least in its 17th-century origins, is not dualistic.

The dialectic world includes both the living and those among the dead who, in a state of dissolution, await a new incarnation. Van Rijckenborgh's idea of subsequent incarnations can only be understood within the framework of his notion that each person is a microcosm. Popular theories of reincarnation, whereby it is the personal ego that reincarnates, are refuted by this view. The only function of the ego is in fact to sacrifice itself in favor of the "resurrection of the original soul," the divine spark at the heart of the human microcosm. The so-called living, having forgotten their divine origin, are imprisoned in this dualist and absurd world, although they also possess a "spirit spark atom," which manifests itself in many as remembrance (or pre-remembrance) and nostalgia. The path to transfiguration, as envisaged by the Lectorium, is a seven-stage process that aims to awaken that divine spark, called "the rose of the heart," and to lead humans back to their original condition, the divine world of the Light.

One finds here the classical picture common to all forms of Gnosticism. This version of Gnosticism, however, organizes itself according to a language and according to models often derived directly from the Cathar tradition. Over and above the debate on the role of Gadal and his neo-Catharism, the dualism of the Lectorium and that of the Cathars are remarkably similar. Both are not only evident in their cosmology but they also inspire human behavior. Human actions can further the progress toward transfiguration or, conversely, can further imprison humans in the dialectic field.

The Lectorium provides an esoteric interpretation of both soul and body, as well as presenting a vision of the future. Here, one finds texts on the coming of a false Christ and an Armageddon that could be regarded as either millennialist or apocalyptic. These labels are misleading, however, since apocalyptic language is used purely within a Gnostic context and is largely symbolic.

Lectorium Rosicrucianum
Bakenessergracht 11-15
2011JS Haarlem
The Netherlands
http://www.lectoriumrosicrucianum.org
Massimo Introvigne and PierLuigi Zoccatelli

See also: Reincarnation; Western Esoteric Tradition.

References

Faivre, Antoine. "Les courants ésotériques et le rapport. Les exemples de la Nouvelle Acropole et de la Rose-Croix d'Or (Lectorium Rosicrucianum)." In *Pour en finir avec les sectes. Le débat sur le rapport de la commission parlementaire*, edited by Massimo Introvigne and J. Gordon Melton, 233–254. Paris: Dervy, 1996.

Van Rijckenborgh, Jan. *The Coming New Man.* Haarlem, the Netherlands: Rozekruis-Pers, 1957.

Van Rijckenborgh, Jan. *Elementary Philosophy of the Modern Rosecross.* Haarlem, the Netherlands: Rozekruis-Pers, 1961.

The Way of the Rosecross in Our Times. Haarlem, the Netherlands: Rozekruis-Pers, 1978.

Legion of Mary

The Legion of Mary is a Roman Catholic lay organization that found its inspiration from its veneration of the Blessed Virgin Mary and its program in a wide variety of charitable activities and support of local parishes.

From its original organization in Ireland, it has spread to most parts of the Catholic world, and is now the largest lay Catholic organization in the church. As such it is a major building block of the world network of Marian devotion that is so much a part of the Roman Catholic infrastructure.

The Legion was founded in 1921 by Frank Duff (1889–1980), a layperson in Dublin, Ireland. Duff promulgated a two-pronged set of objectives, one being the spiritual formation of its members through devotion to the Virgin Mary and the other the building of the church through social service in the members' community.

The devotional life adopted by Legion members is derived from the writings of Saint Louis Marie Grignion de Montford (1673–1716). De Montfort was the author of the classical Marian text, *True Devotion to Mary*. Among de Montford's many accomplishments was the founding the Company of Mary, a religious order organized for evangelism under the protection of the Blessed Virgin.

Members of the Legion are directed into a wide variety of activities, from visitation of the sick and aged, assisting with religious education programs, and nurturing parish activities to evangelism and outreach beyond the parish. A local spiritual director named by the parish priest directs member activities.

Local chapters (praesidia) are associated with other praesidia in a hierarchical organization at the regional (curia), national (senatus), and international levels. The international headquarters remains in Dublin. The life of the organization is described in the organization's *Official Handbook*. The work spread to the United States in 1931 and the first praesidium was formed at Roton, New Mexico.

Legion of Mary
De Montfort House
Morning Star Avenue
North Brunswick Street
Dublin 7
Ireland
http://www.legion-of-mary.ie/

J. Gordon Melton

See also: Mary, Blessed Virgin; Roman Catholic Church.

References
Bradshaw, Robert. *Frank Duff: Founder of the Legion of Mary.* Bayshore, NY: Montfort Publications, 1985.
Official Handbook of the Legion of Mary. Dublin, Ireland: Concilium Legionis Mariae, 1953.

Legion of Mary/Maria Legio (Kenya)

The largest secession from the Roman Catholic Church anywhere in Africa is the Legion of Mary, or Maria Legio, with estimates of membership in the 1990s ranging between 250,000 and 2 million. This movement was founded by Catholic Luos in western Kenya in 1963, the year of Kenya's independence, and its name has been changed many times. The first leaders were laypeople, Simeon Mtakatifu Ondeto (1920–1991) and Gaudensia Aoko. A young woman whose two children had both died on the same day, Aoko began to denounce witchcraft and sorcery. Ondeto established a church headquarters on the holy mountain of Got Kwer, to be called the New Jerusalem and the Holy City, and Aoko began to perform mass baptisms. Within a year, the church had 100,000 members. It retained much Catholic liturgy, including the Latin language, a celibate leadership, an order of nuns, and titles like pope and cardinal.

The Legion of Mary also had many characteristics shared by other spiritual churches, including healing rituals; deliverance from witchcraft; prophecies and spirit possession; prohibitions on dancing and consuming pork, tobacco, and alcohol; and the practice of polygyny.

Aoko left the Legion of Mary in 1965 to found her own movement after Ondeto began restricting the role of women in general and her own role as charismatic founder of the movement in particular. Although she later returned, she was soon again head of her own Legion of Mary movement. Another woman, called Mama Maria, is believed to be the black incarnation of the Virgin Mary. Adherents to the Legion of Mary, called Legios, hold that Mama Maria had returned to heaven in 1966 and is the spiritual mother of Ondeto.

The church initially spread only among Luos but has become increasingly multiethnic, reaching many

Members of the Legion of Mary Catholic movement study in a small classroom in Togo. (Pascal Deloche /Godong/Corbis)

parts of Kenya, Tanzania, and other East African countries. In Tanzania, a schism from this church six months after its founding there resulted in the forming of the African Catholic Church. Ondeto, who died in 1991 and was buried at Got Kwer, became known as Baba Messias and is regarded by some Legios as Christ reincarnated in Africa, the living God. Pope Timothy Blasio Ahitler (1941–1998) was the next leader until his death, when a new pope, Maria Lawrence Pius Jairo Chiaji, was appointed. Since 2004 the leader has been Pope Raphael Titus Otieno.

Allan H. Anderson

See also: Reincarnation; Roman Catholic Church; Spirit Possession; Witchcraft.

References

Anderson, Allan H. *African Reformation: African Initiated Christianity in the Twentieth Century*. Trenton, NJ: Africa World Press, 2001.

Hastings, Adrian. *The Church in Africa, 1450–1930*. Oxford: Clarendon, 1994.

Schwartz, Nancy. "Christianity and the Construction of Global History: The Example of Legio Maria." In *Christianity as a Global Culture*, edited by Karla Poewe. Columbia: University of South Carolina Press, 1994.

Lemba

The Lemba are an African people residing primarily in South Africa and Zimbabwe who claim that they are descendants of Jews who have retained their faith even though cut off geographically for many centuries from the center of Judaism. According to traditions alive among the Lemba, they came from Sena, which many believe to have been a town north of Jericho in Israel. Others claim that the Lemba descend from attendants of the biblical King Solomon, who is said to have traveled to Zimbabwe (the Ophir of 1 Kings 9:28) in search of gold. The Lemba allege that when Solomon returned to Israel (the Hebrew Bible does not record any trip of Solomon to southern Africa), some of his men remained behind, that they intermarried with the Zimbabweans, taught the Africans to worship only one god, Mwali, and spread Jewish traditions through southern Africa.

The Lemba have been associated with the Venda culture that reached its peak in the 14th and 15th centuries, the time of Great Zimbabwe, the magnificent medieval stone city. The Lemba were of lighter skin than the Venda and served as physicians, artisans, and iron workers. They were also somewhat feared as sorcerers. They served with the Venda in wars against the British at the beginning of the 20th century.

A variety of traditional Lemban practices point to Jewish roots (though some claim that they were picked up from Muslim sources). The Lemba circumcise male children. They bury their dead in accordance with Jewish traditions. They hold the first day of the new moon sacred and shave their heads to commemorate it. They do not eat pork. They practice animal sacrifice, but only circumcised males may sacrifice animals for food. Women engage in purification ceremonies after menstruating or giving birth. Non-Lemba women are allowed to marry into the group, but Lemba men may be expelled if they marry outsiders.

It should be noted that the Lemba identify themselves as Jews culturally, but not necessarily religiously. They follow a set of traditional cultural practices that signify to them their Hebrew ancestry. While some have converted to the Jewish faith in recent years, many are Muslims or Christians. It is their unique ritual practices that separate them from their neighbors as a chosen people.

In a series of studies, the first published in 1996, the Lemba claims have been supported by research on their chromosomes, which were discovered to have a remarkable likeness to those of other Semitic people. More important, the researchers found that many Lemba men carry in their male chromosome a set of DNA sequences that is distinctive of the *cohanim,* the Jewish priests believed to be the descendants of Aaron.

There are some 50,000 to 70,000 members of the Lemba community. Their uniting symbol is a flag with a Star of David and the Elephant of Judah. They are not to be confused with Beta Israel, the Jews of Ethiopia.

The Lemba Community
c/o Lawrence R. Matandu
Makereni School
PO Box 249
Mberwengwa
Zimbabwe

J. Gordon Melton

See also: Beta Israel; Judaism.

References
The Jews of Africa." http://www.mindspring .com/~jaypsand/lemba.htm. Accessed June 15, 2009.
Le Roux, M. *The Lemba: A Lost Tribe of Israel in Southern Africa.* Pretoria, South Africa: Unisa Press, 2003.
Parfitt, Tudor. *Journey to the Vanished City.* New York: St. Martin's Press, 1993.
Parfitt, Tudor. *The Thirteenth Gate: Travels among the Lost Tribes of Israel.* London: Weidenfeld & Nicolson, 1987.
Thomas, M. G., T. Parfitt, D. A. Weiss, K. Skorecki, M. le Roux, N. Bradman, and D. B. Goldstein. "Y Chromosomes Traveling South: The Cohen Modal Haplotype and the Origins of The Lemba—The 'Black Jews of Southern Africa.'" *American Journal of Human Genetics* 66 (2000): 674–686.

Lent

For six weeks preceding Easter, Christians have customarily undergone a time of penitential prayer, fasting, and almsgiving to prepare for the celebration of the resurrection of Jesus on Easter Sunday. This season of Lent originally was also a time of preparation for baptismal candidates and those separated from the church who were rejoining the community.

In Latin, this season of the Christian year was called *Quadragesima,* referring to 40 days. With the shift to the vernacular in the Middle Ages, the word "Lent" replaced the Latin term. Lent originates from

Pope Benedict XVI spreads ashes on the head of an unidentified prelate during the celebration of Ash Wednesday mass at the Basilica of Santa Sabina, in Rome, February 17, 2010. Ash Wednesday marks the beginning of Lent, a solemn period of 40 days of prayer and self-denial leading up to Easter. (AP/Wide World Photos)

the Teutonic root for "long" and refers to spring, the time of the year when days lengthen.

Originating in the fourth century of the church, Lent spans 40 weekdays, reminiscent of the 40 days of temptation Jesus spent in the wilderness preparing for his ministry. In the Western church tradition, Lent begins on Ash Wednesday and ends on Holy Saturday, the last day of Holy Week before Easter Sunday. Since Sundays celebrate the resurrection of Jesus, the six Sundays that occur during Lent are not reckoned part of the 40 days of Lent, and are referred to as the Sundays "in" Lent. In the Eastern Orthodox tradition, the 40 days are calculated differently: the fast begins on Clean Monday, Sundays are included in the count, and it ends on the Friday before Palm Sunday.

Ash Wednesday, the seventh Wednesday before Easter Sunday, begins Lent. The name refers to the ancient practice of drawing a cross of ashes in oil on worshippers' foreheads to demonstrate humility before God and mourning for death caused by sin.

There are other holy days within the season of Lent: Clean Monday, the first day of Lent in Eastern Orthodox Christianity; the fifth Sunday of Lent, which begins Passiontide; Palm Sunday, the beginning of Holy Week; Spy Wednesday, recognizing the day Judas betrayed Jesus; Maundy Thursday, in commemoration of the Last Supper; and Good Friday, commemorating Christ's crucifixion and burial.

Throughout Lent, observers fast, though not necessarily every day. Historically, there has been great divergence regarding the nature of the fast. However, traditionally days of fasting include taking one meal a day, in the evening. Often fasters will abstain from meat and wine and the common law of the Roman Catholic Church is to avoid meat, milk, cheese, and eggs. During Holy Week, or at least on Good Friday, it is common to restrict the diet to dry food, bread, salt, and vegetables. Consequently, the custom arose of giving eggs for Easter to break the fast, thus leading to the concept of Easter eggs.

During Lent, the color purple or violet dominates the sanctuary to denote the pain and suffering of Jesus and the world under sin. As well, purple is also the color of royalty, befitting Jesus as the King. Some churches use gray for Ash Wednesday or for special days of fasting and prayer. Commonly, church traditions change the sanctuary colors to red for Maundy Thursday. Good Friday and Holy Saturday may utilize black to symbolize the powers of sin and death overcome by the death of Jesus.

Kevin Quast

See also: Easter; Eastern Orthodoxy; Holy Week; Roman Catholic Church.

References

Adam, Adolf. *The Liturgical Year: Its History and Its Meaning after the Reform of the Liturgy.* New York: Pueblo, 1981.

Regan, Patrick. "The Three Days and the Forty Days." *Worship* 54 (1980): 2–18.

Senn, Frank. *Christian Liturgy: Catholic and Evangelical.* Minneapolis, MN: Augsburg Fortress, 1997.

Stevenson, Kenneth. *Jerusalem Revisited: The Liturgical Meaning of Holy Week.* Washington, DC: Pastoral Press, 1988.

Stookey, Laurence Hull. *Calendar: Christ's Time for the Church.* Nashville: Abingdon, 1996.

Talley, Thomas J. *The Origins of the Liturgical Year.* 2nd ed. Collegeville, MN: Liturgical Press, 1991.

Thurston, Herbert. "Lent." In *The Catholic Encyclopedia.* Vol. 9. New York: Robert Appleton Company, 1910.

■ Lesotho

The African nation of Lesotho, formerly known as Basutoland, is a small country completely surrounded by the Republic of South Africa. Its 11,720 square miles of land is home to 2,100,000 people, almost all of the Sotho linguistic/ethnic group. Sesotho, a bantu language spoken by the Sotho people, is the official language of Lesotho.

Lesotho had its origins in the expansionist policy of Shaka (ca. 1787–1828), a Zulu leader who in 1818 began the process of uniting the Zulu and other Bantu people of southern Africa. Although he conquered the land making up present-day Natal and Transvaal (South Africa), some groups united against him. The most effective counterforce was brought together by Moshoeshoe I (1786–1870), the head of the Bakwene group among the Sotho people. Moshoeshoe united several Sotho and Zulu groups against Shaka. They established themselves along the Drakensberg Mountains and were able to defend themselves in the intermittent wars through the 1820s. Then, in 1839, they had to stave off expansion by the Boer settlers in South Africa. This generation of warfare gave the very different groups a sense of nationhood.

Following the discovery of diamonds in South Africa, British missionaries convinced Moshoeshoe I that the safest course was to allow the British to establish a protectorate over the land to keep back further Boer encroachments. This land remained separate even after the British took control of South Africa. When South Africa attained independence, Britain promised the new country that the several protectorates, including Lesotho, would eventually be integrated into the new republic. However, Britain went back on its agreements after South Africans broke relations with the British government and instituted apartheid. A Constitution was published in 1965, and in 1966 the present state of Lesotho was born.

Christianity entered the country in 1833 when Reformed missionaries representing the Paris Mission of the Reformed Church of France accepted the invitation of Moshoeshoe I to work in the land. They began the process of converting believers from the indigenous religions, the most prominent being a polytheistic faith built around deities (*medimo*) and ancestral spirits (*balimo*). Today less than 10 percent of the population continue to follow the traditional religions.

The work of the Paris Mission led to what is today known as the Lesotho Evangelical Church (Kereke ea Evangeli Lesotho), the second largest religious group in the land. After becoming an autonomous body in 1964, the church has adopted a strong ecumenical outlook, playing a leading role in the formation of the Christian Council of Lesotho and joining the World Council of Churches, the World Alliance of Reformed Churches, and the All Africa Conference of Churches.

The British presence in the region led to the introduction of the Church of England in 1875. Anglican work was organized as a diocese in 1950 and attached to the Church in the Province of South Africa. The Roman Catholic Church entered Lesotho in 1862, when Missionary Oblates of Mary Immaculate from France started a mission. Their work was turned over to Canadians in 1930. A major step in moving beyond the missionary era occurred in 1957 with the consecration of the first indigenous bishop. The Roman Catholic Church is now the largest religious body in the country. The Lesotho Episcopal Conference was founded in 1972.

In the decades leading to World War I, a number of other missionary-minded churches also established work in Lesotho. Many of these, such as the Dutch Reformed Church and the Methodists, came from bases previously established in South Africa. In 1892 the U.S.-based African Methodist Episcopal Church launched a missionary enterprise. During the 20th cen-

LESOTHO

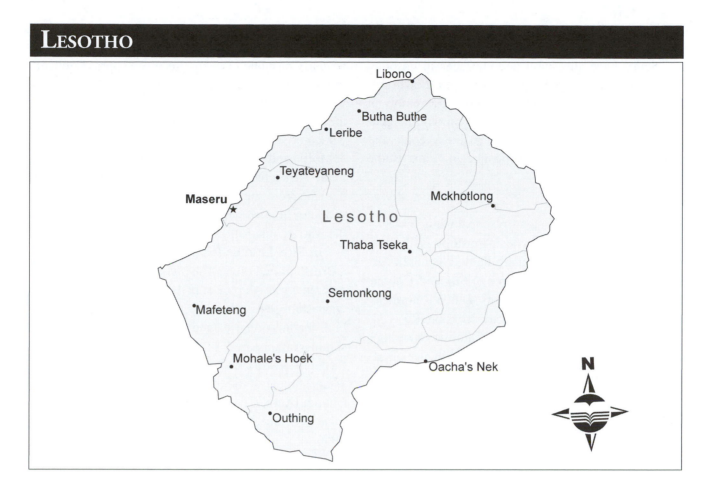

Lesotho

Religion	Followers in 1970	Followers in 2010	% of Population	Annual % growth 2000–2010	Followers in 2025	Followers in 2050
Christians	842,000	1,889,000	92.4	1.14	2,094,000	2,234,000
Roman Catholics	411,000	990,000	48.4	1.27	1,100,000	1,220,000
Protestants	224,000	379,000	18.5	1.69	450,000	550,000
Independents	62,000	218,000	10.7	2.04	270,000	300,000
Ethnoreligionists	181,000	130,000	6.4	−0.88	80,000	60,000
Baha'is	8,700	18,500	0.9	0.99	26,000	45,000
Agnostics	500	4,000	0.2	0.99	6,000	10,000
Hindus	60	1,300	0.1	0.99	2,000	3,000
Muslims	530	1,000	0.0	0.99	1,600	2,500
Atheists	100	600	0.0	1.00	1,000	2,000
Total population	**1,033,000**	**2,044,000**	**100.0**	**0.99**	**2,211,000**	**2,356,000**

tury, the hegemony of the older missionary bodies was challenged by the movement of numerous representatives from the African Initiated Churches (AICs), most from South Africa and other nearby countries. Prominent among these are the Zion Christian Church and the Apostolic Faith Mission of South Africa. Lesotho has also contributed its own additions to the AIC movement with such churches as St. Paul's Church of Africa and the Moshoeshoe Berean Bible Readers Church. Several hundred AIC groups are operating in Lesotho, a number of which have formed the African Federal Council of Churches.

The Seventh-day Adventist Church, the Jehovah's Witnesses, and the Church of Jesus Christ of Latter-day Saints have all established churches in Lesotho. The Baha'i Faith began a period of rapid growth following the formation of its first spiritual assembly in 1964. Islam has made little progress among the general population, but some Asian businesspeople and their families established a mosque in Butha-Buthe in 1972.

J. Gordon Melton

See also: African Methodist Episcopal Church; All Africa Conference of Churches; Apostolic Faith Mission of South Africa; Baha'i Faith; Church in the Province of South Africa; Church of England; Church of Jesus Christ of Latter-day Saints; Dutch Reformed Church; Jehovah's Witnesses; Paris Mission; Reformed Church of France; Roman Catholic Church; Seventh-day Adventist Church; World Alliance of Reformed Churches; World Council of Churches; Zion Christian Church.

References

The Catholic Church of Lesotho at the Hour of Independence. Maseru, Lesotho: Lesotho Catholic Information Bureau, 1966.

Fitzgerald, Emma (Rose Leone), and Julienne Lefebrve (Michel-Archange). *Go Forth . . .: A History of the Sisters of the Holy Names of Jesus and Mary Missionaries in Lesotho.* Congregational Leadership Team of the Sisters, 2002.

Frisbie-Fulton, Michelle. *Historical Dictionary of Lesotho.* Methuen, NJ: Scarecrow Press, 2003.

Machobane, L. B. B. *Basotho Religion and Western Thought.* Edinburgh: Centre of African Studies/ Edinburgh University, 1995.

Mohapeloa, J. M. *From Mission to Church: Fifty Years of the Work of the Paris Evangelical Missionary Society and the Lesotho Evangelical Church, 1933–1983.* Morija, Lesotho: Morija Sesuto Book Depot, 1985.

Lesotho Evangelical Church

The Lesotho Evangelical Church originated in one of the initial thrusts into the heart of Africa by the Paris Mission (of the Reformed Church of France). In 1833 three missionaries—Thomas Arbousset, Eugène Casalis, and Constant Gosselin—received approval to work in the region from King Moshoeshoe I (1786–1870), who at the time was attempting to gather the people of the region into a kingdom. At first the missionaries' work proceeded smoothly. The initial station was erected at Morija and others were opened thereafter. However, South Africa had its eyes on the region, and to protect his land from the superior South African forces, Moshoeshoe aligned with Britain. The mission suffered in the warfare that followed and was eventually closed.

In 1868 Lesotho (then called Basutoland) became a British protectorate. The mission reopened and soon entered a growth phase. In 1887 a theological school was established. The first synod (*seboka*), including both the missionaries and the active graduates of the seminary, appeared in 1898. Natural development through the first half of the 20th century led to the establishment of the independent Lesotho Evangelical Church (Kereke ea Evangeli Lesotho) in 1964. Basutoland became the independent nation of Lesotho in 1966.

In 1970 the prime minister of Lesotho, Leabua Jonathan (1914–1987), suspended the country's Constitution. He attempted to rule as a dictator, pushing aside King Moshoeshoe II (138–1996). The church identified with the opposition. The church newspaper had published detailed stories of life under the new government; its editor was assassinated. The church's vice president was forced to leave the country. Jonathan was overthrown in 1986, but his successor did little better and an unstable period ensued until free elections were held 1993 and a new king was enthroned.

In 2005, the Lesotho Evangelical Church reported 340,500 members in 64 congregations. The highest legislative body is the general synod. The church is a member of the World Alliance of Reformed Churches and since 1956 of the World Council of Churches.

Lesotho Evangelical Church
PO Box 260
Old Busstop, Casalis House
Maseru 100
Lesotho

J. Gordon Melton

See also: Reformed Church of France; World Alliance of Reformed Churches; World Council of Churches.

References

Bauswein, Jean-Jacques, and Lukas Vischner, eds. *The Reformed Family Worldwide: A Survey of Reformed Churches, Theological Schools, and International Organizations.* Grand Rapids, MI: William B. Eerdmans Publishing Company, 1999.

Van Beek, Huibert. *A Handbook of the Churches and Councils: Profiles of Ecumenical Relationships.* Geneva: World Council of Churches, 2006.

Leuenberg Church Fellowship

See Community of Protestant Churches in Europe.

Liberal Catholic Church

The Liberal Catholic Church was established in Great Britain in 1916 as a result of the reorganization of the British Old Catholic movement, introduced into the country by Bishop Arnold Harris Mathew (1852–1919). Bishop Mathew, consecrated to the episcopate of the Old Catholic Church of Utrecht in 1908, presided over an English mission that was independent of the See of Utrecht from 1910 to 1915. In these same years, many English members of the Theosophical Society joined the Old Catholic mission. Following a disagreement with Mathew on the doctrinal themes of the Theosophical movement, the great majority of the mission's members decided to rebuild it on more liberal lines. They sought greater attention to the forms of mysticism that in those decades were influencing Anglicanism and the modernist Christian circles.

The resulting church, formerly known as Old Catholic Church in Great Britain, took the name of Liberal Catholic Church in 1918. The church achieved worldwide growth through the missionary activity of its first presiding bishop, James Ingall Wedgwood (1883–1951), and in many countries it developed through a sort of symbiosis, sometimes highly conflictual, with the Theosophical Society.

A primary spokesman and doctrinal reference for the church is Charles Webster Leadbeater (1854–1934). Already a prolific writer of Theosophical books, Leadbeater was consecrated as a bishop in the Liberal Catholic Church by Wedgwood. He applied his method of extrasensorial perception to the study of Christian sacraments, and his findings were gathered in 1920 in a volume entitled *The Science of the Sacraments.* The liturgy of the Liberal Catholic Church was compiled by Bishops Wedgwood and Leadbeater and, with some minor changes, is still in use today. This liturgy follows in the tradition of Old Catholicism, which preceded the modern liturgical movement in creating a vernacular liturgy on Tridentine lines.

Today the Liberal Catholic Church is present in about 50 countries and organized into ecclesiastical provinces, each directed by a regional bishop and endowed with significant autonomy. The main administrative body is the General Episcopal Synod, headed by a presiding bishop. One of the American churches maintains a site for the international church with links to various dioceses around the world. The total membership in the world is estimated at around 30,000. The current presiding bishop is Most Reverend Graham Wale, elected in 2005.

The unique qualities of the Liberal Catholic Church make it difficult to place in the larger landscape of religious communions. Drawing as it does on both Anglican/Catholic Christianity and Theosophy, it has enjoyed a response from people worldwide while at the same time being somewhat marginalized from mainstream religious movements. Adapting the liturgical heritage of the Old Catholic world, the church offers a wide liberality of thought, in which Theosophical interpretations of Christian doctrines coexist with a search for common Christian roots, studies on psychological and inner effects of the sacraments, and so on. These very different heritages generate a certain level of inner tension within Liberal Catholicism that attracts many spiritual searchers who are confused by the constraints of ancient theologies and mystical doctrines. Some observers foresee that this church, unlike many other "small churches" from the independent Catholic and Orthodox traditions, will perpetuate its well-defined raison d'être and be able to keep a cadre of faithful who are limited in number but clearly defined among spiritual searchers.

Our Lady and All Angels Liberal Catholic Church
Right Reverend William Downey. Regionary Bishop (USA)
1502 East Ojai Avenue
Ojai, CA 93024
http://kingsgarden.org/English/Organizations/LCC
    .GB/LCC.html

Andrea Cassinasco

See also: Old Catholic Church of the Netherlands; Roman Catholic Church; Western Esoteric Tradition.

References

Cooper, Irving S. *Ceremonies of the Liberal Catholic Church*. London: St. Alban Press, 1964.

Norton, Rovnbert. *The Willow in the Tempest: A Brief History of the Liberal Catholic Church in the United States of 1917–1942*. Ojai, CA: St. Alban Press, 1990.

Platt, Warren Christopher. "The Liberal Catholic Church: An Analysis of a Hybrid Sect." Ph.D. Diss., Colombia University, 1982.

Tillett, Gregory J. *The Elder Brother*. London: Routledge and Kegan Paul, 1982.

■ Liberia

The African nation of Liberia is located on the continent's Atlantic coast between Sierra Leone and Cote d'Ivoire. The country also shares a northern border with Guinea. It is home to 3.3 million people, overwhelming members of the several groups that settled the land prior to the 19th century. About 2.5 percent are descendants of the African Americans who migrated there beginning in the 1820s.

The contemporary state of Liberia was originally settled by two major groups of African people, the Kru-speaking groups in the west and the Mende-speaking people (of which the Mandingo are the best known) in the east. There are more than 30 distinct ethnic groups in the country. The coastal region was visited by the Portuguese beginning in the 15th century and became one area from which slaves were collected.

At the end of the 18th century, Liberia was part of Sierra Leone, the area set aside by the British for the relocation of people liberated by their antislavery activity. However, in 1821 the American Colonization Society, an organization devoted to relocating African Americans to Africa, purchased what became Liberia and founded the port city of Monrovia. Some 20,000 African Americans, descendants from various peoples of western Africa, moved to Liberia. They had by this time been largely Americanized and were not well received by the Native inhabitants. Several American scholars coauthored a new Constitution for what in 1847 became the independent country of Liberia. The descendants of the repatriated African Americans formed a ruling elite in the country, a development that has affected its politics to the present.

Although the tropical climate kept many people away from Liberia, the land was rich in resources—from rubber trees to oil and diamonds. The United States intervened on several occasions to protect American economic investments in the country. In 1979 an economic crisis led to a political coup that saw the assassination of President William Tolbert Jr. (1913–1980) the following year. The new president, Samuel Doe (1950–1990), was able to hold office only by suppressing the opposition, a policy that culminated in civil war in 1990. U.S. troops moved into Liberia but were unable to prevent the assassination of Doe. Following his death, a new coalition government that included former rebel leaders was instituted, but fighting continued for another six years. A six-person ruling council assumed authority while elections were planned. Those elections, held in July 1997, led to the overwhelming victory of the National Patriotic Party and its leader, Charles Taylor (b. 1948).

A small contingent in northern Liberia did not accept the elections and continued armed resistance to Taylor's government. Additional opposition soon appeared in the south, and in 2003 the United Nations charged Taylor with war crimes and issued a warrant for his arrest. Taylor subsequently resigned and went into exile in Nigeria. In 2006, Nigeria rejected their asylum and Taylor was arrested. His trial is a continuing pro-

Group of students and staff at a Presbyterian mission school in Liberia, ca. 1895. (Library of Congress)

cess as this encyclopedia goes to press. Meanwhile, elections in 2005 brought a new president, Ellen Johnson Sirleaf, into office. The country remains unstable.

Liberia was included in the territory assigned to the Roman Catholic diocese of Cape Verde as early as 1533, but Catholic priests did not settle in the region. Thus, Christianity's real entrance began with the arrival of the African Americans, many of whom were Christians. Lott Carey and Colin Teague (ca. 1780–1839), remembered as the first African American Christian missionaries, were commissioned by the Richmond (Virginia) African Missionary Convention. Before sailing in 1821, Carey, Teague, and their families and accompanying travelers assembled and constituted themselves as a Baptist congregation. On their arrival on Providence Island, Liberia, they reconstituted them-

selves as the Providence Baptist Church, their meeting place being on high ground overlooking the Mesurado River. Three years later they dedicated a building as their the first sanctuary. The building was the first church building erected in Liberia. Their work was supplemented by that of white missionaries sent by the American Baptists, but eventually the work was assumed by the Lott Carey Baptist Foreign Missionary Convention and the National Baptist Convention, U.S.A.

The Methodist Episcopal Church (now an integral part of the United Methodist Church) sent their first missionary, Melville Cox (1799–1833), to Liberia in 1833. His death only three months after landing portended the problems that most future missionaries would have with the climate. The mission almost died

Liberia

Religion	Followers in 1970	Followers in 2010	% of Population	Annual % growth 2000–2010	Followers in 2025	Followers in 2050
Ethnoreligionists	690,000	1,775,000	41.2	1.96	2,500,000	4,113,000
Christians	432,000	1,764,000	40.9	2.71	3,015,000	5,965,000
Independents	136,000	650,000	15.1	2.94	1,100,000	2,300,000
Protestants	120,000	565,000	13.1	3.37	1,000,000	1,970,000
Roman Catholics	23,700	230,000	5.3	4.00	450,000	1,030,000
Muslims	262,000	691,000	16.0	2.31	1,085,000	2,020,000
Agnostics	0	67,500	1.6	1.39	140,000	300,000
Baha'is	3,000	13,000	0.3	2.30	30,000	60,000
Atheists	0	600	0.0	2.30	1,000	2,000
Total population	**1,387,000**	**4,311,000**	**100.0**	**2.31**	**6,771,000**	**12,460,000**

in the late 19th century but was revived with the support of several prominent bishops. Until the 1920s, attention was focused on the city of Monrovia and the former Americans there, but in 1925 a major work opened at Ganta in the north, and in 1948 another was initiated at Gbarnga. The Liberian work remains organized as a conference within the United Methodist Church (UMC). The UMC work has been supplemented by the work of the African Methodist Episcopal Church and the African Methodist Episcopal Zion Church, which entered Liberia in 1873 and 1876, respectively.

The Presbyterian Church in the U.S.A. (now an integral part of the Presbyterian Church [U.S.A.]) also began work in Liberia in 1833. Like the Baptists, the Presbyterians began their work among the African Americans, a number of whom were appointed as its missionaries. The last of the missionaries were commissioned in 1887, and the Presbytery of Liberia became an independent body in 1928. This was among the first Liberian churches to ordain women. It is now related to the Cumberland Presbyterian Church.

Two years after the Methodists and Presbyterians arrived, John Payne, an American missionary with the Episcopal Church, began to work in Liberia. In 1851 he was named the first missionary bishop of Liberia. Payne quickly escaped the confines of Monrovia and opened work among the Grebo people at Cape Palmas in 1836. Also notable in the Episcopal Church's history was the career of Samuel Ferguson (1847–1916), the first black person appointed to the episcopacy. During his long tenure as bishop (1884–1916), Ferguson devel-

oped an extensive educational system, capped with Cuttington College and Divinity School. The Episcopal Church in Liberia remains a diocese in the Episcopal Church (U.S.A.).

The United Lutheran Church, now an integral part of the Evangelical Lutheran Church in America, began work in 1860 some miles inland from Monrovia along the Saint Paul River. It remained a small effort until the end of the century, when David A. Day (1851–1897) and his wife Emily arrived to assume control. They directed an expansive program that led to the establishment of stations across the country. The Lutheran Church in Liberia was organized in 1948, and in 1967 it was given full control over the extensive medical and education work. It has retained a close relationship with U.S. Lutherans.

Several other Christian groups entered Liberia in the 20th century and have since become as strong as the older churches. These include the Seventh-day Adventist Church, the Fire-Baptized Holiness Church of God (an African American Holiness church), the Assemblies of God, and the Pentecostal Assemblies of the World. The Church of the Lord (Aladura) is the largest of several African Initiated Churches.

The Roman Catholic Church attempted to establish work in Monrovia in the 19th century but was blocked by the predominantly Protestant religious establishment. However, in 1906, missionaries of the Society of Africa Missions—a French Catholic organization founded in 1856 in Lyons by Bishop Melchior de Marion Brésillac (1813–1858)—began work among the Kru-speaking peoples; later, they expanded to other

LIBERIA

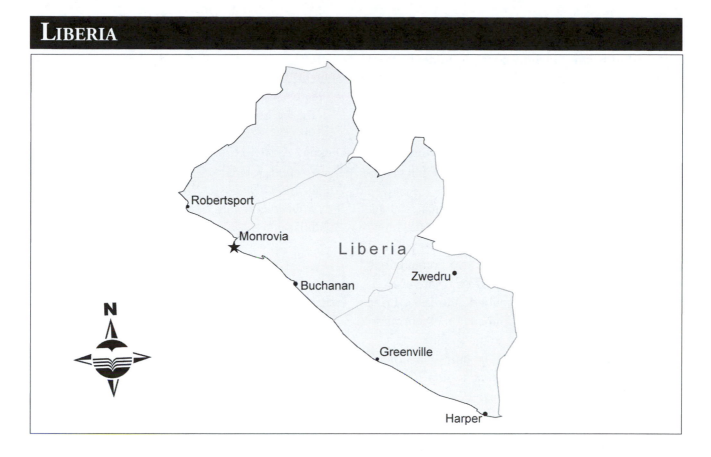

areas. At the end of the 20th century the Catholic Church was the second largest church in the country, second only to the Liberian Baptist Missionary and Educational Convention.

Ecumenical relationships have been strong in Liberia, with the larger Protestant churches sharing support of a variety of educational and charitable institutions. The Liberian Council of Churches is associated with the World Council of Churches (WCC) and includes WCC members such as the United Methodist Church, the Episcopal Church, the Lutheran Church in Liberia, and the Presbytery of Liberia. More conservative churches have formed the Association of Evangelicals of Liberia, which is affiliated with the World Evangelical Alliance.

In spite of the strong Christian missionary activity, less than half of the Liberian people have become Christian. The largest segment, some 40 percent, retain their traditional religions, especially in those parts of the country farthest from the coast. Traditional religions have as major themes the veneration of ancestors, the working of magic, and the prominence of religious

functionaries, popularly known as medicine men, who establish their authority by the demonstration of a spectrum of mystical competence—healing, divining, prognosticating, and so on. Several of the ethnic groups host a spectrum of secret societies to which outsiders are not privy.

Much animosity has been directed toward the traditional religions because of charges that some of their followers practice ritual killing. Ritual killings, in which various body parts are removed from victims and subsequently used in rituals, appear to occur sporadically, though the lack of reliable information is a problem in assessment (the same situation is encountered in other countries). Reports of ritual killing in Liberia may be related to incidents during the civil war of the 1990s, in which faction leaders sometimes ate the body parts of their rivals. One had himself filmed consuming such body parts. In recent years, common criminals have been charged with killing people and selling their body parts.

Islam, primarily of the Sunni Malikite School, has come into the country from the north. The Mandingo have been especially instrumental in the spread of Islam, and the Vai, among other groups, have largely converted to Islam. Muslims now constitute the third largest religious community in the country, making up approximately 16 percent of the population. The national center for Sunni Islam is the National Muslim Council, headquartered in Monrovia. There is also a measurable following of the Ahmadiyya Muslim movement, and both the Qadiriyya and Tijaniyya Sufi orders are strong.

The National Muslim Council participates along with the Liberian Council of Churches in the Interfaith Mediation Council, an effort to counter political forces that attempted to place the two communities in opposition. In 1997 the All Africa Conference of Churches awarded its first Desmond Tutu Peace Prize to the Interfaith Mediation Council for its efforts to bring peace and reconciliation to the country.

The civil war and continuing unrest in Liberia have not made it an attractive home to new religions, and few have attempted to colonize it.

J. Gordon Melton

See also: African Methodist Episcopal Church; African Methodist Episcopal Zion Church; Assemblies of God; Church of the Lord (Aladura); Cumberland Presbyterian Church; Episcopal Church; Evangelical Lutheran Church in America; Liberia Baptist and Educational Convention; Lutheran Church in Liberia; Malikite School of Islam; National Baptist Convention, U.S.A.; Pentecostal Assemblies of the World; Presbyterian Church (USA); Qadiriyya Sufi Order; Roman Catholic Church; Seventh-day Adventist Church; Tijaniyya Sufi Order; United Methodist Church; World Council of Churches; World Evangelical Alliance.

References

Cason, J. W. "The Growth of Christianity in the Liberian Environment." Ph.D. Diss., Colombia University, 1962.

Ellis, Stephen. *The Mask of Anarchy: The Destruction of Liberia and the Religious Dimension of an African Civil War.* New York: New York University Press, 1999.

Gifford, P. *Christianity and Politics in Doe's Liberia.* Cambridge: Cambridge University Press, 1993.

Kane, J. Herbert. *A Global View of Christian Missions.* Grand Rapids, MI: Baker Book House, 1971.

Oldfield, J. R. *Alexander Crummell, 1819–1898 and the Creation of an African/American Church in Liberia.* Lewiston, NY: Edwin Mellen Press, 1990.

Olukoju, Ayodeji. *Culture and Customs of Liberia.* Westport, CT: Greenwood Press, 2006.

Wulah, Teah. *The Forgotten Liberian: History of Indigenous Tribes.* San Jose, CA: AuthorHouse, 2005.

Liberia Baptist and Educational Convention

Baptist work in Liberia has a distinctive history because of its unique place in the emergence of African American Christianity. In 1819, Lott Carey (ca. 1780–1828) of Richmond, Virginia, was able to purchase his freedom from slavery. By all accounts an unusual man, Carey had been converted to Christianity in 1813 and in 1815 had convinced the triennial Convention of American Baptists (now a constituent part of the American Baptist Churches in the U.S.A.) to approve the formation of the African Baptist Missionary Society. The Convention's Foreign Mission Board appointed Carey and Collin Teague (ca. 1780–1839) to work in Liberia. They would be joined by their wives, Teague's son, and another couple, and these seven were to form a seed colony in Liberia. Before they left the States, they constituted themselves a church, later to become the Province Baptist Church in Monrovia, Liberia.

The seven sailed in 1821. During the remaining years of his life, Carey served as pastor of the church, as physician for Monrovia, and as a government official; in 1826 he was named lieutenant governor of Liberia. After his death, additional missionaries were sent by the American Baptists. Meanwhile, in 1845, Southern Baptists left the Triennial Convention and formed the Southern Baptist Convention. In 1846 the new Convention sent John Day (1797–1859), also an African American, to Liberia.

The American Baptists withdrew their support from the Liberian work in 1856, and Southern Baptist support was interrupted by the Civil War in the United States. The Southern Baptists redirected their small missionary budget for Africa to Nigeria in 1875. During this period, lacking support from the United States, the church in Liberia formed the Liberia Baptist Missionary and Educational Convention. The first president of the convention, Joseph James Cheeseman, later became the president of the country.

In 1882 the Baptist Foreign Mission Convention, one of the emerging structures among the African American Baptist community in the United States, provided support for one Liberian missionary. The next year it commissioned six missionaries, who founded a mission among the Vai people. This became the beginning of the Liberian mission of the National Baptist Convention in the U.S.A., formed by the merger of several African American Baptist organizations in 1895. Two years later, some African American Baptists, who withdrew their support from the Foreign Mission Board of the National Baptists, formed the Lott Carey Foreign Mission Convention. The Lott Carey Convention provided support for J. O. Hayes, formerly a National Baptist missionary, to continue his work in Liberia.

In Liberia, the work of the several U.S.-based Baptist organizations (including the Southern Baptists, who re-entered the country in 1960) was absorbed by the Liberia Baptist Missionary Educational Convention, which continues as the dominant Baptist body in the country. In 2009, it reported 72,000 members in 270 congregations. Among leaders of note in the late 20th century was William R. Tolbert, Jr. (1913–1980), who successively became the vice president of Liberia (1951), president of the Liberia Baptist Convention (1958), president of the Baptist World Alliance (1965), and president of Liberia (1971). Tolbert was assassinated in the military coup of 1980, which happened to occur just as the Baptists were preparing to celebrate the centennial of the Convention. Tolbert was still president of the Convention at the time of his death.

The Tolbert assassination began a period of extreme unrest and disruption in Liberia, first under Samuel Doe (r. 1980–1990) and then Charles Taylor (1997–2003). Baptists suffered possibly more than most because of their identification with the late president. Hundreds of thousands were tortured, killed, or exiled, and some stability returned only after Taylor was forced from office and the subsequent election of Ellen Johnson-Sirleaf as the new president in 2005. Baptists have assumed a role in the ongoing national reconciliation efforts.

The Liberia Baptist Missionary and Educational Convention is a member of the Baptist World Alliance.

Liberia Baptist Missionary and Educational
    Convention
PO Box 10
0390 Monrovia
Liberia

J. Gordon Melton

See also: American Baptist Churches in the U.S.A.; Baptists; Baptist World Alliance; National Baptist Convention, U.S.A.; Southern Baptist Convention.

References

Tolbert, William R. "This Matter of Forgiveness." *The Oates Journal.* http://journal.oates.org/special/forgiveness/162-forgiveness-tolbert. Accessed June 15, 2009.

Tyler-McGraw, Marie. *An African Republic: Black and White Virginians in the Making of Liberia.* Chapel Hill: University of North Carolina Press, 2007.

Weeks, Nan F., and Blanche Sydnor. *Liberia for Christ.* Richmond, VA: Missionary Society of Virginia, 1959.

Williams, Walter F. *Black Americans and the Evangelization of Africa.* Madison: University of Wisconsin Press, 1982.

■ Libya

Libya is a large country (679,362 square miles) on the southern edge of the Mediterranean Sea. It sits between Egypt, to its east, and Tunisia and Algeria to its west. Most of the country lies in the Sahara desert, and in the midst of the desert to its south, it shares a border with Niger, Chad, and Sudan. The great majority of its 6.2 million people (2008) reside along its coastal plain.

A mosque in the ancient Berber oasis of Ghadames, Libya. (iStockPhoto)

Libya was settled by Berber Arabs in ancient times and participated in the history of its more famous neighbor, Egypt. It found itself a target of the rising power of the Carthaginian Empire (third century BCE) and later was incorporated into the Roman Empire. Many religious groups, including Christianity, found a home in Libyan cities during the first centuries of the Christian era. During the fourth century, Libyan Christians were divided by the Donatist heresy, and as a result Christianity failed to become the majority religion in the centuries prior to the arrival of the Muslims. Thus, Islam began its period of dominance in the seventh century CE. The Ottoman Empire annexed Libya in 1551.

The modern history of Libya begins with the weakening of the Ottoman Empire. As early as 1837, Muhammad as-Sanusi (ca. 1787–1859) founded a new clandestine Muslim group, the Sanussi, to oppose continued Ottoman rule. The Sanussi still exist as a dissenting Islamic body.

In 1911, Italy seized the Libyan coast concurrently with its declaration of war on Turkey. Following the distraction of World War I, the Italians would spend 15 years trying to consolidate their hegemony in the area. They were not able to annex the land until 1931. During World War II, Libya would be a major battlefield, where Generals Erwin Rommel and Bernard Montgomery would gain immortality. Several years of French and British occupation following the war led to the creation of the modern state of Libya in 1949.

In 1969 a group of army officers under the leadership of 27-year-old Muammar Qaddafi (b. 1942) staged a coup and took control of the government. Two years later, as head of the Revolutionary Command Council (RCC), Qaddafi was named head of state, commander in chief of the armed forces, and chairman of the RCC. On March 2, 1977, the government changed the name of the country from the Libyan Arab Republic to the Socialist People's Libyan Arab Jamahiriya. (Jamahiriya

LIBYA

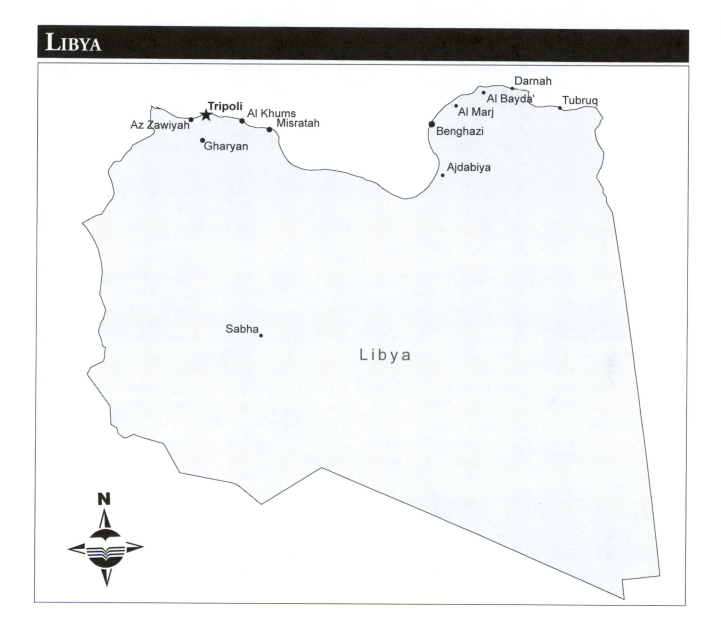

has been defined as Islamic Socialism.) Qaddafi remains in control of the country.

Today, Libya is overwhelmingly Muslim, but several schools of Islam vie for control. The population is largely divided between adherents of the Hanafite and the Shafiite schools, though the Malikite School dominates in Cyrenaica. The Sanussi continue as an important minority voice, a role won not only by its opposition to the Ottomans but its more recent struggle against Italian colonialism. The most prominent centers of the Islamic community are the Department of Arabic Language and Islamic Studies at the University of Libya in Benghazi and the Jamiat al-Dawah

al-Islamiah, an international Muslim missionary organization headquartered at Tripoli. There are a few members of the Kharijite School in Zuwara and the Jabal Nefusa sect in Tripoli.

The first phase of Christian presence in Libya ended gradually under centuries of Islamic dominance. The Roman Catholic Church was reintroduced in the 15th century, but its influence remained minuscule until the 20th century and the years of Italian rule. After World War II the number of Catholics in Libya dropped from more than 100,000 to approximately 40,000, but Catholicism remained a considerable force as the Italian presence remained strong in the country. At the

Libya

Religion	Followers in 1970	Followers in 2010	% of Population	Annual % growth 2000–2010	Followers in 2025	Followers in 2050
Muslims	1,933,000	6,313,000	96.7	2.04	7,785,000	9,284,000
Christians	58,800	171,000	2.6	2.72	218,000	268,000
Roman Catholics	3,600	94,000	1.4	4.58	120,000	145,000
Orthodox	47,000	66,000	1.0	0.74	80,000	90,000
Protestants	3,800	5,500	0.1	0.31	8,000	15,000
Buddhists	400	22,000	0.3	2.06	32,000	50,000
Agnostics	2,000	11,000	0.2	2.05	30,000	45,000
Hindus	0	6,000	0.1	2.05	10,000	15,000
Sikhs	0	2,400	0.0	2.06	5,000	8,000
Chinese folk	0	1,800	0.0	2.06	3,000	6,000
Atheists	0	900	0.0	2.03	1,500	2,500
Baha'is	200	700	0.0	2.05	1,000	2,000
Ethnoreligionists	0	500	0.0	2.06	1,000	2,000
Jews	40	120	0.0	1.98	120	120
Total population	**1,994,000**	**6,530,000**	**100.0**	**2.06**	**8,087,000**	**9,683,000**

end of the 1960s the church consisted of three vicariates and a prefecture. After the coup of 1970s, however, the Italians were expelled from the country, and by 1972 only two Roman Catholic parishes remained and the majority of Libyan Christians were Eastern-rite Catholics.

Protestants began missionary activity in Libya in the 1880s, led by the North Africa Mission, soon followed by the Church Missions to Jews, an Anglican missionary organization. Then in 1936 all non-Catholic missionaries were expelled and were only allowed to return in 1946. All missionaries were again expelled in 1970. All British and American military personnel were expelled in 1974, further reducing the number of Protestants, almost all of whom were expatriates. The remaining Protestant groups are small and most serve small expatriate enclaves.

The Orthodox community began to grow after World War II with the movement of various Arab groups to Libya, especially Egyptians, among whom were many Coptic Christians. As many as 45,000 Coptics may have relocated to Libya before all Egyptians were expelled from the country in 1974. Only a minuscule community remains today.

Through much of the 20th century there was a large Jewish community in Libya, some 37,000 strong.

However, in 1951 almost all of them migrated to the new state of Israel. It is estimated that less than 50 remain in Libya today. There is likewise a tiny number of Chinese Buddhists and members of the Baha'i Faith in Libya.

J. Gordon Melton

See also: Baha'i Faith; Malikite School of Islam; Roman Catholic Church.

References

Horrie, Chris, and Peter Chippendale. *What Is Islam?: A Comprehensive Introduction.* London: Virgin, 1997.

Mason, J. P. *Island of the Blest: Islam in a Libyan Oasis Community.* Athens, OH: Center for International Studies, Ohio University, 1977.

Mayer, Ann Elizabeth. "Islamic Law and Islamic Revival in Libya." In *Islam in the Contemporary World,* edited by Cyriac K. Pullapilly. Notre Dame, IN: Cross Roads Books, 1980.

Ruedy, John. *Islamism and Secularism in North Africa.* New York: Palgrave Macmillan, 1996.

Vanderwalle, Dirk. *A History of Modern Libya.* Cambridge: Cambridge University Press, 2006.

■ Liechtenstein

Liechtenstein is a small country of only 61 square miles located on the Rhine River between Switzerland and Austria. The home to 34,498 people, it shares much of the history of its two neighbors. Liechtenstein became independent in 1719 but was closely linked to the Austrian Empire for the next two centuries. Since the end of World War II, it has been more closely linked to Switzerland.

Christianity came into the area quite early, during the years of the Roman exploration and occupation of the Rhine Valley. As did Austria, Liechtenstein remained loyal to the Roman Church through the Reformation era. Today the Catholic Church remains the dominant religious force in the land, and the several congregations are organized into a deanery attached to the Diocese of Chur (Switzerland).

Protestants came into the area in the 1880s. Most were skilled workers who migrated from Germany and other countries with their families. In 1881 they organized the Evangelical Church. In 1954 the Evangelical Church entered into a *Patronatsvertrag* (patronage agreement) with the Protestant Church of the Canton of Saint Gall in Switzerland, which among other benefits provides access to a pool of pastors. That same year, the Lutheran members of the church left and founded a separate Lutheran organization. Soon afterward they affiliated with the Swiss Lutherans in what is now known as the Association of Evangelical Lutheran Churches in Switzerland and the Principality of Liechtenstein.

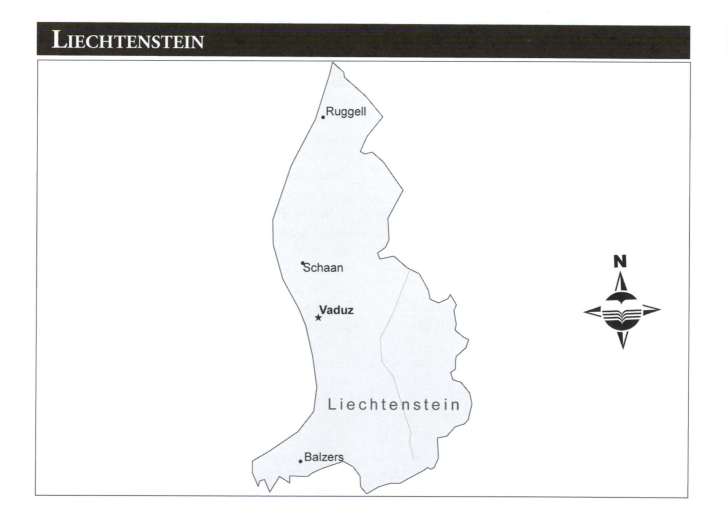

LIECHTENSTEIN

Liechtenstein

Religion	Followers in 1970	Followers in 2010	% of Population	Annual % growth 2000–2010	Followers in 2025	Followers in 2050
Christians	21,200	32,400	89.5	1.00	34,600	37,200
Roman Catholics	19,000	26,600	73.5	0.58	27,800	29,000
Protestants	1,400	3,300	9.1	1.38	4,200	5,500
Marginals	20	120	0.3	0.00	200	400
Muslims	0	2,300	6.4	1.36	3,400	4,500
Agnostics	170	1,400	3.9	1.33	2,200	3,200
Jews	30	50	0.1	0.91	50	50
Atheists	0	30	0.1	3.26	50	80
Baha'is	40	20	0.0	1.92	50	100
Total population	**21,400**	**36,200**	**100.0**	**1.03**	**40,400**	**45,100**

The Seventh-day Adventist Church has a small work in Liechtenstein that is an integral part of the Swiss Union Conference. There is also a small Baha'i spiritual assembly and a recently opened Zen Buddhist center, part of the International Zen Association, headquartered in Paris.

J. Gordon Melton

See also: International Zen Association; Lutheranism; Seventh-day Adventist Church.

References

Beattie, David. *Liechtenstein: A Modern History.* London: I. B. Tauris, 2004.

Eccardt, Thomas M. *Secrets of the Seven Smallest States of Europe: Andorra, Liechtenstein, Luxembourg, Malta, Monaco, San Marino, and Vatican City.* New York: Hippocrene Books, 2005.

Leckey, Colin. *Dots on the Map.* London: Grosvenor House Publishing, 2006.

Wille, H. *Staat und Kirke im Fürstentum Liechtenstein.* Freiburg, Switzerland: University of Freiburg, 1972.

Light of the World Church

This religious tradition, founded in Monterrey, Nuevo León, Mexico, in 1926 by Eusebio Joaquín González (later known as the Apostle Aarón), has blended Mexican mysticism with Pentecostal fervor to create a unique Christian movement that has spread throughout Mexico and to more than 20 countries in the Americas (including the United States and Canada), plus Spain, Portugal, Italy, Germany, and Australia. The Light of the World Church (since 1952 with headquarters in Colonia Hermosa Provincia, Guadalajara, Jalisco, Mexico), grew from 80 members in 1929, to 75,000 in 1972, to 1.5 million in 1986, and to more than 4 million members in 22 countries in 1990, according to church sources.

The official name of this organization is the Church of God, Column and Pillar of Truth, Jesus the Light of the World (Iglesia de Dios, Columna y Apoyo de la Verdad, Jesus La Luz del Mundo), but its followers are popularly known in Mexico as Aaronistas (followers of Aarón). This religious organization has been classified as a Marginal Christian Group by PROLADES due to its unique characteristics, which include its claims to be "the restoration of Primitive Christianity" and that its apostles are "the voice of God on earth."

The Light of the World Church has a strong Mexican nationalistic orientation and has an authoritarian form of church government; it strongly adheres to Old Testament teachings, is legalistic, and upholds high moral standards; and its members are known for their industriousness and honesty. Although there is a strong emphasis on Bible reading and memorization, the prophetic messages spoken by the Apostles Aarón and Samuel are considered as "the fountain of truth." In addition to traditional Protestant hymns and gospel songs (many from the 18th and 19th centuries), some of the songs used refer to the "Anointed One," the "Sent One," or "The Prince," which honor and praise Aarón as the church's First Apostle. The traditional worship style is simple: people kneel to pray, women wear head coverings and long white dresses, no musical instruments are used, the choir sings a capella in four-part harmony, and males and females are separated by a center aisle.

Another unique feature of this movement is that all ordained pastors are required to travel to the Mother Church in Colonia Hermosa Provincia (symbolic of Holy Jerusalem) in Guadalajara on August 14 for an annual celebration of the Lord's Supper, which is held on Aarón's birthday. This event is also an occasion for faithful church members (called "the new spiritual People of Israel") to make a pilgrimage to Guadalajara from within Mexico or from other countries, and to present the Apostle with special gifts. While rejecting Roman Catholicism as an apostate church, Guadalajara has become the new Rome for this movement, and excommunication from the Light of the World Church means that people are "irrevocably lost for all eternity."

Doctrinally, the Light of the World Church has some similarities with the Oneness Pentecostal movement in Mexico but is distinguished by its allegiance to its Supreme Leader, the Apostle Aarón. Historically, Eusebio Joaquín González (an uneducated man of humble origins) was converted in 1926 by an Apostolic fruit vender and became a disciple of two itinerant lay preachers, known as "Saul" and "Silas," who arose within the early Pentecostal movement in northern Mexico during the 1920s.

Eusebio was reportedly baptized by "Saul" on April 6, 1926, in San Pedro de las Colonias (near Monterrey); then he and his wife, Elisa, accompanied the two bearded and barefoot "prophets" for a few months on a preaching journey on foot. At some point, "Saul" is alleged to have spoken the following words of prophecy: "You will no longer be called Eusebio, rather your new name will be Aarón and you will become known in all the world." Later, Aarón testified that this was the moment in which God called him to establish the Light of the World Church as the restoration of the Primitive Church of Jesus Christ, and in December 1926 the City of Guadalajara was selected as his spiritual headquarters (Gaxiola 1994, 167–169).

Between 1926 and 1952, this new religious movement grew from a small group of dedicated followers to an established movement of about 25,000 members. From 1926 to 1934, Aarón and his early disciples traveled on foot to many towns and villages, preaching to the marginalized peasants and forming "house churches" among his followers, who became known as Aaronistas. The first temple of the Light of the World Church was founded in 1934 in the lower-class neighborhood of San Juan de Dios in Guadalajara. By 1938, Aarón had established most of the rules and regulations that would govern the new movement, including the obligatory 5:00 a.m. daily prayer service, and he became known to his followers as "the new Messiah."

In 1942, the Light of the World Church suffered its first major division, when a power struggle among the leaders (Aarón was accused of misusing church finances) resulted in the formation of a rival movement, known as the Good Shepherd Church (Iglesia El Buen Pastor), which is similar in doctrine and practice (Renée de la Torre, 1996, 155).

In 1952, Aarón purchased 14 hectares on the outskirts of Guadalajara, where he and his followers constructed the Colonia Hermosa Provincia as a segregated community to protect church members from worldly temptations and to strengthen the development of a community of faith. During the next few decades, a large central church was built that seated about 3,000 people, around which was developed a walled, self-contained community with its own commercial, medical, educational, and social services. All of these facilities were built by the voluntary labor and tithes of Aarón's faithful followers.

After Aarón's death in 1964, his youngest son, Samuel Juaquín Flores, became the new Supreme Leader and Apostle of the movement; and he began a new era of openness to the larger world by tearing down the stone wall around Colonia Hermosa Provincia, encouraging the growth and development of similar colonies of believers within Mexico and in other countries, and constructing a new, large central church at a cost of more than $5 million—not counting the cost of volunteer labor provided by church members. In 1992, an estimated 150,000 church members gathered for the annual celebration of the Lord's Supper at La Glorieta Central de la Iglesia La Luz del Mundo.

When Aarón died in 1964, the Light of the World Church had 64 churches and 35 missions; under the leadership of Samuel, this movement grew to more than 11,300 churches and missions in 22 countries in 1989, according to Renée de la Torre (1998, 267). This demonstrates the growing social strength and missionary zeal of this autonomous Mexican religious movement.

Despite strong opposition from the Roman Catholic Church, many Protestant denominations, and other religious groups, this independent quasi-Pentecostal organization has achieved significant numerical, socio-economic, and political strength in Mexico (especially in the state of Jalisco), and through expansion to other countries has made its presence and unique message known throughout the Americas.

Apostol Samuel Juaquín Flores
Glorieta Central de la Iglesia La Luz del Mundo
Colonia Hermosa Provincia, Guadalajara,
Jalisco, Mexico
www.laluzdelmundo.com

Clifton L. Holland

See also: Apostolic Church of Faith in Jesus Christ of Mexico; Pentecostalism; Roman Catholic Church; Spiritual Christian Evangelical Church.

References

Berg, Clayton, and Paul Pretiz. *Spontaneous Combustion: Grass-Roots Christianity, Latin American Style.* Pasadena, CA: William Carey Library, 1996.

Gaxiola, Manuel J. *La Serpiente y la Paloma: Historia, Teología y Análisis de la Iglesia Apostólica de la Fe en Cristo Jesús (1914–1994).* 2nd ed. Naucalpan, Estado de México: Libros Pyros, 1994.

Revista Académica para el Estudio de las Religiones, *La Luz del Mundo: un ánalisis multi-disciplinario de la controversia religiosa que ha impactado a nuestro país.* Ciudad de México: Revista Académica para el Estudio de las Religiones, Tomo I, 1997.

Torre, Renée de la. "Pinceladas de una ilustración etnográfica: La Luz del Mundo en Guada-lajara." In *Identidades Religiosas y Sociales en México,* edited by Gilberto Giménez. Mexico City: Instituto de Investigaciones Sociales de la Universidad Nacional Autónoma de México (UNAM), 1996.

Torre, Renée de la. "Una iglesia mexicana con proyección internacional: La Luz del Mundo." In *Sectas o Iglesias: Viejos o Nuevos Movimientos Religioso,* compiled by Elio Masferrer Kan. Ciudad de México: Plaza y Valdés Editores, 1998.

■ Lithuania

Lithuania is a country of Northeastern Europe, the largest from the three Baltic states with the capital at Vilnius and a population of around 3.336 million. The prevailing language is Lithuanian. Ethnically, Lithuania is composed of Lithuanians (84.3 percent), Russians (5 percent), Poles (6.2 percent), and Byelorussians (1.1 percent). There was a large community of Jews before World War II that was hard hit by the Holocaust, and it survives today with fewer than 5,000 members. The mainstream religion is Roman Catholicism. According to the 2001 census 79 percent of the population declared their belonging to the Roman Catholic Church, 4 percent to the Russian Orthodox Church. The membership of other religious communities did not exceed 1 percent of the population: Old Believers (0.78 percent), the Lutheran Church (0.56 percent), and the Reformed Church (0.2 percent). The New Apostolic Church, the Tatar Muslims, Full Gospel/Charismatic churches, Jehovah's Witnesses, Pentecostals, Baptists, and Seventh-day Adventists each have memberships of 1,000 to 3,000 while there are smaller communities of the Church of Jesus Christ of Latter-day Saints, the International Society for Krishna Consciousness, the United Methodist Church, and the Buddhists. There is also a small group of Karaites, who, along with the Sunni Muslim community, have had a presence in Lithuania since the 15th century, when they were brought to Lithuania by the Grand Duke Vytautas, while a variety of Muslims of Tatar, Uzbek, and Azerbaijani background migrated to Lithuania in the 20th century. The Tatar community currently numbers about 5,000.

Hill of Crosses near Siauliai, Lithuania, is a symbol of faith and national identity in the face of oppression. (Corel)

Lithuania has been a part of a Polish-Lithuanian Commonwealth since 1569, and in 1795 was annexed by the Russian Empire. Lithuania was formally re-established as an independent state in 1918. The newly formed Lithuanian state enshrined freedom of religion in its new Constitution; however, there was no strict separation of church and state, and the Catholic Church retained a privileged position, strengthened by a Concordat of 1927 with the Holy See. After a short period of independence Lithuania was annexed by the Soviet Union in 1940, then by advancing Nazi Germany in 1941, and again by the Soviet Union in 1944.

After World War II, Lithuania was kept in the Soviet Union as one of its 15 republics. The independence movement gained momentum again during the perestroika period in the Soviet Union and culminated in the declaration of independence on March 11, 1990, and, after the crashing of a coup in August 1991 weakened the imperialist forces in the Soviet Union, recog-

nition of the declared independence by both the Soviet Union and most states of the world in 1991. Lithuania joined the North Atlantic Treaty Organization (NATO) and the European Union in 2004. After regaining independence Lithuania has experienced vigorous economic growth, though in 2008 the GDP per capita was still only about 60 percent of the average in the European Union.

Modern-day Lithuanians are descendants of a few Baltic tribes, and the premodern indigenous religion of Lithuania was a multifaceted phenomenon belonging to the more generic Baltic family of religions. The sources of ancient Baltic culture are estimated to go back to around 2500 BCE, when autochthonous local cultures were merging with that of the newcomer Indo-Europeans. The pre-Christian religion in the current territory of Lithuania has undergone quite a few changes since those times, but it has kept the basic structure of Indo-European pre-Christian religions.

The cosmology and anthropology of the pre-modern Pagan religion of Lithuania describes the beginning of the world, in which two gods, Dievas and Velnias, create the world together. While creating the world they compete with each other, the world emerging in that constant competition. According to Lithuanian etiological tales, the first human being was created by accident, by a particle of spit from the mouth of Dievas, who only later saw the result of his spit and marveled at what had happened. This pessimistic anthropology permeates the worldview of ancient Lithuanian religion, where human beings are not seen as a result of purposeful divine activity. The vision of the afterlife is more optimistic, though the records about it are very diverse. People who have died would be met by gods and would get the treatment they have earned in this life, either going to *dausos*, the place of eternal bliss, or the place of darkness, governed by Velnias. The deities of the ancient Lithuanian (and Baltic) pantheon had correspondents in the pantheons of other regions. The highest god of the Baltic pantheon was Dievas, who in the later period of the Lithuanian religion became a distant, inactive deity, portrayed in tales as active only in the creation of the world and shortly thereafter. The most important member of the pantheon was Perkunas, god of storm and thunder, perhaps a son of Dievas. The Balts also had a chthonic god, opposite in nature to the heavenly gods, named Velnias, a god of dungeons, magic, and riches. The people also venerated a female deity called Zvoruna or Medeina. Besides the deities common to all the Balts there were different spirits or gods unique to the various tribes. Wizards or witches, warlocks, and medicine women had considerable influence on the common religious life of the people. The ancient shrines in Lithuania, called *alkos*, were constructed of stones on hills or by rivers. Groves were also designated as sacred places, being used to sacrifice to gods and to foretell the future. The remains of a few shrines, known from historic times, are being uncovered by archaeologists. It is in no way certain that the pre-Christian Lithuanian religion was centralized, but there was an important shrine to Perkunas in Vilnius.

Up until the 13th century, the spread of Christianity in Lithuania was prevented by its weak ties with Christian countries, the absence of a strong national state, and confrontation with the Crusaders. In about 1240, Mindaugas (d. 1263) became the ruler of Lithuania, thus uniting the unruly duchies, and in 1251 he was baptized for political reasons (thus gaining the king's title from the pope), though the people and most dukes kept the old faith. Lithuania starting from the 14th century has attracted a large diaspora of Jews, fleeing persecution in Spain and other Western European countries, while in Lithuania they were protected by law to live and practice their faith freely.

Over time, Catholic missionaries, primarily Dominicans and Franciscans, visited Lithuania, where some settled. Apart from a few violent incidents, the Christians and Pagans lived quite peacefully together. The official Christianization of Lithuania began under the Grand Duke of Lithuania Jogaila in 1387, who ruled as king Władysław II of Poland. This movement lasted for about a century. The destruction of the official cult of the Pagan religion also began at that time, though the manifestations of pre-Christian religion survived even into the 16th century, when missionary activity by the Jesuits began. Most of the nobility of Lithuania was baptized in 1387, with the baptism of the people following, while the more independent part of Lithuania, Samogitia, was formally Christianized only about 60 years later.

The Protestant Reformation was brought to Lithuania in the 1520s by the Lithuanian nobles who studied at the universities of Wittenberg and Leipzig, both strong Protestant centers of learning. The Reformation quickly spread through all the strata of society, facing strong resistance from only a small number of clergy who remained loyal to the Roman Catholic Church. The weakened state of the Catholic Church in Lithuania contributed to this rapid spread of the Reformation there, to the extent that by the mid-16th century, Lithuania was predominantly Protestant, with both Lutheran and Reformed influences present. The adherence of the influential Radvila family to Protestantism also contributed significantly to the spread of the Reformation generally.

However, in 1564 the ruler of Lithuania and Poland, Sigismund II Augustus (1520–1572), began implementing the decisions of the Council of Trent, which had been called by the Roman Catholic Church in 1545 to both reform the church and stop the further

LITHUANIA

spread of Protestantism. Jesuit academic and missionary activities played a significant part in the Counter-Reformation that followed the Council. In 1570 the Jesuits established a college in Vilnius, which was later to become a university. With Catholicism regaining ground, the influence of the Protestants gradually faded, remaining strong only in the western and northern parts of Lithuania.

A separate issue was the presence of Eastern Orthodoxy in Lithuania and the Slavic lands within the Grand Duchy of Lithuania, from the 13th to the 16th centuries. To keep political and social peace after the Christianization of Lithuania, Grand Duke of Lithuania Vytautas (1350–1430) strove unsuccessfully to establish a separate administrative unit of the Orthodox Church in Lithuania. Later there were also efforts to unite the Catholic and Orthodox churches within the Grand Duchy of Lithuania and the Kingdom of Poland. These efforts were partially successful and culminated in 1596 with the creation of the union, which was not, however, joined by all Orthodox.

The Catholic-Orthodox problem was never resolved, and it re-emerged in a different form in the 18th century. Following the third division of the Polish-Lithuanian Commonwealth in 1795, by which the Russian Empire had annexed most of Lithuania, the Russians established a policy of assimilating Lithuania culturally, which also meant making it Orthodox. Both Catholic and Protestant churches suffered as a result, but in the end the effort proved unsuccessful. Lithuania retained its sense of nationhood, and both Catholic and Protestant churches played a significant role in preserving Lithuania's national character.

When an independent Lithuania re-emerged in 1918, the country recognized equal rights of all confessions, though the Concordat with the Catholic Church of 1926 established the privileged position of Catholicism, which remained the majority faith. About 5 percent of the population was Reformed or Lutheran, but they had little influence on Lithuanian politics as a whole. Additional Protestant and Free church traditions spread in Lithuania through the 20th century. The

Lithuania

Religion	Followers in 1970	Followers in 2010	% of Population	Annual % growth 2000–2010	Followers in 2025	Followers in 2050
Christians	2,216,000	2,979,000	89.3	–0.15	2,928,000	2,527,000
Roman Catholics	2,060,000	2,640,000	79.1	–0.09	2,566,000	2,181,000
Orthodox	116,000	152,000	4.6	–1.18	150,000	140,000
Protestants	37,200	40,700	1.2	0.61	70,000	90,000
Agnostics	605,000	320,000	9.6	–2.44	150,000	100,000
Atheists	304,000	23,300	0.7	–4.30	10,000	8,000
Muslims	6,000	7,000	0.2	–0.45	8,000	12,000
Jews	9,000	4,800	0.1	–0.45	4,500	4,500
Buddhists	0	700	0.0	–0.46	800	900
Hindus	0	600	0.0	–0.43	700	800
Baha'is	10	300	0.0	0.07	400	500
Ethnoreligionists	0	100	0.0	–0.47	100	100
Total population	**3,140,000**	**3,336,000**	**100.0**	**–0.45**	**3,102,000**	**2,654,000**

Baptists had been in Lithuania from the middle of the 19th century, and the Methodists, Seventh-day Adventists, Pentecostals, and the New Apostolic Church had established communities at the start of the 20th century. The American Bible Student movement (later known as Jehovah's Witnesses) appeared in the 1930s. Western Esotericism took deep roots in the country after one of Lithuania's famous writers, Vydūnas (Vilius Storosta), became an adept of Theosophy.

The Soviet occupation brought repression on all religions, while the persecution of religious minorities was most severe. Some communities were gradually eliminated, including those of the Seventh-day Adventists, Methodists, and Jehovah's Witnesses, and the Baptists were joined together with Pentecostals, in part as an attempt to eliminate their uniqueness and so undermine their existence. Independent, unregistered religious groups were under strict police control, receiving more tolerant treatment only toward the end of the 1970s.

The traditional religious communities faced both persecution and severe limitations on their previously flowering social activities. The Catholic and Reformed churches developed ties to the national resistance movement. Many of the social and religious leaders were exiled and forced to confess atheism. Communist Party membership was required for those taking higher positions in society. Atheist propaganda was widespread.

The restoration of Lithuanian independence in 1990 brought a revival of traditional religions as well as an influx of different religious movements from outside the country. The revival of religion peaked in 1992–1993, with a stabilization or even recession for most religious communities following at the beginning of the 21st century.

There is no state religion in Lithuania, and freedom of religion is established in the country's legal system. There are three levels of legal status for religious communities. Any religious community can be registered to become legal and freely practice their faith if they fulfill certain minimal legal requirements. However, there are nine traditional religions that are "state-recognized" as a part of Lithuanian cultural, social, spiritual heritage: Roman Catholic, Greek Catholic, Evangelical Lutheran, Evangelical Reformed, Russian Orthodox, Old Believer, Jewish, Sunni Islam, and Karaite. This list of privileged religions is final. However, all religious communities are eligible for state recognition—an intermediate status—after they have existed in Lithuania for a few decades. So far, only the Association of the Baptist Churches in Lithuania and the Seventh-day Adventist Church have achieved such status. State recognition gives religious communities some tax privileges, permission to teach religion in public schools, and time on national television. They also enjoy greater social acceptance, as the nontraditional religions are often stigmatized as sects. The most influential religious body in Lithuanian society is the Roman Catholic Church, while other larger communities are based on either a particular ethnic minority group (for example, Russian Orthodoxy being concentrated among ethnic Russians) or a particular region (for example, Lutheranism being concentrated in the southwest part of the country).

Milda Ališauskiene and Donatas Glodenis

See also: Church of Jesus Christ of Latter-day Saints; Dominicans; Eastern Orthodoxy; Franciscans; Free Church; International Society for Krishna Consciousness; Jehovah's Witnesses; Jesuits; Karaites; New Apostolic Church; Old Believers (Russia); Roman Catholic Church; Russian Orthodox Church (Moscow Patriarchate); Seventh-day Adventist Church; United Methodist Church.

References

Beresnevičius, Gintaras. *Religijų istorijos metmenys.* Vilnius: Aidai, 1997.

Beresnevičius, Gintaras. *Lietuvių religija ir mitologija.* Vilnius: Tyto Alba, 2004.

"Communism's Struggle with Religion in Lithuania." *Lituanus* 9, no. 1 (March 1963).

Glodenis, Donatas, and Lahayne, Holger, eds. *Religijos Lietuvoje.* Šiauliai: Nova Vita, 1999.

Musteikis, A. *The Reformation in Lithuania: Religious Fluctuation in the Sixteenth Century.* Boulder, CO: East European Monographs, 1988.

Peškaitis, Arūnas, and Donatas Glodenis. *Šiuolaikinis religingumas.* Vilnius: Vaga, 2000.

Rimaitis, J. *Religion in Lithuania.* Vilnius: Gintaras, 1971.

Suziedelis, S. *The Sword and the Cross: A History of the Church in Lithuania.* Huntington, IN: Our Sunday Visitor, 1988.

Vardys, V. S., ed. *Krikščionybė Lietuvoje.* Chicago: Ateitis, 1997.

Liturgical Year

From as early as the second century CE, the Christian church, following earlier Jewish tradition, has used the seasons of the year to mark sacred times. Around these times it has established festivals and holidays set aside to worship God and mark special moments in salvation history. While Jewish celebration revolves around the exodus from Egypt, the Christian church year focuses on the life and ministry of Jesus.

The Christian calendar is organized around two major feasts: Christmas and Easter. Advent ushers in Christmas and the season ends with the feast of Epiphany. Easter is preceded by Lent and leads to Pentecost. The periods of the year surrounding these two major seasons are known in the liturgical calendars as "Ordinary Time" and focus on various aspects of the Christian faith, particularly the mission of the church in the world.

The timing of all of the other moveable feasts in the Christian year revolves around Easter. The date of Easter itself is set according to a lunar cycle that changes. Consequently, seasons in the liturgical calendar vary in length and dates. As well, the Eastern Orthodox tradition, for example, uses the revised Julian calendar (proposed in 1923 and adopted by most Orthodox churches over the next several decades) rather than the Common Era calendar that has evolved over the last century from the Gregorian calendar. The major events of the liturgical year are as follows.

Advent: First Sunday of Advent through December 24 The beginning of the Christian liturgical year in Western churches, Advent marks the four Sundays before Christmas. The word "advent" comes from the Latin *adventus*, which means "coming." This season just before Christmas is associated with the coming of Jesus as Messiah and marks a time of penitence, preparation, and anticipation.

Advent always contains four Sundays, beginning on the Sunday nearest to November 30 (the feast of Saint Andrew the Apostle). Consequently, Advent may begin as early as November 27 but always ends on December 24. If Christmas Eve is a Sunday, the last Sunday of Advent falls on that day, as Christmas Eve begins at sundown.

Christmas: December 25 through to Epiphany The Christmas season begins with the celebration of the birth of Jesus, Christmas day, or as a vigil on Christmas Eve. The Feast of Christmas lasts 12 days, until Epiphany. The Christmas season is a time of rejoicing in the incarnation. Christmas probably originated in the Roman culture, which celebrated the Winter Solstice on December 25, the shortest day of the year. It was a Pagan celebration of the birth of "The Invincible Sun" as it began its annual journey back north from its southernmost point. It is likely that Christians began celebrating the birth of Jesus at this time as an alternative to the Pagan observance of the Winter Solstice.

Epiphany   Falling on January 6, Epiphany is a Christian feast that celebrates the revelation of God in human form in the person of Jesus Christ. In Greek, the word "epiphany" means "manifestation" and in the Eastern Christian tradition the event is called "Theophany," which means "manifestation of God." In the Eastern tradition, it falls on January 19. Roman Catholics will often celebrate it on the Sunday closest to January 6.

The Western observance commemorates the visitation of the biblical Magi to the child Jesus, stressing the appearance of Jesus to the Gentiles. In many Hispanic and European churches is it also known as "Three Kings Day." Eastern Christians include the baptism of Jesus in their celebration, highlighting Christ's revelation to the world as the Son of God.

Marking the 12th day of Christmas, Epiphany brings to an end the Advent and Christmas seasons.

Ordinary Time after the Baptism: Monday after the Epiphany through to Lent   This season focuses on the early life and childhood of Christ, and then on his public ministry.

Lent: Ash Wednesday through Holy Saturday   The season of Lent begins with Ash Wednesday and lasts until the final Saturday before Easter, Holy Saturday and includes Holy Week, the week before Easter. For six weeks preceding Easter, it is a time of penitential prayer, fasting, and almsgiving to prepare for the celebration of the resurrection of Jesus on Easter Sunday. This season of Lent originally was also a time of preparation for baptismal candidates and those separated from the church who were rejoining the community.

Holy Week, the last week of Lent, commemorates the last week of the earthly life of Jesus Christ. It covers the events of his triumphal entry into Jerusalem, the Last Supper, the arrest, and his death by crucifixion. Beginning with the sixth Sunday of Lent, Holy Week includes Palm Sunday, Spy Wednesday, Maundy Thursday, Good Friday, and Holy Saturday.

Easter: Easter Vigil though Pentecost   The high feast of the Christian church, Easter celebrates the resurrection of Jesus Christ. Even churches that typically do not follow the liturgical calendar observe Easter. Easter Sunday begins a 50-day season of "Eastertide" that includes Ascension Day and leads to Pentecost.

The Easter Vigil is celebrated after night falls on the evening before Easter Sunday. It incorporates a "new light" ceremony in the form of candle-lighting and, often, an outdoor sunrise service. Typically, new converts to the church are baptized on Easter Sunday.

Six weeks into Easter, the church celebrates Ascension Day, a commemoration of the bodily ascension of Jesus into heaven. Until recently this holy day fell on the sixth Thursday after Easter Sunday, the traditional 40 days between the resurrection and ascension in the biblical narrative. However, some Roman Catholic provinces have moved the celebration to the following Sunday to facilitate the obligation of the faithful to receive Mass as part of the feast.

The last day of the Easter season is Pentecost, the festival that marks the birth of the Christian church by the power of the Holy Spirit as recorded in the biblical book of the Acts of the Apostles 2:1–41. The word "Pentecost" means "fiftieth day" and is so-named because it is celebrated 50 days after Easter Sunday.

Ordinary Time after Pentecost: The Day after Pentecost through the Final Day before Advent   The second period of Ordinary Time is the longest liturgical season. Ordinary Time resumes after Pentecost and runs until the final Saturday before Advent. This period of Ordinary Time focuses on Christ's reign as King of kings, and on the age of the church. It is meant to be a time of growth as the church meditates on the teachings of the Bible and their application to the Christian life. This is the present time between the age of the Apostles and the age of Christ's Second Coming. The final Sunday in Ordinary Time is the Feast of Christ the King; the Saturday after this feast is the final day of Ordinary Time. The cycle repeats itself with the beginning of Advent.

Kevin Quast

See also: Advent; Ascension Sunday; Calendars, Religious; Christmas; Common Era Calendar; Easter; Holy Week; Lent; Pentecost.

References

Adam, Adolf. *The Liturgical Year: Its History and Its Meaning after the Reform of the Liturgy.* New York: Pueblo, 1981.

Bonneau, Normand. *Ritual Word, Paschal Shape.* Collegeville, MN: Liturgical Press, 1998.

Bradshaw, Paul F., and Lawrence A. Hoffman, eds. *Passover and Easter: Origin and History to Modern Times.* Notre Dame, IN: University of Notre Dame Press, 1999.

Fink, Peter E., ed. *The New Dictionary of Sacramental Worship.* Collegeville, MN: Liturgical Press, 1990.

Lathrop, Gordon W. *Holy People: A Liturgical Ecclesiology.* Minneapolis, MN: Fortress Press, 1999.

Martimort, Aime Georges, ed. *The Church at Prayer: An Introduction to the Liturgy.* Vol. 4: *The Liturgy and Time.* Collegeville, MN: Liturgical Press, 1986.

Nocent, Adrian. *The Liturgical Year.* Collegeville, MN: Liturgical Press. 1977.

Senn, Frank. *Christian Liturgy: Catholic and Evangelical.* Minneapolis, MN: Augsburg Fortress, 1997.

Stookey, Laurence Hull. *Calendar: Christ's Time for the Church.* Nashville: Abingdon, 1996.

Taft, Robert. "Towards a Theology of the Christian Feast." In *Beyond East and West: Problems in Liturgical Understanding.* Washington: Pastoral Press, 1984.

Talley, Thomas J. *The Origins of the Liturgical Year.* 2nd ed. Collegeville, MN: Liturgical Press, 1991.

West, Fitz. *Scripture and Memory: The Ecumenical Hermeneutic of the Three-Year Lectionaries.* Collegeville, MN: Liturgical Press. 1997.

Living Church of God

The Living Church of God is one of the three largest offshoots of the Worldwide Church of God (WCOG), with an active television, magazine, and booklet outreach.

In the years following the death of founder Herbert W. Armstrong (1892–1986) the WCOG dropped his distinctive teachings one by one under its new pastor general Joseph W. Tkach (1927–1995) and moved closer to standard conservative Protestant teachings. Many WCOG ministers found this difficult to accept. One of these was Roderick C. Meredith (b. 1930), who had been one of Armstrong's earliest students and affiliated with the WCOG since 1949. In 1992, after confrontations with the new leadership of the WCOG, Meredith left to found his own Sabbatarian millenarian church, the Global Church of God, holding firmly to the teachings of the WCOG during Armstrong's lifetime. Because of Meredith's previously high position in WCOG as senior evangelist, many other members left to follow him. The Global Church of God grew to a peak membership of around 7,000.

Armstrong had taught "top-down" church governance, with a single leader having sole authority over the church, and Meredith followed this model. In 1998 the board of the Global Church sought to temper Meredith's authority over his church. After a number of heated meetings and the quite public exchange of accusatory letters, Meredith left his own church and founded the Living Church of God, taking 70 to 80 percent of his ministers and members with him. The Living Church of God is more or less the old Global Church of God under a different name.

The remnant of the Global Church, reduced to fewer than 1,000 members, tried to continue, but they were faced with a dramatic drop in income from members' tithes. This difficulty was only compounded when founding members now with the Living Church demanded the repayment of loans they had made for the start-up funding of the Global Church, which voluntarily entered into a legal equivalent of bankruptcy. Its members re-formed as the Church of God, a Christian Fellowship (CGCF).

In a further twist to the tale, the president of CGCF, Raymond F. McNair (1930–2008), who had led the split from Meredith's original Global Church of God, left CGCF in 2000 and rejoined Meredith's new Living Church of God. He left Meredith's leadership for a second time in 2004 to found his own small church, the Church of God–21st Century (COG21).

In 2001 most CGCF congregations decided to merge with the largest offshoot from the WCOG, the United Church of God. A few remained separate, including the national organizations in Canada (under the name CGCF) and the United Kingdom (still called Global Church of God) and a small group in America that took the name the Church of the Eternal God. The three differently named churches, which are very small, have a joint leadership and literature and linked websites.

Shortly after Meredith left the Global Church of God another minister, David C. Pack, left to found the Restored Church of God, perhaps the most hard-line of all the offshoots from the "Worldwide family." Pack has published a book-length list of 280 teachings that he claims the "new" Worldwide Church has changed from Armstrong's original teachings and a further list of 174 teachings in which he believes all the other offshoots, between them, deviate from Armstrong's truth. A very literature-driven church, it avoided the copyright problems of the Philadelphia Church of God by completely rewriting many of Armstrong's books, along with new ones. The Restored Church of God claims more than 1,000 members.

The Living Church of God claims to hold to all the traditional teachings of Herbert W. Armstrong and the WCOG at the time of his death. Like most of the offshoots, it emphasizes in its literature and broadcasts the need to watch world news to "prove" that these are the end times. The second (or possibly third) largest offshoot from the WCOG, the Living Church of God has TV and radio programs called *Tomorrow's World*, the same name made famous by the WCOG, and publishes a magazine with the same name. It claims a membership of around 7,000 in more than 200 congregations.

The 78-year-old Meredith suffered a mild stroke in 2008 and appointed Richard Ames "to stand in for him as acting chief executive for the duration of his recovery"—one of the very few examples of a WCOG offshoot leader appointing a named deputy, and so a potential successor.

Living Church of God
PO Box 503077
San Diego, CA 92150-3077
www.lcg.org
www.tomorrowsworld.org

Restored Church of God
PO Box 23295
Wadsworth, OH 44282
www.thercg.org

Global (UK), CGCF (Canada), Church of the Eternal God (U.S.A.)
www.globalchurchofgod.co.uk
www.churchofgodacf.ca
www.eternalgod.org

David V. Barrett

See also: Philadelphia Church of God; Sabbatarianism; United Church of God; Worldwide Church of God.

References

Barrett, David V. *The New Believers*. London: Cassell, 2001.

The Journal: News of the Churches of God. 2001–present. Big Sandy, TX: JMC Associates.

Pack, David C. *There Came a Falling Away*. Wadsworth, OH: Restored Church of God, 2000.

Tkach, Joseph. *Transformed by Truth*. Sisters, OR: Multnomah Books, 1997.

Local Church, The

The Local Church is the name assumed in the West by a movement variously known as the Little Flock or the Assembly Hall Churches. The Local Church grew out of the life and thought of Nee To-sheng, better known in the West as Watchman Nee (1903–1972). Nee was born in Shantou, China, and trained in classical Chinese studies. He was converted to Christianity in 1920 under the ministry of Dora Yu (1873–1931), a Methodist missionary who ran a Bible school in Shanghai.

A gathering of members of the Local Church in Taiwan. (J. Gordon Melton)

He was also deeply influenced by the writing of the British-based Keswick Revival and the exclusive Plymouth Brethren. He found himself drawn to the Plymouth Brethren and was associated with them into the 1930s.

Nee began his own ministry with a magazine, *Revival*, in 1923 and finished his first major book, *The Spiritual Man*, in 1928. By this time he had also come to the conclusion that the unity of the church would be best expressed by the establishment of only one church in each city; that is, that denominational competition was unbiblical and the only reason for different churches was geographical—hence the name Local Church. The first "local church" was founded in Shanghai in 1927. Nee also agreed with the ideal previously articulated by several 19th-century missionaries as

"three-self." In order to make the Protestant Christian movement in China independent of foreign churches, missions were urged to work toward three types of independence: self-governance, self-support, and self-propagation. Incarnating such an ideal was, of course, integral to the several indigenous Chinese Christian movements, including the Local Church. From the Brethren, Nee absorbed a dispensational approach to the Bible, seeing human history as unfolding in a series of God's dispensations, during each of which God changed his way of relating to humanity.

The movement's growth was somewhat disrupted by World War II and the Japanese invasion. In 1942 Nee took a job at the pharmaceutical company owned by his brother in order to raise money to support continued evangelical efforts, which had by this time become international. Some saw his taking a secular job as contradictory to his ministry, and the church's elders forbade him from preaching in Shanghai. The issue was not resolved until 1947, when Nee gave the church all of his business assets and withdrew from further secular work. He also encouraged other church members to "Hand Over" their business assets to the church, and the profits from these businesses began to be used to expand the evangelical work.

In the 1930s, Witness Lee (1905–1997) joined the Local Church movement and through the decade became a close associate of Nee. In 1948 Nee sent Lee to Taiwan, where the defeated Nationalist forces were to gather as the Communists took control of the mainland. The church came under attack from the Communist regime in the early 1950s. In 1952 Nee was arrested, and in 1956 he was tried and convicted of corrupt business practices and violations of public morals. He spent the rest of his life in jail. The government recognized only one Protestant church body, the Chinese Protestant Three-Self Patriotic movement, with which all Protestant Christians were required to affiliate. Thus the Local Church was banned in China, and Nee's movement became divided, with some congregations being absorbed into the Chinese Protestant Three-Self Patriotic movement and others continuing as independent congregations outside legal structures.

However, the movement continued to grow outside of China. From Witness Lee's work in Taiwan, the Local Church began to spread throughout Southeast Asia, beginning with the ethnic Chinese communities in the larger cities. In 1962 Lee moved to the United States, learned English, and began to spread the movement among English-speaking residents of California, a first step in making the Local Church a truly international movement.

Lee gained an initial following among evangelical Christians attracted to his emphasis on the spiritual life and the immediate relationship between God and humanity. He continued the theology articulated earlier by Nee, which viewed humans as tripartite beings (body, soul, and spirit) and recognized an intimate relationship between God's Spirit and the human spirit. However, in the 1970s, as Lee expanded upon this mystical theology, trouble developed when some former followers began to suggest that Lee's approach, and some new language he introduced to focus the teachings, represented a loss of distinction between God and humanity and a distortion of traditional Christian teachings on the Trinity.

The seriousness of the theological charges were undergirded by the perception that Lee had gained most of his membership at the expense of other churches. In the early 1980s, the controversy erupted after spokespersons for several Christian counter-cult ministries, led by the Spiritual Counterfeits Project, accused the Local Church of being a cult. Included in their list of objections were several unique practices of the church, such as "Calling upon the name of the Lord," the invocation of God by the loud repetition of phrases such as "O Lord Jesus." (This is the practice that gave one group growing out of the Local Church the appellation "Shouters" in China.) In response, Lee had his theology and the church's practices examined by several trained theologians, who could find nothing heretical, and he attempted to reconcile his differences with his evangelical antagonists. However, the problems had grown with the expansion of Christian counter-cult ministries, and he was unable to resolve them. So in 1985 he sued the Spiritual Counterfeits Project in court and won a large multimillion-dollar judgment for libel and slander. For a period, the court case silenced the church's critics.

Following the court case, Lee began a new effort to encourage the further spread of the Local Church, which had stagnated in the 1980s. He moved to Taiwan for a period and led in the reorganization of the Local Church around a new emphasis on evangelism. He continued to lead the movement until his death in 1997. Since that time, the movement has been guided by a coalition of senior elders.

The Local Churches are organized as autonomous congregations, each led by elders selected from among its own membership. The congregations are tied together by their mutual acceptance of the fundamental doctrines and approach initially articulated by Nee and continued by Lee. Upon his arrival in California, Lee assumed the role of apostle and teacher. He organized Living Stream Ministry as an instrument to provide leadership for all of the local congregations. He published a magazine and a number of books and pamphlets. He also held regular training sessions to educate leaders on both the practical leadership of the churches and theological development of church life. Most church elders were part-time, unsalaried workers, but as the movement grew, some elders were designated as full-time co-workers. Although there are no ordained ministers, the co-workers have assumed many roles typically held by ordained clergy.

Living Stream Ministry continues to serve as the uniting force of the Local Church congregations. During the years of Lee's ministry, the Local Church became a worldwide movement, and it has associated congregations on every continent. Each congregation takes the name of the city in which its members reside. An unknown number of people, reportedly as high as 800,000, continue the ministry of Watchman Nee in mainland China, where a number of leaders have been arrested for preaching outside the established churches. In a 1983 court case, the movement was declared to be counter-revolutionary in but one of a variety of actions to suppress the group, and various international human rights groups have come to its defense. The Local Church in Hong Kong has a large following, necessitating multiple meeting halls, and some 60,000 members are found across Taiwan. Strong congregations are located throughout Southeast Asia, where the movement has moved beyond its base within the Chinese communities, and also across North America. Many Local Churches have their own websites. Worldwide membership is in excess of 1 million.

The belief statement of the Local Churches identifies it with conservative Protestant Free Church beliefs. It strongly affirms the Trinity and the divinity of Christ, substitutionary atonement, and the verbal inspiration of the Bible. Sectarian divisions and denominationalism is eschewed, and the oneness of Christian believers is affirmed. The Local Church places itself in a history of "recovery" of biblical Christianity, which it deems was lost through the centuries after the Apostolic era. The recovery began with Martin Luther and the Protestant Reformation and continued through other movements, including the Methodists and the Plymouth Brethren (now generally called the Christian Brethren). A new phase began with Watchman Nee and his emphasis on the Local Church.

Lee kept up a prodigious schedule of teaching and speaking through the 35 years after his move to the United States. His lectures and sermons were transcribed and published and constitute a large collection of Christian literature. He wrote a multivolume commentary on the Bible and a translation of the Bible, published as the Recovery Version. Recordings of Lee's Bible studies are featured on the Local Church's radio program, *Life Study of the Bible*.

In the late 1990s, critics of the Local Church began to resurface; in response, leadership of the church in Anaheim, California, began anew to convince their critics, all from the evangelical counter-cult movement, of their orthodoxy. Running into opposition on one level, Local Church leaders instituted a suit against John Ankerberg and John Weldon, authors of the *Encyclopedia of Cults and New Religions*, who included the Local Church among the groups they covered. The suit was unsuccessful; however, the effort led to a major re-evaluation of the Local Churches by some of their more prominent critics and the issuance of a statement that they now accepted the Local Church into the circle of their fellowship. Their testimony largely cemented the effort of the Local Churches to re-integrate into the large world of evangelicalism.

The largest number of Christians who have grown from the work originated by Watchman Nee remain in China and Southeast Asia. The American-based Living Streams Ministry has a counterpart in Taiwan, which offers primary assistance to those members who speak Chinese throughout Southeast Asia. It is also attempting to stay in touch with an estimated 1 million "members" still in the People's Republic. Many of these "members" are part of the larger Church of Christ in China; others attend one of the unregistered churches that now dot the landscape. Living Stream Ministry pursues a variety of initiatives to communicate with government officials in China and to establish Watchman Nee's and Witness Lee's place in Chinese Christian history.

Living Stream Ministry
2431 W. La Palma Ave.
Anaheim, CA 92801
http://www.lsm.org/ (in English, Chinese, Spanish, and Korean)
http://www.livingstream.com/

J. Gordon Melton

See also: Chinese Protestant Three-Self Patriotic Movement/China Christian Council; Christian Brethren; Evangelicalism; Luther, Martin.

References

The Beliefs and Practices of the Local Church. Anaheim, CA: Living Stream Ministry, 1978.

Hanegraaff, Hank, Gretchen Passantino, and Fuller Theological Seminary. *The Local Churches: "Genuine Believers and Fellow Members of the Body of Christ."* Fullerton, CA: DCP Press, 2008.

Kinnear, Angus I. *Against the Tide.* Fort Washington, PA: Christian Literature Crusade, 1973.

Lee, Witness. *God's New Testament Economy.* Anaheim, CA: Living Stream Ministry, 1986.

Lee, Witness. *The History of the Church and the Local Churches.* Anaheim, CA: Living Stream Ministry, 1991.

Lee, Witness. *Life Study of the New Testament.* 17 vols. Anaheim, CA: Living Stream Ministry, 1984.

Lee, Witness. *Life Study of the Old Testament.* 15 vols. Anaheim, CA: Living Stream Ministry, 1997.

Lee, Witness. *Watchman Nee: A Seer of the Divine Revelation in the Present Age.* Anaheim, CA: Living Stream Ministry, 1997.

Nee, Watchman. *The Collected Works.* 62 vols. Anaheim, CA: Living Stream Ministry, 1994.

Nee, Watchman. *The Normal Christian Church Life.* Washington, DC: International Students Press, 1969.

Wu, Silas H. *Dora Yu and Christian Revival in 20th Century China.* Boston: Pishon River Publications, 2002.

London Missionary Society

The London Missionary Society (LMS), now a constituent part of the Council for World Mission, is one of several organizations that facilitated the massive expansion of Christianity around the world in the 19th and 20th centuries. It emerged in 1795 in England out of the growing consciousness there of people in the world outside Europe, itself a sign of developing British colonial interests worldwide. Particular inspiration came from the widely published letters sent back to England by William Carey (1761–1834), who had launched a mission in India in 1793.

Thus, in December 1794 a group of ministers and laypeople from the Church of England, the Presbyterian Church, and the Independents or the Congregational Church (the largest number) met to consider the idea of forming a pan-denominational missionary society. In the end, the Congregationalists became the primary supporters of the new LMS, constituted in 1795. Both the Church of England and the Presbyterian Church soon had their own competing missionary structures.

The primary field chosen for work was the South Pacific, then a territory devoid of Protestant church work. The LMS purchased a ship, the *Duff*, and in September 1796 it sent 13 men, 5 women, and 2 children. This first cadre was dispersed between Tahiti and Tonga, with one person staying in the Marquesas. Beginning with this initial band, the Society would dispatch additional missionaries to the Cook Islands and then to most of the larger South Pacific island groups. These first missionaries set a pattern for later missionaries—working with the indigenous population to train a set of local teachers and leaders and translating and publishing the Bible in the local language.

Early in the 19th century, the Society turned its attention to Africa. Two of the most famous people in Christian missionary history, John MacKenzie (1835–1899) and David Livingstone (1813–1873), were LMS missionaries who launched their work in 1840 in South Africa. MacKenzie became a politician and urged British expansion into the lands north of Boer-controlled territory, and Livingstone explored that territory. The Society also pioneered work in China and Mongolia. During its peak years, through the 19th century, the Society supported some 250 missionaries at any given moment.

As a variety of denominational and pan-denominational Protestant missionary societies began working alongside each other, the LMS entered negotiations to cut down on duplication of efforts and direct competition. In this manner, different societies accepted responsibility for different countries or sections of countries. Such agreements worked through much of the 19th century, until the very success of many missionary efforts brought different groups into competition. The origin of the modern ecumenical movement lies, to a great extent, with these attempts to solve the problems of competition and to reduce the introduction of sectarian differences into the mission field from the Americas and Europe.

World War II proved pivotal to the LMS. Following the war, the former colonies of Great Britain became independent, and many territories—like China, the single largest LMS missionary field—were closed to foreign missionaries. Already a number of the missions had matured into independent churches, and beginning in 1947, with the Church of South India, the congregational work in a variety of countries merged with other Protestant missions/churches to form united Protestant churches. Thus in 1966 the LMS and a sister organization, the Commonwealth Missionary Society, merged to form the Congregational Council for World Mission. Then in 1977, a further reorganization and merger included the Presbyterian Board of Missions, founded in 1847, and led to the creation of the Council for World Mission (CWM). The CWM envisions itself as a cooperative, multicultural missionary effort combining the resources of 32 denominational bodies based on continents around the world that now share a partnership relationship. Missionaries are drawn from all of the cooperating churches and may be sent to any country as needed.

Council for World Mission
Ipalo House
32-34 Great Peter St.
London SW1P 2DB
UK
http://www.cwmission.org.uk

J. Gordon Melton

See also: Carey, William; Church of South India.

References

Handbook of the Council for World Mission. London: Council on World Mission, 1984.

Hiney, Thomas. *On the Missionary Trail: A Journey through Polynesia, Asia, and Africa with the London Missionary Society.* New York: Atlantic Monthly Press, 2000.

Kane, J. Herbert. *A Global View of Christian Missions.* Grand Rapids, MI: Baker Book House, 1971.

Van Beek, Huibert. *A Handbook of the Churches and Councils: Profiles of Ecumenical Relationships.* Geneva: World Council of Churches, 2006.

Lourdes

In 1858, Lourdes, a small town in southern France near the Spanish border, became the site of the most well-known modern apparition of the Blessed Virgin Mary. That year, a young girl named Bernadette Soubirous (1844–1879) had visions of the Virgin over a period of six months. The initial vision occurred on February 11, a few days after she had received her First Communion at the local church, her village being a Roman Catholic community. As she searched for wood near a grotto, her attention was drawn to a moving rosebush, and shortly thereafter what she would describe as a young and beautiful woman appeared above the bush. Bernadette immediately dropped to her knees and began to pray and was joined by the woman. The woman then disappeared without saying anything.

The Lady, eventually established to be the Virgin Mary, appeared on 18 subsequent occasions over the next 6 months. Bernadette first heard her speak during the third apparition. During her ninth appearance she instructed Bernadette to dig in the ground. Water would emerge and she was to drink from and bathe in that water. At the spot she dug, a spring began to flow. That spring would then be seen as flowing with healing water available for all. The Lady finally instructed Bernadette to see to the building of a chapel at the grotto.

The local priest, who saw Bernadette as naïve and somewhat ignorant, pressed her to inquire of the identity of the Lady she was seeing and with whom she was conversing, especially after the request to build the chapel was made. Finally, in her last appearance, the Lady identified herself as the Immaculate Conception. At the time, Catholic theologians of the day were pursuing a full inquiry into the viability of the concept of immaculate conception, the idea that the Virgin

Shrine to Our Lady of Lourdes, Palermo, Sicily. (J. Gordon Melton)

Mary had been born without original sin. (Among non-Catholics, the idea of the immaculate conception is often confused with Jesus' birth from a virgin, rather than Mary's birth without sin.) That Bernadette came forward with this somewhat sophisticated idea served to convince the parish priest that she was, in fact, in contact with the Virgin.

The increasingly secularized French public and government officials did not accept Bernadette's claims as readily as the priest. Even as Lourdes gained fame as a healing shrine, government officials occasionally moved against it and at one point closed it for several years.

Through her life, in the years following the visions, Bernadette suffered from a spectrum of illnesses. Her health, in fact, delayed her entrance into a religious order. She was finally accepted only after the local bishop put pressure on the Sisters of Nevers and they found a place for her at the Convent of Saint-Gildard.

During her rather brief career as a nun, she simply grew more ill, and finally passed away on April 16, 1879, at the convent's infirmary.

Many came to view her body, which was allowed to remain on view for three days. She was placed in a coffin on April 19, and it was sealed in the presence of a number of witnesses. Permissions were secured for its movement and on May 30, 1879, the coffin was transferred to the convent's chapel, dedicated to Saint Joseph. In 1909 the coffin was opened, and officials discovered that her body had remained uncorrupted. Once news seeped out, this phenomenon increased her reputation. To this day, her body remains on view at the Nevers chapel.

Meanwhile, though Bernadette remained isolated at the convent, the spring continued to flow and the grotto of the apparitions became the site of a growing number of reported cures. Though tens of thousands of cures were claimed, only a small percentage passed the very strict standards of the medical bureau that was established to examine different cases and assemble records of those that appeared to be medically unexplainable. Over the years the original small chapel was replaced with a large basilica.

Bernadette was canonized in 1933 by Pope Pius XI (r. 1922–1939). A nearby church, the Basilica of Saint Pius X, was dedicated by Angelo Cardinal Roncalli (1881–1963) then the papal nuncio to France and later known as Pope John XXIII. The building, largely underground, can accommodate a crowd of 30,000.

J. Gordon Melton

See also: John XXIII, Pope; Pilgrimage; Roman Catholic Church.

References

Carrel, Alexis. *The Voyage to Lourdes.* New York: Harper, 1950.

Crawford, Kerry. *Lourdes Today: A Pilgrimage to Mary's Grotto.* Ann Arbor, MI: Servant Books, 2008.

McEachern, Patricia. *A Holy Life: The Writings of St. Bernadette of Lourdes.* Ft. Collins, CO: Ignatius Press, 2005.

Neame, Alan. *The Happening at Lourdes: The Sociology of the Grotto.* New York: Simon and Schuster, 1967.

Taylor, Therese. *Bernadette of Lourdes: Her Life, Death and Visions*. London: Burns & Oates, 2003.

Lubavitch Hasidism

In the late 20th century, the Lubavitch emerged as the largest of the Hasidic bodies that survived the Holocaust of World War II, during which many Hasidic bodies ceased to exist and others survived as mere remnants of their earlier life. The Lubavitch community began under Rabbi Schneur Zalman (1745–1813). He had studied with Rabbi Dov Baer, a prominent Hasidic scholar, and Dov Bear's death in 1772 became the catalyst for the founding of the Lubavitch dynasty. Zalman was sent to Lithuania to spread the Hassidic message, and the Lubavitcher community dates its origins from the start of Zalman's teaching in Lithuania.

The son of Rabbi Zalman, also known as Rabbi Dov Baer (1773–1827), or the Mittler Rebbe, succeeded his father and developed the Chabad, as the Lubavitch approach to Hasidism became known. In the late 1820s, he relocated to Lubavitch, Belarus, from which the community's designation is derived. From Dov Baer, the lineage passed to Rabbi Menachem Mendel Schneerson (1789–1866), the son of Rabbi Zalman's daughter. The lineage eventually passed to Schneerson's grandson, Joseph Isaac Schneerson (1880–1950), who brought the movement to the United States. In the 1920s, Rabbi Schneerson founded the Agudas Chassidas Chabad of the United States of America and Canada, first visiting America in 1929. He had resided in Warsaw since the end of World War I, but he was persuaded to leave as the Nazi threat loomed. He took up residence in the United States in 1941.

The Lubavitch teach out of the Kabbalah, the ancient Jewish mystical system. The Kabbalah pictures the world as having emanated from God through several realms of spiritual activity. These spheres (*sephirot*) are pictured on a diagram called the Tree of Life. The name of the Lubavitch teachings, Chabad, is derived from three of the sephirot—Chochmah, Binah, and Daath—wisdom, intelligence, and knowledge. In the Chabad attempt to come into a relationship with the divine, an insistence on study and the intellectual appropriation of truth stands beside a need for faith and belief. As do other Hasidic groups, the Lubavitch use a rite derived from the writings of Rabbi Isaac Luria (1534–1572), a mystic and Kabbalist in Palestine. The prayers of the ritual contain special intentions relating to the mystical union of God and humanity. The Lubavitch also have a commitment to the larger Jewish community and have tried to dispel the low opinion that many Hasids have had of unbelieving and non-practicing Jews in general.

Lubavitchers are known for their music and dancing. Dancing is seen as a basic expression of the inward joy of the divine life. Men dance separately from women, mixed dancing being prohibited. Dancing forms an essential part of Hasidic gatherings, especially the festivals and anniversary occasions.

After World War II, the Rebbe Schneerson initiated a program of expanding the community's school and centers. When his successor, Rabbi Menachem Mendel Schneerson (1902–1994), took over the relatively small movement, he began to build the movement, based on its traditional openness to the whole of the Jewish community. Over the next decades it grew impressively as Jews across the spectrum, from Orthodox to Reform and even unbelief, discovered the movement and affiliated with it. Its work was furthered through the community's publishing arm, Merkos Publication Society; its educational arm, Merkos L'Inyone Chinuch; and its relief organization, Ezrat Pleitim. By the time of Rebbe Menachem Mendel Schneerson's death, the movement had more than 200,000 followers, and centers had been opened in the midst of Orthodox Jewish communities worldwide. Its growth is partially attributed to its acceptance of modern technology, which other Hasidim have tended to reject, and especially to an international network of emissaries who establish missions of outreach.

Toward the end of his life, Rebbe Schneerson, who had led the movement for four decades, suggested that the time of the expected Messiah was at hand. He cited as evidence, among other incidents, the fall of Communism and the U.S. victory in the Gulf War. Some of his followers came to believe that he was the Messiah, and his death in 1994 placed the issue of the future clearly before the community. Following his passing, many refused to speak of him in the past tense, while some insisted that he would somehow cheat death. They refused to discuss a successor, and none had been named as of 2009. Banners and postcards were printed with an oft-repeated slogan, "Long live our master, teacher, and rebbe, King Messiah, forever and ever."

In the meantime, all of the Rebbe's spoken words, including his Sabbath sermons (sometimes four hours in length), were recorded and transcribed. These remain as a body of teachings from which the community can continue to draw inspiration. As a first step in sharing his wisdom, in 1995 a commercial publisher was allowed to publish *Toward a Meaningful Life: The Wisdom of the Rebbe, Menachem Mendel Schneerson.* The headquarters of the Lubavitcher movement is located in Brooklyn, New York, and there are many Chabad websites. As the 21st century begins, there are more than 2,000 Chabad centers serving more than 200,000 members.

Lubavitch Movement Headquarters
770 Eastern Parkway
Brooklyn, NY 11213
http://www.chabadcenters.com/
http://www.chabad.org/

J. Gordon Melton

See also: Hasidism; Orthodox Judaism.

References

Challenge. London: Lubavitch Foundation of Great Britain, 1970.
Dalfin, Chaim. *The Seven Chabad-Lubavitch Rebbes.* New York: Jason Aronson, 1998.
Fishkoff, Sue. *The Rebbe's Army: Inside the World of Chabad-Lubavitch.* New York: Schocken, 2005.
Hilsenrad, Zalman Aryeh. *The Baal Shem Tov.* Brooklyn: Kehot Publication Society, 1967.
Mintz, Jerome R. *Hasidic People: A Place in the New World.* Cambridge: Harvard University Press, 1992.
Schneerson, Menachem Mendel. *I Await His Coming Every Day: Based on Talks of the Lubavitch Rebbe.* Brooklyn, NY: Kehot Publication Society, 1998.
Schneerson, Menachem Mendel. *Toward a Meaningful Life: The Wisdom of the Rebbe, Menachem Mendel Schneerson.* Adapted by Simon Jacobson. New York: William Morrow, 1995.
Warshaw, Mal. *Tradition: Orthodox Jewish Life in America.* New York: Schocken Books, 1976.

Lumbini

Tradition locates the birth place of Gautama Buddha as Lumbini, in what is now Nepal, and in the 20th century it joined the three other sites connected with Buddha's life—Kusinagara, Sarnath, and Bodhgaya—as one of the four major holy places of international Buddhism. Many Buddhists also accept the stories from Buddhist literature that tell of events relative to the birth, which recount how Maya Devi, Buddha's mother, gave birth while traveling to her parents' home in Devadaha. She took a rest in Lumbini under a sal tree. The event is dated as early as 642 BCE, and as late as 566. The infant is also said to have spoken immediately after separating from his mother, "This is my final rebirth." He then took seven steps to the four cardinal points of the compass, and a lotus flower sprang forth with each step.

Scholars of Buddhism have in the last generation called almost every occurrence in Buddha's life into question, including the birth stories, but find themselves on firmer ground when it comes to the later history of Lumbini. Several centuries after the Buddha lived, King Ashoka visited the area (249 BCE) and erected a stele commemorating the event. He also ordered the building of a wall around the village as well as the placement of a stone pillar and four stupas (Buddhist shrines to the dead) to mark the spot. He capped his visit by reducing the taxes that the village would have to pay in the future.

Lumbini remained a Buddhist center under Buddhist hegemony until the ninth century CE. In subsequent centuries, Muslims invaded the area and then Hindus took control of the region. The Buddhist structures were destroyed, and eventually the memory of the location faded. Thus, the 1895 discovery of the Asoka stele by Alois A. Feuhrer, a famous German archaeologist, made news. His find led to further probes that uncovered a temple decorated with scenes of the

The Maya Devi Temple in Lumbini, near the birthplace of the Buddha. (Jun Mu/Dreamstime.com)

Buddha's life, a relatively later temple that had probably been constructed over one of the stupas originally erected by Asoka. Further excavations later in the century uncovered a number of the Buddhist sites. Toward the end of the century, Japanese Buddhists raised money to have the area renovated, and even though located in a remote corner of the world and difficult to reach, Lumbini has re-emerged as a place for Buddhist pilgrimages.

Contemporary pilgrims in Lumbini will find a Tibetan Buddhist monastery, a Nepalese temple (financed in part by U Thant, the Burmese who served as United Nations secretary from 1961 to 1971), and the Maya Devi Temple. The pillar with the Asoka stele remains the most important artifact in the town. The garden, where tradition places the birth of the child who became the Buddha (the Enlightened One) is said to have occurred is now cared for by the devoted faithful, and visitors are invited to take a symbolic wash at the nearby Puskarmi pond in which the infant Buddha got his first bath.

Edward A. Irons

See also: Ashoka; Bodh-Gaya; Buddha, Gautama; Pilgrimage.

References

Majupuria, Trilok Chandra. *Holy Places of Buddhism in Nepal and India: A Guide to Sacred Places in Buddha's Lands*. Columbia, MO: South Asia Books, 1987.

Panabokke, Gunaratne. *History of the Buddhist Sangha in India and Sri Lanka*. Dalugama, Kelaniya, Sri Lanka: Postgraduate Institute of Pali and Buddhist Studies, University of Kelaniya, 1993.

Tulku, Tarthang, ed. *Holy Places of the Buddha*. Vol. 9, *Crystal Mirror*. Berkeley, CA: Dharma Publishing, 1994.

Lusitanian Church/Lusitanian Catholic Apostolic Evangelical Church

The Lusitanian Church is a small Portuguese church founded at the end of the 19th century under the auspices of members of the American Episcopal Church and the Church of England. The church, named after Lusitania, the ancient denomination for the territory that is now Portugal, is a formal member of the Anglican Communion since 1980. It is also affiliated with the World Council of Churches, the Conference of European Churches, and the Conference of Protestant Churches of the European Latin Countries.

After four centuries of almost complete absence, reformist movements saw the relative religious freedom that followed the establishment of a constitutional monarchy in 1834 as an opportunity to assert themselves on Portuguese soil. A few decades later, the introduction of the dogmas of papal infallibility and universal jurisdiction by the First Vatican Council (1870–1871) caused much uproar both among the reformist churches and urban Roman Catholics seduced by Liberalism. In this context, some Spanish priests established in Lisbon several places of worship where they celebrated religious services with Portuguese translations of the English Prayer Book and of the American Book of Common Prayer. Under this influence, some Roman Catholic Portuguese priests and laypeople began to form congregations in various places. In March 8, 1880, these priests and the lay representatives of their congregations met at a synod presided over by Bishop Riley, consecrated in the American Episcopal Church, and celebrated the formalization of the Lusitanian Church. Its members refer to this occasion not as the foundation but as the restoration of their church. They state that the Lusitanian Church is the resumption of the original Christian church that existed in the Iberian Peninsula and was allegedly initiated by early missionaries of the third century or, as some claim, by Saint Paul himself. At the time of the Visigothic invasion in the fifth century CE, the church was already well established, with its own councils and a distinct liturgy. According to this narrative, the Roman Catholic Church only managed to impose a strict papal jurisdiction with the Christian (re)conquest, which began in the ninth century.

From its "restoration" until 1964, the Council of Bishops was formed solely by Irish bishops. The first Portuguese bishop, António Fiandor, was consecrated only in 1958 by three foreign Anglican bishops. The reason for this is that, according to the Lusitanian Church, a legitimate consecration requires historical episcopal succession. Throughout the 1960s, Concordats of Full Communion were established with the American Episcopal Church, the Church of Ireland, the Church of England, and the Old Catholic bishops of the Union of Utrecht.

In 1980, two years after a formal application to the archbishop of Canterbury, the Lusitanian Church was welcomed into the Anglican Communion, of which it is still today an extra-provincial diocese. Following the approval of a new Law of Religious Freedom by the Portuguese Parliament, the Lusitanian Church applied for the status of Established Church, which was granted in 2008. Among other privileges, it can now celebrate religious marriages with civil effects, its donors benefit from a tax deduction, and the church can formalize agreements with the Portuguese state on matters of common interest.

The Lusitanian Church functions as a single diocese divided into two archdeaconries: the South (centering at Lisbon) and the North (centering at Oporto). Most of the 16 congregations cluster around these 2 major cities. The general governing bodies are the bishop, who devotes himself almost entirely to the spiritual leadership of the church; the Synod, consisting of every priest of the church and a lay representative from each parish; and a standing committee, which deals with administration affairs.

Currently, the Lusitanian Church has about 5,000 baptized members and 1,500 communicants, with 8 active priests and 6 active deacons in 16 places of worship. In 1997, 3 women were ordained as deacons. It was the first time in over eight centuries of Christianity in Portugal that women became part of the clergy of a church with the Apostolic ministry.

The doctrine of the Lusitanian Church follows the main parameters confessed by the Anglican Community and expressed in the Lambeth Quadrilateral. Furthermore, it declares itself to be in the historical and doctrinal continuity of the first centuries' churches existing in Lusitania and declines to accept the later additions and changes introduced by the Roman Catholic Church. Its liturgy reflects this alleged heritage. The Portuguese Book of Common Prayer is said to be in accordance with the "Primitive Apostolic Church" and its compilation was largely based on the ancient Missal de Braga.

One of the most visible activities of the Lusitanian Church is its ecumenical effort of promoting interfaith dialogue and the foundation of the Portuguese Council of Christian Churches, along with the Methodists and the Presbyterians. Since its "restoration," the Lusitanian Church has been promoting a ministry of service to the underprivileged and nowadays it includes three institutions with social responsibility (including a day care center, a kindergarten, assistance to the elderly and promotion of social and cultural activities among the blind). Initially, this effort was more focused on the struggle against illiteracy, which by the end of the 19th century was as high as 80 percent in Portugal. Together with every place of worship that was opened, a primary school was also started. Presently, two of those schools are still functioning.

The Lusitanian Church
Rua de Afonso Albuquerque, n° 86
Apartado 392
4431-905 V. N. Gaia
Portugal
http://www.igreja-lusitana.org/

Tiago Santos, Pedro Soares, and Miguel H. Farias

See also: Church of England; Church of Ireland; Episcopal Church; Roman Catholic Church.

References

Lusitanian Church. Vila Nova de Gaia, 1985.

Moreira, Eduardo Henriques. *Esboço da História da Igreja Lusitana*. Vila Nova de Gaia: Sínodo da Igreja Lusitana Católica Apostólica Evangélica, 1949.

Relatório de 1914 da Egreja Lusitana Católica Apostólica Evangélica. Porto, Igreja Lusitana Católica Apostólica Evangélica, 1915.

Soares, Fernando da Luz. *Igreja Lusitana: Caminho para Cristo*. Vila Nova de Gaia: Comissão permanente do Sínodo da Igreja Lusitana Católica Apostólica Evangélica, 1983.

Soares, Fernando da Luz. "The Lusitanian Catholic Apostolic Evangelical Church: A Century of Portuguese Anglican Witness." The Convocation of American Churches in Europe website, 1998. www.tec-europe.org/partners/Lusitanian_partner.htm. Accessed October 6, 2008.

Luther, Martin

1483–1546

Martin Luther, an Augustinian monk, and professor of theology at the relatively new University of Wittenberg, Saxony, began a relatively mild critique of the Roman Catholic Church at the beginning of the 16th century that quickly turned into a complete call for the reformation of the church. The Reformation movement he initiated would find support especially in northern Europe and result in the formation of the Evangelical (Lutheran) Church based in Germany and Scandinavia that would in the subsequent century become a worldwide phenomenon.

Luther was born on November 10, 1483, in Eisenben, Germany. His father, though not of the nobility, was relatively well-to-do and his ambitions for his son included an education. As a youth, Martin was sent to schools in Mansfield, Magdeburg, and Eisenach, which prepared him for entrance to the University of Erfurt in 1501. He graduated four years later with an M.A. Degree. At this point, his college career was diverted by a period of personal soul-searching occasioned by the death of a friend. Feeling his own finitude, he entered the Augustinian Order, within which he combined rumination on his personal spiritual situation with theological studies. He was ordained a priest in 1507. His superiors recognized his intellectual talents and selected him for advanced studies. He earned his bachelor's degree in theology at the University of Wittenberg in 1509.

After completing his doctorate (1512), he stayed at Wittenberg as a lecturer. He initially chose to focus his lectures on the biblical book of Psalms (1513–1515). His studies and lectures led to a belief that Christian salvation focused on a new relationship with God that was based in faith in Christ rather than deeds of merit done by the individual. He concluded that a Christian

Statue of Martin Luther, Worms, Germany. (J. Gordon Melton)

was also a sinner and hence undeserving of God's love. God nevertheless redeemed individuals and out of that new relationship started by God, the individual believer tried to conform his or her life to God's will. While sacraments and good deeds were still an important part of religious existence, they paled in comparison to the new relationship with God.

With this new insight, Luther turned his attention to Paul's letter to the Romans, out of which came his own personal experience of salvation. He came to feel that God had forgiven his sin and that he had received that salvation by faith and faith alone. Luther moved from his intense personal experiences into the middle of a very public controversy. Johann Tetzel (1466–1519), a Dominican monk, traveled through Germany to sell indulgences. Any funds he raised were forwarded to Rome to cover the cost of building St. Peter's Cathedral.

Indulgences fit into a view of salvation that saw individuals pursuing a lifelong effort to become holy.

The average person fell far short, holiness being reached by only a few, the saints, most of whom had abandoned secular occupations for the religious life. The average person would have to continue the process of becoming holy in purgatory, a place of punishment and purgation. Most thought of their family and friends who had previously passed away as now existing in purgatory. One could shorten her or his stay in purgatory through various acts of goodness and/or piety. The church, however, possessed the power to grant "indulgences," pardons that would reduce or even eliminate one's time in purgatory, or the time of a loved one. Tetzel, in particular, offered an indulgence to any who contributed to the construction of St. Peter's.

Luther saw indulgences, especially the commercialization of them by Tetzel, as a practice built on bad theology and a complete misunderstanding of grace, faith, and biblical salvation. He decided to challenge the practice and did so by proposing 95 points for debate. These points were written down and the list, reputedly, nailed to the door of the parish church at Wittenberg on October 31, 1517. The sale of indulgences dropped dramatically. Tetzel attempted to recover by proposing a set of counterpoints. Luther and Tetzel's interaction led to a debate, though Tetzel would be replaced by theologian Johann Eck. The debate was held in 1519 in Leipzig. Luther built his defense by direct reference to the Bible, its text being cited to refute the rulings of popes and church councils. He claimed that both popes and councils had made mistakes. Luther was declared a heretic and excommunicated.

In response to the debate and subsequent excommunication, Luther made his case to a larger audience in three lengthy essays. The *Appeal to the German Nobility* (1520) centered on the idea of the priesthood of all believers. The effect of asserting that every person was a priest had in effect removed some authority from parish priests and recast it in terms of the personal relationship between God and the believer. The whole concept would unfortunately soon be taken in some quite radical (and even violent) ways, much to Luther's consternation. He took up the subject of the church's elaborate sacramental system in *Babylonian Captivity of the Church* (1520) and concluded that only two of the church's sacraments, baptism and the Lord's Supper, met the criteria for continuation. On a lesser but not unimportant point, Luther argued that the cup of wine representing the blood of Christ should be given to the believers when the Lord's Supper was celebrated. Finally, Luther laid out a more systematic and complete understanding of faith in God, salvation, and the Christian life in *The Freedom of the Christian Man* (1520).

Access to one of the new printing presses invented in the previous century by Johann Gutenberg allowed the relatively quick circulation of Luther's writings, and their broad circulation led the emperor of the Holy Roman Empire to summon Luther to the meeting of its governing body, the Diet, which met at Worms. In defending his writings, Luther appealed to the Bible and to reason. The Diet condemned him, but the secular ruler of the region, Frederick, the elector of Saxony (1463–1525), was both very protective of his university and its faculty and strongly opposed the draining of finances from his territory to Rome. In addition, by the time the Diet met, significant support for Luther had developed across northern Germany. Though condemned, Frederick arranged for Luther's disappearance. Luther took the time to produce additional materials supportive of the developing perspective. The major new items produced by Luther at this time were his translation of the New Testament in the German language (1522) and a volume of hymns that included some written by Luther himself (1524).

The progress of Luther's Reformation was called into question by the peasants' revolt, a violent protest by the poorest segment of society using Luther's proclamation of the priesthood of all believers and the freedom of the Christian man. The revolt was put down at a high cost in lives. On May 15, 1525, the peasants were finally defeated at the battle at Frankenhausen, and, in what some saw as the darkest moment of the Reformation, some 50,000 peasants were killed.

The peasants' revolt momentarily slowed but did not stop the Reformation. It occurred in the context of other brutal battles, not the least being those related to the Muslim invasion of Europe. As Luther's movement in Germany developed in the 1520s, Turkish forces moved on Vienna and came close to capturing it.

While the churches in Germany were instituting the changes called for by Luther, a similar movement was developing in German-speaking portions of Swit-

zerland under Ulrich Zwingli (1484–1531). The two Reformation efforts developed along a parallel course, but a significant disagreement emerged between the two leaders over the issue of the sacraments. Zwingli came to believe that baptism and the Lord's Supper were primarily ordinances that continued because they were commanded by Christ. The Lord's Supper was primarily a memorial meal remembering Christ's sacrificial death. In sharp contrast, Luther believed that Christ became present for the believer in the sacramental act. Since they held the great majority of Reformation principles in common, Zwingli met Luther at Marburg in 1529 and the two tried to reconcile their few differences. The Marburg Colloquy, however, was unable to resolve the conflicting views on the sacraments, and the two men went their separate ways.

Unable to reconcile with Zwingli, Luther renewed his attempt to reach an agreement with the Roman Catholics. Through a document largely written by his faculty colleague Philip Melanchthon (1497–1560), in 1530 Luther and his supporters presented a statement of their beliefs to the Lutheran princes of the Diet meeting at Augsburg in 1530. Though the Augsburg Confession was rejected, the Lutheran movement had reached a point of maturity and strength that largely assured its perpetuation.

During the remaining 16 years of his life, Luther spent much of his time to writing, while his colleagues took the lead in the various battles with the Catholic forces. From 1533 to his death in 1546 he served as the dean of the theology faculty at Wittenberg. Meanwhile, on June 13, 1525, Luther had given up his monk's vows of celibacy and married Catherine von Bora (1499–1552). She bore six children, four of whom reached adulthood.

In the later years of his life, Luther completed the German translation of the whole Bible (1534), compiled the Lutheran confessional statement known as the Smalcald Articles (1537), and wrote the *Short Confession Concerning the Lord's Supper* (1544) and a final attack on Roman Catholic authority, *Against the Papacy at Rome Founded by the Devil* (1545). Now considered one of his ill-considered works, he wrote a harsh polemic against the Jewish community, *Jews and their Lies*, published in 1543. Many consider this work a prime example of the anti-Semitism of the era.

Luther's death occurred in the midst of a trip to Eisleben. While there, his health failed him and he was too ill to return to Wittenberg, He died on February 18, 1546.

The Lutheran Reformation destroyed the religious unity of Europe. The movement not only came to dominate much of northern Europe, it created a situation in which further dissent led to the creating of modern Anglicanism in England and the adherents of John Calvin's variant Reformation perspective came to control much of Switzerland, Holland, and Scotland. The whole Reformation would raise considerations of religious toleration and the status of minority dissenting religious groups, most notably the Mennonites and the Unitarians.

J. Gordon Melton

See also: Calvin, John; Dominicans; Lutheranism.

References

Bainton, Roland H. *Here I Stand: A Life of Martin Luther.* Nashville, TN: Cokesbury Press, 1950.

Brecht, Martin. *Martin Luther.* 3 vols. Minneapolis, MN: Fortress Press, 1985, 1990, 1993.

Lohse, Bernhard. *Martin Luther: An Introduction to His Life and Work.* Translated by Robert C. Luther. New York: Abingdon-Schultz; Philadelphia: Fortress Press, 1986.

Luther, Martin. *Luther's Works (LW).* Edited by Jaroslav Pelikan and H. T. Lehmann. 55 vols. St. Louis, MO: Concordia/Philadelphia, PA: Fortress Press, 1955–1986.

Marty, Martin E. *Martin Luther: A Life.* New York: Penguin, 2004.

Lutheran Church in Canada

The Lutheran Church emerged from the reforms initiated by the 16th-century German Reformer Martin Luther (1483–1546). Luther's emphases of justification by grace through faith alone and the authority of the Bible over against tradition and any ecclesiastical authority were embodied in the several Lutheran Confessions (especially the Augsburg Confession) promulgated in the 16th century, which now form the standard of Lutheran belief.

Lutheranism was brought to Canada by German immigrants in the 18th century. The first Lutheran congregation in Canada was established in Halifax, Nova Scotia, in 1752. Most Lutheran churches in Canada, formed primarily in rural Nova Scotia, Ontario, and the Prairie Provinces (Manitoba, Saskatchewan, and Alberta), were organized and affiliated with U.S. Lutheran denominations. Through the 20th century, concentrations of Lutherans developed in Kitchener-Waterloo, Winnipeg, and Edmonton.

The Lutheran Church Canada (LCC) is one of the two main Lutheran bodies in Canada, the other being the Evangelical Lutheran Church in Canada. The LCC has its roots in the Lutheran Church–Missouri Synod (LCMS), which entered eastern Canada in 1854 and western Canada in 1879. By the middle of the 20th century, attempts were being made to create a self-governing church in Canada. The LCC was established in 1959 as a federation of districts within the LCMS, and in 1988 an autonomous church in Canada was founded, comprised of three districts. The denomination continues to keep close ties with the LCMS. Its head office is located in Winnipeg, its two seminaries are in St. Catharine's, Ontario; and Edmonton, Alberta; and it supports a denominational periodical, the *Canadian Lutheran*. The LCC operates an extensive parochial school system across Canada and one university—Concord University College at Edmonton. There are approximately 325 LCC congregations across Canada, with close to 80,000 members.

The LCC has two sacraments, Holy Communion and (infant) baptism. It does not ordain women, and it practices closed Communion. It believes the Bible to be the "written Word of God and the only rule and norm of faith and of practice," and it affirms without reservation the Book of Concord. LCC has observer status with the Evangelical Fellowship of Canada and participates with the International Lutheran Council. Through the Canadian Lutheran World Relief organization, the LCC seeks to be involved in social and justice issues around the world.

Lutheran Church in Canada
3074 Portage Ave.
Winnipeg, Manitoba R3K 0Y2
Canada

http://www.lutheranchurch.ca (in English and
French)

Gordon L. Heath

See also: Evangelical Lutheran Church in Canada;
International Lutheran Council; Lutheran Church–
Missouri Synod.

References

Cronmiller, Carl. R. *A History of the Lutheran
Church in Canada.* Toronto: Evangelical
Lutheran Synod of Canada, 1961.

Pfrimmer, David. "A Lutheran Witness in Canadian
Society." In *Church and Canadian Culture,*
edited by Robert E. VanderVennen. Lanham,
MD: University Press of America, 1991.

Schwermann, Albert H. *The Beginnings of the
Lutheran Church–Canada.* Privately published,
1969.

Lutheran Church in Hungary

The Protestant Reformation began to spread from Germany through the Christian community in Hungary as early as 1518. Well established in the 1520s, over the next generation almost 150 Hungarian students would take their theological studies at Wittenberg with Martin Luther (1483–1546). Magyar translations of the New Testament and Luther's Small Catechism appeared in 1541 and 1550, respectively.

The spread of Lutheranism in Hungary occurred just as Turkish armies were launching an invasion. The decisive battle of Mohács in 1526 was followed by 125 years of Turkish occupation, from 1541 to 1686. After 1550, Lutherans also had to compete with the Reformed Church that also took root in Hungary.

In the 17th century, a Christian-led government returned as Austria slowly pushed the Turkish forces south and Hungary became part of the Austro-Hungarian Empire. Protestants, both Lutheran and Reformed, suffered during this time as Roman Catholics reclaimed numerous parishes and banished Protestant pastors. Pressure was not relieved until Emperor Joseph II (1741–1790) issued an Edict of Toleration in 1781. Lutherans remained a tolerated minority through World War I, but their status was strongly affected by the di-vision of Hungary and the transfer of Transylvania to Romania. In the years after the war, Hungarian Lutherans strongly supported the formation of the World Lutheran Conference and the development of international ties, especially with the United Lutheran Church in the United States.

Following World War II, Hungarian Lutherans gained recognition under the new Marxist government but shared the suffering of all religious groups in the face of an aggressively atheist system. The school system was secularized in 1948, but religious freedom was granted with some imposed limits. A new translation of the Bible into modern Hungarian appeared in 1976. Celebration of significant events, such as the 500th anniversary of Luther's birth in 1983, was permitted. A theology emerged that emphasized the witness to Christian faith through action in situations where religious discourse was not tolerated. Since the fall of Marxism, the church has been granted full freedom and has a new positive relationship to the government. Some of its schools have also been returned.

The Lutheran Church in Hungary adheres to the Augsburg Confession. Over the centuries it has developed a rich liturgical tradition. The church's parishes are divided into two districts or dioceses, both headed by a bishop. The senior bishop is recognized as the presiding bishop. An assembly, presided over by a layperson (the general inspector) and the presiding bishop, is the highest legislative body for the church. Higher education is fostered through the Lutheran Theological Academy in Budapest. There are a number of church-related charitable institutions, including homes for the elderly and for children with disabilities.

In 2006, the church reported 305,000 members and 500 congregations. It publishes two periodicals, *Diakonia* and *Evangélikus Elet.* The ecumenically minded church is also a member of the Ecumenical Council of Churches in Hungary, the Lutheran World Federation, and the World Council of Churches.

Lutheran Church in Hungary
üllöi ut 24
H-1085 Budapest
Hungary
http://www.lutheran.hu/

J. Gordon Melton

See also: Lutheran World Federation; World Council of Churches.

References

Bachmann, E. Theodore, and Mercia Brenne Bachmann. *Lutheran Churches in the World: A Handbook.* Minneapolis, MN: Augsburg Press, 1989.

Van Beek, Huibert. *A Handbook of the Churches and Councils: Profiles of Ecumenical Relationships.* Geneva: World Council of Churches, 2006.

Lutheran Church in Liberia

American Lutheran missionaries, including Morris Officer (1823–1874), began work in Liberia in 1860. However, they had difficulty with the hot and humid weather, and only with the arrival of David A. Day (1851–1897) in 1874 was some continuous leadership for the mission established. Day, a pastor and physician, was able to stay in Liberia for a quarter of a century. He established a station inland from Monrovia on the Saint Paul River and opened a school. As did many pioneer missionaries, he spent considerable time mastering the ways of the people among whom he worked. He offered health services and set up preaching points at settlements across the countryside. In the second generation of the mission, in 1908, a second mission station was opened, this time even farther upriver. As other personnel arrived, additional stations were added. Work concentrated among the Kpelle and Loma peoples, though work has begun among the Gbandi and Pallipo peoples.

During the 20th century, an indigenous leadership was developed, and the most promising ministerial candidates were sent to the United States for seminary training. The Lutheran Church in Liberia was organized in 1948, though it remained subordinate to its American sponsors. In the meantime, American Lutheranism, at one time split into more than 100 separate denominations, was in the midst of consolidating into several large bodies. The Liberian work eventually passed to the Lutheran Church in America (now a constituent part of the Evangelical Lutheran Church in America). In 1967, the Lutheran Church in America granted the Lutheran Church in Liberia full autonomy. It joined both the Lutheran World Federation and the World Council of Churches the next year.

The church adopted a polity combining congregational and presbyterial elements. Work is concentrated along the Saint Paul River from Monrovia to the Guinea border. The Bible has been translated and published in both the Kpelle and Loma languages. The church sponsors a number of elementary and secondary schools that use curriculum material developed in cooperation with the Methodists in Liberia and Sierra Leone. Ministers are trained at the Gbarnga School of Theology, an interdenominational effort sponsored by the Methodist, Anglican, and Lutheran churches. The church admitted women to the ordained ministry in 1982.

Hopes were high for the development of the church, but its work was thoroughly disrupted by civil wars (1989–1996, 2002–2003). In the fragile peace established in 2003, the church has placed priority on national healing and ministry to the traumatized.

In 2005 the church reported 71,196 members in 350 churches.

Lutheran Church in Liberia
PO Box 10-1046
1000 Monrovia 10
Liberia

J. Gordon Melton

See also: Evangelical Lutheran Church in America; Lutheran World Federation; World Council of Churches.

References

Bachmann, E. Theodore, and Mercia Brenne Bachmann. *Lutheran Churches in the World: A Handbook.* Minneapolis, MN: Augsburg Press, 1989.

Van Beek, Huibert. *A Handbook of the Churches and Councils: Profiles of Ecumenical Relationships.* Geneva: World Council of Churches, 2006.

Lutheran Church–Missouri Synod

The Lutheran Church–Missouri Synod is a strict confessional Lutheran church whose origins lie in the de-

Portrait of Carl F. W. Walther, the leading force in the founding of the Lutheran Church—Missouri Synod. (J. Gordon Melton)

veloping history of Protestantism in Saxony. Germany, the home of the Protestant Reformation, was and is predominantly Lutheran, but over the centuries the other major form of Reformation thought, Calvinism, also found adherents; many of Germany's Calvinists (members of the Reformed Church) resided in Saxony.

It was the general agreement among the German states at the time that the ruler determined the faith that the people in his land would follow. In the early 19th century, the ruler of Saxony forced the merger of the Reformed Church in Saxony with the Lutheran Church. However, rather than force Calvinists to accept Lutheranism, he ordered the creation of a new Evangelical Church that would accommodate both Lutheran and Reformed theology and worship.

Although many found this a happy solution, some Lutherans did not, and they formed a movement ad-

hering to a conservative Lutheranism that placed great emphasis upon the Augsburg Confession of Faith and the Small Catechism written by Luther for the instruction of new church members. In 1839 a group of Lutherans who rejected the Saxon Evangelical Church arrived in the United States under the direction of their bishop, Martin Stephan (1777–1846), and settled in Perry County, Missouri.

Soon after their arrival, it was discovered that Bishop Stephan had misappropriated some church funds for personal use, and he was banished. He was replaced by Carl Ferdinand Wilhelm Walther (1811–1887). Walther faulted erroneous theology for Stephan's downfall. He championed orthodox theology in the face of Stephan's errors, especially as they related to the authority of the ministry. Walther advocated congregational rights and responsibility in defending truth. He became the pastor in St. Louis and founded a small school that grew into Concordia Theological Seminary. In 1844 he founded a magazine, *der Lutheraner*, to spread his approach to faith. In 1847 he led in the founding of the Missouri Synod, composed of the 22 ministers and 16 congregations then operating among the settlers.

The synod found favor among German-speaking Lutherans across the Midwestern part of the United States. It found favor among those who preferred an emphasis upon the Lutheran confession rather than the Pietism that predominated in some of the larger Lutheran groups in the eastern United States. The leadership of the Missouri Synod saw an unacceptable doctrinal looseness in these other synods (which would eventually unite into the Evangelical Lutheran Church in America). Through the 20th century, the two approaches would diverge over various issues such as the ordination of women, which the Missouri Synod rejects.

In 2009 the Lutheran Church–Missouri Synod reported 2,418,000 members in 6,155 congregations. It has a congregational polity. Its synod meets every 3 years and oversees an extensive educational program that includes primary and secondary schools, 10 colleges and universities, and 2 seminaries. Throughout the 20th century the church developed a vast missionary program. Many of its world missions have grown into mature autonomous churches with whom the Missouri

Synod retains a partnership. The synod took the lead in forming the International Lutheran Council, which includes many of these partner churches along with other conservative Lutheran churches that agree with the Missouri confessional approach. The church believes that church unity must be based on doctrinal unity and has stayed out of most contemporary ecumenical groups, including the Lutheran World Federation.

Lutheran Church–Missouri Synod
1333 S. Kirkwood Rd.
St. Louis, MO 63122
http://www.lcms.org/index.html

J. Gordon Melton

See also: Evangelical Lutheran Church in America; International Lutheran Council; Lutheran World Federation; Lutheranism.

References

Graebner, A. *Half a Century of True Lutheranism.* Chattanooga, TN: J. A. Fredrich, n.d.
The Lutheran Annual. St. Louis, MO: Concordia Publishing Company, issued annually.
Meyer, Carl S. *A Brief Historical Sketch of the Lutheran Church–Missouri Synod.* St. Louis, MO: Concordia Publishing House, 1938.
Suelflow, August R., ed. *Heritage in Motion: Readings in the History of the Lutheran Church—Missouri Synod (1962–1997).* Moorhead, MN: Concordia College, 1998.
Todd, Mary. *Authority Vested: A Story of Identity and Change in the Lutheran Church-Missouri.* Grand Rapids, MI: William B. Eerdmans Publishing Company, 1999.

Lutheran World Federation

Established in 1947 by representatives of Lutheran churches in 23 countries, the Lutheran World Federation (LWF) in 2009 numbered 140 member churches in 79 countries. It represents approximately 60 million of the estimated 64 million baptized Lutherans in the world; some congregations, though not all, that are associated with the U.S.-based Lutheran Church–Missouri Synod and the International Lutheran Council remain outside the LWF.

Antecedent organizations include the General Council of the Evangelical Lutheran Church in North America (1867), the General Evangelical Lutheran Conference in Germany (1868), and the Lutheran World Convention (1923). The formation of the LWF after World War II served both to extend these efforts and to respond to postwar needs for reconciliation, relief, and service.

Initially regarding itself as a "free association of Lutheran churches," the LWF was organized to foster united witness in the world, common theological research, the ecumenical involvement of Lutheran churches, and a common response to issues of human need and social justice. In 1990 it adopted a new Constitution based on a different self-understanding, one with strong ecclesial overtones: "The Lutheran World Federation is a communion of churches that confess the Triune God, agree in the proclamation of the word of God and are united in pulpit and altar fellowship." This self-understanding is thus built around a theology of communion (Greek: *koinonia*), with increased concern for confessional unity, joint mission and service, theological reflection, and strong ecumenical involvement.

The ecumenical orientation of the LWF is manifest in its close cooperation with the World Council of Churches (WCC), with which most LWF member churches are affiliated. The LWF has also sponsored international, bilateral dialogues with official representatives of the Roman Catholic, Orthodox, Anglican, Reformed, Methodist, Baptist, and Adventist traditions. In Augsburg, Germany, on October 31, 1999—the anniversary of the day Martin Luther nailed his famous Ninety-five Theses to the chapel door at Wittenberg—representatives of the LWF and the Roman Catholic Church signed a "Joint Declaration on the Doctrine of Justification," an agreement that affirms that the mutual condemnations that Lutheran and Catholic leaders declared in the 16th century concerning the article of justification by grace through faith are no longer applicable or church-dividing. This declaration is widely regarded as an ecumenical breakthrough, and conversations with representatives of other Protestant traditions are being pursued by the LWF and the Vatican in the hope that its scope will be widened.

LWF assemblies have been held in Lund, Sweden (1947); Hanover, Germany (1952); Minneapolis, the United States (1957); Helsinki, Finland (1963); Evian-les-Bains, France (1970); Dar es Salaam, Tanzania (1977); Budapest, Hungary (1984); Curitiba, Brazil (1990); and Hong Kong, People's Republic of China (1997). In 2003, the 10th assembly met in Winnipeg, Canada.

The present organizational structure of the LWF was adopted in 1990. The assembly, which normally meets every six years, is the highest legislative authority; a council serves as the governing body and is comprised of 48 elected members, of whom 50 percent are from the so-called northern churches and 50 percent from churches in the so-called two-thirds world. Headquarters for the LWF secretariat are in the Ecumenical Centre in Geneva, and its structure includes three departments in addition to a general secretariat: theology and studies, mission and development, and world service. Nearly 100 staff members serve at the LWF headquarters, and approximately 4,000 persons are employed in LWF world service projects throughout the world. Regional coordinators of LWF now work on four continents: Africa, Asia, Europe, and North America.

PO Box 2100
150, route de Ferney
CH-1211 Geneva 2
Switzerland
http://www.lutheranworld.org

Norman A. Hjelm

See also: International Lutheran Council; Luther, Martin; Roman Catholic Church; World Council of Churches.

References

Brand, E. L. *Toward a Lutheran Communion: Pulpit and Altar Fellowship.* LWF Report 26. Geneva: Lutheran World Federation, 1988.

Nelson, E. C. *The Rise of World Lutheranism: An American Perspective.* Philadelphia: Fortress Press, 1982.

Schjørring, J. H., N. A. Hjelm, and P. Kumari. *From Federation to Communion: The History of the Lutheran World Federation.* Minneapolis: Fortress Press, 1997.

Vajta, V. *From Generation to Generation: The Lutheran World Federation 1947–1982.* LWF Report 16. Geneva: Lutheran World Federation, 1983.

[This entry was adapted from the *Dictionary of the Ecumenical Movement*, rev. ed., with the permission of WCC Publications, Geneva, and the William B. Eerdmans Publishing Company, Grand Rapids, MI.]

Lutheranism

The various Lutheran churches of the world have grown out of the reformist activities launched by a German monk, Martin Luther (1483–1546) in the 16th century. In 1517 Luther challenged what he saw as a distortion of Christian practice, the selling of indulgences, which were believed by Roman Catholics at the time to lessen the time one would spend in purgatory dealing with the consequences of sin prior to going to heaven. A university professor, Luther posted a series of theses that outlined his position and called for a debate. During the ensuing debate, Luther took a further step and asserted that biblical authority transcends that of the church and pope. This assertion led to a papal bull denouncing Luther, which Luther answered in three essays.

As Luther's position developed, he attacked the Roman Catholic doctrine of transubstantiation, limited the sacraments to two (baptism and the Lord's Supper) rather than seven, and elevated the role of the individual over that of the clergy with his understanding of the priesthood of all believers. He also elaborated on his basic principle of scriptural authority and salvation by grace through faith alone. He presented these views to the Diet, the governing body through which the emperor of the Holy Roman Empire exercised his authority, meeting at Worms in 1521 and was condemned. That condemnation set Luther and other Reformers against both secular and church authorities

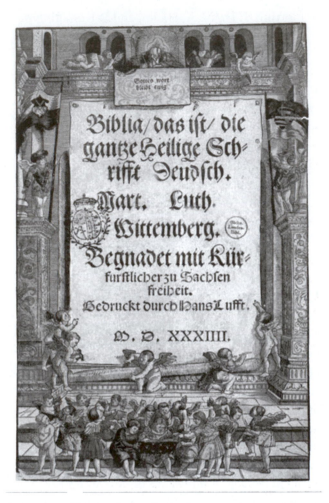

Title page of Martin Luther's German translation of the Bible, finished in 1534. (Saxon State Library/Library of Congress)

and led to a permanent break. Those who stood with Luther became known as the Lutheran or Evangelical Church. (In the French-speaking world, a parallel development led to the Reformed Church, which focused upon the thought of John Calvin of Geneva [1509–1564].)

The Lutheran Reformation became dominant in northern Germany and in areas north and east of Germany, including Scandinavia and Lithuania, though the southern German principalities tended to remain Catholic. During the 19th century, Lutheran missionaries who were connected with a spectrum of missionary societies carried Lutheran belief and practice worldwide, and through the 20th century numerous autonomous Lutheran churches resulted from that activity. Meanwhile, the home base of Lutheranism was devastated by World War II. Out of that war Lutherans worldwide came together in the Lutheran World Federation, initially intended to rebuild those countries ravaged by the war but later participating in a variety of cooperative activities around the globe.

Today Lutherans are characterized by their double emphasis upon Word and Sacrament, that is, biblical authority and preaching coupled with liturgy and the sacrament of the Lord's Supper. Their major doctrinal statement is the Augsburg Confession (1530), though Lutherans have been divided upon the strictness of its interpretation, especially as it stands in relation to Reformed Church confessions and participation in the contemporary ecumenical movement.

Most Lutheran churches around the world belong to the Lutheran World Federation, which has its headquarters in the same building that houses the World Council of Churches. Some more conservative Lutheran churches belong to the International Lutheran Council.

J. Gordon Melton

See also: Luther, Martin; Lutheran World Federation; World Council of Churches.

References

Bachman, E. Theodore, and Mercia Brenne Bachman. *Lutheran Churches in the World: A Handbook*. Minneapolis, MN: Augsburg Press, 1989.

Bodensieck, Julius, ed. *The Encyclopedia of the Lutheran Church*. 3 vols. Minneapolis, MN: Augsburg Publishing House, 1965.

Lagerquist, L. DeAne. *The Lutherans*. Westport, CT: Praeger, 1999.

Lull, Timothy F. *On Being Lutheran: Reflections on Church, Theology, and Faith*. Minneapolis, MN: Augsburg Fortress Publishers, 2005.

Luther, Martin. *Luther's Works*. Edited by Jaroslav Pelikan and H. T. Lehman. 55 vols. St. Louis, MO: Concordia/Philadelphia, PA: Fortress Press, 1958–1967.

Mildenberger, Friedrich. *Theology of the Lutheran Confessions*. Philadelphia: Fortress Press, 1986.

■ Luxembourg

Emerging as a separate entity in the 10th century, modern Luxembourg became fully independent in 1867. Its 998 square miles of land is nestled between France and Germany. It is home to some 486,000 people.

Luxembourg was originally settled at the end of the last Ice Age. Much later, Romans found the region settled by Celts and Germanic peoples. An early Roman center was created at Trier, just east of Luxembourg. In the third century CE, a new border that split the Low Countries (present-day Belgium, the Netherlands, and Luxembourg) divided the region between the German-speaking areas and the Romance language-speaking area controlled by Rome.

The leadership of Luxembourg opposed Spanish rule of the region and sided with rebels who defeated the Spanish in 1576. It later came under the authority of Philip II of France. In 1713, it was incorporated into the Austrian Hapsburg Empire, where it remained until overrun by Napoleon. In 1795 it was again annexed to France.

In 1815 the Congress of Vienna gave Luxembourg to William of Orange, king of the Netherlands, and it was designated a grand duchy. In 1831 Belgium separated from Holland and Luxembourg became separated geographically from the Netherlands. Its territory was divided, the greater portion being assigned to Belgium, the other part being administered independently by the Dutch royal house.

In 1866 the Treaty of London guaranteed Luxembourg's neutrality under the House of Nassau. The duke of Nassau remains the monarch of Luxembourg in what is now a constitutional monarchy. The House of Nassau has ruled the country continuously except for a short period of German occupation during World Wars I and II.

Christianity came to Luxembourg in 698 when Willibrord (ca. 658–739), a missionary from England, established a monastery at Echternach. Catholicism grew, becoming the dominant faith of the regions, and the Roman Catholic Church has remained largely unchallenged through the centuries. Catholicism is still the faith of some 90 percent of the population and stands behind the Christian Socialist Party, several labor

Catholic pilgrims perform a traditional religious dancing procession in Echternach, Luxembourg, in commemoration of the Irish monk St. Willibrord, the founder of the Abbey of Echternach. (AP/Wide World Photos)

unions, and the largest circulating newspaper, the *Luxemburger Wort*. A bishop of Luxembourg was named in 1870, and the office was elevated to archepiscopal status in 1988. The archbishop of Luxembourg resides in Esch-sur-Alzette.

Religious affairs in Luxembourg are handled by the Ministry of Religions. A form of separation of church and state exists, but the Roman Catholic Church is supported by state funds and a course in Catholicism is integrated into the public school curriculum.

The small Protestant community, consisting primarily of expatriates drawn to Luxembourg in the 20th century, has come to play a role in the modern European

Luxembourg

Luxembourg

Religion	Followers in 1970	Followers in 2010	% of Population	Annual % growth 2000–2010	Followers in 2025	Followers in 2050
Christians	323,000	437,000	90.6	0.84	497,000	613,000
Roman Catholics	296,000	427,000	88.4	0.96	480,000	590,000
Protestants	6,700	7,000	1.4	0.81	8,600	10,500
Marginals	1,000	3,400	0.7	−0.60	6,000	8,000
Agnostics	10,800	31,000	6.4	1.67	50,000	75,000
Atheists	3,000	7,200	1.5	0.89	11,000	18,000
Muslims	500	5,000	1.0	0.89	7,000	10,000
Baha'is	1,000	1,600	0.3	0.90	3,000	5,000
Jews	700	760	0.2	0.89	800	800
Total population	**339,000**	**483,000**	**100.0**	**0.89**	**569,000**	**722,000**

business community. The Protestant Church of the Grand Duchy dates to 1813 and the occupation of the area by German soldiers. A Mennonite Church was founded in 1830. There are also churches serving small Dutch-, Greek-, and Russian-speaking communities.

In the late 20th century, Luxembourg began to attract a spectrum of new religions, most notably Sukyo Mahikari, which has its European headquarters at the Grand Chateau at Ansembourg. The New Apostolic Church has come from neighboring Germany, and as in other European Countries, the Jehovah's Witnesses are active in Luxembourg.

J. Gordon Melton

See also: Jehovah's Witnesses; New Apostolic Church; Roman Catholic Church; Sukyo Mahikari.

References

Donckel, F. *Die Kirche in Luxemborg vonden Anfängen biz sur Geganwart.* Luxembourg: Sankt-Paulas Druckerei, 1950.

Eccardt, Thomas M. *Secrets of the Seven Smallest States of Europe: Andorra, Liechtenstein, Luxembourg, Malta, Monaco, San Marino, and Vatican City.* New York: Hippocrene Books, 2005.

Lallemand, A. *Les Sectes en Belgique et au Luxemborg.* Brussels: Editions EPO, 1994.

M

Mabon

See Fall Equinox.

■ Macedonia

The contemporary nation of Macedonia emerged out of the Federated Republics of Yugoslavia in 1991. It includes some 9,781 square miles of land surrounded by Greece, Albania, Serbia, Bulgaria, and the new nation of Kosovo. In 2008, it had just over two million citizens, the majority being Macedonians, a southern Slavic people, but with a significant minority of Albanians, a Paleo-Balkan people.

The history of Macedonia can be traced to the eighth century BCE, when a people calling themselves Macedonians emerged in the Aliákmon River valley and migrated east into present-day Macedonia. The Macedonians became prominent in the fourth century BCE under their king, Philip II (382–336) and his more famous son, Alexander the Great (356–323). During Alexander's reign the Macedonian Empire stretched eastward into India and south into Egypt and North Africa. The empire fell apart in the third century BCE and was finally incorporated into the Roman Empire at the beginning of the second century.

After the fall of the Roman Empire, Macedonia was successively overrun by its neighbors, being at different times a part of the Bulgarian and Byzantine empires, and it was eventually incorporated into Serbia. In the 15th century, it was incorporated into the Turkish Ottoman Empire. Toward the end of the 19th century, enthusiasm for independence rose even as the Otto-

MACEDONIA

man Empire was weakening. Macedonia was coveted by Greeks, Bulgarians, and Serbians, but it remained under Ottoman control until that empire disintegrated in 1908. In 1913, after two wars, Macedonia was divided between Greece and Serbia. Then, following World War I, the northern part of Macedonia was incorporated into Yugoslavia, continuing as a part of the new Yugoslavia after World War II. That part of Macedonia constituted the present nation, which declared its independence in 1991.

Christianity was introduced into Europe in the southern Macedonian city of Thessalonica; indeed, the dream in which the Apostle Paul received the call to come to Macedonia has become a part of Christian lore (Acts 16:9). Christianity penetrated northward, and

The Eastern Orthodox church of St. Jovan Kaneo, perched on a cliff overlooking Ohrid Lake in southern Macedonia, is believed to have been built in the 13th century. (Vanja Genije)

the great majority of Macedonians had become Christian by the fourth century. Through the next centuries, the Macedonian church tended to favor the leadership of Constantinople, and in 1054, when the Roman Catholic and Eastern Orthodox churches divided, the region remained Eastern Orthodox in faith and practice.

An independent Macedonian state arose under the leadership of Czar Samuel (980–1014). During this time the independent Archdiocese of Ohrid emerged. When Samuel's kingdom fell, Ohrid was placed under the authority of Constantinople. In 1219 the Serbian Orthodox Church was formed, and it declared its independence from Constantinople in 1346. The church in Macedonia then came under the hegemony of the Serbian church. That policy continued through the years of Turkish rule, though for a period (1463–1557) the

Turks favored the Ohrid Archepiscopacy and suppressed the Serbian Patriarchate.

The Serbian Patriarchate was re-established in 1557, but it was again suppressed in 1766 when the Ecumenical Patriarchate asserted its power in the region. The Serbian Orthodox Church was granted autonomy in 1832, and a united Serbian Orthodox Church was re-created in 1919; the Orthodox Christians in Macedonia were included in that church. The Patriarchate was re-established in 1920. In 1947, in the aftermath of World War II, a new Yugoslavian government arose, and it forced the creation of a separate Orthodox church to serve the Macedonian Republic within the new Federated Republics of Yugoslavia. In 1959 the government tried to force the Serbian Patriarchate to recognize the new Macedonian Orthodox Church and its leader,

Macedonia

Religion	Followers in 1970	Followers in 2010	% of Population	Annual % growth 2000–2010	Followers in 2025	Followers in 2050
Christians	1,282,000	1,314,000	64.4	0.42	1,305,000	1,155,000
Orthodox	1,240,000	1,282,000	62.8	0.09	1,250,000	1,090,000
Roman Catholics	40,000	17,400	0.9	7.94	26,000	30,000
Protestants	1,600	10,800	0.5	3.67	22,000	28,000
Muslims	178,000	590,000	28.9	0.24	590,000	520,000
Agnostics	78,000	111,000	5.4	−1.64	90,000	60,000
Atheists	30,000	25,000	1.2	0.24	15,000	10,000
Jews	0	1,000	0.0	0.25	1,000	1,000
Total population	**1,568,000**	**2,041,000**	**100.0**	**0.24**	**2,001,000**	**1,746,000**

Bishop Dositej (r. 1958–1981), though for the time being the church was allowed to remain under the authority of the patriarch in Belgrade.

Then in 1967 Dositej declared his complete separation from the Serbian Patriarchate. The autonomous independent church was not recognized by either the Serbian Patriarchate or the Ecumenical Patriarchate until Macedonia became an independent country in the early 1990s. It has now received recognition as a sister body from the other Orthodox bodies as well. The church began to found congregations in North America and Australia in the 1960s, and today its only bishop serving outside of Macedonia resides in Australia. The church is currently led by His Beatitude, archbishop of Ohrid and Macedonia (http://www.m-p-c.org).

Protestantism entered Macedonia in the 19th century. In 1873 the American Board of Commissioners for Foreign Missions extended its work in Bulgaria into Macedonia. It founded some 10 congregations and a school, but following the establishment of Yugoslavia after World War I, the board had trouble responding to the new government. Meanwhile, in 1898 Robert Moller, a Methodist minister from Vienna, came to Yugoslavia. Starting in Croatia, this work slowly spread through the early 20th century. In 1922, the American Board's work in Macedonia was turned over to the Methodists. About that time, a Yugoslavian Mission Conference was formed by the Methodist Episcopal Church (now a constituent part of the United Methodist Church). This church suffered greatly during the German occupation, and following the war many members in Croatia and Serbia left the region. The church

has had an important role in the 1990s and the current president of Macedonia (2001) is a United Methodist layman.

The Baptists extended their work in Yugoslavia into Macedonia in 1928, when one of the Methodist congregations changed its affiliation. At the time the Baptists had legal status in the country, and the Methodists did not. A second Baptist church was opened in Skopje that same year. In 1991 the three active Baptist congregations in Macedonia formed the Baptist Union of Macedonia.

In the early 1990s, two evangelical sending agencies, Partners International and SEND International, launched work in Macedonia. Another agency, Pioneers, based in Florida, has begun work among Macedonian Muslims.

During the years of Turkish rule, many Muslims moved into central Macedonia. Some Christians, not wishing to bear the burdens placed upon them by the Turkish authorities, converted to Islam. The community of Valaades, or Greek-speaking Muslims, survived in some parts of the country until around 1912, when most resettled in Turkey. Today, the Muslim population in the country is composed primarily of the Gypsy, or Romany, people.

There is a small Jewish community at Skopje, and in the 1990s centers of the two Hindu groups, Sahaja Yoga and the International Society for Krishna Consciousness, were opened. There is also a center of the Unification movement and a small group associated with the Ordo Templi Orientis.

J. Gordon Melton

See also: American Board of Commissioners for Foreign Missions; Ecumenical Patriarchate/Patriarchate of Constantinople; International Society for Krishna Consciousness; Ordo Templi Orientis; Sahaja Yoga: Unification Movement; United Methodist Church.

References

Illevski, D. *The Macedonian Orthodox Church: The Road to Independence.* Trans by J. L. Leech. Skopje, Macedonia: Macedonian Review Editions, 1973.

Norris, H. T. *Islam in the Balkans: Religion and Society between Europe and the Arab World.* Columbia: University of South Carolina Press, 1993.

Poulton, Hugh. *Who Are the Macedonians?* Bloomington: Indiana University Press, 2000.

Rossos, Andrew. *Macedonia and the Macedonians: A History.* Stanford, CA: Hoover Institution Press, 2008.

Machu Picchu

Machu Picchu, a medieval Inca site, is located in the Andes mountains about 50 miles northwest of Cuzco, Peru. Probably used as a royal religious retreat center until shortly before the Spanish came into the area in the 16th century CE, Machu Picchu emerged in the late 20th century as an important site for modern Esoteric New Age practitioners to direct their speculation. The site is well away from the primary centers of Inca life, and thus appears to have no practical governmental, economic, or military function. When Spanish forces overran Peru in the 1530s, they missed it. This observation is the basis for the conclusion that it most likely was a religious center. There being no written records of its existence, awareness of the center was lost in Peruvian society and the various Peruvian governments through the 19th century were not aware of its existence. In fact, their hegemony did not extend into the more sparsely populated areas of their formal domain.

It was not until 1911 that Hiram Bingham (1875–1956), an archaeologist working in the country, discovered it after being invited to the site by some local residents. To his surprise, Bingham walked into a site that was largely intact from the time it had been abandoned. Its sudden emergence out of obscurity added to the site's mystique.

Machu Picchu is built around a large central plaza with an adjacent temple. They are surrounded by various buildings, the best guess being that they were living quarters for the rulers, the religious leaders, and other important persons. A large altar stone of unknown purpose dominates the interior of the temple. The site resides on the top of a ridge with a high peak on either side.

The lack of information about the site has transformed it into the focus of wide-ranging speculation. New Agers have suggested that is a place of powerful cosmic energies to which attunement yields a variety of spiritual benefits. Meanwhile, scholars, drawing somewhat on their knowledge of Inca religion, have suggested that the site was the home of a powerful mountain spirit who was worshipped in conjunction with Sun worship. There was also a special group of virginal females (the Chosen Women), who were religious functionaries in the Inca community, and who may have conducted many of their rituals here. Students of archaeoastronomy have weighed in relative to the possible use of Machu Picchu as a site for astronomical observations. They discovered that the Intihuatana stone (also referred to as the "Hitching Post of the Sun"), a protuberance from the temple altar, could be used to indicate several key stellar occurrences, most notably the Spring and Fall equinoxes. At midday on the equinoxes (March 21 and September 21), the Sun is directly above the pillar and the altar momentarily casts no shadow. At that moment, the Sun could be understood as sitting upon the pillar and being briefly "tied" to the altar.

Since the 1980s, specialists in sacred sites within the New Age movement have claimed Machu Picchu to be a particularly powerful site spiritually. They have organized pilgrimages to Peru and touted the remote mountain site as a place of transformation, a location facilitating the gaining of spiritual awareness, and a land of not only geological but spiritual highs. Harking to Chinese ideas of feng shui, tour leaders see the region as the focus of natural energies that flow around the high peaks, through underground openings, and suffusing the nearby valleys.

J. Gordon Melton

Cloud rolls over the Inca ruins of Machu Picchu in the Andes Mountains of Peru. (iStockPhoto.com)

See also: Pilgrimage.

References

Bingham, Hiram. *Lost City of the Incas*. New York: Duell, Sloan, and Pearce, 1948.

Cumes, Carol, and Romulo Lizarraga Valencia. *Journey to Machu Picchu: Spiritual Wisdom from the Andes*. St. Paul, MN: Llewellyn Publications, 1998.

Reinhard, Johan. *Machu Picchu: The Sacred Center*. Lima, Peru: Nuevas Imágenes, 1991.

Waisbard, Simone. *The Mysteries of Machu Picchu*. New York: Avon Books, 1979.

Wright, Ruth M., and Alfredo Valencia Zegarra. *The Machu Picchu Guidebook: A Self-guided Tour*. Boulder, CO: Johnson Books, 2001.

Mackay, George Leslie

1844–1901

George Leslie Mackay is the famous Canadian Presbyterian missionary who came to northern Formosa (Taiwan) in 1872 and preached specifically with Aborigines in mind until his untimely death.

Born on March 21, 1844, to pious Scottish Presbyterians from Upper Canada (Zorra Township, Oxford County, southern Ontario), Mackay embraced the faith at a tender age, and found foreign missionary work his calling. His postsecondary education was Presbyterian through and through; he studied at Knox College (Toronto), Princeton Seminary, and New College (Edinburgh), where his lifelong devotion to "natural theology" was born. Queen's Theological College (Kingston, Ontario) honored him with a doctorate of divinity after almost a decade (1880). Mackay also went on to become the moderator of the Presbyterian Church in Canada in 1894 in absentia. It was his desire to live and die in Taiwan, where he lies to this day in the Mackay family plot adjacent Tamkang Middle School and Aletheia University. In 2004, a monument to his life and work was erected in Woodstock, Ontario. In 2006, Mackay was the subject of a Canadian television documentary, entitled *The Black-Bearded Barbarian of Taiwan*, followed by a Taiwanese opera production of his life at the National Opera in 2008.

Ironically, it was only after much pleading that the Canadian Presbyterian Church agreed to sponsor Mackay, asking only that he choose between Africa, India, and China. Mackay chose northern Formosa—China in effect—because it was "virgin" territory, making him the first Canadian Presbyterian missionary in the region. If his *Diaries* can be believed, he mastered the Native Amoy dialect in a matter of months after arriving in Formosa. He would go on to build 60 churches, including Native presbyters chosen and ordained by him to govern, creating what is now the Northern Synod of the Presbyterian Church in Taiwan (PCT). His ordination of Native preachers proved problematic for some Anglo-Canadians at the time, though he cared very little to ask permission of ecclesiastical precedent and orthodoxy on the matter—whether theological or cultural. Importantly, 70 percent of Taiwan's indigenous population claim allegiance to the Northern Synod.

Education was crucial to Mackay's somewhat unique brand of Native ministry and "Presbyterian Uplift," resulting in two educational institutions of some prominence: Oxford College, now Aletheia University, and Tamkang Middle School, both in Dansui. The so-called Black-Bearded Barbarian Bible Man is equally famous for his work as an amateur dentist in service of Native health reforms, pulling teeth by the tens of thousands in the service of the Lord. Two memorial Presbyterian hospitals have been built in Taipei County since the construction of the first by Mackay in 1882. Moreover, his collection of Formosan native artifacts—considered among the best in the world—is housed at the Royal Ontario Museum (Canada). He died in Taiwan from throat cancer on June 2, 1901.

Mackay is considered by many to be Taiwan's most famous Western missionary and premiere defender of Native culture and thus Taiwanese independence. A man of science and faith, defender and practitioner of miscegenation, proponent of a radical "native ministry" and "indigenized gospel," his beliefs and practices both conformed to and challenged the racial thinking of 19th-century Canadian polite society. His marriage to a Taiwanese slave-girl, Tui Chhang-mia, as well as arranged interracial marriages he performed between select male Chinese and female Taiwanese graduates of Oxford College were consistent with his belief in "civilizing" through miscegenation—his most controversial and significant contribution in some respects. He had three children by Tui Chhang-mia. Bella and Mary, their two older daughters, married prominent Native preachers, whereas George, Jr., the youngest, studied at the University of Toronto and married an Anglo-Canadian woman.

A very private man, Mackay wrote comparatively little—his diaries notwithstanding. It is doubtful that he wrote his autobiography, *From Far Formosa*; his editor, Reverend J. A. MacDonald, claimed full credit after Mackay's death and for good reason. As Mackay scholar James Rohrer writes: Mackay's "correspondence and even his diaries reveal relatively little about his inner life, leaving us in many cases to read between the lines and to conjecture." Mackay had the temperament of a soldier rather than a scholar and, according to his successor William Gauld, spent the bulk of his time "rushing around the country like a madman."

Ironically, Mackay is rarely mentioned in North American histories of the Presbyterian Church and its somewhat unique place, along with his, in the Social Gospel movement. Brian J. Fraser's *The Social Uplifters: Presbyterian Progressives and the Social Gospel in Canada, 1875–1915* makes no mention of him whatsoever. Alvyn Austin's seminal *Saving China: Canadian Missionaries in the Middle Kingdom* devotes a mere five pages to him, much of this less than flattering, and calling the Zorra Boy (Mackay) perhaps "the strangest character nineteenth-century Canada ever produced" (30). There were two Mackays: the indefatigable barbarian missionary abroad and the firebrand at home. Austin also casts doubt on Mackay's medical qualifications.

Mackay scholars per se do not completely agree on the essence of the man and his mission. Dominic

McDevitt-Parks contends that Mackay was an "Orientalist" and thus allegedly a pawn of Western imperialism. His rabid anti-Catholicism may have driven him to build the many chapels he did merely to thwart Dominican priests from the Philippines who came to Formosa in 1886. Mark Eric Munsterhjelm charges him with "cultural genocide" for his role in the destruction of Chinese idols and ancestor tablets. Michael Stainton contends that Mackay's belief in the "southern theory of Taiwanese origins" was essentially anti-Chinese. Finally, James Rohrer contends that Mackay should be seen a charismatic or cult leader and founder of a new Taiwanese "sect" that ran afoul of Christian orthodoxy.

Clyde R. Forsberg Jr.

See also: Dominicans; Presbyterian Church in Canada; Presbyterian Church in Taiwan.

References

Austin, Alvyn J. *Saving China: Canadian Missionaries in the Middle Kingdom.* Toronto: University of Toronto Press, 1986.

Mackay, George Leslie. *From Far Formosa: The Island, its People and Missions.* Ed. by Rev. J. A. MacDonald. Taipei, Taiwan: SMC Publishing, 1896, 1991.

Mackay, George Leslie. *Mackay's Diaries: Original English Version*, Ed. by Neng-Che Yeh et al. Tamsui, Taiwan: The Relic Committee of the Northern Synod of the Taiwan Presbyterian Church, 2007.

McDevitt-Parks, Dominic. "19th-century Anglo-American Representations of Formosan Peoples." Freeman Summer Grant, 2007.

Munsterhjelm, Mark Eric. "Aborigines Saved Yet Again: Settler Nationalism and Narratives in a 2001 Exhibition of Taiwan Aboriginal Artefacts." M.A. thesis, University of Victoria, 2004.

Rohrer, James R. "Mackay and the Aboriginals: Reflections upon the Ambiguities of Taiwanese Aboriginal Christian History." In *Christianity and Native Cultures: Perspectives from Different Regions of the World*. Notre Dame, IN: Cross Cultural Publications, Inc.

Rohrer, James R. "George Leslie Mackay in Formosa, 1871–1901: An Interpretation of His Career." *Journal of the Canadian Church Historical Society* 47 (2005): 3–58.

Rohrer, James R. "Charisma in a Mission Context: The Case of George Leslie Mackay in Taiwan, 1872–1901." *Missiology: An International Review* 36, no. 2 (April 2008): 227–236.

Stainton, Michael. "The Politics of Taiwan Aboriginal Origins." In *Taiwan: A New History*, edited by Murray A. Rubinstein, 27–44. Armonk, NY: M. E. Sharpe, 1999.

■ Madagascar

Madagascar is a large island nation in the Indian Ocean east of the African nation of Mozambique. The fourth largest island on the globe, its land area is 225,000 square miles. There are also several much smaller close-by islands included in the nation of Madagascar, though islands to the north constitute a separate country, the Comoros. The largest group among the country's 20 million people is the Merinas, a people of Austronesian and Malaysian origin who make up approximately one-fourth of the population.

Madagascar appears to have been originally populated by people from Malaysia and Polynesia around the beginning of the Common Era. Some 18 indigenous groups of Malay-Polynesian descent now inhabit the island. The descendants of Bantu Africans, first introduced as slaves, have intermarried and integrated into the general population. The primary groups include the Betsileo, the Sakalave, the Antankarana, the Betsimisaraka, and the Antasaka.

Modern Madagascan history begins in the 13th century, when traders from the Comoros Islands established ports on Madagascar's northern shores. At the beginning of the 16th century, the Portuguese arrived. In their quest for valuables, they destroyed the trading settlements, but after finding no gold or other cash items, they departed.

The arrival of the Europeans became a catalyst for the formation of the first Madagascan kingdoms, one in the east and one in the west. The unification of the island occurred during the reign of King Radama I (1810–1828). Problems with succession following Radama's death facilitated the return of the Europeans,

Celebrants at a rural festival in Madagascar. (Corel)

who took over increasing portions of the land through the 19th century. Eventually Madagascar became a French colony.

In 1947 the struggle for Madagascan independence led to a revolt that was put down harshly, and autonomy was not accomplished until 1960. Fifteen years of political turmoil stood between independence and the establishment of a democratic republic in 1975. The presence of widespread poverty continues to threaten the political process, which in turn slows the processes of economic reform and revival.

Each of the various peoples of Madagascar had their own traditional religion, all of which were related by a common Malay-Polynesian origin. A creator deity (Zahahary) is acknowledged, but primary emphasis is placed upon ensuring survival after death and maintaining a relationship with those who have passed into the next life, that is, one's ancestors. A major ceremony is built around corpses that are moved about, ritually

fed, and invited to dance. Traditional Madagascan belief also includes reliance on magic, with accompanying rejection of witchcraft (malevolent magic) and reliance on the protective effects of amulets. Approximately half of the population remains loyal to traditional religious beliefs.

Christianity was introduced to the island by the Portuguese, but systematic missionary efforts were not launched until the 17th century. Only with the unification of the land under Radama I and his introduction of European culture did the Roman Catholic Church establish permanent structures. The London Missionary Society (LMS) opened work in 1818, and its missionaries developed a written form of the Malagasy language and translated the Bible. In 1836 Radama's successor, Queen Ranavalona I (r. 1828–1861), turned against Christianity, expelled all Europeans, and killed many Christians. However, when the missionaries returned in 1861, they found a growing Christian com-

MADAGASCAR

munity. Queen Ranavalona II accompanied her coronation in 1869 with her conversion to Christianity, which thrived through the rest of the century. Jesuits worked beside Congregationalists, Friends, and, after 1897, Reformed Church missionaries from the Paris Mission. By 1900 there were more than one million Christians.

The Protestant mission was concentrated in the northern part of the island and included numerous elementary schools. The primary churches represented were the Church of England (whose work was later incorporated into the Church of the Province of the Indian Ocean), the Malagasy Lutheran Church, and the Church of Christ in Madagascar (the LMS mission).

These were joined by the Friends Church and the Evangelical Church in Madagascar (the product of the Paris Mission). In 1968 the LMS mission, the Evangelical Church, and the Friends Church united to form the Church of Jesus Christ of Madagascar.

In 1913 the LMS and the Lutherans formed the Missionary Conference, which in 1958 was superseded by the Federation of Protestant Churches in Madagascar. The federation includes the Church of Jesus Christ of Madagascar and the Malagasy Lutheran Church and is related to the World Council of Churches.

Through the 20th century, additional groups representative of the Protestant and Free church perspective arrived to build up the Christian community, including

Madagascar

Religion	Followers in 1970	Followers in 2010	% of Population	Annual % growth 2000–2010	Followers in 2025	Followers in 2050
Christians	3,366,000	11,030,000	51.8	2.98	16,898,000	27,285,000
Protestants	1,351,000	6,651,000	31.2	2.60	9,358,000	14,000,000
Roman Catholics	1,595,000	5,240,000	24.6	4.29	7,500,000	11,500,000
Independents	146,000	940,000	4.4	3.31	1,550,000	2,700,000
Ethnoreligionists	3,437,000	9,722,000	45.6	2.74	12,186,000	15,729,000
Muslims	112,000	420,000	2.0	2.87	650,000	1,000,000
Agnostics	4,000	60,700	0.3	2.87	110,000	200,000
Baha'is	4,000	21,500	0.1	2.86	36,000	75,000
Atheists	0	15,400	0.1	2.86	28,000	40,000
Hindus	1,200	12,600	0.1	2.87	20,000	62,500
Chinese folk	4,000	10,800	0.1	2.87	17,000	40,000
Buddhists	2,000	5,500	0.0	2.87	9,000	20,900
Jews	100	300	0.0	2.88	400	600
Total population	**6,930,000**	**21,299,000**	**100.0**	**2.87**	**29,954,000**	**44,453,000**

the Swedish Assemblies of God, the New Apostolic Church, and the Evangelical Free Church. They were joined by a number of African Initiated Churches, several of which originated from schisms in the LMS mission. The missionaries of the Seventh-day Adventist Church arrived in 1926, and the Jehovah's Witnesses in 1933.

Islam has emerged in Madagascar as a significant minority community, most of whose adherents live on the northwest corner of the island. The Comoros islanders had become predominantly Muslim in the 14th century and became the source of Islam's entrance into Madagascar. The Sunni Shafaiite School is strongest among the Sakalave people. More recently, some Comoros citizens have moved to Madagascar. The Muslim community has been further enlarged by some 15,000 Indo-Pakistani Muslims, among whom are Ismailis and Bohoras, and several thousand Zaydis from Yemen.

The approximately 10,000 Indo-Pakistani people that came to Madagascar were primarily Hindu. There are also a small number of Chinese Buddhists and members of the Baha'i Faith. In 1975 Guru Maharaj Ji, head of the Divine Light Mission (now known as Elan Vital), a teacher in the Radha Soami/Sant Mat tradition, began to gather followers, but his movement was outlawed before the year was out. A minuscule Jewish community, with around 200 members, emerged in the 20th century.

J. Gordon Melton

See also: Assemblies of God; Baha'i Faith; Church of Jesus Christ in Madagascar; Church of the Province of the Indian Ocean; Elan Vital/Divine Light Mission; Friends/Quakers; Jehovah's Witnesses; Jesuits; London Missionary Society; Malagasy Lutheran Church; New Apostolic Church; Paris Mission; Reformed Church of France; Roman Catholic Church; Seventh-day Adventist Church; Shafiite School of Islam; World Council of Churches.

References

Ferrand, G. *Les Musulmans à Madagascar et aux lies Comores.* 3 vols. Paris: E. Leroux, 1891–1892.

Jacobsen, L. D. "Church Growth on the Island of Madagascar." Ph.D. diss., Fuller Theological Seminary, 1967.

Keller, Eva. *The Road to Clarity: Seventh-Day Adventism in Madagascar.* New York: Palgrave Macmillan, 2005.

Madagascar et le christianisme. Historie oecumenique. Paris: Agence de Cooperation Culturelle et Technique, 1993.

Ramambason, Laurent W. *Missiology: Its Subject-Matter and Method: A Study of 'Mission-Doers' in Madagascar*. New York: Peter Lang Publishing, 1999.

Rund, J. *Taboo: A Study of Malagasy Customs and Beliefs*. Oslo, Norway: Oslo University Press, 1960.

Maghi

Maghi, a holiday for Sikhs, commemorates the martyrdom of the Chali Mukte, or Forty Immortals. The remembered incident occurred on December 29, 1705. Today, using the new Sikh Nanashahi calendar, the event is celebrated annually on January 13.

The founding of the Khalsa, the Sikh military order, by Guru Gobind Singh had alerted the Mughal (Muslim) rulers who controlled the Pubjab at the time of the growing strength of the Sikhs and the correlative power of their leader. The Hindu leadership also felt threatened. The initial attempts to suppress the Khalsa were unsuccessful. Much of 1705 was spent fending off the much larger Muslim forces and found the Sikhs in what amounted to a strategic retreat. In December Gobind Singh was visited by a group of 40 Punjabi Sikhs. During their visit, he received word of the imminent approach of a Mughal army led by Wazir Khan. The 40 decided that they could not at that moment support him and they moved away, taking a position by the side of small body of water. As the army became visible, however, they reassessed their situation and turned to face the oncoming force. By sunset all 40 were dead or seriously injured and the Mughal forces retreated. Guru Gobind Singh blessed them as *muktas*, or emancipated ones, and changed the name of the place to Muktsar in their honor.

The largest celebration of Mugli is at Muktsar where an annual fair is held. Around the world, however, Sikhs visit their *gurdwaras* for *kirtan* (hymns), stories of the martyrs, and an end-to-end recital of the holy Guru Granth Sahib, the Sikh holy book.

Maghi is celebrated on the first day of the month of Magh in the Hindu lunar calendar. It follows on the heels of the Hindu mid-winter Lohri festival when bonfires are lit in Hindu fields and yards. The next morning Hindus see as an auspicious occasion to go for a brief swim in the local river or pond.

J. Gordon Melton

See also: Calendars, Religious; Sikhism/Sant Mat.

References
Kapoor, Sukhbor Sing. *Sikh Festivals*. Vero Beach, FL: Rourke Publishing Group, 1989.

Singh, Bhagat Lakeshman. *Short Sketch of the Life and Work of Guru Govind Singh, The Tenth and Last Guru*. Ottawa, ON: Laurier Books, 1995.

Maha Bodhi Society

Established in 1891 in Colombo, Sri Lanka (then Ceylon), the Maha Bodhi Society (MBS) constituted a striking part of the revival of Theravada Buddhism in South Asia around the turn of the century. The Society was founded by the Ceylonese activist Anagarika Dharmapala (1864–1933) with the purpose of regaining control of the Maha Bodhi temple and resuscitating Buddhism in India. This ancient temple marks the site at Bodhgaya, in northeast India, where the Buddha is reputed to have gained enlightenment. It had been adopted centuries later by Hindus for their devotional practices.

The British poet and journalist Sir Edwin Arnold (1832–1904) had visited Bodhgaya in 1885 and lamented publicly that Buddhists had forgotten this "most interesting centre of [Buddhist] faith." Arnold achieved an agreement with the temple's Hindu manager to enable a Buddhist role in the temple's administration. This arrangement was vigorously taken up by Dharmapala, who had visited Bodhgaya in 1891. In a move that was uncharacteristic to Buddhism but in agreement with Arnold, Dharmapala declared Bodhgaya and the temple as the central Buddhist pilgrimage site, encouraging Buddhists the world over to fight for its "rescue." In 1892 the MBS headquarters was moved to Calcutta, and the Society's journal, the *Maha Bodhi*, became established.

To further his cause, Dharmapala untiringly toured the United States, Europe, and East Asia in the next

Maha Bodhi temple in Bodhgaya, Bihar, India. (Luciano Mortula/Dreamstime.com)

four decades, starting with a well-received speech at the World's Parliament of Religions in Chicago in 1893. Overseas branches of the MBS were formed in the United States (1897), Germany (1911), and Great Britain (1926). While in Europe, he initiated into Buddhism C. T. Strauss, the first Westerner to make a formal conversion to the faith. Undoubtedly, Dharmapala can be called one of the first Buddhist "global players," and the MBS the first international Buddhist organization.

Despite Dharmapala's activism, Bodhgaya and the temple remained under sole Hindu supervision during the first half of the 20th century. In 1949 the Bodh Gaya Temple Act reserved four of the nine votes in the temple's administrative board for Buddhists, thereby still securing the Hindu majority. The MBS continued to work for the cause by sending Theravada Buddhist missionary monks from Ceylon/Sri Lanka to Bodhgaya and other Indian places, by publishing the *Maha Bodhi*, and by maintaining hostels for Buddhist pilgrims.

In the late 1990s, the organization had eight centers in North India and five affiliated centers in South India, as well as centers in Sri Lanka, Japan, Korea, Hong Kong, the United States, and the United Kingdom. The Society's self-assured claim to represent all Buddhists in its demand for "rescuing" Bodhgaya certainly cannot be upheld in view of the multiplication of Buddhist schools and traditions at Bodhgaya. These various groups have established monasteries and temples there, particularly since the 1980s. Although the Buddhist presence at the site, with some 40 different organizations as of 2005, has relativized the one-time dominant role of the MBS considerably, Arnold and Dharmapala's Orientalist view of Bodhgaya as the central place of Buddhism has come true a century later.

Buddhagaya Centre
Mahabodhi Society of India
Buddhagaya 824231
Gaya, Bihar
India
http://mahabodhisociety.com/

Martin Baumann

See also: Bodh-Gaya; Buddha, Gautama.

References

Ahir, Diwan Chand. *Buddha Gaya through the Ages.* Delhi: Sri Satguru Publications, 1994.

Guruge, Ananda, ed. *Return to Righteousness: A Collection of Speeches, Essays and Letters of the Anagarika Dharmapala.* Colombo, Sri Lanka: Government Press, 1965.

Sangharakshita, Maha Sthavira. *Flame in the Darkness: The Life and Sayings of Anagarika Dharmapala.* Terawada, Pune, Maharastra, India: Tritarna Grantha Mala, 1980.

Mahasivaratri

On the 14th day of each month of the Hindu lunar calendar, the god Siva (or Shiva), one of the three major deities of the Hindu pantheon, is acknowledged, and the day is called Sivaratri. However, the 14th day of the Hindu month of Magha is designated as Mashiva raatri, and has become a national Hindu holiday celebrated throughout India and the Indian diaspora. It is a solemn occasion in which leaves of the Bael tree, believed to have medicinal value, are offered to Lord Siva and people fast and engage in an all-night vigil.

Mahasivaratri recalls an old story of the Asuras (power-hungry demons) and their half-brothers, the gods. The demons had much power, but because of their lack of piety—they neglected the making of sacrifices and did not visit holy places—they did not acquire great powers within themselves. Meanwhile, the gods made sacrifices, dealt truthfully with each other, visited holy places, and thus increased in power within themselves.

Both the gods and the Asuras knew that they could gain the Amrit, the Water of Life, if they churned up the Ocean of Milk that encircled their world. With the Mountain Mandara for a churning-pole and the giant serpent Vasuki for a churning-rope, the gods and the Asuras churned the Ocean of Milk. As they churned Vasuki spat venom from each of his many heads. The venom broke the rocks around the ocean, creating openings for the ocean to flow over creation, threatening destruction to the worlds of both gods and men.

At that point Siva stepped forward and gathered the venom in a cup and drank it. His wife Parvati, fearing for his life, grabbed his throat so the poison would not enter his stomach. The burn on his throat is still seen to this day as a dark blue marking. His action, however, saved creation and allowed the gods to gain more powers than the demons.

As the churning continued, wondrous things emerged from the primordial Ocean of Milk. Surabhi, the wish-fulfilling cow, came forth. Shri, the goddess of prosperity and fortune, and Dhanavantari, the physician of the gods, came forth. Then the Kaustubha gem that always adorns Vishnu's chest emerged. Finally, the nectar of immortality appeared, and knowing that the demons would want to seize the nectar of immortality, Vishnu took the form of the enchantress Mohini. While the demons were mesmerized with her beauty, she served the nectar to the gods alone. Thus only the gods gained immortality, and when the demons attacked they were routed and the world was once again in the hands of the gods.

Since that time Siva dwells in woodlands filled with flowers. He keeps near him a spear with which he will destroy the worlds at the end of an age, a bow, a battle-axe, and a trident. At one point, his wife Uma covered his eyes with her hands. As a result, the world sunk into darkness. To save the world, Siva developed a third eye on his forehead. When he opened that eye, the light returned to the world. But Siva's throat remains blue from the venom that he drank.

Mahashivaratri is unique as the major Hindu celebration not accompanied by revelry and gaiety. It is rather a solemn event that emphasizes restraint and vows of forgiveness, truth telling, and non-injury to others that must be kept for the full 24 hours. Fasting and staying awake to worship Siva during the entire night fill the hours of observance. One is to recite the mantra of Siva, *om namah shivaya*, and prayers for forgiveness during the evening vigil. If the rites are performed faithfully one is rewarded with worldly success and the heavenly realm of Siva.

Constance A. Jones

See also: Hinduism.

References

Harshananda, Swami. *Hindu Festivals and Sacred Days*. Bangalore: Ramakrishna Math, 1994.

Mukuncharandas, Sadhu. *Hindu Festivals (Origin Sentiments & Rituals)*. Amdavad, India: Swaminarayan Aksharpith, 2005.

Sharma, Nath. *Festivals of India*. New Delhi: Abhinav Publications, 1978.

Welbon, Guy, and Glenn Yocum, eds., *Religious Festivals in South India and Sri Lanka*. Delhi: Manohar, 1982.

Mahasthamaprapta's Birthday

Mahasthamaprapta's (Bodhisattva Great Power, known in Japan as Seishi Bosatsu) is a Mahayana Buddhist bodhisattva best known within the Pure Land Buddhist tradition as a close associate of Amitabha and the Western Paradise. She is most often depicted sitting or standing beside Amitabha, along with Avalokitsevara (Guan Yin). This popular group is known as the Three Saints of the Western Paradise. Mahasthamaprapta's halo of wisdom permeates all creation. She is often seen in feminine form and recognized by the water pitcher on her crown and the lotus bud in her hand. The lotus bud is meant to be used to guide the elect to the Pure Land.

Mahasthamaprapta's birthday is celebrated on the 13th day of the 7th month in the Chinese lunar calendar, just two days before the Ullam-bana Festival. In Japan it is held on July 13. Japanese Pure Land practitioners make note of the fact that Shinran (1173–1263), the founder of the larger Pure Land group, had a vision of Mahasthamaprapta whom he identified with Honen (1133–1212), the founder of Pure Land Buddhism in Japan and Shinran's teacher.

J. Gordon Melton

See also: Amitabha's Birthday; Pure Land Buddhism; Ullam-bana.

References

"The Bodhisattva that Shinran knew in Person." The Way of Shinshu Buddhism. http://www.shinran wasan.info/jw19.htm. Accessed May 15, 2009.

Boheng, Wu, and Cai Zhuozhi. *100 Buddhas in Chinese Buddhism*. Trans. by Mu Xin and Yan Zhi. Singapore: Asiapac Books, 1997.

"The Gentility of the Dharma." The Way of Shinshu Buddhism. http://www.shinranwasan.info/jw118.htm. Accessed May 15, 2009.

The Seeker's Glossary of Buddhism. New York: Sutra Translation Committee of the United States and Canada, 1998.

Vessantara. *Meeting the Buddhas: A Guide to Buddhas, Bodhisattvas, and Tantric Deities.* Birmingham, UK: Windhorse Publications, 1998.

Mahavira

ca. 599–527 BCE

Mahavira was the last in a lineage of 24 *tirthankaras*, enlightened beings, who are recognized as the founders of the Jain religion. A tirthankara is considered to be a person who has conquered his base sensibilities, especially anger, pride, deceit, and desire. Mahavira's life overlapped that of Gautama Buddha, who like him attempted to work a reform of the religion of India of his day, but there is no record of their ever meeting. Among the two major sects of Jains, the Digambara and the Shvetambaras, numerous differences in details concerning Mahavira's life emerge at every major turn.

Mahavira, literally the "Great Spiritual Hero," was born in 599 in Kundgraam, a small kingdom located in what is now the state of Bihar in India. His father, Siddhartha, was the king of Kundgraam and his mother, Trishala, the sister of a local ruler. They named their son Vardhamana ("He who brings prosperity").

Both the Digambara and the Shvetambaras remember that before Mahavira's birth his mother had witnessed 14 auspicious dreams in which she saw successively (1) a white elephant; (2) a white bull; (3) a lion; (4) the goddess Shri (aka Lakshmi); (5) garlands of *mandara* (hibiscus) flowers; (6) the full moon; (7) the rising sun; (8) a beautiful large flag; (9) a vase of fine metal; (10) a lake covered in lotuses; (11) an ocean of milk; (12) a celestial house in the sky; (13) a large pile of gems; and (14) a blazing fire. Digambara Jains, however, believe she also had two additional dreams in which she saw (15) a lofty throne and (16) a pair of fish playfully swimming in a lake. These dreams have now become a standard part of the recounting of Mahavira's life, and contemporary Jains narrate these dreams and re-enact them in dramas as part of their celebration of the five auspicious moments of Mahavira's life.

The Shvetambaras also believe that Mahavira was originally conceived by a Brahmin couple, Rishabhadatta and Devananda, after which the embryo was magically transferred into Trishala's womb. The Digambara reject the story of the transplanted embryo.

Mahavira's saintly career and inherent powers manifested even before his birth. When in his mother's womb, he remained very quiet, demonstrating the Jain virtue of *ahinsa* (non-injury). According to the story he moved only at those moments when he was aware that his mother worried that he might not be alive. His unique future was heralded at his birth. All beings celebrated the birth of a new tirthankara and many marvels and miracles occurred as he was being born. His parents were, of course, followers of the immediately previous Jain Tirthankara and teacher Parshvanatha.

Little is known about Mahavira's childhood. He was raised a prince in a wealthy environment. There are a few stories, such as one that recounts his subduing a ferocious snake, a demonstration of his courage and calmness. The accounts of his young adulthood vary. The Shvetambaras believe that he fulfilled his duties as a householder by marrying a princess named Yashoda and that the couple had a daughter called Priyadarshana. Only after the death of his parents did Mahavira leave the palace and adopt the life of a wandering mendicant. According to the Digambaras, Mahavira never married. He demonstrated an aversion to all worldly matters throughout his life.

When Mahavira was 30 years of age, Mahavira experienced the visit of some (Hindu) deities who urged his renunciation of the world. He chose a symbolic location for the renunciation, a large park under an ashoka tree, already a fabled tree associated with stories of the gods and known in India for its natural beauty (Buddha is said to have been born under an ashoka tree). The act of renunciation, according to the Digambaras, consisted of him removing all of his clothes and pulling out all his hair in five bunches (which remains a norm for contemporary Jain monks and nuns). Afterward he lived as a complete renunciate, which included the life of a naked ascetic. According to

Jain devotees watch a dancer as they celebrate the anniversary of the birth of Lord Mahavira in Allahabad, India. (AP/Wide World Photos)

the Shvetambaras, Mahavira retained a covering over his private parts with a small loincloth he had received from Indra, the king of the gods. He reputedly wore this cloth for 13 months, but when it fell from him, he henceforth lived as a naked mendicant.

Mahavira wandered around India for the next 12 years, including periods during which he abstained from water, food, or both. He proved indifferent to bodily pains and pleasures, seemingly unconcerned if caught in burning sunshine or in pouring rain. The Digambaras assert that he also observed silence for these 12 years.

The Shvetambaras tell the story of Mahavira's encounter with an ascetic, Makkhali Gosala (described as attached to an ancient ascetic order, the anjikas), who attached himself to Mahavira, hoping to attain the yogic powers he manifested. He asked to become his disciple. Gosala traveled with Mahavira and observed

with growing amazement. At some point he left and declared himself a *jina* (spiritual victor). Mahavira later reveals that Gosala not only was not a jina, but that his former disciple had unsuccessfully tried to kill him.

Meanwhile, after this time of ignoring anything done to his body, in a period of intense meditation, Mahavira attains *kevalajnana*, enlightenment, described as an infinite supreme knowledge/intuition. His attainment led to a new status as the 24th and final tirthankara of the era.

The gods constructed a large assembly hall for the new tirthankara. The Digambaras believe that because of his purity, he no longer needed to eat or drink and that he had no need of sleep nor did he age. He sat in meditation in the assembly hall, in the midst of which he uttered a divine sound that carried the essence of the Jain teaching—the beings of every rank from heaven to hell, from human to animal or deity—to all who gathered in the hall in a state of awe. The Shvetambaras teach, in contrast, that only the gods and a few highly select disciples were present for this teaching moment.

It is, however, from this time of his enlightenment that the Jain community began to form, quite apart from Mahavira making any effort to create it. Mahavira lived another 30 years and continued his itinerant life, wandering from place to place. During these years, the community of monks and nuns emerged (the nuns continuing to outnumber the monks to the present). Mahavira's death, at the age of 72, followed his undergoing a series of ever-more-rigorous fasts. Believers hold that his soul journeyed to the top of the universe, where it remains in unlimited consciousness and bliss.

J. Gordon Melton

See also: Asceticism; Buddha, Gautama; Enlightenment; Jainism; Meditation; Monasticism; Yoga.

References

Dundas, Paul. *The Jains.* London: Routledge, 1992.

Jain, Mehesh K. *Lord Mahavira: Life and Philosophy.* New Delhi: Shree Publishers & Distributors, 2003.

Jaini, P. S. *The Jaina Path of Purification.* Delhi: Motilal Banarsidass, 1990.

Lalwani, L. C. *Kalpa Sutra.* Delhi: Motilal Banarsidass, 1979.

Law, Bimala Churn. *Mahavira: His Life and Teachings and Schools and Sects: In Jaina Literature.* Kolkata, India: Maha Bodhi Book Agency, 2002.

Mahayana Buddhism

Buddhism goes back to the historical Buddha (ca. 563–ca. 483 BCE) called the Buddha Shakyamuni. Historically, the development of Buddhism is usually divided into four periods: (1) early Buddhism, from the lifetime of the Buddha until the reign of Asoka (d. 238 or 232 BCE) and the split of the Buddhist order into different branches (*nikaya*); (2) the schools of so-called Hinayana (nikaya); (3) Mahayana Buddhism and its systems; and (4) Vajrayana (or Buddhist Tantrism). Mahayana Buddhism (in Sanskrit, *Mahayana* means, literally, the "Great Vehicle") is now the pre-

A statue of Guan Yin, the Buddhist goddess of compassion. (Kikkeema/Dreamstime.com)

dominant form of Buddhism in Central and East Asia and has also been making its way under its different forms (Tibetan Buddhism, Zen Buddhism, Pure Land Buddhism) into Western countries and cultures.

The early Mahayana sources mainly consist of religious, non-historical literature, and consequently our understanding of the formation of early Mahayana, especially the time and the movement's religious and social background in India, is not clear at all. The common assumption has been that the first step toward (proto-)Mahayana was the schismatic split of the early Buddhist community (*sangha*) into two branches, the Sthaviras (Sanskrit: the "Elder") and the Mahasanghikas (Sanskrit: the "Ones Belonging to the Big[ger] Community"). However, scholars now tend to fix the origin of Mahayana to a later period, probably around the beginning of the Common Era.

Early Mahayana was characterized by a set of concepts that were not necessarily absent in the teaching of Hinayana schools but that gained more prominence in Mahayana circles. Among these was the idea that the ideal soteriological "type" was no longer exclusively the ascetic, self-sufficient *arhat*, that is, the Hinayana saint who had finally reached enlightenment (Sanskrit: *bodhi*) and redemption (*nirvana*). In contrast, the Mahayana ideal was the socially behaving *bodhisattva*, a "being (bearing) enlightenment," who was supposed to undertake any effort, physically and spiritually, to save all living beings before realizing his or her own redemption. Mahayana consequently and early on acknowledged the existence of a plurality of these saviors, including Buddhas, who acted also from beyond this world. This latter notion led to the idea of "paradises" (Pure Lands), where believers wanted to be reborn in order to gain enlightenment and final redemption from the circle of rebirth in the presence and by the teaching of a fully enlightened Buddha.

In religious practice, the concepts of Mahayana paved the way for more soteriological activities of the laypeople: through good deeds one could accumulate merit (Sanskrit: *punya*), which could even be transferred (*punyaparinama*) to other living beings. Even a normal human being bore the germ of enlightenment, and it was one of the goals of the Mahayana religious practice—in an ethical or ritual way or through meditative practice—to unfold this hidden, true nature.

The main philosophical schools of early Mahayana in India were the Madhyamaka ("[Teaching of the] Middle [Way]") of Nagarjuna and the Yogacara ("Practice of the Yoga") / Vijnanavada ("Teaching of [Mere] Consciousness"). With the divergence of different schools in Mahayana, it became necessary, especially in East Asia, to systematize and hierarchize the teachings. Chinese schools like Tiantai, Huayan, and Mizong (esoteric Mahayana, in Japan mainly known as Shingon, "True Word") tried to cope with this task. Besides these, there were schools that emphasized meditative (such as the Chinese Chan Buddhism and the Japanese Zen Buddhism) or devotional practice (like the Chinese Jingtu School and the Japanese Jodo Shu, or Pure Land Buddhism) over systematics.

Max Deeg

See also: Ashoka; Buddha, Gautama; Buddhism; Enlightenment; Pure Land Buddhism; Shingon Buddhism; Theravada Buddhism; Zen Buddhism.

References
Harvey, Peter. *An Introduction to Buddhism: Teachings, History and Practices.* Cambridge: Cambridge University Press, 1990.
Sangharakshita. *The Bodhisattva Ideal: Wisdom and Compassion in Buddhism.* Glasgow: Windhorse, 2000.
Suzuki, D. T. *Outlines of Mahayana Buddhism.* New York: Schocken, 1963.
Williams, Paul. *Mahayana Buddhism: The Doctrinal Foundations.* New York: Routledge, 2008.

Mai Chaza Church/City of Jehovah

One of the more controversial of the African Initiated Churches in Zimbabwe is the City of Jehovah (Guta raJehova) movement, also called the Mai Chaza Church, founded in 1955 by Mai (Mother) Chaza (d. 1960). She was a Methodist who became ill and was divorced from her husband in 1953–1954. After this experience, she claimed to have been resurrected from the dead and stated that in revelations on a holy mountain (called Sinai) she had been called to live a celibate and ascetic life and to preach healing, especially to barren women. Her fame as a healer spread, with people coming to her for healing from all over Zimbabwe and other countries in southern Africa. She preferred to refer to herself as the Mutumwa (Messenger) of God, although followers gave her messianic titles like Muponisi (Savior) and Gwayana (Lamb), and saw her as an African reappearance of Christ.

Chaza faced opposition to her activities and eventually found refuge in the Seke township, near Harare. Here she established the first of seven healing centers created in various parts of Zimbabwe, called Cities of Jehovah, which members enter and may settle in after an elaborate confession procedure. Members of this church, both men and women, wear khaki tunics and shorts with red belts—a radical break with custom for African women, who may also wear white dresses—and they carry sheathed knives as the soldiers of Jehovah.

A book of revelation called the Guta raJehova Bible, in which Mai Chaza's words and deeds are recorded, has virtually replaced the New Testament in the City of Jehovah. Chaza is sometimes depicted as a member of the Trinity. The church opposes traditional healing practices and ancestor rites, monogamy is demanded, African music and dancing are used in liturgy, and infant baptism is practiced. The Eucharist is not celebrated.

When Mai Chaza died in 1960, a succession struggle took place. The minority faction settled in the Mutare area under a Nyamandura. The majority group believed that Chaza's spirit had entered a Malawian man named Mapaulos, who became known as Vamatenga ("someone from heaven"). Like Mai Chaza, Vamatenga was believed to be an incarnation of God, but he did not have the same influence as Mai Chaza. The movement was estimated to have some 60,000 members by 2000.

Allan H. Anderson

See also: Asceticism.

References

Martin, Marie-Louise. "The Mai Chaza Church in Rhodesia." In *African Initiatives in Religion*, edited by David B. Barrett, 109–121. Nairobi: East African Publishing House, 1971.

Scarnecchia, Timothy. "Mai Chaza's Guta re Jehova (City of God): Gender, Healing and Urban Identity in an African Independent Church." *Journal of Southern African Studies* 23, no. 1 (1997): 87–105.

Malagasy Lutheran Church

The Malagasy Lutheran Church (Eglise luthérienne malgache) originated as part of the second phase of Protestant Christian development in Madagascar. Protestant Christianity on the island was pioneered by the London Missionary Society (a Congregationalist organization) and had enjoyed the favor of King Radama I (r. 1810–1828), but following his death in 1835, his successor, Queen Ranavalona I (r. 1828–1861) banished the missionaries and moved to re-establish traditional Malagasy religion. Only after her death in 1860 were the missionaries allowed to return. By this time, however, a translation of the Bible in Malagasy had been made and supporting literature had been printed.

In its conflict with Malagasy indigenous religion, Christian lay practitioners have continued to utilize a Christian rite of exorcism to drive what they believed were demons from new converts. This practice had been widespread in evangelical Christian circles in Asia and Africa.

In 1866 representatives of the Norwegian Missionary Society, the missionary arm of the Church of Norway, began work in the southern part of Madagascar. The work found immediate success and soon spread to a variety of locations, where schools were opened. A seminary for training workers was located in Fianrantsoa. The work was enlarged in 1888 and 1889 by Norwegian Americans sent by the several Norwegian Lutheran churches then operating in the United States (now an integral part of the Evangelical Lutheran Church in America). Through the first half of the 20th century, these three missions developed separately but cooperated in such activities as the seminary and coordinated their evangelistic efforts so as not to duplicate work.

After World War II, the movement for national independence gained significant strength, and the Lutherans responded to the coming changes in 1950 by formally merging their missions into the Malagasy Lutheran Church. Missionaries remained in charge until 1961, when, one year after national independence, the first Malagasy president of the church, Rakoto Andrianarijaona, assumed office.

The church retained an intimate relationship with the supporting missionary agencies and churches in Norway and the United States, which were represented at every level of church organization. A revision of the constitution in 1975 reoriented the relationship between the several churches: The formerly subordinate relationship of the Malagasy church was replaced with a partnership. The missionaries were now integrated into the church structure, and the sending churches reduced their representation in the church's ruling structure. In addition, the Malagasy church was now represented in the administration of the sending churches. The Malagasy church still receives financial support from the Church of Norway and the Evangelical Lutheran Church in America, and in 1978 the Evangelical Lutheran Church in Denmark joined the partnership.

The Malagasy Lutheran Church is headed by a triennial national synod that elects a president and executive committee to oversee administration. It sponsors the Lutheran Printing Press, through which it publishes Bibles, hymnals, and other church literature. It supports a chain of elementary and secondary schools, including one especially equipped to serve the blind and one for those with speaking and hearing disabilities. Since World War II, an extensive medical program has been developed through several hospitals and a set of clinics. The medical units supplement a unique healing program that had been launched in 1894 around Rainisoalambo, a native catechist who was believed to have a gift of healing. Much of the church's growth came from the revival associated with this healing ministry and the diaconal caring program that grew out of it.

In 1975 the church moved its headquarters from southern Madagascar to the capital, a signal of the northward thrust of the church into those areas where Christianity is the weakest. In 2005 the church reported three million members. It is a member of the Lutheran World Federation and the World Council of Churches.

Malagasy Lutheran Church
54 avenue de l'Independance
BP 1741
Antananarivo 1101
Madagascar

J. Gordon Melton

See also: Church of Norway; Evangelical Lutheran Church in America; London Missionary Society; Lutheran World Federation; Malagasy Lutheran Church; World Council of Churches.

References

Austnaberg, Hans. *Shepherds and Demons: A Study of Exorcism as Practised and Understood by Shepherds in the Malagasy Lutheran Church.* London: Peter Lang, 2007.

Bachmann, E. Theodore, and Mercia Brenne Bachmann. *Lutheran Churches in the World: A Handbook.* Minneapolis, MN: Augsburg Press, 1989.

Syrdal, Rolf. *Mission in Madagascar: Studies of our Mission in Madagascar and the Beginnings and Development of the Malagasy Lutheran Church.* Minneapolis, MN: Augsburg Publishing House, 1979.

Van Beek, Huibert. *A Handbook of the Churches and Councils: Profiles of Ecumenical Relationships.* Geneva: World Council of Churches, 2006.

Malankara Orthodox Syrian Church

The Malankara Orthodox Syrian Church traces its history to the legendary travels of the Apostle Thomas to India in the years following the death and resurrection of Jesus. According to tradition, Thomas landed at Cranganore, Kerala, in 52 CE. He is believed to have evangelized the land over the next two decades but was finally martyred at what is known as Saint Thomas Mount.

Through the centuries, the church came into contact with the Apostolic Catholic Assyrian Church of the East, based in Iraq. Information on the existence of this church had been lost during the years after the rise of Islam and its control of the land between Kerala and the main concentration of Christians in Europe. Although the Malankara Church was in full communion with the Assyrian Church, communication was not regular. Then in the 15th century, when Portuguese Roman Catholics arrived, the church quickly established cordial relations with the visitors.

As the Portuguese established themselves in Kerala, representatives of the Roman Catholic Church began to criticize the theology of the Malankara Church. It had a theology that represented a position in the larger church that was condemned in the fifth century by the Council of Ephesus. The Assyrian Church, and hence the Malankara Church, was a Monophysite church that taught that Christ had only one nature, the divine nature. The Council of Ephesus promulgated teachings that Christ had both a human and a divine nature.

The Roman Catholic Church placed considerable pressure on the Malankara Church through the last half of the 16th century, and in 1599, at a synod held at Daimper, the church adopted a series of practices deemed necessary for its alignment with the Church in Rome. Changes included the adoption of Roman vestments, the abandonment of a married priesthood, and the acceptance of Portuguese bishops. Over the next 50 years, there was significant opposition to the changes, and in 1653, the great majority of the church withdrew from communion with Rome. At a synod also held at Daimper, church leaders both formally and symbolically renounced their ties to Rome and the changes that had been wrought in 1599. Those who remained loyal to Rome constituted the Syro-Malabar Catholic Church.

The Malankara Church revived the pre-Roman liturgy and practices and selected a new patriarch, Mar Thoma I (r. 1637–1670), who was consecrated in 1665 by Mar Gregorius (d. 1681) of the Syrian Orthodox Church of Antioch. The two churches enjoyed a cordial relationship for the next several centuries. However, late in the 19th century the relationship between the two churches began to sour. In 1886, Patriarch Ignatius Peter IV (r. 1872–1894) of the Syrian Church called a synod at Mulanthuruthy, India, and laid claim to all the property of the Malankara Church in India. The dispute lasted for more than half a century, during which time the Syrian Church established itself in India. Finally in 1958, the Supreme Court of India refused to sustain the claims of the Syrian Church and awarded all the disputed property to the Malankara Church.

During the lengthy battle with the Syrian Church, the Malankara Church faced other problems as well. First, the Church of England, which had also encountered the Malankara Church following the establishment of British authority in India, began to suggest changes to the church that would bring it more in line with Anglicanism and the orthodox theological tradition that dominated Europe. Through the 19th century, the drive to reform the church along Anglican lines gained considerable support. The Reformist wing of the church eventually left and reorganized as the Mar Thoma Syrian Church of Malabar. On the other hand, in the 1920s several bishops left to found the Syro-Malankara Catholic Church, which has been in full communion with Rome ever since.

The modern Malankara Orthodox Syrian Church is led by the catholicate of the East, an office established by the church in 1912. In the midst of its dispute with the Syrian patriarch, Abdul Messiah, the Indian church leader, announced that the catholicate of Edessa (in Syria), a see that had not existed for centuries, was to be re-established in India. The new catholicate became the first of the new line of Malankara Church leaders.

In the years since World War II, the church has attempted to participate in the new global Christian community. The church is a charter member of the World Council of Churches. It has approximately 2 million members (2005), organized into some 23 dioceses. It sponsors a set of schools, including the Orthodox Theological Seminary, and several medical facilities.

J. Gordon Melton

See also: Apostolic Catholic Assyrian Church of the East; Church of England; Syro-Malabar Catholic Church; World Council of Churches.

References

Chaillot, Christine. *The Malankara Orthodox Church: Visit to the Oriental Malankara Orthodox Syrian Church of India*. Paris, France: Inter-Orthodox Dialogue, 1996.

Frykenberg, Robert Louis. *Christianity in India: From Beginnings to the Present*. New York: Oxford University Press, 2008.

Moffatt, Samuel Hugh. *A History of Christianity in Asia*. Vol. 1, *Beginnings to 1500*. San Francisco: HarperSanFrancisco, 1992.

■ Malawi

Malawi is a small nation in southern Africa east of Zambia and south of Tanzania. Its southern half is surrounded by Mozambique. Much of its border with Tanzania is constituted by Lake Malawi, the southernmost lake in the lengthy Rift Valley that can be traced northward to Kenya. Some 13,900,000 people (2008) live in Malawi's 36,324 square miles of territory.

The land making up the nation of Malawi rose from obscurity in the 10th century as part of the extended territory of the *monomotapa* (ruler) of Zimbabwe. Zimbabwe, desirous of extending its mining operations, had claimed the area to the west and south of Lake

Mission de Shiré (Afrique)
des Pères Montfortains
Un Missionnaire en Tournée

An undated postcard of a Christian missionary near the Shire River in Malawi, Africa. (Rykoff Collection/Corbis)

Malawi. The land had been settled by a variety of Bantu people, especially the Chewas and the Yao. Then the expansion of the Zulus far to the south brought about the decline of the Zimbabwean kingdom and also pushed the Ngoli-Ndwande people into the region.

Western attention to the region began with the explorations of British missionary David Livingstone (1813–1873) and the subsequent assertion of British interest in building a land route linking South Africa to Egypt. In 1891 the British Protectorate of Nyassaland was created. That Protectorate gave way to the independent state of Malawi in 1964. Hastings Kamazu Banda (1906–1997), elected president in the first free elections, soon seized power and continued to rule the country with increasingly dictatorial powers until he was defeated in 1994 in the country's first multiparty elections. The Banda years had been marked by suppression of dissident intellectual, political enemies, and minority religions.

The traditional religions of Malawi have been able to stave off significant missionary efforts from both Christians and Muslims. Approximately 25 percent of the population continues to follow their ancestral faith. Among the more important surviving faiths is that built around the deity Chisumphi, which survives among the Chewa people. The Chewas had held sway over much of Malawi during a period when the Zimbabwean kingdom had been in decline. Worship of Chisumphi was centered on a drum located at the main center of the faith at Kaphirntiwa. He was believed to possess women who functioned as mediums, known as Makewanan.

As Christianity moved into the area, it encountered another belief system among the southern Chewa, built around the deity M'Bona, a god who was once human. Under the impact of the cultural clash, Chewa leaders began to speak of M'Bona as a black Christ and adopted various practices from the Christian church.

David Livingstone issued the call for Christians to evangelize Malawi. The first work, established by the Universities' Mission to Central Africa, an Anglican society, established a station north of Lake Malawi (then known as Lake Nyassa), but it had to be discon-

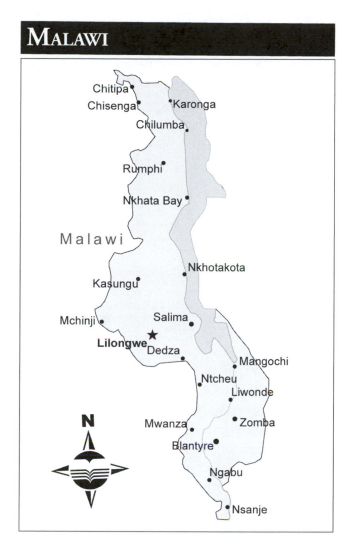

MALAWI

Chitipa
Chisenga
Karonga
Chilumba
Rumphi
Nkhata Bay
Malawi
Nkhotakota
Kasungu
Mchinji
Salima
Lilongwe
Dedza
Mangochi
Ntcheu
Liwonde
Mwanza
Zomba
Blantyre
Ngabu
Nsanje

N

until the end of the 1880s. The White Fathers pioneered this effort. The first Malawian priest was ordained in 1937, and the first bishop was consecrated in 1956. The church experienced rapid growth after World War II and soon surpassed the Presbyterians in membership.

More than 100 different Christian denominations now operate in Malawi. Included are older missionary churches such as the Anglican Church (1879), the Seventh Day Baptist General Conference (1899), and the Churches of Christ (1906). The African Methodist Episcopal Church expanded its work to Malawi in 1924. The Anglican Church has two dioceses in Malawi, now incorporated into the Church of the Province of Central Africa, whose archbishop resides in Botswana.

These denominations have been joined by the newer Holiness and Pentecostal denominations, such as the International Pentecostal Holiness Church (1923), the Assemblies of God (1930), Church of the Nazarene (1957), and the Church of God (Cleveland, Tennessee) (1970). The Wisconsin Evangelical Lutheran Synod is affiliated with the Lutheran Church of Central Africa, established in 1962. More recently the Evangelical Lutheran Church of Malawi (ELCM) was started by a Lutheran layman, Gilbert Msuku, upon his return to Malawi after 17 years of residence in Tanzania. He gathered an initial congregation in Lilongwe, the capital of Malawi, where its headquarters remains. The ELCM is affiliated with the Federation of Lutheran Churches in Southern Africa and the Lutheran World Federation.

Like its neighbors, Malawi is also home to a spectrum of African Initiated Churches, among the most expansive being the African Industrial Mission, founded in 1898, and the African Apostolic Church of Johane Marange, an independent church that began in Zimbabwe. Besides the African Industrial Mission, unique Malawian churches include the Achewa Church (1920), which has Baptist roots, and the Last Church of God and His Christ (1924), founded by former members of the Presbyterian Church.

Malawi has offered strong support to both the Seventh-day Adventist Church and the Jehovah's Witnesses, the latter having made a comeback after its period of suffering in the 1970s. The Greek Orthodox Patriarchate of Alexandria and All Africa has a small

tinued after suffering a series of misfortunes. The Free Church of Scotland, a Presbyterian body, opened more enduring work in 1875, and the Church of Scotland, also Presbyterian, sent missionaries in 1876. In 1926, these two churches joined with the mission founded in 1888 by the Reformed Church of South Africa to form the Church of Central Africa Presbyterian, the largest Protestant church in the country. President Banda was a member of this church and moved against other groups, most especially the Jehovah's Witnesses, who were banned in 1969. The apolitical Witnesses had refused to abide by the law requiring all citizens to be members of the political party led by Banda, and in 1967, many had been savagely beaten for their seemingly unpatriotic stance.

Roman Catholics had first visited Malawi in 1561 but did not establish permanent missionary stations

Malawi

Religion	Followers in 1970	Followers in 2010	% of Population	Annual % growth 2000–2010	Followers in 2025	Followers in 2050
Christians	2,665,000	12,001,000	79.8	2.77	17,410,000	26,553,000
Protestants	960,000	4,115,000	27.4	4.60	5,900,000	9,200,000
Roman Catholics	993,000	3,850,000	25.6	4.52	5,716,000	8,900,000
Independents	194,000	1,900,000	12.6	1.80	3,000,000	4,600,000
Muslims	725,000	1,985,000	13.2	2.62	2,800,000	4,150,000
Ethnoreligionists	1,113,000	940,000	6.3	0.75	950,000	900,000
Agnostics	500	42,000	0.3	2.62	75,000	125,000
Baha'is	8,400	36,000	0.2	2.62	70,000	130,000
Hindus	5,000	31,000	0.2	2.62	45,000	80,000
Sikhs	200	600	0.0	2.61	1,000	2,000
New religionists	200	600	0.0	2.64	1,000	1,600
Jews	80	250	0.0	2.63	300	400
Atheists	0	300	0.0	2.59	1,000	2,000
Total population	**4,518,000**	**15,037,000**	**100.0**	**2.62**	**21,353,000**	**31,944,000**

work associated with its diocese in Zimbabwe. A more substantive Orthodox presence is provided by the Coptic Orthodox Church, which named a bishop for the country in 1920.

The Christian Council of Malawi, an affiliate of the World Council of Churches, dates to 1939. It grew out of the older Consultative Board of Federative Malawi Missions of Nyassaland. There are also two organizations serving primarily African Initiated Churches: the Followers of Christ Association of Malawi and the Reformed Independent Churches Association of Malawi.

Islam has made its most significant impact in Malawi among the Yao people of eastern Malawi, the great majority of whom are now Muslims of the Sunni Shafaiite School. The Malawian Muslim community has expanded in recent decades, receiving financial support from several Arab countries. The first spiritual assembly of the Baha'i Faith in the country was founded in 1964. It experienced early growth in the expatriate Indian community, which includes Hindus, Muslims, and Sikhs. Hindus have organized the Shree Hindu Seva Mandal (a temple) in Blantyre. The Sikh community is centered in Limbe.

J. Gordon Melton

See also: African Apostolic Church of Johane Marange; African Methodist Episcopal Church;

Assemblies of God; Baha'i Faith; Church of God (Cleveland, Tennessee); Church of Scotland; Church of the Nazarene; Church of the Province of Central Africa; Churches of Christ; Greek Orthodox Patriarchate of Alexandria and All Africa; International Pentecostal Holiness Church; Jehovah's Witnesses; Lutheran World Federation; Roman Catholic Church; Seventh-day Adventist Church; Seventh Day Baptist General Conference; Shafaiite School of Islam; White Fathers; Wisconsin Evangelical Lutheran Synod; World Council of Churches.

References

Amanze, Joseph. *African Traditional Religion in Malawi: The Case of the Bimbi Cult.* Zomba, Malawi: Kachere Series, 2002.

Bone, David. S., ed. *Malawi's Muslims: A Historical Perspective.* Zomba, Malawi: Kachere Series, 2000.

Bone, David. S., ed. *Religion in Malawi: Current Research.* Zomba, Malawi: Department of Religious Studies, Chancellor College, University of Malawi, 1983.

Chakanza, J. C. *An Annotated List of Independent Churches in Malawi, 1900–1981.* Zomba, Malawi: Department of Religious Studies, Chancellor College, University of Malawi, 1983.

De Kok, Bergje. *Christianity and African Traditional Religion: Two Realities of a Different Kind.* Zomba, Malawi: Kachere Series, 2004.

Sindima, H. J. *A General Survey of the History of the Independent Church in Malawi, 1900–1976.* Nairobi: AACC, 1977.

Thompson, Jack. *Ngoni, Xhosa and Scot: Religion and Cultural Interactions in Malawi.* Zomba, Malawi: Kachere Series, 2007.

Wishlade, R. L. *Sectarianism in Southern Nyasaland.* London: Oxford University Press, 1964.

■ Malaysia

The modern nation of Malaysia was created in 1963 when the former British colonies of Malaya, Singapore, Sarawak, and Sabah merged to form the Federation of Malaysia (Singapore went its separate way two years later). It lies north of Indonesia, with whom it shares the island of Borneo. West Malaysia shares its northern border with Thailand. Some 25,274,000 people occupy the country's 127,000 square miles of territory. Ethnically, the population includes three significant groups: Malays (50 percent), Chinese (30 percent), and Indians (15 percent).

The Malays settled the land in prehistoric times, and the historical period began with the migration of the Chinese into the region in the second millennium BCE. Indians arrived in the first century CE, when an Indian state emerged on the Mekong River in what is now Vietnam. Chinese Buddhist states emerged along the eastern shore of the Malay Peninsula. In the 15th century, the port of Melaka (or Malacca) was founded on the western shore of the peninsula. This port became the doorway for Islam's entrance into the area, and a century of trade with Muslims coincided with the rise of Islam to dominance among the Malay segment of the population and the replacement of the Buddhist states with Islamic ones.

In 1511, the Portuguese seized Melaka. A century later, the Dutch moved in and replaced the Portuguese. The British then moved into the area by settling along the northern shore of the island of Borneo. The conflict between the Dutch and British, which reached a new peak following the founding of Singapore in 1819,

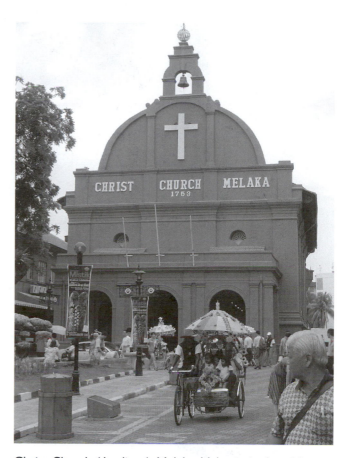

Christ Church (Anglican), Melaka, Malaysia, is the oldest Protestant church in Southeast Asia. (J. Gordon Melton)

led to an 1824 treaty that made Malaya a British colony. From their base at Melaka and Penang, the British encouraged the various sultans who continued to rule over most of the peninsula to form a federation, while the territories on Borneo (Brunei, Sabah, and Sarawak) were turned into protectorates. The British also encouraged the immigration into Malaya first of Chinese and then, in the early 20th century, of Tamils from India. By controlling the economy and employment, the British nurtured a segregated system—the Malays dominating agriculture; the Chinese, mining; and the Indians, rubber production.

The area was occupied by the Japanese during World War II. When the British again assumed hegemony, they began to propose changes in governance, which raised tensions between the several ethnic groups, on several occasions leading to the outbreak of hostilities. Finally, in 1957, a platform for independence was worked out, building on the federation of sultans

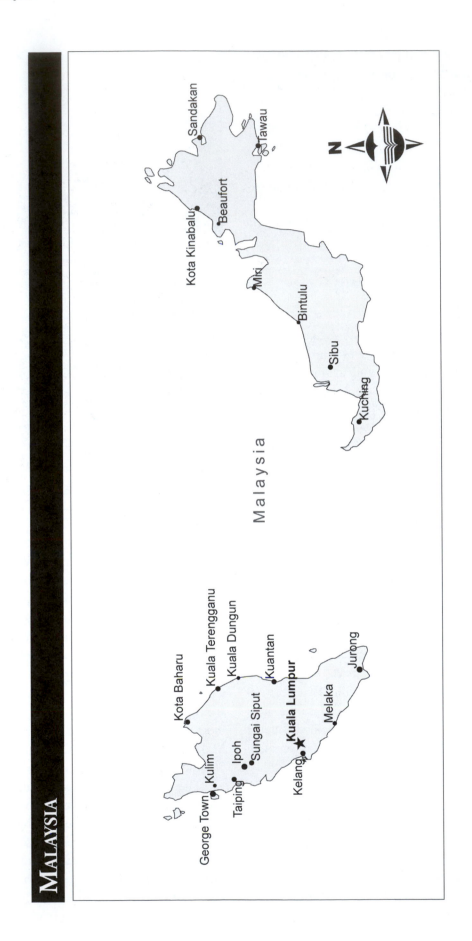

previously established. Malaysia was established as a federation of 11 states. Every five years, one of the sultans from the nine Islamic sultanates is designated as the monarch, sharing power in a constitutional system with a Parliament and popularly elected prime minister. The Chinese and Indians were granted citizenship, but the Malays, as indigenous people, were accorded several special privileges, and Malay was designated the official language.

Today, religion in Malaysia is largely divided along ethnic lines. Malaysia is dominated by Sunni Muslims of the Shafaiite School. Islam was introduced in the 13th century by traders from India (primarily from Bengal and Gujarat) and the Middle East. It replaced the indigenous religions of the Malay peoples as well as the Hinduism and Buddhism of the elites. Aristocrats in the coastal districts were the first to accept the new faith, and the population followed in gradual stages. Diplomatic marriages between the royal classes of different kingdoms further spread the faith. For example, marriages arranged by the sultan in Melaka led to the establishment of Islam on Borneo.

Islam remained dominant during the colonial era, and its continued leadership role is symbolized by the National Mosque in Kuala Lumpur, completed in 1965. Islam was named the state religion in Malaysia in 1957. Each of the nine sultans is head of the faith in his own sultanate. The sultan serving as king is also head of Islam in the two states without a sultan, Melaka and Penang. There is no designated head of the faith in Sarawak or Sabah. Among the king's stated duties is defending the faith, and he also has a set of administrative tasks such as setting the dates for Muslim festivals.

Founded in 1968, the Council for Islamic Affairs, which operates out of the prime minister's office, coordinates the activities of the state councils that advise the sultans and state governments on religious matters. The state and national legislatures have the power to make laws relative to Islam and other religions.

Although Islam of the Shafaiite School predominates, there are measurable communities of Shia Islam and Sufism. The Sufi brotherhoods were prominent among the Muslims who introduced Islam to the region, especially Borneo. There is a small community belonging to the Ahmadiyya Muslim movement, and

the Baha'i Faith is growing primarily from Muslim converts.

Buddhism emerged among the Malaysians of Chinese heritage and still retains the allegiance of the great majority of them. Most follow Chinese Mahayana (Pure Land) Buddhist traditions, often mixed with Daoism. Tian Dao (also known as Yiguandao) is a popular new Daoist movement that includes elements of Buddhism. There are also some Tibetan tantric influences and a few Theravada Buddhists; the urban Buddhist community in particular now manifests the same pluralism as found in other Southeast Asian cities. Thus one would find, for example, centers for groups such as the Falun Gong and the True Buddha School. At the other end of the spectrum, Buddhism fades into Chinese folk religion.

Leading Buddhist organizations include the Malaysian Buddhist Association (Mahayana), the Buddhist Missionary Society Malaysia, Foguangshan Buddhism, the Buddhist Compassion Relief Tzu Chi Association, the Young Buddhist Association of Malaysia, and the Sasana Abhiwurdi Wardhana Society, a Theravada group formed in 1894 for Sri Lankans. The True Buddha School, a Chinese Esoteric Buddhist group from Taiwan, grew significantly in Malaysia through the 1990s, and now has more members in Malaysia than any country.

Hinduism, introduced around the beginning of the Common Era, controlled much of Malaysia through its Hindu rulers prior to the coming of Islam. Today it is the dominant religion of the Indian Malaysians, the majority adhering to Tamil Shaivism. Several of the new Hindu movements entered Malaysia in the 20th century, including the Divine Life Society and the International Society for Krishna Consciousness. A number of Sikhs from India and Pakistan have also made Malaysia their home.

Coming relatively late to Malaysia is Christianity, introduced by the Portuguese when they captured Melaka. The Dutch pushed the Roman Catholic Church aside and introduced Protestantism (the Reformed Church) in the 17th century. However, it was not until the 19th century, during the British era, that the modern Protestant missionary movement targeted the region. Malaysia and Singapore shared a history until 1965, since which they have largely gone their separate ways.

Malaysia

Religion	Followers in 1970	Followers in 2010	% of Population	Annual % growth 2000–2010	Followers in 2025	Followers in 2050
Muslims	5,388,000	15,876,000	56.9	1.97	20,053,000	23,991,000
Chinese folk	2,687,000	5,050,000	18.1	1.94	5,300,000	5,755,000
Christians	582,000	2,530,000	9.1	2.25	3,308,000	4,064,000
Roman Catholics	301,000	1,250,000	4.5	1.64	1,550,000	1,850,000
Protestants	159,000	760,000	2.7	3.09	1,100,000	1,400,000
Anglicans	69,600	230,000	0.8	2.02	290,000	350,000
Hindus	804,000	1,750,000	6.3	1.97	2,100,000	2,450,000
Buddhists	690,000	1,430,000	5.1	1.74	1,650,000	1,900,000
Ethnoreligionists	553,000	950,000	3.4	1.73	850,000	800,000
Agnostics	16,000	105,000	0.4	1.97	200,000	300,000
Baha'is	42,700	78,000	0.3	1.97	100,000	120,000
New religionists	50,800	70,000	0.3	1.97	85,000	100,000
Sikhs	30,000	46,700	0.2	1.97	60,000	75,000
Atheists	8,000	32,000	0.1	1.97	60,000	72,000
Jains	1,200	2,100	0.0	1.96	3,000	4,000
Total population	**10,853,000**	**27,920,000**	**100.0**	**1.97**	**33,769,000**	**39,631,000**

The first Roman Catholic priest settled in Melaka in 1611. In the 1540s, the town was home to one of the more famous Jesuits, Francis Xavier (1506–1552), who introduced Roman Catholicism to much of Asia. The Diocese of Malaysia was established in 1557, abandoned in 1641, and re-established in 1888 (with the bishop residing in Singapore). The Archdiocese of Malaysia and Singapore was separated in 1972. Catholics have their major constituency among the Chinese, Indian, and small Eurasian community. The church has experienced major problems in Sabah as a result of the expulsion of many priests and religious in the early 1970s at the same time that a noticeable increase in Islamic proselytization within the Christian community was evident.

After the British expelled the Dutch from the Reformed Church, the next Protestant missionaries in Malaysia were from the London Missionary Society, a Congregationalist organization. The missionary William Milne (1785–1822) had stopped at Melaka on his way to China, and he stayed to train Chinese Malaysians as missionaries in both Malaya and China. When China was finally opened to Christian missionaries in 1842, the work transferred there.

The Society for the Propagation of the Gospel in Foreign Parts, associated with the Church of England, began work in Malaysia six years after the London Missionary Society, in 1848. It was soon joined by the Church Missionary Society. The Methodist Episcopal Church (now an integral part of the United Methodist Church) began work in Malaysia from its base in Singapore. The effort, originally administered from India, was organized into the Malaysian Mission Conference in 1894 and the Annual Conference in 1902. Meanwhile, in the 1860s, the Christian Brethren launched their missionary efforts.

Through the 20th century, numerous other Christian groups have also initiated work in Malaysia—the Lutherans (Protestant Church of Sabah), the Seventh-day Adventist Church, and the Assemblies of God receiving the best response. Outstanding among missionary efforts, however, is the work of the Borneo Evangelical Mission, which was created in 1928 by a group of conservative Protestants in Melbourne, Australia. Their effort has produced what is now the third largest church in the country, the Evangelical Church of Borneo. It is just behind the Roman Catholic Church and the Methodist Church in Malaysia, and just ahead of the Anglicans, whose three dioceses are now part of the Church of the Province of Southeast Asia (created in 1996).

The Christian community has been increased by the addition of several non-Western groups, most important, the Local Church and the True Jesus Church, both developed early in the 20th century in China. The Tamil-speaking Ceylon Pentecostal Church came to Malaysia from Sri Lanka, and the Mar Thoma Syrian Church of Malabar arrived with members migrating from India. However, even with the development of a variety of different Christian groups, the Christian community remains relatively small compared to the other major traditions. It has had the most success in Sabah and Sarawak as compared to western Malaysia.

Protestant Christians associate with each other across denominational lines through the Council of Churches of Malaysia (founded in 1948 as the Council of Churches of Malaysia and Singapore). It is an affiliate of the World Council of Churches. Conservative Protestants are associated in the National Evangelical Christian Fellowship Malaysia, which is related to the World Evangelical Alliance.

J. Gordon Melton

See also: Assemblies of God; Baha'i Faith; Buddhist Compassion Relief Tzu Chi Association, The; Buddhist Missionary Society Malaysia; Christian Brethren; Church Missionary Society; Church of the Province of Southeast Asia; Church of England; Divine Life Society; Falun Gong; Foguangshan; International Society for Krishna Consciousness; Jesuits; London Missionary Society; Mar Thoma Syrian Church of Malabar; Methodist Church of Malaysia; Pure Land Buddhism; Roman Catholic Church; Seventh-day Adventist Church; Shafaiite School of Islam; Shia Islam; Society for the Propagation of the Gospel in Foreign Parts; Sufism; Tamil Shaivism; Tian Dao; True Buddha School; United Methodist Church; World Council of Churches; World Evangelical Alliance; Young Buddhist Association of Malaysia.

References

Andaya, Barbara Watson, and Leonard Y. Andaya. *A History of Malaysia*. Houndsmills, Hampshire, UK: Palgrave, 2001.

Basri, Ghazalki. *Christian Mission and Islamic Dewah in Malaysia*. Kuala Lumpur: Nurin Enterprise, 1990.

Cheu, Hock Tong. *Chinese Beliefs and Practices in Southeast Asia: Studies on the Chinese Religion in Malaysia, Singapore and Indonesia*. Selangor, Malaysia: Pelanduk Publications, 1999.

Hassan, M. Kamal, and Ghazali bin Basri, eds. *Encyclopedia of Malaysia*. Vol. 10, *Religions and Beliefs*. Singapore: Archipelago Press, 2006.

Hurt, R., L. K. King, and J. Roxborough, eds. *Christianity in Malaysia: A Denominational History*. Salangor Darul Ehran, Malaysia: Palanduk Publications, 1992.

Kennedy, J. *A History of Malaya*. Kuala Lumpur: Synergy Books International, 1993.

Lee, Raymond L. M., and Susan Ellen Ackerman. *Sacred Tensions: Modernity and Religious Transformation in Malaysia*. Colombia: University of South Carolina Press, 1997.

McDougall, C. *Buddhism in Malaya*. Singapore: Donald Moore, 1956.

Putra, T. A. R., et al. *Contemporary Issues on Malaysian Religions*. Petaling Jaya, Malaysia: Pelanduk Publications, 1984.

Malaysia, Islam in

Islam is the dominant religion of Malaysia, though communities of Chinese Buddhists and Asian Indian Hindus and non-Malay Christians exist. Islam came to Malaysia from India and the Middle East through the arrival of Muslim traders.

During its initial growth in the seventh century, Islam identified itself with an emerging Arab culture and was carried from its base on the Arabian Peninsula eastward to the Indus River. In the following centuries, the Indian subcontinent would become a battleground in which Hindus and Muslims would be locked in fierce competition for the souls of the ruling elite and the people, with quite varying results in different areas. Beginning in the 12th century, Islam spread to Malaysia and the neighboring Indonesian archipelago. It was brought by merchants from India and the Muslim lands to the west, where it found a following from persuasion rather than the sword.

The port of Melaka (or Melacca), located on the Malaysian side of the narrow strait that separates Malaysia from Sumatra, was founded in the 15th century. It rulers were the first in the region to convert to Islam and establish it among the people of their land. The prosperity of Melaka, developed from its trade with the Islamic world, tipped the scale among other leaders in the region, and within a short time Islam had become a majority faith and numerous, relatively small sultanates had come into existence. Islam continued to expand even after the Portuguese came to the region in the 16th century.

The Portuguese captured Melaka in 1511. In the mid-1600s, the Dutch entered the region and made an alliance with the sultan of Johor. The Dutch enjoyed a monopoly on trade in the region until the British moved into Malaysia in the late 18th century. After a half century of conflict, in 1824 the Dutch and the English reached an agreement, with the Dutch receiving control of the Indonesian islands and the British receiving control of Malaysia. Until the 1870s, the British did little to interfere with the running of the various states on the Malaysian Peninsula, but in 1874 they imposed the Pangkor Treaty, by which a British advisor was attached to each sultanate. This advisor was to counsel on all matters except Malay religion. The treaty had the unintended consequence of causing the sultans to bring the leadership of the Islamic community into their palaces, launching a tradition whereby the government supplied the top leadership of the religious organizations. As British missionaries moved into the region, Malaysian leaders manifested a noticeable hostility to all things Western, including Christianity.

Growing as it did in a non-Arab context, the form of Islam that became entrenched in Malaysia, Sunni Islam of the Shafiite School, wedded itself to a number of Malaysian cultural practices quite foreign to Middle Eastern Islam. At the beginning of the 20th century, many Malaysian students studied in the Middle East, which they saw as the center of their faith, and absorbed influences from different reformist tendencies. They returned to their homeland to found a movement calling for reform. Shaikh Tahir Jahal al-Din (1869–1957) emerged as the leader of the reformist movement in Malaysia and Indonesia. He called for the establishment of modern Islamic schools and the abandonment of various common practices, which he saw as unlawful innovations.

The reform movement, with a background in Hanafite and even Wahhabi perspectives, did not win the day. However, it did activate the older Shafiite leaders, and in its criticism of the British it is credited with originating the drive for independence that would emerge more visibly after World War II. In the 1950s the Pan-Malayan Islamic Party began to advocate for the establishment of an independent Islamic state.

Following independence in 1957, Islam was named the official religion of Malaysia, and the several sultans in the nine states were named the guardians of the faith in their territory. The country's sovereign is chosen from among the nine sultans. An office of Islamic Development was established in the prime minister's office, and in the 1970s the Islamic Center was opened to give increased attention to the development of the Muslim community. In 1970 the Faculty of Islamic Studies was created at the National University of Malaysia.

The final establishment of modern Malaysia in 1963, complete with the former states of Sabah and Sarawak on the island of Borneo, released the energy of the younger generation. Many affiliated with a new reformist *dawah* (propagation) movement, which saw Islam as a holistic life. Its members demanded a broader application of Islamic law in the land.

The dawah movement has had a visible effect on the government, which established a variety of institutions such as the International Institute of Islamic Thought and Civilization (1987) and changed a number of practices within the government itself so as to embody Islamic values and practices. There is a significant non-Islamic presence in Malaysia; however, it is almost totally limited to Chinese and other non-Malay peoples. Islam is the majority religion on the Malay Peninsula, but it is the minority in Sabah and Sarawak. Proselytization of Muslims is prohibited and conversion of Muslims to other religions is strongly discouraged and carries a variety of penalties.

Department of Islamic Development Malaysia
Menara Pusat Islam
50519 Jalan Perdana
Kuala Lumpur
Malaysia
http://www.islam.gov.my/english/

J. Gordon Melton

See also: Hanafite School of Islam; Shafiite School of Islam; Wahhabi Islam.

References

Andaya, Barbara Watson, and Leonard Y. Andaya. *A History of Malaysia*. Basingstoke, Hamps., UK: Palgrave, 2001.

Bakar, M. A. "Islamic Revivalism and the Political Process in Malaysia." *Asian Survey* 21, no. 10 (1981): 1040–1059.

Hassan, M. Kamel, and Ghazali bin Basri, eds. *Religions and Beliefs*. Vol. 10, *The Encyclopedia of Islam*. Singapore: Archipelago Press, 2005.

Nagata, J. "The New Fundamentalism: Islam in Contemporary Malaysia." *Asian Thought and Society: An International Review* 5, no. 14 (1980): 128–141.

■ Maldives, The

The Maldives is an archipelago in the Indian Ocean southwest of Sri Lanka consisting of some 2,000 small coral islands, fewer than 20 percent of which are inhabited. Their land area is a mere 116 square miles, but is home to 386,000 citizens (2008).

On July 3, 1153, the residents of the island, formerly Buddhists, made their conversion to Sunni Islam, and the ruler assumed the title of sultan. Abul Barakaath Yoosuf Al-Barbary, a Muslim from North Africa, led the conversion process, and Sri Tribuvana Aditiya, the king, assumed the name Sultan Mohamed bin Abdullah and instructed his subjects to adopt Islam. He encouraged the shift of allegiance by destroying the island's Buddhist temples and shrines. It is of interest that many of the mosques are oriented to the rising Sun rather than to Mecca, a seeming remnant of the pre-Buddhist culture of the islands. The Buddhists subsequently built their temples on the same sites, and mosques eventually replaced the Buddhist temples. Due to the scarcity of building materials, no attempt to reorient the buildings occurred.

The hub of the Muslim community is the Islamic Center and Grand Friday Mosque that dominates the skyline of Male, the capital city. Among the more than 20 other mosques in the city is Hukuru Miski, some

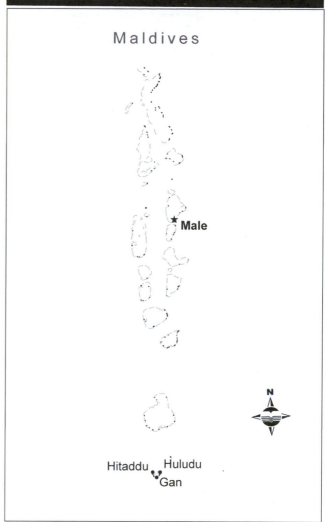

400 years old and famed for the stone carvings it houses. Adjacent to it is the tomb of Abul Barakaath, the island's Muslim pioneer.

In 1887 the sultan agreed that his land would become a British protectorate. Eventually a naval base was set up on one of the islands to protect the vital sea lanes in the region. The Maldives became independent in 1965. Three years later the sultan was forced out of office and a republic replaced his traditional rule. In 1982 the Maldives joined the British Commonwealth.

Sunni Islam is established as the state religion, and proselytizing by other religious groups (including other schools of Islam) is not allowed. There are a small number of members of the Roman Catholic

Maldives

Religion	Followers in 1970	Followers in 2010	% of Population	Annual % growth 2000–2010	Followers in 2025	Followers in 2050
Muslims	121,000	318,000	98.4	1.59	404,000	501,000
Buddhists	0	2,200	0.7	1.59	2,800	3,500
Christians	220	1,400	0.4	−0.31	1,800	2,300
Roman Catholics	120	850	0.3	0.00	1,000	1,300
Protestants	90	420	0.1	−1.28	600	800
Independents	10	20	0.0	0.00	50	100
Hindus	0	1,100	0.3	1.59	1,500	2,000
Agnostics	0	300	0.1	0.60	500	800
Baha'is	20	130	0.0	1.66	300	450
Atheists	0	20	0.0	−0.97	40	60
Total population	**121,000**	**323,000**	**100.0**	**1.58**	**411,000**	**510,000**

Church and the Baha'i Faith, consisting primarily of expatriates.

J. Gordon Melton

See also: Baha'i Faith; Roman Catholic Church.

References

Maloney, C. *People of the Maldive Islands*. Bombay: Orient Longman, 1980.

Metz, Helen Chapin. *Indian Ocean: Five Island Countries*. Washington, DC: U.S. Government Printing Service, 1995.

Yijima, H., ed. *The Islamic History of the Maldive Islands*. 2 vols. Tokyo: Institute for the Study of Languages and Cultures of Asia and Africa, 1982, 1984.

■ Mali

Mali is a landlocked, primarily agricultural country in West Africa, south of the Sahara Desert, and home to the fabled city of Timbuktu. Its 471,000 square miles of territory, the northern third of which is desert, are surrounded by Mauritania, Algeria, Niger, Burkina Faso, Cote d'Ivoire, Guinea, and Senegal. Around half of its 12,300,000 people are from the several groups of the Mande people, the remainder from other African groups.

Settled in prehistoric times, the country is now home to a number of Native peoples, the largest group

being one of the Mande groups, the Bambara. During the first millennium CE a trans-Saharan trade route that linked West Africa with the Nile River valley passed through Mali, and during the 14th century the Mali Empire reached its peak of prosperity. It reached west to the Atlantic (into present-day Senegal and Guinea), north into Algeria, and eastward into what is now Nigeria and Benin. Timbuktu dominated the western end of the trans-African trade. As Mali rose to power, it developed ties to the Muslim world in the Middle East, and Islam and Islamic learning became the dominant cultural forces in the land. The univer-

Detail of the Great Mosque in Djenné, Mali. During the reign of Malian king Sundiata Keita during the 13th century CE, stunning mosques made of earth were constructed throughout the West African empire of Mali. (Corel)

Dogon dancers wearing traditional masks. Living in the central regions of Mali, the Dogon people are known mostly for their culture, which is exemplified by their expressive masks, dances, and architecture. (Travel Pictures Gallery)

sity at Timbuktu rivaled those of Western Europe in the Middle Ages and was an important force in spreading Islam throughout West Africa.

The decline of Mali began at the end of the 15th century. Important in this decline was the diversion of trade from the east to the Atlantic coast and the newly arrived Portuguese traders. As neighboring states grew strong, they took more and more land from Mali, a process that continued until the intervention of the French in the middle of the 19th century. In 1896, after rather brutal attempts to pacify the land, the French annexed Mali and in 1904 made it a part of French Sudan.

Independence came in steps, with Mali becoming autonomous in 1985, part of the Sudanese Republic (with Senegal) in 1959, and fully independent in 1960. The new government, which appeared to have made a good start, was swept away by a coup in 1968 and

since has been plagued by political instability and poverty. The present parliamentary system is based upon that of France.

Although Islam has overwhelmed the religions of most of the Native peoples in Mali, traditional faiths have remained strong among the Kagoro, Bobo, and Minianka peoples, and the beliefs and practices of the Dogon people have become well known, as they have entered into the Western New Age beliefs. Dogon beliefs include an origin myth that ties them to the star system Sirius, a tradition that appears to contain information about the nature of the system that was unknown to secular astronomy until recent decades.

Islam entered Mali as early as the 10th century, and Malian Muslims are primarily of the Sunni Malikite School of Islam. Islam is said to have been established during a drought in the middle of the 11th century, when the ruler, Allakoi Keita, became a

Mali

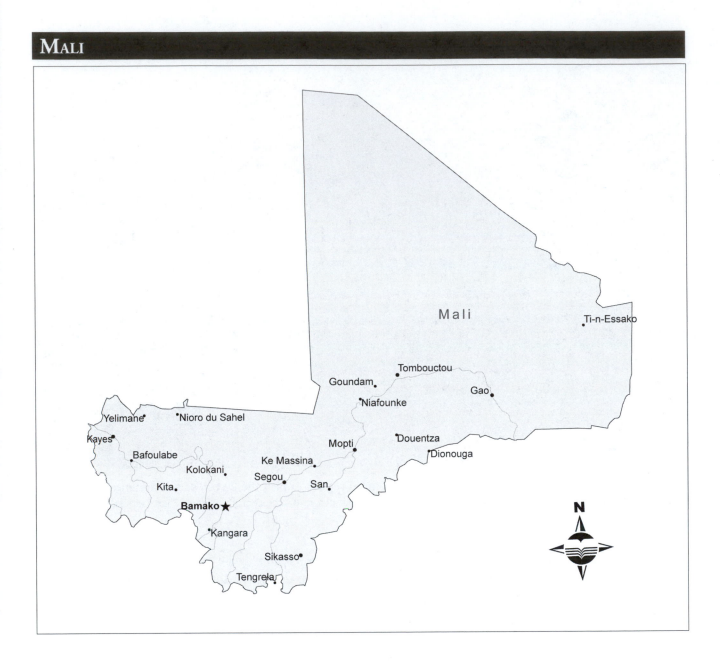

Muslim. Soon afterward the rain began to fall, and in gratitude to God, Keita decided to make a pilgrimage to Mecca. Upon his return to his realm, he was named sultan. The Tijaniyya Sufi Order moved into Mali, where they suffered a major schism, leading to the formation of the Hamaliyya Brotherhood, based in Nioro. By the end of the 20th century, between 70 and 80 percent of the people were Muslim.

Christianity first reached Mali in 1895 with the arrival of the White Fathers, a Roman Catholic missionary order, soon followed by sisters of the affiliate order.

They made slow progress, but in 1921 a vicariate was erected. The first African priest was ordained in 1936, followed by a slow process of building indigenous leadership. The first Malian bishop was consecrated in 1962, two years after Mali became an independent nation. The church has had its greatest success among the Bobo and Dogon peoples.

Protestantism entered the country in 1919 through representatives of the Gospel Missionary Union (GMU), an independent evangelical sending agency founded in the United States in 1892. The Christian and Mission-

Mali

Religion	Followers in 1970	Followers in 2010	% of Population	Annual % growth 2000–2010	Followers in 2025	Followers in 2050
Muslims	3,680,000	11,755,000	87.0	3.08	18,461,000	31,666,000
Ethnoreligionists	1,100,000	1,350,000	10.0	2.72	1,500,000	1,500,000
Christians	85,200	384,000	2.8	2.32	593,000	995,000
Roman Catholics	60,700	270,000	2.0	1.97	415,000	700,000
Protestants	20,100	98,000	0.7	3.27	150,000	250,000
Independents	300	14,000	0.1	2.77	25,000	40,000
Agnostics	0	15,000	0.1	3.02	30,000	60,000
Baha'is	440	1,100	0.0	3.01	2,500	5,000
New religionists	100	700	0.0	3.05	1,500	3,000
Atheists	0	640	0.0	3.04	1,000	1,600
Total population	**4,866,000**	**13,506,000**	**100.0**	**3.02**	**20,589,000**	**34,231,000**

ary Alliance arrived in 1923. The Alliance has had the most success, and its efforts have led to the formation of the Eglise Chrétienne Evangélique du Mali (Evangelical Christian Church of Mali), now the largest of the Protestant bodies. The GMU mission has matured to become the Evangelical Protestant Church of Mali. A spectrum of churches, from the Assemblies of God to the Seventh-day Adventist Church, has appeared, and the Seventh Day Baptist General Conference has a small community.

Given the poverty of the land and the relative difficulty of travel, Mali has not attracted the spectrum of religions found in other countries. There is a small community of the Baha'i Faith and, as is typical of former French colonies, members of the Ancient and Mystical Order Rosae Crucis.

J. Gordon Melton

See also: Ancient and Mystical Order Rosae Crucis; Assemblies of God; Baha'i Faith; Christian and Missionary Alliance; Dogen; Malikite School of Islam; Seventh-day Adventist Church; Seventh Day Baptist General Conference; Tijaniyya Sufi Order; White Fathers.

References

Brenner, Louis. *Controlling Knowledge: Religion, Power, and Schooling in a West African Muslim Community*. Bloomington: Indiana University Press, 2001.

Cardaire, M. *L'Islam et le terrior africain*. Bamako-Koulouba, Mali: IFAN, 1954.

De Villiers, Marq, and Sheila Hirtle. *Timbuktu: The Sahara's Fabled City of Gold*. Walker & Company, 2007.

Harmon, S. A. "The Expansion of Islam among the Bambara under French Rule, 1890–1940." Ph.D. diss., University of California at Los Angeles, 1988.

Macalou, Ousmane Abdoul. *Religion, Magic, Political Power and the Bambara Gods of River Niger*. Stanford, CA: Joint Center for African Studies, Stanford University, 1991.

Soares, Benjamin F. *Islam and the Prayer Economy: History and Authority in a Malian Town*. East Lansing: University of Michigan Press, 2005.

Status of Christianity Profile: Mali. Nairobi, Kenya: Daystar University College, 1988.

Malikite School of Islam

The Malikite School of Islam is one of the four *madhhabs* (schools) of jurisprudence deemed orthodox within the world of Sunni Islam. The school traces its origin to Medina (in present-day Saudi Arabia) and Malik ibn Anas al-Asbahi (713–795), a Yemenite who was born and raised in Medina. His major written work, *Al-muwatta*, was a collection of the *hadith* (the sayings and action of the prophet Muhammad and his companions), which he arranged according to the legal subject to which they spoke. He also made frequent use of the phrase "and this is the rule with us," implying his continuing influence of the *ulama* (the totality of religious scholars) as it existed in Medina. Malik is remembered for opposing the Muslim rulers of his time (of the Umayyad Caliphate) who were asserting the right to make laws without reference to the Koran.

Among Malik's students were Muhammad ibn al-Hasan al-Shaybani (749–ca. 804), later a distinguished scholar of the Hanafite School, and Muhammad ibn Idris al-Shafii (767–820), the founder of the Shafiite School. His thought was carried forward by Yahda al Laythi (d. 848), who preserved *Al-muwatta* for later generations, and Asad ibn al-Furat (d. 828), who compiled what is today the major text identified with the school, *Al-mudawwanah*. The Malikite School held early sway in that part of Arabia near the Red Sea, including Mecca. It also was picked up by pilgrims from North Africa and Spain who came to Arabia on the *hajj* (pilgrimage) to Mecca. North Africa had become separated from the early Arab Muslim Empire and was never integrated into the later Ottoman Empire, except for Egypt. Thus the Malikite School came to dominate across the Mediterranean coast from Libya to Morocco and to be the primary form of Islam that moved across the Sahara and began to penetrate sub-Saharan Africa including Mali, Senegal, Niger, and Nigeria. (The Shafiite School predominates in the Muslim community along the eastern coast of Africa.)

As with the other Sunni legal schools, the Malikites emphasized the primary directives of submission to Allah (God) and the resulting obedience to the Shariah (Islamic law) to be the motivating foundation of their work. They also recognized the Koran and Sunna, the collection of hadith (the sayings and action of the Prophet Muhammad and his companions), as basic texts for the development of a legal system. Malik paid special attention to the consensus of his teachers in Medina and their traditions have had a special authority as the modern consensus of Malikite scholarship has developed. Malik gave some room for the fourth authority for legal rulings in Islam, analogical reasoning (*qiyas*), but gave a much more limited role compared to the Hanifites, primarily on issues not previously treated by the Medina scholars.

Much of the development of the Malikite school depended upon the ongoing process of assembling the hadith and decisions upon which were authentic and which were of dubious origin. Malik and especially his students were also influenced by the Traditionalist movement that developed in the eighth century, which insisted that the authority of tradition should rest upon authentic reports of sayings or actions of the Prophet Muhammad. The Traditionalist movement set issues around which the Malikite School developed while spurring scholarship on the hadith.

J. Gordon Melton

See also: Hanafite School of Islam; Muhammad; Shafiite School of Islam.

References

Coulson, Noel J. *Conflicts and Tensions in Islamic Jurisprudence*. Chicago: University of Chicago Press, 1969.

Coulson, Noel J. *A History of Islamic Law*. Edinburgh: Edinburgh University Press, 1994.

Hallaq, Wael B. *A History of Islamic Legal Theories: An Introduction to Sunni Usul al-Fiqh*. New York: Cambridge University Press, 1997.

Horrie, Chris, and Peter Chippindale. *What Is Islam?* London: Virgin Publishing, 1998.

Khan, Mohammad Hameedullah. *The Schools of Islamic Jurisprudence*. New Delhi: Kita Bhavan, 1997.

Mansour, Mansour Hasan. *The Maliki School of Law: Spread and Domination in North and West Africa, 8th–14th Centuries*. San Francisco: Austin and Winfield, 1994.

Schacht, Joseph. *An Introduction to Islamic Law*. Oxford: Oxford University Press, 1964.

Watt, Montgomery. *The Majesty That Was Islam*. New York: Praeger Publishers, 1974.

■ Malta

The Republic of Malta consists of 5 islands with a total land area of 122 square miles lying south of Sicily in

The Old Parish Church in St. Julian's Bay, Malta, is said to have been built in 1580. (Tyler Olson/Dreamstime.com)

the Mediterranean Sea. Two are uninhabited; of the 3 inhabited islands, Kemmuna is but 0.6 mile in area, and Gozo is 67 square miles. The largest island, Malta, has been the constant target of various groups hoping to control the Mediterranean Basin politically, militarily, or economically. The present population of the Maltese people, now some 404,000 strong, reflects the coming of the Phoenicians, Italians, Arabs, and British at varied points throughout its history.

Though skipped by the basically land-based Arabs as they initially moved across North Africa, Malta came under their control in the ninth century. They held it for two centuries, until it was overrun by the Normans in 1090. The Spanish Kingdom of Aragon reached out for control in the 14th century. In the 16th century, the island was turned over to the Knights of Saint John of the Hospital (now the Knights of Malta), who guarded the island for the next 300 years. In 1798

the French replaced the Knights of Malta but held it for only a short time, until the British were granted hegemony by the important decisions of the Congress of Vienna in 1815. For the next century, Malta was a key part of British dominance of the seaways.

In 1921 the British gave the Maltese a degree of autonomy. Revoked at the beginning of World War II, autonomy was restored in 1947. Independence was finally granted in 1964. Britain retained some responsibility for Malta for a decade, but in 1974, the Republic of Malta was proclaimed. The country has a parliamentary system of government. It joined the European Union in 2004.

With the coming of the Normans, the Roman Catholic Church became the dominant religion of Malta and has remained so to the present. Malta is justly proud of its Christian past, being mentioned in the New Testament as the place the Apostle Paul resided

MALTA

for three months following his shipwreck as he journeyed to Rome. That event is celebrated on the island each February 10. In 451, a bishop from Malta attended the ecumenical council that gathered at Chalcedon.

The Catholic Church is the state religion of Malta, and Catholicism has broad popular support. At the time of independence the church also owned the majority of the island's real estate, a fact that has since then brought it into conflict with the government. In 1983 the government expropriated all the church's properties and secularized all primary education. Two years later, the church signed an agreement with the government that led to the secularization of secondary education.

Although privileging the Roman Catholic Church, the country's Constitution also guarantees freedom to practice other religions. However, almost all other religions on the main island are operative primarily among expatriate communities. Within the English-speaking community, the Church of England, the Church of Scotland, the Salvation Army, and the Methodist Church have congregations. The Church of England has been present since 1798. There is a single congregation of the Greek Orthodox Church under the Ecumenical Patriarchate and also an evangelical congregation associated with the Christian Brethren.

The Jehovah's Witnesses entered the country just before World War II and have carried on a program of proselytization among the general public, though with no spectacular success. For many years there has also been a group associated with the Church of Christ, Scientist.

The Jewish presence on Malta dates to the Roman period, though it all but died out during the period of control by the Knights of Malta. The present community dates from the end of the 18th century, when Malta received Jews who moved from North Africa. The community opened a new synagogue in 1912, but it was demolished in 1979 as part of a development

Malta

Religion	Followers in 1970	Followers in 2010	% of Population	Annual % growth 2000–2010	Followers in 2025	Followers in 2050
Christians	301,000	403,000	98.0	0.68	418,000	409,000
Roman Catholics	297,000	382,000	93.0	0.55	395,000	385,000
Anglicans	3,000	1,000	0.2	−1.89	1,000	1,000
Marginals	230	1,200	0.3	0.70	1,500	2,200
Agnostics	1,000	6,000	1.5	2.11	9,000	13,000
Muslims	0	1,100	0.3	1.11	2,500	3,500
Atheists	500	810	0.2	0.68	1,000	1,200
Baha'is	100	300	0.1	0.70	600	1,000
Jews	50	60	0.0	0.69	60	60
Hindus	50	40	0.0	0.48	100	150
Total population	**303,000**	**411,000**	**100.0**	**0.70**	**431,000**	**428,000**

scheme. There are now approximately 50 Jews on the island. There is an equally small Hindu community on Malta, made up of expatriates from India.

J. Gordon Melton

See also: Christian Brethren; Church of Christ, Scientist; Church of England; Church of Scotland; Ecumenical Patriarchate/Patriarchate of Constantinople; Jehovah's Witnesses; Roman Catholic Church; Salvation Army.

References

Boissevain, Jeremy. *Saints and Fireworks: Religion and Politics in Rural Malta*. Oxford, UK: Berg Publishers, 1965.

Bonnici, M. A. *History of the Church in Malta.* 2 vols. Valletta, Malta: Empire Press–Catholic Institute, 1967, 1968. Vol. 3. Zabbar, Malta: Veritas Press, 1975.

Eccardt, Thomas M. *Secrets of the Seven Smallest States of Europe: Andorra, Liechtenstein, Luxembourg, Malta, Monaco, San Marino, and Vatican City*. New York: Hippocrene Books, 2005.

Gonzi, M. *What Is Happening to Religion in Malta?* Valletta, Malta: Pastoral Research Services, 1969.

Luttrel, Anthony. *The Making of Christian Malta: From the Early Middle Ages to 1530*. Aldershot, Hampshire, UK: Ashgate Publishing, 2002.

Mitchell, John. *Ambivalent Europeans: Ritual, Memory and the Public Sphere in Malta*. London: Routledge, 2001.

Manavta Mandir

Manavta Mandir (Be Man Temple) was founded by Faqir Chand (1886–1981), the chief spiritual successor of Shiv Brat Lal (1860–1939), in 1962 in Hoshiarpur, Punjab, India. Originally designed by Faqir to present the spiritual teachings of Radhasoami in a more ecumenical and nonsectarian fashion, Manavta Mandir represents a radical interpretation of guru-based spirituality. Faqir argued that all gurus of whatever stripe were ignorant about the real cause of the miracles and visions attributed to them. And because of this ignorance (and what Freud called "transference"), the guru gained power, attention, and devotion from disciples who incorrectly imputed omniscience and omnipresence upon such masters, even though they had neither.

In 1939 Faqir succeeded his guru, Shiv Brat Lal, an initiate of Rai Salig Ram (1829–1898), who was the chief disciple of Shiv Dayal Singh (1818–1878), the founder of Radhasoami in Agra, Uttar Pradesh, India. After establishing his main center in Hoshiarpur, Faqir went on yearly trips throughout India and abroad, preaching his unique brand of Radhasoami, which besides the usual moral vows (vegetarianism, sexual purity, no drugs or alcohol, and daily meditation), included a frank admission of ultimate unknowingness. Even after 70 years of meditation and countless admirers, Faqir admitted that he was still unsure what would happen to him after death and did not know whether God really exists.

During his fifth tour of the United States in 1981, Faqir died at the age of 95 in Pittsburgh, Pennsylvania. Shortly before his death, Faqir appointed Dr. Ishwar C. Sharma, a philosophy professor residing in the United States, as his chief spiritual successor at Manavta Mandir. Faqir also appointed several other men and women to serve as initiating gurus in his lineage. Dr. Sharma departed significantly from his guru's teachings and taught a more traditional interpretation of *shabd* yoga and spirituality.

After his wife's death and because of his increasing health problems, Dr. Sharma appointed Shoonyo Maharaj as his spiritual successor. Since Sharma's recent death, Shoonyo has been the chief resident guru at Manavta Mandir.

Today, the Manavta Mandir boasts more than 100,000 followers worldwide.

Manavta Mandir
c/o Be Man Temple
Sutehri Rd.
Hoshiarpur, 146001
Punjab, India
http://www.manavtamandir.com
http://www.faqirchand.net

David Christopher Lane

See also: Radhasoami; Sikhism/Sant Mat.

References

Juergensmeyer, Mark. *Radhasoami Reality*. Princeton, NJ: Princeton University Press, 1991.

Lane, David C. *The Radhasoami Tradition*. New York: Garland Publishers, 1992.

The Unknowing Sage: The Life and Work of Baba Faqir Chand. Walnut, CA: MSAC, 1993.

Mandaeans

The Mandaeans are possibly the only surviving group representing the ancient Mediterranean movement known as Gnosticism. Discovered by Western scholars in the 17th century, the community survives in Iraq, with major centers in Baghdad and Basra and members in the towns along the Tigris and Euphrates rivers between these two cities. Christian missionaries saw

Mandaean Sabian followers prepare for baptism on the banks of the Tigris River in Baghdad in the early morning, May 23, 2003. (AP/Wide World Photos)

them as surviving remnants of the followers of John the Baptist, and the surrounding Muslim community has seen them as "baptizers." This term, used in the Koran, has allowed the group to persist in the otherwise Islamic environment.

The origin of the Mandaeans is somewhat obscure, but they appear to have originated in Palestine as a heretical Jewish sect in the first century BCE. They apparently absorbed material, including the practice of baptism, from the movement begun by John the Baptist and from the early Christians. They appear to have left Palestine toward the beginning of the first century or the beginning of the second century CE. Baghdad became an early center for Mandaeanism following the migration. However, many of their early temples were destroyed in the third century during the period of Zoroastrian ascendancy. Once the Muslims conquered Mesopotamia, the Mandaeans were recognized as a "people of the Book" and hence entitled to official toleration.

In a hierarchical structure, the Mandaean community has been led by the ethnarch, "the head of the people," who oversees the bishops and priests. The office of ethnarch has, however, remained vacant since the beginning of the 20th century. According to the oral history, the destruction of the hierarchy began in 1830, when most of the clerical leaders were killed in an epidemic. At that time, educated laypeople assumed a significant leadership role.

In Mandaean teachings, the cosmos is divided into the world of light (the North) and the world of darkness (the South). Each of the two realms is led by a ruler who heads a hierarchy of powers. The world emerged in the battle between light and darkness (good and evil). Humans are a product of darkness, but they possess a soul, a core of light. At death, the soul is freed and begins a pilgrimage to the realm of light. Baptism is central to Mandaean worship. Unlike Christian baptism, it is not a once-in-a-lifetime event. Baptisms occur each Sunday, and every member participates several times a year.

A set of sacred books is used by the Mandaeans, but the Ginza (Treasure) is the central book. It is centered in the Mass for the dead (*masiqta*), a ceremony marking the release of the soul from the body and its "ascent" on its afterlife journey. The Mandaeans' Jewish roots are also marked by dietary laws, including the ritual slaughter of animals and alms giving. Worship occurs in a sanctuary (*mandi*), a fenced-in area usually built adjacent to a river, the water of which is diverted to provide a baptismal pool with flowing water.

Today an estimated 15,000 to 20,000 Mandaeans exist in the Middle East. Until the beginning of the Iraqi War, almost all lived in southeastern Iraq, with one small community in Khuzistan, Iran. However, since the war began in 2003, the great majority of Mandaeans have fled Iraq for neighboring countries, most often Syria and Jordan. Earlier, several hundred Mandaeans had migrated to the United States in the 1980s, and others had settled in Canada, Australia, New Zealand, and various locations in Europe, including the United Kingdom, Sweden, and the Netherlands.

http://www.mandaean.com.au/home.htm
http://www.geocities.com/usamandaean/who.html (unofficial informational site)

J. Gordon Melton

See also: Gnosticism; Zoroastrianism.

References

Foerster, Werner. *Gnosis: A Selection of Gnostic Texts.* Vol. 2. *Coptic and Mandaean Sources.* London: Clarendon Press, 1974.

"Mandaean Scriptures and Fragments." The Gnostic Society Library Web site. http://www.webcom.com/~gnosis/library/mand.htm. Accessed March 25, 2009.

Rudolph, Kurt. *Gnosis: The Nature and History of Gnosticism.* San Francisco: HarperSanFrancisco, 1987.

Thaler, Kai. "Iraqi Minority Group Needs U.S. Attention." *Yale Daily News*, March 9, 2007. http://www.yaledailynews.com/articles/view/20341. Accessed March 25, 2009.

Manjushri's Birthday

Manjushri (in Japan, Monju-bosatsu) is pictured in the Buddhist sutras (holy books) as the leader of the bodhisattvas. Regarded as a symbol of the perfection of wisdom, he is often pictured, along with Samantabhadra, in attendance upon Gautama Buddha—most notably in the Flower Garland (Adornment) Sutra. He is generally pictured riding a lion and holding a sword symbolic of the sharpness of his discrimination. Manjushri is one of the characters in the Medicine Buddha Sutra.

Manjushri is said to manifest himself on Mount Wutai, in China's Shanxi Province. Stories tell of the visit of an Indian monk in the first century CE who reported a vision of the bodhisattva. Wutai Mountain and the Wisdom Buddha Manjushri are also the subject of various Buddhist scriptures, sutras, and tantras. Mahayana Buddhism began arriving on Wutai Mountain quite early in its transmission to China, and the first temple was constructed during the reign of Emperor Ming Di (r. 58–75 CE). Literally hundreds of monasteries were built over the next centuries. The associations of the mountain with Manjushri were significantly strengthened in the eighth century with the arrival of Padmasambhava, who was spreading Vajrayana Buddhism through nearby Tibet. Manjushri is especially dear to Vajrayana Buddhists. Then in the 12th century, the Mongolians of the Yuan dynasty, as part of their kingdom building, intruded into Tibet and left the Dalai Lama in charge of the country. As the development of Vajrayana Buddhism was encouraged, the Gelugpa School became established at Mount Wutai. The various Buddhist temples that remain on Mount Wutai hold two major celebrations. The first, the Assembly of the Sixth Month, is a time for pilgrims to visit. The second and more important occurs over four days in the fourth month. It focuses on rituals held in 10 of the mountain's largest temples. This ritual cycle marks Manjushri's birthday on the fourth day of the fourth lunar month.

In Japan, celebrations to honor Manjushri can be traced back to the ninth century CE. His veneration is still practiced in Japan. The veneration draws on stories of Manjusri appearing in the guise of beggars. Believers prepare food and drink on this day to feed all beggars. Meanwhile, in the temples, the names of Manjushri and the Medicine Buddha were recited 100 times each, each day. Today this ritual survives in only two temples.

J. Gordon Melton

See also: Bodhisattva; Gelugpa; Mahayana Buddhism.

References

Boheng, Wu, and Cai Zhuozhi. *100 Buddhas in Chinese Buddhism*. Trans. by Mu Xin and Yan Zhi. Singapore: Asiapac Books, 1997.

Einarsen, John, ed. *The Sacred Mountains of Asia*. Boston: Shambhala, 1995.

"Sacred Mountains of China." Places of Peace and Power. http://www.sacredsites.com/asia/china/sacred_mountains.html. Accessed May 15, 2009.

The Seeker's Glossary of Buddhism. New York: Sutra Translation Committee of the United States and Canada, 1998.

"Wutai Mountain Pilgrimage: Manjushri Empowerment, Teachings & Buddhist Qigong." Sacred Journeys. http://www.sacredjourneys.org/schedule/a_wutai.html. Accessed May 15, 2009.

Vessantara. *Meeting the Buddhas: A Guide to Buddhas, Bodhisattvas, and Tantric Deities*. Birmingham, UK: Windhorse Publications, 1998.

Maohi Protestant Church

The Maohi Protestant Church, previously known as the Evangelical Church of French Polynesia (Église évangélique de Polynésie française), dates to the arrival of the first missionaries dispensed to the South Pacific by the newly formed London Missionary Society (LMS) in 1787. The Society sent out 30 representatives, 4 of whom were ordained. The remaining party consisted of spouses and a spectrum of artisans. The original plan called for the team to establish two self-supporting communities on Tahiti and Tonga. Eighteen settled in Tahiti. However, within a year, 11 of these moved on to Australia. The remaining 5 kept the mission going. Their first task was the mastering of the local Tahitian language, "rep maohi." Their work finally bore fruit in 1815 (some sources say 1812) when King Pomare converted and asked to be baptized.

The king's conversion had far-reaching results. He had a large church constructed and urged his people to become Christians. Most followed his lead. The church became institutionalized across Tahiti with the training of lay leadership and the opening of a publishing concern. The missionaries saw to the translation of the Bible that was published in Tahitian in 1838.

The French moved into the area in 1840 and established a protectorate. The authorities soon demanded that French missionaries, primarily Roman Catholic priests, be allowed to work on Tahiti (they were already present on other near-by islands). A number of islanders deserted the Evangelical Church. In 1863, the French Reformed Church, through its Paris Mission, began work on Tahiti. It represented the same Reformed Protestantism as the LMS and in 1883, as the islands were becoming increasing French in language and orientation, the LMS turned all of its work over to the Paris Mission.

Through the 20th century, the Paris Mission spread Protestantism through French Polynesia. In 1963, the

Mission became autonomous as the Evangelical Church of French Polynesia. Through the 20th century, the church developed a mission among the Chinese laborers who arrived in two waves (1856–1866, 1907–1930). It voted to adopt its present name in 2004.

Today, the Maohi Protestant Church continues to dominate the Protestant community and includes a slight majority of French Polynesia's population (251,700) in its membership (130,000 in 2005). They have an additional large congregation among expatriate French Polynesians in Kanaky. There are a variety of small independent churches through the islands, most having been formed by former Evangelical Church leaders.

The Maohi Protestant Church has been a member of the World Council of Churches since 1963 and is an active participant in the Pacific Conference of Churches.

Maohi Protestant Church
BP 113
Blvd. Pomare 403
Paeete, Tahiti
French Polynesia

J. Gordon Melton

See also: London Missionary Society; Paris Mission; World Council of Churches.

References

Bauswein, Jean-Jacques, and Lukas Vischner, eds. *The Reformed Family Worldwide: A Survey of Reformed Churches, Theological Schools, and International Organizations*. Grand Rapids, MI: William B. Eerdmans Publishing Company, 1999.

Van Beek, Huibert. *A Handbook of the Churches and Councils: Profiles of Ecumenical Relationships*. Geneva: World Council of Churches, 2006.

Van der Bent, Ans J., ed. *Handbook/Member Churches/World Council of Churches*. Geneva: World Council of Churches, 1985.

Maori Religion

Aotearoa (New Zealand) was settled late in the first millennium of the Common Era by one or more expeditions from Central Polynesia. These settlers over time developed their own distinctive culture utilizing their Polynesian inheritance. Traditional Maori religion, like Maori society, was tribal in character and varied in detail from region to region. Nonetheless, key concepts and practices were evident throughout the country.

Maori stories of creation often begin with the embrace of the Sky-father, Ranginui, and the Earth-mother, Papa-tuanuku. The offspring of their union and other early descendants include a number of figures common to many regions. Early sources usually refer to these as ancestors (*tupuna*) rather than gods (*atua*). They were, however, invoked in ritual chants (*karakia*), and the line between an ancestor and a god was rather thin. These early ancestors often personify natural elements and forces and human values. Tane (whose name means Man or Male) is the main creator in Maori religion and mythology, and he is usually credited with creating the first human being (often making her his wife) out of soil. Other important figures include Tu-mata-uenga, the archetypal human being and warrior; Rongo, the peacemaker from whom the *kumara* (a highly valued, cultivated sweet potato) originated; Tangaroa, the father of the fish and sea creatures; Tawhirimatea, the father of the winds; and Hine-nui-te-po (literally, Great Woman the Night), the guardian of the dead.

The more recent ancestral dead, especially dead chiefs, are frequently referred to as gods in early sources. These more recent ancestors were thought to continue their interest in tribal affairs even after death. They could be called upon to protect their relatives in times of need, such as war or illness. They also communicated advice and predictions using their living relatives as mediums.

Offerings, often of food, were made to atua. In the case of the more recently dead, the food was offered by suspending it near the sacred place where the body was kept. In the case of earlier ancestral figures, these offerings might be made to carved figures, stones, or other objects representing them. Every community had at least one shrine (*tuahu*) that was the main site where offerings were made to atua and where the priests (*tohunga*) performed rituals. The exact form and location of the shrine varied considerably from region to region, but a typical feature was a mound or hillock.

Maori warriors, bearing the coffin of Maori queen Te Arikinui Dame Te Atairangikaahu, paddle down the Waikato River in Hamilton, New Zealand, August 21, 2006. (AP/Wide World Photos)

The Maori had a cyclic view of life and death. Spirits of the dead were said to go either to Te Po (the underworld) or to Hawaiki (a paradisiacal homeland). Hawaiki was not only the realm of the ancestors but also a source of life and fertility. Like Hawaiki, Te Po was thought to be a place from where infants originated.

A near male relative of the chief often took the role of chief priest. A special role was also accorded one or more high-ranking women. These women performed protective rites and often removed the *tapu* (sacred) at the close of sacred activities such as warfare, house-building, and childbirth. Other men and women also built reputations for their skill in healing, communicating with atua, and prophesying.

The distinction between tapu (sacred) and *noa* (ordinary) was particularly important in Maori religion and ritual. These concepts also reflected and shaped Maori social structure and the division of labor. The lives of *rangatira* (chiefs and their near relatives), who had the closest connection to the tribal gods, were the most ritualized. *Tutua* (ordinary people) pursued their own rituals and observed tapu restrictions to a lesser extent. Enslaved captives (*taurekareka*) seem to have been excluded from this ritual life. Gender also affected one's ritual status. Free men generally had a closer association with tapu and more elaborate ceremonial life than did free women of the same rank.

British missionaries first arrived in the north of New Zealand in 1815. Christianity began to spread rapidly in the 1830s, reaching even those areas of the country remote from Western contact by the mid-1840s. Considerable religious ferment followed, and many new indigenous religious movements developed in the latter half of the 19th century.

The Hauhau Church was the first instance of an organized, independent Maori Christianity. Founded in the early 1860s by Te Ua Haumene, a prophet and visionary, the church was Pentecostal and millennialist in orientation. The guiding principle of Te Ua's faith was goodness and peace (Pai Marire). He supported indigenous traditional practices where he thought them congruent with this principle. Because the Hauhau fought against the British settler government and its supporters, and because of settler outrage at the acts of some militant Hauhau, the popular image of the Hauhau became one of a violent apostate cult. In fact, Te Ua founded a tradition of spiritual vision and biblical prophecy that continued to influence subsequent Maori religious leaders after his death.

In 1996, 60 percent of Maori identified as Christian, constituting the vast majority of Maori who identified themselves as having a religion. More than half of Maori Christians belonged to mainline denominations: Anglican, Catholic, a number of Protestant churches, and the Church of Jesus Christ of Latter-day Saints. Two independent Maori churches continue. A substantial minority belong to the Ratana Church, which was founded in the 1920s by Tahupotiki Wiremu Ratana, a visionary and faith healer. A smaller number adhere to the Ringatu Church, founded in the 1860s by the prophet and military leader Te Kooti Arikirangi Te Turuki. Membership is concentrated in North Island in the Bay of Plenty and East Coast regions, particularly among the Tuhoe, Ngati Awa, and Whakatohea peoples. Within this generally Christian context, Maori continue to draw on older indigenous traditions.

Ratana Church
Waipounamu St.
Ratana Pa, Whangaehu
New Zealand

Adele Fletcher

See also: Ancestors; Anglican Church in Aotearoa, New Zealand, and Polynesia; Church of Jesus Christ of Latter-day Saints.

References

Elsmore, Bronwyn. 1999. *Manna from Heaven: A Century of Maori Prophets.* 2nd ed. Auckland, New Zealand: Reed Books, 1989, 1999.
Head, Lyndsay. "The Gospel of Te Ua Haumene." *Journal of the Polynesian Society* 101, no. 1 (1992): 7–44.
Johansen, J. Prytz. *The Maori and His Religion in Its Non-ritualistic Aspects.* Copenhagen: Munksgaard, 1954.
Orbell, Margaret. *The Illustrated Encyclopedia of Maori Myth and Legend.* Christchurch, New Zealand: University of Canterbury Press, 1995.
Reed, A. W. *Maori Myths & Legendary Tales.* Auckland, New Zealand: New Holland Publishers, 1999.
Shortland, Edward. *Traditions and Superstitions of the New Zealanders: With Illustrations of Their Manners and Customs.* 2nd ed. London: Longman, Brown, Green, Longmans & Roberts, 1856.

Mar Thoma Syrian Church of Malabar

During the second decade of the 19th century, the Malankara Orthodox Syrian Church, a large Orthodox body centered upon the state of Kerala in southern India, came into contact with members of the Church Missionary Society (CMS) who arrived after Great Britain established its hegemony over the subcontinent. For a period, the CMS attempted to work through the Malankara Church but eventually withdrew and began to work independently. However, the CMS assisted in the formation of the Malankara seminary and in 1829 published the Bible in Malayadam.

One British missionary, Abraham Malpan (1796–1843), initiated a movement to reform the Malankara Church. Citing biblical authority, he suggested a number of changes, especially the abandonment of a variety of observances and ceremonial practices that had been added to the church over the centuries, which he considered corrupt. In response, a reformist wing appeared in the Malankara Church, and the conflict was not resolved. The separation of the two factions was formalized late in the 19th century.

By this time a new issue had emerged, namely, the authority of the patriarch of the Syrian Orthodox Church of Malabar, from which the Malankara Church had received its episcopal authority. In the 1880s, the Syrian church asserted a new level of hegemony over the affairs and, more important, the property of the Malankara Church. The reformist group, which took the name

Mar Thoma Syrian Church of Malabar, rejected the patriarch's authority.

Although continuing in the tradition of the Syrian Church, the Mar Thomas Church has revised its liturgy by removing "unscriptural" elements such as the invocation of the saints. It continues to worship in the Syriac language. Through the 20th century it moved closer toward the Church of England in India. In 1937 it established a formal relationship, including a partial intercommunion, with the Church of India, Pakistan, Burma, and Ceylon—the Anglican body that eventually merged into the Church of South India, the Church of North India, and the Church of Pakistan. The Mar Thoma Church is now in full communion with each of these united churches, though it refused to enter the merger, as it wished to continue its unique liturgical heritage. Full communion with the Church of England was granted in 1974.

The Mar Thoma Church has approximately 1.1 million members (2005). It sponsors a broad program of general education, social service, and social reform. It was a charter member of the World Council of Churches.

Mar Thomas Syrian Church of Malabar
Poolatheen
Tiruvalla 689 101
Kerala
India
http://www.marthomachurch.com/

J. Gordon Melton

See also: Church Missionary Society; Church of England; Church of North India; Church of Pakistan; Church of South India; Malankara Orthodox Syrian Church; Syrian Orthodox Church of Malabar; World Council of Churches.

References

Fernando, Leonard, and G. Gispert-Sauch. *Christianity in India: Two Thousand Years of Faith*. New Delhi: Penguin India, 2004.

Moffett, Samuel Hugh. *A History of Christianity in Asia*. Vol. 1, *Beginnings to 1500*. San Francisco: HarperSanFrancisco, 1992.

Neill, S. C. *A History of Christianity in India*. 2 vols. Cambridge: Cambridge University Press, 1984, 1985.

Podipara, Placid C. *The Canonical Sources of the Syro-Malabar Church*. Kottayam, Kerala, India: Oriental Institute of Religious Studies, 1986.

Mara Evangelical Church (Myanmar)

The Mara Evangelical Church is a Protestant body that grew out of the independent efforts of British Congregationalist minister Reginald Arthur Lorrain (ca. 1885–1944) and his wife, who independently began work on the Burma-Indian border in 1907. The Mara people, among whom the Lorrains began their mission, reside in the Chin state of western Myanmar and the Mizoram District of India immediately to the west. They number about 55,000, of which slightly less than half live in Myanmar.

The Lorrains established a church among the Mara in 1907. Their leadership was followed by that of two indigenous leaders, Rev. Mathao (1918–1990) and Rev. K. Teitu (1926–2006). The work in India was set apart following Indian independence in 1947. The church in Myanmar, known simply as the Mara Church until 1960, added the word Evangelical to refer to its self-sustaining nature and enthusiastic engagement in mission. The church adopted a Presbyterian polity and a Calvinist theological outlook. The General Assembly is the highest legislative body of the church.

In 1972, the Mara Church split into two churches, headquartered at Sabawngpi village and Lailenpi village, respectively. The split was healed, but the church retains two headquarters to the present. It is now spreading beyond the boundaries of the Mara community to other ethnic groups. In 2006, the church reported 19,810 members in 97 congregations. It is a member of the World Council of Churches (since 2001) and the World Alliance of Reformed Churches.

GPO Box 366
Yangon
Myanmar

J. Gordon Melton

See also: Congregationalism; World Council of Churches.

References

"Mara Evangelical Church (MEC)." http://www .marachristian.net/?page_id=14. Accessed January 16, 2009.

Van Beek, Huibert. *A Handbook of the Churches and Councils: Profiles of Ecumenical Relationships*. Geneva: World Council of Churches, 2006.

Marian Devotion, World Network of

From its earliest days, the Roman Catholic Church has given an important place to veneration of the Blessed Virgin Mary, the Mother of Jesus. Marian devotion has become the most significant and popular devotion directed toward the saints in the church. Many Catholics believe that at certain times Mary reveals herself to individual Catholics through visions and messages. The places where these apparitions occur generally develop into shrines acknowledged by the church, sometimes of international importance, such as the shrines of Guadeloupe, Fatima, and Lourdes.

Since World War II there has been an exponential increase in the number of apparitions of Mary, and also in the number of apparitions of other saints and Christ, although these are less frequent. In addition to this quantitative change, there has also been a sociographic shift with regard to those receiving the visions: instead of coming to children, the revelations increasingly come to adults. These visionaries not only make the messages public but also interpret them in relation to their own personal views on the church and the world. Adult visionaries are able, especially with

La Conquistadora, Our Lady of the Rosary, Santa Fe, New Mexico. (J. Gordon Melton)

the support of modern media, to distribute messages and interpretations much more widely and intensively and, moreover, they are capable of organizing the resources necessary to create and maintain supportive organizations and pressure groups.

The Catholic Church has become increasingly wary of the boom in such private revelations and devotional activity. Presently, one can distinguish in Catholic culture two devotional circuits. First, activity focuses on sites of acknowledged apparitions—in Mexico around Guadelupe, in France around Lourdes, in Ireland around Knock, and so on. Second, activity focuses on devotions connected with apparitions and private revelations not acknowledged or banned by the church—as in Necedah, Wisconsin; Garabandal, Spain; Conyers, Georgia; and probably the most famous, Medjugorje, Bosnia-Herzegovina.

The various cults in the latter circuit are each independent, but informally they do make up a network. Their collectivity lies in the type of visitors they attract, visitors who generally can be characterized as devotees and believers with conservative or traditionalistic views. These people often visit such sanctuaries in an eclectic manner, participating in the devotional life of each place. But, through their prayer groups, publications, and online medialization, the shrines collectively create a devotional network. On the global level the network is quite informal, there being no institutional umbrella organization apart from website owners and several publishers who tailor their book lists to these interests.

This network of modern divergent devotions is not static, however. There is continued interaction with the institutional church: on the one hand the Catholic Church ignores or impedes these devotions; on the other hand there are also forces within the church that wish to give elements of this *vox populi dei* a stronger role because of its indirect benefits for the church. During the pontificate of John Paul II (r. 1978–2005), this interaction led to the formalization of the devotions of some highly controversial persons (such as Faustina Kowalski and Padre Pio), while some previously "banned" sites of apparitions (such as that of the Lady of All Nations in Amsterdam and the Queen of Love at Schio, Italy) received positive toleration, or at least a level of acknowledgment.

Within the network, the messages given at Fatima (and before that yet, the Rue du Bac visions in Paris in 1830 and at La Salette, France, in 1846) are an important source of inspiration. Central themes such as penitence, prayer (particularly the rosary), war, and the activity of the devil point to approaching apocalyptic times, or the end of time, and a definitive separation of good and evil persons. Since the fall of Communism, new enemies have also been found, including apostasy, social degeneracy, abortion, homosexuality, euthanasia, and the corruption of the church and many of its priests (worldliness, apostasy, sexual abuse), this last concern producing a countermovement, the Marian Movement of Priests. In addition to Fatima, in the course of the 20th century the Italian Franciscan Padre Pio also became an important factor or spiritual guide for many "deviant" devotions.

Important devotions and shrines in the network include, among many others: Kérizine, France (established 1938); Amsterdam, the Netherlands (1945); Montichiari, Italy (1946); Marienfried, Germany (1946); Heroldsbach, Germany (1949); Necedah, Wisconsin (1949); Eisenberg, Austria (1955); Garabandal, Spain (1961); San Damiano, Italy (1961); Akita, Japan (1969); Bayside, New York (1970); Lac-Etchemin, Canada (1971); Medjugorje, Bosnia-Herzegovina (1981); Soufaniyé, Syria (1982); Maasmechelen, Belgium (1982); Melleray, Ireland (1985); Schio, Italy (1985); Manduria, Italy (1992); and Marpingen, Germany (1999).

Among the organizations supporting the world Marian network are the Society of Saint Pius X of Lefebvre (d. 1991); the Apostles of Infinite Love, based in Quebec; Our Lady of the Roses shrine in Bayside, New York; and the Order of Saint Charbel in Australia, which supports the papal claims and Marian contacts of William Kamm, known as the Little Pebble. The network has popular support among Roman Catholics in Africa who have an approved shrine at Kibeho, Rwanda. The Ugandan Marian movement took a tragic turn when the members of the Movement for the Restoration of the Ten Commandments were killed in March 1999. Also, individual priests, fathers, and (titular) bishops like Paul Sigl, Peter Klos, P. van Lierde, Paolo Hnilica, and Emmanual Milingo, proved to be important trait d'unions between the cults.

By its very nature, this informal network has no address of its own, though each of the individual devotional sites do. Relevant international network publishers include the following:

Parvis-Verlag
Rue de l'Eglise 71
1648 Hauteville
Switzerland
http://www.parvis.ch (in French and German)

Miriam-Verlag GmbH
Brühlweg 1
Jestetten
Germany
http://www.miriam-verlag.de (in German)
info@miriam-verlag.de

Segno Ed.
Via E. Fermi 80/1
33010 Tavagnacco (UD)
Italy
http://www.edizionisegno.it (in Italian)

TAN Books and Publishers
PO Box 410487
Charlotte, NC 28241
http://www.tanbooks.com/ (in English)

Peter Jan Margry

See also: Apostles of Infinite Love; Devotion/ Devotional Traditions; Fatima; Homosexuality; Lourdes; Mary, Blessed Virgin; Medjugorje; Roman Catholic Church; Saints.

References

Christian, William, Jr. "Religious Apparitions and the Cold War in Southern Europe." In *Religion, Power and Protest in Local Communities. The Northern Shore of the Mediterranean*, edited by Eric R. Wolf, 239–266. Berlin: Mouton, 1984.

Foundation Marypages. "The Apparitions of the Blessed Virgin Mary." http://www.marypages .com/. Accessed July 1, 2009.

Kohle, Hubert. "Fundamentalistische Marienbewegungen." In *Handbuch der Marienkunde*, edited by Wolfgang Beinert and Heinrich Petri, vol. 2, 60–106. Regensburg, Germany: F. Pustet, 1997.

Marian Library/International Marian Research Institute. "Marian Apparitions of the Twentieth Century." http://www.udayton.edu/mary/ resources/aprtable.html. Accessed July 1, 2009.

Margry, Peter Jan. "La terra di nessuno dei devoti. Devozioni informali tra localismo e transnazionalismo nell'Europa contemporanea." *Sanctorum. Revista dell'associazione Italiana per lo studio della santità, dei culti e dell'agiografia* 1 (2004): 153–178.

Matter, Ellen A., "Apparitions of the Virgin Mary in the Late Twentieth Century. Apocalyptic, Representation, Politics." *Religion* 31 (2001): 125–153.

Peliken, Jaroslav. *Mary through the Centuries.* New Haven, CT: Yale University Press, 1996.

Zimdars-Swarts, Sandra L. *Encountering Mary: Visions of Mary from La Salette to Medjugorje.* New York: Avon Books, 1992.

Maronite Catholic Church

The Maronite Catholic Church, one of several Eastern-rite churches in communion with the Roman Catholic Church, originated in the charismatic ministry of a man later canonized as Saint Maron (d. fifth century). He gathered a religious community in what is today Syria, and his followers founded a monastery west of Antioch (in present-day Turkey). When Muslims came into the area, the community relocated to the mountainous region of Lebanon and survived as a somewhat isolated community. From among their bishops, they elected a leader who assumed the title of patriarch of Antioch and All the East.

Following the establishment of a Crusader kingdom headquartered at Antioch in the 12th century, Maronite church leaders came into contact with bishops of the Roman Catholic Church. Subsequently, in 1182, the Maronites affiliated with the Catholic Church. They retained their Syriac liturgy, with modifications to bring them into alignment with the Church of Rome, and they affirmed those beliefs of the Roman Catholic Church that distinguished it from the Eastern Orthodox churches. The isolated Maronites saw themselves as having never been out of communion with Rome, though no active relationship had existed since the Islamic move into the region.

In the 16th century, the Maronite homeland was incorporated into the Ottoman Empire and periodically suffered persecution from Turkish authorities. The most notable incidence of persecution, a massacre of thousands of Maronites in 1860, led to the intervention of French forces in the area and the formal establishment of French control over Lebanon following World War I. Following the massacre, Maronites also began to migrate away from their homeland, and by the end of the century, they had founded expatriate communities in North and South America and Australia. The establishment of an independent Lebanon in 1944 and the civil war that began in 1975 further encouraged migration.

As of 2008, the Maronite Church reported 3,106,000 members. The church has 10 dioceses in Lebanon and 6 additional dioceses in neighboring countries. Overseas dioceses now exist in Cyprus, Greece, Argentina, Brazil, Mexico, Canada, the United States, and Australia. There are scattered congregations across Europe.

The church is led by Patriarch Nasrallah Cardinal Sfeir (b. 1920). He was elected in 1986 and given his cardinal's hat in 1994. It sponsors two seminaries and a college in Rome. The University of the Holy Spirit at Kasnik offers advanced theological training. There are a number of Maronite religious orders and one missionary community, the Maronite-Lebanese Missionaries. The church is active in the Middle East Council of Churches. Unlike most Eastern-rite churches affiliated with the Roman Catholic Church, there is no Maronite church that exists as an Eastern Orthodox body.

c/o His Beatitude Mar Nasrallah Boutros Cardinal Sfeir
Bkerkē
Lebanon
http://www.bkerke.org.lb/

J. Gordon Melton

See also: Middle East Council of Churches; Roman Catholic Church.

References

Liesel, N. *The Eastern Catholic Liturgies: A Study in Words and Pictures.* Westminster, MD: Newman Press, 1960.

"The Maronite Catholic Church." http://www.cnewa.org/ecc-bodypg-us.aspx?eccpageID=56&Index View=toc. Accessed March 25, 2009.

Roberson, Ronald G. *The Eastern Christian Churches: A Brief Survey*, 5th ed. Rome: Edizioni Orientalia Christiana, Pontificio Istituto Orientale, 1995.

■ Marshall Islands

The Marshall Islands are a group of numerous islands, atolls, and islets in the North Pacific southeast of Hawaii and north of Nauru and Kiribati. The territory under the islands' hegemony, the easternmost part of Micronesia, includes 50 square miles of land and many times the area of ocean. Some 63,000 people (2008) reside on the islands.

Until 1978, the Marshall Islands shared a history with the rest of Micronesia (including the Caroline Islands, Guam, and the Marianas). Since the Spanish first came into Micronesia in the 16th century, these islands had been successively under Spanish, German, U.S., Japanese, and then again, U.S. control. Toward the end of World War II, the Marshalls were the site of some of the bloodiest battles leading up to the Japanese defeat. After the war they were also part of the Micronesian Trust Territory given to the United States. The Marshalls came to have a special role after the Bikini and Kwajalein atolls became the sites of extensive nuclear bomb tests beginning in 1946.

In 1979 a referendum led to the establishment of the Federated States of Micronesia, but the Marshall Islands did not become a part of the new nation. The Marshalls remained in a trust relationship with the United States. The islands were granted local autonomy, but the United States still controlled its security, and for a period it continued to use Kwajalein as a missile-testing site and a dump for toxic wastes. In 1986 the Marshalls became a Free Associated State of the United States. Although it still has a special relationship with the United States, the Marshalls now controls its own foreign policy. In 1990 the nation was admitted to the United Nations.

Roman Catholics arrived in the Marshalls in the 1500s and began the Christian church's warfare against

MARSHALL ISLANDS

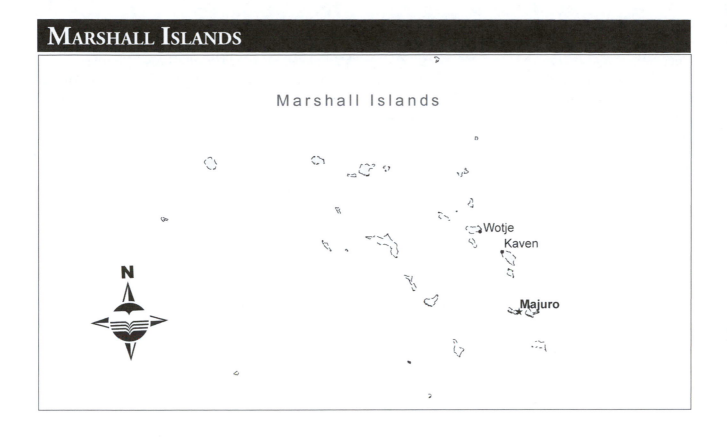

Marshall Islands

Wotje
Kaven

Majuro

Marshall Islands

Religion	Followers in 1970	Followers in 2010	% of Population	Annual % growth 2000–2010	Followers in 2025	Followers in 2050
Christians	19,200	60,300	95.1	1.68	75,000	87,100
Protestants	14,500	59,100	93.2	1.17	70,000	80,000
Roman Catholics	2,000	5,100	8.0	0.11	6,000	6,500
Marginals	340	5,600	8.8	2.72	8,000	10,000
Baha'is	300	1,700	2.7	1.70	2,200	2,500
Agnostics	100	880	1.4	3.07	1,300	2,100
Ethnoreligionists	800	500	0.8	1.72	500	500
Atheists	0	40	0.1	1.71	60	100
Total population	**20,400**	**63,400**	**100.0**	**1.70**	**79,100**	**92,300**

the indigenous religion, a form of polytheism that gave a central place to two deities: the Great Spirit and the Lord of the Nether Regions. That religion has all but disappeared. In 1905 the Catholic work in the Marshall and Caroline Islands was set apart as a separate diocese, with a bishop residing on Guam. More recently, reflecting the different courses taken by those two sets of islands, the work in the Marshalls has been separated from the diocese and placed under an apostolic prefecture.

Missionaries from Hawaii connected to the American Board of Commissioners for Foreign Missions, a Congregationalist organization, arrived in the Marshalls from the Caroline Islands in 1857. That work has grown into the United Church of Christ–Congregational in the Marshall Islands, which became independent following the formation of the United Church of Christ in 1957. It is now a member of the World Council of Churches.

The Church of Jesus Christ of Latter-day Saints opened a mission in the Marshalls in 1977 as part of its general expansion in Micronesia at the time. The work began on the island of Majuro, and it moved on to Kwajalein the following year. Finally it expanded to Arno and Mili, on the eastern edge of Micronesia.

Missionaries of the Seventh-day Adventist Church arrived in Micronesia, including the Marshalls, in 1930. Their work is now part of their Guam Micronesia Mission. The Assemblies of God opened work in 1964. There is one center of the Ahmadiyya Muslim movement on the island of Majuro.

J. Gordon Melton

See also: Assemblies of God; Church of Jesus Christ of Latter-day Saints; Seventh-day Adventist Church; United Church of Christ; World Council of Churches.

References

Barrett, David, ed. *The Encyclopedia of World Christianity*. 2nd ed. New York: Oxford University Press, 2001.

Hezel, Francis X. *The Catholic Church in Micronesia: Historical Essays on the Catholic Church in the Caroline-Marshall Islands.* Honolulu: Micronesian Seminar, 1991. http://www.micsem.org/pubs/books/catholic/index.htm. Accessed March 1, 2009.

Hezel, Francis X. *Strangers in Their Own Land: A Century of Colonial Rule in the Caroline and Marshall Islands.* Honolulu: University of Hawaii Press, 2003.

Ibanez y Garcia, Luis de. *The History of the Marianas, with Navigational Data, and of the Caroline and Palau Islands: From the Time of Their Discovery by Magellan in 1521 to the Present.* Mangilao, Guam: Micronesian Area Research Center, University of Guam, 1992.

Kelin, Daniel A., II. *Marshall Island Legends and Stories.* Honolulu: Bess Press, 2003.

Sam, H. "A New Dawn: Christianity in the Marshall Islands, 1857–1885." M.A. thesis, Pacific Theological Seminary, 1988.

■ Martinique

Martinique, an island in the Lesser Antilles on the eastern edge of the Caribbean Sea north of Trinidad and Tobago, is an overseas department of France. Some 429,500 people (2004) live on the island's 409 square miles of land. Around 90 percent of the present population are descended from the Africans who came to the island beginning in the 17th century.

Martinique was originally inhabited by the Arawak people, but they were displaced by the Carib people around 1000 CE. They called the island Madinina. Columbus visited the island in 1502.

The French first settled on the island in 1635. After slavery was declared legal in 1664, enslaved Africans began to arrive, and the French began to develop the sugarcane business. Through the 1700s, Africans became the major element in the population and were responsible for a series of antislavery revolts. Slavery was abolished in 1794 but was reintroduced by Napoleon in 1802. It is believed that Napoleon's decision was strongly affected by his wife, the Empress Josephine, who was born on Martinique. Slavery was finally abolished in 1848. Chinese and Indian (primarily from Tamil Nadu) laborers were brought to Martinique to replace Africans who refused to work on the plantations.

The island became the site of one of the most famous of modern disasters when on May 8, 1902, Mount Pele erupted and within a matter of minutes killed all but one of the inhabitants of the town of Saint Pierre (approximately 30,000 people).

The Roman Catholic Church came to Martinique with the French and was established by members of the Dominican, Jesuit, and Capuchin orders. A diocese was established in 1850, but the church had a significant problem recruiting priests. In 1909 the island was placed under the Congregation for the Propagation of the Faith at the Vatican, which asked the Holy Ghost Fathers to assume responsibility for the island. Though the overwhelming majority of the population profess the Catholic faith, church attendance is relatively low. The single bishop for Martinique resides in Fort-de-France.

The Reformed Church of France entered the island informally, as French government and military personnel were stationed there, and continues primarily as an expatriate church. The Seventh-day Adventist

The Balata Church near Fort de France, Martinique. (iStockPhoto)

Martinique

Religion	Followers in 1970	Followers in 2010	% of Population	Annual % growth 2000–2010	Followers in 2025	Followers in 2050
Christians	320,000	388,000	96.5	0.49	385,000	324,000
Roman Catholics	306,000	360,000	89.6	0.40	350,000	292,000
Protestants	11,300	33,000	8.2	2.05	35,000	32,000
Marginals	2,000	9,800	2.4	0.88	13,000	14,000
Agnostics	2,700	7,000	1.7	1.67	9,000	12,000
Baha'is	1,000	2,200	0.5	0.88	3,200	4,500
Atheists	1,000	1,800	0.4	0.51	2,400	2,800
Hindus	0	1,000	0.2	0.50	1,400	2,000
Muslims	200	900	0.2	0.52	1,400	2,400
Spiritists	0	440	0.1	0.53	600	700
Chinese folk	0	240	0.1	0.51	400	500
New religionists	200	210	0.1	0.50	300	400
Buddhists	0	160	0.0	0.51	300	400
Total population	**325,000**	**402,000**	**100.0**	**0.51**	**404,000**	**350,000**

MARTINIQUE

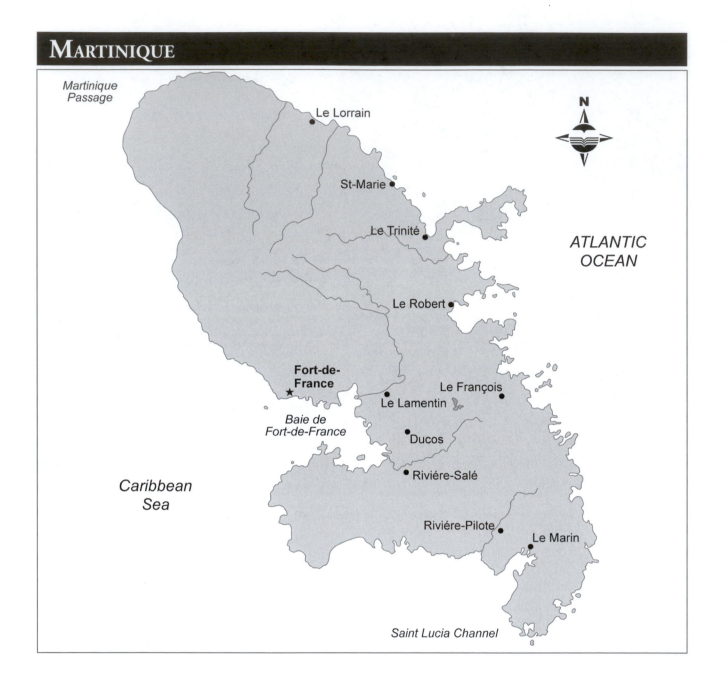

Church began missionary work on the island in 1924. The Martinique Conference was organized in 1974. The conference is now part of the French Antilles–Guiana Union Mission. Both the Baptists and the Jehovah's Witnesses entered Martinique at the end of World War II and have since built a substantial presence. There are also congregations of the Assemblies of God and the Church of the Nazarene.

Possibly the most interesting movement on the island is the Maldevidan religion, a mixture of Hinduism and Catholicism found primarily in the northern part of Martinique. The principal deity is Maldevidan, who is pictured riding a horse and often identified as Jesus Christ. Mari-eman, the principal female deity, is also identified as the Virgin Mary and the mother of Maldevidan. As with Vodou, Maldevidan ceremonies involve drumming, ritual possession by spirit entities, and animal (sheep, roosters) sacrifice.

There is a small Jewish community on Martinique that finds its focus in a single Orthodox center in Fort-de-France. Islam is present in a small community of Syrian expatriates. The first spiritual assembly of the

Baha'i Faith opened in the late 1960s. And as is true of most French-speaking lands, the Ancient and Mystical Order Rosae Crucis has established several lodges.

J. Gordon Melton

See also: Ancient and Mystical Order Rosae Crucis; Assemblies of God; Baha'i Faith; Church of the Nazarene; Roman Catholic Church; Seventh-day Adventist Church; Vodou.

References

Horowitz, M., and M. Klaus. "The Martinique East Indian Cult of Maldevidan." *Social and Economic Studies* 10, no. 1 (March 1961): 93–100.

La Croix, O. "The French Presence and the Church in Martinique and Guadeloupe." In *New Mission for a New People: Voices from the Caribbean*, edited by D. I. Mitchell. New York: Friendship Press, 1977.

Wideman, John Edgar. *The Island: Martinique*. New York: National Geographic, 2003.

Martinism

Martinism is an Esoteric system derived from the teachings of three French masters active between the late 18th and early 19th centuries: Jacques Martinez de Pasqually (1727–1774), Jean-Baptiste Willermoz (1730–1824), and Louis-Claude de Saint-Martin (1743–1803). In 1754, Martinez de Pasqually established the Masonic Order of the Elected Knights Cohen, a new Masonic system with three degrees beyond the three traditional Masonic degrees. The second and third Cohen degrees taught an Esoteric doctrine called "reintegration," which included both Kabbalah and theurgy. A Cohen priesthood enabled initiates to control evil spirits and to communicate with angels. Silence, prayer, and fasting prepared the initiate for the mysterious apparition of la Chose ("the Thing").

Differences do exist between Martinez's system (Martinezism) and the more typically Masonic and Christian teachings of Willermoz, which eventually led to the establishment of the Reformed Scottish Rite of Freemasonry. Saint-Martin joined the Elected Knights Cohen in 1768 and eventually became Martinez's per-sonal secretary. After Martinez's death, Saint-Martin became suspicious of all forms of occultism, and his ideas evolved into an idiosyncratic form of mystical Christianity. The Martinist tradition, in line with these developments, includes both a Martinezist wing, which maintains the Kabbalistic practices, and a Saint-Martinist wing, more interested in mysticism than in theurgy.

In 1891, only one century after Martinez's own initiatives, the Spanish-born French esoteric master Gérard Encausse, called "Papus" (1865–1916), together with Augustin Chaboseau (1869–1946), established an organization known as the Martinist Order. Both Papus and Chaboseau claimed to have been initiated into a chain going back to Martinez and Saint-Martin, although historians dispute their claims. After Papus's death in 1916, the Martinist order fragmented into an extremely complicated series of splinter groups. Most Martinists recognized Charles Détré, known as "Téder" (1855–1918), as Papus's successor, but he died only two years after taking office.

Téder and his successor, Jean Bricaud (1881–1934), changed the rituals in order to make them more Martinezist, closed the doors of their order to non-Freemasons and women, moved the headquarters from Paris to Lyons, and fought attempts by the American Rosicrucian order to create and lead an international federation of Esoteric orders. Favorable to the American order, on the other hand, was another Martinist branch known as the Martinist (and) Synarchist Order, led by Victor Blanchard (1878–1953), who in 1937 transferred his Martinist authority to Harvey Spencer Lewis (1883–1939), founder of the Ancient and Mystical Order Rosae Crucis (AMORC). In 1939, however, the AMORC officially recognized as an allied Martinist order a group known as the Traditional Martinist Order (www.martiniste.org), founded by Chaboseau and Victor-Émile Michelet (1861–1938). This organization has continued its activities to the present day, in close cooperation with the AMORC.

As for Bricaud's order, his successor, Constant Chevillon (1880–1944), renamed it the Martinist Martinezist Order, underlining once again the coveted connection with Martinez. Assassinated by Nazi collaborators in 1944, Chevillon was succeeded by Henri-Charles Dupont (1877–1960). In 1952, Papus's son

Philippe Encausse (1906–1984) re-established a Martinist order in a form similar to his father's, open to both non-Freemasons and women. In 1960 Dupont supervised the merger of his Martinist Martinezist Order with Encausse's Martinist Order, which remains to this day the largest Martinist organization worldwide. In 1942, Robert Ambelain (1907–1997) established a Martinist Order of the Elected Cohens, which after 1960 remained the sole Martinezist organization in the world. In 1962 the Ambelain and Encausse orders entered into a short-lived union, going their separate ways again in 1967. Thus the Martinist scenario appears to be divided today between two large organizations, Encausse's Martinist Order and AMORC's Traditional Martinist Order, as well as a number of smaller Martinezist groups.

Some scholars use the category of Kremmerzian Martinism to indicate the different competing occult orders following the tradition of the Italian esoteric master Giuliano Kremmerz (pseudonym of Ciro Formisano, 1861–1930). Kremmerz was influenced by a number of Esoteric authors connected with a branch of the Martinist tradition in Naples, Italy. Most of the Kremmerz-inspired orders go under the name Brotherhood of Myriam (one is called the Martinist Kremmerzian Order, however) and have a Martinist connection, and in turn Kremmerz influenced several branches of Italian Martinism. Some but by no means all of the Kremmerzian orders appear to be mostly interested in practices of "internal alchemy," including forms of sexual magic.

Among the several contemporary Martinist groups whose relationship to the older Martinist groups is a matter of claims and counterclaims are the Ancient Martinist Order (www.ancientmartinistorder.org), the Martinist Order of Unknown Philosophers (www.moup .org), and the Rose+Croix Martinist Order (www.rcmo .org). There are also several groups calling themselves the British Martinist Order. The Italian- and French-speaking Martinist orders are normally larger than their English-speaking counterparts but some of them are quite secretive and have elected not to maintain a website. One of the largest Italian groups, the Ordine Martinista Antico e Tradizionale, does maintain a website at www.martinismo.eu, while the website www .martinismo.it is operated by the smaller Ordine Mar-

tinista Universale. The oldest Martinist order, Encausse's Martinist Order, may be reached at www .martinisme.org, while the independent French website www.martinisme.fr tries to keep a sympathetic track of the complicated evolution of the various European orders.

Martinist Order (Encausse branch)
5-7, rue de la Chapelle
75018 Paris France
http://www.martinisme.org

The Rose+Croix Martinist Order
3620 W. 10th St. B-150
Greeley, CO 80634-1821
http://www.rcmo.org
British Martinist Order (one of several)

BMO Administration
PO Box 1
Oldham, Lancashire OL4 4WW
United Kingdom
http://www.bmosite.org/
        Massimo Introvigne and PierLuigi Zoccatelli

See also: Ancient and Mystical Order Rosae Crucis; Devotion/Devotional Traditions; Freemasonry.

References

Amadou, Robert, and Alice Joly. *De l'Agent Inconnu au Philosophe Inconnu*. Paris: Denoël, 1962.

Ambelain, Robert. *Le Martinisme, Histoire et doctrine*. Paris: Niclaus, 1946.

Encausse, Philippe. *Science occulte ou 25 années d'occultisme occidentale. Papus, sa vie, son œuvre*. Paris: OCIA, 1949.

Le Forestier, René. *La Franc-Maçonnerie occultiste au XVIIIe siècle et l'Ordre des Elus Coëns*. Paris: La Table d'Émeraude, 1987.

Van Rijnberk, Gérard. *Martinés de Pasqually: Un thaumaturge au XVIIIe siècle*. 2 vols. Hildesheim, Germany: Georg Olms, 1982.

Martyrdom

The original signifier for "martyr," a Stoic term, used in classical antiquity, is Greek *martys* (witness), which has been taken over by Christians into Latin and from there into other languages. The English signifier "martyr" has today conquered the world in the process of globalization. "Truth" or "blood" was sometimes prefixed in the early church to distinguish its specific "witness" from a court witness.

Today there is a vague understanding of what the signifier "martyr" refers to. A person may say: "a martyr is a person who is killed/tortured in hate of his faith/conviction." While this understanding goes back to a technical Christian definition of the cause of martyrdom, to the Latin and Christian formula *in odium fidei* (in hate of faith), its Christian origin has fallen into oblivion.

In the following, an overview of the religious concepts of Judaism, Christianity, and Islam is given with shorter remarks on secular martyrdom. This article replaces "faith" with "conviction" (of a moral or political stand) and suspends the concept of compensation in the next life. Examples are the Chinese Communist Party and the Liberation Tigers of Tamil Ealam, which both cultivate an intensive, secular, martial cult of martyrs.

Judaism Martyrdom is so strong within Jewish religion that it has been called a religion of martyrdom. Modern Jewish theology uses both Hebrew and European languages, among them frequently English. Some important sources by Jewish authors about Jewish martyrs are also in Greek, Latin, and Yiddish. In Hebrew itself, there is no equivalent in one word to Greek *martys*. We find *al qiddush ha-Shem*, "[he died] for the sanctification of the [divine] Name," or simply *leqaddesh et ha-Shem*, "[he died] to sanctify the [divine] Name." This article refers to the Jewish martyr as sanctifier (of the Name).

A Jewish sanctifier is a violence-renouncing person who is killed in hate of his faith, which is evaluated as a sanctification of His Name by Jewish theologians. Modern Jewish use in English makes a clear difference between the sanctifier (violence-renouncing martyr) and the hero (martial martyr). This is reflected in a modern distinction in Hebrew, *Yom HaShoah v'HaGevurah*, which means "Shoa and Heroism Day," but which is freely explained in English by the extended meaning of Remembrance Day or Martyrs and Heroes Day. It takes place annually on the Nissan 27, the day of the Warsaw uprising. In this understanding the martyr

An illustration from the biblical book of Maccabees showing the seven sons of Hannah being martyred for refusing to worship an idol. (Corbis)

is a victim and the hero is a fighter in a resistance movement.

Some of the Jewish sanctifiers today have interpreted their situation according to a prefigured role from the past. This prefiguration of an ideal sanctifier, whose main ambition was to be faithful until death to Jewish culture, was transmitted in rabbinic literature in the first centuries CE. It was based on the writings by Rabbi Aqiva, Rabbi Chananja ben Teradjon, Rabbi Jose ben Joezer, and Rabbi Jehuda ben Baba; on the tradition in 2 Maccabees 6:18–32 and the seven Maccabean martyrs with their mother in 2 Maccabees 7; and on the Midrash of the Ten Martyrs. Already in the Old Testament are statements about prophets who because of their message were despised, persecuted, and even killed. In the book of Daniel, we find the important reflection that death due to persecution results in a "purification" of the group. The dead will also rise from death. This is one example of representational dying that was profiled later through the Jew Jesus.

In the apocryphal book Wisdom of Solomon, from the first century CE, we find the fundamental idea of compensation for suffering and death in the next life. It is a central idea in all religious concepts of martyrdom but is, of course, suspended in secular concepts. Medieval Jewish thinking also knows rewards for the violence avoiding martyrs: the joy of martyrdom, remissions of sins, the passing to paradise without passing hell, the resting at the bosom of Abraham in heaven, the vision of God, the existence in the world of light, and the being in the company of the righteous. The concept of intercession is also available. All this is suspended by secular martyrdom.

The books of the Maccabees describe the heroic armed resistance of the Jews against the attempt to introduce Hellenistic culture in the period 162–163 in Israel. The family of Judas Maccabee opposed the Hellenizing of Jewish culture in connection with political domination and economic exploitation by Hellenized neighboring kings.

Thus, we find both the violence-renouncing martyr, which in Hebrew is given the meaning of and highlighted by the "sanctifier of the divine name," and the martial martyr, who is referred to as "hero," not as "martyr," but when it comes to the use of English the distinction is often suspended. Both are called "martyrs."

Christianity Within the Christian tradition, one has to distinguish between the proto-martyr and the martyr and then between the non-martial martyr and the martial martyr. A person, regularly depicted as an unarmed civilian, has directed his life to witness about his faith, but he has no agenda of seeking a representational and sacrificial death. His agenda is missiological only, not sacrificial. Therefore he is called a proto-martyr by modern theologians. He teaches and preaches, he "witnesses" about Christ. His being killed suddenly interrupts his agenda. From both Israel's past and pre-Christian Greece came concepts of representational sacrificial dying for others that could be com-

bined with the image of the suffering just in Isaiah 53 in connection with missiological activity. This combination became the very heart of all Christian martyrdom.

As a Jew, Jesus saw himself in the tradition of Isaiah 53, of a suffering just person. The ideal persona of a self-sacrificing martyr was foisted upon him by the early church. His life was interpreted by others not just as suffering, but as representational suffering ending in death. The proper way of piety was to imitate Christ, who gave his life to redeem humanity in the eyes of God. This excluded of course armed resistance and indicated a complete trust in God. Jesus became a model for many on how to die as a self-sacrificing non-martial martyr in accordance with John 15:30: "Greater love hath no man than this, that a man lay down his life for his friends." The Eucharist in Christianity preserves this idea and strengthens the church. Here, the famous saying by Augustine and several followers has to be noticed: "The blood of the martyrs is the seed of the church." The idea of John 15:30 has also been made a leading idea in some altruistic secular concepts of martyrdom that replace "church" with "community."

Atonement is one reward of martyrdom: ascending to heaven without waiting for the last day of judgment another. In secular martyrdom the only reward is the experience of satisfaction before dying of having achieved a further step toward the ultimate political aim.

The early church ordered the living to treat the bodies of martyrs with greatest attention. The date of their departure and their anniversaries should be made the object for liturgical celebration. This cult inspired by the cult of the dead in the Hellenistic world developed into elaborate rituals in the mediaeval period. Martyrs were buried in necropolises originally shared by Christians and Pagans. People were careful to unite the dead bodies with the bones of the martyrs. They were buried *ad sanctos*.

Already the early church used a martial language when describing faithful Christians. They were warriors fighting the enemy in a Roman arena or as fighting a regular army led by Satan. This language was available when the church came under the protection of the state through Constantine's intervention. The Christians came into power and had to adopt themselves to

A stained glass window in Belgium shows Jesus Christ carrying the cross along the Via Dolorosa to his crucifixion. (Jorisvo/Dreamstime.com)

the policy of the state in intra-Christian conflicts with Donatists and Arians, and in inter-religious conflicts later, especially with the Muslims. Christians got access to the state monopoly to exercise violence. It was success in battle under the sign of the cross that allegedly made Christianity plausible. The war against the non-believers or Christian heretics was also interpreted as a glorification of God who wishes the defeat of these enemies. A victorious war was verification of the truth of the faith. The medieval warriors, known as Crusaders, were witnesses of the true faith, and, if killed, they were martyrs as described in the life story of, for example, Roland in *La Chanson de Roland/Die Roland-sage*. Today we see a return to the ideal of martyrdom that glorifies the non-violent, victimized, and suffering martyr who dies a representational death in accordance with John 15:30 and exemplified by, for example, Max-

imilian Kolbe (1894–1941), who volunteered to die in place of another.

Most Christian uses of "martyr" are group specific or even sectarian; they reflect the interest of a certain group. Catholics do not recognize a Protestant martyr. In contrast to modern Jewish tradition the martial martyr is marginalized. The World Council of Churches (to which the Catholics do not belong) acknowledged in 1978 Christian martyrs of all confessions and even non-Christian martyrs.

Islam The Arabic word *shahid*, plural *shuhada*, used by Muslims, inspired by the Christian use of martyr as witness, *shahid* meaning also "witness," refers like the Christian signifier to both a witness and to a person being killed in hate of his faith, to a martyr, within an Islamic context. In these meanings, it is also used by

Indian Shiite Muslims carry a replica of a martyr's tomb during an Ashura procession in Ahmadabad, India, January 8, 2009. (AP/Wide World Photos)

militant Sikhs fighting Muslims and Hindus in India fighting Khalistan. The signifier "witness" has also been translated by Christians into Sanskrit, Chinese, Japanese, and many other languages.

In Islam a distinction is made between the martial martyrs who are defined as *shuhada' al-dunya wa l-akhira*, "martyrs in this world and the next," and *shuhada l-akhira*, "martyrs in the next world only." The latter do not die on the battlefield but are slain as civil victims. There are plenty of narrations about violence-renouncing martyrs who were killed while leading the community in prayer or who served God in other ways and who are said to deserve the title *shahid*. These martyrs "in the next world only" correspond well to the Christian proto-martyr type.

The martial martyr has a long tradition in Islam, known already from the military campaigns during the lifetime of the Prophet Muhammad, the first one taking place in Ramadan on March 2, 624. Then the Prophet said, according to later commentators, that whoever would be killed in the battle facing the enemy would enter paradise. This saying is said to be in accordance with the Koran (3:169–170): "Count not those who were slain in God's way as dead, but rather as living with their word, by Him provided, rejoicing in the bounty that God has given them, and joyful in those who remain behind and have not joined them, because no fear shall be on them, neither shall they sorrow."

Late commentators ascribed to Muhammad the view that he promoted three types of martyrs. (1) There is the warrior who goes forth to battle wishing neither to kill nor to be killed. His mere presence should frighten the infidels. (2) There is the warrior who goes forth wishing to kill the enemy, but not be killed himself. This is a situation that most dedicated soldiers all over the world face. (3) There is the warrior who wishes to kill the enemy and to be killed himself. The martyr actively seeks an opportunity to do so, a behavior that is known as *talab al-shahada*, "the quest for martyrdom," which is heard of almost daily from suicide bombers in the contemporary Middle East.

Islam of the medieval period declared the following Muslims martyrs: those who died prematurely, as a result of accident, disease, or some other misfortunes like victimization of bubonic plague, of pleurisy or abdominal disease; those who drown, die in a fire or are struck by a falling house or wall; and women who die in childbirth. There is even a *fatwa* (Islamic legal opinion) written in Jumada in 749 that plague creates martyrs. Plague is caused by a *jinn* (or genie, a supernatural creature) who is an enemy of God. Therefore Muslims who die of plague are victims (not sinners like in a Christian tradition). The plague was regarded as a blessing in disguise. All who died of unnatural deaths, especially plague, are martyrs in a commentarial Muslim tradition.

In the history of Islam, martial martyrs were regularly males, but Islam allowed women supporting roles, such as tending the wounded. Exceptions are mentioned and we find them even today. The martial female martyr in Islam has become an attractive role for some Muslims.

The "canonical" prescriptive passage (Koran 3:169–170) is also a key to understanding what a Muslim *shahid* ultimately should want to achieve, namely, to "rejoice in the bounty of God." According to medieval commentators, the body of a slain martyr should not be washed because on the day of resurrection every wound will exude the fragrance of musk. He should be buried in his bloodstained clothes, which constitute proof of his status on the day of judgment. Coming to the rewards, a martyr will receive, according to the commentators Al-Muttaqi and Sa'id b. Mansur, a wife and forgiveness of sins in paradise.

Peter Schalk

See also: Arius; Constantine the Great; Globalization, Religion and; Muhammad; Ramadan; Roman Catholic Church; Women, Status and Role of; World Council of Churches; Yom HaShoah.

References

Cook, David. *Martyrdom in Islam.* Cambridge: Cambridge University Press, 2007.

Delehaye, Hippolte. *Les origins du culte des martyrs.* Bruxelles: Bureau de la Société des Bollandistes, 1912.

Die Entstehung der jüdischen Martyrologie. Studia post-biblica, 38. Ed. by J. W. van Henten, B. A. G. M. Dehandschutter, and H. J. W. van der Klaauw. Leiden and New York: Brill, 1989.

Fenech, Louis E. *Martyrdom in the Sikh Tradition: Playing the "Game of Love."* New Delhi: Oxford University Press, 2000.

Kohlberg, E. "Medieval Muslim Views on Martyrdom." In *Koninklijke Nederlandse Akademie van Wetenschapen. Mededelingen van de Afdeling Letterkunde, Niuwe Reeks, Deel 60, no 7.* Amsterdam: Koninklijke Nederlandse Akademie van Wetenschapen, 1977.

Martyrdom and Political Resistance. Essays from Asia and Europe. Comparative Asian Studies 18. Ed. by Joyce Pettigrew. Amsterdam: VU University Press, 1997.

"Martyrdom Today." In *Concilium* 163 (March 1983), edited by J-B. Metz and E. Schillebeeckx. New York: The Seabury Press, 1983.

Roos, Lena. *'God Wants It': The Ideology of Martyrdom of the Hebrew Crusade Chronicles and Its Jewish and Christian Background.* Turnhout: Brepols Publishers, 2006.

Schalk, Peter. *Die Lehre der Befreiungstiger Tamililams von der Selbstvernichtung durch göttliche Askese: Vorlage der Quelle, Überlegungen des Anführers. Acta Universitatis Upsaliensis. Historia Religionum 28.* Uppsala: AUU, 2007.

Martyrdom of Guru Arjan

Toward the end of spring each year, Sikhs commemorate the martyrdom of their fifth leader, Guru Arjan Dev Ji (1563–1606), which occurred on the fourth day of the light half of the month of Jyaishtha on the Hindu lunar calendar (May 30, 1606 CE). Today, using the new Sikh Nanashahi calendar, the event is celebrated annually on June 16.

Guru Arjan Dev Ji was born on April 15, 1563, as the youngest of the three sons of the Guru Ram Das Ji (1534–1581). He became the new guru following his father's death in 1581, though still a teenager. Among the accomplishments for which he is remembered is initiating the compilation of the Sikh holy book, the Guru Granth Sahib. Though he was not an aggressive proselytizer, the Sikh community grew during his tenure in office. Many attended upon him at Govindwal, then the center of the Sikh movement.

All was well for the Sikh movement until 1605, when the Mughal emperor Akbar died. His son and successor Jahangir was a fervent Muslim with a vision of turning his land into an Islamic state, which would necessarily include converting the Sikhs. He opened himself to a variety of accusations against Guru Arjan Dev, most significantly to those of Diwan Chandu Shah (whose marriage proposal of the guru's daughter had been refused by Guru Arun Dev). Arun Dev may have sealed his fate when he showed some kindness to Jahangir's rival Khusrau, who ruled Punjab at the time. In any case, Jahangir ordered Guru Arjan Dev's arrest and transport to Lahore. His possessions were also confiscated. Once in Lahore, he was subject to severe torture for six days but refused the emperor's demands. On the last day, he died in the river where he had been taken for a bath.

The martyrdom of Guru Arun Dev is credited with changing the basic character of Sikhs from a passive peaceable people into militant group willing to fight for its own survival and to protect its members from persecution. Arun Dev was succeeded by Guru Har Gobind (r. 1606–1644). He rejected the pacifism and nonviolent stance of previous gurus and organized a small army. He argued that it was necessary to take up the sword in order to protect the weak and the oppressed.

J. Gordon Melton

See also: Calendars, Religious; Pacifism; Sikhism/ Sant Mat.

References

Duggal, K. S. *Sikh Gurus: Their Lives and Teachings.* New Delhi: UBSPD, 2005.

Kapoor, Sukhbor Sing. *Sikh Festivals.* Vero Beach, FL: Rourke Publishing Group, 1989.

Martyrdom of Guru Tegh Bahadur

Guru Tegh Bahadur (1621–1675), the ninth guru of Sikhism, assumed his office on March 20, 1665. He succeeded to the task from his grand-nephew, Guru Har Krishan (1656–1664), who was only five years old when he became the guru and died before his eighth birthday.

Guru Har Krishan did not name a successor, only delivering an ambiguous message that he would be found in Bakala. Several proclaimed themselves the new guru, but eventually the unassuming Tegh Bahadur was singled out and received the support of the community.

He was named guru during the reign of the emperor Aurangzeb (1618–1707), who had the goal of turning India into a Muslim land. He initiated a program of forced conversion in Kashmir. A group of religious leaders agreed, on the advice of the guru, to tell the Mughal authorities that they would willingly embrace Islam if Guru Tegh Bahadur did the same. Aurangzeb ordered his arrest and before leaving for Delhi, Tech Bahadur selected his son, Gobind (later Guru Gobind Singh), as his successor, should it be necessary. He was arrested, detained for three months, and then sent to Delhi in November 1675. He refused

to recant his faith under torture and was eventually beheaded on November 11, 1675. The Gurdwara Sis Ganj Sahib in Delhi was later built over the spot where the execution took place.

The martyrdom of Guru Tegh Bahadur is now celebrated on Maghar 11 on the Nanakshahi calendar, which was accepted by the administrative authorities of the religion in Amritsar in the 1990. Maghar 11 is equivalent to November 24 on the Common Era calendar. Commemoration of Guru Tegh Bahadur's death is one of 12 Gurpurbs, holidays that recall the birth or death of one of the 10 Sikh gurus. Sikhs celebrate the Gurpurbs by performing an Akhand Path, a public reading of the Guru Granth Sahib, the Sikh holy scriptures, in *gurdwaras* around the world. It requires two days to read the entire volume from beginning to end. The reading will thus begin two days before the designated holy day and will end early in the morning of the day of commemoration. Each person chosen to participate will read aloud for two to three hours. The day itself will start early in the morning and include the recitation of prayers, the singing of *kirtans* (holy songs), and speeches on the theme of the day. It will include a communal meal. Though guru for less than two years, Tegh Bahadur made a significant impact on the movement because of his faithfulness under the most severe of circumstances.

J. Gordon Melton

See also: Calendars, Religious; Common Era Calendar; Guru Gobind Singh's Birthday; Sikhism/Sant Mat.

References

Duggal, K. S. *Sikh Gurus: Their Lives and Teachings.* New Delhi: UBSPD, 2005.

Kapoor, Sukhbor Sing. *Sikh Festivals.* Vero Beach, FL: Rourke Publishing Group, 1989.

Mary, Blessed Virgin

The Blessed Virgin Mary, the mother of Jesus of Nazareth, is one of a half dozen women named Mary who appear in the Christian New Testament. She first appears in the Gospel accounts six months after the conception of John the Baptist when she was visited by the angel Gabriel (whom Muhammad would later

Small child next to a statue of the Blessed Virgin Mary at Our Lady of Japan, Tokyo. (J. Gordon Melton)

announce as having visited him with the content of the Koran). At the time Mary was as yet unmarried but was engaged to a carpenter named Joseph. Gabriel told Mary that she was highly honored and would become the mother of Jesus, the Son of the Most High. Given that Mary was a virgin, she would become pregnant by the power of the Holy Spirit. Gabriel also informed her that her cousin Elizabeth was already pregnant (with the future John the Baptist) and Mary proceeded to visit her and share the good news of her situation. Her pregnancy was initially a problem for her future husband, who thought of backing out of the engagement, until the special circumstances were revealed to him in a dream. Following the instructions he had received, Joseph married her.

Shortly before Jesus' birth, the couple traveled to Bethlehem to be counted in a census ordered by Rome. Joseph was descended from King David and thus Bethlehem was his family's home. Mary gave birth to Jesus

under the most humble of circumstances but was soon afterward visited by people to whom his birth had been revealed. Among these were three Wise Men (Zoroastrian astrologers) who had come to Judea looking for someone whose birth had been heralded by a star that had suddenly appeared in the night sky. The Judean King Herod, learning of the child's birth from the Wise Men, decided to kill all the male infants in his realm as he saw the birth of Jesus threatening his throne. Being warned in a dream about this plan, Mary, Joseph, and Jesus left Judea and spent time in Egypt.

When conditions allowed, the family returned to Nazareth and Jesus grew up there. Little is heard of him for the next few decades. One incident stands out. When he was 12 years old, while the family was visiting Jerusalem for the Passover holy day, Jesus disappeared. Mary and Joseph eventually found him discussing serious issues with the elders in the temple.

Elsewhere in the Gospels, Jesus is mentioned as having brothers (James, Joses [or Joseph], Simon, and Judas) and sisters whose names are not mentioned (Matthew 13:55–56; Mark 6:3). Protestants generally assume that while Mary was a virgin when Jesus was conceived and given birth, she later lived a normal married life with Joseph and had additional children. This idea conflicts with the understanding of Mary's perpetual virginity, a doctrine held by the Roman Catholic and Eastern Orthodox churches. They believe that Mary and Joseph never consummated their marriage and that those spoken of as Jesus' brothers and sisters were cousins or even more distant relatives.

Mary appears several times during Jesus' adult ministry. She is, for example, present when he turned water into wine at a wedding (John 2:1–10). She is also seemingly rebuffed when attempting to see Jesus; he refuses by stating that those who do the will of his heavenly Father are his real brothers, sisters, and mother.

Mary finally appears among those who keep watch at Golgotha after Jesus is crucified. While Jesus is hanging on the cross, he commends his mother to the care of his disciple John. She seems to have gone to his home to live from that time. She makes one last appearance, among the disciples in the days following Jesus' resurrection and ascension, but prior to the giving of the Spirit at Pentecost.

In the early years of Christianity, Mary plays into the debates over the way of salvation and the nature of Jesus. In the Apostles' Creed, the earliest statement of Christian belief in creedal form, Jesus is affirmed as having been "born of a virgin." This position is reaffirmed in the fourth-century Nicene Creed and Chacedonian Creed, which nailed down belief of Jesus' dual nature as God and man. Mary's status relative to the Virgin Birth of Jesus would be debated at the Council of Ephesus (451), which affirmed her as *Theotokos*, or Mother of God. Especially since the visit of Constantine's mother Helena to the Holy Land, relics of Mary have been valued. The beliefs of both Eastern and Western Christians prevent the existence of any bodily remains of Mary, but several items associated with her are held at the cathedral at Prado (a piece of ribbon identified as her belt), the cathedral at Chartres (her veil), and the cathedral at Aachen (her shroud).

During the 14th century, in Italy, a house at Loretto was put forth as the house of in which the angel Gabriel made the Annunciation (told Mary that she was to bear Jesus). According to the story, the house was miraculously transported to Tersato, Dalmatia, in 1291 and then to Loretto in 1294. It remains a popular pilgrimage site.

Several traditions have developed concerning Mary's death. Most Eastern Orthodox Christians believe that the Virgin Mary died a natural death, at which time her soul was received by Christ. Her body was buried and three days later was resurrected and taken into heaven as a symbol of the future general resurrection of all believers. They also recognize a site near the Mount of Olives just outside Jerusalem as her burial spot. A small church was built over this site in the fifth century. It was destroyed in the seventh century when Jerusalem was invaded by the Persians. Over the next centuries it was rebuilt and destroyed on multiple occasions, though the crypt remained intact. Though Muslims hold Mary in high respect as the mother of the Prophet Isa (Jesus), in 1187, Saladin destroyed the church that had been erected over the crypt by the Crusaders. Finally in the 14th century, some Franciscans (Roman Catholics) again erected a church over the site. That church is today owned by the Greek Orthodox Patriarchate of Jerusalem, though space in the church is shared with the Armenian Apostolic Church.

A second tradition traces Mary to Ephesus, near which she was taken by the Apostle John to a house on Mount Koressos, in what is today western Turkey, and maintains that she lived there the remaining years of her earthly life. Roman Catholics believe that she did not die but was taken up into heaven. Orthodox and Muslims believed that she died in this house. The site was lost, but was described in visions by 19th-century nun and seer Anne Catherine Emmerich (1774–1824). Using the Emmerich materials, a house was found in the 1890s by two members of the Vincentian Order, founded by Saint Vincent de Paul (1581–1660). They subsequently discovered that people from a nearby village who considered themselves descendants of the Ephesian Christians venerated the house as Mary's final resting place.

Over the centuries, thousands of people have claimed to have been visited by the Virgin Mary, the number rising significantly since early in the 19th century. Several hundred of these apparitions have risen above the mundane and become the basis of new forms of Catholic piety, the source of new revelations, or a new site for pilgrimages. The Roman Catholic rosary, for example, is traced to a 13th-century apparition of Mary to Saint Dominic. The Miraculous Medal was given to Saint Catherine Labouré in her vision of Mary in Paris in 1830.

The scapular is a narrow cloth with an opening for the head that hangs down a person's front and back. Evolving from the aprons worn by agricultural laborers over their clothes, in the medieval period they became the identifying mark of monastic garb. They were later worn by laypeople who wished to show their support for a particular order. In 1251, the Blessed Virgin appeared to Simon Stock, the superior general of the Carmelite Order. She gave him a brown scapular and promised that any who wore it would be saved from eternal damnation. In 1617, Ursula Benincasa (1547–1618), founder of the Congregation of the Oblates of the Immaculate Conception of the Blessed Virgin Mary, had a vision of the Blessed Virgin who showed her a multitude of angels distributing blue scapulars. Her order subsequently made the distribution of the scapular one of its unique activities. Subsequent apparitions have been identified with scapulars of different colors.

Anne Catherine Emmerich is but one of many people who had apparitions of the Virgin and left behind a body of work that included messages to humanity from the Blessed Virgin. Many of the apparitions have relatively brief messages to communicate, most often centered on more fervent devotion or a particular action. But some seers have brought forth lengthy communications delivered over a period of time, some being published as multi-volume texts. Very few of these materials, received in a Roman Catholic context and resembling volumes received by New Age channelers, have received any recognition by church authorities.

The site of many of the 19th- and 20th-century apparitions, from Guadalupe, Mexico; to Lourdes, France; to Fatima, Portugal; to Knock, Ireland, have, especially when given the least bit of approval by church authorities, become popular pilgrimage sites. Even those marginalized by the church—Necedah, Wisconsin; Bayside, New York; and Conyers, Georgia—have been able to sustain a following to the present.

Doctrinal Development The spread of popular piety supported the development of Mariology, a theology of the Virgin Mary, as a subdiscipline of Christian theology. Mariology would explore and define a set of doctrinal affirmations that would become official dogma, that is, a doctrine to which all Roman Catholics are supposed to grant assent. The dogma of the Perpetual Virginity of the Virgin Mary, that Mary remained a virgin throughout her earthly life, was defined quite early and was clearly stated by Augustine and Thomas Aquinas and reaffirmed by the Second Vatican Council (1962–1965). The dogma of the Immaculate Conception, that from her conception, Mary was preserved from original sin, was defined as dogma in 1854 by Pope Pius IX in his encyclical *Ineffabalis Deus*. The dogma of the Assumption of the Virgin Mary, which states that Mary did not die a bodily death but was taken to heaven at the end of her earthly life and now spends her time working for the salvation of all, was put forth in 1950 by Pope Pius XII in his apostolic constitution, *Munificentissimus Deus.*

In addition to these dogmas, there are a number of titles that have been given to Mary—Queen of Heaven, Co-Redemptrix, Mystical Rose—which indicate additional popular beliefs that together have elevated the veneration of Mary into a major aspect of Roman Catholic devotion in the modern world. In addition, Mary has been named as the patroness—protector and intercessor—for a number of organizations, professions, and even countries. She has been named as the patroness of more than 60 countries, not all by any means having a Catholic majority.

Mary has been a primary subject of Christian artists. In the East, a number of sacred icons have Mary as their subject. Several of these have become famous as "weeping" icons. One icon traced back to Helena is called Our Lady of Czestochowa, an icon now located in Poland. In the 1380s, Prince Ladislaus, the regent for King Louis of Poland, prayed to the Virgin asking where her image should be placed, and in a dream she pointed to a hill at Czestochowa. Ladislaus endowed a monastery and left the image with the monks. In the 1430s, when the monastery was attacked, a soldier slashed the cheek of the image three times. He died as he made the third cut. Since that time, attempts to repair the image have been unsuccessful.

In the West, statues of the Virgin have been popular, many depicting the image of the virgin as she appeared in various apparitions. Most of these statues developed special names. Mary also became the subject of 20th-century attempts to build Christina mega-statues. The largest statue of Mary, at 151 feet, is the Virgen de la Paz, located at Trujillo, Venezuela. Other mega statues are the Holy Mother of God the Protectress of the town of Haskovo, Bulgaria, and Our Lady of the Rockies, which sits on the Continental Divide overlooking Butte, Montana.

Mary in Islam In Islamic thought, Jesus is one of the prophets preceding Muhammad, and his mother is given special attention in the Koran. It is noted by Muslim scholars that Mary is granted more attention than any woman mentioned in the Koran. She is in fact the only woman mentioned by name and one of eight persons to have a chapter (the 19th) devoted to her. She is called Mariam, Arabic for Mary. According to the Koran, Mary's mother dedicated her to God while Mary was still in her womb. The angel Gabriel visited Mary to announce her pregnancy with Jesus, though she was a chaste virgin. She has Jesus, alone under a tree, neither Joseph, the visiting Wise Men, nor a manger being mentioned in the Koran. The birth of Jesus has been seen as more like Allah's creation of Adam de novo, rather than as miracle demonstrating Jesus' divinity. Mary is seen as the type of a pious believer who submits to Allah and is told, "O Mary! God hath chosen thee and purified thee—chosen thee above the women of all nations. O Mary! worship thy Lord devoutly: Prostrate thyself, and bow down with those who bow down."

J. Gordon Melton

See also: Augustine of Hippo; Devotion/Devotional Traditions; Islam; Jerusalem; Muhammad; Passover; Statues—Christian; Thomas Aquinas.

References

Ball, Ann. *The Other Faces of Mary: Stories, Devotions, and Pictures of the Holy Virgin from Around the World.* New York: Crossroad Publishing Company, 2004.

Dodds, Monica, and Bill Dodds. *Encyclopedia of Mary.* Huntington, IN: Our Sunday Visitor, 2007.

Durham, Michael S. *Miracles of Mary: Apparitions, Legends, and Miraculous Works of the Blessed Virgin Mary.* San Francisco: Harper, 1995.

Galvan, John. "Jesus and The Virgin Mary in Islam." Islam for Today. http://www.islamfortoday.com/galvan03.htm. Accessed July 1, 2004.

Heintz, Peter. *A Guide to Apparitions of Our Blessed Virgin Mary.* Sacramento: Gabriel Press, 1995.

"The Mary Page (University of Dayton)." http://www.udayton.edu/mary/marypage21.html. Accessed July 1, 2009.

Pelikan, Jaroslav. *Mary through the Centuries: Her Place in the History of Culture.* New Haven, CT: Yale University Press, 1998.

Rubin, Miri. *Mother of God: A History of the Virgin Mary.* New Haven, CT: Yale University Press, 2009.

Zimdars-Swartz, Sandra. *Encountering Mary: From La Salette to Medjugorje.* New York: Harper Perennial, 1992.

Mary I

1516–1558

Mary I (Mary Tudor), queen of England (r. 1553–1558), was the daughter of Henry VIII (1491–1547). She came to power as the Protestant Reformation made a significant impact on the country and she used her power to attempt to bring England back into the Roman Catholic fold. In the process she had a number of Protestant leaders arrested and executed, and drove many more into exile. For centuries afterward, Mary was portrayed as a villain in Protestant literature.

Mary I was born February 18, 1516. She was the only surviving offspring of Henry's brief marriage to Catherine of Aragon (1485–1536), a member of the Catholic Spanish ruling family. While Henry still hoped that he would have a son with Catherine, Mary was generally recognized as the current heir to the throne. However, once Henry moved to annul his marriage to Catherine, Mary fell from his favor. Henry subsequently, in 1533, had a second daughter, Elizabeth, whose mother was Anne Boleyn (ca. 1501–1536).

Catherine died in 1536, and Henry forced Mary to sign a statement renouncing her loyalty to Catholicism. Though having to still endure remarks about her legitimacy, she otherwise enjoyed a brief respite from Henry's anger. The pressure on her was further relieved the following year when Edward VI was born of Henry's next wife, Jane Seymour (1508–1537). In Henry's final will, Mary was named as second in succession to her half-brother Edward VI (1537–1553).

Following her father's death in 1547, she lived quietly away from London, though after the prohibition of the Mass by the Protestant-controlled Council that ran the government given Edward's youth, she defied the Council's leaders and continued Roman Catholic practice in her home. The issue did not prevent her from occasionally paying formal visits to Edward.

Following Edward's death on July 6, 1553, John Dudley, duke of Northumberland (ca. 1502–1553), who as the lord president of the Council had virtually run the country during the reign of the juvenile Edward, attempted to bypass both of Henry's daughters and have his daughter-in-law Lady Jane Grey (ca. 1537–1554) placed on the throne. Mary acted quickly after learning of the plot. She gathered her supporters and arrived in London, where she was acknowledged as the new queen on July 19. She turned on Northumberland and had him arrested and soon afterward executed.

As queen, Mary systematically began the reversal of all the laws and actions taken by her father and then

British queen Mary I signs the death warrant of Lady Jane Grey in 1554. (Library of Congress)

her brother that had moved England away from Rome. She restored several Catholic bishops to their posts and removed the most outspoken Protestant ones. A few, including Nicolas Ridley (ca. 1500–1555), Miles Coverdale (ca. 1488–1569), Hugh Latimer (ca. 1485–1655), John Hooper (ca. 1500–1555), and Thomas Cranmer (1489–1556), were arrested.

Soon after her coronation, she named Reginald Pole (1500–1558) to the post of papal legate to negotiate the issue that had caused the country's formal excommunication and found Philip of Spain an ideal husband. She had Parliament reinstitute the Mass throughout England and then repeal a number of what were perceived as "Protestant" laws.

Finally, Mary suppressed any who opposed her rise to the throne to the point of open rebellion, and from her perspective, now that she occupied the throne, the security of the state seemed to require stern measures. The leaders of the revolt were executed and with them the unfortunate Lady Jane Grey. Any role in the movement by her sister Elizabeth remained ill defined and Mary decided not to move against her.

A year of triumph culminated on November 30, 1554, as Mary participated in a ceremony along with her husband and all the members of Parliament in which Pole absolved England of its past anti-Roman actions. Within a few weeks, Parliament had repealed all the anti-Roman laws, and Roman Catholicism was once again established as the dominant practice throughout the country.

With Catholicism firmly in control religiously, beginning in 1555, Mary turned on the Protestant leadership, Before she left the throne, 277 persons would be burned at the stake for heresy. Cranmer, Latimer, Hooper, and Ridley were prominent among the victims (Coverdale having escaped to the continent). Mary ordered the executions as the only means of ridding England of any Protestant tendencies.

Mary's effort to return England to the Catholic fold permanently was blunted by her poor health. As her attacks on the Protestants continued, the dropsy (edema) from which she had suffered became more severe and she died on November 17, 1558, shortly after the fifth anniversary of her ascendancy to the throne. She would be succeeded by her half-sister Elizabeth, who would move as quickly away from Catholicism as Mary had moved toward it.

In her attempt to heal the divide between her Catholic and Protestant subjects (and in the process create modern Anglicanism) Elizabeth had to deal with the impact of the Marian Exiles, those Protestants who had escaped Mary's wrath by fleeing to the continent. They returned to England fired with Protestant zeal and an intense hatred for the woman whom they blamed for the deaths of so many of their brothers in the faith. They would vilify the one they called "Bloody Mary," the main subject of one of the most renowned of Protestant classics, John Foxe's *Book of Martyrs* (1563). The intense bitterness over Mary was only laid to rest in the radically altered relationship created between Protestants and Catholics in the wake of Second Vatican Council of the 1960s, some 500 years after Mary's reign.

J. Gordon Melton

See also: Church of England; Elizabeth I; Roman Catholic Church.

References

Knighton, C. S., ed. *Calendar of State Papers, Domestic Series Mary I, 1553–1558*. London: Public Record Office, 1998.

Loades, David. *Mary Tudor: The Tragical History of the First Queen of England*. London: National Archives Press, 2006.

Maynard, Theodore. *Bloody Mary*. Milwaukee: Bruce Publishing Co., 1955.

Porter, Linda. *The Myth of "Bloody Mary": A Biography of Queen Mary I of England*. New York: St. Martin's Griffin, 2009.

Prescott, H. F. *Mary Tudor*. New York: Macmillan Company, 1953.

Maryknoll

Maryknoll, officially the Catholic Foreign Missionary Society of America, an American-based foreign missionary society serving the Catholic Church, emerged as a seminary devoted to training missionaries. It subsequently grew, step by step, into a global missionary sending agency.

Maryknoll was founded by Fathers James A. Walsh (1867–1936) and Thomas F. Price (1860–1919). As a young priest, Walsh became interested in foreign missions and founded a periodical, *The Field Afar*, to promote interest in the work. Price, the North Carolinian ordained as a Catholic priest, began his career in home missions but soon expanded his concern to include foreign missionary activity. The two met in 1910 at the Eucharistic Congress held in Montreal and formulated plans for a seminary to train missionaries. They quickly received the approval of the American bishops and in June 1911 traveled to Rome, where Pope Pius X approved their project. The Catholic Foreign Missionary Society of America was a reality before the year ended. The Society was headquartered on a hill (knoll) near Ossining, New York, its name chosen because of Walsh and Price's devotion to the Virgin Mary.

At the time Maryknoll was founded, China was the single country that had received the most Christian missionaries and it was not surprising that China was chosen as the first object of the new Society's attention. Price accompanied the first group of three missionaries —Fathers James E. Walsh (not to be confused with the society's co-founder), Francis X. Ford, and Bernard F. Meyer—as the superior for the work. Price died in Hong Kong a year later of a burst appendix. Father James A. Walsh stayed at Maryknoll as the society's superior general, a post he retained until his death in 1936. In 1933, Walsh and Maryknoll were acknowledged by his being consecrated as the titular bishop of Siene.

Among the many people who worked in the background making Maryknoll a reality was Mary Josephine Rogers (1882–1955). She developed an interest in mission while a student at Smith College, where she organized a Mission Study club. Beginning in 1908, she assisted Walsh, and in 1912 was named the head of the females who were working for the Society. That group gradually began to think of themselves as pursuing a religious vocation, and reorganized in 1920 as the Foreign Mission Sisters of Saint Dominic. The Maryknoll Sisters, as they were popularly termed, became a Pontifical Institute in 1954, at which time its name was changed to Maryknoll Sisters of Saint Dominic. In 1925, Rogers, now known as Sister Mary Joseph, became the Sisters' first mother general, a post she retained until her retirement in 1946. Soon after their founding, the Sisters began working alongside the men in the East and Latin America.

A lay Maryknoll affiliate was added in 1975. Its member Maryknoll Lay Missioners have dedicated themselves to live in economically poorer communities, working to supply basic needs and generally assisting processes that are deemed to be producing a more just and compassionate world. Most lay missionaries are found in Africa, Asia, and the Americas.

The three entities at Maryknoll are distinct branches of the original structure—the Maryknoll Fathers and Brothers, the Maryknoll Sisters, and the Maryknoll Lay Missioners.

Maryknoll Fathers and Brothers spread out globally through the last half of the 20th century—Asia, Africa, and Latin America. They became prominent in South America in the 1960s where many of the brothers emerged as strong supporters of Liberation Theology. The Society has remained on the cutting edge of modern Christian missionary activity as it has made the transition to a decolonialized world and leadership in global Christianity has passed from the hands of Europeans and North Americans. It publication affiliate, Orbis Books, is a major publisher of materials on contemporary Christian missions, missionary theory, and global Christianity.

As of 2009, there are more than 475 Maryknoll priests and Brothers serving in countries around the world, principally in Africa, Asia, and Latin America, while Maryknoll Sisters are to be found in 30 countries around the world.

Maryknoll Fathers and Brothers
PO Box 304

Maryknoll, NY 10545-0304
http://society.maryknoll.org/

Maryknoll Sisters
PO Box 311
Maryknoll, NY 10545-0311

Maryknoll Lay Missioners
PO Box 307
Maryknoll, NY 10545-0307

J. Gordon Melton

See also: Mary, Blessed Virgin; Roman Catholic Church.

References

Byrne, Patrick. *Fr. Price of Maryknoll.* Maryknoll, NY: The Catholic Foreign Mission Society of America, Inc., 1922.

Sargen, Daniel. *All the Day Long.* New York: Longmans, Green & Co., 1941.

Sheridan, Robert. *The Founders of Maryknoll.* Maryknoll, NY: The Catholic Foreign Mission Society of America, Inc., 1980.

Masjid al-Ḥaram Al-

Al-Masjid al-Ḥaram, located in Mecca, Saudi Arabia, is the largest mosque in the world, and in its midst is the Kaaba, a black cubical structure toward which Muslims orient themselves when offering prayers to Allah. Muslims consider it the holiest spot on Earth, the place where the earthly and heavenly realms intersect. It is a high point of the annual pilgrimage (*al-hajj*) in which Muslims come to Mecca, enter the mosque, and circumambulate the Kaaba.

The site of the mosque and Kaaba was in use as a religious site long before Islam arose in the seventh century CE, and various stories are told of its beginnings. Some consider it a product of the angels at the beginning of time. Tradition ascribes its building to the Prophet Ibrahim (Abraham) assisted by his son Ishmael. Some believe the Black Stone located at the eastern corner of the Kaaba to be part of the original structure erected by Ibrahim. After Ibrahim's death, the Kaaba was again filled with idols and remained in that condition until the time of Muhammad. At that

time, the Kaaba was also the site for an annual gathering (the Hajj) of the tribes of the peninsula. It and the surrounding territory were considered an area of nonviolence. The Kaaba was dedicated to Hubal, a deity of the Nabatean people who inhabited northern Arabia.

When Muhammad (570–632) assumed control of Mecca as the leader of the Muslims, he went to the Kaaba and oversaw the destruction of all the idols. At one stage of this process, his son-in-law (and later caliph) Ali Ibne Abi Talib climbed on Muhammad's shoulders to bring down the largest of the idols, that of Hubal. From this point, the Kaaba was integrated into the worship of the Muslims of Mecca.

Following the death of Muhammad, the caliph Omar Ibn al-Khattab (r. 634–644) enlarged the area around the Kaaba by demolishing a number of houses and erecting a wall that enclosed the outdoor prayer area surrounding the shrine. Caliph Uthman Ibn Affan (r. 644–656) enlarged the prayer area and covered it. Successive caliphs continued to enlarge the emerging mosque and added more permanent and aesthetically pleasing decorations. Then in 777, Caliph al-Mahdi (r. 775–785) demolished the existing mosque and saw to the construction of a larger one that incorporated marble columns decorated with gilt teak wooden inlay and three minarets. Caliph al-Madhi's work survived for centuries, but in 1399, the mosque was severely damaged by a fire and had to be rebuilt by Sultan Nasir Faraj bin Barquq (r. 1399–1405).

In 1571, Ottoman Sultan Selim II (r. 1566–1574) commissioned a major renovation of the mosque. At this time, the mosque took on the appearance it still maintains. He saw to the addition of domes over the prayer halls. In 1629, Sultan Murad IV (r. 1623–1640) added the seven minarets.

During the 20th century, the present nation of Saudi Arabia was created and in 1955, the first of what has become as series of expansions and renovations of the mosque, most designed to accommodate the growing number of visitors—especially for the annual Hajj—was begun. King Fahd (r. 1982–2005) added a new wing and an outdoor prayer area on the southeast side of the mosque. He followed between 1988 and 2005 with the addition of new minarets, the king's residence overlooking the mosque, and additional prayer area in and around the mosque. King Abdullah bin Abdul-

Aziz, who succeeded to the throne in 2005, has launched a massive effort to increase the capacity of the mosque by 35 percent. It currently can accommodate 800,000 inside the mosque proper and an additional 1,120,000 immediately outside the mosque.

The current Al-Masjid al-Ḥaram centers on the Kaaba, the 60-foot cube that forms the main reason for Muslims' pilgrimage to Mecca. Surrounding the Kaaba on all sides is a large open area. That area is surrounded by the mosque building itself, a two-story structure that includes a variety of administrative offices and several enclosed prayer halls. Entrance into the area surrounding the Kaaba is through a number of large arched doorways. Outside the building are large areas also set aside for worshippers.

The current structure, including the outdoor and indoor praying spaces, covers an area of 99 acres. While its general capacity is usually two million, it can accommodate up to four million worshippers during the Hajj period.

One event in the modern era disturbed the sanctity of the mosque. In 1979, during the Hajj, a group of extremist Muslims led by Abdullah Hamid Mohammed Al-Qahtani seized control of the mosque. The insurgents declared their leader to be the Mahdi, the prophet who is to arise as the redeemer of Islam. They demanded all Muslims submit to his authority. In the process, a large number of pilgrims became hostages. The takeover lasted for two weeks but finally ended in a gun battle between the militants and the Saudi security forces. A number from both sides were killed in the clash, as were many hostages, before the Saudi forces reassumed control of the mosque.

J. Gordon Melton

See also: Abraham/Abram; Islam; Mecca; Mosques; Pilgrimage.

References

Adawi, Nabil. *The Two Holy Mosques in Saudi Arabia: Historical Context, Modern Developments, and Cultural Significance.* London: Gulf Centre for Strategic Studies, 1994.

King, Geoffrey R. D. *The Historical Mosques of Saudi Arabia.* Reading, MA: Addison-Wesley, 1987.

Trofimov, Yaroslav. *The Siege of Mecca: The Forgotten Uprising in Islam's Holiest Shrine and the*

Birth of Al Qaeda, Garden City, NY: Doubleday & Company, 2007.

Wright, Lawrence. *The Looming Tower: Al Qaeda and the Road to 9/11*. New York: Alfred A. Knopf, 2006.

Master Ching Hai Meditation Association

The Master Ching Hai Meditation Association (also known as God's Direct Contact) emerged in the 1980s around the teachings and person of Master Ching Hai Wu Shang Shih, a Vietnamese teacher in the Sant Mat tradition. Today the organization has centers around the world and sponsors a series of fast food vegetarian-only restaurants (Loving Huts [http://www.lovinghut.com]). These cafés, which can be found throughout North America, Europe, and Asia, serve as mini-centers of Ching Hai's growing ministry. Raised a Roman Catholic in Vietnam, Ching Hai was introduced to Buddhism by her grandmother. As a young adult, Ching Hai moved to England to continue her education and then lived for a short time in France and Germany. While in Germany she married a Buddhist.

During the early years of her marriage, she pursued a spiritual quest at the feet of several different Eastern teachers, after which she left home to find enlightenment. Her quest had been determined by her reading of the Buddhist Surangama Sutra, which spoke of the Quan Yin Method as the surest means to enlightenment, but she could locate no Buddhist teacher who could inform her of the nature of the method. Finally she visited India, where she met Thakar Singh, a teacher in the Ruhani Satsang Sant Mat tradition, who instructed her in the *shabd* yoga of the sound current. The Sant Mat teaches that the world was brought into existence by the Creative Word or divine Sound Current. Through the use of *simran* (repetition of a mantra) and associated meditative techniques (*dhyan* and *bhajan*), individuals can reconnect to the spiritual realms.

Ching Hai concluded that shabd yoga was the Quin Yin Method she had been seeking. After her initiation by Thakar Singh, she moved to Taiwan and began to teach. Through the 1980s she met with an increasingly positive response, and her following expanded through

Southeast Asia and by the early 1990s, around the world. While followers learn and practice shabd yoga, they are also asked to adhere to five precepts: to refrain from (1) taking the life of any sentient beings, (2) lying, (3) stealing, (4) illicit sex, and (5) intoxicants. Followers adopt a vegan or lactovegetarian diet.

Ching Hai is regularly pictured in the movement's literature as wearing designer clothing. In 1995 she created an organization to sell the clothing, which she had herself designed, with the understanding that the income would be used to support humanitarian activities, primarily Vietnamese refugee camps and support of flood victims in Southeast Asia. In December 1999 she attended and spoke at the meeting of the Parliament of the World's Religions in Cape Town, South Africa. The growth of the Master Ching Hai Meditation Association has not always been smooth, however; it has been accused of financial irregularities in Taiwan and has been banned since 1999 in the People's Republic of China, where it has been added to the list of cult-like organizations. Presently, Ching Hai has taken on the honorific "Supreme Master" and has becoming politically active in promoting environmental awareness in her "Be Veg, Go Green, Save the Planet" initiative.

Ching Hai Meditation Association (God's Direct Contact)
PO Box 9
Hsihu, Miaoli 36899
Formosa, R.O.C.
http://www.godsdirectcontact.org/ (English and Chinese)

André Laliberté and David C. Lane

See also: Ruhani Satsang; Sikhism/Sant Mat.

Reference

The Supreme Master Ching Hai. *The Key of Immediate Enlightenment*. 2 vols. Miaoli Hsien, Taiwan/R.O.C.: Meditation Association in China, 1991.

Mata Amritanandamayi Math

The network of centers around the world devoted to extending the ministry of Indian spiritual teacher Mataji Amritanandamayi (b. 1951) (often called "Amma")

People receiving the Darshan (The Embrace) from Mataji Amritanandamayi, or Amma, The Mother. (Frédéric Soltan/ Corbis)

emerged in India in the 1960s. Mataji grew up in Kerala in an atmosphere of family devotion to Krishna, but unlike the other children, at the age of seven she began to compose *bhajans* (holy songs) to him. She identified with him closely and seemed to be able to assume various moods attributed to him or to his consort Devi in a way that facilitated the devotion of others. In the early 1970s, when Mataji had just entered her young adulthood, her neighbors began to recognize her as an enlightened being. Among these was her father, who gave her land upon which to create an ashram (religious community).

Mataji's local ministry began to spread, first throughout Kerala and then all of India. In 1988 she built the first of the unique temples associated with her. These Brahmastanams, or Abodes of the Absolute, are the residence of four deity forms, each installed as part of a single image representing the principle of the Unity of God. In the temples, devotees practice a form of *bhakti* yoga, a spirituality based in devotional service to God, by meditating and singing Mataji's bhajans. Devotion to a wide variety of deity figures, including Jesus, Buddha, the Virgin Mary, and so on, is allowed and even encouraged, as Mataji believes that all religions are spiritual paths that lead to the same One God.

International expansion began in 1987, when Mataji made her first tour in the West, centered on the United States, France, and Switzerland. This tour had been made possible by Western disciples who had encountered her in India. Through the 1990s more than 100 centers emerged across Europe and the Middle East and to Singapore and Australia. In 2008, there were approximately 100 centers in North America.

The Mata Amritanandamayi Math supports several social agencies in India—the Amrita Institute of Medical Sciences and Research Centre in Cochin, Kerala; Amrita Niketanam, an orphanage in Parippally; and Anbu Illam, a home for the aged in Sivakasi, Tamil Nadu. In 1996 Mataji inaugurated a project called Amrita Kuteeram, which within five years (2001) constructed some 20,000 houses in different parts of India. The Math has also instituted a program to provide pensions for widows and elderly women who are not receiving government support. These, and like programs, are seen as a manifestation of Mataji's compassion for all people.

Mata Amritanandamayi Math
Amritapuri, Kollam
Kerala
India
http://www.amritapuri.org/
http://www.ammachi.org

J. Gordon Melton

See also: Hinduism; Meditation.

References

Amritanandamayi, Mataji. *Awaken Children!* 2 vols. Valickavu, Kerala: Mata Amritanandamayi Mission Trust, 1989–1990.

Balagopal. *The Mother of Sweet Bliss.* Valickavu, Kerala: Mata Amritanandamayi Mission Trust, 1985.

"Holy Woman Brings the Mother Spirit to the West." *Hinduism Today* 9, no. 4 (July 1987): 1, 15.

Warrier, Maya. *Hindu Selves in a Modern World: Guru Faith in the Mata Amritanandamayi Mission.* Richmond, Surrey, UK: Routledge-Curzon, 2005.

Mathers, Samuel Liddell MacGregor

1854–1918

A key figure in late 19th-century Esotericism and co-founder of the Hermetic Order of the Golden Dawn, Samuel Mathers was born in London on January 8, 1854. The only child of William Mathers, a merchant's clerk, and his wife Mary Ann, Mathers grew up in Bournemouth in a family environment that was nominally Anglican. After his father died Mathers was sent to Bedford Grammar School. School records show that he was unexceptional as a student, showing none of his future brilliance as a translator of key medieval magical texts.

After leaving Bedford Grammar School, Mathers—like his father before him—began work as a clerk. However, he also developed a keen interest in military history and Freemasonry, and in October 1877, at the age of 23, was initiated as a Mason at Hengist Lodge in Bournemouth. Mathers subsequently gained the three regular degrees—Entered Apprentice, Fellow Draft, and Master Mason—but never became a Lodge Master. He later registered his name with his Lodge as Comte de Glenstrae, a sign that he aspired to more exotic social heights than his conventional and undistinguished background could otherwise provide. Mathers maintained that this title had been conferred on one of his ancestors by King James II. He would later also add MacGregor to his name, claiming that his father was of Scottish descent and that his surname was associated with Clan MacGregor.

According to his future wife Moina it was while working as a clerk that he first began leading "a student's life," although it is likely that this was very much a part-time educational pursuit. Mathers also took up soldiering with the First Hampshire Infantry Volunteers, although according to occult historian Robert A. Gilbert he was never commissioned and it is unlikely that he achieved a higher rank than private. Nevertheless, he translated a military manual from French in order to adapt it to British army requirements and this was a sign of things to come, for Mathers would later revel in this particular skill, translating a number of medieval magical works into English, including Knorr von Rosenroth's *Kabbalah Denudata* (*The Kabbalah Unveiled*); Solomon Trismosin's alchemical treatise *Splendor Solis*; and several magical grimoires, including *The Sacred Magic of Abra-melin the Mage*, the *Key of Solomon*, and *The Grimoire of Armadel*.

In 1881, while still a member of Hengist Lodge, Mathers made a key contact in Dr William Wynn Westcott (1848–1925), who in addition to being a Freemason was also a member of Societas Rosicruciana in Anglia (SRIA). When his mother died in 1885, Mathers left Bournemouth and moved to London's Kings Cross. In London he enjoyed the hospitality extended to him by Westcott, joined the SRIA, and moved in

Hermetic and Theosophical circles. During this period Mathers also spent much of his time in the Reading Room of the British Museum, often arriving in the morning and staying until the early evening, studying and translating various ancient texts. It was here that he met another distinguished occult scholar, Arthur Edward Waite (1857–1942), with whom he soon discovered a mutual interest in all things Esoteric. According to Waite's anonymous tribute to Mathers, published in *The Occult Review* in April 1919—a few months after Mathers's death—Mathers initially spoke to Waite in the Reading Room "in a hushed voice and with [a] somewhat awful accent," announcing that he was a Rosicrucian and a Freemason and that, accordingly, "I can speak of some things, but of others I cannot speak." Mathers clearly loved secrets, and Waite's first impression was that he was somewhat eccentric, but in due course the two men would both become leading members of the Hermetic Order of the Golden Dawn.

As events transpired, Mathers played a key role in the Order's formation in 1888. Wynn Westcott had acquired a Masonic manuscript in cipher form that had been discovered among the papers of a deceased member of the SRIA and he invited Mathers to expand on the Rosicrucian cipher material so that it could form the basis of a "complete scheme of initiation." Mathers subsequently developed the five Masonic grades into a workable system suitable for the practice of ceremonial magic. As a result the Isis-Urania Temple of the Golden Dawn was established in London on March 1, 1888. Mathers, Westcott, and another member of the SRIA—Dr. William Woodman (1826–1891)—were confirmed as leaders of the Order. However, in a comparatively short space of time, Mathers would assume total control. Dr. Woodman died in 1891 and Westcott began redirecting his attention toward the Societas Rosicruciana in Anglia, finally resigning from the Golden Dawn in 1897 because rumors about his involvement in a magical organization were affecting his professional career as a crown coroner. The death of Woodman and the resignation of Westcott left Mathers effectively in control of both the Inner and Outer Orders of the Golden Dawn, even though he and his wife, French artist Moina Bergson (1865–1928), were now based in Paris, having moved there in 1891.

At the time of his assumption of total control of the Golden Dawn, Mathers was engaged in literary research at the Bibliothèque de l'Arsenal, where much of his time was taken up translating the French manuscript of a lengthy and important 15th-century grimoire titled *The Sacred Magic of Abramelin the Mage*. Supported financially by wealthy Golden Dawn member Annie Horniman, a tea heiress and key senior member of the London Isis-Urania Temple, Mathers was presiding over the Ahathoor Temple in Paris while simultaneously attempting to maintain dominance over the various Golden Dawn branches across the Channel. However, when Annie Horniman (1860–1917) queried various aspects of the funding of Mathers's stay in Paris, Mathers accused her of insubordination and expelled her from the Order.

Mathers's increasingly autocratic style and the expulsion of Annie Horniman from the Golden Dawn caused considerable disquiet among Order members and he caused even more consternation soon afterward when he charged senior Order member Mrs. Florence Farr Emery with "attempting to make a schism" in the Golden Dawn and expelled her from the Order as well. The expulsion of Annie Horniman and Mrs. Emery from the Golden Dawn led in turn to years of internal bickering and dissension among Order members, culminating in the fragmentation of the Order itself. Serious rifts appeared around 1903 with the defection of key Order members like Robert William Felkin (ca. 1858–1922) and Arthur Edward Waite (1857–1942), although other members, like J. W. Brodie-Innes (1848–1923), remained loyal to him. Mathers died in Paris on November 20, 1918. The probable cause was Spanish influenza, but according to Mathers's wife, his death resulted from a transcendental encounter with forces on the inner planes that no mortal could survive.

Nevill Drury

See also: Ancient and Mystical Order Rosae Crucis; Crowley, Aleister; Western Esoteric Tradition.

References

Colquhoun, I. *Sword of Wisdom: MacGregor Mathers and the Golden Dawn*. London: Spearman, 1975.

Gilbert, Robert A. *Revelations of the Golden Dawn: The Rise and Fall of a Magical Order*. Slough, UK: Quantum/Foulsham, 1997.

Harper, G. M. *Yeats's Golden Dawn.* London: Macmillan, 1974.

King, Francis. *Ritual Magic in England.* London: Spearman, 1970.

■ Mauritania

The present state of Mauritania lies on the western edge of the Sahara Desert in North Africa, and most of its 398,000 square miles of territory, especially in the north and east, is very sparsely inhabited desert. The majority of its 3,400,000 people live along the Atlantic coast or on the Senegal River that forms much of its southern border with Senegal. Mauritania also shares borders with Mali, Algeria, and the highly disputed Western Sahara territory.

Mauritania gained independence in a process that began following World War II, when it was named a French overseas province. In 1960 autonomy was granted and over the next six years Mauritania struggled to free itself from French economic control. However, the history of the region begins in the fifth century CE, when the Berber people who inhabited the region organized the ancient kingdom of Uagadu, centered on the city of Koumbi-Selah in southern Mauritania, near the Mali border. At its height, Koumbi-Selah was one of the largest cities in the world. During the years of this kingdom, Islam swept across Africa.

In 1076 the armies of the Almoravid Empire, centered on Marrakesh (present-day Morocco), conquered Uagadu, and introduced Islam to Central Africa but left a decade later to concentrate on the conquest of Spain. However, in the next century the Almoravids were replaced by a new Muslim empire, the Almohad, which brought all of Mauritania under its hegemony. This second empire collapsed in the next century, leaving Islam as its enduring legacy.

Over the next centuries, the region experienced intermittent wars between the Berbers and the Arabs.

People coming to Friday prayer in Chinguetti Mosque, Mauritania. (Images&Stories/StockphotoPro)

MAURITANIA

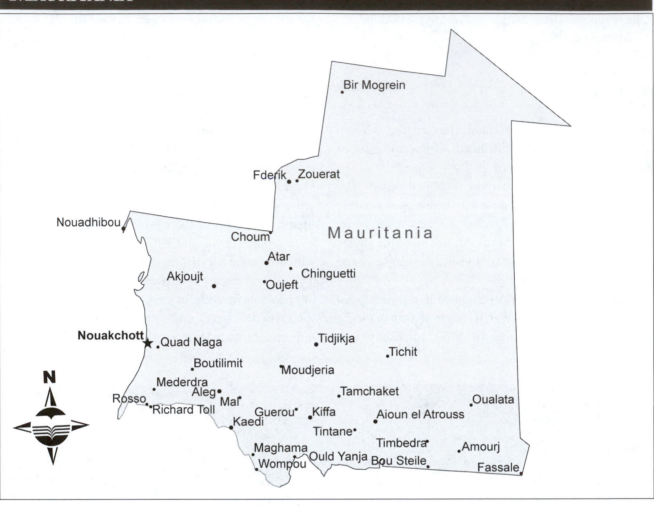

Their conflict came to a head at the end of the 15th century, when the Arabs won the Cherr Baba War. Their victory led to the establishment of a stratified society, with the Arabs (the *hassani*) at the top, the Berbers in the middle, and the residents in the south, the Fulah and the Soninkes, at the bottom. In 1858 the French invaded Mauritania, but they were not able to pacify the land until the 1930s.

Islam has been the religion of the region for a millennium and remains the official religion of the independent nation of Mauritania. As the leader of an Islamic state, the president must be a Muslim. He is assisted by a High Islamic Council. Muslims are prohibited by their religion from converting to another religion. The government provides some support to the Central Mosque in the capital city, but other mosques are supported by their members. Most Muslims in Mauritania are followers of the Malikite School, although Sufi brotherhoods of the Qadiriyya, Tijaniyya, and Shadhiliyya orders are also prominent.

The Roman Catholic Church came into Mauritania with the French army but only established a settled organization at the beginning of the 20th century. The church has been able to continue a presence in the post-French years, primarily serving expatriates from France, Senegal, and the Canary Islands. Protestants attempted to evangelize the country on several occasions but have failed to establish any work apart from the expatriate community. Attempts at proselytization are controlled by a law that bans the publication of any material that is considered against Islam or that contradicts or otherwise threatens Islam. Christian

Mauritania

Religion	Followers in 1970	Followers in 2010	% of Population	Annual % growth 2000–2010	Followers in 2025	Followers in 2050
Muslims	1,142,000	3,333,000	99.1	2.92	4,514,000	6,323,000
Ethnoreligionists	1,000	17,200	0.5	2.92	18,000	20,000
Christians	6,200	8,600	0.3	2.25	10,400	11,600
Roman Catholics	6,200	4,500	0.1	0.00	5,000	5,000
Independents	0	2,000	0.1	5.87	2,500	3,000
Anglicans	0	1,000	0.0	5.15	1,500	2,000
Agnostics	600	3,400	0.1	4.90	5,000	8,000
Baha'is	100	340	0.0	2.87	500	1,000
Atheists	0	280	0.0	2.90	500	700
Total population	**1,150,000**	**3,363,000**	**100.0**	**2.92**	**4,548,000**	**6,364,000**

churches (mostly Catholic) now exist in Nouakchott, Atar, Zouirat, Nouadhibou, and Rosso. The expatriate community of Christians and the few citizens who are considered Christians from birth practice their religion without government interference and may possess Bibles and other Christian religious materials in their homes.

J. Gordon Melton

See also: Qadiriyya Sufi Order; Roman Catholic Church; Shadhiliyya Sufi Order; Tijaniyya Sufi Order.

References

Pazzanita, Anthony. *Historical Dictionary of Mauritania.* Metuchen, NJ: Scarecrow Press, 2008.

Sakho, M. A. *La literature religieuse mauritanienne.* Nouakchott, Mauritania: Imprimerie Nouvelle, 1986.

Status of Christianity Profile: Mauritania. Nairobi, Kenya: Daystar University College, 1988.

Stewart, C. C., with E. K. Stewart. *Islam and Social Order in Mauritania: A Case Study from the Nineteenth Century.* Oxford: Clarendon Press, 1983.

■ Mauritius

Mauritius, an island in the Indian Ocean east of Madagascar, was uninhabited until it was settled by the Portuguese in the 1500s. The independent nation of the same name now includes this island and several nearby islands, the largest of which is Rodriguez Island. Together the islands have 784 square miles of land, which are home to 1,280,000 people.

Abandoned by the Portuguese, Mauritius was resettled in 1598 by the Dutch, who gave it its name. The French recolonized it in 1715, and the British won control in 1814 as part of their prize after the defeat of Napoleon. By 1835, when slavery was abolished, Africans constituted 70 percent of the population. To deal with the labor shortage after the abolition of slavery, sugar plantation owners turned to India. Over the next century almost half a million Indians from Tamil Nadu and Andhra Pradesh in southern India and from various spots in northern India entered the country as indentured servants. They eventually constituted the majority of the island's population, by latest count some 68 percent.

Hinduism is now the dominant religion of Mauritius. The Indian immigrants brought with them the spectrum of traditional Hindu beliefs and practices and have established both Vaishnavism and Shaivism throughout the country. There are also a large number of adherents of the Arya Samaj, a 19th-century reform movement that has found an affinity with American Unitarianism. Most Arya Samaj members have northern Indian heritage.

In the 20th century, a variety of new Hindu movements appeared in Mauritius. The country was an early home of the International Society for Krishna Consciousness, an American movement with roots in

MAURITIUS

Bengali devotional (*bhakti*) yoga. There is also a group attached to the Vedanta Societies/Ramakrishna Math and Mission, also based in Bengal.

The Indians also brought Islam with them. Muslims constitute about 16 percent of the Mauritian population, the great majority being Sunni Muslims of the Hanafite School. There are also Sunnis of the Shafiite school, some Shias, and a few Ismailis, affiliated with the Shiah Fatimi Ismaili Tayyabi Dawoodi Bohra. The largest dissenting group are the Ahmadiyyas, not recognized as orthodox Muslims by the rest of the community.

Christianity was established on Mauritius following the colonization by the French. The Lazarist Fathers, a Catholic order, arrived in 1722. They surrendered their work to the Benedictines in 1819, following the change of political control from France to Great Britain. At the same time, a vicariate was established that included Madagascar, South Africa, and Australia, with Port Louis, the Mauritian capital, as its center. Port Louis was named a diocese in 1852. The Roman Cath-

olic Church is the largest Christian body on the island of Mauritius and claims the allegiance of most of the residents of Rodriguez Island as well.

The Church of England initiated work on Mauritius in 1810 and remains the largest Protestant church. In the 20th century the Church of England granted autonomy to its overseas affiliates and the Mauritian parishes are now part of the Church of the Province of the Indian Ocean. Mauritius has been set aside as a diocese. The archbishop resides in the Seychelles. Shortly after the Church of England was established in Mauritius, missionaries from the London Missionary Society arrived. Their work fed the development of the Church of Scotland, a Presbyterian body. In the mid-19th century, the Church of the New Jerusalem also began a mission, now related to the General Church of the New Jerusalem.

Through the 20th century, a number of Protestant and Free church groups began work, including the Assemblies of God, the Seventh-day Adventist Church, and the Jehovah's Witnesses. The Adventists entered

Mauritius

Religion	Followers in 1970	Followers in 2010	% of Population	Annual % growth 2000–2010	Followers in 2025	Followers in 2050
Hindus	379,000	551,000	42.7	0.91	573,000	539,000
Christians	297,000	435,000	33.7	0.93	476,000	504,000
Roman Catholics	280,000	334,000	25.9	1.79	329,000	336,000
Protestants	5,900	105,000	8.1	4.15	140,000	160,000
Independents	1,300	9,000	0.7	4.56	11,000	13,000
Muslims	132,000	217,000	16.8	0.92	238,000	245,000
Agnostics	1,600	33,500	2.6	0.92	50,000	70,000
Baha'is	6,500	24,800	1.9	0.92	35,000	50,000
Chinese folk	1,600	17,300	1.3	0.92	19,000	20,000
Buddhists	5,800	3,200	0.2	0.92	3,500	3,500
Sikhs	0	3,000	0.2	0.92	3,400	3,600
Ethnoreligionists	0	2,600	0.2	0.91	2,800	3,000
Atheists	400	1,600	0.1	0.92	2,500	4,000
New religionists	100	750	0.1	0.90	1,000	1,500
Total population	**824,000**	**1,289,000**	**100.0**	**0.92**	**1,404,000**	**1,444,000**

Mauritius in 1914, and their Mauritius Conference, now part of the Indian Ocean Union Mission, is now the third largest Christian body on the island.

Other religious groups that have formed congregations on the islands include the Baha'i Faith; the Church of Christ, Scientist; the Christadelphians; and the Church of Jesus Christ of Latter-day Saints (LDS). Since its entrance in 1995, the LDS has built a thriving branch now connected to the South Africa Durban Mission.

The ethnic and religious pluralism on Mauritius has dictated the necessity of interreligious contact, and an interreligious committee has functioned for many years. The country's Constitution guarantees freedom of religion, including the freedom to propagate one's religious views to others. Registered religious groups receive some support from state funds.

J. Gordon Melton

See also: Arya Samaj; Assemblies of God; Baha'i Faith; Benedictines; Christadelphians; Church of Christ, Scientist; Church of England; Church of Jesus Christ of Latter-day Saints; Church of Scotland; Church of the Province of the Indian Ocean; General Church of the New Jerusalem, The; Hanafite School of Islam; International Society for Krishna Consciousness; Ismaili Islam; Jehovah's Witnesses; London Missionary Society; Roman Catholic Church; Seventh-day Adventist Church; Shaivism; Shiah Fatimi Ismaili Tayyabi Dawoodi Bohra; Vaishnavism; Vedanta Societies.

References

Eisenlohr, Patrick. *Little India: Diaspora, Time, and Ethnolinguistic Belonging in Hindu Mauritius.* Berkeley: University of California Press, 2007.

Emrith, M. *History of Muslims in Mauritius.* Vacoas, Mauritius: Editions Le Printemps, 1994.

Hazareesinghg, K. *The Religion and Culture of Indian Immigrants in Mauritius and the Effect of Social Change.* Port Louis, Mauritius: Indian Cultural Association, 1966.

Metz, Helen Chapin. *Indian Ocean: Five Island Countries.* Washington, DC: U.S. Government Printing Service, 1995.

Naqapen, Amei dei n. *The Indian Christian Community in Mauritius.* Port-Louis, Mauritius: Roman Catholic Diocese of Port-Louis, 1984.

Selvon, S., and L. Rivière. *Historical Dictionary of Mauritius.* Metuchen, NJ: Scarecrow Press, 1991.

Mayan Calendar

In the 1990s, an obscure calendar from ancient Meso-America gained some importance among followers of

Calendar from the Mayan civilization, which thrived during the 3rd to 10th centuries, was highly accurate and based on complex mathematical and astronomical calculations. (Corel)

Western Esotericism. The importance of the Mayan calendar was initially proposed by art historian José Argüelles (b. 1939) in his 1987 book, *The Mayan Factor: Path Beyond Technology.* The unexpected success of *The Mayan Factor* among followers of the New Age led him to put out a new calendar for their use, a 13 Moon/28 Day Calendar focused on phases of the Moon, which many New Agers had begun to follow. This calendar runs from July 26 to July 24 of the following year, a total of 364 days. July 25 is left as a "Day out of Time." Argüelles attempted to synchronize his calendar with the Mayan calendar, while drawing on other non-Mayan sources, and make it available to modern people who otherwise live by the Common Era calendar (the modern revised Gregorian calendar used by most countries as the 21st century begins). His

work was highly criticized by his scholarly colleagues, though those criticisms were usually ignored by his New Age audience. Through the several organizations he founded, the Planet Art Network and the Foundation for the Law of Time, he has continued to speculate on the calendar and its modern spiritual and metaphysical implications.

Even before Argüelles, however, speculation concerning the Mayan calendar was made by Michael D. Coe, who in his 1966 book *The Maya* offered the suggestion, in passing, that civilization might end on December 24, 2011. In later editions he revised the date to the now familiar December 23, 2012. The idea was discussed by Frank Waters in his *Mexico Mystique: The Coming Sixth Age of Consciousness* (1975) and again mentioned briefly by Argüelles in both *The Trans-*

formative Vision (1975) and *The Mayan Factor* (1987), but the idea was largely forgotten in the 1990s with the New Age movement in sharp decline.

Then after 20 years of neglect, Daniel Pinchbeck revived speculation about the Mayan calendar and the 2012 date while linking them to a wide variety of beliefs surrounding UFOs, though his best-selling 2006 book *2012: The Return of Quetzalcoatl* was essentially based on his own experiments with mood-altering substances and channeling. He also tempered Michel Coe's original apocalyptic predictions and proposed a shift from materialistic to spiritual consciousness in its stead. By the time Pinchbeck's book appeared, the most popular prophetic Esoteric text of the 1990s, James Redfield's *The Celestine Prophecy*, appeared to have faded in popularity, and within a short time a host of new books appeared discussing and offering alternative speculation about what, if anything, would occur in December of 2012.

While the literature on 2012 generally refers to the Mayan calendar, the Mayans actually had three calendars. Two of these calendars were the Haab' and the Tzolk'in. The Haab' was the 365-day political calendar. It consists of 18 20-day divisions, plus a 5-day period added at the end of the year. These last five days, having been added to bring the year close to the solar year, were to some degree out of the system and viewed as unlucky and unfortunate. The Haab' started at the Winter Solstice and marked out the planning for an agricultural year.

The Haab' was combined with the Tzolk'in, the 260-day religious ceremonial calendar. At the beginning of the Mayan cycle, the Haab' and Tzolk'in would begin running side by side simultaneously. When the Tzolk'in ran out, it would simple begin again. It took 52 years for the Tzolk'in to once again end and begin at the Winter Solstice as did the Haab'. The 52-year cycle would operate for the culture's needs and most concerns, as very few lived to be more than 52 years old. The combined Haab'-Tzolk'in calendars named but did not number the years.

For the recording of events more than 52 years ago, a third calendar was employed, the so-called Long Count calendar. It is this calendar around which modern prophetic speculation has gathered. The Long Count begins counting years from what most believe to be the Mayans' date for creation, which would be August 11, 3114 BCE in the Common Era calendar used in most countries today. The Long Count calendar runs for 5,125 years and hence will run out in 2012 and start over again.

The 2012 date has been correlated with a variety of facts. Some have suggested, for example, that in 2012 the plane of the Solar System will line up exactly with the plane of the Milky Way, thus completing a wobble cycle that takes 5 times the 5,125 years of the Mayan calendar, or approximately 26,000 years.

Prophecies concerning 2012 vary from anticipations of catastrophe to hopes for positive social change and large-scale spiritual transformation for individuals. The expected changes vary from the visible and disruptive alternation of social and natural structures to the invisible and hence difficult to detect changes in human consciousness.

J. Gordon Melton

See also: Calendars, Religious; Western Esoteric Tradition; Winter Solstice.

References

Argüelles, José. *The Mayan Factor: Path Beyond Technology.* Rutland, VT: Inner Traditions/Bear & Company, 1987.

Braden, Greg. *The Mystery of 2012: Predictions, Prophecies and Possibilities.* Louisville, CO: Sounds True, Incorporated, 2009.

Coe, Michael D. *The Maya.* London: Thames & Hudson, 1966, 1987.

Miller, Mary, and Karl Taube. *The Gods and Symbols of Ancient Mexico and the Maya: An Illustrated Dictionary of Mesoamerican Religion.* London: Thames & Hudson, 1993.

Schele, Linda, and David Freidel. *A Forest of Kings: The Untold Story of the Ancient Maya.* New York: William Morrow, 1990.

Pinchbeck, Daniel. *2012: The Return of Quetzalcoatl.* Tarcher, 2006.

Pinchbeck, Daniel, and Ken Jordan, eds. *Toward 2012: Perspectives on the Next Age.* Tarcher, 2009.

Sanderford, Susan K. *What's Up With 2012?* Scotts Valley, CA: CreateSpace, 2008.

■ Mayotte

Mayotte, an island in the Mozambique Channel between Madagascar and Mozambique, has traditionally been considered part of the Comoro Islands. It became the center of French culture during several centuries of French rule. In 1974, when the Comoros Islanders decided to become independent of French rule, the residents of Mayotte voted to remain connected to France. France had established both a naval and an air base on the island. Today, some 216,000 people live on the island's 144 square miles of land.

Meanwhile, the status of the island remains a matter of intense dispute. France has refused to back away from its control of the island in spite of a United Nations resolution in 1991 recognizing the Comoros's claim to the land. The Camoros Islands' claim has been affected by its political instability.

Prior to 1975, Mayotte shares a common history with the Comoro Islands. Both are overwhelmingly Muslim, most residents being Shafaiite Sunnis. However, the Christian presence in Mayotte is stronger than it is in the Comoros, especially since the expulsion of Protestant missionaries there in 1978. The Roman Catholic Church is the largest Christian body, its work being attached to the Diocese of Ambanja (Madagascar). There are only a few thousand members.

J. Gordon Melton

See also: Roman Catholic Church; Shafiite School of Islam.

MAYOTTE

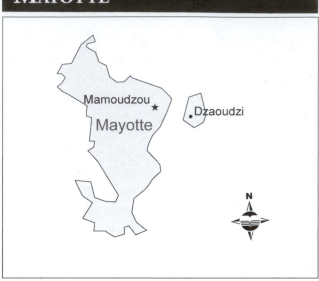

References

Barrett, David, ed. *The Encyclopedia of World Christianity.* 2nd ed. New York: Oxford University Press, 2001.

Beslar, J. "An Ethnography of the Mahorais (Mayotte, Camaro Islands)." Ph.D. diss., University of Pittsburgh, 1981.

Headley, Stephen. *Islamic Prayer Across the Indian Ocean: Inside and Outside the Mosque.* London: RoutledgeCurzon, 2000.

Lambek, Michael. *Knowledge and Practice in Mayotte: Local Discourses of Islam, Sorcery and*

Mayotte

Religion	Followers in 1970	Followers in 2010	% of Population	Annual % growth 2000–2010	Followers in 2025	Followers in 2050
Muslims	42,600	128,000	98.5	2.46	185,000	338,000
Christians	360	940	0.7	1.52	1,100	1,200
Roman Catholics	260	500	0.4	1.90	500	500
Protestants	100	200	0.2	0.00	250	300
Marginals	0	120	0.1	0.00	150	200
Ethnoreligionists	0	580	0.4	2.49	700	900
Agnostics	0	350	0.3	5.69	600	1,200
Atheists	0	50	0.0	2.44	100	200
Total population	**43,000**	**130,000**	**100.0**	**2.46**	**187,000**	**342,000**

Spirit Possession. Toronto: University of Toronto Press, 1993.

Mazdaznan

Mazdaznan is a form of neo-Zoroastrianism which, although declining, is still present in several Western countries. Otto Hanisch (1844–1936), later known under the pen name of Otoman Zar-Adusht Ha'nish, was born in 1844, probably in Teheran, to a Russian father and a German mother. His place of birth was later disputed, and nothing certain is known about his life until he surfaced in 1900 in Chicago. There, he claimed to have been initiated while in Iran (or Tibet) into a mysterious Zoroastrian order. He quickly gathered a number of American followers and in 1917 established, in California, an organization known as Mazdaznan. Among the early followers were Maud Meacham (1879–1959) and Swiss-born David Ammann (1855–1923), the latter being instrumental in spreading Mazdaznan into Europe. Hanisch died in 1936, and his successors are known as Electors.

While Mazdaznan led a comparatively quiet existence in the United States, it became quite controversial in Europe. Critics claimed that Mazdaznan was not a genuinely Zoroastrian religion, putting great stress on Hanisch's idiosyncrasies. Because of his ideas about the Aryan race, Hanisch was accused in several European countries of being racist and anti-Semitic, although he was also critical of Nazism. In fact, the Mazdaznan organization was banned in Nazi Germany as early as 1935.

Crucial to Mazdaznan philosophy is the idea of reconverting Earth into a garden, where God will converse and cooperate with humans. Breathing exercises are also very important, and in fact this practice spread from Mazdaznan to a number of other groups, in German-speaking Europe particularly. Also popular were Mazdaznan songs and ideas about food and diet, which attracted a number of medical doctors to the movement.

The Mazdaznan movement declined steadily through the last half of the 20th century, and as of 2008 no longer has any public presence. Neither the website of the German section (http://www.mazdaznan.de) nor the former American headquarters (http://www.mazdaznan.org) is active. No activity appears to be carried out any longer from the Bonita address, where Mazdaznan remains legally incorporated.

Mazdaznan
4364 Bonita Rd., #617
Bonita, CA 91902-1421

Mazdaznan Canada
94 Autumn Place
St. Catharines, ON
Canada L2P 3W8
http://www.mazdaznan.ca/cart/
Massimo Introvigne and PierLuigi Zoccatelli

See also: Vegetarianism; Zoroastrianism.

References

Ha'nish, Otoman Zar-Adusht. *Avesta in Songs*. Los Angeles: Mazdaznan Press, 1946.

Ha'nish, Otoman Zar-Adusht. *God and Man United. A Study of the Evolution of Religion from 10,000 B.C.* Los Angeles: Mazdaznan Press, 1975.

Ha'nish, Otoman Zar-Adusht. *The Philosophy of Mazdaznan*. Los Angeles: Mazdaznan Press, 1960.

Mecca

Mecca, a city of modern Saudi Arabia, is the geographical center of Islam. The significance of Mecca is based on its being the site of the first shrine built to worship God by Adam and Eve, and the acceptance by Ibrahim (Abraham) to sacrifice his son Ismail were this to be the will of God. It is also the ancestral home of the Prophet Muhammad and so a symbol of his faithfulness to God and to delivering the divine message. It is the site of the annual *hajj*, or pilgrimage ritual, in Islam, and is situated in the Hejaz region of what is today Saudi Arabia. It is the direction toward which Muslims pray and a city that has always been involved in pilgrimages of one sort or another. Vast numbers go on pilgrimage today, and the management of the pilgrimage is a major operation and the responsibility of the Saudi government.

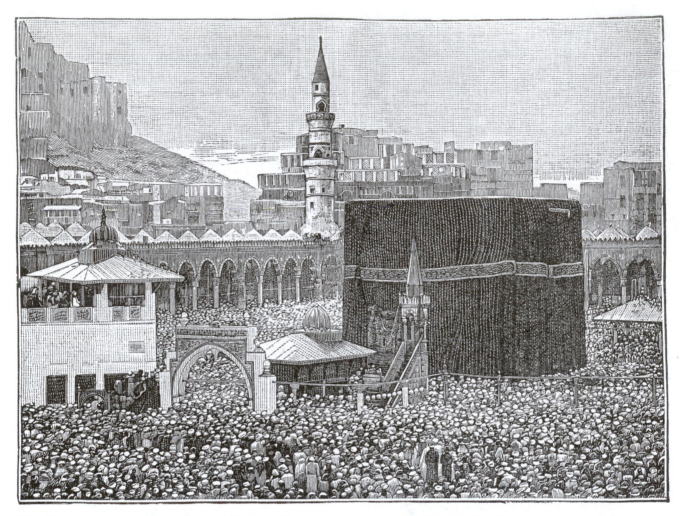

This 19th-century engraving shows the Kaaba at Mecca, in present-day Saudi Arabia. The Kaaba is a shrine that houses the Black Stone of Mecca, the focal point for Muslim prayer and final destination for pilgrims to Mecca. (John Clark Ridpath, *Ridpath's History of the World*, 1901)

Mecca is the site of the Great Mosque in the midst of which is the Kaaba, a black stone said to have been an altar created by Ibrahim and Ismail to worship the one God. This pure monotheism was weakened subsequently by the importation of local deities into the site, which became the center of pilgrimage of Arab tribes. The Quraysh tribe was the dominant force in the city and controlled much of the pilgrimage business, although the extent to which the city was an important economic hub in the spice trade is now controversial. The clan from which Muhammad came, the Hashimites, remained the de facto rulers of the city for a long time, even under the Ottoman Empire, but they were overturned twice subsequently by the Wahhabis, who were supported by the al-Saud family, and eventually Mecca was incorporated into what is today Saudi Arabia. The Saudis are responsible for looking after the two religious sites of Mecca and Medina and organizing the tremendous inflow of pilgrims on the hajj and *umra*. Although Mecca has a tremendous religious significance in Islam, it has never been particularly important politically. Even at the time of the Prophet his main base was Medina not Mecca, and during the various Islamic empires the center of power was always in a capital city far from the Hejaz, in which Mecca is situated. It was largely a center of the pilgrimage and also of scholarship since many pious Muslims stayed there after their pilgrimage, although it has to be said that even in the pursuit of the Islamic sciences Mecca has remained a backwater until recently, the main intellectual centers generally being elsewhere.

The valley in which Mecca lies is called Becca, sometimes linked with the Arabic word *tabakka*, which refers to people crowding together and a lack of water. *Baka* means lamenting, and the local conditions are indeed harsh, with long dry periods being interrupted by sudden and very damaging floods. We are told in the Koran that the first house of God was built there (3:96). It became the *qiblah*, the direction in which Muslims should pray, but initially Jerusalem fulfilled this role, until a later revelation changed the direction.

The hajj is the pilgrimage to Mecca, compulsory for every adult Muslim who can undertake it once in a lifetime (3:91). It takes place in the month of Dhul Hijjah, 70 days after Ramadan. The pilgrimage celebrates three events: the forgiveness and reunion of Adam and Eve, Ibrahim's willingness to sacrifice his son Ismail, and the obedience of the Prophet Muhammad. Adam and Eve were reunited on the plain of Arafat and they are said to have built the Kaaba shrine to worship the one God. It is made of black granite and is now covered with a black cloth with Arabic calligraphy on it. The shrine was rebuilt by Ibrahim to commemorate both the dream he had when he was told to sacrifice his son Ismail to God and the overcoming of Satan. In the end Ibrahim instead sacrificed a ram to God, the origin of the Eid al-Adha festival at the end of the hajj during which sheep are slaughtered. It was here that Ismail and his mother were desperate for water and the Zam Zam spring appeared to save them from death. The water from this spring is still collected today and given to pilgrims, and sent to other parts of the world also. All these events occurred and are commemorated now in the vicinity or actually in Mecca.

Oliver Leaman

See also: Abraham/Abram; Eid al-Adha; Medina; Muhammad; Pilgrimage; Wahhabi Islam.

References

Crone, Patricia. *Meccan Trade and the Rise of Islam.* Princeton, NJ: Princeton University Press, 1987.

Hammoudi, Abdellah. *A Season in Mecca: Narrative of a Pilgrimage.* Cambridge: Polity Press, 2006.

Wheeler, Brannon. *Mecca and Eden: Ritual, Relics, and Territory in Islam.* Chicago: University of Chicago Press, 2006.

Medicine Buddha's Birthday

The Medicine Buddha (Bhaisayja-guru or in Japan, Yakushi-nyorai) is the bodhisattva most known as a healing force in the Mahayana Buddhist tradition. According to Buddhist teachings, prior to attaining enlightenment, Medicine Master made 12 vows to cure all illnesses and lead all people to enlightenment. The circumstances of the making of the vows are revealed in the Medicine Master Sutra, which also speaks of the benefits to be offered to believers who invoke Medicine Buddha's name.

Medicine Buddha is charged with healing all diseases in the sick as well as any deficiencies of wisdom we might have. He is often depicted with the attending bodhisattvas Sunlight (on his left) and Moonlight (on his right) who lead the cadre of bodhisattvas that surround Medicine Buddha. His body is transparent, and he is pictured as wearing a monastic robe and as seated with his legs crossed. His left hand lies in his lap and usually holds the medicine bowl while his right hand forms the charity mudra and holds either a branch with fruit, or just the fruit of the myrobalan, a medicinal plant found in India and other tropical countries. His birthday is celebrated on the 22nd day of the 8th lunar month.

J. Gordon Melton

See also: Bodhisattva; Calendar, Religious; Mudras.

References

Boheng, Wu, and Cai Zhuozhi. *100 Buddhas in Chinese Buddhism.* Trans. by Mu Xin and Yan Zhi. Singapore: Asiapac Books, 1997.

Vessantara. *Meeting the Buddhas: A Guide to Buddhas, Bodhisattvas, and Tantric Deities.* Birmingham, UK: Windhorse Publications, 1998.

Medicine Wheel (Wyoming)

Located high on a peak in the Bighorn Range in Wyoming, Medicine Wheel is an ancient Native American ritual site made of stones laid in a circular pattern, some 80 feet in diameter. At the center of the circle is a horseshoe-shaped cairn, about 12 feet in diameter and 2 feet in height. The central cairn is connected to the outside circle of stones by 28 lines of stones, giving the overall site a resemblance to a modern bicycle wheel. In addition, around the outer ring of stones are six additional unevenly spaced cairns.

The Medicine Wheel is located at a 9,642-feet elevation and is accessible only the 2 warmest summer months. It has been dated to as early as 10,000 BCE or as late as 1700 CE. Since its discovery by European Americans, it has been used and maintained by various groups to the present. The wheel is now seen as an integral part of other sites in the mountainous West, especially the more than 100 wheels that have been found in South Dakota, Wyoming, Montana, Alberta, and Saskatchewan. Near the wheel, at lower altitudes, are a number of sites used for different Native ceremonies, from vision quests to sweat lodges.

Archaeological explorations of the site suggest that the central cairn is the oldest element in the present site. It possibly has at times supported a central pole. In 1974, Jack Eddy opened archaeo-astronomical studies of the site. The placement of the cairns suggested an alignment toward the rising and setting sun at the Summer Solstice. He also checked the alignments with a variety of stars associated with the solstice. He found the cairns marked the rising points of the stars Aldebaran, Rigel, and Sirus, which are known to play important roles in both Cheyenne and Lakota mythology.

In addition, Jack Robinson, an astronomer who visited the site, found an alignment with the rising star Fomalhaut, some 28 days before the solstice, a possible rationale for the 28 "spokes" of the wheel. The rising of Fomalhaut would give people a month's warning of the approaching Summer Solstice. Thus it has been hypothesized that, from about 1200 to 1700 CE, possibly best dates for the circle's construction, that Fomalhaut, Aldebaran, Rigel, and Sirius could have identified the season on the mountain with Fomalhaut rising 28 days and Aldebaran 2 days prior to Summer Solstice, and Rigel rising 28 days after the solstice, and Sirius 28 additional days later, the true end of summer.

In the last generation, the site has enjoyed increasing use by Native Americans across a range of tribal affiliations. Since 1988, two Native organizations, the Medicine Wheel Alliance and the Medicine Wheel Coalition for Sacred Places, have worked with government agencies to preserve the site as sacred space and limit any development of the area. The Forest Service especially had projected improvements that allow greater access. An agreement signed in 1996 between Native Americans and a spectrum of government agencies recognizes Medicine Mountain, and the peak upon which the Wheel rests, as sacred space and radically limits tourist development and any foresting or mining. Twenty-four days each summer, the site will be exclusively for Native ritual use. Most recently, the site has been cordoned off to prevent its deterioration. Native groups have worked to have as large an area around the site as possible declared as protected territory.

J. Gordon Melton

See also: Summer Solstice.

References

Hirschfelder, Arlene, and Paulette Molin. *Encyclopedia of Native American Religions*. New York: Facts on File, 2000.

Magli, Guilio. *Mysteries and Discoveries of Archaeoastronomy: From Giza to Easter Island*. New York: Springer, 2009.

Stanford Solar Center. "Bighorn Medicine Wheel." http://solar-center.stanford.edu/AO/bighorn.html. Accessed July 15, 2009.

Wiklliamson, Ray. *Living the Sky: The Cosmos of the American Indian*. Norman: University of Oklahoma Press, 1987.

Medinah

Medinah was the city to which the Prophet Muhammad retreated when rejected initially by his hometown of Mecca. He built his power base there, and the first mosque, and from there launched his eventually successful campaign to overcome the opposition in Mecca. The Islamic calendar starts with his journey to Medinah and it is today a secondary site of pilgrimage after Mecca, containing important tombs such as those of

Lithograph of people entering the mosque of Medinah, the site of the tomb of Muhammad and the second most holy city of Islam after the spiritual capital, Mecca. (Library of Congress)

the Prophet himself, his daughter Fatimah, and the first two caliphs. It is closed to non-Muslims.

About 200 miles north of Mecca is Medinah, originally called Yathrib, which was a significant city at the time of the Prophet Muhammad. In Arabic "madinah" just means "city" and perhaps it acquired this label because it was the first site of Islamic political power, and indeed Muhammad's arrival in the city constitutes the start of the Islamic calendar. The city is sometimes called Medinat al-Nabi (the city of the Prophet) or Medinat al-munawarrah (the radiant city). Muhammad moved there when driven out of Mecca and found the city a more welcoming environment for the message he was transmitting, although not without difficulties in the form of its stubborn Jewish popula-

tion who were resistant to Islam. We are told that the Constitution of Medinah was written to formulate an agreement between the Muslims and the existing communities in the area, in particular the Jews, and for some time an uneasy peace resulted. When hostilities eventually broke out with the Meccans the Jews were taken to have sided with the enemy of the Muslims and were entirely wiped out in the area, as far as we can tell, destroying any significant opposition to the new Islamic movement.

Medinah is important today for its sites, in particular the Mosque of the Prophet where he is buried and also the grave of the first two caliphs, Abu Bakr and Umar, and the Prophet's daughter Fatimah, and is very much on the pilgrimage route of Muslims when they go on the *hajj* to Mecca. There are said to be other tombs there, of the Prophet's grandson Hasan and the caliph Uthman. The rather elaborate tombs were destroyed by the Saudis; the Wahhabi theology on which the regime is based disapproves of praying at graves and the associated rituals. The first mosque ever built is also there, the Quba Mosque, although it has gone through many changes over time.

Medinah is in a much more favorable part of the Hejaz, with water and surrounded by a plain. It is surrounded by a substantial wall that originates in the 12th century CE and there is also a castle and four gates, of which the Bab al-salam is the most remarkable in design. The city has many houses and gardens, benefiting from the availability of water, and more industrial and technological activities than the other holy city, Mecca. Non-Muslims are not supposed to go to either city, but the exclusion zone in Medinah is far narrower than in Mecca.

Oliver Leaman

See also: Mecca; Mosques; Muhammad; Pilgrimage.

References

Ali Kazuyoshi, Nomachi, and Seyyad Hossein Nasr. *Mecca the Blessed, Medina the Radiant: The Holiest Cities of Islam.* New York: Aperture, 1997.

Dutton, Yasin, Malik ibn Anas, and Muhammad ibn Muhammad Ra'i. *Original Islam: Malik and the Madhhab of Madina.* New York: Routledge, 2007.

Esin, Emel, and Haluk Doganbey. *Mecca the Blessed, Madinah the Radiant.* New York: Crown Publishers, 1963.

Lekker, Michael. "Muhammad at Medina, a Geographical Approach." *Jerusalem Studies in Arabic* 6 (1985): 29–62.

Meditation

The word "meditation" has two distinct meanings. The first refers to philosophical thinking or deliberation that focuses on a particular topic or question, usually of deep existential or metaphysical import (as in the philosopher Descartes' *Cartesian Meditations*). In the second meaning, meditation does not engage the thinking process but, on the contrary, seeks to disengage it. To avoid confusion between the two, the second is sometimes called contemplation. Meditation understood as contemplation is relevant to religious and spiritual practices and will be elaborated upon here. Meditation in this meaning refers to dwelling in a state of consciousness with a single-pointed focus or dwelling in a state of alertness or wakefulness without a particular focus. It also refers to various practices developed for stilling the mind and bringing about these states of consciousness. Meditation practices as we know them today originated in religious contexts, as part of spiritual disciplines designed to help aspirants realize the spiritual goals envisioned by their religions. Today, increasing numbers of people practice some form of meditation, either for spiritual or religious reasons or for other reasons such as general health and well being.

Meditation in the Major Religious Traditions and in Contemporary Life
All the major religious traditions of the world as well as many indigenous religions have developed some form of meditation practices. These vary greatly depending on the cultural context and the purposes assigned to them by the traditions. The common religious objective in all meditation practices is to alter the aspirant's everyday consciousness in which the mind is crowded by thoughts and images and driven by desires and anxieties to a mode in which it is more receptive to and capable of realizing the spiritual goals affirmed by his or her religion.

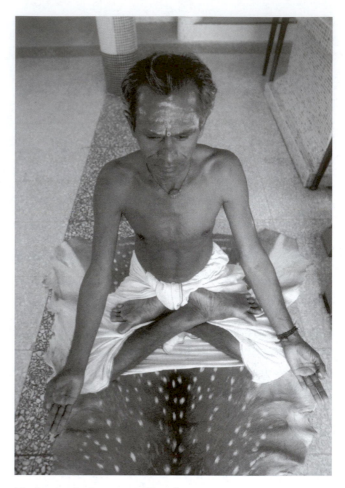

Meditating Indian guru. (Corel)

In monotheistic Western religions (Christianity, Islam, Judaism), God is usually conceived as being ultimately separate from humans, and consequently the highest spiritual goal for human beings is a union (not necessarily oneness) with God. Accordingly, meditation practices in these traditions developed out of the practice of prayer and are designed to deepen the aspirant's devotion and unwavering attention to God. They may consist of chants or repetitions of single words or visualizations that employ images or symbols of God. Contemplative prayers help the aspirant dwell in the qualities of God (such as all-knowing, loving, and merciful). Individuals who seek surrender to God as their life's foremost goal are called mystics in these traditions, and they typically utilize meditation practices along with other practices such as abstinences and privations to attain as direct a connection with God as is possible within the context of their religious beliefs.

Asian religions (Buddhism, Hinduism) tend to conceive of God as ultimately not separate from humans, though many of them acknowledge the presence and importance of God or gods. Meditation practices that are devotional in nature and similar to those in the monotheistic religions abound in these traditions. Additionally, these traditions have elaborate and systematically developed techniques for cultivating the aspirants' mental and spiritual capacities so they may realize God or ultimate reality within their own innermost being. These techniques have had a considerable influence on contemporary Western spirituality, perhaps because they can be relatively easily extracted from their cultural and religious contexts and adapted to contemporary Western cultural and spiritual life.

Meditation has established itself as one of the most important elements in new and contemporary forms of spirituality and also as part of the evolving practices aimed at promoting general health and well being. Beginning in the 1960s in Western popular culture, a variety of meditation practices have been loosely adapted from the Asian and Western Esoteric and to a lesser extent from the Christian and Jewish mystical traditions to fit contemporary lifestyles in which personal meaning and experience is greatly valued. Individuals who embrace traditional Western religions also use meditation to enhance their personal and experiential connection to the beliefs and values of their religion. In addition to these spiritual and religious contexts, contemporary medicine and health science has taken interest in the research and application of meditation.

Types of Meditation Practice Meditation is commonly practiced by sitting still on a cushion or a chair, but it can also be practiced by standing, walking, or lying down. Some practices employ visual imagery and suggestion, as in guided imagery. Most meditation practices that do not involve suggestion fall into one or the other of two basic types, concentrative or opening up, or some combination of the two.

Guided imagery practices may be done individually or in groups with the help of a meditation teacher, guide, or pre-recorded instructions that take the participants on a journey within their minds. The images and meanings suggested typically help calm and soothe the mind and also provide positive affirmations for health and well being. Guided imagery can be done sitting up or lying down, and the effort involved is in following the guidance provided. It is more structured than other types of meditation and for this reason accessible to a wider range of people, including those with health problems and disabilities.

Concentrative meditation, as well as the others described in the sequel, is usually done sitting on a chair or on a cushion with legs folded. Attention is focused on a single object, usually a sound (often referred to by the Sanskrit term *mantra*) or a visual object (*yantra*) such as a concentric image (*mandala*), an image of a deity, or the flame of a candle. The object may also be a natural process such as breathing. Whenever attention veers off of the meditation object, the practitioner brings it back to the object. The objectives of concentrative meditation include calming and stilling the mind and the development of one-pointed concentration and the capacity to abide in whatever the state that is being cultivated. Very deep concentration, which usually requires much practice, can lead to blissful states of stillness called *samadhi*. They may involve experiences of oneness with God or reality—the so-called supramundane states (*dhyana*) the Buddha is said to have experienced while practicing with the yogis with whom he lived in the forest before his enlightenment. In the Hindu tradition, Patanjali's *Yoga-Sutras* is a manual par excellence for concentrative meditation and for cultivating s*amadhi*.

In opening-up meditation, the objective is to relax the narrow focus of intentional consciousness and allow it to open up into a spacious awareness that focuses on nothing in particular yet extends to everything within and around the practitioner without limit. In Zen, the practice of "just sitting," or *shikantaza*, is an example of this type of practice. In Tibetan Buddhism and in other traditions a practice that focuses on the open, limitless sky as the object of meditation is designed to develop this type of expanded, spacious awareness.

The best known meditation practices in the West derive from those developed in the Theravada Buddhist tradition and are known as *vipassana*, or insight meditation. Original descriptions of these can be found in two texts that are part of the Pali canon and are attributed to the historical Buddha. These are the *Anapana-Sati* and the *Satipatthana Sutta*. In the Buddha's time, apparently the aspirants began their training with concentrative practices called *samatha*, and only after developing their skill in abiding with concentrative meditation would they take up opening-up practices called vipassana, in which the aspirant practices mindful attention without selective focus.

Contemporary forms of vipassana taught both in Asia and in the West combine elements of *samatha* and vipassana, with the practitioner focusing on a process that naturally occurs within his or her body and/or mind as a meditation object. Such natural processes include the flow of air around the nostrils or the rising and falling of the abdomen as one breathes, sensations coursing through the body, and the arising and passing of thoughts or mental images within the mind. In concentrative meditation one attempts to still the mind by restricting the movement of thoughts and images, whereas in the combined form attention is returned to the chosen process again and again but is allowed to freely move within its confines. In pure opening-up type of meditation the freedom of the mind's movement is unlimited and attention can easily get lost in thought, whereas in the combined form the restriction of the movement to the process chosen as the object of meditation serves as an anchor for attention.

The objective of vipassana is to cultivate nonreactive openness, or "equanimity," toward whatever happens during the meditation and clear attention that does not get lost in the content of thoughts and images. The cultivation of these qualities in turn enhances the practitioner's capacity for insight into the nature of phenomena, including his or her own thought patterns and emotional reactions. For this reason, vipassana is also referred to as "insight meditation." The major Asian sources for vipassana practice in the West are the Theravada Buddhist traditions in Burma (Myanmar) and Thailand, and many first-generation Western meditation teachers trained with masters from these traditions during the 1960s and 1970s.

Meditation in Contemporary Life The apparent neutrality of vipassana and other Buddhist meditation practices with respect to religious or metaphysical beliefs has allowed their techniques to be adopted not only by Christian and other non-Buddhist religious practitioners but by those within the secular scientific community as well. The therapeutic benefits of vipassana have been recognized in contemporary medicine, and during the 1980s and 1990s the techniques of this meditation approach have been modified and developed into easily accessible forms that do not require knowledge or acceptance of the larger Buddhist worldview or beliefs. These include mindfulness-based stress reduction (MBSR), developed by Jon Kabat-Zinn for treatment of chronic pain and stress, and acceptance and commitment therapy (ACT) developed by Stephen Hayes and colleagues. Modified vipassana practices have also been successfully integrated into cognitive-behavioral therapy—the most commonly employed therapeutic approach today to mental and emotional disorders such as depression and anxiety. Known as mindfulness-based cognitive-behavioral therapy (MBCT), this therapy was developed by Mark Williams, Zindel Segal, and John Teasdale.

The effectiveness of MBSR, ACT, and MBCT in comparison with other treatment modalities has been extensively researched. Research has also pinpointed the basis of their effectiveness increasingly precisely, as having to do with the development of what psychologists call "meta-cognitive awareness" through mindfulness practice. Such awareness allows the practitioner to recognize thoughts in the moment that they arise in his or her mind as simply thoughts and thus remain unaffected by their content or meaning. Depression and anxiety are typically fueled by negative thought content in which patients suffering from these conditions get absorbed. Meta-cognitive awareness developed through mindfulness practice can help patients break free of such absorption and the associated tendency to relapse into depression or anxiety.

Kaisa Puhakka

See also: Asceticism; Buddha, Gautama; Devotion/ Devotional Traditions; Vipassana International Academy; Yoga; Zen Buddhism.

References

Beck, Charlotte J. *Everyday Zen: Love and Work*. New York: HarperCollins, 2007.

Das, Lama Surya. *Awakening the Buddha Within: Tibetan Wisdom for the Western World*. New York: Broadway Books, 1998.

Davich, Victor. *Eight Minute Meditation: Quiet Your Mind, Change Your Life*. New York: The Berkeley Publishing Group, 2006.

Feuerstein, Georg. *The Yoga-sutra of Patanjali: A New Translation and Commentary*. Rochester, VT: Inner Traditions International, 1989.

Goldstein, Joseph. *Insight Meditation: The Practice of Freedom*. Boston: Shambhala, 2003.

Hart, William. *Vipassana Meditation as Taught by S. N. Goenka*. New York: Harper & Row, 1987.

Hayes, Steven C., Victoria M. Follette, and Marsha M. Linehan, eds. *Mindfulness and Acceptance: Expanding the Cognitive Behavioral Tradition*. New York: Guilford Press, 2004.

Kabat-Zinn, Jon. *Wherever You Go, There You Are: Mindfulness Meditation in Everyday Life*. New York: Hyperion, 1995.

Khema, Ayya. *Being Nobody, Going Nowhere*. Boston: Wisdom Publications, 1987.

Kornfield, Jack, and Paul Breiter. *A Still Forest Pool: The Insight Meditation of Achaan Chah*. Wheaton, IL: Quest Books, 1993.

Laird, Martin. *Into the Silent Land: A Guide to the Christian Practice of Contemplation*. New York: Oxford University Press, 2006.

Mendenhall, Sarah. *Guided Imagery Meditation: The Artistry of Words*. Bloomington, IN: AuthorHouse, 2008.

Mund, Todd. *Christian Growth through Contemplation*. Lincoln, NE: iUniverse, Inc., 2003.

Nhat Hahn, Thich. *Breathe, You Are Alive: The Sutra on the Full Awareness of Breathing*. New York: Parallax Press, 1990.

Nhat Hahn, Thich. *The Miracle of Mindfulness*. Boston: Beacon Press, 1987.

Roehmer, Lizabeth, and Susan Orsillo. *Mindfulness and Acceptance-based Behavioral Therapies in Practice*. New York: Coleman Barks, 1995.

Rossman, Martin. L. *Guided Imagery for Self-healing*. Publishers Group West, 2000.

Sekida, Katsuki. *Zen Training: Methods and Philosophy*. Boston: Shambhala, 1985.

Taimni, I. K. *The Science of Yoga: Translation and Commentary on Patanjali's Yoga Sutra*. Wheaton, IL: Quest Books, 1981.

Underhill, Evelyn. *Mysticism: A Study in the Development of Spiritual Consciousness*. New York: Meridian, 1911/1974.

Wallace, B. Alan. *Buddhism with an Attitude: The Tibetan Seven-point Mind Training*. Ithaca, NY: Snow Lion, 2003.

Williams, Mark, John Teasdale, Zindel Segal, and Jon Kabat-Zinn. *The Mindful Way through Depression: Freeing Yourself from Chronic Unhappiness*. New York: Guilford, 2007.

Wynne, Alexander. *The Origin of Buddhist Meditation*. New York: Routledge, 2007.

Medjugorje

The authenticity of the apparitions that have taken place since 1981 in Medjugorje, Bosnia-Herzegovina (then a part of the Marxist Socialist Federal Republic of Yugoslavia), is among the most contentious topics in the contemporary Roman Catholic Church. In 1981 2 boys and 4 girls, then between 10 and 17 years old, began receiving daily messages from Mary, who appeared under the title of Queen of Peace (feast day: June 25). These messages continue today. Like those of the apparitions at Fatima, Portugal, their themes include conversion, penance, prayer, the rosary, the family, and, particularly, peace. At first the Tito regime acted against the devotion and against Franciscan Jozo Zovko, the "counter-revolutionary" parish priest and spiritual advisor to the visionaries. After 1984 the government did not interfere with the cultus, possibly in part because of the hard currency that its pilgrims brought in, at that time primarily from Italy, Austria, and France.

A controversy about this Marian devotion also arose within the church. In this region of Europe, the Franciscan Order has a strong tradition of local pastoral care. The Fathers, popular for their spiritual care, refused to turn over parts of their pastoral responsibilities to the bishop of Mostar-Duvno. Against the background of this controversy, the bishop had growing doubts about the authenticity of the apparitions and messages, and suspicions of manipulation by the Franciscans who controlled the parish and the seers arose.

Over the years many influential persons in the Catholic Church, right up through Pope John Paul II (r. 1978–2005), have spoken out on the cultus, while others have expressly refused to take a position on it. The church is caught in a field of interests, which

Statue of Our Lady of Medjudjorge, Bordeaux, France. (J. Gordon Melton)

include those of the adherents who really "see" Mary, other Catholics who consider it all the work of Satan, yet others who hypothesize pious deception on the part of the visionaries and their advisors, and still others who assume machinations by the Franciscans are involved. Whichever view is correct, three diocesan investigative committees have declared the appearances and messages inauthentic, and in 1998 the Vatican itself also accepted that standpoint.

However, over against the negative position of the church hierarchy stands a massive following of devotees and believers who find considerable strength in the shrine. In 1987 a total of about 5 million pilgrims had visited Medjugorje; in 1991 that number had reached 15 million, and in 2009, more than 60 million, including thousands of priests and hundreds of (arch-) bishops. The vast majority of the visitors are Catholics of conservative or traditional outlook. Because of the opposition of the hierarchy, organized devotional ac-

tivity exists in a problematic spiritual vacuum, and links have arisen with other contested apparitions and devotions around the world, such as the Lady of All Nations in Amsterdam.

The spiritual and theological autonomy of the devotion is further stimulated by a powerful relation between the devotion to Our Lady of Peace and the Charismatic movement, a revivalist endeavor that tends to disassociate itself from institutional ecclesiastical structures. Charismatic prayer groups, initiated from Medjugorje, function as models for other groups elsewhere in the world and serve to further spread word of the Medjugorje apparitions. Intensive mission activities are supported by world tours by the visionaries and the Fathers themselves. Since 1997 a dedicated radio station, Radio MIR [peace] Medjugorje, helps spread the messages. Medjugorje prayer groups, foundations, committees, magazines, and websites have been established all over the world and branch shrines have been created, giving the millions of devotees who cannot come to Medjugorje opportunities for frequent and nearby devotion.

As a result of the massive growth of interest in Medjugorje, it is no longer possible for the movement to retreat from its position and continued rejection by the Vatican is less likely. The movement's position is strengthened by the constant reference to the "fruits" its activity has borne for the Catholic Church, such as conversions, vocations for the priesthood, and miraculous healings. Since 2000, when the Belgian cardinal Godfried Danneels—influential in the church hierarchy —argued for reopening the discussion of Medjugorje, more clerics pleaded for officialization, but as of 2009 their efforts were in vain; the deadlock between the Vatican and the local Franciscans and their pressure groups still continues.

St. James Parish
Zupni Ured
88266 Medjugorje
Bosnia-Herzegovina
http://www.medjugorje.hr (official website)
http://www.medjugorje.org/
http://www.medjugorje.com/

Information Center MIR Queen of Peace
Gospin Trg 1

88266 Medjugorje
Bosnia-Herzegovina

Peter Jan Margry

See also: Charismatic Movement; Devotion/ Devotional Traditions; Fatima; Marian Devotion, World Network of; Mary, Blessed Virgin; Roman Catholic Church.

References

Bax, Mart. *Medjugorje: Religion, Politics, and Violence in Rural Bosnia.* Amsterdam: VU Uitgeverij, 1995.

Claverie, Élisabeth. *Les guerres de la vierge. Une anthropologie des apparitions.* Paris: Gallimard, 2003.

Craig, M. *Spark from Heaven: The Mystery of the Madonna of Medjugorje.* London: Hodder & Stoughton, 1988.

Jones, E. Michael. *The Medjugorje Deception: Queen of Peace, Ethnic Cleansing, Ruined Lives.* South Bend, IN: Fidelity Press, 1998.

Laurentin, René, and René Lejeune. *Messages and Teachings of Mary at Medjugorje: Chronological Corpus of the Messages.* Milford, OH: The Riehle Foundation, 1988.

Margry, Peter Jan. "Marian Interventions in the Wars of Ideology: The Elastic Politics of the Roman Catholic Church on Modern Apparitions." *History and Anthropology* 20, no. 3 (2009).

Sivric, Ivo. *The Hidden Side of Medjugorje: A Theologian's Observations.* Vol. 1. Saint Francis du Lac, Ca: Psilog, 1989.

Skrbis, Zlatko. "The Apparitions of the Virgin Mary of Medjugorje: The Convergence of Croatian Nationalism and Her Apparitions." *Journal of the Association for the Study of Ethnicity and Nationalism* 11, no. 3 (2005): 443–462.

Zimdars-Swartz, Sandra L. *Encountering Mary: Visions of Mary from La Salette to Medjugorje.* New York: Avon Books, 1992.

Meenakshi Temple (Madurai)

The Meenakshi Sundareshvarar temple complex, one of the largest in India, is located at Madurai, in the state of Tamil Nadu, at the southern tip of India. Madurai, one of India's older cities, traces its origin to the story of Indra, the king of the gods, who after fighting the demon Vrtrasura, was wandering the fields and forests of southern India. At one spot, he found a *linga* of Siva and began to worship it. A local resident who saw him then reported the occurrence to the local king, who immediately ordered a temple be built on the site. Around the temple a city grew. Madurai had its ups and downs over the years, but reached its zenith under the Nayak dynasty (1559–1736 CE).

The temple's original site seemed certainly to have been dedicated to the goddess Minakshi and worship of her in the region was from ancient times. The first Meenakshi Sundareshvarar temple was built by Maaravaramban Kulasekara Pandyan (r. 1258–1308), who ruled the ancient Pandyan kingdom that covered much of South India. It was later abandoned and fell into ruins. A new temple structure was begun by Viswanath Nayakar, the first king of the Nayak dynasty, in the 16th century and completed by one of his descendants, Tirumalai Nayakar, in the 17th century.

The temple complex is on a set-aside site measuring 700 feet by 850 feet. The outer wall is punctuated with 4 towers at the 4 entrance ways, each tapering upward to a height of some 120 feet. These are all elaborately decorated with multi-colored stucco carvings of a myriad of people and scenes from Hindu mythology.

Within the courtyard, the main temples take up a space of 225 feet by 150 feet. The modern temple also contains, in addition to the inner sanctum with the goddess's image, a linga for Siva worship, as well as a large statue of Siva as Nataraja, the Lord of the Dance. Visitors will also find the overarched area of the eight Shaktis (female deities); a golden lotus pond adjacent to the Meenakshi shrine in which devotees may bathe; the hall of parrots, where they are heard as singing praises of the two main divinities of the temple—Siva and Meenakshi, and the 1,000 pillar hall with the wall paintings that picture scenes from the Purana (Hindu holy texts) that relate the story of Siva's adventures.

Each spring, the temple is a focal point for the Chittirai Festival, at which the story of the wedding of Siva and Minakshi is re-enacted and celebrated. On the 10th day of the 12-day festival, large temple carts

A lake in the courtyard of the Sri Meenakshi Hindu temple in Madurai, India. (Sergey Kushnir/Dreamstime.com)

with the 2 lovers are carried around the temple. In Hindu lore, Meenakshi is the brother of the deity Vishnu and, of course, has a prominent place in their marriage. The temple also includes statues and pictures of Vishnu.

Constance A. Jones

See also: Hinduism; Pilgrimage; Temples—Hindu.

References

Fuller, Chris. *A Priesthood Renewed: Modernity and Traditionalism in a South Indian Temple.* Princeton, NJ: Princeton University Press, 2003.

Fuller, C. J. *Servants of the Goddess: The Priests of a South Indian Temple.* New York: Cambridge University Press.

Harman William P. *The Sacred Marriage of a Hindu Goddess.* Bloomington: Indiana University Press, 1989.

Hudson, D. Dennis. "The Two Chitra Festivals of Madurai." In *Religious Festivals of South India and Sri Lanka*, edited by Gray R. Welbon and Glenn E. Yocum. Delhi: Manohar, 1982.

Meiji Jingu

The Meiji Jingu, a Shinto shrine located in Tokyo, is the leading center of national Shinto in Japan. It was built in 1920 to honor the life and accomplishments of the Emperor Meiji (1852–1912) and his wife, the Empress Shoken (1850–1914). Born on November 3, 1852, Emperor Meiji oversaw what was considered a prosperous era in Japan generally, and he was viewed as leading a transition period that took the country from the premodern to the modern world. Not the most popular ruler within the Buddhist community, during his half century (1867–1912) on the throne, he had led in re-establishing Shinto as the state religion and creating initiatives to integrating it into the identity of the Japanese people. He was initially buried in Kyoto, his birthplace. Empress Shoken was born on May 28, 1850, in Kyoto. During her reign as empress, she became best known for her promotion of the Japanese Red Cross. Like her husband, she too was buried in Kyoto.

Following the deaths of the emperor and his wife, by which time World War I was in full progress, the Japanese leadership began to consider how they could properly honor their deceased rulers. The decision to construct the site and the subsequent effort to build it could be seen as the culmination of a half century of regulations that had been put in place to guide the rise of Shinto to its place within Japanese society and the downgrading of Buddhism.

The Japanese military served as the official sponsors for the site, which was designed to visibly focus the faith in the divinity of the emperor. State Shinto was elevated to a role beyond mere religion. All gave it homage and were otherwise left free to choose a religious faith, albeit from among the relatively small number of religions that had been recognized by the government. Individual citizens were expected to show themselves as proper Japanese by publicly assenting to and showing appropriate behavior, at least minimally, relative to the state Shinto system. The designation of the emperor as divine created numerous problems for both Buddhists and Christians.

The shrine, located in the midst of a large park, was completed and ready to receive the souls of the royal couple in 1920, their souls being enshrined on November 1. One enters the park through Japan's largest *tori* (gate). There are three main buildings: the Outer Shrine, the Inner Shrine, and the Main Shrine. Believers will upon entering the site initially engage in a brief purification ceremony that includes rinsing their hands and gurgling water. Once inside, they may do one or more of a variety of devotional actions, such as making an offering, acknowledging the deity spirits (*kami*), and/or engaging in an act seeking one's fortune. The nearby Treasure Museum houses a selection of the couple's personal possessions along with a photo exhibition of their life.

The shrine was destroyed during World War II, and, following the war, the United States insisted that the emperor's role be transformed from absolute monarch to symbol of Japanese unity (similar to the role of the British monarch). Under pressure, in 1946, the emperor issued a formal renunciation of his role as divine spirit (kami). Shinto was also discontinued as the state-supported faith. After a decade of getting used to the new order of religious life, in 1958, the government undertook the project of rebuilding the shrine.

Today, while continuing as a center of Shinto practice—it is the site for 11 Shinto festivals annually—the Meiji Shrine has become a major recreational magnet for Tokyo residents and tourists. The large surrounding garden includes an art museum and a variety of sports facilities for baseball, tennis, golf, swimming, and others. For nature buffs, the park includes more than 300 species of trees native to Japan that were brought from across the country. The shrine attracts several million visitors annually.

Edward A. Irons

See also: Pilgrimage; Shinto.

References
Kasahara, Kazuo. *A History of Japanese Religion.* Tokyo: Kosei Publishing, 2001.
Reader, Ian, Esben Andreasen, and Finn Stefansson, eds. *Japanese Religions: Past and Present.* Honolulu: University of Hawaii Press, 1933.

Melkite Catholic Church

The Melkite Catholic Church is a Byzantine Catholic church centered in Syria and Lebanon. It is termed "Byzantine" because its liturgy is derived from the Greek liturgy developed by the Ecumenical Patriarchate and widely utilized by the several Greek churches in the Middle East. It is Catholic in that it is in full communion with the Roman Catholic Church. The Melkite Church emerged in the 18th century in Syria following a schism within the Syrian Orthodox Church of Antioch. Antioch is an ancient center of Christianity and the seat of one of the four ancient patriarchates of Eastern Orthodoxy.

In 1724 a schism developed in the Syrian Church when two parties, one centered in Aleppo and one in Damascus, each elected a patriarch. The ecumenical patriarch stepped in and declared the candidate of the Aleppo party to be the new patriarch of Antioch. The other candidate, Cyril VI, was deposed and forced into exile in Lebanon. Then, four years later, in 1729, Pope Benedict XIII (1649–1730) recognized Cyril as the new patriarch of Antioch, and authorized his forming a new jurisdiction, the Melkite Catholic Church. (The word "Melkite" derives from the word for king in the Syriac and Lebanese languages.) The new church retained its Eastern liturgy and traditions (including the ordination of married priests) and adopted the several changes that would bring it into alignment with Roman Catholic doctrine, especially on those matters in which the Roman Catholic Church and Eastern Orthodoxy have disagreed since the 11th century.

The Melkite Catholic Church has approximately one million members worldwide. The church is centered in Syria and Lebanon and has expanded into Palestine and Egypt. Its patriarch was given the additional titles of patriarch of Jerusalem and patriarch of Alexandria (two of the sites of the other ancient Christian patriarchates). In 1848 the church was granted recognition by the authorities of the Ottoman Empire and headquarters were moved to Damascus from its original site in Sidon, Lebanon. Beginning late in the 19th century, Melkite Christians joined in the dispersion of Syrians and Lebanese around the world. Communities were established in Brazil, Venezuela, Canada, and the United States, all of which evolved into new dioceses.

The church is currently headed by Patriarch Gregory III Laham (b. 1933). He took office in 2000. It supports eight religious orders, a seminary at Raboué, Lebanon, and a theological institute in Harissa, Lebanon. For many years it sent its candidates for priesthood to Saint Anne's Seminary in Jerusalem, operated by the White Fathers, but that school closed in 1967. In 2008 it reported 1,347,000 members worldwide. The church is active in the Middle East Council of Churches.

Melkite Catholic Church
BP 22249
Damascus
Syria
http://www.pgc-lb.org/english/index.shtml
http://www.melkite.org/ (U.S. Eparchy of Newton)

J. Gordon Melton

See also: Ecumenical Patriarchate/Patriarchate of Constantinople; Middle East Council of Churches; Roman Catholic Church; White Fathers.

References

Descy, Serge. *The Melkite Church: An Historical and Ecclesiological Approach.* Newton, MA: Sophia Press, 1993.

Liesel, N. *The Eastern Catholic Liturgies: A Study in Words and Pictures.* Westminster, MD: Newman Press, 1960.

Roberson, Ronald G. *The Eastern Christian Churches: A Brief Survey.* 5th ed. Rome: Edizioni Orientalia Christiana, Pontificio Istituto Orientale, 1995.

Mencius

ca. 372–289 BCE

Mencius is the second most famous figure in Confucianism. A great teacher, Mencius lived during the Warring States period of Chinese history, characterized by a weak imperial dynasty and feudal wars. The constant bickering and alliance-building associated with this warfare was under the banner of an eventual unification under one state. The old gentry families had lost power, leaving the way for ambitious newcomers to rise through the social ranks. In this general atmosphere of confusion and collusion the intellectual challenge was to find a new set of world values beyond those dealing with individual goodness.

Very little is known of Mencius's life. Scholars disagree over his dates. He seems to have been born in what is now Shandong Province, not far from Qufu, where Confucius was born. It was suggested that he was a pupil of Confucius's grandson, Zisi.

Mencius and his followers often traveled to different states and so observed the social climate carefully. In contrast to his great adversaries, the Mohists, who preached a doctrine centered on efficient state functioning in order to maximize the general welfare, Mencius emphasized the Confucian virtues of humanity (*ren*) and righteousness (*yi*). For Mencius humanity was innate and central to each individual. Righteousness grew

The Chinese philosopher Mencius taught that humans are innately good but would act nobly only if and when they had peace of mind. Such statements are contained in The Book of Mencius, the standard commentary on the teachings of Confucius. (Ivy Close Images/StockphotoPro)

from that sense of humanistic compassion. By focusing on righteousness, Mencius deepened Confucian doctrine, which had previously focused on the relationships between individuals and how to regulate those through virtues. For Mencius the focus became the relationship between the individual and the group or social environment. Righteousness became a social virtue as well as a personal virtue. Adhering to righteousness would ensure fairness and social wellbeing.

Mencius concluded early on that humans are basically good, something Confucius had only indirectly implied. His position allowed later thinkers such as Li Ao and Wang Yangming to develop intriguing theories

of human nature. Confucianism continues to be associated with the tenet of innate goodness.

Edward A. Irons

See also: Confucius; Confucianism.

References

Cho-yun Hsu. "The Unfolding of Early Confucianism: The Evolution from Confucius to Hsun-tzu," In *Confucianism: The Dynamics of Tradition*, edited by Irene Eber, 23–37. New York: Macmillan, 1986.

McGreal, Ian, ed. *Great Thinkers of the Eastern World*. New York: HarperCollins, 1995.

Mennonite Church in the Netherlands

The Protestant Reformation called for a break between church and state and for a church consisting of those adults who had turned to God with faith. One radical movement within the Reformation, Anabaptism, began in Switzerland. Anabaptists took their name from the second baptism they offered to adherents who had previously been baptized as infants. Their new ideas led both the Roman Catholic Church and Protestant churches to attempt their suppression. The course of the movement was deeply affected by an incident at Münster, Germany, where the most radical branch of the movement attempted to set up the kingdom of God and awaited Christ's intervention as secular authorities tried to retake the city.

Anabaptism was brought to the Netherlands by Melchior Hoffman (ca. 1500–1545), a leader who differed from some of his Anabaptist colleagues by his emphasis on the imminent end of the world. It was in the Netherlands that the movement was to be revived and reformed by a Dutch convert, Menno Simons (1496–1559), who would lend his name to the movement. As a Roman Catholic priest, he had begun to study the Bible on the question of the sacraments and concluded that the Roman Catholic doctrines of infant baptism and the physical presence of Christ in the Eucharist were not supported by scripture. He came to the fore as a dissident leader in the mid-1530s, when he spoke out against the Münsterites. By 1536 he fully identified with the more moderate Anabaptists, and the next year he was ordained as their leader.

Simons assumed the task of articulating a theology to defend the idea of a separated church. This theology emphasized biblical authority and the justification of believers by faith in Christ. The immediate question, however, was survival, and Simons attempted to answer all the major attacks made on the group by leaders in the established churches.

Indeed, life for a Mennonite leader was still dangerous, and Simons had to be on the move constantly. The community suffered repression and produced a number of martyrs. Persecution in Holland finally ended in 1674 with the country's independence from Spain, and Holland emerged as the most tolerant nation in Europe. Galenius Abrahamsz de Haan (d. 1706) was the dominant leader of the Mennonite Church through the end of the 17th century. In 1699 he wrote an important defining statement of the Mennonite position. As the community prospered, it also was able to aid in other, less hospitable locations around the continent.

In the relatively tolerant climate of the 18th century, the church declined radically from 180,000 to fewer than 30,000 members. Many members converted to Dutch Reformed faith, and others left for America. To deal with the decline, in 1811 an all-Mennonite conference, the Algemeene Doopsgezinde Societeit, was founded. By midcentury the decline had been stopped, and some growth occurred through the 20th century. In 1847 a group had organized the Mennonite Missionary Association to focus interest on foreign missionary activity. The first missionary was sent to Java in 1851. In the 1950s it was superseded by the European Mennonite Evangelism Committee, a cooperative effort of the Dutch, French, German, and Swiss Mennonites.

At present, the Dutch Mennonites constitute the largest Mennonite body in Europe, with 10,200 members. The Algemeene Doopsgezinde Societeit is a member of the World Council of Churches and cooperates with the Mennonite World Conference.

Algemeene Doopsgezinde Societeit
Singel 454
NL-1017 AW
Amsterdam

The Netherlands
http://www.ads.nl/ (in Dutch)

J. Gordon Melton

See also: Mennonite World Conference; Roman Catholic Church; World Council of Churches.

References

Dyck, Cornelius J. *An Introduction to Mennonite History*. Scottsdale, PA: Herald Press, 1967.

Hamilton, Alastair, Sjouke Voolstra, and Piet Visser, eds. *From Martyr to Muppy: A Historical Introduction to Cultural Assimilation Processes of a Religious Minority in the Netherlands: The Mennonites*. Amsterdam: Amsterdam University Press, 2002.

Hoekstra, E. G., and M. H. Ipenburg. *Wegwijs in religieus en levensbeschouwelijk Nederland. Handboek religies, kerken en stromingen.* 3rd ed. Kampen, the Netherlands: Kok, 2000.

Krahn, C. *Dutch Anabaptism: Origin, Spread, Life and Thought (1450–1600)*. The Hague: Martinus Nijhoff, 1968.

Lapp, John A., and C. Arnold Snyder, eds. *Testing Faith and Tradition: Global Mennonite History Series: Europe*. Intercourse, PA: Good Books, 2006.

Mellink, A. F. *Documenta Anbaptistica Neerlandica*. Leiden: E. J. Brill, 1975.

Mennonite Church, U.S.A.

The Mennonite Church, U.S.A., the largest of the Mennonite bodies in North America, was founded in 2002 by the merger of the Mennonite Church and the General Conference Mennonite Church.

The Mennonite Church was the oldest of the several Mennonite groups in the United States. Mennonites came to America as early as 1643, though it was not until 40 years later that the first Mennonite settlement appeared—in Germantown, Pennsylvania (now part of Philadelphia). This early community became known for its stance against the introduction of slavery into the American colonies and it influenced later opposition to slavery by the Friends (Quakers).

Mennonite boy, Lancaster, Pennsylvania, 1942, descendent of the original German settlers of Pennsylvania. (Library of Congress)

Mennonite ecclesiastic organization emerged as needed. In 1725 the congregations in Pennsylvania called a conference in which the major issue was the publication of an English translation of the Confession of Dortrecht, the primary statement of Mennonite beliefs. It was not until the 19th century, however, as the Mennonites moved to different sections of the country and issues of accommodating to American life began to emerge, that a regular conference structure developed. The conferences created a biennial General Assembly, the highest legislative body in the church.

Traditionally, the Mennonite Church was a rural church whose members worked primarily in agriculture. However, during the last half of the 20th century, it developed a significant urban membership. That change was accompanied by a more liberal approach to traditional behavioral norms, especially manifest in the abandonment of the "plain clothing" that has distinguished many Mennonite groups. Members also began to use modern conveniences, including automobiles and electricity (still eschewed by more conservative Mennonites).

In the mid-19th century, John H. Oberholtzer (1805–1895), a young Mennonite minister, began to anticipate the direction that the Mennonite church would take in the 20th century. Meanwhile, he found himself in conflict with his brethren in the Franconia District (located in Pennsylvania). He began to protest the plain, collarless coat worn by most ministers, which he saw as an arbitrary requirement having nothing to do with the Mennonite faith. He then argued for the adoption of a written constitution so that proceedings could be conducted more systematically. Finding but little support, Oberholtzer withdrew from the Franconia District in 1847. That same conference then proceeded to expel him. Sixteen ministers and several congregations left with him and formed a new conference.

The new denomination quickly moved to adopt a more liberal view of the ban (or shunning, the practice of avoiding contact with those who have withdrawn or been excluded from the fellowship), opened communication with other Mennonite groups, allowed intermarriage with persons of other denominations, and, eventually, provided salaries for their clergy. Oberholtzer also founded the first Mennonite newspaper in America, the *Religioeser Botschafter* (later *Das Christliche Volksblat*).

From the beginning, Oberholtzer envisioned the union of all Mennonite congregations then—and still —divided into many factions. At the same time, thousands of Mennonite immigrants were moving to America and bringing into existence new churches. In 1855, Daniel Hoch (1805–1878), a minister to several Mennonite churches in Ontario, Canada, aligned with an Ohio congregation under the leadership of Reverend Ephraim Hunsberger (1814–1904) to form the Conference Council of the Mennonite Communities of Canada—West and Ohio. In Lee County, Iowa, two isolated congregations united and called for a systematic evangelistic effort among Mennonites who had

now resided some distance from the main body of believers in the East. Representatives of some of the above groups met in 1860 in Iowa and invited Oberholtzer to attend. He was selected to chair the gathering that proceeded to form the General Conference Mennonite Church. They adopted Oberholzer's vision of uniting all the Mennonite congregations in the United States and Canada.

Both the Mennonite Church and the General Conference shared a common belief in accord with most Mennonite bodies. As the two groups began talk of uniting, a summary "Confession of Faith in a Mennonite Perspective" had been adopted by both groups in 1995. This 24-article confession affirms the church as a Trinitarian body in the mainstream of Christian belief relative to affirmations on biblical authority, creation, salvation in Jesus Christ, and the church of believers. It describes three ordinances: baptism, the Lord's Supper, and foot washing. It also retains the traditional position of the Mennonites as a peace church and emphasizes the role of the family. The issues that had led the Oberholzer group to leave in the 1880s had long since been decided.

The united church is organized around a congregational polity, and congregations are located in 21 regional conferences. The national church commissions in the two churches that oversaw publishing, support of work in other countries, education, home missions, social concerns, and congregational life in the two former churches have been merged. They carry on a large mission program with congregations on every continent. In the United States, home mission work is conducted among Native Americans, African Americans, Jews, the Spanish-speaking, Asian refugees, and the deaf. There are four church-wide ministry agencies: Mennonite Mission Network, Mennonite Education Agency, Mennonite Publishing Network, and Mennonite Mutual Aid. The new church sponsors four colleges, two universities, and two theological seminaries.

In 2006 the Mennonite Church, U.S.A. had approximately 109,174 members in 935 congregations. The church cooperates with the Mennonite World Conference.

Mennonite Church, U.S.A.
722 Main St.

PO Box 347
Newton, KS 67114-0347

500 S Main St.
PO Box 1245
Elkhart, IN 46515-1245
www.mennoniteusa.org/

J. Gordon Melton

See also: Amish; Friends/Quakers; Mennonite World Conference.

References

Dyck, Cornelius. *An Introduction to Mennonite History: A Popular History of the Anabaptists and the Mennonites.* Lancaster, PA: Herald Press, 1993.

Hostetler, Beulah Stauffer. *American Mennonites and Protestant Movements: A Community Paradigm.* Scottdale, PA: Herald Press, 1987.

Kaufman, Edmund G. *General Conference Mennonite Pioneers.* North Newton, KS: Bethel College, 1973.

Kraybill, Donald B., and C. Nelson Hostetter. *Anabaptist World USA.* Scottsdale, PA: Herald Press, 2001.

Krehbiel, H. P. *The History of the General Conference of the Mennonite Church of North America.* 2 vols. Newton, KS: Author, 1889–1938.

The Mennonite Encyclopedia. 4 vols. Scottsdale, PA: Mennonite Publishing House, 1955–1959.

Springer, Nelson P., and A. J. Klassen, eds. *Mennonite Bibliography, 1631–1961.* 2 vols. Scottdale, PA: Herald Press, 1977.

Waltner, James H. *This We Believe.* Newton, KS: Faith and Life Press, 1968.

Wenger, John Christian. *The Doctrines of the Mennonites.* Scottsdale, PA: Mennonite Publishing House, 1950.

Wenger, John Christian. *The Mennonite Church in America.* Scottsdale, PA: Herald Press, 1966.

Mennonite World Conference

The Mennonite World Conference is an ecumenical association uniting Mennonites globally. The Mennonites are the main group inheriting the tradition of the Swiss Brethren and other 16th-century groups that rejected the idea of a state-aligned church as well as infant baptism (thus they are called Anabaptists). From the earliest times, Mennonites have been pacifists and activists in peacemaking endeavors.

The Mennonite World Conference grew out of suggestions circulated in the years immediately prior to World I that communication and fellowship should be facilitated among the many churches of the Mennonite heritage (including some such as the Brethren in Christ that do not have the word "Mennonite" in their name). Tabled during the war, the proposals finally came to fruition in 1925, with the first international gathering of Mennonites, which was held in Switzerland on the anniversary of the first Anabaptist baptism in 1625. The initial conference was attended primarily by German, Dutch, French, and Swiss delegates. Only one North American was at the Conference.

The idea of cooperative activity among Mennonites grew considerably after World War II with the transformation of Mennonite missions into autonomous churches and the development of a consciousness of the Mennonite family as a global community. As the 21st century begins, some 84 Mennonite and Brethren in Christ churches from 49 countries on 5 continents cooperate through the Mennonite World Conference.

The Conference promotes international meetings; cooperative action in social service, issues of world peace and community reconciliation; the creation of professional networks of pastors, educators, women, peace workers, and historians; and the communication of news, testimony, and teaching from churches around the world. The Conference has two headquarters, one in France and one in Canada. Its website includes an extensive directory of Mennonite and Brethren in Christ churches worldwide, and well as other demographic data.

Mennonite World Conference
8, rue du Fossé des Treize
67000 Strasbourg
France

Mennonite World Conference
50 Kent Ave.
Kitchener, Ontario N2G 3R1

Canada
http://www.mwc-cmm.org/

J. Gordon Melton

See also: Anabaptism; Brethren in Christ; Mennonites; Paraguay, Mennonites in.

References

Beecher, Claude, et al. *Testing Faith and Tradition.* Intercourse, PA: Good Books, 2006.

Bender, Ross T., and Alan P. F. Sell, eds. *Baptism, Peace, and the State in the Reformed and Mennonite Traditions.* Waterloo, ON: Wilfrid Laurier University Press, 1991.

Checole, Amelu, et al. *Anabaptist Songs in African Hearts.* Intercourse, PA: Good Books, 2006.

Mennonite World Handbook: Mennonites in Global Mission. Carol Stream, IL: Mennonite World Council, 1990.

Snyder, C. Arnold. *From Anabaptist Seed.* Kitchener, ON: Pandora Press; Scottsdale, PA: Herald Press, 1999.

An Amish man, accompanied by a youth, guides a horse-drawn plow in Lancaster County, Pennsylvania. (AP/Wide World Photos)

Mennonites

The Mennonite movement emerged in the 1540s as the more moderate and theologically sophisticated branch of the Anabaptist movement that had begun in Switzerland two decades earlier. As the Protestant Reformation divided Christianity into three larger communities, the Roman Catholic Church, Lutheranism, and the Reformed movement, Anabaptism emerged as a fourth option. It accepted the Reformation emphases on the authority of the Bible and the centrality of justification of the believer by faith in Christ. However, it differed from all three by its critique of the sacraments, which it replaced with two ordinances. Baptism was not for everyone but was limited to those adults who made a profession of faith. The Lord's Supper was a memorial meal recalling the events of the crucifixion and resurrection of Christ.

In the intense atmosphere of the Reformation's first decade, the decentralized Anabaptist movement was carried away by theological radicalism. Most important, it very nearly became a millennial movement. One of the most important leaders, Melchior Hoffman

(ca. 1500–1545), developed an emphasis on the imminent Second Coming of Christ. Hoffman's imprisonment in 1533 occasioned the rise of Jan Matthys of Haarlem (Netherlands) (d. 1534), who found support for his millennial ideas in Münster, Germany. Matthys called upon the people to prepare Münster, by force if necessary, for the coming kingdom of God. The city armed for the battle to come, which came in the form of a siege. Matthys was killed early in the fighting and was replaced by an even more radical leader, Jan Beuckelson of Leiden (ca. 1509–1536). Beuckelson proclaimed himself King David returned, introduced polygamy, and ruled the city as an Oriental potentate. The city eventually fell, and with it, seemingly, the Anabaptist cause.

However, in Holland, a former Roman Catholic priest named Menno Simons (1492–1561) became convinced of the Anabaptist basics. Simons emerged as the anti-Münster spokesperson, and with his theological training he was able to work out a viable alternative. He developed the ideal of the believers' church, a

Christianity consisting of those people who have experienced faith and choose in their adult life to live as Christ's disciples. The church should operate apart from the state and accept only the faithful who are willing to accept its discipline for baptism and membership. Simons articulated the importance of love and nonresistance as signs of the Christian life, the latter leading to pacifism and an unwillingness to bear arms. In place of the sword and other coercive powers of the state, he instituted the ban as a means of chastising errant members. Members had to radically limit their contact with anyone under the ban, a rule that most affected spouses, who could neither eat nor sleep with a spouse who had been banned until he or she had been reinstated.

The Mennonites suffered severely under intolerant governments, which were especially upset with their refusal to serve in the military, and they were forced to move from place to place as rulers came and went and occasional campaigns of repression and persecution arose. Military service was foremost among issues that led the first Mennonites to accept the invitation to settle in Russia and Pennsylvania at the end of the 17th century, and thus the center of Mennonite life shifted away from Western Europe. But by the 19th century conditions in Russia became increasingly hostile as the czarist government put aside the agreement that first led the Mennonites to migrate there. Thus many Russian Mennonites (and the related Hutterites) began to move to North America and develop a new set of communities in Canada and the United States.

The Mennonites in North America survived the crisis of World War I, when authorities had trouble understanding and appreciating their pacifist ways, and the continent became the new center of their community. However, in the relatively free conditions of both the United States and Canada, the small Mennonite community, which numbered only several hundred thousand, splintered into numerous denominations. Two of the larger Mennonite bodies, the Mennonite Church and the General Conference Mennonite Church, recently united to form the Mennonite Church, U.S.A. On the more conservative side are the Old Order Mennonites and the Amish who have attempted to perpetuate the agricultural and communal aspects of church life in 18th-century Europe. In the 19th and 20th cen-

turies, Mennonites spread to Africa and South America, and they have had a significant impact in Paraguay. Attempts to assist the smaller Mennonite communities around the world and to provide some sense of fellowship and unity among the many Mennonite groups led to the formation of the Mennonite World Conference.

There are an estimated 850,000 Mennonites in the world as the 21st century begins. This number includes 266,100 U.S. Mennonites, 114,400 Canadians, 112,906 in the Democratic Republic of the Congo, and 76,670 in India. More than 320,000 Mennonites reside in Africa and Asia. In the 1990s, more than 75,000 Mennonites moved from Russia to Germany. The Mennonite Central Committee was founded in the 1920s to serve Mennonites in the former Soviet Union and now operates as an inter-Mennonite relief agency in the global context.

J. Gordon Melton

See also: Amish; Hutterites; Mennonite Church, USA; Mennonite World Conference; Roman Catholic Church.

References

The Complete Writings of Menno Simons, 1491–1561. Scottsdale, PA: Herald Press, 1956.

Dyck, Cornelius J. *An Introduction to Mennonite History.* Scottsdale, PA: Herald Press, 1967.

Kraybill, Donald A. *Who Are the Anabaptists: Amish, Brethren, Hutterites, and Mennonites.* Scottsdale, PA: Herald Press, 2003.

The Mennonite Encyclopedia. 5 vols. Scottsdale, PA: Herald Press, 1955–1959.

Mennonite World Handbook: Mennonites in Global Mission. Carol Stream, IL: Mennonite World Council, 1990.

Roth, John D. *Beliefs: Mennonite Faith and Practice.* Scottsdale, PA: Herald Press, 2005.

Snyder, C. Arnold. *Anabaptist History and Theology: An Introduction.* Scottsdale, PA: Herald Press, 1995.

Mennonites in Paraguay

See Paraguay, Mennonites in.

Meron, Mount

Mount Meron is the highest mountain in pre-1967 Israel and is the site of the graves of important Kabbalists and also supposedly of earlier Jewish commentators. It is today the site of a ceremony that has become very popular among orthodox Jews where boys receive their first haircut.

Mount Meron is the site of the grave of Shimon bar Yochai, a second-century CE rabbi and official author of the *Zohar*, a major Kabbalistic text. The mountain is a place of pilgrimage for orthodox Jews who are particularly numerous at the festival of Lag B'Omer, where it is the tradition for their sons at the age of three to have their first haircut. The Aramaic word, *hillula*, meaning "festivity," was originally used to designate a marriage party. Among Jews originally from Muslim countries, the hillula generally commemorates the death of a sage, whose soul is regarded as having been reunited with its Creator. The classic instance of the hillula is that marking the traditional anniversary of the death of Rabbi Simon Bar Yohai, which is celebrated at his putative burial place and that of his son Eleazar in Meron, in northern Israel. Crowds as large as 100,000 people attend the festivities and large bonfires are lit and burn throughout the night. Mount Meron is the major mountain in Galilee, rising to about 4,000 feet, and is also the official burial site of a number of prominent rabbis, in particular the distinguished commentators Hillel and Shammai and many of their students. There is also a very old synagogue there, and the putative burial place of Shimon is covered now with a domed building. The celebration of Lag B'Omer, a festival in between Passover and Pentecost (Pesach and Shavuot), is a huge event for the Orthodox community in Israel. The festival represents the period of the ending of a great epidemic that killed many Torah students, and also the death of Shimon bar Yochai. He and his son are supposed to have spent 13 years hiding from the Romans in a cave where they were visited by Elijah and instructed in the mysteries that are hidden in the written Torah, which then became the *Zohar*, or "glittering." Although the *Zohar* was undoubtedly written by someone else, this story has served to make Mount Meron a popular site for those interested in the Kabbalah. It is also much valued by the Mizrachi community in Israel, Jews who originated in the Middle East.

Oliver Leaman

See also: Passover; Shavuot; Synagogues.

Reference

Heilman, Samuel. *Defenders of the Faith: Inside Ultra-Orthodox Jewry*. New York: Penguin, 1992.

Messianic Judaism

Messianic Judaism is a movement originating in 19th- and 20th-century Protestant missions to the Jews as well as the countercultural religious and ethnic ferment of the 1960s and 1970s. Jewish- and Gentile-born adherents accept Yeshua (Jesus) as Savior and Son of God as well as other tenets of evangelical theology, but utilize Jewish practices to express this faith. Today, hundreds of congregations throughout the world affirm this unique Jewish/Christian religious identity.

In the 19th and early 20th centuries, Protestant missionaries used Jewish symbols and language to communicate the message of salvation to Jewish audiences, and sponsored separate congregational worship for new Hebrew-Christian converts. By the 1950s, several Hebrew-Christian congregations existed under Protestant denominational control that kept potentially dangerous "Judaizing" to a minimum. Hebrew Christians were still eventually expected to integrate fully into existing church structures.

In the 1960s and 1970s, however, the growing interest among young adults in ethnic identity and religious meaning led to new developments. Martin "Moishe" Rosen, founder of Jews for Jesus, affirmed that Jewish identity need not be washed away by baptism. Although new converts were still expected to join Christian churches, the missionary organization utilized Jewish symbols effectively to reach Jewish youth. By 1975, the Hebrew Christian Alliance of America changed its name to the Messianic Jewish Alliance of America as a symbol of self-acceptance and as a successful evangelization tool. More important, key leaders such as Martin Chernoff began to form congregations to maintain Jewish identity; "assimilating" into churches was now rejected. "Jesus" became "Yeshua," churches "synagogues," and Protestant hymns were replaced with Jewish-sounding music and Israeli dancing. A Jewish calendar was followed, with Christological messages inserted into each holiday using altered Jewish liturgy.

This lifestyle alteration led to deeper theological discussions concerning the place of Jewishness in the movement and divides congregations into several groups. The two largest are the Union of Messianic Jewish Congregations (UMJC) and the International Alliance of Messianic Jewish Congregations, founded in the mid-1980s, which accept charismatic worship and a modicum of Jewish practices amended to fit evangelical faith. While some congregations are independent, others are formed, funded, and belong to Protestant denominations. All adherents agree, however, that Jesus was a Jew and Son of God, Jewish identity is God-given, and Jewish practices enrich their faith. Today these two movements, along with the International Federation of Messianic Jews (a Sephardic organization) include 172 congregations. With the approximate average congregational size of 60 members, and each congregation approximately 60 percent Gentile, this movement involves around 6,000 born Jews in the United States, with estimates of perhaps the same number in Israel and far less in small congregations worldwide.

Despite these small numbers, American Jews actively oppose the Messianic movement. While evangelical churches often support Messianic Judaism as an effective outreach method and a unique "ethnic" expression of Christianity, Messianic Jewish proselytizing angers American Jews. Jews for Judaism, based in Los Angeles, is the most prominent organization fighting what it sees as Messianic deception of ignorant and vulnerable Jews with the message that one can be both Jewish and Christian.

Recently, however, the UMJC seems to be focusing on drawing closer to the normative Jewish community. Dr. Mark Kinzer, a prominent Messianic rabbi in the organization, argued in *Postmissionary Messianic Judaism* (2005) that all Jews continue a covenantal relationship with God and do not need to be "saved" by Messianic Jews. A Jesus-believing Jewish movement without an evangelistic mission would certainly divide Messianic Jews from evangelical Christianity and from many fellow Messianic Jews and might even create new relationships with the American Jewish community. Any actuation of this idea could significantly reshape the direction and future of the Messianic movement.

The International Alliance of Messianic Jewish
    Congregations
PO Box 20006
Sarasota, FL 34276-3006

Union of Messianic Jewish Congregations
529 Jefferson St. NE
Albuquerque, NM 87108

International Federation of Messianic Jews
PO Box 271708
Tampa, FL 33688

Carol Harris-Shapiro

See also: Evangelicalism; Judaism.

References

Cohn-Sherbok, Daniel. *Messianic Judaism*. New York: Continuum Publishing Group, 2000.

Cohn-Sherbok, Daniel, ed. *Voices of Messianic Judaism: Confronting Critical Issues Facing a Maturing Movement*. Baltimore: Lederer Books, 2001.

Harris-Shapiro, Carol. *Messianic Judaism: A Rabbi's Journey through Religious Change in America*. Boston, Beacon Press, 1999.

Karabelnik, Gabriela. "Competing Trends in Messianic Judaism: The Debate over Evangelicalism." Unpublished senior thesis, Yale University, 2002.

Kinzer, Mark S. *Postmissionary Messianic Judaism*. Grand Rapids, MI: Brazos Press, 2005.

Methodism

The Methodist movement grew out of the life and work of John Wesley (1703–1791), an Anglican minister who in 1738 had an intense religious experience that culminated in a period of spiritual searching. Once he settled his own faith questions, Wesley began an itinerant ministry throughout England and Ireland that

Portrait of George Whitefield, colonial Protestant preacher of the Great Awakening. (Library of Congress)

led to the establishment of a host of religious societies or revitalization groups within the Church of England. Wesley called people to a personal experience of the faith into which many had already been baptized and to a life of growth in grace toward holiness or perfection. As the movement grew, Wesley commissioned a number of lay preachers to assist him.

Methodism grew for several decades as a fellowship within the Church of England, and in the 1760s it spread to the American colonies, where Wesley sent preachers to nurture the gathered believers. The crisis of the American Revolution and the establishment of the United States led Wesley to assume the role of a bishop, as he ordained ministers to facilitate the formation of an independent American Methodist organization. In 1784 the American leaders organized the Methodist Episcopal Church, now a constituent part of the United Methodist Church, and accepted orders from Wesley through his representative, Thomas Coke (1747–1814). The Methodists were the only group in

the decades prior to the American Civil War to systematically welcome African Americans into membership, and three large predominantly African American churches grew from that effort: the African Methodist Episcopal Church, the African Methodist Episcopal Zion Church, and the Christian Methodist Episcopal Church.

British Methodists remained a fellowship within the Church of England until 1795, when the Wesleyan Conference was reorganized as a dissenting church. Through the 19th century, both the Methodist Episcopal Church and the Wesleyan Conference would experience a number of schisms, and a spectrum of Methodist bodies would arise in both the United States and the United Kingdom. The U.S. Methodists would also become the fertile ground upon which the Holiness Movement and then Pentecostalism would develop. During the 20th century, the larger Methodist bodies in both countries would go through a series of mergers, resulting in the United Methodist Church in the United States and the Methodist Church in the United Kingdom.

In the 19th century, the several Methodist churches became active participants in the worldwide spread of Protestantism, and the movement spread to Africa, the South Pacific, and Asia. To a lesser extent, it was established across Europe. Many of the churches that resulted from that movement are members of the World Methodist Council.

Methodists inherited a Calvinist theological tradition, but Wesley adopted the form developed by Dutch theologian Jacob Arminius (1560–1609) that rejected the emphasis upon predestination. The Wesleyan emphasis on the free grace of God led to a focus on evangelism and resulted in Methodism becoming the largest religious grouping in the United States in the early 19th century. Wesley also developed a doctrine of perfection as the goal of the Christian life, leading to an emphasis on both holy living and social action.

J. Gordon Melton

See also: African Methodist Episcopal Church; African Methodist Episcopal Zion Church; Arminius, Jacob; Christian Methodist Episcopal Church; Church of England; Holiness Movement; Methodist Church, Great Britain; Pentecostalism; United

Methodist Church; Wesley, John; World Methodist Council.

References

Collins, Kenneth J. *John Wesley: A Theological Journey*. Nashville: Abingdon Press, 2003.

Harmon, Nolan B. *Encyclopedia of World Methodism*. 2 vols. Nashville: United Methodist Publishing House, 1974.

Heitzenrater, Richard P. *Wesley and the People Called Methodists*. Nashville: Abingdon Press, 1994.

Richey, Russell E., Jean Miller Schmidt, and Kenneth E. Rowe. *Marks of Methodism*. Nashville: Abingdon Press, 2005.

World Methodist Council. Handbook of Information, 2002–2006. Lake Junaluska, NC: World Methodist Council, 2003.

Methodist Church, Ghana

Methodism was introduced to what is now the nation of Ghana in 1835, when the Wesleyan Methodist Missionary Society in England responded to the request of a Ghanaian who had previously organized several groups for Bible study. Joseph R. Dunwell (1806–1835) arrived on January 1, 1835, but unfortunately he died six months later. His successors also succumbed to the climate and shared a similar fate. Then in 1838, John Birch Freeman (1809–1890), an African who had lived in England, arrived in Ghana with his wife. He worked among the Mfantse-speaking people along the coast and the Ashanti people farther inland, and from his base in Ghana he introduced Methodism to many places along the West African coast.

Once planted, the church grew steadily and by the end of the century had become one of the largest churches in the country. It developed an extensive educational system that included both primary and secondary schools. It supports the cooperative Trinity College with the Presbyterian and Anglican churches.

The church was granted autonomy in 1961. Since that time it has increased its membership from around 80,000 to around 800,000 (2005). Work is divided into 13 districts. The church is an active member of the Ghana Council of Churches, the World Methodist Council, and the World Council of Churches.

Methodist Church, Ghana
E252/2 Liberia Rd.
PO Box 4043
Accra
Ghana

J. Gordon Melton

See also: World Council of Churches; World Methodist Council.

References

Bartels, F. L. *The Roots of Ghana Methodism*. Cambridge: Cambridge University Press, 1965.

Harmon, Nolan B. *Encyclopedia of World Methodism*. 2 vols. Nashville: United Methodist Publishing House, 1974.

Southon, A. E. *Gold Coast Methodism*. London: Hodder & Stoughton, n.d.

Van Beek, Huibert. *A Handbook of the Churches and Councils: Profiles of Ecumenical Relationships*. Geneva: World Council of Churches, 2006.

World Methodist Council. Handbook of Information, 2002–2006. Lake Junaluska, NC: World Methodist Council, 2003.

Methodist Church, Great Britain

The Methodist Church of Great Britain is the primary body continuing the Methodist movement launched by the ministry of John Wesley (1703–1791). During his lifetime, Wesley had called together the preachers who worked with him into regular conferences, where they resolved both doctrinal issues and more practical matters about ordering the Methodist religious societies, the local organizations that would at a later date become congregations. Although Wesley took steps to establish the American work as a separate organization, he was always careful to view the British work as a movement within the Church of England. As early as 1752, he began to hold a separate conference for the Methodist preachers in Ireland.

In 1791 the conference assumed control of the movement. Four years later it authorized the serving of the sacraments in the society meetings, an act that is generally considered to mark the formal separation of Methodism from the Church of England and the point at which the Methodist Church became a separate denomination in Great Britain and Ireland. This act also brought the Methodists under a set of British laws regulating dissenting Christian churches, though by this time those laws were falling into obsolescence.

In 1797 the debate over the church's constitution led one group to break away and form the Methodist New Connexion, seeking a more democratic organization. In the Wesleyan Conference, which retained its hold on the movement, only the ministers were members of the conference. Jabez Bunting (1779–1858), who emerged as the leading minister of the conference, founded the Wesleyan Methodist Missionary Society in 1814. He held the movement together but opposed any move to democracy. As a result, the Wesleyan Methodist Association (1837) and the United Methodist Free Church (1857) were set up by dissenting groups. Lay representation was finally granted in the 1870s.

Through the 19th century, the Methodists remained theologically conservative, and although organizationally separate from the Church of England, they were supportive of its role as the country's national church. They were known for their religious fervor and their commitment to social reform, rather than their theological prowess. In 1896 they joined with the other dissenting churches in an ecumenical endeavor, the National Council of Evangelical Free Churches.

Pan-Methodist union in Great Britain was raised as an issue as the ecumenical Methodist conferences began to meet in 1881. After the meeting in London in 1901, three of the smaller British Methodist bodies began a process that led in 1907 to the creation of the United Methodist Church. In 1918 the Wesleyan Methodist Conference invited the Primitive Methodists (a British group that had imported American-style revivalism and camp meetings to England) and the United Methodists to consider a larger merger. A plan of union was approved by the three churches in 1928 and 1929, but it took three more years to complete the process, which included the approval of Parliament. The united body was called the Methodist Church.

The Wesleyan Conference had been a pioneer in world missions even prior to the founding of the Wesleyan Methodist Missionary Society. As early as 1794, Thomas Coke (1747–1814) published *A Plan of the Society for the Establishment of Missions Among the Heathen*. Because the American work had developed in an independent direction after the American Revolution, Coke turned his attention to building Methodism throughout the Caribbean. The work began on Antigua, from where it spread to other islands. Early in the 19th century, he began to advocate the establishment of work in Africa, and in 1811 George Warren (d. 1812) was appointed to Sierra Leone. In 1813 Coke gave the last of his savings to that cause; he died the following year on his way to Ceylon (Sri Lanka).

Methodism spread as the British Empire expanded, and throughout the 19th century, Wesleyan missions turned Methodism into a global movement. Work was successively opened in Cape Colony, Ceylon, Australia, New Zealand, and the South Pacific Islands. In the 1840s Thomas Birch Freeman (1809–1890) led in the spread of Methodism along the West African coast. In the 20th century many of these missions would grow into the autonomous church bodies that now carry the tradition in most countries of the world.

In 2005 the Methodist Church of Great Britain reported 293,661 members in its 5,900 congregations in England, Scotland, and Wales. It is the largest of the Free churches in the United Kingdom. It is a member of the Council of Churches for Britain and Ireland, the World Methodist Council, and the World Council of Churches. The conference in Ireland evolved into the Methodist Church in Ireland in the early 19th century; it has always included the Methodists of Northern Ireland.

J. Gordon Melton

Methodist Church of Great Britain
25 Marlebone Rd.
London NW1 5JR
United Kingdom
http://www.methodist.org.uk/

See also: Church of England; Wesley, John; World Council of Churches; World Methodist Council.

References

Davies, Rupert, and Gordon Rupp, eds. *A History of the Methodist Church in Great Britain*. 4 vols. London: Epworth Press, 1965–1992.

Harmon, Nolan B. *Encyclopedia of World Methodism*. 2 vols. Nashville: United Methodist Publishing House, 1974.

Turner, John Munsey. *Modern Methodism in England*. London: Epworth Press, 1997.

Methodist Church, Nigeria

The beginnings of Methodism in Nigeria can be traced to several Africans who had spent time in the Americas as slaves before being freed and returned to Sierra Leone by the British. In 1838 they made their way back to their homeland at Abeokuta, in the southwestern part of present-day Nigeria. They subsequently asked that a missionary be sent to their people.

His Royal Highness Samuel Ademola II, seventh Alake of Abeokuta, with his daughter at the Methodist Missionary Society in London, 1937. (Hulton-Deutsch Collection/Corbis)

In 1942 Thomas Birch Freeman (1809–1890), the British African missionary who introduced Methodism to much of West Africa, traveled to Abeokuta and established a mission station there and at Badagry. In its first generation, the work spread in the territory west of the Niger River, growing so successfully that a separate district was set apart in 1878. By 1913 the mission had more than 6,000 members. Meanwhile, in 1893 two British ministers from the Primitive Methodist Church arrived in Nigeria from their center on the island of Fernando Póo. They settled at Archibong and began to build a missionary movement east of the Niger.

These two missions were brought together in 1932 by the union in the United Kingdom of the Wesleyan Methodists and the Primitive Methodists to form the Methodist Church. The mission established an expansive system of primary and secondary schools and opened a number of medical facilities, including a colony at Uzuakoli for those suffering from Hansen's disease (leprosy).

The mission became the independent Methodist Church, Nigeria in 1962. Joseph Soremekun was elected as the first president of the new church. In 1976 the church adopted an episcopal governance system. Churches are grouped into circuits, and circuits are grouped into dioceses, each headed by a bishop. The bishop presides at the annual synod meeting. Dioceses are grouped into six archdioceses, which meet annually under the archbishop. The conference of the whole church meets biennially and is presided over by the church's prelate. In 2005, the church reported two million members.

The Methodist Church, Nigeria oversees two colleges, Immanuel College at Ibadan, cosponsored with the Anglican Church of the Province of Nigeria, and Trinity Theological College at Umuahia, cosponsored with the Anglicans and the Presbyterian Church of Nigeria. The church is ecumenically minded, and it is a member of the World Council of Churches and the World Methodist Council.

Methodist Church, Nigeria
Wesley House
21/22 Marina
PO Box 2011
Lagos
Nigeria

J. Gordon Melton

See also: Methodist Church, Great Britain; World Council of Churches; World Methodist Council.

References

Ajanaju, Olufemi. *Methodist Church Nigeria Today & by the Year 2000*. Lagos: Free Enterprise Publishers, 1996.

Barclay, Wade Crawford. *History of Methodist Missions*. 3 vols. New York: The Board of Missions and Church Extension of the Methodist Church, 1949–1950.

Copplestone, J. Tremayne. *History of Methodist Missions*. Vol. 4, *Twentieth-Century Perspectives*. New York: The Board of Global Ministries, The United Methodist Church, 1973.

Harmon, Nolan B. *Encyclopedia of World Methodism*. 2 vols. Nashville: United Methodist Publishing House, 1974.

World Methodist Council. *Handbook of Information, 2002–2006*. Lake Junaluska, NC: World Methodist Council, 2003.

Methodist Church, Sri Lanka

The Methodist Church in Sri Lanka originated early in the 19th century, when Britain ruled the island nation, then called Ceylon. Thomas Coke (1747–1814) had motivated British Methodists (now the Methodist Church [UK]) to develop an Indian mission, giving the last of his savings to the Wesleyan Conference to help sway them to accept his vision. At the end of 1813 he sailed for Ceylon, but unfortunately he died on the voyage before reaching his destination. Six ministers accompanied Coke, and after their arrival they made two important decisions. They agreed to open schools (a suggestion of the British governor) and subsequently settled in locations on the island in both predominantly Buddhist and predominantly Hindu communities.

The group was soon joined by William Harman, who settled in Colombo and opened a printing establishment. The first church in Sri Lanka, and the first Methodist church in all of Asia, was opened in Co-

Wesleyan mission house in Sri Lanka (formerly Ceylon). (The Print Collector/StockphotoPro)

lombo in 1816. An extensive school system using Ceylonese teachers was established, and from the school came many of the early converts and many ministers. The elementary schools led to the formation of secondary schools, colleges, and a theological school. The work grew slowly but steadily through the century. Of interest was a Christian-Buddhist debate in 1873 in which a Methodist, David de Silva, participated. The debate attracted the attention of Henry Steel Olcott (1832–1907) of the Theosophical Society, leading to

his conversion to Buddhism and to his support of Anagarika Dharmapala (1864–1933) in his development of the Maha Bodhi Society.

Through World War II the work in Ceylon continued as a district attached to the work in India. Ceylon became independent in 1948, but not until 1964 was a separate Ceylon Conference constituted. At that time the conference became autonomous as the Ceylon Methodist Church. F. S. de Silva was its first president. He was followed by Daniel T. Niles (1908–1970), one of the most famous Asian Christians of the 20th century and a president of the World Council of Churches. The church was invited to join in the formation of a United Church of Ceylon (now the Church of Sri Lanka), but the necessary majority need to support the effort failed to appear.

In 1972 Ceylon withdrew from the British Commonwealth and renamed itself Sri Lanka. The Methodist Church changed its name soon thereafter. In 2005 the Methodist Church, Sri Lanka, reported 32,000 members in what is still a predominantly Buddhist country. The church is a member of the World Methodist Council and the World Council of Churches.

Methodist Church, Sri Lanka
252 Galle Rd.
Colombo 3
Sri Lanka

J. Gordon Melton

See also: Maha Bodhi Society; Methodist Church, Great Britain; World Council of Churches; World Methodist Council.

References

Barclay, Wade Crawford. *History of Methodist Missions.* 3 vols. New York: The Board of Missions and Church Extension of the Methodist Church, 1949–1950.

Copplestone, J. Tremayne. *History of Methodist Missions.* Vol. 4, *Twentieth-Century Perspectives.* New York: The Board of Global Ministries, The United Methodist Church, 1973.

Goh, Robbie B. H. *Sparks of Grace: The Story of Methodism in Asia.* Singapore: Methodist Church in Singapore, 2003.

Small, W. J. T. *The History of the Methodist Church in Ceylon.* London: Kelly, 1913.

World Methodist Council. *Handbook of Information.* Lake Junaluska, NC: World Methodist Council, 1997.

Methodist Church, Upper Myanmar

In 1887 the Wesleyan Methodists in England (now known as the Methodist Church [UK]) responded to the opportunity to establish work in Upper (or northern) Myanmar (then called Upper Burma) by sending two missionaries and two Sri Lankan ministers. They began to establish churches in the dry zone of Upper Burma, also building a number of accompanying schools and medical facilities. The work grew steadily and quietly through the mid-20th century. It became the autonomous Methodist Church in Upper Myanmar in 1964.

In 1948 Burma became an independent country. In 1962 the government was overthrown in a military coup and the new leader, General Ne Win (1911–2002), instituted a socialist regime that discarded the democratic guarantees of the country's Constitution. In 1966 he ordered all foreign missionaries to leave the country.

Fortunately, by 1966 the church had largely become an indigenous institution among the Burmese people. After the church became independent in 1964, the emergence of the indigenous leadership led to an increase in membership, which grew by one-third in 1967 alone. So, unlike its American Methodist counterpart in the southern part of the country (now called the Methodist Church of the Union of Myanmar), the church did not suffer the loss of a large number of English-speaking members and quickly recovered from the departure of the missionaries. It did lose its schools and the Methodist Leprosy Home and Hospital, all of which were nationalized.

The Methodist Church, Upper Myanmar, is led by a president rather than a bishop following the British Methodist practice. It is a member of the World Methodist Council, the Christian Conference of Asia, and the World Council of Churches. Now known as the Methodist Church, Upper Myanmar (Myanmar having become the name of the country in 1990), it is not to be confused with the Methodist Church, Lower Myanmar (also known as the Methodist Church of the Union of Myanmar), the other Methodist church operating in the country. The church reported 27,543 members in 2005.

Methodist Church, Upper Myanmar
PO Box 9
28th Street, between 68th and 69th Street
Mandalay
Myanmar

J. Gordon Melton

See also: Methodist Church, Great Britain; Methodist Church in the Union of Myanmar; World Council of Churches; World Methodist Council.

References

Barclay, Wade Crawford. *History of Methodist Missions.* 3 vols. New York: The Board of Missions and Church Extension of the Methodist Church, 1949–1950.

Copplestone, J. Tremayne. *History of Methodist Missions.* Vol. 4, *Twentieth-Century Perspectives.* New York: The Board of Global Ministries, The United Methodist Church, 1973.

Goh, Robbie B. H. *Sparks of Grace: The Story of Methodism in Asia.* Singapore: Methodist Church in Singapore, 2003.

Harmon, Nolan B. *Encyclopedia of World Methodism.* 2 vols. Nashville: United Methodist Publishing House, 1974.

World Methodist Council. *Handbook of Information.* Lake Junaluska, NC: World Methodist Council, 1997.

Methodist Church in Brazil

In 1835 the Tennessee Conference of the Methodist Episcopal Church (MEC, now an integral part of the United Methodist Church) sent Fountain E. Pitts (1808–1874) to survey the situation in Brazil, Uruguay, and Argentina. While in Brazil, Pitts organized a congregation of English-speaking residents of Rio de Janeiro. Following his return to the United States, the church then commissioned Justin Spaulding (1802–1965) to expand the small beginning. He was joined in 1839 by Reverend (and later Bishop) Daniel P. Kidder (1815–1891), his wife, Cyndy Kidder, and two teachers. However, when Cyndy Kidder died and left her husband with an infant, he returned to the States and the mission only lasted a few more years.

The reopening of the work came by an unusual means, following the American Civil War. Confederates who were unwilling to swear allegiance to the U.S. government left for Brazil, where they founded several expatriate communities. Joining the exodus was Reverend Junius E. Newman (1819–1895), of the Alabama Conference of the Methodist Episcopal Church, South (MECS, now a constituent part of the United Methodist Church). He settled in the Province of São Paulo, where most of the Americans had moved. He began preaching in several locations and in 1871 organized the first church. He also began to ask for additional personnel. The General Conference of the MECS sent the first set of missionaries in 1876. At about the same time, an independent layman, William Taylor (1821–1902), became interested in Brazil as part of an overall effort to build a mission in South America. The MEC would later make him a bishop and his work would later be absorbed into the expanding mission of the MECS.

In 1986 Bishop John C. Granbery (1829–1907) organized the Brazil Annual Conference (the basic organizational unit in Methodism), known within Methodism as the smallest conference ever formed, there being only three ministerial members. Growth was steady from that year forward, in spite of opposition from the Roman Catholic Church and deaths from yellow fever. It was assisted by three Brazilian converts, Bernardo and Ludgero Miranda and Felipe de Carvaiho, who became preachers of note.

At the beginning of the 20th century, the conference asked for a resident bishop. The action was opposed by the MECS General Conference and did not occur until 1930, when the work was set apart as the autonomous Methodist Church in Brazil. In 1935 the first Brazilian bishop, Cesar Dacorso, was elected. A council was created to continue the fraternal relations between the Brazilian Church and the parent body. In succeeding years, the MECS assisted with funds to open a publishing house and to extend the educational program. A theological school opened in 1942 in São Paulo. In 1955 the annual conferences were designated as regions. Today there are six.

The church's General Conference is the highest legislative body. The College of Bishops administers the policies and decisions of the General Conference, which are collected in three documents, the Social Creed, the Plan for Life and Mission of the Church, and the Guidelines for Program. The Methodist Church in Brazil was the first organization in Latin America to join the World Council of Churches and is also a member of the World Methodist Council. In 2005, the church reported 163,424 members.

Methodist Church in Brazil
Avenida Piassanguaba 3031
Bairro
Planalto Paulista
04060 004 Sao Paulo, SP
Brazil

J. Gordon Melton

See also: Roman Catholic Church; United Methodist Church; World Council of Churches; World Methodist Council.

References

Barclay, Wade Crawford. *History of Methodist Missions.* 3 vols. New York: The Board of Missions and Church Extension of the Methodist Church, 1949–1950.

Copplestone, J. Tremayne. *History of Methodist Missions.* Vol. 4, *Twentieth-Century Perspectives.* New York: The Board of Global Ministries, The United Methodist Church, 1973.

Harmon, Nolan B. *Encyclopedia of World Methodism.* 2 vols. Nashville: United Methodist Publishing House, 1974.

Van Beek, Huibert. *A Handbook of the Churches and Councils: Profiles of Ecumenical Relationships.* Geneva: World Council of Churches, 2006.

Methodist Church in Chile

The Methodist Church in Chile began with the 1887 plan of William Taylor (1821–1902), a layman in the Methodist Episcopal Church who wanted to organize missions along the west coast of South America. The first group of missionaries landed in Chile the following year, just as what was to become known as the Nitrate War was about to break out. The war led to the annexation of what is now the northern third of Chile from Bolivia and Peru, and as a result the initial work that had been established in Iquique had to be abandoned. More permanent work was established in Valparaiso and Santiago. The work spread as additional missionaries arrived.

The missionaries gathered in 1880 to create a conference structure and elect a president. This work was independent of the Methodist Episcopal Church. How-ever, at the 1884 General Conference, Taylor was suddenly raised from layman to minister and was then elected bishop. He was sent to Africa as a missionary bishop. The Methodist Episcopal Church then moved to adopt his independent work in Chile, which in 1889 became the Chile district of the Cincinnati (Ohio) Conference. James P. Gillialand was named the first district superintendent.

The work in Chile was integrated with a Methodist mission in Argentina in 1892, and the South America Annual Conference was created in 1893. Later Chile was set apart as an annual conference (the basic organizational unit in Methodism). The church entered a growth phase, though it experienced a major schism in 1909, when churches and members influenced by Pentecostalism left to found the Methodist Pentecostal Church of Chile. This schism took with it the most conservative wing of the church.

In 1924 the work in South America was set apart as a central conference, which meant that rather than bishops from the United States coming to South America to head the conference sessions, resident South American bishops were to be elected. The first bishops for the central conference were elected in 1932. The work suffered greatly from a massive earthquake in 1939, in which two Methodist schools, Concepción College and Colegio Americano, and a number of church buildings were destroyed. An earthquake in 1960 likewise did severe damage to church property.

In 1968, the year of the merger that created the United Methodist Church, the Chilean Conference joined in the request of the other South American conferences for independence. The uniting conference granted that request, and the completion of the process occurred at the Annual Conference meeting in 1969. That meeting was held in connection with the last meeting of the Latin American Central Conference and the creation of a new Methodist ecumenical structure, the Council of Latin American Evangelical Methodist Churches.

In 2006, the Methodist Church of Chile reported approximately 10,000 members in 90 churches. The church is headed by a bishop. It is a member of the World Council of Churches and the World Methodist Council. In the meantime, the Pentecostal Methodist movement, divided into a number of denominations, has become the largest segment of Chilean Protestantism—the 800,000-member Pentecostal Methodist Church of Chile being the largest organization.

Methodist Church of Chile
Sargento Aldea 1041
Casilla 67
Santiago
Chile

J. Gordon Melton

See also: Methodist Pentecostal Church of Chile; United Methodist Church; World Council of Churches; World Methodist Council.

References

Barclay, Wade Crawford. *History of Methodist Missions.* 3 vols. New York: The Board of Missions and Church Extension of the Methodist Church, 1949–1950.

Copplestone, J. Tremayne. *History of Methodist Missions.* Vol. 4, *Twentieth-Century Perspectives.* New York: The Board of Global Ministries, The United Methodist Church, 1973.

Harmon, Nolan B. *Encyclopedia of World Methodism.* 2 vols. Nashville: United Methodist Publishing House, 1974.

World Methodist Council. Handbook of Information, 2002–2006. Lake Junaluska, NC: World Methodist Council, 2003.

Methodist Church in Fiji and Rotuma

Methodism was brought to Fiji in 1835, after negotiations among various British Protestant groups working in the South Pacific had led to the assignment of the islands to the Methodists. Thus, in 1835 William Cross (d. 1842) and David Cargill (d. 1843), previously working on Tonga, replaced two missionaries of the London Missionary Society who had set up work in Fiji in 1830. Their work was initially assisted by several Fijians they had met while on Tonga. In 1841 the work on Rotuma, just north of Fiji, was assigned to the Fiji Mission.

The Methodists arrived during the reign of Na Ulivau, who had united the islands into one community. The missionaries made little progress until 1854, when they effected the conversion and baptism of Ratu Seru Cakobau, Na Ulivau's son and successor. Ratu Seru Cakobau developed a great love for Western culture, at one point offering his kingdom for annexation by the United States. Caught in the grip of an impending civil war, Washington ignored his overtures. Great Britain accepted his invitation in 1874. They began to bring Indian laborers to the island, which in 1892 prompted the Methodists to begin an Indian mission there.

In 1854 the Australian Methodists (now a constituent part of the Uniting Church in Australia) assumed responsibility for the work in Fiji, and work continued under their guidance until 1964. It then became one of the independent island conferences affiliated with what was known as the Methodist Church of Australasia. As each of the island groups gained political independence, the conferences became national churches and the Methodist Church of Australasia was discontinued.

The Methodist Church in Fiji and Rotuma follows the beliefs of other Methodists, as embedded in the writing of John Wesley (1703–1791) and the Methodist Articles of Religion. The church has strong fraternal relationships with the Uniting Church in Australia, the United Methodist Church (U.S.A.), and the Methodist Church in Great Britain.

As the church became established, it became a missionary sending organization. The first missionaries from Fiji arrived on New Guinea in 1875. Subsequently, Fijian missionaries served in Papua, the Solomons, and northern Australia. In 1924 it founded the Navuso Agricultural School.

Over the years, beginning with its close relationship with Ratu Seru Cakobau, the church was often identified with the Fijian government. The church had developed the country's educational system, which was taken over by the government in 1846. That close relationship became something of a problem as the Indian segment of the islands came to numerical majority. Methodists, the largest Christian group in the islands, became second to the Hinduism brought from India.

This identification with the government has been critical to the public understanding of the church, beginning with the government coup in 1987 and in subsequent years, as the conflict between the native Fijians and Indian-Fijians has flared. The church was accused of identifying with the coup leaders in 1987 and of attempting to replace the religious freedom enjoyed in the islands with a government preference for Christianity. The same accusation emerged in 2000, when a native Fijian, George Speight (b. 1957), attempted a second coup. The church had to publicly distance itself from the coup attempt and the taking of hostages, while at the same time minister pastorally to supporters of the coup, many of whom were Methodists. Speight was himself identified with the Seventh-day Adventist Church.

The church reported 213,000 members in 2006. This ecumenically minded Methodist body is a member of the Fiji Council of Churches, the Pacific Conference of Churches, the World Methodist Council, and the World Council of Churches.

Methodist Church in Fiji and Rotuma
GOP Box 356
Suva
Fiji

J. Gordon Melton

See also: London Missionary Society; Methodist Church, Great Britain; Seventh-day Adventist Church; United Methodist Church; Uniting Church in Australia; Wesley, John; World Council of Churches; World Methodist Council.

References

Barclay, Wade Crawford. *History of Methodist Missions.* 3 vols. New York: The Board of Missions and Church Extension of the Methodist Church, 1949–1950.

Copplestone, J. Tremayne. *History of Methodist Missions.* Vol. 4, *Twentieth-Century Perspectives.* New York: The Board of Global Ministries, the United Methodist Church, 1973.

Harmon, Nolan B. *Encyclopedia of World Methodism.* 2 vols. Nashville: United Methodist Publishing House, 1974.

World Methodist Council. Handbook of Information, 2002–2006. Lake Junaluska, NC: World Methodist Council, 2003.

Methodist Church in India

Methodist interest in India began with British minister Thomas Coke (1747–1814), who died at sea on his way to Ceylon and to establish work at Madras. James Lynch (1775–1858) and others who were traveling with Coke settled in Ceylon (Sri Lanka) and initiated the Methodist Church Sri Lanka. In 1817 Lynch moved on to Madras and initiated an extensive Methodist work associated with the British Methodists. More than 100 years later, as India was attaining its independence, that work would merge with missions from several other Protestant churches to become the Church of South India and the Church of North India. Methodists from the United States, associated with the Methodist Episcopal Church (MEC) (now a constituent part of the United Methodist Church), arrived in 1856. Among the volunteers were Reverend William Butler (1818–1899) and his wife, Clementina Rowe. They had moved to the United States from Ireland, where Butler had been the assistant to James Lynch after Lynch's stay in India. The Butlers began their work in Lucknow and Bareilly, and were able to take advantage of the East India Company's new impetus to found schools in the country. The company gave both official sanction and resources for the development of the mission's extensive education program, which included primary and secondary schools and several colleges.

By 1864 an annual conference (the basic unit of organization in Methodism) was organized and four Indian ministers were received as members. In 1870 the famous lay-preacher and future Methodist bishop William Taylor (1821–1902) began his four-year stay in India, during which time the mission was energized and expanded. The conference began to experience spurts of growth, as whole groups of people would often make the decision to become Christians together. These group conversions, sometimes inappropriately termed "mass movements," led to the rapid growth of the church in northern India. In 1870 the movement was first joined by the female missionaries of the newly formed Woman's Foreign Missionary Society. The first of these missionaries were Isabella Thoburn (1840–1901), the sister of the missionary and future-bishop James Thoburn (1836–1922), and Clara A. Swain (1834–1910), one of the first American fe-

Methodist bishop Edgar Bentley Thorp attending the inauguration of the Church of South India. (Time & Life Pictures/Getty Images)

male physicians. Isabella Thoburn founded the first college for women in India, today known as Thoburn College. Swain formed the first hospital for women in the country, which also today bears the name of its founder.

In 1884 the MEC General Conference passed legislation that allowed the formation of a semiautonomous central conference in areas of the world where there were multiple annual conferences. The South Asia Central Conference was organized in 1885 in India and covered work eastward to Malaysia and eventually the Philippines. The central conference assumed the duty of electing bishops in the area, and in 1930 the first

Indian national, Jasvant Rao Chitambar, was elected to the episcopacy.

The church in India remained affiliated with the United Methodist Church formed in the United States in 1968, but in 1980 it received permission to consider reorganization as an independent body. It voted in favor of independence, and in 1981 the Methodist Church in India came into existence. It continues its cordial and interactive relationship with the United Methodist Church and maintains the structure that was set in place during the days of the central conference.

In the late 1990s the Methodist Church in India reported 648,000 members. Its 2,460 congregations are organized among 12 district conferences. It is a member of the World Council of Churches.

Methodist Church in India
Methodist Centre
21 YMCA Rd.
Mumbai Central
Bombay 400 008
India

J. Gordon Melton

See also: Church of North India; Church of South India; United Methodist Church; World Council of Churches.

References

Barclay, Wade Crawford. *History of Methodist Missions.* 3 vols. New York: The Board of Missions and Church Extension of the Methodist Church, 1949–1950.

Copplestone, J. Tremayne. *History of Methodist Missions.* Vol. 4, *Twentieth-Century Perspectives.* New York: The Board of Global Ministries, The United Methodist Church, 1973.

Matthews, James K. *South of the Himalayas: One Hundred Years of Methodism in India and Pakistan.* New York: Board of Missions of the Methodist Church, 1955.

Goh, Robbie B. H. *Sparks of Grace: The Story of Methodism in Asia.* Singapore: Methodist Church in Singapore, 2003.

World Methodist Council. Handbook of Information, 2002–2006. Lake Junaluska, NC: World Methodist Council, 2003.

Methodist Church in Indonesia

The Methodist Church of Indonesia is a multicultural church with a multicultural origin. It began with the arrival of Hong Tean, a Chinese layman who settled in Medan, Sumatra, where he established a school. His work was soon supplemented by the arrival of C. F. Pyekett, a Methodist minister from the United States. Pyekett then facilitated the addition of S. S. Pakianathan, a Malaysian pastor, who spoke Tamil. In 1907, Pakianathan moved to Palembang to work with John R. Denyes, who had also come to Sumatra from Malaysia. Over the succeeding decades, additional missionaries arrived and the work spread. By 1940, there were 60 congregations with some 2,500 members, most Indonesians of Chinese and Indian heritage. An autonomous Sumatra annual conference, independent of the Methodist Church (in the United States), was created in 1964. Following the merger of the Methodist Church and the Evangelical United Brethren in 1968, the Evangelical United Brethren work begun on Sulawesi in the 1950s was integrated into the Methodist church in Indonesia.

Outreach has continued to be focused in education and most congregations support an elementary school. In some districts the children in school outnumber the church membership. Work remains multi-linguistic. While Indonesian is a basic language, especially for the schools, worship is carried out in more than a dozen languages.

Since becoming an independent body, the church has spread to all parts of Indonesia, though its strength remains in Sumatra. It has strength on Bali, South Sulawesi, around Pontianak in Kalimantan, and the suburbs of Jakata (Java). In 2005, it reported 119,000 members. Its 469 congregations were organized into 2 annual conferences and 12 districts. It is led by its bishop, R. P. M. Tambunam. It is a member of the World Methodist Council and the World Council of Churches.

I Jl. Kartini No. 31
Medan 20252
Sumatra Utara
Indonesia

J. Gordon Melton

See also: United Methodist Church; World Council of Churches; World Methodist Council.

References

Harmon, Nolan B. *Encyclopedia of World Methodism.* 2 vols. Nashville: United Methodist Publishing House, 1974.

Van Beek, Huibert. *A Handbook of the Churches and Councils: Profiles of Ecumenical Relationships.* Geneva: World Council of Churches, 2006.

World Methodist Council. Handbook of Information, 2002–2006. Lake Junaluska, NC: World Methodist Council, 2003.

Methodist Church in Ireland

John Wesley (1703–1791), the founder of the Methodist movement, made his first visits to Ireland in 1747, prompted by the fact that some Methodist preachers had already organized a Methodist religious society in Dublin. Both he and his brother Charles spent a great deal of time in Ireland through the rest of the decade, and Wesley returned there on 19 subsequent occasions. Wesley held the first Irish conference in 1752, and either he or Thomas Coke (1747–1814) presided each year through the rest of the century. In the years after Wesley's death, Coke worked with the conference that became the inheritor of Wesley's authority.

Following Coke's death, the relationship of Irish Methodists to the Roman Catholic Church, the Anglican Church of Ireland, and the dissenting Free churches dominated its discussions. In 1816 the conference gave permission for the celebration of the Lord's Supper at the local Methodist societies. When that action had been taken in England some years earlier, it had signaled the movement's separation from the British Methodists. Those Methodists in Ireland who opposed this action formed the Primitive Wesleyan Methodist Connexion and kept their identification with the Church of Ireland. By the 1870s that relationship was no longer operative, and in 1878 the two branches of Irish Methodism united to form the present Methodist Church in Ireland.

In the meantime, Irish Methodists kept a cordial relationship with British Methodists. Rather than cre-

Methodist church in Howth, Dublin, Ireland. (iStockPhoto)

ating a separate missionary society, they supported the Wesleyan Methodist Missionary Society, through which they made their contribution to the worldwide spread of Wesley's movement. The Irish Methodists founded their first school in 1784, and elementary education remained an important concern through the 19th century. In 1868 the Methodist College at Belfast was opened. The Wesleyan Connexional School (secondary school) evolved into Wesley College, Dublin. During this time Irish Methodists had to continually overcome the effects of the immigration of its members, especially to the United States.

Methodist organization is based in the annual conference, now consisting of an equal number of ministers and laypeople. The Methodist Church in Ireland maintains a traditional and somewhat unique relationship with the Methodists in the United Kingdom. The president of the Methodist Church of Great Britain presides as president of the Irish conference, and eight Irish ministers sit in the British conference. The Irish elect the vice president of the conference, who acts as president of the church except when the conference meets.

In 2005, the Methodist Church in Ireland reported 60,000 members. From the 19th century to the present, in large part due to the immigration patterns, Methodism has shifted is center from Dublin and southern Ireland to the Belfast area. In 2002 the church entered into a covenant relationship with the Anglican Church of Ireland. It is a member of the World Methodist Council and the World Council of Churches.

The Methodist Church in Ireland
1 Fountainville Avenue
Belfast BT9 6AN
United Kingdom
http://www.irishmethodist.org/

J. Gordon Melton

See also: Roman Catholic Church; Wesley, John; World Council of Churches; World Methodist Council.

References

Cole, R. Lee. *Methodism in Ireland.* Belfast: Irish Methodist Publishing, 1960.

Cooney, Dudley Lewistone. *The Methodists in Ireland: A Short History.* Dublin: Columba Press, 2001.

Jeffrey, F. *Irish Methodism: An Account of Its Traditions, Theology, and Influence.* Belfast: Epworth House, 1964.

Vickers, John A. *A Dictionary of Methodism in Britain and Ireland.* London: Epworth Press, 2000.

World Methodist Council. Handbook of Information, 2002–2006. Lake Junaluska, NC: World Methodist Council, 2003.

Methodist Church in Kenya

Methodist work in Kenya was initiated in 1857 by the United Methodist Free Churches, one of several splinter groups among the British Methodists that had come into existence as part of the struggle of laypeople to gain a greater voice in the running of the church. The United Methodist Free Churches commissioned missionaries to work in East Africa in 1862. The 19th-century mission was largely confined to the coastal region, but around 1912 work was established in the center of the country, north of Mount Kenya. As the mission developed, schools, medical facilities, and programs in agriculture were started.

Early in the 20th century, the United Churches would participate in a series of mergers, leading in 1932 to the formation of the present Methodist Church and bringing the African mission with it. The Kenyan church became autonomous in 1967, four years after Kenya became an independent country. The next year the government assumed hegemony over all schools in the country, including the Methodist schools, though a cooperative management arrangement was retained. The church now works with more than 200 schools and in addition sponsors agricultural training institutes, technical schools, and special schools for the physically disabled. It co-sponsors the ecumenical Theological College at Limuru. In the 1990s it opened a major new national venture, Kenya Methodist University.

Following the British model, the church was originally headed by a president, but it has since moved to an episcopal system. The church is currently led by a presiding bishop, and a bishop heads each of the 10 synods (districts). In 2005, the church reported 450,000 members. It is a member of the World Methodist Council and the World Council of Churches.

Methodist Church in Kenya
PO Box 47633
Nairobi
Kenya

J. Gordon Melton

See also: Methodist Church, Great Britain; World Council of Churches; World Methodist Council.

References

Harmon, Nolan B. *Encyclopedia of World Methodism*. 2 vols. Nashville: United Methodist Publishing House, 1974.

Nthamburi, Zablon John. *A History of the Methodist Church in Kenya*. Nairobi: Uzima Press, 1982.

World Methodist Council. Handbook of Information, 2002–2006. Lake Junaluska, NC: World Methodist Council, 2003.

Methodist Church in Samoa

The Methodist Church in Samoa dates to the arrival of a Samoan chief on Tonga in 1826 and his conversion by the Methodist missionaries he found there. Upon his return to Samoa in 1828, he began to preach and raise churches. Peter Turner, the first European Methodist to arrive and settle in Samoa, found a thriving Methodist movement of more than 2,000 believers. About that same time representatives of the London Missionary Society (LMS), a Congregationalist organization that had established work in Samoa in 1830, and the Methodist leadership in Tonga agreed to divide the land upon which they would work. To avoid competition, the LMS would work on Samoa and the Methodists would work in Tonga. Turner was asked to withdraw from Samoa.

In part because communication at the time was slow and primitive and in part because they identified with Methodism, the Methodists of Samoa did not accept the decision to join with the LMS work. Thus they found themselves cut off from the mainstream of Methodist life. Then in 1855, the Methodist Church in Australia became independent of the mother church in Great Britain. John Thomas (1796–1881), the leader of the Methodist missionaries in Tonga, became the advocate of the Samoan Methodists, and the Australians voted to resume relations with the small group. Thomas argued that the new independent body was not bound by the agreement their British forebears had made with the LMS. Martin Dyson arrived in Samoa in 1857 and was succeeded by George Brown (1835–1917), who was most successful in building the church while keeping cordial ties to the LMS missionaries. The LMS remained by far the larger body.

The church continued to grow even after the division of Samoa in 1899, when the eastern islands were set apart as American Samoa. In 1964, two years after the western islands became the independent nation of Samoa, Samoan Methodists became the independent Methodist Church in Samoa.

Worshippers at the front of a congregation in a Methodist church in Western Samoa. (Nik Wheeler/Corbis)

At the end of the 20th century, the Methodist Church in Samoa reported approximately 36,000 members. The majority of members live in Samoa, but there are congregations across American Samoa and in the United States, where many Samoans have migrated. The church is a member of the World Council of Churches and the World Methodist Council.

The Methodist Church in Samoa
PO Box 1867
Apia
Samoa

J. Gordon Melton

See also: London Missionary Society; World Council of Churches; World Methodist Council.

References

Barclay, Wade Crawford. *History of Methodist Missions.* 3 vols. New York: The Board of Missions and Church Extension of the Methodist Church, 1949–1950.

Copplestone, J. Tremayne. *History of Methodist Missions.* Vol. 4, *Twentieth-Century Perspectives.* New York: The Board of Global Ministries, The United Methodist Church, 1973.

Harmon, Nolan B. *Encyclopedia of World Methodism.* 2 vols. Nashville: United Methodist Publishing House, 1974.

World Methodist Council. Handbook of Information, 2002–2006. Lake Junaluska, NC: World Methodist Council, 2003.

Methodist Church in Singapore

The Methodist Church in Singapore began in 1885 with the arrival of William F. Oldham (1854–1937) and James M. Thoburn (1836–1922) of the Methodist

Episcopal Church (now an integral part of the United Methodist Church). Oldham established a multiethnic congregation, and a building was erected before the year was out. A school for Chinese members was opened, and members of Tamil (Indian) background soon organized a Tamil-speaking congregation and school. These became the start of an extensive education system serving the Chinese and Indian communities within the small island state. The missionary thrust soon carried the Methodists across the Malaysian Peninsula.

The work in Singapore was originally included in the South India Annual Conference. In 1902 the Malaysia Annual Conference was organized. In 1950, the church in the region took a step toward independence with the establishment of the Southeast Asia Central Conference, which elected its own bishop. Autonomy finally arrived in 1968 when the Methodist churches and institutions in Malaysia and Singapore were set apart as the Methodist Church in Malaysia and Singapore. This was the same year that the United Methodist Church was formed in the United States. In 1976 the Malaysian and Singapore works were separated and the Methodist Church in Singapore was formed. Theodore R. Doraisamy was the new church's first bishop.

In 2005, the Methodist Church in Singapore reported 32,236 members. The church continues to support an extensive educational system. Ministers are trained at Trinity Theological College, a joint venture of Methodists, Anglicans, Presbyterians, and Lutherans. Members are organized in three conferences, one serving mostly Anglo members, one primarily serving the Chinese, and one serving Tamil members. The church is a member of the World Council of Churches and the World Methodist Council.

The Methodist Church in Singapore
10 Mount Sophia
Singapore 228459
http://www.methodist.org.sg/

J. Gordon Melton

See also: United Methodist Church; World Council of Churches; World Methodist Council.

References

Barclay, Wade Crawford. *History of Methodist Missions*. 3 vols. New York: The Board of Missions and Church Extension of the Methodist Church, 1949–1950.

Copplestone, J. Tremayne. *History of Methodist Missions.* Vol. 4, *Twentieth-Century Perspectives.* New York: The Board of Global Ministries, The United Methodist Church, 1973.

Doraisamy, T. R. *Forever Beginning 2. One Hundred Years of Methodism in Singapore.* Singapore: Methodist Church in Singapore, 1986.

Goh, Robbie B. H. *Sparks of Grace: The Story of Methodism in Asia.* Singapore: Methodist Church in Singapore, 2003.

World Methodist Council. Handbook of Information, 2002–2006. Lake Junaluska, NC: World Methodist Council, 2003.

Methodist Church in the Caribbean and the Americas

The Methodist Church in the Caribbean and the Americas incorporates the work launched in the late 19th century by British Methodists in the Caribbean and Central America. In the years immediately after the American Revolution, after overseeing the process of setting up an independent American Methodist church, Thomas Coke (1747–1814) emerged with a world missionary vision. As early as 1784 he published the *Plan of the Society for the Establishment of Missions among the Heathen.* Following up on that plan, in 1786 he made his first trip to the West Indies, landing in Antigua on Christmas Day. There he visited an Antiguan slave owner named Nathaniel Gilbert (d. 1774), who for several decades had pursued a Methodist-inspired Christian work among the Africans on his land. In his second trip in 1789, Coke visited Jamaica, where William Hammett (d. 1803), the first Methodist missionary in the region, would be assigned. From Antigua and Jamaica, Methodism spread to other Caribbean islands, especially the Bahamas (1799) and Trinidad and Tobago (1812). Methodism became identified with the antislavery cause in the Caribbean, and many former slaves joined the church after their emancipation.

Methodism ventured to Guyana in the persons of two laymen, who moved there from Nevis in 1801. The first minister was assigned by the British Conference

A 19th century Methodist church in Philipsburg on the island of St. Maarten in the Antilles. (Ramunas/Dreamstime.com)

Leeward Islands, Panama, and Costa Rica combined to form the Methodist Church in the Caribbean and the Americas. The Bahamas were added in 1968. The church's work now extends throughout the Caribbean, including some 62,000 members (2005) in some 35 nations. The church is a member of the World Council of Churches and the World Methodist Council.

Methodist Church in the Caribbean and the Americas
Methodist Conference Center
Scott's Hill
PO Box 9
St. John's Antigua

J. Gordon Melton

See also: Methodism; World Council of Churches; World Methodist Council.

References

Forever Beginning: Two Hundred Years of Methodism in the Western Area. Kingston, Jamaica: Literature Department of Methodist Church, 1960.

Walker, F. Deaville. *The Call of the West Indies.* London: Cargate Press, 1910.

World Methodist Council. Handbook of Information, 2002–2006. Lake Junaluska, NC: World Methodist Council, 2003.

Methodist Church in the Union of Myanmar

in 1815. Much of his effort was directed to the slave population, and he joined the Moravians in the attempt to overcome the plantation owners' opposition to missionary activity. Work then extended to British Honduras (now Belize) when a Methodist layperson asked the British Conference to appoint a minister to the region. Thomas Wilkinson arrived in 1825.

The work in the various British colonies around the Caribbean developed somewhat independently. In 1885, an autonomous West Indian Conference was formed, but it was disbanded in 1904, and the work returned to the direct control of the British Conference. Then in 1967, a new effort at independence was inaugurated when Jamaica, Guyana, Honduras, and the South Caribbean and the sub-district that included Haiti, the

Methodist work in Myanmar (then Burma) began in 1873, when James M. Thoburn (1836–1922), a missionary (and later bishop) in India, responded to requests for support from Indian Methodists who had relocated to the Burmese city of Rangoon (now Yangon). In 1879 William Taylor (1821–1902), an independent Methodist lay evangelist, sent a colleague, Robert E. Carter, to Rangoon, and Thoburn acted quickly to coordinate the two efforts. Soon a building was secured and services were begun in Tamil and Telegu, both Indian languages. The Burma work was seen as an outpost of the South India Conference, assigned to the new Bengal Conference in 1888.

Although based in the Indian expatriate community, the work soon extended to the Amoy-speaking people and the Chinese community. Because of this growth, it was designated as a mission conference in 1901 and an annual conference (the basic unit of organization in Methodism) in 1927. In 1951 the Indian government opened the Andaman Islands to civilian settlement, and a number of the Burmese Indian Methodists moved there to found the first Christian community.

In the early 1960s, as Burma moved to national independence, the Burma Annual Conference of what was then the Methodist Church (1939–1968) (now a constituent part of the United Methodist Church) requested autonomous status. That request was granted by the 1964 General Conference. The independent Burma Methodist Church was constituted in 1965. Lim Si Sin was elected as the first bishop. The church had approximately 2,800 members (adults and children) at the time, and it sponsored a string of elementary and secondary schools across the country. The church was organized into four districts according to language groups.

Burma had become an independent nation in 1948. However, in 1962 General Ne Win (b. 1911) overthrew the government and abrogated the democratic government and Constitution. Through the 1960s, a number of the English-speaking Methodists left the country, and in 1966 all missionaries were expelled by the new Socialist government. In the 1980s the country passed through difficult economic times and was cited for numerous human rights violations. In 1990 the name of the country was changed to the Union of Myanmar. During the 1990s the government massacred members of various ethnic groups residing in Burma. The Methodist Church, based as it has been in the ethnic communities, suffered accordingly.

In 1986, the church opened a theological institute for the training of ministers. Early in the new century it reported approximately 2,000 members (adults and children). It is a member of the World Methodist Council and the Christian Council of Asia, but it is not a member of the World Council of Churches. The church is also known as the Methodist Church of Lower Myanmar, not to be confused with the Methodist Church Upper Myanmar, the product of British Methodist missionary activity.

The Methodist Church in the Union of Myanmar
c/o Methodist English Church
47 Baho Road, Thazin Lane
Ah lone Township
Yangon
Myanmar

J. Gordon Melton

See also: Methodist Church, Upper Myanmar; United Methodist Church; World Council of Churches; World Methodist Council.

References

Barclay, Wade Crawford. *History of Methodist Missions.* 3 vols. New York: The Board of Missions and Church Extension of the Methodist Church, 1949–1950.

Copplestone, J. Tremayne. *History of Methodist Missions.* Vol. 4, *Twentieth-Century Perspectives.* New York: The Board of Global Ministries, The United Methodist Church, 1973.

Harmon, Nolan B. *Encyclopedia of World Methodism.* 2 vols. Nashville: United Methodist Publishing House, 1974.

Goh, Robbie B. H. *Sparks of Grace: The Story of Methodism in Asia.* Singapore: Methodist Church in Singapore, 2003.

World Methodist Council. Handbook of Information, 2002–2006. Lake Junaluska, NC: World Methodist Council, 2003.

Methodist Church in Zimbabwe

British Methodists Owen Watkins (1842–1915) and Isaac Shimmin introduced Methodism into present-day Zimbabwe (then Southern Rhodesia) in 1891. They had responded to an offer from Cecil Rhodes (1853–1902) of 100 pounds sterling per annum for the Wesleyan Methodists (now the Methodist Church in Great Britain) in support for such an endeavor. Rhodes's British South Africa Company had also made a grant of land for the development of missionary stations. The original stations were opened at Epworth near Salisbury and at Sinoia in the Lamagundi District. The following year, stations were opened at Nengubo (or

Waddilove), Kwenda, and Bulawayo. The work was assigned to the Transvaal District of the South African Conference.

The most notable Methodist leader of the first generation was John White (1866–1933), who served for almost 40 years and became known for his defense of the resident Zimbabweans in the face of an often abusive colonial regime. He also developed the Waddilove Institute, where the first Zimbabwean ministers were trained. In 1904 the first African ministers were ordained by the church.

The church grew steadily through the 20th century in the area west and south of Salisbury. It developed a cooperative relationship with an American Methodist mission (now an integral part of the United Methodist Church) that had begun in 1897 and concentrated its work north and east of Salisbury. In 1964 the church became a charter member of the Christian Council of Rhodesia, which earned the wrath of the government by declaring its disapproval of the country's unilateral declaration of independence in 1965. In 1968 it joined other members of the Council in forming a college.

The Methodist Church in Zimbabwe became independent of the British Conference in 1977. It organized in a manner similar to the parental body and was led by a president rather than a bishop. That changed in 1989, when Farai J. Chirisa was named the church's first bishop. At the beginning of the new century, the church reported 111,900 members. It is a member of the World Council of Churches.

Methodist Church in Zimbabwe
Central Ave.
PO Box 712
Causeway, Harare
Zimbabwe

J. Gordon Melton

See also: Methodist Church, Great Britain; United Methodist Church; World Council of Churches; World Methodist Council.

References

Barclay, Wade Crawford. *History of Methodist Missions.* 3 vols. New York: The Board of Missions and Church Extension of the Methodist Church, 1949–1950.

Copplestone, J. Tremayne. *History of Methodist Missions.* Vol. 4, *Twentieth-Century Perspectives.* New York: The Board of Global Ministries, The United Methodist Church, 1973.

Harmon, Nolan B. *Encyclopedia of World Methodism.* 2 vols. Nashville: United Methodist Publishing House, 1974.

World Methodist Council. Handbook of Information, 2002–2006. Lake Junaluska, NC: World Methodist Council, 2003.

Methodist Church of Cuba

The Methodist Church of Cuba originated among Cubans living in Key West, Florida, in the 1870s. Around 1883 several of these Cubans, including the Reverends Enrique B. Someillan (1856–1928) and Aurelio Silvera, returned to their homeland and began to lead worship services. The first church was opened in Havana in 1888. There were 194 members. Other Cuban pastors arrived soon afterward to help expand the work.

Spain's defeat in the Spanish-American War in 1898 forced it to relinquish control of the island, which became an independent country. Immediately after the war, Bishops Warren A. Candler (1859–1941) and Walter R. Lambuth (1854–1921) of the Methodist Episcopal Church, South (MECS, now a constituent part of the United Methodist Church) went to Cuba to inspect and reorganize the work there. Two missionaries arrived in 1899 to further expand the work geographically. The Cuba Mission of the MECS was organized in 1907. It became a mission conference in 1919. In 1939 the MECS united with the Methodist Episcopal Church and the Methodist Protestant Church to create the Methodist Church (1939–1968), then the largest Protestant church in the United States. The Cuban work became the Cuba Annual Conference of the merged body.

In 1959 Fidel Castro became the prime minister of Cuba, and relations between Cuba and the United States have since remained hostile. In 1962 most of the U.S. missionaries were withdrawn, leaving the church in a somewhat weakened condition. Women became an even more important part of church leadership and were welcomed as lay ministers. In 1964 the General Conference of the Methodist Church, partially in response to the needs of the Cuban Methodists now worshipping under a regime hostile to religion, passed a resolution allowing the Cuban work to become autonomous. In 1968 the newly independent church reorganized as the Methodist Church of Cuba. It recognized one of its recently deceased leaders, Angel Foster, as its first bishop, and then elected Armando Rodriguez as its new bishop.

Although somewhat hampered by the Castro regime, the church has revived, joining the World Council of Churches and the World Methodist Council, and participating in missionary activities in Colombia and other areas that lack a Methodist church. Early in the new century, the church had approximately 10,000 members.

Calle K. #502
Entre 25Y27 Venado
Ciudadde la Habana, 10400
Cuba

J. Gordon Melton

See also: United Methodist Church; World Council of Churches; World Methodist Council.

References

Barclay, Wade Crawford. *History of Methodist Missions.* 3 vols. New York: The Board of Missions and Church Extension of the Methodist Church, 1949–1950.

Copplestone, J. Tremayne. *History of Methodist Missions.* Vol. 4, *Twentieth-Century Perspectives.* New York: The Board of Global Ministries, The United Methodist Church, 1973.

Harmon, Nolan B. *Encyclopedia of World Methodism.* 2 vols. Nashville: United Methodist Publishing House, 1974.

Wingeier, Philip. *Cuban Methodism: The Untold Story of Survival and Revival.* Stone Mountain, GA: Dolphins & Orchids Publishing, 2007.

World Methodist Council. Handbook of Information 2002–2006. Lake Junaluska, NC: World Methodist Council, 2003.

Methodist Church of Malaysia

The Methodist Church of Malaysia traces its beginnings to the visit of William F. Oldham (1854–1937) and James M. Thoburn (1836–1922) (both later bishops) to Singapore in 1885. They founded a church under the auspices of the South Indian Conference of the Methodist Episcopal Church (MEC), now a constituent part of the United Methodist Church. From its base in Singapore, then part of the Straits Settlement, work was launched northward into the Federation of Malaysia. The work grew quickly and in 1889 was named the Malaya Mission of the newly formed Bengal (India) Conference; in 1894 it was set apart as the Malaysia Mission Conference. It became an annual conference (the basic organizational unit in Methodism) in 1902.

Important to the work was William G. Shellabear (1852–1947), an Englishman who met Oldham in Singapore. A talented linguist, Shellabear was soon fluent in Malay and several dialects. Until he was overcome by the hot and humid weather, he gave valuable service translating Christian literature into Malaysian. Meanwhile, in 1890 Benjamin F. West and H. L. E. Leuring traveled through Dyak (Iban) country in Sarawak.

Then in 1901 a number of Chinese, including some Methodists from the China mission, were forced out of their homes by the Boxer Rebellion. Bishop Frank W. Warne (1854–1932) accompanied them and assisted in their resettlement in Sarawak. New congregations of Methodists arose almost immediately. As a result, James M. Hoover (1872–1935) was transferred from the Malaysia Conference to Sarawak, where he would remain for the next 35 years. As he spoke Malaysian, he was able to begin work among them and then extend his evangelistic efforts to the Dyak (Iban) people. Work was especially fruitful among the ethnic Chinese, who constitute a sizable minority in Malaysia. In 1936 the Chinese work was set apart as a second Malaysia Mission Conference. It became an annual conference in 1948.

In 1968, as U.S. Methodists moved to reunite into the United Methodist Church, the work in Malaysia was granted permission to become an autonomous church. That year, the Malaya Chinese Annual Conference, the Singapore-Malaya Annual Conference, the Tamil

Christians sing during a prayer service at Kuala Lumpur Wesley Methodist Church in Malaysia. (Viviane Moos/Corbis)

Provisional Annual Conference in West Malaysia and Singapore, the Sarawak Annual Conference, and the Sarawak Iban Provisional Annual Conference in East Malaysia united to form the new Methodist Church of Malaysia and Singapore. Dr. Yap Kim Hoa was elected as the first bishop. The conferences continued as units in the new church. The work in Singapore was set apart as the Methodist Church in Singapore in 1976. In 1996, the Methodist Church of Malaysia moved to establish mission conferences to organize the Chinese work in Sabah and the Sengoi work on the peninsula of Malaysia.

In 2005, the Methodist Church of Malaysia reported 97,197 members. It is a member of the World Methodist Council and the World Council of Churches.

Methodist Church of Malaysia
69 Jin 5/31
46000 Petaling Jaya
Senlangor, D.E.
Malaysia

J. Gordon Melton

See also: United Methodist Church; World Council of Churches; World Methodist Council.

References

Barclay, Wade Crawford. *History of Methodist Missions.* 3 vols. New York: The Board of Missions and Church Extension of the Methodist Church, 1949–1950.

Copplestone, J. Tremayne. *History of Methodist Missions.* Vol. 4, *Twentieth-Century Perspectives.* New York: The Board of Global Ministries, The United Methodist Church, 1973.

Goh, Robbie B. H. *Sparks of Grace: The Story of Methodism in Asia.* Singapore: Methodist Church in Singapore, 2003.

Harmon, Nolan B. *Encyclopedia of World Methodism.* 2 vols. Nashville: United Methodist Publishing House, 1974.

World Methodist Council. Handbook of Information, 2002–2006. Lake Junaluska, NC: World Methodist Council, 2003.

Methodist Church of Mexico

The Methodist Church of Mexico traces its beginning to the country's Constitution of 1857, which included provisions for the separation of church and state and for the freedom of religion. U.S. Methodists immediately expressed an interest in establishing missions in Mexico, but this work awaited the outcome of the American Civil War and the readjustments of the church in the war's aftermath. In 1871 Bishop Matthew Simpson (1811–1884) of the Methodist Episcopal Church (now a constituent part of the United Methodist Church) led the process of allocating church funds for a missionary to Mexico. As a result, Bishop Gilbert Haven (1821–1880) went to Mexico the next year. He was soon joined by William Butler (1818–1899), who was designated as the superintendent of the soon-to-be established mission. Butler opened the first church on Christmas Day, 1873.

At the 1873 Louisiana Conference of the Methodist Episcopal Church, South (MECS, now also a constituent part of the United Methodist Church), money was raised to send Bishop John C. Keener (1819–1906) to Mexico to launch another mission. Keener secured the first church of the MECS mission, a former monastery chapel. Alejo Hernandez (1842–1875), a Mexican who had been converted during a stay in Brownsville, Texas, returned to Mexico City to become the pastor of this Methodist congregation. He was the first native Mexican preacher of the Methodist Episcopal Church, South. J. L. Daves arrived in 1875 as the superintendent of the movement.

Although church and state were formally separated in Mexico, the Catholic Church remained a strong establishment and the building of Protestant churches was plagued by obstacles. However, by the end of the century, churches and associated schools and medical facilities had been established in most of the major cities. In 1930, anticipating the union in the United States of the Methodist Episcopal Church and the Methodist Episcopal Church, South (which occurred in 1939), the missions of the two churches in Mexico united and became the Methodist Church of Mexico. For a number of years the two missions had held an annual joint national convention.

Shortly after the union, the new church published a Discipline, the book of church law, and established two annual conferences, the basic organizational unit in Methodism. Bishops are elected for four-year terms. Currently the church is divided into six episcopal areas that include parishes in all but two of the states of Mexico.

Education has been an important emphasis since the beginning of the church, and in addition to its system of primary and secondary schools, the church founded several institutions of higher learning, including Colegio Palinore in Chihuahua and the Union Theological Seminary in Mexico City, the latter created in cooperation with the Christian Church (Disciples of Christ) and the Congregational Church (now a constituent part of the United Church of Christ). It currently oversees a university and two theological seminaries.

In 2005, the Methodist Church of Mexico reported 50,000 members in 400 churches. It is a member of the World Methodist Council and the World Council of Churches.

Methodist Church of Mexico
Cuernavaca 116
Col. San Benito
CP 83191 Hermosillo, Sondra
Mexico

J. Gordon Melton

See also: Christian Church (Disciples of Christ); United Church of Christ; United Methodist Church; World Council of Churches; World Methodist Council.

References

Baker, Betty M. *Mexico Methodism: A Continuous Ministry Since 1832.* Mexico United Methodist Church, 1976.

Barclay, Wade Crawford. *History of Methodist Missions.* 3 vols. New York: The of Missions and

Church Extension of the Methodist Church, 1949–1950.

Copplestone, J. Tremayne. *History of Methodist Missions.* Vol. 4, *Twentieth-Century Perspectives.* New York: The Board of Global Ministries, The United Methodist Church, 1973.

Lee, Elizabeth M. *Methodism in Mexico.* New York: Board of Missions of the Methodist Church, n.d.

World Methodist Council. *Handbook of Information, 2002–2006.* Lake Junaluska, NC: World Methodist Council, 2003.

Methodist Church of New Zealand

The Methodist Church of New Zealand (Te Haahi Weteriana o Aotearoa) traces its beginning to the arrival of Samuel Leigh (1785–1852), who had also introduced Methodism into Australia. Leigh settled at Kaeo in the 1820s, where he established an initial station, called Wesleydale. The station was destroyed by Maori warriors in 1827, and the missionaries moved their work to Mangungu, from which it spread throughout the island. Despite the animosity of their initial encounter with the missionaries, many Maoris became Methodists.

The Methodist missionaries played a significant role in facilitating the signing of the 1840 Treaty of Waitangi, which placed New Zealand under British protection and guaranteed the Maori a broad set of rights. However, the mission was hurt significantly in the fighting between the Maoris and the Pakela people, and the mission never really recovered. By the mid-1900s, there were approximately 15,000 Maori Methodists.

In the meantime, Methodism spread among the European settlers in New Zealand. In 1854 oversight was transferred from England to Australia, and in 1873 a New Zealand Conference was established. Also, several schismatic Methodist churches, the United Methodist Free Churches, the Bible Christian Church, and the Primitive Methodist Church, had spread to New Zealand from England. In 1896 the United Methodist Free churches and the Bible Christians merged into the Methodist Conference. On January 1, 1913, the New Zealand Methodists became autonomous from Australia as the Wesleyan Methodist Church of New Zealand.

A month later, that church merged with the Primitive Methodists to form the presently existing Methodist Church of New Zealand.

The church continues the beliefs and practices of the parent bodies in Australia (now part of the Uniting Church in Australia) and the United Kingdom (now the Methodist Church [UK]). A college for training ministers was founded in 1912. Prior to 1913, New Zealanders also supported the Australian missions on several South Pacific islands. In anticipation of autonomy, the New Zealand church was assigned hegemony over the mission in the Western Solomon Islands. After World War II, the New Zealanders cooperated with the Australians in work in New Guinea, the personnel of which included Solomon Islanders.

Today, the Methodist Church of New Zealand has associated work in Samoa, Tonga, and Fiji. In 2005 it reported 18,548 members in 158 parishes. It is a member of the World Methodist Council and a founding member of the World Council of Churches.

In 1972, a new recognition of the importance of the Maori membership was made with the designation of a Maori Synod (the Taha Maori). Then in 1983, the church officially committed itself to continue a bicultural program in which the Maori culture is equal to that of the more dominant Anglo culture.

Methodist Church of New Zealand
Morley House
21/22 Marina
PO Box 931
Christchurch 8015
New Zealand

J. Gordon Melton

See also: Methodist Church; Uniting Church in Australia; World Council of Churches; World Methodist Council.

References
Harmon, Nolan B. *Encyclopedia of World Methodism.* 2 vols. Nashville: United Methodist Publishing House, 1974.

Lewis, Jack. *The Search for Unity: Methodism and Ecumenism in New Zealand.* Christchurch: Wesley Historical Society (New Zealand), 1983.

World Methodist Council. *Handbook of Information, 2003–2006*. Lake Junaluska, NC: World Methodist Council, 2003.

Methodist Church of Peru

The Methodist Church of Peru (Iglesia Metodista del Peru) grew out of the visits of William Taylor (1821–1902), an American Methodist layman, to the west coast of South America in 1877. Taylor established work at Iquique, but soon afterward that part of Peru became the subject of a war between Chile and Peru and was annexed to Chile. In the 1880s, Francisco G. Penzotti (1851–1925), a Methodist and agent of the American Bible Society, began to travel through Peru, distributing Bibles. In 1890 he was arrested and became the focus of international concern about freedom of religion in the country. His work resulted in the first Methodist congregation in Peru being organized in 1889 in Callao.

The next year, Thomas B. Wood (1844–1922), a Methodist who had been working in Argentina and Uruguay, arrived in Peru. He had been designated the superintendent of the new Western District of the South American Conference of the Methodist Episcopal Church (now a constituent part of the United Methodist Church). With his daughter, Elsie Wood, he founded several schools, the first Protestant institutions in the country. Although the educational work grew, evangelism was hampered through the first generations of this mission. By 1945 there were still only some 400 members. However, in the decades after World War II, missionaries moved into the countryside and the church began to grow among several of the native peoples, especially the Campa people. In the 1960s the work in Peru was named a provisional conference of the Methodist Episcopal Church.

In 1961 the church added to its school system the Panamericana Normal School, which focused on the training of teachers for its elementary and high school system. Meanwhile, other work was growing into five institutions of higher education: Colegio America del Callao, Colegio Alverado, Colegio Andino, Colegio Americo de la Victoria, and Colegio Daniel Alcides Carrion. The Peruvian conference also supported a theological center, Comunidad Biblico Teológica Wenseslao Bahamonde.

At the same time, the conference developed a new emphasis on social service and social change. In 1965 it issued a document unique among South American Protestants called the "Manifesto to the Nation," outlining the church's role as an active force in affecting the social and economic order. This document, which argued that effective revolution should spring forth from the power of God, was issued in the midst of large-scale social protest over what many perceived as an unjust social system.

By 1968 the work in Peru had been organized as an annual conference in the Methodist Church (1939–1968). That same year the Methodist Church entered into the merger that produced the United Methodist Church, which gave its South American conferences the option of becoming autonomous. The Peruvian Conference opted for independent status. The new Methodist Church of Peru was organized in 1970. Dr. Wenceslao Bahamonde was elected as the church's first bishop. The church's theological training center is named in his memory.

In 2005, the church reported 8,000 members in 130 congregations. It is a member of the World Methodist Council and, since 1972, the World Council of Churches.

Methodist Church of Peru
Apartado 1386
Lima 100
Peru

J. Gordon Melton

See also: United Methodist Church; World Council of Churches; World Methodist Council.

References

Barclay, Wade Crawford. *History of Methodist Missions*. 3 vols. New York: The Board of Missions and Church Extension of the Methodist Church, 1949–1950.

Copplestone, J. Tremayne. *History of Methodist Missions*. Vol. 4, *Twentieth-Century Perspectives*. New York: The Board of Global Ministries, The United Methodist Church, 1973.

Harmon, Nolan B. *Encyclopedia of World Methodism*. 2 vols. Nashville: United Methodist Publishing House, 1974.

World Methodist Council. *Handbook of Information, 2002–2006.* Lake Junaluska, NC: World Methodist Council, 2003.

Van Beek, Huibert. *A Handbook of the Churches and Councils: Profiles of Ecumenical Relationships.* Geneva: World Council of Churches, 2006.

World Methodist Council. Handbook of Information, 2002–2006. Lake Junaluska, NC: World Methodist Council, 2003.

Methodist Church of Puerto Rico

The Methodist Church of Puerto Rico is a product of the Protestant missionary movement on the island following its transfer to American control in 1898. The Methodist Episcopal Church (now an integral part of the United Methodist Church) transferred Charles W. Drees (1851–1926), previously stationed in Uruguay, to Puerto Rico in 1900. The first church was organized in Guyana in 1902. That same year, the Puerto Rico Mission was formally organized. It evolved into a mission conference in 1913. In 1939, the year of a major merger of the branches of American Methodism, it reported 2,800 members. The next year the work was named a provisional annual conference. By the time of the formation of the United Methodist Church in 1968, the conference reported 11,800 members and was recognized as a full annual conference. In 1972, it began a process of becoming autonomous, a process completed in 1992, though it retains a strong fraternal relationship to its parent body.

In 2005, the church reported 12,000 members in 100 congregations. It maintains a variety of educational and social service ministries, and is ecumenically active. It is a member of both the World Methodist Council and the World Council of Churches.

Methodist Church of Puerto Rico
Box 23339, UPR Station
San Juan, PR 00931-3339

J. Gordon Melton

See also: United Methodist Church; World Council of Churches; World Methodist Council.

References

Harmon, Nolan B. *Encyclopedia of World Methodism*. 2 vols. Nashville: United Methodist Publishing House, 1974.

Methodist Church of Sierra Leone

Methodism in Sierra Leone began with the efforts of U.S. Methodists to extend their ministry into Canada. In 1781 William Black (1760–1834) was assigned to pioneer work in Nova Scotia, where he discovered at Sherburne and other communities a number of Africans who had been brought to Canada by the British army at the end of the American Revolution. They had supported the British in return for a promise of freedom.

With the help of British antislavery organizations, the Africans living in Nova Scotia were offered transportation to the new colony of Sierra Leone. In 1792 many accepted the opportunity and were taken to Freetown, including some 200 Methodists. Soon thereafter they began to correspond with the Wesleyan Methodists in England (now the Methodist Church [UK]), and, in 1811, George Warren (d. 1812) was finally assigned as a missionary. He arrived with three schoolmasters, who began the Methodist educational enterprise in Sierra Leone.

Warren died some eight months after his arrival in Sierra Leone, but the church survived and grew over the next decade. In addition to the former slaves from Nova Scotia, the missionaries served other groups in Sierra Leone. A number of Maroons, former slaves who had escaped plantation life in Jamaica only to be recaptured and transported to Sierra Leone in 1800, came under the influence of the Methodists, as did the "recaptures," those slaves captured in the process of being transported to the Americas and returned to Africa. What looked like the blossoming of a prosperous mission, however, quickly disintegrated. In 1821 the older members of the Methodist church in Freetown argued with the missionaries, who then attempted to dissolve the congregations. They continued as an independent

Parishioners worship at Zion Wilberforce Church in Freetown, Sierra Leone, 1975. (National Geographic/Getty Images)

organization. Then the Maroons (1835) and "recaptures" (1844) left the Freetown society because they felt they were being treated as second-class citizens.

The Methodists had thus split into four separate groups: the original Freetown society, the Wesleyan mission, the Maroon church, and the "recaptures" church (known as the West African Methodist Church). In addition, in 1841, following public excitement over the *Amistad* incident, American Methodists founded a fifth Methodist church among the Mende people at Sherbro, Sierra Leone. This work now exists as the Sierra Leone Conference of the United Methodist Church.

Eventually, the problems of the Freetown society and the Maroon church with the Wesleyan mission were resolved, and they reunited. The West African Methodist Church, however, affiliated with the United Methodist Free Churches in the United Kingdom. In 1932 the Wesleyans in England merged with the United Methodist Free Churches to create the Methodist Church of Great Britain. In Africa, their two affiliates also merged, but in 1934, the West African Methodist Church again went its separate way.

The Wesleyan mission experienced a period of growth in the 1930s, when it also began work in Mende country. Because of this opening, the missionaries launched work on a Mende edition of the Bible, published in 1959, and opened a hospital at Segbwema. In 1967 the former mission became an independent church, the Methodist Church of Sierra Leone. It has continued in a working relationship with British Methodists.

Like all religious bodies in the country, the Methodist Church of Sierra Leone has suffered from the civil war that has continued through the 1990s into the new century. Many church members have been killed, and many church facilities have been damaged or destroyed.

In 2005, the church reported 50,000 members, serving a constituency of 1.5 million. It is a member of the World Methodist Council and the World Council of Churches.

Methodist Church of Sierra Leone
4 George St.
PO Box 64
Freetown
Sierra Leona

J. Gordon Melton

See also: Methodist Church, Great Britain; United Methodist Church; World Council of Churches; World Methodist Council.

References

Harmon, Nolan B. *Encyclopedia of World Methodism.* 2 vols. Nashville: United Methodist Publishing House, 1974.

Marke, C. *The Origins of Wesleyan Methodism in Sierra Leone.* London: Charles H. Kelly, 1913.

"The Spirit of Amistad in the United Methodist Church." Website of the General Board of Global Ministries, United Methodist Church. Online.

http://new.gbgm-umc.org/about/history/mission/africa/index.cfm?i=8445. Accessed December 15, 2008.

Walker, James. *The Black Loyalists: The Search for a Promised Land in Nova Scotia and Sierra Leone 1783–1870*. Toronto: University of Toronto Press, 1992.

World Methodist Council. *Handbook of Information. 2002–2006*. Lake Junaluska, NC: World Methodist Council, 2003.

Methodist Church of Southern Africa

The Methodist Church of Southern Africa traces its origins to a small religious society founded in 1806 in Cape Town by members of the Seventy-second Regiment of the British army under the leadership of George Middlemiss. A decade later Barnabas Shaw (1788–1857) arrived in Cape Town to serve as the minister for the Methodists. However, Shaw wanted to work among the Native Africans and soon left Cape Town to establish the Leliefontein mission station some 250 miles north among the Namaqua. As other missionaries arrived, work was concentrated in what is now known as Namibia and Bechuanaland. The Namibian work was eventually turned over to the Lutheran-based Rhenish Mission, and the work in South Africa was expanded among both white settlers and the Native population.

In 1820 William Shaw (1798–1872) arrived to become the chaplain to a group of settlers. His work became a second beginning for Methodism. He organized a series of preaching stations eastward all the way to Durban, many located in hostile territory. The work among the Native population was slow, but the church grew as more British settlers arrived. Shaw organized the Wesleyan Methodist Church, which experienced sporadic growth. A Methodist congregation was often the first English church to appear in the new settlements, attracting members of a variety of Protestant churches. As Presbyterian, Congregational, and Anglican congregations emerged, these members would leave the Methodist Church to rejoin their own denominations. In 1862, the church launched a mission among the new settlers from India.

A Methodist church in Stellenbosh, South Africa. (Inna Felker/Dreamstime.com)

The church grew up as a mission of the British Wesleyan Conference. As the districts multiplied, triennial meetings were held, beginning in 1873. In 1883 the districts were tied together by what was called the Affiliated Conference. Ties to Great Britain were loosened until complete autonomy was granted in 1927 with the formation of the Wesleyan Methodist Church of South Africa. A merger in 1932 with the Primitive Methodist Mission and with the work in the Transvaal that had not joined in the 1927 reorganization led to the formation of the present Methodist Church of South Africa.

The South African church followed the belief, practice, and organization of the Methodist Church of Great Britain. Until 1988 it was headed by a president, who was elected at the annual conference, the basic organizational unit in Methodism. After 1988 the district heads were redesignated as bishops, and a presiding bishop, elected for a three-year term, replaced the national president.

In 2005 the Methodist Church of Southern Africa reported a membership of 1,700,000. It has jurisdiction over Methodist work in Mozambique and Namibia. Its extensive educational and medical programs were lost when the government nationalized the schools and hospitals. In 1978 the church was outlawed in Transkei, and Methodists there reorganized as the United Methodist Church of Southern Africa. Most of that church reunited with the main body when the ban was lifted in 1988. The church is a member of the World Council of Churches and the World Methodist Council. It currently supports the Federal Theological Seminary of Southern Africa, a cooperative venture with Congregationalists, Presbyterians, and Anglicans.

Methodist Church of Southern Africa
PO Box 1771
Sasolburg 1947
South Africa

J. Gordon Melton

See also: Methodism; Rhenish Mission; World Council of Churches; World Methodist Council.

References

Barclay, Wade Crawford. *History of Methodist Missions.* 3 vols. New York: The Board of Missions and Church Extension of the Methodist Church, 1949–1950.

Copplestone, J. Tremayne. *History of Methodist Missions.* Vol. 4, *Twentieth-Century Perspectives.* New York: The Board of Global Ministries, The United Methodist Church, 1973.

Harmon, Nolan B. *Encyclopedia of World Methodism.* 2 vols. Nashville: United Methodist Publishing House, 1974.

South African Methodism—Her Missionary Witness. Cape Town: Methodist Publishing House, 1966.

World Methodist Council. *Handbook of Information, 2002–2006.* Lake Junaluska, NC: World Methodist Council, 2003.

Methodist Church of the Union of Upper Myanmar

See Methodist Church, Upper Myanmar.

Methodist Church of Togo

The Methodist Church of Togo began in the 1840s, when Thomas Birch Freeman (1809–1890) arrived as a representative of the Wesleyan Methodists in Great Britain. Freeman, the son of an African father and a British mother, developed a friendship with a chief of the Mina people at Anécho, who granted him permission to begin preaching to the people and to establish a school. Birch's original work was soon supplemented by other Methodists who were moving along the coastal communities from Nigeria to the Gold Coast. As the work developed, it was seen as part of the developing church in Dahomey (present-day Benin). That identification was increased by the French takeover from the Germans after World War I.

In 1957 the Dahomey and Togo work was set aside as a separate district of the Methodist Church of Great Britain. After Benin gained its independence in 1974, the Togo work became part of the Protestant Methodist Church of Benin. It separated from the church in Benin and again became a district of the Methodist Church in Great Britain. It voted to become fully autonomous in 1995, an action that was completed in 1999. It has remained focused on serving the Mina people, and thus has not grown, as have the Presbyterian Evangelical Church of Togo and the Assemblies of God mission.

In 2005, the Methodist Church of Togo reported 45,000 members. It is a member of both the World Methodist Council and the World Council of Churches.

Methodist Church of Togo
BP 49
Lomé
Togo

J. Gordon Melton

See also: Methodist Church, Great Britain; Protestant Methodist Church of Benin; United Methodist

Church; World Council of Churches; World Methodist Council.

References

Barclay, Wade Crawford. *History of Methodist Missions.* 3 vols. New York: The Board of Missions and Church Extension of the Methodist Church, 1949–1950.

Copplestone, J. Tremayne. *History of Methodist Missions.* Vol. 4, *Twentieth-Century Perspectives.* New York: The Board of Global Ministries, The United Methodist Church, 1973.

Harmon, Nolan B. *Encyclopedia of World Methodism.* 2 vols. Nashville: United Methodist Publishing House, 1974.

World Methodist Council. *Handbook of Information, 2002–2006.* Lake Junaluska, NC: World Methodist Council, 2003.

Methodist Pentecostal Church of Chile

The Methodist Pentecostal Church of Chile (Iglesia Metodista Pentecostal de Chile) developed early in the 20th century, when the Pentecostal experience emerged within the Methodist Church of Chile (then still a district in the American-based Methodist Episcopal Church). In 1909 Willis C. Hoover (1856–1936), a missionary who pastored a Methodist church in Valparaiso, was influenced by the spread of Pentecostalism through Europe and India soon after its emergence in Los Angeles, California. He began to correspond with Pentecostal leaders in other countries and instituted prayer meetings and Bible study around the issue of the baptism of the Holy Spirit and the experience of speaking in tongues. Those in attendance soon professed to manifest the gifts of the Spirit.

The Pentecostal movement spread from Hoover's congregation to other Methodists in Chile, and in 1911, bowing to pressures from the United States, the leaders of the church in Chile expelled Hoover and his Pentecostal followers, who then reorganized as the Methodist Pentecostal Church. The church suffered through a period of discrimination until 1925, when a new Constitution established the separation of church and state in Chile. The church experienced a growth phase through the 1930s, expanding across Chile and into Argentina, Uruguay, Paraguay, Bolivia, and Peru. In the years since World War II, the church's membership has doubled annually, and it has become one of the most successful indigenous churches in South America. The Jotabeche Pentecostal Evangelical Church in Santiago is one of the largest congregations of any kind in the world, rivaling in size the Yoido Full Gospel Church in Seoul, Korea. The church has also experienced a number of schisms that have effectively spread Pentecostalism farther, as several of the daughter churches have also grown into large bodies.

Methodist Pentecostal Church of Chile
Bernal del Mercado 139
Santiago Casilla 213-2
Santiago
Chile

J. Gordon Melton

See also: Methodism; Pentecostalism; Yoido Full Gospel Church.

References

Barclay, Wade Crawford. *History of Methodist Missions.* 3 vols. New York: The Board of Missions and Church Extension of the Methodist Church, 1949–1950.

Copplestone, J. Tremayne. *History of Methodist Missions.* Vol. 4, *Twentieth-Century Perspectives.* New York: The Board of Global Ministries, The United Methodist Church, 1973.

Harmon, Nolan B. *Encyclopedia of World Methodism.* 2 vols. Nashville: United Methodist Publishing House, 1974.

Hoover, Willis C. *History of the Pentecostal Revival in Chile.* Trans. Mario G. Hoover. Santiago: Imprenta Eben-Ezer, 2000.

Metropolitan Community Churches

See Universal Fellowship of Metropolitan Community of Churches.

Mevlevi Sufi Order

The Mevlevi Sufi Order was founded by mystic and philosopher Jalal ad-din ar-Rumi (ca. 1207–1273) in Konya, Turkey. Rumi was born into a learned family in Balkh, Afghanistan. In the face of Mongol incursions into the region, his family moved on several occasions before finally settling in Konya. Rumi succeeded his father as a professor in religious sciences in 1231. Rumi is considered the most eminent poet produced by the Sufi movement, the height of his work being his momentous mystical work, *Mathnawi*.

The Mevlevi Sufis adopted their name from the term "Mevlana," or "our Master." Their main Sufi tenets consist of unconditional love and tolerance, positive reasoning, charity, and spiritual enlightenment through love of all of God's creation. According to Rumi, human beings consist of the tripartite components of spirit, reason, and love. The spiritually advanced Mevlevi Sufis are supervised by the leading sheikh (*celebi*) as they whirl in circles during a devotional liturgy (*sema*); hence they have been called the Whirling Dervishes. Their dancing represents the mystical journey of turning oneself completely toward the One. Through eternal love, devotion, integrity, and generosity, the Mevlevis aspire to maintain their focus on the divine.

The international headquarters of the Mevlevi order is in Konya, Turkey. Members are found primarily in Turkey, Syria, and Central Asia, but in recent years they have also established centers in Europe and North America. Today, the order is headed by Faruk Hemden Celebi (b. 1950), a direct descendant of Rumi who succeeded to his post in 1996 following the death of his father, Celaleddin Bakir Celebi (1926–1996). Celaleddin Celebi (celebi, literally well-mannered gentleman, is the title given the order's leader) was responsible for bringing the order to the West with the appointment of Edmund Kabir Helminski as the order's representative in North America. Helminski founded the Threshold Society, which has become a major force for the publishing and circulation of Mevlevi literature in the English-speaking world. In 1994, in honor of the success of the Threshold Society, the Threshold Center in Brattleboro, Vermont, was designated Konya West by the Order.

The Whirling Dervish Festival held each December in Konya, Turkey, honors Jalal ad-din ar-Rumi, the 13th-century poet and Islamic philosopher who founded the Mevlevi Order of Whirling Dervishes. (Corel)

Threshold Society
270 Quarter Horse Lane
Watsonville, CA 95076
http://www.sufism.org/

Qamar-ul Huda

See also: Sufism.

References

Chittick, William. *The Sufi Path of Love: The Spiritual Teachings of Rumi*. Albany: State University of New York Press, 1983.

Hakim, Khalifa Abdul. *The Metaphysics of Rumi: A Critical and Historical Sketch*. 2nd ed. Lahore, Pakistan: The Institute of Islamic Culture, 1959.

Harvey, Andrew. *Light upon Light: Inspirations from Rumi.* Berkeley, CA: North Atlantic Books, 1996.

Lewis, Franklin. *Rumi: Past and Present, East and West.* Oxford: Oneworld Publications, 2000.

Mevlana Cealeddin Rumi. http://www.mevlana.net. Accessed February 1, 2002.

Schimmel, Annemarie. *The Triumphal Sun: A Study of the Works of Jalaloddin Rumi.* Albany: State University of New York Press, 1993.

■ Mexico

The United Mexican States (Estados Unidos Mexicanos) constitute one of the largest countries (an area of 761,606 square miles) in the Americas, located geographically in North America between the United States of America in the north and Guatemala and Belize in the southeast. It is bordered on the east by the Gulf of Mexico (part of the Caribbean Sea) and on the west by the Pacific Ocean. Mexico's population in mid-2000 was estimated at 97.5 million and in mid-2008 at 109 million, third in size in the Americas after the United States and Brazil.

The nation is composed of a diversity of ethnic groups: *mestizos* (mixed Spanish-Indian blood who are native Spanish-speakers), 88 percent; Amerindians (239 living languages among 13 linguistic families), 9 percent; and others (including North Americans, Europeans, Afro-Americans, Middle Easterners, and Asians), 3 percent. The predominant Amerindian languages are Náhuatl, Maya, Mixteco, Zapoteco, Otomí, Tzeltal, Tzotzil, Totonaco, Chol, Mazahua, and Huasteco.

Although Mexico continues to be dominated by the Roman Catholic Church (second-largest Catholic population in the world, after Brazil), those claiming affiliation with Roman Catholicism declined at the end of the 20th century—from 89.7 percent of the total population in the 1990 census to 88 percent in the 2000 census. Protestant adherents increased from 5 percent in 1990 to 5.7 percent in 2000; those affiliated with "other religions" increased from 1.4 percent in 1990 to 1.9 percent in 2000; and those with "no religious affiliation" (or providing "no answer") increased from 3.9 percent in 1990 to 4.4 percent in 2000.

The present Constitution provides for freedom of religion relative to both belief and the practice of ceremonies and acts of worship. Congress may not enact laws that establish or prohibit any religion. The Constitution provides for the separation of church and state, and the 1992 Law of Religious Associations and Public Worship defines the administrative policies and remedies that protect the right to religious freedom. A provision was added to the Constitution in 2001 that established, for the first time, a constitutional prohibition against any form of discrimination, including discrimination against persons of the basis of religion.

As of March 2009, the Government's Office of Religious Affairs reported a total of 7,073 officially registered religious associations (ARs) in Mexico. A previous report, issued in June 2005, listed 6,373 ARs, which can be classified as follows: Christian/Roman Catholic (2,962, or 46.5 percent), Christian/Orthodox (21), Christian/Protestant (3,298, or 51.8 percent), Christian/Other (65), and non-Christian (27).

When the Spanish conquistadors arrived in Mexico in the early 1600s, they discovered some of the greatest cultures of human history, beginning with the Olmec civilization that began about 1200 BCE and continuing through the Aztec Empire that dominated the central region of the country with its elaborate ceremonial and political center (Tenochtitlan) built on a man-made island in Lake Texcoco in the Valley of Mexico. Around 9,000 years ago, ancient Amerindians domesticated corn and initiated an agricultural revolution, which led to the formation of many complex civilizations. Between 1800 and 300 BCE, many of these matured into advanced Mesoamerican civilizations that are credited with many innovations, including cosmology, astronomy, writing, mathematics, government, militaries, engineering, and medicine. These civilizations were organized around cities and pyramid-temples.

Mexico is said to have had five major civilizations: the Olmec, Teotihuacan, Toltec, Aztec, and Maya. At their peak, an estimated 350,000 Aztecs presided over a wealthy tribute-empire comprised of around 10 million people, almost half of Mexico's estimated population of 24 million in 1500. After 4,000 years, the existing civilizations were destroyed after the arrival of the Spaniards in 1519.

Our Lady of Guadalupe Church, Santa Fe, New Mexico, is the oldest shrine to Gaudalupe in the United States. (J. Gordon Melton)

Conquistador Hernán Cortéz (1485–1547) landed in Mexico at a site that later became the modern city of Veracruz and with his small army of 508 Spaniards supported by thousands of Tlaxcalteca allies conquered the Aztecs in 1521. He established Spanish rule on the ruins of the Aztec capital of Tenochtitlan, renamed Mexico City. In 1519, Tenochtitlan was the largest city in the world with a population of about 350,000; by comparison, the population of London in 1519 was only 80,000 people. When the Spanish arrived, there were an estimated 25 million Amerindians in the territory known today as Mexico.

During the Spanish colonial period (1521–1821), the majority of its Amerindian population was decimated by warfare, famine, and disease. Formal independence from Spain was recognized in 1821. The

U.S.-Mexican War (1846–1848) ended with the ceding of almost half of Mexico's national territory, including present-day Texas, New Mexico, Arizona, and California. French forces invaded Mexico in 1861 and ruled briefly until 1867. The Mexican Revolution of 1910–1917 resulted in the death of an estimated 10 percent of the nation's population.

Between 1521 and 1821, the government aligned with the Roman Catholic Church. The Catholic Church also tried to build on ancient Native worship. The persistence of Amerindian cultures and belief systems is a vital force in modern Mexican society, as seen by the prevalence of practices such as shamanism (intermediaries between the human and spirit worlds), magic and witchcraft (*bujería*), herbal healing (*curanderismo*), and "folk saints and healers" throughout Mexico.

After independence from Spain in 1821, the Roman Catholic Church began to lose its place of privilege. Citizens were no longer obligated to pay tithes or to work for the church as serfs in a feudal society. The Catholic Church did, however, maintain its monopoly on religion in Mexico as affirmed by the Constitution of 1824, which declared that religion "will perpetually be Catholic, Apostolic, and Roman." Full diplomatic relations were maintained with the Vatican until broken in 1867, following the period of French intervention.

From Independence to the Mexican Revolution (1821–1910), the Catholic Church sided with the more Conservative political parties, though certain liberal-minded elements within the church identified with the revolutionary struggle of the peasants. Through the 19th century, the Catholic Church was aligned with Conservative politics and opposed both the Liberal movement and Freemasonry, which had gained popularity among the wealthy elite. Church leadership opposed the reform movement led by Benito Juárez (1806–1872) and welcomed the French occupation of Mexico in 1862.

Although church-state tensions eased considerably during the Conservative administration of Porfirio Díaz (1876–1910), they flared up again after the Revolution of 1910–1917. The Constitution of 1917 established a separation between church and state, guaranteed a secular public education, and prohibited the clergy from participating in the nation's political life and from owning property.

The Cristero War (1926–1929) was an attempt by conservative Catholic forces to invalidate anti-Catholic elements of the Constitution. Catholics resorted to armed violence against the government of President Elías Calles (1877–1946). The conflict ended in 1929, when President Emilio Portes Gil (1890–1978) promised a new respect for religion, which allowed the Catholic clergy to resume their religious work throughout the country.

In the decades after the Mexican Revolution, the Institutional Revolutionary Party (PRI, Partido Revolucionario Institucional) came to power. It controlled national politics from 1929 until 2001. In 2000, after 70 years, the PRI lost the presidential election to an opposition candidate, Vicente Fox Quesada, who won under the banner of the National Action Party (PAN, Partido de Acción Nacional), which has close ties to the Catholic Church. However, the continued non-PAN majority in Congress prevented him from implementing most of his proposed reforms during his term in office (2000–2006). In 2006, PAN candidate Felipe de Jesús Calderón Hinojosa, a self-described devout Roman Catholic, won the presidency for a six-year term (2006–2012).

The Roman Catholic Church   The military conquest of Mexico by Spanish forces was generally perceived as the triumph of Catholicism over the Amerindian deities, and particularly as the disintegration of the Aztec worldview that required continuous human blood sacrifice to sustain the universe. The defeat of Amerindian religious leaders and the destruction of their sacred temples and images by Cortés' army were seen as a spiritual conquest over a fundamentally-flawed brand of religion by agents of a superior religion. However, most of the Spanish friars were more ambivalent about associating their own missionary enterprise with Spanish military conquests.

The evangelization of the Amerindian tribes of Mexico by Roman Catholic missionaries began with the arrival of the Franciscans (1524), the Dominicans (1526), and the Augustinians (1533). Between 1594 and 1722, the Jesuits worked among the Amerindians in northern Mexico, During the 17th and 18th centuries, the Franciscans organized a vast mission empire that included 11 districts: from Sierra Gorda and Tampico in the northeast to Sonora, Arizona, New Mexico, and Alta California in the northwest. The Dominicans established two important mission centers in Sierra Gorda (1686) and Baja California (1772).

The first Catholic bishopric erected in Mexico was the See of Yucatán, under the patronage of the Virgin Mary as La Nuestra Señora de los Remedios. In 1526, Pope Clement VII (r. 1523–1534) named Father Julian de Garces as the first bishop of New Spain. In 1545, at the request of Spanish King Charles V (r. 1516–1556), Pope Paul III (r. 1534–1549) separated the dioceses of New Spain from the metropolitan See of Seville and established the Archdiocese of Mexico. During the Spanish colonial period (1520–1821), Catholic missionaries systematically established churches in nearly every village of Mexico.

Virgin of Guadalupe carved in a cottonwood tree. Also known as The Lady of Guadalupe, she is of significant importance to Mexican Catholics. (Corel)

Today, the Virgin of Guadalupe is a symbol of Mexican national identity, while the chapel to Our Lady of Guadalupe at Tepeyac hill (now a suburb of Mexico City) built in 1555–1556, has become the most sacred site for Catholics in Mexico. Future generations of clerics embellished the legend of Our Lady of Guadalupe, so that by 1648 Mexican peasants considered the shrine to have supernatural significance and to be a sign of divine approval for regarding themselves as the "new chosen people" (a cosmic race) that God had selected through the agency of the Virgin Mary, who, according to the legend, miraculously appeared to a shepherd at Tepeyac in 1531.

Special celebrations are held annually at these shrines, three of the most important being those dedicated to La Virgin de Juquila in the state of Oaxaca, to Nuestro Señor Jesucristo y San Miguel de las Cuevas de Chalma in the state of Mexico, and to La Virgin de Guadalupe in the Federal District.

There are a variety of "folk saints" in Mexico that have not been canonized by the Catholic Church but that are treated as sacred by many believers. One of the most popular folk saints is José Fidencio Síntora Constantino, known as El Niño Fidencio (b. 1898). He became known to the Mexican press during the Cristero War (1926–1929), when Catholics were persecuted during the administration of President Plutarco Elías Calles. El Niño Fidencio is popularly identified with the Christ Child, and is reported to have received his calling as a child, and as a young man received the gift of healing and achieved fame as a healer (*curandero*).

Another folk saint that has been popularized throughout Mexico is La Santa Muerte (Saint Death). Her larger-than-life statue, which devotees keep in glass boxes at road-side sanctuaries, is usually draped in lace-trimmed satin; her hooded, grinning skull is crowned with a rhinestone tiara, and the bony fingers that protrude from beneath her cloak are adorned with glittering rings. Stories of prayers answered and miracles performed have fueled the spread of this popular cult, whose worship is said to date to the mid-1960s among rural villagers. Prisoners, petty thieves, corrupt policemen, and powerful drug traffickers are believed to be devotees of La Santa Muerte, who appeals to the faith of simple working-class Mexicans who daily face hunger, injustice, corruption, and crime in some of Mexico's toughest neighborhoods.

The independent Traditional Mex-USA Catholic Church is led by its self-appointed bishop David Romo Millán, a principal leader of the Iglesia de la Santa Muerte. Jesús Romero Padilla is the guardian of one of the movement's main sanctuaries, located in Tepito in the Federal District; he is reported to lead processions honoring La Santa Muerte in Puebla, Toluca, Veracruz, and Oaxaca.

Yearly, there is a special celebration in honor of the dead, called Culto a los Muertos, which is celebrated from October 21 to November 2. In many villages, towns, and cities across the country, Mexican peasants bring a variety of offerings—flowers, food, drink, and candles—to a family altar in their homes or to the gravesides of their dead relatives, and there is a celebration with music, dances, masks, and other symbols of death and fireworks in their honor.

For many Mexicans, affiliation with the Catholic Church has become less of a social obligation than during previous decades, with fewer than 20 percent of Catholics regularly attending Mass. During the 1990s, numerous public opinion polls revealed increasing numbers unhappy with the Vatican's official policy regarding birth control, divorce, remarriage, abortion, the role of women in the church, obligatory celibacy for priests and nuns, the absolute authority of the pope, the authoritarianism of the bishops, and the lack of lay participation in church matters.

Today, the Roman Catholic Church in Mexico is divided administratively into 15 regions and 22 jurisdictions: 14 archdioceses, and 5 territorial prelatures. Eastern-rite Catholics are found in two eparchies and an apostolic exarchate: Nuestra Señora de los Mártires del Líbano en México (the Maronite Eparchy with about 148,250 adherents); Nuestra Señora del Paraíso en México (the Greek-Melkite Eparchy, with about 4,600 adherents); and America Latina e Messico, Faithful of the Oriental Rite (the Armenian Apostolic Exarchate with about 12,000 adherents).

The Mexican Episcopal Conference is composed of 157 members (the papal nuncio, cardinals, archbishops, and bishops) and presided over by Monsignor Carlos Aguilar Retes, the archbishop of Tlalnepantla. The archbishop of Mexico City (Federal District) is Cardinal Norberto Rivera Carrera, who was appointed archbishop in June 1995 and elevated to cardinal in 1998.

The Protestant Movement   After the Constitution of 1857 formalized Liberal reforms, which limited the power of the Roman Catholic Church and broadened individual freedoms, a spectrum of Protestant groups began to penetrate Mexico. By 1900, at least 15 U.S. Protestant denominations from America entered Mexico, many having begun along the U.S.-Mexican border. Others arrived on the coastlands (Veracruz), and a few in Mexico City and other major cities.

One of the first independent missionaries to begin Protestant work along the border (1852, in Brownsville, Texas) was Melinda Rankin (1811–1888), a Presbyterian who later joined the American and Foreign Christian Union and established Protestant schools in Matamoros, Tamaulipas (1862–1863), and Monterrey, Nuevo León (1866). The first Protestant church organized in Mexico City (1861) was a German Lutheran congregation. In 1862, an independent Baptist missionary, James Hickey, arrived in Monterrey from Texas and began the task of evangelizing and establishing a church (1864) that was later pastored by Thomas Westrupp. By 1870, there were two Protestant churches in Monterrey, one affiliated with the American Baptist Home Mission Society (Westrupp) and the other related to the American Cumberland Presbyterian Church, pastored by John Parks. In 1868, the Protestant Episcopal Church established a relationship with an independent Catholic church (non-papal), known as the Mexican Church of Jesus, which had been organized in 1859 in Mexico City. By 1870, there were 23 Episcopal-Church of Jesus congregations in the Valley of Mexico.

During the period 1870 to 1900, at least 15 additional U.S. Protestant mission agencies inaugurated work in Mexico. The Society of Friends (Quakers) arrived in Matamoros, Tamaulipas, in 1871, near the Texas border. Three missionary couples affiliated with the Northern Presbyterian Church arrived in Mexico City in 1872, and eventually began work in Zacatecas, San Luis Potosí, and Guanajuato. The American Board of Commissioners for Foreign Missions (Congregational Church) sent two missionary couples to Guadalajara in 1872, and five missionary couples were sent to Monterrey in 1873 to work with congregations formed by Melinda Rankin and Juan Sepulveda that grew out of the early Baptist and Presbyterian efforts. In 1872, both the Methodist Episcopal Church (North) and the Methodist Episcopal Church (South) began work in Mexico City, after purchasing from the government properties that formerly belonged to the Catholic Church. In 1874, the Southern Presbyterians began work in Matamoros, Tamaulipas. The Associated Reformed Presbyterian Church arrived in 1878, the Southern Baptist Convention in 1880, the Plymouth Brethren (also known as Christian Brethren) in 1890, the Seventh Day Baptist General Conference in 1893, and the Christian Women's Board of Missions (Disciples of Christ) in 1895.

Between 1900 and 1949, at least 45 Protestant church bodies or mission agencies were established in Mexico. The revolution of 1910 proved a significant watershed in Protestant church life. Most, if not all, of the Protestant missionaries in Mexico left the country soon after the beginning of hostilities and did not return until after the conflict ended in 1917. In that year, the mainline U.S. Protestant mission agencies (those affiliated with the Federal Council of Churches) that had previously initiated work in Mexico constructed a "comity" plan, whereby the various agencies were assigned to different geographical areas of the county in an effort to avoid competition and the duplication of efforts, though they left Mexico City open to all. However, the so-called Cincinnati Plan did not work out well in practice, as most Mexican denominational leaders, pastors, and their church members had already developed strong denominational loyalties and refused to adhere to the plan.

Many presently existing Pentecostal churches and denominations in Mexico trace their origins to the work begun by the Swedish Free Mission/Filadelfia Swedish Pentecostal Churches, founded in 1924 by Axel Anderson in Coyoacán, who was later assisted by other Swedish missionaries, such as Charles Armstrong and Gunhild Gustaffson. The Swedish Pentecostals looked for guidance from Reverend Lewi Petrus (1884–1974), the pastor of the Filadelfia Church in Stockholm, which in 1929 was reported to be the largest Pentecostal church in the world with 3,500 members. According to Manuel Gaxiola, Lindy Scott, and other sources, the Mexican denominations that grew out of this movement include the following: the Independent Evangelical Church in Mexico (IEIM), the Independent Evangelical Church in the Mexican Republic (IEIRM), the Independent Pentecostal Christian Church (ICIP), and the Independent Pentecostal Fraternity (FRAPI–composed of eight autonomous church associations).

Between 1950 and 1980, another 94 Protestant mission agencies began work in Mexico, and scores of new denominations came into existence under national leadership. During the 1940s and 1950s there were many reports of the severe persecution of evangelicals by fanatical Catholics, especially in rural areas and within Amerindian communities.

During the 1960s and 1970s, the Charismatic Renewal movement (CRM) began and flourished in Mexico. An ecumenical bridge between Catholics and Protestants in Latin America in the late 1970s and early 1980s was the John 17:21 Fellowship associated with David du Plessis. A Latin American branch of this Fellowship was established in Guatemala City after a major earthquake occurred there in 1976; the coordinator was the Reverend Robert Thomas of Los Altos, California. In Mexico, Thomas worked closely with Friar Alfonzo Navarro Castellanos and the Catholic Missionaries of the Holy Spirit (MSpSC) to form UCELAM (Christian Union for Evangelizing Latin America) in 1978, which held annual ecumenical CRM conferences in Mexico City for a decade or more. Some of the UCELAM teams included evangelicals such as Bob Thomas, Paul Northrup (secretary of the Latin American John 17:21 Fellowship), Bill Finke, and Juan Carlos Ortiz (an early leader in the Argentine CRM between 1967 and 1978), who spoke to many ecumenical audiences in the United States and Latin America during the 1980s.

The Current Situation Statistics on the various Protestant denominations in Mexico at any point in time has been difficult for most researchers and church historians to find. One of the first sources of information about this was *The Missionary Review of the World* (May 1911, vol. 24), which reported 469 organized local churches with 16,250 members in 1888. In 1910, another source reported 23,940 baptized Protestant church members in Mexico: Methodists (12,500), Presbyterians (5,700), Baptists (2,630), Congregationalists (1,540), Christian Churches–Disciples of Christ (900), and Quakers (670).

However, in 1936, the total membership of these same denominations was reported to be 22,882, which reflects some of the difficulties encountered during the Mexican Revolution and the Depression years. Nevertheless, some of the newer denominations reported the following membership statistics in 1936: Assemblies of God (6,000), Adventists (4,000), Swedish Pentecostals (4,000), Nazarenes (2,000), Pentecostal Holiness (1,300), Pilgrim Holiness (1,200), and Mexican Indian churches (560), for a total of about 19,000 members. These are partial statistics because other denomi-

A statue of Fray Junipero Sera (of California mission fame) and the Templo de la Santa Cruz in Queretaro, Mexico. (Arturo Osorno/Dreamstime.com)

nations (with an estimated total of 6,000 members) were known to exist in 1936 that were not included in the study published by the International Missionary Council in 1938. The total Protestant membership in Mexico for 1936 was estimated to be 48,000 but did not include the Mennonite colonies.

Today, there are an estimated 80,000 Mennonites (adherents) in Mexico. They live in several areas, particularly in the states of Chihuahua and Durango. During the 1920s, the Mexican government wanted to settle the barren northern region with industrious farmers such as the Mennonites. In 1922, at the invitation of President Alvaro Obregón, 20,000 Mennonites left Canada and settled in the state of Chihuahua. The Mexican government agreed to sell them land at reasonable prices and level no taxes for 100 years if the

Mennonites would produce the bulk of cheese needed for northern Mexico. President Obregón granted the Mennonites full control of their schools including retaining their language, independence of religion in both home and schools, and exemption from military service. In 2006, there were a total of about 26,000 Mennonite church members in Mexico.

By 1962, there were about 276,000 Protestant church members in Mexico, according to a study conducted by Dr. Donald McGavran; however, there was no mention of the Mennonite colonists. At that time, the largest denominational families were the following: Presbyterian (42,000), Methodist (33,000), Adventist (22,700), Church of God (Cleveland, Tennessee) (15,500), Swedish Pentecostals (15,000), Assemblies of God (15,000), Movement of Independent Evangelical Pentecostal Churches (Movimiento Iglesia Evangélica Pentecostés Independiente [MIEPI]) (10,000), and scores of other groups with less than 10,000 members each.

In 1960, the Mexican national census reported the Protestant population at 578,515. A study by William Read, Victor Monterroso, and Harmon Johnston on Protestant church growth in Latin America, published in 1969, reported that the total Protestant membership in Mexico was about 430,000 in 1967, of which 64 percent was Pentecostal and 36 percent non-Pentecostal. Obviously, the number of Pentecostal church members had increased faster than that of the non-Pentecostals in the 30-year period 1936–1966.

The size of the Protestant population in 2000 was 5.7 percent of the total population, compared to 4.9 percent in 1990, 3.3 percent in 1980, and 1.8 percent in 1970, based on statistics from the Mexican national censuses. By comparison, the percentage size of the Protestant population in Mexico is much lower than in the counties of Central America where Protestants are between 15 and 35 percent of the national population in each country; however, in terms of actual population, the number of Protestants in Mexico is very large, an estimated 6,322,000 in mid-2008, fourth in size in the Americas after the United States (150 million), Brazil (30 million), and Canada (9.5 million).

Based on information from a variety of sources, the largest Protestant denominations in Mexico today are believed to be the following in order of relative size

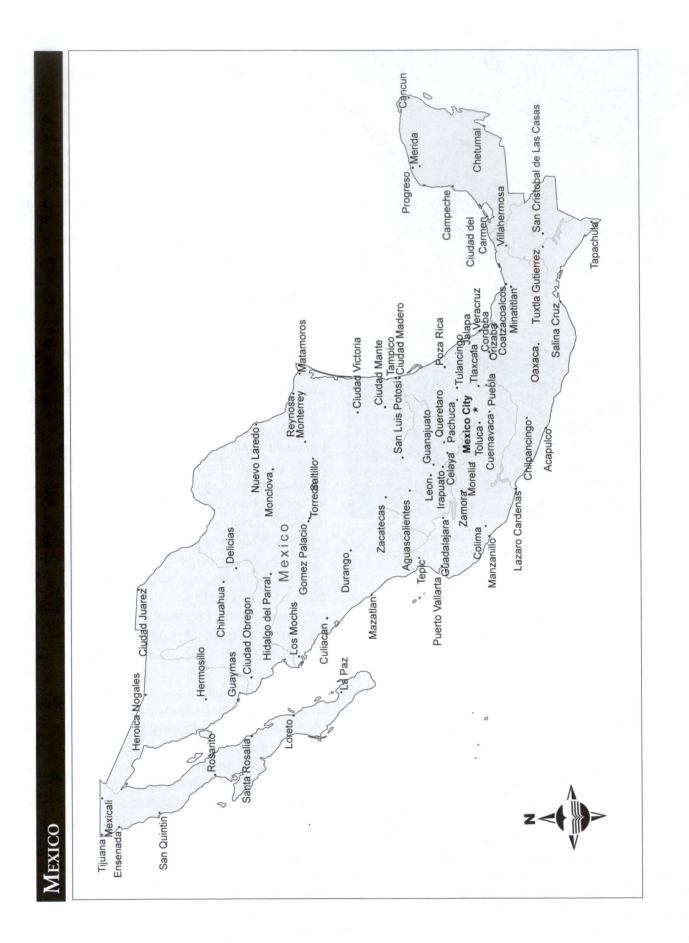

Mexico

Religion	Followers in 1970	Followers in 2010	% of Population	Annual % growth 2000–2010	Followers in 2025	Followers in 2050
Christians	51,018,000	105,583,000	95.7	0.87	117,604,000	122,760,000
Roman Catholics	47,029,000	98,500,000	89.3	0.87	107,000,000	108,263,000
Protestants	693,000	4,325,000	3.9	1.78	6,500,000	8,100,000
Independents	1,176,000	3,687,000	3.3	2.40	5,500,000	8,000,000
Agnostics	854,000	2,900,000	2.6	1.80	5,000,000	7,000,000
Ethnoreligionists	50,000	1,240,000	1.1	0.90	1,200,000	1,200,000
Muslims	15,000	220,000	0.2	0.89	400,000	650,000
Jews	35,000	125,000	0.1	0.89	125,000	125,000
Atheists	20,000	120,000	0.1	0.89	200,000	300,000
Baha'is	15,100	37,500	0.0	0.89	60,000	80,000
Buddhists	15,000	25,700	0.0	0.89	40,000	60,000
New religionists	2,000	14,600	0.0	0.89	25,000	40,000
Chinese folk	3,000	12,000	0.0	0.89	20,000	35,000
Hindus	0	9,800	0.0	0.89	15,000	20,000
Sikhs	1,000	5,500	0.0	0.89	6,500	8,000
Total population	**52,028,000**	**110,293,000**	**100.0**	**0.89**	**124,695,000**	**132,278,000**

by membership: National Council of the Assemblies of God (more than 5,000 congregations and 650,000 members in 2000); National Presbyterian Church (4,800 congregations and 624,000 members in 2008); Seventh-day Adventist Church (more than 2,852 congregations and 597,540 members in 2007); Independent Evangelical Church in Mexico (IEIM, founded by Swedish Pentecostal Axel Anderson); Interdenominational Christian Church in the Mexican Republic (ICIRM, Pentecostal); National Baptist Convention of Mexico (more than 1,700 congregations and 272,000 members in 2009); Church of God in the Mexican Republic (IDRM, a split from the Assemblies of God); Apostolic Church of Faith in Jesus Christ (more than 1,400 congregations and 150,000 members in 2008—Oneness Pentecostal); Movement of Independent Evangelical Pentecostal Churches (MIEPI); Church of God (Cleveland, Tennessee); Spiritual Christian Evangelical Church (362 churches and 578 preaching centers, with an estimated 62,500 members—Oneness Pentecostal); Methodist Church of Mexico (400 congregations and 52,000 members in 2006); Church of the Nazarene (616 churches and 40,000 members in 2008); Centers of Faith, Hope and Love of the Missionary Revival Crusade (245 centers, some of which have over 10,000 members each—Pentecostal); Independent Pentecos-

tal Fraternity (FRAPI); Independent Evangelical Church in the Mexican Republic (IEIRM, a Swedish Pentecostal split from IEIM); National Evangelical Pentecostal Church (INEP); Universal Pentecostal Church of Jesus (in Morelos, Guerrero, and Veracruz); and independent Christian Churches/Churches of Christ (affiliated with Churches of Christ in Christian Union).

Several ecumenical organizations operate among Protestants in Mexico. The Latin American Confraternity of Evangelicals (CONELA) members in Mexico include the Secretariat of Social Communication of the Evangelical Christian Church of Mexico (Secretaría de Comunicación Social de Iglesias Cristianas Evangélicas de México [SECOSICE]); and the Mexican Evangelical Confederation (Confraternidad Evangélica Mexicana [CONEMEX]), founded in 1982. The only CLAI (Latin American Council of Churches) members in Mexico are the German Lutheran Church and the Methodist Church (affiliated with the United Methodist Church in the U.S.A.). The Methodist Church of Mexico is the only Mexican-based church that is a member of the World Council of Churches, though a variety of Protestant churches are related through their American affiliates. The World Evangelical Alliance work in Mexico through two national bodies: the Secretaría de Comunicación Social de Iglesias

Cristianas Evangélicas de México (SECOSICE) and the Associate Alliance: Confraternidad Evangélica Mexicana (CONEMEX).

Eastern Orthodox and Independent Catholic Jurisdictions Eastern Orthodox jurisdictions in Mexico include both the large church representing the older Middle Eastern and Eastern European jurisdictions and some of the new western jurisdictions: The Greek Orthodox Archdiocese of Mexico and Central America affiliated with the Ecumenical Patriarchate based in Istanbul was founded in 1996 in Mexico. It is led by Arzobispo Atenagoras (Anesti). This jurisdiction is also known as Sacro Arzobispado Ortodoxo Griego de México (Greek Orthodox Holy Mission). The Greek Orthodox Patriarchate of Antioch and All the East (commonly known as the Antiochian Orthodox Church) was founded in Mexico in 1943 under the leadership of Amín Aboumrad, who reported to Archbishop Samuel David in Toledo, Ohio; St. George's Orthodox Cathedral was built in Colonia Roma Sur, Delegación Alvaro Obregón, DF, between 1944 and 1947. In 1966 Antonio Chedraui became the first bishop of Mexico, and in 1996 he was appointed as the metropolitan archbishop of Mexico, Venezuela, Central America, and the Caribbean. Russian Orthodox are found in the Catholic Orthodox Church in Mexico (affiliated with the Orthodox Church in America) under the leadership of Presbyter Desiderio Barrero Sermeño; the Orthodox Apostolic Catholic Church (Russian Orthodox Patriarch of Moscow) based in the Parish of the Protection of the Holy Mother of God in Nepantla, state of Mexico; and the Russian Orthodox Church Outside Russia (ROCOR) (Patriarch of Moscow) under Archbishop Kyrill of the Western Diocese of North America. The related but smaller Ukrainian community is found in the Ukrainian Orthodox Church of Patriarch Moses of Kiev. Its congregations are associated together in the Archdiocese of Mexico and All Latin America under Archbishop Daniel de Jesús (Ruiz Flores).

Among several independent Western Orthodox churches operating in Mexico is the Eastern Orthodox Catholic Church (Iglesia Católica Ortodoxa Oriental), Archdiocese of the Americas & Diaspora, whose episcopal orders derive from Syrian and Russian Orthodox successions. It uses the Divine Liturgy of Saint John Chrysostom with the Syriac-Greek Typicon. This church is administered by a Synod of Bishops headquartered in Cleveland, Ohio; Cyril Cranshaw is the bishop of Central and South America (which includes Mexico).

The Coptic Orthodox Church of Alexandria, whose members derive primarily from Egypt, are under Patriarch Shenouda III. Its Mexican community founded the first church in the 1990s, as St. Mary and St. Mark's Coptic Orthodox Church in Tlaycapan, state of Morelos.

There are several small independent Western Roman Catholic-derived groups, among the most important being the Mexican National Catholic Church, which was founded in the 1920s to take the place of the temporarily disenfranchised Roman Catholic Church. It emerged in Massume under Bishops José Juaquín Pérez y Budar, Antonio Benicio López Sierra, and Macario López y Valdez.

More recently, the Mexican Apostolic Catholic Church, also known as the "Church of Mr. President," was founded in 1979 in Mexico City by excommunicated Catholic Bishop Eduardo Dávila de la Garza as an independent Mexican Apostolic Church. This church does not recognize the pope; rather, it claims that the president of the Republic of Mexico is its highest authority. The basic characteristic of this movement is a belief in the miracle of the *hostia sangrante* ("bleeding communion wafer") that is reported to have taken place in 1978 in the parish of Our Lady of Guadalupe, located in a poor neighborhood on the east side of Mexico City.

Other Christian Churches Although some of the non-Protestant Christian groups were probably included in the "Protestant-Evangelical" category in the 1990 and 2000 censuses, the two main denominational families are the Jehovah's Witnesses and the Church of Jesus Christ of Latter-day Saints. The official 2005 Report of Jehovah's Witnesses Worldwide listed 11,192 congregations with a peak attendance of 593,802 in Mexico. The 2000 Mexican census reported 1,057,736 Jehovah's Witnesses adherents, which means that the Jehovah's Witnesses in Mexico are the second largest worldwide to JWs in the United States.

The largest of the several Mormon groups in Mexico, the Church of Jesus Christ of Latter-day Saints (popularly called Mormons), based in Salt Lake City, Utah, first arrived in the Casas Grandes Valley of Chihuahua in 1885 and eventually established nine agricultural colonies: six in the state of Chihuahua and three in Sonora. In February 2000, they dedicated a new temple in Juárez to serve its 25,000 members in that state.

The Community of Christ (until recently known as the Reorganized Church of Jesus Christ of Latter-day Saints), based in Independence, Missouri, has eight congregations scattered across the country that are associated with the congregations in Texas under the guidance of the Texas-Mexico mission Center in McAllen, Texas.

When the Church of Jesus Christ of Latter-day Saints abandoned the practice of polygamy, a variety of dissenting groups established work in Mexico, which has been relatively tolerant of them. Included among these groups are the Church of the Firstborn in the Fullness of Times (known as the LeBaron Mormon Polygamist movement), which settled in Chihuahua in 1922); United Order Front (now known as the Fundamentalist Church of Jesus Christ of Latter-day Saints); and the Apostolic United Brethren (a split from the United Order Front). The Church of Christ (Temple Lot), now based in Independence, Illinois, has an origin independent of both the Community of Christ and the Utah church. The 2000 Mexican census reported a total of 205,229 adherents for all Latter-day Saint groups. In contrast, the official Church of Jesus Christ of Latter-day Saints website reported 1,158,236 members in 1,977 congregations for 2007.

Also present in Mexico are the Children of God (now called The Family International), the Christadelphian Bible Mission, Christian Science (Church of Christ, Scientist), Growing in Grace Ministries International (based in Miami, Florida), Mita Congregation (from Puerto Rico), the People of Amos Church (a split from Mita Congregation under Nicolas Tosado Aviles in Puerto Rico), Voice of the Cornerstone (a Branham-related group from Puerto Rico), the God is Love Pentecostal Church, and the Universal Church of the Kingdom of God (both from Brazil), among others.

Another significant religious tradition, founded in the city of Monterrey, Nuevo León, in 1926 by Eusebio Joaquín González (known as the Prophet Aarón, who died in 1964), has blended Mexican mysticism with Pentecostal fervor to create the Light of the World Church (its full name is the Church of the Living God, Column and Pillar of Truth, Jesus the Light of the World). Since 1952, its headquarters have been located in Colonia Hermosa Provincia, Guadalajara, state of Jalisco. In 1942, the Light of the World Church experienced a division that led to the founding of the Church of the Good Shepherd, led by José María González, with headquarters in Toluca de Lerdo, capital of the state of Mexico. Similar to the mother church, this denomination holds an annual celebration of the Lord's Supper (Communion) in April during Holy Week with the participation of pastors and lay representatives from all of its local congregations in Mexico, the United States, and Central America.

In 1965, Abel Joaquín Avelar, a son of Eusebio Joaquín (the Prophet Aarón), left the Light of the World Church in Guadalajara, moved to Mexico City, and founded his own organization, the Church of Jesus Christ (Iglesia de Jesucristo), which now has at least 22 organized churches. The leader of this denomination has taken the title apostle of the church and has an Apostolic Council composed of 12 members.

The Christian Apostolic Church of the Living God, Column and Pillar of Truth was founded in 1978 in Cuernavaca, Morelos, by Francisco Jesus Adame Giles, who claimed to have a dream or vision in 1978 in which he reported that "an angel appeared to me and called me to preach the Gospel and announce the Kingdom of God." In 1989 he formed a community of followers in Colonia Lomas de Chamilpa on about 16 square miles of land, north of Cuernavaca, with himself as the maximum authority. This community of an estimated 400 families is now called Provincia Jerusalén; its members are prohibited from smoking, drinking, and dancing, and women may not use makeup or wear jewelry or slacks. Adame has a dominant role in their lives—spiritually, socially, and economically; this group claims to be neither Protestant nor a sect, but rather "Israelites of the New Israel of God." The movement claims to have about 50,000 followers in the states of Morelos, Oaxaca, Veracruz, Guerrero, Mexico, Puebla, Guanajuato, and Baja California Norte.

Other Religions Religions not associated with the Christian tradition include some 60 registered religious associations that represent the spectrum of the world's religions: Judaism, Islam, Baha'i Faith, Buddhism, Hinduism, Sikh, Sant Mat, Chinese religions, and Shinto. Relatively small, these organizations have pioneered a presence for the various groups with roots in the Middle East (Islam, the Baha'i Faith) and Asia (Buddhism, Hinduism, Sant Mat). Buddhism is represented by the Centro Budista de la Ciudad de México, Casa Tibet México, Soka Gakkai de México; Jodo Shinshu Hongwanji-Ha Misión de México; Jodo Shinshu Hongwanji-Ha Ekoji de México; and Centro Zen de México. Hinduism movements include the Sociedad Internacional Para la Conciencia de Krishna en México, Iglesia del Señor Chaitanya/Sri Chaitanya Saraswat Ashram de Mexico, and the Movimiento Hare Krishna-Iskcon. The Sant Mat tradition includes the Organización Espiritual Mundial Thakar Singh; Eckankar de México; and the Movimiento del Sendero Interno del Alma (Movement of Spiritual Inner Awareness [MSIA]).

The Western Esoteric Tradition is represented by Freemasonry, Servants of Light School of Occult Science, Rosicrucians (Ancient and Mystical Order Rosae Crucis, AMORC; Fraternitas Rosicruciana Antigua, FRA; Rosicrucian Fellowship), the Grand Universal Fraternity (headquarters in El Limon, Aragua, Venezuela), GFU Network (led by Jose Manuel Estrada Vasques, with headquarters in Morelos, Mexico), the Universal Gnostic Movement of Mexico (founded by Victor Manuel Gomez Rodrígues, known as Samael Aun Weor after 1956, with headquarters in Mexico City), the International Gnostic Movement (headquarters in Guadalajara, Mexico), the Universal Christian Gnostic Church, the Gnostic Movement Cultural Association, the Quetzalcoatl Cultural Institute of Psycho-Analytical Anthropology (Loreto, Zacatecas, Mexico), the New Acropolis Cultural Association, the Cafh Foundation, Wicca, and the International Pagan Federation of Mexico. Also, a variety of Satanist groups are known to exist in Mexico.

Additional Esoteric presence can be found in the more than 27 Spiritualism associations, several Theosophical groups, the Church of Scientology, and the Unification Church (Holy Spirit Association for the Unification of World Christianity), among others. One Mexican national religious tradition blends Catholicism with Spiritualism (communication with the dead through the use of mediums and séances): the Marian Trinitarian Spiritualist Church, founded by Roque Jacinto Rojas Esparza (1812–1869) in Mexico City in 1866. Rojas allegedly received a message from the biblical prophet Elijah (Elías in Spanish), who named him "the prophet of the First Period." After Rojas's death in 1869, the movement split into several factions; these groups are known today as the Prophet Elijah (Elias) movement, which included at least 47 registered religious associations in 2009.

"Popular religiosity" (syncretistic) is practiced by a majority of the Hispanic population, which is also present among numerous Amerindian religions (animist) that have blended elements of Catholicism to create several varieties of popular religiosity. The Amerindian groups are scattered throughout the national territory, with the largest concentration in the state of Oaxaca in southern Mexico. Religious shrines, images, and sacred places form part of the religious landscape in Mexico, some of which are dedicated to the Virgin Mary (la Virgin de Guadalupe), the Christ Child, the Black Christ, Saint Death (La Santa Muerte), and revered "folk saints and healers," such as the Niño Fidencio cult (José Fidencio Sintora Constantino, 1898–1938) in Guanajuato, and the Juan Soldado cult (Juan Castillo Morales) in Baja California.

A revitalization movement among Amerindian tribes in the northern and central regions of Mexico (along the western Sierra Madre mountain range) is called the Peyote religion, due to its use of the peyote cactus, which is a psychotropical plant that produces "altered states of consciousness" during shamanic rituals. According to authoritative sources, this practice dates to about 7000 BCE in Mexico. The Native American Church of Itzachilatlan was founded by Aurelio Dias Tepankai in Yoricostio, Michoacán. Similar religious organizations exist in the United States, which have blended Christianity with the Peyote religion, such as the Native American Church in North America with headquarters in Box Elder, Montana.

Among the Afro-American population, elements of African-derived religions from the Caribbean may exist, such as Vodou (Haiti), Santeria (Puerto Rico and

Cuba), Myalism-Obeah, and Rastafarianism (British West Indies).

The Inter-Religious Council of Mexico was founded in Mexico City in 1992 with representatives from the following traditions: Roman Catholic, Greek Orthodox, Anglican, Lutheran, Presbyterian, Mormon, Buddhist, Hindu, Sikh, Jewish, and Sufi-Muslim. In 1999, the coordinator of the council was Jonathan Rose, the Jewish representative.

Clifton L. Holland

See also: American Baptist Churches in the U.S.A.; American Board of Commissioners for Foreign Missions; Ancient and Mystical Order Rosae Crucis; Apostolic Church of Faith in Jesus Christ of Mexico; Armenian Catholic Church; Assemblies of God; Augustinians; Benedictines; Christian Brethren; Christian Church (Disciples of Christ); Church of Christ, Scientist; Church of God (Cleveland, Tennessee); Church of God of Prophecy; Church of Jesus Christ of Latter-day Saints; Church of Scientology; Church of the Nazarene; Cistercians; Cumberland Presbyterian Church; Dominicans; Ecumenical Patriarchate/Patriarchate of Constantinople; Evangelical Covenant Church; Family International, The; Franciscans; Freemasonry; Gnostic Movement; Greek Orthodox Patriarchate of Antioch and All the East; International Church of the Foursquare Gospel; International Pentecostal Holiness Church; Jehovah's Witnesses; Jesuits; Latin American Council of Churches; Light of the World Church; Maronite Catholic Church; Mary, Blessed Virgin; Melkite Catholic Church; Mennonites; Methodist Church of Mexico; Mita Congregation; Movement of Spiritual Inner Awareness; New Acropolis Cultural Association; New Age Movement; Pentecostalism; Roman Catholic Church; Russian Orthodox Church Outside Russia; Salvation Army; Santeria; Seventh-day Adventist Church; Seventh-Day Baptist General Conference; Southern Baptist Convention; Sufism; Unification Movement; United Methodist Church; Universal Church of the Kingdom of God; Vodou; Wesleyan Church; Western Esoteric Tradition; Wiccan Religion; Witchcraft; Women, Status and Role of; World Council of Churches; World Evangelical Alliance.

References

Barry, Tom, ed. *Mexico: A Country Guide.* Albuquerque, NM: The Inter-Hemispheric Education Resource Center, 1992.

Bastian, Jean-Pierre. *Protestantismo y Sociedad en México.* Mexico City: CUPSA, 1983.

Blancarte, Roberto. *Historia de la Iglesia Católica en México.* Mexico City: Fondo de Cultura Económica, 1992.

Dussel, Enrique, ed. *Historia General de la Iglesia en América Latina.* Tomo V, *México.* México, DF: Ediciones Paulinas, 1984.

Fernández Olmos, Margarite, and Lizabeth Paravisini-Gebert. *Creole Religions of the Caribbean: An Introduction from Vodou and Santería to Obeah and Espiritismo.* New York: New York University, 2003.

Gaxiola, Manuel J. "Las Cuatro Vertientes del Pentecostalismo Mexicano." http://esnuestra historia.wordpress.com/historia/.

Giménez, Gilberto, ed. *Identidades Religiosas y Sociales en México.* Mexico City: Universidad Nacional Autónoma de México, 1996.

Grimes, Barbara F., ed. *Ethnologue: Languages of the World.* 12th ed. Dallas, TX: Summer Institute of Linguistics, 1992.

McGavran, Donald, ed. *Church Growth in Mexico.* Grand Rapids, MI: William B. Eerdmans Publishing Company, 1963.

Pardo, Osvaldo F. *The Origins of Mexican Catholicism.* Ann Arbor: University of Michigan Press, 2006.

Poole, Stafford. *Our Lady of Guadalupe: The Origins and Sources of a Mexican National Symbol, 1531–1797.* Tucson: University of Arizona Press, 1995.

PROLADES-RITA database: "A Chronology of Protestant Beginnings in Mexico." http://www .prolades.com/cra/regions/nam/mexico/ chron-mex.pdf.

PROLADES-RITA database: "Religion in Mexico." http://www.prolades.com/cra/regions/nam/ mexico/mex-rd.htm.

Read, William R., et al. *Latin American Church Growth.* Grand Rapids, MI: William B. Eerdmans Publishing Company, 1969.

Scott, Lindy. *Salt of the Earth: A Socio-Political History of Mexico City Evangelical Protestants (1964–1991)*. Mexico City: Editorial Kyrios, 1991.

Scheffler, Lilian. *Magia y Brujería en México*. Mexico City: Panorama Editorial, 1994.

U.S. Department of State. *International Religious Freedom Report 2008*. http://www.state.gov/g/drl/rls/irf/2008/108532.htm.

VELA. *Panorama Evangélico Nacional 2008: Congregaciones Evangélicas de la República Mexicana*. México, DF: Visión Evangelizadora Latinoamericana (VELA) y Sociedad Bíblica de México, 2008.

■ Micronesia, Federated States of

The Federated States of Micronesia emerged as a new country out of the several island groups of Micronesia, islands of the Pacific north of Papua New Guinea, and the Solomon Islands. Together, the islands have 271 square miles of land, upon which some 108,000 people (2008) reside. The great majority of the people are of one of several Micronesian ethnic groups.

The term "Micronesia" (meaning "small islands") describes three archipelagos: the Marshall Islands, the Marianas Islands, and the Caroline Islands. They were inhabited in prehistoric times by Micronesians of various groupings. The first Europeans, Ferdinand Magellan (ca. 1480–1521) and his crew, visited the Marianas in 1521. They would be named for Queen Maria Ana of Austria (1667–1740) during her time as regent to the Spanish throne. The Spanish claimed hegemony over the islands and in 1885 were able to keep the Germans from trying to place a protectorate over them. The United States received Guam from Spain in 1898 as a result of the Spanish-American War. Spain then sold the rest of the Marianas to Germany.

Japan occupied Micronesia in 1914 and actually launched the attack on Pearl Harbor from a base there. Before the war was over, several of the islands, like Saipan, became famous battlegrounds. At the end of World War II, the United Nations Security Council gave the islands to the United States as a trust. The UN mandated that the U.S. government manage the trust so as to prepare the islands for independence. In 1975, as a result of a referendum, the Marianas were set aside as the Northern Marianas. In 1978, following another referendum, the Federated States of Micronesia, constituting the Caroline Islands, came into being. Palau and the Marshall Islands stayed out of the federation and now exist as independent countries. In 1982 the U.S. government signed an agreement with the Federated States that gave them local autonomy but assigned to the United States responsibility for defense and foreign relations. There are four states in the Federated States of Micronesia—Chuuk, Yap, Pohnpei, and Kosrae.

The traditional religions of Micronesia followed a polytheism that recognized a variety of deities under a supreme being known as Ialulep. The traditional religions have largely been replaced by Christianity, but they continue to exert influence through the survival of traditional healing practices.

Christianity came to Micronesia in 1668 with the opening of the first Roman Catholic Church mission. The missionaries had their greatest success among the Chamorros of the Marianas, who developed their own form of Spanish Catholicism. Work in the Marianas grew into a separate diocese headquartered at Agana, the capital of Guam. The work on the Carolinas and Marshalls was combined in a vicariate. More recently, the Caroline Islands were set aside as a separate diocese and the Marshalls as an apostolic prefecture.

In 1852 the American Board of Commissioners for Foreign Missions (ABCFM), an association of American Congregationalists, sent a party of American and Hawaiian missionaries to the Caroline Islands, where they opened missions on Kusaie and Ponape. In 1857 they extended the work to the Marshall Islands. In 1865, administration of the Micronesian mission was assigned to the Hawaiian (Congregationalist's) Church's Board of Missions. German missionaries from the Liebenzell Mission entered and opened stations on the Truk Islands (or Chuuk), Palau, and the Yap Islands. They had come at the request of the ABCFM missionaries after Germany had asserted its claim to the area. The Germans worked cooperatively with the American missionaries until World War I, when all missionaries

FEDERATED STATES OF MICRONESIA

Federated States of Micronesia

Palikir

Colonia

N

Micronesia, Federated States of

Religion	Followers in 1970	Followers in 2010	% of Population	Annual % growth 2000–2010	Followers in 2025	Followers in 2050
Christians	57,600	107,000	94.5	0.58	118,000	125,000
Roman Catholics	20,000	70,100	62.0	−0.48	75,000	76,000
Protestants	27,200	50,000	44.2	0.79	52,000	54,000
Marginals	320	4,500	4.0	1.76	6,500	8,000
Ethnoreligionists	3,000	3,500	3.1	−0.42	3,000	3,000
Agnostics	0	850	0.8	2.20	1,500	2,500
Baha'is	610	500	0.4	−1.72	500	500
Buddhists	0	500	0.4	0.57	1,000	1,500
New religionists	0	420	0.4	0.51	600	800
Chinese folk	200	340	0.3	0.55	500	700
Atheists	0	60	0.1	0.82	100	200
Total population	**61,400**	**113,000**	**100.0**	**0.55**	**125,000**	**134,000**

had to leave. They returned in 1925 and remained through World War II. Their work matured into the Protestant Church of East Truk.

The ABCFM was superseded by the United Church Board of World Missions in 1957, when the Congregational-Christian Churches in the United States united with the Evangelical and Reformed Church to form the United Church of Christ. The United Church of Christ continued to support the work in Micronesia. In 1986, at the time the new Federated States of Micronesia was being formed, the mission work was reorganized as the United Church of Micronesia, modeled in both doctrine and polity after the United Church of Christ. The United Church of Micronesia included four churches, the United Church of Christ in Kosrae, the United Church of Christ in Pohnpei, the United Church of Christ in Chuuk, and the United Church of Christ-Congregational in the Marshall Islands.

Through the 20th century, a number of U.S. churches across the Protestant-Free Church spectrum opened work in Micronesia. The Seventh-day Adventist Church, which arrived in 1930, now assigns the work to their Guam-Micronesia Mission. More recent arrivals include the General Baptists (1947), the Assemblies of God (1960), the United Pentecostal Church International (1965), the Baptist Bible Fellowship International (1972), and the Conservative Congregational Christian Church, an offshoot of the United Church of Christ (1984). The Baptist Bible Fellowship International mission began at the request of

Ermut Ikea, the mayor of Puluwat (one of the Chuuk Islands).

In addition, a variety of independent evangelical and fundamentalist missionary agencies have started missions in Micronesia in recent decades. The Jehovah's Witnesses came in 1965, and the Church of Jesus Christ of Latter-day Saints (LDS) in 1976. Beginning its work on Pohnpei, the LDS extended its mission to include Chuuk and Yap in 1977 and Kosrae in 1985. By 1996 the church could report some 3,000 members.

Several indigenous religious movements surfaced in the 20th century. The first was Modekne, an attempt to synthesize Christian elements with the traditional religion on Palau. From its first appearance there, it spread through the islands, its appeal being attributed to its emphasis on healing, until it was suppressed by the government in 1945. It continues as an underground movement.

Following World War II, the Baha'i Faith came to Micronesia, and some Chinese Buddhist/Daoist worship is present among Chinese expatriates.

J. Gordon Melton

See also: American Board of Commissioners for Foreign Missions; Assemblies of God; Baha'i Faith; Baptist Bible Fellowship International; Church of Jesus Christ of Latter-day Saints; Jehovah's Witnesses; Roman Catholic Church; Seventh-day Adventist Church; United Church of Christ; United Pentecostal Church International.

References

Haynes, D. E., and W. L. Wuerch. *Micronesian Religion and Lore: A Guide to Sources, 1526–1990*. Westport, CT: Greenwood Press, 1995.

Hezel, F. X. *The Catholic Church in Micronesia: Historical Essays on the Catholic Church in the Caroline-Marshall Islands*. Chicago: Micronesian Seminar/Loyola University Press, 1991.

Hezel, F. X. *Strangers in Their Own Land: A Century of Colonial Rule in the Caroline and Marshall Islands*. Honolulu: University of Hawaii Press, 2003.

Mueller, K. W. "The Protestant Mission Work on the Truk Islands in Micronesia: A Missiological Analysis and Evaluation." M.A. thesis, Fuller Theological Seminary, 1981.

Trompf, Gary. *The Religions of Oceania*. New York: Routledge, 2004.

Wiltgen, Ralph M. *The Founding of the Roman Catholic Church in Melanesia and Micronesia, 1850–1875*. Eugene, OR: Pickwick Publications, 2008.

Mid-Autumn Festival

The Mid-Autumn Festival occurs in the middle of the second of the three lunar months that make up the autumn season in China—the seventh, eighth, and ninth months. As the months are measured from new moon to new moon, the middle of the month is always at a full moon. In a time before electricity, the moon was a more important illuminating force than in recent times, and the coming of a full moon at the time of the year when there were few clouds to obscure it and people were at the end of a long farming season were reasons enough for a pause to celebrate.

Buddhists contributed to this festival oriented on the moon by contributing several legends from India that introduced a connection between the moon and rabbits. According to one popular story, the Buddha summoned animals to him as he was preparing for the end of his earthly existence, but only 12 animals showed up to say goodbye. He acknowledged their presence by naming the years of the 12-year cycle in Chinese astrology after them. Of these, the fourth to arrive before the Buddha was the rabbit. Another story tells of Buddha's prior incarnation as a rabbit. One day while traveling with an ape and a fox, he encountered a hungry beggar. The three left to find some food. The ape and fox returned with some, but the rabbit found nothing. In his determination to be of service, however, the rabbit made a fire and then jumped into it so that he would become food for the beggar. The beggar turned out to be the god Indra; he rewarded the rabbit by sending him to the moon.

Picked up by the Daoists, the rabbit on the moon was pictured as standing under a magical tree making the elixir of immortality. This image would be integrated with another story of Hou Yi and his wife Chane E who lived in ancient China during the reign of the long-lived Emperor Yao (2358–2258 BCE). Hou Yi was a member of the imperial guards known for his skill as an archer. At one point during Emperor Yao's reign, suddenly 10 suns appeared in the sky. Their combined heat made life unbearable and the emperor asked Hou Yi to get rid of them. With his arrows, he was able to get rid of nine of them. As a reward, he was summoned to the throne room of the Queen Mother of the West who resided in the Kunlun Mountains, a very real set of mountains in Western China that in places form the northern border to Tibet. To the Daoists this mountain was a heavenly place. Though geographically placed on Earth, it was analogous to the Buddhists' Pure Land. When Hou Yi visited there, he was given a pill of immortality, but told to prepare himself with prayer and fasting before taking it. His wife, however, discovered the pill and took it. She found she could fly, and to escape her husband's anger flew to the moon.

On the moon, Chang E coughed and part of the pill flew out of her mouth. The pill became a jade rabbit and she a toad. Hou Yi in the meantime erected a new home on the sun. He is reunited with his wife monthly in the full moon.

These legends continue to inform what has become a family holiday in modern Chinese society, in both the People's Republic and the diaspora. It is a time to reunite with friends and family and enjoy a characteristic Chinese delicacy, the moon cake. Moon cakes come in a variety of shapes and are filled with sweets, meats, or salty fillings.

Transparent dragon in a Mid-Autumn Festival street parade in Singapore's Chinatown on September 13, 2008. Farmers celebrate the end of the summer harvesting season on this date. (Espion/Dreamstime.com)

The primary ritual of the Mid-Autumn Festival is conducted by women on the 15th day of the lunar month as the full moon reigns above. It occurs around an open-air altar decorated with a picture of the moon goddess and some representation of the rabbit. Different food substances are brought to the altar, a wine glass filled, and incense lit. The culmination of the ritual involves the women of the house bowing, what in Chinese is a kowtow, before the goddess. The ceremony ends with the burning of the moon goddess's picture, the act of burning not being a destructive act but one of communion and communication.

J. Gordon Melton

See also: Buddha, Gautama; Daoism.

References

Kaulbach, B., and B. Proksch. *Arts and Culture in Taiwan*. Taipei: Southern Materials Center, 1984.

Latsch, Marie-Luise. *Traditional Chinese Festivals*. Singapore: Greaham Brash, 1984.

Liming, Wei. *Chinese Festivals: Traditions, Customs, and Rituals*. Hong Kong: China International Press, 2005.

Windling, Terri. "The Symbolism of Rabbits and Hares." *Journal of Mythical Arts* (Winter 2007). http://www.endicott-studio.com/rdrm/rrRabbits.html. Accessed May 16, 2009.

Middle East Council of Churches

The Middle East Council of Churches brings together the many divergent streams of Christianity that have operated through the centuries in the region of Christianity's birth. Protestants were among the last of the large international Christian communions to try to establish themselves in what is largely a Muslim-dominated region of the world (along with the Jewish-dominated country of Israel).

Early in the 20th century, Protestants raised the issue of Christian unity in a series of international conferences, most notably at Edinburgh in 1910. In the Middle East these conversations led to the meeting of the United Missionary Council in Jerusalem in 1924 and the Council of West Asia and North Africa (1927). These meetings led to the formation of the Near East Christian Council (1929). The Near East Council existed for 35 years as an exclusively Protestant organization, but in 1964 the Syrian Orthodox Church joined. That action prompted a name change to the Near East Council of Churches.

The action of the Syrian church came after more than three decades of conversations between Protestants and both the Eastern Orthodox and the non-Chalcedonian Orthodox (generally referred to as the Oriental Orthodox). That conversation followed the same dialogical effort that was leading to Orthodox participation in the formation of the World Council of Churches. Both Protestants and Eastern Orthodox accept the theological decisions of the Seven Ancient Ecumenical Councils of the church, while the Oriental Churches do not accept the promulgation of some of those councils (though in substance they have not specifically rejected the position articulated by those councils).

Though the World Council was formed in 1948, the conversation proceeded as a slower speed in the Middle East, where the claims and counterclaims of the various churches created the greatest number of immediate issues. Continued dialogue led in 1972 to the drafting of a constitution for an organization that included all three communions. That organization came into being in 1974 as the Middle East Council of Churches. It first general assembly was held on the island of Cyprus. In 1990, the Roman Catholic Church, manifest in both its Latin-rite diocese and its Eastern-rite dioceses, joined the Council.

The Council operates with an understanding that it is the meeting ground of four Christian family communions, the four being the Protestants, the Eastern Orthodox, the Oriental Orthodox, and the Roman Catholic. Each communion is represented equally at the general assembly (which convenes every five years) and the Council's governing bodies, and each communion appoints its own representatives to the Council.

The Council has been quite active in the many conflictual issues that have made the Middle East an area of constant turmoil and unrest. Most notably, it has tended to support the cause of the Palestinians within Israel. It has also supported efforts to bring peace and reconciliation in Iraq. As the most representative Christian organization in the region, it has led efforts at dialogue to bring understanding among the various communions and to represent them within the larger Muslim world. Equally notable has been its attempt to dialogue with those evangelical and Free churches that have most recently entered the area and often become the focus of issues brought on by their zealous proselytizing.

The Protestant churches that had originally formed the Near East Christian Council also saw a continued need to maintain a special relationship among themselves following the organization of the Middle East Council of Churches. Without lessening their commitment to the new Council, they also formed the Fellowship of Middle East Evangelical Churches as an organization to affirm their common life and provide for action on their specific concerns.

In 2008, the Council reported 27 member denominations based in 12 countries and representing some 14 million members.

The Middle East Council of Churches
Makhoul Street, Deeb Building
PO Box 5376
Beirut
Lebanon

J. Gordon Melton

See also: Eastern Orthodoxy; Roman Catholic Church; World Council of Churches.

Reference

Van Beek, Huibert, comp. *A Handbook of Churches and Councils: Profiles of Ecumenical Relationships*. Geneva: World Council of Churches, 2006.

Midway Island

Midway became famous as the site of the decisive naval battle of the war in the Pacific during World War II. Midway is a single atoll of a mere 2.4 square miles with two islands, Sand Island and Eastern Island. Midway was annexed in 1867 by the United States and administered by the U.S. Navy. Until 1993 as many as 2,300 people, almost all military personnel, resided on the islands. In that year, however, the naval facility was closed and hegemony over the atoll was transferred to the Fish and Wildlife Service of the U.S. Department of the Interior. Midway is now a wildlife refuge and only some 40 people reside on the atoll as permanent residents.

There are no permanently organized churches or religious groups on Midway.

J. Gordon Melton

References

Barrett, David, ed. *The Encyclopedia of World Christianity*. 2nd ed. New York: Oxford University Press, 2001.

Bissio, Roberto Remo, et al. *Third World Guide 93/94*. Montevideo, Uruguay: Instituto del Tercer Mundo, 1992.

The World Factbook 2000: Midway Islands. Washington: Central Intelligence agency, 2002. http://www.faqs.org/docs/factbook/print/mq.html.

Milarepa

1052–1135

Milarepa, a native Tibetan, was one of the pioneers spreading Vajrayana Buddhism in Tibet and one of the founders of the Kagyu School of Tibetan Buddhism.

Milarepa was born into an upper-class family in Upper Tsang in northern Tibet. He was orphaned as a child. He began his religious life attempting to work black magic on his aunt and uncle, who adopted him and treated him most cruelly. He seems to have had some success in gaining a degree of retribution on the couple, but came to regret what he had done and turned away from his negative course.

As a young man, he found his way to a famous lama in central Tibet, Rongton Lhaga, who sent him

A close-up view of a Buddhist *tanka* representing Milarepa. Milarepa is generally considered one of Tibet's most famous yogis and poets. (iStockPhoto)

to southern Tibet to study with Marpa Lho-brag-pa (1012–1097), a student of the Indian Vajrayana teacher Naropa. Marpa sensed that Milarepa was to be an outstanding student, and before seeing him, made him pass a set of difficult tests. Milarepa, desirous of becoming Marpa's student, performed all that was asked of him and was finally allowed to take his refuge vows from Marpa. Marpa noted that Naropa also made his young students go through a series of tests to show their perseverance and respect for their future teacher.

Milaerapa joined with Marpa's three other leading students Ngok Choku Dorje, Tsurton Wanggi Dorje, and Meyton Chenpo in learning the basics of Vajrayana Buddhism, which includes mastering a number of techniques that open the invisible spiritual world and experiencing a series of initiations that bring the student into a relationship with various deities. Marpa gave Milarepa the Chakrasamvara initiation, during which Milarepa was able to see first the face of the deity and then the entire mandala in which Chakrasamvara appears surrounded by a retinue of other spiritual beings. After the initiation, Marpa offered a prophecy utilizing a four-handled pot, which Milarepa had presented to Marpa at an earlier date. In the prophecy he likened the four handles to his four main students while singling out Milarepa, for whom he saw a particularly fruitful future.

Milarepa remained with Marpa for another 12 years, during which time he learned the full spectrum of Tantric Buddhist practices that had been passed to Marpa. Marpa recognized him as having reached full enlightenment (termed *vajradhara*) and gave him the religious name by which he is still known.

Milarepa departed from his teacher and settled in Drakar Taso, which became the base from which he would travel across Tibet for the rest of his life. He composed a number of poems/songs that conveyed his teachings in a form his students could easily remember. Unlike Marpa and Naropa, who had spent much time with a few students, Milarepa drew a large number of disciples who would spread the Kagyu dharma across the country and eventually to neighboring Nepal and Bhutan. His most prominent student was Gampopa (1079–1153), who founded the Kagyu monastic lineage.

J. Gordon Melton

See also: Kagyupa Tibetan Buddhism; Tantrism; Vajrayana Buddhism.

References

Garma C. C. Chang, trans. *The Hundred Thousand Songs of Milarepa.* Boston: Shambhala, 1999

Evans-Wentz, W. Y., ed. *Tibet's Great Yogi Milarepa: A Biography from the Tibetan.* London: Oxford University Press, 1951.

Kunga Rinpoche, Lama, and Brian Cutill, trans. *Drinking the Mountain Stream: Songs of Tibet's Beloved Saint, Milarepa.* Somerville, MA: Wisdom Publications, 2003.

Lobsang Lhalungpa, trans. *The Life of Milarepa.* Boston: Shambhala, 1985.

Mission 21

See Basel Mission.

Mission Covenant Church of Sweden

The Mission Covenant Church is a Scandinavian expression of the free religious impulse represented by the 18th-century evangelical revival in England and the Pietist movement in Germany. Essential to the Scandinavian revival was the work of Karl Olof Rosenius (1816–1868), editor of the periodical *Pietisten*. He organized conventicles—informal meetings outside the supervision of the state church—and led in the development of a new hymnology. A renewed emphasis on the spiritual life in Sweden in the mid-19th century led in 1855 to the formation of a new congregation separate from the state-supported Church of Sweden. Other congregations emphasizing the free association of committed believers were soon organized, and in 1878, when these groups established a formal relationship, they agreed upon a congregational polity. Growth was somewhat inhibited by the high level of immigration of members to the United States.

The Mission Covenant Church looked upon the Bible as its sole rule of faith and life, neither composing nor adopting a creedal statement. A Protestant theological perspective much influenced by both its Lutheran heritage and Methodism developed, but through the 20th century a Reformed perspective came to dominate. However, theology was always subordinated to the spiritual life. The church refrained from Baptist independency and continued to practice infant baptism.

At the end of the 1990s the Mission Covenant Church of Sweden reported approximately 70,000 members. The church developed an extensive mission program, often in cooperation with its sister church in America, and its missionary efforts resulted in the development of related autonomous churches around the world, from India and Japan to Ecuador and the Congo. These churches now fellowship through the International Federation of Free Evangelical Churches. The Mission Covenant Church of Sweden continues to provide support for its sister churches in poorer countries.

The pressure to provide training for ministers early in the 20th century resulted in the organization of a seminary in 1908. Known since 1994 as the Stockholm School of Theology, the school is now a cooperative effort, jointly supported with the Baptist Union of

Sweden. The church also supports Svenska Missions-förbundets Ungdom (Mission Covenant Youth), which has emerged as a broadly supported youth work with units throughout the country.

The general assembly is the highest legislative body in the church. Between meetings of the assembly, an executive board administers its policies. In 2005, the church reported 63,000 members. Its 790 congregations are organized into 7 districts, each of which is led by a superintendent. The church was a founding member of the World Council of Churches and also joined the World Alliance of Reformed Churches.

Mission Covenant Church of Sweden
PO Box 6302
Tegnérgatan 8
S-11381 Stockholm
Sweden
http://www.smf.se/ (in Swedish)

J. Gordon Melton

See also: Church of Sweden; International Federation of Free Evangelical Churches; World Alliance of Reformed Churches; World Council of Churches.

References

Bauswein, Jean-Jacques, and Lukas Vischner, eds. *The Reformed Family Worldwide: A Survey of Reformed Churches, Theological Schools, and International Organizations.* Grand Rapids, MI: William B. Eerdmans Publishing Company, 1999.

Van Beek, Huibert. *A Handbook of the Churches and Councils: Profiles of Ecumenical Relationships.* Geneva: World Council of Churches, 2006.

Missionaries of Charity

The Missionaries of Charity are an ordered community of the Roman Catholic Church that has become world famous because of the attention directed to its founder, Mother Teresa (1910–1997). She was born Agnes (or Gonxha) Bojazhiu into an Albanian family residing at Skopje, now the capital of Macedonia. When she was 18, she became a nun with the Sisters of Loreto. In 1929, after learning some English, she

Portrait of Mother Teresa, 20th-century Catholic nun and founder of the Missionaries for Charity religious order. (Zatletic/Dreamstime.com)

entered the novitiate at Darjeeling, India, and two years later she was assigned to work in Calcutta.

In 1946 Mother Teresa experienced a new calling to serve the poor of Calcutta. Two years later, with the blessings of her order and church authorities, she left the Sisters of Loreto and settled in the slums of Calcutta. Several women who came to assist her became the nucleus of a new order that was formally approved as a diocesan congregation in 1950 and as a pontifical institute in 1965.

Over the next several decades the order grew rather quietly, with its first activities directed toward Calcutta's street children and then toward the dying, for whom Mother Teresa opened hospices. The order's concern grew for the homeless and those with the most despised diseases, such as Hansen's disease and AIDS. The order also expanded into other countries, and by the time of Mother Teresa's death it included more than 2,300 sisters serving in more than 80 countries. In 1984, Mother Teresa led in the founding of a male auxiliary to the order she led, the Missionaries of Charity Fathers. Members are priests who assume the traditional monastic vows of chastity, poverty, and obedience, along with a fourth vow of "Wholehearted and Free Service to the Poorest of the Poor."

Mother Teresa was succeeded by Sister Nirmala Joshi, who served two terms as superior general of the order (1997–2009). She was succeeded by the current leader, Sister Mary Prema. There are novitiates in Rome, Italy; Manila, the Philippines; Warsaw, Poland; Tabora, Tanzania; and San Francisco, California.

Mother Teresa's work began to attract international attention, especially in Roman Catholic circles, in the 1970s, and she became the recipient of a series of awards, including the Pope John XXIII Peace Prize (1971), the Nehru Prize for her promotion of international peace and understanding (1972), and the Balzan Prize for promoting peace and brotherhood (1979). These were capped by the Nobel Peace Prize in 1979, which made her one of the most well-known women in the world. Even before her death, there were calls to canonize Mother Teresa, and they were acted upon soon after she passed away. In 2003, a mere six years after her passing, Pope John Paul II (r. 1978–2005) beatified Mother Teresa, the final step before canonizing her as a saint.

Missionaries of Charity, Motherhouse
c/o Sr. Nirmala, MC
54A, Acharya Jagadish Chandra Bose Rd.
Calcutta 700 016
India
http://www.mcpriests.com/ (Missionaries of Charity Fathers)

J. Gordon Melton

See also: John XXIII, Pope; Roman Catholic Church; Saints.

References

Collopy, Michael. *Works of Love Are Works of Peace: Mother Teresa of Calcutta and the*

Missionaries of Charity. San Francisco: Ignatius Press, 1996.

Kumar, Sinita. *Mother Teresa of Calcutta*. London: Weidenfeld and Nicolson, 1998.

Le Joly, E. *Mother Teresa of Calcutta: A Biography*. San Francisco: Harper & Row, 1983.

Serrou, R. *Teresa of Calcutta: A Pictorial Biography*. New York: McGraw Hill, 1980.

Missionary Sisters of Our Lady of Africa

The Missionary Sisters of Our Lady of Africa, commonly called the White Sisters, is a Roman Catholic female order established in the 19th century to assist in the rapidly developing missionary efforts especially in North Africa. In 1868, the archbishop of Algiers, Charles M. Lavigerie (1825–1892), had founded the Society of Missionaries of Africa (the White Fathers) who launched work among the Muslim population of the French colony. It quickly became evident that women were needed to reach the women of the country who had limited contacts with males outside their family. Thus in 1869 Archbishop Lavigerie began to open houses in several European countries for women called to missionary work. Novices went through a lengthy probationary period that included both an examination of their calling and preparation for life in Africa. Within a few years they began to take their place beside the male missionaries. They spread to French-speaking Canada in 1903.

The order maintains a special relationship with Islam, in part derived from its origins in North Africa. Like their male counterparts, the members of the order adopted the white dress common among the Arabs as their habit, which resulted in their nickname, "the White Sisters." Lavigerie envisioned the work of the two orders as launching missions and quickly training African converts to assume responsibility for their own progress. To accomplish the task, missionaries had to be aware of the language and culture of the people among whom they would work. To meet this ideal, members of the White Sisters begin their religious life with a 9-month postulancy followed by an 11-month novitiate during with time they are schooled in African languages and culture.

Currently, the order has a number of houses across France, with additional centers in Germany, Belgium, Switzerland, England, the Netherlands, Poland, and Spain, and a general house in Rome. Branches are also found in North America: in Canada, the United States, and Mexico. Work is focused in 16 countries in Africa. The order peaked in 1966, at which time it had 2,163 members. It has declined to close to 1,000 by the beginning of the 21st century. In 2008, approximately 900 sisters are stationed at locations around the world, with about half at the various locations in Europe, and a fourth in Africa.

Missionary Sisters of Our Lady of Africa
Sœurs Missionnaires de Notre Dame d'Afrique
24, quai Fernand Saguet
94700 Maisons-Alfort
France
http://soeurs-blanches.cef.fr/index.php

J. Gordon Melton

See also: Roman Catholic Church; White Fathers.

References

Lacayo, Beverly. *100 Years in Zambia: What Is God Teaching Us When One Culture Meets Another?* The Missionary Sisters of Our Lady of Africa, 2001.

Renault, Francois, *Cardinal Lavigerie: Churchman, Prophet, and Missionary.* London: Athlone Press, 1994.

Missione–Luigia Paparelli, La

1908–1984

Luigia Paparelli was born in Scranton (Pennsylvania) on December 7, 1908. In the 1940s, she met Basilio Roncaccia (the founder of the Divine Mission, who claimed to have received the "divine mission" of sharing with his followers his newly found healing power) in Rome. Roncaccia and Paparelli shared a devotion to the Holy Trinity, and the idea of helping those who suffered, but their practices were different, and they separated quite soon. A charismatic figure, Paparelli gathered a significant number of followers around her. The first "sign" of her future mission dates back,

in fact, to 1937 when, afflicted by a somewhat mysterious illness, the Lord, she claimed, had visited and miraculously healed her. Seven years of penance followed, and on October 13, 1944, Paparelli had a new mystical experience and interpreted it as the Sacred Heart of Jesus giving her the mission to "heal bodies in order to save souls." The first cure ascribed to Paparelli's miraculous powers took place in October 1944. In that year, she established a group called the Luigia Paparelli Mission (Missione Luigia Paparelli) and started calling her followers the "Brothers of the Mission." Paparelli became, for her followers, "the Master," divinely invested with powers to heal and exorcise. She "signed" the sick with a cross on the forehead, lips, heart, and the afflicted part of their bodies, in the name of the Holy Trinity. Paparelli also instructed those "signed" by her to visit a Catholic church in order to confess and receive holy Communion. In 1970 the Office of the Cardinal Vicar of Rome stated in a letter that Paparelli's phenomena and "signs" were "superstitious" and could in fact "promote a form of superstition detrimental to religion." In such phenomena, the declaration went on to say, there was "nothing supernatural." The Mission continued to grow, however, and assumed the name La Missione–Luigia Paparelli (slightly different from the original) following Paparelli's death. She died surrounded by the Brothers of the Mission, on August 28, 1984, in Valmontone (Rome).

Luigia Paparelli stated emphatically that she did not regard herself as the founder of a new religion; her faith, she said, was "the one and only religion of Jesus Christ, based on the Ten Commandments." Rather, Paparelli's teachings and her supernatural phenomena created a large community of believers who still regard themselves as Roman Catholics, but whose individual perception of their Catholicism differs from person to person and from place to place. Some Brothers of the Mission would simply claim that their feeling toward Paparelli is one of deep gratitude. For other Brothers, however, Paparelli is nothing less than divine and some of them also have an exclusive faith in her healing powers, to the exclusion of all mainstream medicine. These fringes of the larger movement live their lives quite separately from society as a whole, and often break ties with their own families in consequence. The relationship between the Mission and the Roman

Catholic hierarchy is different in terms of the various attitudes held by Paparelli's followers and by local parish priests and bishops.

After Paparelli's death, problems of succession generated several divisions. According to some witnesses, the Master, before her death, "called" Rina Menichetti Frizza (1928–2002) from Orvieto (Central Italy) to whom Paparelli addressed her last words. Those Brothers of the Mission who were called Apostolini ("Little Apostles") recognized Menichetti as Paparelli's spiritual heir. There are, however, other Brothers of the Mission who assign no particular role to Menichetti.

Menichetti continued to welcome followers to her Orvieto house until her death. In her house she also enjoyed spiritual visions of the Master (Paparelli), whose messages she immediately wrote down for the Brothers. Menichetti told of her encounters with the Master who "[took] her on her coach" to "her Kingdom" together with God the Father and the Virgin Mary. In Menichetti's visions, Paparelli claims that she is the Son (not "the Daughter") of the Father, and that the Brothers should anticipate her return: "My return will be your liberation." At the end of each "conversation," Menichetti received a blessing from the "Holy Trinity": "In the name of the Father, Luigia the Son, the Holy Spirit, and the Virgin Mary."

After Menichetti's death most of the Brothers of the Mission that recognized Menichetti as Paparelli's spiritual heir think there is no successor with the same charisma; a minority of Brothers recognize another person as Menichetti's spiritual heir.

The stated aim of the Mission is the promotion of the "Catholic, Apostolic and Roman religion." Its main centers are located in Gambassi (Tuscany) and San Venanzo, (Umbria), both in central Italy. "Temples" of the Mission, with statues of Jesus, the Virgin Mary, the Holy Trinity, and Luigia Paparelli herself, have been built, and are regarded as sacred places where both special yearly festivals and traditional Catholic feasts are celebrated. There are other centers in Italy, in Rome (Lazio), Marche, and Sicily, and in several other countries too (Norway, Denmark, Sweden, Switzerland, France, the United States). Brothers of the Mission, and "Little Apostles" in particular, do not proselytize. The Mission's message is normally spread by some-body who has been healed, and who, in turn, propagates its powers of healing. The Brothers of the Mission in Italy and abroad total approximately 10,000. The movement does not maintain a website.

Via Montefalconi 21
50050 Gambassi terme (Firenze)
Italy

Raffaella Di Marzio

See also: Roman Catholic Church.

References

Note: Rina Menichetti's visions from July 8, 1986, to April 8, 1988, are privately circulated.

Di Marzio, Raffaella. "Gruppi ispirati a Basilio Roncaccia e a Luigia Paparelli." In *Enciclopedia delle Religioni in Italia,* edited by Massimo Introvigne, Pier Luigi Zoccatelli, Nelly Ippolito Macrina, and Verónica Roldán, 66–75. Leumann (Torino): Elle Di Ci, 2001.

Massimo Introvigne, Pier Luigi Zoccatelli, Nelly Ippolito Macrina, and Verónica Roldán. "Movimenti cattolici di Frangia in Italia: dalla Missione Divina di Basilio Roncaccia a Luigia Paparelli." In *Identità religiosa, pluralismo, fondamentalismo*, edited by Mario Aletti and Germano Rossi, 161–167. Torino: Centro Scientifico Editore, 2004.

Pia Società San Paolo. *Chiese e sette protestanti in Italia.* Roma: Edizioni Paoline, 1956.

Mita Congregation

The Mita Congregation, a Puerto Rican-based Christian Pentecostal church, was founded by Juanita García Peraza (1897–1970). When she was eight years old, García Peraza became ill with ulcers and was nursed back to health with prayer. Once well, she began to attend a Pentecostal church, the Pentecostal movement having just come to the island. She grew to womanhood, married, and bore four children. As a young woman, she had a vivid religious experience: she was visited by the Holy Spirit, who informed her that her body was needed to carry out God's work. After she accepted this calling, she was given a choice.

Her life trial would either be persecution or illness, and she chose the latter. One night a short time later, as she looked out the window, she saw a shooting star, which approached her and landed on her forehead. At that moment she became the incarnation of the Holy Spirit. She was also told the name of God for the new era: Mita. She subsequently began to perform a spectrum of miracles. She saw her experience as fulfillment of a prophecy in Revelation 2:17.

In the late 1930s García Peraza came into conflict with the Puerto Rican Pentecostal leaders, who were all male. One day while "in the Spirit," she designated Teófilo Vargas Sein as the First Prophet of God for the new era, renaming him Aarón. As the conflict grew, she was tried for heresy. In the midst of the trial, she and 11 followers walked out of the Pentecostal church, and in 1940 she founded the Free Church. She later designated a site in San Juan where a temple would be built as the headquarters for the movement.

From the basic Pentecostal theology, Mita, as García Peraza became known, developed a new perspective. Drawing on an ideal initially articulated by Joachim of Fiore (ca. 1135–1202), she divided history into three eras, that of Jehovah, God the Father; that of Jesus, God the Son; and now that of Mita, God the Holy Spirit and Mother. Members draw a distinction between García Peraza, the human woman, and Mita, the God who worked through her. Aarón, who succeeded her, is seen as having become the channel through which the Holy Spirit (Mita) continues to speak.

The special work of Mita has been to gather the scattered children of God, which is done under the three banners of Love, Freedom, and Unity. The new era initiated by Mita serves to relativize and somewhat supersede the revelation that previously came through Christ. In the new era, baptism, the Eucharist, and many of the trappings of the Roman Catholic Church (the dominant religious body in Puerto Rico) have been left behind. Mita's followers also see the arrival of Mita as equivalent to the Second Coming, fulfilling the prophecy of Jesus in John 14:16 concerning the coming Comforter. She is also identified with the woman in Revelation 12:1–2.

Mita's movement originally developed among the working classes of San Juan. Developed along with the church is a corporation, Congregación Mita, Inc., through which numerous businesses have been organized, membership in the church coinciding with membership in an economic cooperative. As the movement grew, a variety of businesses were formed apparently with a long-term plan of community self-sufficiency. These have diversified to include farms and cattle ranches in rural areas and both retail and wholesale businesses in the cities. Over the years the businesses have prospered and have also given birth to various social services, including health and counseling services, a nursing home, and several schools. Rather than withdrawing from society as many communal groups do, the Mita Congregation is thoroughly integrated into the surrounding community.

Once established in Puerto Rico, the church expanded to Colombia and the Dominican Republic, where it has had equal success, and from there to Mexico, Venezuela, Costa Rica, El Salvador, Curaçao, and Panama. The church has also followed the migration of Latin Americans to North America, where congregations have been planted in Spanish-speaking communities across the continent. In 1990, in commemoration of the 50th anniversary of the founding of the movement, a new temple was dedicated in San Juan. It seats 6,000 people.

Mita Congregation has established its headquarters in Hato Rey, Puerto Rico, inland and south of San Juan. It has approximately 50,000 members, the largest number of which is in Colombia. There are six congregations in the United States and one in Canada.

Mita Congregation
Calle Duerte 235
Hato Rey, 60919
Puerto Rico

J. Gordon Melton

See also: Pentecostalism; Roman Catholic Church.

Reference

Camayd-Freixas, Erik. "The Cult of the Goddess Mita on the Eve of a New Millennium: A Socio-Anthropological Look at a Caribbean Urban Religion." *Latin American Issues* 13 (1997).

Modernity

The term "modernity" is generally held by the social sciences to describe the forces, structures, and historical patterns of the period from the late 16th century forward. This article begins with a discussion of the political, economic, and cultural building blocks of the modern period; it then provides a general outline of the ideas of modern sociological theorists insofar as they relate to religion; and finally, it touches on the particular patterns of religion in response to modernity. Modernity and its conceptual child, globalization, are the core constructs that every sociological theory must address in the contemporary world, but it is important to remember that modernity was neither inevitable nor simply a natural evolution in human history. Modernity was constructed, and it has become the most powerful force in human history.

The explosive growth of the world's population from 400 million in 1500 to 1.6 billion in 1900, a number that has now quadrupled, reflects that radical transformation of the globe through the period that we call modernity, but what explains this transformation? The answer begins with the age of European discovery and the world-changing shifts that occurred politically, economically, and religiously. The Spanish colonization of the Americas facilitated the largest transfer of wealth from Central and South America in human history. The Spanish Empire, lasting more than 300 years, conquered the Aztec and Incan empires, extracting much of their gold and silver and enabling Spain and the rest of Europe to become the wealthiest nation-states in human history. This wealth, along with the new agriculture learned in the Americas, allowed for the capital investments that led to the Industrial Revolution and simultaneously produced gains in foodstuffs that enabled the quadrupling of the world's population. Spanish expansion, as well as French, Dutch, and English colonization, solidified European power; monetized industries; enabled the expansion of the arts and sciences; facilitated modern Christian missions; and produced the economic, cultural, and social capital that constructed the modern world. During this period of colonization, religion and empire partnered to Christianize the world dominated by Europe. Roman Cathol-

icism was spread in the Spanish and French colonial possessions, and the English were not far behind in seeding their colonies, particularly the United States, with the Anglican and Protestant religions.

This baseline of colonialism not only secured resources but also set the table for the development of new political ideas that marked and enabled modernity to thrive. Intellectual and political leadership produced the French Revolution (1789), putting forward a universalist vision of reason that sought to displace religion and its authority with the power of liberty and an egalitarian spirit. This ideology set in motion a series of attempts at representative government throughout Europe and eventually across the globe. A similar egalitarian and democratic mode of revolution mobilized the English and American revolutions of 1642 and 1776. These revolutions, different from the French, integrated religion and reason, leading to various forms of accommodation between church and state. Indeed, religious liberty became a critical feature of democracy, even as it had a mixed history in England and Europe. In the American context church and state were eventually separated, producing open cultural and religious markets that Protestant entrepreneurs would exploit as they churched America and sought to Christianize the world.

Max Weber and Emile Durkheim are the key theorists of religion and modernity. Weber, the German sociologist, interpreted the forces of modernity as rationalizing instruments of culture and religion. The compartmentalization of public and private life separated religious human ideals from the cultural, economic, and political spheres. Each sphere had its own rationality, and religion could and would no longer be an explanation that made rational sense outside the confines of the human heart. Modernity, for Weber, was a quintessential force of disenchantment, whereby the universe was no longer explained by God's actions in it, nor did providential forces drive history.

Durkheim, the French sociologist, used the theory of differentiation to explain and describe the forces of modernity. For Durkheim modernity was marked by divisions of labor, the specialization of roles and responsibilities, and dominated by forms of instrumental rationality that sought profit over meaning and

Portrait of Max Weber, sociologist who conceptualized the theory of the Protestant work ethic and wrote about its influence on capitalism. (Library of Congress)

Portrait of Emile Durkheim, late-19th- and early-20th-century French sociologist. Considered the founding father of modern sociology, Durkheim revolutionized the discipline by adopting the rigorous scientific methodology of the natural sciences. (Bettmann/Corbis)

results over purpose. Unlike Weber, Durkheim argued that this loss of overall social solidarity created social anomie in which modern people experienced chaos and a lack of overall meaning. For society and culture to function properly, culture needed a sacred canopy—something like religion, though Durkheim never found or proposed a replacement for it.

In the 20th century, Peter L. Berger was the foremost theorist of religion and modernity. He took up where Durkheim left off, theorizing that, without a sacred canopy, religion would decline and lose its vitality and efficacy in modern life. However, Berger's prediction of secularization as the main result of mo-

dernity ran into empirical disconfirmations at the end of the 20th century. Indeed, Berger confessed that he was wrong. Other sociologists of religion, such as Rodney Stark and Roger Finke, used economic theory and empirical analysis to propose a contrary theory. Modernity, precisely because it creates so many more options and open religious markets, gives access to religious entrepreneurs who, because they have no state-sponsored religious bureaucracies, have fewer barriers to overcome but must work harder to share their religious "goods."

Modern Religious Trends Predictions that modernity would lead to the death of religion were premature. The modern era has ushered in a multitude of innovative new religious sects; some lead to new global religions such as the Church of the Latter-day Saints, Falun Gong, or any number of less well known new religious movements across the globe. Moreover, more traditional religions, like Islam and Christianity, have taken on new strength and vitality as they have flourished in various regions of the world. In Islam, new surveys show that Muslims, despite what many suspected were the corrosive effects of modern life, perceive their religion as very important. In fact, Muslim countries usually rate the importance of religion as higher than even the United States, a country that is supposed to be exceptionally religious. Again, religion and modernity are not mutually exclusive.

Christianity has adapted to modernity with success as well. At the end of the 19th century, it experienced an explosive new trend in the faith; Charismatic and Pentecostal forms of piety focused on more experiential and egalitarian modes of spiritual experience and authority. Its impact on Asia, Latin America, and Africa has been world changing. The Roman Catholic Church no longer dominates Latin America, and in some countries, such as Guatemala, more than half of their population is now Protestant. Indeed, Africa went from having nearly no Christians in 1900 to more than 360 million Christians in 2000. Some have suggested that the center of Christianity is no longer in the Anglo American or European context, but indeed in Asia, Latin America, and Africa—it has become, not unlike Islam, a global faith.

Modernity, far from being the death knell of religions, has rather become a context for enormous religious change and innovation. The tendency in the past was to write about the golden age of Christendom in the Middle Ages. We now know it was a myth—there appears to be little evidence for mass piety in that period of European history. Thus, the relative lack of modern Christian practice in Europe may simply be consistent with its history. England, however, seems to have experienced a real decline in the Christian faith and practice; empirical evidence supports this claim. In this way, England has become more like the rest of Europe than like its cousins, the Americas. There may be less religious and church affiliation, but one of the marks of modernity, at least in the United States, is the explosion of people who claim to be spiritual but not religious. Many now argue that they are neither members nor attendants of religious services, yet, they have high rates of belief in God as well as prayer. How to judge and define religion in the modern period is one of the real challenges of the era.

The modern market in religion appears to be more open to innovation and change than ever before. That this indicates a decline in religious affiliation per se is clear. But the claim that modernity means the death of religion is no longer plausible. Religion in modern life is as robust and powerful as it ever has been for good and for ill. We have not only had tremendous outbreaks of violence done in the name of God, across all the religions, but we have seen signs of the good that religions produce in caring for others on levels both small and large. In the modern world, where globalism creates new opportunities to communicate and share information, religion is more than ever an active partner in framing how we shape our cultures, societies, and politics.

James Wellman

See also: Church of Jesus Christ of Latter-day Saints; Falun Gong; Globalization, Religion and; Pentecostalism; Roman Catholic Church; Secularization.

References

Berger, Peter L. *The Desecularization of the World: Resurgent Religion and World Politics.* Grand Rapids, MI: William B. Eerdmans Publishing Company, 1999.

Bruce, Steve. *Politics and Religion.* Cambridge: Polity Press, 2003.

Cole, Juan. *Engaging the Muslim World.* New York: Palgrave Macmillan, 2009.

Finke, Roger, and Rodney Stark. *The Churching of America, 1776–2005: Winners and Losers in our Religious Economy.* Piscataway, NJ: Rutgers University Press, 2005.

Freston, Paul. *Evangelicals and Politics in Asia, Africa and Latin America.* Cambridge: Cambridge University Press, 2001.

Wright, Ronald. *What Is America? A Short History of the New World Order.* Cambridge: De Capo Press, 2008.

Wellman, James K., Jr., ed. *Belief and Bloodshed: Religion and Violence across Time and Tradition.* Lanham, MD: Rowman and Littlefield, 2007.

■ Moldova

Moldova, which emerged as an independent country with the breakup of the Soviet Union in 1991, is sandwiched between Romania and Ukraine. It was once united with what is now the Romanian province of Bucovina in the Principality of Moldova. The modern nation includes some 13,066 square miles of territory upon which live some 4,300,000 people (2008). Since independence, Russian armed forces have had a continued presence in Transnistria, the sliver of Moldovan land east of the Dniester River. The majority of people who reside in the area are Ukrainians and Russians, and they have asserted their independence as a Transnistria republic.

The eastern European nation of Moldova has for centuries been home to the Vlach people, closely related to the Romanians. They emerged out of the silence of many centuries in the mid-1300s, when Vlach people northeast of Wallachia formed their own kingdom and separated themselves from Hungarian rule. Their territory was established between the Danube and Dniester rivers and northwest of the Black Sea. Running through the middle of the land was the Prut River. The Vlachs enjoyed great success through the 15th century under Stephen the Great (1435–1504), reaching eastward into modern Ukraine east of the Dniester River. But the Vlach Kingdom constantly had to defend its borders from its neighbors and from the expanding Ottoman Empire. Early in the 1500s, it was overrun by Turkish forces and turned into a vassal state.

In the 18th century, Moldova aligned itself with Russia in an attempt to overthrow Ottoman rule. By the early 19th century, Russia had gained hegemony over Moldova and expelled the Turkish residents. The land between the Dniester and Prut rivers became an autonomous region within Russia, Bessarabia, and then in 1873 it became a Russian province. During the 20th century the population soared, from 250,000 to 2.5 million. A process of Russification led in 1966 to the discontinuance of the Moldovan language in the schools.

In the years immediately following World War I, an independent Moldova was established with Romanian assistance, but Moldova became contested territory between Romania and the Soviet Union. The land west of the Dniester and Prut rivers became part of Romania, and that to the east of the Dniester was made a part of the Ukraine. In 1940 the Soviet Union annexed Bessarabia and created the Federated Republic of Moldova, with the approximate borders of the present state of Moldova.

Moldova proclaimed its independence from the Soviet Union in 1991. The land to the west (between the Prut River and the Carpathian Mountains) is a part of present-day Romania and the Moldovan land to the east of the Dniester River remains a part of the Ukraine.

Christianity spread along the western shore of the Black Sea in the third century CE, and from there it moved north and west along the rivers. By the time a Moldovan nation emerged in the 14th century, Orthodox Christianity oriented toward Byzantium had been established there. The church in Moldova was influenced first by the Romanian Orthodox Church, but beginning in the 18th century, the Russian Orthodox Church (Moscow Patriarchate) (ROC) had a greater impact. After Moldova was incorporated into Russia, the Moldovan church was incorporated into the Russian Orthodox Church. During the years of harshest repression of religion in the Soviet Union, the Moldovan church was least affected, and a larger percentage of its churches remained open than in other parts of the Soviet Union.

By the time of the country's independence in 1991, the church in Moldova had been thoroughly integrated into Russian Orthodoxy and remains so to the present. There are four dioceses of the ROC in Moldova, which function under the Moscow Patriarchate as the Orthodox Church of Moldova. It has close to 1,000 parishes. In 1992, some Moldovan priests left the church to form the independent Bessarabian Orthodox Church and sought to place themselves under the Romanian Patriarchate in Bucharest. The government has, however, refused to recognize this splinter.

More than 95 percent of the nation's 4.5 million citizens identify with the Orthodox Church. There are, however, many Romanian-speaking people in Moldova, and there is a diocese of the Romanian Orthodox Church with headquarters at Chisinau. There is also a diocese of the Russian Old Believers Church.

German Baptists came to Moldova in 1876 and baptized nine believers in Turtino (now in Ukraine). A

MOLDOVA

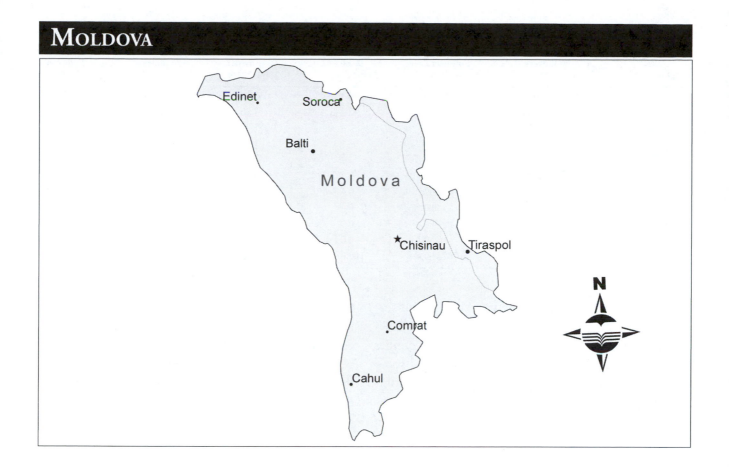

church was formed three years later as part of the larger Baptist community in the Ukraine. In 1907 three German-speaking Baptist churches in Bessarabia formed the first Moldovan Baptist association. The German Baptists continued to grow until World War II, when most Germans left the region.

The first Russian Baptist congregation was formed in 1908 in Chisinau. A Russian Baptist association was formed in 1920. By 1942 there were 347 Baptist churches and 18,000 members. In 1944 the Moldovan Baptists were forced into the All Union Council of Evangelical Christians–Baptists, the umbrella group for evangelical churches in the Soviet Union. Following independence, Baptists in Moldova organized the independent Union of Evangelical Christians–Baptists of Russia.

The Seventh-day Adventist Church also began work in Moldova, which in 1989 was organized as the Moldova Union Conference. The Conference reported some 7,000 members as the 21st century began. Jehovah's Witnesses had opened work early in the 20th

century, but in 1951 they were deported from the region. Before the fall of the Soviet Union, they quietly began to return and evangelize and by the mid-1990s they had 80 kingdom halls.

Islam entered with the Turkish forces at the end of the 15th century, and a Muslim community grew up during the years of Turkish hegemony in the region, mostly among Turkish expatriates. Most of the Turks (and hence most of the Muslims) were expelled by the Russians, but a few thousand remain. Some 3.5 percent of the population speaks Gagauz, a Turkish dialect.

Jews began settling in Moldova in the 15th century. The community grew rapidly during the 19th century, from some 20,000 to more than 220,000. It continued to grow through the first half of the 20th century. Although Jews in the region had been perennially subjected to various forms of anti-Semitism, serious trouble began in 1940 with the exile of many Jewish leaders to Siberia. Nazi forces overran the area in 1941, and between 1941 and 1944, most of the remaining Jews were either killed or deported.

Moldova

Religion	Followers in 1970	Followers in 2010	% of Population	Annual % growth 2000–2010	Followers in 2025	Followers in 2050
Christians	1,665,000	3,568,000	96.3	−1.11	3,393,000	2,808,000
Orthodox	1,549,000	3,444,000	92.9	−1.20	3,203,000	2,636,000
Protestants	32,800	88,000	2.4	1.90	130,000	130,000
Marginals	200	42,000	1.1	1.92	50,000	50,000
Agnostics	1,068,000	80,000	2.2	−6.12	60,000	40,000
Jews	55,000	27,000	0.7	−5.71	20,000	15,000
Atheists	800,000	16,000	0.4	−6.37	10,000	8,000
Muslims	7,000	15,000	0.4	−3.88	12,000	10,000
Baha'is	0	600	0.0	−0.31	1,000	2,000
Ethnoreligionists	0	250	0.0	−1.29	300	300
Total population	**3,595,000**	**3,707,000**	**100.0**	**−1.33**	**3,496,000**	**2,883,000**

After the war, exiles returned and along with survivors re-established the Jewish community. In 1989 migrations to Israel began, and the majority of younger Jews have left the country. By the mid-1990s, some 65,000 Jews resided in Moldova, the largest community residing in Chisinau. Most Jews are Russian-speaking in a land where the majority of the population speaks Romanian.

J. Gordon Melton

See also: Jehovah's Witnesses; Old Believers (Russia); Romanian Orthodox Church; Russian Orthodox Church (Moscow Patriarchate); Seventh-day Adventist Church; Union of Evangelical Christians–Baptists of Russia.

References

Barrett, David, ed. *The Encyclopedia of World Christianity*. 2nd ed. New York: Oxford University Press, 2001.

Dima, Nicolas. *From Moldova to Moldova: The Soviet-Romanian Territorial Dispute*. New York: East European Monographs/Columbia University Press, 1991.

The Republic of Moldova. Chisinau: Moldpres, 1995.

Molokans

The Molokans (milk drinkers), also spelled Molokons, one of the most prominent of the 19th-century Russian Christian sectarian groups, were named for their practice of drinking milk during Lent, a practice forbidden to the members of the Russian Orthodox Church (Moscow Patriarchate). The Molokans generally trace their beginning to the career of Simeon Uklein (b. 1733), the nephew of a noted Doukhobor leader. He grew dissatisfied with Doukhobor attitudes toward the Bible, and in the mid-18th century he began to preach in Tambov, southeast of Moscow. He proclaimed the Bible as his only authority, and by around 1780, the Molokans had arisen as an independent body.

Uklein was not a Trinitarian. Rather he taught that God the Father is the one God, that Christ is his Son and clothed with angelic flesh, and that the Holy Spirit is of the same substance as the Father but inferior to him. He also held that at the time of resurrection all believers will receive a new body, different from their present one. Uklein suggested that Christians should obey the secular law when it does not contradict divine law. He ran into trouble with the Russian authorities because he opposed war and advised believers to refrain from military service. He denied the need for sacraments and ritual. Water baptism was replaced with instruction in the Word. Molokans opposed the veneration given to icons.

Concerned about both the Molokans and the Doukhobors, the Russian government began to push them out of central Russia southward to the Ukraine and then farther south into the Caucasus (present-day Georgia, Armenia, and Azerbaijan) and Central Asia. Repression of the group initially peaked in 1826, when the Molokans refused to be recruited in the army or to pay taxes.

Under repression they quickly reassessed the tax issue, but when pressed into the army would only take non-combat duties (hospitals, cooking, etc.). By the 1840s, the Russian government estimated that some 200,000 Molokans could be found in the Tambov region alone.

In the 1830s, a spiritual awakening spread through the Molokan communities. It was characterized by the practice of jumping about in spiritual ecstasy. It also coincided with the appearance of several charismatic prophets, some of whom had a millennial, apocalyptic message that tended to attract believers. The jumping phenomenon split the Molokans into two major groups: the Postoyannye (Steadfast), who rejected the jumping, and the Pryguny (Jumpers).

The Molokans may have had as many as half a million members by the middle of the 19th century. The problems with the government reached a new peak in 1878, when the government attempted to introduce universal military service, and this became a matter of most intense concern when the Molokans refused to bear arms during the Russo-Japanese War (1904–1905). At this time, many Molokans began immigrating to the United States. Some 2,000 Pryguny migrated to Southern California between 1904 and the beginning of World War I. Several hundred Postoyannye moved to Hawaii in 1904, relocating to San Francisco, California, the next year. Today, some 2,000 Postojannye reside in California and Oregon, and some 10,000 Pryguny reside in Southern California, Arizona, and Baja California, Mexico. There are also seven Molokan centers in Australia.

The Molokans have survived in Russia, over the years becoming the foundation upon which a number of other groups built their Russian ministries. Many Molokans joined the Mennonites, Baptists, and evangelical Christians. The Soviet government was no kinder to the Molokans that the Russian czarists had been. As the 21st century begins, however, more than 150 Molokan communities exist in Russia and the countries of the former Soviet Union, especially Azerbaijan. Most Molokans who were in the Caucasus have been driven out and have relocated in the southern part of Russia. In Russia, some coordination of the Molokan communities is being provided by the Community of Spiritual Christians–Molokans. In 1926, the Pryguny Molokans in southern California organized into the United Molokan Christian Association. There are an estimated 20,000 Molokans worldwide.

Community of Spiritual Christians–Molokans
c/o Head Minister Timofei Schetinkin
Kochubeevka, Stavropol'slii krai
Russia

United Molokan Christian Association
16222 Soriano Dr.
Hacienda Heights, CA 91745-4840

J. Gordon Melton

See also: Doukhobors; Russian Orthodox Church (Moscow Patriarchate).

References

Dunn, Ethel, and Stephen P. Dunn. *The Molokan Heritage Collection.* Vol. 1. *Reprints of Articles and Translations.* Berkeley, CA: Highgate Road Social Science Research Station, 1983.

Klibanov, A. I. *History of Religious Sectarianism in Russia (1860s–1917).* Trans. Ethel Dunn. Oxford: Pergamon Press, 1982.

Mohoff, George W. *The True Molokan.* Montebello, CA: the author, 2003.

"Molokan Home Page." http://gecko.gc.maricopa .edu/clubs/russian/molokan/. Accessed December 19, 2001.

■ Monaco

Monaco, a small principality of only one square mile, is located on the French Mediterranean coast between Nice, France, and San Remo, Italy. Well known for its casinos, it attained a high profile after its prince married American movie star Grace Kelly (1929–1982). The majority of the 32,496 Monacans (2008) are of French heritage, but in the 20th century, Monaco became a metropolitan community, with residents from many national backgrounds having moved there from Italy and the several French-speaking countries.

Christianity spread along the French coast beginning in the first century. A Roman Catholic parish was established in 1247 as part of the Diocese of Nice. The Diocese of Monaco was established in 1887, though there are still a relatively small number of parishes.

Monaco

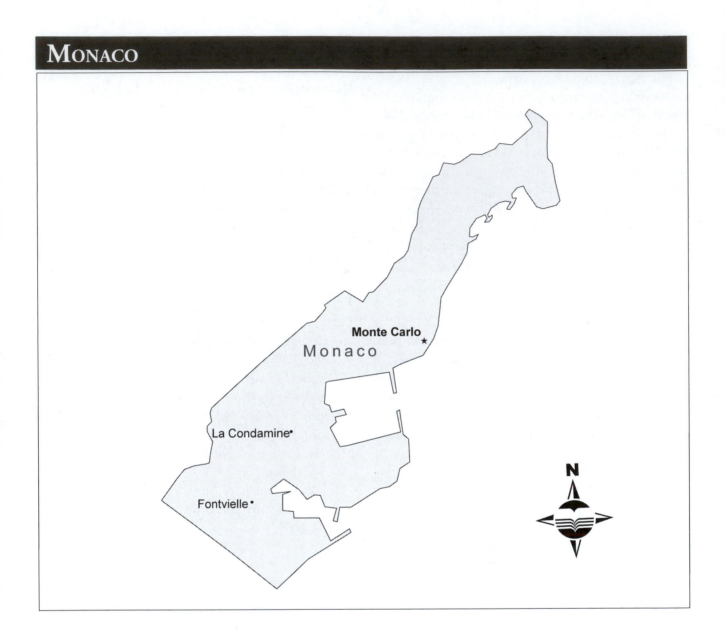

Monaco

Religion	Followers in 1970	Followers in 2010	% of Population	Annual % growth 2000–2010	Followers in 2025	Followers in 2050
Christians	23,300	28,500	86.2	0.10	28,500	29,100
Roman Catholics	21,700	27,200	82.3	0.07	27,100	27,800
Protestants	1,000	700	2.1	2.53	800	800
Anglicans	450	300	0.9	−1.28	300	300
Agnostics	0	3,000	9.1	2.49	4,500	5,500
Atheists	0	760	2.3	0.32	1,200	1,500
Jews	400	560	1.7	0.29	600	630
Muslims	0	150	0.5	0.28	280	400
Baha'is	30	70	0.2	0.33	120	200
Total population	**23,700**	**33,000**	**100.0**	**0.30**	**35,200**	**37,300**

Protestantism was established in 1925 when the Church of England created Saint Paul's Anglican Church, which serves English-speaking residents and the many tourists who come to Monaco annually. Saint Paul's is attached to the Diocese of Europe. Greek residents organized a parish of the Greek Orthodox Church under the Ecumenical Patriarchate in 1957. French Protestants organized a congregation affiliated with the Reformed Church of France in 1959.

There is a small Jewish community in Monaco, but no synagogue has been erected. The Baha'i Faith organized in the mid-1950s. Many other different religious organizations are now represented among Monaco's diverse residents, but few have enough members to hold public worship or organize a center.

J. Gordon Melton

See also: Baha'i Faith; Church of England; Ecumenical Patriarchate/Patriarchate of Constantinople; Reformed Church of France; Roman Catholic Church.

References

Barrett, David, ed. *The Encyclopedia of World Christianity*. 2nd ed. New York: Oxford University Press, 2001.

Eccardt, Thomas M. *Secrets of the Seven Smallest States of Europe: Andorra, Liechtenstein, Luxembourg, Malta, Monaco, San Marino, and Vatican City*. New York: Hippocrene Books, 2005.

Pemberton, H. *The History of Monaco, Past and Present*. Boston: Adamant Media Corporation, 2002.

Monasticism

Monasticism is a form of religious life in which one renounces the world and chooses to live by specific means to reach salvific goals. It is marked by renunciation of and separation from routine social life. In most cases, potential members (novices) are tested for understanding and compliance to community expectations before being allowed to swear permanent vows. Physical separation in distinct, purpose-built structures is common, as is symbolic separation. The monk may wear distinctive clothing (a habit) or a tonsure (the specific emblematic pattern in which hair is removed) or take a religious name replacing that given at birth. These criteria preclude discussion of quasi-monastic forms found in various religions.

Monasticism's roots are lost in time's shrouds. The Greek "monos," meaning "alone," becomes "monk" (or "monarchist") in English. Early monks seceded from society for spiritual purposes. Over time, hermits gathered followings, which were organized into communities. "Cenobitic" (or "common") monasticism became Christianity's norm; it also figures in Buddhism and Jainism.

The oldest continually-practiced monastic forms arose in South Asia, in Buddhism and Jainism. Their precise developmental relationship eludes academic consensus. Both, along with ascetic Brahmanism, may be differing elaborations of a pre-existing regional thread of asceticism. Both seek release from karmic bondage. Discussion of intellectual dependency and direction of influence may reveal as much about the Western Enlightenment's fixation on "first" manifestations of ideas or practices as it does the primitive sources of Indian asceticism. Common in theme, however, is the hermits' practice of congregating in fixed locations during the three-month summer rainy season.

Buddhist Monasticism Buddhism granted monasticism a particular role in the process of attaining *nirvana* (freedom from suffering). Monachists devote themselves to seek total emptiness and loss of self. Chanting and breathing practices prescribed in their scriptures aided the monachists' search.

Buddhist monasticism is an extension of the original *sangha* (community) gathered around Gautama. Derivative sanghas, however, did not possess authoritative leadership. Initially only men were accepted; a tale exists of Buddha's reluctant acceptance of women.

The rulings of the First Three Buddhist Councils ground current practice for Theravadan Buddhists (the dominant form in Ceylon, Burma, and Thailand), although this idea remains controversial—Theravadans alone recognizing the third council. The first, around 486 BCE, recounts an attempt to preserve the recently deceased Buddha's teaching by reciting the sangha's key disciplinary rules (the *Vinayapataka*, or Book of Discipline). All Buddhist groups acknowledge this council's existence, but debate its content. Fortnightly

Buddhist monks, Kuming, China. (J. Gordon Melton)

communal reading from the *Vinaya* remains central to most Buddhist monachism. The second council, approximately 386 BCE, centered on 10 points allegedly deviating from the *Vinaya*, including the propriety of accepting monetary gifts. This partisan account of Buddhism's first schism foregrounds tensions between mobile ascetics and proponents of stable communities.

The Theravadan sangha consisted of six categories: monks and nuns, novices of both sexes, laymen and laywomen; both Chinese and Tibetan Mahayana sanghas add male and female categories of probationers, a status lower than novice. *Bhikkhu* (monk) and *bhikkhuni* (nun) literally translate as "almsman" and "almswoman." Sanghas are the embodiment of *dhamma* (teaching). Over time, initiation or ordination rites became more intricate. Likewise, monasteries evolved from park-like spaces reserved for monks during the

rainy season hiatus to elaborate buildings with designated rooms for varying purposes.

Buddhism entered China roughly two millennia ago; it flourished in Japan from the 500s, where it introduced monasticism. The 1868 Meiji Restoration brought monastic suppression, with confiscation of property and encouragement of monachists' marriage.

Jaina Monasticism Mahavira, the great Jain teacher, was Buddha's contemporary. He recognized four branches of Jain practice: monks, nuns, laymen, and laywomen. Jainism elevates monastic mendicancy to a central role in achieving "emancipation" (*moksha*). In light of the genuine risk of starvation, mendicants' self-chosen begging is viewed as heroic, bringing contact with spiritual reality. Begging benefits not merely mendicants, but provides an avenue for donors' generosity, reducing both persons' negative karma. Ideally, death would occur during meditation after prolonged fasting.

Two major monastic divisions exist: Svetambara (white-clad) and Digambara (sky-clad). Both subscribe to the five basic Jaina tenets, differing profoundly over the interpretation of renunciation of personal property. The numerically inferior Digambaras include clothing among forbidden items. The division occurred somewhere after the fifth century BCE. Differing explanations are offered, but the core issue was Digambara accusations that clothed opponents' failure to take a vow of nudity indicated lax discipline. Renunciation of clothes is often gradual, as novices progress spiritually. Similarly citing renunciation of property, Digambara decline alms-bowls, eating only food placed in their up-turned palms. Digambara nuns, who cannot achieve moksha without reincarnation as men, do not practice nudity.

The Svetambara canon includes the *Ayara-*, *Kappa-* and *Vavahara-suttas*, which define the scope of monks and nuns' disciplined life. More than 100 pages are devoted to the process of begging. Svetambara reject nudity as an attempt to restore insignificant details of Mahavira's work. So strong is concern not to damage life that Sthanakvaki- and Terepantha-Svetambara wear mouth-coverings to avoid damaging tiny beings with their breath. Renunciation of sexual activity is based not only on denying pleasure but upon belief that female genitalia teem with microscopic life that is pulverized during intercourse. Similarly, alcohol is rejected not only for its effects but because microbes are destroyed during fermentation. Both branches allow whisks for the sweeping of sleeping areas to remove insects that might become crushed. Forgoing travel in the rainy season lessens the likelihood of harming water-borne creatures.

The Terepantha-Svetambara founded a research institute in the 1970s to promote much-needed academic reflection on Jaina monasticism.

Christian Monasticism Christian monasticism was polygenetic, arising simultaneously and independently in several locations. Whatever its New Testament-era role, the Qumran community's eradication by Romans broke any institutional link with Christian monasticism. Marking Christian monasticism is a persistent "restorationist" theme, attempting to re-create the perceived community from Acts 2.

Evidence suggests the existence, easterly outside the Roman Empire, of an ascetic tradition predating Egyptian developments. Tatian (ca. 120–180) and his eremitic encratic (literally "self-controlled") followers were considered heretical in the West, but their heightened strictness matched that of other regional religions. Ascetics undertook wandering mission journeys, separating themselves "to" mission, rather than "from" society. By the third century, celibate, single-minded community observance in Syria began with the "Sons and Daughters of the Covenant." Persian monastic community dates from the fourth century, with revitalization in the sixth, including the foundation of the Great Monastery on Mount Izla.

Egyptian hermits, perhaps reacting to relatively comfortable late third-century conditions, fled to the desert. Their story is shadowy until Athanasius (ca. 293–373) wrote his *Life of Antony*, a hagiography revealing typical early practices. Monastic vows were a second or true baptism. The Edict of Milan brought both rejoicing at the empire's apparent conversion and concern over lax discipline. Christian Platonists' elision of learning and asceticism grounded the movement; some see it as continuing early pacifism, monks' acting on the majority's behalf. Monastic community developed around 320, under Pachomius (ca. 292–348 CE). This cenobitic monasticism envisioned a third option between direct struggle with the world and withdrawal to undertake solely spiritual battles. His pragmatic *Rule* provided ad hoc advice for daily issues.

In Asia Minor, monasticism unfolded under the influence of Macrina (324–379) and Basil (330–379). Disdaining eremiticism as selfish, they promoted church reform through a service-based life with decentralized leadership. Basil's widely translated *Asceticon* was not a true "rule," but a guiding conglomeration of scriptures and ideas. Orthodox monastic spirituality extensively used icons from the sixth century. Imperial edicts in the eighth and ninth centuries, essentially equating icon veneration with idolatry, mandated iconoclasm (destruction of icons). Resistance by iconophiles, who defended their devotion on Christological grounds, led to their persecution.

Portrait of Saint Basil the Great, a fourth-century Christian leader and bishop of Caesarea. Basil was instrumental in the development of Eastern Christian monasticism. (André, Thevet, *Les Vrais Pourtraits et Vies Hommes Illustres,* 1584)

Several monastic figures attempted to bridge East and West. Indirect evidence of a native-Western ascetic and eremitic proto-monastic tradition comes from Jerome (ca. 347–420), who rendered Pachomius's *Rule* into Latin. Ambrose (ca. 340–397), co-founder of Just War Theory, which banned monks from combat, was influenced by Athanasius and in turn influenced Augustine (354–430). Augustine, a key North African monastic promoter, prepared an unsystematic set of canons. The first known Latin rule, it influenced Benedict (480–547).

Monasticism, as governed by *The Rule of St. Benedict* (hereafter *RB*), and the papacy are medieval Christianity's two defining institutions. *RB* is the high-water mark in a process, not a lone genius's innovation. Benedict of Nursia originally sought a hermit's life. Gradually gathering a following, he and his sister Scholastica (ca. 480–547) founded houses on Monte

Casino's Pagan hill-shrine site. *RB*'s life of reclusive prayer dovetailed with Pope Gregory the Great's (r. 590–604) emphasis on purgatory and the idea of the Mass's being a sacrifice. Monks' financial needs were met by patrons' endowing perpetual recitation of Masses to secure release from purgatory. With papal support, *RB* spread throughout Western Christendom, the Middle Ages' second-most copied document. The Council of Tours (567) mandated cloistered life for monks.

RB's twin pillars, permanence (or stability) and obedience, assume a leadership principle, possibly borrowed from secular models, parallel to theories of papal power. Abbots stand in Christ's authority; inferiors' obedience is expected to be absolute, abbots alone are responsible for errors. As imperial institutions crumbled and society atomized, Benedictine abbeys' resiliency and economic self-containment created their massive social significance. Tiny libraries provided a slender thread preserving Western knowledge. Their near monopoly on literacy earned wide political influence. Drawing upon Psalm 119, *RB* punctuated daily life with eight services, between 2:00 a.m. and 6:30 p.m. To communal worship were added four hours of private prayer or study and six hours of manual labor. Bells called monks to prayer; a lectionary cycled through the Bible annually. Their spartan meatless diet provided one daily meal in winter, two in summer.

Celtic monastic communities, predating Patrick (ca. 387–493), resembled Greek semi-eremitism. Clusters of hermit's cells formed monastic villages, but disciplined community was absent. Monasticism's alleged centrality to Irish ecclesiology (abbots' governing regions instead of bishops) has been challenged by recent historiography. Cuthbert of Lindisfarne (ca. 634–687) founded the Iona community and left an advice-oriented *Rule*. Pilgrimage, antithesis of stability, featured prominently. Monks wandered in groups, voluntary exile contributing to personal spiritual journeys. Controversy with Romans peaked at the Synod of Whitby (663), spawning the overwriting of Celtic rules by *RB*. The Iona network switched by 716; the palimpsest was completed in Ireland in the late 1100s, propelled by dual forces of Cistercian reform and Norman invasion.

By 800, *RB* was not universal. *RB*'s Roman nature suited Charlemagne's (742–814) plans to unite his empire religiously. Benedict of Aniane's (750–821) reformed *RB* spread under Charlemagne's son, Louis (778–840). After Louis's death, observance declined. Occasional flourishing centers merely underscored overall decay. Making matters worse, Vikings stole most Northern European monasteries' endowments.

Reform at Cluny, around 909, evinced increasing task specialization, both spiritually and logistically. Priors aided abbots; sacrists cared for increasingly elaborate chapel contents and ornaments. Reading increasingly displaced manual labor; daily reading of *RB*'s chapters occurred in an eponymous chapter house.

The Crusades constituted militant and mobile monastic forms. Bound by the code of chivalry and ideas of "holy war," Crusaders undertook armed pilgrimages. Motivated by indulgences, promises of remission of sins' penalties, and eschatological hopes, they mounted campaigns of conquest. Modified monastic rules resulted in vows of obedience, poverty, and celibacy, but not geographical stability or renouncing violence. These orders became major landowners, later seizing Rhodes and Malta after being ejected from Palestine.

Reorganization restricted women's roles. Whereas Hilda of Whitby (ca. 614–680) had governed a joint male-female monastery in the seventh century, 12th-century abbesses' power was limited and subject to male oversight. Men outnumbered women probably on the order of three or four to one. Hildegard von Bingen (1098–1179), mystic and writer, was a rare late medieval prominent female monachist.

When this monastic resurgence began, no carefully defined orders existed. Reform flowered into new Benedictine forms. The emergent orders' interpretation of *RB* differed from the mainstream. "White monks" (denoting undyed as opposed to black habit cloth) rode the crest of a late 10th-century wave of asceticism.

The 1084 founding of an abbey in Chartreuse (Latin: Carthusia) marked the Carthusians' return to minimalist pre-Benedictine practices. Semi-eremitic monks lived in clustered cells, eating and praying alone, shifting emphasis from liturgy to private devotions. The order's rigor ensured it remained small.

In 1098, the Benedictines at Citeaux (Latin: Cistercium) began following the unaltered *RB*. Never as ascetic as Carthusians, these Cistercians nevertheless eschewed architectural and liturgical decoration, reacting to perceived Cluniac excesses. Cistercian houses ranged from 12 to 140 monks and 40 to 500 lay brothers. Brothers covered most manual labor. Around 1200, half of monks were priests; proportions rose thereafter. Their intellectual center developed at Clairvaux, under Bernard (1090–1153), whose revisionism limited *RB*'s authoritarian absolute abbacy. Cistercians often settled unoccupied areas, seeking seclusion and purity, but secular settlements built up around the innovative and successful monasteries. Cistercians' 1119 papal charter made them the first formal order. Cistercian houses multiplied rapidly across Europe: from 19 in 1122 to 529 by 1200.

Early medievals tended to believe only monks and nuns merited redemption. By roughly 1100, hope arose that the faithfully married might be saved. Despite this optimism, the number of monachists increased, outstripping general population growth by a factor of four. Europe's monasteries numbered in the thousands, having garnered broad community support. Previously, chief benefactors were kings and princes; now less wealthy folk pooled resources to found monasteries. There was also more wealth to mobilize, as better weather, land reclamation, and improved agricultural practices increased food supplies. Infant mortality dropped; surviving children often were entrusted to monasteries. Paralleling early church fears of laxity in the face of prosperity, lingering concern over biblical warnings of rich people's spiritual peril motivated gifts. By the 13th century, as much as one-third of some jurisdictions' land belonged to monasteries.

Monastic reform must be viewed in the context of papal reform, particularly the 12th and 13th centuries' Lateran Council series. The Fourth Lateran Council (1215) recognized mendicant orders, Dominicans and Franciscans. Renouncing fixed incomes, wandering Europe preaching and begging food, mendicants held to obedience but not stability. They constitute a separate monastic category, precursor of modern active orders. Mendicant orders remained urban, as only cities provided sufficient concentrations of donors.

Founded by the Castilian noble Dominic de Guzman (1170–1221), Dominicans attracted intelligent young ascetics. Within Dominic's lifetime, women had a parallel order. Exempted from physical labor and soon expected to attend university, friars preached and taught theology. Commitment to orthodoxy made them invaluable Inquisitors. Their most famous member was Thomas Aquinas (1225–1274). They maintained a strong missionary emphasis, from Italy to Lithuania to China.

Francis of Assisi (ca. 1181–1226), a prosperous cloth merchant's son, played both wastrel and warrior before making a pilgrimage to Rome. Called by a voice while praying in a derelict church, he bought and repaired it, the first of many. His was not a spiritualized imitation of Christ, but concrete emulation. As such, Francis set down no elaborate fixed rule, like *RB*. A passionate denouncer of pride and greed, Francis downplayed learning or dogma. His Gray Friars (or Friars Minor) were anti-worldly, poor in spirit, possession, office, and learning. Papal pressure resulted in three successive *Rules*, each increasingly ordered and hierarchical. By the early 1300s, there were roughly 1,400 houses, possibly one-fifth for women.

The same era witnessed the eclipse of monasteries' educational role by emerging universities. Monastic schools' practical learning was supplanted by a scientific approach, aiming to meet the demands of business and secular government. Monarchs encouraged universities because they provided a steady stream of reliable, secular administrators. These bureaucracies simultaneously freed government for direct ecclesiastical involvement and nurtured nascent nationalism. Quasi-monastic expressions of the Modern Devotion, such as the Brethren of the Common Life, also set the stage for the Reformation.

Orthodox monasticism proved an important institution for preserving the Orthodox Church during the era of Turkish rule following the fall of Constantinople (Istanbul) in 1453. Latin churches in the region were suppressed; Orthodox properties were confiscated, then sold back to them. Thriving communities continue to this day.

Protestantism rejected monasticism, whether on principle (Lutherans and Reformed) or opportunistically (Anglicans). Henry VIII's seizures of monastic property in the 1530s forced English monasticism underground until the 1828 Catholic Emancipation. Numerous Protestant communitarian groups (Anabaptists, English Civil War radicals, Moravians, and American utopianists), although quasi-monastic are beyond this entry's scope.

The Catholic Reformation's medieval character is partly demonstrated by the founding of the Society of Jesus (Jesuits) by Ignatius Loyola (1491–1556), who sought papal recognition in 1540. A crippled former soldier, Loyola framed *Spiritual Exercises* by which spiritual mentors direct seekers into a life of unhesitating obedience. Obedience dominated Ignatius's personal piety, blending Renaissance individualism with ecclesiastical subservience. Jesuits differed from the other orders, having no distinctive habit or fixed hours of prayer and adding a vow of direct obedience to the pope. Jesuit seminaries prepared priests to reclaim territory lost to Protestants. Another keynote was missions beyond Europe, from Brazil to Japan. As other orders penetrated East Asia, conflict ensued over mission strategy. Jesuits advocated indigenization, but Franciscans and Dominicans insisted upon replicating European patterns, a debate known as the Chinese Rites Controversy.

In Europe's Enlightenment and Revolutionary eras, monasticism suffered. From France to Italy to the Habsburg Empire, waves of suppressions, secularization, and persecution winnowed monastic populations. Nineteenth-century stability witnessed the emergence of new monastic orders, a trend cresting in the mid-20th century. More than 30 congregations of active Benedictine sisters sprang up in a century and a half.

The Second Vatican Council impacted monasticism. Of the almost one and a half million Catholic monachists in 1967, fewer than 5 percent belonged to traditional contemplative orders. Popular culture advocates for activist orders over contemplative, although the recent trend is to stronger cenobitic recruitment despite its being at cross-purposes with Western hyper-individualism and anti-authoritarianism. Women outnumber men three to one, but all orders are declining. While the American monastic population remains above 1900 levels, the movement's mean age is high, with new vocations not replacing dying members. Lay oblate numbers, however, increase. Financial solvency is a growing parallel problem, prompting more double (male-female) monasteries. In Asia and Africa, contemplative orders are growing. Dialogue was initiated with non-Christian monachists.

Current Protestant monasticism remains limited. German Lutheran monasticism recommenced with the 1947 founding of the Evangelical Sisters of Mary. Anglo-Catholic contemplative communities are still the minority, but increasingly popular. From the 1970s, a few evangelicals dabbled with communitarianism. Increasing numbers of evangelical Protestants have been exploring monastic spirituality and choosing life as oblates.

C. Mark Steinacher

See also: Athanasius; Augustine of Hippo; Benedictines; Buddha, Gautama; Cistercians; Communalism; Dominicans; Franciscans; Hildegard of Bingen; Istanbul; Jainism: Jesuits; Mahavira; Sthanakvaki Jain Tradition; Terepanth Svetambara Jain Tradition; Theravada Buddhism; Thomas Aquinas.

References

Benn, James Alexander, Lori R. Meeks, and James Robson, eds. *Buddhist Monasticism in East Asia: Places of Practice.* New York: Routledge, 2009.

Dunn, Marilyn. *Emergence of Monasticism: From the Desert Fathers to the Early Middle Ages.* New York: Wiley-Blackwell, 2003.

Harmless, William. *Desert Christians: An Introduction to the Literature of Early Monasticism.* New York: Oxford University Press, 2004.

Kim, Sunhae, and James W. Heisig, eds. *Monasticism, Buddhist, and Christian: The Korean Experience.* Grand Rapids, MI: William B. Eerdmans Publishing Company, 2008.

Lawrence, Christopher Nugent. *The Age of the Cloister: The Story of Monastic Life in the Middle Ages.* Mahwah. NJ: HiddenSpring, 2003.

Rankin, Aidan. *The Jain Path: Ancient Wisdom for the West.* Berkeley, CA: O Books, 2006.

■ Mongolia

Mongolia is an Asian country sandwiched between Russia and the People's Republic of China. A relatively large country, its 600,000 square miles of territory are eclipsed by those of its neighbors. It also has a relatively sparse population of only 2,996,081 people.

The Mongols are a group of peoples tied together by a common ancestry, culture, language, and residence in the land between China and Siberia. As early as the fifth century BCE, the Huns established themselves in the valleys of the Selenga River. Over the succeeding centuries a Hun Empire emerged and became a major competitor against the Chinese Empire to the south. In the fifth century, the Huns under Attila (ca. 406–453) turned their attention eastward and conquered most of Europe. Attila's successors were displaced by the Turks.

The Mongolians reached a new zenith under Genghis Khan (ca. 1162–1227), whose kingdom stretched from Beijing to Tibet and Turkistan. As so often occurred, his successors were unable to keep his empire together. During the succeeding centuries, Mongolia and China were periodically at war. In the 17th century, some Mongolians sided with the Manchurians who took control of China in 1644, and over the next 100 years, Mongolia was almost totally absorbed into China.

At the end of the 19th century, Mongolia became an object of dispute between Russia, China, and Japan, and following the Russo-Japanese War (1904–1905), Russia recognized Japanese hegemony over Inner (southern) Mongolia. In 1911, northern or Outer Mongolia revolted against China and proclaimed its independence. It again became a battleground between China and the troops of the czar at the time of the Russian Revolution. In the midst of continuing war, some Mongolians turned to Bolshevik Russia for help. In 1921 a combination of Russian and Mongolian troops seized Urga (now Ulaanbaatar), the capital of Outer Mongolia. Three years later, the People's Republic of Mongolia was proclaimed. It was able to resist the Japanese attempt to invade in 1939, and the assistance provided by the Soviet Union at that time cemented the cordial relationships that continued in subsequent decades. In 1992 a new Constitution moved Mongolia from the one-party system and domination by the People's Revolutionary Party and introduced a variety of democratic reforms. Meanwhile, Inner Mongolia has become an autonomous region of the People's Republic of China.

Religious life in Mongolia was radically changed during the reign of Atlan Khan (1543–1583), who believed that the Mongols needed a unifying religion.

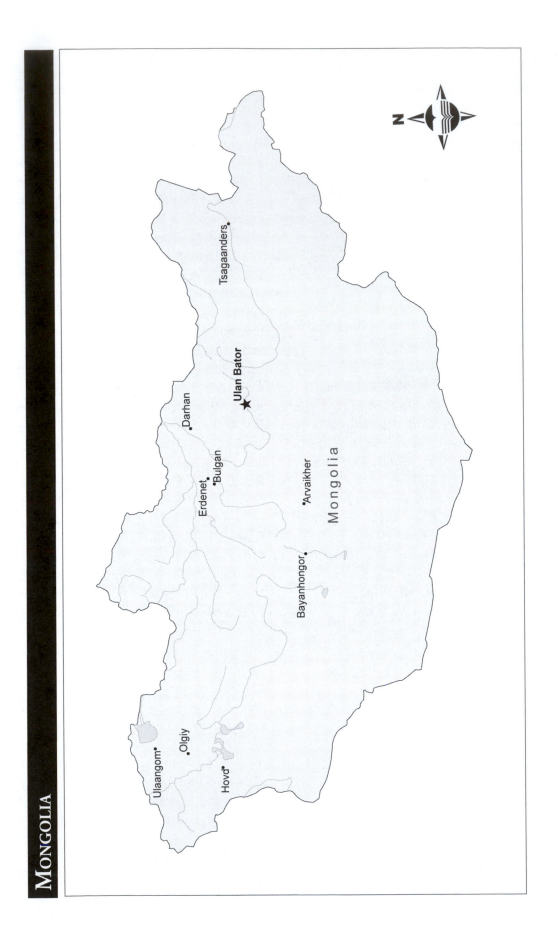

MONGOLIA

After considering Chinese religion, he rejected it because of the possibility of Mongolia being absorbed by the Chinese. Instead he chose Tibetan Buddhism. He invited a Tibetan religious leader, Sonam Gyatso (1543–1588), to whom he granted the title of Dalai Lama (Ocean of Wisdom), to lead the religion. Sonam Gyatso is remembered today as the third Dalai Lama, as the title was posthumously bestowed on his two predecessors.

Thus Tibetan Buddhism was wedded to the Mongol state. In this process, one of the heirs of the Khalkas, the leading Mongol group in Outer Mongolia, was claimed to be the first reincarnation of the Living Buddha of Urga. His successors, seen as the third most important Tibetan Buddhist leader after the Dalai Lama and the Panchen Lama, remained in power until 1921, when the office was reduced to a puppet status. The political status of the Living Buddha was completely eliminated in 1924.

Tibetan Buddhism had been present among the Mongols from the time of Genghis Kahn's grandson, Kublai Khan (1215–1294), who became emperor in 1259. He installed lamas as religious advisors to his court and supported the rise of Tibetan religious leaders into political control of their homeland. The integration of previously existing shamanistic and magical practices into the new Buddhism among the Mongol peoples also contributed to the creation of Tibetan Buddhism as a separate branch of the Buddhist family.

As in Tibet, leadership in the Mongolian Buddhist and political realm was focused upon a set of lamas, venerated as incarnations of different bodhisattvas (highly evolved souls). When such a lama passed away, his successor, believed to be his reincarnation, was sought among the recently born male children of the region. Once designated, the infant would be taken to the local monastery for training.

At the time of the emergence of a Communist government in the 1920s, there were more than 2,500 temples and monasteries in the land and more than 120,000 Buddhist priests (lamas). Beginning in 1929, however, the new secular government began the suppression of Buddhist worship. During the 1930s more than 20,000 monks were killed and more than 800 temples and monasteries destroyed or secularized. Lamas were integrated into the rest of the population. The heavy suppression of Buddhism was only relieved in the 1960s—one symbol of the new policy being the construction of the Gandan Monastery at Ulaanbaatar. It houses a community of some 100 monks and a new temple for the Living Buddha. The monastery serves as headquarters of the Asian Buddhist Conference for Peace, which holds conferences for foreign Buddhists, published a journal that circulated internationally, and hosted visits by the Dalai Lama in 1979 and 1982.

Buddhism has experienced a remarkable comeback in Outer Mongolia in the generation since World War II and now claims more than 20 percent of the population as adherents. During the 1990s, the new monastic communities formed a Buddhist Association to assist with the Buddhist revival. This revivalist movement owes much to a Ladaki monk, Bakula Rinpoche, who also is the Indian ambassador to Mongolia. He established a Buddhist school in Ulaanbaatar to train young monks and an associated temple. He is also credited with the idea of forming the Buddhist Association. In mid-1999, the Foundation for the Preservation of the Mahayana Tradition also became involved in the effort to revive Mongolian Buddhism.

In the meantime, the pre-Buddhist shamanistic religion has never been displaced as a living tradition among the Mongol people, and today it continues to claim the allegiance of almost one-third of the people. It grew considerably when Buddhist structures were dismantled, though the largest segment of the population think of themselves as atheist or nonreligious.

Christianity was originally introduced among the Mongols in the seventh century but in its original form did not survive. The Roman Catholic Church was introduced in the 13th century, and the Russian Orthodox Church (Moscow Patriarchate) came during the years of Russian influence. In 1817 the London Missionary Society, a Congregationalist organization, sent two missionaries who succeeded in translating the Bible into Mongolian, though few converts were ever made. This second wave of Christianity was formally suppressed in 1924, and virtually no Christians could be found in the country until the faith was introduced again in the 1990s.

The largest Christian group, the Mongolian Partnership, was initiated from Hong Kong by several cooperating evangelical agencies. There is one parish of

Mongolia

Religion	Followers in 1970	Followers in 2010	% of Population	Annual % growth 2000–2010	Followers in 2025	Followers in 2050
Ethnoreligionists	438,000	913,000	33.7	1.39	1,307,000	1,488,000
Agnostics	494,000	735,000	27.2	0.05	600,000	400,000
Buddhists	27,000	675,000	24.9	1.57	900,000	1,170,000
Atheists	268,000	200,000	7.4	0.22	100,000	50,000
Muslims	22,000	120,000	4.4	−0.83	100,000	100,000
Christians	3,500	47,100	1.7	5.98	84,600	150,000
Protestants	0	20,000	0.7	6.72	40,000	80,000
Independents	100	14,000	0.5	5.64	23,000	38,000
Marginals	0	9,000	0.3	11.11	16,000	25,000
Chinese folk	3,000	17,000	0.6	0.88	20,000	30,000
Baha'is	0	60	0.0	1.20	200	400
Total population	**1,256,000**	**2,707,000**	**100.0**	**0.88**	**3,112,000**	**3,388,000**

the Russian Orthodox Church Outside of Russia, and the Jehovah's Witnesses have initiated a work.

The other measurable religion in Mongolia is Islam, mostly of the Hanafite Sunni School, which is practiced by ethnic Uzbeks, Kazakhs, and Ulghurs who reside in the western part of Mongolia. The Baha'i Faith began work in the 1990s following the collapse of the Communist government.

J. Gordon Melton

See also: Baha'i Faith; Foundation for the Preservation of the Mahayana Tradition; Hanafite School of Islam; Jehovah's Witnesses; London Missionary Society; Roman Catholic Church; Russian Orthodox Church (Moscow Patriarchate); Russian Orthodox Church Outside of Russia.

References

Bodio, Stephen A. *Eagle Dreams: Searching for Legends in Wild Mongolia*. Guilford, CT: Lyons Press, 2002.

Heissig, W. *The Religions of Mongolia*. Trans. G. Samuel. Berkeley: University of California Press, 1980.

Moses, L. W., and S. A. Halkovic Jr. *Introduction to Mongolian History and Culture*. Bloomington, IN: Research Institute for Inner Asian Studies, Indiana University, 1985.

Sabloff, Paula L. W. *Modern Mongolia: Reclaiming Genghis Khan*. Philadelphia: University of Pennsylvania Museum Publication, 2001.

Montenegrin Orthodox Church

The Montenegrin Orthodox Church is a relatively new Eastern Orthodox Church that emerged in the wake of the disintegration of the former Socialist Republic of Yugoslavia. Orthodoxy in Montenegro dates to the 13th century, when Saint Sava worked with the Serbian ruler to create a strong Orthodox presence throughout the realm then under Serbian control. Before Montenegro regained its independence, Orthodoxy had largely replaced Roman Catholicism in Montenegro. Once it gained independence, an autonomous Montenegrin Church was established in communion with the Ecumenical Patriarchate. For several centuries, until the mid 19th century, the nation had a theocratic government whose head of state was an Orthodox bishop.

Serbia re-established control over Montenegro at the end of World War I, and in 1920 the Montenegrin Autocephalous Orthodox Church, to which the great majority of the population belonged, was abolished, and the Serbian Orthodox Church assumed control over the church's administration and property. Montenegro remained in union with Serbia through the 1990s and into the middle of the first decade of the new century. However, through these turbulent times, many in Montenegro yearned for the same independence from Serbia that was being asserted by Macedonia, Bosnia-Herzegovina, and Kosovo. That independence was finally gained in 2006.

Meanwhile, in 1993, a small group of Orthodox believers, aligned with the Liberal Alliance of Montenegro, a political party that emerged as the first group advocating an independent Montenegro, declared the re-establishment of the Montenegrin Orthodox Church as the new legitimate representative of Orthodoxy in Montenegro. This action was staunchly opposed by the Ecumenical Patriarchate.

The first leader of the church was Metropolitan Antonije (1919–1996, born Antonije Abramović). He was succeeded by Metropolitan Mihailo (b. 1938 as Miraš Dedeić), a former priest in the Greek Orthodox Church in Italy and now the archbishop of Cetinje (the site of the old capital of Montenegro and its ecclesiastical center). As voices grew for national independence, the new church attempted to assert its continuity with the previous Montenegrin Church and hence its right to the property it believed was illegitimately seized by the Serbian Orthodox Church in 1920.

The Montenegrin Church had some success beginning in 1997. Metropolitan Mihailo was consecrated by bishops from the Bulgarian Alternative Orthodox Church, which had challenged the legitimacy of the Bulgarian patriarch (who had held office during the Communist era). The Bulgarian Alternative had also found support in the post-Communist Bulgarian government. Also in 1997, the pro-Serbian government that had been in power in Montenegro was voted out of office and the new authorities quickly registered the Montenegrin Orthodox Church as a civil organization. Four years later the church was recognized as a nongovernmental organization by the Montenegrin Ministry of the Interior. Its gains were the result of rediscovering provisions of an obsolete (but still operative) law on the Legal Position of Religious Communities that had been retained from the former Socialist Republic of Yugoslavia.

Montenegro finally became independent in 2006, and the Montenegrin Church moved to register itself in Serbia, looking to gain support from ethnic Montenegrins residing there. Though initially rebuffed, in 2007 it won its case before the Serbian court.

The new Montenegrin Church continues to assert its legitimacy but as of 2009 had made no real headway in even partially replacing the Serbian Orthodox Church in the new nation. It is to be noted that almost half of the Montenegrin Orthodox believers are ethnic Serbians.

In the meantime, the Bulgarian government turned against the Bulgarian Alternative Orthodox Church, and in 2004, government authorities removed the priests of the group from all the church facilities they had held for the previous decade. Due to that action, the Montenegrin Church lost its major hope of a powerful international ally. Today the Montenegrin Orthodox Church is in communion with a spectrum of small Orthodox churches, including the Bulgarian Orthodox Church, the Chiesa Ortodossa in Italia, and the Ukrainian Orthodox Church-Kiev Patriarchy.

The Serbian Orthodox Church has challenged the status of the Montenegrin Orthodox Church. The Serbian Church sees the ecclesiastical unity of Serbian and Montenegrin Orthodoxy that begins with the conversion of Montenegro by Saint Sava. Now that the country is independent, it remains to be seen if there will be a move to separate the Orthodox faithful from the Serbian Church either through the government's privileging the Montenegrin Orthodox Church, which has failed to gain any widespread public support, or through separate action.

Montenegrin Orthodox Church
Gruda b.b.
81250 Cetinje, Crna Gora
Montenegro

J. Gordon Melton

See also: Bulgarian Orthodox Church; Chiesa Ortodossa in Italia; Montenegrin Orthodox Church; Ukrainian Catholic Church.

References
Montenegrin Association of America. http://www.montenegro.org/. Accessed May 15, 2009.

Montenegrin Orthodox Church. http://www.moc-cpc.org/.

Morrison, Kenneth. *Montenegro: A Modern History.* London: I. B. Tauris, 2009.

■ Montenegro

Montenegro is a small country in southeastern Europe on the Adriatic Sea. It is bounded by Albania, Kosovo,

The Monastery of Ostrog, a monastery of the Serbian Orthodox Church, is placed against an almost vertical background high up in the large rock of Ostroska Greda, in Montenegro. (Sasa Golub/Dreamstime.com)

Serbia, and Bosnia and Herzegovina. Its population of 620,000 (2009) resides on its 5,233 square miles of territory. Ethnically, the country primarily consists of Montenegrins (43 percent) and Serbians (32 percent). Serbian is spoken by twice the number who speak Montenegrin.

Slavic people began to settle what is now Montenegro as early as the sixth century CE. By the ninth century, a large percentage of the Slavs had become Christians (Roman Catholic), and the region existed as a vassal state called Duklja within the Byzantine Empire. In 1042, Duklja's King Vojislav won a decisive battle against Byzantium, and Duklja became an independent state. The fall of the Vojislavljevic dynasty in the 12th century led to a period in which what would become Montenegro struggled for independence, first from neighboring Serbia and then from the Ottoman Empire.

In the 14th century, the Crnojevic dynasty moved to maintain independence as the Ottoman armies established hegemony over their neighbors. Serbia fell following the Battle of Kosovo in 1389, Bosnia fell in 1463, and then Herzegovina in 1483. Ivan Crnojevic (1465–1490) allied himself with the city-state of Venice and was able to stop the Ottoman advance. In 1482, he established a new capital in a strategic location that evolved into the long-term capital, Cetinje. He also brought the first printing press into the southern Balkans, though it would be his successor and son, Djuradj Crnojevic (r. 1490–1496), who would become renowned for printing the first books originating in southeastern Europe.

Montenegro was able to maintain its independence through the next centuries and entered the 20th century as the Kingdom of Montenegro. It joined the allied cause in World War I, during which time Monte-

MONTENEGRO

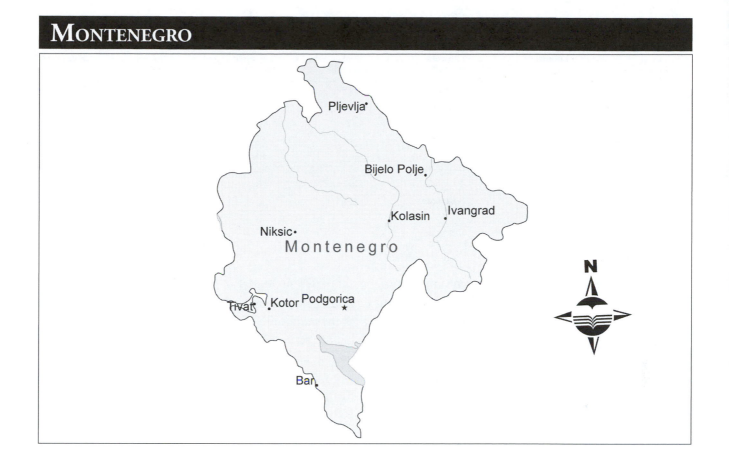

negro was occupied by Austria. King Nikola and his family fled to Italy. In 1918, Nikola's son-in-law and king of Serbia, Petar Karadjordjevic, had his army occupy Montenegro. Instead of reestablishing his father-in-law's throne, however, he annexed Montenegro and forbade Nikola's return. Though Montenegrins staged a national uprising against the Serbian annexation, they were eventually absorbed into the Kingdom of Serbs, Croats, and Slovenes, which evolved into the Kingdom of Yugoslavia in 1929. Following World War II, it was included in the Socialist Federal Republic of Yugoslavia. Yugoslavia fell apart in 1992. Montenegro initially joined Serbia in the Federal Republic of Yugoslavia, which was increasingly unstable and evolved by 2003 into Serbia and Montenegro. In May 2006, Montenegro held a referendum on it relation with Serbia and more than 55 percent of the people voted for a break. Thus, on June 2, 2006, Montenegro formally declared itself an independent state.

As Montenegro emerged as a visible state in the 11th century, its population included Pagans who fol-

lowed traditional Slavic religions; Bogomils, a Gnostic faith that had emerged in the southern Balkans; and Latin-rite Roman Catholic Christians. In the 12th century, with the fall of the Vojislavljevic dynasty, the influence of Constantinople became dominant, and there was considerable pressure placed on converting the region to Eastern Orthodoxy. With the further suppression of the Pagans and Bogomils, Eastern Orthodoxy had become the dominant religion by the time of the rise of the Ottoman Empire. During the Crnojevic dynasty, when books began to be printed, most were Christian books for use by the Orthodox faithful. The place of the Orthodox Church was even more firmly secured after the end of the Crnojevic dynasty. The country turned to the church, and for 180 years (1516–1697) Montenegro was ruled by their Vladikas (that is, the bishops), who were selected by popular assemblies. In 1697, the new Vladika Danilo Petrovic established the rulership of Montenegro in a single family, the Petrovics. The rulers, as orthodox bishops, were celibate, and thus the office of ruling Vladika passed

Montenegro

Religion	Followers in 1970	Followers in 2010	% of Population	Annual % growth 2000–2010	Followers in 2025	Followers in 2050
Christians	262,000	471,000	78.5	−0.89	496,000	494,000
Orthodox	226,000	425,000	70.9	−0.93	443,000	446,000
Roman Catholics	31,400	24,700	4.1	−2.96	24,200	22,300
Protestants	2,500	10,500	1.8	2.21	12,100	13,500
Muslims	62,900	99,000	16.5	−1.93	100,000	98,000
Agnostics	141,000	25,000	4.2	−10.66	15,000	10,000
Atheists	52,400	5,000	0.8	−8.25	2,000	1,500
Total population	**519,000**	**600,000**	**100.0**	**−1.93**	**613,000**	**603,000**

from uncle to nephew. That continued into the middle of the 19th century, when the new ruler Danilo Petrovic, instead of seeking ordination, secured the endorsement of the czar of Russia to rule as the prince of Montenegro. Thus the country smoothly transitioned to secular rule, which remained in place until World War I.

Following the annexation of Montenegro to Serbia, in 1920, the Montenegrin Autocephalous Orthodox Church, to which the great majority of the population belonged, was abolished and the Serbian Orthodox Church assumed hegemony over its property and assimilated its leadership into its own hierarchy.

As early as 1993, a group of Orthodox believers in Montenegro declared the re-establishment of the Montenegrin Orthodox Church, proclaimed to be the legitimate representative of Orthodoxy in Montenegro. Though this action was opposed by the Ecumenical Patriarchate, in 1997, Metropolitan Mihailo (b. 1938) was selected to lead the church with the title of archbishop of Cetinje. Over the next decade, the groups attempted unsuccessfully to assert its rights to the property still in the hands of the Serbian Orthodox Church. It was finally registered as a civil organization in 1997 and in 2001 as a nongovernmental organization recognized by the Montenegrin Ministry of the Interior under provisions of an obsolete law on the Legal Position of Religious Communities from the former Socialist Republic of Yugoslavia. Following Montenegro's declared independence, the Montenegrin Church attempted to register itself in Serbia, and in 2007 was supported in that effort by the Serbian courts. The new Montenegrin Church has attempted to assume the role of the autonomous church since prior to World War II, but has so far (2009) been rebuffed. It may have sealed its fate by aligning itself with the Bulgarian Alternative Orthodox Church, a dissenting group in Bulgaria that has been unsuccessful in challenging the Bulgarian Orthodox Church. Bishops of the Bulgarian group consecrated Metropolitan Mihailo to his office. The Montenegrin Church also remains alienated from the Ecumenical Patriarchate.

As the first decade of the 21st century draws to a close, the majority of Montenegrins (including the minority of ethnic Serbians residing in the country) adhere to the Orthodox Church, now a part of the jurisdiction of the Serbian Orthodox Church. In 2003, the most recent census reported 460,383 members (74.24 percent of the population). The church is currently headed by Metropolitan Amfilohije, the archbishop of Cetinje and metropolitan of Montenegro and the Littoral. The Serbian Orthodox trace their Montenegrin history to 1219 and the founding of the first diocese in the old capital by Saint Sava (ca. 1175–1235). Today, there is a second eparchy (diocese) based in Podgorica, the country's present capital.

The second largest Christian body in Montenegro is the Roman Catholic Church. The 2003 census reported 21,972 members (or 3.54 percent of the population). Catholics in Montenegro are almost entirely followers of the Byzantine or Eastern Greek rite and ethnically of Croatian or Albanian background. In 2003, Rome named an Apostolic Exarchate for the Greek Catholics of Serbia and Montenegro, headed by Bishop Djura Džudžar (b. 1954), though most of the faithful he oversaw were in the region of Vojvodina, Serbia.

Islam, the second largest religious community in Montenegro, consists largely of followers of the Hanafite School of Sunni Islam who reside in the extreme northern corner of the country, near the Bosnian border, and in various cities where Albanians and Bosnians have clustered. In 2003, the census reported 110,034 Muslims, making then about 18 percent of the population.

There are small groups of Protestants (less than one percent of the population), most notably members of the Reformed Christian Church in Serbia and Montenegro and the Slovak Evangelical Church of the Augsburg Confession in Serbia and Montenegro.

J. Gordon Melton

See also: Bulgarian Alternative Orthodox Church; Bulgarian Orthodox Church; Hanafite School of Islam; Montenegrin Orthodox Church; Roman Catholic Church: Serbian Orthodox Church.

References

Montenegrin Association of America. http://www.montenegro.org/. Accessed May 15, 2009.

Morrison, Kenneth. *Montenegro: A Modern History.* London: I. B. Tauris, 2009.

Roberts, Elizabeth. *Realm of the Black Mountain: A History of Montenegro.* Ithaca, NY: Cornell University Press, 2007.

■ Montserrat

Montserrat is an island of the Lesser Antilles on the northeastern edge of the Caribbean Sea, southwest of Antigua. Its 39 square miles of land is dominated by the Soufriere Hills Volcano, an active volcano that drove the majority of the population to leave in 1995 and has had multiple eruptions in successive years. The present population is a mere 5,000 (2008).

Montserrat was originally inhabited by the Carib people and was first sighted by Columbus in 1493. It was colonized in the 18th century by Irish people, driven from Saint Kitts, who began to plant sugarcane and cotton. They also imported slaves to work their plantations. The slaves were liberated in the middle of the 19th century, by which time they made up 90 percent of the population, the Caribs having all but disappeared.

Montserrat is still a colony of the United Kingdom, having previously been included with other colonies in the West Indian Federation. When the Federation was dissolved in 1962, Montserrat's government was given semiautonomous status, though the governor is still appointed from London.

With the passing of the Caribs, Christianity became the dominant religion of Montserrat, and Anglicanism its first and foremost representative. Anglicanism claims approximately one-third of the 5,000 residents of the island. The Methodists entered in 1820 and have about 20 percent of the islanders as members. The Anglican diocese is attached to the Church in the Province of the West Indies, and the Methodists are part of

Montserrat

Religion	Followers in 1970	Followers in 2010	% of Population	Annual % growth 2000–2010	Followers in 2025	Followers in 2050
Christians	11,300	5,700	95.3	2.47	6,100	6,300
Protestants	4,400	3,400	56.7	1.27	3,800	3,900
Anglicans	4,000	1,500	25.0	0.00	1,600	1,600
Roman Catholics	1,300	400	6.7	0.00	400	400
Agnostics	130	180	3.0	6.32	300	400
Baha'is	150	90	1.5	2.64	150	250
Spiritists	0	10	0.2	2.71	20	30
Hindus	0	10	0.1	3.71	20	40
Total population	**11,600**	**6,000**	**100.0**	**2.57**	**6,600**	**7,000**

MONTSERRAT

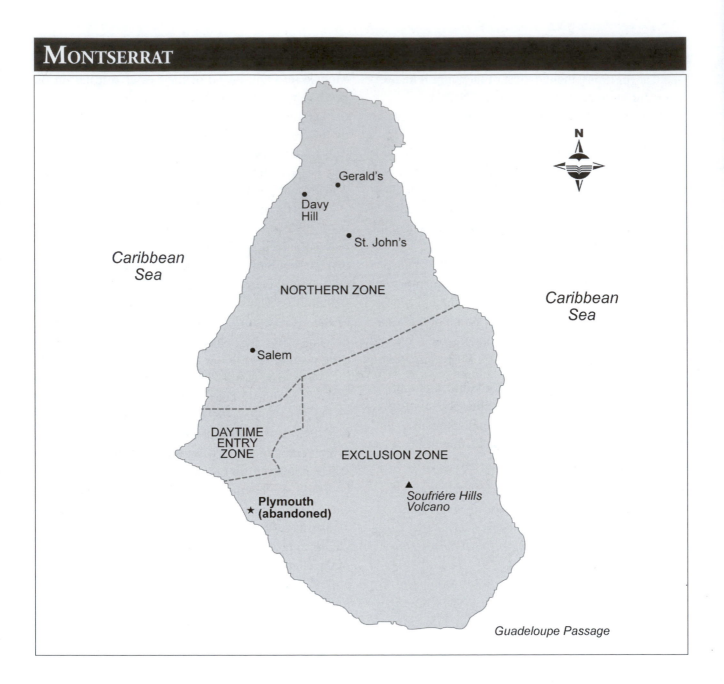

the Methodist Church in the Caribbean and the Americas, both headquartered on Antigua. In like measure, the Roman Catholic Church on Montserrat is an extension of the Diocese of Saint John's, also on Antigua.

Canadian Pentecostals came to Montserrat in 1910 and have built a thriving work, still related to the Pentecostal Assemblies of Canada. Subsequently, missionaries from the Seventh-day Adventist Church, Pilgrim Holiness Church (since 1968 part of the Wesleyan Church), and the Church of God of Prophecy have also started churches. The Jehovah's Witnesses and the Baha'i Faith have a limited presence on the island.

J. Gordon Melton

See also: Baha'i Faith; Church in the Province of the West Indies; Church of God of Prophecy; Jehovah's Witnesses; Methodist Church in the Caribbean and the Americas; Pentecostal Assemblies of Canada; Roman Catholic Church; Seventh-day Adventist Church; Wesleyan Church.

References

Boix, Maur M. *What Is Montserrat: A Mountain, A Sanctuary, A Monastery, A Spiritual Community.* L'Abadia de Montserrat, 1985.

Demets, B. A. *The Catholic Church in Montserrat, West Indies, 1756–1980.* Plymouth, Montserrat: Montserrat Printery, 1980.

Dobbin, J. D. "Religion and Cultural Identity: The Montserratian Case." *Caribbean Issues* 4, no. 1 (1980): 71–83.

Fergus, Howard A. *Montserrat: History of a Caribbean Colony.* Oxford: Macmillan Caribbean, 1994.

Lawrence, G. E. *Montserrat and Its Methodism.* Bristol, England: G. E. Lawrence, 1967.

Moon, Sun Myung

b. 1920

Sun Myung Moon, a native of Korea, is the founder of the Unification Church, the Family Federation for World Peace, and a host of other religious, political, and social organizations that together constitute the Unification movement. He was born on January 6, 1920, in what is now North Korea. His followers claim that Jesus appeared to him on April 17, 1935, and asked him to fulfill the mission begun by Jesus. As such, Rev. Moon claims to be the Lord of the Second Advent, which is Unification terminology for the one who is the promised Second Coming of Christ mentioned in the New Testament.

Reverend Sun Myung Moon and his wife, Hak Ja Han, are shown during the traditional invocation of a blessing at a mass wedding in Seoul's Chamsil gymnasium. At this ceremony, 6,000 couples from about 80 countries were married on October 14, 1982. (AP/Wide World Photos)

Moon studied engineering in Japan from 1941 to 1943 but returned to Korea to focus on his spiritual calling. He was married for the first time in 1943 and a son was born in April 1946. Two months later he left his wife and son behind to travel to North Korea. He was arrested twice and finally freed on October 14, 1950. He reunited with his family in 1952, but his marriage ended the next year. He started the Holy Spirit Association for the Unification of World Christianity in 1954 and sent the first missionary to America in 1959. He married Hak Ja Han in 1960 and she has given birth to 13 children. She and her husband are known as True Parents among followers.

Moon moved to the United States in 1971 and became a controversial figure after he supported embattled U.S. President Richard Nixon. He was a target of an emerging anti-cult movement and was imprisoned for income tax evasion in 1984. Even from jail he led the Unification movement and his far-flung enterprises worldwide. He viewed his imprisonment as a Calvary experience and his release in 1985 as parallel to resurrection. Based on his campaign against Communism, he took credit for the fall of the Berlin Wall in 1989 and said that his political insight led to the Allied victory in the first Gulf War. He is the founder of *The Washington Times* and has established universities in both the United States and Korea. In 2008 he passed leadership to his youngest son and his oldest surviving son.

Moon's thought is expressed in his work *Divine Principle* and through the thousands of sermons that he has delivered over the last five decades. His religious views were shaped by his Presbyterian roots and elements of shamanism. He also was impacted by several new religious movements that focused on Korea as the locus for God's end-time work. His followers are taught that Jesus ultimately failed in achieving full redemption and that Moon has had to restore God's broken heart. Unificationists are also taught that being grafted into Moon's family takes away sin and creates a new family of God. Unificationists engage in special wedding and marriage rituals as part of the salvation process and in recent years have paid for the liberation of their ancestors.

James A. Beverley

See also: Ancestors; Unification Movement.

References

Barker, Eileen. *The Making of a Moonie*. Oxford: Basil Blackwell, 1984.

Beverley, James A. "Spirit Revelation and the Unification Church." In *Controversial New Religions*, edited by James R. Lewis and Jesper Aagaard Petersen. New York: Oxford University Press, 2005.

Breen, Michael. *Sun Myung Moon: The Early Years*. West Sussex, UK: Refuge, 1997.

Chryssides, George. *The Advent of Sun Myung Moon*. New York: St. Martin's, 1991.

Hong, Nansook. *In the Shadow of the Moons*. Boston: Beacon Press, 1998.

Inglis, Michael, ed. *40 Years in America*. New York: HSA, 2000.

Introvigne, Massimo. *The Unification Church*. Salt Lake: Signature Books, 2000.

Moon, Sun Myung. *As a Peace-Loving Global Citizen*. Washington: Washington Times Foundation, 2009.

Moral Re-Armament

See CAUX-Initiatives for Change.

Moravian Church, Eastern West Indies Province

Interest in the plight of Africans in the West Indies launched the entire Moravian missionary enterprise. In 1731 in Copenhagen, the Moravian leader, August Spangenberg (1704–1792), encountered an African man named Anthony, who told him of the deplorable conditions faced by Africans in the West Indies. Spangenberg's decision to respond to these conditions led Leonhard Dober (1706–1760) to offer his services as a missionary to the Dutch West Indies, thus becoming the first Protestant missionary of the modern era. Dober began his work on St. Thomas. It was soon extended to St. Croix (the site of a bloody slave revolt in 1833) and St. John, the Virgin Islands then being in Danish hands. In 1734 a team of 18 missionaries arrived on St. Thomas, and Dober turned the work over to them and returned to

Germany with his first convert, an orphan boy named Carmel Oly, whose freedom Dober had purchased.

The work grew in spite of opposition from most of the plantation owners and the high toll of lives among the Moravians unable to cope with the climate. When Count Nikolaus Ludwig von Zinzendorf (1700–1760), the Moravian bishop, visited the islands in 1739, he found the missionaries in prison as a result of a conflict with the local Dutch Reformed Church minister. On a more positive note, he also found some 800 African converts.

In 1772 the islands were hit by a major hurricane that destroyed much property; indeed, bad weather would periodically produce temporary setbacks throughout the history of the mission. However, as the work was established in the Danish East Indies, it built up enough momentum to carry the mission to the neighboring islands of Barbados (1765), Antigua (1771), St. Kitts (1777), and Tobago (1790). The effort on Tobago, then a French possession, was halted almost as soon as it began by the unrest at news of the French Revolution. The revolution also stimulated efforts that grew in England for the abolition of slavery. With the abolition of slavery on Haiti in 1793, hope for freedom spread throughout the Caribbean. Through the 19th century, one by one, the islands would become free states.

In 1830 the centennial of the mission was marked when the Danish king recognized the Moravians and granted them equal status with the state church (Lutheran). The next step in the mission's growth would be its maturation into an autonomous church, a process that began in 1879 when the West Indies work was organized as a province, accepted the challenge to become self-supporting, and established a semiautonomous governing board. The Europeans continued to provide some financial support, but they set a schedule to gradually decrease it. In 1886 the theological seminary was established at Nisky on St. Thomas.

In 1899 the Moravians moved to restructure their international fellowship as a federation. This restructuring brought a new level of independence to the island church. In 1922 the Moravian British Province assumed responsibility for the work in the West Indies. In 1931 the International Missions Board was abolished. Finally, in 1967, the work in the Eastern West Indies was set apart as a fully autonomous province.

The Moravian Church, Eastern West Indies Province, is at one with beliefs and practices of Moravians worldwide. It now includes work in the U.S. Virgin Islands, St. Kitts, Barbados, Antigua, and Trinidad and Tobago. In 2005 it reported 20,000 members in 53 congregations. It is a member of the World Council of Churches.

Moravian Church, Eastern West Indies Province
PO Box 504
Cashew Hill
Antigua
http://www.candw.ag/~moravians/welcome.htm

J. Gordon Melton

See also: World Council of Churches.

References

Gillespe, Michelle, and Robert Beachy, eds. *Pious Pursuits: German Moravians in the Atlantic World*. Oxford: Berghahn Books. 2007.

Hamilton, J. Taylor, and Kenneth G. Hamilton. *History of the Moravian Church: The Renewed Unitas Fratrum, 1722–1957*. Bethlehem, PA, and Winston-Salem, NC: Interprovincial Board of Christian Education, Moravian Church in America, 1967.

Maynard, G. O. *A History of the Moravian Church: Eastern West Indies Province*. Port of Spain, Trinidad: Yuille's Printerie, 1968.

Moravian Church, European Continental Province of the

The Moravian Church continues the attempts at reformation of the Roman Catholic Church that were made by Jan Hus (ca. 1373–1415). Because of his oratorical skills as the preacher at the Bethlehem Chapel in Prague, Hus gained a popular following. His calls for reform came just as the papacy was divided between two claimants to Peter's chair and Prague was divided between its German-speaking and Bohemian-speaking populations.

After his excommunication in 1410, Hus became a popular hero among the populace. He attacked corruption in the church and its granting of indulgences as a means of raising money, and he upheld the authority of the Bible as a standard by which the church and its leadership could be judged. In 1414 Hus was invited to present his views at the Council of Constance, called by the Roman Catholic Church to deal with issues of reform. Though he was granted safe passage, when he arrived the protection was withdrawn, and he was condemned and executed.

Hus was condemned in part for his belief that the Eucharist, the sacrament recalling the sacrificial death of Jesus, should be served to the people in both kinds, that is, bread and wine, rather than just as bread, the common practice at the time. After Hus's death, the serving of the Eucharist in both kinds became characteristic of his followers, known as Hussites, and the Roman Catholics were unable to suppress the revolt immediately. A temporary compromise was worked out in 1436. Amid the spectrum of opinion in Bohemia and neighboring Moravia arose a new mediating group, the Unitas Fratrum.

During the 16th century, the Reformed Church (with teachings based on John Calvin's [1509–1564] theology) emerged in Bohemia and Moravia and held sway until the beginning of the 17th century. Then after the Thirty Years' War, Protestant leaders in Prague encountered Catholic leadership in the Holy Roman Empire bent on Counter-Reformation. In 1620 a Catholic army defeated the Bohemian forces and began to impose Catholicism anew throughout the land. In 1652 the expulsion of all Protestants from Catholic-controlled lands was implemented. Many members of the Unitas Fratrum went underground, and others fled their land. They settled first in Poland, and then, after 1722, they found refuge on the Prussian estate of Count Nikolaus Ludwig von Zinzendorf (1700–1760), where they founded the village of Herrnhut. Here they developed an order to rule both their spiritual and secular lives. The acceptance of this new order in 1727 by the Czech brethren marks the beginning of the reorganized Moravian Church.

Within the church, new ministerial leadership soon developed. Zinzendorf wanted the church to remain as an ordered community within the Lutheran Church, while many of the community's leaders looked for the development of a revived separate Moravian church. In 1835 the ancient episcopal lineage was passed to the community by Daniel Ernst Jablonski (1660–1741), a German Calvinist who had been consecrated by the Polish Moravians. Zinzendorf was consecrated in 1837. In 1845 the Moravian Church was more formally organized as a new episcopal body. It was recognized by the Church of England and the British Parliament in 1749.

The Moravian Church would develop two important emphases. First, the church developed in Germany just as a scholastic approach to Protestantism was becoming dominant, and in reaction the Moravians absorbed the lively spirituality of the Pietist movement, which had spread through Germany in the 17th century from the University of Halle. Thus, Moravians would become known for their heart-felt religion, which would have a significant effect upon a youthful John Wesley (1703–1791), the founder of Methodism.

Second, beginning with Zinzendorf's encounter with natives of the Danish West Indies and Greenland in 1731, the movement became enthusiastic proponents of a missionary enterprise. The Moravians sent the first missionaries to the West Indies in 1732 and to Greenland the next year. Through the rest of the century, the work would spread to England and the American colonies. Within the first generation, missions would follow to Labrador, South America, and Egypt. Stemming from this effort, the Methodists and then the Baptists would begin their own mission programs, and from this new venture would come the world-changing missionary enterprise of the 19th century, which would carry Protestantism around the globe.

During the mid-1700s, Zinzendorf assumed both temporal and spiritual powers as the leader of the Moravian Church. After his passing in 1760, the church organized its General Synod as the highest legislative body and appointed an executive board to administer the affairs of the synod. The executive board would in time evolve into the Unity Elders' Conference. Doctrinally, the church saw itself in general agreement with the Augsburg Confession (Lutheran), though there was no attempt to enforce assent to every sentence of this lengthy statement. A brief statement of essential beliefs was accepted in 1775. In practice, the church made or confirmed many of its practical decisions, especially concerning the deployment of personnel, by the casting of lots.

Through the early decades of the 19th century, the Moravian Church continued to expand globally. Partly because of the slowness of response from Europe, the church faced an increasing number of requests for grants of self-government from mission centers abroad. In 1857 the church established four provincial synods—one in continental Europe, one in England, and two in the United States, one in the North and one in the South. These provinces were given limited autonomy.

In 1879 the mission in Jamaica organized as a governing board with a proto-provincial organization, indicating that in the future, missions would grow to become discrete provinces. The 20th-century problems of continuing financial support for the ever-growing world membership, the transformation of Europe in the wake of two World Wars, and the changing perspective on missions within ecumenical Christianity led the Moravians in 1957 to extend the process of dividing the church's membership geographically into autonomous provinces. Meanwhile, in Europe, the work was divided into two independent provinces, setting off the work in what was then the German Democratic Republic of Germany, including the headquarters church at Halle. The European work was again combined after the reunification of Germany in 1990.

The Continental Province continues to have responsibility for Moravian life in Europe apart from the British Isles. The Moravian Church in the United States maintains an Internet site with links to Moravians around the world. The church has been active ecumenically and is a member of the European Council of Churches and Samen Kerk in Nederland (SKIN or the Church Together in the Netherlands). It was once a member of the World Council of Churches but, as of 2006, is no longer a member.

European Continental Province of the Moravian
    Church
Zusterplein 20
NL-3703 CB Zeist
The Netherlands
http://www.moravian.org/ (Moravian Church in
    America website)

J. Gordon Melton

See also: Calvin, John; Church of England; Roman Catholic Church; Wesley, John; World Council of Churches.

Reference

Hamilton, J. Taylor, and Kenneth G. Hamilton. *History of the Moravian Church: The Renewed Unitas Fratrum, 1722–1957*. Bethlehem, PA, and Winston-Salem, NC: Interprovincial Board of Christian Education, Moravian Church in America, 1967.

Moravian Church in America

The Moravian movement, first established in Europe as a descendant of the reformism of Jan Hus (ca. 1373–1415), was brought to North America in 1735, when a group under the leadership of Bishop August Gottlieb Spangenberg (1704–1792) moved to the new colony of Georgia. Because of the group's pacifism and refusal to serve in the militia, they left Georgia for Pennsylvania, where they initially settled on land owned by Methodist evangelist George Whitefield (1717–1770). They purchased 500 acres for the original settlement of what became Bethlehem, Pennsylvania, in 1741, and shortly thereafter obtained another 5,000 acres for the settlement they called Nazareth. Later, other settlements were created in neighboring New Jersey and Maryland, all positioned to carry out the primary goal of the movement from Germany, the evangelization of the Native Americans.

Spangenberg then led a group to North Carolina, where a large tract of land became the site of three settlements—Bethabara, Bethania, and, most important, Salem (now known as Winston-Salem). Over the next century, Bethlehem, Pennsylvania, and Winston-Salem, North Carolina, emerged as the center for the spread of the movement throughout North America and the headquarters of what would later become the two provinces (Northern and Southern) of the American church. The Moravian Church in America became autonomous following the international Unity Synod of Moravian leaders in 1848. The church found its best response in communities of German immigrants, especially in the Midwest. Then, at the end of the 19th century, it spread into Canada.

Moravian church building in Winston-Salem, North Carolina. (iStockPhoto)

During its earlier years, the church adopted a communal organization that had been proposed by Spangenberg. The pooling of economic resources, which lasted for about two decades, allowed the church and its members to prosper quickly and led to a close communal life that persisted for several generations after the communal living experiment ended.

The Moravians retain the essentials of Protestant Christianity, but they have adopted a motto to govern their approach to theology: "In essentials unity; in nonessentials liberty; in all things love." They accept the Bible as the source of Christian doctrine. Central to the Moravian life is what is termed "heart religion," a personal relationship with Jesus being more important than doctrinal purity. They continue to hold simple communal meals called love feasts and developed an early emphasis on music.

The Moravian Church in America has two headquarters: one for the Northern Province and one for the Southern Province. The Northern Province is divided into an Eastern District, Western District, and Canadian District. Of the church's 22,000 members, approximately half live in the states of Pennsylvania and North Carolina. The church regularly participates in the meeting of the Unity (the international Moravian movement), which is held every seven years. The Moravian Church supports the Moravian College and Theological Seminary in Bethlehem, Pennsylvania. It is a member of the World Council of Churches.

Moravian Church in America, Northern Province
1021 Center St.
Box 1245
Bethlehem, PA 18016-1245

Moravian Church in America, Southern Province
459 S. Church St.
Winston-Salem, NC 27108
http://www.moravian.org/

J. Gordon Melton

See also: World Council of Churches.

References

Allen, Walter H. *Who Are the Moravians?* Bethlehem, PA: Walter H. Allen, 1966.

Customs and Practices of the Moravian Church. Bethlehem, PA: Moravian Church in America, 2003.

Fogleman, Aaron Spencer. *Jesus Is Female: Moravians and Radical Religion in Early America.* Philadelphia: University of Pennsylvania Press, 2008.

Hamilton, J. Taylor, and Kenneth G. Hamilton. *History of the Moravian Church: The Renewed Unitas Fratrum, 1722–1957.* Bethlehem, PA and Winston-Salem, NC: Interprovincial Board of Christian Education, Moravian Church in America, 1967.

Weinlick, John R. *The Moravian Church through the Ages.* Bethlehem, PA: Moravian Church in America, 1988.

Moravian Church in Great Britain and Ireland

Moravian work in Great Britain formally began with the establishment of a religious society in London in 1742, from which it quickly expanded. Groups in Wiltshire, Yorkshire, and the Midlands had formed out of the preaching activity of several independent preachers affiliated with the Moravian movement: John Cennick (1718–1755), Benjamin Ingham (1712–1772), and Charles Delamorte. The first Moravian school was opened in 1742 in Essex. In 1746 Cennick visited Ireland and raised a congregation of some 500 members in Dublin. A number of congregations emerged among the Protestants in the north.

In 1749 Count Nikolaus Ludwig von Zinzendorf (1700–1760), the Moravian leader, arrived in England to negotiate a statement from the government recognizing the church and granting its ministers and members exemption from military service on the grounds of conscientious objection. He presented documents to a parliamentary commission to the effect that the Moravian Church continued the ancient church of Bohemia and Moravia and was aligned doctrinally with the German Lutherans. Based upon a favorable report by the commission, Parliament passed legislation, signed by the king, recognizing the Moravian Church as an "Ancient Episcopal Church." The church was thus accorded the status of a sister church of the Church of England and Zinzendorf was acknowledged as a bishop.

The British Moravians, now under the superintendency of Peter Böhler (1712–1774), experienced a period of rapid growth that in some ways paralleled that of the Methodists. A British synod of what would become the Province of Great Britain convened for the first time in 1752. The church expanded into Scotland in 1765 after members from Ireland moved there.

The British Moravians became intricately involved in the support of the church's worldwide mission program. When financial problems hit the church on the European continent in 1817, the British organized the London Association in Aid of the Missions of the United Brethren, which reached out to the missionary-minded friends of the Moravians. The association was to prove invaluable in the extension of Moravian missions in the 19th and 20th centuries.

In 1818 the Unity Elders' Conference, then the central authority in the international church, moved to establish a provincial conference to administer the affairs of the British work. The first session, which met in 1824, was called upon to face both a decline in membership and a general pessimism that had swept through the congregations. Through the next decades, growth would be slight. In 1847, in light of its stagnation, the British provincial synod proposed that it be allowed to dissent from the Augsburg Confession and that its use of the drawing of lots, a time-honored practice among the Moravians, be discontinued for some decisions. A decade later the synod prepared to implement the change wrought by a new constitution. Over the next century, the church would drop many of its peculiar features, inherited from Germany, and adopt an organizational life more like that of other British churches.

In 2006, the church reported 1,700 members in 34 congregations. Though relatively small in numbers, through the 20th century the British Moravians built a strong ecumenical base. In 1919 they joined the Federation of Evangelical Free Churches of England, and in 1950, the British Council of Churches (now the Churches Together in Britain and Ireland). The church is a member of the World Council of Churches.

Moravian Church in Great Britain and Ireland
5 Muswell Hill
London N10 3TJ
UK
http://www.moravian.org.uk/

J. Gordon Melton

See also: World Council of Churches.

References

Hamilton, J. Taylor, and Kenneth G. Hamilton. *History of the Moravian Church: The Renewed Unitas Fratrum, 1722–1957.* Bethlehem, PA, and Winston-Salem, NC: Interprovincial Board of Christian Education, Moravian Church in America, 1967.

Mason, J. C. S. *The Moravian Church and the Missionary Awakening in England, 1760–1800.* London: Royal Historical Society, 2002.

Stead, Geoffrey, and Margaret Stead. *The Exotic Plant: A History of the Moravian Church in Britain, 1742–2000.* London: Epworth Press, 2004.

Moravian Church in Jamaica

The impetus for Moravian work in the West Indies came in the 18th century directly out of the church's international center in Germany. The West Indian effort had spread through the easternmost islands but had not opened a station on Jamaica. Then in 1754, two plantation owners, John Foster Barham and William Foster, who resided in England and also happened to be Moravians, asked for missionaries to minister to the Africans residing on their lands in Jamaica. Zacharias George Caries and two companions pioneered the work, and with the initial support of Foster and Barham, they soon gained the support of other plantation owners.

The work got off to a slow start; there were frequent changes of personnel, disease took its toll, and on occasion the converts returned to the religions they had brought from Africa. Then in 1834, slavery was ended in all British colonies. The church had taken special efforts to prepare its members for the new era. Some 26 schools had been opened. Membership shot upward in the years immediately after emancipation. In 1847 a conference structure replaced the rule of the mission's superintendent.

Representatives from Jamaica attended the 1863 conference on St. Thomas (Virgin Islands), where the process of transformation in the Caribbean toward more indigenous leadership and eventual self-support was discussed. The Jamaicans agreed to move toward self-support if the European church would continue to supply financial support for building and the travel of missionaries. As a first step, in 1876 a seminary was opened at Fairfield. In 1879 the work was reorganized as a separate province with semiautonomous status. The first bishop, Peter Larsen, was consecrated in 1901.

Most of the congregations were located in the western and especially the southwestern part of the island. The church developed under the most trying of conditions, including epidemics, hurricanes, and a devastating earthquake in Kingston in 1907. The bad times drew together the various denominations represented on the island, and in the 1920s union negotiations began between the Moravians and the Methodists, Presbyterians, Disciples of Christ, and Congregationalists. Though they did not bring union, these discussions did bring closer relations and a new commonly supported seminary.

Soon the work had grown enough to enable Jamaican Moravians to give more systematic attention to their responsibility for the church's world mission. In 1925 the Moravian Missionary Society held its initial gathering and focused concern for the missions in West Africa and Egypt.

The independent province of the Moravian Church in Jamaica was set apart in 1967. In 2005, it reported 30,000 members. It is at one with the beliefs and practices of Moravians worldwide. It is a member of the World Council of Churches.

Moravian Church in Jamaica
3 Hector St.
PO Box 8369
Kingston C. S. O.
Jamaica
http://www.jol.com.jm/moravian/

J. Gordon Melton

See also: World Council of Churches.

References

Hastings, S. U. *Seedtime and Harvest: A Brief History of the Moravian Church in Jamaica 1754–1979.* Moravian Church, 1979.

Hamilton, J. Taylor, and Kenneth G. Hamilton. *History of the Moravian Church: The Renewed Unitas Fratrum, 1722–1957.* Bethlehem, PA, and Winston-Salem, NC: Interprovincial Board of Christian Education, Moravian Church in America, 1967.

Warner-Lewis, Maureen. *Archibald Monteath: Igbo, Jamaican, Moravian.* Kingston, Jamaica: University of West Indies Press, 2007.

Moravian Church in Nicaragua

In 1947 the Moravians sent missionaries to the Caribbean coast of what is today Nicaragua. They landed at Bluefields, then the capital of a kingdom of Native people, the Miskitos, which included other groups as well. The Anglicans had previously established a small work in the region, but the Moravian missionaries were appalled by the polytheism and polygamy they saw practiced there. They were welcomed by the Miskito king, who assigned them some land on which to begin their mission.

The work was substantially supplemented in 1856 with the arrival of African converts from Jamaica. Two

A Nicaraguan girl plays with a discarded tire in front of the Moravian Church of the community, February 13, 1998, in Pearl Lagoon on the Caribbean coast of Nicaragua. (AP/Wide World Photos)

years later they were given the first of several boats, which improved their movement up and down the coast. The mission progressed through the rest of the century in spite of several destructive hurricanes, diseases, political changes, and the opposition of many traders who made their living off of the Native population. In the 1880s the missionaries progressed in their mastery of the Miskito language, culminating in a translation of the four Christian Gospels and the book of Acts in 1889. A grammar and dictionary soon followed.

The mission had a major setback in 1900, when the Nicaraguan government mandated that all instruction in grammar schools would be in Spanish and given only by teachers who had passed the government exams. The missionaries, being unprepared to comply, closed the numerous schools they had founded, and the schools did not reopen until 1910. This difficulty was offset somewhat in 1902 by the consecration of the first bishop for the evolving church, August Hermann Berkenhagen.

The Moravian Church in America assumed responsibility for the church during World War I. Through the 20th century, the church moved to develop indigenous leadership. The first Nicaraguan bishop was consecrated in 1949, and the church became autonomous in 1974.

In 2006, the church reported 82,944 members. It supports a hospital at Bilwaskarma, an extensive school system (including a seminary and university in Puerto Cabezas), and through the Institute for Social Development of the Moravian Church in Nicaragua, it supports a range of economic and developmental projects in remote villages. It is a member of the World Council of Churches.

Moravian Church in Nicaragua
Apartado 3696
Managua
Nicaragua
http://www.moravianmission.org/nicaragua.htm

J. Gordon Melton

See also: World Council of Churches.

References

Hamilton, J. Taylor, and Kenneth G. Hamilton. *History of the Moravian Church: The Renewed Unitas Fratrum, 1722–1957*. Bethlehem, PA, and Winston-Salem, NC: Interprovincial Board of Christian Education, Moravian Church in America, 1967.

Robertson, C. Alton. *The Moravians, the Miskitu, and the Sandinistas on Nicaragua's Atlantic Coast: 1979–1990*. Bethlehem, PA: Moravian Church in America, 1998.

Van der Bent, Ans J., ed. *Handbook/Member Churches/World Council of Churches*. Geneva: World Council of Churches, 1985.

Moravian Church in Southern Africa

As early as 1736, Moravian attention focused upon the Hottentot people of South Africa. These people, small of stature in comparison with both other African peoples and European settlers, were treated by many as less than human. Georg Schmidt (1709–1785), a former butcher turned evangelist, spent a year studying Dutch, and then traveled to Cape Town in 1737 to establish a rural mission at Genadendal. After a promising beginning, however, he was forced to return to Europe because of the Moravian clash with Reformed authorities in Holland.

Moravians did not return to South Africa until 1792, when they took up where Schmidt had left, even finding several people who had been converted by him. However, the quick improvement in the life of the Hottentots caused jealousy to arise among the European settlers. The hostile climate was not helped by the British occupation of Cape Town in 1795, but the British protected the colony that developed and gradually the settlers were won over as they benefited by the changes introduced into the Hottentot life. In 1800 a church that could accommodate 1,500 people was constructed. The missionaries worked constantly to counter the negative images of the Hottentots held by the Europeans.

By 1816 the work was well established and the Moravians made plans to start a fresh venture among the Bantu-speaking people along the White River some 400 miles from Cape Town. The mission, called Enon, survived even though it was largely destroyed by armed raiders soon after opening. Work also expanded to the

Tambookie people in Kaffraria. Subsequent stations, called Elim and Shiloh, were also opened in the 1820s and provided attention to the Fetkannas.

Gradually the original station at Genadendal grew into a small town with a gristmill and shops that included a variety of artisans. In 1838 a normal school (for the training of teachers) was opened, and other Protestant groups began to send their people for training. A printing press began to publish a periodical and produced a Harmony of the Gospels in the Bantu language. The work grew steadily over the next decades, the government often inviting the Moravians to open stations in specific locations. The missionaries also sent people to the leper colony set up on Robben Island in 1845.

In 1865 the now extensive work in South Africa was divided into two provinces. The attempt to build indigenous leadership finally culminated in the first ordinations of native South Africans in 1883. After 1900, the pressure to develop local leadership would be significantly increased by the church's international leadership, but it was continually thwarted by wars and the developing racial policies of the colonial government. It would not be until 1951 that a stable institution for ministerial training would be opened.

In 1910 the four distinct colonies located on the southern tip of Africa were united into the Union of South Africa. Although this move softened ties between the Dutch settlers (the Boers) and the British authorities, it created some deep racial divisions between Native Africans and the European settlers. Despite this, the Moravians extended their work among the different African peoples and placed particular importance on the establishment of schools wherever possible. The school system would be nationalized in 1955.

In 1899 Ernst van Calker, the superintendent of the South Africa East Province, was consecrated as its first bishop, and in 1909 a new church constitution was adopted. It was not until 1921 that a constitution and church order was effected for the Western province. After World War II, efforts to draw the two provinces together were launched, and in 1951 both provinces participated in the formation of a seminary. In 1956 representatives of both provinces met at Port Elizabeth and merged the two provincial boards into one

South Africa Board, to be consulted on matters of mutual interest and concern. The united province became fully independent in 1967. In 2005, it reported 80,000 members.

The Moravian Church in Southern Africa has a long history of Christian ecumenical endeavor, its two provinces having participated in the first General Mission Conference in South Africa in 1904. It joined the National Council of Churches in South Africa and is a member of the World Council of Churches.

Moravian Church in Southern Africa
PO Box 24111
Lansdowne 7779
South Africa

J. Gordon Melton

See also: World Council of Churches.

References

Hamilton, J. Taylor, and Kenneth G. Hamilton. *History of the Moravian Church: The Renewed Unitas Fratrum, 1722–1957*. Bethlehem, PA, and Winston-Salem, NC: Interprovincial Board of Christian Education, Moravian Church in America, 1967.

Kruger, Bernard. *The Pear Tree Bears Fruit: The History of the Moravian Church in South Africa-West*. Genadendal, South Africa: [Moravian Book Depot], 1984.

Moravian Church in Suriname

Moravians received an invitation to begin work in the Dutch territory of Suriname in 1836, and two years later missionaries arrived and settled on a plantation on the Berbice River. Their primary work was among the Africans on the plantation and nearby. Work expanded in 1848 with the arrival of Theophilus Salomon Schumann, a linguist who had mastered the language of the Native people, the Arawak. He soon translated the Bible into their language. The mission ran into trouble, however, when the local traders told the Arawak that the Moravians planned to sell them into slavery and told the authorities that the Moravians were inciting the Arawak to rebellion. Once the problem was solved,

Schumann moved into the interior and began his life's work among the Arawak people. He died an untimely death in 1760, after which the mission to the Arawak died away and the church in the capital, Paramaribo, took center stage.

The work among the Africans was continually thwarted by whites who saw it as subversive of the slave system. By the beginning of the 1800s, the original mission still counted only a few hundred people as members. Work in the interior was slow because of the inability of the missionaries to adjust to the climate. By the 1820s, work was limited to the capital and a few nearby estates.

However, a growth period followed the smallpox epidemic of 1820 and the fire that destroyed Paramaribo in 1821. Afterward, the plantations opened their doors to the missionaries. The Dutch Society for the Promotion of Christian Knowledge among the Negroes of Surinam gave them boats to facilitate their travel to the growing number of plantations. The work was also assisted by the translation of a portion of the New Testament into the new language, Sranana Tongo, which the Africans had developed. By mid-century, the work claimed some 5,000 adherents. Overcoming significant opposition, they began schools for the Africans that were able to also train a set of teachers, who had greater access to their fellow slaves. In 1856 the mission took on a new responsibility at the request of the government—fulfilling the spiritual needs of those suffering from Hansen's disease (leprosy) at the hospital at Batavia.

In 1857 the mission gained a convert named John King, of the Matuari people, who had arrived at the mission door one day, prompted by a dream. King studied with the missionaries over the next four years and was ordained in 1861. He then spent the next 35 years taking Christianity to the residents of the interior. His efforts led to the conversion of the chief of his people and the development of a strong Moravian presence in the interior.

As in other lands, Moravian membership on Suriname rose in the years immediately after the emancipation of the slave population, about 60 percent of which identified with the church. Some 25,000 former slaves became Moravian in the decade during the transition to complete freedom (1863–1873). The mission also moved to evangelize the Chinese and Asian Indians who came into the country to replace the former slaves who left the plantations.

The changes adopted by the Moravian Church as a whole in 1899, to restructure their international fellowship as a federation, led the mission in Suriname to move toward autonomy. A new constitution was approved, and businesses that had been developed to support the work of the mission were formally separated from it. Shortly thereafter, the work was divided into the Old or Creole Mission and the New Mission. The former moved toward self-support, and in 1911 a church conference under the leadership of a resident bishop, Richard Voullaire, assumed authority. The development of indigenous leadership was assisted by the opening of a school to train teachers and ministers in 1902. Full autonomy came in steps through the next decades, held back by the general poverty of the land and political events, not the least of which was the German invasion of the Netherlands during World War II. The Old Mission became an autonomous Moravian province in 1963.

Although the Creole Mission also moved toward autonomy, it worked among the peoples residing in the interior, primarily Africans who had escaped plantation life during the days of slavery and re-established an African-like existence, complete with their traditional African faith. Some groups resisted any relationship to the church, but they finally developed more positive relationships as they saw the mission as a source for education and medical assistance. The mission also developed a following among immigrants from East India, China, and Java, the latter forming some 17 percent of the Surinamese population at the beginning of the 20th century.

In a joint venture with other Protestant groups, the Moravian Church in Suriname sponsors Bethesda, a hospital specializing in the treatment of Hansen's disease. The church is a member of the World Council of Churches. In 2006, it reported 40,000 members.

Moravian Church in Suriname
PO Box 219/1811
Paramaribo
Suriname

J. Gordon Melton

See also: World Council of Churches.

References

Hamilton, J. Taylor, and Kenneth G. Hamilton. *History of the Moravian Church: The Renewed Unitas Fratrum, 1722–1957*. Bethlehem, PA, and Winston-Salem, NC: Interprovincial Board of Christian Education, Moravian Church in America, 1967.

Van Beek, Huibert. *A Handbook of the Churches and Councils: Profiles of Ecumenical Relationships*. Geneva: World Council of Churches, 2006.

Moravian Church in Tanzania

In 1885 Germany was given hegemony over territory in east central Africa. The Moravian Church saw this action as an occasion for extending its missionary activity, and in 1891 it commissioned a team of missionaries to the new colony. They built their first station in Rungwe, in what was then called Tanganyika (now part of Tanzania), among the Konde people, a branch of the Bantu. Several additional stations were established in the southern highlands, but it was not until 1897 that the missionaries received their first convert. The missionaries developed the stations as self-supporting villages, utilizing the many skills that they brought with them from their homeland, such as farming and raising donkeys. In 1900 a clear separation was made between the mission and the economic enterprises that supported it. Simultaneously, the church inherited an older missionary station in western Tanganyika (south of Lake Victoria) from the (Anglican) Church Missionary Society. This work expanded rapidly, as the missionaries took advantage of government policy limiting each area to a single missionary group. The first converts were received into the church in 1903.

In 1912 the missionaries in the south expanded their services to include a medical facility, and they also supported the centers set up to assist those suffering from Hansen's disease. Some worked with workers from other missions on translating the Bible and other literature into more of the many languages spoken in the colony. By 1913 the Moravian missionaries could report that from their nine main missionary stations, they had developed more than 1,000 preaching points and had a membership of 1,955. Meanwhile some 800 children attended the schools they had established. Work in the west proceeded more slowly. Though the number of stations expanded, some schools were opened, and a headquarters was established at Tabora, the number of converts was small.

In 1916 the British invaded East Africa. They interned all of the missionaries in the southern highlands, and the work of the mission was turned over to the Free Church of Scotland (now a constituent part of the Church of Scotland). The church had few personnel and quickly expanded the role of the African teachers. Meanwhile, Belgium invaded the western territory being worked by the missionaries. Most were interned and sent back to Europe.

In 1923 the British allowed the first Moravians to return to Tanganyika, and in 1926 formal control of the mission was passed back into Moravian hands. Dutch Moravians assumed leadership in the west, and British Moravians in the south. As personnel and financial support arrived, stations were reopened and refurbished. The church focused attention on the school program, which was greatly expanded. In 1943 a teacher-training school was opened in cooperation with the Church Missionary Society.

During the 1930s, the mission emphasized the development of a self-supporting indigenous church. One step in that direction was the ordination of the first African ministers in 1935. This action proved fortuitous, as all the missionaries were again interned in 1939. A Danish couple sent from Great Britain was able to fill some of the need created by the internments, and they were joined by two more colleagues from South Africa the following year. They were able to work in conjunction with 13 African ministers. After the war further steps toward the maturity of the mission were taken, as it accepted responsibility for paying the salaries of all the ministerial staff.

Work expanded in the decades after World War II. As the African leadership evolved, three synods were organized, one in the west and two in the south. These were then linked by a Joint Board, designed to oversee and coordinate all the Moravian work in the newly independent nation of Tanzania. Each synod elected a provincial board, and the three boards came together to form the Joint Board.

The Joint Board of the Moravian Church in Tanzania now oversees the largest Moravian church in the world, with some 500,000 members (2005). It is a member of the World Council of Churches.

Moravian Church in Tanzania
PO Box 747
Mbeya
Tanzania

J. Gordon Melton

See also: Church Missionary Society; Church of Scotland; World Council of Churches.

References

Hamilton, J. Taylor, and Kenneth G. Hamilton. *History of the Moravian Church: The Renewed Unitas Fratrum, 1722–1957*. Bethlehem, PA, and Winston-Salem, NC: Interprovincial Board of Christian Education, Moravian Church in America, 1967.

Van Beek, Huibert. *A Handbook of the Churches and Councils: Profiles of Ecumenical Relationships*. Geneva: World Council of Churches, 2006.

■ Morocco

The Kingdom of Morocco is located on the northeast corner of Africa, immediately south of Spain and the Island of Gibraltar. It shares borders with the disputed Western Sahara territory and Algeria. The west border of its 172,317 square miles of territory faces the Atlantic Ocean; the central part of the country is mountainous; while the far west reaches into the edge of the Sahara Desert. The bulk of Morocco's 34,343,000 citizens (2008) reside in the northeast corner of the country between the mountains and the sea.

Morocco was originally home to various Berber people. They were incorporated into the Roman Empire and later, after Rome fell, the land was overtaken by the Arab Muslims who swept into the area in the eighth century on their way to Spain. In the 11th century, an Islamic movement among Berbers who had established themselves in present-day Senegal estab-

lished control of all of the land between Senegal and Gibraltar. Their Almoravid Empire lasted for a century (1062–1147), only to be replaced by the Almohad Empire (1147–1258). The Almoravids took control of southern Spain and helped create the rich culture generally associated with Granada and Cordoba. Modern Morocco was largely shaped by Spain's conquest of the Iberian Peninsula in the 15th century and the annexation of Algeria by the Ottoman Empire a century later.

Morocco remained an independent state into the 20th century, but in the decades prior to World War I it became a tantalizing target for colonization by various European nations. In 1912 Morocco became a French protectorate, while Spain retained Sahara, to the south of Morocco, and a small bit of land immediately south of Gibraltar. Tangiers was declared an international city. French rule was never accepted, however, and nationalist opposition grew over the next four decades until the French finally recognized Moroccan independence in 1956. In stages the country gained control of Tangiers and the remaining Spanish territory to the north.

Muhammad V (1909–1961) ascended the throne of independent Morocco in 1957. He was succeeded in 1961 by Hassan II, who ruled until his death in 1999. Hassan's rule was marked by his attempt to claim Sahara, the former Spanish territory to the south. He invaded Sahara and, along with Mauritania, occupied the region. In 1976 Spain renounced its claim in favor of Morocco and Mauritania, but the Saharans proclaimed their own independence. The border between the two countries remains a disputed boundary. After King Hassan's death on July 23, 1999, his son, Muhammad VI, ascended the throne.

Islam became the dominant religion in Morocco late in the first millennium CE, and today most Moroccans are Sunni Muslims of the Malikite School. Sufi Brotherhoods are also present in significant numbers, especially the Qadiriyya and the Kattaniyya.

The king, known as the "Commander of the Faithful," is seen as the center of the Muslim community. Among his assigned duties is ensuring that Islam is properly respected. The Muslim community is given focus in the Université Ben Youssef at Marrakech and the Université al-Qarawiyin, with campuses at Rabat,

Koutoubia Mosque in Marrakech, Morocco, 12th century. Construction on the Almohad structure began about 1150 and was completed during the reign of al-Manur (1184–1199). (Jupiterimages)

Fez, and Marrakech, both dedicated to Arabic and Islamic studies. The latter institution dates to the ninth century.

The Jewish community in Morocco predates the introduction of Islam, and over the centuries it has enjoyed a largely tolerant setting in which to develop, though there have been times of persecution. The community grew noticeably at the end of the 15th century, following the expulsion of Jews from Spain and Portugal. During the transition to independence, the great majority of Jews migrated to Israel, Canada, France, and Spain. The community shrunk from 250,000 to 30,000 members. It continued to decline through the last quarter of the 20th century and at the beginning of the new millennium numbered only 13,000. The Jewish community is centered at Casablanca, though there are smaller groups in Tangiers, Fez, and other cities.

Christians came to Morocco during the days of the Roman Empire. Christian churches thrived in the northern part of the territory (Tangiers, Rabat, and Fez). Through the centuries these churches were rent by both the Donatist and the Arian controversies and were finally overwhelmed by Islam. An attempt to reintroduce Christianity was made by priests of the Franciscan Order in 1220, who actually built a following that justified the formation of a diocese at Marrakech in 1234. The diocese was suppressed in 1566, and the Roman Catholic Church barely survived. By the beginning of the 19th century there was only one priest in the whole country.

As the French began to operate in the country, a new attempt to grow the church was initiated, and in 1859 a prefecture was created. There was steady growth through the 20th century. The Vicariate of Rabat,

A Berber sounds a traditional instrument in present-day Morocco. (Corel)

created in 1923, became an archdiocese in 1955. As the transition to independence was made, the church suffered greatly from the migration of many of its expatriate members. Membership declined from 420,000 in 1955 to 100,000 in 1970. However, church leaders supported independence, and consequently the new government looked with favor upon Christianity.

Protestants first entered Morocco in 1884, with missionaries from the North Africa Mission, an interdenominational missionary agency. They were joined by the Gospel Missionary Union in 1894 and the Emmanuel Mission Sahara in 1926. These two groups were expelled in 1969. After the declaration of the French protectorate, the Reformed Church of France entered the country and formed what became the Evangelical Church of Morocco (Eglise Evangélique au Maroc), now the largest of the several Protestant bod-

ies. Several other groups such as the Assemblies of God, the Seventh-day Adventist Church, the Christian Brethren, and the Jehovah's Witnesses have attempted to build a following, but with limited response. Unable to do direct evangelism, several groups keep a Christian ministry alive through the operation of various humanitarian projects, the most famous being the Tullock Memorial Hospital and Nurses Training School in Tangiers, operated by the North Africa Mission.

Anglicans established work in 1929 through the efforts of the Bible Churchman's Missionary Society. Beginning as an extension of the Diocese of Sierra Leone, the Anglican parishes are now part of the Diocese of Egypt under the jurisdiction of the Episcopal Church in Jerusalem and the Middle East. Morocco is also home to a range of Orthodox churches, which emerged through the century as groups of expatriates

Morocco

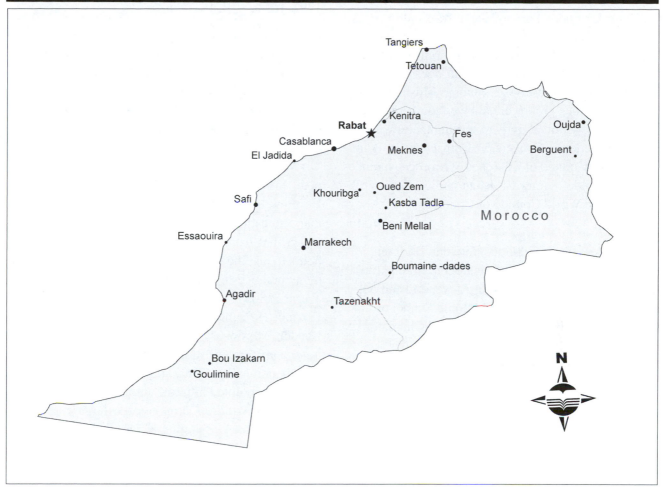

Morocco

Religion	Followers in 1970	Followers in 2010	% of Population	Annual % growth 2000–2010	Followers in 2025	Followers in 2050
Muslims	15,012,000	31,845,000	98.8	1.14	37,111,000	41,598,000
Agnostics	3,000	310,000	1.0	1.07	500,000	700,000
Christians	131,000	54,100	0.2	−0.10	63,600	69,800
Roman Catholics	100,000	20,000	0.1	−1.73	20,000	20,000
Independents	23,200	27,000	0.1	1.21	35,000	40,000
Protestants	5,000	3,800	0.0	1.60	5,000	6,000
Baha'is	2,200	32,400	0.1	1.14	45,000	60,000
Jews	31,100	4,200	0.0	1.13	4,000	4,000
Atheists	1,200	800	0.0	−2.90	1,000	1,000
Total population	**15,181,000**	**32,247,000**	**100.0**	**1.13**	**37,725,000**	**42,433,000**

settled in the country from Russia, Belorus, and other North African nations. These churches are members of the Greek Orthodox Patriarchate of Alexandria and All Africa.

The Moroccan Constitution guarantees freedom of religion to all, but such freedom does not include the freedom to proselytize among Muslims. Non-Muslim religious groups are allowed to operate freely as long as they limit activity to serving their own present constituencies. Conversion from Islam is against the law. The Council of Churches of Morocco includes the several older, larger Christian bodies and is affiliated with the World Council of Churches.

J. Gordon Melton

See also: Assemblies of God; Christian Brethren; Episcopal Church in Jerusalem and the Middle East; Greek Orthodox Patriarchate of Alexandria and All Africa; Jehovah's Witnesses; Malikite School of Islam; Qadiriyya Sufi Order; Reformed Church of France; Roman Catholic Church; Seventh-day Adventist Church; World Council of Churches.

References

Geertz, C. *Islam Observed: Religious Development in Morocco and Indonesia*. New Haven, CT: Yale University Press, 1968.

Holme, L. R. *Extinction of the Christian Churches in North Africa*. New York: Burt Franklin, 1969.

Hoffman, Katherine E. *We Share Walls: Language, Land, and Gender in Berber Morocco*. New York: Wiley-Blackwell, 2008.

Howe, Marvine. *Morocco: The Islamist Awakening and Other Challenges*. New York: Oxford University Press, 2005.

Munson, H., Jr. *Religion and Power in Morocco*. New Haven, CT: Yale University Press, 1993.

Pennel, C. R. *Morocco since 1830: A History*. New York: New York University Press, 2001.

Shahin, E. E. A. "The Restitution of Islam: A Comparative Study of the Islamic Movements in Contemporary Tunisia and Morocco." Ph.D. diss., Johns Hopkins University, 1990.

Zeghal, Malika. *Islamism in Morocco: Religion, Authoritarianism, and Electoral Politics*. Princeton, NJ: Markus Weiner, 2008.

Morrison, Robert

1782–1834

Robert Morrison was a pioneer Protestant Christian missionary in Asia and the first Protestant missionary to work in China. His work prepared the way for both an indigenous Christian missionary movement in China and the development of the largest of the 19th-century missionary programs developed by the Protestant Church.

Morrison, of Scottish heritage, was born near Morpeth, Northumberland, England, on January 5, 1782. He grew up at Newcastle-upon-Tyne. After his primary education, his parents apprenticed him to a shoemaker, but from an early age he devoted his leisure hours to reading religious materials. After completing his apprenticeship and becoming an adult, he spent a year (1803–1804) at the Independent Academy at Hoxton. He subsequently applied for support to the London Missionary Society, an interdenominational missionary organization primarily supported by the Congregationalists. They suggested he study Chinese, and then appointed him to Canton (now Guangzhou).

The East India Company, the large British importing company operating in East Asia, was strongly opposed to Christian missionaries entering into the territories where it operated. They showed their displeasure at his appointment to Canton by refusing to take him to China on one of their ships. Morrison developed an alternate route that began in America. In 1807, James Madison, then the U.S. secretary of state, gave Morrison a letter of introduction to the American consul in Canton. The owner of Oliphant & Co. provided him with his needed transportation to China.

Once in Canton, Morrison's situation changed significantly, and soon he was on the payroll of the East India Company as a translator and was provided the time (and legal permission to remain in Chinese territory) to complete both a Chinese grammar text (originally published in 1814) and a translation of the New Testament (also published in 1814). He also met and in 1809 married Mary Morton, whose father was a physician for the Company.

Morrison went to work on producing an edition of the Bible in Chinese. He was joined in the effort to produce a Chinese edition of the Hebrew Bible by

William Milne and his wife in 1815. The publication of the Bible, along with several translation books, was extremely helpful to future missionaries all across China.

Morrison's translation and publishing work proceeded in a somewhat clandestine manner as China had promulgated laws prohibiting the publishing of any religious books. Morrison lived quietly and adopted local dress. In the meantime, the Milnes had moved to Malacca, on the Malaysian coast, and in 1820 Morrison assisted them in opening an Anglo-Chinese college where Native evangelists could be trained. Their few Chinese converts could do the preaching work that the non-Chinese were prohibited from doing.

In 1821 the East India Company published the six-volume *Chinese Dictionary* Morrison had compiled. As his wife had died that year, he made a return visit to England, where in 1823 the Royal Society recognized his accomplishment by electing him a fellow. He remained in England for several years, during which time he met and married his second wife, Eliza Armstrong. In 1826 the couple returned to China, where Morrison picked up his work translating and publishing. He died in Canton on August 1, 1834, and was buried in the Protestant cemetery in Macau.

Like other pioneer Christian missionaries, Morrison made few converts, He baptized his first, Tsai-A-Ko, in 1814. However, he is remembered for producing the tools from which hundreds of missionaries who followed him would work. By the 20th century, China was the site of the largest Protestant missionary effort in the world. It survived the attempt to destroy it by the authorities of the People's Republic of China after the Chinese Revolution. As the 21st century begins there are more than 20 million Protestant Christians in China.

J. Gordon Melton

See also: London Missionary Society.

References

Broomhall, Maurice. *Robert Morrison, a Master-builder.* London: Livingstone Press, 1924.

Morrison, Robert. *A Dictionary of the Chinese Language.* 6 vols. London: Black, Parbury and Allen, 1815–1823.

Morrison, Robert. *A parting memorial: consisting of miscellaneous discourses, written and preached in China; at Singapore; on board ship at sea, in the Indian Ocean; at the Cape of Good Hope; and in England; with remarks on missions, &c. &c.* London: W. Simpkin and R. Marshall, 1826.

Rubenstein, Murray A. *The Origins of the Anglo-American Missionary Enterprise in China, 1807–1840.* ATLA monograph series no. 33. Lanham, MD: Scarecrow Press, 1996.

Moscow

During the first half of the second millennium CE, Moscow rose out of obscurity to become the center of Russia and of the Russian Orthodox Church (Moscow Patriarchate). So important had the ecclesiastical establishment in the city become that shortly after the fall of Constantinople to the Ottoman Turks in 1453, the idea emerged that it had now become the Third Rome, that is, the heir to the Byzantine (Roman) Empire. Currently Moscow is the capital of the Russian Federation and, with 10.5 million inhabitants (2009), one of the largest cities in the world.

The first reference to Moscow dates from 1147 when it was just an obscure settlement on the Moscow River in the principality of Rostov, northwest of what was to become Russia. By the 12th century, Christianity had already had two centuries to make itself the dominating religious influence. Originally centered in Kiev, in 988 Christianity became the official religion of the early Eastern Slavic state under Grand Prince Vladimir I (ca. 956–1015). Ecclesiastically, he aligned his regime with Byzantium and an archbishop metropolitan with authority from Constantinople residing in Kiev arose to head the church.

Moscow would take its first steps toward its future prominence in the last half of the 12th century. In 1156, Prince Yury Dolgoruky (ca. 1099–1157) built fortifications to protect the town. They proved ineffective against invasions in 1177 and in particular in 1237–1238, when the Mongol warriors passed through the region. Each invasion resulted in Moscow being burned and many of its inhabitants being killed, but the city was then repopulated and rebuilt. By the end of the 13th century, under Prince Danill Aleksandrovich (1261–1303), Moscow had become a prosperous center of a

14th century, the Grand Duchy of Moscow emerged as the most prominent Russian principality and in 1380 its Prince Dmitry Ivanovich (1363–1389) formed a united Russian army and secured an important victory over the Golden Horde in the Battle of Kulikovo. However, the fight for liberation from the Mongols took another 100 years. In 1382, Khan Tokhtamysh overran and sacked the city, though he was unable to breach the new fortifications of the Kremlin. It was only in 1480 that Ivan III (1462–1505) finally defeated the Mongol army, freed the country from their control, and made Moscow the center of power in Russia.

The city's new might and stability did not mean the end of its traumas. In 1571, the khan of the Crimea, one of the successors of the Golden Horde, attacked and sacked and burned the city, sparing only the Kremlin. In 1610 the Polish Lithuanian army began a two-year occupation of the city. In 1812, the city was burned as Napoleon's army approached, most likely as the result of an attempt to deny it to the invader, compounded by the chaos of its residents' evacuation. In 1941, Adolf Hitler tried and failed to take the city.

Moscow's ascendance to political power was accompanied by its rise as the ecclesiastical center of Russia, at the expense of Kiev. In 1299, the metropolitan of Kiev moved his residence to Vladimir, Moscow's rival, but shortly after to Moscow. From 1325, when Peter (d. 1326), still officially metropolitan of Kiev, established his seat in Moscow, the city became the center of the Russian Orthodox Church. In 1448, five years before the fall of Constantinople, Jonas (d. 1461) was declared the metropolitan of Moscow. In 1589, Job (d. 1607) was consecrated as the patriarch of Moscow and All Russia, and the Russian Church became jurisdictionally equal to its Constantinople progenitor.

As Moscow emerged in prominence, it also became the home to monasteries, prominent churches, and cathedrals. The oldest monastic community was at Novospassky Monastery founded in the 12th century during the reign of Prince Yury Dolgoruky, considered to be the founder of Moscow. Also laying claim to being the city's oldest monastery is the Danilov Monastery, founded in 1282 by Prince Danill. Monastic activities were later neglected and the buildings fell into disrepair. Thus in 1330, the monks were relocated and

Novospassky Monastery (New Monastery of the Savior) is one of the fortified monasteries surrounding Moscow from the southeast. (Vladislav Rumyantsev/Dreamstime.com)

small independent principality, though still under the authority of the Mongol regime.

Moscow's relatively stable position after the withdrawal of the Mongol army attracted large numbers of refugees from other parts of what is now Russia. Under Ivan I (1288–1340), Danill's son, the Principality of Moscow surged in front of the rival principalities of the region. Under Ivan I (called "Kalita," or "Money Bag," in old Russian) Moscow got the exclusive right to collect taxes from other Russian lands for the Golden Horde, the Mongolian state. By acting as the Mongol's enforcement arm in the region and paying an additional amount of tribute, Ivan gained the khan's agreement that the Moscow Principality would not be divided among his sons, but would pass entirely into the hands of his eldest son, Simeon (1316–1353). Through the

it would be two centuries before the site was revived as a monastic center. The most tragic episode in the monastery's history was when in 1930 it was turned into a children's prison by the Soviet government. It was returned to the Russian Orthodox Church in 1983 and became the residence of the Moscow Patriarchate, the governing body of the church.

The transfer of ecclesiastical power led to construction of churches and monasteries inside the Kremlin, which is the fortified center of Moscow. These included the Dormition Cathedral (1327), the monastery Church of the Saviour's Transfiguration (1330), and Archangel Cathedral (1333). A second building spree at the end of the century, under Ivan III, was intended to symbolize and celebrate Moscow's rise as the center of a powerful new state (the word "Russia" came to be used during Ivan III's reign). Apart from the new Kremlin walls and towers (still in place), this added new ecclesiastical buildings, such as Annunciation Cathedral, the Chudov Monastery, and Ascension Convent.

Earlier, Metropolitan Peter saw to the opening of the Vysokopetrovsky Monastery on a site outside the Kremlim walls. Metropolitan Alexei (1354–1378) built two monasteries during his long tenure as head of the Russian church. With high fortified walls, each new monastery added to a ring gradually being built around the Kremlin. Alongside their religious function, the monasteries would now also have a purely secular function as the first line of defense against future invaders. The Andronikov Monastery, located a short distance from the Novospassky Monastery, was built in 1360, following Alexei's return from Constantinople. It is said that, having encountered a violent storm while on the Black Sea during his return trip, Alexei had vowed to build a church if he survived. A short time later, he left Moscow to treat the ailing wife of the Mongol khan and the khan rewarded him with a grant of land in Moscow upon which he erected the Chudov Monastery. This monastery attained religious fame as the home of the 14th-century icon painter Andrei Rublev (ca. 1360–ca. 1430) and was saved from demolition during the Communist era by being transformed for a time into the Andrei Rublev Museum of Early Russian Art.

By the early 16th century, when the concept of the Third Rome was first elaborated by Filofey (Philotheos), a monk from the city of Pskov in the Russian northwest, Moscow was already a city of numerous Orthodox churches and monasteries. Its most internationally famous ecclesiastical building, however, would not be built until the reign of Ivan IV ("the Terrible") who, in the 1550s, commissioned a new cathedral to replace Trinity Cathedral located next to the moat that ran beside the Kremlin. The church was constructed to celebrate Ivan's conquest of the Kazan Khanate, the decisive victory of which fell on the feast day of the Intercession of the Virgin, and so named his new church the Cathedral of the Intercession of the Virgin on the Moat. However, at the time, the recently deceased holy man Basil the Blessed (1468–1552) was enjoying great popularity with the city's residents (including Ivan himself), and the church came to be called St. Basil's, the name by which it is known today. St. Basil's is a Moscow architectural landmark, famous for its nine colorful towers, each in a different pattern, and its intricate complex design.

The erection of St. Basil's came on the heels of the 1534 construction of the Novodevichy Convent and Monastery that celebrated another Russian military victory: the recapture of Smolensk from the Lithuanians in 1524. Toward the end of the century, Boris Godunov (ca. 1551–1605), who served as regent of Russia for a number of years and in 1598 became czar, commissioned the Donskoi Monastery to honor an icon of the Mother of God, which many believed was responsible for the deliverance of Moscow from a series of attacks by Mongols through the century. Continuing the construction of commemorative church buildings on the occasion of military victories would be the Kazan Cathedral, built to celebrate Russian victory over the Poles and Lithuanians in 1612. Though destroyed by the Soviet government, it has recently been rebuilt.

The erection of new monumental religious structures would be put to an end by the movement of the capital of Russia to St. Petersburg by Peter the Great (1682–1725) in 1712. It would remain the capital until 1918. During this period, only one new monumental project would be undertaken in Moscow, the Cathedral of Christ the Savior, the new cathedral church of the patriarch of Russia, originally opened in 1883 to commemorate Russia's victory over Napoleon. Joseph Stalin (1878–1953) ordered this symbol of Russian

Orthodoxy and popular patriotism pulled down in the 1930s, and its reconstruction became one of the first projects of the Russian Orthodox Church and Moscow authorities in the 1990s, after the fall of the Soviet Union.

However, until 1917, construction of ecclesiastical buildings continued in the ever-expanding city, reflecting changes in architectural tastes, social structure, and economic prosperity. In the late 19th century the city was commonly referred to as a place of "forty forties" churches, as it was believed to have had at least 1,600 golden cupolas, their abundance reflected in many works of Russian arts and literature. According to the available statistics, at the beginning of the 20th century Moscow had around 450 churches. At the same time, while remaining a recognizably Russian Orthodox city, it was becoming increasingly multi-religious.

From the mid-16th century, Protestants (Lutherans, Calvinists, and Anglicans) were invited by czars as much-needed professionals and settled in Moscow, initially segregated in a special district called the German Quarter (Nemetskaya sloboda). At the beginning of the 20th century, there were around 25,000 Catholics and roughly the same number of Protestants in Moscow (out of around 1.3 million of its inhabitants). Over the centuries, there also emerged Muslim, Jewish, Armenian, and other communities. The first two Protestant churches (a Lutheran one and a Calvinist one) were built not far from the Kremlin in the mid-16th century under Ivan IV, but they were demolished shortly after the czar had grown fearful of their "heretical influence." Despite numerous restrictions and obstacles, from the late 18th century, however, non-Orthodox faiths began to be architecturally represented in Moscow. In 1791, the first Catholic church, St. Ludwig, was erected in Moscow (to accommodate religious needs of refugees from post-1789 France), followed by an Anglican church, St. Andrew's, in 1884. There is reliable evidence of a mosque being opened in 1823, but there may have been even an earlier mosque in the city. After many delays and much resistance, the first synagogue was opened in Moscow in 1906.

The Bolshevik assault on religion resulted in closures of religious communities, demolition of churches, and desecration of ecclesiastical buildings by turning them into secular offices, storage houses, and even prisons. By the mid-1980s, there remained no more than 20 functioning churches in Moscow. St. Andrew's church was confiscated by the Bolsheviks in 1920, the mosque was closed down in 1939; the synagogue and St. Ludwig's Church functioned throughout the Soviet period, though under severe restrictions and with much reduced space. At the same time, beginning in 1930, the Soviet government carried out a large-scale program of Communist "visual propaganda," which, among other things, was designed to replace the Orthodox image of the city with Communist symbolism. The most ambitious project within this program involved construction of the Palace of Soviets on the spot of the demolished Cathedral of Christ the Savior. The palace was supposed to be 1,033 feet high and topped with a 328-foot statue of Lenin, founder of the Soviet state. For technical reasons, however, the project never went beyond excavation works for creating the foundation; in the late 1950s, a large outdoor swimming pool was built there instead.

After the fall of the Soviet Union in 1991, Moscow became a hub of post-Soviet religious resurgence. It has around 900 registered religious organizations, and hundreds of groups operate without registration. Around 50 different religions are represented in the city. The Russian Orthodox Church dominates in the city, in terms of both the number of its congregations (320, or 30 percent) and, in particular, architecturally. Many churches and monasteries were restored and new churches built, including in residential areas constructed during the Soviet period. However, the city's religious profile has changed considerably toward more diversity, with around 250 Protestant congregations (more than 30 prayer houses), 25 Muslim (6 mosques), 15 Jewish (5 synagogues), 16 Buddhist (3 temples), 12 Catholic (3 churches), and dozens of New Religious movements and New Age groups currently present in the city. However, this new diversity has also caused concerns and controversies over the Russian Orthodox profile of the Russian capital. This partly explains the disputes over construction of some non-Orthodox buildings, such as mosques and a Krishna temple. Some congregations have been legally challenged by Moscow city authorities, which resulted in a ban and later refusal to register the Salvation Army, which was later declared unlawful by the European Court of Human Rights. The Salvation Army's Moscow branch has now been reregistered. In 2004, the Moscow congregation of the Jehovah's Witnesses was legally "liquidated" as a religious organization.

J. Gordon Melton and Marat S. Shterin

See also: Calvinism; Cathedral of Christ the Savior; Cathedrals—Christian; International Society for Krishna Consciousness; Jehovah's Witnesses; Lutheranism; Monasticism; Roman Catholic Church; Russian Orthodox Church (Moscow Patriarchate); Salvation Army.

References

Brooke, Caroline. *Moscow: A Cultural History.* New York: Oxford University Press, 2006.

Krasovskii, Mikhail. *Moscow Church Architecture.* Moscow: G. Lissner, 1911.

Murrell, Kathleen Berton. *Moscow: An Illustrated History.* New York: Hippocrene Books, 2003.

Pospielovsky, Dimitry. *The Orthodox Church in the History of Russia.* Crestwood, NY: St. Vladimir's Seminary Press, 1998.

Vladimirskaia, Norma. *Art and History of the Kremlin of Moscow.* New York: Bonechi Books, 2000.

Voyce, Arthur. *The Moscow Kremlin: Its History, Architecture and Art Treasures.* Berkeley: University of California Press, 1954.

Moses

Moses was the leader of the Israelites in their departure from Egypt and plays a central role in receiving the covenant from God. He is often identified as the main lawgiver in Judaism, and also represents the law in other religions such as Islam and Christianity. Moses is the main human figure in the Jewish Torah, the first five books of the Bible, often called the Five Books of Moses. He leads the Jews out of Egyptian slavery, directs them during their 40 years in the desert, brings the law down from Mount Sinai, and organizes the entry into the land of Canaan.

The name Moses, or Moshe in Hebrew, plays on a link with the word for drawing out of water (Exodus 2:10). He was born around the 13th century BCE to Amram and Jochabed with a sister Miriam and brother Aaron. During a time of persecution of Jewish males he was hidden in a basket and placed in the river, only to be rescued and subsequently brought up by Pharaoh's daughter. He fled to Midian after killing an Egyptian in defense of a fellow Israelite, marrying Zipporah, and having two sons. Here he again defended the weak, resisting aggression against the daughters of his father-in-law Jethro. On Mount Sinai he experienced the presence of God through a burning bush and received the orders to lead the Hebrews from Egypt. Moses protested his inadequacy and was told to take his brother Aaron with him to help in his task. Pharaoh resisted Moses' mission, although Moses carried on trying to change his mind, and the Egyptians were punished with the 10 plagues. With the last, the death of the Egyptian firstborn, Moses succeeded in leading the Israelites out of Egypt and evading the Egyptian attempt at recapturing them. He took them through the Red (Reed) Sea into the Sinai desert and returned to Mount Sinai, where a detailed covenant was established with God and the whole of the community. His people constantly let him down, yet he persisted in caring for them and guiding their route to the Promised Land. Moses then continued to lead the Israelites to the land of Canaan, but died at Mount Nebo without himself entering.

One of the rather charming aspects of Moses is his apparent modesty. He was frightened by the presence of God in the burning bush and refused to look at him, and admitted to not knowing the divine name or being able to carry out the task he was set. When his mission to Pharaoh was at first unsuccessful and the Israelites turned against him, he complained to God for sending him (Exodus 5:22) as the Hebrews complained to him about God's plans for them. Even when they escaped from Egypt and discovered the pursuing Egyptian army they blamed Moses. Moses followed God's instructions throughout the exodus and served as the conduit for divine assistance for the Hebrews throughout this long period when they were threatened by enemies, both human and natural. When Moses was delayed on Mount Sinai, where he received the details of the law, the people revolted against monotheism and constructed the Golden Calf, an event that caused

Moses to smash the tablets he brought down with him. Eventually, after punishing the leaders of the revolt, he returned to Mount Sinai with blank tablets and God dictated the terms of the covenant.

Moses was also involved in constructing the tabernacle that contained the tablets of the law, and continued to intercede on behalf of the Hebrews on the occasions when they were attacked and the even more frequent occasions when they turned against God and refused to trust in the eventual success of their mission. Even Moses himself at Numbers 20:10 is shown to be very human in carrying out an order by God to tell a rock to produce water, when the Israelites were yet again complaining of lack of sustenance. He struck the rock twice and water did indeed gush out, but the implication was that he had carried out the miracle, not God, and for this he is told at Numbers 20:12 that he will not be allowed to enter the land of Israel, although other reasons are also given in the commentatorial tradition. Even when at 120 years old he saw the land from Mount Nebo and pleaded for admittance, God did not relent. Moses gathered the Israelites and reminded them of their trials in the desert and summarized some of the basic principles of the law they received on Mount Sinai. At the end of the Bible, Moses is referred to as a unique prophet, someone whom God knew face to face, and who was engaged in performing the most remarkable events. Yet unlike many of the other major figures in Judaism, his burial place is known to no one.

Moses as Musa figures as a major character in the Koran, the most frequently mentioned human being (137 references). The account of his life and achievements is broadly in line with the Jewish Bible. He is referred to as both a prophet and a messenger in accordance with the significance of his role for the Israelites. He is also the most mentioned Old Testament character in the New Testament, often referred to as representing the law and prefiguring Jesus. He has frequently become part of modern theological debates, such as whether or not he was in fact Jewish (Freud thought he was an Egyptian) and what meaning his prophecy has for the three religions that regard him as significant.

Oliver Leaman

See also: Judaism; Sinai, Mount.

References

Buber, Martin. *Moses: The Revelation and the Covenant.* Amherst, NY: Prometheus Books, 1998.

Freud, Sigmund. "Moses and Monotheism: Three Essays." In *The Standard Edition of the Complete Psychological Works of Sigmund Freud,* vol. 23, 36–53. Trans. James Strachey. London: Hogarth Press, 1964.

Walzer, Michael. *Exodus and Revolution.* New York: Basic Books, 1986.

Wheeler, Brannon. *Moses in the Qur'an and Islamic Exegesis.* London: Routledge, 2002.

Wildavsky, Aaron. *Moses as a Political Leader.* Jerusalem: Shalem, 2005.

Mosques

Mosques are the gathering places for worship within the Muslim community. The mosque is primarily a house for prayer, especially on Friday at noon, the main time for the community to gather. *Masjid,* another word for mosque, means literally a "place for prostration," referring to the posture assumed during prayer. The term "masjid" is often used to refer to smaller mosques. Traditionally, Muslims consider that prayer done in the mosque is more valuable than that done daily in the home or elsewhere.

The most important aspect of the area of a mosque, the *musallah,* or prayer room, is the *qibla,* the direction in which the believer orients himself or herself for *salat,* the prayer of Islam. The qibla is always aimed toward Mecca, or more precisely toward the Kaaba, the most holy place in Islam. The wall containing the qibla is perpendicular to the qibla. The Kaaba is the large cube-shaped building (approximately 50 feet high, 40 feet long, and 33 feet wide) cut from stone, located in the midst of the Grand Mosque in Mecca. Its four corners are oriented on the four cardinal directions, and the Black Stone, a sacred rock, is in its eastern corner.

Worshippers in the mosque face Mecca while praying. Mecca was not always the direction for worship.

The Sultan Salahuddin Abdul Aziz Shah Mosque, popularly termed the Blue Mosque, is the second largest mosque in Southeast Asia and the state mosque for the state of Selangor, Malaysia. (J. Gordon Melton)

For a few years (622–624 CE), the qibla was Jerusalem. Worship in Orthodox Judaism is also oriented toward Jerusalem. The change is noted in the Koran.

Each mosque must clearly show the qibla, the most common means being through a niche in one wall called a *mibrab*. The mibrab symbolizes the doorway into paradise. The area immediately in front of the mihrab is under a roof, and doors that worshippers use to enter the prayer hall are located on the wall not containing the mihrab. Near the mihrab is the *minbar*, an elevated chair used by the imam to deliver the sermon each Friday. The floor is usually covered with one or more rugs.

At the entrance into the mosque, shoes are removed and a place, the *sardivan*, is provided for ritual ablutions. Here the worshipper washes face, hands, and feet according to instructions found in the Koran (sura 5:6), "O you who believe! When you rise up to pray, wash your faces and your hands as far as the elbows, and wipe your heads and your feet to the ankles." Those in a state of ceremonial impurity are instructed to bathe their whole body. If no water is available, for example, if one is in the desert, a symbolic substitute (sand, earth) may be used.

The evolution of the mosques begins in Medina, where the courtyard of the prophet Muhammad's home became an initial gathering place for the first Muslim community in 622. Here the original qibla faced Jerusalem, though soon changed to face Mecca, and worship conducted under a covered space. The roof of

Muhammad's house was the original place from which the daily calls to prayer were made by Bilal, an early convert, who acted as the first *muazzin*. It is considered the precursor of the minarets (towers) that are now attached to every mosque. Muhammad's wives resided in houses to the left of the courtyard. The Medina mosque quickly acquired a variety of functions central to the community.

In 630 Muhammad made his return to Mecca and he and his companions took control of the city, and most important, of the Kaaba. The items representative of various other religions that accumulated around the Kaaba were removed and the area transformed into the Grand Mosque and geographic center of Islam. By this time, additional mosques had begun to appear throughout the Arabian Peninsula. Very quickly, mosques would be created wherever the religion spread and it spread rapidly during its first century.

At some point during his years in Mecca, Muhammad was miraculously transported to Jerusalem, from where he visited heaven. After the Muslim Caliphate expanded to include Palestine, the Aqsa Mosque was constructed on the Temple Mount in Jerusalem over the spot it is believed where Muhammad led the former prophets and the angels in prayer immediately prior to his ascent into heaven. The original mosque was a rectangular prayer hall with its long axis oriented on another site on the Temple Mount, the Dome of the Rock. All three mosques, the one at Muhammad's home and burial place in Medina, the Grand Mosque in Mecca, and the Aqsa Mosque in Jerusalem, constitute the three most holy sites on earth for all Muslims. Other sites, especially the mosques in Karbala and Najaf, are particularly revered by Shia Muslims.

In the Middle East, most mosques are closed to non-Muslims, a regulation that evolved through the first century of Islam parallel to an increasing emphasis on the sanctity of the mosque. The sanctity of the mosque in Saudi Arabia has led to whole sections of Mecca and Medina being off limits to non-Muslims and the whole region being closed to tourists. In the West, where Muslims are a distinct minority, mosques are usually open to non-Muslim visitors, and have to be available to a variety of non-Muslims from fire marshals to building code inspectors. Ideally, all mosques are open to all Muslims, but as divisions have appeared

in the Muslim world, in practice, there are boundaries that are largely respected. Thus Shia Muslims and Sunni Muslims do not share the same mosques. There are also mosques for Kharijis, and increasingly Islamists are somewhat segregated. Ahmadiyya Muslims are considered sectarians by the larger Islamic world and do not mix with other Muslim groups. These boundaries are most neglected in the larger more famous mosques.

The architecture of the mosque developed from a very simple area for worship with only a few essentials to much more elaborate and complex structures. Designs and decorations were kept simple, both to maintain theological purity and to avoid confusion between the mosques and the structures of other religions. Minarets proved a functional addition and were added fairly early, possibly as early as 665. The oldest minaret still in existence is at Kairouan, Tunisia. It was built between 724 and 727, about a century after the Medina mosque. Rooms were added as the mosque took on multiple functions and it became the residence of local holy men.

The early mosques were built by the government and owned by the ruler who authorized it and his successors. Later, besides the government, a wealthy donor would supply the funds. Its maintenance would be paid out of tax money and/or derived from various endowments. Administration would be in the hands of officials appointed by the ruler, the donor if she or he so chose, or a local *nazir* (administrator) who was usually the judge of *sharia* law. As the arbiter of legal matters, a nazir was a most powerful person in the Muslim community. In more secularized settings, or where the Muslims form a minority community, the mosque is usually paid for, constructed, and afterward maintained by those people who will be its support community once built.

The ruler was also (and is some Muslim countries remains) the official worship (prayer) leader, the imam, in the mosques of his domain. In practice, he rarely acted in that capacity, and in his stead, a *khatib*, literally the one who delivers the sermon, was appointed to act as imam. That person could also be a judge. In larger mosques, one would find several khatibs.

As they developed, mosques served many social functions, but began to evolve institutionally. Schools (*madrasses*) were added for training the young in Is-

The Islamic Society of North Texas has a large mosque in suburban Dallas. (J. Gordon Melton)

lamic belief and practice and some of these evolved into universities, the al-Aksa University in Cairo being possibly the most prominent example. Mosques also housed law courts, lodging for travelers, and even hospitals. Some of these functions are being lost as society evolves and new secularized structures assume control of educational, legal, and medical facilities and different arrangements are made for travelers.

While women have an important role in Islam, their role differs markedly from that of men. This difference shows up at the mosque. The Friday prayers and sermon has been considered to be compulsory for all male Muslims. In some Muslim countries, women are not welcome at mosques, and mosques can be closed to women, though such prohibitions are absent from the Koran and the *hadith*. In mosques where women are welcome, in more secularized Muslim countries

or in the West, women may be segregated and during Friday services seated in the rear of the mosque or in a separate room divided from the prayer hall by a screen that allows sound to pass freely through it.

In only a few mosques in the West do women join men in the main prayer hall and otherwise participate in the administration and management of the mosque. This issue has joined the veiling of women and their access to education and employment as major issues for those concerned with the status and role of women in Islam.

Besides the three major holy sites, a number of mosques have become famous for their historical importance, cultural identifications, and/or architectural significance. Notable among these are the many mosques of Cairo beginning with the Mosque of Amr, the oldest mosque in the city; the al-Azhar Mosque, the primary mosque of the Fatimid rulers in the 10th century, out of which al-Azhar University emerged; the 13th-century An-Nasir Mohammed Mosque, the oldest building inside the Citadel; the Mosque of Sultan Hassan, completed in 1363; and the 19th-century Mosque of Muhammad Ali.

The largest mosque in the world is al-Masjid al-Haram, the Grand Mosque of Mecca, which surrounds the Kaaba. It is an open-air mosque that has been repeatedly enlarged to accommodate the faithful as the movement has grown. One obligation of all able-bodied male Muslims is to make at least one pilgrimage to Mecca. The mosque can currently accommodate some 800,000 people both inside and immediately outside. During the *hajj* (pilgrimage) that capacity is increased to four million. In 2007, the current ruler of Saudi Arabia, King Abdullah bin Abdul-Aziz (b. 1924), initiated plans to increase the normal capacity to 1,120,000.

The Mosque of the Prophet in Medina is both the second holiest and the second largest mosque in the world. Like the mosque in Mecca, it has also been repeatedly renovated and enlarged. As a result, the current prayer hall can accommodate up to a half million worshippers. Muhammad's tomb is contained within the mosque and rests under a unique Green Dome in the center of the mosque.

Four other mosques are notable for their size, being able to accommodate as many as 100,000 worshippers in their main prayer hall: the Faisal Mosque in Islamabad, Pakistan, and the largest mosque in South Asia; the Imam Reza shrine, a *sahia* mosque in Mashhad, Iran; Istiqlal Mosque, (Independence Mosque) in Jakarta, Indonesia, the national mosque of Indonesia, the world's most populous Muslim nation; and the largest mosque in Southeast Asia; the Hassan II Mosque located in Casablanca, Morocco, and the largest mosque in Africa. Each of these mosques are products of the late 20th century.

A number of Muslim countries have impressive national mosques, designated either officially or unofficially, like the Masjid Negara, the national mosque of Malaysia, located in Kuala Lumpur. The Great Mosque of Djenné, Mali, is most unusual, being constructed entirely of mud brick. It is the largest mud brick building in the world. The Id Kah Mosque located in Kashgar, Xinjiang, is the largest mosque in China.

From Afghanistan, Islam spread along the Silk Road through central Asia to China. Along that route, which became dominantly Muslim, are a number of cities, all of which have been notable centers of Islamic life. Prominent mosques include the Khast Imam Mosque at Tashkent; the Bibi Khanym Mosque at Samarkand, the Maghak-i 'Attari Mosque and Bukhara; the Azadi, Khezrety Omar, and Iranian mosques in Ashgabat; and the mosque/mausoleum complex of Sultan Sanjar in Merv, once the largest city in the world.

Minarets also grew taller as rulers discovered that they could also serve as observation posts from which possible invading hostile forces could be seen, though that motive seems superfluous relative to what is now the tallest minaret in the world found at the new Hassan II Mosque in Casablanca, Morocco. It reaches upward of 689 feet. The tallest brick minaret in the world (238 feet) is the Qutb Minar located in Delhi, India, and built between 1193 and 1385. It was constructed of red sandstone and covered with intricate carvings and verses from the Koran. For a time it served as the minaret for the Quwwat-ul-Islam mosque, the earliest extant mosque built by the Delhi sultans.

The Minaret of Jam, built in 1194 by Sultan Ghiyath al-din Mohammed Ibn Sam (1163–1202) in the province of Ghur, in what is now Afghanistan, is the second tallest minaret in the world. The tower is unique in that it sits in an isolated area of the country and was lost to history, the Ghurid dynasty and the society that supported it having been destroyed and dispersed by the Mongols. Even the site of the Ghurid capital remains unknown. The Minaret of Jam appears to have been the direct inspiration for the Qutb Minaret. It was rediscovered in 1957 by Ahmed Ali Kohzad, the president of the Afghan Historical Society, and French archaeologist André Maricq.

The United Nations Educational, Scientific and Cultural Organization (UNESCO) has recognized the cultural significance of the mosque and added a number of them to its list of World Heritage Sites, including the minaret at Jam, Afghanistan; the Historic Mosque City of Bagerhat, Bangladesh; and the Great Mosque and hospital at Divrigi, Turkey. Many more are included in the designation of historical sections of cities from Cairo to Bukhara.

J. Gordon Melton

See also: Cairo; Great Mosque, Djenné, Mali; Jerusalem; Mecca; Medina; Orthodox Judaism.

References

Frishman, Martin, and Hasan Uddin Khan, eds. *The Mosque: History, Architectural Development, and Regional Diversity.* New York: Thames and Hudson, 1994.

Grabar, Oleg. *The Formation of Islamic Art.* New Haven, CT: Yale University Press, 1973.

Holod, Renata, and Hasan Uddin-Khan. *The Mosque and the Modern World: Architects, Patrons, and Designs since the 1950s.* London: Thames and Hudson, 1997.

McCauley, David. *The Mosque.* New York: Houghton Mifflin, 2003.

Welzbacher, Christian. *Euro Islam Architecture: New Mosques in the Occident.* Amsterdam: Sun Publishers, 2008.

Mother Meera, Disciples of

Mother Meera, born Kamala Ready (1960) in Chandepalle, Andhra Pradesh, is an Indian female guru who since the 1980s has gained a large following in the West. When she was 12, her uncle Balgur Venkat Reddy declared her to be the incarnation of the original and supreme female power, Adiparashakti, and took her to live with him at the ashram of Sri Aurobindo Ghose (1872–1950). There, she gathered some fame and came to be regarded as an avatar, or a divinity in human form who comes to save the world. Avatars (as opposed to gurus) are believed to be purely and originally divine and devoid of any sinful human nature. Kamala took the name Meera and was called Mother by her disciples. Among the early disciples of Meera was Adilakshmi, a woman about 20 years her senior, who is still Meera's closest associate, and Andrew Harvey, whose books gained Meera early popularity in the West, but who subsequently broke his association with her.

In the early 1980s, Meera, Balgur Venkat Reddy, and Adilakshmi visited disciples in Germany, where Meera married and settled. Reddy died in 1985, but Meera's fame has spread throughout Europe, the United States, and Australia. Every year, she receives tens of thousands of visitors who come for *darshan* (spiritual encounter or audience). Characteristic of Meera's darshan is the complete silence in which it occurs. Her darshan room has no icons or music, and she does not deliver any teachings or meditation instruction. Disciples approach one by one, kneel in front of Mother Meera, and place their head in her hands. After pressing the temples for a few moments, she looks the disciple straight in the eyes. This is believed to undo spiritual blockages and to release spiritual energy in the disciple.

Though there are very few teachings, the writings by and about Mother Meera reflect a mixture of the teachings of Aurobindo with popular Hindu devotion. Though Mother Meera is herself the central focus of this devotion, disciples are encouraged to realize their own divine nature through surrender to the Mother. It is the absence of any systematic teaching, organized ritual, or institution that appears to be part of the appeal of Mother Meera in the West.

Mother Meera
Oberdorf 4a
D-65559 Dornburg-Thalheim
Germany
http://www.mothermeera.com

Catherine Cornille

See also: Devotion/Devotional Traditions; Hinduism; Meditation.

References

Adilakshmi. *The Mother.* Thalheim, Germany, 1987.

Cornille, Catherine. "Mother Meera, Avatar." In *The Graceful Guru. Hindu Female Gurus in India and the United States,* edited by K. Pechilis, 129–148. Oxford: Oxford University Press, 2004.

Goodman, Martin. *In Search of the Divine Mother.* San Francisco: Thorsons, 1998.

Harvey, Andrew. *Hidden Journey: A Spiritual Awakening.* London: Rider, 1991.

Linebaugh, Sonia. *At the Feet of Mother Meera.* Philadelphia: Xlibirs Corporation, 2005.

Mother Meera. *Answers.* 2 vols. Ithaca, NY: Meeramma Publications, 1991, 1997.

Mother of God Centre

The Orthodox Church of Mother of God Derzhavnaya ("Majestic"), commonly known as the Mother of God Centre (MGC), is an indigenous Russian new religious movement that emerged as an underground group in the late 1980s in the Soviet Union and was officially registered in 1992 in the wake of the introduction of the 1990 Law on Freedom of Religions. To some extent, it started as a breakaway movement from the Russian Free ("Catacomb") Orthodox Church, which in turn had splintered from the Russian Orthodox Church (Moscow Patriarchate) and operated underground since the 1920s.

MGC was founded and is currently led by Archbishop Ioann Bereslavski (Veniamin Yakovlevich Bereslavski, b. 1946). In the mid-1980s, he was baptized and took monastic vows in the Free (Catacomb) Church, and soon after was ordained a priest and then a bishop. According to Archbishop Ioann, in 1984 the Mother of God appeared before him and revealed the true meaning of Christianity and the sufferings of the Russian people and their church. Since then he has been having continuous revelations, which constitute the basis of his ever-evolving theology and define the dynamics of the movement he leads.

While claiming allegiance to the Eastern Orthodox tradition (the Nicene Creed, the Apostolic succession, and the decisions of the seven ecumenical councils), MGC reinterprets it in a revivalist and millenarian fashion in light of the church's "Marian faith." This "renewed faith" is based on a series of miraculous 20th-century appearances and revelations of the Virgin Mary, in both Eastern Orthodox and Roman Catholic contexts, which taken together are believed to constitute "the White New Testament" or "the New Covenant." According to Ioann Bereslavski, the New Covenant signifies that the world has entered the "era of the Holy Ghost," in which God no longer dominates the world but reunites with it. "Charismatic gifts" of spiritual knowledge and divine life are no longer limited to the official church authorities but can be found in an infinite variety of sources and manifestations: from the centuries-old Russian tradition of monastic sainthood of Saint Nil Sorski and Saint Serafim Sarovski, through Russian classical literature and the philosophy of Leo Tolstoy and Nicolas Berdyaev, to the 20th-century martyrdom of Nicolas II monks of the Solovki Islands. From the late 1990s, following a series of visits and pilgrimages abroad, MGC widened its repertoire of charismatic gifts to include elements of Western sacred mythology, beliefs, and practices, such as the legend of the Holy Grail and mysticism of the Cathars.

The theology and mythology of MGC, however, remain Russocentric and particularly focused on the drama of Russian modern history. In his early prophecies, Bereslavski claimed that the Virgin Mary in her revelation in 1917 in Fatima, Portugal, predicted that Russia would become the battlefield of the final "cosmic" confrontation between the evil of Communism and God as embodied in the Orthodox Church. However, he asserted, the Moscow Patriarchate betrayed the Virgin's salvationist mission through collaboration with the Communist regime, which was symbolized in the image of the three-headed Dragon, representing the Communist Party, the KGB, and the Moscow Patriarchate. The defeat of the 1991 Communist coup signified the end of the first two heads, and the severance of the last head will make possible the salvation of humanity through acceptance of the "True Marian Faith."

In its early days, MGC bore an imprint of its origins in the monastic tradition of the Catacomb Orthodox Church on the one hand, and of youthful idealism of its first—predominantly male—members on the other. Salvation could only be achieved through "seeking sainthood," that is, following strict asceticism and separation from "the world." In social terms, this meant living in small semi-underground communities led by authoritarian sages (starets), separation from the biological parents, engaging in exhausting fasting and prayers, and avoiding—and at times harshly treating—women. However, from the mid-1990s this monastic revivalism gradually gave way to a more accommodating stance, with interest in engagement with the wider world, more open communities with flexible criteria for membership, and establishing contacts with other Christian churches and world religions.

The revivalist interpretation of the Orthodox tradition by MGC can be seen in its liturgical practice: the canonical Orthodox liturgy is complemented by the "plastic prayer," which is silent prayer accompanied by highly expressive gesticulation, and by exuberant rhythmical music, dance, and colorful dress. In contrast to the Old Slavonic of the Russian Orthodox Church, MGC uses modern Russian as its liturgical language.

MGC has seven bishops, including head Archbishop Ioann (Bereslavski). The movement holds an annual Church Council, which is a major religious festival for all its participants and sympathizers. Its infrastructure includes several small monasteries, a school, a theological academy, and a publishing house, New Holy Russia Publishers, which annually produces dozens of books and two periodicals—*The Virgin's Mercy* (formerly *The Knight of Faith*) and *The Oasis of Peace*.

There is no formal membership. It is estimated that the movement has never attracted more than a few hundred core followers and around 3,500 to 4,000 more loosely affiliated participants in various parts of Russia, around 400 of whom reside in Moscow. Since the early 1990s, the movement has been involved in the World Network of Marian Devotion. It now has followers in Croatia, Bulgaria, Italy, and some other European countries.

In the early 1990s, MGC was subject to controversy and became one of the main targets of anti-cult groups and the Moscow Patriarchate. The anti-cult groups mainly focused on allegations of hypnosis and assault on the family, which caused several investigations by the Office of the General Prosecutor. No evidence of criminal or antisocial activity was found. Several official documents of the Russian Orthodox Church mention MGC among the most dangerous "totalitarian sects" whose teachings and practices are unacceptable for both theological and moral reasons. In its early days, some anxieties were caused by MGC's political activities encouraged by its messianic anti-communism, and its staunch opposition to the "Communist Church." At that time, the movement's monarchist political views encouraged several of its members to proselytize in some units of the Russian army in order to "re-educate" officers in the spirit of Marian faith and the Russian monarchist tradition. Although the subsequent moderation of the movement contributed to its removal from the list of primary anti-cult targets,

it remains high on the church's counter-cult agenda. Also the negative publicity created by the mass media is likely to have contributed to the recent instances of violence against MGC and unlawful detention of its members.

MGC is a prominent example of indigenous religious innovation in response to the opportunities and frustrations of the transitional period in Russia. In a way, MGC has created a religious mythology for post-Communist Russia, drawing on elements of the country's traditional religious culture, as it survived the Soviet period and was transformed after the collapse of Communism.

Marat S. Shterin

See also: Asceticism; Marian Devotion, World Network of; Mary, Blessed Virgin; Roman Catholic Church; Russian Orthodox Church (Moscow Patriarchate); Saints.

References

Baklanova, G. *Pravoslavnaja Tserkov' Bozhiei Materi "Derzhavnaja."* Moscow: Agent, 1999.

Filatov, S. "Sects and New Religious Movements in Post-Soviet Russia." In *Proselytism and Orthodoxy in Russia: The New War of Souls,* edited by J. Witte Jr. and M. Bourdeaux, 163–184. Maryknoll, NY: Orbis Books, 1999.

Shterin, Marat. "New Religious Movements in the New Russia." *Nova Religio* 4, no. 2 (April 2001): 310–321.

Mountains

Humans have imputed sacredness to mountains for a number of reasons. Most obviously, mountains are high, reaching into the heavens—the realm of the gods. Mountains often are remote as well, and thus inaccessible to the majority of people, adding to their sense of mystery. The striking beauty of many mountains only adds to the awe people have felt, and still feel, when viewing them. In addition, mountains frequently provide the elements necessary for life: water (as the sources of rivers and springs), food (through the plants and animals found on their flanks), and minerals (both common and precious). As a result, most cultures

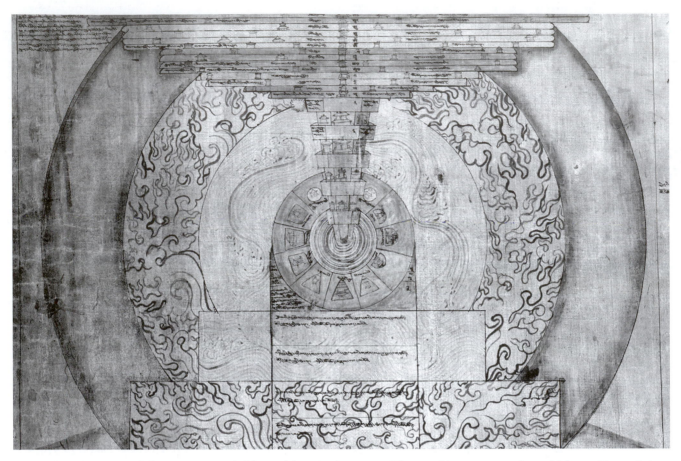

A Buddhist depiction of the universe with Mount Meru in the center. The world system consists of Mount Meru, sitting on top of four elemental disks, with the realms of all the gods above. At the very bottom is the black disk of wind, above it is the red disk of fire, next is the white disk of water, finally there is the yellow disk of earth. (iStockPhoto)

have imputed to mountains—both mythical and real—sometimes towering and sometimes merely higher than their surroundings—a sense of the sacred.

Because their tops stretch high above the surrounding lands, mountains have been viewed as the *center of the universe*, linking Earth with both heaven and hell, by many of the world's cultures. The prototypical *axis mundi* (world center) is Mount Meru (or Sumeru) of Indian mythology, which influenced both Hindu and Buddhist beliefs. Harney Peak serves a similar function for the Sioux (Lakota) of North America, as does Gunung Agung for the Balinese, while the Kaaba is the highest point on Earth and center of heaven according to Islamic tradition. Indeed, the highest point on Earth, atop the cosmic mountain, functions in many cultures as the "cosmic navel" as well, the site at which the world was created.

Veiled by clouds, mountains also have been considered *dwelling places of deities* by large numbers of religions and cultures. Often the god said to live on a particular mountain has a direct association with the geography or geology of the peak (such as the storm gods of various ancient Near Eastern civilizations or the volcano goddess Pele of Hawaii). In other cases, mountains are home to a chief deity; Hindus, for example, believe Mount Kailas in Tibet to be the home of Siva, the god of destruction. Still other mountains are considered the homes of multiple deities, such as Mount Olympus, home of the ancient Greek pantheon, or the mythical Mount Kunlun in China.

Some mountains, such as Mount Kailash, are seen not merely as divine dwelling places but also as *temples* at which to worship their associated deities. The physical reality of the mountain and its spiritual significance become united in the mind of the devotee, who sees and experiences the peak in multiple ways simultaneously. In some cultures the linkage could be so complete that a mountain became an *object of worship* in its own right. The association made by ancient Chinese between Mount Yue and the life-giving water that came down from it was so strong that they offered sacrifices to the mountain to ensure abundant rain and crops. In Japan, Mount Miwa was venerated as the body of a deity, while in Africa the Kikuyu worship Mount Kenya as the brightness of the supreme deity.

Even mountains not revered as temples in their own right could, by virtue of their proximity to heaven, become *homes to shrines* dedicated to worship and sacrifice. On Crete, for example, are numerous peak sanctuaries at which ashes and other remains of offerings have been found. Palestine likewise was home to "high places" that God commanded the Israelites to destroy during the conquest of Canaan but that later became rivals to the Jewish temple in Jerusalem. Interestingly, in order to be accessible to a wide range of people (such as the elderly and the infirm), mountain shrines were sometimes sited neither on the tallest nor the most remote peaks.

Mountain shrines, of course, are hardly a thing of the past. Adam's Peak in Sri Lanka, for example, is the site of an impression resembling a footprint that various traditions say was made by the Buddha (Buddhists), Siva (Hindus), Adam (Muslims), or Saint Thomas (Christians). Furthermore, the sacred spaces of mountains often served as *models for temples* located at some distance from them. Structures as varied, and as far-flung, as the step pyramids of the Americas, the ziggurats of Mesopotamia, the stupas and chedis of south and southeastern Asia, and the pagodas of east Asia all derive their appearances from, and act as replicas of, sacred mountains.

Their closeness to the heavens also makes mountains *sites of divine revelation*. This is particularly true for the world's great monotheistic religions. On Mount Sinai, cloaked in fire and smoke, Moses received from God the Ten Commandments and the rest of the law for the Jewish nation. On the Mount of Transfiguration, Jesus' appearance shone as God declared him his chosen son, overwhelming the three disciples who ac-

companied him. And on Mount Hira Muhammad heard the first words of the Koran.

Not all mountains derive their sacredness from direct associations with the divine, however. For example, a wide variety of cultures have stories of a flood that destroys all except a remnant of humanity (although the reasons for the flood differ). Some of them—from Hawaii, the Andes of South America, and the Great Plains of North America, for example—describe mountains that serve as *refuges from the flood* for the people fleeing the coming destruction. In order to spare the refugees, some of the mountains actually grow taller so that they rise above the floodwaters.

Other stories tell of heroes who escape the flood in boats that later come to rest on mountain peaks. In the Judeo-Christian tradition, Noah and his family took refuge in an ark that eventually came to rest on Mount Ararat. The hero Utnapishtim's boat ran aground on Mount Nimush (or Nisir) in the Mesopotamian Gilgamesh epic. Deucalion and his wife Pyrrha landed on Mount Parnassus according to Greco-Roman tradition, while Hindus tell how Manu, the first man, was saved by building a boat that Vishnu, incarnated as a fish, pulled to a mountain that subsequently was named Manu's Descent.

Some cultures saw in the loftiness and remoteness of mountains a *connection with the afterlife*. To the ancient Japanese, mountains acted both as the realm of the dead and as the gateway to it from the land of the living, besides being places where the denizens of the two could meet. As a result, mountains also served as burial places in Japan. Likewise, ancient Chinese considered Mount Kunlun in the west the gateway to heaven. Others constructed artificial "mountains" in which to bury their dead, including the earthen burial mounds built by the original peoples of North America and the pyramids of the ancient Egyptians.

Albert W. Hickman

See also: Emei Shan; Fiji, Mount; Heng Shan; Jiu-Hua Shan; Kailas, Mount/Lake Manasarovar; Lakota; Muhammad; Olympus, Mount; Putuo Shan; Sinai, Mount; Song Shan; Tai Shan; Wu Tai Shan.

References

Bernbaum, Edwin. *Sacred Mountains of the World.* Berkeley: University of California Press, 1997.

Bonnefoy, Yves, comp. *Mythologies.* Ed. Wendy Doniger. 2 vols. Chicago: University of Chicago Press, 1991.

Einarsen, John, ed. *The Sacred Mountains of Asia.* Boston: Shambhala Publications, Inc., 1995.

Eliade, Mircea. *The Myth of the Eternal Return: Cosmos and History.* Trans. Willard R. Trask. Princeton, NJ: Princeton University Press, 2005.

Movement for the Restoration of the Ten Commandments, The

The Movement for the Restoration of the Ten Commandments (MRTC) was a small movement in Uganda that suddenly made international news in March 2000 when hundreds of its members were murdered. MRTC traced its origin to visions of the Virgin Mary given to a young Ugandan woman, Credonia Mwerinde (1952–2000). As early as 1981, the Virgin told Mwerinde in a series of messages to renounce the sin in her life, change her ways, and prepare for a future mission. The messages also lamented the abandonment of the Ten Commandments by Christians, and they attacked the kind of malevolent magic that had spread from Rhodesia since the 1950s by the Mchape (witchcraft eradication) movement.

In the late 1980s, two other female visionaries, Angelina Migisha (1947–2000) and Mwerinde's niece Ursula Komuhangi (1968–2000), identified with Mwerinde. In 1989 the three recruited to their cause Joseph Kibwetere (1932–2000), who had independently received a vision of the Virgin. MRTC was essentially established by these four people. Kibwetere, a Roman Catholic layman, functioned as a bishop for the group. Eventually eight additional leaders, all designated apostles, were chosen.

The visions shared by these 12 apostles described apocalyptic events that would befall the people in the near future. Beginning in 1989, the group began to share their visions publicly, and in 1991 they published them in a book, *A Timely Message from Heaven: The End to the Present Times*, which announced the initiation of MRTC as a movement calling all believers back to observance of the Ten Commandments. The

apostles were very loosely connected with the larger global network of groups that also received messages from the Virgin Mary.

MRTC's apocalyptic teaching became more defined through the 1990s. The group taught that the present generation would soon be brought to an end. They compared the Earth to a tree that had become barren. One vision predicted three days of darkness, during which all the faithful were to go into a sanctuary prepared for this purpose, shut the doors, and remain secluded. At the end of that time, three-quarters of the world's population would be dead. The remainder would inherit a new redeemed Earth.

Kibwetere was reported to have predicted significant changes at the end of 1999. These reports appear to be false, as the group was in fact focused on the end of 2000, the actual end of the millennium. Indeed, in January 2000 MRTC leadership sent a letter to the Ugandan government announcing that its mission was concluding and that there would be no year 2001.

The movement was headquartered at Kanungu, a village in the Rukungiri District of Uganda. Members constructed a complex of buildings, and eventually Kanungu became known as Ishayuriro rya Maria (Rescue Place for the Virgin Mary). They adopted a highly disciplined life that included celibacy and a simple uniform dress of green, black, and white. The movement also developed a form of sign language that replaced speech as much as possible (except during worship services), and contact with nonmembers was minimized.

Much about the movement remains unknown and is not likely to be discovered. However, MRTC leaders evidently made a decision early in 2000 to end the movement's existence by systematically orchestrating the deaths of its membership. It has been further hypothesized that their decision may have been occasioned by the demand of some members for the return of their donations to the movement. Whatever the motivation, the deaths occurred in two phases. Members were killed at various movement centers around the country. Deaths occurred by poison, strangulation, and stabbing. Some 400 members were killed and buried in mass graves at 6 different locations. The members residing in Kanungu were killed on March 17.

In the days prior to the climactic event, word circulated that the Virgin was about to appear and members were urged to prepare for their deliverance at her hands. They slaughtered cattle, purchased a large supply of Coca Cola, indulged themselves with food, and purchased a supply of gasoline. Some members sold property and destroyed personal items. On the evening of March 15, they gathered for a party at which the food and drink were consumed. Two days later they gathered at their sanctuary, where the windows were already boarded up as prescribed in an early revelation. Shortly thereafter, there was a violent explosion and consuming fire from which no one escaped.

Initially, the reports of the event talked of a "ritual mass suicide." But during the investigation of the event, the bodies of those who had been killed at the other MRTC sites around the country were also discovered. Only when these hundreds of additional bodies were uncovered did the interpretations shift to homicide. The final count of victims was 780. MRTC leaders who planned the event seem to have perished in the fire with the believers, though their bodies have not been identified. Uganda issued warrants for their arrest, but no sign of any survivors have appeared. Given the group's location and the limited resources available for its investigation, many questions about the group and its final days will probably never be answered. The movement was one of thousands of new African indigenous movements that began to appear at the end of the 19th century. There was little indication that the movement was headed toward a disastrous end.

J. Gordon Melton

See also: Roman Catholic Church.

References
Kabazzi-Kisirinya, S., R. Nkurunziza, K. Deusdedit, and B. Gerard, eds. *The Kanugu Cult-Saga: Suicide, Murder, or Salvation?* Kampala, Uganda: Department of Religious Studies, Makerere University, 2000.
Mayer, Jean-François. "Field Notes: The Movement for the Restoration of the Ten Commandments of God." *Nova Religio* 5, no. 1 (October 2001): 203–210.
A Timely Message from Heaven: The End of the Present Times. Rukungiri, Uganda: The Movement for the Restoration of the Ten Commandments of God, 1991.

Movement of Spiritual Inner Awareness

The Movement of Spiritual Inner Awareness (MSIA) is a contemporary metaphysical Christian group founded by John-Roger Hinkins in 1971. MSIA is sometimes classified as "New Age," and its Sound Current practices are closely related to practices found in the Radhasoami tradition.

Hinkins, informally referred to as "J-R," was born Roger Hinkins in 1934 to a Mormon family in Rains, Utah. He received his bachelor of science degree in psychology at the University of Utah and in 1958 moved to Southern California, where he became an English teacher at Rosemead High School. In 1963, while undergoing surgery, he fell into a nine-day coma. Upon awakening, he announced that a new spiritual personality, named John, had merged with his old personality. The name John-Roger acknowledges this new transformed self.

Around this time John-Roger was a seeker exploring a variety of different spiritual teachings, including the Agasha Temple of Wisdom founded and led by Reverend Richard Zenor (1911–1978), correspondence courses of AMORC, the Ancient and Mystical Order Rosae Crucis, and Eckankar, a Sant Mat-inspired group (Introvigne 1998). He began to teach and counsel informally and, by the late 1960s, held gatherings as an independent spiritual teacher. In 1971, he formally incorporated the Movement of Spiritual Inner Awareness. He also founded a number of additional organizations out of MSIA, including Prana (now Peace) Theological Seminary and College of Philosophy (1977), Baraka Holistic Center (1977), and Insight Seminars (1978). The John-Roger Foundation was created in 1982 in order to coordinate the several programs initiated by MSIA. The Foundation also initiated the Integrity Day celebrations, an effort to promote global transformation through the enrichment and upliftment of individuals. Beginning in 1983, the Foundation held an annual Integrity Award banquet, giving awards to individuals for their achievement, until 1988.

MSIA teachings reflect a blend of traditional Asian faiths—Hinduism, Buddhism, and especially Sikhism. However, the organization regards itself as a mystical Christian group, and its literature explicitly and repeatedly asserts that "Jesus Christ is the head of the Church of the Movement of Spiritual Inner Awareness" (Lewis 2009, 240).

MSIA advocates the idea that the individual soul incarnates on the physical, material world to learn its true nature. "MSIA teaches Soul Transcendence, which is becoming aware of yourself as a Soul and as one with God, not as a theory but as a living reality. MSIA offers an approach to living that focuses on how to incorporate spirituality into your everyday life (MSIA 1999).

In common with Sant Mat groups, MSIA pictures the cosmos as composed of many different levels or planes. Originally, these levels evolved from God along a vibratory "stream" until creation reached its terminus in the physical plane. The Sant Mat tradition teaches that individuals can be linked to God's creative energy, and that this stream of energy will carry them back to God. The Mystical Traveler Consciousness—a key MSIA concept that originally manifested through John-Roger—accomplishes this link-up during initiation. Once this initial link is made, however, the individual gains its benefits through the practice of various spiritual exercises, particularly the repetition of the mantra "Hu" and the chanting of other sacred initiatory names of God.

Each individual is seen as being involved in a movement of spiritual inner awareness, of which MSIA is an outward reflection. Individuals who wish to develop a total awareness, including freedom from the cycle of reincarnation, seek the assistance of the Mystical Traveler, who is believed to exist simultaneously on all levels of consciousness in total awareness. The consciousness can teach them how to reach awareness and assists them in understanding and releasing themselves from their karmic responsibilities and is believed to have the psychic ability to read the karmic records of each individual.

Some of the several New Age healing techniques focusing on different aspects of the self have been adopted by MSIA. These include "aura balancing," which is a technique for clearing the auric (magnetic) field that exists around each individual; "innerphasings," a technique through which the individual can reach into the subconscious and bring to consciousness and remove the dysfunctional patterns learned early in life; and "polarity balancing," which releases blocks in the physical body.

What might be termed membership in MSIA is accomplished when the individual is enrolled in a series of monthly lessons, referred to as Soul Awareness Discourses. After studying the Discourses for specified periods of time, an individual may apply successively for the four formal initiations that mark a person's spiritual progress. Independently of the initiation structure, one may also become an MSIA minister. The basic MSIA gathering is the home seminar. MSIA ministers do not normally minister to congregations; rather, they are involved in some type of service work, which constitutes their ministry.

In 1978, John-Roger and Russell Bishop developed Insight Training Seminars (Insight Seminars), a program built around an intense transformational experience. "The Seminars literally guide participants into the awareness of how life can be better—for themselves and others—when they are living compassionately, making choices from the perspective of what we call their 'heart.' The process is so profound that it transforms the way they look at, and live, their lives. It creates a greater experience of loving, inner peace, health, wealth, success, happiness, and joy that becomes a template for how life can be—if they choose it" (Insight Seminars 2009). The Insight Seminars emphasize the individual's ability to move beyond self-imposed limitations. Insight became a separate organization, independent of MSIA, in 1978. Insight claims that more than one million people around the world have participated in the Seminars since their inception.

John-Roger founded the University of Santa Monica (USM), which has also developed into a separate institution that offers a Soul-Centered Graduate Curriculum through the principles and practices of Spiritual Psychology (http://www.universityofsantamonica.edu/). A second educational institution, Peace Theological Seminary and College of Philosophy (PTS), on the other hand, has become an integral part of MSIA outreach. Today, PTS is the primary setting for MSIA seminars and workshops. PTS has expanded the program, adding master's and doctoral degrees. According to its course catalogue, the purpose of PTS is "to facilitate learning the lessons of the physical and spiritual worlds. We maintain that our primary relationship is with our own Soul and we provide educational opportunities that support students in becoming more aware of the Divine in themselves. The teachings in PTS courses are very ancient, but presented in a straight forward, modern day presentation."

In 1988, the mantle of the Mystical Traveler consciousness was passed to John Morton, one of John-Roger's students. Morton has increasingly taken the primary role in MSIA events and remains the Spiritual Director of MSIA today.

As the anti-cult movement developed in the late 1970s, it paid little attention to MSIA; then a small group compared it to the more visible religious groups that had called it into existence. In 1988, the *Los Angeles Times* and *People* magazine attacked MSIA. Criticism centered on charges by former staff members that John-Roger had sexually exploited them, a charge John-Roger denied. After the issues were aired, the controversy largely died. Then in 1994, MSIA was again the subject of media attention when multimillionaire Michael Huffington ran for the U.S. Senate and it was learned that Arianna Huffington, his wife, was an MSIA member. About the same time, Peter McWilliams, an MSIA minister who had coauthored a series of popular books with John-Roger, dropped out of the movement and authored a bitter anti-MSIA book, *LIFE 102: What To Do When Your Guru Sues You*, which attracted some media attention. Shortly before his death in 2000, McWilliams appeared to have reconciled his differences with the organization. (Refer to his online letter at: http://www.life102.com/.)

As of early 2009, more than 4,000 people were studying the Soul Awareness Discourses, of which some 2,600 were in the United States.

Movement of Spiritual Inner Awareness
Peace Theological Seminary and College of
    Philosophy

3500 W. Adams Blvd.
Los Angeles, CA 90018
http://www.msia.org
http://www.pts.org

James R. Lewis

See also: Reincarnation; Sikhism/Sant Mat.

References

[Hinkins], John-Roger. *Inner Worlds of Meditation*. Los Angeles: Mandeville Press, 1997.

[Hinkins], John-Roger. *Spiritual Warrior*. Los Angeles: Mandeville Press, 1998.

[Hinkins], John-Roger, and Mark Lurie. *Interviews with John Morton and John Roger: Religious Scholars Interview the Travelers*. Los Angeles: Mandeville Press, 1999.

Insight Seminars. 2009. Insight Seminars website. http://www.insightseminars.org/.

Introvigne, Massimo. 1998. "The Origins of the Movement of Spiritual Inner Awareness (MSIA)." http://www.cesnur.org/testi/msia.htm.

Lewis, James R. 2009. "Did Jesus Die for our Karma? Christology and Atonement in a Contemporary Metaphysical Church." In *Alternative Christs*, edited by Olav Hammer. Cambridge: Cambridge University Press.

Lewis, James R. *Seeking the Light*. Los Angeles: Mandeville Press, 1997.

MSIA. *An Introduction to The Movement of Spiritual Inner Awareness*. Los Angeles: Peace Theological Seminary and College of Philosophy, 1999.

■ **Mozambique**

Mozambique is an East African country between South Africa and Tanzania. To the west it shares borders with Malawi, Zambia, and Zimbabwe. To the east its long shoreline faces the Mozambique Channel, which separates the country from Madagascar. Its 309,500 square miles of territory is home to 21,285,000 people (2008), almost all descended from various African Native peoples.

Great Mosque and beach, Mozambique. (JMN/Cover/Getty Images)

Bantu peoples began to move into what is today Mozambique in the early centuries of the Common Era. They spread through the region and developed both agriculture and mining. Then in the 10th century, a prince from Shiraz, Persia (present-day Iran), founded the city of Sofala near present-day Beira, which became a trading center through which goods moved from the interior (Zimbabwe) to the spreading Islamic culture along the African coast. The area flourished until the Portuguese arrived and destroyed it in their attempt to take over the trade. The first European to see Mozambique, Vasco da Gama (ca. 1460–1524), sailed along the coast in 1498. The Portuguese returned two years later and began the destruction of Mozambique and the Arab settlements northward up the coast.

Finally expelled from the lands to the north in the 18th century, the Portuguese in Mozambique turned to the slave trade. During the 19th century, the Portuguese ruled the coast but had little influence inland. They tried to assert their hegemony in the interior, including several failed attempts to connect Mozambique with Angola (a plan that countered British plans to connect South Africa with Egypt). In their attempt to gain authority over the interior, they gave many land grants (Portuguese: *prazos*) to Portuguese colonists, and these ultimately became virtually independent lands. Finally, between 1890 and 1920 Portugal asserted its control over both the landholders (*prazeiros*) and the various Native peoples.

Independence movements developed after World War II. A 1960 demonstration that led to the deaths of 500 people convinced many that there would be no peaceful transition. In 1962, Eduardo Mondlane (1920–1969) was able to unite several groups into the Front for the Liberation of Mozambique (FRELIMO), which in 1965 launched a civil war. The war continued until the revolution in Portugal in 1974. The independent republic of Mozambique was established the next year.

The new government began to reorganize the country along Socialist lines, and in 1977 it proclaimed Marxism-Leninism as the nation's ideology. The country was soon involved with neighboring countries, supporting Zimbabwe's fight for independence and opposing the apartheid regime in South Africa. In the 1980s South Africa aligned with dissident former-supporters of Portuguese rule, the Movement of National Resistance (RENAMO), and attacked Mozambique. The war continued through the 1980s and hundreds of thousands of people left the country.

Peace talks began under the auspices of Italy and the Roman Catholic Church. After a decade of conflict, FRELIMO and RENAMO agreed to a partial cease-fire in 1990, and finally, in October 1992, a general peace accord was signed. A UN peacekeeping force oversaw the cease-fire and the transition to multiparty elections, which took place in 1994. In the mid-1990s, more than 1.7 million refugees who had sought asylum in neighboring countries returned to Mozambique—the largest repatriation ever seen in sub-Saharan Africa.

Traditional religions still hold sway in much of rural Mozambique, especially in the northern two-thirds of the country. During the 20th century, a variety of revivalist movements appeared in response to the white culture. One prophetic group arose among the Hlengwe around 1913. It was built around belief in Mwirimi, the Supreme Being, who was believed to possess prophetic leadership. The movement included a campaign to rid the area of malevolent magic, tobacco smoke being the magical agent utilized. As the movement gained strength, the Portuguese moved to suppress it.

Islam came to Mozambique in the 10th century with the establishment of the city of Sofala. During the next centuries, the coastal region was controlled by representatives of the sultan in Zanzibar. To this day, many people who reside in the coastal area and along the Zambesi River are Muslim. In the 19th century, a new wave of Muslim belief entered the area. The Yao people, who operated as traders between Lake Malawi and the Muslim coastlands south of Zanzibar in Tanzania, converted to Islam. Today the Yao and related ethnic groups (including the Makua and the Makonde, the last hold-outs against the Portuguese pacification of the country) include some eight million people in Mozambique and neighboring Malawi and Tanzania.

Most Yao people are Sunni Muslims of the Shafaiite School, but there are also three other distinct factions of Muslims. The Sufis in Mozambique retain the Islam that was adopted at the time the Yao originally converted. They have kept many traditional rituals, over which Islamic practice has been added. They practice a form of Sufi worship called the *dhikr* (remembrance of God), which among the Yao includes a circle dance designed to produce an ecstatic state. A second group, the Sukutis (the quiet), rejected the dhikr. They are closer to the Sunnis but, like the Sufis, do not place a great emphasis on studying the Koran or on Islamic law. Finally, the Sunni community has in the last generation experienced a new wave of reform generated by teachers from Kuwait. They have emphasized orthodoxy and the study of Arabic, the Koran, and Islamic law. They reject all practices not sanctioned by the Koran.

Christianity was introduced to Mozambique by the Dominicans in 1506. They were later assisted by the Jesuits and Augustinians in building the Roman Catholic Church in Mozambique. They concentrated their efforts along the southern coast and in the Zambesi River valley. It was not until the end of the 19th century that stable work was established north of the Save River and began to penetrate inland, and in spite of the long history of Roman Catholicism, a bishopric was not established until the 20th century. The process of placing priests in all parts of the country was not completed until the 1930s. However, today, the Roman Catholic Church is the largest Christian group in Mozambique. It is organized into three archdioceses and nine dioceses.

Protestant Christianity was introduced by missionaries of the American Board of Commissioners for Foreign Missions (Congregationalists) in 1881, but the Board eventually decided to relocate its missionaries elsewhere. In the meantime, as a result of the Berlin Treaty of 1885, authorities became more open to admitting non-Catholic missionary personnel. Bishop William Taylor (1821–1902) of the Methodist Episcopal Church (now an integral part of the United Methodist Church) moved to secure the Congregationalist stations in 1889 and 1890, making them into the beachhead for a new missionary thrust. Originally attached to the Congo Mission, this work became a mission

MOZAMBIQUE

conference in 1920 and an annual conference in 1954. It remains a part of the United Methodist Church.

During the 1880s, the Episcopal Methodists were joined by missionaries from the Free Methodist Church of North America, the Methodist Church, Great Britain, and the Swiss Reformed Church. In the 1890s, Anglican missionaries of the Church of England visited the Yao people in northeast Mozambique and established work in 1893. Of the minority of Yao who have not accepted Islam today, many are Anglican.

The Anglican work is now a diocese of the Church in the Province of South Africa.

After World War I, a host of European and North American churches initiated work in Mozambique. The Free Baptist Union (based in Sweden) entered southern Mozambique in 1921. Its work grew and prospered, and in 1968 it was in place to absorb the work originally begun by the Church of Scotland in northern Mozambique. That work has passed through several hands and eventually came under the direction of the

Mozambique

Religion	Followers in 1970	Followers in 2010	% of Population	Annual % growth 2000–2010	Followers in 2025	Followers in 2050
Christians	2,610,000	11,925,000	52.7	2.92	16,819,000	23,349,000
Roman Catholics	1,553,000	5,100,000	22.5	3.71	7,550,000	11,000,000
Independents	54,300	3,050,000	13.5	1.41	4,000,000	5,000,000
Protestants	378,000	2,800,000	12.4	3.46	3,900,000	5,600,000
Ethnoreligionists	5,925,000	6,690,000	29.6	1.42	6,780,000	8,370,000
Muslims	900,000	3,870,000	17.1	3.01	5,100,000	7,000,000
Agnostics	5,000	90,000	0.4	2.07	150,000	250,000
Hindus	6,500	36,000	0.2	2.45	50,000	80,000
Atheists	0	20,000	0.1	2.19	50,000	60,000
Baha'is	1,000	3,700	0.0	2.45	5,000	7,500
Jews	200	200	0.0	2.41	200	200
Total population	**9,448,000**	**22,635,000**	**100.0**	**2.45**	**28,954,000**	**39,117,000**

South Africa General Mission (SAGM, now known as the Africa Evangelical Fellowship). The government moved to close the mission and refused entry to SAGM missionaries. Thus, the Swedish Baptists came to oversee the northern missions. The resultant United Baptist Church faced a rough period during the civil war, but in the 1990s it had an explosive growth. It is now the largest Protestant church in the country, with some 4 million adherents.

Among the larger Protestant groups as the 20th century came to a close were the Presbyterian Church of Mozambique, the Full Gospel Church of God (Igreja do Evangelho Completo de Deus), which resulted from several Pentecostal efforts, and the Jehovah's Witnesses. Protestant Christians associate with each other across denominational lines through the Christian Council of Mozambique, an affiliate of the World Council of Churches. Conservative Protestants are associated in the Associação Evangélica de Moçambique, which is related to the World Evangelical Alliance.

Neither the Portuguese colonial government nor the Marxist government of independent Mozambique was supportive of African Initiated Churches. Nonetheless, more than 100 indigenous, African-led churches and movements have appeared in Mozambique. Many, including the African Apostolic Church of Johane Marange and the Apostolic Faith Mission of South Africa, originated in neighboring countries. The African Portuguese Church was the first Mozambique-founded Christian church.

Jews began to enter Mozambique at the end of the 19th century. Though split between Sephardic and Ashkenazi, they were able to build a small synagogue in 1926. But they were never was able to hire a rabbi. Following independence in 1975, most Jews left the country. The synagogue was confiscated and turned into a warehouse, and organized Jewish life in Mozambique was abandoned. Then, in 1989, a local non-Jewish businessman organized a campaign for the return of the synagogue to the city, with the idea that it would become a monument to the former Jewish community. Instead it became the start of a revival of services among the small group of Jews remaining in the country.

During the 1990s, Mozambique became the scene of a unique adventure by the World Plan Executive Council, the organization established by the Maharishi Mehesh Yogi for the saturation of the world with Transcendental Meditation (TM). Following the general peace agreement of 1992, Dutch representatives of the council offered TM to the new Mozambique government as a means of bringing order and quelling future conflict. Initially, TM was taught to various military personnel as the start of an attempt to produce the "Maharishi Effect," which is believed to occur when a critical mass of meditators is reached, a number high enough to radiate peace and harmony throughout the nation. The country's president, Alberto Joachím Chissano (b. 1939), discovered TM in 1992 and continues to meditate twice daily. As of 2002, he remains an avid supporter of the program, which he holds up as a "non-religious" activity and hence an appropriate program for government support. He authorized the creation of the Prevention [of War] Wing of the military, and beginning in 1994, all military and police recruits were ordered to meditate for 20 minutes, twice a day. In 2001, for reasons not altogether clear, government support for TM was withdrawn, and it is no longer compulsory within the army, though a number of people continue to meditate.

J. Gordon Melton

See also: African Apostolic Church of Johane Marange; American Board of Commissioners for Foreign Missions; Apostolic Faith Mission of South Africa; Church in the Province of South Africa; Church of England; Church of Scotland; Dominicans; Free Methodist Church of North America; Jehovah's Witnesses; Methodist Church, Great Britain; Presbyterian Church of Mozambique; Roman Catholic Church; Shafiite School of Islam; United Baptist Church; United Methodist Church; World Council of Churches; World Evangelical Alliance.

References

Azevedo, Mario. *Historical Dictionary of Mozambique.* Methuen, NJ: Scarecrow Press, 2004.

Garcia, A. *Historia de Moçambique cristão.* Lourenço Marques: Diario Grafica, 1969.

Harries, Patrick. "Christianity in Black and White: The Establishment of Protestant Churches in Southern Mozambique." *Lusotopie* (1998): 317–333. http://www.lusotopie.sciences pobordeaux.fr/harries.pdf. Accessed March 1, 2009.

Ndege, George O. *Culture and Customs of Mozambique.* Westport, CT: Greenwood Press, 2006.

Thorold, Alan. "Metamorphoses of the Yao Muslims." In *Muslim Identity and Social Change in Sub-Saharan Africa,* edited by Louis Benner. Bloomington: Indiana University Press, 1993.

West, Harry M. *Kupilikula: Governance and the Invisible Realm in Mozambique.* Chicago: University of Chicago Press, 2006.

Mudras

The term *mudra* derives from a set of words in ancient India that carried ideas of authority, the imprint left from a seal, and the way of holding the fingers. The meaning evolved to designate hand gestures or positions that enhance the spoken word and convey a mystical or occult meaning. In Hindu paintings and statues, the deities are pictured with what appears to the observer with unusual or strained hand gestures, some as if a movement has been caught in the middle, at other times with fingers entwined in a complicated pattern.

Mudras are used quite commonly in Hindu *pujas*. In creating mudras, each finger has been assigned a relationship to one of the five classical elements: thumb, *agni*/fire; forefinger, *vayu*/air; middle finger, *akash*/ether; ring finger, *prithvi*/earth; little finger, *jal*/water. Mudras are further classified as Aasanyukta (single-handed mudras) or Sawyakta (double-handed).

The oft-seen abhaya, or fearlessness gesture, is a good example of an Aasanyukta mudra. It is made simply by lifting the right hand to shoulder height with the palm open and face forward. It represents benevolence, the absence of fear, and the granting of protection. The pankaj, or potus, mudra is a simple Sawyakta mudra. The two hands are brought together in such a way that the fingers are separated and pointed upward, with the two thumbs and the two little fingers touching each other. The person making the symbol is, like the lotus that is detached from the mud below it, detached from the world while in meditation. The pankaj mudra also emphasizes the fire and water elements represented by the thumb and little finger.

Within Buddhism mudras have become marks of identity of the deity being personified. Thus in statuary and paintings, the different Buddhas and bodhisattvas can often be identified, amid dozens of very similar representations, by the mudra she or he assumes. Within Vajrayana, or Esoteric, Buddhism, these mudras are symbolic of various aspects of Esoteric reality. Mudras are designed to evoke both meaning and power among those who understand their significance.

Of the many mudras, five have become central to the presentation of images of the Buddha and bodhisattvas. The dharmachakra mudra, for example, recalls

Standing Buddha statue, Penang, Malaysia, with hands showing mudras. (J. Gordon Melton)

the Buddha's first sermon at Sanath. Both hands are pictured with the thumb and forefinger touching to form a circle (the Wheel of the Dharma), and the three remaining fingers extended, to which additional meaning is ascribed. The bhumisparsha mudra recalls the Buddha's enlightenment, with the right hand touching the Earth and the left hand placed flat in the lap. The varada mudra, emphasizing the Buddha's charity and compassion, shows the left hand, palm up and fingers extended. The dhyana mudra is made with the left hand placed in the lap, a symbol of wisdom (a feminine virtue). Various symbolic objects may then be placed in the open palm. The abhaya mudra, usually pictured with a standing figure, shows the right hand raised and the palm facing outward. The left hand is at the side of the body, often with the palm also facing outward.

In Esoteric Buddhism, the five Dhyani Buddhas are central deity figures. They are not thought of as historical figures who have reached enlightenment, but are transcendent beings symbolizing universal principles. Each Dhyani Buddha is associated with a spectrum of attributes and symbols. Each one, for example, represents one of the five basic wisdoms, and thus each one can transform one of the five deadly poisons into one of the wisdoms. When pictured in Tibetan iconography, the five Buddhas are commonly shown sitting cross-legged in the meditative position and at first glance appear to be exactly the same, especially in statuary where the colors that often distinguish the five Buddhas have been lost. What really distinguishes the five Buddhas, however, are the mudras; each one is always shown with one of the basic mudras traditionally identified with the wisdom they embody. The Buddhas and the mudras they demonstrate are: Vairocana, dharmachakra or wheel-turning mudra; Akshobhya, bhumisparsa or witness mudra; Ratnasambhava, varada or charity mudra; Amitabha, dhyana mudra; and Amogasiddha, abhaya or fearlessness mudra. The most ubiquitous bodhisattva in Asia is Guan Yin (aka Avalokitesvara) who will be shown with a range of mudras or their variations. In one form of the 1,000-armed Guan Yin, each hand is arranged to show a different mudra.

Those who understand mudras will recognize that the Zen Buddhist practitioner while engaged in *zazen,* or sitting meditation, places her or his hands in what is known as the cosmic mudra. One hand rests on top of the other, with palms open and up. The joints of the two middle fingers rest on top of the other, and the tips of the thumbs are touching lightly.

In Esoteric Buddhist practice, unique hand positions indicate to the faithful the nature and the function of the deities, Buddhas, and bodhisattvas on which they gaze. Mudras thus symbolize divine manifestation. Teachers use them in rituals and spiritual exercises as aids to the invocation of the deity. When understood in its magical context, the use of mudras by the practitioner facilitates the flow of the invisible forces within the earthly sphere. Some hypothesize that the sequence of hand postures that manifest in ritual contexts may stand behind their entry and evolution in Indian Classical dance. Esoteric Buddhists see mudras as physical movements that alter perception and deepen awareness. Their use can assist the awakening of the *chakras* (energy centers believed to exist along the spine) and the flow of *kundalini* (the energy that travels along the spine and accompanying enlightenment).

J. Gordon Melton

See also: Bodhisattva; Guan Yin's Birthday; Meditation; Sarnath; Zen Buddhism.

References

Bunce, Frederick W. *Mudras in Buddhist and Hindu Practices: An Iconographic Consideration.* New Delhi: D. K. Printworld. Pvt. Ltd., 2005.

Chandra, Lokesh. *Mudras in Japan.* Vedam eBooks, 2001.

De Kleen, Tyra. *Mudras: The Ritual Hand-poses of the Buddha Priests and the Shiva Priests of Bali.* 1924; rpt.: New Hyde Park, NY: University Books, 1970.

Hirschi, Gertrud. *Mudras: Yoga in Your Hands.* Weirs Bach, ME: Weiser Books, 2000.

"Mudra." Mystical Myth. http://www.bellaterreno.com/art/a_religion/buddhism/buddhist_mudra.aspx. Accessed May 15, 2009.

Saunders, E. Dale. *Mudra: A Study of Symbolic Gestures in Japanese Buddhist Sculpture.* London: Routledge & Kegan Paul, 1960.

Thrungpa, Chogyam. *Mudras.* Berkeley: Shambhala, 1972.

The prophet Muhammad is depicted in this painting from the Tomb of Harun in Isfahan, Iran. (Art Directors.co.uk/Ark Religion.com/StockphotoPro)

Muhammad

ca. 570–632

The Prophet of Islam, Muhammad, is regarded by Muslims as the final prophet bringing God's most complete revelation to humanity. His life was apparently full of military as well as spiritual success, and he established Islam on solid foundations from which it was to rapidly become one of the world's major religions. His life and character are taken to be exemplary for Muslims, although he is not in any way regarded as anything more than a human being. It is a central claim of Islam that he did not write the Koran, but merely received it and passed on that revelation to the local community in Arabia, from which it spread throughout the world. He was also a remarkably astute political leader, creating a highly effective military force and a strong society in an environment in which initially he experienced much hostility.

Muhammad is generally accepted to have been born around 570 CE, to a mother who died soon after his birth; his father had died earlier. He was raised by a grandfather and later his uncle Abu Talib. In the traditional Muslim accounts he is said to have visited Syria twice as a trader with Abu Talib and his commercial background was also emphasized by his marriage around 595 to Khadija, a female trader. The archangel Gabriel (Jibril) is said to have visited Muhammad on Mount Hira near Mecca on the 17th night of Ramadan in 610 and sura 96 is taken to have been the very first revelation from God. He is described in the Koran as illiterate and so should never be accused of having written the Book. He did not immediately begin to communicate God's message to the Meccans; there was a pause of three years, and the early reception was not favorable, although he did acquire some supporters.

The attack on idolatry struck at the heart of the main business of Mecca, which was to support the tribal and religious practices in the area that were thoroughly polytheistic at that time. Muhammad came in for much abuse. In 620 we are told that Muhammad was taken to Jerusalem by Jibril on the back of Buraq, a winged horse, and from there was taken up into the heavens where he met some earlier messengers. Two years later he left for Yathrib, later called Medina, which was less hostile than his hometown, and here he forged the first state based on Islam, increasingly distinguishing itself from Judaism and Christianity as the local Jews and Christians apparently resisted the message of Islam. For eight years Muhammad was involved in protracted military campaigns with the Meccans, and he seems to have been an impressive military commander, not unwilling on occasion such as the War of the Trench in 626–627 to take ruthless measures against his opponents. He also conducted raids to the north before returning in triumph to Mecca in 628 and capturing territory in the wider area also.

In 629 Muhammad made a pilgrimage to Mecca and appears to have won over his clan, taking control of the city the next year and destroying the idols in the Kaaba, the main shrine in Mecca. His final pilgrimage was in 632, after which he returned to Medina, where he died and was buried. The evidence for the historical account that has been given here is entirely based on Islamic sources, and the *hadith*, the reported statements of the Prophet and his Companions, widen this account to include various miracles and extraordinary events that are absent from the Koran, the revelation that Muhammad was to deliver to the Arabs and ultimately to the whole of humanity. In the Koran he is named at the seal of the prophets (33:40), as the last prophet, the heir of Jesus (61:6) and Moses (46:10), and the symbol of divine mercy (9:61 and in many other places).

His character is said to have been mild and patient, but he does not appear in the Koran to be perfect, as later on his followers took him to be. Some of the references to him in the Koran seem to describe arrangements designed for his convenience, as when he is allowed to marry women who would ordinarily not be available to him or when people are told not to visit him before mealtimes and are advised not to linger afterward. Muhammad has served as the great exemplar of how Muslims should live, down to how they should perform their ablutions, what they should eat, how their beards should be cut, and the statements he made that have been collected in the hadith have acquired a powerful status in many forms of Islam. In Shia Islam the idea that the family of the Prophet has a special status became canonical, leading to the divide between those who believed that the ruler could be anyone selected by appropriate processes, the Sunni, while the party of Ali, shi-at Ali, argued that only someone related to the Prophet and his descendants could legitimately rule, instancing first Ali, his cousin and son-in-law.

In just the same way that Muslims have a very high regard for the Prophet, the detractors of Islam are critical of him, citing his apparent enthusiasm for conflict and conquest, and pouring scorn on his claims to have received a revelation. In earlier centuries he was often depicted as especially evil, or mad, and in later centuries criticized for his heavy involvement in military campaigns and bloodshed, by contrast with Jesus. It is difficult to know precisely what form his life took since there is no evidence apart from what is found in the religious accounts provided in Islamic tradition. He certainly appears to have been a forceful political leader, while at the same time capable of energizing a society that was wedded to ideas of which he disapproved.

Oliver Leaman

See also: Ali ibn Abi Talib; Jerusalem; Masjid al-Ḥaram, Al-; Mecca; Medina; Moses; Shia Islam.

References

Cook, Michael. *Muhammad.* New York: Oxford University Press, 1983.

Motzki, Harald, ed. *The Biography of Muhammad: The Issue of the Sources.* Leiden: E. J. Brill, 2000.

Peters, F. E. *Muhammad and the Origins of Islam.* Albany: State University of New York Press, 1994.

Ramadan, Tariq. *In the Footsteps of the Prophet: Lessons from the Life of Muhammad.* New York: Oxford University Press, 2007.

Rubin, Uri., ed. *The Life of Muhammad.* Aldershot: Ashgate, 1998.

Watt, W. Montgomery. *Muhammad: Prophet and Statesman.* London: Oxford University Press, 1961.

Mülheim Association of Christian Fellowships

The Mülheim Association of Christian Fellowships (Mülheim Bewegung), the original Pentecostal association in Germany, traces its beginning to a series of meetings held in Kassel in 1907. The meetings were facilitated by two women who had come to Germany from a Pentecostal revival in Norway, led by Thomas B. Barratt (1862–1940). The revival centered on participants' reception of the Pentecostal baptism of the Holy Spirit and the manifestation of the gifts of the Spirit (as mentioned in 1 Corinthians 12), such as prophecy, healing, and speaking in tongues. The local evangelical (Lutheran) leader, Heinrich Dallmeyer, at first tried to work with the group but later rejected the manifestation of the gifts as diabolical. Observation of the Pentecostals over the next year led a number of other evangelical leaders to reject the new movement as well, some refusing to accept the highly charged emotional nature of the meetings, others focusing on theological differences.

One major concern was the "Methodist" theology assumed by the Pentecostals, who taught an approach to salvation that included three stages: justification (the making right of a believer before God), followed by sanctification (the believer becoming holy in the sight of God), and the baptism of the Holy Spirit. Lutheran theology assumes that justification and sanctification occur at the moment of faith, and Lutherans had no theology to account for a subsequent baptism of the Holy Spirit. In 1909 a group of evangelical leaders issued the Berlin Declaration, a strong denunciation of the new movement.

The declaration slowed but did not stop the spread of Pentecostalism, and Free church congregations arose over the next years. Among the ministers who emerged as leaders were Eugen Edel, Jonathan Paul, Emil Humburg, and A. Frieme. Though the churches originally attempted to remain a spiritual movement that influenced life in both the established church and the various Protestant Free churches, many of the churches came together in 1913 to form the Mülheim Association, which in stages emerged as a separate church body.

The Mülheim Association is not only the oldest but also the largest Pentecostal body in Germany. It also developed somewhat independently of the Pentecostal movement in the English-speaking world. For example, it rejected one of the major doctrinal foundations of Pentecostalism, which tied the baptism of the Holy Spirit to the visible evidence of speaking in tongues. The movement was also open to contemporary approaches to biblical scholarship and tried to reconcile with Reformation theology. As such, prior to the Charismatic revival in the 1970s, it often found itself at odds with the larger international movement.

The Mülheim Association survived the Nazi era and the division of Germany following the war. Today it is headquartered in Niedenstein, Germany. The Association has been in decline, and by the end of the 1990s it reported 3,180 members.

Mülheim Association of Christian Fellowships
Hauptstrasse 36, D-34305
Niedenstein
Germany

J. Gordon Melton

See also: Evangelical Church in Germany; Pentecostalism.

References

Burgess, Stanley M., and Eduard van der Maas, eds. *The New International Dictionary of Pentecostal and Charismatic Movements.* Grand Rapids, MI: Zondervan, 2002.

Eggenberger, Oswald. *Die Kirchen Sondergruppen und religiösen Vereinigungen.* Zürich: Theologischer Verlag, 1994.

Hollenweger, Walter J. *Pentecostals: The Charismatic Movement in the Church.* Minneapolis, MN: Augsburg, 1972.

Muridîyya

Muridîyya is the Arabic version of the name of a Muslim brotherhood or Sufi order (Arabic: *tariqa*) that was

Muslim pilgrims gather at the Grand Mosque of Touba in Senegal for prayers. Thousands of disciples of the Muslim Muridîyya brotherhood visit Touba as part of the annual Magal pilgrimage in the holiest week of the Muridîyya calendar, commemorating the 110th anniversary of the departure into exile of their spiritual guide Sheikh Ahmadou Bamba. (© Pierre Holtz/epa/Corbis)

founded toward the end of the 19th century by the charismatic Sheikh Ahmadou Bamba (ca. 1853–1927) in Senegal (West Africa). In French, the official language of Senegal, the order is known as Mouridisme, and in English the followers of this Sufi order are referred to as Mourides. The basic meaning of the Arabic word *murid* from which these terms are derived is *aspirant*, that is, one who seeks after progress on the mystical path of Islam.

Probably no Muslim community in sub-Saharan Africa has been the subject of more attention, both academic and non-academic, than the Muridîyya. This seems to be one of the reasons why their importance

and influence tend to be exaggerated. Although reliable statistical data is not available, it is likely that about one-third of the Muslim population in Senegal can be counted as followers of Bamba. We can thus estimate the membership of the Muridîyya at about three million in 2001. Outside Senegal, the Muridiyya has recruited few followers. However, Senegalese Mourides can now be found in many francophone African countries and in countries of the Middle East. Since the 1970s, they have established important diaspora communities in Europe, particularly in Italy, France, and Spain, and in the United States, most notably in New York and Chicago. The influence of Ahmadou Bamba has been further extended by the efforts of additional teachers such as Sheikh Abdoulaye Dieye, who founded the independent Islamic Society of Mourids of Reunion, from whence he has built an international following.

The life of Ahmadou Bamba is surrounded by countless legends that remain tremendously popular among Senegalese Muslims. Some of these legends have found their way into modern Senegalese literature, popular music, and arts such as glass painting. Bamba can in fact be described as a national saint of Senegal, and his portrait can be seen on the walls of shops and private houses all over the country. It is possible to distinguish four phases in the development of the Muridîyya: the founding years (ca. 1880–1912), the transition from rejection to acceptance of colonial rule (1912–1927), the cooperation with two successive political regimes and the expansion of peanut cultivation (1927–1970), and finally, the shift from agriculture to modern business and the establishment of diaspora communities around the world (ca. 1970 to the present).

Bamba emerged as a religious leader after the death in 1882 of his father—a religious scholar, teacher, and advisor to a local ruler. In 1887, he founded the village of Touba in the region of Baol, which later became the capital of the Muridîyya. At that time, he had not yet established his own Sufi order, but practiced the recitation formulas (*awrad*, singular *wird*) of other orders, such as the Qadiriyya, the Shadhiliyya, and the Tijaniyya.

Around the same time, the French succeeded in destroying the local kingdoms of the Wolof, the primary ethnic group in Senegal. In this situation, Bamba's mysticism became the rallying point for a rapidly increasing number of followers, mostly of Wolof origin. As members of the former ruling elite and the warrior class were part of Bamba's entourage, Bamba himself came under suspicion of being the possible leader of an anti-colonial revolt. As a result, he was exiled in 1895. Bamba spent seven years in Gabon and, after a brief stay in Senegal, another four years in Mauritania. He returned to Senegal in 1907.

The exile of Bamba did not lead to a decrease in the number of his followers, as the French had hoped. Nevertheless, from about 1910 on, relations between the Muridîyya and the French gradually improved. Bamba repeatedly declared his loyalty to the French cause and urged his followers to obey the orders of the administration. During World War I, Bamba recruited 500 soldiers from among his disciples, and these were sent to Europe in order to fight for the French army. However, Bamba was never permitted to live in Touba again. When he died in 1927, the administration gave permission to bury him at Touba, where his tomb became the destination of an annual pilgrimage.

After the death of Ahmadou Bamba, his eldest son took over the leadership of the Muridîyya, at that time numbering about 100,000 people, most of them Wolof. Up to the present day, the brotherhood's supreme leader (called the Khalife général) is one of Bamba's two surviving sons. Under this new leadership the Muridîyya continued to expand rapidly into the so-called new territories, that is, into hitherto uncultivated areas of the Senegalese hinterland. New rural communities were established in these areas, and the members of these communities committed themselves to the cultivation of peanuts. The severe drought in the early 1970s and the later dramatic drop in the price of peanuts occasioned the move of many followers into the urban centers of Senegal, where they set up business enterprises in the modern sector, some migrating to Europe and the United States.

The doctrine of the Muridîyya does not essentially deviate from what might be called standard Islamic mysticism, although a difference has been noted between the "official" doctrine and its popular interpretation. The former stresses compliance with the Islamic norms related to prayer, fasting, and so on and emphasizes the necessity of a "spiritual education" that in turn is based on the disciple's total obedience

and submission to his master. The Muridîyya also assign a central role to the Prophet Muhammad. On several occasions, Bamba claimed to have had an encounter with the Prophet, who Sufis usually believe can still appear and talk to whomever he wishes. According to Muridîyya hagiography, the first of these encounters took place in 1893. After that time, Bamba stopped practicing the liturgy (wird) of the other Sufi orders and began to present himself as the "servant of the Prophet." For the Muridîyya, this encounter meant that Bamba had acceded to the position of the supreme Muslim saint (*qutb al-aqtâb*).

In popular imagery, the position of Bamba as the supreme qutb gave rise to the belief that Bamba and his living representatives can guarantee success in this world and salvation in the hereafter. Moreover, the members of a group within the Muridîyya known as Baye Fall hold that they will go to paradise only on account of their total commitment to their spiritual master, without needing to comply with the ritual norms of Islam. This commitment usually takes the form of work for a Muridîyya leader, be it in the peanut fields or in a modern profession. The Baye Fall justify their conduct by pointing to the alleged sayings of Bamba, including "Work is prayer," and "Work for me, then I will pray for you." Indeed, the extraordinary spiritual value attached to physical work—not only by the Baye Fall, but also by many other followers—is perhaps the most peculiar feature of Muridîyya doctrine.

A spectacular event in Muridîyya community life is the annual pilgrimage (*magal*) to the Holy City of Touba, which is a kind of state within a state and during the 1990s developed into one of the biggest Senegalese cities. In recent years, the magal has brought together some two million people—including some of Senegal's most prominent politicians—who exalt the memory of Ahmadou Bamba. Another distinctive practice of the Muridîyya relates to ritual: the Mourides regularly meet in groups to recite Bamba's religious poetry, known as *khassaites* (from Arabic *qasa'id*, singular *qasida*, poem). Some of this poetry is in praise of the Prophet Muhammad, and other poems can be described as vulgarizations of mystical teachings.

Muridîyya Headquarters
c/o Son Excellence le Khalife Général de Mourides

Touba

Senegal

http://touba-internet.com/top_contacts.htm (in
    French)

http://www.toubaislam.org/ (in French and English)

Ruediger Seesemann

See also: Islam; Muhammad; Shadhiliyya Sufi Order;
Sufism; Tijaniyya.

References

Bamba, Ahmadou. *Dîwân fî l-'ulûm ad-dîniyya.
    Recueil des poèmes en sciences religieuses.*
    2 vols. Casablanca: Dar el Kitab, 1989.

Bamba, Ahmadou. *Les itinéraires du Paradis.* Trans.
    Serigne Sam Mbaye. Casablanca: Dar el Kitab,
    1984.

Cruise O'Brien, Donal B. *The Mourides of Senegal.*
    Oxford: Clarendon, 1971.

Dieye, Sheikh Abdoulaye. *Ocean of Wisdom.* St.
    Louis, Réunion: Islamic Society of Mourids of
    Reunion, n.d.

Dumont, Fernand. *La pensée religieuse d'Amadou
    Bamba.* Dakar: Nouvelles Editions Africaines,
    1975.

Mbacké, Serigne Bachir. *Les bienfaits de l'Eternel
    ou la biographie de Cheick Ahmadou Bamba
    Mbacké.* Trans. Khadim Mbacké. Dakar: Imp.
    Saint-Paul, 1995.

Schmidt di Friedberg, Ottavia. *Islam, solidarietà e
    lavoro. I muridi senegalesi in Italia.* Torino, Italy:
    Ed. della Fondazione Giovanni Agnelli, 1994.

Seeseman, Rüdiger. *Ahmadu Bamba und die Entste-
    hung der Murîdîya.* Berlin: Schwarz, 1993.

Musama Disco Christo Church

The Musama Disco Christo Church (MDCC) is one
of the spiritual churches in Ghana. In 1919 Prophet
Jemisemiham Jehu-Appiah (1893–1948), born Joseph
W. E. Appiah, a former Methodist preacher and
schoolteacher, had a vision of three angels who sent
him on a mission. He was filled with the Spirit and
began to perform miracles, establishing the Faith
Society with the assistance of a woman named Abena
Bawa, whom he renamed Hannah Barnes. This prayer
and Bible study group within Methodism became distinguished by its practice of prophecy, healing, and
speaking in tongues. In 1922 the group's members
were dismissed from the Methodist Church, Ghana,
for alleged "occult practices."

Appiah and Barnes then founded the Musama
Disco Christo Church (Army of the Cross of Christ), a
name given by heavenly revelation. They established
the holy city of Mozano (my [God's] town), which
Appiah was given by the local chief to develop his
own settlement. Appiah based his complex church
organization on the traditional Fanti court and became
the Akaboha I. Hannah Barnes, the Akatitibi (queen
mother), was taken up into heaven and given instructions, including the revelation that she would marry
Akaboha I, which she did after the prophet received a
similar revelation. The movement spread and Akaboha
I gave new heavenly names—each one unique and
never repeated—to the thousands who joined, a practice that continues today. Members speak a special language in greeting and wear distinctive copper rings and
crosses. Akaboha I died in 1948 and was succeeded by
his son Matapoly Moses Jehu-Appiah (1924–1972),
who was credited with a miraculous birth and became
Akaboha II. In 1951 a new holy city, New Mozano,
was established.

The MDCC is noted for its ban on ancestor rituals
and its use of medicines. It has an elaborate system of
angels, whose names are to be mentioned in prayer.
The MDCC has complex rituals, involving several sacred objects, including an ark of the covenant in a holy
shrine that only the Akaboha and senior ministers can
enter to offer prayers and make petitions. The church
has other sacred places and fast days, and its rituals
involve sacrificial animals, candles, incense, rosaries,
and elaborate ceremonial gowns. Healing rituals include the use of anointing oil and holy water. The office of the Akaboha, who is also called the General
Head Prophet, is hereditary in the Jehu-Appiah family,
and the Akaboha has both spiritual and political duties.
On the death of Akaboha II in 1972, his eldest son
Prophet Miritaiah Jonah Jehu-Appiah became Akaboha III. Another son of Akaboha II, Jerisdan Jehu-
Appiah, has established the MDCC in Britain.

The MDCC, together with the Twelve Apostles
and the African Faith Tabernacle, are the largest of the

spiritual churches in Ghana, with about 125,000 affiliates each in 1990.

Musama Disco Christo Church
c/o Mozano
PO Box 11
Gomoa Eshiem
Ghana

Allan H. Anderson

See also: Methodist Church, Ghana.

References

Ayegboyin, Deji, and S. Ademola Ishola. *African Indigenous Churches: An Historical Perspective.* Lagos, Nigeria: Greater Heights Publications, 1997.

Bakta, G. C. *Prophetism in Ghana: A Study of Some 'Spiritual' Churches.* London: SCM, 1962.

Jehu-Appiah, Jemisemiham. *The History of the Musama Disco Christo Church.* Koforidua, Ghana: Fanzar Press, 1939. Trans. Jerisdan H. Jehu-Appiah, 1998.

Muslim Brotherhood

The Muslim Brotherhood, al-Ikhwan al-Moslemoon, is one of the most important movements of contemporary Islamism, the revival of ultraconservative Islam with the aim of re-creating governments ruled by Islamic law throughout the Middle East. The Brotherhood was founded as a youth movement in 1928 in Egypt. Its founder, Hassan al-Banna (1906–1949), was a Muslim cleric concerned about the current drift of the Islamic public away from what he saw as Orthodox belief and practice, and he wanted to woo the next generation to the traditional Muslim way as defined in the Koran, the Muslim holy book, and the *hadith*, the accounts of the Prophet Muhammad and his companions. Both are considered the authorities for the formation of a Muslim lifestyle.

The call for a return to the Koran appealed to many Muslims, and the Brotherhood built a large base nationally. In the 1930s, however, it began to focus more clearly on political issues, in part occasioned by the pullout of British forces from Palestine and the resulting conflict between Jewish settlers, many advocating a Jewish homeland, and Muslim Palestinians. The Brotherhood openly favored the Palestinian cause. The situation in Palestine called attention to the weakness of the Egyptian government, which was heavily influenced by Great Britain.

By the end of the 1930s, al-Banna had outlined a program for the Brotherhood summarized in "The Twenty Principles for Understanding Islam," which was included in his book *The Message of the Teachings.* According to al-Banna, Islam speaks to all of the spheres of life; from personal conduct to the running of government and the business world, the basics are plainly laid out in the Koran and hadith. Recognition of Allah's existence is the primary attribute of the Muslim. Everything that has been introduced into the community that is without a base in the Koran or hadith should be abandoned, especially the popular practices of folk magic. Further, the divisions of the four Sunni legal schools are considered relatively unimportant, and wasting time on minor legal matters should be discontinued. And, most important, from belief comes action, for although good intentions are important, they must generate righteous deeds.

As part of its program, the Brotherhood became involved on a more clandestine level in the conflict between Palestinians and the new Jewish settlements in Palestine that escalated after the formation of the nation of Israel. In 1948 members of the Brotherhood joined the forces that attempted to block Israel's stabilization. Meanwhile, in Egypt, it attempted to change the government by assassinating various officials, including one prime minister. The violence in Egypt came back on the Brotherhood in 1949 when al-Banna was himself assassinated.

The death of al-Banna set the context for the rise of Sayyid Qutb (1906–1966). Qutb was in the United States when al-Banna was killed, but upon his return to Egypt he devoted his life to the Brotherhood cause, having integrated the ideas of al-Banna with those of Indian Muslim leader Sayyid Abul A'la Mawdudi (1903–1979), founder of Jamaat-e-Islam. Mawdudi had projected the ideal image of a state administered by Muslims who adhere to the Koran and hadith and who would enforce Islamic law upon the land. Likewise,

Muslim Brotherhood leaders mark the centenary of Imam Hassan al-Banna. Banna founded the Muslim Brotherhood movement in Egypt in 1928. (© Jamal Nasrallah/epa/ Corbis)

Qutb looked for nothing less than a total reformation of Egyptian government and society.

Qutb became the chief editor of the Muslim Brotherhood's periodical and authored the first books that represented this new perspective, built around al-Banna's theme of Islam as a complete way of life. In 1954, Gamal Abd an-Nasser (1918–1970) led the coup that overthrew the Egyptian government, but rather than move toward an Islamic regime, he declared a Socialist and nationalist government. He also had been the victim of a failed assassination attempt by the Brotherhood, and soon after assuming the presidency he moved to crush them. He was additionally motivated by the fact that the Brotherhood was the one significant political force that could oppose his plans

for a new Egypt. Included in the mass arrests that ensued was Qutb, who would spend the next decade in jail. While in jail, he penned his major work, published soon after he was released. In *Ma'alim fi al-tariq* (later translated into English as *Milestones*), he condemned the Nasser government as essentially un-Islamic and laid the foundation for the broad program of reform since advocated by the Brotherhood. Based upon his reading of the book, Nasser again moved against the surviving remnants of the Brotherhood. The top leaders, including Qutb, were arrested and executed.

In *Milestones*, Qutb explained the need for Muslim opposition to Western decadence, symbolized most clearly in the West's moral turpitude, its merchandising of women and sex, and its racism. One sign of Egypt's problem, he wrote, was the influx of Western degeneracy. More important, Qutb merged Mawdudi's call for an Islamic revolution with a Leninist approach, calling for an Islamic vanguard to organize and overthrow the un-Islamic political powers. Although stopping short of explicitly calling for the use of force and violence to implement his program, he provided a platform by which the use of violence could be justified.

In Egypt, the presidency of Anwar Sadat (1971–1981) created hope. He released all the remaining Brotherhood prisoners and promised to implement Islamic law in Egypt. The Brotherhood in turn pledged to renounce violence. Sadat's public movement away from many of Nasser's policies somewhat concealed his own attempt to create a middle ground between the visions for Egypt of Nasser, on the one hand, and of Qutb, on the other. The Brotherhood's support of Sadat ended with the Camp David Accords and peace with Israel in 1979. A variety of militant factions emerged, including one named Islamic Jihad, accused of Sadat's assassination two years later.

Eventually, after renouncing violence, the Brotherhood was allowed to become active again as a popular religious movement. It also integrated itself into the Egyptian government as a conservative Islamic political party. Although the writings of al-Banna and Qutb continue to inspire its members, the elements of its most radical past appear to have been largely inherited by other newer groups, not the least of which is al-Qaeda, the movement led by Saudi Arabian terrorist Osama bin Laden (b. 1957). Bin Laden's primary contact with the Brotherhood has come from his association with leaders of the Islamic Jihad, including Ayman Al-Zawahiri, who sits on al-Qaeda's Majlis-e Shura (consultative council), and other leaders like Abd al-Salam Faraj and Sheikh Omar Abdel Rahman, who contributed substantially to the Islamic perspective that bin Laden has come to hold, which legitimizes terrorist activity. Through the 1980s, Rahman carried the Brotherhood's banner, calling for an Egyptian state ruled by Islamic law. Under government pressure, he left Egypt and relocated to the United States. He is now in a U.S. prison after being convicted of charges related to the 1993 bombing of the World Trade Center.

In 1987 the Brotherhood supported the merger of several Egyptian political parties to form the Labour Islamic Alliance. Members of the Brotherhood won more than half of the Alliance's 60 seats in the national legislature, the People's Assembly, which has more than 400 members. However, in 1995, the Hosni Mubarak government again moved against the group on the grounds that it gave support to violence-prone militants. The government closed Brotherhood offices and confiscated its assets. In 1999, 20 of its most senior leaders were arrested, and as the 21st century begins its public presence in Egypt has come to an end.

At the same time, the Brotherhood claims to exist in more than 70 countries. People sympathetic to the Brotherhood in England maintain a website, http://www.ikhwanweb.com/. In other Middle Eastern countries, it has had very different histories. It has been most successful in Jordan, where since 1989 it has developed a political party, the Islamic Action Front, and has been very active in national politics under its spiritual leader Abdul Majeed Thneibat. The Syrian branch, on the other hand, was brutally suppressed by the Syrian army following its involvement in an insurrection in 1982. Some of its members were finally released from prison as part of the celebration of the Syrian president's 25th anniversary in power, but the group remains marginalized and suspect.

J. Gordon Melton

See also: Islamism; Jamaat-e-Islam; Muhammad.

References

Esposito, John, ed. *Voice of the Resurgent Islam.* New York: Oxford University Press, 1983.

Lia, Brymjar. *The Society of the Muslim Brothers in Egypt: The Rise of an Islamic Mass Movement, 1928–1942.* Reading, UK: Ithaca Press, 1998.

Moussalli, Ahmad S. *Radical Islamic Fundamentalism: The Ideological and Political Discourse of Sayyd Qutb.* Syracuse, NY: University of Syracuse Press, 1994.

Qutb, Sayyid. *Milestones.* Beirut, Lebanon: The Holy Koran Publishing House, 1978.

Wiktorowicz, Quintan. *The Management of Islamic Activism: Salafis, the Muslim Brotherhood, and State Power in Jordan.* Albany: State University of New York Press, 2001.

Muslim World League

The Muslim World League was founded in 1962 as a relief organization working in several predominantly Muslim countries. However, over the years a secondary goal, that of advancing Muslim unity internationally, has come to dominate its program. The League has also devoted considerable time and energy to promoting Islam throughout the world and to defending Muslims, especially in those countries in which they are a minority.

The Muslim World League has its headquarters in Mecca, Saudi Arabia, in a building given by King Fahd bin Abdul Aziz (1923–2005), and the Saudi government continues to support the work of the League financially. That work is guided by a Constituent Council, composed of 62 members—all prominent scholars and thinkers from throughout the Muslim world. The executive branch of the Council, the Secretariat-General, is charged with implementing the Council's policies. The World Supreme Council of Mosques consists of 20 members representing various Muslim peoples and minority groups plus 30 additional members who seek the restoration of the mosque's role to what it was during the early days of Islam. The World Supreme Council also strives to gain freedom to propagate Islam in various countries of the world and to preserve Muslim religious endowments (charitable funds). The Islamic Jurisprudence Council is a group of scholars and jurists who study Islamic problems and attempt to suggest solutions based upon their study of the Koran, the Sunna, and the consensus of the Muslim scholarly community.

Among the more interesting structures associated with the League is the Commission on Scientific Signs in the Holy Qur'an and Sunna, which was suggested by the World Supreme Council of Mosques. This commission is a body of Islamic scholars who investigate and circulate information on the scientific and natural phenomena discussed in the Koran and Sunna in the light of modern science.

The League's headquarters and several of its national chapters sponsor websites. It has opened offices in more than 30 countries around the world, including both those in which Muslims predominate and those in which they are a minority. It publishes the weekly *World Muslim League Journal*.

Muslim World League
PO Box 537
Makkah al-Mukarramah (Mecca)
Saudi Arabia
http://www.themwl.org/

Gary Burlington

See also: Islam; World Muslim Congress.

Reference
Waines, David. *An Introduction to Islam*. Cambridge: Cambridge University Press, 1995.

Mutima Walowa Wa Makumbi

Emilio Mulolani Chishimba (b. ca. 1921), a Zambian of Bemba ethnicity, founded the movement known as Mutima Walowa Wa Makumbi (Sweet Heart of the Clouds) in 1951. *Sweet Heart* represents the mystical experience of God available to believers through Chishimba. *Clouds* is a double reference to the barren spirituality of Europeans (that is, white, rainless clouds practicing a male-focused Christianity) in contrast to the fecund spirituality of Africans (that is, black, rain-bearing clouds practicing a balanced male/female Christianity).

In 1950, 14 years before Zambian independence, Chishimba, a Roman Catholic lay leader, received a revelation from the Virgin Mary. Her message, which revealed the selection of Chishimba as her representative on Earth, upheld God's androgynous nature and announced the Virgin's status as savior for Africa and her seniority over Jesus—revelator of God's male aspect and savior of Europeans—as well as the elevation of Africans over Europeans in world spiritual leadership. Chishimba rejected the bishops' authority, substituted a traditional Bemba meal for the Eucharist, and replaced gendered congregational seating with mixed-gender seating. He encouraged overnight worship gatherings, egalitarian relations between the sexes, and fasting leading to direct encounters with God. The Mutimas separated from the Roman Catholic Church in 1958.

Chishimba taught that a true relationship with God restores the innocence of Eden. He therefore promoted nude baptism. His church supported Simon Kapwepwe's (1922–1980) political message of African isolationism against the internationalism of Dr. Kenneth Kaunda's (b. 1924) postcolonial government. As a result of public outrage over nudity and government fears of internal stability, Chishimba's church was banned in the 1970s; believers were arrested and many followers defected. Chishimba dropped nude baptism but continues to teach its validity in principle. The church is still illegal in Zambia.

The story of Chishimba's birth is a paradigm through which he understands the Bible and the relationship between Africans and Europeans. Chishimba's mother, Chilufya, married a European named Stuart and gave birth to two children. Abandoned by her husband, Chilufya then married a Bemba, by whom Chishimba was born about 1921. Later Chilufya returned to Stuart. Chishimba was given to foster parents because Stuart threatened to drown him.

As Chishimba points out, the story of Rebekah's twins (Genesis 25 and 27) parallels his own. Chilufya, like Rebekah, gave birth to children representing two nations. The biblical prediction that the elder sibling would serve the younger supports the idea that Chishimba must usurp the spiritual position of the pope, while Africa must become the epicenter of Christianity. Jesus' words—"The first will be last" (Luke 13:30)—further confirm this view.

The lunar calendar regulates Mutima holy days. Believers consider the seventh day holy. Worship is influenced by the Catholic Mass but venerates the female aspect of God manifested in Mary. Vegetarianism, prayer, and fasting are encouraged. Accepting church teaching, adherence to the Mutima ethical code, and suffering to liberate androgynous souls from gendered bodies all produce salvation. Chishimba is revered as Guide and Parent in whom the female aspect of God resides. He is the final religious authority and the source of all church liturgy.

A laity and celibate clergy comprise the church. The highest clerical rank is that of Apostle, a position open to women. Other church ranks are Disciple, some of whom are celibate while others lead a lay life and may marry more than one wife; Servant, a lay rank with authority over mundane issues at the local level; and Freed One, members without rank. Clergy live in rural and urban communes known as Queen's Villages and are supported by their own labors, lay contributions, and church-managed businesses. The church is administered hierarchically at the national, provincial, and local levels.

The Mutima Church is confined to Zambia and its membership numbers are unknown. Hugo Hinfelaar (1994) estimates the number at 5,000, but church leaders claim the number to be 50,000 to 100,000.

Gary Burlington

See also: Mary, Blessed Virgin; Roman Catholic Church; Women, Status and Role of.

References

Chishimba, Emilio Mulolani. *Kambelenge Nga Ni Mpelwa Ukucushako Amenso Ya Mubili Pa Kumfwa Icafikila Munyinefwe Umo Mu Calo Ca Zambia*. N.p., n.d.

Garvey, Brian. *Bembaland Church: Religious and Social Change in South Central Africa, 1891–1964*. New York: E. J. Brill, 1994.

Hinfelaar, Hugo F. *Bemba-Speaking Women of Zambia in a Century of Religious Change (1892–1992)*. New York: E. J. Brill, 1994.

■ Myanmar

Myanmar (formerly Burma) is a multicultural country of 50 million people, with a new "siege-proof" capital deliberately located deep in the remote countryside at Nay Pyi Taw, 199 miles north of Rangoon (Yangon).

Ruined pagodas of the former city of Bagan (Pagan), Myanmar. The site was an important Buddhist ceremonial center. (© Rfoxphoto/Dreamstime.com)

Approximately 70 percent of the country is Ba-ma (Burmese), and the remaining 30 percent are members of various other ethnic communities. Official statistics claim 90 percent are Buddhist, 5 percent Christian, 3 percent Muslim, 0.5 percent Hindu, and 1 percent continue to follow premodern traditional faith. More likely estimates are 12 percent Muslim and 3.5 percent Hindu. In either case, demographic certainty about religion is difficult because many people do not want to tell the censor the truth lest it work against them. Myanmar is a troubled religious plurality, and combined with the latent, simmering power of a huge Buddhist *sangha* (monks' order), 300,000 strong, this makes religion a serious political issue.

Important religious minorities notwithstanding, Buddhism is clearly the largest and most influential

MYANMAR

faith in Myanmar. Most Burmese and many from the minority communities are Theravada Buddhist. The religion has had a presence in Myanmar for more than 1,000 years, and it coexists alongside a rich indigenous, apotropaic, magical animism (*nat* and spirit worship, the close involvement of Baydin Sayas or astrologers with official life). Early Pyu and Mon Buddhist kingdoms in lower Burma were replaced with the rise of

Pagan, a golden age of Buddhism lasting from 800 to 1300 CE, followed by the Ava period (to 1550), the Toungoo (to 1750), and finally the Konbaung (dissolved by the British in 1885).

The British ignored Buddhism, leaving the still-medieval theological and clerical structure ill-equipped to meet modernity and to work out its own destiny. Even so, Buddhism became a potent ingredient of

Myanmar

Religion	Followers in 1970	Followers in 2010	% of Population	Annual % growth 2000–2010	Followers in 2025	Followers in 2050
Buddhists	20,410,000	36,851,000	73.6	0.89	40,879,000	43,552,000
Ethnoreligionists	3,000,000	5,200,000	10.4	0.25	5,000,000	4,500,000
Christians	1,350,000	4,002,000	8.0	1.83	4,828,000	5,498,000
Protestants	963,000	2,600,000	5.2	1.74	3,200,000	3,600,000
Roman Catholics	268,000	660,000	1.3	0.72	800,000	900,000
Independents	87,200	780,000	1.6	3.81	1,000,000	1,200,000
Muslims	1,000,000	1,900,000	3.8	0.89	2,150,000	2,300,000
Hindus	450,000	855,000	1.7	0.80	940,000	1,000,000
Confucianists	0	750,000	1.5	0.89	900,000	1,000,000
Agnostics	50,000	250,000	0.5	0.89	350,000	450,000
Chinese folk	80,000	132,000	0.3	0.89	145,000	160,000
Baha'is	11,200	85,000	0.2	0.89	140,000	200,000
Atheists	26,000	21,000	0.0	0.89	35,000	40,000
Jains	500	2,500	0.0	0.89	5,000	7,000
Sikhs	5,000	1,400	0.0	−6.97	1,000	1,000
Zoroastrians	200	700	0.0	0.92	700	700
Jews	200	20	0.0	0.85	30	30
Total population	**26,383,000**	**50,051,000**	**100.0**	**0.89**	**55,374,000**	**58,709,000**

nationalist ambitions, with key figures like the monks U Wissara (d. 1929) and U Ottama (d. 1939) taking leading roles in defying colonial rule in the 1920s and 1930s. The assassination of Bogyoke Aung San (ca. 1914–1947) was a crucial tragedy because he alone had worked out a vision for the newly independent nation that brought together the various religio-ethnic constituencies.

The first prime minister of the independent Myanmar was U Nu (1907–1995), a well-meaning ardently pro-Buddhist but somewhat unrealistic leader. Unfortunately, the army (Tatmadaw) used his zeal for religion as an excuse to seize power in 1962. The new government withdrew recognition of Buddhism as the state religion. It also ordered all religions to register with the government. In 1966 the government nationalized all religious schools (except seminaries) and medical facilities, and ordered all foreign missionary workers (mostly Christians) to leave the country.

Attempts by the several military regimes to "purify" Buddhism through reform councils (in 1965, 1980, and 1985) have brought the sangha under nominal government control. Yet in 1988 and 1990, the sangha showed vital support for the democracy move-

ment, even "overturning the begging bowl" (*patta ni kauz za na kan*) to prevent the military from making merit the most crucial Buddhist ritual aim. Further, in September 2007, a mass protest suddenly erupted led entirely by Buddhist monks (and thereby named the Saffron Revolution). Tens of thousands of monks paraded in monsoon conditions citing the Metta Sutta and briefly offering the hope of regime change. The event, as close to an uprising as Myanmar has had since 1988, was put down by the state in the usual brutal manner, with many monasteries closed and monks sent home. But the Buddhist sangha again showed its key place in society in the aftermath of the May 2008 Cyclone Nargis, which devastated the Ayeyarwaddy delta, killing thousands and leaving 2.4 million homeless and in danger. The Myanmar military government refused most international aid and even discouraged internal private donors, leaving the sangha alone as the only initial conduit for help: providing food, shelter, medical care, and compassion. Despite the present state's Peace and Development Council's dislike of sangha autonomy, the junta knows that its authority must at least in part be established on its identification with Buddhism. An increasing engagement with the religion for political purposes is paradoxically evident, with emoluments showered on cooperating monks and public displays of the junta's religious piety.

Various Buddhist organizations in Myanmar reflect the several schools of thought within the country's Theravada Buddhism. The largest number identify with the Thudharma, and the Shewgyin and Dwara sects are also important minorities. In the late 20th century, several Burmese meditation masters, most notably Mahasi Sayadaw (1904–1982), U Ba Kin (1899–1971), and Satya Narayan Goenka (b. 1924), built large international followings. These have become embodied in such groups as the Insight Meditation Society, the International Meditation Centres, and the Vipassana Meditation Centres.

Of the minority faiths, Hinduism retains a close connection with Buddhism, despite serious pogroms against Indian expatriates in the past. Most of the remaining Hindus are descendants of immigrants from Tamil-, Bengali-, and Telegu-speaking parts of India.

Christianity is chiefly represented by the Roman Catholic Church and an assortment of Protestant denominations linked with the Myanmar Christian Council. Christianity continues to grow, in part through natural increase and because of missionary success among the hill tribes. The first Christian missionaries entered the country in the 16th century. Representatives of the Church of England came in 1825 and the result of their activity is now manifest in the Church of the Province of Myanmar, created in 1970. Of the various Protestant and Free Churches that opened work through the 19th and 20th centuries, that of the American Baptists attained legendary status as a landmark of the Protestant missionary movement. The Myanmar Baptist Convention now has almost 500,000 members, but a total Baptist affiliation is estimated at one million.

Islam in Myanmar is comprised of three distinct constituencies, all largely Sunni: the distressed and persecuted Rohingyas in the Arakan region on the Bangladeshi border, the Indian Muslims, and the mixed-marriage Burmese Muslims (called Zerbadees). There is a single Jewish synagogue in Yangon. Established in 1896, it now serves a small community of 25 to 50 persons. Taken together, religion is still a commanding force in this country, one of the poorest on Earth where millions live in extreme poverty and fear, and which has endured so much in recent decades.

J. Gordon Melton

See also: Church of England; Church of the Province of Myanmar; International Meditation Centres; Insight Meditation Society; Myanmar Baptist Convention Theravada Buddhist.

References

Houtman, Gustaaf. *Mental Culture in Burmese Crisis Politics: Aung San Suu Kyi and the National League for Democracy*. Tokyo: Institute for the Study of Languages and Cultures of Asia and Africa, 1999.

Mendelson, E. Michael. *Sangha and State in Burma*. Ed. by John P. Ferguson. Ithaca, NY: Cornell University Press, 1973.

Sarkisyanz, Emmanuel. *Buddhist Backgrounds of the Burmese Revolution*. The Hague: Martinus Nijhoff, 1965.

Spiro, Melford E. *Buddhism and Society: A Great Tradition and Its Burmese Vicissitudes*. Berkeley and Los Angeles: University of California Press, 1982.

Suu Kyi, Aung San. *Freedom from Fear and Other Writings*. London: Penguin, 1991.

Yegar, Moshe. *The Muslims of Burma: A Study of a Minority Group*. Wiesbaden, Germany: Otto Harrassowitz, 1972.

Myanmar Baptist Convention

The Baptists were the first Protestants to enter Burma (since 1989 known as Myanmar). The mission work actually began when Adoniram Judson (1788–1850), who had arrived in India under the auspices of the Congregationalist organization the American Board of Commissioners for Foreign Missions, converted to the Baptist faith and upon his arrival in Calcutta was rebaptized by a British Baptist. Judson settled in India but was forced out by the authorities and in 1813 relocated to Rangoon (now Yangon). He eventually received the support of the American Baptists; in fact, his work became the occasion for the formation of the Triennial Convention (now a constituent part of the

American Baptist Churches in the U.S.A.), through which American Baptists built their international missionary endeavor.

Judson set out to master the Burmese language and produced the first Burmese grammar text and later the standard Bible translation. The British Baptists in India gave Judson a printing press in 1816, which allowed him to found the Baptist Mission Press. Judson would go on to publish the Bible in four additional languages.

Growth really began in 1828 with George Boardman (1801–1831) and his wife, Sara Hall Boardman, who began work with Ko Tha Byu, a convert from among the Karen people. The three soon had a flourishing work among the Karen. Work was later developed among the Zomi and Kachin. Members were also received among the Burmese and the Shan. To assist the mission, the Burman Theological Seminary (1936) and the Karen Theological Seminary (1845) were opened. These various missions were combined in 1865 into the Burma Baptist Convention. Among the first activities of the Convention was the founding of Rangoon Baptist College, later Judson Baptist College. In 1880 representatives from the Karen people in Burma began work among their people residing in Thailand, resulting in the establishment of the Karen Baptist Convention in that country.

Early in the 20th century, Dr. Gordon S. Seagrave (1897–1965) began his career as a medical missionary in the northeast part of the country near the Chinese border. The story of his work under relatively primitive conditions was told in two books, *Waste-Basket Surgery* (1938) and *Burma Surgeon* (1943).

The mission suffered greatly through the mid-20th century. During World War II, the Japanese invasion led to the wide-scale destruction of property, which was slowly rebuilt after the war. In 1965 church property was again lost when all of the church's schools (including Judson College) and medical facilities were nationalized. In 1966 missionary personnel were deported, though the leadership and administration of the convention had already been turned over to the Burmese in the 1950s. The loss of the missionaries, however, seemed to spur growth. In 1963 there were around 216,000 members. In the next 30 years the membership more than doubled, and growth has continued to

the present. In 2005 the Convention reported more than 650,000 baptized members and more than 600,000 additional unbaptized members.

The Convention is a member of the World Council of Churches, the Baptist World Alliance, and the Myanmar Council of Churches.

Myanmar Baptist Convention
143 Minye Kyawswa Rd., Lanmadaw
PO Box 506
Yangon
Myanmar

J. Gordon Melton

See also: American Baptist Churches in the U.S.A.; American Board of Commissioners for Foreign Missions; Baptist World Alliance; World Council of Churches.

References
Seagrave, Gordon S. *Burma Surgeon*. New York: W. W. Norton, 1943.
Seagrave, Gordon S. *Waste-Basket Surgery*. Philadelphia: Judson Press, 1931.
Tegenfield, Herman G. *A Century of Growth: The Kachin Baptist Church of Burma*. South Pasadena, CA: William Carey Library, 1974.
Torbet, Robert G. *Venture of Faith*. Philadelphia: Judson Press, 1955.
Van Beek, Huibert. *A Handbook of the Churches and Councils: Profiles of Ecumenical Relationships*. Geneva: World Council of Churches, 2006.

Myôchikai Kyôdan

Myôchikai Kyôdan, a Japanese new religion, was founded by Miyamoto Mitsu (1900–1984) in 1950. Along with her husband, Kohei, Miyamoto joined Reiyukai in 1934 and practiced rigorously. In 1945 Kohei died, and in 1950 Mitsu broke away and became independent of Reiyukai, taking 300 followers with her.

Myôchikai Kyôdan has a sanctuary in Chiba Prefecture, and a religious pilgrimage to this sanctuary is important in the movement's practices. The main ceremonies held there are the Kaishu (Miyamoto Mitsu) ceremony in the spring and the Daionshi (Miyamoto Kohei) ceremony in autumn. Myôchikai Kyôdan values the Lotus Sutra, ancestor worship, and repentance. Members are admonished to venerate their ancestors by offering them memorial rites utilizing the Lotus Sutra on a daily basis.

The current leader of Myôchikai Kyôdan is Miyamoto Takeyasu. Its headquarters are in Tokyo, Japan. In 2000 it reported 1,070,813 members.

Myôchikai Kyôdan
3-3-3 Yoyogi

Shibuya-ku, Tokyo 151-0053
Japan

Keishin Inaba

See also: Reiyukai.

References

Inoue, Nobutaka, et al., eds. *Shinshûkyo Kyodan Jinbutsu Jiten*. Tokyo: Kobundo, 1996.

Komoto, Mitsugi. "The Place of Ancestors in the New Religions: The Case of Reiyûkai-Derived Groups." http://www2.kokugakuin.ac.jp/ijcc/wp/cpjr/newreligions/komoto.html. Accessed March 25, 2009.

Index

Abbasids, 463, 855, 1497, 1521, 2608, 2788, 2789, 2903
Abd al-Aziz ibn Sa'ud, **3–4,** 3 (image)
Abd-al-Wahhab, Mohammad ibn, 3083, 3084
Abduh, Muhammad, **4–5,** 19, 20
Abeel, David, **5–6**
Abell, Theodore, 1365
Aboriginal cult. *See* Lionza, Maria, Aboriginal cult of
Aboriginal religions, **8–10,** 9 (image)
   and Aboriginal artwork, 9–10
   and the Dreaming cosmology, 8
   and knowledge of the law, 8–9
   response of Aboriginals to Christianity, 9
Abraham/Abram, **10–13,** 12 (image), 1594
   Genesis account of, 10–11
   status of in Islam, 11–12
Abraham, K. E., 681
Abu Bakr, 76, 348
Abu Hanifa, **13**
Abyssinia. *See* Ethiopia
AD2000 and Beyond Movement, **14–15**
   criticism of, 15
Adamski, George, 2917
Adejobi, Adeleke, 716
Adidam (Adidam Ruchiradam), **15–16**
   alternate names of, 16
Adler, Cyrus, 781–782
Advent, **16–18,** 17 (image)
Adventism, **18–19,** 18 (image)
Afghani, Jamal al-Din al-, 4, **19–20,** 1525–1526
Afghanistan, **20–24,** 21 (image), 22 (map), 23 (table), 1522
   Buddhism in, 22–23
   Christianity in, 22

Indians (Sikhs and Hindus) living in, 21
influence of the Taliban in, 21
intervention of the United States in, 23
Jews in, 22
Northern Alliance of, 21
presence of al-Qaeda in, 23
relationship with the Soviet Union, 20–21
Africa Inland Church, **24–25**
Africa Inland Mission (AIM), 24, 777, 1627, 2815
African Apostolic Church, 34
African Apostolic Church of Johane Marange (AACJM), **25–26,** 25 (image)
African Brotherhood Church (ABC), **26–27**
African Church, Nigeria, **28**
African Church of the Holy Spirit, **28–29**
African Greek Orthodox Church, 42
African Independent Pentecostal Church (AIPC), **29–30**
African Initiated (Independent) Churches (AICs), 26, 27, **30–36,** 31 (image), 33 (image), 35 (image), 48, 136, 338, 645, 812, 1210–1211, 1781, 2012
African/Ethiopian churches, 33–34
   in Botswana, 2702–2703
   different types of, 30–33
   in Ghana, 2699–2700
   in Kenya, 2115–2116, 2700–2702
   Pentecostal/Charismatic churches, 35–36
   in Rwanda, 2485
   spirit/prophet-healing churches, 34–35

in Togo, 2877
in Zambia, 3177
in Zimbabwe, 3187
African Israel Church, Nineveh (African Israel Nineveh Church [AINC]), **36–37**
African Methodist Episcopal Church (AMEC), **37–39,** 38 (image), 40
African Methodist Episcopal Zion Church (AMEZ), **39–41**
African Orthodox Church (AOC), 29, **41–43**
African Protestant Church, **43**
African traditional religions, **43–50**
   creation myths of, 44, 45–46
   and dynamism (power and power specialists), 46–48
   spirituality of (ancestors and the spirit world), 48–50
   and theism (concept of God and of lesser divinities), 44–46
Aga Khan, 1334 (image), 1335, 1491, 1534
Agassiz, Louis, 821–822
Agca, Ali, 1104
Agnosticism, **50–51,** 50 (image), 2943
Agonshu, **51–53,** 52 (image), 1568–1569
Agrippa. *See* Nettesheim, Heinrich Cornelius Agrippa von
Ahidjo, Alhaji Ahmadou, 484
Ahmad, Hazrat Mirza Tahir, 47
Ahmad, Mirza Ghulam Hazrat, **54–56,** 55 (image), 57, 2171
Ahmadiyya Anjuman Islaat Islam Lahore, **56–57**
Ahmadiyya movement, **57–59,** 58 (image), 2171–2172
Aitken, Anne, 888

European, 1015, 2168
in Hungary, 1369
in Latvia, 1692
neo-Paganism, 945, 2421, 2753, 2928, 3120
in Portugal, 2275
in Ukraine, 2924, 2925
Pakistan, **2169–2174,** 2170 (image), 2172 (map), 2173 (table)
the Ahmadiyyas in, 2171–2172
ancient Pakistan, 2169–2170
Christianity in, 2173
Islam in, 2171, 2172–2173
modern state of, 2170–2171
Roman Catholicism in, 2174
separation of Bangladesh from, 2171
Palau, **2174–2176,** 2175 (map), 2176 (table)
Palm Sunday, 1432
Palo Mayombe, **2176–2177**
Palau, Luis, 1037–1038, 1038 (image)
Palestine, 1535, 1590, 1994
See also Israel, occupied territories of
Pali Canon, 417, 440
Panama, **2177–2188,** 2178 (table), 2181 (map), 2184 (image)
Anglicanism in, 2183
Assemblies of God in, 2182–2183, 2185
Baptists in, 2183–2184
Catholic Charismatic Renewal movement in, 2182
Eastern Orthodoxy in, 2185–2186
economy of, 2177–2178
history of U.S. intervention in, 2178–2180
minor sects in, 2186–2187
Pentecostalism in, 2184
Protestantism in, 2184–2185
Roman Catholicism in, 2178, 2180–2182
Panchen Lama, 579 (image)
Pangestu, **2188–2189**
Pannenberg, Wolfart, 2551
Pantheism, **2189–2190**
Paparelli, Luigia, **1918–1919**
Papua New Guinea, **2190–2194,** 2191 (image), 2192 (map), 2193 (table)
indigenous religions in, 2193
Lutheranism in, 2190–2191

wide spectrum of Christian denominations in, 2191, 2193
Paraguay, **2194–2205,** 2195 (image), 2199 (map), 2203 (table)
the Colorado Party of, 2196, 2197
dominance of Roman Catholicism in, 2194
Jesuit missions in, 2199–2200
Mennonites in, 2205–2206
non-Christian religions in, 2203–2204
Protestant movements in, 2202–2203
Roman Catholicism in, 2198–2202
social progress of due to immigration, 2195–2196
under the dictatorship of Stroessner, 2197–2198
under the dictatorship of Francisco López, 2196–2197
under Spanish colonial rule, 2196
Paramahamsa, Ramakrishna, 1430, 3046, 3047–3048
Parham, Charles Fox, 159–160, 159 (image), 212, 406, **2206–2207,** 2221, 2225
Paris Mission, **2207–2208,** 2295
Parker, Quanah, 2038
Parks, John, 1899
Parr, John Nelson, 215
Parsons, Jack, 699, 2150
Parsons, Levi, 2791–2792
Paryushana, **2208–2209**
Pashupata Saivism, **2209**
Pasqually, Jacques Martinez de, 1813
Passover, **2209–2212,** 2210 (image)
among Jewish Christians, 2211–2212
Christian Passover, 2211
See also Pesach
Pasundan Christian Church, **2212**
Patanjali, **2213,** 3158, 3163
Patotsav, **2213–2214**
Patterson, J. O., 680
Patterson, John Coleridge, 652, 2751
Paul VI (pope), 2563, 3023
Paul, 633, 634, 1231, **2214–2216,** 2214 (image)
conversion of, 2215
education of, 2214–2215
journeys in Greece, 1247, 2215
martyrdom of, 2216
missionary journeys of, 2215–2216

Paul, Joseph, 270
Paulceus, Joseph, 680
Payne, John, 1716
Peace of Augsburg, 1020
Peace Theological Seminary and College of Philosophy (PTS), 1980–1981
Peacocke, Arthur, 2551
Pelagius, 238
Penn, William, 711, 1155, 1157–1158
Pennepack Baptist Church, 90
Pendell, Larry, 2221 (image)
Pentecost, 924, **2216–2217**
Pentecostal Assemblies of Canada, **2217–2218**
Pentecostal Assemblies of the World, **2218–2219**
Pentecostal Church of Chile, **2219–2220**
Pentecostal Church of God, **2220–2222,** 2221 (image)
The Pentecostal Mission (TPM), **2222–2223**
Pentecostal Mission Church, **2222**
Pentecostal Missionary Union (PMU), 216
Pentecostal World Fellowship, **2223–2225**
Pentecostalism, 153–154, 159–160, 215, 368–369, 392, 393–394, 773, 836–837, 1160, **2225–2227,** 2226 (image), 2523
in Honduras, 1352–1353
in Nigeria, 2109
in Norway, 2121
in Panama, 2184
in the Republic of Korea, 1649
in Scandinavia, **2227–2228**
in Uruguay, 3031
See also Charismatic movement; People of God; Spirituality, Pentecostal; True Jesus Church
People of God, **2228–2229**
People's Republic of China (PRC), annexation of Tibet, 573, 574, 1619
Peoples Temple, **2229–2231,** 2230 (image)
suicide pact taken by members of, 2231
Perennialism, **2231–2232**
Perfect Liberty Kyodan, **2232–2233**
Perl, Jacob, 1670